SINGER
sewing book

SINGER
sewing book

Revised Edition

Jessie Hutton
Gladys Cunningham

Book design, art direction and
production supervision
Claire F. Valentine

Published by THE SINGER COMPANY · New York, New York

Portions of the section entitled
The Many Faces of Knits were
first published in a slightly different
form as chapters in the book entitled
"Singer Sewing Series for Home and Fashion."

LIBRARY OF CONGRESS CATALOG CARD NUMBER: 72-5727

PRINTED IN THE UNITED STATES OF AMERICA
PUBLISHED SIMULTANEOUSLY IN CANADA

SECOND EDITION

SECOND PRINTING

NA 5840-A

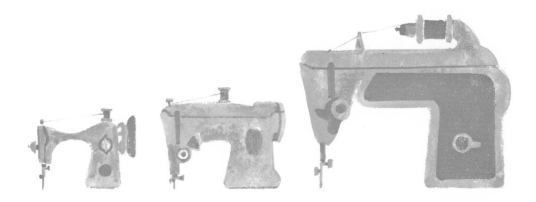

You are about to begin an adventure in creativity: you are going to sew. And you are going to sew well. You may open this book as a beginner, eager to make an absolutely smashing dress; or you may open it as an experienced sewer, determined to master tailoring. Whatever your reason, we believe the book will satisfy you, for it aims to teach the novice basic sewing skills and help the advanced seamstress perfect her ability.

Sewing today is an exciting and rewarding pastime. Whether you sew for economy or fashion, you have at your disposal superb fabrics in brilliant colors and interesting textures and weaves; you have patterns by famous designers; and you have a versatile and compliant helpmeet—your sewing machine.

Begin your adventure with a simple dress, and follow the rules explicitly. When you have mastered them, decide where you can cut corners without sacrificing good workmanship. (Many of the basic principles of sewing must never be omitted.) Each time you make a dress, select a design that is a little more difficult. Gradually work up to bound buttonholes, set-in pockets, and finally suits and coats. Follow the same principle when sewing for your home. Start with a simple curtain or bedspread and advance to draperies, slipcovers, and designs featuring decorative detail. If you are skilled in sewing, use this book to broaden your knowledge — to acquaint yourself with the new construction methods that today's fabrics and fashions demand.

Sewing is an art and, as such, demands the discipline of an art. Bring to it desire, enthusiasm, and imagination, and it will give you in return a satisfaction that is unique: the joy of creating something that is truly yours.

Acknowledgments

Many talented persons have applied their skills and abilities
to making this book informative, useful, and attractive.

Jacket Design—Ralph Castenir

Editorial
Editorial supervision—Elna Wallace

Special thanks are due to Mary Skemp Perkins, who provided
creative editorial assistance to Miss Cunningham in the
preparation of the first edition of the SINGER Sewing Book.
Kathleen Fredrick contributed helpful editorial review.
Kathleen Coyle edited a substantial portion of *The Many
Faces of Knits*.
Proofreading—Kathleen Coyle, Mary Littell, Christine Scanlon Tracey,
Jean Crawford Weir.

Text Illustration
Drawings for the text were made by A. Bernasconi, Sr., Helen Disbrow,
Ralph Castenir and Derek Moore. Valerie Allen and Harold Skelton
did most of the color-separation overlays. Anthony Schmidt was most
cooperative in supplying sewing machine drawings.
Edward Hauser did most of the illustrations for *The Many
Faces of Knits,* and the color-separation overlays were
made by Myron and Joel Goetz.

Color Photographs
Design and execution of sewing projects—Ruth Kirkpatrick, June King,
Marjory Firrantello, Edith Paul, Barbara Ann Swenson, Maybelle Bronca,
Luci Ciancia.
Photographic and mechanical supervision—Sherman Deutsch
Photography—Rudy Muller Studio
Line drawings—Ester Larsen, Robert Flinn, Helen Disbrow.
Color-wheel mechanical—Charles Palmer
Permission to reproduce the beautiful interior photographs in the
four-color pages is gratefully acknowledged. The source is given
under each illustration.

Our appreciation is extended to the following for their generous
assistance in providing material and information—
Margaret Brindle—F. Schumacher & Company; Conso Products, Inc.;
Kirsch Company, Inc. and Man-made Fiber Products Association.

THE SINGER COMPANY

Contents

Color Plates

A Place To Sew

To FIND IN SEWING the pleasure that is waiting there, you need a cheerful, comfortable, neatly organized sewing area where you can keep your sewing machine and sewing supplies. The ideal place, of course, is a room where you can leave the machine open, the pressing board up, and the work spread out when you have to stop. But most women have to compromise and sequester a corner where they can.

Much, of course, depends on the space available and the time you spend in sewing. If you sew in the evening, you may be able to find a place in the family room where you can work while the rest of the household is busy with television, a record player, homework, reading, or a hobby. A large closet might be outfitted with your sewing and pressing supplies and the dining-room table might double as your cutting table. Or, if you have a light and modern laundry area that is large enough for all your sewing equipment, you might make that your sewing studio.

Study the layout of your own house. You are sure to come up with several good ideas. If you cannot have a room of your own for sewing, make the best compromise—one that offers the most convenience to you with the least disruption to family life. Remember, if you have only a short time to sew, you do not want to spend most of it getting out your sewing and putting it away. And the pleasure possible in sewing will certainly be diminished if you have to sew in one room, press in another, and store your sewing supplies in still another.

ARRANGING YOUR SEWING AREA

Wherever the space you have found for your sewing nook, you can, with skillful planning, arrange your sewing equipment and tools for long sewing sessions. The success with which you do this will be apparent in your sewing results.

Sewing and Pressing Area

Place your sewing machine near a window if possible so that you may have the benefit of natural daylight. Use a stool or straight chair without arms so that you can move your own arms and body freely as you work.

Since pressing as you sew is essential, place the pressing board and other pressing equipment close to the machine. Be sure the section is well lighted. The light on your machine is focused on the stitching area; to illuminate the section for both sewing and pressing, place a floor lamp or table lamp nearby.

Keep a wastebasket handy for scraps and threads. If you keep your working area neat as you go along, you will find that you can quickly clean up when you have finished sewing.

If you have a dress form, place it near the sewing unit so that it is handy for fitting and assembling your garments. (Store it in the closet when you have finished.)

Pattern Layout and Cutting Area

You will need a smooth surface. A bedboard, which can be supported with two bridge tables, or a ping-pong table is quite satisfactory since both are about 60 inches long. The bedboard can be stored between the mattress and box spring and the ping-pong table can be folded when not in use.

Locate the table so that you can walk around at least two sides. Use it not only when laying out the pattern and cutting but also when marking the cutout garment and when basting the sections together.

If you have to use the dining-room table, be sure to protect it with heavy brown paper or a stiff table pad. (And don't let sewing interfere with family meals.)

1

For fitting you will need a full-length mirror (a three-way mirror is better) so that you can inspect the fit of your garments as you try them on during various stages of construction. A mirror on a closet door solves this nicely. Other members of the family will probably appreciate it too when they are dressing.

Storage Area

The storage area should be near the sewing area if possible. The amount of space needed will depend on your sewing supplies and tools and the kind of sewing you do. You may need two or three drawers in a chest or linen closet to store fabrics, interfacings, trimmings, patterns, and related items. A sewing basket or sewing box is ideal for the smaller items such as scissors, needles, pins, bobbins, thread, thimbles, pin cushion, snaps, tape measure, and the like. You can keep the basket on a closet shelf.

All your pressing equipment should be stored together so that it is readily accessible when you are sewing.

You should have closet space for hanging dresses, coats, and suits that are under construction and for hanging lengths of fabric that you may buy ahead and make up later. You should also keep on hand several padded hangers. As soon as darts are basted, pin the seam edges of the dress together and hang the dress on the padded hanger instead of folding or laying it on the table or bed. This will keep the fabric free of wrinkles and save you time later because you will not have to press the dress before you start working on it again.

Store sewing books on the closet shelf or in a bookcase; store fashion magazines on a shelf or in a magazine rack.

When storage space is limited, you might consider a storage wall. Secure a pegboard with hooks inside a closet door and use it for small tools such as a yardstick, tape measures, scissors, and the like.

EQUIPMENT AND SUPPLIES

Besides a good sewing machine, your place to sew should be outfitted with many small tools and sewing supplies. They will facilitate your sewing and help you attain a professional look in your finished product. Purchase quality tools and supplies, take care of them properly, and store them so that you can quickly locate what you need when you start to sew. You will be repaid with good service, convenience, and praiseworthy sewing results.

The following are essential for good sewing:

Thread. Have on hand silk, mercerized, and synthetic thread in an assortment of colors for sewing, basting, and making tailor's tacks. Also have a large spool of white basting thread as well as thread that matches the color of the fabric you are sewing. (Leftover spools of thread may be used for tailor's tacks.)

Hand-sewing needles. Buy good-quality steel needles to be sure of perfect sewing performance. Keep them in the package to prevent rust. Needles are available in sizes from 3 to 10; the selection depends on the weight and character of the fabric. There are also many types of needles to choose from; here the selection depends on the kind of stitching you expect to do. The following will guide you:

Straw and *Milliner's* needles are long and slender with round eyes. Because of their length, slender shaping, and flexibility, they produce good results when multiple stitches are woven onto the needle as in basting, hand shirring, overcasting, and similar stitching.

The *Betweens* are the very short, round-eyed needles. Use them, as tailors do, to make the fine, short, sturdy, invisible stitches that are a mark of good tailoring.

The all-purpose *Sharps* are medium-length, round-eyed needles. Use them for general sewing.

Crewel needles are similar to the Sharps in length but have a long, oval eye for easy threading and for carrying multiple strands as in hand embroidery.

Darners are long needles with long, oval eyes that are designed to carry multiple strands of thread. Because of their length, many stitches can be woven onto the needle with a single stroke.

Upholstery needles are curved and are made for stitching into a cushioned surface. The curved needle rises out of the cushion with each stitch, thus facilitating stitching that would be difficult with a straight needle.

Machine needles. Keep an assortment of sizes from 9 to 18. Select the size that is suited to the weight and character of your fabric. *Fabric, Thread, Needle, and Stitch Length Chart,* page 24, gives complete information on selecting the proper needle for the fabric used. A machine needle should be changed after it has been used to stitch two or three garments since it becomes bent and burred from use.

Pins. Select fine, slender dressmaking pins with needlelike points and smooth blades. Always keep them separate from household pins since they will become bent and burred if used for purposes other than sewing.

Tape measure. Select a tape measure with metal tips, 60 inches in length, reversible, and numbered to read from each end. Linen, plastic, and plastic-coated tape measures are best because they will not stretch.

Gauges. Keep several 6-inch sewing and knitting gauges for measuring short distances.

Rulers. Have one *18-inch ruler* and a *yardstick* for measuring fabric grain line on pattern layout, and a *folding ruler* or *steel tape* for measuring windows for curtains and draperies.

Thimbles. Be sure that thimbles fit well, and use one in all hand sewing and basting.

Scissors. You will use three kinds; (1) *Bent-handle dressmaker's shears* with 6- or 7-inch blades for cutting. These shears have a small ring handle for the thumb and a large ring for two or three fingers. (2) *Light trimmers* for trimming seams and for small jobs. These have a small ring handle for the thumb and a large ring for two or three fingers. (3) *Small embroidery scissors* for cutting threads and buttonholes. Left-handed sewers should use *left-handed shears* for greater ease and accuracy in cutting.

Pinking shears. Use them only for finishing seam edges.

Pressing equipment. You will need a steam iron, sleeveboard, seamboard, ironing board, press-mitt and tailor's ham, three kinds of press cloths, sponge, paintbrush, clothes brush, and pressing pad. *Pressing as You Sew,* on page 64, explains how you will use this equipment.

Pin cushion. Use for needles and a few pins.

Emery cushion. Use it to sharpen needles and remove rust.

Extra bobbins. Keep a good supply on hand for your machine. Always have one bobbin wound with black thread and one with white for ready use in mending.

Awl or stiletto. Use it to punch holes for eyelets.

Tweezers. They are handy for removing tailor's tacks and short basting threads.

Bodkin. Have one for inserting cord in casing. It is also useful when you are forming a thread shank while sewing buttons.

Scalloped rulers. Get an assortment of sizes to simplify marking scallops.

Skirt marker. It is a must for marking hemlines.

Embroidery hoops. Keep two or more, 6 inches and smaller, for darning and embroidery.

Tailor's chalk or chalk pencil. You will need this for transferring pattern markings to some fabrics, for marking adjustments in garments, and for marking the width of hems.

Tracing wheel and dressmaker's tracing paper. These are useful for transferring pattern markings on interfacing, underlining, and some fabrics.

Beeswax. Keep a piece on hand for waxing thread before you sew buttons on coats, jackets, waistbands, and tough fabrics. It strengthens the thread and prevents snarling and snagging. Use it also for smoothing the surface of the iron.

Staple notions. Keep an assortment of snaps, hooks and eyes, elastic, straight seam binding, bias seam binding, and zippers.

Buttons. It is wise to have several cards of pearl buttons of various sizes, which can be used for blouses and children's clothes and for many mending jobs. Also, keep a box for buttons that you have removed from discarded garments; they may be used again.

Besides these supplies, a small "reference" library is strongly recommended. It should contain: 1. The instruction book for your machine. 2. This sewing book. 3. A scrap book or folder of fashion clippings and interiors from newspapers and magazines for ideas that you would love to copy or use for inspiration. Also, watch for new sewing aids to appear on notion counters from time to time. You may find some item that can help you save time and make your sewing more professional.

Your Sewing Machine

IF YOU ARE AN EXPERIENCED SEWER, you know how valuable and essential a good sewing machine is to a well-run home. You also know how important it is to keep your machine in first-class condition. (Information on caring for your machine appears at the end of this chapter.)

In addition, you should realize that advances in fabrics have caused many changes in your stitching needs. To the familiar fabrics loomed of natural fibers—cotton, silk, wool, and linen—have been added many man-made or synthetic fibers. The blending of natural and synthetic fibers and new finishing methods have revolutionized the appearance and properties of fabrics. Double-knit, stretch, bonded, permanent press, and many other fabrics have increased the stitching range you will require from your machine.

Added to all these fabric developments are the ever fickle whims of fashion, which have changed sewing methods.

Fashion emphasis on simple, straight seams places emphasis, in turn, on the quality of stitching that holds the seam. Knit and stretch fabrics, for example, require greater seam strength and flexibility. In loosely woven and textured fabrics, the seam should be finished by machine to prevent raveling and eliminate bulk. (Machine finishing will also save time.) Underlining and lining, which are now widely used to help retain the shape of the fabric and give added body, require stitching through several layers of unlike fabrics. This makes the feeding qualities of your machine more important.

Your sewing is simplified if your machine is easy to thread and if you can adjust the needle-thread tension, pressure, and stitch length with a minimum of effort. You should be able, with minor adjustments of one or more of these, to stitch the newest fabrics without puckered seams or skipped stitches.

Sewing machine manufacturers have kept pace with fabrics, fashion sewing, and modern living. And sewing machines today offer many features that facilitate your sewing tasks.

Deluxe zig-zag machines offer finger-tip switch from straight stitching to zig-zag stitching for finishing seams, buttonholing, blindstitching hems, sewing buttons, and mending as well as doing decorative stitching. Simple zig-zag machines have limited zig-zag features and are less expensive. Straight stitch machines are designed to do excellent straight stitching and detailed sewing and to make buttonholes with the aid of a Buttonholer.

Some machines have other features that make sewing more pleasant—for example, a slant needle for maximum vision, a horizontal spool pin that permits the thread to unwind without drag from the spool, and a push-button bobbin that lets you fill the bobbin directly from the needle. Some machines will even chain stitch for easy-to-remove temporary stitching. In fact, modern sewing machines do more practical stitching jobs than you can imagine.

Many machines are light enough to carry as portables; or they can be placed in attractive cabinets that match or blend with your furniture.

The type of machine you need will depend on the extent to which you use a machine and the kind of sewing you do. Remember that your sewing machine is the main equipment in your place to sew. Arrange all sewing tools and supplies around it.

Caring for Your Machine

Just as a good craftsman is meticulous about the care of his tools, so should you be about the care of your sewing machine. By accustoming yourself early to removing dust and lint regularly, to oiling the machine frequently, and to having it cleaned at reasonable intervals, you will be assured of a faithful sewing companion—one that will give you pleasure, satisfaction, and service. Suggestions on dusting and oiling the machine are given below; as for cleaning, your Singer Center can render this service whenever you wish.

Removing Dust and Lint

Many fabrics, when sewed, drop lint and particles of fiber or filling. These, mixed with dust and moisture from the air, collect around the bobbin case and feed dog. Lint and dust also collect around the moving parts of the machine.

Expose the working parts by removing the throat plate and face plate (on some machines the slide plate should be removed), and brush away the dust and lint. A special lint brush and a piece of cheesecloth are ideal for this job.

Oiling the Machine

Oiling keeps the machine running freely and prevents friction and wear. If the machine is used all day and every day, it should be oiled daily. If it is used moderately, it should be oiled every week or two. *Always remove the dust and lint before oiling the machine.* If the machine has not been used for some time, oil it the day before you start to sew to be sure that no oil will soil the fabric.

To locate the oiling points, refer to the diagram in the instruction book. Use just a drop or two of oil at each point; never drench the machine

with oil. After the machine has been thoroughly oiled, run it slowly for several minutes to allow the oil to work into the moving parts. Then remove the excess oil from the thread-handling parts with clean cheesecloth or any other lintless fabric. Polish the take-up lever, the thread guides, and the area around the needle and presser foot. Pass the cloth between the tension discs, being careful to avoid catching the take-up spring.

If you are going to give the machine an extended rest, remove the lint and oil the machine before placing it in storage. Lint absorbs moisture from the air and holds it against the metal parts, increasing the risk of rust damage in humid climates or over a long period of nonuse.

Some machines have gears that are lubricated instead of oiled; motors equipped for gear drive should be lubricated only once a year. Motors with grease tubes require lubrication every six months, however. On many machines, the motor is sealed and requires no lubrication.

Read carefully the instruction book accompanying your machine. It will tell you exactly how to care for it—whether to oil or lubricate it, where to apply the lubricant, and how often. A word of caution: always buy a high-quality oil or lubricant made specifically for sewing machines.

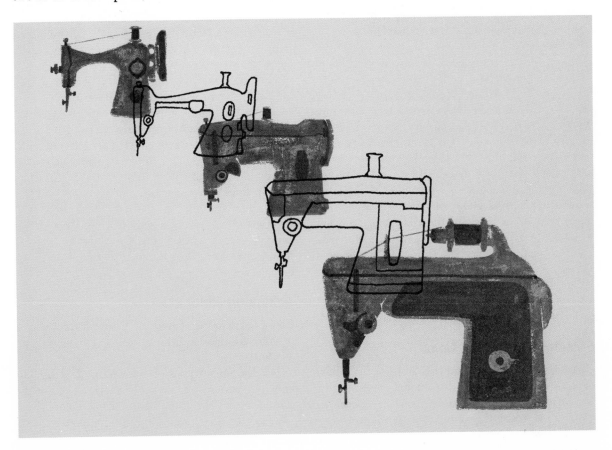

What You Should Know About Color and Fabric

EAGER AS YOU MAY BE to get started on sewing, you should sit back for a moment and consider where you are going. Essential to planning a wardrobe is a knowledge of color and fabrics. This chapter will acquaint you with the fundamentals. Then you are on your own.

ABOUT COLOR

Color can be exciting. Used wisely—and imaginatively—it will give your wardrobe a lift, contribute to the smartness of your costume, and enhance your appearance by flattering your eyes and adding a glow to your skin tone and a radiance to your hair.

Since color has a strong influence on everyday life, you should know a few facts about it before you begin. Then you can be your own watchdog. Simply explained, color has three attributes: hue, shade, and tint. Hue denotes the pure or "true" color, which may be described as red, yellow, or blue, or intermediates between two of these, as orange, green, and violet. If you add varying degrees of grey or black to the true color, you get a *shade* or a color value darker than the true color; if you add varying degrees of white, you get a *tint* or a color value lighter than the true color. The color wheel, plate 17 opposite page 340, illustrates the principle, and the text on page 338 tells you many of the rules of color.

Selecting the Right Color

One season's fashions may be a splash of color, another's may be subdued. Although it is easy to be carried away by a vivid, brilliant, or new shade, you should resist the temptation until you have satisfied yourself that the color is right for you. Put personal preferences aside for a moment. Here are some tests you can apply in selecting a color:

Is the color becoming to you? It should compliment your skin tone and bring out the beauty of your hair and eyes. Let your mirror be the judge. At the fabric counter, drape the fabric over one shoulder; study yourself in both natural and artificial light to see what the color does for you. Or, buy a package of assorted colors of construction paper. Round out a section to fit your neckline and try different colors against your face to determine which are the most becoming. Make a memo of those colors in your sewing notebook, or on the color bibs.

Is the color flattering to your figure? Light, bright, or vivid shades of almost any color tend to make the figure appear larger or heavier; on the other hand, darker, subdued tones of the same color have a slenderizing effect. This does not mean that if you are stocky or overweight, you must always choose dull colors. Rather, you should select fashion lines that minimize your figure.

Remember, too, that the chic black dress is always in fashion and certainly is a must for almost every woman's wardrobe. It can be worn all year round and changed or accented with colorful jewelry or a scarf.

Achieving Color Harmony

Color harmony is important to the attractiveness of your costume and the rules for achieving it are explicit.

Of the many types of color harmony, the best known is perhaps the monochromatic, which is the use of various shades and tints of one color.

You can also obtain interesting effects by combining different textures, weaves, and fibers of the same color. Before combining them, however, be sure that they look well together and are comparable in weight. Never mix two prints, two plaids, or a print and plaid. Also make sure that your repetition of one color does not produce a monotonous effect. If it does, try adding a slight or decided contrast.

Combining contrasting colors is another way of achieving a richness in your ensemble. But watch out! Two colors may give a pleasing contrast; three or more may introduce complications that destroy the harmony you are seeking. A sharp contrast in color is usually effective; however, use the strong, contrasting color sparingly. Complementary colors lie opposite each other in the color wheel, Plate 17. Combining two of these colors produces a striking effect with proper balance of color, and a negative effect with improper balance.

These, then, are the rules. But like all rules, fashion occasionally breaks them and combines clashing colors and prints. In this she is being true to her role of shocking the eye once in a while and thus jolting her followers into a new awareness of the beauty and possibilities of color.

To use such shocks skillfully, however, first learn the rules. Then you are at liberty to break them just as the modern painter does when he splashes color on a canvas, seemingly heedless of line and form.

A Word about Accessories and Cosmetics

Accessories play a major role in color harmony. Rather than have all your accessories of a contrasting color, choose shoes and handbag to match, or hat and gloves to match, or hat, shoes, and handbag to match. Vivid colors are often more dramatic when worn with conventional black accessories.

If a limited budget prevents you from having several sets of accessories, the wise thing is to choose a color for your coat and accessories which will blend with the other colors you are apt to choose for dresses and suits. This basic color will enable you to achieve color harmony without exceeding your budget. It will also give continuity to your wardrobe.

About cosmetics: Train yourself to select them as carefully as the colors you wear, for they can kill an otherwise harmonious appearance. As skin tone and fashion colors change, so should make-up. Manufacturers of cosmetics keep pace with fashion colors; beauty consultants at cosmetic counters know how to match shades of cosmetics with skin tone and colors. Do not hesitate to seek their advice at regular intervals.

Always remember this: If you learn to use color to your best advantage in every way, friends will compliment you and not the dress.

ABOUT FABRICS

You cannot sew successfully without a knowledge of fabrics, for fashion is found in fabrics as surely as it is found in pattern designs. Fabrics are available in a variety of weaves, textures, and colors. Often they are so exciting that you must choose a simple pattern design that will not detract from their beauty.

Unlike choosing a color, however, choosing a fabric calls for more than your eye or common sense to guide you. You must know whether the fabric is suitable for your use, whether its durability justifies your expenditure of time and money, whether its upkeep is practical for your situation.

Without being overly technical, this section will give you some fabric facts that will help you select the fabric best suited to your requirements.

Fibers

Fabric is made up of either *natural fibers* or *man-made fibers* that are spun into yarns and woven together on various types of looms. The natural fibers are *cotton, linen, silk,* and *wool.* Cotton fiber is made from the cotton plant, linen fiber from the flax plant, silk fiber from the cocoon of the silkworm, and wool fiber from the fleece of sheep or lamb or the hair of certain goats or camels.

Man-made fibers are those synthetic or manufactured fibers that are produced through chemistry. Their list is long and, since new types appear on the market almost every year, never quite complete. The chart that follows gives the generic classification, the trade-mark name, and the manufacturer of some of the more familiar fibers or yarns. (The manufacturers listed produce only the basic fibers; they do not make the fabric containing these fibers.)

It is wise to make a note of the fiber content of the fabrics you buy and file it for future reference. You should know what special qualities or service you may expect from the fabric and whether it is sunfast, tubfast, or preshrunk. Look for this information on the label or hang-tag. It is important in the care and handling of the fabric, particularly in dry cleaning or washing and in pressing. Also, stitching techniques and the type of thread used depend to a large extent on the fabric—and the behavior of the fabric depends on the fibers and the finish.

MAN-MADE FIBERS OR YARNS
(Synthetics)

Generic Classification	Trademark Name	Manufacturer or Source
ACETATE	ACELE	E. I. duPont de Nemours & Co., Inc.
	ARNEL	Celanese Fiber Company, Division of Celanese Corporation
	AVISCO	FMC Corporation, American Viscose Division
	CELANESE	Celanese Fiber Company, Division of Celanese Corporation
	CELAPERM	Celanese Fiber Company, Division of Celanese Corporation
	CHROMSPUN	Eastman Kodak Company, Tennessee Eastman Company Division
	ESTRON	Eastman Kodak Company, Tennessee Eastman Company Division
ACRYLIC	ACRILAN	Monsanto Company, Textiles Division
	CRESLAN	American Cyanamid Company, Fibers Division
	ORLON	E. I. duPont de Nemours & Co., Inc.
	ZEFKROME	Dow Badische Company
	ZEFRAN	Dow Badische Company
GLASS FIBER	BETA	Owens-Corning Fiberglas Corporation
	FIBERGLAS	Owens-Corning Fiberglas Corporation
	PPG FIBER GLASS	PPG Industries, Inc. Fiber Glass Division
	UNIFAB	Ferro Corporation Fiber Glass Division
METALLIC YARNS	CHROMEFLEX	Metal Film Company, Inc.
	FAIRTEX	Fairtex Corporation
	LUREX	Dow Badische Company
	MALORA	Malina Company, Inc.
	METLON	Metlon Corporation
	MYLAR	E. I. duPont de Nemours & Co., Inc.
MODACRYLIC	DYNEL	Union Carbide Corporation Fibers and Fabric Division
	VEREL	Eastman Kodak Company, Tennessee Eastman Company Division
NYLON	ANTRON	E. I. duPont de Nemours & Co., Inc.
	CELANESE	Fiber Industries, Inc., Marketed by Celanese Fibers Company, Division of Celanese Corporation
	CHEMSTRAND	Monsanto Company, Textiles Division
	BLUE C NYLON	Monsanto Company, Textiles Division
	CAPROLAN	Allied Chemical Corporation, Fibers Division
	ENKA	American Enka Corporation
	QIANA	E. I. duPont de Nemours & Co., Inc.

Generic Classification	Trademark Name	Manufacturer or Source
OLEFIN	DPL	Dawbarn Division, W. R. Grace & Company
	HERCULAN	Hercules Incorporated, Fibers & Film Department
	VECTRA	Vectra Company, Division of The National Plastic Products Company, Inc.
POLYESTER	AVLIN	FMC Corporation, American Viscose Division
	BLUE C	Monsanto Company, Textiles Division
	DACRON	E. I. duPont de Nemours & Co., Inc.
	FORTREL	Fiber Industries, Inc., Marketed by Celanese Fibers Company, Division of Celanese Corporation
	KODEL	Eastman Kodak Company, Tennessee Eastman Company Division
	VYCRON	Beaunit Corporation, Beaunit Fibers Division
	IRC	Midland-Ross Corporation, IRC Fabrics Division
RAYON	AVISCO	FMC Corporation, American Viscose Division
	AVRIL	FMC Corporation, American Viscose Division
	AVRON	FMC Corporation, American Viscose Division
	BEMBERG	Beaunit Corporation, Beaunit Fibers Division
	COLORAY	Courtaulds North America, Inc.
	CUPIONI	Beaunit Corporation, Beaunit Fibers Division
	ENGLO	American Enka Corporation
	ENKA	American Enka Corporation
	ENKROME	American Enka Corporation
	FIBRO	Courtaulds North America, Inc.
	FORTISAN	Celanese Fiber Company, Division of Celanese Corporation
	JETSPUN	American Enka Corporation
	NUB-LITE	Beaunit Corporation, Beaunit Fibers Division
	PURILON	FMC Corporation, American Viscose Division
	RAYFLEX	FMC Corporation, American Viscose Division
	STRAWN	Midland-Ross Corporation, IRC Fibers Division
	ZANTREL	American Enka Corporation
SARAN	ROVANA	Dow Badische Company
	VECTRA	Vectra Company, Division of The National Plastic Products Company, Inc.
	LUS-TRUS	Southern Lus-Trus Corporation
SPANDEX	LYCRA	E. I. duPont de Nemours & Co., Inc.
	VYRENE	UniRoyal Fiber and Textile Division of UniRoyal, Inc.
VINYON	AVISCO	FMC Corporation, American Viscose Division

Yarns

Next, fibers are spun into yarns. Yarns may be made from short or "staple" fibers or from long or "filament" fibers, and the construction may be simple or complex. One of the natural fibers or one of the man-made fibers may be used alone; or two or more fibers may be blended or mixed to give durability and beauty to the fabric or to facilitate the manufacturing process. The number and size of the fibers, the tightness of the twist, the roughness or smoothness of the yarn are some of the many factors that determine the characteristics of the fabric made from the yarn.

Processing techniques can be varied to produce novelty yarns such as bouclé, ratiné, nub, seed, slub, spiral or corkscrew, or looped, which are unusual in texture or appearance or both. Textured yarns may be formed from man-made fibers. Through certain processing techniques the filaments are coiled, crimped, curled, or looped. These yarns are called textured, bulk, or stretch yarns.

Woven Fabrics

Each fabric begins with the yarn threaded lengthwise on the weaving loom. Next, the filler yarn is woven crosswise, over and under the lengthwise threads. The lengthwise yarn is called the "warp," and the crosswise or filler yarn is called the "weft" (old term "woof"). The extreme outside finished edges, which are parallel to the lengthwise yarns, are called "selvage." These woven threads form the true lengthwise and crosswise grains of the fabric.

By varying the number of yarns on a loom, it is possible to produce many different weaves and achieve interesting textures and effects. It is often difficult to distinguish one man-made fiber from another or from the natural fibers because the weaves are so much alike. Rayon may look like silk, cotton may look like wool tweed. The weave of the fabric plays a greater part in determining the appearance of the final product than fiber or finish.

Familiar Types of Weaves

Here is a description of the common types of weaves that you may be using in your sewing. These standard weaves can be varied to produce many interesting effects.

Plain· weave. In this, the simplest and most common of all weaves, the horizontal threads (weft or filler) pass alternately over and under successive vertical threads (warp). Muslin and taffeta are examples. Variations are the basket weave and the rib weave.

Twill weave. This is more closely woven than a plain weave. In it, the warp and filler threads are interlaced to form a diagonal ridge or rib on the face of the fabric. Gabardine is an example. Fancy designs can also be produced; the herringbone is a common variation.

Satin weave. Threads are interlaced at irregular intervals, with one set of threads floating over the opposite set of threads. The floats lie parallel to each other thus forming a smooth, lustrous finish. Cotton sateen and damask are examples.

Leno weave. This is a porous, open-looking weave used to produce lightweight, gauzy fabrics—for example, marquisette.

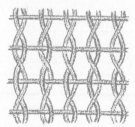

Jacquard weave. This is an intricate, figured weave made on a Jacquard loom. Examples are damasks, brocades, and tapestries.

Dobby weave. This weave is produced by placing a dobby attachment on the loom. It is simpler and less expensive than the Jacquard weave and consists of small, geometric designs that are repeated frequently throughout the fabric.

Double-cloth weave. More than one set of warp and filler yarns are used in weaving to produce a fabric with two distinct faces—for example, double damask.

Pile weave. Three sets of yarns are interlaced in such a manner that the third set forms cut loops that stand up densely on the surface. Examples are velvet, velveteen, corduroy, and plush. An exception is terry cloth, which has uncut loops, usually on both sides of the fabric.

Finishes

Many fabrics are given a "finish" after they are woven to increase their body, to prevent shrinkage (sanforized) or wrinkling (pre-cured or permanent-press type), to impart crispness to the surface, or to make them wash-and-wear, water repellent, stain resistant, mothproof, drip-dry, or crease resistant. It is unnecessary—and almost impossible—to list the many finishes manufacturers are able to produce; however, they can be described as dull, shiny, stretch, rough, soft, smooth, coarse, fine, lustrous, hard, laminated, or napped.

Napped fabrics (such as wool broadcloth, duvetyn, doeskin, and flannel) have fuzzy or hairlike fibers lying in one direction. This effect is achieved in the finishing process by a revolving brush that is used to raise the fibers of the cloth to the surface.

Stretch Fabrics

Stretch fabrics are woven fabrics that have been made to "give" with the body and then recover their normal dimensions. Do not confuse them with knit fabrics.

Stretch characteristic can be given to classic fabrics such as denim, tweed, gabardine, twill, corduroy, seersucker, batiste, and broadcloth, as well as to many of the newer fabrics. It can also be given to all-cotton fabrics; to blends with natural fibers, rayon, or acetate; or to all wool.

The amount of stretch a fabric will deliver varies; so do the processes of achieving stretch.

There are three kinds of stretch fabrics:

Lengthwise (warp) stretch, which is recommended for pants and slacks.

Crosswise (filling) stretch, which is used for blouses, shirts, jackets, coats, sport dresses, skirts, and shorts.

Lengthwise and crosswise, or two-way stretch, which is used mostly in swimsuits.

Some of the stretch fabrics are woven to look the same lengthwise as crosswise even though they stretch only in one direction. They can be used in any garment. Always examine the fabric carefully before purchasing it to be sure that the stretch goes in the direction you want. See page 218.

Stretch fabrics can be given wash-and-wear or water-repellent qualities.

Knit Fabrics

Knit fabrics are made of interlocking loops of yarn. There are two types of knit construction, warp and weft knits.

Warp knits, which are made on flat-bed machines, are generally tighter, flatter, and less elastic than weft knits. In warp knitting, multiple yarns (all part of a single system of yarns) run vertically and parallel to each other. The fabric is constructed by manipulating all of these warp yarns at the same time into loops that are interconnected. Tricot and raschel are common types.

Weft knits, which are made on either circular or flat-bed knitting machines, are constructed in much the same way as hand knits, with one yarn at a time running in a horizontal direction. The most familiar types are jersey, rib knits, double knits, and jacquards. See *The Many Faces of Knits,* page 417.

Blends and Combinations

Techniques of blending and combining fibers have revolutionized the fabric world and simplified in many ways the homemaker's life. Although most consumers apply the term "blend" to any fabric containing more than one kind of fiber or yarn, there is a difference between blends and combinations. *Blended fabrics* are made of yarns in which two or more fibers have been mixed before spinning; the yarns may be used either as warp or filler or as both. *Combination fabrics* are made by combining different yarns, each of a single fiber, in the weaving process. In other words, the warp yarn may be of one fiber and the filler of another. Examples are silk/wool; silk/cotton/linen (two or more natural fibers); cotton/Dacron polyester (natural and man-made fibers); or Orlon acrylic/rayon/nylon (two or more man-made fibers).

Bonded and Laminated Fabrics

Like blends and combinations, the terms "bonded" and "laminated" are often used interchangeably by the shopper. And they are similar in one respect—both describe fabrics that are made of two layers.

In *bonded* fabrics, two layers of fabric are permanently joined either by an adhesive or by a thin layer of urethane foam, which is heat-set to form a bond.

Although almost any fabrics can be bonded, the most common bonds are of lining and face fabric. Acetate tricot seems to be favored for the lining; the face fabric may be wool, synthetic, a blend of wool and man-made fibers, loopy tweed with a mohair look, and knits. Bonding makes lace suitable for a tailored costume; the bonded lining adds stability to the fabric and prevents stretching.

Bonded fabrics are appropriate for dresses, coats, suits, and sportswear. See page 220.

In *laminated* fabrics a backing of synthetic *foam* is bonded, or heat-set, to adhere permanently to a *face fabric*. Laminates have warmth without weight and require no interfacing; however, they should be lined to protect the foam backing. You will find laminated wool, jersey, cotton, and synthetic fabrics that are appropriate for jackets, coats, sportswear, rainwear, children's wear, and coat linings. Most of them can be washed or dry-cleaned. See page 221.

Nonwoven Fabrics

Nonwoven fabrics have no grain. They are made by pressing fibers together. Examples are felt, plastic film, Pellon, Keyback, and Interlon.

Selecting Fabric

The judgment and taste you exercise in coordinating the fabric with the pattern can determine the success of your finished product. On the back of the pattern envelope you will find a list of fabrics appropriate for the design. This is a good guide if you are in doubt.

Suits and tailored dresses require firm fabrics with body. Dresses with shirring, draping, or gathers require soft fabrics.

Remember too that a print, plaid, or design should be in proportion to your figure. A small figure should not wear large stripes, plaids, or prints. A large figure may wear large prints; however, a large plaid will emphasize figure proportions. Narrow stripes will make the figure appear taller, broad stripes will make it appear shorter. Large prints and plaids on the tall, thin figure will break the height.

The finish of the fabric also affects the appearance of your figure. For slimness, choose fabrics with a smooth, dull finish. The bulk of heavyweight or rough-finished fabrics makes the figure look larger. If handled with too much fullness, such fabrics may overpower a small figure and add weight to a full figure; simply handled they may be very flattering.

The following list will help you select suitable fabrics for various garments.

Daytime and Tailored Dresses

Jersey	Corduroy
Silk	Velveteen
Gingham	Linen
Broadcloth	Surah
Dotted Swiss	Barathea
Crepe—Silk or Rayon	Shantung
Wool Crepe	Cotton
Pima Cotton	Honan
Raw Silk	Piqué
Heavy Sheers	Tie Silk
Cotton and Dacron	Faille
Blend	Double Knit

Soft, Draped Dresses

Sheer Woolens	Chiffon
Soft Silk	Surah
Jersey	Barathea
Voile	Lace
Nylon	Velvet
Blends or Combinations	
of Natural and Synthetic Fibers	

Sportswear

Flannel	Velveteen
Denim	Gingham
Chintz	Seersucker
Sailcloth	Polished Cotton
Cottons	Stretch Fabrics
Woolens	Bonded Fabrics
Corduroy	Madras
Blends or Combinations	
of Natural and Synthetic Fibers	

Cocktail or "After 5"

Suits	Dresses
Moiré	Taffeta
Peau de Soie	Brocade
Satin	Faille Taffeta
Taffeta	Peau de Soie
Ottoman	Heavy or Firm Lace
Brocade	Velvet
Bengaline	Velveteen
Velvet	Matelassé
Velveteen	Metallic
Metallic	Surah
Matelassé	Chiffon
Wild or Raw Silk	Moiré

Evening Dresses

Lace	Peau de Soie
Chiffon	Dotted Swiss
Taffeta	Organdy
Velvet	Net
Velveteen	Brocade
Piqué	Metallic
Cottons	Surah
Sheers	Moiré
Silks	Satin

Dressmaker Suits

Linen	Tussah
Faille	Heavy Cottons
Silk and Wool Blends	Corduroy
or Combinations	Duvetyn
Silk and Cotton Blends	Seersucker
or Combinations	Double Knit
Lightweight Wool	

Tailored Suits

Woolens—
    Medium or Heavyweight

Tweed	Ottoman
Wool Broadcloth	Douppioni
Twill	Wild or Raw Silk
Flannel	Gabardine
Linen	Glen Checks
Heavy Cottons	Tussah
Silk and Wool Blends	Bengaline
or Combinations	Double Knit

Coats

Coating	Corduroy
Wool Broadcloth	Velveteen
Flannel	Suede Cloth
Camel's Hair	Fur Fabric
Vicuna	Brocade
Cashmere	Jersey Coating
Silk Faille	Worsted
Ottoman	Tweed
Nubbed Wool	Douppioni

Fabric Width

Fabric widths vary greatly, and before buying a fabric you should refer to the back of the pattern envelope to see how many yards you will need of the fabric width you have chosen. Linens, velveteens, and corduroys are 36 inches wide; cottons, 36 to 39 inches; silks and synthetics usually 39 to 42 inches; wools, 54 to 60 inches; and felts, 36 to 70 inches. Jersey is usually circular and about 56 inches all around; double knit is a flat knit about 54 inches wide. Imported silks are often only 27 inches wide and imported cottons may be 50 inches wide. Most interfacings are from 25 to 50 inches wide.

Know the Right Side of the Fabric

Simple as it may seem, knowing the right side of the fabric can be tricky.

In satins and polished cottons, the lustrous face is on the right side; in pile and napped fabrics, the longer threads or pile is on the right side. Cottons and linens are usually folded right side out. The weave of many fabrics will help you identify the right side; so will the selvage, which is smoother on the right side than on the wrong. Often you must examine the selvage closely, however, to detect the "smoother" side. Many cottons, plaids, and solid colors can be used on both sides.

Grain Lines

In any sewing you do, you must consider the grain lines of the fabric because they have a direct influence on the way the garment fits and hangs.

The *lengthwise grain* of the fabric is the thread parallel to the selvage and is known as the "warp" thread in weaving. It is marked on all pattern sections and must be observed when laying and cutting any garment or article.

The *crosswise grain* is at a right angle to the lengthwise grain; it runs from selvage to selvage and is known as the "weft" thread in weaving. In most fabrics there is some "give" in the crosswise grain, but very little in the lengthwise grain.

The *true bias* of the fabric is the diagonal line formed by folding the lengthwise grain parallel to the crosswise grain. The maximum amount of "give" in any fabric is found in the true bias.

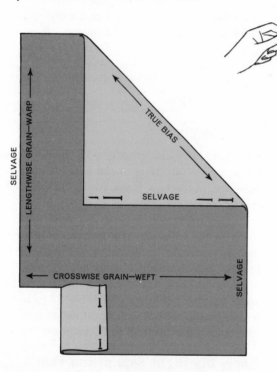

Preparing the Fabric for Cutting

Here you are concerned with three questions:
1. Are the fabric ends (crosswise grain) straight?
2. Does the lengthwise grain need straightening?
3. Has the fabric been shrunk?

Straightening Fabric Grain

In the manufacturing process—perhaps during finishing, printing, or rolling—some fabrics are pulled "off grain," and you must straighten them before

cutting the garment so that the grain lines are correct; otherwise your garment will not fit and hang as it should.

To straighten the fabric ends, find the crosswise grain of the fabric as follows:

—Snip through the selvage edge with scissors.

—With the fingers, grasp one thread that runs across the weave.

—Pull it gently, allowing the fabric to gather on the thread.

—Cut carefully along this pulled thread only as far as you can follow it clearly.

—Grasp it again (or the one next to it) in your fingers and repeat the pulling and cutting until you have reached the other selvage.

Some fabrics will tear easily and you can clip the selvage and tear quickly across from selvage to selvage to straighten the ends. However, drawing a thread is preferred because tearing sometimes pulls the fabric "off grain."

To determine whether the fabric grain needs straightening, place the fabric on a flat surface and fold it with the selvages together. Pin the edges together along the straightened end. If the fabric lies flat when the selvages are together, the two grains are at a right angle and need no further attention. If not, the fabric must be straightened.

To straighten the fabric grain is simple.

—First, straighten the ends as explained above.

—Then, gently pull the fabric on the true bias (as illustrated at the top of opposite page) and gradually work down the full length of the fabric.

—Repeat along the length, if necessary.

Pressing with steam is helpful in straightening some fabrics; or you may have to dampen the fabric and then straighten it.

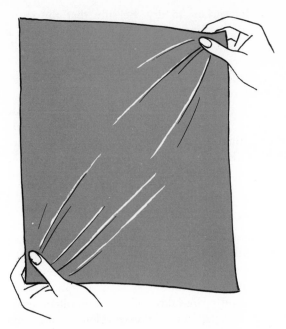

If dampening is necessary, proceed as follows:

On cottons and linens, use a damp sponge to moisten the fabric, then pull gently.

On wools, place a wet sheet over the fabric and leave it long enough to moisten the wool (about two or three hours). Be sure that the fabric lies flat and that there are no wrinkles in either the fabric or the sheet. Pull gently to straighten the fabric.

If fabrics such as chintz, polished cotton, and those with crush-resistant finish cannot be straightened because of their finish, square off the crosswise grain with a ruler. Place the fabric flat on a table with the selvage parallel to the side of the table. Lay a ruler across the cut end of the fabric so that it forms a right angle with the selvage, and draw a line with chalk from selvage to selvage; then cut on this line. Use only the lengthwise grain as a guide when cutting the garment. These fabrics are quite satisfactory as they will not lose their shape in

wearing, hanging, or pressing.

If a print or plaid is finished "off grain," the design will not match at the seamline when the garment is cut on the true grain. Examine the fabric closely before making a purchase. If it is printed "off grain," do not buy it.

Checking the Fabric for Shrinkage

Most fabrics are preshrunk and information to that effect usually appears on the descriptive hang-tag or on the selvage. Look for the labels "preshrunk," "Sanforized," or, in the case of fine wools, "ready for the needle" or "sponged."

If one of them is used, it means that the fabric will not shrink more than 1 inch per yard; if you fail to find any information, ask the saleswoman. Fabrics that have not been preshrunk must be shrunk before cutting except wool crepe and silk crepe.

To shrink a fabric, clip the edge every 2 or 3 inches along each selvage. If the selvage is not cut, it will draw up in the shrinking process.

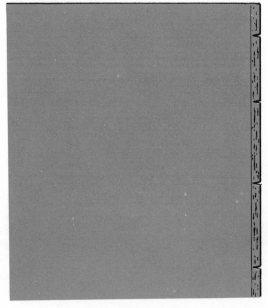

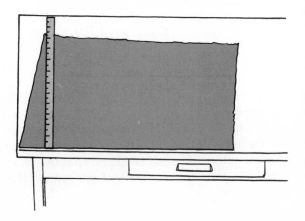

For *cottons, linens,* and other *washable fabrics,* open the fabric its full width and form deep folds (about 18 inches) on the crosswise grain. Place the fabric in the bathtub, cover it with lukewarm water, and leave it immersed for an hour. At the end of an hour, drain the water from the tub. Then press the water out of the fabric with your hands. (Do not wring or wrinkle the fabric.) Hang the fabric lengthwise over the shower rod or the clothesline. Be sure that it is straight and smooth. Remove as much water as you can with a towel. Before the fabric is completely dry, press it on the wrong side. Glide the iron with the lengthwise grain. Press out the center fold.

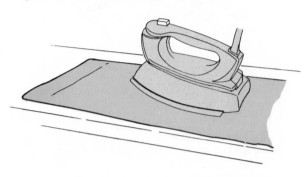

If you are uncertain about the necessity of shrinking washable fabrics, make a test: Cut a swatch on the true lengthwise and crosswise grains and make a note of its length and width. Shrink the swatch as instructed above. After pressing, measure again. If the swatch is smaller than the original size, you will have to shrink the fabric.

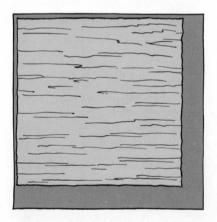

For *woolens,* fold the fabric lengthwise on the straight grain and place it between the folds of a wet sheet. Fold on the crosswise grain in deep folds. Avoid wrinkles in the fabric and wet sheet. Cover the folded sheet with a towel so that the top section will not dry, and leave for eight or ten hours. Then remove the sheet and spread the fabric on a flat surface to dry. Be sure that the grains are straight. When dry, press on the wrong side with a press cloth or cheesecloth between the fabric and iron. Press out the center fold.

(Woolens can also be shrunk by a dry cleaner if they are not "ready for the needle."

Be sure to shrink *woven interfacings* that are not preshrunk as well as *belting* and *grosgrain* ribbon that will be used in washable garments. Follow the immersion method described above.

Interfacings

Interfacing is a third thickness of a carefully selected fabric that is cut in the same shape as the section interfaced and placed between the facing and garment section.

An interfacing adds body to the collars, cuffs, facings and peplums of dresses, blouses, suits, and coats, and it adds strength to the areas around buttonholes and buttons. It is also used to mold and hold the shape in certain sections of the garment. It gives a professional look to anything that is well made.

Pattern envelopes usually include a separate pattern for the interfacing or instruct you to cut it the same as the garment section. Woven interfacing, which has a lengthwise and crosswise grain, must be cut with the same grain as the garment; non-woven interfacing has no grain and can be cut with the pattern laid in any direction.

Interfacing is available in a variety of textures and weights and should be selected with care. Consider the firmness and weight of the fabric to be interfaced as well as the style of the garment. Lay the interfacing between two layers of your fabric and manipulate the materials so that you can judge the final effect. Before buying interfacing, make sure that:

—It can be washed or dry-cleaned as the rest of the garment.

—The weight is appropriate for the fabric.

—The quality of the interfacing equals the quality of the garment fabric.

The following table shows you the variety of interfacing fabrics that are on the market. Use it as a guide only in shopping; you should examine the interfacing carefully before you buy, for several types may be correct for your garment, depending on the effect desired. Note that one fabric is missing from the list—that is self fabric, which is frequently used as interfacing, especially if the garment fabric is sheer.

FABRICS FOR INTERFACINGS

FABRIC	TYPE	DESCRIPTION	COLORS	WEIGHT	USE	CARE
Armo[1]† "Acro"	Woven	Hair canvas	Ecru	Medium	Washable dresses, suits, and coats	Machine wash-and-wear; dry-cleanable
Armo[1] P-27	Woven	Hair canvas	Natural	Light	Tailored dresses and lightweight suits	Dry-clean only
Armo[1] P-17	Woven	Hair canvas	Natural	Medium	Suits and medium-weight coats	Dry-clean only
Armo[1] P-20	Woven	Hair canvas	Natural	Heavy	Heavy suits and coats; also under-lining for bouffant jackets and coats	Dry-clean only
Armo[1] "Fino"	Woven	High-quality worsted hair canvas	Natural	Medium	Light- and medium-weight suits and coats	Dry-clean only
Armo[1] "Finolight"	Woven	High-quality hair canvas	Sand	Light	Silk and lightweight wool suits	Dry-clean only
Instant Armo[1] P-93	Woven	Hair canvas iron-on	Natural	Heavy	Heavy suits and coats	Dry-clean only
Instant Armo[1] P-94	Woven	Worsted hair canvas iron-on	Natural	Medium	Medium- and heavy-weight suits and coats	Dry-clean only
Batiste	Woven	Fine cotton	All colors	Light	Soft silk, cotton, and linen dresses and blouses	Washable; shrink before using
Bravo[2]	Woven	Canvas	Natural, white	Medium	Silk and light- to-medium-weight wool suits and coats	Dry-clean only
Bravo-Set[2]	Woven	Canvas	Eggshell	Light	Suits and coats made of silk, light- and medium-weight wools, and blends	Washable; dry-cleanable
Capri[3]	Woven	Closely woven	Black, white	Light—soft finish; Light—crisp finish	Soft silk and cotton dresses and blouses Medium-weight fabric for firm shapes	Washable; dry-cleanable
Everflex[3]	Woven	Mesh	Black, white, natural	Medium	Silk and medium-weight wool suits	Washable; dry-cleanable
Formite [Z] [1]	Woven	Sheer canvas	Black, white, natural	Medium	Dress-weight fabrics, knits, and sportswear	Washable; dry-cleanable

†Numbers indicate owners of trademark names, as shown on page 19.

(continued on following page)

FABRIC	TYPE	DESCRIPTION	COLORS	WEIGHT	USE	CARE
Hymo[2]† "Regular"	Woven	Hair canvas	Natural	Medium	Suits and medium-weight wool coats	Dry-clean only
Hymo[2] "Special"	Woven	Hair canvas	Natural	Heavy	Medium-to-heavy wool suits and coats	Dry-clean only
Interlon[2]	Non-woven	Has no grain line	Black, white	Light / Regular / Heavy	Soft, fluid shapes / Soft, yet firm shapes / Heavy fabrics—firmly molded shapes	Washable; dry-cleanable
Keybak[3]	Non-woven	Visibly porous	Black, white	Light / Medium / Heavy	Soft, fluid shapes / Soft, yet firm shapes / Heavy fabrics—firmly molded shapes	Washable; dry-cleanable
Keybak[3] Hot Iron	Non-woven	Visibly porous	Black, white	Medium	To reinforce small areas	Washable; dry-cleanable
Kyrel[4]	Non-woven	Has no grain line	Black, white	Light	Lightweight dresses and blouses	Drip-dry; dry-cleanable
Adheron Kyrel[4]	Non-woven	Iron-on	Black, white	Light	To reinforce small areas	Drip-dry; dry-cleanable
All Bias Kyrel[4]	Non-woven	Has "give" in any direction	Black, white	Very light	Loosely woven or stretch fabrics where shape is needed	Drip-dry; dry-cleanable
Lawn	Woven	Semi-sheer	All colors	Light	Soft, lightweight dresses and blouses	Washable; shrink before using
Marquisette	Woven	Mesh	All colors	Very light	To add body to delicate fabrics	Washable; dry-cleanable; shrink before using
Muslin	Woven	Medium; heavy	White or unbleached	Medium	Cotton dresses and blouses, as well as sleeve hems and bottom hems of suits and coats	Washable; dry-cleanable; shrink before using
Organza	Woven	Sheer silk	All colors	Very light	To add body to delicate chiffons and other sheer fabrics	Dry-cleanable
Pelomite[5]	Non-woven	Iron-on	Black, white	Light	To reinforce small areas	Washable; dry-cleanable

†Numbers indicate owners of trademark names, as shown on page 19.

(continued on following page)

FABRIC	TYPE	DESCRIPTION	COLORS	WEIGHT	USE	CARE
Regular Pellon[5]	Non-woven	Has no grain line	Black, white	Light / Medium / Heavy	Light, soft shapes / Light, yet firm shapes / Firmly woven shapes	Machine wash-and-wear; dry-cleanable
"All Bias" Pellon[5]	Non-woven	Has "give" in any direction	Black, white	Light, Medium	Loosely woven or stretch fabrics where shape is needed	Wash-and-wear; dry-cleanable
Poplin	Woven	Dress fabric	All colors	Medium	Soft, yet firm shapes for cottons and linens	Washable; shrink before using
Steflex[2] "All-Purpose"	Woven	Iron-on	Black, white	Medium	To reinforce small areas	Washable; dry-cleanable
Staflex-[2] for-Wools	Woven	Canvas iron-on	Natural, white	Medium	Medium- and heavy-weight wool suits and coats	Dry-clean only
Sta-Shape[2] SS/50	Woven	Tailor's canvas	Black, white, natural	Light	Medium-weight suits and coats; also underlining for bouffant jackets and coats	Washable; dry-cleanable
Sta-Shape[2] SS/65	Woven	Canvas	Natural	Medium	Medium-weight suits, coats, and tailored dresses	Dry-clean only
Sta-Shape[2] SS/77	Woven	Hair canvas	Natural	Medium	Medium- and heavy-weight suits and coats	Dry-clean only
Super Siri[1]	Woven	Closely woven	Black, white	Super soft / Soft / Firm	Cotton dresses and blouses; also used for underlining / Soft, yet firm shapes / Lightweight suits and sportswear	Machine wash-and-wear; dry-cleanable
Taffeta	Woven	Silk or rayon	All colors	Light	Soft silks and woolens; also used as underlining for lace and chiffon as well as woolens	Dry-clean only
Veriform[2] "Basic Liner"	Woven	Mesh	Black, white, natural	Medium	Heavy cottons, silks, and soft woolens; also used as underlining in suits and separate skirts	Washable; dry-cleanable

[1] David B. Carmel & Company
[2] Stacy Fabrics Corp.
[3] Chicopee Mills, Inc.
[4] Kimberly-Stevens Corporation
[5] Pellon Corporation

Underlining and Lining

Underlining and lining are a second thickness of fabric that supports the garment fabric and gives it extra resistance to strain. Both help to hold the shape of dresses, suits, coats, shorts, and at-home wear. *Underlining and Lining,* beginning on page 95, describes how to underline or line dresses of various styles and of various fabrics.

Underlining and lining should be selected with care. The fiber content need not be the same as that in the dress fabric, except in sheer fabrics; however, the colors should match.

Fabrics that are appropriate for underlining and lining—or are made expressly for them—are: silk organza, China silk, taffeta (silk or rayon), batiste, voile, peau de soie, silk crepe, silk and acetate underlining, acetate sheath lining, UnderCurrent, and SiBonne (synthetic underlining), all of which are available in colors. Silk and acetate underlining and acetate sheath lining resemble China silk but are less expensive. SiBonne is available in a soft or crisp finish. Veriform, an underlining with a soft or crisp finish, is available in black and white and is suitable for underlining or lining many opaque fabrics.

The table below suggests types of fabrics that can be used for underlining and lining different dress and suit fabrics.

DRESS OR SUIT FABRICS	SUGGESTED UNDERLINING AND LINING FABRICS
Soft silks and lightweight rayons that will be dry-cleaned	Silk organza, China silk, UnderCurrent[1], SiBonne[2], silk and acetate underlining, acetate sheath lining — all available in colors.
Heavy and medium-weight silks, wools, and rayons	Silk organza, China silk, UnderCurrent, SiBonne, taffeta, silk and acetate underlining, acetate sheath lining — all available in colors.
Cottons that will be dry-cleaned	Batiste, voile, China silk, UnderCurrent, SiBonne, organza — all available in colors. (Shrink batiste and voile.)
Sheer wools and chiffons	Taffeta, peau de soie, silk crepe, satin — all available in colors.
Lightweight wools	China silk, organza, silk and acetate underlining, UnderCurrent, SiBonne, acetate sheath lining — all available in colors.
Jersey and loosely woven fabrics	China silk, silk and acetate underlining, UnderCurrent, SiBonne, acetate sheath lining, voile, batiste — all available in colors. (Shrink batiste and voile.) If skirt is full, use taffeta.
Wool suit skirts	China silk, silk and acetate underlining, UnderCurrent, acetate sheath lining, SiBonne, crepe with which jacket is lined — all available in colors.
Linens that will be dry-cleaned	Voile, batiste, SiBonne, UnderCurrent, China silk, silk and acetate underlining — all available in colors. (Shrink voile and batiste.)
Lace	Taffeta, satin, peau de soie, polished cotton, silk organza, net, marquisette, chiffon — all available in colors.

Some of the fabrics suggested for interfacing are also used for underlining and lining, particularly for gored and circular skirts and suits and coats that are bouffant—for example, hair canvas, Siri, Pellon, or Veriform "Basic Liner."

[1] UnderCurrent—Trademark of David B. Carmel & Company
[2] SiBonne—Trademark of Stacy Fabrics Corp.

Beginning To Sew

IF YOU ARE A BEGINNING SEAMSTRESS, you may sometimes think that your sewing machine was built only to outwit you. But be patient. This carefully constructed piece of equipment requires some understanding. Those of you who have sewn for a while know that if you take a little time to master your machine, you will have a versatile and willing partner in creativity.

GETTING TO KNOW YOUR MACHINE

The operation of any sewing machine is simple if you understand the function of the principal parts and know how to thread the machine and regulate the three elementary controls: tension, pressure, and stitch length. Your instruction book contains information on these essential points. Do not hesitate to refer to it frequently.

The principal parts of the *Touch & Sew°* sewing machine by Singer are illustrated below. Although your machine may be of a different model or make, it has many features in common with all machines, and the explanations that follow will be applicable to it.

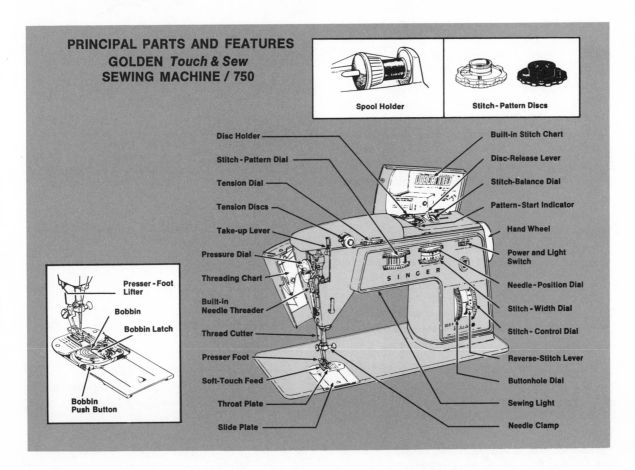

PRINCIPAL PARTS AND FEATURES
GOLDEN *Touch & Sew*
SEWING MACHINE / 750

Spool Holder

Stitch-Pattern Discs

Disc Holder
Stitch-Pattern Dial
Tension Dial
Tension Discs
Take-up Lever
Pressure Dial
Threading Chart
Built-in Needle Threader
Thread Cutter
Presser Foot
Soft-Touch Feed
Throat Plate
Slide Plate

Presser-Foot Lifter
Bobbin
Bobbin Latch
Bobbin Push Button

Built-in Stitch Chart
Disc-Release Lever
Stitch-Balance Dial
Pattern-Start Indicator
Hand Wheel
Power and Light Switch
Needle-Position Dial
Stitch-Width Dial
Stitch-Control Dial
Reverse-Stitch Lever
Buttonhole Dial
Sewing Light
Needle Clamp

SINGER

Threading the Machine

In threading the machine, you are concerned with four operations: (1) winding the bobbin, (2) threading the bobbin case, (3) threading the needle (or upper threading), and (4) raising the bobbin thread. Always follow the diagram shown in the instruction book given with your machine.

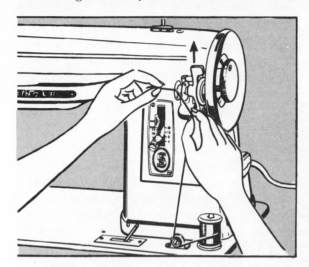

Winding the bobbin. Many machines have the conventional bobbin winder on the right hand side as in the illustration above. The *Touch & Sew* machine, which is illustrated on page 21, has push-button bobbin winding—that is, you wind the bobbin with the needle thread without removing it from the machine. Refer to your instruction book.

Here are the basic rules:

1. Start with an empty bobbin so that the new thread can pass through the eyelet on the side. *Never wind one color over another.*

2. Select a thread identical to the one used for upper threading.

3. Wind it evenly in level layers across the bobbin.

4. Do not wind the bobbin so full that it will be tight in the bobbin case; it should fit in easily.

If you observe these rules, you will find that the bobbin thread will feed evenly to the very end of your stitching. This is important because it influences the quality and regularity of your stitch.

Threading the bobbin case. On some machines the bobbin thread leads off in a clockwise direction; in others it is counterclockwise. Refer to your instruction book and follow the directions carefully. If you thread the bobbin case improperly, the thread will usually slip out of the threading notches and from under the tension spring.

Threading the needle. Upper threading is simple if you follow this sequence:

1. Raise the take-up lever to its highest point.

2. Lead the thread from the spool pin through the threading points as shown in diagram—(1) thread guide, (2) needle-thread tension discs, (3) thread guide, (4) take-up lever, (5) thread guides, and (6) needle. The direction for threading the needle varies. Some machines are threaded from left to right, others from right to left, and others from front to back.

3. Draw enough thread through the eye of the needle to start sewing.

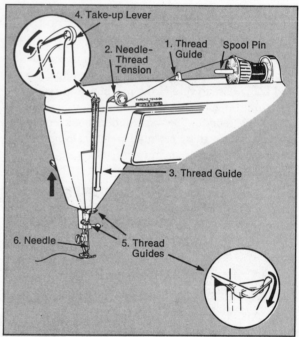

Raising the bobbin thread. You must now draw the bobbin thread through the needle hole in the throat plate. To do that:

1. Hold the needle thread lightly with the left hand.

2. Turn the hand wheel toward you until the needle goes down and up again and the take-up lever returns to its highest point.

3. Pull the needle thread; the bobbin thread will follow and form a large loop.

4. Undo the loop with your finger.

5. Place both needle and bobbin threads under the presser foot and lay them diagonally to the right.

You are now ready to sew. If you want to begin at once, turn to page 27, which starts you off with a simple seam.

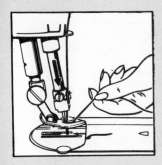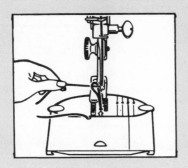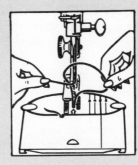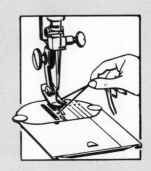

Regulating Stitch Length

The length of your stitch depends on the weight and texture of the fabric you are sewing as well as the type of sewing you are doing. Form the habit of testing the stitch length on a swatch of the fabric.

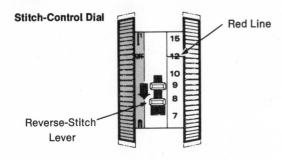

Stitch-Control Dial · Red Line · Reverse-Stitch Lever · 15 12 10 9 8 7

Delicate fabrics require a *short, fine stitch*.

Heavy fabrics require a *long, heavy stitch*.

For topstitching, the stitch length should be shorter than inside stitching when fine thread is used, longer when heavy thread is used.

Curved seams require a shorter stitch than that used for straight stitching. If you are using a 12 stitch length for straight stitching, you will need a 15 stitch for curves to give the seams greater elasticity and strength.

Bias and *semi-bias cut seams* also require a short stitch since they must have more elasticity than seams following the lengthwise or crosswise grain of the fabric.

Scallops require a shorter stitch than curves to maintain a smooth, rounded contour and permit close blending of seams.

Bound buttonholes and *pockets* are made with a short stitch to ensure strength and durability—generally a 20 stitch length.

When stitching is used to *control fullness* at the sleeve cap, at the elbow of long sleeves, at the top of a hem, or at a point where one seam edge is eased to another, a slightly longer stitch is required than the one used for straight stitching.

The three types of *temporary stitching* require different stitch lengths. For regular machine basting, use a 6-to-8 stitch length. For chainstitching, which is available on some sewing machines, use a 10-to-12 stitch length. For speed basting, which is also available on some models, you have a wide choice. You can choose any length from 6 to "fine" and produce a basting stitch up to 2 inches long.

In some *zig-zag sewing*, such as decorative satin stitching and buttonholes, use a "fine" stitch setting. For other zig-zag sewing, use longer stitches.

If you compare different grades of clothing, you will notice that quality garments are stitched with a short stitch and appropriate weights and types of thread and that economy clothing is often stitched with a longer stitch and less durable thread.

To determine the stitch length appropriate for your fabric, test the stitch on a swatch of fabric.

For directions on setting the stitch length selector on your machine, check your machine instruction book as well as the diagram shown here. A stitch length selector that is clearly marked is easy to set.

Selecting the Thread

The rules that guide thread selection are easy to observe:

Select a thread two shades darker than the fabric. Since thread on the spool appears to be darker than it actually is, draw a strand over the fabric to make sure you have the right color.

Select the proper thread for your fabric. There are three types of general-purpose thread: polyester core with mercerized cotton wrap, mercerized, and spun polyester. When fine thread is appropriate, choose silk, nylon twist, or fine spun polyester for lingerie.

When stitched, the thread must set into the weave of the fabric. A thread that is too heavy will remain on the surface and give shorter serv-

FABRIC	THREAD	NEEDLES	
		TYPE	SIZE
DELICATE — tulle, chiffon, fine lace, organza	Fine mercerized cotton Fine synthetic thread	Catalog 2020 (15x1)	9††
LIGHTWEIGHT — batiste, organdy, jersey, voile, taffeta, crepe, chiffon velvet, plastic film	50 mercerized cotton "A" silk Synthetic thread Polyester core/cotton	Catalog 2020 (15x1)	11
MEDIUM WEIGHT — gingham, percale, pique, linen, chintz, faille, satin, fine corduroy, velvet, suiting, knits, deep-pile fabrics, vinyl	50 mercerized cotton 60 cotton "A" silk Synthetic thread Polyester core/cotton	Catalog 2020 (15x1)	14
MEDIUM HEAVY — gabardine, tweed, sailcloth, denim, coatings, drapery fabrics, vinyl, deep-pile fabrics	Heavy-duty mercerized cotton 40 to 60 cotton Synthetic thread	Catalog 2020 (15x1)	16
HEAVY — overcoatings, dungaree, upholstery fabrics, canvas	Heavy-duty mercerized cotton 24 to 40 cotton Synthetic thread	Catalog 2020 (15x1)	18
ALL WEIGHTS — decorative top stitching	"D" silk††† (Buttonhole twist)	Catalog 2020 (15x1)	18
ALL WEIGHTS — decorative hemstitching	50 mercerized cotton "A" silk Synthetic thread	Catalog 2020 (15x1)	18
SYNTHETIC KNITS AND STRETCH FABRICS — polyester double knit, nylon tricot, jersey, spandex, ciré tricot, panné velvet	"A" nylon 50 mercerized cotton "A" silk Polyester core/cotton	Catalog 2045 Ball Point (Yellow Band) Catalog 2021 Ball Point	14 11
LEATHER — suede, kidskin, capeskin, lambskin, lined leathers	50 mercerized cotton Synthetic thread "A" silk Polyester core/cotton	Catalog 2032 (15x2)	11 14 16
LIGHT AND MEDIUM WEIGHTS — decorative twin-needle stitching	50 mercerized cotton	Catalog 2028 (twin)	14

†Does not apply to chainstitching. ††Size 9 needle recommended for sewing only. For bobbin winding, use larger size needle. †††Use with 50 mercerized cotton or "A" silk in bobbin.

ice and less strength than a fine thread that imbeds itself in the texture of the fabric.

Consult the chart above for further suggestions on thread selection.

Selecting the Sewing Machine Needle

In selecting the needle, remember that: (1) You must consider both the thread and the fabric. (2) The eye of the needle must be large enough for the thread to pass through freely; a needle too fine for the thread will cause the thread to fray. (3) The needle blade must be fine enough to enter the fabric without marring it with a large puncture, yet heavy enough to pierce the fabric without being bent or deflected. (4) A needle too fine for the fabric may break.

Regular, general-purpose needles are available in sizes 9, 11, 14, 16, and 18. Ball-point needles, which separate the yarns rather than piercing them when penetrating the fabric, are recommended for knits. A special wedge-point needle is available for sewing real and fake leather fabric.

Always have a supply of all sizes on hand to meet your needs. A bent needle causes the fabric to draw to one side, feeding in a curve rather than a straight line. A blunt needle can cause pulls in the fabric.

Also take care to position the needle properly in the needle clamp. If you do not, your machine will skip stitches or not stitch at all.

Refer again to the chart above for further information on needle selection.

Regulating the Pressure

Pressure is the force the presser foot exerts on the fabric when it is being stitched. Pressure is important because it influences the straightness of your seams, the uniformity of stitch length, and the even handling of both layers of fabric. The pressure should be heavy enough to prevent side creepage and light enough to carry the fabric without marking it. *Too light a pressure* will cause irregular feeding, which affects the quality of the stitch and evenness of seams. *Too heavy a pressure* will affect the stitch length and seam quality and mar a smooth surface or pile fabric.

Regulate the pressure according to the fabric. Generally, heavy fabrics require heavy pressure; medium-weight fabrics require pressure midway between light and heavy; and lightweight fabrics require light pressure. Surface finish and texture must also be considered; soft fabrics, for example, require less pressure than crisp.

To test for pressure, take two layers of fabric cut on the lengthwise grain and stitch without thread. If all seam edges are handled evenly, the pressure is correct; if they are not, turn the pressure dial or thumb screw until they are and until the fabric moves easily under the presser foot without showing feed marks.

To decrease pressure, turn the thumb screw counterclockwise.

To increase pressure, turn the thumb screw clockwise.

If you have a Singer machine with a pressure dial inside:

To decrease pressure, turn the dial to a lower number.

To increase pressure, turn the dial to a higher number.

PRESSURE DIAL

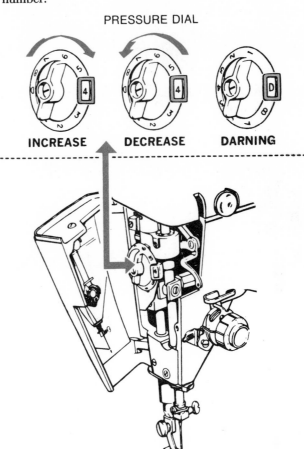

INCREASE   DECREASE   DARNING

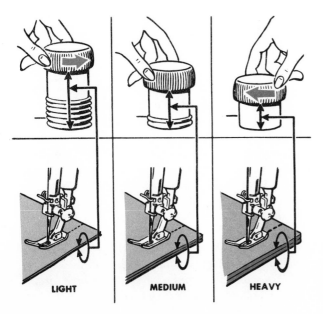

LIGHT   MEDIUM   HEAVY

Regulating the Tension

Tension controls the threads as they interlock to form a stitch on the sewing machine. There are two tensions—the upper, which controls the needle thread, and the lower, which controls the thread from the bobbin case or shuttle. A perfectly locked stitch can be formed only when the two tensions are in balance and the two threads are drawn into the fabric to the same degree. The tensions should be heavy enough to pull the threads to the center of the fabric and form a good stitch.

Both tensions correct

To determine whether your tension adjustment is correct, test the stitch on a scrap of your fabric with the needle and thread you are going to use. You will find that a seam stitched with balanced tensions is twice as strong as one stitched with unbalanced tensions. It is easy to verify this by making the following **strength-of-seam test:**

—Use a size 14 needle.

—Thread the machine with size 50 mercerized thread, using a light color for the upper threading and another color for the bobbin.

—Set a stitch length at 10 or 12.

—On a square of fine muslin or the equivalent, stitch on the bias and on both the lengthwise and crosswise grains.

—Inspect the lines of stitching. They should not pucker and the stitch formation should appear well set on the top and underside of the muslin. If the lines of stitching pucker, you are likely to find also that they are not equally set on the top and underside and look like this:

Loose upper tension
Tight lower tension

Tight upper tension
Loose lower tension

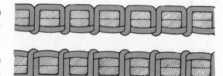

—*To determine whether the upper tension is too tight or too loose,* use the following test. Grasp the bias line of stitching between the thumb and index finger. Space the hands about 3 inches apart and pull with an even, quick force until one thread breaks. If the broken thread is the color of the needle thread, you know that the upper tension is too tight. If the broken thread is the color of the bobbin thread, you know that the upper tension is too loose. If both threads break together and require more force to break, you know the tensions are balanced.

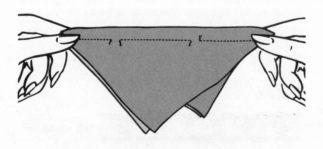

To decrease tension, turn the thumb nut counterclockwise. Each lower number denotes less tension.

To increase tension, turn the thumb nut clockwise. Each higher number denotes increased tension.

TENSION DIAL

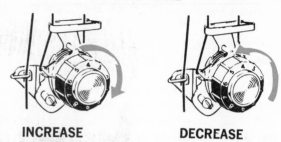

INCREASE   DECREASE

—Repeat the test until both threads break together.

Bobbin-thread tension. The tension on the bobbin thread is regulated by the small screw on the bobbin case or shuttle. It is seldom necessary for you to change it since you can usually obtain a balanced stitch by varying the tension on the needle thread.

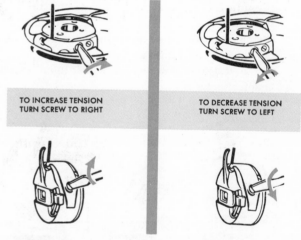

TO INCREASE TENSION
TURN SCREW TO RIGHT

TO DECREASE TENSION
TURN SCREW TO LEFT

Here are some simple rules to guide you in adjusting the upper tension for different types of threads and fabrics:

To sew with silk thread. Set the upper tension from one to two points lower than when stitching with mercerized thread. The bobbin tension remains the same.

To sew with heavy cotton or linen thread. In general, increase the upper tension when sewing with this weight of thread on dense fabrics. The bobbin tension remains the same.

To sew with certain sewing machine accessories. Follow the instructions given in this book for the specific accessory. Sometimes an adjustment of the upper tension is necessary.

To sew on zig-zag machines. Loosen the upper tension when doing decorative, closely spaced satin stitches. Wide, closed stitching requires a lighter needle-thread tension than narrow stitching. See page 266.

To stitch special fabrics. Nylons, dense fabrics, polished cottons, some resin-treated wash-and-wear fabrics, and others of similar close weave usually require tension adjustment. Always test your stitch on a scrap of your fabric.

YOUR FIRST STEPS IN SEWING

Your machine is threaded and ready to go. If this is your first venture into serious, creative sewing, you should allow yourself a period of practice before you try a pattern.

First, familiarize yourself with simple stitching. Work carefully and correctly from the start. The good habits you form now will make all your later work easier and more professional looking. Proof of your efficient handling of the sewing machine will be found not only in an evenly controlled acceleration of the machine and a perfectly formed and positioned first stitch in a seam, but in the exact assembling of seams, collars, facings, and pockets, and a competence in all the intricate details of sewing.

Begin your practice period with the "exercises" described here.

Posture and Speed Control

Correct posture at the machine enables you to work comfortably and well. Follow these rules:

1. Sit back on the chair or stool squarely in front of the needle. Do not lean against the chair back; instead, bring your body forward slightly.

2. Place both feet flat on the floor, with one foot forward. If your machine has a knee control, place the left foot forward and press the right knee against the control. If your machine has a foot control, place the right foot forward and press on the control.

3. Position the bulk of the fabric to the left of the needle and the seam edge to the right.

4. Place the left hand lightly on top of the fabric so that your fingers can control it. Make sure that the weight of your left arm is not resting on the fabric since this will cause uneven feeding.

5. Place the right hand 3 or 4 inches in front of the needle so that your fingers can guide the edge.

6. Gradually press on the foot or knee control until you reach a slow, even speed. Never try to sew too fast. Skillful machine operation depends on your ability to sew easily, rhythmically. You can work up to a high speed later when you are stitching long, straight seams.

How to Start and End a Seam

To start and end a seam, take these steps in sequence:

1. Raise the take-up lever to its highest point by turning the hand wheel toward you.

2. Place both needle and bobbin threads under the presser foot and lay them diagonally to the right.

3. Place the fabric under the presser foot with the bulk of the fabric to the left and the seam edge to the right.

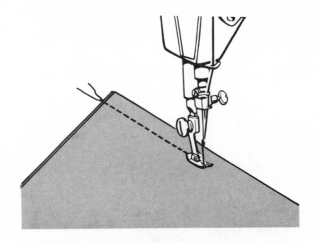

4. Lower the needle into the fabric where the first stitch is to begin. Hold the thread ends and lower the presser foot.

5. Stitch with a slow, rhythmic speed.

6. When you reach the end of the seam, turn the hand wheel to raise the take-up lever to its highest point.

7. Raise the presser foot and removed the fabric by drawing it to the back and left.

8. Clip the thread ends on the thread cutter.

The Seam Guide and throat plate guidelines will help you keep the stitching parallel to the seam edge. See page 81.

How to Reinforce a Seam with Backstitching

Follow the procedure described on previous page. At step 4, lower the needle into the fabric about ½ inch from the seam end and backstitch to the end of the fabric. Then stitch forward to end of the seam and finish with backstitching to reinforce the end.

How to Guide and Support the Fabric

Most fabrics need to be guided only in front of the presser foot. Exceptions are fabrics of unusual

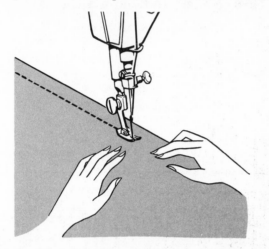

texture and weave, filmy sheers, crepes, knits, tricots, and the like. For them, gently apply tension

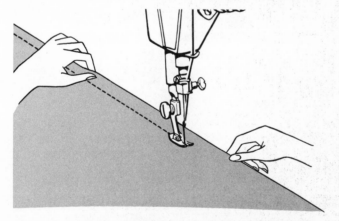

to the seam by holding the fabric in front and in back of the presser foot as illustrated at bottom of previous column. Never pull the fabric when sewing. If you are sewing fabric of unusual texture on a zig-zag machine, use the straight-stitch throat plate and presser foot for close control.

How to Pivot

You need to "pivot" when stitching corners on collars, lapels, shaped necklines, bound buttonholes, and pockets. Here is what you do:

1. Stitch to the interesecting seamline at the corner.

2. With the needle in the fabric, turn the hand wheel forward to bring the needle to its upward stroke. Just before the needle leaves the fabric, raise the presser foot and turn the fabric, pivoting on the needle.

3. Lower the presser foot and stitch.

4. To avoid bulk at the point of a collar or lapel, take from one to three stitches diagonally between the intersecting lines of stitching. See page 91. Practice pivoting a few times. You will find that it is easy.

How to Stitch Curved Seams

Curved seams should be stitched slowly. To guide the fabric on small curves, such as scallops, stop the machine with the needle in the fabric, lift the presser foot slightly, and turn the fabric just enough to follow the seamline.

Practice stitching and guiding straight seams, curved seams, and corners until you have mastered them.

The chapter beginning on page 81 tells you how to make many different kinds of seams.

BASIC TECHNIQUES FOR HAND SEWING

Some hand sewing is required in almost all the work you will be doing. If you already know how to sew by hand, check yourself against the guides given here. You may find some suggestions that will improve your technique or your deftness.

Threading the Hand Needle

1. With sharp scissors, cut the thread end on an angle. Avoid breaking, biting, or tearing the thread, for then you will have trouble threading it through the needle eye.

2. Hold the needle in the left hand and the thread end tightly in the right hand between the thumb and index finger. Then pass the thread through the needle eye, and with the same motion, transfer the needle into the grip of the right thumb and index finger. With the left hand, draw the thread end from the eye about halfway down the remaining supply of thread.

3. Always sew with a short thread. For finishing stitches, use less than a 24-inch length; for basting, use a slightly longer thread. A thread that is too long will tangle and weaken from being pulled through the fabric repeatedly; also, it requires tiring arm motions to draw each stitch in place. With the exception of sewing on buttons, snaps, and hooks and eyes, you will seldom need to use a double thread in hand sewing. Some prefer a single thread for all operations.

Tying a Knot

To prevent the longer thread end from pulling through at the beginning of the stitching, form a secure knot as follows:

1. Hold the thread end between the thumb and first finger of the left hand.

2. Use the right hand to bring the thread over and around the finger tip of the left hand, crossing it over the thread end.

3. Hold the longer thread taut while pushing the thumb toward the finger tip. This causes the thread to roll around the loop.

4. Slip the loop off the finger tip and at the same time pull against the longer thread held in the right hand to set the knot.

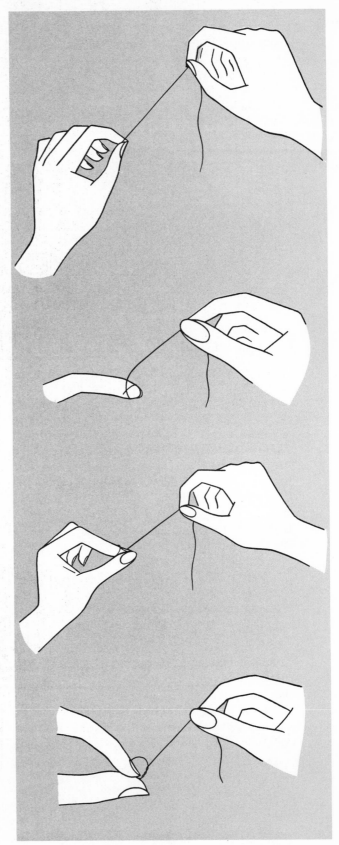

Using a Thimble

Do not allow yourself to develop the habit of sewing without a thimble. A thimble will prevent your finger from being roughened and sore and will enable you to sew better and faster.

Thimbles are available in sizes 5 to 12 in both metal and plastic. It is easy to select an inexpensive one that fits your finger snugly.

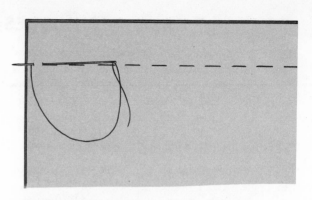

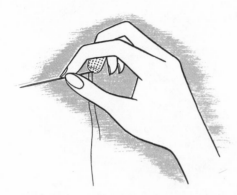

The thimble is worn on the second finger of the right hand and is used to direct and force the needle through the fabric. At first it may seem to be awkward and uncomfortable. If so, make hand stitches on a heavy, dense fabric such as drill cloth. You immediately will feel the need for the protection a thimble gives. If you continue to find sewing with a thimble awkward, make sure you are using a needle of appropriate length for the work you are doing. In general, use a long needle for long stitches or running stitches and a short needle for short, single stitches. Check the description of needles on page 2 to determine the best size and style for your work.

Fastening Stitches

The fastening stitch is used at the end of a line of basting to hold the stitches in place. To fasten a line of basting, take one short backstitch. This is easy to remove when the permanent stitching has been completed.

To fasten a line of fine hand stitching, bring the needle through to the underside. Take one backstitch, catching only a single thread in the fabric;

pull the needle through, leaving a small loop in the thread. Take another small backstitch, then pass the needle through the thread loop of the first stitch and set the knot close to the fabric. Repeat if greater security is needed.

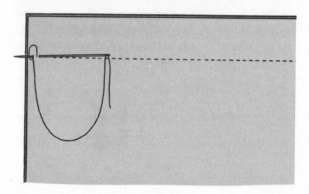

Removing Kinks and Twists

The simple process of pulling thread through fabric often causes the remaining supply of thread to twist. Some threads twist more readily than others —for example, buttonhole twist. And some hand sewing operations, such as fine overstitching, tend to cause greater twisting and kinking than straight running stitches.

To remove the excessive twist without unthreading the needle, merely hold the thread end in the left hand while sliding the needle down against the fabric. Then without holding the thread end, slide the needle upward on the thread to a sewing position. This motion pushes the extra twist to the end of the thread and the remaining work can be completed without troublesome knotting and kinking.

Pattern Preliminaries

Buying the right pattern is a challenge, for it requires that you reconcile the often conflicting demands of fashion, figure, practicability, and purse. Selecting the correct size may pose a prob- lem too, especially if you are buying a pattern for the first time.

Read carefully the suggestions given here. They offer practical guides to keep you out of trouble.

SELECTING A PATTERN STYLE

Whatever you make should reflect current style and fashion. With that in mind:

Study the fashions in magazines, newspapers, and store windows as well as in the pattern cata- logs. Choose a pattern from the latest fashions *but do not follow fashion blindly.* The extremes in high fashion are attention getting but quickly out- dated.

Look for lines and styles that dramatize your best points. Do not be misled by an attractive style modeled by a 20 year old if you are twice that age, or by a style that emphasizes all the wrong proportions of your figure. Remember that vertical lines give an illusion of tallness, a full skirt draws attention to large hips, a bloused bodice makes a full bust look larger, and a "V" neckline makes a pointed chin more pronounced.

Consider wearability, practicability, and pur- pose. Can the garment be worn year-round? Will it be fashionable for more than one season? Will it require special accessories? Does it suit the occasion?

If you already have the fabric, be careful to choose a pattern that suits its texture and weight.

DETERMINING THE CORRECT PATTERN SIZE

Clothes that look well, fit well. And proper fit begins with the selection of the correct pattern size. To determine that, take body measurements accurately. Wear a good foundation garment, the lingerie you normally wear, and the same style of shoes you will wear with the finished garment.

Taking Your Measurements

Measurements must be taken with the correct lo- cation of these seams in mind:

The *shoulder seam* begins at the neckline, 1 inch behind the ear lobe, and extends across the top of the shoulder to the arm joint.

Side seams are perpendicular to the floor, hang- ing straight from underarm to lower edge. Locat- ing this seam is known as "forming a plumb line" from the underarm.

The *natural armhole, or armscye, seam* falls straight down from the arm joint for 2½ to 3 inches, depending on size, then curves under the arm about 1 inch below the armpit.

The natural neckline or beadline hugs the base of the neck closely, crossing just above the pit of the throat and the prominent vertebra at the back of the neck.

The waistline is the smallest part of the torso. To locate it readily when taking your measure- ments, pin a ¼-inch tape or elastic around your waist before you start. Always measure *to* the bot- tom of this tape for bodice length and *from* the bottom for skirt length.

The bustline measurement is taken across the fullest part of the bust and from the back, with the tape very slightly raised.

The bodice length is measured from the shoulder seam at the neckline, over the fullest part of the bust, to the waistline.

The hipline measurement is taken over the full- est part of the hips and from the front. If the distance from waistline to hipline (measure at side seam) varies from the standard 7 inches, show the correct figure on your measurement chart.

Recording Your Measurements

The illustrations below show you exactly where to take the measurement for each part of your body. *Measure from the right side, unless otherwise indicated,* and enter each measurement in the space provided on the Measurement Chart. As your figure changes with time, correct the recorded measurements.

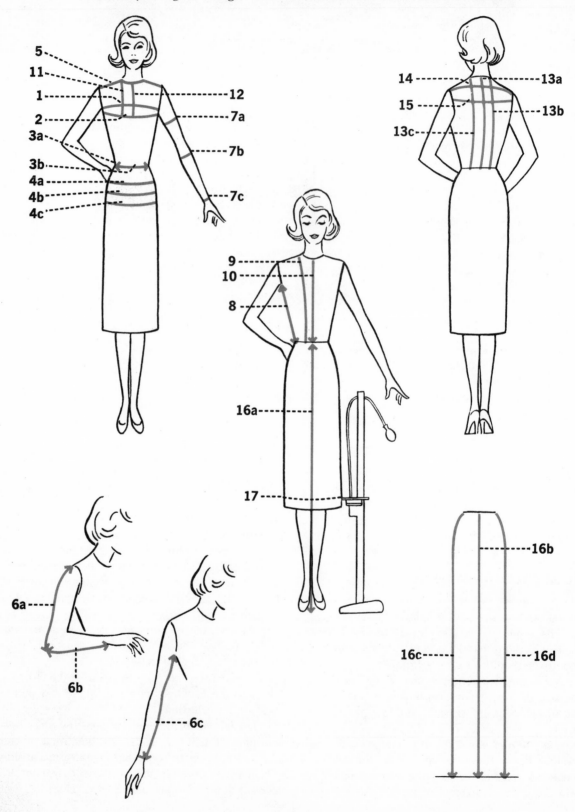

MEASUREMENT CHART

	YOUR OWN MEASUREMENT (INCHES)	USUAL ALLOWANCE FOR EASE (INCHES)	PATTERN MEASUREMENT† (INCHES)
1. CHEST — Tape straight across back			
2. BUST — Fullest part; tape slightly higher in back		3	
3. WAISTLINE —			
a—Locate natural waistline. Place tape or elastic band around waist		1	
b—Across front, side seam to side seam			
4. HIPLINE —			
a—3″ below waist; mark with pins			
b—7″ below waist		2	
c—9″ below waist		2	
5. SHOULDER LENGTH —			
Neck to seam line — Right			
Neck to seam line — Left			
6. SLEEVE LENGTH —			
a—Shoulder to elbow			
b—Elbow to wrist			
c—Inside from underarm seam to wrist			
7. SLEEVE WIDTH —			
a—Upper arm		2 to 3	
b—Lower arm (below elbow)			
c—Wrist			
8. UNDERARM TO WAISTLINE —			
1″ below armpit — Right			
1″ below armpit — Left			
9. SHOULDER TO WAISTLINE — H.P.††		½ to 1	
10. CENTER FRONT — Neck to waistline			
11. SHOULDER TO BUSTLINE — H.P.††			
12. CENTER FRONT TO BUSTLINE			
13. BACK LENGTH —			
a—Neckline to waistline		½ to 1	
b—Shoulder (H.P.††) to waistline—Right			
c—Shoulder (H.P.††) to waistline—Left			
14. SHOULDER TO SHOULDER			
15. BACK WIDTH — 4″ below neckline with arms forward and raised slightly		½ to 1	
16. FULL LENGTH — Waistline to floor			
a—Center front			
b—Center back			
c—Left side			
d—Right side			
17. SKIRT LENGTH PLUS HEM ALLOWANCE			

†Consider seam allowance in checking with pattern
††Highest point

Basic Rules for Pattern Size

Pattern sizes are based on actual body measurements and allow enough ease for comfort and proper fit. The amount of ease will vary with the style and with the manufacturer. Some pattern companies may allow more ease than others; however, this does not mean that you cannot use all makes of patterns.

Pattern sizing has recently been changed to correspond more closely to standard ready-to-wear sizing. However, patterns with former sizing may be available for some time. All patterns using the new sizing will be clearly indicated on the envelope.

Generally, you will take one or two sizes larger in a pattern than in ready-to-wear. Check your measurements with those on the back of the pattern envelope, and *select your pattern by bust measurement* and make any needed adjustments in other places. It is easier to adjust the waist and hip than the shoulder and bust. (Remember that an "up-lift" bra will very often raise the bustline enough to measure a size larger.)

If, however, the bust is larger in proportion to the other measurements, take a chest measurement. If the difference between bust and chest is 4 inches or more, buy your pattern one size smaller than the bust measurement and enlarge it through the bust. The smaller size is recommended for this reason: It is important that your pattern fit well through the shoulders and armholes; therefore, to retain shape and fit, that area should be changed as little as possible. If you buy a pattern by the larger (bust) measurement, you will also have to cope with a longer shoulder line and deeper armholes than you may need. The smaller size pattern, however, will probably match your measurements more closley.

If only the bust is large in proportion to the rest of your body, and if you prefer not to alter the bustline, buy two patterns, one by bust measurement, the other a size smaller. Use only the front bodice of the larger pattern and all other pattern pieces of the smaller pattern. Increase the darts at underarm, shoulders, and waistline so that the front and back sections are equal at the seams.

For skirts. In general, select the pattern by waist measurement. However, if hips are full, buy the pattern according to hip measurement since it is easier to adjust the waistline than the hipline.

For pants. Buy the pattern according to hip measurement.

Always purchase the same pattern size for dresses, suits, and coats.

TYPES OF PATTERNS AVAILABLE TO YOU

Girls'	Size 7 to 14	Designed for underdeveloped figure. **Not an age.**
Young Junior/Teen	Size 5/6 to 15/16	Designed for the developed pre-teen and teen figures; about 5'1" to 5'3" without shoes.
Junior Petite	Size 3JP to 13JP	Designed for the well-proportioned, petite figure with shorter waist and larger bust than the Junior pattern; about 5' to 5'1" without shoes.
Junior	Size 5 to 15	Designed for the well-proportioned, short-waisted figure; about 5'4" to 5'5" without shoes.
Misses'	Size 6 to 18	Designed for the well-proportioned, developed figure with normal waist length; about 5'5" to 5'6" without shoes.
Women's	Size 38 to 46 (sometimes to 48 and 50)	Designed for the larger, more fully mature figure; about 5'5" to 5'6" without shoes.
Half-Size	Size 10½ to 20½ (sometimes to 24½)	Designed for the shorter woman with fully developed figure and a short backwaist length. Waist and hips are larger in proportion to bust than the "Misses'" and "Women's" patterns. About 5'2" to 5'3" without shoes.

Types of Patterns Available to You

To lessen the need for pattern adjustment, pattern companies have designed patterns *proportioned to conform with many figure types.*

The table on the opposite page, which was made up from information found on the last pages of pattern catalogs, calls your attention to what is available. This is a general summary; not all companies show these exact proportions for each figure type. The illustration below shows the difference in pattern proportion.

Pattern companies have also developed *patterns that combine two sizes in one pattern.* This should make it easier for certain figure types to obtain the right fit. Two of these improvements are discussed here.

The standard size pattern with cutting guidelines for two sizes of patterns (your size and the size smaller or larger). If you measurements require the smaller size bodice and the larger size waistline and hipline, you can use the cutting guidelines that agree with your figure proportions. This is only one example of the possible combinations you may select for the two sizes.

The standard size pattern with additional cutting guidelines for a smaller and a larger size at waistline and hipline. You can use the cutting guidelines that conform to your measurements.

Each of these pattern innovations also has complete instructions for other combinations of bust, waist, and hip measurements.

The difference in pattern proportions is illustrated below in five front-bodice patterns for different figure types. Size 12 is used for each except the "Junior," which is size 11, and the "Half-Size," which is size 12½.

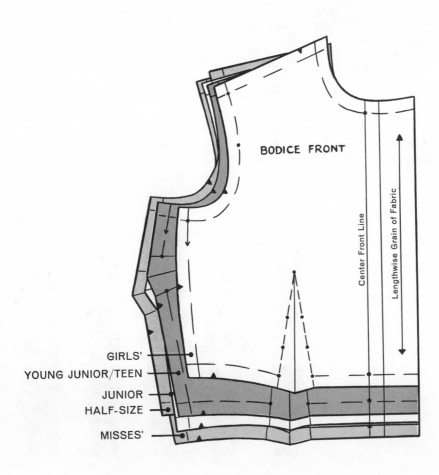

GIRLS'

YOUNG JUNIOR/TEEN

JUNIOR

HALF-SIZE

MISSES'

BODICE FRONT

Center Front Line

Lengthwise Grain of Fabric

Recognizing Your Figure Type

It is important that you recognize your figure type before selecting your pattern size. Each figure illustrated in the two groups here measures the same in the bustline; however, height, width of shoulders, hips, and height of bustline differ. It can readily be seen that certain pattern adjustments will be necessary. If the proper pattern is selected, however, those adjustments can be kept to a minimum.

Study the illustrations and find the figure type that most closely approaches yours. Use the size and adjustment suggestions as a guide.

In the first group shown, each figure type is Size 12, but figure proportions are quite dissimilar.

Average figure should select Size 12 "Misses'" pattern since she has no figure problem.

Short figure with small waistline and high bust should select the "Junior" pattern, Size 11.

Tall figure should select Size 12 "Misses'" pattern and lengthen both bodice and skirt.

Figure with wide shoulders and narrow hips should select Size 12 "Misses'" pattern and widen the bodice through the shoulders and narrow the skirt through the hips.

Figure with large hips and narrow shoulders will probably obtain a better fit by selecting Size 10 "Misses'" pattern and enlarging through the hips.

Figure with narrow hips and average shoulders should select Size 12 "Misses'" pattern and narrow the skirt through the hips.

Each figure type illustrated in the group at the bottom of the page is Size 40. The pattern size is proportioned for the more mature figure.

Average figure should select Size 40 "Women's" pattern since she has no figure problem.

Short figure with narrow shoulders and large waistline should consider the "Half-Size" pattern, Size 20½.

Tall figure should select Size 40 "Women's" pattern and lengthen both bodice and skirt.

Figure with a high, large bust should select Size 38 "Women's" pattern and adjust the bustline in both width and length.

Figure with a low bust and large waistline and hips should select Size 40 "Women's" pattern and lower the dart at underarm and enlarge through waistline and hips.

Figure with narrow hips and broad shoulders should select Size 40 "Women's" pattern and widen the bodice through the shoulders and narrow the skirt through the hips.

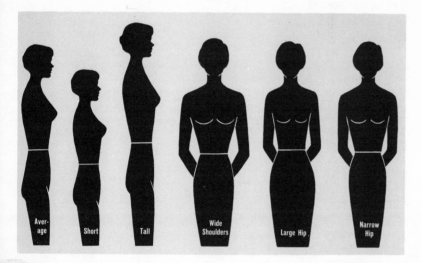

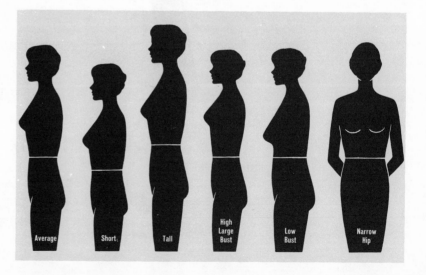

Plate 1
Decorative bands and borders
add individuality to simple clothes.
Left: Three decorative stitch
patterns accent a child's linen dress.
Right: A combination of
stitch patterns turns a
simple faille top into a
Russian peasant
blouse.

Above:
Satin zig-zag
stitch and an open
stitch pattern form a leaf
design on double organdy hem.

Left: Black velveteen diamonds
appliquéd on wool in the style of Chanel.

Right: A combination of stitch patterns used both
to apply and to decorate metallic braid on chiffon.

Plates 2 and 3   **Varied table fare**

Above left: Diamond stitch pattern motifs arranged in flower-like design.

Above right: Shadow appliqué of white and a single shade of green organdy; various layers are cut away to obtain two shades of green.

Below left: Linen appliquéd on organdy.

Below right: Linen appliquéd band. First a band of background color is appliquéd in the center of a dark green band and the arrowhead stitch pattern is centered. The decorative band is then appliquéd across the ends of the place mat.

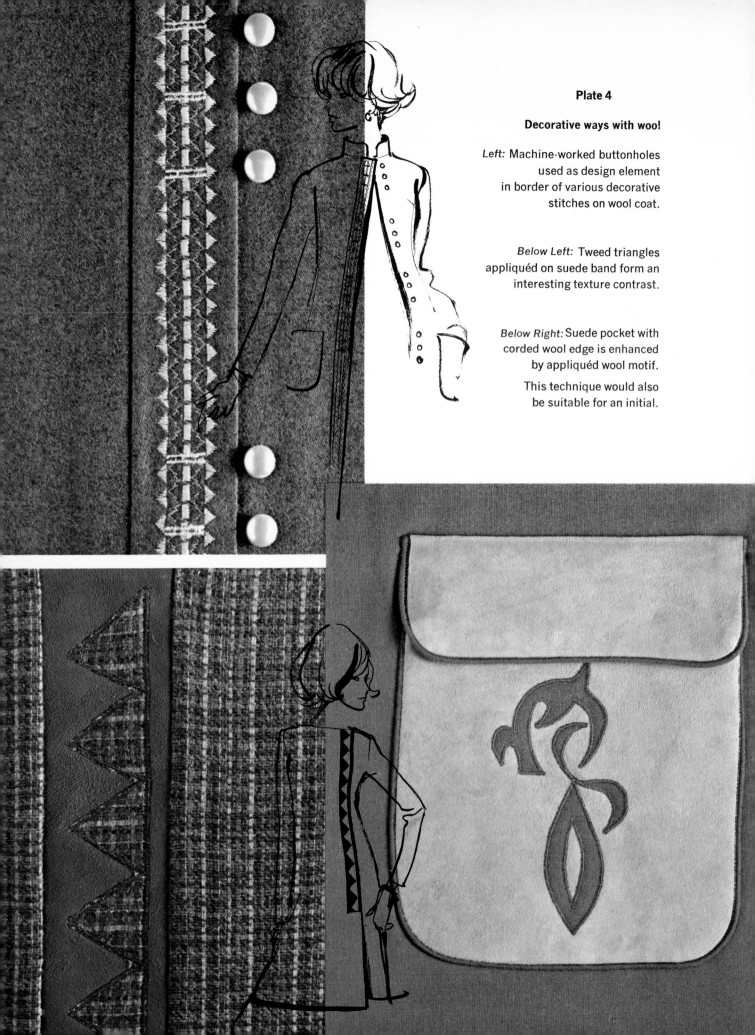

Plate 4

Decorative ways with wool

Left: Machine-worked buttonholes used as design element in border of various decorative stitches on wool coat.

Below Left: Tweed triangles appliquéd on suede band form an interesting texture contrast.

Below Right: Suede pocket with corded wool edge is enhanced by appliquéd wool motif.

This technique would also be suitable for an initial.

Fitting the Pattern to Your Figure

ALL THE WORK you have done so far has been a build-up to the steps you are about to take. For now you are ready to open the pattern envelope and begin.

To bring the pattern into complete conformity with your figure, proceed as follows:

1 Check the pattern against the measurements you recorded on your chart

2 Try on the tissue pattern

3 Adjust the pattern where necessary.

CHECKING THE PATTERN AGAINST YOUR MEASUREMENTS

The pattern envelope shows different versions of the pattern. Choose the one you prefer, and then read carefully the pattern guide inside the envelope. Select the pattern pieces you need for the version you have chosen and replace the others in the envelope.

Press all pattern pieces with a lukewarm iron

to remove the creases. Be careful not to use too hot an iron, for it will cause tissue patterns to curl.

Measure the pattern from seam allowance to seam allowance in the same places that body measurements were taken. When there is no center seam or opening, measure from seam allowance to center line. *Never include seam allowances in pattern measurements.*

When comparing the pattern measurements with your body measurements, do not expect them all to match exactly. All pattern companies allow ease for comfort and body movement, and some allow more than others. In addition, some styles call for more ease than others. To make sure that you retain the style of the design, as well as the necessary ease, *do not overfit.*

The check list below indicates where pattern measurements should be the same as body measurements and where you should allow for ease. Compare the pattern measurements with your own—allowing for ease where required—and note any necessary adjustments on the pattern. In noting your adjustments, remember that only half the

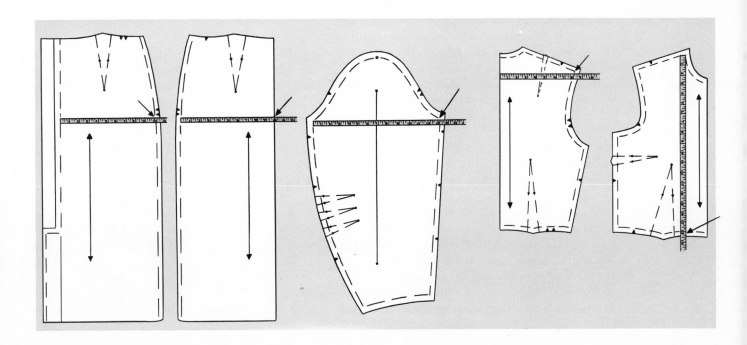

pattern in given. Therefore, in all girth measurements, make *one-fourth* the amount of the adjustment in the front section and *one-fourth* in the back section. If only the front or back section requires changing, make *one-half* the amount of the adjustment in the one pattern section.

Shoulder length must be identical to your body measurement. Measure length of shoulders on the pattern front, not on the back, since the back shoulder seam has ease or a dart.

Across the back, from armhole to armhole, allow ease for freedom of arm movement.

In the bustline, allow between 2 and 3 inches for ease, depending on the style of the pattern. A smoothly fitted garment will require 3 inches of ease; a loosely fitted one, a little more. For a strapless evening dress or sun dress, where you need just enough ease to breathe freely, 2 inches should be sufficient. In such dresses, additional darts are usually provided at the upper edge for ample freedom across the bustline and a snug fit at the upper edge.

The waistline should fit snugly. Add about 1 inch to your total measurement. However, this may be adjusted according to individual preference.

The length of the pattern from shoulder to waistline must be from ½ to ¾ inch longer than the body measurement. Some pattern styles require as much as 2 inches for ease.

Darts must conform with the contour of your figure. If they are poorly fitted, your dress will be uncomfortable and will not look well. For specific instructions on the correct position of darts, see page 100.

Buttons and buttonholes should be spaced in harmony with the individual figure. If you lengthen or shorten the pattern, or change the bustline, change the spacing of buttonholes. If you plan to use buttons larger than the size designated on the pattern, make the proper allowance in the measurement between the center line and the finished edge. This is fully explained under *Position of Buttonhole,* page 107.

The high hipline measurement, which falls about 3 inches below the waistline, requires a minimum ease of 1 inch in girth.

The regular hipline measurement, which usually falls about 7 inches below the waistline, requires between 2 and 4 inches for ease. Allow enough ease so that you can sit down without straining the seams. A skirt that fits too tightly will rip at the seam or cause the woven threads in the fabric to separate. When you are sitting, it will wrinkle across the front; when you are standing, it will

cup under the buttocks.

The length of the skirt pattern should be the measurement from waistline to hemline plus sufficient allowance for the hem.

TRYING ON THE TISSUE PATTERN

Although a tissue pattern fits a little differently from the fabric, this fitting will enable you to prove that the pattern adjustments you noted are necessary. It will also help you determine whether the style is suitable for your figure type.

In every step of fitting, wear a good foundation garment, the lingerie you normally wear, and shoes with the correct heel height.

To prepare the tissue pattern for fitting, trim the pattern margins from the armhole and neckline seams. Pin in darts, tucks, and ease allowance. Pin shoulder seams, side seams, and seams within the bodice or skirt sections by placing pattern sections, wrong sides together, with seam edges even. Place the pins parallel to the seamline, taking the seam allowance indicated on the pattern (usually ⅝ inch). Pin bodice and skirt sections together.

Try the pattern on the right side of the figure. If shoulder pads or shapes will be worn in the garment, slip them in place under the tissue pattern.

Check the fit. The shoulder seam should be directly on top of the shoulder, and side seams should hang straight from armpit to lower edge. If the pattern has a set-in sleeve, the underarm seam of the armhole should fall at least 1 inch below the armpit. If this seam is fitted too high, it is uncomfortable; if fitted too low, it causes strain across the sleeve. A round, high neckline should fit snugly. The pattern has an extended seam allowance, which makes the neckline seem smaller than it will be in the finished dress.

ADJUSTING THE PATTERN

Rules to Remember

1. When you need to lengthen or widen a pattern, use tissue paper for the adjustment. Cut it 1 inch wider than the adjustment so that the pattern will overlap the tissue ½ inch on each side of the adjustment.

2. Pin the pattern to the tissue, placing the pins parallel to the adjustment. If the pattern is one you may use more than once, machine-baste after pinning.

3. When making a pattern piece smaller with the use of tucks or darts, remember that the width of the tuck or dart should be just half the amount to be removed.

4. When making pattern pieces wider or narrower, and only half the pattern is given, divide the amount of the adjustment into fourths, and add or subtract one-fourth in both the front and the back of the pattern. If only a front or back section requires adjustment, add or subtract one-half the amount of the adjustment in the section that needs it.

5. Always measure the pattern again after making adjustments.

To Lengthen the Pattern

Slash across the pattern on the printed lengthening line. Place a piece of tissue underneath. Spread the pattern the necessary amount and pin it to the tissue. Keep the grain line straight. If the grain line does not extend as far as the lengthening line, extend it the full length of the pattern before slashing. Adjust the facing the same amount.

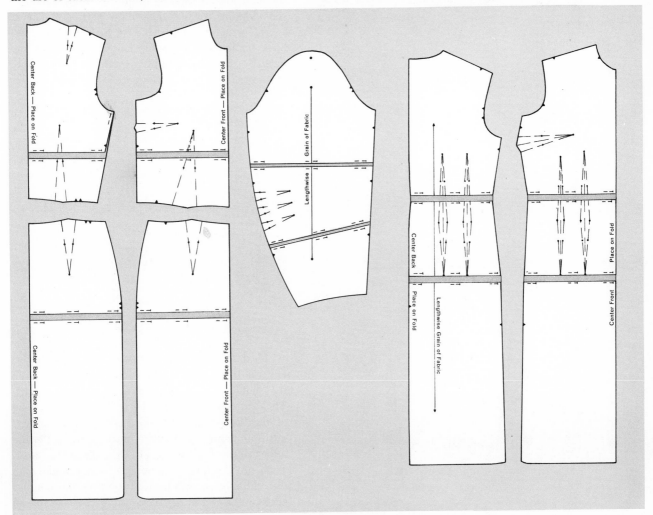

To Shorten the Pattern

Fold the pattern on the printed shortening line and pin in a tuck, even in width, of the necessary amount. Remember that the width of the tuck should be just half the amount to be removed. For example, to shorten a pattern ½-inch, make a ¼-inch tuck. Keep the grain line straight. Adjust the facing the same amount.

Full Bust

When a pattern fits everywhere except over a very full bust, buy the pattern by chest measurement and adjust the bustline. You will need extra length and width. Two methods are shown:

Method 1: With shoulder dart (Below left) Draw a line from the center of the waistline dart to the fullest part of the bust and another from the shoulder to the fullest part of the bust. Then draw a horizontal line across the fullest part of the bust. Place a large piece of tissue underneath and slash the pattern on these lines. Pin the upper center section to the tissue and spread the pattern, using the point where the lines cross as a pivot. Add the necessary amount on the horizontal line and one-half the amount needed on the vertical line. Pin the remaining three sections in position. Keep the grain line straight and the pattern flat. Adjust the facing the same amount on the horizontal line.

To take up excess width, add a dart at the shoulder as indicated by the dotted lines. The dart should point toward the fullest part of the bust. Increase the underarm dart so that the front and back bodice are the same length; keep waistline darts the same length but increase the width (note the dotted lines). Trim the outer edge of the tissue.

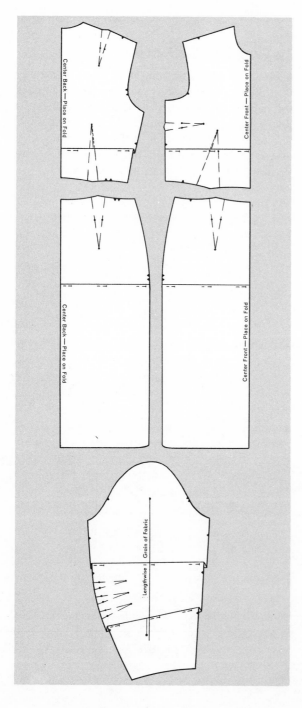

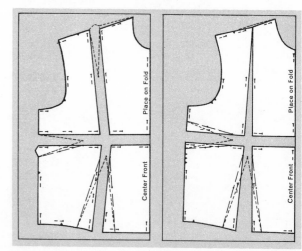

Method 2: Without shoulder dart (Above right) Draw a line over the fullest part of the bust from the shoulder to the center of the waistline dart. Then draw a horizontal line across the fullest part of the bust. Place a large piece of tissue underneath and slash the pattern on these lines. Pin the upper center front section to the edge of the tissue. Then pin the lower center front section, allowing the additional length necessary. Bring the shoulder edges of the two upper sections together and spread

the pattern at the bustline, adding one-half the width necessary. Pin to tissue. Spread the lower side section and pin to tissue. Keep the grain line straight and the pattern flat. Adjust the facing the same amount on the horizontal line.

Keep underarm and waistline darts the same length but increase them the necessary amount in width, as shown by the dotted lines. Straighten the shoulder line. Trim off the outer edges of the tissue.

Flat Bust

Adjust the necessary amount by folding a tuck across the chest, decreasing in width at the armhole. Pin in place. Make a corresponding dart in front of the sleeve so that the armhole and sleeve will fit correctly. Remember, the width of the dart is just half the amount to be removed.

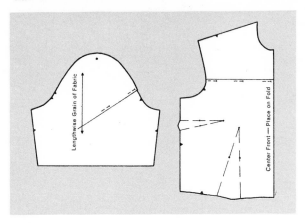

Hollow Chest

Fold a dart across the chest, tapering toward the armhole. Pin in place. Remember, the width of the dart is just half the amount to be removed. Straighten the center front as shown by the dotted lines. No sleeve adjustment is necessary since the point of the dart ends at the armhole.

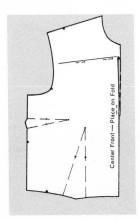

Low Bust

A low bust requires lowering the dart at the underarm. Slash across the pattern the length of the dart, about 1 inch below the armhole; then slash down toward the waistline. Place the tissue underneath and pin it to the pattern at the upper edge of the slash. Slide the dart section down until the point of the dart is aligned with the fullest part of the bust. Pin to tissue. Form a tuck in the pattern below the dart so that the pattern will lie flat.

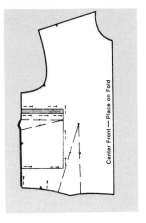

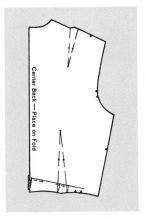

Erect Back (Above)

Slash across the pattern just above the waistline. Lap and pin the slashed edges the necessary amount, tapering to a point at the side seam. Straighten the center back and dart as illustrated by the dotted lines.

(Continued)

If the pattern is too long from shoulder to armpit, pin a tuck across the shoulder. Dart the back of the sleeve to correspond with the bodice so that the sleeve and armhole will fit correctly. Straighten the grain line on the sleeve as indicated by the dotted lines.

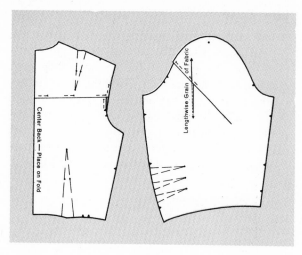

Round Shoulders

Slash across the pattern from the center to the armhole at the fullest part of the back. Place the tissue underneath and raise the pattern at the neck to add the necessary amount across the shoulders. Add the amount required at center back to keep it straight. Pin the pattern to the tissue. Fold a dart at the neckline to take up the amount added and to retain size.

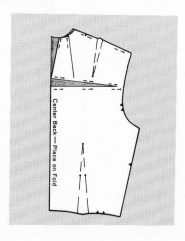

Square Shoulders

Slash across the pattern front and back, from the armhole toward the center, just below the shoulder line. Place a piece of tissue underneath and raise the shoulder line the necessary amount. Pin the pattern to the tissue. Raise the armhole at the underarm the same amount to retain size. Straighten the dart at the shoulder as illustrated by the dotted lines.

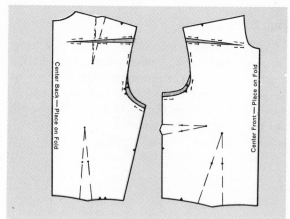

Sloping Shoulders

Slash across the pattern front and back, from the armhole toward the center, just below the shoulder line. Lap and pin the slashed edges the necessary amount at the armhole, tapering to a point. Lower the armhole the same amount at underarm to retain the shape and size of the armhole as illustrated by the dotted lines. Straighten the shoulder dart.

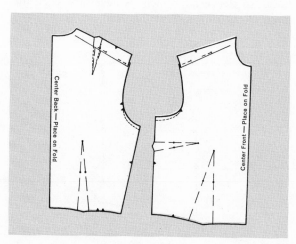

Broad Shoulders

Slash the pattern front and back, from the center shoulder down as far as the armhole notches. Then slash across almost to the armhole edge. Place the tissue underneath and spread the outer edge of the shoulder the necessary width. Pin the pattern to the tissue. Straighten the shoulder line as illustrated by the dotted lines.

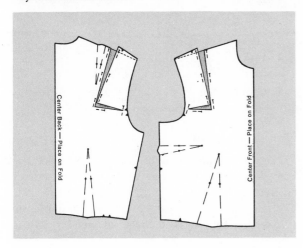

For kimono sleeves, place a large piece of tissue under pattern front and back, and cut it the same shape as the shoulder and sleeve of the pattern. Slash the pattern from shoulder to waistline. Spread the pattern and add the necessary amount at the shoulder. Bring the slashed edges together at the waistline. Pin the pattern to the tissue. Adjust the sleeve edges as illustrated by the dotted lines and the tissue to retain the original contour.

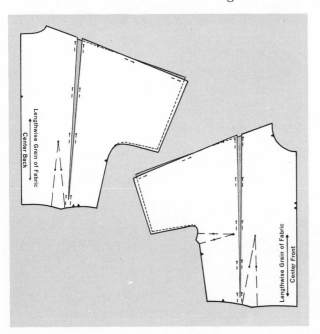

Narrow Shoulders

Slash the pattern front and back from the center shoulder line diagonally to the notches in the armhole. Lap and pin the slashed edges the necessary amount at the shoulder. Adjust the shoulder seam as illustrated.

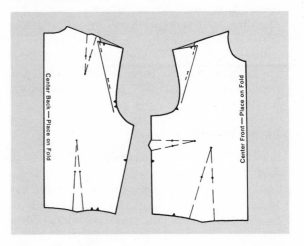

For kimono sleeves, place the tissue under the pattern front and back and cut it the same shape as the shoulder and sleeve of the pattern. Fold and pin a dart at the shoulder to take up the necessary amount. Adjust the edges to retain the original shape, as illustrated by the dotted lines.

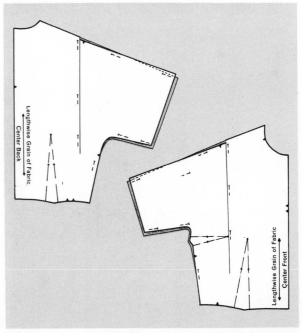

To Lengthen Back Bodice (Right)

If you need extra length in the back and under-arm but not in the front below the bust, slash across the back bodice on the lengthening line. Place the tissue underneath and spread the pattern the necessary amount. Pin it to the tissue. Slash across the front bodice almost to the center line. Place the tissue underneath and spread the pattern at the underarm seam the same amount as the back bodice, tapering to a point at the center front. Pin the pattern to the tissue. Straighten the center front, front darts, and side seams, as illustrated by the dotted lines.

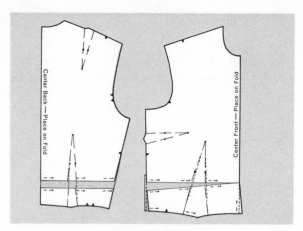

Large Waistline

For this you must adjust both the bodice and the skirt. To adjust the bodice, slash the pattern front and back from the waistline toward the shoulder. Place the tissue underneath. Spread both front and back bodices to add the necessary width. Divide the required amount into fourths and add one-fourth to each section. Pin the pattern to the tissue.

To adjust the skirt, slash the pattern front and back from the waistline down toward the hipline. Place the tissue underneath and spread the pattern to correspond with the bodice section. Pin the pattern to the tissue.

When the fullness is only at the front or back, add one-half the amount of the adjustment to only the one pattern section.

Small Waistline

Take up the same amount in both the bodice and the skirt in the front and back of the pattern by increasing the depth of each waistline dart or tuck. To decrease the waistline 1 inch, for example, increase the two darts in the front and the two in the back ⅛ inch in depth.

If you need to decrease still more, take up at the side seams. Either make the side seams deeper or slash the pattern, bodice and skirt, from the waistline and lap the slashed edges the necessary amount. A seam allowance ¼ inch deeper at the sides, or a ¼-inch lapped slash will decrease the waistline 1 inch.

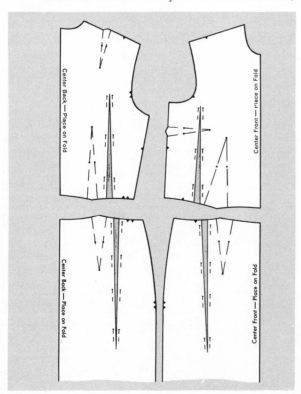

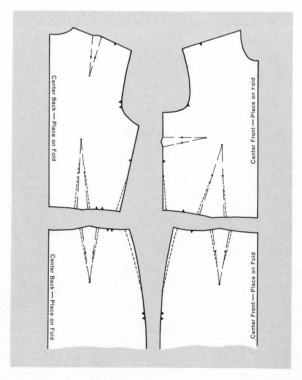

Large Arm

On each side of the sleeve, draw a horizontal line about 3 inches long, beginning at the underarm; from this, draw a vertical line to the lower edge on each side. (If the sleeve is short, carry the vertical slash to the end of the sleeve.) Slash on these lines and place the tissue underneath. Spread the pattern, adding one-half the necessary amount on each side. Pin the pattern to the tissue.

To adjust the armhole seam, slash from the armhole almost to the waistline on the front and back bodice. Place the tissue underneath and spread the pattern sections to correspond with the sleeve adjustment. Adjust the armhole seam as illustrated.

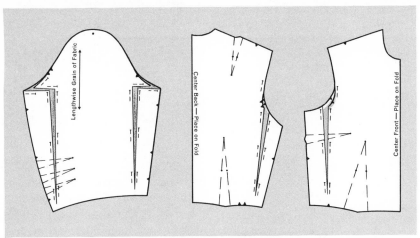

Large Upper Arm

To enlarge the upper part of the sleeve, use either of these methods:

Method 1: Place the sleeve over tissue of the same size and trim the tissue to match the cap of the sleeve. Slash the pattern from the shoulder line to the lower edge. Then spread each side of the pattern to add the additional width. Pin the lower sections of the pattern to the tissue. Bring the slashed edges of the cap together at the top and fold a dart on each side so that the pattern will lie flat. Pin the pattern to the tissue. Keep the grain line straight. Lower the armhole in the bodice at the underarm to fit the adjusted sleeve.

Method 2: Slash the sleeve from the shoulder line to the lower edge. Place the tissue underneath and spread the pattern to add the necessary width. Pin the pattern to the tissue. Lower the armhole in the bodice at the underarm to fit the adjusted sleeve.

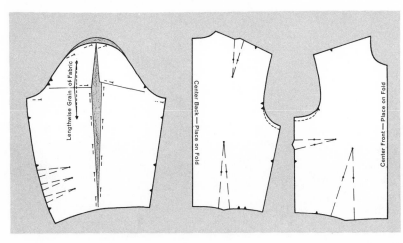
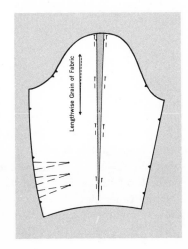

Small Arm (Below left)

Fold a small tuck, lengthwise, through the center of the sleeve and increase the underarm seam the necessary amount. Raise the armhole at the underarm the same amount so that the sleeve and armhole will fit correctly, as illustrated for "Square Shoulders," but omit the slash to raise the shoulder line.

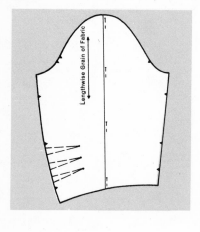

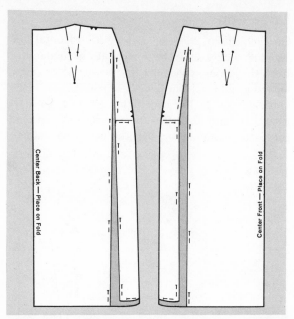

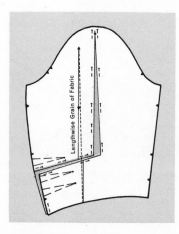

Fullness at Elbow (Above right)

Extend the grain line the full length of the sleeve. Slash the sleeve across the elbow to the center; then slash up to the top of the sleeve. Place the tissue underneath and spread the pattern the necessary width. Pin the pattern to the tissue. Increase each dart by dividing the number of darts into the amount of the increase.

Straighten the grain line by drawing a straight line between the two ends as illustrated by the dotted lines. Increase the outer edge at the elbow as shown.

Full Hips (top of next column)

Slash the front and back skirt, near the side seams, from the lower edge to the waistline. Keep the grain line straight. Place the tissue underneath and pin it to the inside edge of the slash. Spread the outer edge of the pattern to add the necessary width at the hipline. Add one-fourth the amount needed to both the front and the back of the skirt. Pin the other slashed edge of the pattern to the tissue from the waistline to the hipline. Form a dart in the pattern below the hip, tapering to the

side seam, as illustrated, to remove excess fullness at the lower edge. Pin the edge to the tissue below the dart. Add the necessary length to the lower outside edge to compensate for the dart.

Narrow Hips

Remove excess width from the skirt front and back and divide the amount into fourths. At the hipline, form a lengthwise tuck in the skirt front and back to take up one-fourth the amount in each section. Taper the tuck to a point at the waistline but keep it the same width from hipline to lower edge. Make the adjustment near the side seam to avoid crossing darts and grain line.

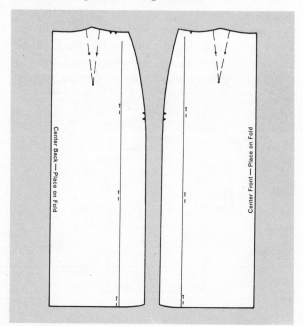

Large Derrière

Extend the grain line the full length of the pattern. To add width across the hips and length at the center back, draw a line through the center of the waistline dart to the hemline. Draw another line from the center back to the side seam at the fullest part of the hips. Place the tissue underneath. Slash the pattern on the drawn lines. Spread the upper sections of the pattern to add one-half the necessary width across the hips. Pin the edges to the tissue.

Spread the lower center section to add the necessary length to the center back. Pin it to the tissue. Spread the lower outside section to add length and width; join the upper and lower sections at the seam edge. Pin to the tissue. Form a dart below the hipline to avoid excess fullness at the hem edge. Pin lower section to tissue. Add length to the lower outside edge, as illustrated, to keep the pattern even.

Adjust darts to fit the waistline, and straighten the seamline at the point of adjustment, as illustrated by the dotted lines.

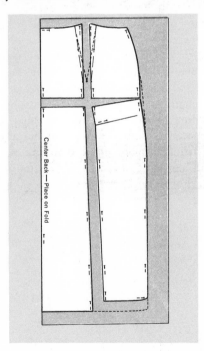

Swayback

Use either of these methods:

Method 1: Slash across the skirt from the center back to the seam edge about 2 inches below the waistline. Lap and pin the slashed edges at the center back (usually about ½ inch), tapering to a point at the seamline. Use cellophane tape to hole the point in place. Add, as illustrated, to the center back to keep it straight. Straighten darts as shown by the dotted lines.

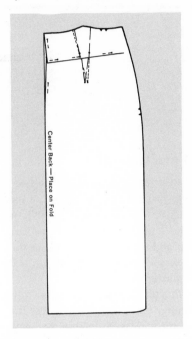

Method 2: You may also adjust for a swayback after you have cut the skirt. To do that, measure ½ inch down from the waistline edge of the fabric at the center back and place a pin. Then form a line with pins, gradually tapering to the seam edge at each side, as illustrated. Baste along this line. Do not trim off the edge at this time. In fitting and joining the skirt to the bodice, form a seam ⅝ inch below the basted line. Trim off the excess seam allowance after you have made the permanent line of stitching.

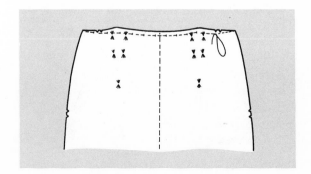

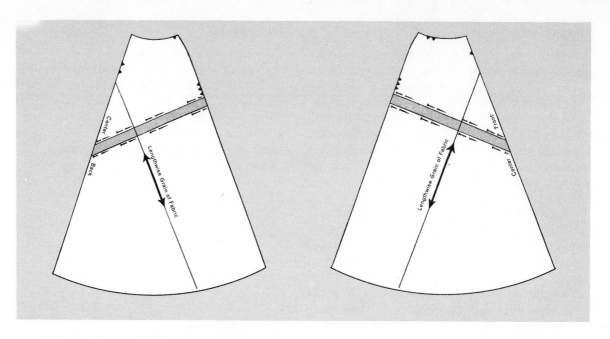

Gored or Flared Skirt

To lengthen. Extend the grain line of the front and back skirt the full length of the pattern. Draw a line across the pattern at a right angle to the grain line and slash on this line. Place tissue underneath and spread the pattern far enough to add the necessary length. Keep the grain line straight. Pin the pattern to the tissue.

To shorten. Follow the same instructions for lengthening, but fold a tuck across the pattern to take up the necessary length. Remember that the width of the tuck is just half the amount to be removed.

To enlarge waistline. Slash the front and back pattern sections lengthwise, from the waistline to the lower edge. Place tissue underneath. Spread the pattern and add one-fourth the necessary width to both the front and the back. (When extra width is needed at the waistline, it is usually needed the entire length of the skirt to retain the grain line and contour of the pattern.)

If the skirt has a matching bodice, make corresponding adjustments in the bodice. See *Large Waistline*, page 44.

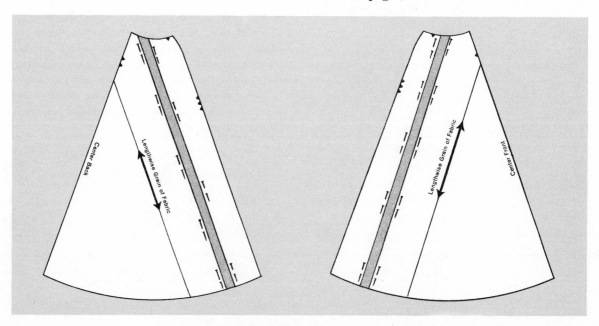

Shorts and Slacks

Buy the pattern by the hip measurement and make adjustments in the crotch and waist as illustrated below.

Method 1, Model seated: Measure at the side seam from the waistline to the chair seat. (Chair seat should be firm). Add ½ inch for ease on small sizes and 1 inch on large sizes. *Recommended for the average figure.*

To measure the pattern, extend the grain line on the front and back sections the full length of the pattern. Draw a line at a right angle to the grain line, from the point where the seams join at the crotch to the side seam, as illustrated. Measure the pattern from the waistline to the drawn line as shown. If there is a difference in pattern and body measurements, adjust both the front and the back pieces. Pin the pattern pieces together and try on.

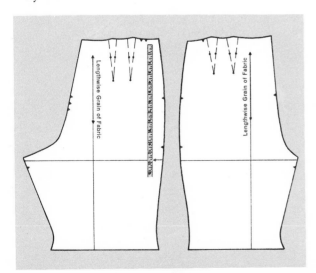

Method 2, Model standing: Measure the crotch from the front waistline, between the legs, to the back waistline. Add 3 inches for ease. *Recommended for the rounded figure.*

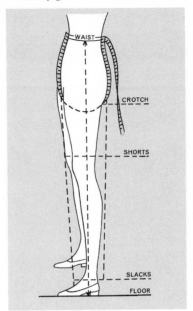

To measure the pattern, pin the front and back sections together at the crotch. (Fold under the seam allowance on one side and lap over the seam allowance on the other). Measure around the crotch from the back waistline to the front waistline *at the seamline* not the seam edge. (Stand the tape on edge to get an accurate measurement of the curve of the crotch.) If there is a difference between body measurement and pattern measurement, adjust as follows:

If the figure is equally proportioned, adjust both front and back. If the figure is large in the back,

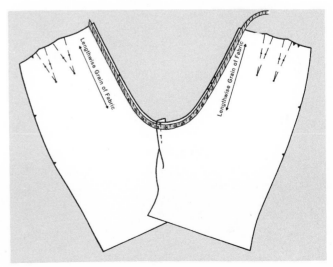

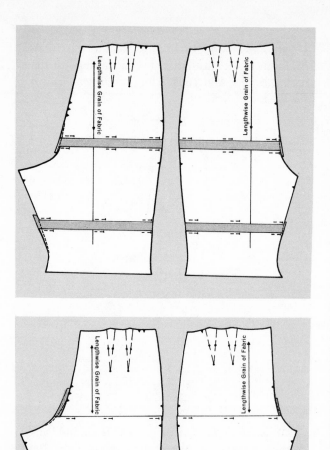

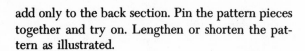

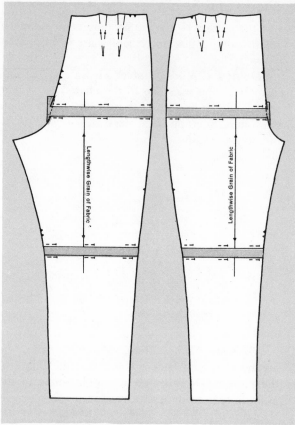

add only to the back section. Pin the pattern pieces together and try on. Lengthen or shorten the pattern as illustrated.

For length of slacks, measure from waistline to floor at front and side seams. Then measure the number of inches desired from the floor and subtract from the total length. Add the necessary amount for hem or cuff. The belt is not included in full-length measurements.

Laying Out the Pattern and Cutting

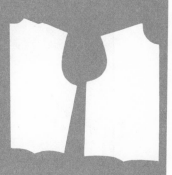

BEFORE LAYING THE PATTERN PIECES on the fabric, be sure that you have completed the following steps;

1) Pressed your pattern and made all necessary pattern adjustments. See page 37.

2) Shrunk the fabric, if necessary, and straightened the fabric ends. See page 14.

3) Pressed out all creases and wrinkles in the fabric. See pressing instructions, page 64.

The guides given here cover the three steps you will take now:

1 Working with your pattern layout

2 Cutting the fabric

3 Transferring notches and markings to the fabric sections.

PATTERN LAYOUT

Rules to Remember

1. Clear a large, flat surface to accommodate your work. A dining-room table (protected with brown paper), a cutting board, a bedboard placed on the bed, or a ping-pong table, makes an excellent cutting surface.

2. Study the cutting layouts shown in the instruction guide included with your pattern. Select and circle the layout for the view you have chosen

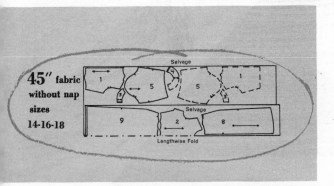

as well as for your pattern size and for the width and type of fabric you are using.

3. Consider the type of fabric you will be working with. Some plaids and florals have an "up" and "down" to the design and must be matched. Napped and pile fabrics have the nap or pile running in one direction and therefore must be cut with all pattern pieces laid in the same direction. Satin, wool broadcloth, and similar weaves often show a varied degree of sheen in different directions; when in doubt, stay on the safe side by laying all pattern pieces in one direction.

4. Lay the pattern pieces printed side up unless otherwise instructed.

Solid Colors or Small Prints

When the cutting layout shows a *double thickness,* fold the fabric right sides together. Pin edges together along the ends and selvages. Slash the selvage edges if they draw.

When the cutting layout shows a *single thickness,* lay the fabric right side up and the pattern printed side up. When right and left sides are cut separately, be sure *to turn the pattern pieces over to cut the second half of the garment;* otherwise you will have two bodice or skirt sections for the same side, or two sleeves for one arm.

When the layout shows a combination of *single and double layers of fabric,* make sure that you lay the correct pattern pieces on the single or double layer and that they face the direction shown in the layout.

Some layouts show the fabric opened to its full width and folded on the crosswise grain, right sides together. Napped, pile, plaid, and floral fabrics cannot be cut by this layout. See page 53.

The lengthwise grain line printed on the pattern must always parallel the fabric selvage. Place each pattern piece accurately on the fabric, and

CUTTING THE FABRIC

Rules to Remember

1. Use bent-handle dressmaker's shears with 6- or 7-inch blades. *Do not use pinking shears;* they are for seam finishing only.

2. Keep the fabric flat on the table and cut along the "cutting line" or edge of the pattern. Cut with long smooth strokes but do not close the shears to the point. Doing that will produce irregular edges. Leave pattern pieces pinned to the fabric until all markings have been made.

pin at one end of the grain line marking. Use a tape measure or yardstick to measure, and adjust the pattern position so that the distance from grain line marking to selvage is the same at both ends. Then complete pinning along the grain line.

For pattern pieces designated "place on lengthwise fold of fabric," place the fold line *exactly* on the lengthwise fold of the fabric, and pin along the fold. (This designation appears when there is no center or back seam or opening in a bodice or skirt section.)

After you have accurately located the grain line, smooth out the pattern so that it will lie flat on the fabric. Pin pattern sections to the fabric along the edges, using plenty of fine, sharp pins to keep the fabric from slipping. Pin with the grain of the fabric and within the seam allowance. Re-check each grain line placement.

Lay and pin all pattern pieces before you start cutting.

3. Cut the notches after cutting each garment section except when they are cut outward. See *Notches,* page 56.

4. Cut out the entire garment at one time. Also, cut the interfacing and underlining before beginning to sew. The underlining is usually cut by the same pattern as the garment after all markings have been made on the fabric.

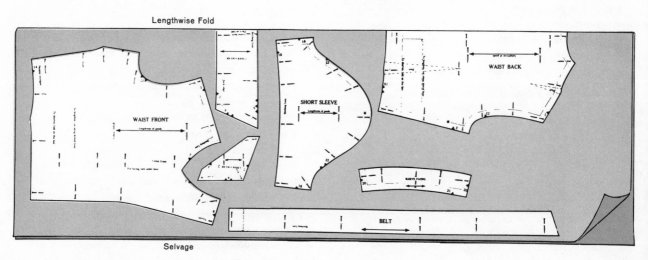

Plaids

If the pattern is appropriate for plaids, the pattern envelope will usually indicate how many yards of fabric you need. If it does not, buy an extra ¼ to ½ yard of fabric, depending on the size of the plaid.

A word about your pattern: To work successfully with plaids, avoid selecting a pattern with diagonal bustline darts, shoulder darts, or shaped joinings within a bodice or skirt. Too many seam joinings will break the continuity of the plaid. If the pattern shows darts at the waistline, convert them to tucks or gathers so that the plaids will match.

The plaid must match exactly in color and stripe at side seams, center seams or openings, shoulder seams, waistline, armholes, and sleeves. Therefore, during dress construction, slip-baste all seams following the instructions on page 62. This will enable you to match the plaids successfully and will prevent the fabric from slipping during the stitching.

EVEN PLAID

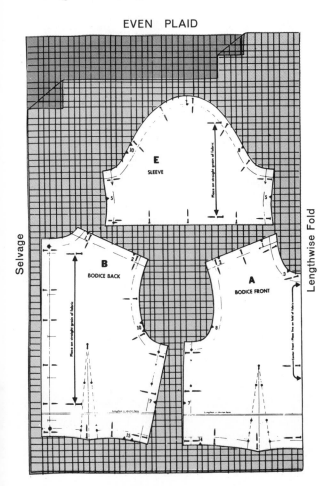

Plaids may be *even* or *uneven*. Your pattern layout will depend on the type of plaid you have selected.

Even Plaids

Even plaids repeat their design on *both the lengthwise and the crosswise stripes.* They are identical in color, right and left and up and down. To work with them, follow these rules:

1. Fold the fabric, right sides together, so that the center of the plaid or the center of a bold lengthwise stripe falls on the center back and center front of the bodice and skirt. The upper and lower layers of the folded fabric must match exactly in color and stripe; pin them together along the stripe lines to prevent slipping during cutting.

2. Lay the pattern pieces on the fabric in either direction. Notches that will be joined together must be placed on the same color stripe. Matching notches occur at side seams, shoulder seams, armholes, sleeves, and waistline. Be careful to match at the *seamline*, not the seam edge. Match crosswise stripes of the sleeves and bodice.

Uneven Plaids

Plaids may be *uneven* in *lengthwise* or *crosswise* directions or in *both.*

When *only the crosswise stripes* of the plaid are *uneven,* follow these rules:

1. Fold the fabric lengthwise, right sides together, so that the center of the plaid or the center of a bold lengthwise stripe falls on the center back and center front of the bodice and skirt. The upper and lower layers of the folded fabric must match exactly in color and stripe; pin them together along the stripe lines to prevent slipping during cutting.

2. Lay all pattern pieces on the fabric in *one direction.* Notches that will be joined together must

be placed on the same color stripe. Match at the *seamline*, not the seam edge. Match crosswise stripes of the sleeves and bodice.

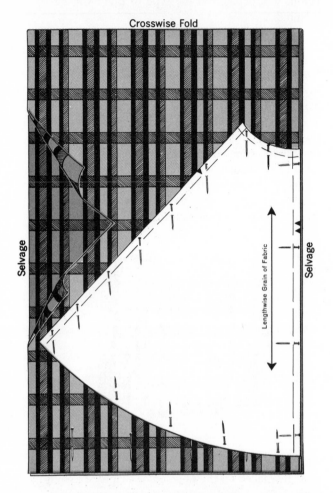

Crosswise Fold

Selvage

Lengthwise Grain of Fabric

Selvage

When *only the lengthwise stripes* of the plaid are *uneven,* they can be matched only when the pattern has a center seam or opening in the front and back of both bodice and skirt.

1. Open the fabric its full width and fold on the crosswise grain, right sides together. Match the identical stripes in the upper and lower layers of the folded fabric and pin them together along the stripe lines to prevent slipping during cutting.

2. Lay the pattern pieces on the fabric in *one direction* with the center of the plaid or the center of a bold lengthwise stripe falling on the center back and center front of the bodice and skirt. Notches that will be joined together must be placed on the same color stripe. Match the *seamline,* not the seam edge. Match the crosswise stripes of the sleeves and bodice.

When both *lengthwise and crosswise stripes* are *uneven,* they can be matched only when the fabric

has no right or wrong side and when the pattern has a center seam or opening in the front and back of both bodice and skirt.

1. Use the pattern layout "with nap"; lay the fabric right side up.

2. Lay all pattern pieces in *one direction* on *a single thickness of fabric,* with the center seam on a prominent lengthwise stripe. Notches that will be joined together must be placed on the same color stripe. Match at the *seamline,* not the seam edge. Match the crosswise stripes of the sleeves and bodice. Cut this half of the garment.

3. For the second half, lay the pattern on the fabric with the first half still pinned to it, matching identical lengthwise and crosswise stripes. Cut the second half of the garment. Cut notches and make markings through the two layers of fabric.

4. Reverse one side of each garment section when joining seams because there is no right or wrong side to the fabric.

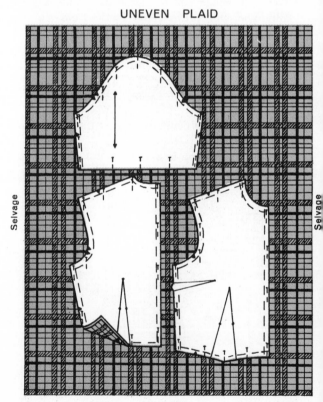

UNEVEN PLAID

Selvage

Selvage

Stripes

Stripes may be *even* or *uneven.* They are cut the same as plaids. In placing the pattern on the fabric, be sure that notches that will be joined together fall on the same stripe.

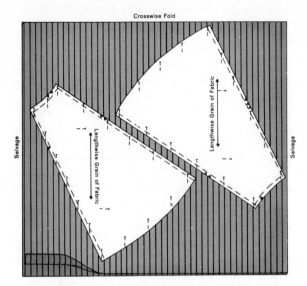

If the garment is cut on the bias, select a pattern with a center seam or opening in the front and back and follow these rules:

1. Fold the full width of the fabric on the crosswise grain, right sides together.

2. Lay the pattern with the grain line parallel to the selvage. Notches that are to be joined together must be on the same stripe. Stripes must be matched at side seams and center seams or center openings. Match at the *seamline,* not the seam edge.

3. During dress construction, slip-baste all seams.

When the stripes are *uneven,* lay the pattern pieces on the fabric in *one direction.*

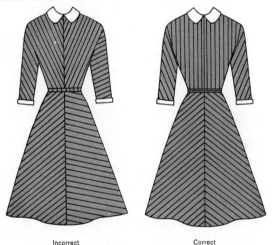

Incorrect   Correct

Checks

Checks ¼ inch or more in size *must* be matched; smaller checks are more attractive when matched. Follow instructions for cutting plaids.

Florals, Prints, and Jacquards

Many floral fabrics have an "up" and "down" to the motif, and when they do, you must lay all pattern pieces in *one direction.*

To achieve a pleasing effect with medium or large motifs, make sure that they fall above the bustline instead of directly over it, approximately in the same position in the front as in the back, and in the same place on each sleeve. Match at the seamline whenever possible.

As with plaids, avoid patterns that require many seams within the bodice and skirt. Simple lines are more appropriate for prints, both large and small.

Incorrect   Correct

Pile Fabrics

Pile fabrics such as velvet, velveteen, and corduroy should be cut with the pile standing up to emphasize the rich, dark tone. To determine the direction of the pile, brush the fabric with the fingers. If the surface is smooth, you are brushing with the pile; if rough, you are brushing against the pile. Use the "rough" direction for the top of your pattern layout; and lay all pieces in the *same direction,* following the "with nap" instruction guide with the pattern. Use fine needles to pin the pattern to the fabric.

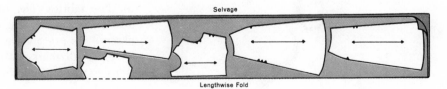

Napped Fabrics

Napped fabrics such as wool broadcloth, duvetyn, vicuna, and cashmere, have fuzzy fibers running in *one direction*. Often the direction is visible to the eye. If it is not, brush the fabric with your fingers as for velvet.

Cut napped fabrics with the *nap running down.* Lay all pattern pieces in *one direction*. Use fine needles to pin the pattern to the fabric.

TRANSFERRING NOTCHES AND MARKINGS

The notches and markings on the pattern are your key to successful dress construction. Each has a special meaning and each must be transferred to the fabric while it is still pinned to the pattern.

Notches

Notches are guides for joining the garment sections. They indicate which edges are seamed together and where the ease is located. On some patterns they are numbered to indicate the sequence in which the seams are sewn. Like notches are always joined.

Notches may be cut *inward* or *outward*, depending on the fabric you are using and your personal preference. Fabrics that fray readily or seam formations requiring an untrimmed, smooth seam edge, such as a French seam or a flat felled seam, should be cut with notches outward. Some beginners prefer to cut notches outward as a precaution against cutting too deeply into the seam allowance. Patterns designate both inward and outward methods.

To Cut Notches Inward

After cutting the pattern piece, lift the fabric and fold it in the center of the notch. With the scissor points toward the outer edge, as illustrated, cut the notch only ⅛ inch deep. Be careful not to

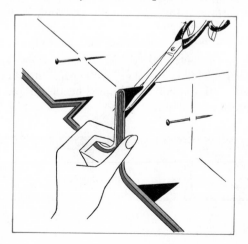

cut too deeply because this will weaken the seam allowance.

To Cut Notches Outward

Notches are cut outward as the garment is cut, following the markings that project beyond the seam edge. Cut them the exact shape of the pattern or you will not get an accurate joining. Use outward notches on chiffons and other sheer fabrics.

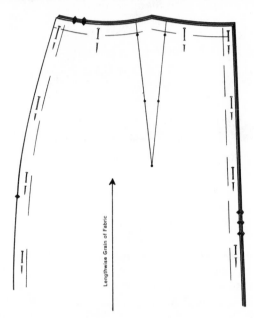

Other Methods for Marking Notches

If the fabric ravels easily, make a tailor's tack (see below) at the point of each notch. Or, if you are an experienced sewer, clip in ⅛ inch from the edge of the fabric at the point of each notch, using scissors that cut sharply at the point. This is a timesaving method. However, watch closely for these clipped edges when assembling the garment.

Markings

Dots, squares, triangles, or crosses on the pattern indicate the position for darts, buttonholes, tucks and pleats, seam allowances, joining points for gussets and yokes, and other construction details. To transfer these markings from the pattern to the fabric, use tailor's tacks, chalk, chalked thread, tracing wheel and tracing paper, or pins. The safest of these is tailor's tacks, which are preferred for fine fabrics. The other methods are quicker and can be safely used on many fabrics if you observe the precautions noted here.

Since all markings must be accurately made, transfer them while each pattern piece is pinned in position.

Tailor's Tacks

Tailor's tacks are markings that will not rub off, press off, or mar the fabric. To make them, use a double thread about 24 inches in length and in a contrasting color to the fabric. Do not knot the end. Use a different color for each symbol, then it is simple to join like colors. Although regular mercerized thread is suitable, some sewers prefer embroidery or darning thread because it is soft and clings to the fabric. Follow these rules:

1. At the point to be marked, take a small stitch through the pattern and double thickness of fabric, leaving about a ¾-inch thread end.

2. Take a backstitch in the same place, and leave a loop a little shorter than the thread end. Clip the thread, leaving a ¾-inch thread end.

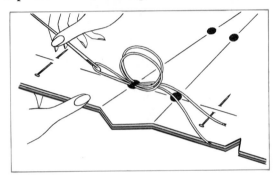

Continue in this manner until all markings have been finished.

If a group of tailor's tacks are made close to-gether, such as in darts, move from one marking to another without clipping the thread between the marks.

Before removing the pattern, clip the threads between the tacks. Remove pins, and carefully remove the pattern by pulling the threads through the tissue so that the tailor's tacks are not disturbed.

3. Raise the upper layer of fabric slightly, and clip the threads between it and the bottom layer, leaving thread tufts in both layers of fabric.

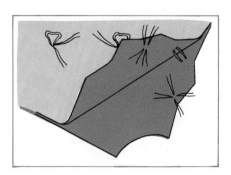

Chalk

Tailor's chalk may be used when there is no danger of marring the fabric. Since it rubs off easily, use it only when the construction will be done immediately. (Always mark the wrong side of the fabric.) Chalk is available in several colors, with or without a wax base.

1. Place a pin through the pattern and double thickness of fabric at the point of the marking. Carefully slip the tissue pattern over the heads, then the points of the pins.

2. With tailor's chalk, mark the fabric over the pins on one side. Turn the section over and chalk the other side in the same place.

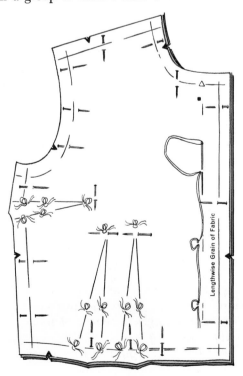

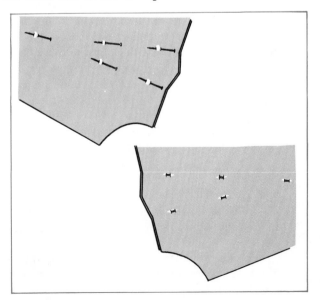

Chalked Thread

Chalked thread is thread that has been coated with tailor's chalk. Use it as you would tailor's chalk above.

Thread a needle, using a double thread about 12 inches long. Do not knot the end.

1. Pull the thread around the square of tailor's chalk several times until it is well coated, even to the end.

2. Take a stitch in each marking through the pattern and double thickness of fabric. As the chalked thread is pulled out, it leaves a tiny chalked marking in each thickness of fabric. Re-chalk the thread frequently.

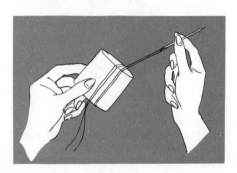

Tracing Wheel and Tracing Paper

Dressmaker's tracing paper is available in white, blue, red, yellow, and orange. Several colors are combined in one package. If you plan to use it, observe these cautions:

1. Use white tracing paper whenever possible. If you need a color, choose one near the color of the fabric but sufficient in contrast to make visible marks.

2. *Always mark the wrong side of the fabric* since the marks remain on the fabric until it is washed or cleaned. Although they can be removed from almost any fabric with a household dry cleaner such as carbon tetrachloride, energine, or benzine, on·many delicate fabrics good judgment dictates that you choose a safer method of marking.

3. Work on a flat surface. If you use a table, cover it with heavy cardboard so that it will not be marred by the tracing wheel.

4. Mark lightly with the tracing wheel. Do not press down too hard because the points of the wheel will mar the fabric.

5. Use small pieces of tracing paper and move them from one section to another as you are marking.

Practice using the tracing wheel and tracing paper on a swatch of the same fabric before marking the garment.

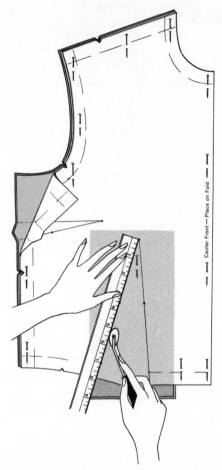

To mark a double thickness of fabric, which you will have when you cut with the fabric folded right sides together, use two pieces of tracing paper. Place one, right side up, under the botton layer of fabric. Remove enough pins to slip the second piece of tracing paper, right side down, between the pattern and top layer of fabric. (See illustration above.)

Use a ruler to keep the lines straight as you mark with the tracing wheel. Move the tracing wheel along the exact line of the darts or other details with one smooth, even stroke so that you do not change their shape. *Do not "saw" back and forth.*

If the fabric is heavy, you may have to mark one layer at a time.

To mark the right side of the fabric, as you must for pockets, buttonholes, and similar details, mark the wrong side with the tracing wheel and tracing paper and then baste along the marked line to transfer the markings to the right side.

To mark a single thickness of fabric, which you will have when you cut with the right side of the fabric up, place a piece of tracing paper, right side up, under the fabric and mark.

Marking with Pins

Pin markings are not suitable for fine fabrics or patterns with intricate details. Use this method only when the darts, tucks, or other details will be basted immediately after each section is marked. Do not pin and set aside and later expect to find the pins in place.

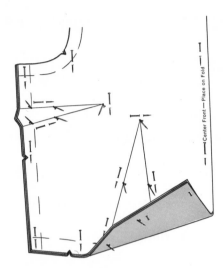

From the pattern side, plunge a pin through the pattern markings and two layers of fabric. Push the pins down so that the heads are tightly against the pattern.

Turn the section over and place a second pin through in the same point as the first pin.

Remove the pattern, carefully pulling the pinhead through the pattern.

When the two layers are separated, the fabric is pin-marked on both the left and the right sides.

Center Line Markings

The center line of both front and back sections of the skirt and bodice is a guide for fitting as well as for joining facings and collars at the neck, lapping two sections when there is an opening, positioning buttonholes, joining the bodice and skirt, and folding the hem smoothly. Mark the center line after you have completed *all* other markings. Use a thread of contrasting color to the fabric and the other markings.

On folds, make long basting stitches in the fold, using a single thread. Knot the end of the thread at the beginning and take one backstitch at the end. (See top right.)

For openings, baste through the pattern and two layers of fabric along the center line, using a double thread. Make the stitches small and about 2 inches apart, leaving a loop between the stitches. Clip the looped thread between the stitches and carefully lift the pattern from the fabric, leaving

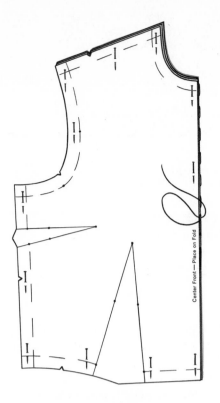

the thread markings in the fabric.

Raise the upper layer of fabric and clip the thread between the two layers. Fold on the line of thread tacks, and pin. Make long basting stitches in the fold, following the instructions above. Remove the thread tacks.

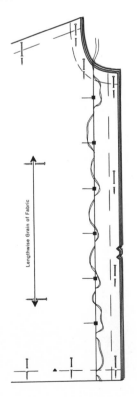
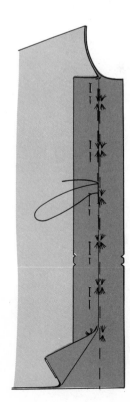

59

Assembling Your Work

WITH THE FABRIC SECTIONS before you, with pins handy, and with a threaded needle and a threaded machine waiting to be used, the moment has come to put your creation together. Your work will proceed in this sequence:

1 Stay stitching
2 Basting.

STAY STITCHING

Stay stitching is a line of machine stitching, placed through a single thickness of the seam allowance, ½ inch from the seam edge. It is used to hold the original shape of necklines, shoulder lines, waistline, and hiplines, and to prevent them from stretching when fitting and handling the garment. Stay stitching is not always a necessary step in dress construction. Some sewers like to stay-stitch fabrics that stretch easily or that will be pin-basted.

For your stitching, use matching thread and the appropriate stitch length for stitching seams in your fabric. Chain stitching can also be used to stay-stitch seams. See page 63.

Direction of Stay Stitching

Neckline—from shoulder to center
Shoulder line—from neckline to armhole
Waistline (skirt and blouse)—from side seams to center
Hipline and bias skirt seams—from lower edge to waistline
"V" neckline—from point of "V" to shoulder line

BASTING

Basting is a temporary stitch made to hold two or more pieces of fabric together before final stitching. It facilitates seaming and fitting and contributes to the appearance of good workmanship in the finished product. Basting may be done by hand, by machine, or by pins. In all cases, it is removed after each seam is completed.

Hand Basting

Use a long, slender needle and a single strand of thread not more than 30 inches in length and contrasting in color so that it can easily be seen in the fabric. You may use regular "basting" thread, which is soft and lightly twisted, or mercerized thread. Use silk thread for fine fabrics when basting on the top side to hold two or more layers in position during final pressing—for example, along the finished edge of a facing, the fold for a hem, and similar details. In these cases silk is preferred because it does not leave a mark after pressing and will not mar fine fabrics at the needle puncture.

When basting sections of a garment, work on a flat surface such as a table or lap board. Place the seam edges together; pin at each end, at notches, and at the center. Then distribute the pins at equal intervals, working toward the seam ends. Place the

pins at right angles to the seamline, with heads to the seam edge. Do not ease or stretch the seam.

Knot the longer end of the thread at the beginning of the basting line and fasten the line with a short backstitch at the end. Hand-baste, using one of the methods illustrated.

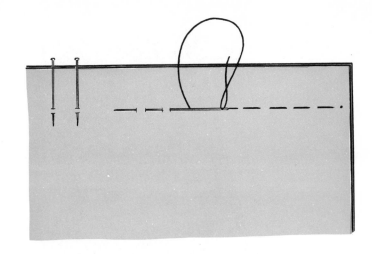

Uneven Basting

Uneven basting may be used to baste regular seams on all fabric and *should* be used to mark the stitching line for top-stitching zippers, seams, facings, and the like.

Working from right to left, make a short stitch on the underside of the fabric and a long stitch on the top side. To remove, clip every 3 to 5 inches and pull out.

Even Basting

Even basting may also be used to join side seams on any fabric. It is the preferred basting method for fabrics with a smooth finish and for areas that require close control—for example, set-in sleeves.

Working from right to left, take several long running stitches on the needle before pulling it through. To remove, clip every 3 to 5 inches and pull out.

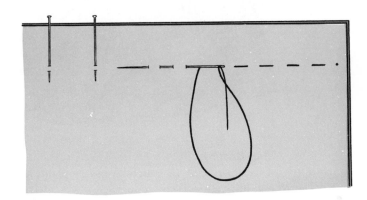

Diagonal Basting

After the facing edges of collars, lapels, cuffs, scallops, and similar construction details have been stitched, blended, and turned, they are held in place for pressing with *diagonal basting*. This is usually done with silk thread. Diagonal basting is not used to indicate a stitching line or to hold a seam when fitting.

Working from right to left and with the needle pointed toward you, take a short stitch at a right angle to the edge through all layers of fabric. The stitch length should be from ¼ to ⅜ inch, depending on the thickness of fabric. Place succeeding stitches in the same way, spacing them ⅛ to ¼ inch apart. A diagonal stitch will appear on the upper side and a straight stitch, at a right angle to the edge, on the underside.

Diagonal basting is also used to hold interfacings and underlinings firmly against the fabric during assembly steps. In this application, the spacing between the short stitches may be as much as an inch.

To remove diagonal basting, clip the diagonal thread every three or four stitches, and pull out.

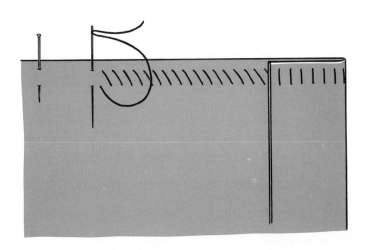

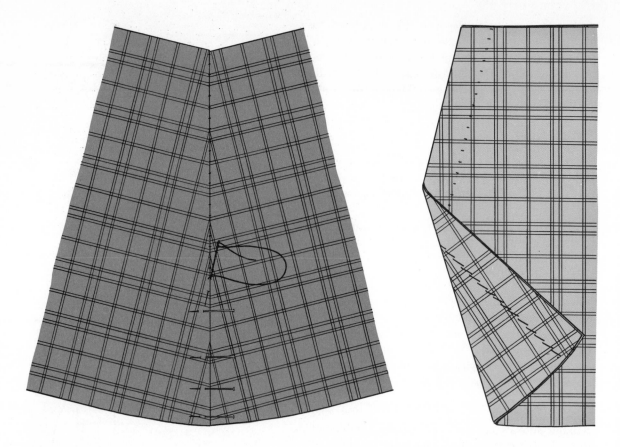

Slip Basting

Use slip basting to match stripes or plaids and to join intricate curved sections.

Work from the right side of the garment; fold under the seam allowance on one edge and pin. (Baste if necessary.) Lap the folded edge over the seam allowance of the joining section, being careful to match each stripe or plaid. Place pins at right angles to the folded edge, with heads toward the seam edge. Space the pins about ½ inch apart, depending on the size of the stripe or plaid.

Insert the needle, from the wrong side, up through the three thicknesses of fabric near the folded edge, and pull through. Then from the top side, directly opposite the previous stitch, insert the needle through the single thickness and bring it up through the three thicknesses and near the folded edge. A long stitch appears on the underside and a short stitch appears under the folded edge. The long stitch is usually from ¼ to ⅝ inch in length but may vary with the shape of the joining, the pattern of the stripe or plaid, or the texture of the fabric.

If you used a basting thread to retain the fold, remove it before stitching. Machine-stitch the seam from the wrong side through the center of the short basting stitches.

To remove the basting, clip the longer basting threads every two or three stitches and pull out. Use tweezers if your fingers cannot grasp the threads.

Machine Basting

Machine basting is quick and easy, but it should be used only on fabrics where the needle puncture will not show.

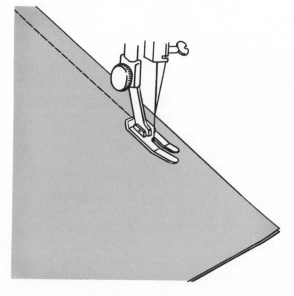

Pin the seam edges together as instructed for hand basting. Adjust the stitch length selector on the machine for a 6 to 8 stitch length and stitch on the seamline. To remove, clip the top thread at intervals of four or five stitches, then pull the bottom thread.

Pin Basting

Pin basting may be used on straight seams in fabrics that are easy to handle.

Place pins at right angles to the seamline, with the heads toward the edge; if you are going to use the Seam Guide, place the points toward the seam edge. The pins should just nip into the fabric at the stitching line; they should not extend under both sides of the presser foot and should never be placed on the underside of the fabric in contact with the feed of your machine. Machine-stitch on the seamline, using a hinged presser foot.

Chain Stitching

The chain stitch is made by the needle thread alone. On top it looks like regular stitching, on the underside you can see that it is a series of interlocking loops that can be removed with just a pull on the thread end. This makes chain stitching a convenient method of basting seams for fitting, marking construction guidelines, inserting

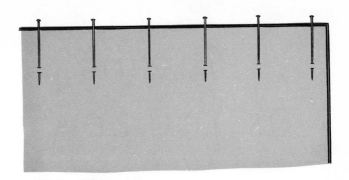

"growth tucks" in children's clothes, and applying removable trimming.

Chain Stitch accessories are provided with some machines by Singer. Check your instruction book for the many sewing jobs you can do with chain stitching.

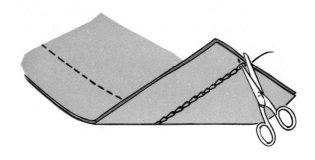

Pressing as You Sew

PRESSING OFTEN SEEMS TO BE an unnecessary interruption in your work. This is far from the truth, however, and you should disabuse yourself of that notion now, for *pressing is an integral part of sewing.*

After stitching seams, darts, tucks, facings, and hems, you must press them. You must also press garment sections before joining them. If you do this faithfully as you sew, a touch-up here and there is all you will need when you have finished your work.

Form the habit of pressing correctly and at the proper time, as instructed in this chapter, and you will attain a perfection in finish and fit in your sewing which equals that of custom-made clothes.

The instructions that follow explain what you should know about:

1 Pressing equipment
2 Fundamentals of pressing
3 Pressing different kinds of fabrics
4 Pressing various construction details.

PRESSING EQUIPMENT

Begin with proper pressing equipment conveniently arranged near the sewing machine. This will encourage you to use the methods professionals use. Once you have established a routine, you will find these methods valuable timesavers. They produce good results immediately and eliminate the "doing-over" that is discouraging to the experienced sewer as well as to the beginner.

The following equipment is basic and essential for good pressing:

Iron. The undisputed "first" of good pressing tools is your iron. Select one with a dependable fabric dial so that you are always sure of using the degree of heat appropriate for your fabric.

A steam iron is a good investment and may be used for both pressing and ironing. On some fabrics and in some areas of pressing, steam from the iron may supply enough moisture; generally, however, you will need additional moisture for an expert pressing job.

Ironing board. A sturdy board that you can easily adjust to several heights is the next requirement. Make sure that your board has a smooth, padded surface.

Sleeveboard. This small ironing board, which is used on your regular ironing board, is required for pressing sleeves, seams, and all fine details. The ironing board supports the weight of the garment and prevents unfinished areas from stretching or wrinkling.

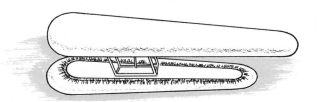

Seamboard. This board, which is also placed on the ironing board, is used for pressing seams open on facings and especially at points. It is excellent for worsteds and other fabrics with a hard finish which must be pressed on a firm surface if you want to get a flat, sharply pressed seam.

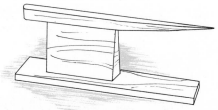

Press mitt. This is essential for pressing darts, the top of set-in sleeves, and curved seams where the contour and fit of the garment must be preserved. Place the press mitt on the small end of the sleeveboard.

Tailor's ham. The tailor's ham is used on the ironing board for pressing and shaping curved seams, darts, collars, and lapels on suits, coats, and other tailored garments. It may be purchased at a notions counter and where tailors' supplies are sold.

You can also make one quickly, easily, and inexpensively. Purchase about ½ yard of drill cloth and shrink it before cutting. Make a paper pattern, egg-shaped, about 14 inches long and 10 inches in width at the wide end. Then cut two pieces of drill cloth by the pattern. Pin them together and stitch ½ inch from the edge, leaving a 5-inch opening. Backstitch at each end of the stitching. Press, then turn to the right side. Fill with clean, sifted sand or sawdust, packing the filling firmly into the cover. Turn the raw edge under on one side and lap the folded edge over the opposite edge; close the opening with hand stitching.

Press cloths. You will need three kinds of press cloths to properly press the range of fabrics used by most women who sew: (a) a chemically treated press cloth for pressing heavy fabrics; (b) a double thickness of cheesecloth as a thin, starch-free press cloth, for pressing medium and lightweight fabrics; and (c) wool woven interlining fabric for top pressing on all fabrics.

You will also need a yard length of good quality cheesecloth. Use it, moistened, when pressing cottons and linens; place it over the dry press cloth to provide uniform moisture when pressing silks, woolens, and many construction details. To moisten the cheesecloth, dip it in water, then wring as dry as possible.

Wooden pounding block. Use this to flatten the edges of faced lapels and collars, hems, facings, and pleats on tailored garments made of heavy or bulky fabrics. Steam the area first, then quickly apply the pounding block. After a little practice you will be able to determine the amount of pressure needed.

Sponge and small camel's hair paintbrush. Use these to moisten the seams of woolens.

Clothesbrush. Use this for brushing napped fabrics after pressing.

Pressing pad. You will need a pressing pad when pressing monograms, lace, and construction details such as zippers, corded buttonholes, and pockets in napped fabrics.

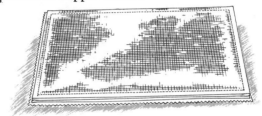

To make a pad, take three or four thicknesses of wool interlining about 20 inches long and 14 inches wide, and stitch them to a backing of drill cloth. Place the pressing pad on the ironing board with the layers of wool interlining right side up.

FUNDAMENTALS OF PRESSING

Pressing demands a different technique from ironing. In pressing there is little motion of the iron when it is in contact with the fabric. In ironing, you glide the iron over the fabric in the direction of the fabric grain to remove wrinkles and to restore the shape of a garment or fabric that has been laundered. The amount of heat, moisture, and pressure required will vary with the fiber content. Here are the rules to follow in pressing:

1. Always test the fabric for pressing. If necessary, make a seam or dart in a swatch of the same fabric and press it to determine how much heat and moisture the fabric requires. Labels are not always at hand and some fabrics are difficult to classify.

2. Place the garment in position for pressing, making sure that the fabric is straight and smooth. Lift the fabric with both hands when it is necessary to move it.

3. Always press on the wrong side to guard against shine.

4. Use a press cloth on all fabrics, except cottons and linens; place it between the iron and the fabric. The kind of press cloth to use and the amount of moisture required will depend on the fabric.

5. Place the iron lightly over the section to be pressed and allow the steam to enter the fabric. Use minimum pressure on the iron and press in the direction of the fabric grain. This helps to retain the shape. Lift the iron to move to another section.

Do not overpress. It will take the life out of the fabric and cause shine. Overpressing results when you use too hot an iron, leave the iron in one place too long, use an inadequate press cloth, apply too much moisture, or press too frequently.

HOW TO PRESS DIFFERENT KINDS OF FABRICS

Fiber, texture, and thickness determine how a fabric is pressed. Fiber content dictates the temperature of the iron, texture dictates the method of handling the fabric.

Nylon, Dacron, and similar fabrics require little heat. Set the heat control to the lowest temperature. Press the fabric on the wrong side, using a thin press cloth. The iron will not steam at this low setting. If moisture is required, place a single thickness of a moist cheesecloth over the dry press cloth.

Rayon requires a low heat, slightly more than nylon. Set the heat control on "Rayon." Press the fabric on the wrong side using a thin press cloth. Generally, steam from the iron will supply sufficient moisture. For heavy seams on which you will need more moisture, place a single thickness of a moist cheesecloth over the thin, dry press cloth.

Silk requires slightly more heat than rayon. But guard against too hot an iron, for it will weaken the fiber and discolor pastels and white. Set the heat control on "Silk." Press the fabric on the wrong side. For lightweight silk, use a thin press cloth. The steam iron should give sufficient moisture. For added moisture on thick seams, place a single thickness of a moist cheesecloth over the thin dry press cloth. On medium and heavyweight silks, use a double thickness of moist cheesecloth over the thin, dry press cloth for extra moisture.

Lightweight cotton requires slightly more heat than silk. Set the heat control on "Cotton." Press on the wrong side. You may place the iron directly on the fabric unless you are using a dark color. To provide uniform moisture on seams, facings, and similar construction, cover with a moist cheesecloth; press dry.

Wool requires more heat than lightweight cotton. Turn the heat control to "Wool." Press on the wrong side using a heavy press cloth or a double thickness of cheesecloth, covered with a moist cheesecloth. *Do not press entirely dry.* (Overdrying will produce a shine.) If you are working with a napped fabric, brush it with a clothesbrush, while there is still a moist steam, to raise the nap after pressing.

Linen and heavy cotton require a very hot iron. Set the heat control on "Linen." Press on the wrong side. You may place the iron directly on linen except when the fabric is of a dark color. To prevent shine on thick seams and dark colors, use a thin press cloth covered with damp cheesecloth for added moisture. Press dry.

Velvet and velveteen are steamed. *Do not bring the iron in contact with the fabric or you will flatten the pile.* Stand the iron on its heel and place a damp turkish towel over the soleplate. Hold the wrong side of the velvet close to the towel and move it back and forth to allow the steam to penetrate the fabric.

You can also steam velvet and velveteen on a velvet pressboard, which has fine fiber needles, or you can use a wool-faced pressing pad for steaming. Place the velvet face down over the pressboard or

pressing pad. Hold the steam iron close to the fabric—not on it—and brush the fabric lightly to distribute the steam. Press the seam open with the finger tips, and steam it by holding the iron close to it. Keep your fingers dry; to avoid finger marks, lift the velvet only when it is dry.

Blends require varying degrees of heat, depending on the fiber content. The fiber requiring the lowest heat determines the proper temperature for the fabric. Press blends on the wrong side, using a thin press cloth. For a blend of Dacron and cotton, steam from the iron should supply sufficient moisture. For a blend of Dacron and silk, you will need additional moisture; use a single thickness of a moist cheesecloth over a thin press cloth. For a blend of silk and wool, which requires more steam than silk and Dacron, use a heavy press cloth covered with a moist cheesecloth.

Crepe weaves may present a problem since they tend to draw in when damp and stretch when under pressure. Place the pressing pad *under* the crepe, and the cheesecloth or wool press cloth *over* the fabric to retain the crinkle in pressing. The iron temperature is governed by the fiber content.

HOW TO PRESS VARIOUS CONSTRUCTION DETAILS

Rules to Remember

1. Remove pins and basting stitches before pressing. Pins mar the fabric and the soleplate of the iron; basting stitches leave an imprint. If you need a basting to hold two or more layers of fabric together during pressing (for example, facings), use silk thread and diagonal basting as instructed on page 61.

2. When pressing the first detail of a garment, press the entire section and not merely the area around the seam or dart. In many cases, there is a slight shrinkage of the fabric even though it has been preshrunk.

Seams

Always use a sleeveboard when pressing seams or a seamboard if you have one.

Plain Seam

A plain seam should be pressed as follows:

Step 1: Press the seam in the same position as it was stitched. This will give you a smooth seam and imbed the stitching. To prevent shine, place the proper press cloth over all fabrics except light-colored cottons, which need no protection.

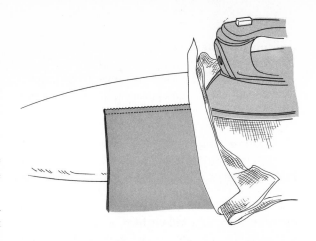

Step 2: Place the seam over the sleeveboard so that you can see the detail clearly and the bulk of the garment can rest on the ironing board. Use the fingers and the *point of the iron* to open the seam. The fingers should work about 2 inches ahead of the iron. Use a moist sponge or camel's hair paintbrush to apply moisture in seams of woolens before pressing them open.

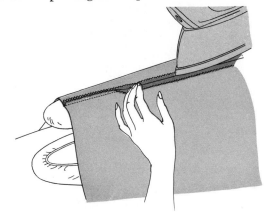

Step 3: Press the seam open, using a press cloth between the iron and fabric. See page 66, *How to Press Different Kinds of Fabrics,* for the amount of

moisture and the weight of press cloth you need. For heavy fabrics, place a strip of brown paper under the seam allowance to prevent the imprint of the seam edge from appearing on the right side of the fabric.

Curved Seam

A curved seam must be blended before it is pressed. See *Seam Blending,* page 89. For the first pressing, follow Step 1 above. Then place the curved seam over the curve of a press mitt (which has been placed on the end of a sleeveboard) or over the curve of a tailor's ham. Follow the pressing instructions in the second and third steps for the *Plain Seam.*

ing and press again. The final pressing occurs after you have made the second line of stitching; press the same as in the first step. Use a press cloth and moisture required by the fabric.

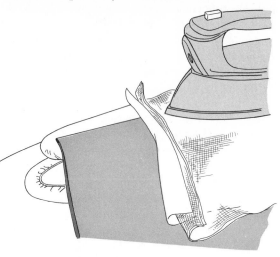

Flat Felled Seam

The flat felled seam is usually formed on the right side of the fabric and must be pressed with a press cloth between the iron and fabric. Trim

French Seam

The French seam is first pressed in the same position as it was stitched, then pressed open with the *point of an iron.* Remember, this seam is on the right side of the fabric and must be protected with a press cloth to guard against shine. After trimming the seam allowance and turning to the wrong side, fold sharply on the first line of stitch-

off the edge of one seam allowance, then press the seam open the same as the French seam. Fold on the seamline and press both seam edges in the same direction, with the longer edge on top. After turning the edge under and stitching a second time, press again from the wrong side, covering with a press cloth. (See the two illustrations at bottom of previous page.)

Lapped Seam

A lapped seam is pressed on the wrong side after the edge on one side has been folded under and basted. Press only the very edge on curved seams. Cover the fabric with the proper press

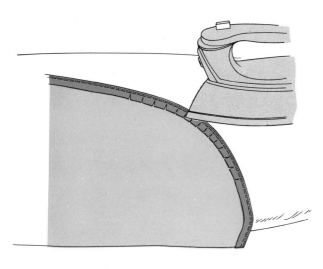

cloth and use moisture. Press again on the wrong side after the seam is lapped and stitched. If top pressing is required, place the wool press cloth over the fabric.

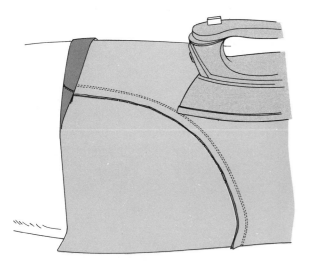

Darts

Darts should be pressed with care, for pressing further molds the dart to bring shape and roundness to the garment.

1. Press the dart flat, as it was stitched, *carrying the crease only as far as the stitching*. Protect the fabric with the proper press cloth and use the sleeveboard.

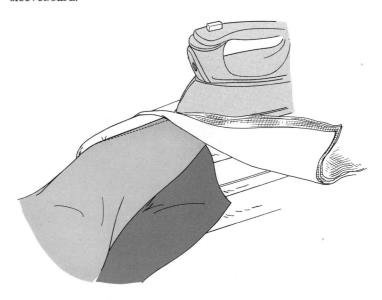

2. Place the dart over the curve of a press mitt, which has been placed on the small end of a sleeveboard, or over the curve of a tailor's ham. Darts are pressed *toward the center* of skirt front and back, blouse front and back, and shoulders; they are pressed *downward* at the underarm and elbow. Turn your dart in the proper direction and if the fabric is heavy, slip a strip of brown paper under the dart to prevent the imprint of the dart from appearing on the right side of the fabric. Cover the dart with the appropriate press cloth and use the amount of moisture required by the fabric. Press toward the point of the dart. Then press the entire section of the garment, using a press cloth.

Darts in Heavy Fabrics

Darts in heavy fabrics are slashed and pressed open. After pressing the dart flat, as stitched, place the dart over the curve of a press mitt or tailor's ham. Open the dart with the *point of the iron*.

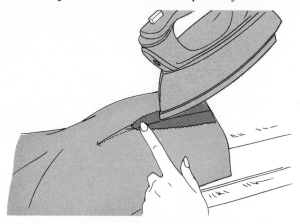

Place a strip of brown paper under each side of the dart, cover with the appropriate press cloth, and use the proper amount of moisture. Press the dart open.

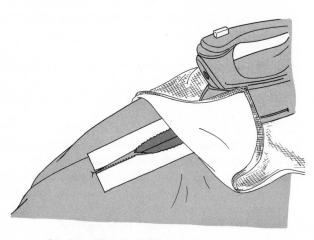

Contour Darts

Contour darts are slashed at the waistline to within ¼ inch of the stitching to relieve strain.

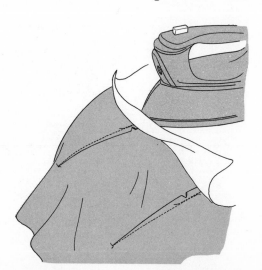

Press them in two operations: (1) press one-half the dart over the curve of a press mitt or tailor's ham the same as the conventional dart above; (2) reverse the garment and press the other half. Protect the fabric with a press cloth and use the moisture required by the fabric.

Tucks and Gathers

Tucks

Tucks are first pressed in the same position as they were stitched. Do not allow the point of the iron to go beyond the stitching. Then press the tucks in the proper direction, which is usually toward the center. When tucks are formed on the outside, the pattern may show them pressed either toward or away from center. Protect the fabric with the correct press cloth and use the proper moisture for the fabric.

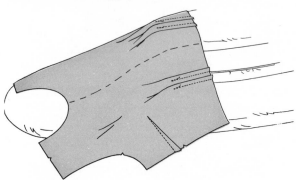

Gathers

Gathers are pressed by moving the point of the iron upward to the stitching. Lift the iron and repeat. The pressing can be done best with the iron directly against the wrong side of the fabric; for that reason, control of the iron's heat is very important. Since gathers are customarily made in soft fabrics, steam from the iron should give sufficient moisture.

Buttonholes and Pockets

To achieve professional-looking buttonholes and pockets, you must not only follow scrupulously the sewing instructions but press at every step of construction. There are several excellent methods of making bound buttonholes and pockets. (Refer to *"Buttonholes"* or *"Pockets."*) The pressing technique illustrated here is one you should master since it is basic to most buttonholes and can be applied as well to pockets, which follow a construction sequence closely related to that of buttonholes.

The first pressing is done after the fabric patch is stitched in place for the buttonhole or pocket. Place the work, wrong side up, over the sleeveboard. Cover with the proper press cloth and press, using moisture appropriate for the fabric.

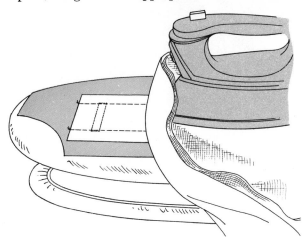

After slashing through the center and to each corner, turn the facing to the wrong side. Place the work, wrong side up, over the sleeveboard. Fold back the facing and pull the triangular ends away from the opening to square the corners. Apply moisture with a moist cheesecloth, and press away from the opening with the *point of the iron.* If the corners are slashed deeply enough, they will be square.

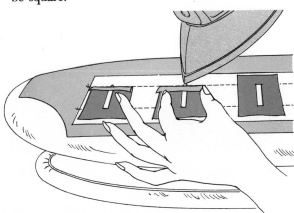

On each side of the buttonhole, fold the patch back, apply moisture with a moist cheesecloth, and press the seam allowances away from the opening, with the point of the iron touching the stitching. Press the entire length of the patch to crease the fold beyond each end of the stitching.

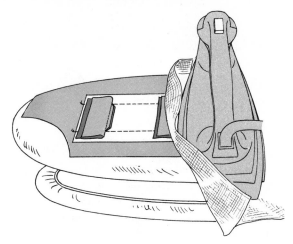

After basting the folds in place to fill the opening, press on the wrong side, using the proper press cloth and the appropriate amount of steam. Slip brown paper between the buttonhole seam allowances and garment to prevent the imprint of the

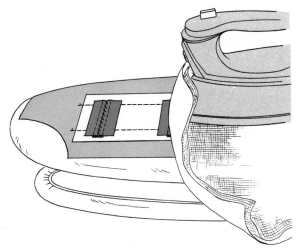

seam allowance from appearing on the right side of the fabric.

Follow the same pressing rules after the final

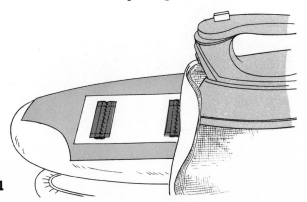

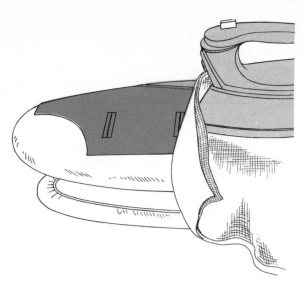

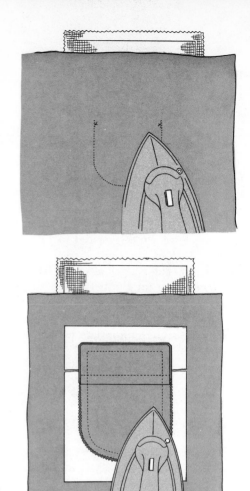

stitching and after the garment facing has been hemmed to the buttonhole as illustrated above.

For the final pressing of corded buttonholes, corded pockets, patch pockets, and pockets with a flap, place the wool-faced pressing pad on the ironing board. (See above right.) Slip brown paper between the garment and pocket pouch and between the garment and pocket flap as shown at right. If it is necessary to do any pressing on the right side, cover the garment with a wool press cloth.

Neckline Facing Seams

Press the seam in the same position as stitched after you have trimmed and slashed the seam allowances. Use the proper press cloth and moisture required by the fabric.

Place the seam over the seamboard and open it with the *point of the iron.* Apply moisture with a moist sponge or paintbrush. Carefully control the heat of the iron so that you can press without a press cloth in this step.

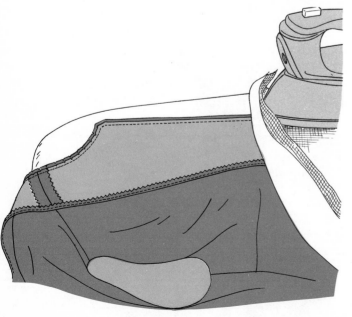

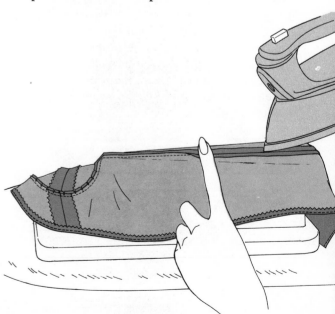

On the curve of the neckline, press just a small portion at a time. Lift the garment with both hands to move it.

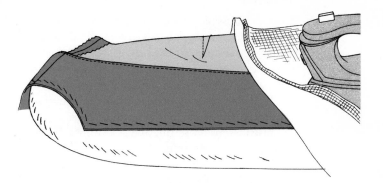

Turn the facing to the underside, then ease it under slightly at the stitching line and baste. Use silk thread and diagonal basting to hold the facing securely in place on silks and woolens. Silk thread will not leave an imprint on the fabric. Press on the underside; cover with a wool press cloth and use the amount of moisture appropriate for the fabric.

Outside curved seams as in collars and cuffs are pressed open over the heel of the seamboard.

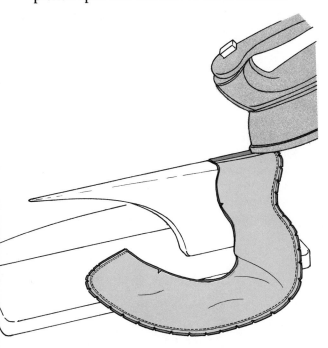

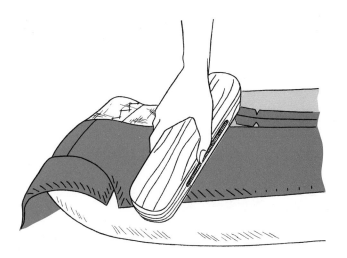

To press faced lapels and collars on tailored suits and coats that are made of heavy or bulky fabrics, steam the area until you have plenty of live steam, then quickly pound the finished edge of the garment with a wooden pounding block. This will force out the steam and leave a flat edge without shine. (See above.)

Sleeves

Correct pressing makes the difference between a homemade and a professional-looking sleeve. The underarm seam is pressed as it was stitched, the same as a plain seam; then the sleeve is placed over a sleeveboard, and the seam is pressed open.

Your first pressing of a set-in sleeve comes after pin-fitting the sleeve in the armhole. See page 159 for instructions on setting the sleeve into the armhole. Follow these rules:

1. Remove the sleeve from the armhole. Use a press mitt on the small end of the sleeveboard. Place the sleeve cap over the press mitt and secure it with pins. Cover the seamline with a dry press cloth and moist cheesecloth. Move the *point of the iron over the seam allowance* to shrink out the fullness. Be careful not to press beyond the stitching and overflatten the sleeve.

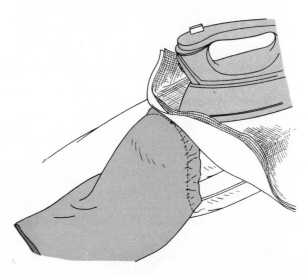

2. After you have stitched the sleeve into the armhole, press the armhole seam allowances over the small end of the·sleeveboard. Use the *point of*

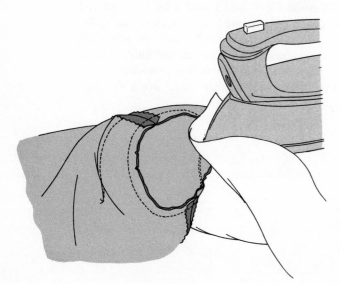

the iron and press into the sleeve *only as far as the stitching*, never beyond it. Turn the seam allowance into the sleeve without further pressing.

In heavy fabrics, such as coating, press the seam open. In a puffed sleeve, as in children's clothes, the seam should be turned into the sleeve.

Plackets

The universally accepted placket closing is the zipper. See page 176 for instructions on various types of zipper insertions. Your first pressing comes after closing the opening with machine basting. Press

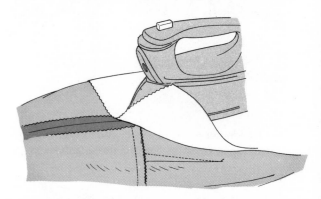

the curved seam open in the machine-basted area; place it over the curve of a press mitt, which has been placed on the small end of the sleeveboard or over the curve of a tailor's ham.

Your second pressing step comes after the final hand or machine stitching. Place the wool-faced pressing pad on the ironing board with the wool interlining upward. Lay the garment, right side down, on the pad. Place a dry press cloth, then a moist cheesecloth, on the wrong side of the garment and press along the stitching line. Do not

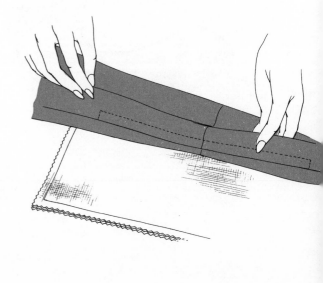

press over the metal chain or synthetic coil of the zipper, for you may mar the fabric, zipper, and soleplate of the iron.

After you have removed the machine basting, you may need a touch-up pressing. Place a strip of brown paper between the placket opening and the metal chain or synthetic coil of the zipper. Protect the fabric with a wool press cloth and press only the stitching line.

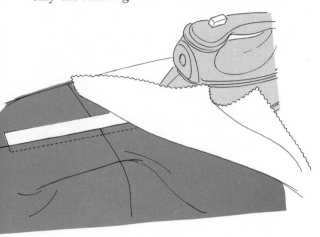

Hems

Hems should not be visible in the finished garment. To achieve this, you must not only mark, fold, and finish the hem properly (see page 187), but *press* it carefully.

The first pressing step occurs after you have folded the hem and basted ¼ inch from the fold. Place the garment, wrong side up, over the end of the ironing board; cover with the proper press cloth and apply the moisture required by the fabric. Do not glide the iron; lift it from one section

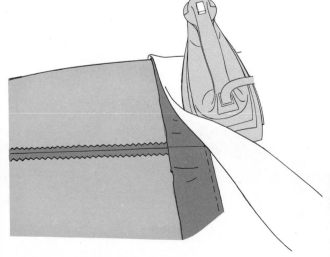

to the other, pressing lightly and forcing steam through the press cloth to form a sharp crease at the fold.

If the fabric is heavy or bulky, steam the hem edge; then use the wooden pounding block, following the directions for *Faced Lapels and Collars*, on page 73.

Fashion may dictate a **soft hem fold** for fabrics such as double knits, loosely woven woolens, raw silks, and bonded fabrics. In such cases, press the hem *very lightly* so that you do not flatten the fold.

Hems in Gored and Flared Skirts

Gored and flared skirts have fullness at the top of the hem which is controlled with machine stitching. To shrink out any excess fullness before applying seam binding, place the free edge of the hem over the curve of a press mitt (which has been placed over the small end of the sleeveboard) or over the curve of a tailor's ham. Cover with the same press cloth and use the same amount of moisture required in the first step. Press to shrink out the fullness.

After you have stitched the seam binding in place or completed the appropriate finish, press the hem on the wrong side in the position it will be hand-stitched, using a press cloth. Move the iron upward from the bottom of the hem to the top of the seam binding.

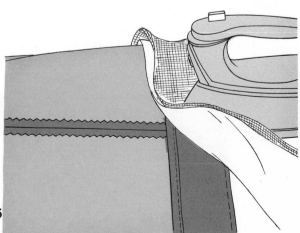

When the garment is of a heavy fabric, slip a strip of brown paper between the skirt and hem before pressing. This prevents the imprint of the hem edge from appearing on the right side of the garment.

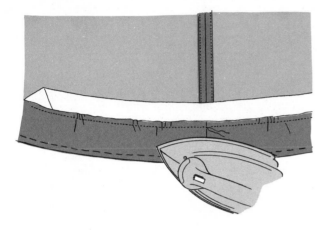

Press napped fabrics over the wool-faced pressing pad.

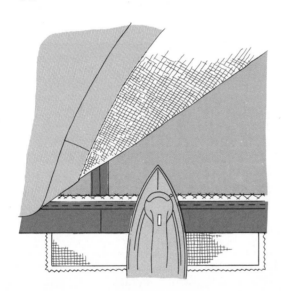

After the final hand stitching, cover with a press cloth, use moisture for steam, and press lightly on the wrong side.

Hem Across Pleat

When the skirt has a pleat, press the seam open in the area of the hem. See page 191 for instructions on slashing the seam allowance before pressing it open.

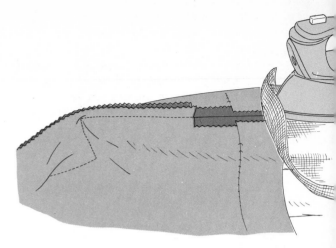

After you have finished the hem, turn the skirt to the wrong side, turn the pleat away from the skirt and press.

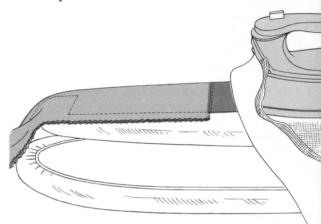

To sharpen the edge of a pleat, turn the garment to the right side. Place the pleat section over the sleeveboard with the underfold of the pleat up. Cover with the wool press cloth and press the length of the pleat. For instructions on pressing pleated skirts, see page 211.

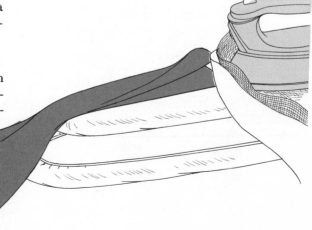

Fitting as You Sew

FITTINGS ARE PLEASANT STEPS in sewing that show you how your work is progressing. Even though you adjusted the tissue pattern to your measurements before cutting the fabric, you are apt to find that minor changes are required when you fit the fabric.

Be critical. The success of your garment depends as much on its fit as on the suitability of the pattern design and fabric. Fashions can be copied, but the garment becomes individually yours when it fits your figure properly. For a good fit, the fabric grain lines must fall correctly in the proper places on your figure. This is explained below in *Understanding Balance Lines.*

In addition to acquainting you with balance lines, this chapter also takes you through the basic fittings. A word of advice: Do not feel bound to fit your dress only at the intervals given here. You may want to fit it more often—especially if the pattern is intricate or you are not sure of an adjustment or are a beginner. Sometimes it is necessary to try on only the bodice or skirt section to test the fit. Fit as often as you feel you should before making the permanent line of stitching. Remember, changes made at the proper time are easier and quicker, and your dress is sure to be a success.

UNDERSTANDING BALANCE LINES

The lengthwise and crosswise grains of the fabric must be in proper relation to the individual figure for any garment to fit well. The positions of the key grain lines are known as "balance lines."

The grain lines are in the correct positions on the tissue pattern. However, if your figure does not conform to standard measurements, adjustments are necessary. In adjusting the pattern and in fitting your dress, you must retain the correct position of the balance grain lines on your figure so that your dress will fit as it should.

The illustrations and text here point out the correct position of balance lines on a sheath dress.

Bodice Front

Chest—about 4 inches below the base of the neck, on the *crosswise grain.*

Bust—across the fullest part of the bust, on the *crosswise grain.*

Waist—about 1½ inches above the waistline, on the *crosswise grain.*

Center Front—center of body, from base of neck to waistline, on the *lengthwise grain.*

Bodice Back

Shoulder—about 4 inches below the prominent vertebra, on the *crosswise grain.* (This corresponds with the chest on the bodice front.)

Underarm—about 1½ inches below the armhole, across the shoulder blades, corresponding with the bustline, on the *crosswise grain.*

Waist—about 1½ inches above the waistline, corresponding with the front grain line, on the *crosswise grain.*

Center Back—center of body, from prominent vertebra at neck to waistline, on the *lengthwise grain.*

(Continued on next page)

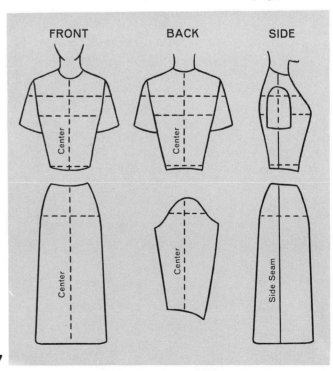

Sleeves

Center—from shoulder line marking to center of wrist, on the *lengthwise grain*.

Sleeve Cap—about 3 inches below the shoulder line, across the sleeve cap at a right angle to the lengthwise grain. This line is on the *crosswise grain* and corresponds with the chest and shoulder grain line of the bodice.

Skirt—Front and Back

Center Front and Back—center of body from waistline to hemline, on the *lengthwise grain*.

Hips—across the fullest part of the hips, usually about 7 inches below the waistline, parallel to the floor, on the *crosswise grain*.

The *side seams* of bodice and skirt must hang perpendicular to the floor although they are seldom cut on the straight grain of the fabric. In full skirts, the center front and back seams may be bias and the side seams may be straight grain, with a slight curve from the waistline about 4 inches down. All four seams must hang straight from waistline to hemline.

Always mark the center line on the fabric with hand basting. It is wise to baste the horizontal balance lines when sewing on fine fabrics, and it is especially important if you are a beginner in sewing.

When a muslin shell is made for use in fitting, draw the balance lines on the muslin before constructing the shell. In this way, you can easily determine whether the balance lines are in the correct position. If adjustments are necessary, make them in the muslin shell. Then make the same adjustments in the tissue pattern before cutting into the garment fabric. See *Muslin Shell,* page 315.

As you and your dress proceed through the basic fittings described below, keep an eye on the balance lines and make sure that they are in the correct position on your figure.

PIN FITTING

Assembling Your Dress

Before pin-fitting your dress, you should have completed these steps:

1) Transferred all markings from pattern to fabric.

2) Stay-stitched if necessary.

3) Basted darts and tucks.

4) Machine-stitched where needed to control any gathered fullness.

5) Basted sectional seams together so that you have four pieces: upper front, upper back, skirt front, and skirt back.

Work on a flat surface. Pin bodice sections together at the shoulder line and underarm seams, and skirt sections together at the side seams. Place pins parallel to the seamline with the fabric right side out and seam edges extended. Leave an opening on the left side of both bodice and skirt for the zipper. Turn under the waistline seam allowance of the skirt and pin.

Fitting Your Dress

Try on the garment, right side out, in front of a full-length mirror if possible. Wear the lingerie and shoes you will wear with the finished garment. And don't forget make-up. It will help you visualize how the dress will look on you. If you plan to wear shoulder pads or shapes, insert them (and be sure to use them in every step of fitting).

If there is a center opening, lap the opening (with center lines coinciding) and pin together at buttonhole markings. Pin seams together in the opening for the zipper. Pin the bodice and skirt together at waistline, with the skirt seam allowance overlapping the bodice seam allowance; be sure to match center lines, darts, and side seams. Adjust the shoulder line to your figure and be certain that the basted center lines of the garment coincide with the center of your figure.

If you are a newcomer to dressmaking, you will probably be carried away by the fact that "it" actually looks like a dress. But let your eye roam critically over the several parts of the work. You will observe that the fabric fits a little differently from the tissue pattern. The need for minor adjustments, which you could not easily detect in fitting the tissue pattern, will become apparent now. As you make them, note them for future reference, for you will want to incorporate them in patterns you use later.

In studying your pin-fitted garment in front of the mirror, remember these points and consider them in your fitting:

1. The neckline has an extended seam allowance, which makes it seem smaller than it will be when the neckline is finished.

2. All ease allowances must be correct as outlined in checking and fitting the pattern. See page 37. Do not overfit the garment. The amount of fullness allowed in the pattern will differ with the style.

Fit the fabric for right- and left-figure differences, which occur most frequently at shoulders, waistline, and hipline. The paragraphs below explain how to make some of the usually needed adjustments.

Bodice Adjustments

Observe and change when necessary the position of the waistline, placement of side seams and shoulder line, and alignment of buttonholes.

Check the length of the shoulder seam. Bring the arms forward to test the ease across the back, from armhole to armhole.

Sloping shoulders will cause the balance line to drop at the armholes and form wrinkles. To correct, re-pin the shoulder seams, making them slightly deeper as you approach the shoulder tips. This means lowering the armhole so that the sleeve will fit as it should. Baste the position of the new seamline. Lay the pattern on the fabric with the shoulder seamline of the pattern on the basted line of the fabric, and recut the armhole. Both shoulders are seldom identical and it may be necessary to change only one.

If square shoulders are the problem, the balance line swings up at the armholes and causes wrinkles to form diagonally toward the bustline and below the back neckline. Re-pin the shoulder seams, making them deeper at the neckline and tapering to a shallow seam allowance at the shoulder tips.

Bustline darts may need adjustment. Check the length and location of the darts. If there is fullness below the bustline and the balance line seems to drop below the fullest part of the bust, raise the underarm darts enough to bring the points in line with the fullest part of the bust; if there is fullness above the bustline and the balance line is above the fullest part of the bust, lower the underarm darts.

A small, flat bust will cause the balance line to sag at the center front. Decrease the underarm darts enough to correct the balance line position and achieve a smooth effect. Now the bodice front will be longer than the bodice back at the underarm seams. *It is a common mistake for a beginner to make the bodice too short;* therefore, try on the dress again to prove the adjustment is correct. Then make a tuck across the tissue pattern, decreasing the length of the bodice front the same amount as you decreased the darts. Lay the pattern on the bodice front, and recut the lower edge of the fabric.

Skirt Adjustments

Difference in hips. It is not unusual for the side seams to fit differently on the right and left sides of the skirt because one hip is higher or larger than the other. Be sure that the side seams hang straight from waistline to lower edge. The skirt should have enough ease at the hipline for you to sit comfortably and enough ease below the hipline so that the skirt will not cup.

A swayback will make the grain line sag at the center back and cause wrinkles below the waistline. To correct, raise the waistline of the skirt in the center back from ½ to ⅝ inch. Mark the adjusted seamline with basting, gradually tapering to the regular waistline seam allowance as you approach the side seams. Sometimes it is necessary to lift the skirt on only one side at the waistline.

If the skirt hikes in the front and the side seams jut forward, raise the back and sides of the skirt at the waistline just enough to bring the balance line in correct position and the side seams in a straight line to achieve a smooth effect.

Skirt darts should extend to the fullest part of the hips. It may be necessary to lengthen or shorten the darts to conform with the contour of your figure.

Observe the length of the skirt and the amount allowed for the hem.

Pin-mark any adjustments. Remove the garment and mark the adjustments with bastings.

You are now ready for some serious seaming. Before you begin, it may be wise to read over the pressing advice given in *Pressing As You Sew,* page 64.

Garment Construction to Be Completed

The steps in construction to complete before this fitting are as follows:

1) Stitch and press all darts.

2) Make bound buttonholes if your pattern calls for them.

3) Baste, stitch, and press seams that occur within front and back sections.

4) If underlining is used, stitch and press the darts, then baste the underlining to the wrong sides of the garment sections.

5) Stitch and press shoulder seams.

6) Apply the interfacing, and finish the neckline and front or back opening.

7) If your dress has sleeves, baste the darts or control any fullness at the elbow. Baste the sleeve underarm seam.

8) Try the sleeve on the right arm, right side out, with the arm flexed to allow for muscle expansion. If there is a marked difference between the right and left arms, fit both sleeves.

9) Baste any adjustments and refit the sleeve. Stitch and press sleeve underarm seams.

10) Baste the side seams in the bodice and in the skirt, right sides together, observing the adjustments made in the pin fitting.

11) Pin and baste the sleeves into the armholes.

12) Baste bodice and skirt together at the waistline, right sides together, observing any changes made in the pin fitting.

Fitting Your Dress

Try on the dress, right side out, to verify the adjustments noted in the pin fitting before stitching the side seams.

1. Lap and pin the opening. Position the seams and center lines correctly on your figure.

2. Tie a tape measure or a strip of fabric, about 1 inch wide, around your waist to locate the normal waistline. The seam should fall beneath the tape. Check the waist length, the ease allowances in all girth measurements, the placement of side seams and shoulder line, and the hang and true fit of the sleeves. The balance lines in the sleeves and bodice should correspond.

3. Bring the arm forward to test the ease across the back, from armhole to armhole, for freedom of arm movement. Insufficient ease will cause strain across the sleeve and be uncomfortable, and the sleeves will pull out at the seamline after you have worn the garment a few times. If shoulder seams are too long, the sleeves will drop off the shoulders and be uncomfortable. Bend the arms to be sure you have allowed enough ease in the sleeves for comfort. Pin-mark any adjustments. Baste the new adjustments and try on the garment again to prove them.

SUBSEQUENT FITTINGS

Fitting to Check Sleeve and Waistline

Before this fitting, remove the waistline and sleeve bastings. Stitch and press the side seams in the bodice and skirt. Baste sleeves into the armholes again and baste bodice to skirt, right sides together, observing any changes made in the preceding fitting.

Now, try on the dress; lap and pin the opening. Observe the bodice length, the fit in the waistline, the placement of the ease in the sleeves; determine the sleeve length. If you are satisfied, proceed with the final stitching.

Your Final Fitting

Before the final fitting, sew sleeves into armholes, join skirt and bodice at the waistline, and sew in the zipper.

Try on the dress and test the fit. If you are satisfied, mark the hemline.

Seams, Seams, Seams

Seams do more than hold your dress together. Plain seams can express the lines of your dress through subtle shaping. Properly formed, they are almost invisible. Decorative seams can emphasize line in the dress design.

This chapter explains what you should know about seams to achieve the effect you want. The material is grouped in five sections:

1 General rules and helps in seaming
2 Different kinds of seams
3 Seam blending, beveling, or grading
4 Seam finishes
5 Understitching.

GENERAL RULES AND HELPS IN SEAMING

A seam results when one or more lines of stitching are used to join two or more pieces of fabric. The steps in forming a seam are these:

1. Pin the seam edges together at ends, at notches, and at center, finally working between center and ends.

2. Hand-baste the seam. If your fabric is easy to handle and if you are sufficiently skilled in stitching, you can use pin basting instead of hand basting.

3. Stitch the seam with thread the exact color of the fabric. Set the stitch selector for the stitch length appropriate for your fabric (refer to the *Fabric, Thread, Needle, and Stitch Length Chart* on page 24) and then test the stitch on a swatch of the fabric. Stitch along one side of the basting thread, close to it but not through it. Backstitch at each end of the seam to secure the threads and to prevent the seam from raveling. Remove the basting thread.

4. Finish the seam edges. See page 91.

5. Press the seam in the same position as it was stitched and then press it open unless the pattern instructs otherwise.

Seam Guidelines

The Seam Guide and throat-plate guidelines help you guide the stitching straight and parallel to the seam edge. The Seam Guide is adjustable for spacing stitching at any distance between ⅛ and 1¼ inches from the edge of the fabric. The throat-plate markings progress at ⅛-inch intervals, starting at ⅜ inch and extending to ¾ inch from the needle at the right. Since most patterns have a ⅝-inch seam allowance, the ⅝-inch line is more prominent than the other markings on the throat plate.

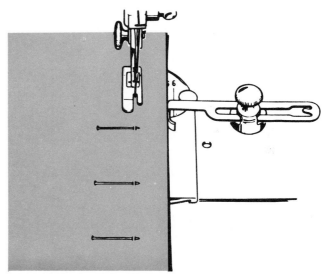

Directional Stitching

There are also rules on the direction you should follow in stitching seams. In general, shoulder seams are stitched from the neckline to the armhole; bodice seams from underarm to waistline; sleeve seams from underarm to wrist; skirt seams from hem to waistline. There are exceptions, however; for example: pile fabrics such as velvet, velveteen, and corduroy are cut with the pile standing up, and all seams should be stitched upward with the pile (from lower edge to top edge).

Your pattern will indicate the types of seams you are to use, and below you will find instructions for forming them. Unless otherwise stated, all seams are stitched from the wrong side of the fabric.

Plain Seam—Straight

The plain seam is formed with the right sides of fabric together. Place the seam under the needle, with the edges to the right. Position the needle about ½ inch from the back edge and lower the presser foot. Backstitch to the edge of the fabric for reinforcement; then stitch forward to the end of the seam and backstitch to reinforce it. Raise the presser foot and remove the fabric. Form the habit of using the Thread Cutter located at the back of the presser bar assembly and just above the presser foot.

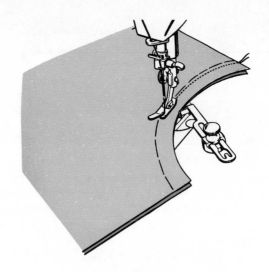

Plain Seam—Curved *(Top right)*

Curved seams require special attention in handling and shaping. Use a shorter stitch than for a straight seam. If you used a 12 stitch length for straight seams, use a 15 stitch length for curved seams to ensure extra elasticity and strength and to prevent seam failure under strain. Position the Seam Guide at an angle so that you get a uniform seam edge.

Curved seams must be blended so that they will lie flat. See instructions on page 89.

Bias Seam

Hand-baste bias seams, leaving the threads loose at the ends. Allow your work to hang overnight before stitching. Always use a shorter stitch length for a bias seam. Fabric requiring a 12 stitch length on a straight seam requires a 15 stitch length on a bias seam to increase the elasticity of the seam. Stitch with the grain.

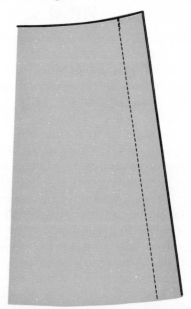

Seam with Bias Edge and Straight Edge

To join a bias edge to a straight edge, pin and baste with the bias section on top. Stitch with the bias edge against the feed to ensure a smooth, even joining. *(See illustration at top of next page.)*

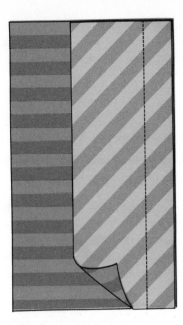

Double-Stitched Seam

Use this seam in sheer fabrics and lace for curved as well as straight seams.

Place the first row of stitching on the seamline. Press. Place the second row of stitching within the seam allowance, about ¼ inch from the first row, using a fine multiple-stitch zig-zag. Straight stitching may also be used. Trim the seam allowance close to the outside row of stitching.

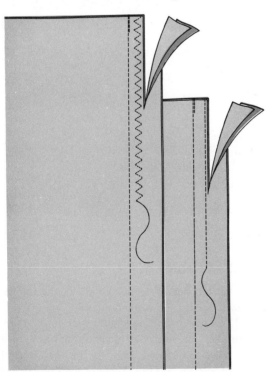

Lapped Seam

Use lapped seams when joining sections of interfacing and interlining to eliminate bulk.

Lap one edge over the other, with the seamlines meeting in the center. Stitch through the center, using a multiple-stitch zig-zag or straight stitching. If the seam edges are too wide, trim after stitching.

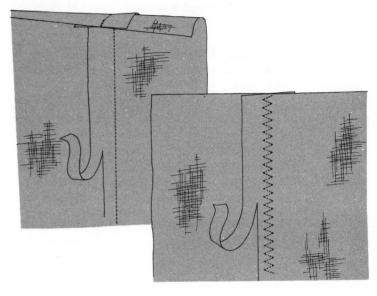

Abutted Seam

Use abutted seam in nonwoven interfacings and interfacings of hair canvas, muslin, and similar fabrics.

Trim away the seam allowance on both sections. Bring the two edges together and pin over an underlay of a lightweight fabric. The underlay should be 1 inch wide and slightly longer than the

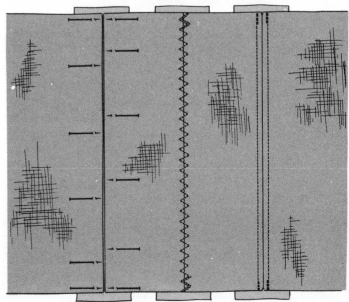

seam. Stitch from the right side, using the multiple-stitch zig-zag, widest stitch width, and 20 stitch length. Backstitch at each end. Be sure the abutted line is aligned with the center of the presser foot. Straight stitching may also be used on each side of the abutment.

Ease in a Seam

A seam with slight ease often occurs at the shoulder or elbow where a long seam edge joins a shorter one.

Working from the long side, pin the edges together, matching at the ends of the seam and at the notches. Between the notches, ease the long side to the short side by inserting pins at frequent intervals, distributing the fullness evenly. Hand-baste, then stitch with the full side against the feed.

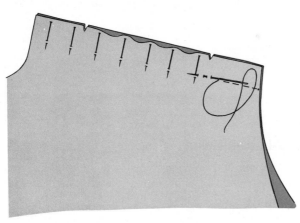

Seams that Cross

Seams that cross occur at the shoulder line, waistline, and underarm, and where darts join a seam or tuck.

Press the seams open and finish the edges as required by the fabric. To ensure accurately matched seams that cross, pin with a fine needle, with only the point nipped into the fabric at the stitching line; then pin on each side on the seamline. The

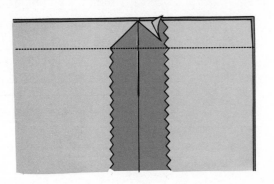

needle prevents one seam from slipping beyond the other during stitching and will not mar delicate fabrics. Blend away the excess seam allowance at the point where the seams cross.

Top-Stitched Seam

Top stitching is used as a styling point along the finished edge of a garment or along the seam within a garment.

When preparing a curved, top-stitched seam, stay-stitch near the seamline on both the overlap and the underlap. Fold under the seam allowance on the overlap and pin, baste, blend, and press. Lap the folded edge a full seam's width over the underlap, then pin and baste. Remove the first basting. Top-stitch from the right side, close to the folded edge. If the stitching is ¼ inch or more from the edge, mark the stitching line with basting as instructed for *Top Stitching,* page 335.

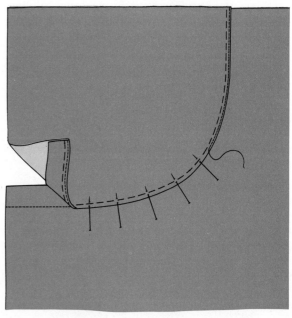

Tucked Seam

Use tucked seams as a styling accent in blouses, dresses, skirts, and other apparel.

Working from the right side, fold under the seam allowance on one side and pin; baste, if necessary. Lay the folded edge on the seamline of the second section and pin, keeping the raw edges even on the underside. Baste the tuck, maintaining an even distance from the folded edge to the basting line. Then stitch, following the even basted line. Trim off the seam edge on the undersection. The Quilter is an aid when stitching this seam because the guide keeps your stitching straight and parallel to the folded edge.

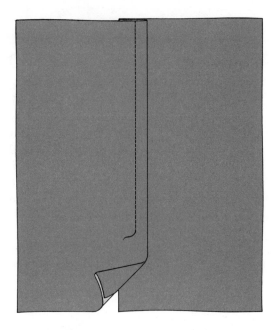

Self-Bound Seam

Use self-bound seams in sheer curtains, children's clothes, blouses, and the like.

Make a plain seam and press it as stitched. Trim one edge to within ⅛ inch of the stitching. Turn under the other edge and pin it to the seam at the line of stitching, enclosing the first edge. Stitch near the folded edge.

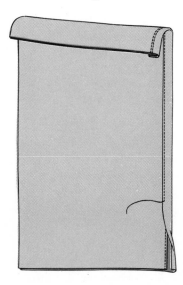

Hemmed Seam

A hemmed seam is appropriate when a fine, narrow seam is required, such as in sheer curtains and children's clothes.

When using this seam in a garment, the fitting must be done first and seam edges trimmed to ¼ inch. Attach the Hemmer Foot to the machine in place of the regular presser foot. With right sides of the fabric together, place the upper layer ⅛ inch to the left of the lower layer. Insert the edge into the scroll of the Hemmer and stitch so that the wide edge is hemmed over the narrow edge. See Hemmer Foot, page 283.

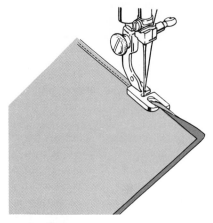

Lingerie Seam

With zig-zag stitching, you can make dainty lingerie seams durable and rip-proof. This method is particularly good where flat bias seams are desired.

After straight-stitching the bias seam on the wrong side, press as stitched. Pink, and then press both seam allowances in the same direction. From the right side, stitch with a fine zig-zag stitch, allowing the needle to enter the seamline, then the seam thickness.

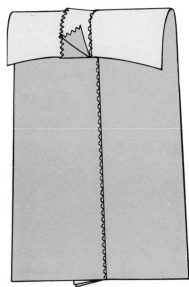

Catch-Stitched Seam *(Right)*

A catch-stitched seam is used where the garment is interfaced or underlined. This is an excellent means of preventing seam edges from rolling when the garment is dry-cleaned. Use it in shoulder seams and notched collars, and where collar and facings join.

Trim the interfacing or underlining seam allowance close to the stitching. Press the plain seam open, then catch-stitch the seam edges by hand. Working from left to right, with the needle pointed to the left, catch only one or two threads in the seam allowance, then only a single thread outside the seam allowance and in the interfacing or underlining. Alternate the stitches along the seamline. The stitches are not visible from the top side.

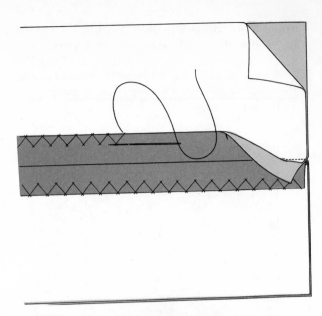

French Seam

Use a French seam in sheer fabrics, blouses, children's clothes, and lingerie. It is not appropriate for curved seams.

A French seam is a seam within a seam and, when finished, is usually ¼ inch or less in width. Place the wrong sides of the fabric together and stitch about ¼ inch from the seamline. Press as stitched. Trim seam allowances to within ⅛ inch of stitching and press the seam open. Turn the

right sides of the fabric together; fold on the stitching line, and press. Then stitch on the seamline.

The Edge Stitcher may be used in making a French seam. The slot in the accessory assures a straight line of stitching. See page 284 for instructions on using the *Edge Stitcher*.

Mock French Seam

Use this seam in sheer and lightweight fabrics, children's clothes, and blouses, in place of the conventional French seam. Both straight and curved seams may be finished in this way.

Stitch along the seamline with right sides of the fabric together. Press as stitched. Trim the seam edges slightly if they are too wide. Fold both seam edges to the inside and stitch them together.

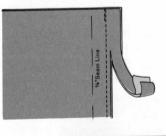

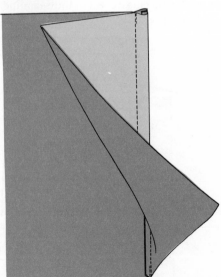

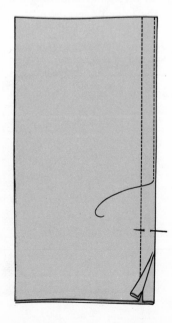

Flat Felled Seam

Men's and boys' wear usually calls for flat felled seams. They are also used in give a tailored appearance to women's sportswear. It is a matter of preference which side of the seam is made on the right side. One side reveals an inside seam paralleled by stitching, and the reverse side reveals a top-stitched seam paralleled by a row of stitching.

With right sides of the fabric outward, take the full seam allowance with the first row of stitching. Press the seam open, then press both seam allowances to one side, keeping the right side of the stitching on top. Trim the under seam allowance to one-half its width. Turn the upper seam allowance edge evenly over the trimmed edge; then top-stitch.

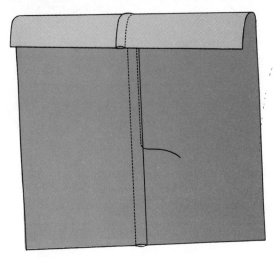

Opinions differ on the handling of flat felled seams. On men's wear, the seam edges that are blended are usually (1) the back seams on side seams and sleeve seams, (2) the sleeve seam edge on shoulder seams, (3) the garment section on yoke

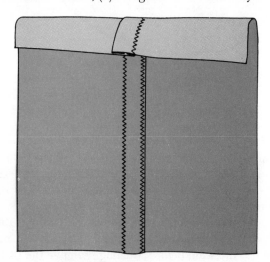

seams, and (4) the front seam on shoulder seams.

Zig-zag stitching gives strength and durability to flat felled seams. You can substitute it for straight stitching, following the directions given above. Use a 15 stitch length and a medium-width zig-zag stitch.

Slot Seam

Slot seams are used as fashion seams in skirts, blouses, dresses, suits, coats, and children's clothes made of heavy or medium-weight fabrics.

Pin and machine-baste on the seamline, leaving one long thread at each end. Press as stitched, then press the seam open. Clip the machine basting on one side at four- to five-stitch intervals. Cut an underlay of the same or contrasting fabric 1 inch wider than the two seam edges. Working from the wrong side, center the underlay over the seam and pin in position. Baste from the right side. Then from the right side, stitch along each side an equal distance from the seam depression. The distance may be from ¼ to ½ inch, depending on the fabric. If less than ¼ inch, gauge the distance with

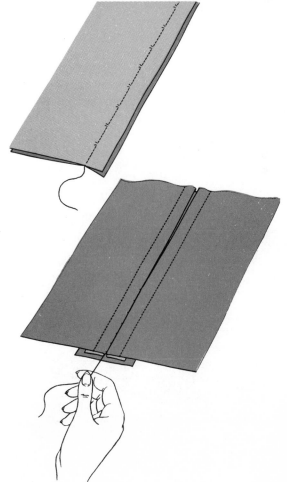

the presser foot; if more than ¼ inch, mark both stitching lines with basting as instructed for *Top Stitching*, page 335. Remove the machine basting by pulling the long thread, and remove any short threads that are visible.

The Quilter is convenient for top stitching. The space guide on the Quilter is guided into the depression of the machine-basted seam, ensuring an accurate stitching line parallel to the fold. See the instructions below for *Welt Seam*.

Welt Seam

Welt seams are style seams that are often found in suits and coats made of firm fabrics.

Form a plain seam on the wrong side, using the stitch length appropriate for the fabric. Press first as stitched; then press the seam open. Trim 3/16 inch from one seam edge, and press both seam edges to one side so that the wide edge covers the narrow edge. Baste flat. From the right side, stitch an even distance from the seam depression. If the distance is greater than ¼ inch, mark the stitching line with basting as instructed for *Top Stitching*, page 335.

The Quilter is excellent for this top stitching since it gauges the stitching, keeping it straight and parallel to the seam depression. Insert the removable space guide from the right side of the Quilter and adjust it for the desired distance. If the fabric is heavy, tilt the space guide so that its wall will accommodate the layers of fabric. As you sew, guide the seam depression against the space guide.

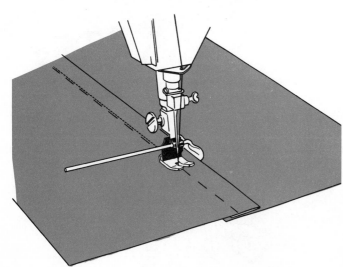

Hairline Seam

A dainty hairline finish is desirable for enclosed seams of sheer collars and facings.

Set your zig-zag machine for a short stitch length and a narrow stitch width, and use a filler cord of either heavy-duty thread or buttonhole twist. Unwind a sufficient amount of the filler cord to prevent strain or tension on the cord. Lead the end of the cord through the right eyelet on the Special Purpose Foot. Draw the cord under and in back of the foot. Stitch on the seamline, covering the filler cord. Press, and trim away the seam

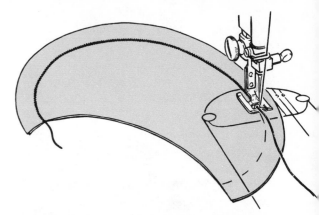

allowance close to the stitching. Turn to the right side and press. Seam allowances that would ordinarily show through are eliminated.

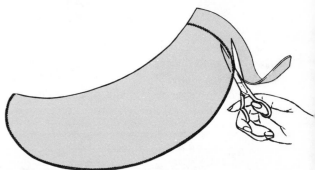

Seams in Chiffon

Carefully hand-baste seams in chiffon. Using a 15 to 20 stitch length, test the stitching on a swatch of the chiffon. The quality of the stitching depends on the machine and the softness of the fabric. Stitch slowly, and apply gentle tension on the seam by holding it both in front and in back of the presser foot.

If your machine does not stitch chiffon satisfactorily with the above method, place tissue paper under the seam before stitching. Remove the tissue paper by gently pulling it away from one side of the stitching, then from the other.

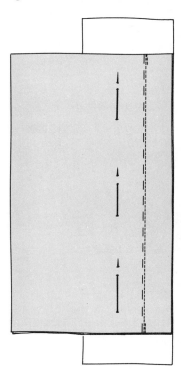

Seams in Knit Fabrics

Because of their loop construction, knit fabrics are not always seamed and finished in the same way as woven fabrics. The kind of seam that is most appropriate for a specific knitted fabric will depend on the amount of stretch in the fabric, the weight or thickness of the fabric, the kind of garment it will be used for, and the position of the seam within the garment. The technique for easing one seam to another is quite different from that appropriate for woven fabrics. Also, the kind of seam finish, if one is required, and the seam width will vary from those appropriate for woven fabrics. See *Knits,* beginning on page 417.

Seams in Kimono Sleeves

To make seams in kimono sleeves, see *Kimono Sleeve—without Gusset,* page 162; or *Kimono Sleeve —with Gusset,* page 164.

SEAM BLENDING, BEVELING, OR GRADING

To blend, bevel, or grade a seam means to remove the bulk so that the seam will lie flat. The procedure varies depending on whether the seam is enclosed or fitted and whether it is an inside curve, an outside curve, a straight seam, or square corner or point. Seams that require blending are stitched and then blended according to the methods described here.

Fitted Seams

Fitted seams are found at the shoulder line where the neck is built up, in a princess-line bodice, at the waistline in suit jackets, in yokes, and in seams extending over the bust and hipline. These seams are usually pressed open and the edges are finished as required by the fabric.

Fitted seams may be inside or outside curves. Do not trim them, but blend them as follows:

Inside curves. Slash into the seam allowance far enough to relieve the strain imposed by the seam edge so that it will lie flat. The depth of the slash and the number of slashes will vary with the degree of the curve and texture of the fabric; however, the slashes usually extend to within ¼ inch of the stitching and are made at evenly spaced intervals. There are times, however, when only one slash is necessary.

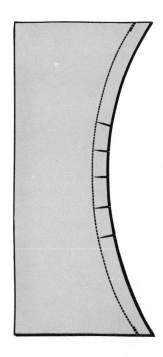

Outside curves. Cut narrow notches or wedges out of the seam allowance, sufficient in depth to remove only the portion of the seam edge that may overlap when the seam is pressed open. Avoid cutting out a wedge so large that it will produce a saw-tooth effect in the seam edge that will press through and mark the right side of the fabric. Cut the notches at evenly space intervals. The frequency and spacing depend on the degree of the curve and the texture of the fabric. When the curve is slight and the fabric flexible, it may not be necessary to blend the seam.

Often an inside curve is seamed to an outside curve. This requires slashing the inside curved edge and notching the outside curved edge.

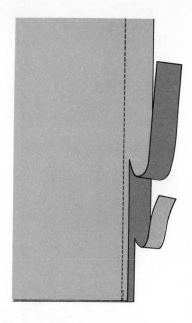

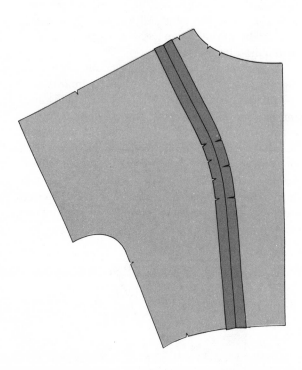

Enclosed Seams

Enclosed seams are found in facings. They may be straight, as in front and back facings of blouses, dresses, jackets, and coats; or curved or shaped as in necklines, collars, cuffs, shaped yokes, pockets, and similar construction. Blend them as follows:

Straight seams. Trim the interfacing close to the stitching if it is included in the seam. Blend the facing seam allowance to ⅛ inch and the garment seam allowance to ¼ inch. Press, then press the seam open. Turn to the right side; ease the facing under slightly at the seamline and baste. Use diagonal basting and silk thread. Press flat. *(See illustration at top of next column).*

Inside curves. If interfacing is included in the seam, trim it close to the stitching. Blend the facing seam allowance to ⅛ inch and the garment seam allowance to ¼ inch. Slash these blended seam edges to within ⅛ inch of the seamline at evenly spaced intervals. This relieves the strain imposed by the seam edge and prevents pulling. Press the seam open. Then, turn to the right side; ease the facing under slightly at the seamline and baste. Use silk thread and diagonal basting. Press flat.

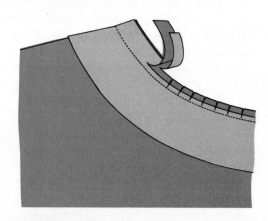

Outside curves. If interfacing is included in the seam, trim it close to the stitching. Blend the facing seam allowance to ⅛ inch and the garment seam allowance to ¼ inch. Cut notches in the seam allowance at evenly spaced intervals to remove the bulk. Cut away only enough to permit the seam to lie flat so that you do not have a saw-tooth effect in the seam edge. Press, then press the seam open over the curved edge of a seamboard, a press mitt, or the finger. Turn to the right side;

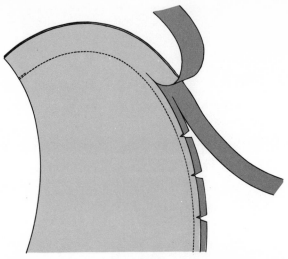

ease the facing under slightly at the seamline and baste. Use silk thread and diagonal basting. Press flat.

Square corners and points. Square corners and points require diagonal stitching across the point to allow enough space to smoothly enclose the seam edge that turns to the inside. The number of diagonal stitches varies with the weight of the fabric. Lightweight, crisp fabrics may require only one stitch across the point and heavy fabrics may require as many as three.

Stitch to within one or two stitches of the intersecting seamline. Pivot with the needle in the

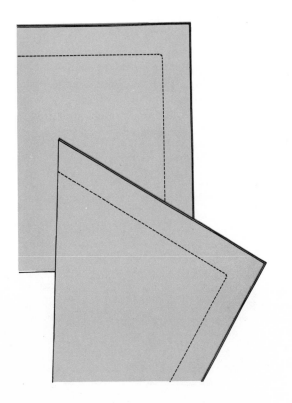

fabric, but on its upward stroke, and turn the fabric so the stitching is directed diagonally across the corner; then take one, two, or three stitches. Pivot again, turn the fabric, and stitch, following the seamline.

If interfacing is included in the seam, trim it close to the stiching. Blend the seam allowance on the facing to ⅛ inch and on the garment to ¼ inch. Trim away the seam allowance diagonally across the point and very close to the stitching; then trim away the seam allowance diagonally at the sides of the point. Press the seam open before turning to the right side. Ease the facing under slightly at the seamline and baste. Use silk thread and diagonal basting. Press.

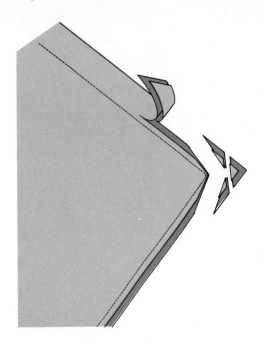

SEAM FINISHES

Seam edges are "finished" to prevent them from raveling during use and in washing or dry cleaning; to improve the appearance of the inside of your garment; and to strengthen the seam itself.

Seams in a garment should be finished during the assembly process and before being crossed by another seam. The seam finish must be without bulk so that it is not visible when the garment is worn and does not form a ridge on the right side when the garment is pressed.

You should know a variety of seam-finishing methods so that it will be easy for you to select the one best suited to your needs. When in doubt, try several different methods on test seams before making up your mind.

Pinked Seam

Use a pinked seam on fabrics that will not fray or ravel.

After stitching a plain seam, pink the seam edges with pinking shears. Remove only the seam edge. Cut with a medium stroke; do not fully open the shears or cut entirely to the point. Press the seam in the same position as it was stitched, and then press it open.

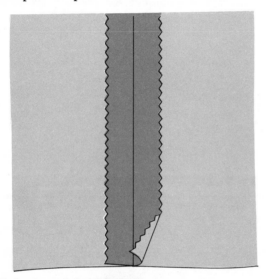

Pinked and Stitched Seam

This seam finish may be used on almost any fabric that will ravel.

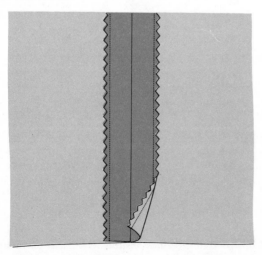

Form a plain seam. Place a line of stitching about ¼ inch from the seam edge, using a 20 stitch length. Pink the edges. The stitching will prevent the seam from raveling and curling.

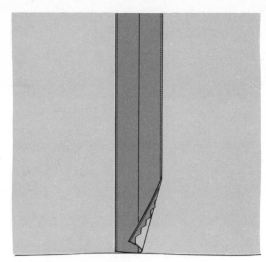

Edgestitched Seam (Above)

Use this finish on lightweight and medium-weight fabrics as well as on unlined jackets and boleros.

Stitch a plain seam. Press the seam flat, then press it open. Pink the edges; then fold them under ⅛ to ¼ inch and stitch on the folded edge. The Edge Stitcher will help you keep this stitching straight and parallel to the edge. For instructions on using it, see page 284.

Open Bound Seam (Below)

Binding is an excellent finish for fabrics that tend to fray, such as tweed and heavy, coarse weaves, as well as for unlined jackets and coats. Instructions for using the *Binder* may be found on page 282.

Form a plain seam. Press the seam, then press it open. With the Binder on the machine and silk bias seam binding, bind each seam edge, using either straight stitching or an open zig-zag stitch. To prevent seam edges from stretching or fraying

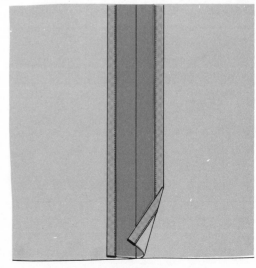

in loosely woven fabrics, place a row of stitching ⅛ inch from the seam edge before applying the binding.

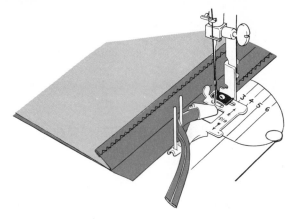

Net Bound Seam

Delicate fabrics that fray easily, such as chiffon velvet, and sheer metallic, may have seam edges bound with nylon net, which prevents fraying without adding bulk.

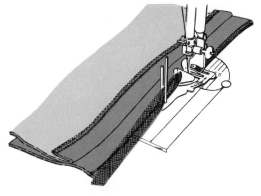

Cut the net into ½-inch strips and insert, unfolded, into the Binder. Feed seam edges into the Binder with napped or right side up. Stitch, using a medium-width zig-zag stitch.

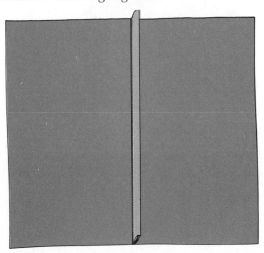

Plain Bound Seam *(Bottom, previous column)*

This seam is practical for household items such as cushions, simple slipcovers, and articles made of plastic.

After stitching a plain seam, trim the seam edges to a scant ¼ inch. Press. Insert both edges into the Binder and stitch, keeping the seam edges well into the scroll as you sew.

Machine Overedged Seam

The blindstitch zig-zag provides an excellent finish for tweed, raw silk, double knit, and heavy woolens.

Form a plain seam. Press the seam as stitched, then press it open. Use the blindstitch zig-zag, and form the stitches over the edge of the seam. Both the stitch length and the stitch width settings vary with the fabric.

When both seam edges are turned in the same direction as in a sleeve armhole and pocket pouch, press the plain seam as stitched. Trim the seam allowance to about ¼ inch. Then stitch the edges together, using the blindstitch zig-zag.

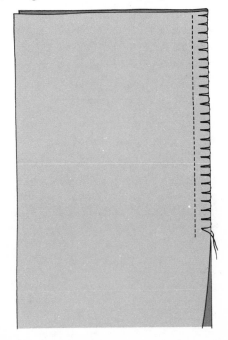

Zig-Zag Seam

Zig-zag stitching is an ideal seam finish for jersey, double knit, and other fabrics with "give" because the stitch is as flexible as the fabric. Either the plain or multiple-stitch zig-zag may be used.

After forming a plain seam, press it open. Select a plain zig-zag stitch, medium stitch width, and between 15 and 20 stitch length. Stitch near the seam edge but not over it. Press. Trim off the seam edge close to the stitching.

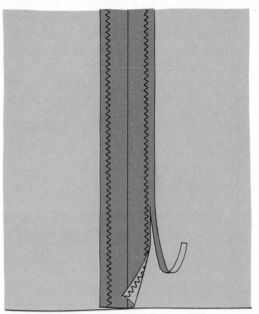

For the multiple-stitch zig-zag, select a wide stitch width and a short stitch length (in the "fine" area), and stitch close to the seam edge. Press.

Seams Overcast by Hand

If the fabric has a tendency to ravel and a machine finish would be too harsh, finish the seam edge by hand.

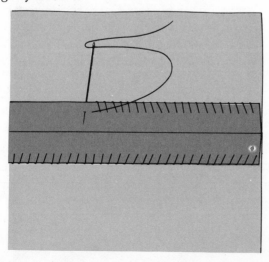

Form a plain seam and press it open. By hand, make slanting stitches over the seam edge, about ¼ inch apart and about ⅛ inch in depth, depending on the weight of the fabric. Do not pull the threads too tightly.

When the seam is pressed open, overcast the edges separately. When both seam edges are turned in the seam direction (sleeve and waistline seams are examples), overcast the two edges together.

UNDERSTITCHING

To prevent a facing edge from rolling beyond the garment edge, you must stitch the seam allowances to the facing on the underside.

Before doing this you will have completed a certain amount of garment construction—namely: the facing will be stitched in place and the seam blended and pressed; then the facing will be turned to the underside and eased under slightly at the seamline before pressing again.

To understitch, turn facing and seam allowances away from the garment and stitch from the right side, through facing and seam allowances, close to the seamline. Since this stitching is not on the right side of the garment, it is invisible in the finished work.

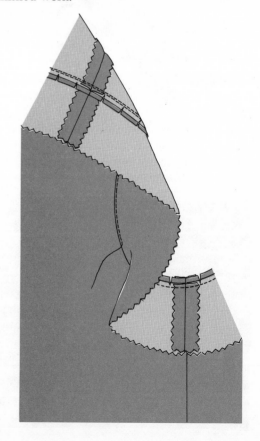

Underlining and Lining

ADDING AN UNDERLINING OR LINING to your dress is one way of achieving a custom-made look in your clothes. Many fabrics and fashion styles require either one or the other to retain the shape and add body to the garment.

Simply defined, underlining and lining are a *second thickness* of carefully selected fabric that is used to support the garment fabric and add resistance to strain. *Underlining* is sewed into the seams with the garment fabric. Hand stitches that hold down facings and hems are made in the underlining instead of the garment fabric. *Lining* is constructed separately and attached to the skirt at the waistline seam or to the dress at the neckline, armhole, and waistline seams.

Do not confuse underlining and lining with interfacing. See page 134. When a garment is underlined or lined, interfacing is included in such areas as facings, collars and cuffs, lapels, and the like.

Whether or not you underline or line a gar-ment is a decision you should make when you are planning your dress and selecting a pattern. The type of underlining or lining you select depends on the fabric you are using as well as the effect you wish to achieve. For example, a sheer fabric such as organza makes an ideal underlining for soft silks and woolens, peau de soie, and imported cottons that will be dry-cleaned. It allows them to retain their naturally soft, luxurious feeling, which would be lost if a bulky or heavy underlining were used. For a closely woven wool or raw silk, a heavier fabric such as China silk or SiBonne may be a good choice—and lining rather than underlining may be preferable. Lay your dress fabric over the underlining or lining fabric so that you can judge the final effect.

Almost any fabric may be underlined; generally, however, only firm and opaque fabrics are lined. For guides on fabrics to use as underlining or lining, see page 20.

HOW TO UNDERLINE DRESSES AND SKIRTS

You may underline the entire dress or just a section of it. The underlining in skirts may extend to the fold of the hem, to the top of the hem, or to about 12 inches below the hipline.

Underlining a Dress

Cut the underlining by the same pattern pieces and on the same grain as the garment. Notch and mark each section the same as the dress fabric, and place the corresponding pieces together.

Stitch the darts and seams within the bodice and skirt sections separately in the dress fabric and underlining unless the fabric is sheer. See page 97. Finish seam edges, and press.

Place the fabric, wrong side up, on a flat surface; lay the underlining over it. Both pieces must be smooth and wrinkle-free. Pin them together along the center line, side seams, and waistline. Place several rows of diagonal basting within each section, as illustrated below and on the following page, to hold the two layers of fabric together.

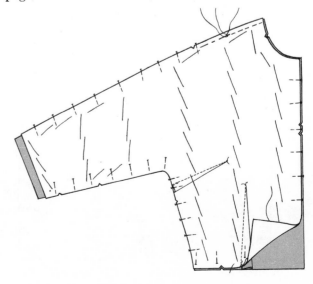

95

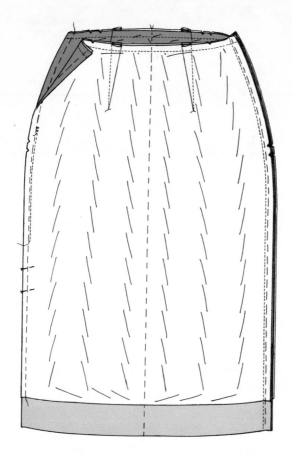

At the waistline of the skirt and bodice, machine-stitch the underlining to the dress fabric ½ inch from the seam edge. Handle the fabric and underlining as one piece of fabric in assembling the garment.

Hemming Underlined Garments

When the underlining extends to the top of the hem, pink the lower edge of the underlining; then fold it under ¼ inch and stitch near the folded edge, using the multiple-stitch zig-zag.

When the underlining extends to the fold of the hem, fold the hem over the underlining and hand-stitch in place, making the stitches through only the underlining and hem.

Hem the skirt, using the method suitable for the fabric. See *Hems and Hem Finishes* page 187.

Underlining a Skirt with a Pleat

When there is a pleat in the skirt, you should extend the underlining to the top of the hem.

In the skirt fabric, stitch the darts and seam for the pleat, following the instructions accompanying the pattern.

In the underlining, stitch the seam above the pleat from the waistline to the top of the pleat, leaving a slit in the pleat area. Trim off excess fabric, allowing a ⅝-inch seam allowance. Pink the seam edges and lower edge of the underlining

Use silk thread and make the stitches from ⅜ to ½ inch in length and about 2 inches apart. Do not draw the thread tightly. *Do not remove these bastings until the hem is finished.* (If the two fabrics are of different lengths, the skirt will not hang evenly.) Hand-baste a scant ⅝ inch from all seam edges in the bodice and side seams of the skirt.

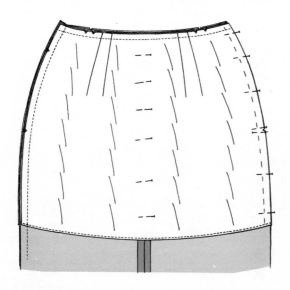

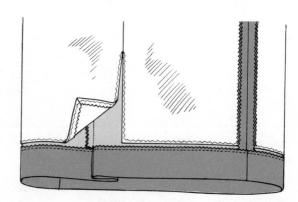

back and front. Fold the pinked edges under ⅝ inch and stitch around the lower edge and both sides of the slit, using the multiple-stitch zig-zag for added strength. Stitch the darts. Baste the fabric and underlining together, following the instructions for *Underlining a Dress,* above, and handle as one in assembling the garment.

Underlining Sheer Fabrics

Fabrics such as chiffon and lace should be underlined with a smooth, firm, opaque fabric, similar in fiber content to the sheer. Colors should match or complement each other to create an illusion of color intensity or variation. Two underlining methods are given here; select the one appropriate for the style of your dress and the effect you wish to achieve.

Method 1: A complete underlining, stitched as one with the garment fabric, permits you to treat a sheer as a heavier fabric and to use patterns with darts and styling seams since the underlining conceals them in the finished dress.

Place underlining sections, right side up, on a flat surface and the sheer dress fabric, right side up, over them. Baste together, following the directions for *Underlining a Dress*, page 95. Hand-baste through the center of darts to hold the two layers of fabric together. Pin, baste, and stitch the darts through the two layers. Handle the fabric and underlining as one in assembling the garment.

To create the illusion of a sheer yoke and sleeves or of strapless, bare shoulders, underline the upper part of the bodice with net or chiffon and the lower part of the bodice with a firm, opaque fabric. Join the two fabrics above the bustline.

Method 2: If the dress has a full skirt, the bodice section may be underlined and the skirt section lined—that is, the two fabrics in the skirt can be seamed and hemmed separately and joined only at the waistline.

Treat the bodice section as instructed above. For the skirt, follow the instructions given on page 99, *Lining a Sheer Skirt*.

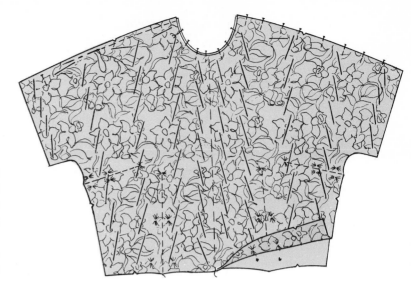

HOW TO LINE DRESSES AND SKIRTS

When dresses or skirts are lined, they are finished as nicely on the underside as on the top side. The top fabric and lining are constructed separately and are placed wrong sides together so that the seam allowances are hidden. In dresses, the lining is joined to the top fabric at the neckline, armhole, or waistline seams; in skirts it is joined to the top fabric at the waistline. Do not confuse these linings with those used in tailored coats and suits which are covered in *Graduate to Tailoring*, pages 325 and 329.

Lining a Dress

In a blouse or sheath dress that is collarless and sleeveless, the lining can serve as a one-piece neckline and armhole finish. In a collarless garment with set-in sleeves, it can serve as a neckline finish. In both cases you eliminate the regular facing, which would only add unnecessary bulk.

If the dress is collarless and sleeveless, cut the lining by the dress pattern. Stitch the underarm seams separately in the dress and in the lining. Finish the seam edges and press the seams open. *Leave the shoulder seams open.* Apply the lining to the dress, following the instructions for the *One-piece Neckline and Armhole Facing,* page 141. But substitute the full-length lining for the facing in the instructions.

Hem the lining and dress separately, making the lining 1 inch shorter than the dress. To add a decorative touch, you can make a narrow hem in the lining and sew lace edging to the hemmed edge.

If the dress has sleeves, cut the lining by the dress pattern. Stitch the shoulder and underarm seams separately in the dress and in the lining. Finish seam edges. Press the seams, then press them open.

Turn the dress wrong side out and the lining right side out. Place the lining inside the dress, right sides together. Pin and baste the lining to the dress around the neckline, matching center lines, notches, and shoulder seams. Stitch.

Trim the lining seam allowance to ⅛ inch and the dress seam allowance to ¼ inch. Slash the seam allowances on curves and clip off corners where seams cross at the underarm. Press.

Turn the lining through the neck opening and over the wrong side of the dress; then turn the dress to the right side. Ease the lining under slightly at the seamline and baste. Press, then remove bastings. Understitch the seam to prevent the lining from rolling out of place (see page 94). Press. Arrange the lining smoothly against the underside of the garment fabric, then baste around the armholes. Handle as one fabric when you sew in the sleeves.

Hem the lining and dress separately, making the lining 1 inch shorter than the dress.

Lining a Skirt

The skirt and lining are constructed separately and joined only at the waistline seam. This is an excellent treatment for heavy woolens and firmly woven cottons that will be dry-cleaned.

Cut the lining by the same pattern pieces and on the same grain as the skirt. Notch and mark each section the same as the skirt fabric.

Stitch and press the darts and all seams in the

skirt and sew in the zipper. Then stitch and press the darts and all seams in the lining. Make the opening for the zipper the same length in the lining as in the skirt fabric.

Place the lining inside the skirt, wrong sides together, and pin together at the waistline, matching seams, darts, and markings. Turn the skirt to the wrong side with the lining on the top side. At the end of the placket opening in the lining,

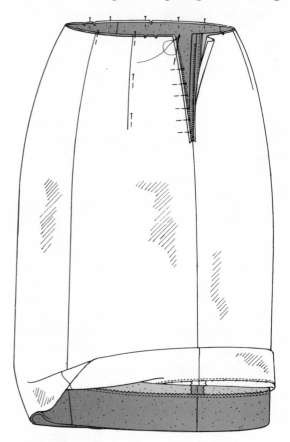

slash diagonally on each side, ¼ inch beyond the seamline. Fold under the edges and pin them to the zipper tape, as illustrated. Slip-stitch in place. Stitch the skirt and lining together at the waistline, ½ inch from the seam edge. Apply the waistband.

Hem the skirt and lining separately, making the lining 1 inch shorter than the skirt.

Lining a Slit Skirt

In the method explained here, the slits in the lining do not correspond with those in the skirt. If the skirt is slit in the back, as in the illustration, the lining is slit at each side seam; if the skirt is slit at the side seams, the lining is slit in the center front or center back. Then a facing is stitched to the lining, directly under the slits of the skirt, which leaves a pleasing finish.

Cut the lining by the same pattern pieces and on the same grain as the skirt. Notch and mark each section the same as the skirt fabric.

Construct the skirt, leaving the seams open the depth of the slits plus hem. Reinforce with backstitching. Machine-baste the seams together in the slits.

Construct the lining so that the seams will face the seams in the skirt. Stitch darts and the full length of the seams that correspond with the slits in the skirt.

Cut a facing of the skirt fabric 5 inches longer than the slit plus hem and seam allowance, and 8 inches wide so that it will extend 4 inches on each side of the slit. (The skirt illustrated has two slits in the back and required only one piece of the fabric for the facing. It was cut 8 inches wider than the distance between the two slits.) Fold under the seam allowance at the top and each side of the facing. Press.

Center the facing right side up on the top side of the lining, keeping the lower edges even; pin. Baste, then stitch near the folded edges. (If the slits in the skirt are at the side seams, center the facings over the side seams of the lining.)

Pin the front and back lining sections together at the side seams. Stitch, leaving the seams open the depth of the slits. Reinforce with backstitching. Machine-baste the seams together in the slits. Finish the seam edges. Press, then press the seams open.

Turn the lining to the right side. Place it inside the skirt, with the faced side of the lining to wrong side of the skirt. Pin together at the waistline, matching seams and markings. Finish, following the instructions above under *Lining a Skirt*.

Hem the skirt and lining separately, keeping them the same length. See *Hem in Slit Skirt*, page 191.

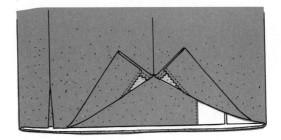

Lining a Sheer Skirt

To create an interesting variation, the lining is sometimes fitted closely to the figure and the sheer top skirt is billowy or flowing, which creates a misty effect. Such treatment requires careful handling and finishing of all seams.

Seam the sheer fabric and lining separately; use a fine French seam in the sheer fabric. Place the lining inside the sheer skirt, with the right side of lining next to the wrong side of the skirt. Join them at the waistline (see page 98), then join the skirt to the underlined bodice. Hem the two fabrics separately. A narrow hem is essential for the sheer full skirt—make either a hand-rolled hem or a hem with horsehair briad. See pages 197 and 192. Make a 2-or 3-inch hem in the closely fitted lining.

If both the sheer and the lining are circular or flared, they must also be hemmed separately to keep the sheer from sagging and blousing over the lining. Make a narrow hem in each.

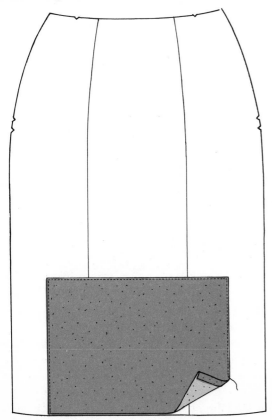

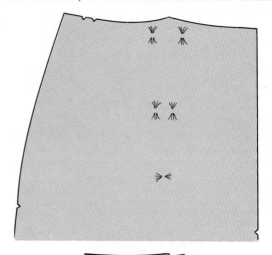

Darts, Tucks, and Gathers

DARTS, TUCKS, AND GATHERS are three friends you will meet often in apparel construction. Darts are preferred in firm fabrics; tucks in smooth, drapable fabrics; and gathers in soft, sheer fabrics. All three have a functional and decorative use in sewing; each in its own way gives fit and contour to a garment. For purely decorative applications of tucks and shirring, see pages 235 and 243.

DARTS

Beginning Tips on Darts

Darts provide fullness at the bust, hip, shoulder, and elbow. They must point toward the fullest curve of the figure but must not extend as far as the curve.

It may be necessary to change the position of darts to conform with the contour of your figure. Darts extending from waistline to bustline are sometimes moved closer to the center or farther apart to bring them directly under the fullest part of the bustline. To accommodate a lower bustline, darts extending from underarm toward the bustline should be placed lower than indicated on the pattern.

The length of darts in a skirt may also have to be adjusted for better fit. A short figure may require shorter darts, and a very tall figure longer darts. If darts in the bodice are moved closer to the center or farther apart, then the darts in the skirt must be moved to correspond with them.

Darts are usually formed on the wrong side of the garment. They are stitched on the right side only when they are styling points and the continuous-thread dart is used. See page 101.

Stitching a Dart

How you handle the fabric when forming and stitching a dart has a direct influence on the result. Since darts should be barely visible when completed, they must be tapered gradually to the point so that there is no bulge where the dart ends.

Fold the dart and match markings; start pinning at the seam edge, then at the point, and at intervals between. Place the pins at right angles to the seamline, with the heads toward the folded

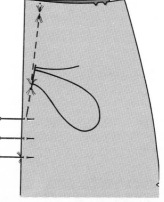

edge. Baste from the seam edge to the point. Remove the tailor's tacks. Start stitching near the seam edge and reinforce with backstitching, tapering gradually to the point where the last three or four stitches parallel the fold in the dart, *just a thread's width from the fold*. Continue stitching off the fabric to form a chain about ½ inch beyond the point. Clip the thread ends about 2 inches from the point. Tie the thread chain into a single knot, using a pin to set the knot close to the fabric.

(Illustrated at top of next column)

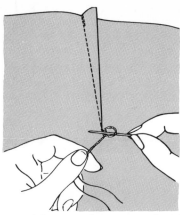

In heavy fabrics such as tweed and flannel, darts are frequently slashed and pressed open. If the fabric is one that ravels or frays easily, overcast the slashed edges. On firm fabrics that do not fray easily, finish with pinking shears.

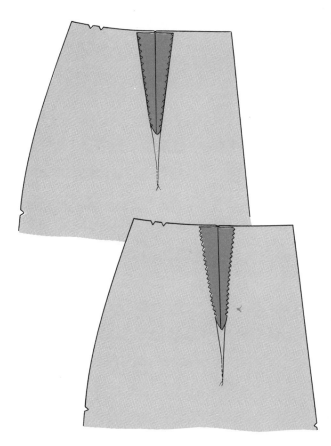

Pressing Darts

Pressing further shapes and molds the dart after stitching. Darts are pressed toward the center in skirt back, blouse front and back, and shoulder; and downward at the underarm and elbow. Use the curved surface of a press mitt or tailor's ham.

First press the dart flat as it was stitched, carrying the crease only as far as the stitching. Protect the fabric with a press cloth. Then place the dart over the tailor's ham or press mitt. Turn the dart in the proper direction. Cover it with a press cloth, and use the amount of steam required by the fabric. Press toward the point of the dart.

Continuous-Thread Darts

The continuous-thread dart is used (1) on "outside" darts, that is, when the fold of the dart is on the outside of the garment; and (2) on inside darts when the fabric is sheer. The stitching begins *at the point* rather than the seam edge as in the conventional dart, and no thread ends are left to be tied in a knot at the point.

Thread the bobbin thread through the needle in the opposite direction from the usual threading, and tie it to the upper thread in a single knot. Rewind the spool until the knot has passed all threading points and is a sufficient distance from the last thread guide nearest the spool to provide enough thread to stitch the full length of the dart.

Position the tip of the needle into the point

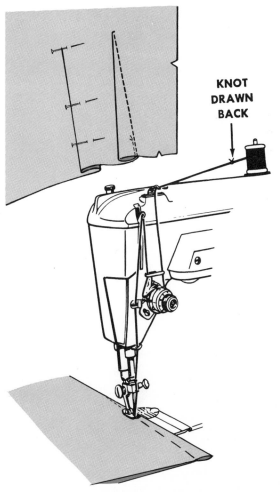

KNOT DRAWN BACK

...rt, *just a thread's width from the fold.*
...slack out of the thread by turning the
...wer the presser foot and stitch, carefully
...he point while stitching toward the seam
...inforce the seam edges with backstitching.
...l the machine for each dart.

...*Touch & Sew* machine has push-button
...winding, which simplifies threading for
continuous-thread darts. The bobbin stays in the
machine and is wound with thread directly from
the needle, which gives a continuous thread. If
you have a *Touch & Sew* machine, wind an empty
bobbin with enough thread to make a single dart
(usually about one yard). Stitch as instructed above.
Wind an empty bobbin for each dart.

Skirt Darts

Darts in the back skirt extend to the fullest part
of the hips and are pressed toward the center.
Darts in the front skirt are smaller and may be
in groups of two. Skirt and bodice darts must
meet at the waistline.

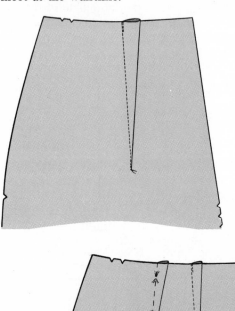

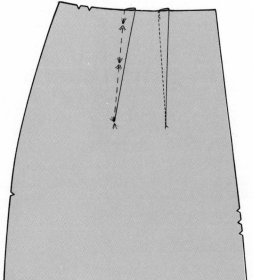

Underarm Darts

Underarm darts point to the fullest part of the
bustline and may be on a horizontal or diagonal
line. They are formed in the same manner as the
conventional dart. Press flat as stitched; then press
downward over a press mitt.

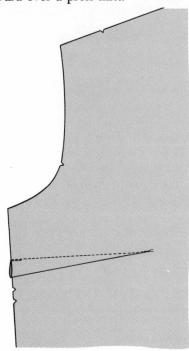

Shoulder Darts

Shoulder darts are usually narrow and about 4
inches in length, depending on the size of the
pattern. They are stitched in the same manner
as the conventional dart and pressed toward the
center over a press mitt.

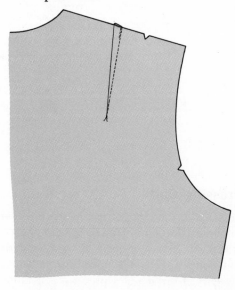

Elbow Darts

Close-fitting sleeves that extend below the elbow are usually darted for ease at the elbow. The darts are stitched in the same manner as the conventional dart. Press flat as stitched; then press downward over a press mitt.

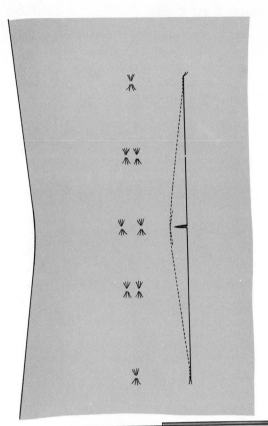

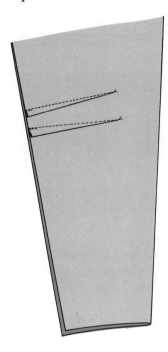

Contour Darts

Darts that fit the waistline and taper to a point at each end are known as "contour" darts. They are used in suits, princess-line coats and dresses, and overblouses.

To form the dart, fold the fabric and match markings; pin at the waistline, at each point, and at intervals between. Baste.

Stitch the dart in two steps, beginning at the waistline and stitching to the point each time. Overlap the stitching about ¾ inch at the waistline. Tie the thread ends at each point. Slash to within ¼ inch of the stitching at the waistline to relieve the strain. Press flat as stitched; then press each end over a press mitt.

The continuous-thread method may be used when stitching the contour dart. Follow the instructions for *Continuous-Thread Darts*. Start stitching from one of the points to ⅜ inch beyond the waistline. Rethread the machine (or, on a *Touch & Sew* machine, rewind the bobbin). Repeat the operation from the other point, overlapping the stitch about ¾ inch at the waistline. Slash and press the same as above.

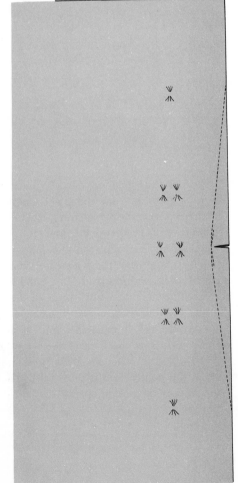

Diagonal Bust Darts

Diagonal darts may originate at the underarm seam or at the waistline, and they always point diagonally toward the fullest part of the bust. They may have the conventional fold or a cutout section where seam edges are joined.

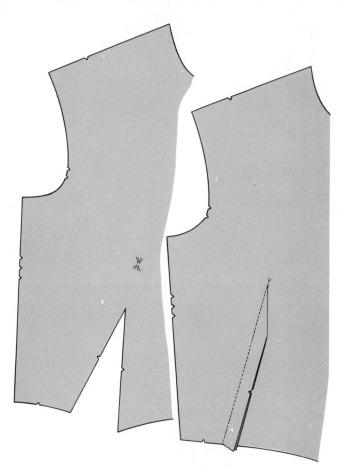

To make the diagonal dart, begin at the waistline or underarm seam and place the seam edges of the dart together, matching markings. Pin at the wide end, at the point, and at intervals between, easing the seam on the long side. Baste. Begin stitching from the wide end; reinforce with backstitching, and gradually taper the stitching to the point where the last three or four stitches parallel the fold *and are just a thread's width from it*. Then tie the thread ends into a single knot, using a pin to set the knot close to the fabric.

Press flat as stitched; then press both edges toward the center over a press mitt. The seam in the dart may be pressed open if the fabric is heavy.

Interfacing Darts

To shape darts in interfacing and eliminate bulk, cut out the dart allowance on the stitching line. Bring the two cut edges together and pin over an underlay of a lightweight fabric such as organza. Cut the underlay 1 inch wide and slightly longer than the dart. Stitch from the right side.

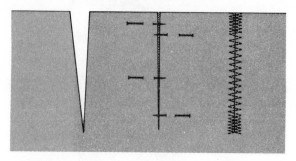

When using a zig-zag machine, select the multiple-stitch zig-zag, widest stitch width, and 20 stitch length. Align the abutted line with the center of the presser foot.

If you use straight stitching, stitch on each side of the abutted line. Reinforce with backstitching at each end. Press over the curved surface of a press mitt.

TUCKS

Tucks for Contour

Contour tucks are found at the front shoulder line, front and back waistline of the bodice, and the front section of the skirt. They are used to provide fullness and are usually formed on the wrong side of the garment. (They may, however, be formed on the right side as a styling point. See *Continuous-Thread Tucks* below.)

Tucks extending down from the shoulder seam

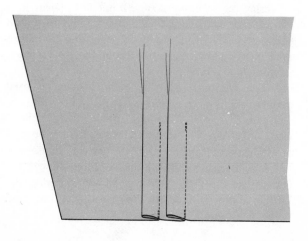

and up from the front waistline should be directly in line with the fullest part of the bust. Tucks in the front skirt section should match the tucks in the bodice section when joined.

Fold the tuck, match the markings, and keep the seam edges even. Pin and baste.

Start stitching at the seam edge and reinforce with backstitching. Continue stitching to the end of the tuck, then backstitch again for reinforcement.

Continuous-Thread Tucks

When the fold of the tuck is formed on the right side of the garment to provide a style accent, the continuous-thread tuck is used so that no backstitching shows. (Threads may be drawn to the underside and tied, but the continuous-thread method is more durable and attractive.)

Pin and baste the tuck, keeping the seam edges even. Begin the continuous-thread stitching at the end of the tuck farthest from the seam edge (below the bustline) and finish it at the seam edge with backstitching.

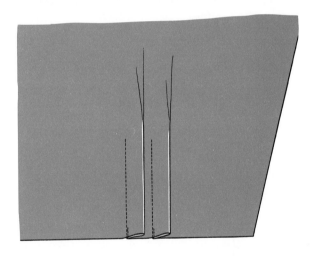

Position the tuck under the needle and lower the presser foot. Hold the needle thread loosely with the left hand while turning the hand wheel with the right hand to form a stitch. Draw the bobbin thread up through the fabric. Thread the bobbin thread through the needle in the opposite direction, following the instructions for *Continuous-Thread Darts* on page 101. Then, position the point of the needle in the fabric and pull the slack out of the thread by turning the spool. Stitch slowly to the seam edge and reinforce with backstitching.

For instructions on pressing tucks, see page 70.

GATHERS

Gathering to Control Fullness

Patterns for soft or sheer fabrics may indicate gathering to control fullness at the shoulder, at the waistline of the bodice or skirt, at yoke joinings in a bodice or skirt, at the shoulder or cuff of sleeves, and at other styling points. The pattern should indicate the number of rows of stitching.

Use an 8 to 10 stitch length in medium-weight fabrics and a 12 to 15 stitch length in soft or filmy fabrics. Loosen the upper tension enough to draw the bobbin thread. (Do not forget to return the tension to its previous setting.)

Place the first row of stitching in the seam allowance a scant ⅝ inch from the seam edge; place the second row in the seam allowance about ½ inch from the seam edge. Neither of these rows will be visible in the finished garment. Additional lines of gathering, which will be visible in the finished garment, may be placed ⅛ to ¼ inch apart. Space the first additional row the selected distance from the first row of stitching at the ⅝-inch position.

At one end, draw the threads through to the underside. Tie by forming a single knot in the two strands of thread and set the knot tightly against

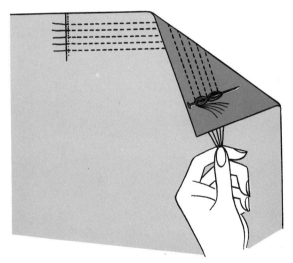

the fabric. Hold these thread ends and fold the fabric at the end of the rows of stitching. Stitch close to the fold, forming a pin tuck across the end, extending it from the seam edge to the last row of stitching. Cut off the ends of the gathering threads ½ inch from the stitching.

At the other end of the stitching, anchor the threads on the right side of the garment by forming a figure eight around a pin. One thread for each row of stitching remains on the wrong side

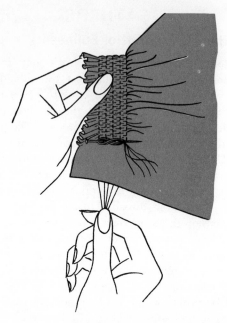

of the garment. Tightly twist these threads together and pull, and at the same time ease the fabric back on the stitches to form uniform gathers. Finish the second end by drawing threads to the underside and tying. Cross with a pin tuck.

Gathered Skirts

In gathered skirts, use heavy-duty mercerized or nylon thread on the bobbin because it will not break while you are easing the fullness across the width of the skirt.

First stitch the side seams and put in the zipper. Pin-mark the waistline at the zipper opening and at the right side seam. Then place the stitching for the gathers as instructed above; however, stitch the front and back sections separately. Extend the stitching from the right side seam to the zipper opening in each section, and leave 3-inch thread ends. (The pin tuck is eliminated in this method.)

Match markings on the skirt with those on the waistband or bodice, and pin. To gather each skirt section between the markings, pull the bobbin thread at each end of a section and ease the fullness toward the center. Pull threads to the underside and join the broken lines of stitching by tying the four threads together into a single knot close to the stitching. See illustration on page 306. Pin the skirt to the waistband or bodice at close intervals, then stitch.

Buttonholes without Tears

THE THOUGHT OF MAKING BUTTONHOLES has been known to throw the budding seamstress into a panic. It need not. What may seem like the bane of dressmaking will soon become a pleasant routine if you approach the task cautiously but courageously.

Remember first that buttonholes may be decorative as well as functional. Properly positioned, they contribute to the fit and comfort of your garment.

This chapter tells you about the preparatory steps and explains how to make the several kinds of buttonholes—fabric bound, corded, machine-worked (using either the zig-zag machine or the Buttonholer), and hand-worked. The type of buttonhole you make depends on the fabric, the style of the garment, and your preference and skill. Corded and bound buttonholes are usually preferred in women's dresses, suits, and coats; machine-worked buttonholes are used in sportswear and children's clothes as well as men's and boys' wear; hand-worked buttonholes are found in babies' clothes and blouses of soft, fine silk, linen, or cotton.

PREPARATORY STEPS

Position of Buttonhole

The rules for positioning buttons and buttonholes apply to all types of buttonholes:

—Buttonholes in women's and girls' clothes are placed on the right side of the garment; in men's and boys' wear, on the left side.

—*Horizontal* buttonholes are placed to extend ⅛ inch beyond the center line basting; *vertical* buttonholes are placed so that the center line basting falls in the center of the buttonhole.

—Buttons are sewed on the opposite side of the garment with the center of the button positioned exactly on the center line basting. When the garment is buttoned, the center lines on the

right and left sides coincide. If a closing overlaps more or less than the pattern indicates, the fit of the garment is altered.

—The pattern usually designates the button size the garment is designed to carry. The space from the center line basting to the finished facing edge must be from three-quarters to once the diameter of the button. With this spacing, the button will not extend beyond the facing edge when the garment is buttoned. If you plan to use a button size different from that indicated on the pattern, take this into account when cutting the garment so that you allow the proper distance between the center line and finished edge. Adjust facing width the same amount.

—Spaces between buttonholes should generally be equal, although fashion may show a different arrangement, especially in loosely fitted garments. Your pattern will designate the spacing required. However, if you have had to adjust the pattern—that is, lengthen or shorten the bodice or skirt, or alter the bustline—or if you use a button larger or smaller than the size indicated on the pattern, you will have to modify the buttonhole spaces accordingly.

Normally, buttonholes should be spaced in harmony with the figure. When they are incorrectly spaced, the closing gaps, giving the appearance of a poorly fitted garment.

—*The three key points for positioning buttonholes* are at the fullest part of the bust, the neckline, and the waistline.

Mark the position of the buttonhole at the fullest part of the bust, then at the neckline (and then at the waistline if you are making a coat, jacket, overblouse, or princess-line dress).

After locating these key points, space additional buttonholes evenly between them.

If the pattern has buttons all the way down the front, place the last buttonhole about 4 inches from the hem edge.

—Determine the positions of the buttonholes and mark the fabric while the pattern is still pinned to it. During the first fitting, check the positions to prove that they are accurate.

Length of Buttonhole

Since the length of the buttonhole depends on the size of the button, *select buttons before making buttonholes.* To determine the length, measure the diameter plus the thickness of the button. To test the length, cut a slash in a double thickness of fabric swatch. If the button slips through the slash easily, the size is correct.

Always make a test buttonhole in a swatch of the fabric you are working with. Fold the fabric, duplicating a facing, and include the same type of interfacing you will use in the garment. Buttonholes should be long enough so that the button slips through easily, yet snug enough so that the garment stays buttoned.

BOUND AND CORDED BUTTONHOLES

In making bound buttonholes, you have a range of methods from which to choose: the patch, one-piece, two-piece piped, and corded. All produce attractive durable buttonholes. The two-piece piped method is recommended for loosely woven fabrics; for all other fabrics, the selection is up to you.

Bound buttonholes are not difficult when you follow the directions given here. They are made through the garment fabric and either a stay or lightweight interfacing before the facing is attached.

Use a stay of a lightweight fabric such as batiste lawn, or silk organza to reinforce the stitching around the buttonhole when you are using a *heavyweight* interfacing. *Never make bound buttonholes through hair canvas or heavy interfacing.*

When the interfacing is of a *lightweight* fabric such as batiste, lawn, organdy, it may serve as a stay as well as an interfacing.

Position the stay or lightweight interfacing on the wrong side of the garment, and pin. Then baste guidelines for the position and size of the buttonholes as instructed below.

When making a series of bound buttonholes, always carry through the same step for each buttonhole before proceeding to the next step. Press carefully after completing each step.

Always make a test buttonhole in a swatch of

the same fabric you are using in the garment regardless of how many buttonholes you have made previously.

Guidelines for Bound Buttonholes

Study the lines **A, B,** and **C** on the diagram. These lines of basting are made on the true grain of the fabric and are your guidelines for stitching the buttonholes. For basting, use thread contrasting in color to that of the fabric so that it can be easily seen and removed.

On the right side of the garment, place a vertical line of machine basting ⅛ inch outside the center line basting—as at **A.** (The center line should have been hand-basted before the pattern was removed from the fabric.) Measure the length of the buttonholes and place the second vertical line of machine basting the measured distance from **A**—as at **B.** Machine-baste the position of each buttonhole on a horizontal line, extending each end of the stitching about ¾ inch beyond the vertical markings—as at **C.** Use hand basting if machine basting will mar the fabric.

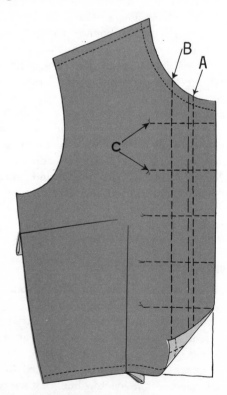

Patch Method

The patch method requires additional markings for accurately stitched buttonholes. First, machine-baste the vertical and horizontal guidelines, **A, B,** and **C,** as instructed above. Then on the stay or

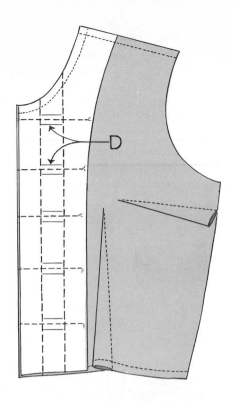

patch over each buttonhole marking, right sides together. Pin in position; baste if necessary. See bottom of previous column.

3. On the wrong side, stitch around the buttonhole, following the markings. Use a 20 stitch length. Begin at the center of one side and stitch to the end; leave the needle in the fabric, raise the presser bar, and turn the fabric on the needle. Lower the presser bar and stitch across the end, taking four or five stitches. Continue stitching around the buttonhole, turning each corner in the same way; make the same number of stitches at each end and overlap about four stitches at the starting point. Press.

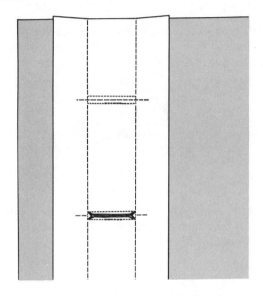

lightweight interfacing on the underside, draw a pencil line on each side of and ⅛ inch from the horizontal basting—as at **D.** This is the stitching line. If the fabric is bulky, draw the lines farther from the basting but not more than ¼ inch.

1. For each buttonhole, cut a patch of fabric on the crosswise grain or on the true bias, 2 inches wide and 1 inch longer than the finished buttonhole. Crease lightly through the center, following the crosswise grain (or true bias) of the fabric.

2. On the right side of the garment, center a

If you have a Singer Buttonholer for your zigzag machine, it will perform this basic stitching. It controls the buttonhole length and width and eliminates turning the fabric.

4. Remove basting threads across each end of the buttonhole. Carefully cut through the center of the buttonhole to within ¼ inch of each end; then cut diagonally to each corner. Do not clip through the stitching.

5. Draw the patch through the opening to the underside.

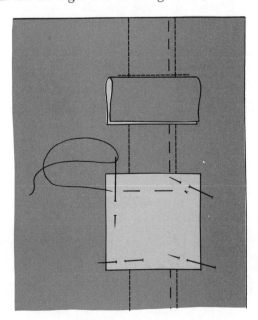

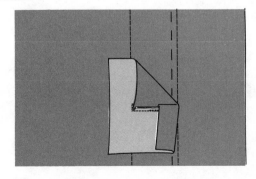

6. Carefully pull out the triangular ends to square the corners. If the slashes are made deep enough into the corners, the opening will be smooth. Press the triangular ends and side seam allowances away from the opening. See *Pressing as You Sew,* page 71.

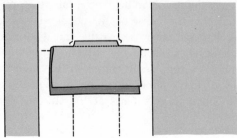

7. Fold each side of the patch to form pleats that meet at the center of the buttonhole and cover the opening. Carry the folds to the edge of the

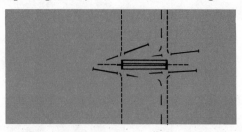

patch. From the right side, baste along the center of each fold, then overcast the folds together. Remove machine-basted guidelines. Press.

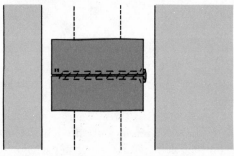

8. Place the garment right side up on the machine, fold it back, and stitch the pleats to the seam allowances. First stitch across the triangular ends on the original stitching line, beginning and

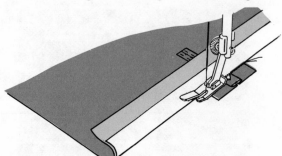

ending the stitching at the raw edge of the patch. Then stitch along the seams on each side, *just a hair's width from the original stitching line,* beginning and ending at the raw edge of the patch. The side stitching crosses the end stitching and squares the corners. The stitching is not visible on the right side.

9. Remove all hand bastings except the overcasting holding the pleats together. Press. Trim the patch to within ¼ inch of the stitching.

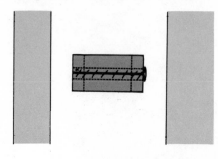

Treating Heavy Interfacing

If the garment is interfaced with fabric such as Armo or any other hair canvas, use a stay of lightweight fabric under the buttonholes. Attach the interfacing to the garment after the buttonholes have been made. Be sure the interfacing lies

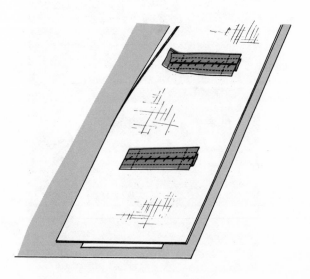

smoothly against the fabric. Pin around each buttonhole. From the right side, insert pins straight through each of the four corners to mark the position of the buttonhole on the interfacing. Using the pins as a guide, cut out a piece from the interfacing, barely outside the pin mark, which is slightly longer and wider than the buttonhole. Pull the seam edges of the buttonhole through the opening in the interfacing.

Finishing the Back of Buttonholes

Finish the back of buttonholes *after you have attached the facing* to the garment. Baste the facing to the garment around each buttonhole, then finish it using one of the three methods illustrated below.

Method 1: Use this method if the fabric does not ravel easily and if the facing side of the buttonhole will not be visible when the garment is open. From the right side, insert pins straight through each of the four corners to mark the position of the buttonhole on the facing. On the underside, cut the facing between the pins to within ¼ inch of the ends; then cut diagonally to the corners. Use the point of the needle to turn under the edges, and slip-stitch the facing in place. The facing side has the same rectangular shape as the front of the buttonhole.

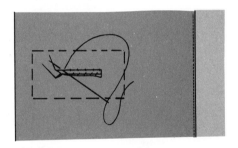

Method 2: This method is preferred for tweeds and fabrics that ravel easily. From the right side, insert a pin straight through each end of the buttonhole. Cut the facing between the pins. Turn under the edges with the point of the needle and slip-stitch the facing in place, forming an oval shape.

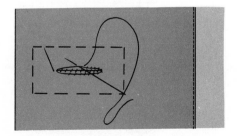

Method 3: If the facing side of the buttonhole will be visible at times (as in coats or suits that may be worn closed at the neckline or open with lapels), it must be as neat as the garment side.

After you have attached the facing (see pages 134 and 135), pin it in place around the buttonhole. Mark the buttonhole position on it by inserting pins straight through the four corners from the right side of the garment. Then from the facing side, insert pins straight through the facing in the same places. Remove pins on the top side and around the buttonhole. Carefully separate the facing from the garment, leaving the facing pin-marked. Hand-baste the outline of the buttonhole, using the pins as a guide.

Finish with a faced rectangular opening. Select organza the exact color of the garment fabric. To cut, stitch, and turn the organza patch to form the opening, follow *Steps 2 through 5 on page 113* for the *Two-Piece Piped Method*. Then trim off the edges of the organza ⅜ inch from the opening.

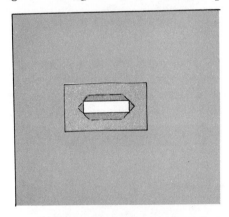

Pin, then baste, the facing in place again. The opening in the facing should be the exact size of the finished buttonhole in the garment, and the buttonhole stitching should not be visible. Be sure the organza does not show on the right side of the facing. Slip-stitch in place, making invisible stitches.

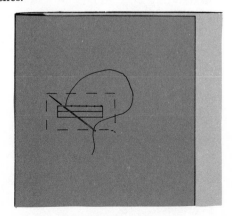

One-Piece Method

Position the stay or lightweight interfacing on the underside, then baste guidelines to mark buttonhole positions as described on page 108.

1. For each buttonhole, cut a strip of fabric on the crosswise grain, 1 inch wide and 1 inch longer than the finished buttonhole.

2. Form the buttonhole strip by accurately folding the cut edges to the center, wrong side together, and baste along each fold. This will form a folded strip ½ inch in width. Cover with a press cloth, and press. Remove basting.

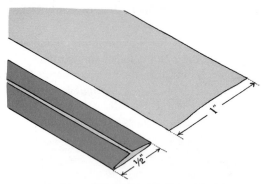

3. On the right side of the garment, center a buttonhole strip over each buttonhole marking, and pin at each end. Hand-baste through the center of each fold to hold the strip in place.

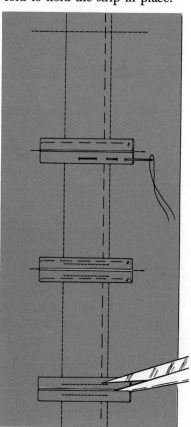

4. Stitch on each side of the buttonhole, using a short stitch. Position the stitching in the exact center between the fold and the cut edge on each side. Begin and end the stitching exactly on the basted lines designating the buttonhole length. Remove hand basting. Draw the threads through to the underside and tie. Press. See *Pressing as You Sew*, page 71.

5. Remove the horizontal basting designating the buttonhole position. Cut through the center of the *buttonhole strip only.*

6. Working from the underside, carefully cut between the two lines of stitching, through the garment and stay, to within ¼ inch of the ends of the buttonhole; then cut diagonally to each corner. The basted guidelines across the ends will prevent fraying at the corners until the ends are stitched to the strip.

7. Draw the strip through the opening to the underside, with the folded edges meeting at the center of the opening. Carefully pull the triangular ends away from the opening to square the corners. Press. Overcast the folded edges together.

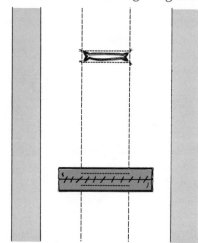

8. Place the garment right side up on the machine; fold it back and stitch the triangular ends to the strip at each end of the buttonhole. Remove the vertical basted guidelines. Trim ends of the

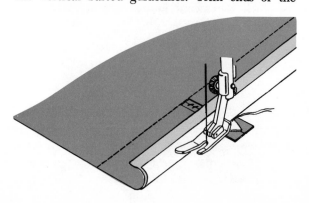

buttonhole strip to within ¼ inch of the stitching. Press.

Treat the interfacing as described on page 110. Finish the back of the buttonhole after the facing is attached, as instructed on page 111.

A corded effect may be given to buttonholes by cutting the strip on the true bias. Follow the same procedure given above for the *One-Piece Method* up to *Step 8*. From the underside, draw wool yarn through the pleats; a single or double strand may be used. Then stitch across the ends.

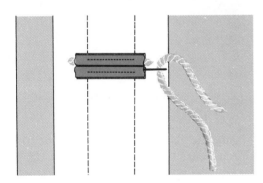

Two-Piece Piped Method

Use this method when the fabric is heavy, bulky, or loosely woven. Since such fabrics require heavy interfacing, always apply the interfacing *after* making the buttonholes to eliminate bulk.

1. Position a stay of lightweight fabric on the underside, and baste guidelines to mark buttonhole positions as described on page 108. Then on the stay on the underside, draw a pencil line on each side of and about 3/16 inch from the horizontal basted line. This marks the stitching line.

2. Cut a patch of organza 2 inches wide and 1 inch longer than the finished buttonhole. (The organza must match the fabric exactly in color.) Center the patch over the buttonhole marking on the right side of the fabric. Pin; baste if necessary.

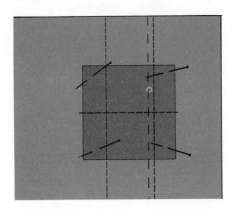

3. Turn the garment to the wrong side and stitch around the buttonhole, following the markings and using a 20 stitch length. Begin the stitching at the center of one side; at the corners, pivot the fabric on the needle; make the same number of stitches (four or five) across the ends; and overlap about four stitches at the starting point. Press. Carefully remove the basted guidelines through the center and across the ends of the buttonhole.

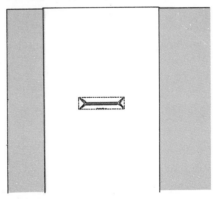

4. Cut through the center of the buttonhole to within ¼ inch of each end; then cut diagonally to each corner.

5. Turn the organza patch through the opening to the underside. Carefully pull out the triangular ends to square the corners and press them away

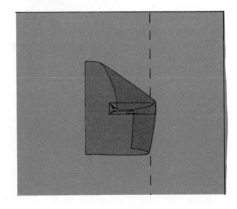

from the opening. Turn the seam allowances and organza patch away from the opening along the sides, fold on the stitching line, and press flat against the fabric. You now have a faced rectangular opening.

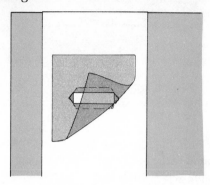

6. *For the piping,* cut two strips of garment fabric on the crosswise grain, 1½ inches wider and 1 inch longer than the finished buttonhole. Place them right sides together and machine-baste through the center, following the fabric grain line. Leave threads at each end so the basting can be easily removed.

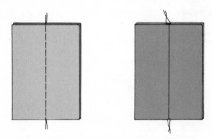

7. Press, then press the basted seam open. Be sure to place a press cloth between the fabric and iron because you are pressing on the right side of the fabric. (You should now have each strip folded, wrong sides together, and the two strips temporarily basted together along the folds.)

8. With the garment right side up, place the strip over the wrong side of the opening with the basted seam centered and the ends extending ½ inch beyond the opening. Pin the strip in place with fine needles close to the ends of the opening.

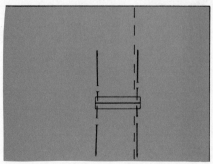

9. Place the garment right side up on the machine; turn back the edge and stitch the seam allowances and organza patch to the strip. Use a 20 stitch length and place the stitching barely beyond the previous stitching so that the organza patch will not be visible on the top side of the garment. First pin the triangular ends to the strip

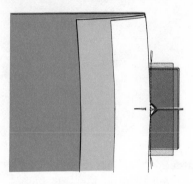

with fine needles and stitch across the ends; then, just before stitching along each side, remove the needles on the top side and pin the seam allowances

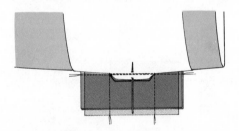

and organza to the strip on the underside to prevent them from slipping during the stitching. Trim the ends of the strip to within ¼ inch of stitching; along the sides, trim the seam allowance on the top layer of the strip to ¼ inch and on the bottom layer to ⅜ inch. Before pressing, slip brown paper between the garment and seam allowance to prevent the outline of the seam allowance from pressing onto the fabric.

Treat the interfacing as described on page 110. Finish the back of the buttonhole after the facing is attached, following the directions on page 111. Remove the basting joining the buttonhole strips.

Corded Buttonholes

Additional markings are required for accurate corded buttonholes. First, machine-baste the vertical and horizontal guidelines, as instructed on page 108. Then on the stay or lightweight interfacing on the underside, draw a pencil line on each side and 3/16 or 1/4 inch from the buttonhole marking.

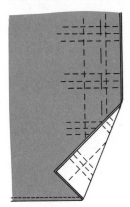

Machine-baste on these lines to transfer the markings to the right side. The spacing of these lines from the buttonhole marking will vary, depending upon the size of the cord and the weight of the fabric used.

Prepare the corded strips from a true bias cut 1 inch wide and sufficient in length for all the buttonholes to be made. To determine the length of the corded strip needed, allow twice the length plus 2 inches for each buttonhole.

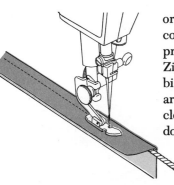

Use No. 9 cable cord or twine string for the cording. Replace the presser foot with the Zipper Foot. Fold the bias strip, right side out, around the cording. Stitch close to the cording, but do not crowd. Press.

1. For each buttonhole, cut two corded strips 1 inch longer than the buttonhole. Position two

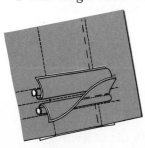

strips over each buttonhole marking, aligning the corded edges with the outside markings and keeping the raw edges toward the center. Hand-baste in position.

2. Stitch on each side of the buttonhole, placing the stitching between the cord and previous line of stitching. Use a short stitch, and adjust the Zipper Foot to the left of the needle. Begin and end the stitching exactly on the guidelines designating the buttonhole length. Remove hand bastings. Pull the threads through to the underside and tie. Remove all horizontal basting lines. Press See *Pressing as You Sew,* page 71.

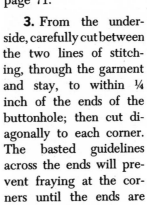

3. From the underside, carefully cut between the two lines of stitching, through the garment and stay, to within ¼ inch of the ends of the buttonhole; then cut diagonally to each corner. The basted guidelines across the ends will prevent fraying at the corners until the ends are stitched in place.

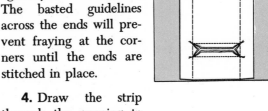

4. Draw the strip through the opening to the underside, with the corded edges meeting at the center of the opening. Carefully pull the triangular ends away from the opening to square the corners. Press. Overcast the corded edges together.

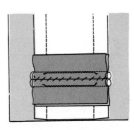

5. Place the garment right side up on the machine; fold it back and stitch the traingular ends to the corded strip at each end of the buttonhole. Replace the Zipper Foot with the presser foot for this operation. Remove the vertical guidelines. Trim the ends and sides of the corded strip to within ¼ inch of the stitching. Press. Treat the interfacing as described on page 110. Finish the back of the buttonhole after the facing is attached as described on page 111.

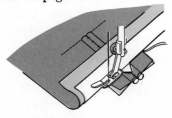

Buttonholes in a Seam

Buttonholes in a seam are often found on a horizontal line at the waistline of a jacket, where the peplum joins the bodice, and in yoke seams across the bodice; and on a vertical line where a binding or an extended facing is used. Where there is no seam, additional buttonholes are made, using one of the conventional methods shown earlier in this chapter.

1. Carefully mark the position of the buttonhole in the seam. With right sides of fabric together, pin and baste a ⅝-inch seam in the garment.

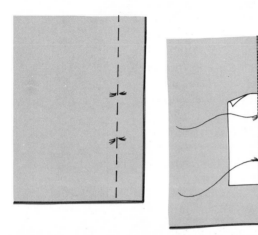

2. Cut two stays for each buttonhole 1 inch longer than the buttonhole and 1¼ inches wide for reinforcement. Use batiste, organza, or a similar fabric, and cut the stays on the same grain as the garment. Place one on each side of the seam over the buttonhole marking, keeping seam edges even. Pin.

3. Beginning at the end of the seam, stitch to the buttonhole marking. Leave thread ends long enough to tie. Then from the opposite end of the buttonhole, stitch the entire length of the seam or

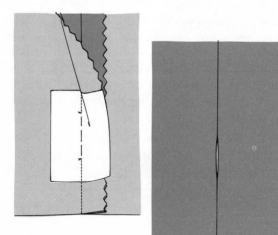

to the marking for the next buttonhole. At each end of the buttonhole, pull the threads to one side and tie. Remove tailor's tacks, if used, and basting, except across the buttonhole opening.

4. Press the seam, then press it open. Trim the stay on each side of the buttonhole to within ⅜ inch of opening.

5. Treat the interfacing as instructed on page 110. Finish the back of the buttonhole *after the facing is attached*, as described on page 111.

WORKED BUTTONHOLES

Machine-worked and hand-worked buttonholes are made after the garment is finished. For machine-worked buttonholes you may use either the zig-zag machine or a straight stitch machine with a Buttonholer.

Use interfacing in the buttonhole area for reinforcement. It is essential if the fabric is loosely woven or is one that stretches easily (for example, a knit), for it holds the fabric firmly so that you can make a neat buttonhole; it also keeps the finished buttonhole in shape.

Determine the buttonhole position and length as described on pages 107 and 108.

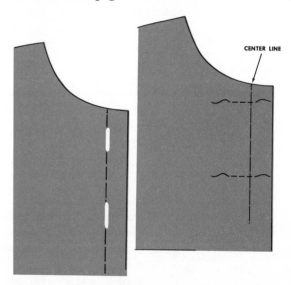

With Zig-Zag Machine

Worked buttonholes of any length and varying widths can be made quickly and easily on a zig-zag machine.

To determine the length of the cutting space (the opening through which the button passes), refer to page 108. The length of the finished buttonhole is the cutting space plus ⅛ inch at each

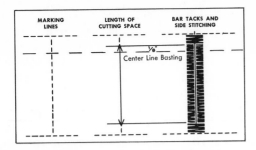

MARKING LINES	LENGTH OF CUTTING SPACE	BAR TACKS AND SIDE STITCHING

Center Line Basting

end for bar tacks. After determining the size of the buttonhole, mark the buttonhole size with either chalk or hand basting along the thread of the fabric.

Set the selectors on the machine for a plain zig-zag stitch, and set the stitch length selector for satin stitching. Work a sample buttonhole in a scrap of the same fabric used in the garment. Fold the fabric, duplicating the facing, and include the same type of interfacing used in the garment. Follow the instructions for making buttonholes in the instruction book accompanying the machine.

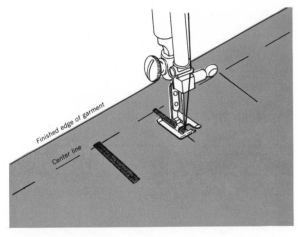

Finished edge of garment

Center line

Corded buttonholes. Both size 8 pearl cotton and buttonhole twist make suitable filler cords for corded buttonholes.

Unwind a sufficient amount of the filler cord to prevent tension or strain on the cord. Lead the end of the cord through the left eyelet of the Special Purpose Foot. Draw the cord under and in

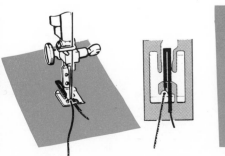 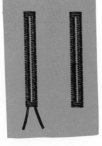

back of the foot. Proceed with stitching as for regular buttonholes. The zig-zag stitches are made over the filler cord.

With the Buttonholer

Mark the end position as well as the line of the buttonhole along the thread of the fabric. Use chalk or hand-baste. To determine the buttonhole position and length, see pages 107 and 108.

Select the size template required for the buttonhole and insert it in the Buttonholer. Regulate the stitch width and cutting space required according to the fabric.

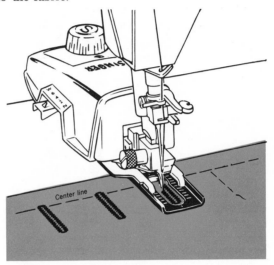

Center line

Then make a test buttonhole in a swatch of the same fabric used in the garment. Fold the fabric, duplicating the facing, and include the same type of interfacing used in the garment. Follow the directions given in the instruction book accompanying the Buttonholer. See also *Buttonholer,* page 287.

Hand-Worked Buttonholes

Hand-worked buttonholes may be made on a horizontal or vertical line. If horizontal, they have a fan at the outside end near the edge of the garment, which carries the strain, and a bar tack at the inside end. If vertical, they have a bar tack at each end.

Use the buttonhole stitch and thread that matches the fabric exactly in color. Work with a thread about 18 inches in length and rethread the needle for each buttonhole because the thread will wear when repeatedly pulled through the fabric.

Determine the buttonhole position and length as described on pages 107 and 108. Then follow the instructions below, beginning with a practice buttonhole in a swatch of your fabric.

Horizontal Buttonhole

1. Carefully mark the length and line of the buttonhole with chalk or hand basting along the true grain of the fabric. Pin the layers of fabric together to prevent them from slipping.

2. Machine-stitch around the buttonhole for reinforcement. Use a 20 stitch length and place the stitching 1/16 inch from the buttonhole marking; take two or three stitches across the ends. In heavy fabrics, place the stitching about ⅛ inch from the marking. Take care that the stitching is straight and evenly spaced because it is a guide for the depth of the hand stitches (however, this stitching is not visible in the finished buttonhole). A fine hand running stitch, although not so firm, may be substituted for machine stitching. Press. If the fabric is one that will fray, overcast the edges.

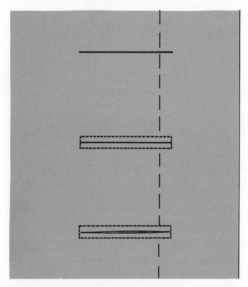

3. Cut the buttonhole between the two lines of stitching, using sharp, pointed scissors.

4. *Work from right to left.* Hold the fabric, needle, and thread in the position shown in the illustrations. With the right side of the garment up, *start working at the inside end.* Bring the cut buttonhole over the first finger of the left hand.

Do not knot the end of the thread. Take two small backstitches at the end to fasten the thread. Clip off the thread end after several stitches have been made. Bring the thread to the left, then to the right, to form a loop around the point where

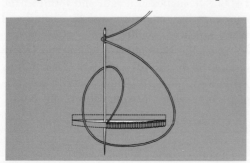

the stitch will be made. Insert the point of the needle through the opening and up through the fabric just below the machine stitching. Keep the thread in back of both the point and the eye of the needle. Hold the lower edge of the loop with the left thumb until you draw up the thread for the stitch. Pull the needle through the fabric, then away from you, to place the purl of the stitch on the cut edge of the buttonhole. Pull the thread gently yet firmly enough to make smooth, flat stitches. Continue making buttonhole stitches until you reach the outside end. Keep the spacing between the stitches uniform and the depth as even as possible.

5. Fan the stitches at the outside end. Place about five or seven stitches in the fan and make them slightly longer than the side stitches so that they will appear to be the same length.

Work down the opposite side to the inside end. Turn the buttonhole to the right as you work around it.

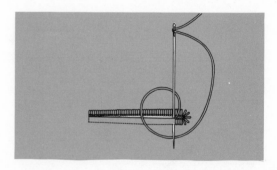

6. Make a bar tack across the inside end by taking two straight stitches through the fabric.

7. Complete the bar by working over the stitches, using a blanket stitch. Make the stitches through the fabric and under the bar. Fasten the thread on the underside with two backstitches.

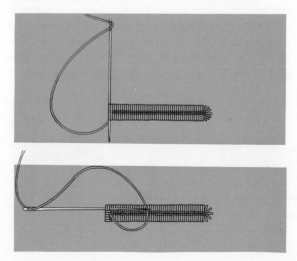

Vertical Buttonhole

Vertical buttonholes are set so that the center line basting falls in the center of the buttonhole.

1. Mark the length and line of the buttonhole on the true lengthwise grain of the fabric.

2. Machine-stitch around the buttonhole for reinforcement. Use a 20 stitch length and place the stitching 1/16 inch from the buttonhole marking; take two or three stitches across the ends.

3. Cut the buttonhole between the two lines of stitching.

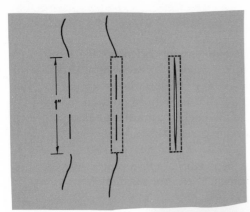

4. Place the garment right side up. Start working at the lower end, using the buttonhole stitch as described in *Step 4,* page 118. Make a bar tack across the upper end by taking two straight stitches through the fabric. Complete the bar by working across the stitches, using the blanket stitch. Make the stitches through the fabric and under the bar.

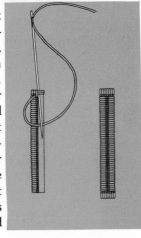

5. Work down the opposite side and finish the lower end with a bar tack. Fasten the thread on the underside with two backstitches.

Tailored Buttonhole

Tailored buttonholes have an eyelet at the outside end near the edge of the garment. The shank of the button fits into the eyelet opening. This prevents the overlap from bulging when the garment is buttoned.

1. Mark the position of the buttonhole with hand basting, chalk, or pencil on the crosswise grain of the fabric.

2. Cut the buttonhole on the marked line. At the outside end, near the edge of the garment,

make two small slashes about ⅛ inch in depth or punch a small hole, using a stiletto.

3. Overcast around the cut edges to keep them from fraying and to hold the layers of fabric together. Make the stitches about ⅛ inch in depth.

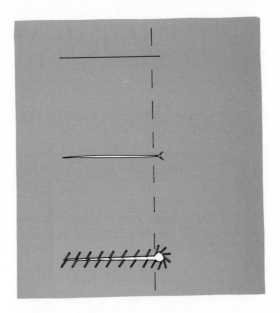

4. Start at the inside end, and place a strand of buttonhole twist along the edges of the buttonhole. Fasten the ends by forming a figure eight around a pin. Use buttonhole twist in the needle. Take one backstitch at the inside end to tie the thread. Follow the instructions on page 118 for *Steps 4 and 5,* and make buttonhole stitches over the twist. Fan the stitches at the eyelet end.

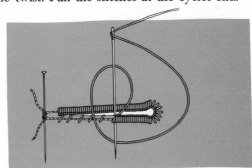

5. Make a bar tack across the inside end by taking two straight stitches through the fabric. Complete the bar by working over the stitches, using a blanket stitch. Make the stitches through the fabric and under the bar. Fasten the thread on the underside with two backstitches.

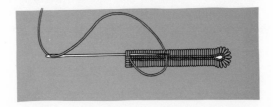

Pick a
Pretty Pocket

THE FASHION INTEREST in pocket styles fluctuates from the subtle set-in pocket to the bold patch pocket. Whatever the style, the secret of pocket making lies in accurately marking and stitching your pocket and pressing each step as it is completed. Pockets are not difficult if you remember that.

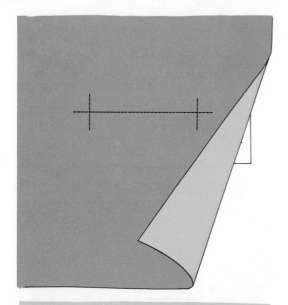

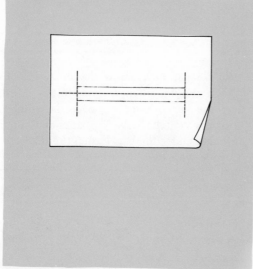

The pattern usually designates the position of pockets in a garment; however, if you decide to add them, do so in the planning stage so that you can measure and mark their position on the pattern. Make the pockets after the pin fitting, before assembling the garment pieces.

Always make a practice pocket in a swatch of the garment fabric before proceeding to work on the garment itself. For instructions on pressing, see page 71.

SET-IN POCKETS

Guidelines for Pockets

Mark the position of the pocket with tailor's tacks before removing the pattern from the garment section.

Place an underlay of batiste, muslin, lawn, or similar fabric under the stitching line to reinforce the opening and retain the shape of the pocket. Cut the underlay 1½ inches wider than the pocket opening and about 3 inches long. Center it over the markings on the wrong side of the garment, and pin.

From the right side, machine-baste across the ends of the pocket to mark the width. Then machine-baste through the center, extending the stitching about ¾ inch beyond the ends, to form guidelines. Follow the grain of the fabric unless the pocket is on a diagonal line. Use thread contrasting in color so that it can easily be seen and removed. Hand-baste if machine basting will mar the fabric.

On the wrong side, draw pencil lines on each side of and ¼ inch from the center basting to designate the stitching line. This distance may vary depending on the style of the pocket.

(Additional markings are required for a *corded pocket* and are illustrated under the instructions for making the pocket.)

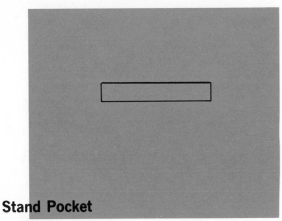

Stand Pocket

Mark the guidelines of the pocket as instructed on opposite page.

Cut a piece of fabric on the lengthwise grain twice the pocket depth plus twice the depth of the stand, and 1 inch wider than the opening. Crease the pocket section crosswise, 1 inch above the center.

1. On the right side of the garment, place the pocket section, right sides together. Align the crease with the marking on the garment, extending the long end of the pocket below the marking. Pin. Baste, if necessary.

2. On the wrong side, stitch around the pocket, following the guidelines. Use a short stitch and begin the stitching at the center of one side; pivot the fabric on the needle at the corners and take the same number of stitches across each end. Overlap about six stitches at the starting point. Do not stitch on the bastings. Remove the basted guidelines, and press.

3. Cut between the two lines of stitching, through all thicknesses, to within ½ inch of the ends; then cut diagonally to each of the four corners. Do not clip through the stitching.

4. Draw the pocket through the opening to the wrong side. Pull out the triangles at the ends to square the corners. Press the triangular ends and seam allowances along the side away from the opening.

5. Fold the lower section of the pocket to form a pleat to cover the opening. Check both the right and wrong sides to be sure that the pleat is even and covers the opening. Hand-baste on the folded edge, carrying the basting to each end of the pocket. Press the folded edge. Overcast the fold to the top edge of the opening. (Pin the upper section of the pocket to the garment to keep it out of the way for the next step.)

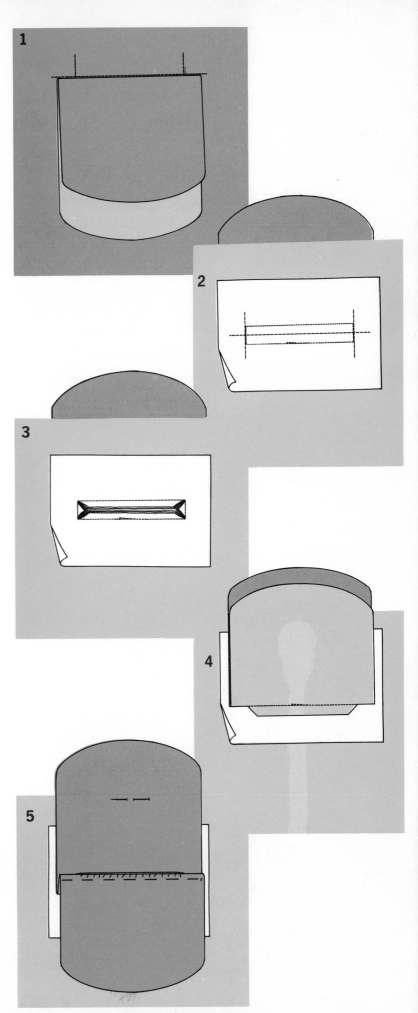

121

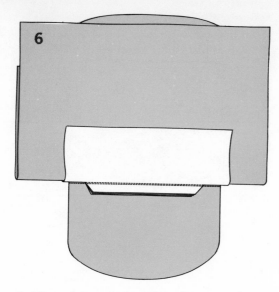

6. Place the garment right side up on the machine; fold back the edge and stitch the seam allowances to the lower pocket section to hold the pleat in place.

7. Turn down the upper section of the pocket and pin it to the lower section. Press the top seam open.

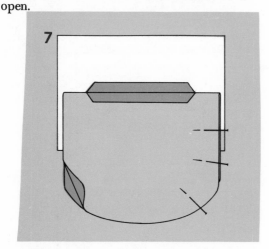

8. Place the garment right side up on the machine; fold back the edge and stitch the two-pocket sections together. Stitch across the triangle at one end, around the pocket, and across the triangle at the opposite end. Stitch the triangular ends on the original line of stitching. Tie thread ends.

Trim seam allowances evenly and finish the

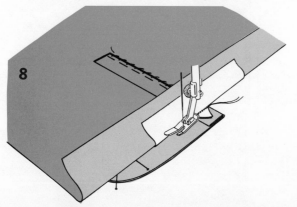

edges according to the fabric. Remove all bastings and press. Trim underlay to within ½ inch of stitching.

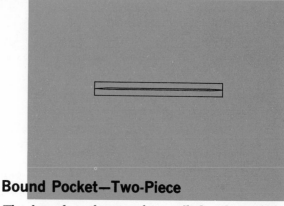

Bound Pocket—Two-Piece

The bound pocket is often called a buttonhole pocket because it is made exactly like a buttonhole.

Mark the guidelines of the pocket as instructed on page 120.

Cut one pocket section the depth of the pocket plus 2 inches, and 1 inch wider than the opening. Cut another section the depth of the pocket plus the seam allowance, and 1 inch wider than the opening. (To avoid bulk in suits, coats, and garments of heavy fabric, you may cut the lower section [the short one] from the lining fabric or a lightweight fabric matching in color.)

1. On the right side of the garment, place the long section of the pocket, right side down, extending the edge 1½ inches below the marking. Pin. Baste, if necessary.

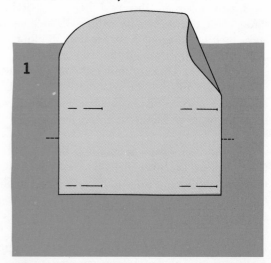

2. On the wrong side, stitch around the pocket, following the guidelines. Use a short stitch and begin stitching at the center of one side; pivot the fabric on the needle at the corners and take the

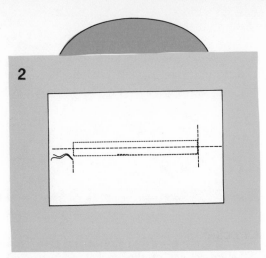

2

same number of stitches across each end. Overlap about six stitches at the starting point. Remove the basted guidelines at the ends, and press.

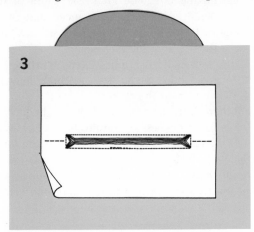

3

3. Cut between the two lines of stitching, through all thicknesses, to within ½ inch of the ends; then cut diagonally to each of the four corners. Do not clip through the stitching.

4. Draw the pocket through the opening to the underside. Pull out the triangular ends to square the corners. Press the triangular ends and seam allowances along the sides away from the opening.

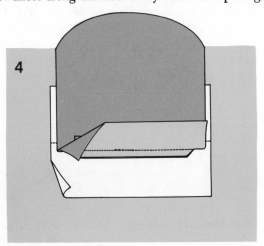

4

5. Fold the pocket section to form a pleat on each side that meets at the center and covers the opening. Check both the right and wrong sides to be sure that the pleats are even in width. Baste along the center of each fold, then overcast the folded edges together. Carry the basting to the raw edge of the pocket section. Remove the center basted guideline, and press.

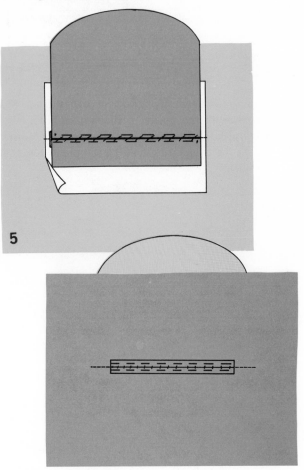

5

6. Place the garment right side up on the machine; fold back the edge and stitch the seam allowances to the pleats. First stitch across the triangular ends on the original stitching line; then stitch across the seam at the top, *just a hair's width from the original stitching line*. The side stitching crosses the end stitching and squares the corners.

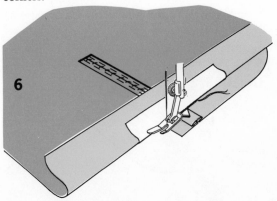

6

7. Place the second pocket section under the bottom seam, right side up; then stitch the seam allowance to the pleat and lower pocket section in one operation.

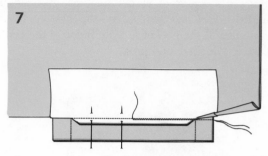

8. Turn down the lower pocket section. The underside of the pocket is illustrated. Stitching is not visible on the right side. Remove all bastings except the overcasting holding the pleats together. Press.

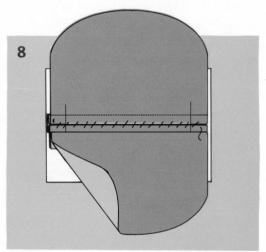

9. Turn down the upper section of the pocket and pin it to the lower section. Place the garment right side up on the machine. Fold back the edge of the garment and stitch the two pocket sections together. Stitch across the triangle at one end, around the pocket, and across the triangle at the opposite end. Stitch the triangular ends on the original line of stitching. Tie thread ends.

Trim seam allowances evenly and finish the edges according to the fabric. Remove all bastings and press. Trim underlay to within ½ inch of the stitching.

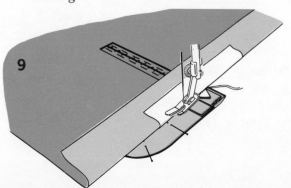

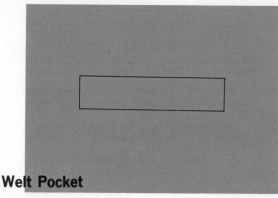

Welt Pocket

Mark the guidelines of the pocket as instructed on page 120.

Welt. If a pattern for the welt is not included, cut one on the crosswise grain the width of the pocket opening plus seam allowances, and twice the depth of the finished welt plus seam allowances. (Allow ¼ inch for each seam.)

If the fabric is not firmly woven, interface the welt to give added body. Two methods may be used, depending on the fabric.

Method 1: In cottons and lightweight fabrics, use a double thickness of muslin, batiste, or lawn for the interfacing. Shrink it; then cut it the same as the welt. Fold through the center and crease with the iron. Turn the welt wrong side up and place the fold of the interfacing along the center of the welt. Stitch close to the interfacing fold.

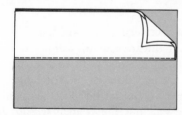

Method 2: In coats, suits, and garments of heavy fabric, interface with hair canvas. Shrink the interfacing; then cut it the width of the welt and one-half the depth. Trim off the seam allowance on each end and along the lower edge. On the wrong side of the welt, place the edge of the interfacing along the center of the welt. Pin and baste. Catch-stitch in place.

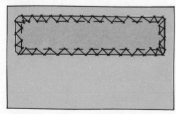

For Methods 1 and 2, fold the welt in half on the crosswise grain, right sides together. Stitch

124

across the ends. Backstitch at each end for reinforcement. Cut diagonally across corners at the
top edge. Trim the facing seam allowance to ⅛
inch. If Method 1 is used, trim the interfacing
seam allowance close to the stitching. Press.

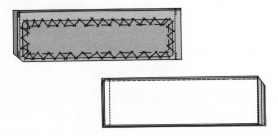

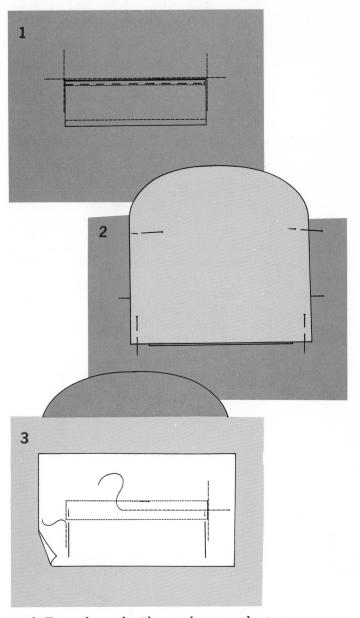

Turn the welt right side out. Fold on the stitching line; pull out the corners and press. Machine-
stitch a scant ¼ inch from the lower edge to hold
the layers of fabric together.

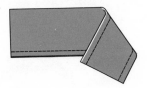

Pocket. Cut one pocket section the depth of
the pocket plus 2 inches, and 1 inch wider than
the opening. Cut another section the depth of
pocket plus seam allowance, and 1 inch wider than
the opening. (To avoid bulk in suits, coats, and
garments of heavy fabric, you may cut the lower
section [the short one] from the lining fabric or a
lightweight fabric matching in color.)

To make the welt pocket, proceed as follows:

1. Turn garment right side up. Place the welt
below the pocket marking, right side down, with
the raw edge on the center basting line. (The ends
must be even with the guidelines. Adjust if necessary.) Pin and hand-baste. On the underside, pin
at each corner, using fine needles to prevent the
welt from slipping as you stitch in *Step 3.*

2. On the right side of the garment, place the
upper pocket section (the long one) over the marking, right sides together, extending the edge 1 inch
below the center marking. Pin. Baste, if necessary.

3. From the wrong side of the garment, stitch
around the pocket opening, following the guidelines. Use a short stitch and begin stitching at the
center of the upper side; pivot the fabric on the
needle at the corners and take the same number
of stitches across each end. Overlap about six
stitches at the starting point. Check the right side
to be sure the end stitching does not extend beyond the welt. Remove all bastings, and press.

4. From the underside, cut between the two
lines of stitching, through all thicknesses, to within
½ inch of the ends. Cut diagonally to each of the
four corners. Do no clip through the stitching.

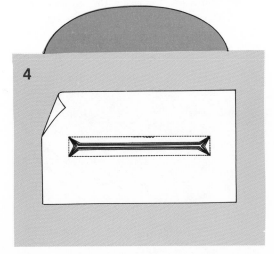

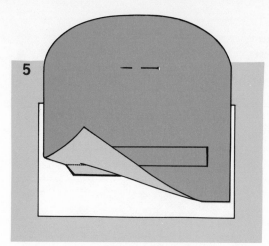

5. Turn the pocket through the opening to the underside. Pull out the triangular ends to square the corners, and turn the welt up on the right side to cover the opening. Press the triangular ends and seam allowances along the sides away from the opening. Turn the extended lower edge of the pocket away from the opening and press. (Pin the upper pocket section to the garment to avoid catching it in the stitching of the next step.)

6. Place the garment right side up and fold back the lower edge. Place the lower pocket section under the opening, right side up, keeping the cut edges even along the lower edge of the opening. Turn back the seam allowances, and stitch the pocket section together close to the previous stitching. Begin and end the stitching at the outer edges of the fabric. Press; then turn down the lower pocket section and press again.

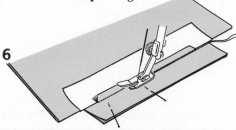

7. Turn down the upper pocket section and pin the two sections together. Trim both sections to the same length. Place the garment right side up on the machine. Fold back the edge and stitch the pocket sections together. Stitch across the triangle at one end, around the pocket, and across

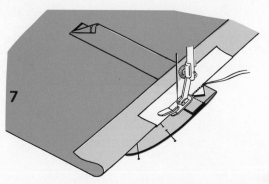

the triangle at the opposite end. Stitch the triangular ends on the original line of stitching. Tie the threads. Remove all bastings and press.

Finish seams as required by the fabric. Trim underlay to within ½ inch of the stitching.

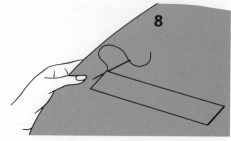

8. On the right side, slip-stitch the ends of the welt to the garment.

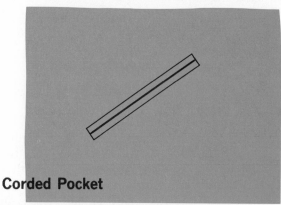

Corded Pocket

Mark the guidelines of the pocket as instructed on page 120. Then mark additional lines for the position of the cording. The position of these lines is determined by the size of the cord; take twice the width of the cord plus 1/16 inch. (Size 40 cord, for example, will require a distance of 5/16 to ⅜ inch, depending on the thickness of the fabric.) On the underside, draw a pencil line on each side of and 5/16 inch (or the necessary distance) from the center basting. This designates the position of the corded strip. Machine-baste on these lines to transfer the markings to the right side.

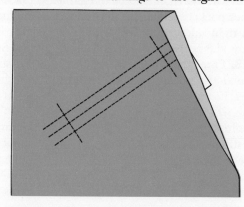

Cording. Refer to *Cording,* page 244, for instructions on cutting the bias strip and covering the cord. For each pocket, cut two corded strips the width of the pocket plus 1 inch; avoid seams within the strips.

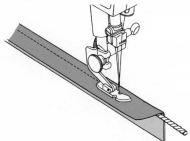

Pocket. Cut two pocket sections the depth of the pocket plus 1 inch, and 1 inch wider than the opening. (You will use them in *Steps 6 and 8.*)

To make the corded pocket, proceed as follows:

1. On the right side of the garment, place a corded strip on each side of the pocket markings. Align the corded edges with the outside markings, keeping the cut edges toward the center. Pin close to the cord. Check the underside to be sure that the pins are midway between the outside and center markings. (Use fine needles to pin heavy fabric.) Hand-baste, close to the cord, the entire length of the corded strip.

2. Using a short stitch, stitch the cording in place, placing the stitching between the cord and previous line of basting. Begin and end the stitching exactly on the end guidelines. Adjust the Zipper Foot to the left of the needle for this operation.

Check the underside to be sure the line of stitching on each side is midway between the center and outer guidelines. Pull the threads through to the underside and tie. Remove all bastings except those across the ends. Press.

3. From the underside, cut between the two lines of stitching through the garment and underlay, to within ½ inch of the ends; then cut diagonally to each of the four corners. Do not clip through the stitching, and hold the corded strips out of the way to avoid cutting into them.

4. Turn the cut edges of the corded strips through the opening to the underside, with the corded edges meeting at the center to cover the opening. Pull out the triangular ends to square the corners. Press the triangular ends and seam allowances along the sides away from the opening. Overcast the corded edges together.

5. Place the garment right side up on the machine; fold back the edge and stitch the triangular ends to the cording. Remove machine basting across the ends, and press.

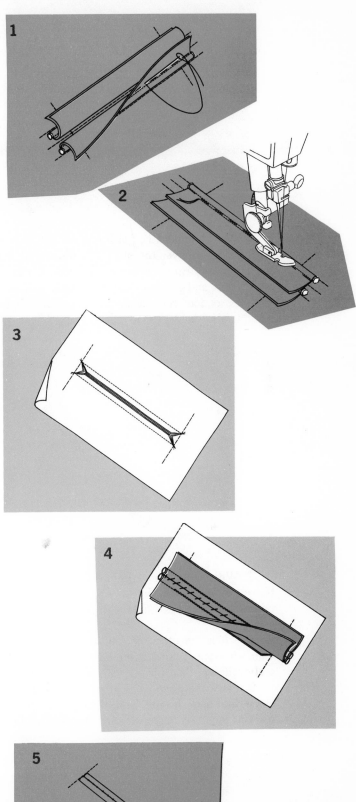

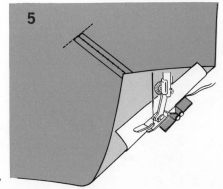

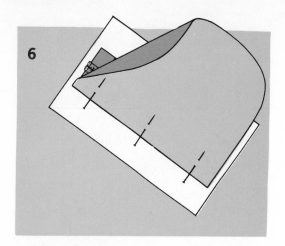

6. On the underside, place one pocket section, wrong side up, over the pocket as illustrated. Pin to the lower seam allowance. (To avoid bulk in suits, coats, and garments of heavy fabric, you may cut this section from the lining fabric or a lightweight fabric matching in color.)

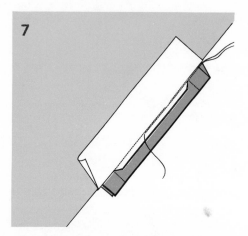

7. With the garment right side up, fold back the edge and stitch the seam allowances to the pocket section. Press. Fold the pocket section down, and press.

8. Stitch the other pocket section to the top seam allowances in the same way. Press. Fold this section down; then pin the two sections together.

9. Place the garment right side up on the machine; fold back the edge and stitch the two pocket sections together. Begin stitching at the edge above

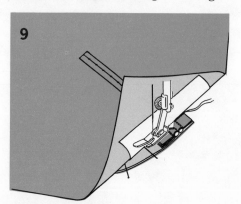

the triangular point, around the pocket, and across the triangle at the opposite end. Stitch the triangular ends on the original line of stitching. Press.

Finish the seam edges according to the fabric. Trim the underlay to within ½ inch of the stitching. Remove the overcasting holding the two corded edges together.

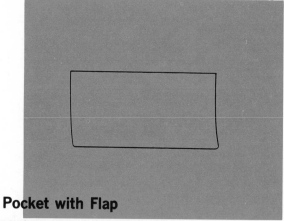

Pocket with Flap

Mark guidelines of the pocket as instructed on page 120.

Flap. Cut the flap and the facing the width of the opening plus seam allowances, and the depth desired plus seam allowances (¼-inch seam allowances are sufficient in most fabrics). Round the lower corners, if desired.

Interface the flap to give the added body necessary. Two methods are given below. Select the one most suitable for your fabric.

Method 1: In cottons and lightweight fabrics, interface with muslin, batiste, or lawn. Shrink, then cut a double thickness of interfacing the same size as the flap. Pin the interfacing to the wrong side of the flap. Baste, if necessary.

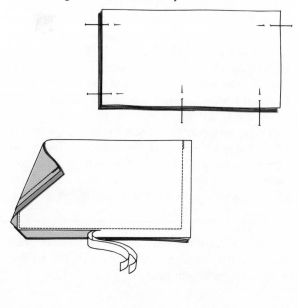

Method 2: Interface woolens, heavy silks, and similar fabrics with preshrunk hair canvas. Cut the interfacing the same size as the flap. Trim off the seam allowance plus ⅛ inch. Center the interfacing over the wrong side of the flap and baste. Catch-stitch in place around the edges. Press.

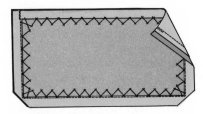

For Methods 1 and 2, pin the facing to the flap, right sides together. Stitch on the seamline, leaving the upper edge open. Backstitch at each end. Clip off corners at the lower edge. Trim the facing seam allowance to ⅛ inch and the flap seam allowance to ¼ inch. If *Method 1* is used, trim the interfacing seam allowance close to the stitching. Turn the flap right side out. Pull out the corners. Ease the facing under slightly at the seamline and baste. Press. Top-stitch if desired. Stitch across the cut edges a scant ¼ inch from the edge to hold the layers of fabric together. Remove bastings.

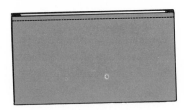

Pocket. Cut one pocket section the depth of the pocket plus 2 inches, and 1 inch wider than the opening. Cut another section the depth of the pocket plus seam allowance, and 1 inch wider than the opening. (To avoid bulk in suits, coats, and garments of heavy fabric, you may cut the lower section [the short one] from the lining fabric or a lightweight fabric matching in color.)

To make the pocket, proceed as follows:

1. Turn the garment right side up. Place the flap above the pocket marking, right side down, with the raw edge on the center basting line. The flap ends should just touch the end bastings. Baste. On the underside, use fine needles to pin each corner to prevent the flap from slipping as you stitch in *Step 3.*

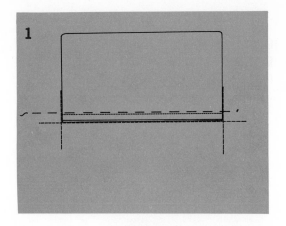

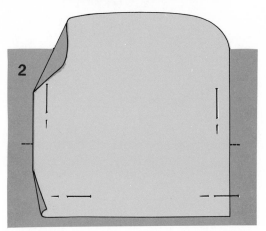

2. On the right side, place the long pocket section, right sides together, over the opening, extending the lower edge 2 inches below the center basting. Pin in place.

3. From the wrong side, stitch around the pocket opening; use a short stitch and follow the guidelines. Start stitching at the center of the lower side; pivot the fabric on the needle at the corners and make the same number of stitches at each end. Overlap about six stitches at the starting point. Check to be sure the end stitching does not extend beyond the ends of the flap. Remove all bastings and press.

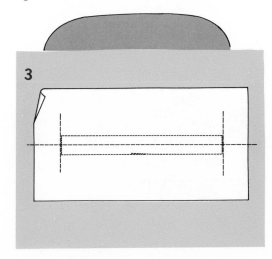

4. From the underside, cut between the two lines of stitching, through all thicknesses, to within ½ inch of the ends; then cut diagonally to each of the four corners. Do not clip through the stitching.

5. Turn the pocket through the opening to the underside. Pull out triangles at the ends to square the corners. Press triangular ends and seam allowances along the sides away from the opening. Turn

down the flap before pressing the seam across the top. Pin the upper pocket section to the garment to avoid catching it while stitching *Step 7*.

6. Fold the pocket extension, which is below the opening, to form a pleat that covers the opening. Hand-baste on the fold. Press.

7. Place the garment right side up; fold back the lower edge and pin the free edge of the pleat to the seam allowance. Place the lower pocket section underneath, right side up, and pin. Stitch the pleat and pocket section to the seam allowance at the same time. Press the seam; then turn down the lower pocket section and press. Trim the seam allowances to different widths to avoid forming a ridge on the right side when pressing.

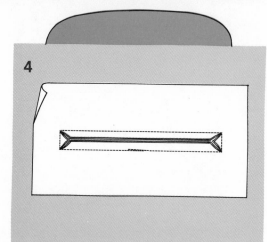

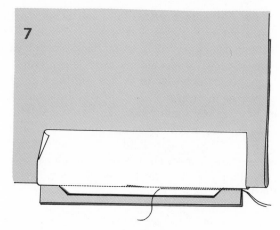

8. Turn the upper pocket section down and pin the two sections together. Trim both sections to the same length. Place the garment right side up; fold back the edge and stitch the two pocket sections together. Stitch across the triangle at one end, around the pocket, and across the triangle at the opposite end. Stitch the triangular ends on the original line of stitching. Tie thread ends and press.

Finish seam edges as required by the fabric. Trim underlay to within ½ inch of the stitching.

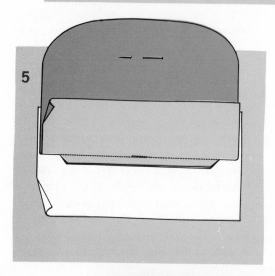

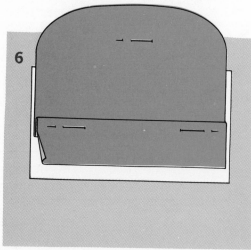

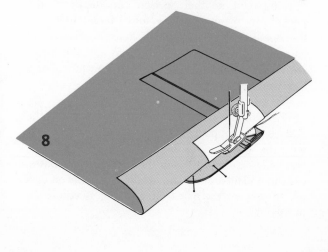

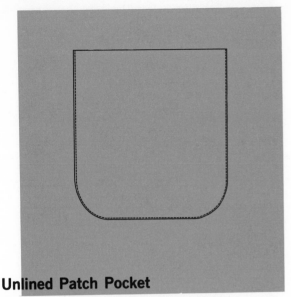

Unlined Patch Pocket

Mark the position of the pocket with tailor's tacks before removing the pattern from the garment. If the addition of pockets is your idea, mark their position on the pattern; then mark the garment. Follow the fabric grain unless the pocket is on a diagonal line.

Cut the pocket the width and depth desired plus seam allowances and a hem at the top. Round the lower corners, if desired.

1. Fold under the top edge of the pocket ¼ inch and stitch near the fold. Press. Fold the top hem to the right side. Pin and stitch across the ends on the seamline. Backstitch at each end. Press. Stitch around the curve of the pocket, ½ inch from the edge, to control the fullness of the seam allowance. Leave thread ends long enough to draw. (Loosen the upper tension, if necessary. Do not forget to return the tension to its previous setting.)

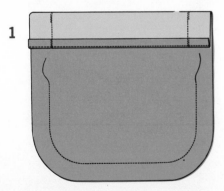

2. Trim the seam allowance to within ¼ inch of the stitching and cut diagonally across corners at the top of the hem.

3. Turn the hem to the wrong side. Fold on the

stitching line, pull out corners, and press. Draw bobbin thread, easing the fabric back on the stitches around the curved edge. Adjust the fullness for a smooth curve.

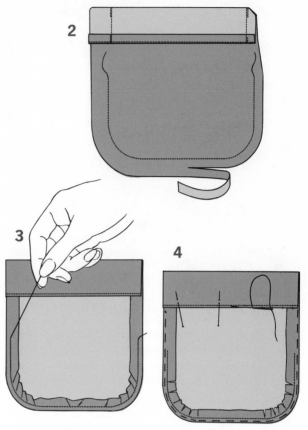

4. Turn the edges under on the seamline and baste. Notch the seam allowance on the curve to remove bulk so that the seam will lie flat. Press. Pin the hem in place at the top and slip-stitch.

5. Pin and baste the pocket over the markings on the right side of the garment. Stitch close to the edge or slip-stitch in place. Pull threads to the underside and tie. Remove bastings and press.

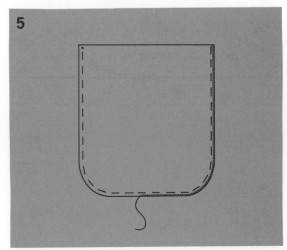

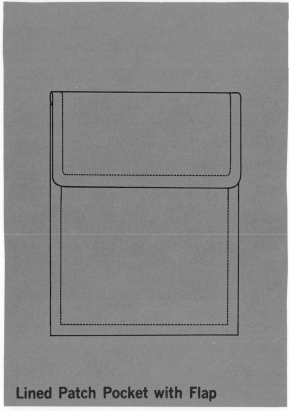

Lined Patch Pocket with Flap

Mark the position of the pocket the same as above.

Pocket. Cut the pocket and lining the depth and width desired, plus seam allowances. Use a lining of the same fabric or, if the fabric is heavy, use a lighter weight lining, matching in color.

1. Pin the lining to the pocket, right sides together. Stitch around the pocket, leaving a 2½-inch opening for turning. Backstitch at the beginning and ending of the seam and take one stitch across each corner for a smooth turning. Press.

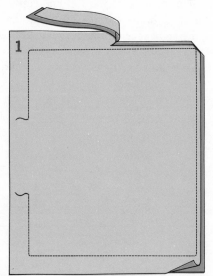

Blend lining seam allowance to ⅛ inch and pocket seam allowance to ¼ inch. Cut diagonally across the corners, close to the stitching. Press.

2. Turn the pocket through the opening to the right side. Pull out the corners. Ease the lining under slightly at the stitching line and baste. Slip-stitch the open edges together. Press.

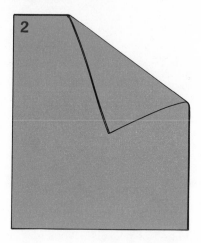

3. Pin and hand-baste the pocket over the markings on the right side of the garment. Place a second basting exactly ⅜ inch from the edge to mark the stitching line. Use a gauge to measure and to keep the line even. The Quilter may also be used to gauge the stitching line. See *Top Stitching*, page 335, and *Welt Seam*, page 88.

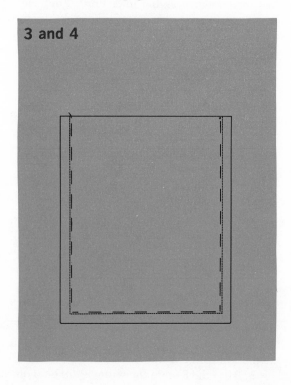

4. Stitch the pocket to the garment along the ⅜-inch line; pivot the fabric on the needle at the corners. Draw threads to the underside and tie. Remove bastings, and press.

If top stitching is not used, slip-stitch the pocket to the garment.

Flap. Cut the flap and facing the width of the pocket and depth required, plus seam allowances. Round the lower corners, if desired.

5. Interface the flap to give the added body necessary. See *Pocket with a Flap,* page 128, and use either *Method 1 or 2,* depending on the weight of the interfacing and the fabric used.

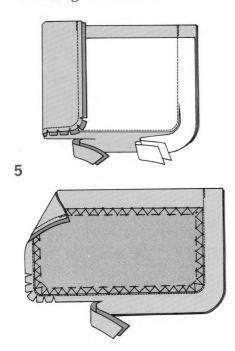

For Methods 1 and 2, pin the facing to the flap, right sides together. Stitch on the seamline, leaving the upper edge open. Backstitch at each end. Press.

Trim the lining seam allowance to ⅛ inch and the flap seam allowance to ¼ inch. If Method 1 is used, trim the interfacing seam allowance close to the stitching. Notch the curved edges. Press.

6. Turn the flap to the right side. Ease the lining under slightly at the stitching line and baste. Press. Pin the cut edges together and baste ⅝ inch from the edge. Top-stitch the flap ⅜ inch from the edge, following the direction for the pocket.

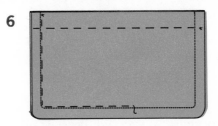

7. Pin and baste the flap to the garment, right sides together, placing the seamline ½ inch above the pocket. Stitch. Pull threads to the underside and tie. Press the seam. Turn under the cut edge and slip-stitch in place. Turn the flap down over the pocket.

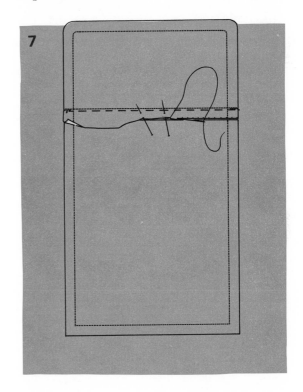

Neckline Finishes

How to finish a neckline depends on several things—pattern design, fabric, and in some instances even personal preference. Many different types of finishes are possible. You may, for example, face the neckline (and the front opening, too, if you have one); you may bind or cord it; or you may add a collar.

Interfacing

For almost all the work you will be doing in neckline finishing, you will need to interface. Interfacing is a third layer of fabric placed between the facing and garment section. It gives added body to the neckline and front or back opening and to collars and around buttonholes. In selecting interfacing be sure to choose one appropriate in type and weight for your fabric and style. Also, *shrink before cutting*. See page 16 for specific guides on the kind of interfacing to use.

Before you begin to work on the neckline, be sure that darts are stitched and pressed, shoulder seams stitched, seam edges finished, and seams pressed open.

Leave the underarm seams open because it is easier to finish the neckline when these seams are not joined and the work is flat.

FACED NECKLINE FINISHES

Faced Neckline and Front Opening

The type of interfacing you are using—whether lightweight or heavyweight—governs the method you should follow in attaching the interfacing to the neckline and front opening. If separate pieces for the interfacing are not included in the pattern, use the facing patterns as a guide. Cut the pre-shrunk interfacing and follow the appropriate instructions below.

Facing with Lightweight Interfacing

Interfacing. Join the interfacing pieces for the back and front sections at the shoulder line with a lapped seam, using the multiple-stitch zig-zag to eliminate bulk. See *Lapped Seam*, page 83.

Pin and baste the interfacing to the wrong side of the garment, keeping the seam edges even. (Bound buttonholes may be made through the garment and lightweight interfacing before the facing is stitched in place.)

Facing. Join facings for the back and front sections at the shoulder seams. Stitch, then press. Finish seam edges and press seams open.

Pin and baste the facing to the garment, right sides together, matching markings and shoulder seams. Stitch on the seamline, taking one stitch

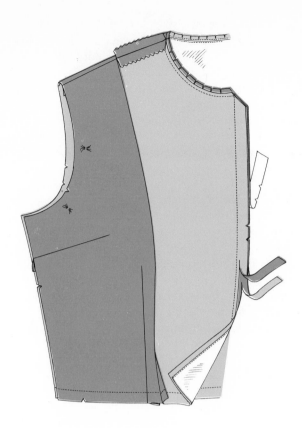
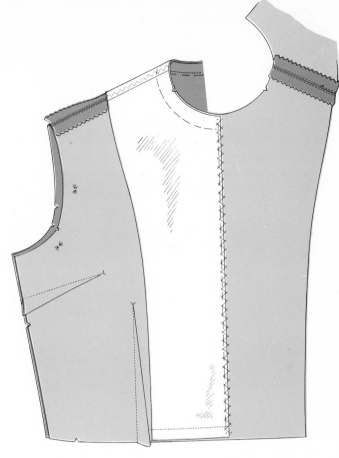

diagonally across the corners for a smooth turning.

Trim the interfacing seam allowance close to the stitching; then trim the facing seam allowance to ⅛ inch and the garment seam allowance to ¼ inch. Cut diagonally across the corners close to the stitching. Slash the seam allowance on the neckline curve at even intervals and clip off corners where seams cross at the shoulder line. Press, then press seams open.

Turn the facing to the underside. Pull out the corners to square them; ease the facing under slightly at the seamline and baste with silk thread. Use diagonal basting on woolens and silks. Press.

Finish the free edge of the facing. For lightweight fabrics, pink the edge, then fold under ¼ inch and edgestitch. For heavy fabrics, pink the edge, then stitch ⅛ inch from the edge, or stitch seam binding over the right side of the edge. The multiple-stitch zig-zag is ideal for finishing jersey, double knit, and similar fabrics. If bound buttonholes are used, you must finish the back of the buttonholes. See page 111. Tack the facing to the garment shoulder seam allowances.

When the front facing and bodice are cut-in-one, turn the facing to the underside and press. Then turn the facing away from the garment. Trim off the front seam allowance on the interfacing.

Pin the interfacing to the wrong side of the garment, aligning the front edge with the crease for the facing. Baste the interfacing in place at the neckline and front opening; catch-stitch it in place along the front opening, and machine-stitch it to the waistline ½ inch from the seam edge.

On washable blouses and children's clothes you may eliminate the catch stitch. Buttons and buttonholes will hold the interfacing in place along the front opening; however, be sure to remove the bastings holding the interfacing after sewing on the buttons and making the buttonholes.

Finish the neckline, following the instructions given above.

Facing with Heavyweight Interfacing

Interfacing. Heavy interfacing such as hair canvas, Siri, Formite, or Pellon is used in dresses of heavy fabric and in suits and coats to give extra body to certain areas. Bound buttonholes are made *before* the heavy interfacing is attached to the garment.

To eliminate bulk, do not sew the interfacing in with the seam but attach it by one of the following methods:

Method 1: Mark the seam allowance at the shoulder line of the back and front pieces of the interfacing; mark the neckline and front sections a measured ¾ inch from the edge (⅝-inch seam al-allowance plus ⅛ inch). Trim off along the marked line. Clip off corners to avoid bulk when turned.

Join the interfacing pieces for the back neckline and front sections at the shoulder line with an abutted seam, and stitch, using the multiple-stitch zig-zag. See *Abutted Seam,* page 83.

Cut a strip of organza or a similar lightweight fabric 1½ inches wide on the lengthwise grain, using the pattern to shape the front and neckline edges.

Pin the organza strip over the interfacing, extending the edge ¾ inch beyond the interfacing. Then stitch in place, using the multiple-stitch zig-zag or two lines of straight stitching. Press.

Pin, then baste, the interfacing to the wrong side of the garment, keeping the organza strip and garment edges even. *(Illustrated lower left)*

This method ensures a thin seam since the organza, instead of the interfacing, is included in the seam.

Method 2: Mark the seam allowance at the shoulder line of the front and back pieces of the interfacing; mark the neckline and front sections a measured ¾ inch from the edge (⅝-inch seam allowance plus ⅛ inch). Trim off along the marked line; clip off the corners. Join at the shoulder line with an abutted seam, using the multiple-stitch zig-zag. See *Abutted Seam,* page 83.

Pin the interfacing to the wrong side of the garment, ¾ inch from the edge. Baste. Catch-stitch the interfacing to the garment, using matching thread. As the stitches are made, catch one thread in the fabric barely outside the seam line and only through the interfacing on the opposite side.

(For instructions on cutting the interfacing and slipping buttonholes through the cut opening, refer to page 110.)

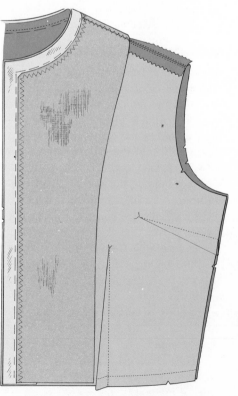

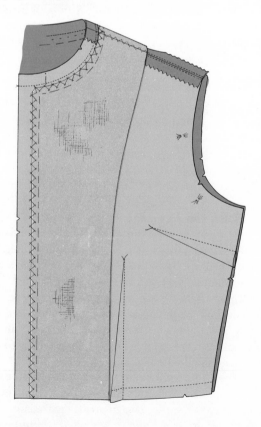

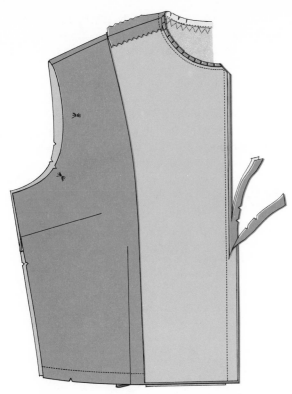

Facing. For Methods 1 and 2, join the facing for the back neckline and front sections at the shoulder line. Stitch. Finish the seam edges, then press the seam open.

Pin and baste the facing to the garment, right sides together; match markings and shoulder seams.

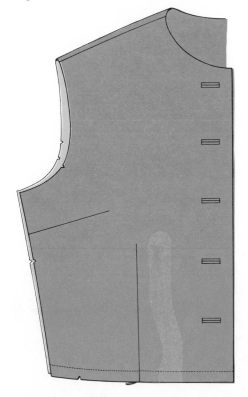

Stitch, taking one stitch diagonally across the corners for a smooth turning.

Trim the facing seam allowance to ⅛ inch and the garment seam allowance (and organza in *Method 1*) to ¼ inch. Cut diagonally across the corners close to the stitching. Slash the seam allowance on the neckline curve at even intervals and clip off the corners where seams cross at the shoulder line. Press, then press the seam open. On soft woolens and fabrics that fray easily, press before blending the seam.

Turn the facing to the underside. Pull out the corners to square them; ease the facing under slightly at the seamline and baste with silk thread. Use diagonal basting on woolens and silks. Press.

Finish the free edge of the facing, following the directions on page 135.

If your garment is lined, you will not need to finish the facing edge. If bound buttonholes are used, you must finish the back of the buttonholes. See page 111.

Slip-Stitched Facing

When a narrow facing is turned to the right side of the garment, use a slip stitch rather than top stitching to hold it in place.

For added body, place the interfacing between the top facing and garment. Use self fabric or a lightweight fabric such as organza or batiste, depending on the fabric in the garment. Cut the interfacing by the facing pattern.

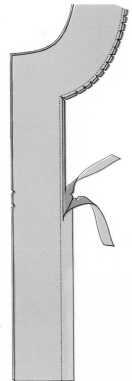

Self-fabric interfacing. Place the facing and interfacing, wrong sides together, and pin along the inside edge as illustrated. Baste if necessary. Stitch on the seamline; pivot the fabric on the needle at the inside corners.

Trim the interfacing seam allowance to ⅛ inch and the facing seam allowance to ¼ inch. Clip into the corner almost to the stitching and notch the seam on the outside curve. Press, then press seam open.

Turn the facing and interfacing to the right side of the garment. Ease the facing under slightly at the seamline and baste, using diagonal basting and silk thread. Press.

On the wrong side, position the facing with the right side next to the garment and pin *only* the outside edge of the facing in place. Stitch on the seamline, taking one or two stitches diagonally across the point for a smooth turning.

Trim the interfacing edge to a generous ⅛ inch beyond the stitching of the facing seam. Carefully baste the interfacing to the facing. Leave this basting until the facing is finished on the top side.

baste the free edge of the facing to the garment. Slip-stitch in place. Remove all bastings and press.

Lightweight interfacing. Pin the interfacing to the wrong side of the facing. Stitch a scant ⅝ inch from the edge of the facing, as illustrated. Press.

On the wrong side of the garment, position the facing, to which the interfacing is attached, with the right side next to the garment, and pin along the outside edge. Baste, then stitch on the seamline.

Trim the interfacing seam allowance close to the stitching. Trim the garment seam allowance to ⅛ inch and the facing seam allowance to ¼ inch. Clip diagonally across the corners close to the stitching, and slash the seam on the inside curve. Press, then press the seam open.

On the free edge of the facing, trim the interfacing edge close to the stitching and trim the facing edge to within ¼ inch of the stitching. Clip

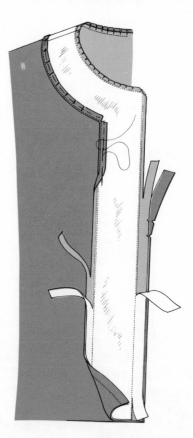

Trim the garment seam allowance to ⅛ inch and the facing seam allowance to ¼ inch. Clip diagonally across the corners close to the stitching. Slash the neckline seam allowance on the inside curve. Press, then press the seam open.

Turn the facing to the top side of the garment. Ease the garment side under slightly at the stitching line and baste. Pin and

into the corner almost to the stitching. Turn free edge to the wrong side, barely beyond the stitching and baste. Notch the seam allowances on the outside curve so that they will lie flat. Press.

Turn the facing to the top side of the garment and finish, following the procedure given for self-fabric interfacing.

Faced Scallops

You may use scalloped facings in both heavy and lightweight fabrics, but avoid them in sheers because of the distracting shadow effect in the seams. Faced scallops accent the edges of front and back openings, sleeves, and hemlines of jackets and skirts. When handled correctly, they give a feminine look to your ensemble.

Interface shaped and bias edges with a lightweight fabric. Baste the interfacing to the wrong side of the fabric.

Lightly draw the scallops on the wrong side of the facing, using the scalloped ruler as a guide. Don't forget a seam allowance. (Plastic scalloped rulers are available in various sizes and simplify the marking when scallops are not shown on the pattern.) *Do not cut the scallops.* Pin and baste the facing to the garment, right sides together.

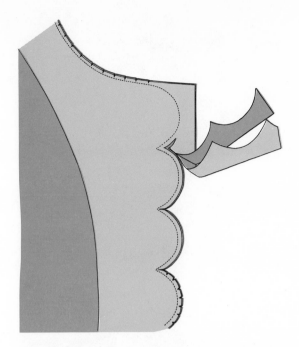

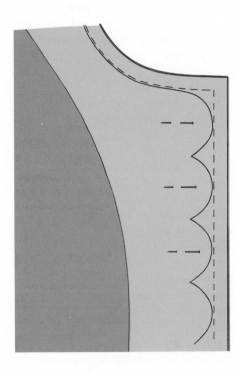

Use a short stitch and a lighter than regular pressure adjustment so that you can turn the fabric freely. Stitch on the traced outline of the scallops, taking one stitch across the point between each scallop. This space provides width when you are cutting and prevents the point between the scallops from pulling in the finished work. Remember that exactness in stitching assures a well-shaped scallop. The Quilter greatly facilitates stitching small scallops because of its open, short toe.

If the interfacing is included in the seam, trim it close to the stitching. Blend the garment and facing seam allowances to a scant ⅛ inch on small scallops and to a generous ⅛ inch on large scallops. Blend one edge shorter than the other except on small scallops. Slash at the point, almost to the stitching. Cut notches from the seam allowances at evenly space intervals. Press.

Turn the facing to the underside, gently working the seam edges between the thumb and finger to bring the stitching line to the very edge. Baste the edges with silk thread to retain the shape of the scallops until after pressing.

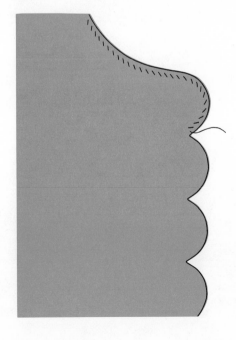

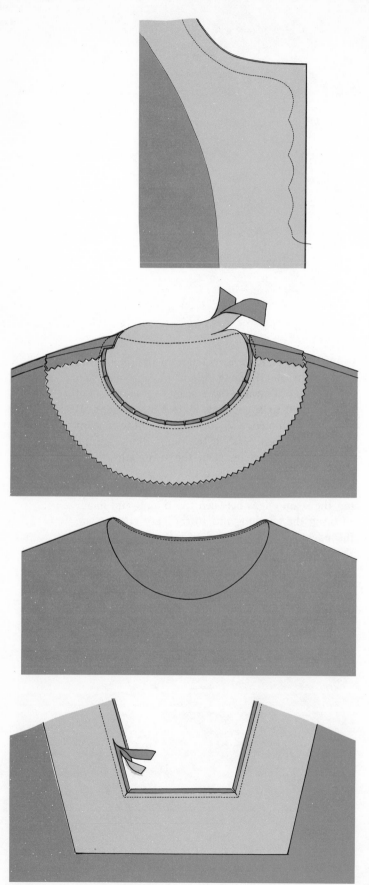

If you have a zig-zag machine, you will find that it greatly simplifies the stitching of small scallops. Set the selectors for the scallop pattern and adjust the stitch length and stitch width, which vary the length and depth of the scallop. Always start stitching at the beginning of a scallop unit. See page 266. As you sew, the fabric passes straight under the presser foot and the needle follows a scallop pattern. Press, blend the seams, and turn the facing as instructed on previous page.

Round Neckline with Fitted Facing

Cut the facing and preshrunk interfacing to match the edge to be faced.

Join the interfacing at the shoulder seams, using a lapped seam. See *Lapped Seam*, page 83. Baste the interfacing to the wrong side of the garment.

Join front and back facings at the shoulder seams. Finish the seam edges and press the seams open.

Turn the garment to the right side. Pin the facing to the neckline, right sides together, matching markings, center lines, and shoulder seams. Stitch, using a short stitch around the curved neckline.

Trim the interfacing seam allowance close to the stitching; trim the facing seam allowance to ⅛ inch and the garment seam allowance to ¼ inch. Slash into seam allowances on the curve and cut off corners where seams cross at the shoulder line. Press.

Turn facing to the underside, ease it under slightly at the seamline, and baste. Press, then remove bastings. Understitch the seam to prevent the facing from rolling out of place.

Finish the free edge of the facing, following the directions on page 135. Tack the facing to the garment shoulder seam allowances.

Square and V-Neckline with Fitted Facings

Follow the instructions for a round neckline, but pivot the fabric on the needle at the corners to square them, and clip diagonally into the seam allowances at the corners so that the facing will turn smoothly.

One-Piece Neckline and Armhole Facing

If a one-piece facing is not included with your pattern, cut one using the blouse pattern as a guide. Lay the front and the back pattern pieces over a paper as wide as the pattern and long enough to extend 4 inches below the armhole at the underarm seam. Cut around the neckline, shoulder, armhole, and underarm to 4 inches below the armhole. Remove the pattern pieces. Trim off the lower edge of the facing pattern about 4 inches from the armhole and neckline edges. Cut the facing by this pattern.

Stay-stitch the neckline and armholes if you are not using interfacing. If you are using interfacing, you can omit stay stitching because the interfacing, which is cut the same shape as the neckline and armholes, is sufficient support.

Cut the interfacing by the facing pattern, and baste it to the underside of the garment with the cut edges even at the neckline and armholes. Stitch the underarm seams of the garment, right sides together, and include the interfacing. Finish the seam edges and press the seams open. *Leave shoulder seams open.*

Pin and stitch the underarm seams of the facing, right sides together. Trim the seam allowances to one-half their width and press the seams open. *Leave shoulder seams open.* Trim ⅛ inch off the armhole edges from the shoulder to the notches of the facing only. This will permit the neckline and armhole edges to roll under slightly at the seamline after the facing is turned. The result will be a neat, smooth finish because the facing will not be visible along the edges. To finish the free edge of the facing, pink it, then turn it under ¼ inch and edgestitch. For heavy fabrics, pink, then stitch near the edge, using a short stitch.

Two methods of applying a one-piece facing are illustrated. Select the one you prefer and feel competent to do. *Use the same method when underlining a collarless and sleeveless blouse or dress.*

Method 1: Fold under the seam allowance on the shoulder seam of the facing; baste.

Turn the garment to the right side. Pin the facing to the front and back neckline and each armhole, right sides together. Match notches, center lines, and underarm seams, and keep the cut edges even. Baste if necessary. Turn garment to the wrong side and stitch from the facing side.

Begin and end the stitching ⅝ inch (seam allowance) from the shoulder edge and backstitch at each end. Compare front and back shoulders to be sure that the distance between the neckline and armhole stitching is the same. Remove bastings.

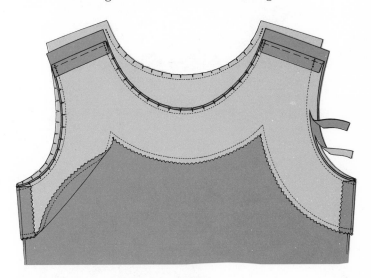

Trim the interfacing seam allowance close to the stitching. Trim the facing seam allowance to ⅛ inch and the garment seam allowance to ¼ inch. Slash the seam allowances on curves and cut off corners diagonally where seams cross at the underarm. Press.

Turn the facing to the wrong side, ease it under slightly at the seamline, and baste. Press. Remove bastings.

Understitch the neckline and armhole seams to prevent the facing from rolling out of place. Begin and end the stitching about 2½ inches from the shoulder line.

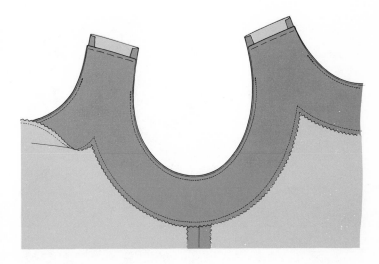

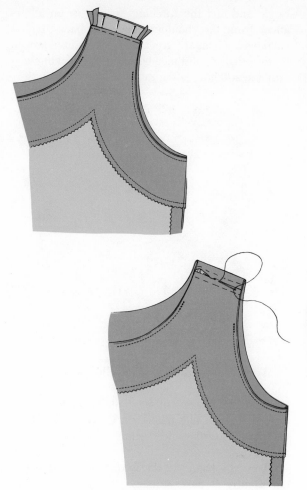

Turn the garment to the wrong side. Pin the shoulder seams of the front and back bodice together. Stitch on the seamline and backstitch at each end. Press the seams open, then slip them under the open facing seam. Slip-stitch the folded edges of the facing together. Tack the outer edges of the facing to the underarm seam allowances.

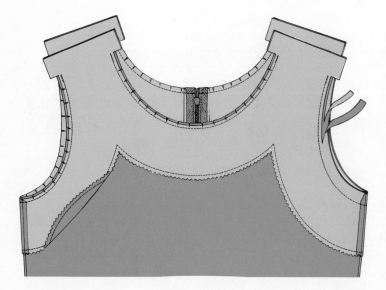

Method 2: Prepare the dress and facing, following the directions beginning on page 141. If there is a neckline opening, sew in the zipper before applying the facing.

Turn the dress to the right side. Place the facing over the dress, right sides together, and pin along the seamline of the neck and each armhole. Match center lines, underarm seams, and notches; keep the cut edges even. Baste if necessary.

Turn the dress to the wrong side. Stitch around the front and back neckline and armholes from the facing side, beginning and ending the stitching 1½ inches from the shoulder edge. Backstitch at each end. Compare front and back shoulders to be sure that the distance between the neckline and armhole stitching is the same.

Trim the interfacing seam allowance close to the stitching. Trim the facing seam allowance to

⅛ inch and the garment seam allowance to ¼ inch where stitched. (Leave the full seam allowance above the stitching until you have stitched the shoulder openings.) Slash the seam allowances almost to the stitching and at frequent intervals. Clip diagonally across corners where seams cross at the underarm. Press seams.

Turn the facing to the underside. Ease it under slightly at the seamline and baste. Press, then remove the basting.

Turn the dress to the wrong side so that right sides of the dress are together. Pin the front and back shoulder seams of the dress together. (They are the two inside edges.) With the front of the dress toward you, slip your fingers up between the facing and the garment. Grasp the shoulder seam edges of both facing and garment (four of them); pull down on the edges and at the same time turn the front facing back to bring the shoulder seam into view. This procedure turns the front shoulder of the garment and facing right sides together and pulls the back shoulder and facing into the front one. The two shoulder seam edges that were previously pinned together are on the bottom, and the two facing edges are above, right sides together.

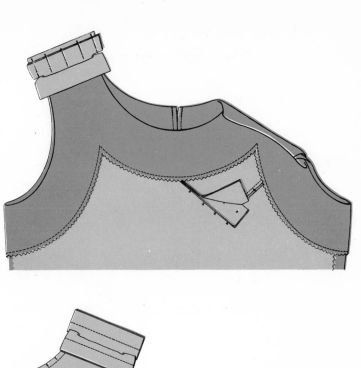

Stitch the shoulder seam of the garment, taking the regular ⅝-inch seam allowance. Then, pin and stitch the facing shoulder seam. Press seams.

Pull the back part of the shoulder seam farther into the front one so that the shoulder seam allowances are in full view and the unstitched portion of the neckline and armhole seams can be stitched. Press the shoulder seams open. Use a seamboard, and slip the pointed end through the open seam on each side of the garment; press.

Pin the neckline edges together and the armhole edges together; then stitch across the openings, overlapping the previous stitching on each side of the shoulder seam. Blend seam allowances, and press.

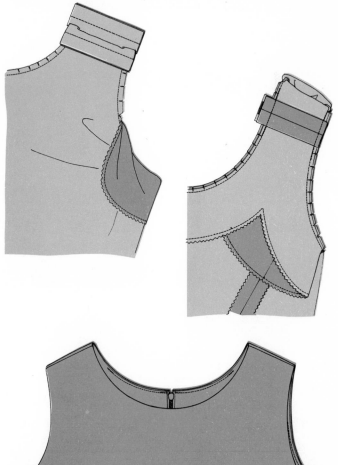

Turn the front facing to the wrong side of the dress, then pull the back shoulder into position. Press. Stitch the opposite shoulder.

Understitch the neckline and armhole, following the directions given for Method 1. Tack the outer edges of the facing to the underarm seam allowances.

Faced Slash Opening

Mark the position of the slash. *Do not cut.* Stitch around the opening for the slash, using a short stitch. Begin at the neckline, a scant ¼ inch from the center, and gradually taper to 1/16 inch at the point; take one stitch across the point. Continue stitching up the opposite side, gradually tapering to a scant ¼ inch from the center at the neckline. This stitching is not visible in the finished work.

Cut the facing the same as the edge to be faced and about 2 inches longer than the front opening. Join the seams at the shoulder line. Finish the seams and press them open.

Turn the garment to the right side. Pin and baste the facing to the neckline, right sides together. Match markings, shoulder seams, and center lines.

Place the work under the needle with the facing next to the feed. Stitch the neckline seam from one shoulder line to within ¼ inch of the center front marking. Take one stitch diagonally, then stitch down one side of the center front marking, gradually tapering to 1/16 inch at the point. Take one stitch across the point, then continue up the opposite side in the same manner and around the neckline, overlapping a few stitches at the starting point. The width at the point provides space for cutting and prevents pulling at the point in the finished work.

Blend the facing seam allowance to ⅛ inch and the garment seam allowance to ¼ inch. Clip into the seam allowance on the curve and cut off corners where seams cross at the shoulder line. Cut between the two rows of stitching, almost to the point of the slash, then cut off corners at the top of the slash, close to the stitching.

Turn facing to the wrong side. Pull out the corners to square them. Fold on the seamline and baste. Press. Remove bastings.

Understitch the neckline seam to prevent the facing from rolling out of place. Do not understitch around the slash.

(Continued)

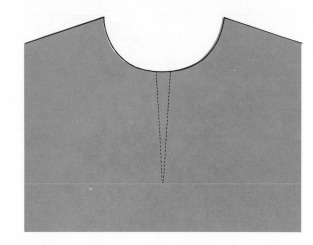

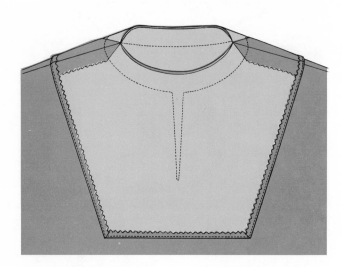

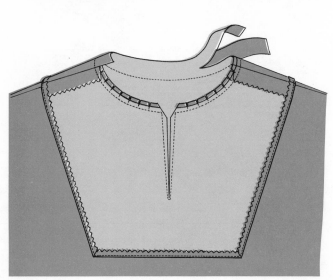

To stay the point of the slash, fold a 1½-inch length of straight seam binding through the center and press. Pin it to the underside of the facing with the upper edge exactly at the point of the slash. Stitch near the top edge of the seam binding.

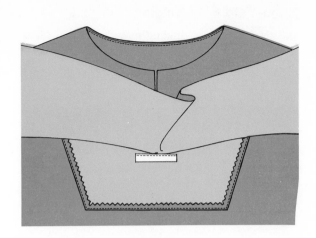

BOUND AND CORDED NECKLINE FINISHES

Double-Fold Bias Binding

A double-fold bias binding is used as a neckline finish on blouses, dresses, and children's clothes. It is also applied to the edge of sleeves and at the waistline of a garment. The bias binding may be of self or contrasting fabric. The finished width is usually about ¼ inch.

If binding is not specified on the pattern, trim off the neckline seam allowance. Stay-stitch 3/16 inch from the edge. (This stitching is not visible in the finished work.)

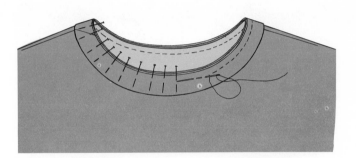

Cut a strip on the true bias, six times the width of the finished binding. See *Cutting Bias Strips*, page 244. Fold it through the center, wrong sides together, and finger-press lightly.

On the right side of the garment, pin the double bias strip around the neckline, matching seam edges. Stretch the binding slightly on this inside curve. Join the bias on the lengthwise grain at the shoulder line. See *Joining Bias Strips*, page 244. Baste. Stitch a scant ¼ inch from the edge, using a short stitch, and overlap a few stitches at the starting point. Press the seam only.

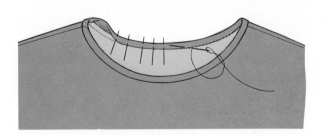

Fold the binding over the seam edge to the stitching line on the underside, enclosing the cut edges. Pin. Finish by hand, using a slip stitch.

When there is an opening at the neckline, fold the facing for the opening to the underside and press. Pin and baste it to the neckline of the garment.

Turn under the end of the binding ¼ inch before folding it through the center. Align the folded end with the folded edge of the opening. Treat the neckline and facing as one, and pin the double bias strip around the neckline, matching seam

edges. Fold the binding under ¼ inch at the opposite end. Then finish, following the procedure given above. Slip-stitch the folded edges of the binding together at each end.

Single-Fold Bias Binding

The single-fold bias binding may be used in place of the double-fold. The finished width is usually about ¼ inch.

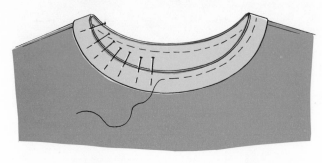

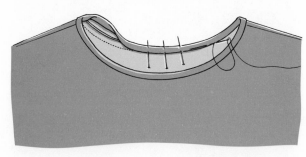

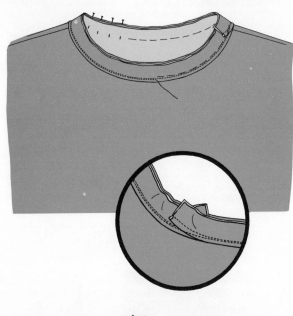

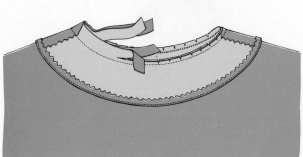

Trim off the neckline seam allowance if binding is not specified on the pattern. Stay-stitch 3/16 inch from the edge. (This stitching is not visible in the finished work.)

Cut a strip on the true bias four times the finished width. See *Cutting Bias Strips,* page 244.

On the right side of the garment, pin one edge of the bias strip to the neckline, right sides together. Match the seam edges, and stretch the binding slightly along the edge when the seam is on inside curve. Join the bias on the lengthwise grain at the shoulder line. Baste. Stitch a scant ¼ inch from the edge, using a short stitch, and overlap a few stitches at the starting point. Press.

Turn under the cut edge of the binding ¼ inch and finger-press. Fold the binding over the seam edge to the stitching line on the underside, enclosing the cut edges. Pin. Finish by hand, using a slip stitch.

When there is an opening at the neckline, follow instructions given under *Double-Fold Bias Binding* on page 145.

Corded Neckline

A fine, dainty, corded neckline in a smart finish for blouses, dresses, and children's clothes. It is a detail that is often found on expensive ready-to-wear garments. The covered cord may be made of self or contrasting fabric.

Follow instructions on page 245 for preparing the cording.

Pin the cording to the right side of the neckline, keeping the stitching of the cording on the seamline. The seam allowance on the cording is full and requires easing so that the cord will lie smoothly along the curve. Allow ⅝ inch at each end of the cording for joining at the shoulder line. Pull out the cord from its bias cover and clip off ⅝ inch at each end so the cord will just meet at the joining. Ease the two ends of the bias slightly toward the seam as illustrated. Adjust the Zipper Foot to the right of the needle. Stitch, using a stitch shorter than for straight stitching. *Do not crowd the stitching against the cord.* Press the seam.

Pin and baste the facing over the neckline, right sides together, matching the shoulder seams and center lines. Place the work under the needle with the first stitching uppermost so that you can use it as a guide. Stitch, crowding the stitching between the cord and the previous stitching; overlap a few stitches at the starting point.

Trim the corded seam allowance to ⅛ inch and the garment and facing seam allowances to ¼ inch. Clip into the seam edge on the inside curves at even intervals. Clip off corners where seams cross at the shoulder line. Press.

Turn the facing to the underside. Fold on the seamline and press. Finish free edge of the facing and tack it to the shoulder seam allowance.

To eliminate bulk, the facing is often omitted, especially if the fabric is double knit or heavy, and the garment is underlined. As the cording is stitched to the neckline, crowd the stitching between the cord and previous line of stitching. Trim the neckline seam allowance to ¼ inch and slash it at even intervals. Trim the cording seam allowance that will be next to the garment to ⅛ inch. Press, then turn the seam allowances to the underside and press. Pin the wide seam allowance to the garment; then catch-stitch, making stitches through the seam allowance and the underlining. (These stitches are not visible on the top side.)

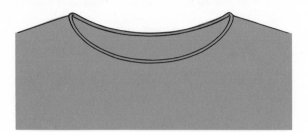

When there is an opening at the neckline, stitch the facing to the opening, blend the seams, and press. Pin cording to the neckline, extending the end ⅝ inch beyond the facing seam on each side. Start stitching at the facing seam and continue around the neckline to the opposite facing seam. Tie the threads. (Below left).

Pull out the cord at each end and clip off ⅝ inch. Then fold the bias ends diagonally toward the neckline seam and stitch in place, as illustrated. Press.

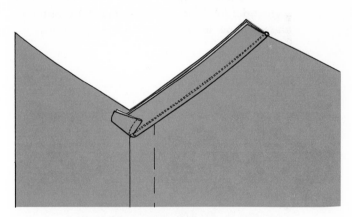

Pin and baste the facing to the neckline, right sides together. Stitch, blend the seams, and press, following the procedure given above.

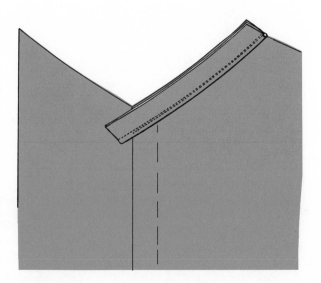

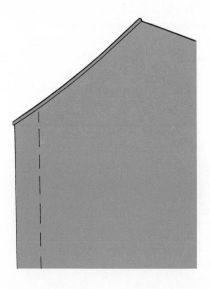

Before attaching a collar, make sure that you have: 1) stay-stitched the neckline of the garment; 2) stitched, finished, and pressed the shoulder seams and darts; 3) attached the facing and interfacing to the front opening, leaving the neckline edge free. Refer to *Faced Neckline and Front Opening*, page 134. Leave the underarm seams open for convenience in finishing the neckline.

Several methods of constructing and attaching a collar are described below. Choose the one that best suits your garment and fabric.

Collar with Bias Facing

This method may be used for cotton fabrics and children's clothes.

Cut preshrunk interfacing by the same pattern as the undercollar, and baste it to the wrong side of the undercollar, matching markings.

Pin and baste the top collar to the undercollar, right sides together, matching markings. Stitch on the seamline, leaving the neckline edge open.

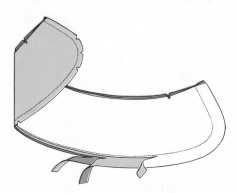

Trim interfacing seam allowance close to the stitching. Trim seam allowance on the undercollar to ⅛ inch and on the top collar to ¼ inch. Notch the outside curved edges. Press.

Turn the collar to the right side. Work the seam edges between the thumb and finger and ease the undercollar slightly to the underside at the seamline; then baste. Press. Top-stitch if desired.

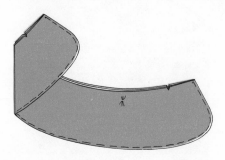

Attaching the Collar

Turn the garment to the right side. Pin and hand-baste the collar and the interfacing to the neckline edge, matching markings, shoulder line, and center lines. Roll the collar as it will be worn, allowing sufficient ease in the top collar for it to fit smoothly over the roll. Fold the front facing back over the right side of the collar and pin.

Cut a true bias strip 1¼ inches wide and long enough to extend around the neckline. Pin it over the collar at the neckline, allowing ¼-inch seam on the bias and extending the ends of bias strip ⅜ inch over the front facings. Stitch around the neckline in one continuous line from one front edge to the other. Backstitch at each end for reinforcement.

Trim the interfacing seam allowance close to the stitching. Trim collar and garment seam allowances to ¼ inch. Slash the seam allowance on the neckline curve at even intervals and cut diagonally across the corners close to the stitching. Cut off corners where seams cross at the shoulder line. Press.

Turn the front facings and the bias strip to the underside. Fold the bias under ¼ inch and pin it to the garment across the back of the neckline. Finish by hand, using a hemming stitch. Tack the front facings to the shoulder seam allowance. Press.

Notched Collar with Back Facing

Use this method for a better finish and for fabrics that will require dry cleaning.

The notched collar may be cut in one or two pieces.

One-piece collar. Crease the collar crosswise through the center. Cut preshrunk interfacing one-half the width of the collar; clip off the corners. Pin the interfacing to the wrong side of the collar just below the crease. Fold the collar in half, right sides together, and stitch across the ends. Trim the interfacing seam allowance close to the stitching. Trim the seam allowance on the undercollar to ⅛ inch and on the top collar to ¼ inch. Cut diagonally across the corners close to the stitching.

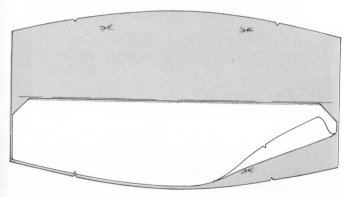

Turn collar to the right side. Pull out the corners and ease the undercollar slightly to the underside at the seamline; baste. Press.

Two-piece collar. Cut preshrunk interfacing the same as the collar. Pin and baste it to the wrong side of the undercollar. Clip off the corners of the interfacing to avoid bulk when the collar is turned.

Lay the top collar over the undercollar, right sides together, matching markings. Pin and baste. Stitch on the seamline, leaving the neckline edge free. Take one stitch diagonally across the corners to allow for a smooth turning. Trim the interfacing seam allowance close to the stitching. Trim the seam allowance on the undercollar to ⅛ inch and on the top collar to ¼ inch. Cut diagonally across the corners close to the stitching. Turn the collar to the right side. Pull out corners and ease the undercollar slightly to the underside at the seamline. Baste and press.

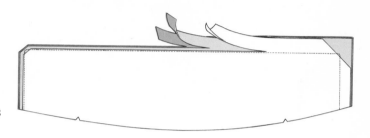

Attaching the Collar

After joining the front and back facings at the shoulder seams, stitch the facing to the garment, right sides together, along the front seams, leaving the neckline edges free. Press. Blend the seams and press them open. Slash into the neckline seam allowance almost to the stay stitching.

Pin and baste the undercollar and the interfacing to the neckline, matching markings, shoulder line, and center lines. Stitch in a continuous line, beginning ⅛ inch from one collar edge and stitching

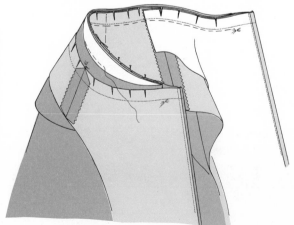

to within ⅛ inch of the opposite collar edge.

Turn the facing over the right side of the garment and pin it to the neckline from the front edge to the collar edge. Pin and baste the neckline facing to the top collar, matching markings and center lines. Stitch in a continuous line, beginning ⅛ inch from one collar edge and stitching to within ⅛ inch of the opposite collar edge.

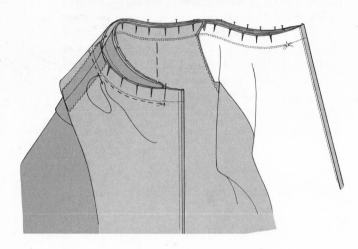

Stitch the facing to the neckline from the front edge into the collar ⅛ inch, joining the previous line of stitching. Trim the interfacing seam allowance close to the stitching. Trim the facing seam allowance to ⅛ inch and the garment and the collar seam allowances to ¼ inch. Slash the seam allowances on the neckline curve at even intervals and cut diagonally across the corners close to the stitching. Cut off corners where seams cross at the shoulder line. Press, then press seams open.

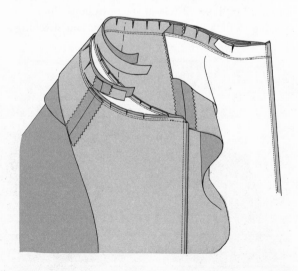

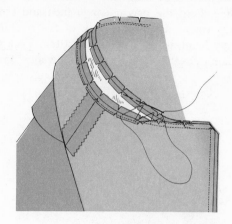

Roll the collar over the left hand, shaping it as it will be worn, and pin through all thicknesses at the roll line. Allow sufficient ease for the top collar to fit smoothly over the undercollar. Bring the top and undercollar seams together, matching shoulder seams and center lines. Pin, then staystitch together by hand.

Turn the facing to the underside. Finish the free edge of the facing and tack it to the shoulder seam allowances.

Notched Collar without Back Facing

Clip into the garment neckline seam allowance almost to the stay stitching.

Construct the notched collar as directed on page 149.

Pin the undercollar and the interfacing to the

neckline across the back from shoulder seam to shoulder seam, leaving the top collar free. Match markings and center lines. Then pin the undercollar, top collar, and interfacing to the neckline from shoulder to center front on each side, matching markings.

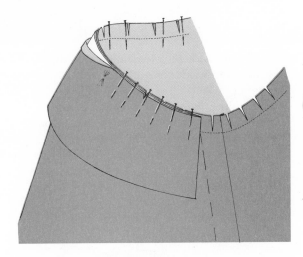

Turn the front facing over the collar, right sides together, and pin, matching markings. Baste from front edge to shoulder seam. Slash the top collar the depth of the seam allowance at each shoulder line, then baste the undercollar and interfacing to the neckline across the back. Continue basting to the opposite edge.

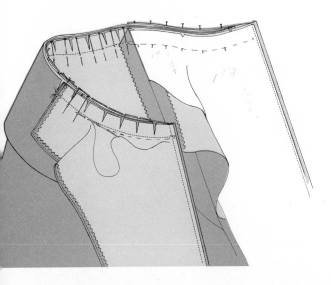

Stitch in a continuous line from one front edge to the other, leaving the top collar free across the back. Trim the interfacing seam allowance close to the stitching. Trim the garment and collar seam allowances to ¼ inch. Slash the seam allowance on

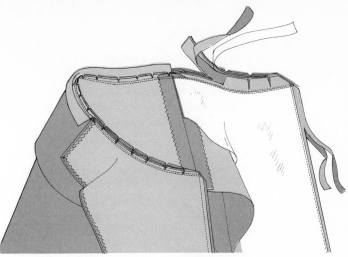

the neckline curve at even intervals and cut diagonally across the corners close to the stitching. Cut off corners where seam cross at the shoulder line. Press. Turn the facing to the underside.

Turn the seam allowance into the collar across the back neckline. Roll the collar over the left hand, shaping it as it will be worn, and pin through all thicknesses at the roll line. Allow sufficient ease for the top collar to fit smoothly over the undercollar. Turn under the free edge of the top collar and pin it to the stitching line across the back. Slip-stitch in place. Tack the front facings to the shoulder seam edges.

Velvet Overcollar

An overcollar of velvet or velveteen will complement coats, suits, and sometimes dresses for women and children.

A velvet collar covers the finished collar and the entire garment should be completed before applying it.

Follow *Method 1* when the edge of the collar

forms a border around the velveteen as in the Peter Pan collar; follow *Method 2* when the velveteen covers the collar completely as in the illustration of the notched collar.

Method 1: Cut the velvet collar by the garment collar pattern, then trim off ¼ inch on the outer edge. Stay-stitch around the neckline and outer edge of the collar ½ inch from the edge. Fold under the ⅝-inch seam allowance and baste ¼ inch

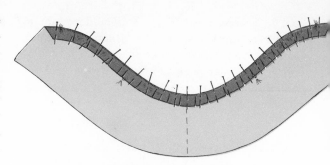

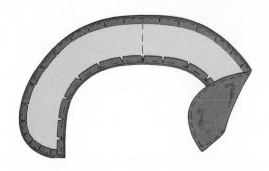

from the folded edge. Notch the seam allowance on the outside curve and slash it on the neckline curve so that the seams will lie flat.

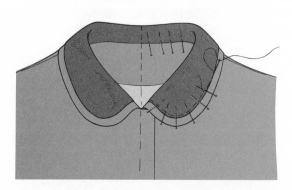

Place the velvet collar over the finished collar on the garment, matching center lines, shoulder line, and neckline seams. Pin at the neckline. Roll both collars over the left hand, shaping them as they will be worn, and pin through all thicknesses at the roll line. Allow sufficient ease for the velvet to fit smoothly over the finished collar. Then pin the outer edge of the velvet collar in place—a generous ¼ inch from the edge of the finished collar. Pin at the center back, front edges, then at intervals between. Slip-stitch velvet collar in place, catching only the upper layer of the finished collar.

Method 2: Cut the velvet collar by the pattern used for the garment collar. Stay-stitch around the neckline, ½ inch from the edge. Fold under the ⅝-inch seam allowance and baste ¼ inch from the

folded edge. Slash the seam allowance on the inside curve of the neckline and notch it on the outside curve so that the seams will lie flat.

Place the velvet collar over the finished collar on the garment, matching center lines, shoulder line, and neckline seams. Pin at the neckline. Roll both collars over the left hand, shaping them as they will be worn, and pin through all thicknesses at the roll line. Allow sufficient ease for the velvet to fit smoothly over the finished collar. Then pin the collars together near the outer edge.

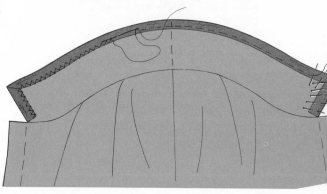

Fold the velvet collar over the collar edge and pin it in place on the underside. Pin at the center back, front edges, then at intervals between. Miter corners. Baste.

Catch-stitch the velvet collar in place on the underside, then slip-stitch it in place at neckline on the right side.

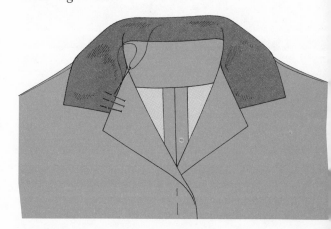

Waistline Joinings and Waistbands

BEFORE YOU JOIN THE BODICE AND SKIRT, you should have completed these steps:

1) Stay-stitched the waistline of both the bodice and the skirt.

2) Stitched the bodice underarm seams and the skirt side seams, finished the seam edges, and pressed the seams open.

The opening for the placket may be on the left side, as illustrated, or in the center back.

To Join Bodice to Plain or Gored Skirt

Turn the skirt to the wrong side and the bodice to the right side. Place bodice inside the skirt, right sides together, and pin at the waistline, matching center lines, seams, darts, and notches. Baste.

Stitch around the waistline from one edge of the placket opening to the other. Reinforce with backstitching at each end. Press.

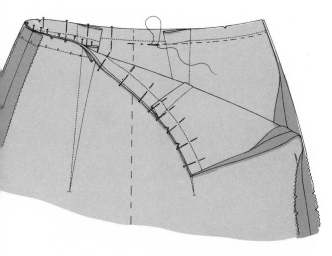

Turn the seam allowances away from the garment. On the bodice side, stitch preshrunk straight seam binding to the seam allowance barely below the first line of stitching. Begin and end the stitching about 1¼ inches from each side of the opening. Press. (The seam binding prevents the seam from stretching.) Clip off corners where seams

cross on the right side and at darts. Press. Turn the seam allowance down toward the skirt.

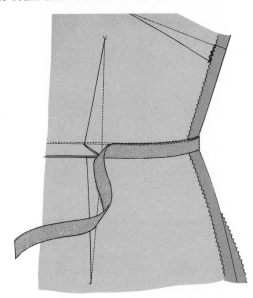

After the zipper is inserted, turn under the ends of the seam binding and tack them to the zipper tape.

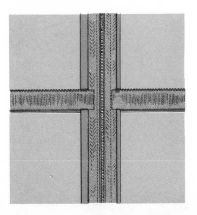

To Join Bodice to Gathered Skirt

Turn the skirt to the wrong side and the bodice to the right side. Place the bodice inside the skirt, right sides together. Pin the bodice and skirt together at the waistline, matching center lines, side seams, and markings. Adjust the gathers to fit the waistline and pin. Baste. Turn to page 106 for instructions on *Gathered Skirts*.

Stitch the seam with the bodice next to the feed. Place a second row of stitching in the seam allowance ¼ inch from the first line of stitching. Pink the edges.

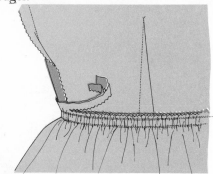

If the fabric is loosely woven, overcast the edges either by hand or by machine, using the blindstitch zig-zag. Turn seam allowance up against the bodice.

To Stay the Waistline

To prevent stretching and to allow for ease in fitting, stay the waistline of a skirt with seam binding.

Cut preshrunk straight seam binding to the

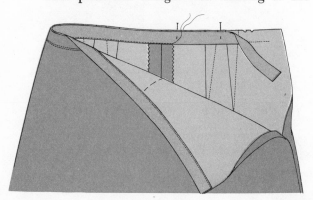

waistline measurement plus seam allowances. Pin it to the wrong side of the skirt waistline, keeping edges even and the seam binding within the seam allowance so that the stitching will not be visible in the finished garment. Evenly distribute the slight ease in the skirt. Stitch the binding to the skirt. Press.

To Attach Waistband to Skirt

Before attaching a waistband to the skirt, the waistline of the skirt should be stay-stitched; darts and seams stitched, finished, and pressed; and the zipper inserted in the placket on the left side or center back. See *Skirt Placket Zipper in Lapped Seam*, page 179.

The method used in joining a waistband to a skirt will vary, depending on the style of the garment, weight of the fabric, and personal preference. The band should be interfaced for added body. The band extension may either overlap on the front side, underlap on the back side, or lap on both sides. The width of the finished band is usually 1 inch to 1¼ inches.

Method 1: Cut the fabric for the waistband on the lengthwise grain as follows: twice the *finished width* plus seam allowances, and *the length* of the waistline measurement plus 2 inches for seam allowance and overlap on the front side of the closing and 2½ inches for seam allowance and underlap on the back side of the closing.

Fold the waistband lengthwise through the center, wrong sides together, and crease.

Cut the interfacing of nurses cloth or muslin twice the width of the finished waistband, less ¼ inch, and the same length. Fold it lengthwise through the center and press. Cut one end to a point.

Stitch the interfacing to the wrong side of the waistband back section barely below the crease and then along the opposite edge, leaving a seam allowance in the band at the pointed end.

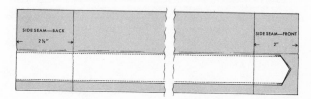

Mark the wrong side of the waistband 2 inches from the pointed edge for the overlap, and 2½ inches from the opposite end for the underlap. The length between the two markings should be the waistline measurement.

Open the zipper. Place the waistband over the waistline of the skirt, right sides together, extending the pointed end 2 inches beyond the front edge of the placket, and pin. Extend the opposite end 2½ inches beyond the back seam of the placket opening, and pin. (This end should extend the width of the zipper underlay.) Pin waistband to waistline at the right side seam, allowing the same amount of ease in the front and back of the skirt.

Match the front seamline of the placket opening with the right side seam, and pin. Fold the front section of the waistband and pin-mark the center. Match the back seamline of the opening with the right side seam, and pin. Pin-mark the center back of the waistband in the same way as the front. Pin the band to the skirt at center front and back. Evenly distribute the ease in the skirt between the markings, and pin. Baste. Stitch on the seamline, and backstitch at each end. Clip off corners where seams cross at the right side and at darts. On firmly woven fabrics, trim the waistline seam allowance to ¼ inch.

Remove bastings, and press. Turn the waistband away from the skirt and press the seam allowances toward the waistband.

Fold the pointed end of the waistband in half, right sides together, and pin across the end and along the lower edge as far as the placket opening. Stitch barely outside the interfacing, taking one stitch across the point for a smooth turning. Reinforce each end of the seam with backstitching. Fold the opposite end, right sides together and pin; stitch across the end. Trim the seam allowances to ¼ inch and press. Turn the waistband to the right side and press the ends.

Fold the waistband in half and pin along the fold. Turn under the seam allowance on the free edge of the waistband and pin to the seam at the waistline, enclosing the seam allowances. Finish by hand, using a hemming stitch. Make the stitching through the waistband and seam allowance only so that it will not be visible on the top side. Press. If top stitching is desired, stitch around the waistband from the top side.

Sew on hooks and eyes, as illustrated. Make the stitches through the underside of the waistband and interfacing. If you want a button instead of hooks and eyes for the waistband closing, work a buttonhole near the point and sew the button in position at the opposite end. If a bound buttonhole is used, make it before attaching the interfacing to the waistband. However, sew on hooks and eyes at the end of the underlap to hold it in position on the underside.

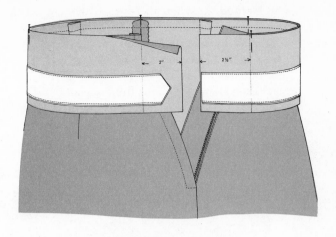

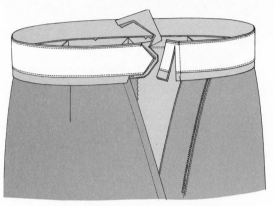

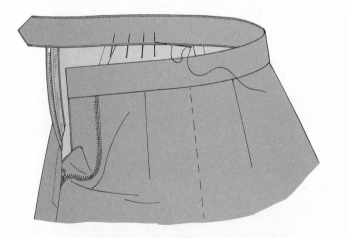

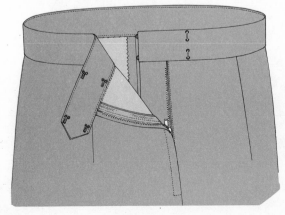

Method 2: When there is no overlap on the front seam, cut the waistband on the lengthwise grain as follows: twice the *finished width* plus seam allowances, and the *length* of the waistline measurement plus 1 inch for depth of the point and seam allowance on the front side and 2½ inches for underlap and seam allowance on the back side.

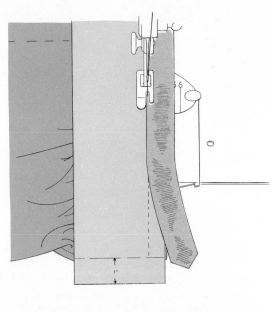

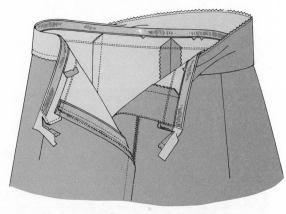

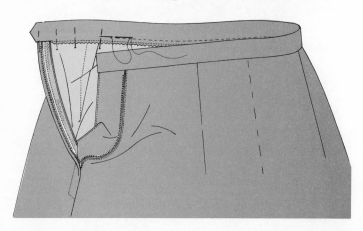

Mark the waistband at these intervals. The length between the two markings should be the waistline measurement.

Open the zipper. Place the waistband (without interfacing) over the waistline of the skirt, right sides together, extending the end 1 inch beyond the front edge of the placket opening, and pin. Extend the opposite end 2½ inches beyond the back edge of the placket opening, and pin. (This end should extend the width of the zipper underlay.)

Finish pinning the waistband in place as instructed in *Method 1.* Baste.

For the interfacing, use a heavy grosgrain ribbon 1 inch in width or a fine quality of belting. Cut it the same length as the waistband and cut one end to a point.

Lap the grosgrain or other interfacing over the waistband side of the seam allowances, keeping the edge even with the seamline. Pin. Stitch on the edge of the interfacing with the skirt next to the feed. Backstitch at each end. Remove bastings and press.

Turn the waistband away from the skirt and press the seam allowances and interfacing toward the waistband. Trim seam allowances under the interfacing to ¼ inch and clip off corners where seams cross at the right side and at darts.

Pink the free edge of the waistband, then stitch ¼ inch from the edge, using a 20 stitch.

Fold the pointed end of the waistband, right sides together, and pin across the end. Stitch barely outside the interfacing. Take one stitch across the point for a smooth turning. Reinforce the ends with backstitching. Fold the opposite end, right sides together, and pin. Trim the end of the interfacing to the seamline of the waistband. Stitch across the end of the waistband. Trim the seam allowances to ¼ inch and press. Turn the ends to the right side, ease out the corners, and press.

Turn the free edge of the waistband over the interfacing and pin to the seam at the stitching line on the underside, enclosing the seam allowances. At the front seam, fold under the raw edges of the waistband as far as the zipper tape. Finish by hand with a backstitch, catching only into the seam allowance and waistband so that the stitches will not be visible on the top side. Sew on hooks and eyes as illustrated in *Method 1.*

To Attach Waistband on Knit Fabric

To assure a snug fit in knit fabrics and still allow as much "give" in the waistband as in the fabric, use 1-inch elastic inside the waistband instead of grosgrain or fine belting. Use zig-zag stitching for flexibility.

Follow the instructions in *Method 2* on cutting the waistband and pinning it to the skirt.

Cut the elastic 1 inch shorter than the waistband and cut one end to a point. Lap the elastic over the waistband side of the waistline seam allowance, keeping the edge even with the seamline, and pin. Distribute the ease evenly in the front and back skirt section. Stitch near the edge of the elastic, stretching the elastic between the pins as you sew. Use a medium-width plain zig-zag stitch and 12 stitch length. Backstitch at each end for reinforcement.

Trim the seam allowance under the elastic to ¼ inch and clip off corners where seams cross at darts and at the right side seam. Turn the waistband away from the garment and press the seam allowance and elastic toward the waistband. Finish the free edge of the waistband with the multiple-stitch zig-zag.

Fold the pointed end of the waistband, right sides together, and pin. Stitch across the point, barely outside the elastic. Fold the opposite end, right sides together, and pin. Trim elastic end even with the seamline of the waistband. Stitch across the end of the band barely outside the elastic. Trim seam allowances to ¼ inch and press. Turn ends to the right side and press.

Fold the waistband smoothly over the elastic and pin to the seam at the stitching line on the underside, enclosing the seam allowances. Baste. Stitch from the top side, stretching the elastic as you stitch so that it will remain stretchable after the stitching is finished. Use a medium-width plain zig-zag stitch and a 12 stitch length. Sew on hooks and eyes as illustrated in *Method 1*. Make the stitches through the underside of the waistband and elastic. Or, work a buttonhole and sew on a button.

To Attach Elastic at the Waistline

Your pattern design may show the bodice and skirt of a dress, or the bodice and peplum of a jacket, cut-in-one and belted at the waistline to form soft gathers. To ensure that the gathers are evenly distributed, stitch narrow elastic to the underside of the waistline.

Mark the waistline of the garment. Fit the elastic for the desired snugness at the waistline, allowing 1 inch for finishing at the opening.

Divide the garment waistline and elastic into quarters, allowing ½ inch at each end of the elastic

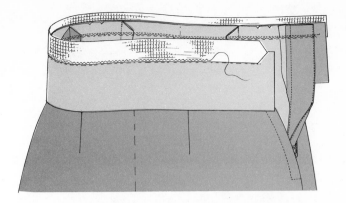

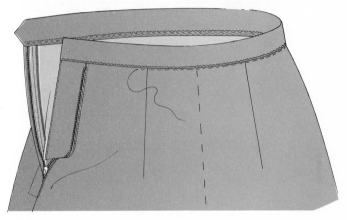

for finishing.

Pin the elastic to the underside of the garment waistline at the quartered intervals; fold ends of the elastic under ½ inch and pin to facing or zipper tape on each side of the opening. Stretch the elastic between the pins as you stitch so that it will remain stretchable after the stitching is finished. A narrow multiple-stitch zig-zag or two rows of straight stitching may be used. Fasten the ends of the elastic securely with hand stitches.

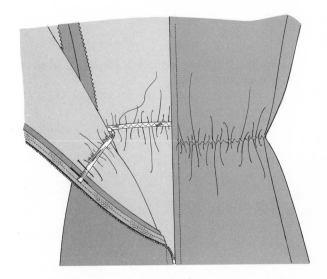

Sleeve Styles and Finishes

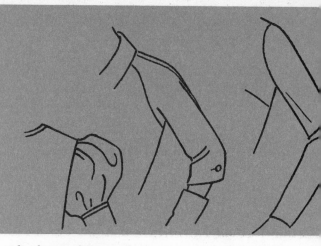

Look to the sleeve for fashion. Construct it with care. It signals the difference between a home-made and a professional-looking garment.

Your pattern design specifies the style and fin-ish of your sleeve and gives you explicit directions to follow. The paragraphs below will help you work carefully and confidently.

CONSTRUCTING DIFFERENT SLEEVE STYLES

Guidelines and Cautions

—Transfer accurately from pattern to fabric all *markings in the sleeve and armhole.*

—Never omit pinning and basting.

—The shoulder length of the bodice is important to the fit of the sleeve, especially the plain, set-in sleeve.

The fashion of the pattern may show the garment shoulder line extending beyond the natural shoulder line. Do not fit the fashion out of this sleeve. If the natural shoulder line is the fashion of your pattern, however, be sure that it is the correct length for your figure. If it is too wide, the sleeve will hang off the shoulder, giving the garment a homemade appearance; if it is too narrow, the sleeve will draw and may rip at the seam. There should always be sufficient ease for movement.

—If your pattern calls for shoulder pads or shapes, the allowance for them has been made in the pattern.

—Do not overlook proper pressing of the sleeve during construction.

Sleeve styles are numerous and almost every one is illustrated here. Variations should be constructed along the same lines as those described below.

Set-in Sleeve

Carefully check and match notches in the sleeve cap with those in the armhole to avoid constructing two sleeves for the same arm.

Three-quarter and full-length sleeves have full-ness at the elbow, which is controlled with darts or gathers. Stitch darts and press them downward over a press mitt. See *Elbow Darts,* page 103.

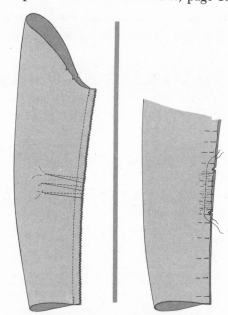

If gathers are indicated, control the fullness with a row of stitching between the notches, bare-ly outside the seamline. Fold the sleeve, right sides together, and pin on the seamline, matching mark-ings. Draw the thread to ease in the fullness at the elbow; distribute the fullness evenly between the notches. Baste, then stitch underarm seams and finish seam edges. Press the seam; then slip the sleeve over a sleeveboard, and press the seam open.

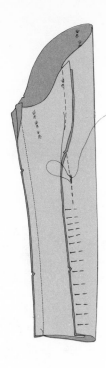

The two-piece sleeve is generally used in suits and coats. There is a slight ease in the upper sleeve section at the elbow. When joining sleeve sections, control the ease by pinning the seam at ¼-inch intervals between the notches. After the seam is basted and stitched, shrink the fullness by pressing.

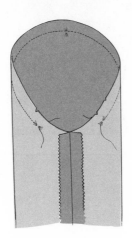

Setting Sleeve into Armhole (Above)

Turn the sleeve to the wrong side and, from the inside, place one or two lines of stitching around the cap of the sleeve between the notches to control the ease. Place the first line barely outside the seamline, in the seam allowance. Use the same length stitch as used in stitching the garment and leave thread ends long enough to draw. (Loosen the upper tension just enough to draw the bobbin thread to ease the fullness. Do not forget to return the tension to its previous setting.) If two lines of stitching are used, place the second line in the seam allowance, 3/16 inch from the first line of stitching.

Turn the sleeve to the right side. With the wrong side of the garment toward you, slip the sleeve into the armhole, right sides together. Pin, matching underarm seams, notches, and shoulder line. Working with the sleeve toward you, draw the bobbin threads at each end of the stitching, easing in the fullness from the notches to within ½ inch of the shoulder line. Draw the threads enough to fit the sleeve cap to the armhole. (The ½ inch at the shoulder line is on the straight grain of the fabric and should not be eased.) *Roll the seamline of the sleeve and armhole over the fingers and distribute the sleeve ease evenly.* Pin the sleeve

in the armhole at close intervals, taking only a small nip at the seamline.

Turn the garment to the right side and lay the shoulder over the hand to check the "hang" of the sleeve. Be sure the ease is in the correct place. The center lengthwise grain of the sleeve should fall in a straight line and the crosswise grain should fall at right angles to it. See *Understanding Balance Lines,* page 77.

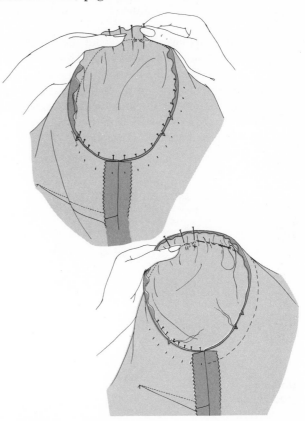

With the sleeve toward you, baste, using a short stitch.

If you are working with wool, it may be necessary to shrink out the fullness at the sleeve cap

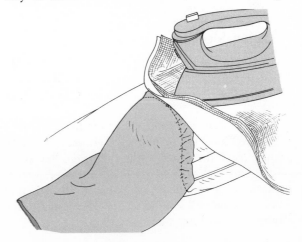

before basting. See *Pressing*, page 74. Re-pin the sleeve in the armhole the same as before, then baste.

Try on the garment before sewing in the sleeve. Pin the bodice and skirt sections together so that the bodice will not slip out of place. Check the true fit of the sleeve. Make any necessary adjustments.

Stitch from the sleeve side, barely beyond the stitching used to control the ease. Begin the stitching at the underarm seam and continue around the sleeve, overlapping stitches about 1 inch at the underarm seam. Remove basting. Trim the seam allowance to one-half its width. Clip off the corners where seams cross at the underarm and shoulder. The first row of stitching, used to control the fullness, may be removed if desired. See *Sleeves*, page 323 for additional information.

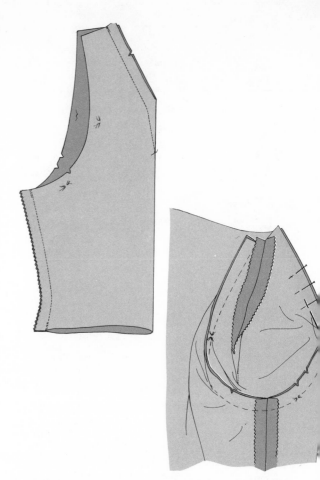

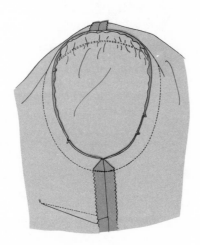

Press into the sleeve as far as the stitching. Turn the seam allowance into the sleeve. In heavy coat fabric, use only one line of stitching to control the ease. Press the seam, then press it open. See *Pressing*, page 74.

Raglan Sleeve

Pin, baste, and stitch the dart at the shoulder, matching markings. A dart in this position is usually slashed and pressed open. See *Darts*, page 101.

Stitch the underarm seams of the sleeve and bodice. Finish the seam edges and press the seam open. Turn the sleeve to the right side. Pin to the front and back bodice, right sides together, matching markings and underarm seams. Baste. Stitch in one continuous line from one neckline edge to the other. Remove bastings.

Slash the seam allowances on the inside curve and notch them on the outside curve. Clip off corners where seams cross at the underarm. Finish seam edges as required by the fabric. Press the seam open from the neckline to the curve at the underarm. Turn seam allowances toward the sleeve at the underarm.

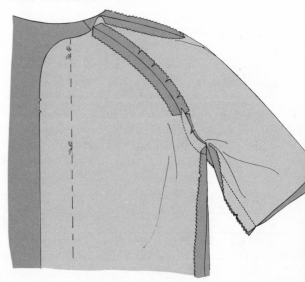

Epaulet Sleeve

The epaulet sleeve has a yoke extending over the shoulder from the top of the sleeve cap to the neckline.

At the cap of the sleeve, where the epaulet begins, stay-stitch the point where the seam allowance will be slashed. Use a short stitch and take one stitch across the point. Press. Stitch the underarm seams of the sleeve and bodice. Finish the seam edges and press the seam open.

Turn the sleeve to the right side. With the wrong side of the bodice toward you, place the sleeve into the armhole, right sides together. Pin, matching underarm seams, shoulder markings, and notches. Then with the sleeve toward you, pin at close intervals. Baste in one continuous line from one side of the shoulder to the other.

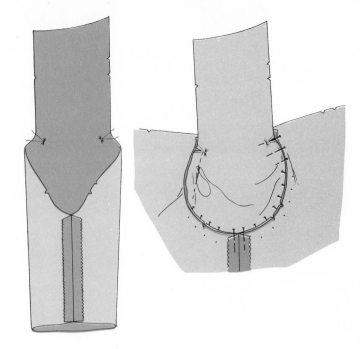

At the shoulder line of the sleeve, slash almost to the stay-stitched point. Pin the epaulet to the shoulder line of the bodice on each side, matching markings. Be sure that the corners do not pucker. Baste with a short stitch. Check the right side to be sure that the corners are square.

Stitch from the sleeve side in a continuous line from one neckline edge to the other. Pivot the fabric on the needle at the corners; take one stitch across the point; pivot again and continue stitching. Smooth out the fabric at the point so that a pleat is not formed. Remove bastings. Clip off the corners where seams cross at the underarm. Press the seam as stitched, then press the seam edges toward the epaulet. In the sleeve section, turn seam allowances toward the sleeve.

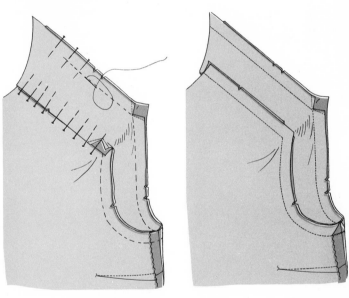

Puffed Sleeve

Puffed sleeves are found in children's clothes, blouses, many shirtwaist dresses, and lingerie.

Stitch underarm seams. (A French seam is frequently used in children's clothes and garments made of sheer fabric.)

Turn the sleeve to the wrong side and, from the inside, place two lines of stitching around the cap of the sleeve between the notches. Place the first line of stitching barely outside the seamline in the seam allowance and the second line in the seam allowance, about 3/16 inch from the first.

At the lower edge of the sleeve, place a line of stitching between the markings. Gather and finish the lower edge.

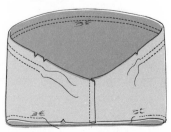

Turn the sleeve to the right side. With the wrong side of the garment toward you, slip the sleeve into the armhole, right sides together. Pin, matching underarm seams, notches, and shoulder lines. With the sleeve toward you, draw the threads for both rows of stitching at the same time, and gather the sleeve between the notches to fit the armhole. Distribute the fullness evenly, and pin. Baste, using a short stitch.

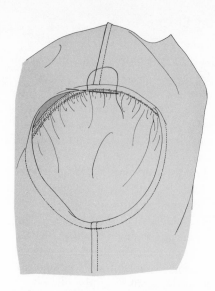

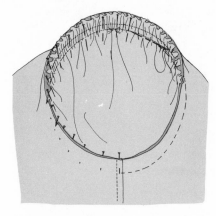

Stitch from the sleeve side, barely beyond the first line of gathering stitches and overlap the stitching about 1 inch at the underarm. Stitch again on the second line of gathering stitches. Trim the seam allowance close to the second line of stitching. Press. Finish the seam edges with binding or overcast them together, using the blind-stitch zig-zag. Turn the seam allowances toward the sleeve.

on the bodice side; fold this seam allowance over the sleeve seam allowance to the stitching line, enclosing the cut edge. Pin. Slip-stitch to the sleeve seam barely above the stitching. This seam finish is barely visible through sheer fabric.

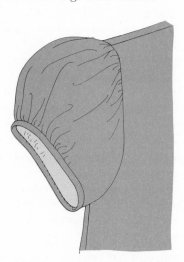

Kimono Sleeve—without Gusset

To prevent the seam from breaking under strain, use a stay, following one of the methods given here.

Method 1: Pin, baste, and stitch the seam, using a shorter stitch on the curved section. Slash the seam allowances almost to the stitching line on the curve to relieve the strain. Press the seam, then press it open.

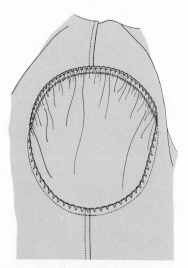

Use straight seam binding over the open seam from the hem fold in the sleeve to the lower edge of the bodice. Turn the seam allowance away from the garment and stitch the binding to each side of the seam allowance. Stitch again through the

In sheer fabrics, place the second line of stitching around the cap of the sleeve, ⅛ inch from the first line, and use only one line of stitching to sew in the sleeve. Trim the seam allowance on the sleeve side to ¼ inch. Turn the cut edge under ⅛ inch

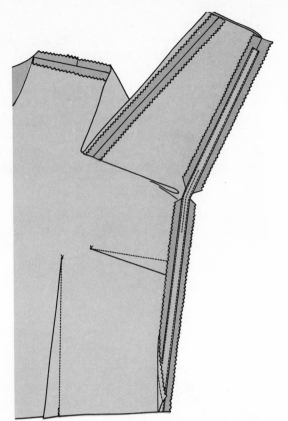

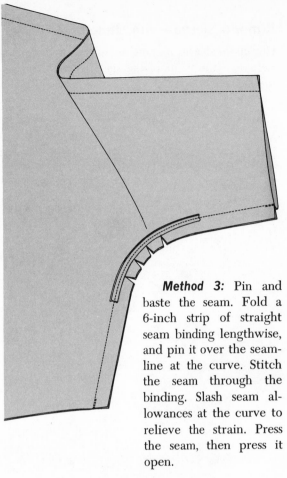

curve on one side, close to the seamline. The binding is stitched only to the single seam allowance and is not visible from the right side. Press seam open.

Method 3: Pin and baste the seam. Fold a 6-inch strip of straight seam binding lengthwise, and pin it over the seamline at the curve. Stitch the seam through the binding. Slash seam allowances at the curve to relieve the strain. Press the seam, then press it open.

Method 4: On **knit fabrics,** after stitching the underarm seam, baste straight seam binding over the curved section of the open seam. Then, from the right side, stitch the binding to the curved section of the seam, using a narrow zig-zag stitch (generally, a 12 to 15 stitch length and medium stitch width).

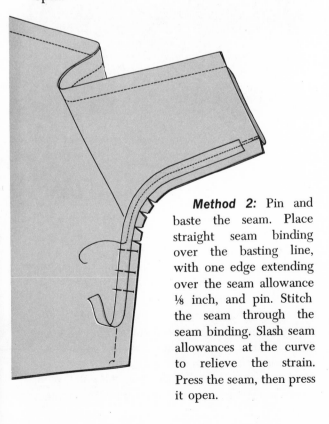

Method 2: Pin and baste the seam. Place straight seam binding over the basting line, with one edge extending over the seam allowance ⅛ inch, and pin. Stitch the seam through the seam binding. Slash seam allowances at the curve to relieve the strain. Press the seam, then press it open.

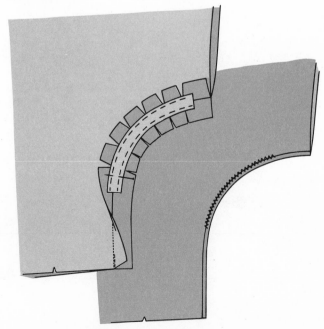

Kimono Sleeve—with Underarm Gusset

Gussets in sleeves may be one-piece or two-piece. Reinforce the point of the slash with a facing of the seam fabric cut 2 inches wide and 2½ inches long. If the fabric is heavy, use straight seam binding of the same color as the fabric.

Mark the position of the gusset at the underarm seam. On the right side, pin the facing right side down over the point of the slash, extending the top edge ½ inch beyond the point. From the wrong side, stitch the facing to the garment, following the seamline and using a short stitch. At the point, pivot the fabric on the needle and take one stitch across; then pivot again and stitch down the other side. Press.

Slash halfway between the stitching lines to within a few threads of the point. Turn the facing on the stitching line to the wrong side. Press. The reinforcement forms a wider seam allowance at the point.

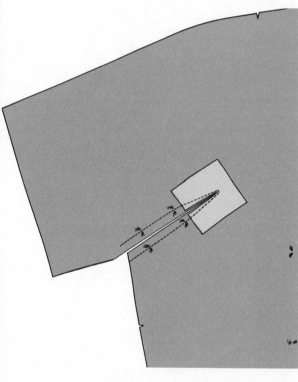

One-piece gusset. Stitch the underarm seams of the sleeve and bodice. Finish the seam edges as required by the fabric. Press the seams, then press them open.

Pin and baste the gusset to the slashed edges, matching markings at the point and at the seamline. Stitch with the gusset next to the feed. On one side, stitch from the underarm seam to the sleeve seam; take one stitch across the point; pivot again and stitch down the other side. On the other

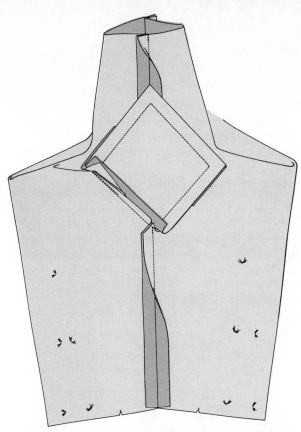

Stitch with the gusset next to the feed. Follow the seamline to the point; pivot the fabric on the needle and take one stitch across the point; then pivot again and stitch down the other side. Press the seams, then press the seam allowance away from the gusset. Stitch the underarm seam in a continuous line from the sleeve edge to the waistline. Backstitch at both ends. Finish the seam edges as required by the fabric. Press the seam, then press it open.

To prevent pulling. To prevent the gusset from being pulled out at the point of the slash, which can happen with frequent wearings, use straight seam binding over the shoulder from one point of the gusset to the other.

Turn one end of the straight seam binding under ¼ inch and pin it to the gusset seam allowance and reinforced facing, near the stitching line.

side, stitch from the sleeve seam to the underarm seam. Pull threads through to the underside and tie. Press seam allowances away from the gusset.

Two-piece gusset. Pin and baste one gusset section to the slashed edges of the front bodice and the second gusset section to the back bodice, matching markings at the point and at the seamline.

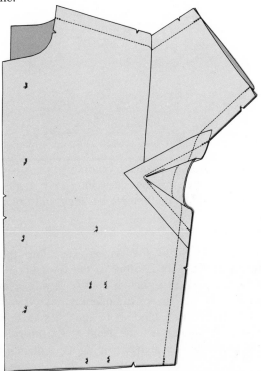

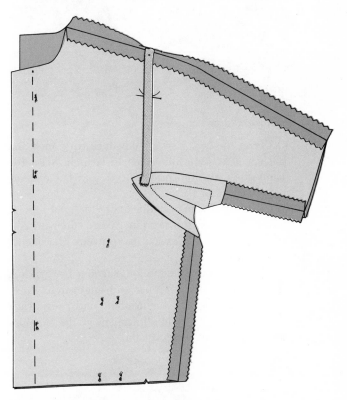

Bring the binding over the shoulder and down to the same point on the opposite side, and pin. Pin a 1/16-inch tuck, under the binding, in both the front and the back of the bodice. Then adjust the length of the binding to fit smoothly over the shoulder line. Pin the binding to the shoulder seam allowance, then tack it in place at each point and at each side of the shoulder seam allowance. Remove the pin tucks, which will allow just enough slack in the garment to prevent pulling.

Armhole with Fitted Facing

Cut the facing the same as the edge to be faced. Join seams at the shoulder and at the underarm. Finish seam edges, and press seams open.

Turn the garment to the right side. Pin the facing to the armhole, right sides together, matching notches and seams at the shoulder and underarm. Baste. Stitch around the armhole on the seamline, overlapping a few stitches at the starting point. Press.

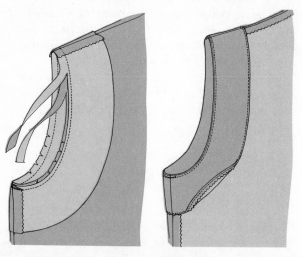

Trim the facing seam allowance to ⅛ inch and the garment seam allowance to ¼ inch. Slash the seam allowance on inside curves and cut off corners where seams cross.

Turn the facing to the underside and ease it under slightly at the seamline. Baste, then press.

Understitch the seam to prevent the facing from rolling out of place. Press.

Finish the free edge of the facing by pinking; then turn it under ¼ inch and edgestitch. Press. Turn the facing into the armhole and press. Tack the facing to the seam allowances at the shoulder seam and the underarm seam.

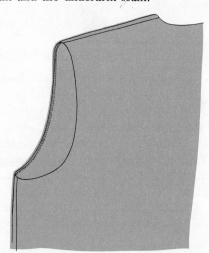

FINISHING THE SLEEVE

To ensure a correct sleeve length, long sleeves or those varying in length between the elbow and wrist are finished at the lower edge after the sleeve is sewed into the armhole. Short sleeves may be finished before they are sewed into the armhole.

Hemmed Edge—Short Sleeve

Fold the hem evenly to the underside and baste ¼ inch from the fold. Press. Pin, then stitch seam binding ¼ inch from the free edge of the hem. Join the binding by folding the end under ¼ inch and overlapping ½ inch at the seam. Press.

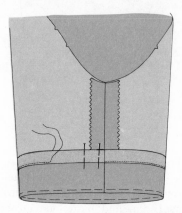

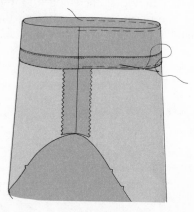

Pin the free edge of the binding to the sleeve. Baste. Slip-stitch in place, catching only a single thread of the fabric. Remove bastings, and press.

Wrist Closing

Turn the sleeve to the wrong side. Pin, then stitch, straight seam binding to the front edge of the wrist opening ⅛ inch from the *seamline*, extending it ½ inch above the opening.

Pin, then stitch binding to the back edge of the wrist opening, ⅛ inch from the *seam edge*, extending it ½ inch above opening. Clip diagonally into this seam allowance from the top of the binding to the opening. Press.

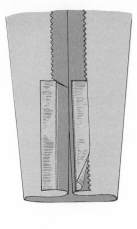
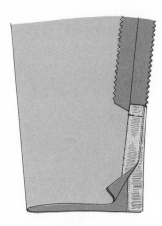

At the back edge of the opening, fold the binding to the underside and pin the free edge to the sleeve. Finish by hand, using a hemming stitch. At the top of the opening, stitch the front and back seam edges together the depth of the seam allowance.

At the front edge of the opening, fold the binding to the underside and pin the free edge to the sleeve. Finish by hand, using a hemming stitch.

At the lower edge of the sleeve, pin, then stitch, binding ¼ inch from edge, extending the ends ¼ inch beyond the edges of the opening. Press. Cut diagonally across corners of the sleeve seam al-

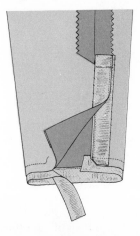
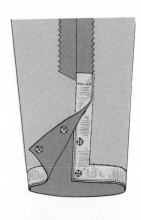

lowance close to the stitching. Fold the binding to the underside, miter the corners, and baste the free edge to the sleeve. Press. Finish by hand, using a hemming stitch. Remove bastings and press. Sew on small snaps.

Zipper Closing

Select a fine neckline zipper, about 4 to 6 inches long, for a wrist closing. Apply the zipper following the instructions for the *Neckline or Sleeve Zipper in Slot Seam*, on page 181. Then open the zipper and finish the lower edge of the sleeve with straight seam binding, following the method described above.

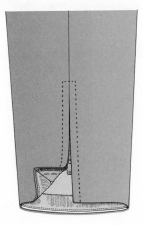

Vent Closing

The vent closing is frequently used in the back seam of two-piece tailored sleeves. It is also used in jackets at center back or side seams.

Sleeve Seams

Mark the line of the fold for the vent closing and for the hem at the lower edge of the sleeve. If a bound buttonhole is used in a three-quarter length sleeve, make the buttonhole before seaming the sleeve.

Join the seams of the upper and lower sleeve sections, leaving the back seam open below the

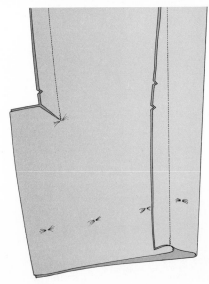

marking for the vent. Reinforce seam ends with backstitching. Clip diagonally into the seam allowance of the under section from the cut edge to the top of the opening. (This wide seam allowance in the opening will extend under the front seam allowance when the vent is finished.) Press seams, then press them open, carrying the crease in the back seam of the upper section to the lower edge of the opening. Fold the bottom hem to the underside, and press.

The Interfacing

Cut preshrunk muslin interfacing on the true bias, ½ inch wider than the hem and long enough to extend around the sleeve; extend one end the depth of the opening. Place the interfacing on the wrong side of the sleeve with the lower edge along the hem fold and the extended edge along the lengthwise fold of the opening on the upper section. Pin, then baste. Catch-stitch each edge of the interfacing along the hem; make a tiny stitch barely outside the interfacing, catching only a single thread in the fabric; then make a stitch on the opposite side through the interfacing only. Space the stitches about ⅝ inch apart. Do not pull the threads too tightly. Remove bastings. The interfacing along the fold of the opening will be held in place when the buttons are sewed on; you may catch-stitch it if you wish, however, and you should catch-stitch it if you do not plan to use buttons on the opening.

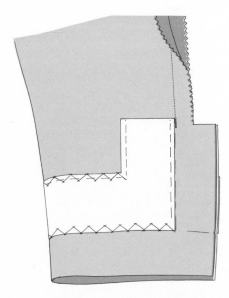

The Hems

Bottom hem. Fold the bottom hem over the interfacing and baste ¼ inch from the fold. Press. Pin, then baste the free edge of the hem to the

interfacing. Catch-stitch in place from the back edge to the lengthwise fold in the opening on the upper section, making the stitches through the hem and interfacing only. The stitches are not visible on the right side, and the interfacing above the hem will not be visible when the lining is in place.

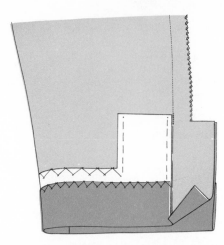

Side hem and opening. On the upper section, trim the bottom hem to ¼ inch from the cut edge to the lengthwise fold in the opening. Miter the corner to the point where the lining will overlap the hem. Press. Fold the seam allowance in the opening to the underside and pin in place. Slip-stitch the mitered corner in place, then catch-stitch the free edge of the seam allowance to the interfacing the depth of the opening.

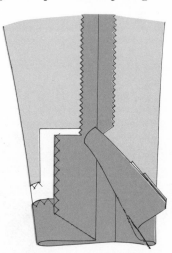

Turn the sleeve to the right side. Lap the upper section over the under section the depth of the seam allowance in the opening and pin. Be sure the lower edges are even.

Work from the wrong side and catch-stitch the edge of the back seam allowance in place from the lower edge to the top of the interfacing.

Make fine stitches through the seam allowance and interfacing only. Tack the seam edges to the interfacing at the top of the opening. Remove all bastings and press.

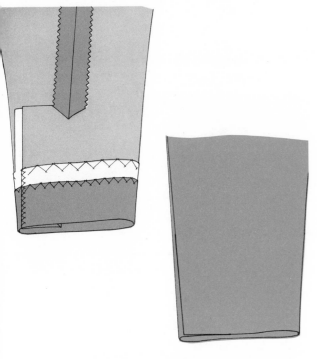

Turn the sleeve to the right side and sew on buttons through all thicknesses of fabric. The interfacing above the hem will not be visible when the lining is hand-sewed in place.

Hemmed Cuff

The hemmed cuff is an excellent finish for blouses and children's clothes. The cuff and sleeve are cut-in-one, with the cuff section shaped to turn back smoothly over the sleeve.

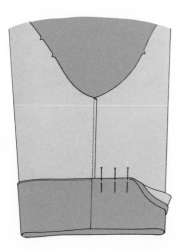

After you have stitched the underarm seam, fold the cuff hem to the underside and press. Baste before pressing if necessary. Fold the free edge of the hem under ¼ inch, and finger-press. Pin the free edge to the sleeve, matching seams. Stitch near edge. (In the illustration the sleeve is turned to the wrong side so that the work may be easily seen.)

Turn the sleeve to the right side. Turn the cuff back over the sleeve, ½ inch below the stitching.

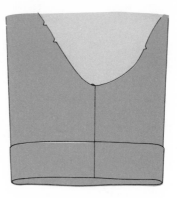

Turn-Back Cuff

The ends of the cuff may be stitched together, as illustrated here, or left open. When the ends are left open, construct the cuff in the same manner as a collar and attach it to the sleeve, following the instructions given below.

Stitch the ends of the cuff together on the undercuff and on the upper cuff. Reinforce with back-stitching. Press, then press seam open.

Cut preshrunk interfacing by the cuff pattern. The sewing and handling instructions for attaching it to the cuff vary, depending on the weight of the interfacing and the fabric in the garment. Follow the appropriate method below.

With lightweight interfacing. Join interfacing

ends with a lapped seam, using the multiple-stitch zig-zag to eliminate bulk. See *Lapped Seam*, page 83.

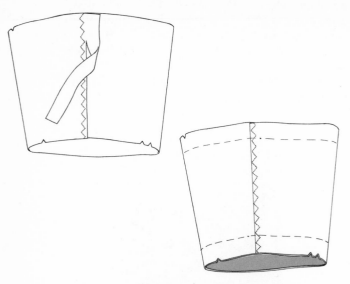

Turn the undercuff to the wrong side and slip interfacing over it, matching seams. The interfacing should fit smoothly over the cuff. Pin, then baste each edge of the interfacing to the cuff.

Turn the undercuff right side out with the interfacing to the inside. Slip the upper cuff over the undercuff, right sides together, matching markings and seams. Pin along the top edge, easing the upper cuff between the markings. Baste, then stitch, overlapping a few stitches at the starting point.

Trim the interfacing seam edge close to the stitching; then trim the seam allowance of the undercuff to ⅛ inch and of the upper cuff to ¼ inch. Notch the seam edges on the outside curve and clip off corners where seams cross. Press.

Turn the cuff to the right side with the upper cuff to the top. Ease the undercuff slightly to the underside at the seamline and baste. Press.

With heavyweight interfacing. Trim off the seam allowance plus ⅛ inch on the upper and lower

edges of the interfacing, and trim off the seam allowance at each end.

Cut two strips of organza 1½ inches wide—one the shape of the top of the cuff and the other the shape of the bottom. Lay the organza strip over the upper edge of the interfacing, extending it ¾ inch beyond the interfacing edge. Pin. Follow the same procedure at the lower edge. Then stitch, using the multiple-stitch zig-zag. Press. Join ends with an abutted seam. See *Abutted Seam*, page 83.

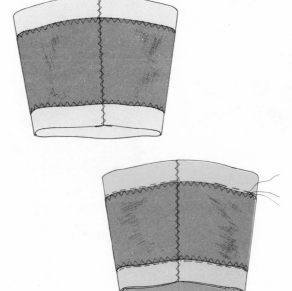

Turn the undercuff to the wrong side and slip the interfacing over it, matching seams. The interfacing should fit smoothly over the cuff. Pin, then baste each edge of the interfacing to the cuff.

Turn the undercuff right side out with the interfacing to the inside. Slip the upper cuff over the undercuff, right sides together, matching markings and seams. Pin along the top edge, easing the upper cuff between the markings. Baste, then stitch, overlapping a few stitches at the starting point.

Trim the undercuff seam allowance and organza strip to ⅛ inch and the upper cuff seam allowance to ¼ inch. Notch seam allowance on the curve and clip off corners where seams cross. Press.

Turn the cuff to the right side with the upper cuff to the top. Ease the undercuff slightly to the underside at the seamline, and baste, using diagonal basting and silk thread. Press.

Attaching Cuff to the Sleeve

Turn the sleeve and cuff to the right side. Slip the cuff over the sleeve. Pin, then baste the undercuff and interfacing to the lower edge of the sleeve, matching markings and seams. (Fold back the upper cuff about 1 inch to keep it out of the way for the next step.) Stitch from the sleeve side, overlapping a few stitches at the starting point.

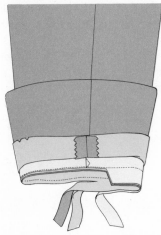

Trim the interfacing seam allowance close to the stitching; trim the undercuff seam allowance to ⅛ inch and the sleeve seam allowance to ¼ inch. Clip off corners where seams cross and slash the curved seam allowance of the cuff. Press, then press the seam open.

If a sleeve facing is not shown with the pattern, cut one about 3 inches deep, using the sleeve pattern as a guide. (The facing must not be deeper than the cuff.) Stitch the ends together, then press the seam open. Pin and baste the facing to the free edge of the upper cuff, matching markings and

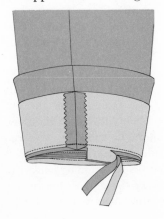

seams. Stitch, overlapping a few stitches at the starting point.

Trim seam allowance to ¼ inch. Clip off corners where seams cross and slash the curved seam allowance at evenly spaced intervals. Press, then press the seam open.

Slip the fingers of the left hand between the sleeve and cuff and pin the cuff sections together about ½ inch above the lower edge. Stay the open seams of the two cuffs together, allowing sufficient ease in the upper cuff for it to fit smoothly over the fold of the interfacing and undercuff. This prevents the undercuff from wrinkling and slipping out of place at the top.

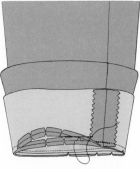

If the garment is unlined, finish the free edge of the facing, then turn the facing into the sleeve, and pin the free edge to the sleeve. Finish by hand, spacing the stitches about 1 inch apart.

When a facing is not used, follow the above method up to instructions for cutting the facing. Turn the cuff away from the sleeve and press the seam allowances toward the cuff. Turn the cuff back over the sleeve. Slip the fingers of the left hand between the sleeve and cuff and pin the cuff sections together about ½ inch above the lower edge. Fold under the seam edge on the upper cuff and pin it to the sleeve at the stitching line, enclosing the seam allowances inside the cuff. Allow sufficient ease in the upper cuff for it to fit smoothly over the fold for the interfacing and undercuff. Finish by hand, using a hemming stitch. (Work inside the sleeve.)

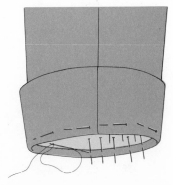

French Cuff

The French cuff is a popular sleeve finish for tailored dresses, blouses, and shirts. It is cut twice the finished width and is folded crosswise through the center to form a double cuff that is open at the ends. It requires four buttonholes for cuff links or for buttons joined with French tacks.

If bound buttonholes are used, make them before stitching the cuff.

Cuff. Cut preshrunk interfacing by the cuff pattern. Baste it to the wrong side of the upper-cuff. Clip off the four corners of the interfacing to eliminate bulk when the cuff is turned.

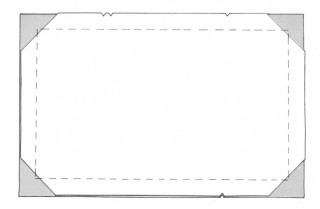

Pin the upper cuff over the undercuff, right sides together, matching markings. Baste if necessary. Stitch around three sides, leaving open the edge that will join the sleeve. Take one stitch across the corners for a smooth turning and backstitch at each end of the seam. Remember to construct one cuff for the left sleeve and one for the right. Remove all bastings and press.

Trim the interfacing seam edge close to the stitching. Trim the undercuff seam edge to ⅛ inch

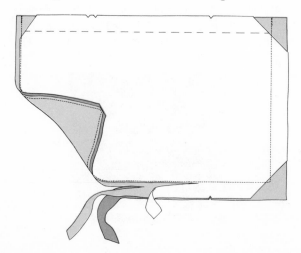

and the upper cuff seam edge to ¼ inch. Cut diagonally across corners, close to the stitching. Press. Turn the cuff to the right side. Pull out corners to square them. Ease the undercuff slightly to the underside at the seamline and baste. Press.

Sleeve. Mark the position for the opening in the sleeve and finish it with a continuous bound placket before stitching the underarm seams. See page 185.

Turn the sleeve to the wrong side and, from the inside, place two lines of stitching around the lower edge to gather the fullness. Place the first line of stitching a scant ⅝ inch from the seam edge and the second line in the seam allowance, ¼ inch from the first line. Use the same stitch length you used in stitching the garment and loosen the upper tension slightly. (Do not forget to return the tension to its previous setting). Leave thread ends long enough to draw.

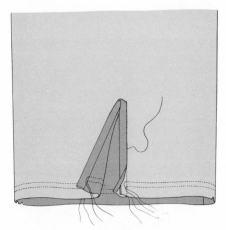

Attaching Cuff to Sleeve

Turn the sleeve to the right side. On the right side, wind the thread ends around a pin, forming a figure eight at each end of the stitching. Place the cuff over the sleeve, with the upper cuff and right side of the sleeve together. Pin the upper cuff and interfacing to the sleeve, matching markings and extending the placket binding beyond each end of the cuff.

Working with the wrong side of the sleeve toward you, draw both threads at the same time and gather the sleeve to fit the cuff. Distribute the fullness evenly, then pin the sleeve to the cuff at close intervals. Pull the gathering threads to the underside and tie.

Fold the placket binding back over the gathers, and pin. Baste the cuff to the sleeve. Stitch from the sleeve side, barely beyond the first line of

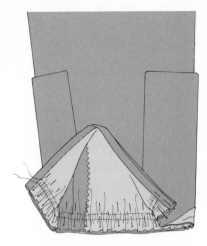

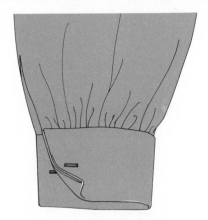

and machine-worked buttonholes in fine cottons or woolens. Cut buttonholes and insert cuff links.

gathering stitches. Backstitch at each end. (Do not catch the undercuff on the stitching).

Trim the interfacing seam edge close to the stitching. Trim the cuff seam edge to ⅛ inch and the sleeve seam edge to ¼ inch. Press the seam, then turn the cuff away from the sleeve and press the seam edges toward the cuff.

Fold the cuff smoothly through the center. Slip the fingers of the left hand between the fold to be certain there is enough ease in the upper cuff for it to fit smoothly over the fold of the interfacing and undercuff. Pin through all thicknesses, about ½ inch above the fold. Fold the free edge of the cuff under ¼ inch and pin it to the sleeve at the stitching line, enclosing the gathered seam allowance inside the cuff. Slip-stitch in place.

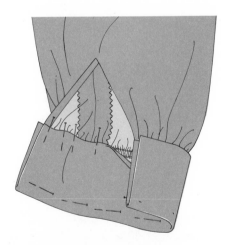

Check the position of buttonholes on both cuff layers to be sure that they coincide and then work a buttonhole at each end of both the cuff sections, using hand-worked buttonholes in soft, silk fabrics

Cuff Cut-in-One with the Sleeve

The cuff cut-in-one with the two-piece sleeve is generally found in suits and coats. Since it is most often a soft cuff, it requires a light or medium-weight interfacing. The cuff opening is in the back seam of the sleeve.

Mark the sleeve for the turn of the cuff.

Join the upper and lower sleeve sections at the front seam, right sides together. Press the seam open.

Cut preshrunk interfacing by the cuff pattern. Trim off the seam allowance plus ⅛ inch on the top edge and at each end. Cut a strip of organza 1½ inches wide to fit across the top edge and the ends of the cuff, using the pattern to shape the outer edges. Pin the organza strip over the interfacing, extending the edges ¾ inch beyond the interfacing. Clip off the corners of the interfacing to eliminate bulk when the cuff is turned. Stitch, using the multiple-stitch zig-zag. Press.

Pin the interfacing over the wrong side of the undercuff, which is cut-in-one with the sleeve. Baste in place along the lower edge and each end of the cuff.

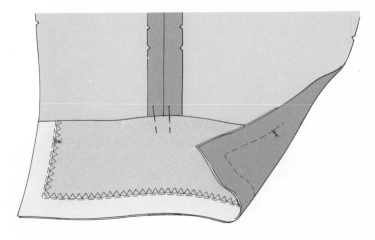

Join the upper and lower sleeve sections at the back seam, leaving the seam open below the marking for the cuff. Backstitch at each end of the seam. Press, then press the seam open.

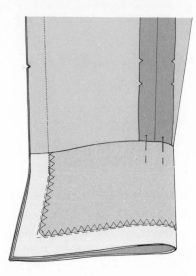

Turn the sleeve to the right side. Place the upper cuff over the undercuff, right sides together. Pin in place along the edge and ends, matching markings. Pin at the points and markings, then at intervals between, easing the upper cuff between the markings.

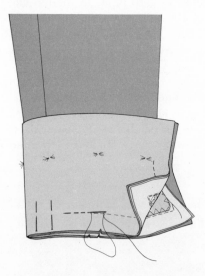

Stitch from the interfacing side, beginning at one end of the cuff opening and continuing around the cuff to the opposite end. Take one stitch across the corners for a smooth turning. Pull the threads to the underside and tie. Remove basting.

Pin the upper cuff seams together above the opening, then stitch. Press the seam open. Trim

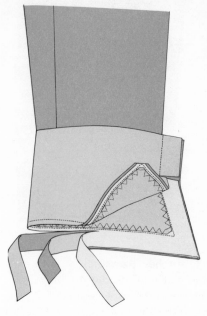

the undercuff seam edge and organza strip to ⅛ inch and the upper cuff seam edge to ¼ inch. Cut diagonally across corners, close to the stitching. Press.

Turn the cuff to the right side. Pull out the corners to square them. Ease the undercuff to the underside slightly at the seamline, and baste, using diagonal basting and silk thread. Press.

With the sleeve right side out, turn the cuff back over the sleeve. Slip the fingers of the left hand between the sleeve and cuff and pin through all thicknesses, ½ inch above fold. Turn the free edge of the cuff into the sleeve, allowing sufficient ease in the upper cuff for it to fit smoothly over the fold of the interfacing and undercuff. Tack the free edge to the sleeve seam allowances. Remove all bastings. The lining, when it is attached, will hold the cut edge of the cuff in place.

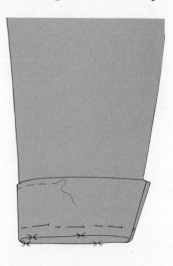

Double-Fold Bias Binding

A double-fold bias is used as a sleeve finish in blouses, dresses, and children's clothes. The same type of finish is also used at the neckline. The finished width of the binding is usually ¼ inch; the sleeve edge may be straight or gathered as in the puffed sleeve.

Trim the seam allowance on the lower edge of the sleeve to a scant ¼ inch. Gather the lower edge of the sleeve as indicated on the pattern.

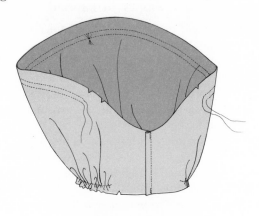

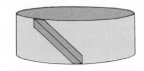

Cut a strip on the true bias six times the width of the finished binding. See *Cutting Bias Strips*, page 244.

Join the bias strip on the lengthwise grain to fit the sleeve edge, taking a ¼-inch seam. Press the seam open.

Fold the bias through the center, wrong sides together, and finger-press lightly. Pin the double bias over the right side of the sleeve, keeping the cut edges even. Baste. Stitch from the sleeve side a scant ¼ inch from the edge, using a short stitch and overlapping a few stitches at the starting point. Press.

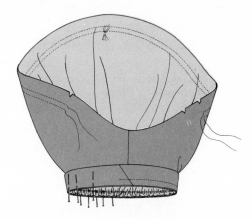

Turn the sleeve to the wrong side. Fold binding over the seam edge to the stitching line on the underside, enclosing the cut edges. Pin. Finish by hand, using a slip stitch.

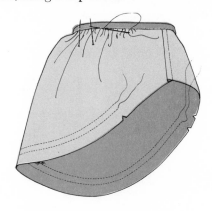

175

Homeward Bound:

Zippers, Hems,
Belts, and Buttons

YOUR DRESS at last looks almost ready to wear. The adjustments and fittings and the basting and stitching are over. All that is lacking now are the final details—a zipper, a hem, maybe a belt, and some buttons.

ZIPPERS AND PLACKETS

There are several ways of inserting zippers; the one you select depends on the location of the zipper in the garment and the type of garment. Generally zippers are either concealed in a lapped seam with only one line of stitching visible or centered under a slot seam with two lines of stitching visible. The lapped seam application is used

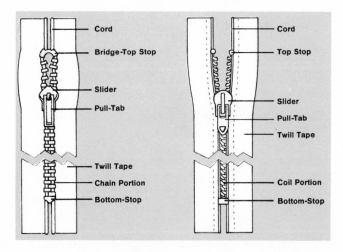

in side seam closings for dresses, skirts, and shorts. It is also popular for center back closings when long zippers are used. The slot seam application is used in neckline, sleeve, and center back or front closings. It is sometimes used for side closings instead of a lapped seam.

The pattern envelope will designate the length and type of zipper to buy. To ensure a neat, professional zipper application, follow the step-by-step methods given below.

Dress Placket Zipper in Lapped Seam

Before you put in the zipper, the bodice and skirt sections should be joined at the waistline. The left side seam should be open above and below the waistline. The placket opening should be ½ inch longer than the metal or synthetic portion of the zipper. Check the ends of the permanent stitching on both the skirt and bodice to be certain that they are reinforced with backstitching.

Inspect the fit of the dress; the side seams should hang straight from underarm to hemline.

If the waistline is small and the hips rounded, the seam below the waistline will be curved and applying the zipper will require a little extra care. If the waistline is comparatively large and the hips flat, the seam will be fairly straight, and the zipper application will require less caution. Compare the front and back seams of the opening to make sure they are the same length. Chalk or hand-baste exactly on the seamline on each side of the opening. Select a dress placket zipper of the correct length (9, 10, or 12 inches).

1. Turn the dress to the wrong side. Pin the

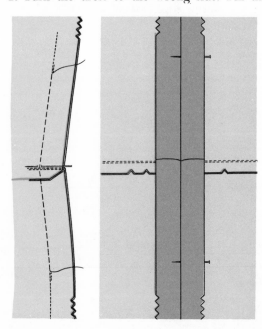

seams together, carefully matching the waistline seams. Machine-baste on the seamline the exact length of the opening. Clip off corners where seams cross at the waistline.

If the placket seam allowance is less than ¾ inch, stitch seam binding to the seam edge on the front side.

2. Press the seam open over the curve of a press mitt to retain the shape of the hipline. Press the zipper tape.

Mark the ends of the permanent stitching by placing pins across the seam but not through the dress.

3. Fold under the back seam allowance ⅛ inch from the machine-basted seam and place the fold over the right side of the zipper tape, with the bridge-top stop ⅛ inch below the top of the opening; pin. Roll the zipper and folded edge over the fingers of the left hand to ease the seam, then pin the folded edge to the zipper tape. The bottom stop should fall ⅛ inch above the opening in the skirt. This allows ¼ inch for ease throughout the length of the zipper. Pin the seam allowance to the tape above and below the opening. Hand-baste.

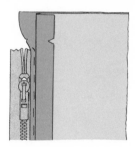

4. Replace the presser foot with the Zipper Foot and adjust the foot to the left of the needle.

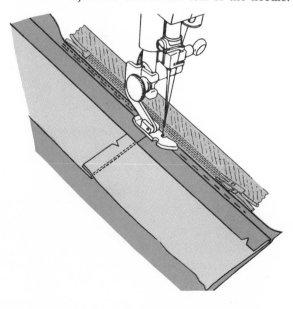

Turn the pull-tab up to lessen bulk in stitching. Stitch from the bottom to the top near the edge of the fold. *Remove hand basting* and *turn the pull-tab down.*

5. Turn the dress to the right side. Turn the zipper and back seam allowance flat against front seam allowance. Place the fingers of the left hand under the zipper; press the zipper in position. Work from the right side and roll the zipper and seam over the fingers of the left hand to ease the fabric. Pin through all thicknesses, placing pins at right angles to the seam, through the fabric, and under the chain portion of the zipper. Alternate the direction of the pins to distribute the slight ease evenly.

Hand-baste a measured distance of ⅜ to ½ inch from the machine-basted seam, using a long and short basting stitch. Use the basting as a guide in stitching.

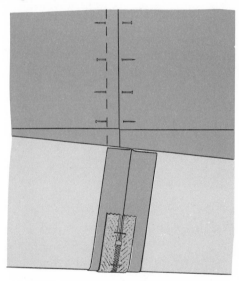

6. Adjust the Zipper Foot to the right of the needle. From the right side of the garment, stitch across the lower end, up along the zipper, following the even line of basting, and across the top end. Pull the thread ends to the underside and tie.

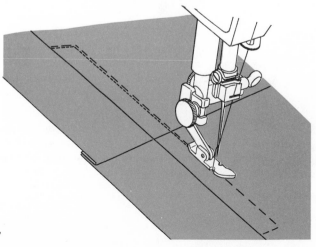

7. Remove the hand basting. Turn the dress to the wrong side and remove the machine basting under the back seam allowance by clipping every four or five stitches, then pulling the long thread. Press the work over the curve of a press mitt to retain the shape of the hipline. Cover it with a wool press cloth to protect the fabric from shine.

A dress placket handled in this way is almost invisible because the front seam overlaps the zipper ⅛ inch and the placket has been shaped to fit the curve of the hip.

Hand-Finished Zipper Application

To add a professional touch, you can hand-sew the zipper with backstitches at the final step instead of top-stitching by machine. If you are working with chiffons, sheers, velvets, or any other delicate fabrics, you *must* hand-sew because machine stitching is too harsh.

1. To finish with hand sewing, follow the instructions given above up to Step 6, which is top stitching.

2. With a fine needle and matching thread, start working at the bottom of the zipper. Fasten the thread end with two backstitches on the underside of the zipper tape. Bring the needle through from the underside at the seamline. Take a backstitch

seam allowance to the zipper tape for added support.

Remove the hand basting and the machine basting under the back seam allowance. Press.

Blindstitched Zipper Application

Blindstitching the final step of a zipper application gives a fine finish that is almost invisible. The placket seam allowance should be ⅞ inch and may be made wider when the garment is cut.

1. Follow the instructions beginning on page 176, up to *Step 6,* which is top stitching.

Select the blindstitch zig-zag on the zig-zag machine, 15 stitch length, and narrow stitch width. Adjust the Zipper Foot to the right of the needle.

2. Turn the dress to the wrong side. Place the lower end of the zipper tape over the feed of the machine and turn back the front section of the dress to the basting line, creating a soft fold. Position the work so that the straight line of stitching

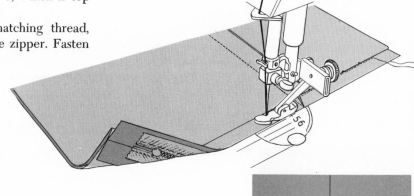

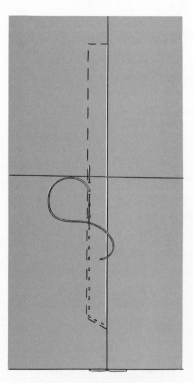

across only one or two fabric threads; then bring the needle up through all thicknesses a scant ⅛ inch from the backstitch. Begin each additional backstitch just outside the preceding stitch. The stitches on the underside will be twice as long as those on the top side. Continue the stitches across the bottom end, up the side along the basted line, then across the top end. Push the needle through to the underside, and fasten the thread with two backstitches in the tape.

3. Turn the dress to the wrong side and machine-stitch the edge of the front

is made through the seam allowance and zipper tape, and the sideward stitch pierces only a few threads of the soft fold. Stitch slowly. Pull the thread ends to the underside and tie.

Hand-sew the front seam allowance to the zipper tape below the bottom stop and above the bridge-top stop. Remove both machine and hand bastings. Press.

No-Pin, No-Baste Method

To use this method of applying a zipper, follow the rules below:

1. Turn the dress to the wrong side. Pin, then machine-baste the side seams together the exact length of the opening. Press the seam open over the curve of a press mitt to retain the shape of the hipline. Stay-stitch ⅜ inch from the seam edge on each side of the placket opening. Mark the length of the opening with pins.

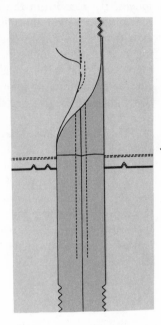

2. Adjust the Zipper Foot to the right of the needle. Open the zipper and place it face down over the back seam allowance, with the edge of the teeth at the seamline and the bottom stop at the end of the opening. Stitch the tape to the seam allowance from bottom to top alongside the zipper.

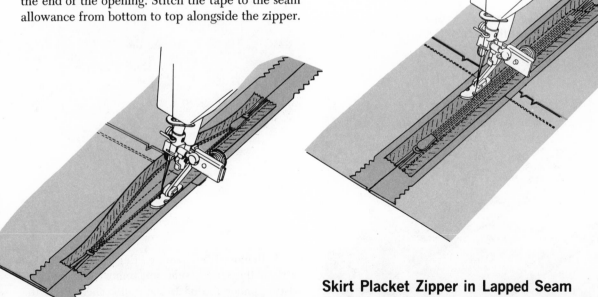

3. Adjust the Zipper Foot to the left of the needle. Close the zipper and turn it face up.

Smooth back the seam allowance at the edge of the zipper and stitch it to the tape.

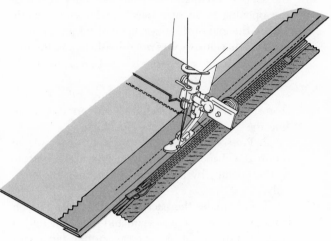

4. Turn the dress to the right side and work on the underside. Turn the zipper face down, flat over the front seam allowance. Stitch across the lower end, up the front along the zipper tape guideline, then across the top end. Pull the thread ends to the underside and tie. Remove machine basting under the back seam allowance. Press.

Skirt Placket Zipper in Lapped Seam

A skirt placket zipper is used in shorts and slacks as well as skirts. It is a heavy zipper designed to withstand strain and is applied before the waistband.

A skirt must be fitted in the same careful way as a dress. The opening in the left seam should be 1 inch longer than the metal or synthetic part of the zipper. Compare the front and back seams of the opening to be sure they are the same length. Check the end of the permanent stitching to make certain that it is reinforced with backstitching. Chalk or hand-baste exactly on the seamline on each side of the opening.

1. Turn the skirt to the wrong side. Pin the seams together and machine-baste on the seamline the exact length of the opening.

2. Press the seam open over a press mitt to retain the shape of the hipline. Mark the bottom of the opening by placing a pin through the seam only.

3. Fold under the back seam allowance ⅛ inch from the machine-basted seam and place the folded edge over the right side of the zipper tape with the pull-tab ¾ inch (⅝-inch seam allowance plus ⅛ inch) below the seam edge at the top, and the

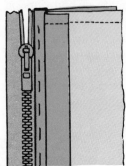

bottom stop ⅛ inch above the lower end of the opening; pin. This allows ⅛ inch for ease throughout the length of the zipper. Roll the zipper and folded edge over the fingers of the left hand and pin the folded edge to the zipper tape. Hand-baste.

4. Replace the presser foot with the Zipper Foot, and adjust the Zipper Foot to the left of the needle. *Turn the pull-tab up to lessen bulk when stitching.* Stitch from the bottom to the top near the edge of the fold. Remove *hand basting.*

5. Turn the skirt to the right side. Turn the zipper and back seam allowance flat against the front seam allowance with the *pull-tab still turned toward the top.* From the right side, roll the zipper and seam over the fingers of the left hand to ease the fabric. Pin through all thicknesses, placing pins at right angles to the seam, through the fabric, and under the chain portion of the zipper. Alternate the direction of the pins to distribute the slight ease evenly. See illustration on page 177, *Step 5.*

Hand-baste a measured ½ inch from the machine-basted seam, using a long and short basting stitch. Use the basting as a stitching guide.

6. Adjust the Zipper Foot to the right of the needle. Stitch across the lower end, then up along the zipper, following the even line of basting, to the waistline. Pull the thread ends to the underside and tie. (If hand sewing is used instead of machine stitching, follow the directions on page 178.)

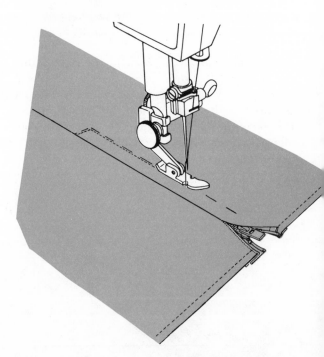

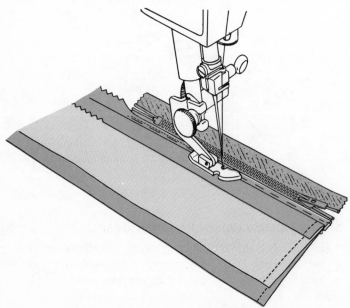

7. Remove the hand basting. Then, turn the skirt to the wrong side and remove the machine basting under the back seam allowance. Press the work over a press mitt to retain the curve of the hipline. Cover it with a wool press cloth to protect the fabric from shine. Trim the tape even with the waistline seam edge.

To Attach Underlay

An underlay is usually placed under the zipper to improve the fit of the skirt. It gives support to the underlap of the waistband and also helps prevent the zipper from clogging.

The underlay may be either a double or a single lengthwise strip of the same fabric cut the length of the zipper tape. If single, cut it 2½ inches wide, using the selvage of the fabric for the finished edge. If double, cut it 5 inches wide, and fold it lengthwise through the center; stitch near the fold and cut edge. Pink the edge.

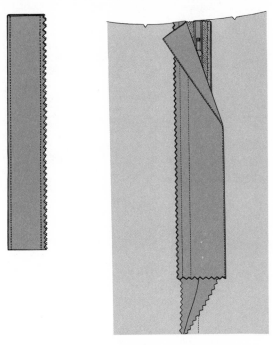

Turn the skirt to the wrong side. Place the underlay over the zipper tape, keeping the cut edges even with the back seam edge. Pin only to the seam allowance. Turn the seam allowance and underlay away from the skirt and stitch the underlay to the seam allowance. Tack the lower end of the underlay to the front seam allowance. The skirt is now ready for the waistband.

Neckline or Sleeve Zipper in Slot Seam

A neckline zipper is usually inserted in a center front or back seam at the neckline of a dress, hostess robe, or blouse or in a sleeve seam at the wrist. An extra fine neckline zipper is available for the closure.

Apply a neckline zipper before joining the front and back bodice at the shoulders and underarms since it is easier to work on a flat section than a partially assembled garment.

The length of the opening should be 1 inch longer than the metal or synthetic part of the zipper. (The seam allowance at the neckline is ⅝ inch, and ⅜ inch provides space for crosswise stitching at the bottom and top of the zipper.) You will not have to allow for ease since the zipper is usually set into a straight grain seam. The seam below the opening should be permanently stitched and the end reinforced with backstitching.

1. Turn the garment to the wrong side. Pin the seams together and machine-baste the exact length of the opening.

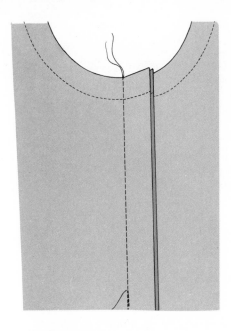

2. Press the seam, then press it open. Mark the end of the opening with a pin on the right side.

3. Turn the garment to the right side. Turn the zipper *pull-tab up to lessen bulk when stitching*. Pin the zipper in position, with the machine-basted seam centered directly over the chain portion. Place the pull-tab at the top, ¼ inch below the ⅝-inch seam allowance at ·the neckline, and the bottom stop ⅛ inch above the lower end of the opening. Place pins at right angles to the seam, through all thicknesses, and under the chain portion of the zipper. Alternate the direction

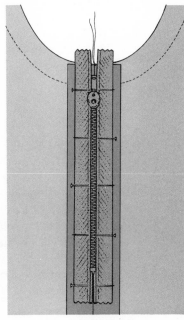

of the pins. Hand-baste, on each side, a measured ¼ inch from the center seam. Use the basting as a guide in stitching.

4. Replace the presser foot with the Zipper Foot, and adjust the foot to the left of the needle. On the right side of the garment, stitch around the zipper ¼ inch to the left of the center seam, using the measured basting as a guide. Pivot the fabric on the needle at the corners and take the same number of stitches on either side of the center seam.

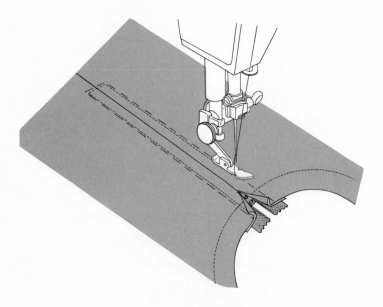

If the final step is hand-sewed instead of machine-stitched, follow the directions on page 178; however, machine-stitch the edge of the seam allowance to the zipper tape on each side for added support.

5. Remove both hand and machine bastings. Press carefully. Trim the zipper tape even with the neckline seam edge. The garment is ready for the neckline finish.

Zipper in Center Back Lapped Seam

Before applying the zipper in a center back closing, join the dress sections at the shoulder line, underarm, and waistline seams.

Leave an opening 1 inch longer than the metal or synthetic part of the zipper. (The neckline seam allowance is ⅝ inch, and ⅜ inch provides space above and below the zipper.) You will not need to allow for ease since a center seam is usually on the straight grain of the fabric. Check the end of the permanent stitching in the skirt to make

sure that it is reinforced with backstitching. Compare the right and left seams of the opening; they must be the same length.

To Finish Neckline

Before inserting the zipper, finish the neckline as instructed here to eliminate bulk across the top of the zipper.

1. Pin the facing to the neckline. Start stitching ¾ inch from the seam edge that is on the right-hand side when the dress is worn, and continue to within 1¼ inches of the seam edge on the left-hand side, taking a ⅝-inch seam.

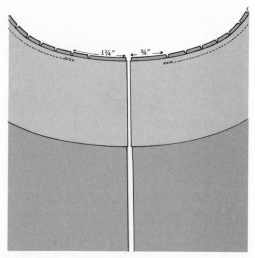

2. Trim the facing seam allowance to ⅛ inch and the garment seam allowance to ¼ inch; then clip into the curved seam allowance. Press; then press the seam open. Turn the facing to the underside, ease it under slightly at the seamline, and baste. Press. Understitch the seam to prevent the facing from rolling out of place. Fold and press the garment and facing on the seamline, from the stitching to the center opening.

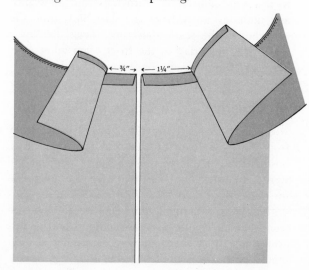

To Insert the Zipper

Trim the waistline seam allowance that is on the right-hand side when the dress is worn, to ¼ inch from the center seam edge to a depth of ¾ inch, and trim the seam allowance on the opposite side to ¼ inch from the center seam edge to a depth of 1¼ inches. This removes bulk under the zipper seam.

1. Turn the dress to the wrong side. Turn the neckline facing away from the garment. Pin the center seams together, carefully matching waistline seams and folded seams at the neckline. (Be sure the seam edges of the opening are the same length.) Machine-baste the exact length of the opening. If the seam allowance that is on the left-hand side when the dress is worn is less than ⅝ inch, stitch seam binding to the edge.

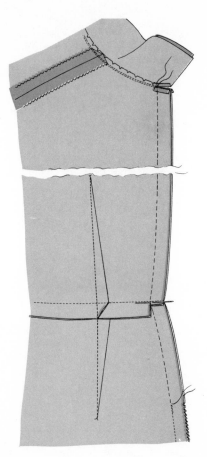

2. Press, then press the seam open. Mark the bottom of the opening by placing a pin through the seamline only.

3. On the right-hand side when the dress is worn, fold the seam allowance under ⅛ inch from the machine-basted seam. Pin the folded edge over the right side of the zipper tape, with the pull-tab at the top, ¼ inch below the folded neckline

seam, and the bottom stop ⅛ inch above the end of the opening. Pin the seam allowance to the zipper tape below the opening. Hand-baste.

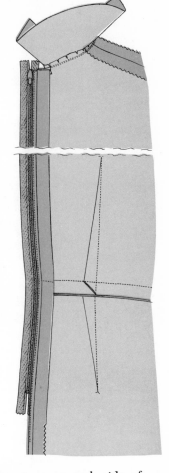

4. Adjust the Zipper Foot to the left of the needle. *Turn the pull-tab up* to lessen bulk when stitching. Stitch from the bottom of the zipper up to the neckline, close to the folded edge. Tie thread ends at the neckline. Remove hand basting.

5. Clip into the zipper tape on each side of the neckline, almost to the cord; then trim close to the cord up to the end of the tape.

Turn the ends of the tape away from the pull-tab and tack them to the seam allowance, using matching thread. Clip off the ends of the tape to ½ inch. This eliminates bulk at the neckline.

(Continued)

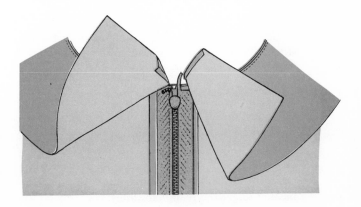

6. Turn the dress to the right side. With the *pull-tab still turned up*, turn the zipper and seam allowance flat against the left-hand side of the seam allowance. Press the zipper against the seam with the left hand. Working from the right side, place pins at right angles to the seam, through all thicknesses, and under the chain portion of the zipper. Alternate the direction of the pins.

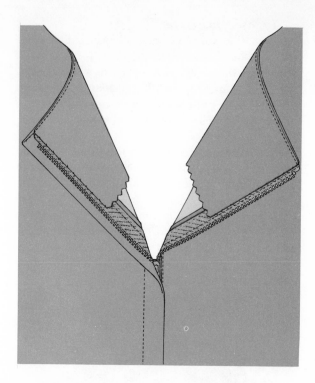

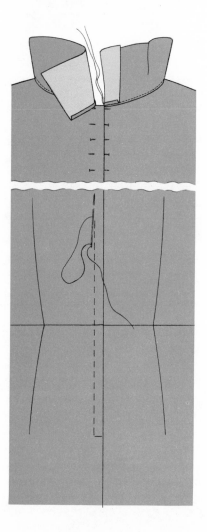

Hand-baste a measured ½ inch from the machine-basted seam, using a long and short basting stitch. Use the basting as a guide in stitching.

7. Adjust the Zipper Foot to the right of the needle. On the right side of the dress, stitch across the lower end and up the side to the neckline, following the evenly basted line. Pull threads to the underside and tie. (When hand sewing is used instead of machine stitching, follow the directions on page 178.) Remove hand basting, then turn the dress to the wrong side and remove the machine basting under the seam allowance.

8. Fold under the center ends of the neckline facing, and trim the seam allowances to ½ inch. Pin the folded edges to the zipper tape and finish by hand, using a hemming stitch. Slip-stitch the edges together at the neckline where the fabric fold covers the zipper. Press.

Sew a hook to the underside of the fold covering the zipper at the neckline and make a thread eye on the opposite side. See *Thread Eye*, page 207.

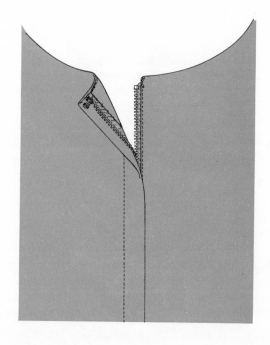

Continuous Bound Placket

The continuous bound placket may be in a seam or slash. It is found in sleeve openings where a cuff or band is used and in children's dresses.

Placket in a Slash

1. Mark the position for the slash, and stay-stitch around the point, using a 20 stitch length. Take one stitch across the point to allow space for a smooth turning. Press. Slash the opening to within about two threads of the point.

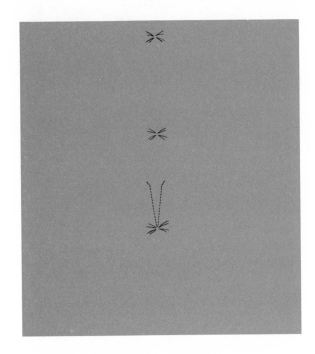

2. Cut a strip of fabric on the lengthwise grain, 1¼ inches wide and twice the length of the opening. If the fabric is heavy, cut the strip 1½ inches wide.

At one end, pin the strip to the opening, right sides together, keeping the cut edges even. *Draw the point of the slash back 3/16 inch from the edge of the strip* and pin at the point; then pin at the opposite end, keeping the cut edges even. Pin at intervals between. Baste.

3. From the garment side, stitch ¼ inch from the *edge of the strip*, beginning at the end and stitching to the point. With the needle in the fabric, raise the presser foot and fold the garment back, forming a "V" at the point; then lower the foot and stitch to the opposite end of the opening. Reinforce the ends with backstitching. Press, then

turn the strip away from the garment and press the seam allowance over the strip.

4. Fold under the free edge of the strip ¼ inch and crease. Then fold the strip over the seam edge to the stitching line on the underside, enclosing the seam allowances. Pin. Either machine-stitch or finish by hand, using a short hemming stitch. Press.

(Continued)

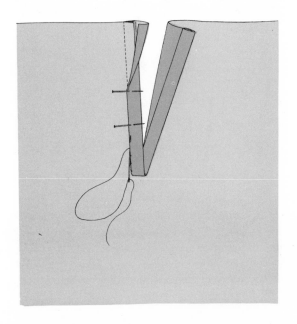

Fold the strip under on the side that will overlap, as illustrated. Press. The fabric strip is not visible in the closing.

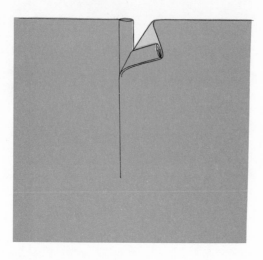

Placket in a Seam

1. Stitch the seam below the opening. Reinforce the end with backstitching. Clip into the seam allowances at the end of the opening, then trim the seam allowances to ¼ inch from this point to the end of the opening. Press the seam open below the placket opening.

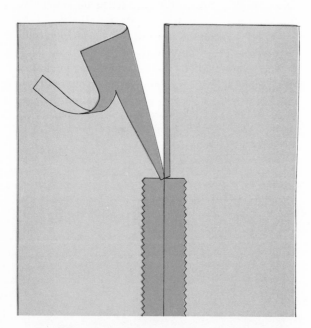

2. Cut a strip of fabric on the lengthwise grain 1½ inches wide and twice the length of the opening. Pin the strip to the opening, right sides together, keeping cut edges even. Pin at one end, at the point of the opening, then at the opposite end. Pin at intervals between.

3. Stitch from the garment side, taking a ¼-inch seam. Reinforce the ends with backstitching. Press, then turn the strip away from the garment and press the seam allowance over the strip.

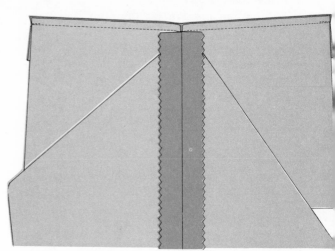

4. Fold under the free edge of the strip ¼ inch and crease. Then turn the strip over the seam edge to the stitching line on the underside, enclosing the seam allowances. Pin. Either machine-stitch or finish by hand, using a short hemming stitch.

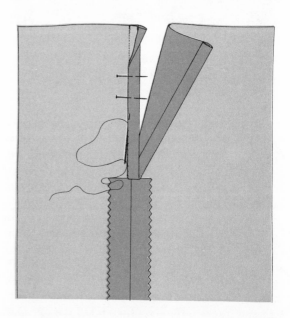

Fold the strip under on the side that will overlap, as illustrated in the slash above. Press. The fabric strip is not visible in the closing.

HEMS AND HEM FINISHES

The hem is your last step in finishing the garment. It is usually finished by hand and the stitches should be invisible on the right side. However, a narrow hem, which is preferred for ruffles and sashes, may be finished either by machine or by hand. Proper pressing is essential in making a smooth hem; do not overlook it.

The hem in a skirt should never be obvious but should be wide enough to hang in smooth, graceful lines. A slim skirt usually requires a hem of greater width than a full skirt. The hem width designated on the pattern is generally the width you should use since it is appropriate for the style of the garment and the fabric recommended. If you want a wider hem than that shown on the pattern—for example, to create a shadow effect in a full-skirted dress made of sheer fabric—allow for the extra width when cutting the garment.

Although fashion dictates to some extent the length of skirts, do not follow it blindly but consider your figure proportions as well.

Checking the Fit of the Dress

Try on the dress for the final inspection, wearing the foundation garment, slip, and shoes you will wear with the dress. Review the general fitting. Be certain that the front and back center line bastings are in place and hang perpendicular to the floor; that the waistline joining is comfortably positioned. If any adjustment in fit is necessary, make it before marking the skirt length. A skirt that hangs well is the result of correct pattern adjustments, careful cutting with the grain of the fabric, and proper pressing.

If your dress has a bias or semi-bias skirt, always allow it to hang overnight with the side seams hand-basted, threads loose at the ends, before stitching any seams. Then, after the skirt is assembled, hang it again overnight before taking the skirt length so that all the sag is evident at the points where the true bias occurs.

Preparing the Hem

To ensure a smooth and inconspicuous hemline, follow closely the steps given below. They are basic for all hems. Step 4, however, will vary with the fabric, the style of the skirt, and individual preference.

Step 1: Mark the Hemline

Mark the skirt an even distance from the floor. Use either a pin- or chalk-type skirt marker. To

avoid any unnecessary shifting of posture or position, have the person taking the skirt length move around the model. If the lining is attached to the waistline only, mark the hemline in the skirt and in the lining separately.

For full-length evening dresses, have the model stand on a stool or platform that will allow the dress to hang freely over the edge.

Step 2: Fold the Hem

Turn the hem on the chalk or pin line and place pins at right angles to the folded edge. The fold of the hem should follow an even line. Should slight irregularities occur, owing to the sway of the body or the unevenness of the floor, adjust the hem fold accordingly. However, *do not make radical adjustments*. Ease the hem down slightly at the seams to allow for the fold over the seam allowances.

Baste with silk thread ¼ inch from the folded edge. Press to sharpen the crease, gliding the iron along the lengthwise grain of the fabric. See *Hems*, page 75.

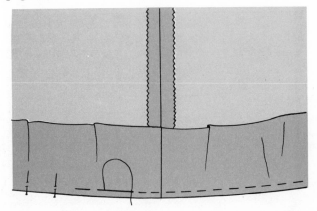

Step 3: Even the Hem Width

Lay the skirt against a flat surface with the right side down and work from the hem side. Measure and chalk-mark the desired hem width. Then cut away the excess width. Trim all seam allowances to one-half their width from fold to hem edge.

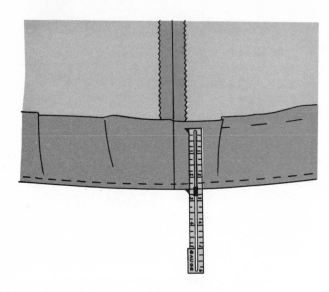

Step 4: Finish the Hem

A variety of methods for finishing hems are given below. Choose the one you prefer, keeping in mind the fabric you are working with and the shape of the skirt at the hemline.

Finishes for Skirt Hems

Edgestitched Hem

Edgestitching provides a sturdy hem finish for cottons that must withstand repeated laundering and for linings and underlinings that are hemmed separately from the skirt.

1. Prepare the hem for the finish, following the three steps outlined above.

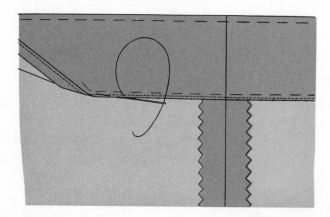

2. Fold the free edge of the hem under ¼ inch and stitch near the edge of the fold. Press. Pin the hem to the skirt, matching seams and center lines. Hand-baste. Finish by hand, using a slip stitch. See page 228. Remove bastings, and press.

Pinked Hem—Blind Catch Stitch

The pinked hem is suitable for fabrics that do not fray readily and are likely to show a line on the outside of the skirt if other hem finishes are used—for example, silk, crepe, jersey, double knit, and firmly woven woolens. The blind catch stitch is invisible and holds the hem securely without strain. This is also known as a *French hem.*

1. Prepare the hem for the finish, following the three steps outlined on page 187.

2. Pink the free edge of the hem, then stitch ¼ inch from the edge, using a 20 stitch length.

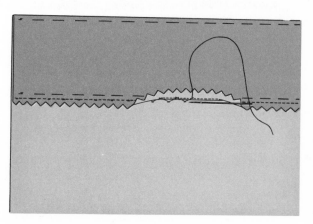

3. Pin, then hand-baste the hem to the skirt just below the stitching line, matching seams and center lines. With the left hand, fold back the pinked edge along the basting and blind catch-stitch below the hem edge and between the hem and skirt. Work from left to right with the needle pointed to the left. Hold the hem edge between the thumb and index finger. Make a stitch in the underside of the hem edge, then make a stitch in the skirt, catching only a single thread of the fabric. Alternate the stitches in a zig-zag fashion. Do not tighten this hand stitch, but knot the stitches frequently. Remove bastings, and press.

Bound Hem

Hems in heavy or napped woolens and fabrics that fray easily are often finished with a bound edge of rayon or silk bias binding. They are not noticeable when the garment is worn.

1. Prepare the hem for the finish, following the three steps outlined on page 187.

2. Bind the free edge of the hem, using the Binder and a medium-width open zig-zag stitch. Press.

3. Pin the free edge of the hem to the skirt, matching center lines and seams; then, hand-baste just below the binding. Blind catch-stitch between the hem and skirt, as instructed for a *Pinked Hem —Blind Catch Stitch*, above. Knot the stitch at frequent intervals. Never pull the thread tight enough to dent the right side of the fabric. Remove bastings, and press over a pressing pad.

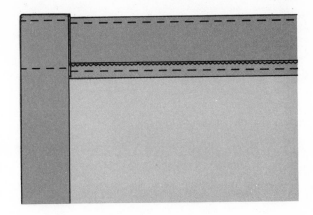

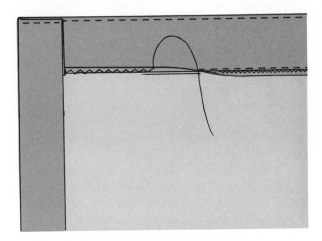

Blindstitched Hem

Blindstitching provides a durable hem finish that is almost invisible on the right side of the garment. It is especially suited to children's clothes, straight and full skirts, and curtains. Taped, bound, edgestitched, or unfinished hem edges may be blindstitched by machine with equal ease.

1. Prepare the hem for the finish, following the three steps outlined on page 187.

2. When straight or bias seam binding is used, pin the binding to the hem ¼ inch from the free edge. Stitch, using a narrow zig-zag stitch and 12 to 15 stitch length. Press.

3. Hand-baste the hem to the skirt ¼ inch from the free edge.

4. Use the blindstitch zig-zag; select a narrow to medium stitch width and 12 to 20 stitch length. (The selection is determined by the weight and texture of your fabric.) The blindstitch zig-zag produces four straight stitches separated by a single sideward stitch to the left.

Place the hem edge over the feed of the machine; turn back the bulk of the fabric to the bast-

ing line, creating a soft fold. Position the work so that the straight stitches are made on the hem edge and the sideward stitches pierce only one or two threads of the soft fold.

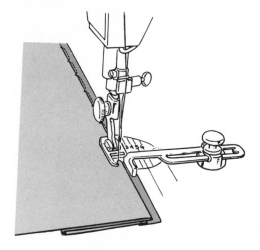

Attach the Seam Guide to the machine and adjust it over the right toe of the presser foot so that it rests next to the soft fold. When stitching, feed the fold against the edge of the guide. After you have finished, swing the Seam Guide out of position before raising the presser foot. Remove bastings, and press.

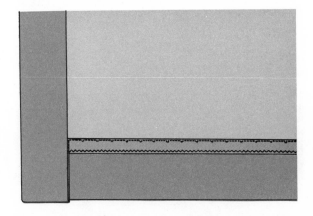

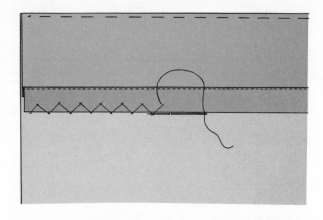

Catch-Stitched Hem

The catch-stitched hem is suitable for loosely woven woolens and raw silk. The hem edge may be finished with pinking as described on page 188 or with straight or bias seam binding and then catch-stitched in place.

1. Prepare the hem for the finish, following the steps outlined on page 187.

2. Finish the free edge of the hem.

3. Pin, then hand-baste the hem to the skirt ⅛ inch from the finished edge, matching center lines and seams. Catch-stitch in place. Work from left to right with the needle pointed to the left. Take a stitch in the binding, then one in the skirt over the edge of the hem, catching only a single thread in the fabric. Continue alternating the stitches. Press.

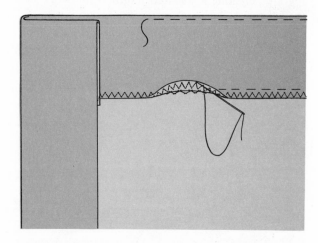

Zig-Zag Hem—Double-Knit Fabric

The zig-zag hem finish is ideal for skirts made of double knits because it prevents fraying and the stitching has as much "give" as the fabric.

1. Prepare the hem for the finish, following the three steps outlined on page 187.

2. Finish the free edge of the hem with a row of multiple-stitch zig-zag, blindstitch zig-zag, or plain zig-zag stitch placed near the edge. Use a fine stitch length and the widest stitch width. Press. Trim the edge close to the stitching.

3. Pin, then hand-baste the free edge of hem to the skirt just below the zig-zag stitching, matching seams and center lines. Finish with a blind catch stitch between the hem and skirt, as instructed for the *Pink Hem—Blind Catch Stitch*, page 188.

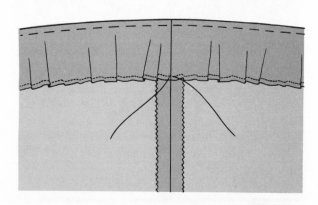

Gored and Semiflared Skirts

1. Prepare the hem for the finish, following the three steps outlined on page 187.

2. Control the fullness that exists with a line of stitching placed exactly ¼ inch from the free edge of the hem and extending from seam to seam. Pin the hem to the skirt, matching seams and center lines. Draw the bobbin thread and ease the fullness between the seams. Be careful not to draw in the top of the hem too much. The hem must conform exactly to the body of the skirt.

3. Place the hem over the curve of a press mitt and shrink out the fullness by pressing with steam.

4. Bias seam binding is often used on a hem with fullness. For silk and synthetic fabrics, use rayon or silk bias binding. Preshape the seam bind-

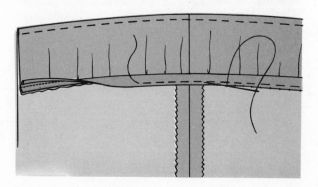

ing by steam pressing; pin, then stitch it to the hem edge, barely covering the control line of stitching. At the joining, fold under the end and overlap the binding about ⅜ inch. Press. (Binding may be applied as an inside seam, as illustrated, or it may be top-stitched.)

5. Pin the free edge of the hem to the skirt, matching seams and center lines. Hand-baste ⅛ inch from the edge. Finish by hand, using a blind hemming stitch. See page 228. When finished, fasten the threads with two tiny backstitches in the hem edge. Remove bastings and press.

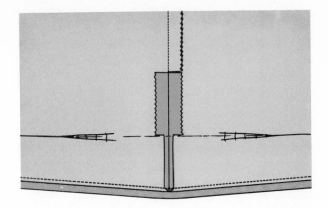

Hem across Pleat in Skirt *(Upper right)*

Seams on the inside fold of a pleat must be blended and pressed open in the hem area to eliminate bulk.

1. After you have marked the hem, press the seam open to the point where the hem will be sewed to the skirt. Blend the seam edges within the hem area to one-half their width. Slash seam allowances to within a few threads of the stitching at the top of the hem.

2. Proceed to form the hem, and finish according to the method best suited to the fabric.

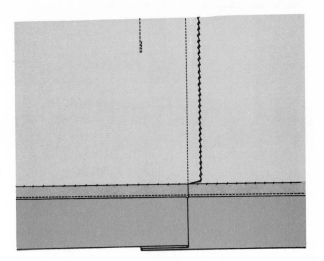

Hem in Slit Skirt

The pencil-slim skirt, without a pleat, is often slit at the seams to allow for greater freedom of movement. (For instructions on lining the skirt, see page 98.) To hem the skirt, proceed as follows:

1. Check the end of the seam above the slit to be certain that it is reinforced with backstitching. Pin, then machine-baste the seams together in the slit, beginning exactly at the top of the slit.

Stay-stitch ½ inch from the seam edge on each side of the slit. Press, then press the seam open.

(Continued on following page)

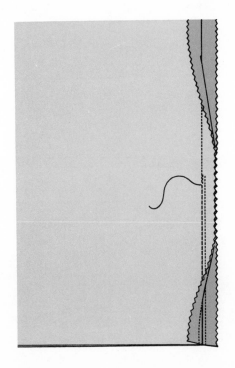

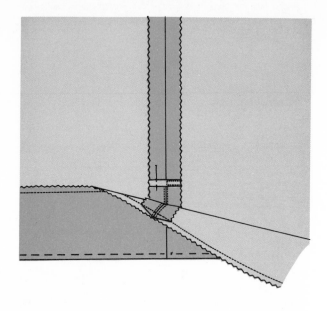

2. Cut a strip of preshrunk straight seam binding to fit the width of the open seam allowance. Fold through the center and press. Pin the binding to the seam allowance, keeping the lower edge even with the top edge of the machine-basted opening. Turn the seam allowance away from the skirt, and stitch the binding to one side of the seam allowance, as illustrated; then stitch the opposite side the same way. Follow this procedure for slits in the lining. The stays reinforce the ends in the slits and prevent ripping.

3. Prepare the hem for the finish, following the steps outlined on page 187.

4. Remove the machine basting in the slit. Finish the hems in the skirt and lining separately, following the method best suited to the fabric. Ease the hem under slightly on each side of the slit, and pin. Slip-stitch in place.

Hem in Circular Skirt

To ensure a smooth hemline, the hem in a circular skirt should be narrow. A wide hem is bulky. Use rayon or silk bias binding for the finish. Before marking the hem, hang the skirt for 24 hours to allow for any "stretching" of the fabric.

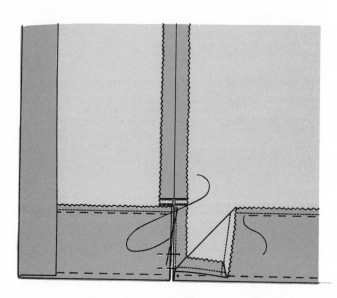

1. Mark the hem as instructed in *Step 1*, page 187. Trim away the excess fabric ⅜ inch below the marking.

2. Pin bias seam binding ¼ inch from the edge of the skirt, right sides together. Apply seam binding as an inside seam, as illustrated. Stitch, guiding the fabric in both the front and the back of the needle to prevent puckering or stretching. Clip off corners where seams cross. Press.

3. Turn the binding to the underside, then fold the skirt ⅛ inch beyond the binding and hand-baste. Press.

4. Hand-baste the hem to the skirt near the edge of the binding. Finish by hand, using a blind hemming stitch or slip stitch. Remove bastings and press.

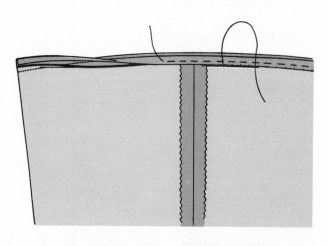

Horsehair braid is often used to give stiffness to circular hems in evening, cocktail, and wedding dresses. Prepare the hem the same as above.

1. Baste 1-inch horsehair braid to the right side of the hem, edges even. Stitch ⅛ inch from the edge. Press. *(Illustrated at top of next page)*

2. Turn the horsehair braid to the underside; fold the hem ⅛ inch beyond the stitching line, and pin. The lower edge of the horsehair will extend to the hem fold. *(Continued)*

3. Work on the right side, and hand-sew the horsehair to the skirt, barely above the ⅛-inch hem, using a fine backstitch. See page 230.

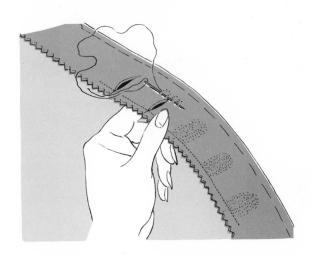

Spliced Hem

Heavy woolens sometimes resist the shaping and easing required to assure a smooth circular hem. Should this be the case, use the following method. (This type of skirt usually has a lining that extends to within an inch of the hem fold.)

1. Prepare the hem for the finish, following the three steps outlined on page 187.

2. Cut narrow wedges in the hem at regular intervals, several inches apart. Do not cut deeper than 1 inch from the hem fold.

Bring the cut edges together with a line of machine stitching ¼ inch from the free edge. Darn the slashes together with matching silk thread or a thread drawn from the weave of the fabric.

3. Pink the free edge. Finish with a blind catch stitch between the hem and skirt as instructed on page 188.

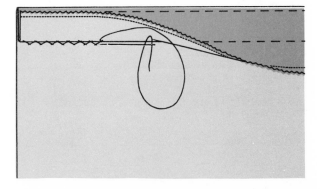

Double-Stitched Hem

Wide hems, or hems in heavy fabrics, sometimes tend to sag because one line of stitching is insufficient for the weight of the hem. To prevent this, stitch the hem twice—once through the center and again at the free edge. The two rows of stitches distribute the weight of the hem, and the hem is not visible in the finished skirt.

1. Prepare the hem for the finish, following the three steps outlined on page 187.

2. Finish the hem edge, using the method best suited to the fabric. Pin, then hand-baste the center of the hem to the skirt, matching center lines and seams. Fold back the hem on the basting line, and blind catch-stitch between the hem and the skirt as instructed for a *Pinked Hem—Blind Catch Stitch*, page 188. Be careful not to pull the stitches too tight or they will dent the right side of the garment.

3. Pin, then hand-baste the free edge of the hem to the skirt, matching center lines and seams. Finish by hand, using a blind catch stitch between the hem and the skirt.

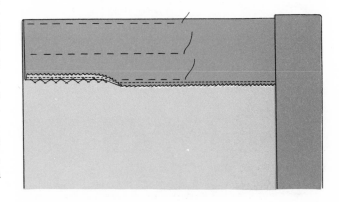

Soft Hemline

Interface the hem if you want it to have a soft or slightly padded look. Use a fabric that does not crease easily—either hair canvas or lamb's wool. For additional softness in the hem fold, the garment should be underlined and the underlining should extend to the hem edge.

1. Prepare the hem as described under *Step 1,* page 187. Hand-baste the line of the hem but do

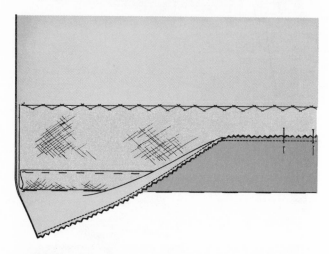

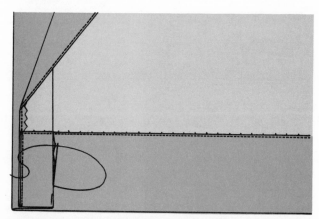

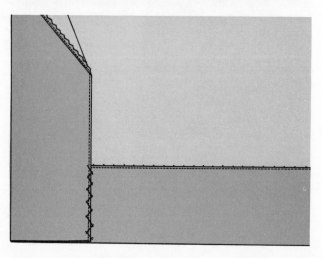

not fold or crease it. Mark the hem width as described under *Step 3,* page 188, and finish the free edge as required by the fabric.

2. Cut the interfacing on the true bias 2 inches wider than the hem and the length required plus 1 inch for seam allowances. Allow enough extra length so you can join the bias on straight grain. See *Joining Bias Strips,* page 244. Turn the interfacing up 1 inch along one edge, creating a soft fold. (Do not crease.) Pin, then hand-baste ¾ inch from the soft fold. Make small stitches, spacing them about ¼ inch apart; secure the thread ends because this is permanent basting that will prevent the interfacing from wadding at the hemline.

Place the interfacing over the underside of the garment and align the soft fold with hemline basting. Join ends on straight grain by lapping 1 inch and basting together. Pin the interfacing in place along top edge and catch-stitch. Make a stitch through interfacing and underlining, then a stitch in only the underlining over the interfacing edge so that stitches will not be visible on the top side. Continue alternating the stitches. Press.

3. Turn the hem over the interfacing and hand-baste in place, using silk thread. (The interfacing is 1 inch wider than the hem.) Finish by hand, using the blind catch stitch. Make the stitches through only the hem and interfacing. To keep the hem fold soft, do not press it, but do press along the line of the hand stitches. Remove all bastings.

A garment with this type of hem is generally lined, and the lining extends to within an inch or two of the hem fold, covering the interfacing.

Hem at Corners

When the skirt of a garment is open all the way down the front or back, the opening is faced and you have a corner to deal with.

1. Prepare the hem for the finish, following the three steps outlined on page 187. However, extend the hem across the facing at the opening.

2. Finish the hem, using the method best suited to the fabric. (The edgestitched finish is shown in the illustration.) Remove bastings and press.

3. Fold the facing to the underside and press. Pin through the center of the facing, catching the hem beneath. Place the pins parallel to the facing edge. Fold the facing back on the pinned line and stay it to the hem by hand to prevent it from slipping out of place. Turn the free edge against the hem and pin; then catch-stitch it to the hem.

Since the hem is not cut out under the facing, the skirt can be lengthened later if necessary.

Hem with Mitered Corner

Hems in linens are usually mitered at the corners to remove bulk.

1. Fold the hem along all edges, measuring the width evenly. Press. Fold under ¼ inch on the free edge and press.

2. Turn the hem away from the fabric. Turn the corner toward the inside, folding the lengthwise grain to the crosswise grain with the diagonal fold crossing exactly at the junction of the lengthwise and crosswise folds of the hem. Press. The diagonal fold indicates the exact position for stitching the miter.

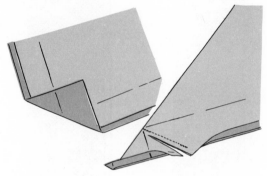

3. Fold the lengthwise hem over the crosswise hem, right sides together, matching the crease on the diagonal line. Pin, then stitch, extending the stitching as far as the first fold of the hem. Backstitch at each end.

4. Blend the seam to ¼ inch and clip off the corner at the hem fold. Press, then press the seam open over the pointed end of a seamboard.

5. Turn the hem to the underside and carefully hand-baste the free edge in place. Linens may be finished with hemstitching, a decorative zig-zag stitch, machine stitching, or hand stitching.

Narrow Hem Finishes

A narrow hem is used on ruffles, ties, scarves, lingerie, aprons, blouses, sashes in children's clothes, and circular skirts of evening and cocktail dresses. The hem may be finished by hand or by machine, depending on where it is used and the type of fabric.

Machine-Stitched Hem

A machine-stitched hem is used to finish the edges of lingerie, ruffles and sashes in children's clothes and aprons, and ruffles in curtains. The Hemmer Foot is a must for this, for it forms a perfectly turned narrow hem without requiring any basting or pressing on your part. See *Hemmer Foot*, page 283.

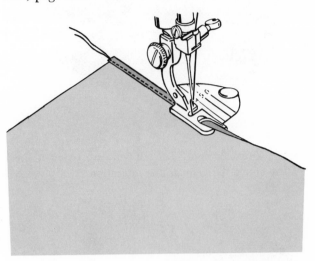

Cut the edge of the fabric evenly on the lengthwise or crosswise grain or on a true bias. To prevent the fabric from stretching when it is cut on the bias, place a row of stitching near the edge, using a short stitch. Press, then trim as close to the stitching as possible before placing the fabric in the Hemmer Foot.

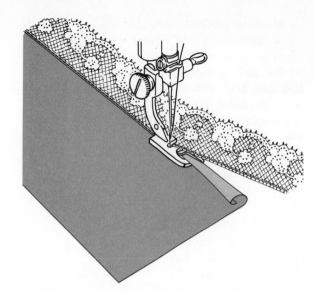

You can apply lace, if you are using it, over or under the hem in one operation.

You can also turn and decorate hems in one operation on a zig-zag machine. Select patterns that will form on the fold of the hem and adjust

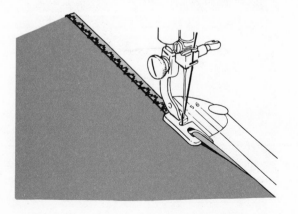

the machine for the appropriate stitch length and stitch width; then hem from the right side of the fabric.

A *soft shell edge* makes an attractive finish for lingerie and many delicate fabrics. To obtain this effect, set the selectors on the machine for either the blindstitch or the multiple-stitch zig-zag; then hem with the fabric right side up.

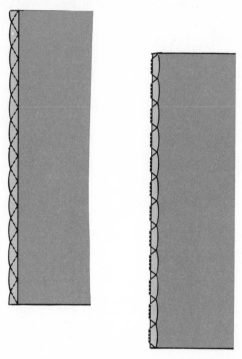

To make a ¼-inch hem or one slightly wider, use the presser foot and turn the fabric by hand the entire length of the hem. The edge of the fabric must be cut evenly. Make a double-fold hem so that the cut edge will not be visible through the fabric. (*Illustrated at top of next page*)

You can turn the hem easily if you work on an ironing board. As you turn and measure each fold, pin through the fabric into the ironing board pad, then press.

1. Turn a measured scant ¼ inch to the underside and pin along the cut edge. Press the fold. Then make the second turn a measured ¼ inch from the fold and pin along the first fold; press the second fold.

2. Stitch near the folded edge, using a shorter stitch than that used to stitch the garment. If the hem is slightly wider than ¼ inch, baste before stitching.

If you plan to finish the hem with decorative zig-zag stitching, baste the hemline to form a guide for the top stitching (except on sheer fabrics where the hem edge is visible through the fabric). Select

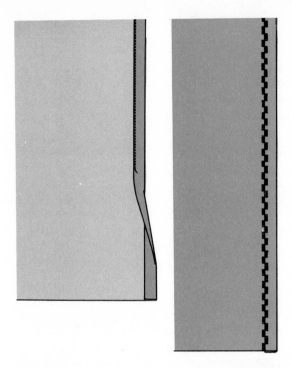

3. Fold the edge to the wrong side, barely beyond the stitching. Use a fine needle and matching thread. Working from right to left, or toward you, take a stitch through the fold; then, ⅛ inch from the fold, take a stitch diagonally in the garment, catching only a single thread. Continue, alternating the stitches and spacing them about ⅛ inch apart. After making about six stitches, pull the thread to draw the fold down and form a neatly rolled hem.

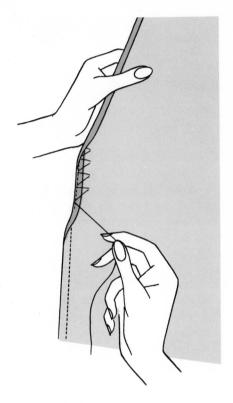

the stitch pattern desired, set the stitch length selector for satin stitching, and stitch from the right side of the fabric.

Hand-Rolled Hem

A hand-rolled hem is a delicate finish, suitable for chiffon, crepe, velvet, lace, wool, and many other fabrics. It is the preferred hem finish for scarves and full-skirted evening, cocktail, and wedding dresses.

1. Mark the hem as instructed under *Step 1* on page 187.

2. Machine-stitch ⅛ inch below the marking for the hem, using a short stitch. Trim off the seam allowance a scant ⅛ inch below the stitching. Press.

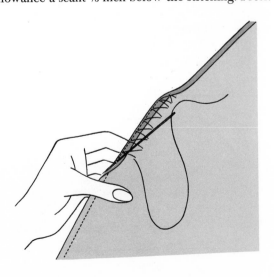

Blouse Hems

A tuck-in blouse requires a tidy, unobtrusive finish at the lower edge so that it will lie smooth under the skirt. Two excellent methods are suggested.

1. For fabrics that are lightweight or that will fray easily, pink the lower edge of the blouse and fold it under ¼ inch. Stitch near the fold; then stitch again ⅛ inch from the hem fold.

2. For fabrics that will not fray, pink the edge and stitch ⅛ inch from the pinked edge, using a 20 stitch length.

Overblouses should be finished with a hem ½ inch to 2 inches wide. Either machine or hand stitching may be used.

Belts can be a special point of interest in your costume, providing a decided contrast in color or texture, or they can be a demure and utilitarian addition, blending in with the whole. Often you can alter the appearance of your dress by merely changing the belt.

The paragraphs below explain how to make several different kinds of belts and the carriers that hold your belt in place.

Belt with Stiffening

If your pattern or preference demands a stiff belt, you must use a stiffening called "belting" inside your belt.

1. Cut the belting 4 inches longer than the waist measurement, and shape one end. Cut the fabric on the lengthwise grain, 1 inch longer than the belting and twice the width plus seam allowances. Fasten a safety pin on the right side of the fabric about 1½ inches from the shaped end. This will be used later to turn the belt to the right side.

2. Use the Zipper Foot in place of the presser foot on the machine. Adjust the toe to the right of the needle. Fold the fabric around the belting, wrong side out; turn the end with the safety pin toward the point. Stitch along the side, close to the belting. Press seam.

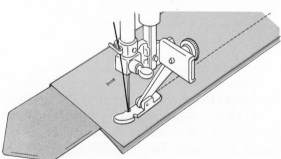

3. Move the fabric around the belting, bringing the seam to the center. Press the seam open, then trim the seam allowances to ¼ inch. Stitch the point barely outside the edge of the belting. Backstitch at each end. Trim the seam edges to ¼ inch. Withdraw the belting.

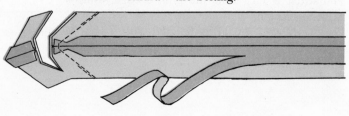

4. Turn the belt fabric to the right side by pushing the safety pin toward the open end and working the belt back over it. Work the end of the belt between the thumb and finger to bring the stitching to the very edge for a smooth point. Center the seam and press the entire belt.

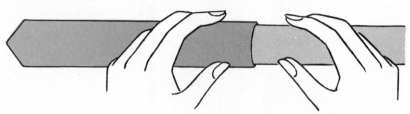

5. Insert the belting, cupping the edges slightly between the thumb and forefinger to facilitate your work. Press. If top stitching is desired, stitch around the right side of belt, close to the edge. Sew on the buckle.

Lined Soft Belt

1. Cut the fabric on the lengthwise grain 4 inches longer than the waist measurement and twice the width of the finished belt plus seam allowances. Fold lengthwise, wrong sides together, and crease.

Cut the interlining of lawn, nurses cloth, or organdy on the lengthwise grain, the length of the fabric and twice the finished width. Crease lengthwise through the center. Shape one end to a point, then cut off the end of the point to eliminate bulk when turned.

2. Place the folded edge of the interlining along the crease on the wrong side of the belt, with the point ¼ inch from the end. Stitch in place along each side and around the point. Press. Fasten a

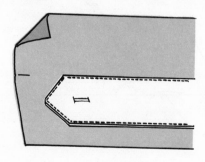

safety pin through the lining and fabric near the shaped end. This will be used later to turn the belt to the right side.

3. Fold the belt, right sides together, and pin

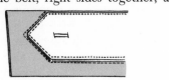

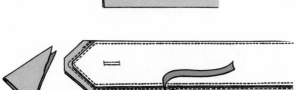

the seam edges together. Stitch just outside the edge of the interlining along the side and shaped end, taking one stitch across the point. Backstitch at each end. Trim seam edges. Press seam.

4. Turn the belt to the right side by pushing the safety pin toward the open end and working the belt back over it.

Carefully fold on the stitching line and press. If top stitching is desired, stitch around the right side of belt, close to the edge.

Contour Belt

Maintaining the contour of the belt is your primary concern here. If you need to adjust the length of the belt, measure your waistline and add 5 inches. Measure the pattern and note the difference between the measurements. **To shorten,** take half the amount to be shortened from each end. **To lengthen,** add half the amount to be lengthened to each end. Construct the belt as follows:

1. Cut the belt and lining of the same fabric, using the pattern as a guide. Stay-stitch the top section of the belt ¼ inch from the seamline, in the seam allowance. Stay-stitch the lining barely outside the seamline in the seam allowance.

2. Use a double thickness of heavy Pellon for the interfacing. Pin the pattern over the Pellon and trace the outline of the pattern along the *seamline.* Place several lines of stitching across the two layers of Pellon to hold them together, using

the multiple-stitch zig-zag or straight stitching. Press. Cut out the Pellon interfacing, following the drawn lines.

3. Work on a flat surface with the wrong side of the top belt fabric up, and the pointed end to the left. Center the interfacing over the belt fabric and pin through the center. Fold the seam edge of the fabric over the interfacing and pin, working from the center to the outer edges. Clip into the seam edges on the inside curve almost to the stay stitching, and cut notches in the seam edges on the outside curve so that the seams will lie flat. Miter the corners at the pointed end. Baste.

4. Catch-stitch the fabric seam allowance to the interfacing, making the stitches through the seam allowance and interfacing only so that they are not visible on the right side. Press.

...

(Continued on following page)

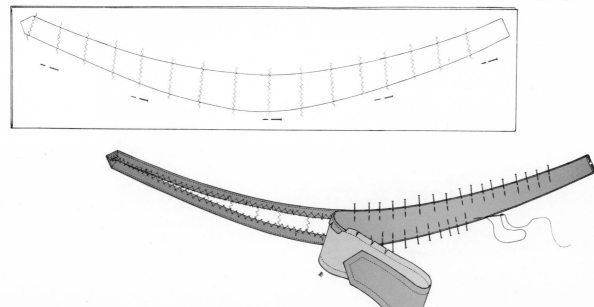

199

5. Trim the seam allowance to ⅜ inch on all edges of the belt lining except the straight end that will be sewed to the buckle. Clip into the seam allowance on the inside curve and notch the seam allowance on the outside curve. Center the lining over the belt, wrong sides together, and pin through the center the length of the belt. Fold under the cut edge of the lining and pin barely below the belt edge. Slip-stitch in place.

If top stitching is desired, stitch around the right side of the belt, close to the edge.

Narrow Tie Belt

The narrow tie belt may be from 1 inch to 1½ inches in finished width when cut on the lengthwise grain and about ½ inch when cut on the true bias. The ends should be long enough to lap or tie in a knot or bow. A wide seam allowance is used as an interlining in the instructions below.

1. Cut the belt on the lengthwise grain or on the true bias, the length of the waistline measurement plus the length desired for the tie, and four times the finished width.

2. Fold the fabric lengthwise through the center, right sides together, and pin. Baste through the center of the folded belt. Stitch 1/16 inch from the basting toward the cut edge. The seam allowance (from stitching line to cut edge) is ⅛ inch less than the width of the finished belt (from stitching line to folded edge); this difference will allow the seam allowances to fit smoothly inside the fin-

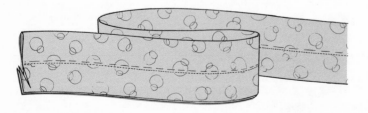

ished belt. (The Seam Guide adjusted the desired distance from the needle will help you guide and stitch the fabric evenly.)

3. Press, then fold one cut edge back on the stitching line and press the seam open. Clip off the corners diagonally from stitching to cut edge. If you are working with a lightweight fabric, leave both edges of the wide seam allowance for the interlining; however, if less thickness is required for the interlining, trim one edge of the seam allowance to ¼ inch.

4. Fasten a safety pin on the inside of one end, near the fold. Turn the belt to the right side by pushing the pin toward the open end and working the fabric back over it.

5. Carefully fold on the stitching line, and baste. Press. Turn the open ends into the belt ¼ inch, and pin. Slip-stitch the folded edges together.

Sash Belt

The illustrated sash belt fits around the waistline, is crossed in the back and tied in the front. It is an attractive treatment for taffeta, satin, and many cottons. The sash is made of a double thickness of fabric that is cut on the true bias. Though the width may vary, a 9-inch finished sash is most becoming. The sash requires 1⅛ yards of 40-inch fabric so that only one joining is necessary.

1. Cut the sash on the true bias twice the length of the waistline measurement plus the length for the tie, and twice the finished width plus seam allowances. See *Cutting Bias Strips*, page 244.

2. Fold the sash through the center, right sides together, and pin. Shape the ends, and pin. Baste. Stitch, leaving a 4-inch opening near the center for turning the belt to the right side. Take one stitch across the points and backstitch at each end of the seam. Trim one seam edge to ⅛ inch and the other to ¼ inch. Clip off the corners at the points, close to the stitching.

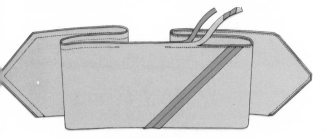

3. Turn the sash to the right side through the opening in the seam. Fold on the stitching line, and baste. Press. Slip-stitch the edges of the opening together. Remove bastings.

Corded Belt

Cording of various sizes may be used in belts. A single large cord or a braid of several cords is equally attractive. The cord is covered with a bias strip of soft satin or crepe. See *Tubular Cording*, page 247.

1. When braiding the cords, leave an unbraided length at each end for a tassel effect. At the end of the braiding, tie one tubular cord in a knot around the remaining cords. Tack the knot in place on the underside to prevent it from coming loose.

2. Trim the ends evenly. Pull out ½ inch of the cord and clip it off. Turn the ends of the fabric to the inside and slip-stitch them together, or knot

each end. Ease the knot down to within ½ inch of the end. Tuck the cut fabric ends under the knot with a heavy needle, and tack in place, taking care that the stitches are not visible.

Cummerbund with Featherboning

1. Cut the fabric for the cummerbund on the true bias the length of the waistline measurement plus 2 inches for seam allowances and overlap, and about 9 inches in width. See *Cutting Bias Strips*, page 244. Cut the lining of the same fabric, the length and width of the cummerbund. If the fabric is heavy, cut the lining of soft silk of the same color.

2. Fold the cummerbund, extending the front section 1 inch beyond the back section (the front of the waistline is always larger than the back); and pin near the fold. Baste along the fold to mark the position of the seam on the right side.

3. Place the lining over the top fabric, right sides together, and pin on the seamline. Baste across the left front end and along each side. (Leave the opposite end open for turning the cummerbund to the right side.) Stitch the basted edges, taking a ½-inch seam; however, at the lower edge leave an opening of ¾ inch at the closed end and

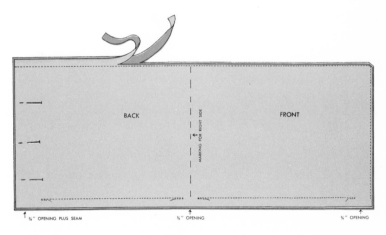

at the marking for the right side seam, and ¾ inch plus ½-inch seam allowance at the open end as illustrated. Reinforce each seam end with backstitching. (These three openings are necessary for the stays, which you will insert between the two layers of fabric.)

4. Trim lining seam edges to ⅛ inch, top fabric seam edges to ¼ inch, and trim both seam edges across the openings to ¼ inch. Press. Turn the cummerbund to the right side. Fold on the stitching line and baste. Press. *(Continued)*

5. At the open end, turn the seam edges to the inside ½ inch, and pin together. Baste and press. Stitch from the right side, close to the edge. Stitch again a scant ⅜ inch from the first row of stitching to form the casing for the stay. Pull threads to the underside and tie. Stitch the opposite end

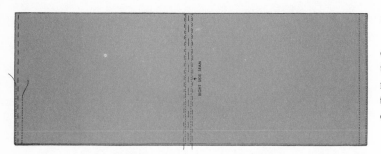

in the same way to form the casing there.

6. At the right side seam, pin and baste on each side of the marking to keep the bias from stretching while stitching. Space the bastings about ½ inch apart. Stitch on each side of the marking, spacing the lines of stitching a scant ⅜ inch apart. Pull threads to the underside and tie. Press. Remove bastings.

7. Cut three stays of featherboning 3½ inches in length. Remove the casing on the featherbone.

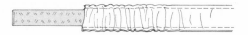

At the lower edge of the cummerbund, slip a featherbone stay into each opening between the rows of stitching and work the stay up to the top edge. Stitch the featherboning in place about ⅛ inch from the top edge. Stitch very slowly, turning the hand wheel by hand. Turn the fabric on the needle and stitch again on the first line of stitching. Pull threads to the underside and tie.

Ease the fabric back on each featherbone stay until the end of the stay is at the lower edge and under the fold of the seam. Stitch across the end of the stay the same as before. Distribute the fullness evenly. Slip-stitch the open edges of the casing together. Use four hooks and eyes to fasten the ends.

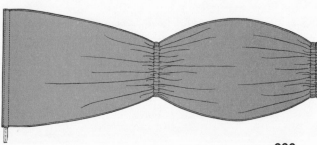

Belt Carriers

Belt carriers are used to hold a belt in position. They may be hand-worked with a blanket stitch or chain stitch, or they may be made of fabric.

Blanket-Stitch Carriers

1. Pin-mark the position for the carriers at the side seams, above and below the beltline.

2. Use a double strand of thread and knot the ends together. On the underside of the garment, take two backstitches to tie the thread at the top marking. Bring the needle through to the top side, then take a stitch at the opposite marking, leaving enough slack in the thread to fit over the belt.

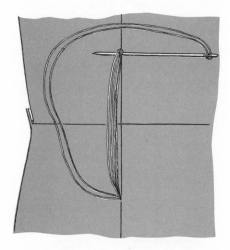

Work back and forth two or three times, always allowing the same amount of slack. Blanket-stitch over the strands of thread, drawing the stitches firmly. Fasten the thread securely on the underside with two backstitches.

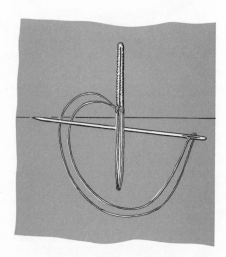

Chain-Stitch Carriers

1. Mark the position for the carrier the same as above.

2. Use a double thread and knot the ends together. On the underside, take two backstitches in the seam at the top marking. Bring the needle through to the top side, then take a small stitch and draw the thread part way through, leaving a 2-inch loop. Hold the loop open with the needle. Reach through the loop with the thumb and one

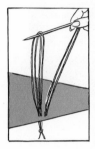
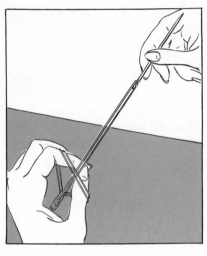

finger of the left hand and grasp the needle thread, pulling it through to form a new loop. Draw the released loop down to the fabric. Continue chaining for the length required. Pass the needle through the last loop to lock the chain. Stitch through the fabric and fasten the thread with two backstitches on the underside.

You can make chain-stitch carriers quickly by machine if you have the Chain-Stitch Accessories. Refer to the instruction book accompanying the machine and to page 63.

Fabric Carriers

Fabric carriers add a styling note to the waist and serve a utilitarian purpose as well. They are found on the waistbands of skirts, shorts, and slacks and in side seams of dresses. Generally, four to six carriers are used around the waistline. They vary from ¼ to ½ inch in width, depending on the fabric and garment.

1. Cut a strip of fabric on the lengthwise grain, twice the finished width plus ½ inch for seam allowances, and more than sufficient in length for the number of carriers required.

2. Fold the strip lengthwise, right sides together, and stitch a scant ¼ inch from the edge. Trim the seam edges to ⅛ inch. Ease the seam to the center of the strip and press open with the fingers. Stitch across one end.

3. Turn the strip right side out. (Use an orange stick with a straight end.) Turn the stitched end to the inside, then ease the strip back over the orange stitck. Clip off the stitched end. Ease the seam to the center and press.

4. Cut each carrier long enough to fit over the belt with ease plus 1 inch for seam allowances. Fold under ½ inch at each end and press.

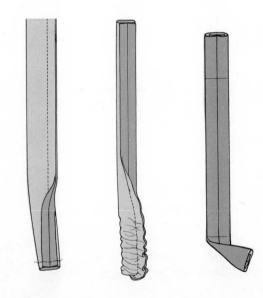

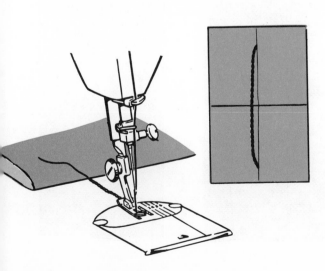

5. Mark the position for the finished end of the carrier on the garment. Place the carrier right

side up, with the cut end ⅛ inch inside the marking. Stitch ⅛ inch from the edge. Backstitch at each end; do not stitch beyond the edges of the carrier. Trim the end close to the stitching and press.

6. Fold the carrier back on the stitching line and press. Stitch ⅛ inch from the fold, using a closely spaced zig-zag stitch. Finish the opposite end in the same manner.

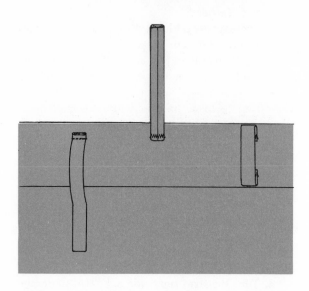

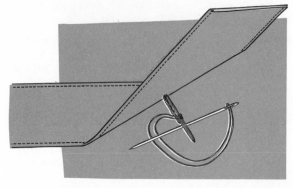

Belt Attached with French Tacks

A French tack may also be used to hold a belt in place. See *French Tacks*, page 208 for instructions.

BUTTONS AND FASTENINGS

Positioning Buttons

Buttons are positioned *on the center line* of the garment, opposite the buttonholes.

1. Lap the buttonhole side of the garment over the button side, *matching center lines,* and pin together between the buttonholes.

2. Mark the position of the button by placing a pin straight through the outer end of a horizontal buttonhole at the center line marking, and through the center of a vertical buttonhole. Carefully lift the buttonhole over the pin. The pin marks the position for the center of the button.

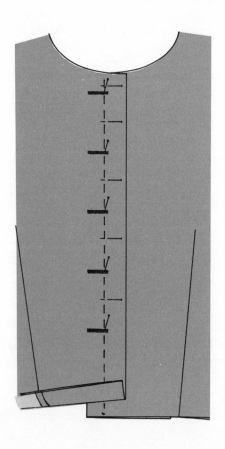

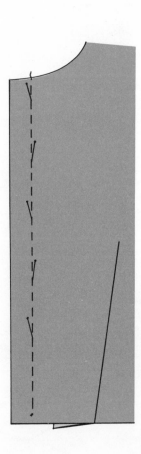

Sewing on Buttons

Buttons may be sewed on by hand or with a zig-zag sewing machine. Whether or not you make a thread shank depends on the garment and the thickness of the fabric. A shank is not necessary on skirts, blouses, washable dresses, and pajamas; it is necessary on suits, coats, and garments of heavy fabric. The shank raises the button from the surface of the garment, allowing space for the layers of fabric on the buttonhole side to fit smoothly under the button. Mercerized or cotton thread is generally used on lightweight and washable fabrics; buttonhole twist is preferred for suits, coats, garments made of suede, and the like.

Buttons without a Shank

Use thread matching the button in color. Knot the long end of the thread. Position the button over the marking and *on the center line* of garment.

Bring the needle through the fabric from the underside and up through one eye of the button. Place a pin across the button between the eyes, then bring the needle down through the second eye and back into the fabric. Take about six stitches; then fasten the thread with two or three overcast stitches around the threads on the underside.

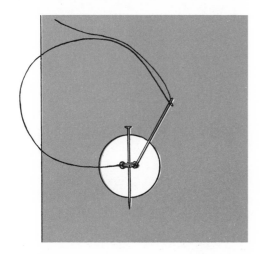

Buttons with four eyes may be sewed in various ways for decorative effects.

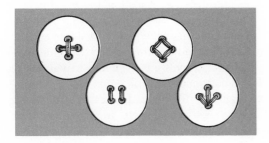

Buttons with Thread Shank

For coats, suits, and garments that will be worn open, make the stitches through the garment and interfacing, but not through the facing. Knot the long end of the thread.

1. On the right side of the garment, take a stitch through the top layer of fabric and interfacing at the position for the button and on the center line of the garment. Bring the needle up through one eye of the button. Place a bodkin or smooth toothpick across the button between the eyes, then bring the needle down through the second eye. Take a stitch through the top layer of fabric and interfacing. Make about six stitches the same way. On the last stitch, bring the thread down through the eye.

2. Remove the bodkin, then pull the button away from the fabric and wind the needle thread evenly around the threads between the fabric and button to form the thread shank. Fasten the thread securely with two overcast stitches.

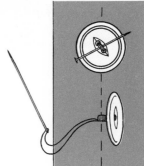

Reinforced Button

On garments made of suede, leather, or heavy coating, where the underside must be as neat as the top side, sew a small button on the underside so that the stitches will be inconspicuous. This gives added strength and prevents the thread from cutting the suede or leather.

Use buttonhole twist and knot the end of the thread.

1. Position the top button. Bring the needle through the fabric from the underside and up through one eye of the button. Place a bodkin across the button between the eyes. Then bring the needle down through the second eye and fabric, and through the eye of the bottom button. Make about six stitches through the eyes of the top and bottom buttons at the same time. On the last stitch, bring the thread down through the eye of the top button.

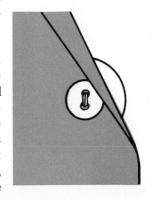

2. Remove the bodkin, pull the top button away from the fabric and finish the thread shank between the top button and fabric as described above.

Machine-Sewed Buttons

A zig-zag machine may be used to sew on buttons with or without a thread shank. Refer to the instruction book accompanying your machine for directions.

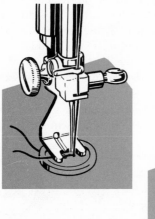

Snap Fasteners

Snap fasteners are usually placed at the neckline and waistline to hold the facing edge flat when buttons are used; at the pointed end of the waistband with hooks and eyes; and at the waistline of blouses and the closing for long, closely fitted sleeves. They are seldom used alone.

Snaps are available in various sizes. Select a size that is not too heavy for the fabric. A small snap is preferred in dressmaking.

1. Mark the position for the snap on the overlap about ⅛ inch from the finished edge so that it is not visible when the garment is worn.

2. Sew the ball part of the snap to the underside of the overlap. Take about six stitches through the hole, then carry the thread under the snap to the next hole. Make the stitches through the facing and interfacing only so that they are not visible on the right side of the garment. Fasten the thread securely with two overcast stitches around the threads.

3. Chalk the ball and press it against the underlap to mark the position of the socket. (On some fabrics, merely pressing the ball against the underlap will mark the position.) Sew the socket to the underlap in the same manner as the ball section.

Lingerie Strap Holder

Strap holders are used at the shoulder seam to hold lingerie straps in position.

Use straight seam binding about 1½ inches long. Fold under the ends and press, then fold through the center and press. Stitch on each side. Mark the position for each end of the strap at the shoulder seam. Hand-stitch one end to the seam allowance at the marking near the armhole.

Sew one part of the snap to the free end of the strap and the other part to the seam allowance.

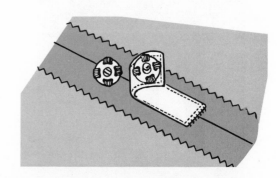

Hooks and Eyes

Hooks and eyes are placed at the waistband closing of a skirt, at the neckline when a zipper is used, at a closing where the edges meet, and at the waistline and neckline when a button is used.

Hooks and eyes are available in various sizes. Select small, fine ones for lightweight fabrics and a medium size for heavy fabrics. A straight eye is generally used when there is an overlap, and a round eye when edges meet.

Overlap in a Waistband

1. Sew the hook to the underside of the overlap of the waistband, placing the end far enough from the edge so that it will not be visible when the garment is worn. Make about six stitches through each loop, then carry the thread under the hook and take several stitches through the end to hold it flat. Do not stitch through to the right side of the garment. Fasten the thread with one or two overcast stitches.

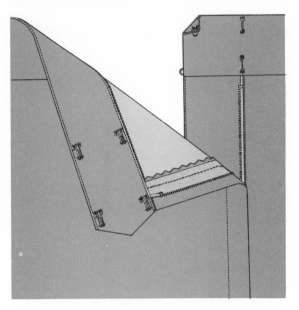

2. To mark the position for the eye, lap the closing and pin-mark the underlap directly opposite the end of the hook. Center the straight eye over the marking and sew through each loop.

3. On the underlap, sew a round eye at the end of the band. Fasten the hook in the eye, then sew it in place on the underside of the front band section.

When Edges Meet

1. When edges of a closing meet, mark the position for the hook and eye on each side of the closing. Sew a round eye on one side, extending the edge slightly, or make a thread eye, following the instructions given below.

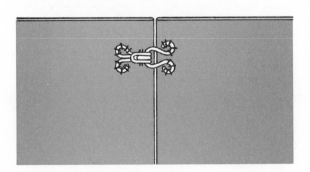

2. Fasten the hook in the eye, then bring the garment edges together to determine exactly where you should sew the hook on the opposite edge. Sew the hook in place. Be sure the stitches do not show through on the right side of the garment.

Thread Eye

A thread eye is generally used at a neckline closing with a zipper and at a waistline closing with a button.

1. Sew the hook to the underside of the overlap, placing the end far enough for the edge so that it will not be visible when the garment is worn.

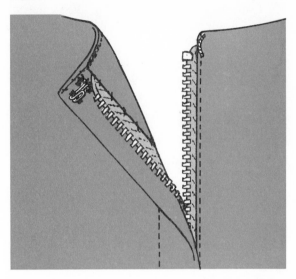

2. To mark the position for the eye, lap the closing and pin-mark the underlap directly opposite each side of the hook end.

3. *To make a thread eye,* use thread matching the fabric in color. Knot the long end of the thread. Bring the needle through from the underside at one end of the marking for the eye. Then take a stitch at the opposite end. Work back and forth two or three times, then blanket-stitch over the strands of thread, firmly drawing the stitches. Fasten the last stitch securely on the underside.

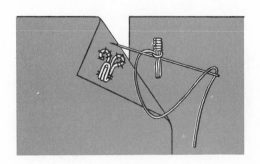

Thread Loops

Thread loops are often used with buttons at a neckline opening in a dress or blouse.

1. Determine the spacing for the buttons and mark the edge of the garment. Center the button on the marking and pin-mark the position for the loop on each side of the button.

2. Use a single strand of matching thread and knot the long end of the thread. At the top marking, bring the needle through the fabric from the underside near the edge of the opening; then take a stitch in the edge at the bottom marking, leaving a loop large enough to slip easily over the button. Work back and forth two or three times, keeping the loops even. Blanket-stitch over the strands of thread, firmly drawing the stitches. Fasten the threads securely on the underside.

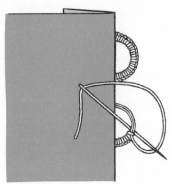

French Tacks

French tacks are used when two fabric surfaces must be connected with a certain ease allowance —for example, linings at the lower edge in coats or draperies, or the lower edge of facings in coats. They are placed at the seams and intervals between. French tacks may also be used in attaching a belt to a garment or joining buttons to form cuff links.

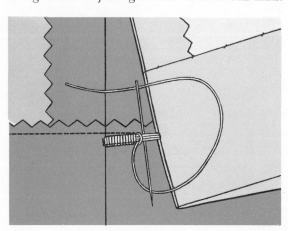

1. Use a double strand of silk or mercerized thread or a single strand of buttonhole twist. Knot the end of the thread. Take a stitch near the top of the garment hem (through the hem and seam allowance), then a stitch directly opposite in the lining, leaving a ¼- to 1-inch slack in the thread. Work back and forth two or three times, allowing the same amount of slack.

2. Blanket-stitch over the strands of thread, firmly drawing the stitches. When finished, fasten stitches securely in the fabric with one or two overcast stitches.

Eyelets

Eyelets are used in belts, in cuffs that require cuff links, and for lacings. They may be hand-worked or machine-worked with the Buttonholer.

Hand-Worked Eyelets

1. Mark the position for the eyelets. Punch a hole in the fabric with a stiletto. (It may be necessary to cut out the excess fabric with sharp, pointed scissors. Do not make the hole too large.)

2. Use a single strand of silk or mercerized thread, or buttonhole twist. Bring the needle up through the fabric from the underside a scant ⅛ inch from the edge of the hole, leaving about 1 inch of the thread on the underside. Work around the hole and over the 1-inch thread on the underside with blanket stitches, forming the purl on the outer edge. Keep the stitches as even as possible. When finished, fasten the thread securely on the underside with one or two overcast stitches.

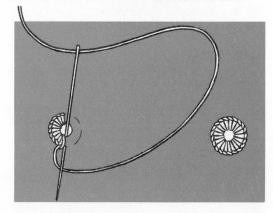

Pleats and Godets

PLEATS AND GODETS ARE STYLING POINTS that appear and disappear at intervals, depending on the whim of fashion. Both add fullness and interest to a skirt.

FORMING PLEATS

In your sewing you will come across many kinds of pleats. This chapter deals with the four most common ones: side pleats, inverted pleats, box pleats, and pleated skirts.

Side Pleats

Side pleats run in one direction—from right to left. They are often used to provide fullness at the lower edge of a pencil-slim skirt.

If the pattern you are using does not extend the pleat allowance the entire length of the skirt,

do so by marking the fabric with chalk before cutting.

1. Mark the position of the pleat and the seamline above the pleat with tailor's tacks. Pin and baste the seamline and the extension for the pleat. Then stitch close to the basting. Remove bastings and press.

Baste the fold line for the pleat and remove tailor's tacks.

2. Working from the wrong side, turn the pleat and seam allowance to the left side. Cut out the top layer of fabric above the pleat, leaving a ⅝-inch seam allowance. This eliminates bulk. The second layer of fabric will hold the pleat in position so that you do not need to stitch across the top of the pleat on the right side.

3. Press the seam open above the pleat. Turn the pleat and seam allowance to the left side and press. Press lightly in the hem area since the crease is reversed in the hem when it is folded.

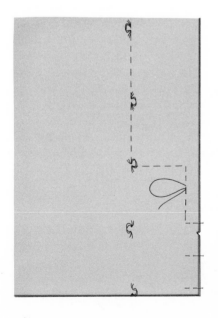 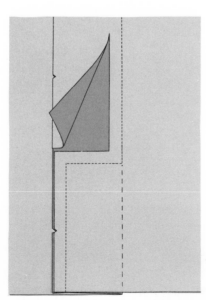 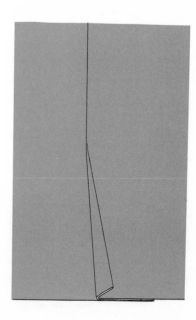

Inverted Pleat with Underlay

An inverted pleat is formed by folding two pleats toward each other. When an underlay is used on the underside of an inverted pleat, there is a seam instead of a fold on each side of the pleat that is concealed by the depth of the pleat.

If the pattern does not extend the pleat allowance the entire length of the skirt, do so by marking the fabric with chalk before cutting.

1. Mark the position of the pleat and the seamline above the pleat with tailor's tacks.

Pin and baste the entire length of the seam and pleat. Then stitch the seam from the waistline to the top of the pleat, reinforcing the ends with backstitching. Remove bastings along the stitching but not in the pleat area. Press. Then press the wide seam open the entire length of the seam and pleat. Press lightly in the hem area.

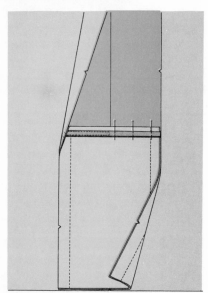

2. Place an underlay over the pleat section, right side down, extending the edge ⅝ inch above the top of the pleat. Pin and baste the underlay to each side of the pleat section. Stitch seams, and press.

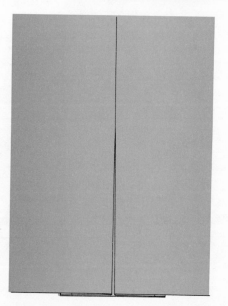

3. To stay the top of the pleat, cut straight seam binding the width of the pleat. Fold it lengthwise through the center, and press. Turn the pleat away from the skirt. Pin the stay across the pleat with the lower edge exactly at the top of the pleat. Stitch the underlay and stay to the pleat from seam edge to center. Treat the opposite side in the same way. This eliminates the need for stitching across the top of the pleat on the right side and also prevents the seam from ripping above the pleat. Press, then remove bastings.

Box Pleats

A box pleat is formed by folding two side pleats in opposite directions to make a panel. Transfer the markings for the pleats, following the instructions given for a *Pleated Skirt;* then lay in the pleats.

Pleated Skirt

When the entire skirt is pleated, each pleat in the pattern is marked with two vertical lines from the waistline to the lower edge. One line designates the top fold for the pleat, the other the position of the fold that forms the pleat. Each pleat is made proportionately deeper at the waistline. The depth of the pleats conceals the seams within the skirt.

1. Transfer the markings to the fabric with tailor's tacks, using contrasting colors of thread to designate the two lines that form the pleat. This will simplify your work later when you begin to lay in the pleats, for you can fold one color to the other. *Be sure to use the correct marking on the pattern to form the top fold for each pleat.*

2. Before forming the pleats, stitch the seams within the skirt, and press. Determine the skirt length and finish the hem at the lower edge.

Three methods are suggested for forming the pleats. Use the one best suited to your fabric. Always work on a flat surface, and remember to press. See page 66 for information on pressing various types of fabric.

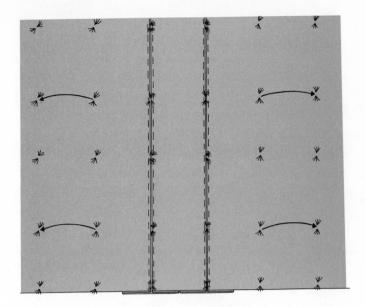

Method 1: Use this method of pleating for medium-weight fabrics with body that crease easily.

Work on the right side of the fabric. Lay in the pleats, matching markings. Place pins at right angles to the pleats. Baste near the fold, using silk thread. Press from the wrong side. Be sure to use the appropriate press cloth and moisture, and glide the iron the length of the pleat.

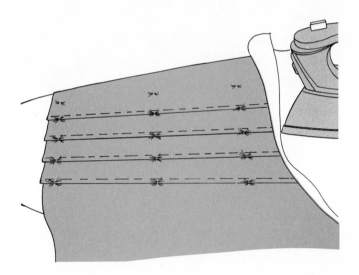

Method 2: Use this method on woolens that resist creasing and on heavy fabrics where pressing the fold of the pleat against the fabric is apt to form a ridge under the fold.

Work on the right side of the fabric. Pin, then baste the top fold for each pleat, using silk thread. Press from the underside of the fold to form a sharp crease. Since this step requires pressing on the right side of the fabric, use a wool press cloth and moist cheesecloth as protection.

Lay in the pleats, matching markings. Pin, then baste, using silk thread. Press from the wrong side, as instructed in Method 1, and crease the under fold for the pleat.

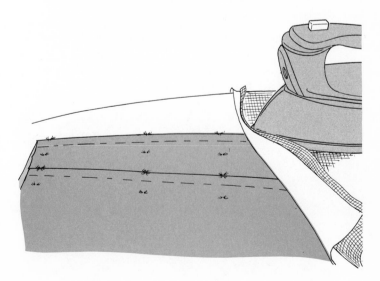

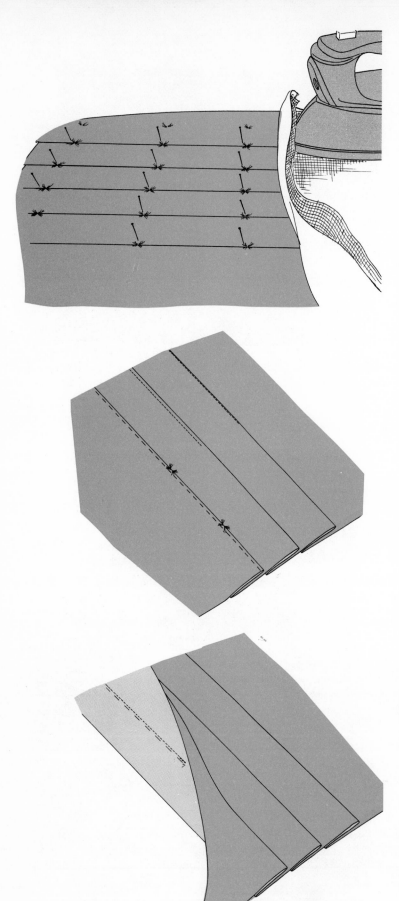

Method 3: Use this quick and easy method for cottons and similar fabrics.

Work on the ironing board. Turn the fabric right side up and lay in each pleat, matching markings. Pin straight through the fabric into the ironing board. Press between pins. Since the pressing is done from the right side, use the appropriate press cloth and moisture required by the fabric. Remove pins, and press again.

Stitching Pleats

Pleats may hang freely from the waistline or may be stitched from waistline to hipline. They may be top-stitched or stitched from the underside. Do the stitching after you have applied the zipper and before you attach the waistband.

After you have basted and pressed your pleats as described in any one of the methods above, follow the instructions given here.

Top-stitched Pleats

Pleats may be either edgestitched or stitched about ¼ inch from the edge. Since they are made proportionately deeper at the waistline, they overlap in this area.

Pin-mark the length to be stitched on each pleat. On the underside, fold back the pleat that precedes the line of stitching; then on the right side, stitch the pleat in place from the marking up to the waistline. Stitch each pleat in the same way. Pull threads to the underside and tie. Press. Attach the waistband; then remove all bastings for the pleats.

Pleats Stitched on Underside

Remove the bastings from the waistline to about 3 inches below the hipline. Turn the skirt to the wrong side. Then turn the pleat away from the skirt and mark the length for the stitching with chalk. Pin and baste in the crease designating the top fold of the pleat. Then stitch in the crease from the marking up to the waistline. Reinforce each end with backstitching.

Turn the pleats in the direction they were pressed. Then press from the wrong side.

Apply the waistband before you remove the bastings.

Pleated Ruffles

The small pleats required for ruffles can easily be made with the Ruffler. See page 281 for instructions.

As the Ruffler forms each pleat at the seamline, finger-press the entire length of the pleat. Then

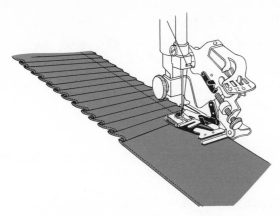

press with an iron. For fabrics that you cannot finger-press satisfactorily, use an iron after pleating the ruffle. Work on the ironing board and form the pleat from the stitching line to the outer edge; then place a pin straight through the outer edge and into the ironing board. Pin each pleat in the same way. Press.

INSERTING GODETS

Godets may be set in a cutout of the skirt or in a seam. They should be stitched in place before you stitch the side seams since it is easier to work with a flat piece of fabric.

Godet in a Cutout

When setting in a godet, you will be working with two curves—an outside curve, which is in the godet, and an inside curve, which is in the cutout of the skirt.

1. Stay-stitch a scant ⅝ inch from the seam edge of the cutout for the godet. Press. Slash the seam allowance on the curve almost to the stitching.

2. On the underside, pin the center of the godet to the center of the cutout, right sides together. Then, on each side, pin from the center to the lower edge. Carefully shape the inside curve of the cutout around the outside curve of the godet and ease the godet slightly around the curve, keeping seam edges even. Hand-baste on each side from center to lower edge, using a fine stitch. Check the right side to be certain that the curve is maintained on both pieces of fabric. Hang the garment overnight to allow for any stretching in the godet.

3. Place the godet next to the feed and stitch slowly in a continuous line from one edge to the other. Finish seam edges as required by the fabric. Press the seam, then press it away from the opening.

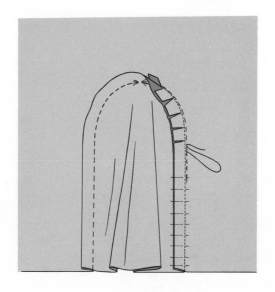

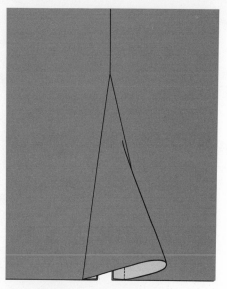

Godet in a Seam

Stitch the seam above the opening for the godet and reinforce each end with backstitching. Finish the seam edges. Clip into the seam allowances at the top of the opening, almost to the stitching. Press; then press the seam open.

1. Position the godet in the opening, right sides together, matching the marking at the point with the end of the seam above the opening; pin at the point. Pin and baste one side from the point to the lower edge; keep seam edges even. Do not stretch the bias seam in the godet.

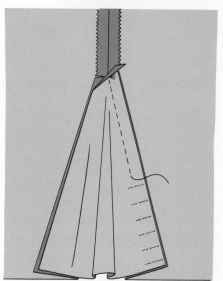

2. Stitch on the garment side, from the lower edge to the point, joining the stitching in the seamline above the godet. Pin, baste, and stitch the opposite side in the same way.

At the point of the godet, pull all threads to the underside and tie them together in a single knot. Remove bastings and press. Finish seam edges.

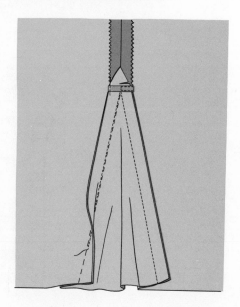

3. To stay the seam at the point, cut straight seam binding the width of the open seam edges. Fold the binding lengthwise through the center and press. Pin the stay across the godet and garment seam allowances, keeping the lower edge of the stay exactly at the top of the stitched point. Turn the seam allowances away from the garment and stitch from seam edge to seamline; treat the opposite side in the same manner. Clip off seam allowances at the point ¼ inch from the stitching.

Fabrics that Require Special Handling

THERE IS A WIDE ARRAY OF FABRICS that demand special attention in sewing. To mention a few—knits, silks, soft leather and suede, and stretch. Techniques used in stitching and handling vary with the fabric. Although these fabrics require a little more time and patience, if you follow the suggestions given here as well as the usual methods of good dressmaking, your finished garment is certain to become one of your favorites.

Instructions for the various sewing techniques referred to in this chapter can be found in other parts of this book. Check the alphabetical index.

SILK FABRICS

Silk can go anywhere. Ranging in weight from sheer chiffon to heavy tweed, it is suitable for all types of garments. "Light and gentle" describes the hand for working with silk.

Preparing to Sew

Pattern. You can select almost any pattern for silk provided you also select the correct weight of silk for the garment. Heavy silks are suitable for tailored dresses, suits, and coats; soft silks for blouses and dresses; and sheer silks, such as chiffon or lace, for softly draped styles and full skirts. Unless completely underlined, however, sheer silks will not be pleasing to the eye if neckline and sleeve facings are used or if styling seams and darts are obvious.

Cutting. Do not try to cut silk on a highly polished surface and certainly not on the carpet or floor. A cork or felt surface is preferred, but sheeting pinned tightly over your usual cutting table or board will make a good substitute.

Use fine pins or, better still, needles, when pinning the pattern to the fabric. Place them close together and within the seam or dart allowance.

Use sharp scissors of medium length. Your careful cutting will be reflected in the accuracy of seam width and garment proportions. On sheer silk, cut notches outward so that they will not interfere with the seam construction or final finishing.

Markings. Use tailor's tacks only.

Underlining and lining. For the custom-made look you desire, you should either underline or line silk fabric. The chapter on underlining and lining contains comprehensive instructions. See page 95. Select such fabrics as China silk, silk organza, silk crepe, or silk taffeta.

Interfacing. Select the interfacing the same way as you would for any fabric of similar weight. If the silk is sheer, use self-fabric or silk organza; match the fabric color exactly.

Stitching and Handling

Basting. Hand-baste seams and darts. Avoid temporary machine stitching that must later be removed since many silks will show needle marks. Baste with silk or soft mercerized thread contrasting in color, and use a size 8 or 9 hand-sewing needle of appropriate length.

Thread and needle. Machine-stitch silk fabric with silk thread as the expert always does. Use a size 11 machine needle in lightweight silks and a size 14 on heavy or rough-surfaced silks. In most cases, the needle thread tension must be lessened one to two points or until the stitching looks the same on the top and underside and does not pucker.

Stitch length and pressure. Use a 15 to 20 stitch length for sheer and soft silks and a 12 stitch length for medium and heavy silks.

The pressure exerted by the presser foot on the fabric should be light, no heavier than needed to carry the fabric gently and evenly under the foot.

Stitching. Medium and heavy silks require guiding only in front of the needle during the machine stitching. Crepe weaves and chiffon require gentle support; when stitching them, hold the seam in back of the presser foot as well as in front of the needle. Do not pull the fabric under the foot; merely place it under slight tension. When stitching with a zig-zag machine, use the straight-stitch throat plate and presser foot for best results.

Darts. If the silk is underlined, construct the darts in the silk and underlining separately unless the fabric is sheer. On sheer fabrics, make the darts through both layers at once so that they will not be distracting. Unstitched darts, gathers, and shirring are generally more pleasing in a sheer fabric than the conventional stitched dart.

Seams and seam finishes. Select a finish that will give the seam as little bulk as possible. Some closely woven silks require no seam finish; others you may prefer to pink. Finish rough, open weaves that tend to ravel with either the blindstitch zig-zag or the multiple-stitch zig-zag.

Sheer silks, such as chiffon, require narrow French seams. The hairline seam is a neat finish for enclosed seams in facings and collars, and fine double-fold bias binding makes a more pleasing neckline and sleeve finish than a shaped facing.

Zipper closing. Follow the conventional method of inserting the zipper until the final step. Then, instead of top-stitching, hand-sew, using a fine, short backstitch, or machine-stitch using the blind-stitch zig-zag. The method you choose is more a matter of preference than of necessity.

Buttonholes. Machine-worked, hand-worked, or bound buttonholes are appropriate for all silks except sheers, where buttonholes should be avoided. Always use an underlay of a firmly woven lawn or muslin to reinforce the stitching around the buttonholes.

Hems. Seam tape is acceptable for the hem edge finish, but a pinked edge with a line of machine stitching ¼ inch from the edge is preferred. Rough, open weaves that tend to ravel may be finished with the blindstitch zig-zag or multiple-stitch zig-zag.

Always hand-sew the hem with silk thread, using the French method, which places the stitches between the hem and garment and not over the hem edge.

If the silk is sheer and the lining is joined only at the waistline, hem the silk and lining separately. A double-fold hem is a favorite. It adds weight to the bottom edge, improves the hang of the skirt, and eliminates the turned, raw edge that would normally show through. However, it can be used only if the hemline is straight, not flared. Double the hem allowance; if you want a 4-inch hem, allow 8 inches. Turn a 4-inch hem and press, then turn 4 inches again. Slip-stitch the hem in place, catching only one thread of the skirt in each stitch and slipping the needle inside the fold between the stitches to conceal the thread. When the hemline is circular or flared, make a narrow machine-stitched or hand-rolled hem, or use horsehair braid. Hem the sheer silk and underlining separately to avoid sagging and to prevent the sheer from blousing over the underlining.

Pressing. Follow the instructions given for pressing silk on page 66.

Lining. Coats and jackets should be lined in the usual way. Always select a lining of crepe or taffeta.

KNIT FABRICS

Knit fabrics have as many different faces and characteristics as woven fabrics, and for that reason no single set of sewing guidelines can be applied to all knits. *The Many Faces of Knits,* page 417, describes the construction of knit fabrics and the uses and characteristics of the various types of knits. It includes guidelines for stitching and suggestions for many different seams and constructions appropriate for the fabrics in each knit group.

Firm, stable knits — such as double knits and warp knits of polyester, wool, or blends of polyester and wool or cotton — are the most popular fashion knits. They are the easiest to sew, and they react more like woven fabrics than any of the other knits. For a capsule review of how to sew them, read the suggestions below.

Preparing to Sew

Pattern. Many styles of suits, dresses, and coats make up well in firm knits. In selecting your pattern, pick one with simple, uncluttered lines. Some patterns are designated "suitable for knits"; other patterns include firm knits or double knits in the list of suitable fabrics on the pattern envelope. Do not choose a pattern designated "stretchable knits only" if you are working with a firm, stable knit. Smart ways to accent double knits and firm warp knits include matching fabric, braid, or satin binding; topstitching; and welt seams.

Shrinking. Washable knits, such as polyester and polyester-and-cotton blends, should be laundered before cutting to remove the excess finishing solution, which imparts permanent-press qualities. Wool double knits should be sent to the tailor/dry cleaner for shrinking unless labeled washable. Prepare them for shrinking by folding on a lengthwise rib, right side out, squaring the ends with a table, and basting the ends and edges. (Knits that are finished out-of-square can seldom be straightened by pulling diagonally.)

Cutting. Lay out the pattern following a "with nap" pattern layout. Knits have an up-and-down direction because of their loop construction and will reflect light differently in the crosswise and lengthwise directions. If the fabric has a deep center crease, it seldom can be pressed out, so avoid including the crease in a prominent part of the garment. If the crosswise courses of the knit do not run perpendicular to the lengthwise rib, or if a design in one direction is not perpendicular to one in the other direction, expand all half pattern sections with tissue paper into whole pattern sections; cut the fabric singly, using the most prominent direction of a fabric as the "grain line."

Use ball-point pins, preferably within dart and seam allowances. To avoid stretching, do not let the fabric hang over the edge of the cutting table. Cut with sharp, heavy-blade shears. Cut extended notches.

Markings. Use hand basting for center lines and tailor's tacks for internal markings. Tracing paper and a tracing wheel do not perform well on most firm knits.

Underlining and lining. Both are optional and impart different characteristics to a garment. Underlining and lining cancel the comfort of a knit fabric. They increase the stability of the fabric and cause the garment to hang free of the figure just like a woven fabric. Select a thin, soft, supple fabric for a softly draped look or a thin, crisp fabric for a mounted look. Suit jackets may be lined with either a color-matching single knit or a tricot to preserve the give of knit.

Interfacing. Collars, cuffs, pocket flaps, and front facing areas should be interfaced in firm knits. Select a thin, supple woven interfacing or an all-polyester nonwoven interfacing for minimum support; a lightweight hair canvas for tailored shaping; or time-saving press-on interfacing (fused to the underside of the outside section) for a crisp effect.

Stitching and Handling

Basting. Hand basting ensures a smooth seam and enables you to test the fit of the garment before machine-stitching the seams. Machine basting with the Even Feed machine foot, or speed basting (if your sewing machine has this feature), will give you the same advantages as hand basting.

Thread and needle. Select strong thread for machine stitching. Silk, nylon, spun polyester, and polyester-core threads are suitable. They provide both stretch and strength. Use a size 14 ball-point needle (Singer No. 2021 or 2045). Regulate tensions to produce a balanced stitch.

Kind of stitch. For plain seams in firm knits, a 12 length straight stitch made with a strong thread is suitable. For seams that will be subjected to strain, the straight stretch stitch is recommended. Use one of the overedge stitches for finishing hem and facing edges.

Presser-foot pressure. Use medium or normal presser-foot pressure.

Stitching. For straight stitching, use the straight-stitch presser foot and throat plate. Guide and support the fabric while stitching by holding the seam under tension in back of the presser foot and in front of the needle. Or use the Even Feed foot instead to ensure that the seam ends come out even without basting or guiding and supporting the seam.

Stabilize seams that must not stretch, such as shoulder, neckline, and waistline seams, with woven-edge seam binding.

Armhole seams for set-in sleeves should be double-stitched, first on the seamline with a straight or straight stretch stitch, then ¼ inch outside the seamline with a straight stitch or a zig-zag overedge stitch. Trim seam allowance outside second stitching.

Topstitching with buttonhole twist is a fashion accent recommended for firm knits. Use a size 16 or 18 needle to carry the buttonhole twist, and thread the bobbin with either silk or mercerized thread. Increase the needle-thread tension slightly to set the stitch firmly. The Even Feed foot will improve the feeding of the fabric layers for all topstitched detail. Topstitching may also be done

with the same thread used for constructing the garment.

Darts. To eliminate bulk in small darts, slash through center and press open. Trim the inside layer of slanted bustline darts to ½ inch and press downward.

Seam blending. Blend, grade, or bevel seam allowances inside collars, cuffs, and similar constructions in the same way as on woven fabrics.

Seam finishes. Press plain seams open. Edges do not ravel and do not require a seam finish.

Buttonholes. Bound or machine-worked buttonholes are appropriate. Always make buttonholes through firm woven or all-polyester non-woven interfacing or stay.

Hems. To ensure an even and accurate hemline, allow knit garment to hang at least 24 hours before hemming. Mark, fold, and baste the hem in the same way as on woven fabrics. Finish the hem edge with a zig-zag overedge stitch or a straight stitch ¼ inch from edge. Blindstitch hem by hand. For deep hems, place the first row of blind hemming stitches at the center of the hem width and the second row ¼ inch from the hem edge.

Pressing. Always use a thin press cloth between the iron and the fabric. A slightly dampened cheesecloth will produce sufficient steam with the iron on the silk setting. Steam-press polyester thoroughly as you sew. Little or no pressing is required after laundering if thorough pressing is done during the construction of the garment.

STRETCH FABRICS

Since the stretch characteristic has been added to fabrics primarily for comfort in action plus neatness of fit, the direction in which the stretch is used in a garment is important. Stretch should run across the shoulders in blouses, shirts, dresses, and jackets; from waistline to ankle in pants or slacks; and from side to side in skirts and shorts. Examine the fabric carefully *to be sure that the stretch goes in the right direction* for your garment.

Some fabrics are woven to look the same lengthwise as crosswise even though they stretch in only one direction. They can be used for any garment, but you must cut the fabric with the stretch running in the proper direction, as stated above. For a description of stretch fabrics, see page 11.

Preparing to Sew

Pattern. Select a pattern in your usual size, with slim, simple styling. In adjusting the pattern to your fitting requirements, remember that you may not need quite so much ease allowance for body action as you do when using a firm fabric.

Shrinking. It is advisable to shrink the fabric before cutting since laundering may cause it to shrink more in the stretch direction than a firm fabric.

Cutting. Lay the pattern pieces on the fabric in the direction of the desired stretch. Use fine pins with sharp points, and place them perpendicular to the direction of the stretch. Cut, following the same procedure you use for regular fabrics. A 1-inch seam allowance is recommended for lightweight or medium-weight twill weaves and heavy stretch fabrics. Simply cut 1 inch from the seamline marking on the pattern.

Markings. Use either tailor's tacks or tracing wheel and dressmaker's tracing paper. Tailor's tacks are recommended for heavy fabrics since the tracing wheel may not mark the bottom layer of fabric.

Interfacing. Interface the garment in the same way as one made of regular fabric.

Stitching and Handling

Basting. Hand basting is recommended for stretch fabrics. It saves time in the long run because it enables you to test the fit of the garment before machine stitching; also, it ensures an even seam width when stitching. Baste darts from the wide end toward the point, leaving a 4-inch thread end at the point. After fitting the garment, clip the seamline bastings at 4-inch intervals to allow for stretching the fabric during the machine stitching.

Thread and needle. Select strong thread for machine stitching. Nylex, Nymo, and Dacron are all excellent because they provide strength plus give to seams. Silk thread may also be used. Select size 14 machine needle.

Regulate the tension to produce a balanced stitch, otherwise strength is sacrificed.

Stitch length and pressure. Use a 12 stitch length. The pressure exerted by the presser foot on the fabric should be medium.

Stitching. Seams on the stretch grain require special handling. Make a test sample on your fabric before actually stitching on the garment. Do not forget to clip seamline bastings at 4-inch intervals. As you sew, stretch the fabric by holding it in front and in back of the presser foot; in other words, keep the fabric under tension while stitching. If you are using Nymo, Nylex, or Dacron thread, all of which have a certain amount of elasticity, stretch the fabric slightly during the stitching. If you are using silk thread, stretch the fabric the full amount of the built-in stretch. Use medium to slow speed. Backstitch at each end of the seam for reinforcement. After stitching a seam, stretch it the full amount to be sure that the thread

will not break under strain. If you have a slant-needle zig-zag machine, you can use the Overedge Foot and *Fashion* disc, which will produce a flexible stitch that will stretch with the fabric.

In some seams stretch is undesirable, such as those at the neckline, waistline, and shoulders. Stay them with straight seam binding.

Seam finishes. Press the seam open and finish the edges with a plain zig-zag stitch, wide stitch width, and 12 stitch length; or with a multiple-stitch zig-zag, wide stitch width, and "fine" stitch length. Pink the seam edges if the fabric is firmly woven. Blend seams inside collars, cuffs, facings, and similar construction in the usual way.

Waistband on skirt and pants. Cut the band on the lengthwise grain of the fabric and interface it with grosgrain ribbon. If you want stretch in the band, cut the band on the stretch grain and interface it with elastic that has been fitted for the desired snugness. (Remember, the waistline of the garment must also be on the stretch grain.) Stretch both the elastic and fabric as you sew, using a medium width zig-zag stitch.

Zipper closing. Insert the zipper in the conventional way. Do not stretch the fabric since the zipper tape will not stretch. A side closing or fly front is preferred for skirts, shorts, slacks, or pants.

Buttonholes. Machine-worked or bound buttonholes are suitable. Always stay buttonholes with a backing of a firmly woven fabric.

Hems. Finish the hem edge the same way as the seam edges. Then blindstitch the hem in place, using the machine. If the hem is along the stretch grain, use a plain zig-zag stitch, medium stitch width, and 12 stitch length instead of the blindstitch.

Pressing. Press carefully to avoid stretching the fabric. Use the regular steam setting on the iron. Place the iron lightly over the section to be pressed and allow the steam to enter; lift the iron and move to another section. Do not glide the iron in the direction of the stretch grain. To avoid the imprint of the seam edge on the fabric, slip a strip of brown paper under the seam allowance.

Lining. Select a stretch fabric for the lining, if you are using one; otherwise you will lose the "stretch" advantage of your garment.

In bonded fabrics (see description on page 12), the face fabric and lining are bonded together. This means that you can make a garment in less time than with other fabrics because only a single cutting and sewing operation is required.

Preparing to Sew

Pattern. Bonded fabrics are appropriate for dresses, suits, and coats with tailored lines. Avoid circular skirts and softly draped styles. Top stitching is a smart way to accentuate the lines of the garment.

Cutting. A fabric that has an "up" and "down" to the design should be treated the same way as any floral fabric. If the face fabric is knit, treat the rib as the true lengthwise grain and follow the directions for knit fabric. When you are unable to straighten the fabric because of the bonded lining, square off the crosswise grain with a ruler and use only the lengthwise grain as a guide in cutting. See page 15. These fabrics are quite satisfactory because the bonded lining retains the shape of the fabric.

Always fold the fabric wrong sides together, and lay the pattern on the right side. Use plenty of fine pins.

Markings. Mark with tailor's tacks or chalk pencil.

Interfacing. Preshrunk muslin and batiste are preferred for tailored dresses. Hair canvas may be used for suits and coats.

Stitching and Handling

Basting. Pin or hand-baste all seams, darts, and the hem to ensure an even seam. Basting will also permit you to test the fit of the garment before stitching.

Needle and thread. Silk, mercerized, or synthetic thread may be used for the machine stitching. A size 14 needle is required. Regulate the tension to produce a balanced stitch.

Stitch length and pressure. Select a 12 stitch length. The fabric requires medium pressure.

Stitching. Guide and support the fabric in front and in back of the foot. Do not pull the fabric as it passes under the foot; merely place it under slight tension. This will allow give in the seam and prevent puckering. Where sleeve and bodice are cut-in-one, stitch underarm seams with a narrow, open zig-zag stitch to allow for greater ease in the seam.

To emphasize the seamline, make slotted seams or press seams open and top-stitch on each side ½ inch from the seamline. Stabilize seams at shoulders, neckline, and waistline with straight seam binding to prevent stretching. If set-in sleeves are chosen, stabilize the armhole seams also; pre-shape the binding by steam pressing and pin it over the seamline. After setting the sleeve into the armhole, finish the seam allowance with zig-zag stitching as described on page 323. Corners should be blunt. Either round the corners slightly, or take two or three stitches across the point to allow sufficient width for turning.

Darts. Slash through the center of darts and press them open to eliminate bulk.

Seam blending. Blend seams inside collars, facings, and similar construction, in the usual way to eliminate bulk.

Seam finishes. Seam edges require no finish since the cut edges will not ravel.

Finishing the edges. Tailored binding or braid is a fashionable finish for the neckline, sleeves, and all outside edges of dresses, jackets, and coats.

Waistline joining. Follow the procedure for knit fabrics, page 218.

Buttonholes. You may use machine-worked or bound buttonholes. Always use an underlay such as batiste or muslin to reinforce the stitching around the buttonholes.

Hemming. Finish the free edge of the hem with pinking, then stitch close to the edge, using a 20 stitch length. Make a French hem—that is, a catch stitch below the hem edge and between the hem and garment.

Pressing. Use the regular steam setting on the iron. Cover the fabric with a lightweight press cloth, and press from the wrong side. For extra moisture on seams, use a moist cheesecloth over the press cloth. Faced edges may be tapped gently with a wooden pounding block to flatten them. Press the hem lightly so that the fold will not be sharply creased.

Laminates are relatively easy for the home sewer to handle. For a description of them, see page 12.

Preparing to Sew

Pattern. Choose a simple, bulkless style with a minimum of darts and seam details. Styles with center front and back seams or openings are preferred. Adjust the pattern to your individual requirements. Cut off the pattern margin on the cutting line before placing the pattern on the fabric.

Cutting. Lay the pattern pieces on the right side of the fabric so that the fabric grain line is always visible. For accuracy in cutting, cut only a single layer of fabric at a time. When the fabric is folded with wrong sides together, the foam sticks together. (A lightweight fabric, however, can be cut double.) Place pins parallel to the seamline. Follow the same cutting procedure used for regular fabrics. Large, bent-handle cutting shears give a cleaner edge to seams than smaller scissors. Cut all notches outward.

Markings. Use tailor's tacks only.

Interfacing. Laminated fabrics do not require interfacing.

Stitching and Handling

Basting. Seams, darts, and hems should be hand-basted to prevent the fabric from slipping during machine stitching. Basting also allows you to test the fit of the garment before stitching.

Thread and needle. You may use silk or mercerized thread for machine stitching. Dacron, Nymo, and Nylex threads are also satisfactory and stronger than mercerized thread. Usually, a size 14 machine needle produces the best results. Regulate the tension to produce a balanced stitch.

Stitch length and pressure. Select 10 to 12 stitch length. The pressure on the fabric should be medium.

Stitching. Before machine stitching, baste straight seam binding or a strip of crisp lawn about ⅝ inch wide over the foam sides so that both the presser foot and feed dog are in contact with the lawn or seam binding and not with the foam.

This prevents the foam from sticking to the presser foot and feed and produces a smooth seam. After the stitching is completed, trim lawn to ¼ inch to eliminate bulk yet strengthen the seam.

Corners must be blunt, not pointed. Either round corners slightly, or place two or three stitches across the point to allow sufficient width at the point for a smooth turning.

Darts. Slash through the center of darts, and press them open to eliminate bulk.

Seams. Press the seam open. Top-stitch on each side of, and about ¼ inch from, the seamline. Trim the seam allowance on the underside to ¼ inch. This will produce a neat, tailored finish as well as strengthen the seam. A welt seam is also appropriate. See pages 335 and 88.

If the fabric is heavy, stitch the top collar and facing to the undercollar and garment with the foam sides together. Trim the seam allowance to ½ inch, and bind the edges with a bias strip or braid. See *Tailored Binding*, page 334.

Seam blending. Blend seams inside collars, cuffs, facings, and similar construction in the usual way to eliminate bulk.

Buttonholes. Always stay buttonholes with a backing of a firmly woven muslin or lawn. Machine-worked or bound buttonholes are suitable.

Hems. You may sew the hem in place by machine or by hand. Fold and baste the hem in the conventional manner. Place several parallel rows of top stitching in the hemline, spacing them about ¼ inch apart.

If a hand finish is desirable, finish the hem edge by stitching seam binding over the cut edge. Then finish by hand, using a blind hemming stitch. Make the stitches through the entire fabric, catching only one thread on the right side of the fabric. Stitches made through foam alone will not hold.

Pressing. Laminates require little pressing. Finger pressing is effective. Light steam pressing, with a press cloth between the fabric and iron, helps to sharpen seams.

Lining. Garments made of laminated fabrics should be lined to protect the foam backing. Follow the method used in lining a jacket or coat.

WASH-AND-WEAR FABRICS

The term "wash-and-wear" as used here means any fabric that is washable and requires little or no ironing after washing. It can be of cotton, nylon, Dacron, Orlon, Acrilan, Arnel, and other fibers, or a blend of synthetic and natural fibers.

When selecting a wash-and-wear fabric, bear this in mind: The fabric must be finished *straight of grain*—that is, the crosswise threads must be at right angles with the lengthwise threads (or selvage edge). If they are not, it means that the fabric has been finished off grain and cannot be straightened; therefore, they must be squared off with a ruler and cut with only the lengthwise grain as a guide. See page 15. Obviously, this fabric fault impairs the quality of the garment.

Preparing to Sew

Pattern. A wide variety of styles are appropriate for wash-and-wear fabrics. Avoid those with seam details; select a design that calls for single seam construction rather than multiple thickness.

Cutting. If the manufacturer folded the fabric through the center, press out the crease before cutting. If the crease cannot be pressed out, arrange the pattern pieces to avoid the crease so that it does not appear in the finished garment. Pin the pattern to the fabric with fine, sharp-pointed pins. (Blunt pins may mar some fabrics permanently.) Cut with sharp scissors.

Markings. Use either tailor's tacks or a tracing wheel and dressmaker's tracing paper. Do not use a wax chalk since the marking cannot be removed from wash-and-wear fabrics.

Interfacing. Always select fabric of the wash-and-wear type or of nylon taffeta or marquisette.

Stitching and Handling

Thread and needle. On cotton fabrics having a wash-and-wear finish, mercerized thread is most acceptable. Wash-and-wear blends of natural and synthetic fibers may be stitched with mercerized, Nylex, Nymo, or Dacron thread, depending on the fiber make-up of the blend. (Check the fabric label for fiber content.) The size of the needle is determined by the thread: size 14 for mercerized thread; size 11 for Nylex, Nymo, and Dacron.

Stitch length and pressure. As a rule a 12 stitch length is preferred. Pressure should be heavy enough to carry the fabric without showing the print of the feed.

Stitching. Since many wash-and-wear fabrics are blends of two or more fibers, it is wise to test your stitching on a swatch of your fabric. If the seams pucker after being stitched with one of the synthetic threads, you must adjust the tension. Begin by changing the upper tension to a lower number; then if the stitch is not locked in the center of the fabric, it may be necessary to loosen the lower tension slightly. (A dense or tightly woven fabric usually requires a heavier upper tension.)

Stitch slowly. Check seams immediately after stitching and then a few hours later. Synthetic threads have a "recovery" factor. Although the seam may appear to be smooth and without pucker immediately following stitching, a few hours later the thread may recover its set dimension and cause a pucker. Seams that are smooth after stitching and before pressing will remain smooth through many washings. This is the secret of sewing wash-and-wear.

VELVET, VELVETEEN, AND CORDUROY

Velveteen is fashionable for daytime, sports, and formal wear; velvet is used primarily for formal wear. Corduroy, which is generally less expensive than the other two, is practical for sportswear and children's clothes. These pile fabrics are also used in robes, bedspreads, curtains, and slipcovers.

Pile fabrics have an "up" and "down." To determine the direction of the pile, follow the instructions on page 55.

Preparing to Sew

Pattern. Many pattern designs are appropriate for velvet, velveteen, and corduroy. The most effective, however, are those with simple lines that show off the rich tone of the fabric. Avoid too many styling seams within the garment. Unpressed pleats are suitable. Always cut off the pattern margin on the cutting line before placing the pattern on the fabric.

Fitting. It is important to fit and adjust the pattern exactly to your requirements before you cut pile fabrics. Any alterations after cutting affect the pile and are noticeable. If your pattern design is intricate, cut, stitch, and fit a muslin shell on which you can make all corrective adjustments before cutting the fabric.

Cutting. Lay the fabric on a smooth, flat surface with the pile side (right side) up. For sections where you must lay the pattern on a fold, be sure to fold the fabric lengthwise with the pile side on the outside. You must lay all pattern pieces in one direction with the pile running up. To avoid marring the pile, pin the pattern to the fabric with long, fine needles instead of pins.

Markings. Make tailor's tacks only, with silk thread.

Interfacing. Use preshrunk muslin, batiste, or a similar fabric for interfacing; silk organza is excellent for a soft velvet. Interface suits and coats with a fine grade of hair canvas, following *Method 1*, on page 136.

Underlining and lining. You may underline or line the entire garment or just a portion of it. Cut the underlining or lining by the same pattern pieces and on the same grain as the garment. Select such fabrics as silk crepe or China silk and match the fabric exactly in color.

Stitching and Handling

Basting. Always baste with silk thread. Fit the garment and make all necessary adjustments before machine stitching. Avoid temporary machine stitching that must later be removed; it will mar the pile.

Thread and needle. Stitch velvet with silk thread and velveteen and corduroy with silk or mercerized thread. Use mercerized thread on washable velveteen and corduroy that are made into children's clothes. Most pile fabrics require size 14 needle; however, a size 11 is frequently used to stitch velvet. When stitching with silk thread, decrease the needle thread tension one or two points, or until the stitching looks the same on the top and underside.

Stitch length and pressure. A 12 stitch length is correct. The pressure exerted by the presser foot should be somewhat lighter for pile than for a flat woven fabric of the same thickness—just heavy enough to carry the fabric without showing the print of the feed.

Stitching. The rule is to stitch with the pile. Since the pile runs up, this means that seams are stitched from the bottom to the top. A plain seam, pressed open, is preferred.

Seam finishes. Several methods of finishing the seam edges are appropriate. They are: pinking; binding with nylon net; overcasting by hand; or overedging by machine, using the blindstitch zig-zag. Do not allow edges of the fabric to pucker.

Darts. Slash through the center of darts and press them open to eliminate bulk.

Underlining and lining. A pencil-slim skirt should be completely lined to retain its shape. Page 95 describes how to use underlining and lining. Use the method where underlining and skirt are joined only at the waistline.

To eliminate bulk in velvet, velveteen, and corduroy, omit the facing at the neckline and at the lower edge of short sleeves and let the lining serve in its place.

Line the bodice from the neckline to about two inches below the armhole. First stitch and press the shoulder seams separately in the velveteen and lining. Place velveteen and underlining sections right sides together. Pin, baste, and stitch around the neckline, following the seamline. Blend the seams and press. Turn the underlining to the underside and ease it under slightly at the seamline; baste flat against the velveteen. Press. Handle as one fabric in the balance of construction.

To line short sleeves, stitch underarm seams separately in the velveteen and lining; then, at the lower edge of the sleeve, stitch the velveteen to the lining, right sides together. Blend seams and press. Turn the sleeve to the right side, with the lining on the underside. Ease the lining under slightly at the seamline; baste and press. Baste the two fabrics together at the sleeve cap and handle as one in the balance of construction.

Zipper closing. Hand-sew the final step of the zipper to give your dress the couturier touch. Follow the conventional method of inserting the zipper up to the final step. Then, finish by hand, using a short backstitch. See page 178.

Hems. The free edge of the hem may be finished with silk seam binding or bound with nylon net. Always hand-stitch the hem with silk thread. Place the stitches between the hem and garment and not over the hem edge. On a circular skirt, where a narrow hem is essential, use a hand-rolled hem.

Pressing. Follow the instructions given on page 66.

LACE FABRICS

Lace fabrics may be made of cotton, rayon, wool, linen, silk, or other fibers. They may be expensive or inexpensive, depending on what fibers they contain and whether they are made by hand or by machine.

Fashion dictates the uses of lace. It may advocate lace fabrics for wedding, late afternoon, and evening dresses; for daytime dresses, blouses, stoles, jackets, and evening coats; for tailored garments and beach coats. The lace must, of course, be appropriate for the occasion. Silk laces are used primarily for formal wear; most of the other lace fabrics may be used for other occasions as well as for formal wear.

Preparing to Sew

Pattern. To emphasize the design of the lace, choose simple style lines. The pattern should have a minimum of darts and seam details; too many break the continuity of the design of the lace. Styles with bodice and sleeve cut-in-one are excellent. Avoid neckline and sleeve facings unless you plan to underline the lace with an opaque fabric; cut the facings of matching fine net or tulle to eliminate bulk. Do not use styles requiring faced front and back openings unless the facing and bodice are cut-in-one, which will eliminate the seam. Avoid shoulder pads or shapes, even when in fashion, if you are using a sheer underlining.

Cutting. The design of the lace must be matched. Some laces have an "up" and "down" to the design and must be cut with all pattern pieces laid in the same direction. See the directions for *Florals, Prints and Jacquards,* page 55. Always fold the lace wrong sides together. Use sharp pins. (Some sewers prefer needles to avoid snagging or marring the lace.) As a further precaution, pin within the seam allowances and gathered areas. Cut all notches outward so that they will not interfere with seam construction or final finishing. Shears should be sharp and not excessively large.

Markings. Use tailor's tacks only.

Underlining and lining. Underlining is necessary to support the delicate network of threads in lace fabrics. Lining, however, is sometimes used in full skirts if there is little openwork in the lace and the texture is firm. Select a smooth, firm fabric. Opaque fabrics such as taffeta, satin, peau de soie, polished cotton, or wool crepe will place the lace in the category of a heavy fabric. If you wish to maintain the sheerness of the lace, underline with

silk organza, fine net, marquisette, or chiffon, and make a special slip of opaque fabric to wear with the dress. In a dress-and-jacket ensemble, the dress may be underlined with an opaque fabric and the jacket with fine net or organza. Wool crepe is an appropriate underlining for wool lace.

Generally the underlining should match the lace exactly in color, although a subtle contrast may occasionally be used effectively—for example, off-white with white, écru with white, or a shade darker than the color.

Underlining and Lining beginning on page 95, describes the techniques you should follow.

Stitching and Handling

Basting. Use a size 8 or 9 hand sewing needle and baste all seams to prevent the lace from slipping during machine stitching. If there is a design to be matched at the seamline, slip-baste.

Thread and needle. Select silk thread for the machine stitching on silk, wool, or synthetic lace, and mercerized thread for cotton and linen. These threads require a size 14 needle; however, use a size 11 if you can do so without thread breakage. Stitching synthetic laces with synthetic thread will permit you to use a size 11 needle.

Stitch length and pressure. In stitching the fine openwork of lace, use a 15 stitch length and light pressure—no heavier than needed to carry the fabric evenly under the presser foot without marring the lace.

Stitching. Medium-weight laces require guiding only in front of the needle during machine stitching; soft and silk laces require a little more support. Gently control the fabric both in front and in back of the foot, taking care not to pull or stretch the lace.

Darts. Use darts only if your underlining is opaque; it will conceal the darts in the finished garment. If your underlining is sheer, change darts to soft gathers.

Seams and seam finishes. An opaque underlining will prevent the seam allowances from showing through the lace, so you may use a plain seam in your dress. Pink the seam edges and press the seam open. If you are using a sheer underlining, however, or are attaching the skirt and underlining at the waistline only, you must use a fine, narrow seam and conceal the seam edges. Use a French seam or, to eliminate bulk, a double-stitched seam.

Seam blending. Blend curved seams in the usual way to eliminate bulk.

Finishing the edges. A fine double-fold bias binding makes a pleasing finish for the neckline, sleeves, and front or back opening. Use it rather than shaped facings. Satin, taffeta, and organza, matching the lace exactly in color, are all excellent fabrics for the binding.

Zipper closing. Insert the zipper by hand to give the couturier touch. Buy a fine zipper and follow the conventional method of applying it up to the final step. Then, instead of top stitching, hand-sew, using a short backstitch. To vary from the conventional zipper application, use the slot seam method. Center the zipper under the machine-basted seam; hand-sew ¼ inch from the center seam.

Fastenings. Do not make buttonholes in lace; thread loops are better suited to the fabric. Choose small buttons; large buttons are inappropriate and too heavy for lace.

Hems. If the lace has a border or scalloped edge, use that as the finish. In circular skirts, where a lining is used, hem the two fabrics separately. A narrow hem is essential; either make a hand-rolled hem or use horsehair braid. If the lace is underlined with an opaque fabric, form a hem of average width. Finish the free edge with a multiple-stitch zig-zag, or pink it and stitch ¼ inch from the edge, using a 20 stitch length. Then make a French hem by catch-stitching below the hem edge and between the hem and the garment.

Pressing. Use the regular steam setting on the iron. Place a wool-faced pressing pad on the ironing board with the wool-facing side up. Lay the lace, right side down, on the pad. (A turkish towel may be substituted for a pressing pad.) Cover the lace with a thin press cloth; if additional moisture is required for seams, place a moist cheesecloth over the thin press cloth before pressing. If you follow these suggestions, you will not flatten the raised design of the lace during the pressing.

SOFT LEATHER AND SUEDE

Acquaint yourself with the approximate size and shape of the skins you contemplate using. Remember that many skins have thin areas and you must avoid placing them in garment sections subject to strain. Unless you are experienced in selecting and handling skins, limit your sewing to small apparel items and trims. It takes a knowing eye and sound judgment to select skins of the correct weight and regularity for large garments.

Preparing to Sew

Pattern. Select a design with seams that will accommodate the size and dimension limitations of your skins. Other seaming, unless it contributes to styling, is not attractive.

Fitting. You must do all fitting *before* you cut the suede or leather. Adjust the pattern; cut, stitch, and fit a muslin shell; then make all corrective fitting adjustments *in the shell.* Trim all seam allowances to ⅜ inch for economy in cutting the leather *unless* you plan to place top stitching more than ¼ inch from the edge, or to use a welt seam. The narrow seam allowance will also eliminate bulk in the finished garment.

Cutting. Lay the muslin pattern pieces on the wrong side of a *single layer* of suede or leather. Do not fold the skins or cut two pieces at one time. Be sure to turn the pattern pieces over to cut the second half so that you will have a right and left side. Since leather has no grain, the pattern pieces may be laid either lengthwise or crosswise on the skins, depending on which direction gives you the most even distribution of thickness. Note, however, that *all pieces must be laid in the same direction.* Since suede has an up and down, you must lay all pattern pieces lengthwise on the skins and in one direction with the nap running down. To determine the direction of the nap, brush the suede with your fingers as you would velvet and napped fabrics. See pages 55 and 56. Do not pin into the body of the garment since punctures will permanently mar the leather. Either pin within the seam allowance or use cellophane tape to hold the muslin pattern in position. Use sharp scissors. Cut all notches outward or mark them with chalk on the underside of the leather.

Markings. Mark darts, buttonholes, center lines, and styling points with chalk on the wrong side of the skin. Do not use a tracing wheel; it will mar the leather. To transfer markings, turn back a portion of the pattern and fold along the line of the dart, buttonhole, or other marking; chalk-mark the skin along the line of the fold. Use a ruler to keep lines straight. Reinforce thin spots with "press-on" mending tape on the wrong side of the skin.

Underlining and lining. Suede and leather garments should be lined. Synthetic linings such as SiBonne, UnderCurrent, Veriform, rayon taffeta, and acetate sheath lining are appropriate.

Interfacing. Interface collars, cuffs, and front facing areas with hair canvas or a nonwoven interfacing. Follow directions given for *Method 1* on page 136. For additional shape retention, extend the front section of the interfacing to the armhole.

Stitching and Handling

Basting. Although seams may be pinned or basted, be careful to make the pin or needle punctures within the seam allowance. Paper clips are a safe substitute. Or, you may find that you can handle the seaming without pinning or basting, depending on your sewing skill.

Thread and needle. Use either silk or heavy-duty mercerized thread for machine stitching. Select size 14 machine needle for medium-weight skins, size 11 needle for fine leather and thread, and size 16 for heavier leather and thread. A wedge-point needle, designed expressly for stitching leather, is available at your Singer Center in the sizes mentioned. The narrow wedge point pierces the leather cleanly, ensuring a neat, uniform stitch.

Regulate the tension to produce a balanced stitch. In most cases the upper tension should be slightly higher for leather than for medium-weight woven fabrics.

Stitch length and pressure. Regulate the stitch length to 12 for lightweight and medium-weight leathers, and to 10 for heavier weights. The pressure should fall within the medium range and carry the leather without showing the print of the feed.

Stitching. Preshrink straight seam binding and use it for staying seams and points of strain. Hold the tape gently against the upper side of the leather and against the presser foot as you sew the seam. The tape will strengthen the seam and prevent the leather from sticking to the presser foot. Stitch slowly and handle the leather lightly. Do not pull the leather as it passes under the presser foot, for this may stretch it. After the seams are stitched, slash the edges of the tape at even intervals to prevent them from pulling. Be sure your garment

fits correctly before you begin stitching because ripped seams have needle holes that will permanently mar the skins.

Corners must be blunt, not pointed. Either round the corners slightly or place two or three stitches across the point to allow sufficient width for turning.

Seams and seam blending. To enhance center front and back seams and yoke seams, use welt seams, or press the seam open and top-stitch on each side an equal distance from the seamline.

Blend seams inside collars, cuffs, facings, and similar construction in the usual way. To prevent facings and seams from rolling out of place, glue the seam allowances in place. Use rubber cement, "Sobo" glue, or a similar liquid adhesive suitable for leather, fabric, or a combination of two materials. Spread the glue on the underside of the seam allowance; then finger-press the seam allowance against the garment.

Darts. Slash through the center of darts, and press them open to eliminate bulk.

Lining. Line the skirt, following the method given on page 98 where lining and skirt are joined only at the waistline.

Avoid facings and hems in a waistcoat or vest. The lining can serve as facing as well as support the suede. See *One-Piece Neckline and Armhole Facing*, page 141. Before joining shoulder and underarm seams, place the suede and lining sections right sides together. Stitch around the neckline, front opening, lower edge, and armholes following the seamline. Blend seams, turn to right side, ease underlining under slightly at the stitching line, and press. Join shoulder and underarm seams of suede with machine stitching, and press seams open. Then, on the lining, fold under the seam allowance on one side and lap it over the opposite seam allowance, and pin. Slip-stitch in place. Top-stitch around the neckline, front opening, lower edge, and armholes, gauging the stitching from ¼ to ⅝ inch from the finished edge.

Buttonholes. Machine-worked, hand-worked, or bound buttonholes are suitable. Stay them with a backing of firmly woven muslin or lawn between the facing and top fabric.

If you are making bound buttonholes, follow the *One-Piece Method.* See page 112. Instead of basting the buttonhole strip in place, place cellophane tape across the ends, and use a 12 stitch length in the stitching.

The facing treatment is different from the method used for woven fabrics. Stitch the facing in place in the usual way. Then, from the right side of the garment, machine-stitch around the buttonhole just inside the seam on the buttonhole strip and across the ends through the facing. Slash the facing and trim away the suede or leather inside the stitching line.

Hems. The depth of the hem should be no greater than 1½ or 2 inches, and the hem must conform exactly to the body of the skirt. Use chalk to mark the hemline on the wrong side of the leather. For an invisible finish, glue the hem in place. See *Seams and Seam Blending* above. Lay the skirt right side down on a flat surface and work from the hem side. Spread glue along the underside of the hem as far as the fold line. Turn the hem; then finger-press it against the skirt. Begin at the center front or back and work toward the side seams, matching seams and center lines.

Pressing. Seams in leather and suede should be pressed with a warm, not hot, iron (do not use steam). Cover the area with brown paper, and press on the wrong side. Seams may also be tapped lightly with a wooden pounding block to compress them.

Lining. Suede and leather jackets must be lined. Crepe, faille, and China silk are suggested fabrics.

FIBERGLASS

Fiberglass is a synthetic fabric that is ideal for curtains, draperies, and bedspreads. It is available in a variety of weaves, either translucent or opaque. It will not shrink, stretch, or sag, and needs no ironing. There is no problem in stitching it when a few simple rules are followed.

Instructions for constructing home furnishings begin on page 338 of this book.

Preparing to Sew

Cutting. To cut a plain fabric, always draw a thread from the fabric to indicate the cutting line. Cut printed designs on the patterns. If the fabric is cut off grain, curtains and draperies will not hang well.

Lining. Fiberglass draperies are seldom lined. The translucent beauty of the unlined fabric is preferred by many decorators. If a lining is used, however, it should also be of fiberglass so that it will not shrink, stretch, or sag. When extra opaqueness is desired, make an underdrapery instead of a lining, and hang it from a separate rod so that it can be opened and closed independently.

Be sure to use washable, preshrunk stiffening in the heading.

Stitching and Handling

Thread and needle. Select mercerized, Dacron, Nymo, or Nylex thread for the machine stitching. Use a new, sharp machine needle, size 11 for translucent fiberglass and size 14 for heavy or rough-surfaced fiberglass.

Regulate tensions to produce a balanced stitch.

If the seam puckers, it may be necessary to loosen the upper tension.

Stitch length and pressure. A 10 to 12 stitch length is satisfactory for sheer as well as opaque fiberglass. The pressure must be light—no heavier than required to carry the fabric gently and evenly under the presser foot. If the pressure is too heavy, the print of the feed shows on the fabric and the feed may cut the threads of the fiberglass.

Stitching. Pin the seam edges together. Stitch slowly and guide the fabric gently behind the presser foot and in front of the needle. Let the machine do the work. When using a straight stitch on a zig-zag machine, use the straight stitch throat plate and presser foot for best results.

To prevent the edges from raveling and to achieve a finished underside, make French seams on all fiberglass fabrics.

It is wise to experiment with stitch length, tension, and pressure, and with guiding the fabric on a swatch of fiberglass before you begin your work. You will find that with a little practice you can handle the fabric expertly.

Seam finishes. Seam edges in glass curtains and draperies should be enclosed and do not require finishing. Finish the seam edges of bedspreads with the blindstitch zig-zag.

Hems. Make a double-fold hem in sheer fabrics to eliminate the turned raw edge that would normally show through. Pin hems in place before stitching. Stitch hems in sheer fabrics with a straight stitch and hems in heavier and rough-surfaced fabrics with either a straight stitch or the blindstitch zig-zag.

Hand Sewing—
Plain and Fancy

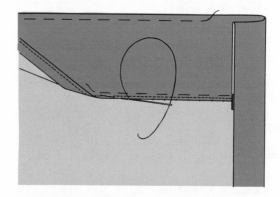

HAND SEWING IS STILL AN ESSENTIAL PART of dressmaking. In professional, well-made wearing apparel, hems are finished by hand. In children's clothes and table linens, decorative fashion details are added by hand to provide an attractive accent. To achieve the custom-made look in home decoration, hand sewing is preferred in many areas.

This chapter tells you how to make many of the basic hand stitches. If any of them are unfamiliar to you, practice making them on a swatch of fabric before you attempt to use them in your work. All the decorative or embroidery stitches described here may be used individually or in various combinations to produce a design; they may be worked in matching or contrasting thread, or in two or more colors of thread.

A Word about Thread

Hems should be finished with mercerized, silk, or synthetic thread, depending on the fabric; the thread should match the fabric exactly in color.

Hand embroidery stitches may be made with single or multiple strands of sewing thread, six-strand floss, synthetic or silk floss, pearl cotton, buttonhole twist, and wool or synthetic yarn. The selection depends on the fabric, the size of the stitch, and the effect desired. Choose colorfast threads to trim children's clothes and household linens that will be laundered.

Slip Stitch

The slip stitch is almost invisible. It is used when one edge is turned under as in hems, bias binding, curved seams, top facings, coat or suit linings, and similar places.

Baste the folded edge in position. For stitching, use mercerized, silk, or synthetic thread matching the fabric exactly in color. Knot the long end of the thread.

Work toward you, or from right to left, with the hem fold between the thumb and index finger of the left hand. Bring the needle up through the fold. Directly opposite and barely outside the fold, take a stitch, catching only one thread of the fabric; then slip the needle through the fold a stitch length. Continue making the stitches, spacing them from ¼ to ⅜ inch apart. In seams that may be subject to excessive strain, space the stitches a scant ⅛ inch apart. Do not pull the threads taut. When completed, fasten the thread with two tiny backstitches in the hem edge or seam.

Blind Hemming Stitch

This is the stitch most frequently used for hemming. The edge may be finished with seam binding or edgestitching.

Baste the hem in place. For stitching, use mercerized, silk, or synthetic thread matching the fabric exactly in color. Knot the long end of the thread.

Work toward you, or from right to left, with the hem fold between the thumb and index finger of the left hand. Bring the needle up through the hem edge. Directly opposite and barely outside the hem, take a stitch, catching only one thread

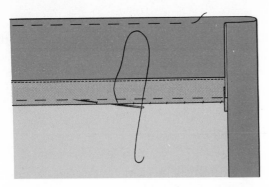

of the fabric; then direct the needle diagonally up through the hem edge. Continue making the stitches, spacing them from ¼ to ⅜ inch apart, depending on the fabric. Do not pull the thread taut. When completed, fasten the thread with two tiny backstitches in the hem edge. The stitches are invisible on the right side.

Hemming or Whipping Stitch

The hemming or whipping stitch is another popular stitch for hemming. The edge may be finished with bias seam binding, edgestitching, or straight seam binding.

Baste the hem in place. For stitching, use mercerized, silk, or synthetic thread matching the fabric exactly in color. Knot the long end of the thread.

Work toward you, or from right to left, with the hem edge between the thumb and index finger of the left hand. Bring the needle up through the edge of the hem and take a stitch in the fabric over the hem edge, catching only a single thread of the fabric; then bring the needle out through

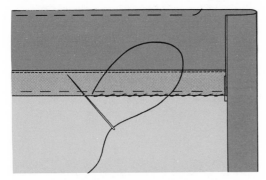

the hem edge. When completed, fasten the thread with two tiny backstitches in the hem edge. The stitch is invisible on the right side and long slanting stitches are visible on the wrong side.

Overhand Stitch

The overhand stitch is a tiny stitch used to join lace, insertion, and grosgrain ribbon.

For stitching, use a short, fine needle and fine

thread. Knot the long end of the thread.

Place the lace or ribbon right sides together. Pin or baste the edges to prevent them from slipping. Make small over-and-over stitches along the edge of the seam. Space the stitches about 1/16 inch apart.

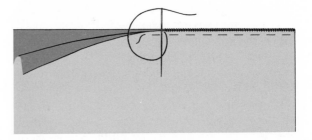

Catch Stitch

The catch stitch is used in hemming, in seaming lapped joinings on the underside, in attaching interfacings to garments, and in hand-sewing darts and tucks in suit and coat linings.

Baste the hem, facing, tuck, dart, or edge in place. For stitching, use mercerized, silk, or synthetic thread. Knot the long end of the thread.

Work from left to right, with the needle pointed to the left. Hold the hem edge between the thumb and index finger of the left hand. Make a stitch in the hem or facing, catching one or two threads in the top layer of fabric; then make a stitch barely outside the hem edge, catching only a single thread of the under layer of fabric. Alternate the stitches along the edge in a zig-zag fashion. The threads will cross between the stitches. When finished, fasten the thread with tiny backstitches in the hem.

When using a catch stitch to sew darts and tucks in coat and suit linings, work on the right side of the fabric and make the stitches through all thicknesses of fabric, near the top fold for the tuck or dart.

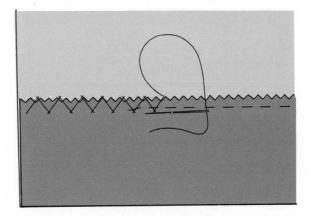

Backstitch

The backstitch is a small stitch that is used when top stitching by machine would be too harsh—for example, in the final stitching of the zipper in sheer, delicate fabrics or fine woolens. It is also used in other areas of dress construction where machine stitching would be difficult (for example, in lapped seams in interfacings) and in the repairing of ripped seams.

For stitching, use the same kind of thread you used for the machine stitching. Fasten the thread with two backstitches on the underside. Work toward you, or from right to left. Bring the needle up through the fabric to the right side. Insert it one or two fabric threads behind the place where the thread came out, and bring the needle forward and out a scant ⅛ inch from the backstitch. Begin each additional stitch just outside the preceding stitch. (The stitches on the underside will be twice as long as those on the top side.) Make the stitches through all layers of fabric. When completed, fasten the thread on the underside with two tiny backstitches.

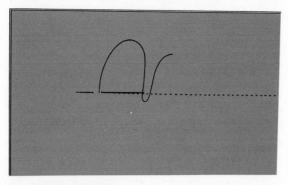

Running Stitch

The running stitch is used for seaming, tucking, mending, gathering, and other kinds of delicate sewing.

For stitching, use a long, slender needle, size 7 or 8, and mercerized, synthetic, or silk thread matching the fabric exactly in color. Knot the long end of the thread.

Work from right to left, with the fabric edge between the thumb and index finger of the left

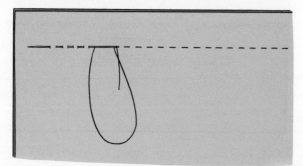

hand. Weave the point of the needle in and out of the fabric five or six times before pulling the thread through. Make small, even stitches. When finished, fasten the thread with one or two tiny backstitches.

Handpicked Stitch

Handpicked stitching adds a smart touch to collars, cuffs, lapels, pockets, and fashion seams of coats, suits, and tailored dresses. The garment should be completed before you add this fashion detail.

On the right side, baste the line for the stitches ⅜ to 1 inch from the finished edge, depending on the fabric, the design of the garment, and personal preference. Use a gauge to measure the distance as you baste.

For stitching, use buttonhole twist matching the fabric exactly in color. Knot the long end of the thread.

Work toward you with the needle pointed in the same direction. Bring the needle up through the interfacing and top layer of fabric. Insert it 1/16 inch behind the place where the thread came out, through the top layer of fabric and interfacing; then bring it out a generous ⅜ inch from the backstitch. (With this spacing, the finished stitches should be about ¼ inch apart.) Do not draw the threads taut; the backstitch should lie beadlike on the fabric surface. Remove the bastings as you work. When completed, fasten the thread between the layers of fabric with two tiny backstitches. The stitches are not visible on the underside.

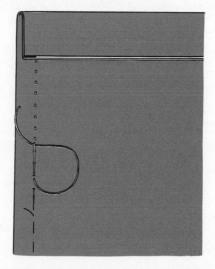

If your costume has lapels, you must transfer the stitches to the opposite side of the seam at the

turn of the lapel. At this point, and on the back-stitch, bring the needle through all layers of fabric to the opposite side of the seamline and continue making the same stitches.

Padding Stitch

The padding stitch is used primarily in tailoring to hold two layers of fabric together to prevent slipping—for example, to hold the interfacing in place along the roll line of lapels and collars.

Baste the interfacing in place. Work toward you and on the wrong side, with the needle pointed to the left. For stitching, use thread matching the fabric exactly in color. Hold the work between the thumb and fingers of the left hand and take a short stitch from right to left through the interfacing

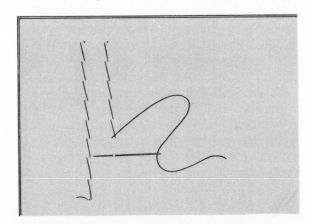

and fabric, catching only one thread in the fabric. Space the stitches about ⅜ inch apart. The long slanting stitches on the wrong side are visible but the short crosswise stitches on the right side are not.

Buttonhole Stitch

The buttonhole stitch is used for a decorative finish on edges as well as for hand-worked buttonholes. As a decorative finish, the stitches may be almost any depth; in buttonholes, however, they should be from 1/16 inch to 1/8 inch in depth and closely spaced.

For the stitching, see *A Word about Thread*, page 228. Work from right to left. Hold fabric, needle, and thread in the position shown in the illustration.

With the right side of the fabric up, bring the edge over the first finger of the left hand. Take two backstitches at the edge to fasten the thread. Bring the thread to the left and then to the right to form a loop around the edge where the stitch will be made. Insert the point of the needle from the underside up through the fabric, keeping thread behind both the point and the eye of the needle. Hold the loop with the left thumb and pull the needle up through the fabric, then away from you to place the purl of the stitch on the edge of the fabric. Keep the stitches as even as possible.

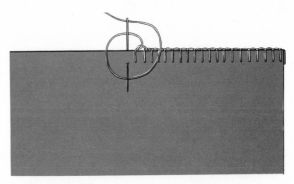

Blanket Stitch

The blanket stitch is often used to decorate children's clothes, lingerie, and household linens. It is an excellent edge finish for babies' receiving blankets, sacques, and kimonos. It is also used for hand appliqué.

Fold and baste the hem.

For stitching, select thread appropriate for the

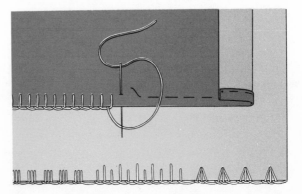

fabric. Take two backstitches on the underside in the hem fold to fasten the thread. Work from left to right, with the right side of the edge toward you. Hold the thread down with the thumb and insert the needle from the right side, barely catching the top edge of the hem; then bring it out from under the edge and over the thread. Draw the thread through by pulling it toward you, forming the blanket stitch. Do not pull the thread taut. When completed, fasten the thread on the underside with two tiny backstitches in the lower edge of the hem. The stitches may be evenly spaced, closely spaced in groups of three, or varied in length to form a pattern or a fan-shaped design.

Chain Stitch

The chain stitch is an outline stitch used in children's and babies' clothes as well as in linens and lingerie.

Knot the long end of the thread. Work from right to left. Bring the needle up through the fabric to the right side. Hold the thread against the fabric with the left thumb. Insert the needle close to the point where the thread came out and bring it out over the thread just a stitch length to form a loop. Keep the thread to the left of the needle. Begin each successive stitch inside the loop to form a chain. The length of the stitch will depend on the fabric. Do not pull the thread taut. When finished, fasten the thread on the underside with two tiny backstitches.

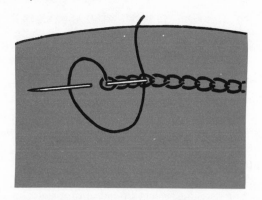

Cross-Stitch

The cross-stitch is one of the oldest decorative stitches. It may be used on household linens, blouses, children's clothes, and collar and cuff sets as well as on canvas in needle-tapestry work.

The cross-stitch is usually made over a stamped transfer design; however, if the design of the fabric is a small ¼-inch check, you may use it as a pattern. If you are working with hopsacking or a

similar coarse weave, you can make even cross-stitches by counting the fabric threads for each stitch.

Work from left to right with the needle pointed toward you. Bring the needle up through the fabric to the right side of the lower left corner of the cross, leaving a thread about ½ inch long; catch that thread under the stitches as they are made to fasten it. Carry the thread diagonally to the right, insert the needle in the upper right corner, and bring it out at the lower left corner of the next cross. A diagonal stitch will appear on the right side and a straight stitch on the underside. Continue making the same stitches across the work. Then work back over the stitches in the opposite direction to form the crosses. Be sure that the crosses touch. The stitches should be firm so that the threads lie smooth on the surface.

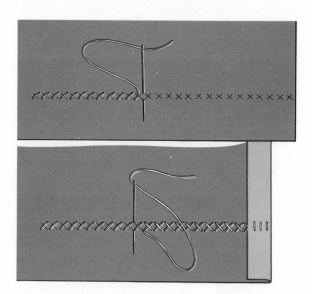

Featherstitch

The featherstitch, also known as the "brier" stitch, is appropriate for decorating household linens, children's and babies' clothes, and is used in stitching darts and tucks in suit and coat linings.

Baste or chalk the line of the stitch on the right side of the fabric. Work toward you and bring the needle up through the fabric to the right side where the stitch is to begin. Hold the thread down with the thumb and take a small stitch on the right side of the line, slanting the needle toward the line and passing the thread under the needle. Make the same kind of stitch on the left side of the line, slanting the needle toward the line. Continue alternating the stitches on the right and left, keeping the stitch length, spacing, and slant of the needle the same in each stitch. Draw the thread firmly enough to keep it flat, yet loosely enough to curve it slightly. When completed, fasten the thread on the underside with two tiny backstitches.

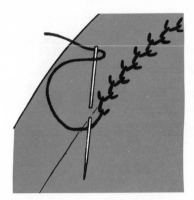

French Knot

The French knot is a familiar embroidery stitch in the center of flowers. Groups of knots are also used to form designs. They are generally placed close together and combined with other stitches.

Knot the long end of the thread. Bring the needle up through the fabric at the point where the knot is to be made. Hold the needle close to the fabric and wind the thread two or three times around the point. Hold the thread taut around the needle and insert the needle through the fabric close to the point where the thread came

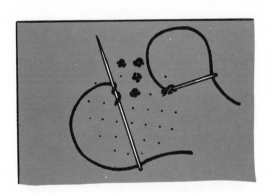

out. Place your thumb over the knot to hold the twist in place and pull the thread through to the underside, bringing the knot snugly against the fabric. Then bring the needle up through the fabric for the next French knot. When the work is finished, fasten the thread on the underside with two tiny backstitches.

Lazy Daisy

The lazy daisy is a loop stitch used to form a daisy petal.

For stitching, select a thread size that is appropriate for the size of the petal.

Bring the needle up through the fabric at the center end of the petal. Loop the thread to the left. Insert the needle close to the point where the thread came out, and then bring it out over the thread at the opposite end of the petal. Insert the needle barely outside the petal loop and bring it out again at the center where the next petal begins. Do not draw the thread taut. When the lazy daisy is finished, fasten the thread on the underside with two tiny backstitches. French knots placed in the center enhance the design.

Outline Stitch

The outline stitch may be used to form a border, to make flower stems and leaf veins, or to outline a design.

Lightly mark or transfer the design to the fabric. Knot the long end of the thread.

Work from left to right with the needle pointed to the left. Bring the needle up through the fabric

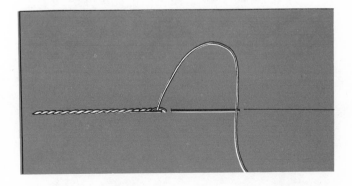

from the underside. Make small backstitches, lapping each stitch slightly by bringing the needle out about 1/16 inch behind the previous stitch. Hold the thread down with the thumb as you pull the threads through. Keep the thread above the needle; insert the needle and bring it out on the line of the design. When completed, fasten the thread on the underside with two backstitches.

Hand Hemstitching

Hemstitching is used in table linens, lingerie, and babies' clothes.

Measure the hem allowance and draw about three or four threads from the fabric parallel to the hem. The number of threads drawn will depend on the weave of the fabric and the width desired for the hemstitching. Fold the fabric edge under ¼ inch; then fold and baste the hem, keeping the folded edge barely below the drawn work.

For stitching, use a fine mercerized thread. Knot the long end of the thread. Work from right to left on the wrong side. Bring the needle up through the hem edge so that the knot will be between the hem and top fabric. Slide the needle under several threads of the fabric; loop the thread to the left under the point of the needle. Pull the thread through and draw up the stitch tightly by

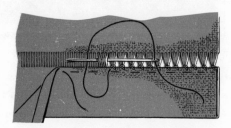

pulling the thread toward you. Then take a stitch in the edge of the hem fold, catching only a single thread of the fabric. Repeat the stitch until one edge is finished. Keep the same number of fabric threads in each group.

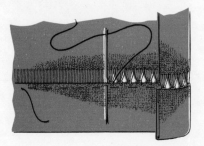

For double hemstitching, turn the work and make the same kinds of stitches on the opposite edge, picking up the same threads in the fabric to form a bar. Fasten the thread on the underside with two small fastening stitches.

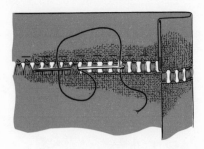

Fagoting

Fagoting is a decorative stitch used to join sections in blouses, dresses, lingerie, collars, and cuffs.

Fold under the seam allowance on the cut edges, and press. Hand-baste the folded edges to heavy paper for support. The distance between the edges is the width of the fagoting.

For stitching, use pearl cotton, buttonhole twist, or a similar thread. Knot the long end of the thread. Bring the needle up through the fabric fold. Carry the thread diagonally across the opening, and insert the needle up through the fabric fold on the opposite side; pull the thread through. Pass the needle under the thread, diagonally across the opening, and up through the fabric on the opposite side. Continue alternating the stitches across the opening. Evenly spaced stitches are essential. When finished, fasten the thread on the underside. Remove the basted paper, and press.

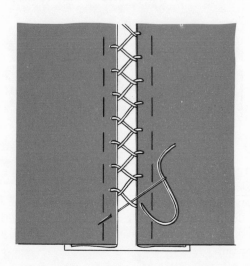

Decorative Touches

A DECORATIVE TOUCH THAT ADDS INTEREST and femininity to your costume marks you as a competent, creative seamstress. It transforms a simple dress into a special dress, a plain-looking blouse into a lovely one, and much more.

The many fashion "extras" you can apply in sewing are described in this chapter. They include tucks, ruffles, shirring, cording, appliqué, smocking, quilting, beads and sequins, lace edging and insertion, and braid. Some of them can be used in home decorating as well as in wearing apparel.

TUCKS

Tucks are always in fashion in dresses, blouses, neckwear, children's clothes, and lingerie. They are equally at home in sheer and heavy fabrics. They may be very narrow, as a dainty "pin tuck," or an inch or more wide. They may be machine-stitched or hand-stitched.

Since the beauty of a tuck depends on its absolute accuracy, you must stitch exactly along the woven thread of the fabric. The Tucker and Edge Stitcher are two accessories that will help you. The Tucker makes tucks from ⅛ to 1 inch in width and ensures tucks of equal width and spacing from start to finish; the Edge Stitcher guides the width for tucks from "pin" width to ¼ inch. See pages 286 and 284. Both are timesavers and contribute a great deal to the attractiveness of your work.

To Estimate Fabric Width Requirements

If the pattern calls for tucks, it will allow sufficient width for the size of the tuck specified. If you decide to add tucks to the dress as a point of interest, you will need extra fabric as follows:

When the tucks and spaces are equal, fabric twice the finished width is required. When the fold of the tuck touches the stitching of the previous tuck, as in a blind tuck, three times the finished width is required.

If an entire section such as a pocket, yoke, or collar, is to be pin-tucked, you should *tuck the fabric first and then cut out the section according to the pattern.*

To Mark the Position of Tucks

Tucks are usually made on the lengthwise grain of the fabric since it is always firmer than the crosswise grain and lends itself well to tucking. Occasionally, however, a design calls for crosswise tucking to emphasize style lines.

Draw a single thread from the fabric to mark the position for each tuck. Fold and press the fabric on the drawn thread the entire length of the tuck. If tucks are ¼ inch or wider, hand-baste along the line of each tuck to prevent the layers of fabric from shifting during the stitiching.

To Stitch Tucks

Rules to Remember

Always stitch tucks so that the stitching uppermost under the needle is visible when the garment is worn (unless you are applying lace in the tucking operation as on page 237). When tucks are used on both sides of the garment section, they are turned in opposite directions from the center, and you must alternate the direction of the stitching on the right and left sides.

Be sure that tensions are balanced. Since tucks are top stitched, they require a shorter stitch than that used for inside, straight seams. See the *Fabric, Thread, Needle, and Stitch Length Chart,* page 24. The thread should either blend perfectly with the fabric in color and texture or be a decided contrast.

Always make a few practice tucks in a swatch of your fabric to be certain that the stitch length, tuck size, and spacing are satisfactory.

Pin Tucks

Pin tucks, as their name implies, are only as wide as a pin. They are generally spaced about 3/16 inch apart in groups of three or five, with a wider space between each group. Lace is often inserted between the groups.

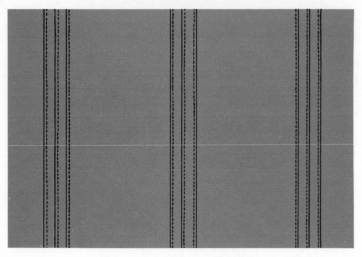

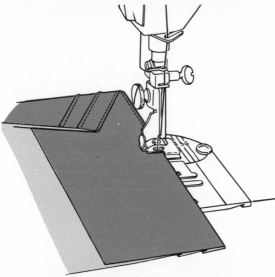

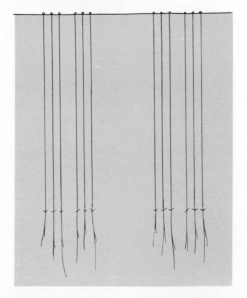

Mark the position for each tuck, following the instructions given above. Adjust the Edge Stitcher, see page 285, so that the stitching falls very close to the folded edge of the fabric. Stitch slowly, guiding the fabric. Press.

When the tucks extend only a few inches into the garment section, as in the yoke of a baby's dress or shoulder of a blouse or dress, pull the threads through to the underside and tie the two threads together at the end of each tuck.

Hand-Stitched Tucks

Hand-stitched tucks are found in babies' clothes and sheer blouses.

Mark the position for each tuck, following the instructions given on page 235. Hand-stitch, using a long, slender needle, fine thread, and a very small running stitch. When finished, fasten the thread on the underside of the fabric. Press.

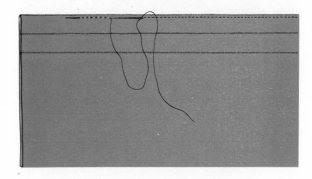

Tucks and Space of Equal Width

When spacing and tucks are equal, you will need twice the finished width in the fabric. The space between the markings for each tuck is four

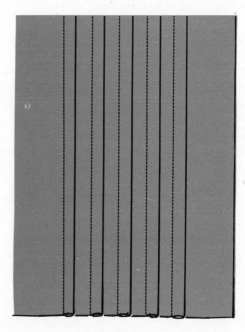

times the width of the finished tuck, or 1 inch for a ¼-inch tuck.

Mark the position for the tucks, following the instructions on page 235. Stitch, using either the *Edge Stitcher* or *Tucker*. See pages 285 and 286. Press.

Blind Tucks

In blind tucking, the fold for the tuck touches the stitching of the previous tuck. The tucks may be of almost any width; the 1-inch tuck is illustrated. The space between the markings for each tuck is three times the width of the finished tuck.

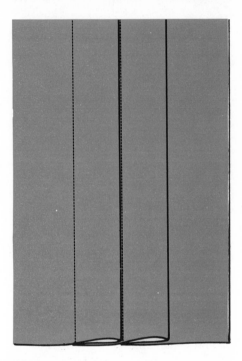

Mark the position for the first tuck, following the instructions given on page 235.

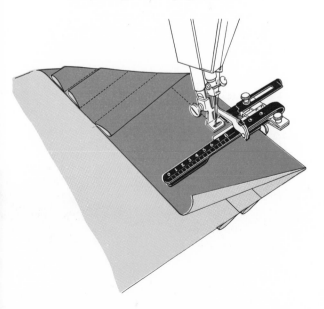

On most fabrics, the space scale on the Tucker will mark the position of the second and succeeding tucks as the present one is being stitched. If the fabric is one that the scale will not mark, you must mark the position for all the tucks before you begin to stitch. See *Tucker* page 286. Use the Tucker and adjust it for the desired width of tuck and spacing. Stitch slowly, guiding the fabric. Press.

Decorative Tucks

Decorative tucks are made by using the Tucker on a zig-zag machine.

Mark the position for the first tuck, following the instructions given on page 235. Adjust the Tucker for the desired width of the tuck and spacing. Select a stitch pattern appropriate for tucks and stitch slowly, guiding the fabric. Press.

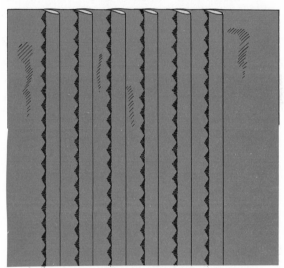

Tucks with Lace

You can make ¼-inch tucks and apply lace underneath with a single line of stitching when you use the Edge Stitcher. *(Continued)*

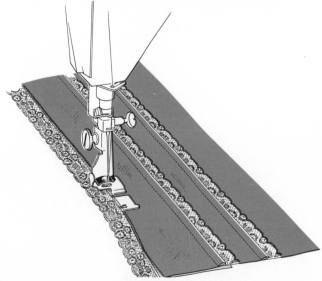

Select lace wide enough to extend beyond the tuck but not dwarf it. Mark the position for each tuck, following the instructions on page 235.

Use the Edge Stitcher with the lug adjusted far enough to the left to place the stitching on the selvage of the lace. Insert the folded edge from the right in slot 5, and the lace edge from the left in slot 1. Stitch slowly, guiding the fabric and the lace. Press the tuck over the lace.

Smocked Tucking

Smocked tucking, a variation of straight tucking, provides a texture contrast on the yoke or pockets of a dress or blouse made of plain fabric.

Tuck the fabric on the lengthwise grain, making ⅛- or ¼-inch tucks spaced ¼ inch apart, using the Edge Stitcher. See page 284.

For the crosswise stitching, use the Edge Stitcher. Adjust it so that each side is the same distance from the needle. Alternate the direction of each row of stitching, keeping the rows the same distance apart. The Edge Stitcher turns the tucks in the same direction of the stitching, creating a smocked effect.

When the stitching is completed, press. Cut the tucked section by the plain pattern piece.

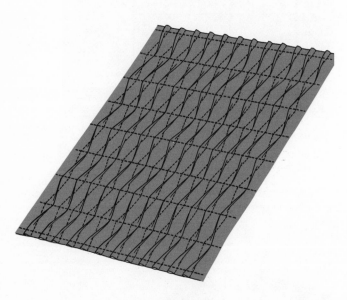

Shell Tucks

Shell tucks are an attractive treatment for babies' dresses and blouses. Usually ⅛ to ¼ inch in width, they can be stitched by hand or by machine. Use silk, batiste or a similar soft fabric.

Hand Stitched. Mark the position for the tucks as instructed on page 235. Machine-stitch the tucks, using a line of straight stitching and either the Tucker or Edge Stitcher to keep the stitching an even distance from the edge.

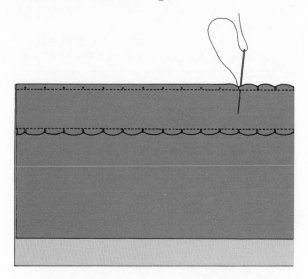

Lightly mark the size of each shell or scallop at equal intervals—generally ¼ to ⅜ inch apart. Use a fine needle and knot the end of the thread. Bring the needle up through the tuck at the first marking; take two stitches across the tuck, drawing the thread tightly to form a scallop. Slip the needle between the two layers of fabric in the tuck and bring it out at the marking for the next stitch. When finished, fasten the thread on the underside of the fabric. Press.

Machine Stitched. Mark the position for each tuck as instructed on page 235. Baste if necessary. Set selectors on the machine for the blindstitch zig-zag. Make a test on a sample of your fabric to find the right needle thread tension, stitch length, and stitch width.

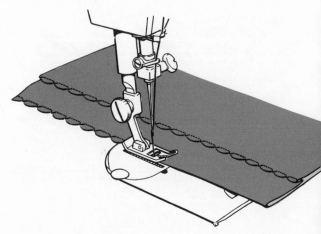

Place the prefolded tuck under the presser foot, with the fold toward the left. Stitch slowly, guiding the fabric by hand so that the sideward stitches do not pierce the folded edge. Press.

Scalloped Tucks

Dainty, scalloped tucks are used extensively as self-trimming on blouses, dresses, lingerie, and children's clothes.

In your planning, allow sufficient width in the fabric for the tucks, as instructed on page 235, plus an additional ½ inch for seam allowances on the edge of the scallops.

Fold and crease the fabric on the line for the tuck, with right sides together. Trace the scallop on the fabric, placing the edge of the scallop ¼ inch from the fold to allow for seaming.

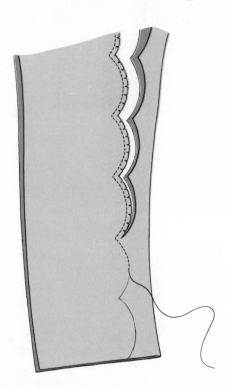

Use a short stitch and the Quilter if you have one. (The open construction and short toe of the Quilter greatly facilitate the stitching of small scallops.)

Stitch around the scallops exactly on the traced line, taking one stitch across the point between each scallop. This extra stitch gives you width when cutting and prevents pulling at the point between the scallops in the finished work.

On small scallops, blend the seam allowances to a scant ⅛ inch; on large scallops, blend them a generous ⅛ inch, and blend one edge shorter than the other. Slash at the point almost to the stitch-

ing. Cut notches in the seam edges at evenly spaced intervals. Press.

Turn the scallops to the right side. Gently work the seam edges between the thumb and finger to bring the stitching to the very edge. Baste the edges with silk thread to retain the shape of the scallop until after pressing.

Using the desired width, stitch the tucks an even distance from the edge with a line of straight stitching. Press.

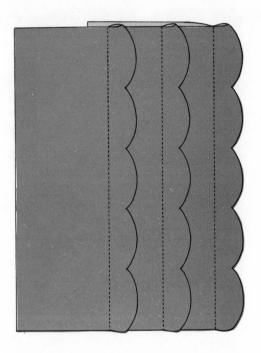

You can also stitch small scallops easily on the zig-zag machine. Set the selectors for the scallop pattern. The stitch length and stitch width vary the length and depth of the scallop; select the length and width you want. As you stitch, the fabric passes straight under the presser foot, and the needle follows a scallop pattern. Always start each row of stitching at the beginning of a scallop unit. See page 266 for instructions. Press, blend seams, and turn the scallops as instructed above.

To Press Tucks

To imbed the stitching, press the underside of each tuck in the same position as it was stitched. Then on the wrong side, press the tucks to one side, flat against the fabric. (Normally, tucks are turned away from the center of the garment.) Cover the fabric with the appropriate press cloth and use the amount of moisture required.

Ruffles add a feminine touch to blouses and dresses. They are also a pleasing trimming on lingerie and children's clothes, and on curtains and bedspreads.

To Prepare the Fabric

Ruffles on garments are usually cut on the crosswise grain or true bias. Ruffles on sheer curtains are cut on the lengthwise grain to keep seaming to a minimum. The texture of the fabric makes a difference in the fullness—soft and medium-weight fabrics are more adaptable to ruffles than firm fabrics.

Double or triple fullness may be required for the ruffle depending on the width of the ruffle as well as the texture of the fabric. Wide ruffles require more fullness than narrow ruffles. It is always wise to cut and ruffle a little more length than the estimated requirement.

Cut the fabric two to three times longer than the length of the finished ruffle.

Before gathering the ruffle, finish the outer edge either by machine, using the Hemmer Foot; by hand; or by one of the pattern stitches on the zig-zag machine that is suitable for an edge finish. You may apply lace at the same time you machine-stitch the hem.

To Gather the Ruffle

The Ruffler enables you to gather the fabric quickly, easily, and evenly. See *Ruffler*, page 280, for instructions.

After you have adjusted the setting of the Ruffler, test the fullness on a swatch of the same fabric you are working with.

To ruffle organdy or chintz, dampen the fabric along the seamline with a small, moist sponge and gather while damp.

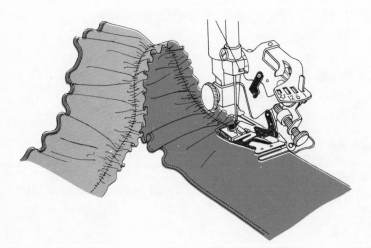

To Apply the Ruffle

To an Edge

Pin the ruffle to the edge, right sides together, extending the straight edge a scant ½ inch beyond the gathering stitches of the ruffle. Pin at close intervals. Baste if necessary. Stitch with the ruffle side up, just beyond the gathering stitches.

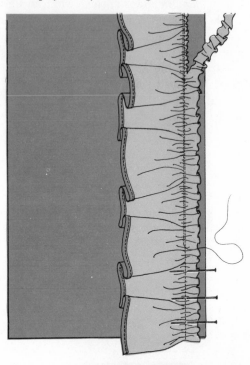

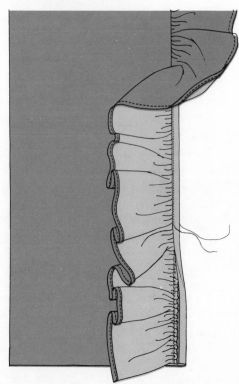

Trim the seam allowance on the ruffle to ⅛ inch. Fold the straight edge under ⅛ inch, then fold it over the seam edges to the stitching line on the underside, enclosing the cut edge. Pin. Stitch near the first fold. Press. Turn the ruffle away from the garment and press the seam toward the garment.

The fabric may be gathered and stitched to a straight edge in one operation. See page 281.

For a Lingerie Edge

Pin the ruffle to the edge, right sides together, keeping the edges even. Stitch with the ruffle uppermost under the needle.

Trim the seam allowance to ¼ inch. Overcast the cut edges together, using the blindstitch zigzag. Use a fine stitch length and medium stitch width.

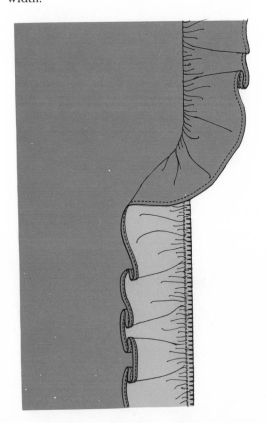

In a Straight Seam

Pin the ruffle to the seam edge, right sides together, extending the straight edge a scant ½ inch beyond the gathering stitches of the ruffle. Stitch from the ruffle side on the gathering stitches. Press the seam.

Place the attached ruffle over the second seam edge, right sides together. Pin at close intervals. Baste if necessary.

Place the work under the needle with the first line of stitching uppermost so that you can use it as a guide. Stitch barely beyond the previous line of stitching. Press. The stitching is not visible on the right side.

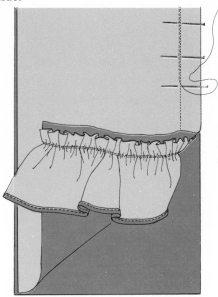

To a Faced Edge

When a ruffle is added as a decorative trim to the edge of a collar or cuff, it is set between two layers of fabric and often must be eased around a corner.

Pin the ruffle to the outer edge of the top collar or cuff, right sides together. About ½ inch on each side of the corner, ease the gathers closer together with the thumb as you pin. This will give the extra fullness needed around the corner. Baste if necessary. With the ruffle side up, stitch on the gathering stitches. Press the seam.   *(Continued)*

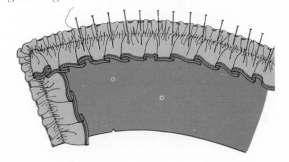

Place the edge of the attached ruffle over the undercollar or cuff, right sides together, matching markings. Pin and baste, leaving the neckline edge, or lower edge of the cuff, open. Smooth out the ruffle so that only the seam allowance is caught in the stitching.

Place the first line of stitching uppermost under the needle; stitch barely beyond it. Press the seam.

Trim the seam allowances on the undercollar and ruffle to ⅛ inch and the seam allowance on the top collar to ¼ inch. Clip off the corners and notch into the seam allowances on the outside curve. Turn the collar to the right side, and press.

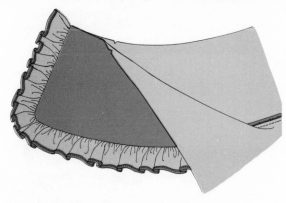

To Attach Pinafore Ruffles

Shoulder ruffles in the bodice of a pinafore are shaped at each end; that is, they are wider through the center and taper almost to a point at the ends.

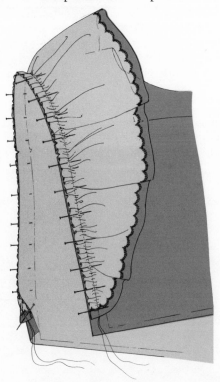

Therefore, they must be gathered to fit the bodice length. You will often find it necessary to adjust the fullness of the ruffle after you have gathered it.

Loosen the upper tension slightly on your machine and use the Ruffler to gather the fabric. See page 280 for instructions on using the Ruffler. Leave long threads at each end of the seam. (Do not forget to return the tension to its previous setting.)

Pin the ruffle to the pinafore, matching markings. Work from the center to the outer edges, and adjust the ruffle to fit the pinafore by easing the fabric back on the bobbin thread.

Stitch and blend the seam allowances as instructed above for a ruffle applied to a faced edge.

To Attach Ruffle with Heading

Finish both edges before gathering the ruffle. See *Ruffle with Heading*, page 281 for instructions.

Turn the straight edge of the garment to the underside and make a ⅛-inch double fold. Press. Pin the ruffle to the right side of the edge at closely spaced intervals, centering the gathering stitches over the double fold. Stitch from the ruffle side on the previous line of stitching. The folded edge and ruffle are held in place with one line of stitching.

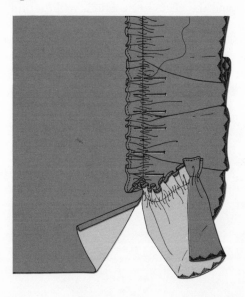

SHIRRING

Rows of shirring often appear as a styling point at the shoulder line, waistline, and lower edge of sleeves. Sometimes an entire section, such as a yoke or pocket, may be shirred for a decorative effect.

Soft fabrics—batiste, voile, silk, net, and fabrics of similar textures—lend themselves better to shirring than firm fabrics. Crisp sheers, however, can be shirred if they are steam-pressed to soften the finish and stitched while damp. The true bias or crosswise grain of the fabric is more easily shirred than the lengthwise grain. Shirring by machine is quick and produces strong, even stitches.

Shirring with the Gathering Foot

You can achieve many lovely effects with simple rows of evenly spaced shirring made with the Gathering Foot. For instructions on how to use foot and the stitch length required, see page 285.

Draw a single thread or crease the fabric on the crosswise grain at selected intervals for the spacing desired. Stitch on each of these lines, using the Gathering Foot. If you are spacing your rows ½ inch apart, you can gauge the distance by the edge of the foot.

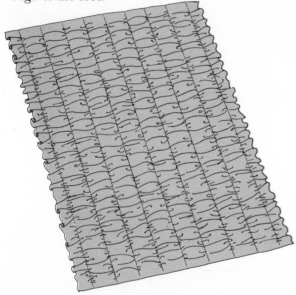

When you are shirring an entire section such as a yoke or pocket, shirr the fabric, then cut the section according to the pattern. Always test the fullness on a swatch of your fabric before working on the garment.

Waffle Shirring

Waffle shirring gives texture interest to smooth-surfaced fabrics. It has a broad application on cottons, silks, woolens, and rayons, and is particularly interesting for details on children's dresses, blouses, and lingerie.

With the Gathering Foot, stitch on the crosswise grain of the fabric and then on the length-wise grain. Use a stitch length short enough to produce only a slight fullness.

Controlled Shirring

When a section of a seam is to be shirred and stitched to a straight seam, the shirring must be "controlled" so that the seams, when joined, are of the same length. See *Gathering to Control Fullness*, page 105.

Use a stay of the same fabric to prevent strain on the shirring. Cut the stay ½ inch deeper than the rows of shirring and wide enough to fit across the entire garment section when shirred.

Place the stay over the wrong side of the shirred section, keeping the seam edges even. Pin and baste in position. Stitch the stay into the seam when the garment sections are joined.

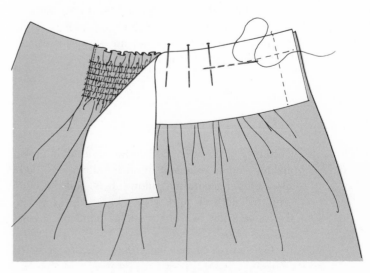

Shirring with Elastic Thread

Elastic shirring is appropriate for lingerie, children's clothes, and washable skirts. It requires no special machine accessory.

Wind the bobbin with elastic thread, using the bobbin winder on the machine. The elastic thread will stretch slightly as it is wound on the bobbin. If you have a *Touch & Sew* machine, wind the bobbin by hand, stretching the elastic thread slightly. For a heavy fabric where greater strength is required, wind double strands of elastic thread on the bobbin. Use mercerized thread for the top threading of the machine.

Select a 10 to 12 stitch length, depending on the fabric. Always test the fullness on a swatch of the same fabric used in the garment. In stitching the second and subsequent rows, stretch the elastic in the previous rows as you sew so that the shirring will be even. Rows spaced ¼ inch apart may be gauged by the edge of the presser foot.

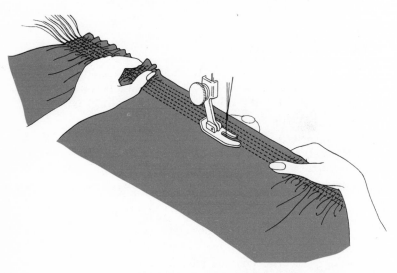

At each end of the stitching, tie the elastic and needle threads together by forming a single knot in the two strands of thread; use a pin to set the knot tightly against the fabric.

CORDING

Cording is a versatile and handsome detail in dressmaking and an excellent finish for slipcovers, bedspreads, and decorative pillows. It is made by covering a length of cord with a bias strip of either the same color as your work at hand or a contrasting color.

Corded seams may be either delicate or bold,

depending on the size of the cord. If you are going to use corded seams, make a corded "welting," which can be stitched into the seam or onto an edge. If you are going to use the cording for button loops, trimming, or frogs, you will make what is called "tubular" cording. Instructions for both are given here. But first you must cut and join your bias strips.

Cutting Bias Strips

The true bias is the diagonal line of a square of fabric. Fold the crosswise grain of the fabric to the lengthwise grain; this forms a true bias. Cut along the fold.

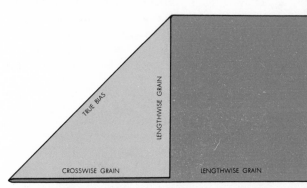

How wide to make your bias strips depends on the size of the filler cord. Cut the strips 1¼ inches plus three times the width of the cord. Use a ruler and measure the required width from the true bias edge of the fabric. Mark the line with tailor's chalk. Measure and mark as many strips as you will need, then cut on the markings.

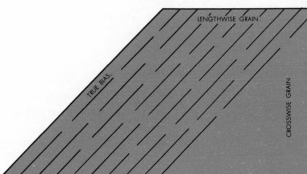

Joining Bias Strips

If you need only a short length of cording, avoid piecing it; however, if you need a long, continuous length, you will have to join bias strips.

All bias strips are joined on the lengthwise grain so that the seams will be less noticeable. If one end of your bias strip is on the crosswise grain, fold this fabric end on the lengthwise grain and cut.

Join the lengthwise ends; offset the width of the joining seam and stitch, taking a ¼-inch seam. Be careful to match any prominent weave, stripe, or design of the fabric. Press the seams open.

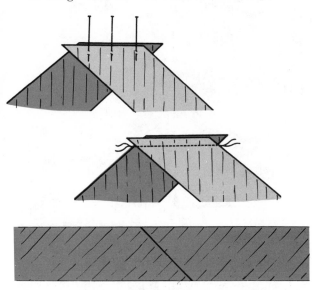

Corded Seams

Covering the Cord

Replace the presser foot with the Zipper Foot and adjust it to the left of the needle.

Bring the bias strip around the cord, right side

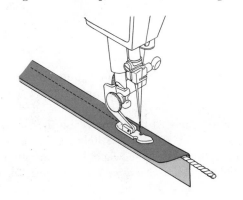

out, keeping the seam edges even. Use a slightly longer stitch than that ordinarily used for seaming the fabric. Stitch close to the cord, but do not crowd the stitching against the cord. You have now formed a "welt." Press the stitching.

A chain stitch is an ideal stitch for fabrics that are cut on the bias since the loop formation of the stitches makes them less taut than regular straight stitches. If your machine has Chain Stitch Accessories, refer to the instruction book accompanying the machine and to page 63.

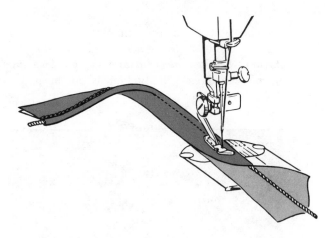

If sheer fabric is used to cover the cord, underline the bias strip with an opaque fabric, such as taffeta or polished cotton, that matches the sheer fabric in color. Cut bias strips of the underlining. Place the sheer bias strip, right side up, over the right side of the underlining and handle the two as one in covering the cord. Follow the above procedure.

Applying the Cording to a Straight Seam

Pin the cording to the right side of the single seam edge, keeping the previous line of stitching over the seamline. Adjust the Zipper Foot to the right of the needle. Stitch with the same stitch length used when covering the cord. Press the stitching.

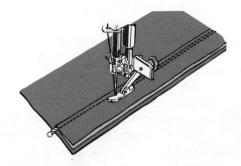

Pin and baste the second seam edge over the cording, right sides together. Place the work under

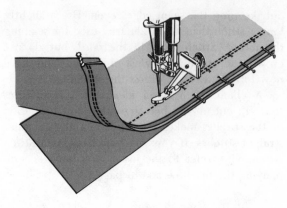

Trim the corded seam allowance to ⅛ inch and the garment and facing seam allowances to ¼ inch. Notch the seam allowance on the curve at regular intervals. Press. Turn the facing to the underside. Fold on the seamline and press. Finish the free edge of the facing. All stitching is on the underside of the finished garment.

the needle with the first stitching uppermost so that you can use it as a guide. Stitch, *crowding the stitching between the cord and the previous line of stitching.* Press. All stitching is on the underside of the finished garment.

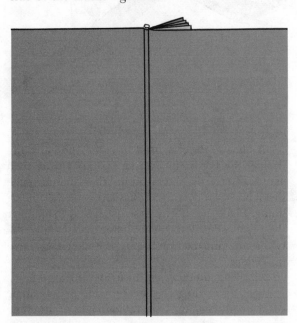

Applying the Cording to Curves

Inside curves. See *Corded Neckline,* page 146.

Outside curves. Pin the cording to the right side of the garment, keeping the previous line of stitching on the seamline. Clip into the corded seam allowance almost to the stitching so that the cord will lie smooth around the curve. Baste, if necessary. Adjust the Zipper Foot to the right of the needle. Stitch, using a stitch shorter than that for straight seams. Press.

Pin and baste the facing over the cording, right sides together. Place the work under the needle with the first line of stitching uppermost so that you can use it as a guide. Stitch, crowding the stitching between the cord and the previous line of stitching. Press.

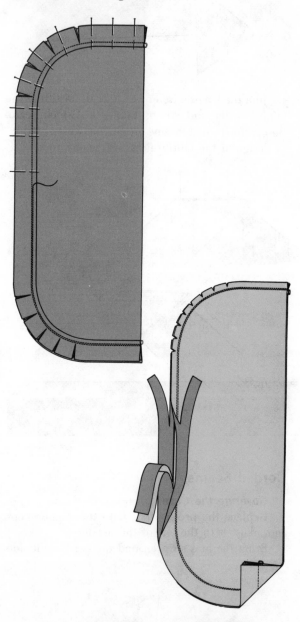

Applying the Cording to Square Corners

Pin the cording to the right side of a single seam edge, keeping the previous line of stitching on the seamline. At the corner, slash the bias edges almost to the stitching. Stitch the seam as instructed for a straight seam; take one stitch diagonally across the corner for a smooth turning. Press.

Lay the facing over the cording with the right sides together, and pin. Place the work under the

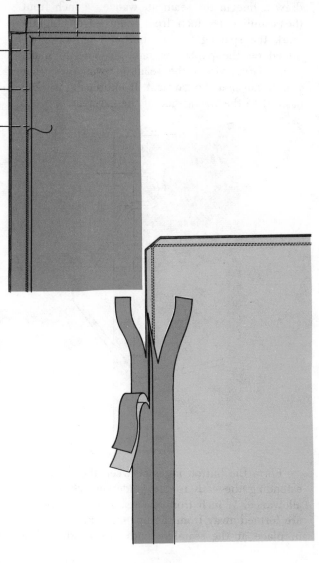

the stitching between the cord and the previous line of stitching. Press.

Cut diagonally across the corner close to the stitching. Trim the corded seam allowance to ⅛ inch and the garment and facing seam allowances to ¼ inch. Press, then turn to the right side and press.

TUBULAR CORDING

To Make Tubular Cording

Cut a true bias strip 1 inch wide plus three times the width of the filler cord. Cut one end to a point.

Use a filler cord twice the length of the bias strip. Machine-stitch the center of the cord to the wrong side of the pointed end. Stitch from the point to about ⅜ inch from it.

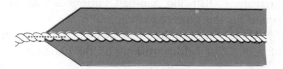

Turn about ⅜ inch of the pointed end and the filler cord to the right side of the bias, then fold the bias in half around the cord. The remaining half of the cord extends from the point.

Adjust the Zipper Foot to the right of the needle. Use a short stitch. To avoid stitching the turned-under point, form a funnel at the point and taper it for about 1 inch; then crowd the stitching against the cord and, at the same time, stretch the bias slightly. One half of the filler cord is covered and one half extends beyond the funneled end. Press, then trim the seam allowances to ⅛ inch.

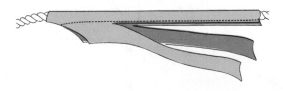

(If your machine has Chain Stitch Accessories, use them for stitching fabrics that are cut on the bias. See page 63.)

Work the bias back over the extended cord while pulling the encased cord. *Do not twist.* The

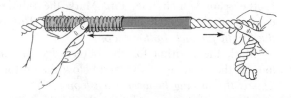

stitches will not break if you have used a short stitch and have stretched the bias in the stitching.

Button Loops

Button loops are in and out of fashion. When they are "in," they may be found at openings in the neckline, sleeves, and front bodice; in jackets and in lingerie. Ball and half-ball buttons are appropriate for this type of closing.

Always make a test button loop in a swatch of your fabric before working on the garment.

Length and Spacing of Button Loops

To determine the length and spacing of button loops, make a paper diagram. Draw a straight line ⅝ inch from the edge to represent the seamline. Draw a second line in the seam allowance, ¼ inch from the first line and parallel to it to represent the position of the loop ends.

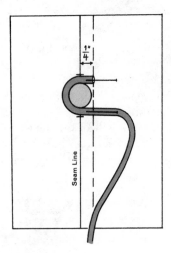

Place the exact center of the button on the seamline. Bring the tubular cording around the top edge of the button *with the seam to the inside of the loop.* Pin the end of the cording on the marking you made ¼ inch from the seamline. Form the loop to the left, around the button and back to the seam ¼-inch line. Pin. Mark the tubular cording at the ¼-inch line as illustrated. *This is the length for each button loop.*

Mark the position for the outer edge of the loop at the seamline, above and below the button. *This is the spacing between each loop.*

Measure the space and mark the fabric at these intervals. Measure the determined amount for each loop and mark the tubular cording at these intervals. Clip through the seam allowance and into the cord at each marking, but not far enough to separate the loops.

Stitching of Button Loops

Turn the garment to the right side. Baste or draw a line in the seam allowance, ¼ inch from the seamline (⅜ inch from seam edge). Lightly mark the spacing for the button loop as determined on the paper diagram. Be sure to make your marks within the seam allowance so that you do not mar the garment. If interfacing is used, baste it to the wrong side of the garment.

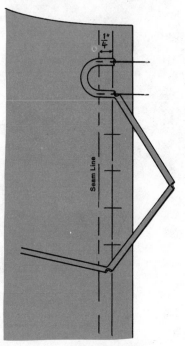

Form the button loops between the markings, extending the ends to the guideline in the seam allowance, ¼ inch from the seamline. (The loops are formed away from the opening.) Pin the loops in place at the seamline with fine needles. The

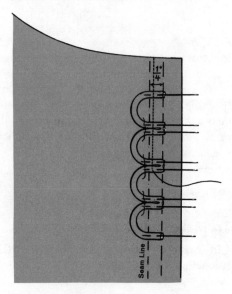

248

outer edges of the loops should touch. Tack the loops together so that they hold their shape until the stitching is completed. Stitch the loops to the garment 1/16 inch outside the seamline. This stitching is not visible in the finished work.

Pin and baste the facing over the garment, right side together. Place the work under the needle with the previous stitching uppermost so that you can use it as a guide. Stitch on the ⅝-inch seamline to conceal the previous line of stitching.

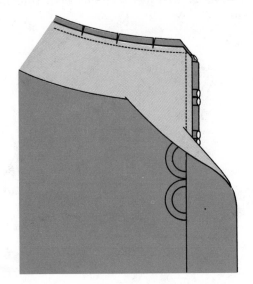

Trim the facing seam allowance to ⅛ inch and the garment seam allowance to ¼ inch. Press.

Turn the facing to the underside. Fold on the seamline, and press. When the facing is turned, the loops will extend beyond the opening edge.

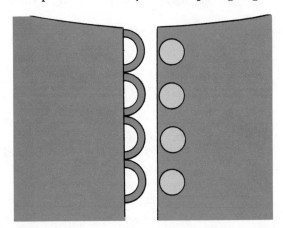

Frogs

Tubular cording may be looped into many interesting designs to form frogs.

Loop tubular cording into the desired design, keeping the seam on the underside. Determine the length needed for each loop and pin-mark the cord-

ing at these intervals. Do not cut. Allow a ¼-inch seam allowance at each end. Pull out the cord at the ends and clip off ¼ inch.

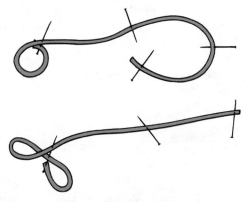

Form the first loop and insert a pin up from the underside to hold the loop in place. Then slip each consecutive loop over the end of the pin as illustrated. Leave the last loop free to slip over the button.

Tack the loops together at the crossing on the underside, concealing the end. Make the tack through the first two loops and catch only the underside of the third loop. Determine the length required to slip over the button, then form the last loop and tack it to the underside, concealing the end.

Make a frog for each side of the opening. Pin them on the right side of the garment, then tack them in place on the underside. Use half-ball, full-ball, and shank buttons with frogs.

Buttons

To make buttons of tubular cording, fold under the end, then wind the cording into a circle the desired size, keeping the seam on the underside. Pin through the side to hold the cording in place and hand-stitch it on the underside. Bring the outer end to the underside and tack. Sew the buttons on the garment with a thread shank.

Other Tubular Trimming

You can make tubular scrolls. Follow the instructions above for the button; however, allow enough tubular cording for two buttons. Begin at the center of the cording; at one end wind the cording clockwise and at the other end wind it counterclockwise.

You can loop tubular cording into a graceful design and apply it to your dress as you would braid. You can also use it for spaghetti trimming in belts and bows.

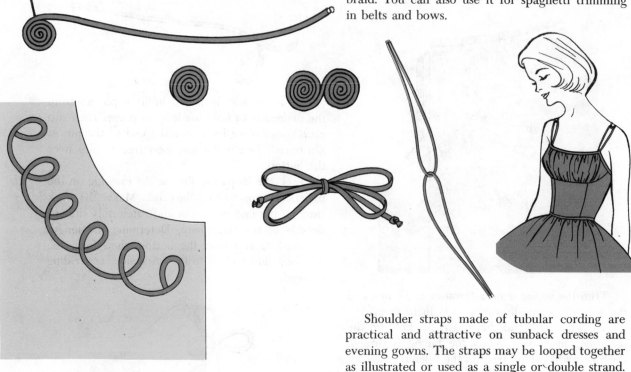

Shoulder straps made of tubular cording are practical and attractive on sunback dresses and evening gowns. The straps may be looped together as illustrated or used as a single or double strand.

APPLIQUÉ

Appliqué is the loving touch in sewing. It offers an unlimited opportunity for self-expression and adds beauty and interest to wearing apparel, linens, and fabric furnishings.

You can create your own design or buy pattern motifs and appliqué transfers ready for tracing. Fabrics of like textures or of different textures and weaves combine equally well.

Printed linen handkerchiefs or drapery fabric, chintz, and other fabrics with a definite design, make interesting appliqués.

Appliqué may be done by machine or by hand. Machine appliqué, however, is preferred since the work may be accomplished with greater ease and accuracy. The zig-zag machine ensures close evenly spaced stitches and enables you to stitch many intricate designs, too difficult for hand work.

Transferring the Design

Transfer the design on a swatch of fabric slightly larger than the design, using one of the methods given below:

1. If you are using a hot-iron transfer, carefully follow the instructions on the back of the pattern envelope.

2. If you are not using the hot-iron method, trace the design on heavy paper or lightweight cardboard, and cut it out. Position the cutout on a swatch of fabric slightly larger than the design. Mark lightly around it with pencil or chalk.

3. If the fabric is not too heavy, place the pattern for the design over a windowpane and secure it with cellophane tape. Hold the fabric swatch over the design and trace lightly around it.

4. On heavy fabrics, place dressmaker's tracing paper between the design and the fabric. Then trace lightly around the design.

5. Place sheer fabrics such as organdy over the design, then lightly trace the design on the fabric with pencil or chalk.

Do not cut out the fabric after tracing the design.

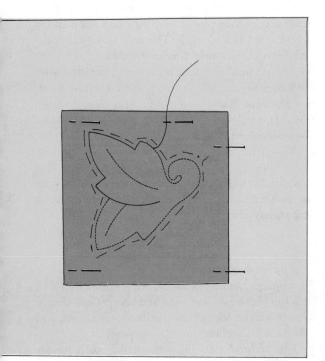

Machine Appliqué

A closely spaced zig-zag stitch is the most versatile in appliqué work. Although you may vary the width of this stitch to accommodate fabric weaves and textures, never allow the stitch to be too wide.

Preparation *(Lower left)*

Carefully position the fabric design on the article to be decorated and pin it in place. Hand-baste near the design outline.

Outline the design with straight stitching; use a short stitch. Stitch any lines shown within the design. Remove bastings, and press.

Replace the presser foot on the machine with the Special Purpose Foot designed for use in appliqué work. Set the selectors for a narrow zig-zag stitch and shorten the stitch length for satin stitching. See *Satin Stitching*, page 266.

Before starting the work, study the design to determine which section you should complete first. Avoid crossing the lines of stitching whenever possible since this may break the continuity of the design.

Simple Appliqué

Two methods may be used in the appliqué stitching. Choose the one appropriate for your fabric. Remember a test sample is always advisable.

Method 1: Use a closely spaced zig-zag stitch. Stitch over the straight stitch outline. Stitch any lines shown within the design first. Pull the threads to the underside and tie. Press. Cut away the fabric on the outer edge close to the stitching, using embroidery scissors.

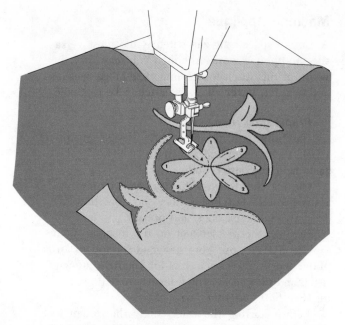

Method 2: Trim the outside edge of the fabric close to the straight stitching. For added body, baste an underlay of lawn on the wrong side of the fabric, under the design.

Overedge the design with a closely spaced zig-zag stitch. A smooth, lustrous finish results, which requires no additional trimming. Pull the threads through to the underside and tie. Press. Trim the underlay on the wrong side close to the stitching, using embroidery scissors.

To make smooth, rounded corners, stop the machine with the needle in the outside edge of the fabric; lift the foot, turn the fabric slightly, and take two stitches, turning the hand wheel by hand. Repeat several times. To make square, open corners, pivot the fabric on the needle when the needle is on the inside edge.

Corded Appliqué

Corded appliqué is an ideal finish for a motif of lace. Use gimp, fine crochet thread, buttonhole twist, or heavy-duty thread for the filler cord.

Select wide lace edging with a definite floral design. If you are applying the lace to an edge, extend the fabric edge at least 1 inch beyond the line of the appliqué stitch. Choose a motif from the lace and position it separately above the edging; hand-baste in place.

Either *Method 1 or 2* described above may be used for corded appliqué. *Method 1* is recommended for intricate lace designs. The only change in procedure is the introduction of the filler cord, over which appliqué stitching is formed. Insert the filler cord into the eyelet on the Special Purpose Foot. See *Hairline Seam*, page 88 for threading instructions. This stitching technique gives a raised, three-dimensional effect.

When the work is finished, removed the bastings. From the right side, cut away the excess lace close to the stitching; from the wrong side, trim the excess fabric ¼ inch from the stitching, using embroidery scissors. Press.

Appliqué Monograms

Appliqué monograms add a luxurious touch to bath towels, shower curtains, and bedspreads. Heavy fabrics such as slipper satin, chintz, Glosheen, and taffetta are excellent for this purpose.

Use *Method 1* for monogramming bath towels and either method for bedspreads and shower curtains. Corded appliqué is also an effective finish.

Shadow Appliqué

Shadow hems and designs are lovely for table linens and children's clothes of crisp organdy or fine linen.

Baste the hem the full depth of the design and miter all corners. Lightly trace the design for the hem and motif on the right side of the article to be appliquéd. See page 251.

Cut a swatch of the same fabric slightly larger than the motif. Pin it over the wrong side of the motif. Hand-baste about ¼ inch from the lines of the motif and the hem.

Follow the instructions for *Corded Appliqué* and stitch around the design, using a fine filler cord; remove bastings and press.

Cut away the outer edges of the fabric on the underside close to the stitching, using embroidery scissors. Press.

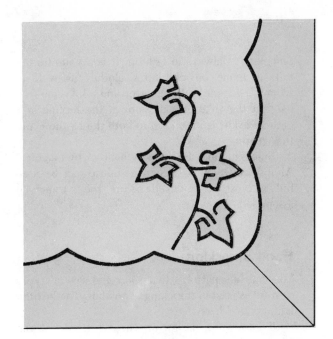

Hand Appliqué

The cut edges of the design are folded to the underside in hand appliqué.

Trace the design to be appliquéd on a swatch of fabric slightly larger than the motif. See page 251.

Cut out the design ¼ inch from the marking. Fold the cut edges to the underside ¼ inch and hand-baste. Miter the corners; notch the seam edges on outside curves, and clip into them on inside curves so that the seams will lie flat. Steam-press.

For stitching, use one or two strands of six-strand floss and a fine needle, and blanket-stitch over the edge of the design. Uneven as well as even stitches may be used. Fasten the threads on the underside. Remove bastings, and press. Stems and lines within the design may be embroidered.

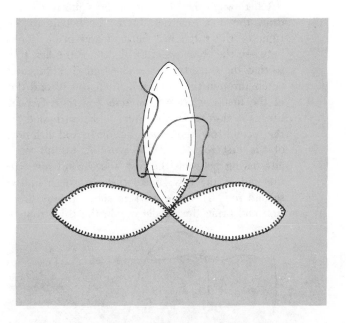

Carefully position the fabric design on the article to be decorated and pin. Hand-baste about ¼ inch from the edge. Remove the first bastings on the folded edge.

If you prefer an invisible finish, slip-stitch the design in place instead of using the blanket stitch.

253

SMOCKING

Smocking is always in fashion. It is a youthful detail—at home on children's clothes as well as women's lingerie and soft cotton and silk. A smocked band at the yoke of a dress or at the hipline of a gathered skirt lends charm to both the costume and the wearer.

Smocking may be done by hand or by machine. Almost any type or design of fabric can be used but it must be smocked before the garment is assembled.

Hand Smocking

You can buy patterns that show the several types of stitches used in smocking. The honeycomb stitch is illustrated here.

Transfer the design on the right side of the fabric. If you are working with a small check or plaid, you may use it as a guide.

Six-strand floss is suitable for both cotton and silk fabrics; on silk, however, you may prefer a silk floss. Use two or three strands in the needle and knot the long end of the threads. Choose a thread color that matches your fabric or, for a pleasant change, one that contrasts with it.

Work from left to right with the needle pointed to the left. Bring the needle up through the fabric between the first two dots of the second row. Take a small stitch through the second dot and a small stitch through the first dot in the same row; then draw the dots together. Insert the needle to the right of the stitch just finished and bring it out between the second and third dots of the first row so that the thread is under the fold. Take a small stitch through the third dot, then the second dot in the first row; draw the dots together. Repeat the procedure over the third and fourth dots of the second row; then over the fourth and fifth dots of the first row. Continue working in this way, alternating between the first and second rows, to the end of the row; make the last stitch in the second row. Turn the work in the opposite direction and bring the needle out in the third row to

the right of the last stitch. Work over the dots in the third and fourth rows; then the fifth and sixth rows, as illustrated. Continue until the smocking is completed.

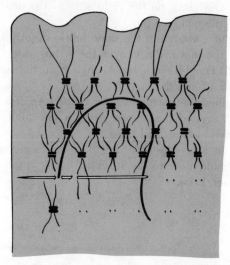

When drawing the stitches together, always pull the threads either up or down at right angles to the stitches to form even pleats or folds. When each row is finished, gently pull the fabric lengthwise to straighten the pleats.

To press with a steam iron, pin the top row of the smocking securely to the ironing board; place a pin above each stitch. Hold the iron about 1 inch above the smocking and allow the steam to penetrate the fabric while you gently pull the smocking from the bottom.

To press with a dry iron, follow the instructions for velvet, page 66.

Machine Smocking

Machine smocking resembles hand smocking when the rows are accurately stitched. It is quick and easy and any one of the three methods given below may be used.

Method 1: Use matching thread and loosen the upper tension slightly so that the bobbin thread may be drawn later to gather the fabric.

From the right side of the fabric, place a row of stitching in the seam allowance, ½ inch from the edge. This stitching is not visible in the finished work. Place a second row of stitching barely beyond the ⅝-inch seam allowance, and a third row ⅛ inch from the second row. Place additional rows in groups of two, spaced ⅛ inch apart, and allow ½ inch between groupings.

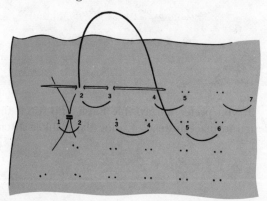

Gather the fabric to the desired width. See *Gathering to Control Fullness*, page 105.

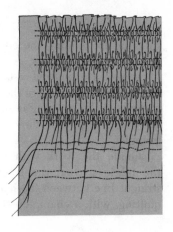

Cut an underlay of lawn or organdy the length and width of the shirring. Position it on the underside, over the shirring. Pin it in place from the right side.

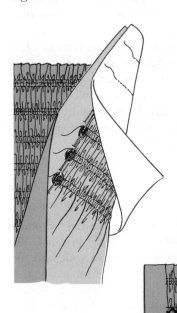

Select one of the zig-zag stitch patterns and stitch between the rows that you spaced ⅛ inch apart, using thread contrasting in color. For an interesting effect, select two stitch patterns and alternate them in stitching the rows.

Method 2: Use the Gathering Foot and heavy-duty thread for both the bobbin and the upper threading. Stitch following a design. See *Gathering Foot*, page 285 for instructions on its use.

Method 3: Use heavy-duty thread for both the bobbin and the upper threading and about 10 stitch length. Stitch from the right side, following a design similar to the one illustrated. You may use different colors of thread in stitching alternate rows. (If you are using a heavy thread only on the bobbin, stitch from the wrong side of the fabric.)

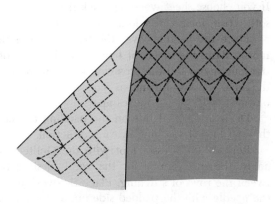

After you have stitched the design, wind the bobbin with elastic thread and place several rows of stitching across the work, spacing them in harmony with the design. See *Shirring with Elastic Thread*, page 244.

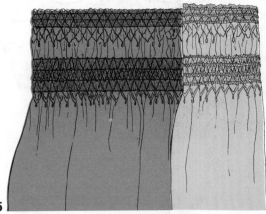

255

Quilting is the art of stitching two or more thicknesses of fabric together in a planned design. A light padding is stitched to the underside of the fabric to produce a soft, puffed effect that is becoming to some wearing apparel and to many fabric furnishings.

Your sewing machine enables you to quilt quickly and easily and to achieve a variety of effects. The Quilter Foot, which has an open construction and short toe, simplifies the stitching of padded fabrics. Its adjustable and removable space guide may be placed to the right or left of the needle. This makes it especially adaptable to diagonal quilting.

Select the thread, needle, and stitch length appropriate for your fabric. (Do not use a long stitch.) The pressure should be slightly heavier than that for medium-weight fabrics.

Diagonal Quilting

Outing flannel, canton flannel, sheet wadding, or lightweight interlining makes a practical padding. If you choose sheet wadding, back it with voile or soft batiste for greater durability.

Place the padding over the wrong side of the fabric. Baste the layers of fabric together on both the lengthwise and the crosswise grains to prevent the layers from shifting as you sew. Space the basting rows about 2 inches apart.

Draw a diagonal line on the padding to mark the first line of stitching in each direction.

Replace the presser foot with the Quilter and adjust the space guide for the width desired between the rows of stitching. Place the work under the needle with the padded side up, and stitch on the drawn line. Space each successive row of

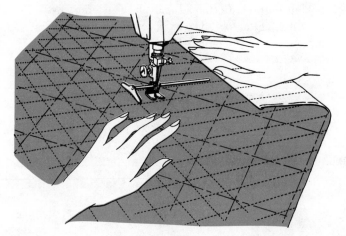

stitching by guiding the edge of the space guide along the previous row, as illustrated.

If you are quilting a large piece, work from the center to the edge of the fabric. After you have completed the stitching in one direction, stitch the lines in the opposite direction to form squares or triangles.

Guide the work with both hands placed on the fabric so that the lengthwise grain forms a straight line between the hands. This ensures even quilting, with a characteristic soft puff.

Pattern Quilting

Floral and scroll designs may also be stitched with the Quilter. The space guide is removed, however.

Prepare the fabric following the instructions for diagonal quilting, but transfer the design to the padding before basting the two layers of fabric together. Then stitch around the outline for the design as instructed for trapunto quilting below.

If the fabric has a floral or scroll design, the pattern in the fabric can be your quilting design. Stitch it from the top side, using either straight stitching or zig-zag stitching.

Trapunto Quilting *(Illustrated on next page)*

Trapunto quilting is a form of quilting in which small designs are made to stand out in relief. The fabric is backed with soft batiste, voile, silk organza, or organdy. Trace the motif on a swatch of the backing. Carefully plan the position of each motif so that the design is attractively spaced. Baste the backing on which the design has been traced to the wrong side of the fabric.

Raise the space guide of the Quilter or remove it entirely. The short open toe permits you to follow the curved lines easily and accurately. Choose thread that matches the fabric in color, and use a short stitch.

After stitching each portion of the design from the wrong side, pull the threads to the underside and tie. If the design has large leaves, flowers, or scrolls, place a second row of stitching inside the design, about ⅛ inch from the first row.

When the stitching is completed, pad the design with strands of wool yarn carried by a tapestry needle or darning needle. (Wool yarn should be used because of its resiliency.) Pass the needle

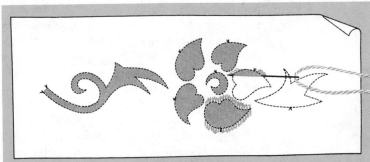

through the backing from one stitching line to the other. It often is necessary to use several strands of yarn to fill a section of the motif.

Clip both ends of the yarn close to the stitching. Gently stretch each portion of the design on the bias to conceal the ends of the yarn on the inside of the backing.

Lace and other transparent fabrics are often backed with satin or taffeta and the design padded with silk yarn to produce a delicately tinted pattern.

BEADS AND SEQUINS

Beads and sequins are glamorous accents on cocktail and evening dresses, sweaters, blouses, scarves, and evening bags. They may be used alone or combined with decorative zig-zag stitching as illustrated on page 276. A variety of fabrics may be used for this work.

Beading by Machine

Small beads may be sewed in place by machine. Use a medium-width, open-spaced zig-zag stitch and the Zipper Foot. Stitch the beads in place before you assemble the garment sections so that you have only a small section to deal with.

The spaces between the sections within the design must be far enough apart for the Zipper Foot to work between them. In straight or block designs, however, several rows may be stitched close together. (For small, intricate designs, bead by hand.)

Transfer the motif for the beading to a backing of organdy, voile, or lawn. If the garment is underlined, transfer the design to the underlining. Carefully position the backing on the wrong side of the fabric and pin near the design. Use matching thread and machine-stitch on the lines of the design to transfer it to the right side of the fabric.

String bulk beads on a double strand of matching mercerized or silk thread, using a fine needle. Knot the ends together. Pass the needle through the first bead, then between the two strands of thread near the knot. This will prevent the beads from slipping beyond the knot. After you have strung the beads, arrange them smoothly; then

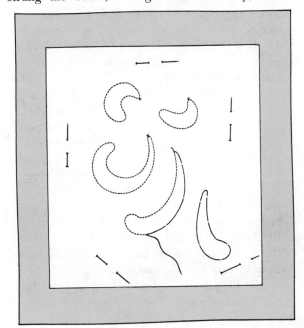

pass the needle through the last bead a second time to prevent the beads from slipping on the thread.

Adjust the machine for a medium-width zig-zag stitch in central needle position and 15 stitch length. Use either silk or mercerized thread matching the fabric exactly in color.

Place the beads directly over the line of the design and adjust the Zipper Foot far enough to the left or right to ride against the beads. This adjustment enables you to position the zig-zag stitching over the beading thread. As you sew, hold the beads in place with the index finger, close to the needle. The threads are drawn between the beads, making the stitching invisible.

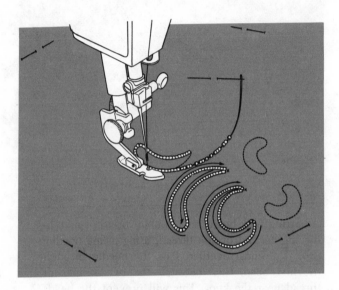

On scroll designs, start the stitching on the inside curve with the Zipper Foot adjusted to work inside the design; stitch to the beginning of the outside curve. Stop the machine *with the needle in the fabric*, adjust the Zipper Foot to the opposite side, then work outside the design, as illustrated. (It is necessary to remove the foot to make this adjustment since the needle is in the fabric.) In the illustration, dotted lines and arrows indicate the direction of the stitching and the position of the Zipper Foot in relation to the beads.

After stitching each portion of the design, draw the thread ends to the underside and tie them together in a single knot set close to the fabric. Clip the bead threads about 4 inches from the design and remove all beads on them except one to cover the knot. With a needle, bring the thread ends through the first bead at the beginning for a smooth joining; then bring the needle through to the underside of the fabric and fasten the threads with several backstitches.

Beading by Hand

Round beads, pearls, and bugle beads can be sewed in place by hand. Baste or lightly trace the design on the right side of the fabric, then follow one of the methods described below.

Method 1. Use a needle fine enough to slide through the beads without splitting them and select thread matching the fabric in color.

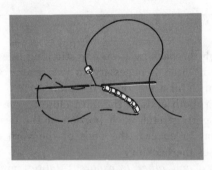

Fasten the thread on the underside of the fabric with two tiny backstitches. Bring the needle up through the fabric. Pass the needle through a bead; take a backstitch and bring the needle out exactly a bead length from where the thread came out. Start each successive backstitch against the previous bead to place the beads close together. Draw up the thread tightly enough for the beads to lie flat against the fabric. When completed, fasten the thread on the underside with tiny backstitches.

Method 2: String the beads on mercerized or nylon thread, leaving a 4-inch thread end to fasten on the underside.

Use a second thread, matching the fabric exactly in color, and a fine, short needle to couch on the beads. Fasten the thread on the underside of the fabric with two tiny backstitches. Hold the

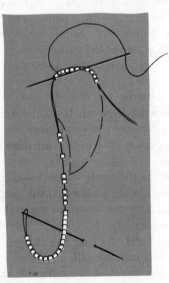

beads in position and bring the needle up through the fabric on the left side of the beading thread. Bring the thread to the right, between the beads, and take a slanting stitch over the beading thread, bringing the needle out on the left side of the beading thread at the end of the next bead.

When completed, fasten the needle thread on the underside with tiny backstitches. Clip the beading thread about 4 inches from the design and remove the excess beads. Use a needle to bring the end threads to the underside. Tie them in a single knot set close to the fabric.

Sewing on Sequins

Outline the design first, then fill in the center. Use a fine needle and a thread matching the sequins exactly in color.

Fasten the thread on the underside of the fabric with tiny backstitches. Bring the needle up through the fabric and through a sequin. Hold the sequin flat against the fabric, right side up, and take a stitch in front of it. Pass the needle through a sequin from the right side and take a backstitch as illustrated. Draw up the thread and at the same time turn the sequin right side up. The sequins will overlap and the stitches will be hidden. The stitch length on the underside must be the same size as the sequin. When finished, fasten the threads on the underside with tiny backstitches.

To add a bead to the center of a sequin, bring the needle up through the fabric and through a sequin. Pass the needle through a bead, then down through the sequin and fabric. Draw up the thread and take a tiny backstitch to fasten it. (The bead acts as an anchor, holding the sequin in place.) Bring the needle up through the fabric at the point where the next sequin will be sewed. This method is excellent when sequins are not sewed close together.

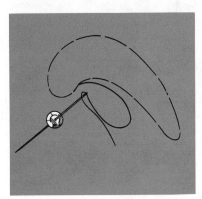 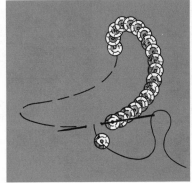 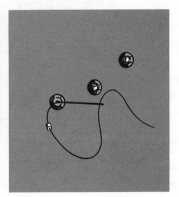

LACE EDGING AND INSERTION

Lace adds a delicate trimming to blouses, women's and children's dresses, babies' clothes, lingerie, and household linens.

You may apply lace to the edge of the fabric or set it into the fabric. Lace edging and insertion of cotton, silk, linen, rayon, nylon, wool, and other fibers are available in a variety of widths, patterns, and types.

The delicate network of threads in lace requires special sewing techniques. Whether you stitch the lace by hand or by machine depends on your fabric, the position of the lace on the garment, and personal preference. In all cases, use a short stitch and fine needle and thread. In handwork, the needle should be short as well as fine. *Always press the lace before applying it to the fabric.*

Gathering Lace

To gather lace, gently draw the top thread of the selvage and ease the lace back on the thread to the desired fullness. Be careful to distribute the fullness evenly.

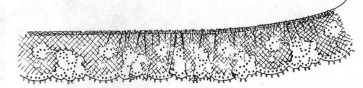

Applying Lace Edging

Lace over Rolled Edge

Straight lace. Baste the lace over the seam allowance of the fabric; both lace and fabric should be right side up. Trim the seam allowances under the lace to a scant ¼ inch. On the underside, roll the edge of the fabric and make small stitches through the rolled hem and lace. On the right side, the lace is over the hem.

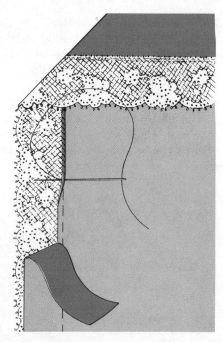

Gathered lace. Baste the gathered lace on the seamline of the fabric, right sides together. Trim the fabric seam allowance to a scant ¼ inch. Roll the fabric edge over the stitching line, and make small stitches through the rolled hem and lace. When finished, turn the lace over the rolled hem.

If you want the rolled hem on the top side in the finished work, baste the gathered lace on the seamline of the fabric, *wrong sides together* instead of right.

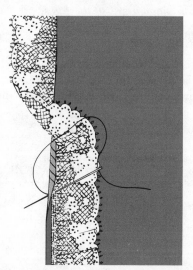

Gathered Lace under Rolled Edge

Place a line of stitching ⅛ inch from the seamline, using a short stitch. Press. Trim off the edge close to the stitching.

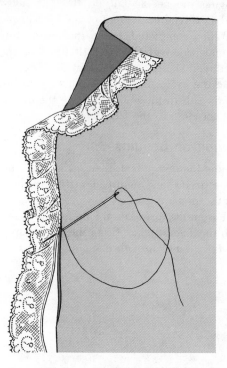

Roll the fabric to the underside as you sew the lace in place. Place the gathered lace over the rolled hem, right side down, and make small stitches through the lace and rolled hem. On the right side, the lace is under the hem.

Lace on Finished Edge

By hand. The fabric edge may be finished with a hem or facing. Lay the lace over the finished edge, right sides together, keeping the edges even. Pin. Working from the lace side, make very small

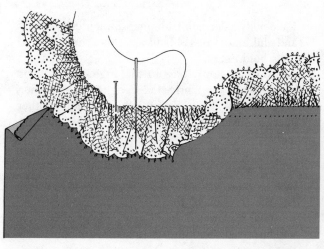

260

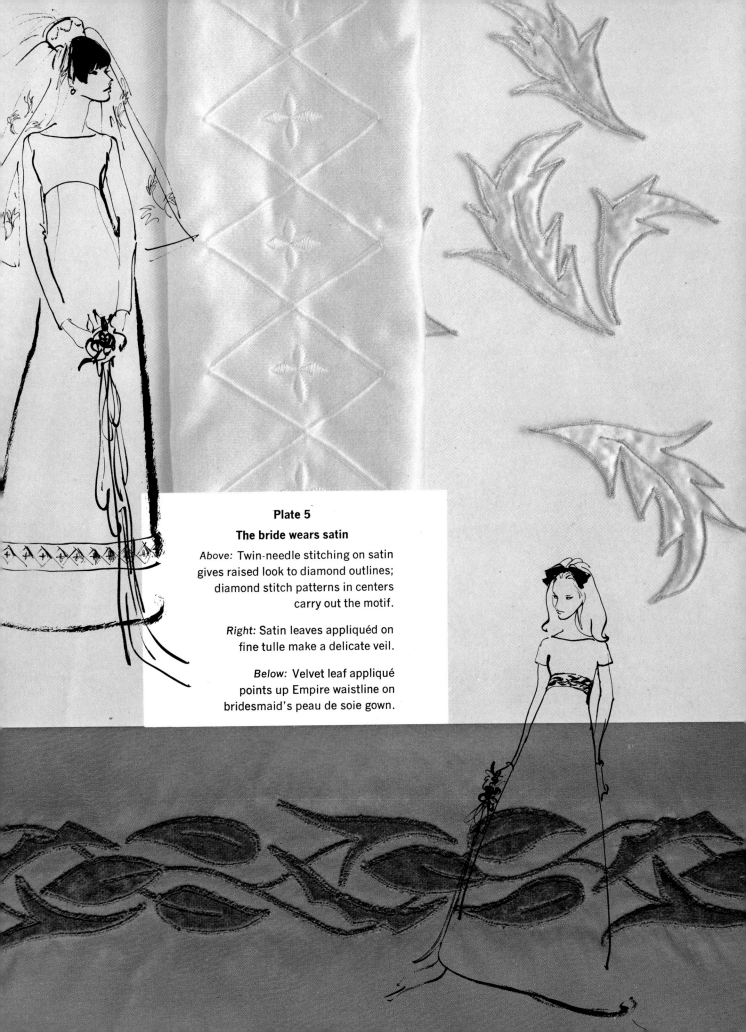

Plate 5

The bride wears satin

Above: Twin-needle stitching on satin gives raised look to diamond outlines; diamond stitch patterns in centers carry out the motif.

Right: Satin leaves appliquéd on fine tulle make a delicate veil.

Below: Velvet leaf appliqué points up Empire waistline on bridesmaid's peau de soie gown.

Plates 6 and 7

Sheer elegance in hems and a border

Top: Three rows of twin-needle stitching
produce raised design on silk organza hem.

Bottom left: Border of delicate rows of zig-zag stitching
is enhanced by edge-stitched scallops.

Bottom right: Shadow hem. The edge of organza
on the underside is cut away,
above design, after stitching.

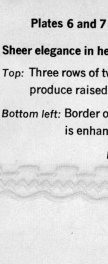

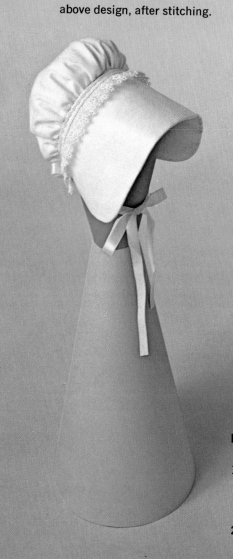

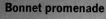

Bonnet promenade

1) Pique with Irish
   lace attached by a band
   of yellow zig-zag stitching.

2) Flannel tam with corded edge, ribbon
   trimmed with decorative stitch patterns.

3) Pique cap with flag appliqué,
   satin-stitched flagstaffs.

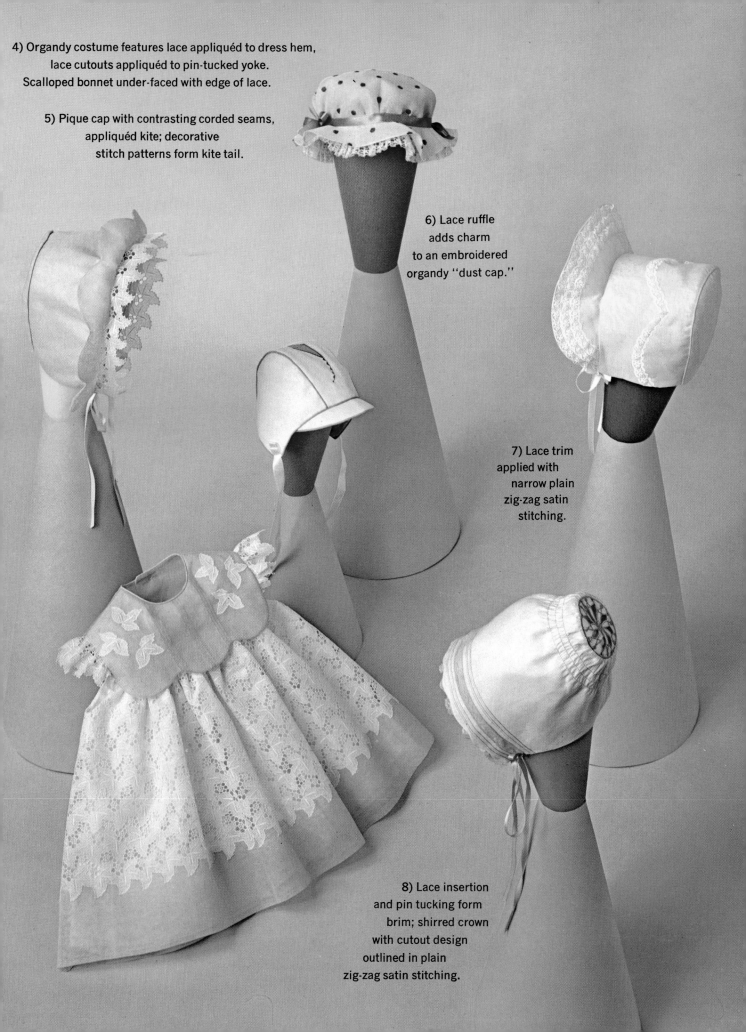

4) Organdy costume features lace appliquéd to dress hem, lace cutouts appliquéd to pin-tucked yoke. Scalloped bonnet under-faced with edge of lace.

5) Pique cap with contrasting corded seams, appliquéd kite; decorative stitch patterns form kite tail.

6) Lace ruffle adds charm to an embroidered organdy ''dust cap.''

7) Lace trim applied with narrow plain zig-zag satin stitching.

8) Lace insertion and pin tucking form brim; shirred crown with cutout design outlined in plain zig-zag satin stitching.

Plate 8

Night-blooming flowers

Left:
Appliquéd lace cutouts
form a delicate tracery
on a taffeta
evening gown.

Below:
Midnight black
zig-zag stitching
on stark white satin
becomes exotic
with the addition
of hand-sewn bugle
and round beads.

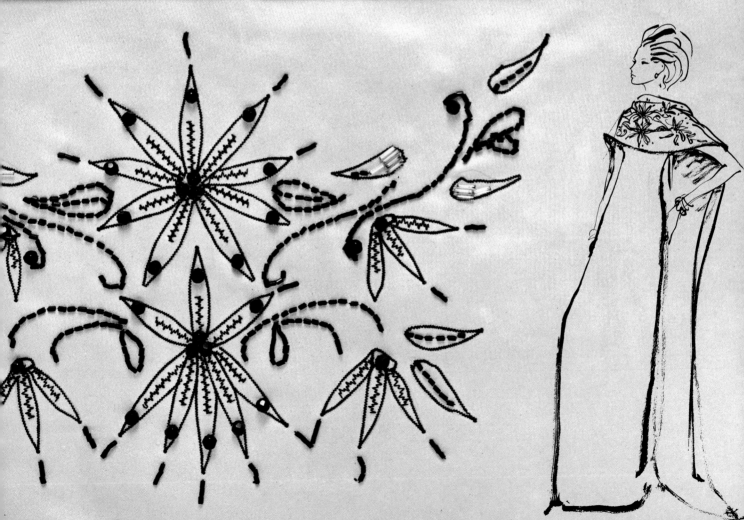

overhand stitches over the edge. The stitches should be loose enough so that the seam may be spread open when it is finished.

By machine. Lace edging and a narrow hem may be sewed in place with one line of machine stitching when the Hemmer Foot is used. The lace may be stitched over or under the fold for the hem. See *Hemmer Foot*, page 283.

Joining Lace Edging and Lace Insertion

By hand. The lace edging may be straight or gathered. Match the lace patterns when cutting the lace into lengths. Lay the right sides of the lace together, keeping the edges even, and pin. Work from the gathered side and make small over-hand stitches over the edge. The stitches should be loose enough so that the lace and insertion may be spread open when the stitching is finished. Two rows of insertion may be joined in the same way.

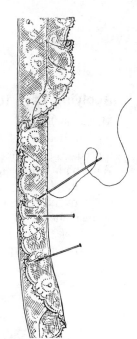

By machine. Match the lace patterns when cutting the lace into lengths. Replace the presser foot

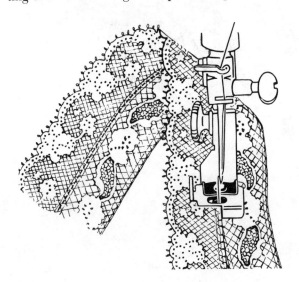

with the Edge Stitcher. Place one piece of lace in slot 1 and the other in slot 4. (The edges will barely overlap.) Adjust the lug to position the stitching close to the lace edge, and guide the lace against the slots as you sew. See *Edge Stitcher*, page 284.

Joining Lace Insertion and Fabric Bands

Fold the edge of the fabric under ½ inch, and press. Replace the presser foot with the Edge Stitcher. Place the fabric band in slot 1. Adjust the lug to position the stitching close to the folded edge. Insert the lace in slot 4 with the fabric band overlapping it slightly. Stitch, guiding the band and lace against the edges of the slots as instructed above. See *Edge Stitcher*, page 284.

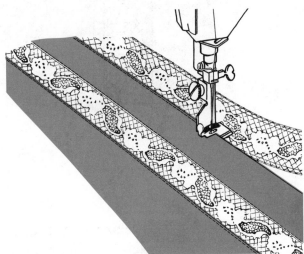

Inserting Lace

Pin each edge of the lace insertion in place; both lace and fabric must be right side up. Machine-stitch on each side of the insertion close to the edge. Press. If the fabric is to remain under the

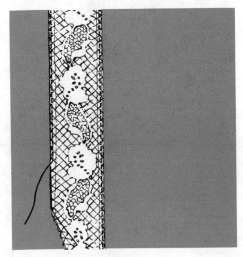

lace, the work is finished. If a lace insert is desired, trim the fabric under the lace to within ⅛ inch of the stitching. Turn the fabric edges away from the lace, and press.

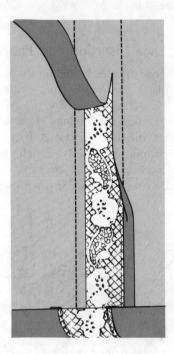

inch from the edge; baste the insertion where it is to fall in the garment. Select one of the decorative zig-zag stitches and set the stitch length for satin stitching. Position the work under the needle so that when the needle is on the extreme right stroke, it catches the selvage of the lace edging. Stitch. Then stitch down one edge of the insertion in the same way. Turn the fabric and stitch the other edge of the insertion from the opposite end. This procedure places the points of the design in opposite directions. Press. Trim the fabric under the lace close to the stitching.

Applying Lace to Curved Area

Mark the line on the right side of the fabric for the position of the lace. Draw the thread on the top edge of the lace and shape it to fit the curve. With both fabric and lace right side up, pin and baste in position. The lace may be stitched in place by hand, using a short overhand stitch or by machine. A narrow open-spaced zig-zag stitch or one of the decorative zig-zag stitches may be used instead of straight stitching.

Using Decorative Stitching with Lace

Many of the decorative zig-zag stitch patterns can be used effectively as both a finished and a trimming for lace edging and insertion.

Baste the lace edging over the fabric about ½

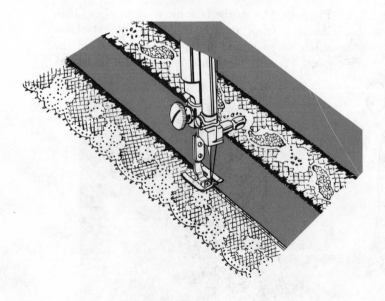

Applying Lace to Square Corner

Miter the lace insertion at the corner and press. Join with overhand stitches across the miter. On the underside, cut away the excess at the corner.

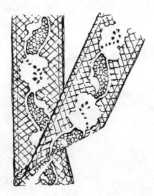

Stitch the lace edging and insertion together. The lace edging is generally gathered around the corner. About ½ inch from the corner, draw the top thread of the lace edging and gather it just enough so that it will lie flat when turned down. Catch the loop of the drawn thread under the overhand stitches as the lace and insertion are joined.

If lace edging is used alone, you may miter it at the corner instead of gathering it.

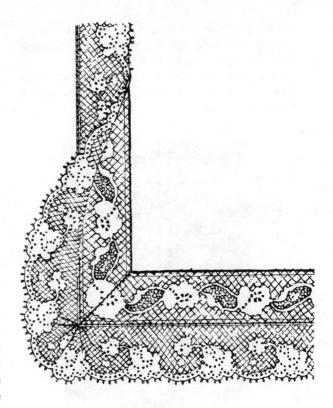

ENTREDEUX AND BRAID

Entredeux

Extredeux, sometimes called veining or beading, is a narrow insertion of open embroidered design. It is used between fabric edges in blouses, lingerie, and babies' and children's clothes. The wider width can be laced with ribbon.

Place the entredeux over the fabric, right sides together, with the embroidered edge on the seamline. Stitch close to the embroidery. Press; then press the seam edge away from the entredeux. On the underside, trim seam edges to ⅛ inch, and overcast them together.

(Continued on next page)

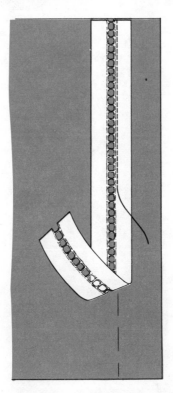

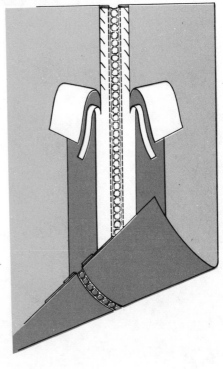

If top stitching is desired, fold the seam allowance to the underside and press. Lap the fabric over the entredeux, keeping the fold close to the embroidered edge. Stitch close to the fold. Trim, then overcast the seam edges on the underside the same as above.

Braid

Braid is used to edge collars, cuffs, lapels, and pockets and to accent other parts of a dress.

Finish the edges in the usual way before applying the braid. Carefully pin the braid over the finished edge; shape it to conform to curved edges, and miter square corners. Baste. Slip-stitch each edge of the braid in place.

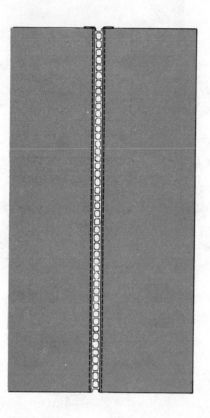
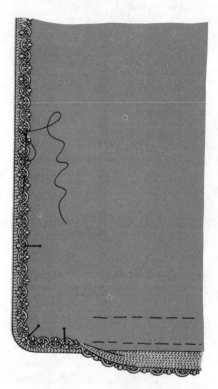

Zig-Zag Sewing

ZIG-ZAG SEWING HAS FOUND a solid place in dress construction and home and family maintenance sewing. That is not the end of the story, however. To stimulate your creative imagination, this chapter explains how you can also use your zig-zag machine for decorative sewing and fashion detailing. The opportunities for self-expression and originality are almost unlimited. You can enhance the appearance of clothing, household linens, and fabric furnishings without adding to their cost; you can achieve lovely effects in a formal evening dress or a simple apron or cottage curtain.

Like most women you are probably more creative than you realize. Learn to look for suggestions in ready-to-wear and in newspaper and magazine fashions; learn to use as design sources such unlikely material as wallpaper, children's coloring books, and printed fabrics. Decorative zig-zag sewing is easy, but do not make the mistake of overdecorating. Plan your placement of stitch patterns carefully, considering the fabric and the age of the person for whom the garment is intended or the type of household article you are making. If you do, your results will be pleasing and rewarding.

Many of the machine accessories may be used in zig-zag sewing. Check the instructions for accessories, beginning on page 280. For guides on how to use the zig-zag stitch in dress construction and family maintenance sewing, consult the alphabetical listing under *Zig-Zag Sewing* in the index.

Planning Preliminaries

The decision to use decorative zig-zag stitching must be made when the garment or article is in the planning stage. Often the stitching will extend through a seam allowance and must, therefore, be applied before the seam is stitched. Or the decorative stitching may be confined to a small section of the garment as for a motif or monogram; then it is easier to handle the small section under the needle than the finished garment.

Mercerized or silk sewing thread may be used in decorative stitching. It may blend with the fabric in color or be a decided contrast in shade or color. Subtle color contrasts are more tasteful and are usually preferred to bold contrasts, which tend to cheapen the appearance of a garment. Do not hesitate to experiment, however. Even the experts find that they can always learn something new about color combinations.

To Prepare the Work for Stitching

You can do decorative zig-zag stitching on almost any fabric. On soft fabrics you must add a backing to ensure firm satin stitching, and on many other fabrics you will achieve better results when a backing is used. Crisp lawn, organdy, or organza is suitable for this purpose. When the work is completed, the backing is cut away close to the stitching with small, sharp scissors.

To prepare your work for stitching, take these steps:

1. Steam-press the fabric so that it will be wrinkle-free.

2. Transfer the design to the fabric.

3. Cut the backing on the same grain as the fabric and at least 4 inches wider than the decorative stitching that will be applied.

4. Press the backing and position it carefully on the wrong side of the fabric, where the stitching will be applied. Pin, then baste in place.

5. After you complete each line of decorative stitching, press the work on the wrong side before proceeding with any additional stitching.

To Prepare the Machine

Some zig-zag machines have built-in discs and one or two selectors that may be set for any stitch pattern you want. Others have an assortment of discs (or cams), and you insert one for each stitch pattern.

The *stitch length selector* regulates the space between the stitches. The *stitch width selector* regulates the width of some stitch patterns and completely changes the pattern of others. The instruction book accompanying the machine explains how to select the stitch patterns as well as how to adjust the stitch length, stitch width, and tension.

Satin Stitching

For decorative zig-zag stitching the stitch length should be very short so that the zig-zag stitches are placed close together. A series of closely spaced zig-zag stitches that form a smooth, satinlike surface is known as "satin stitching." It is used for almost all the decorative work described in this chapter.

A Special Purpose Foot, designed for use in satin stitching, is generally provided with the machine. The foot has a raised center section that allows mounds of satin stitches to move freely under it. It also has an eyelet through which a filler cord or decorative thread may be inserted. Use this foot in your decorative stitching.

To adjust the stitch length for satin stitching. Move the stitch length selector to the "fine" area. Then run the machine at slow speed and gradually tighten the thumb nut until the stitches are closely spaced and form a smooth surface on your fabric.

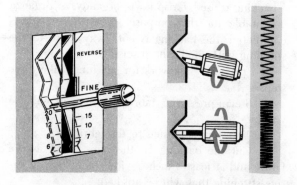

To adjust the tension for satin stitching. Satin stitching requires a lighter needle-thread tension than straight stitching or open-spaced designs. The wider the satin stitch, the lighter the tension required. A properly balanced satin stitch should lie flat across the fabric. Any tightness or

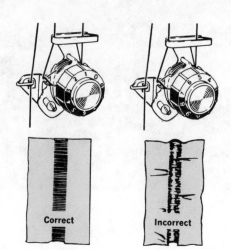

Correct   Incorrect

puckering usually indicates too high a needle thread tension.

Test stitching. To be sure that you have the correct tension setting, stitch length, and stitch width, test your stitching on a swatch of the same fabric you are using in your work. Use a backing if your fabric requires one.

On the same swatch, make a stitching test to determine which stitch pattern you wish to use. If you are planning to use two or more patterns, decide which ones may be combined attractively and how they should be spaced.

To Find the Beginning of a Pattern Unit

When you use a decorative stitch pattern in a motif or monogram, you must always start stitching at the beginning of a pattern unit. To do this, stitch on a scrap of fabric until you come to the end of a complete pattern unit—that is, to the end of the diamond, arrowhead, or whatever pattern you are using. Now you are ready to start stitching

at the beginning of the next unit. Remove the scrap of fabric from under the presser foot and position the motif or monogram under the needle, aligning the marking with the center of the presser foot. Lower the foot, and stitch. After you have stitched one portion of the design, pull the threads through to the underside and tie them. This sequence is recommended for all precise design placement.

DECORATIVE ZIG-ZAG STITCHING

The stitch patterns may be applied in a simple or an elaborate way. Either is attractive. It would be impossible to illustrate all of the many interesting, pleasing, and practical applications you can devise. The suggestions that follow give you an idea of what you can do. They also present instructions that are basic to the placement of *all* stitch patterns.

Applying a Trimming

Braid, Ribbon, and Rickrack

Metallic braid or narrow velvet ribbon adds an unusual and dramatic touch when combined with one of the decorative stitch patterns as either finish or trim. If a backing is required, baste it to the wrong side of the fabric. Then baste the braid or ribbon in position. Select one of the decorative stitch patterns, and set the stitch length selector for satin stitching. Stitch down one side of the braid or ribbon; then turn the fabric and stitch down the other side from the opposite end. This procedure places the points of the stitch pattern in opposite directions. In the illustrations, only the points of the stitching catch into the metallic braid, and the satin stitches are on the edge of the velvet ribbon with the points extending into the fabric. When finished, remove bastings and press. Trim the backing close to each side of the stitching.

Braid and decorative stitching are an effective trimming on hand towels, pillows, and other household articles. For a stitch pattern such as the one illustrated, position the work under the needle with the edge of the braid aligned with the center of the presser foot. Stitch as instructed above. Press.

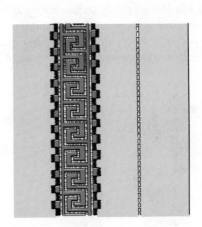

For a simple treatment on children's clothes, aprons, and cottage curtains, add rickrack—either a single row or two colors braided together. Baste the rickrack in position. Align the center of the rickrack with the center of the presser foot, and sew in place using a decorative stitch pattern or an open zig-zag stitch. Press.

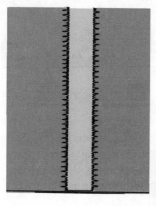

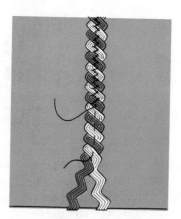

Bias Strip with Lace or Rickrack

Decorative stitching combined with bias tape and lace or bias tape and rickrack is an interesting treatment for little girls' dresses, blouses, and lingerie. *(Illustrated on next page)*

Open up the binding and stitch the rickrack or lace to each side of the cut edge. Extend the edge of the rickrack about ⅛ inch beyond the binding edge; keep the edges of the binding and lace even, and match the patterns in the lace. Fold the binding edge back in place; the lace or rickrack will extend beyond it. Press.

Baste the binding in position on the garment. Select a stitch pattern, and set the stitch length selector for satin stitching. To place the stitching on each edge of the binding, as illustrated with rickrack, position the work under the needle so that when the needle is on the extreme left stroke it catches the left edge of the binding; then turn the work and stitch down the other side of the binding from the opposite end.

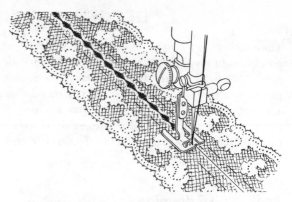

Bias Binding with Net Ruffles

Bias binding applied with decorative stitching adds a dainty touch to net ruffles on petticoats.

Replace the presser foot with the Binder and insert in it either silk or rayon bias binding. Carefully select a stitch pattern that complements the binding. Set the stitch length selector for satin stitching, and bind the edge. Press. See page 282 for instructions on using the *Binder*.

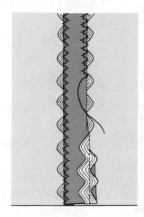

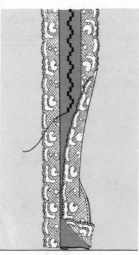

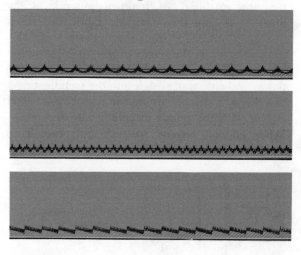

To place one row of stitching through the center, as illustrated with lace, align the center of the binding with the center of the presser foot, and stitch. Remove bastings, and press.

Lace with Decorative Stitching

Baste two strips of lace in position on the garment with the inside edges of the lace touching. Match the patterns in the lace. Baste a backing of crisp lawn to the underside. Select the stitch pattern, and set the stitch length selector for satin stitching. Align the center of lace with the center of the presser foot, and stitch. Remove bastings and press. Trim the backing close to the stitching. *(Illustrated at top of next column).*

Stitching Designs

Geometric Design

A geometric design with an interlaced effect will enhance the appearance of a full-skirted dress made of organdy, organza, or linen. It is also appropriate for such household articles as place mats and hand towels.

Trace the design lightly on the right side of the fabric. See page 251. Baste a backing of crisp organdy or lawn on the underside of the design for added body. Study the design to determine which sections you should stitch first. Select a narrow, plain zig-zag stitch, and set the stitch length selector for satin stitching. Align the markings of the design with the center of the presser foot, and stitch around each edge. Press.

Next, select an open-spaced stitch pattern, and stitch midway between the two previous lines of stitching. Pull the threads through to the underside and tie. Remove bastings; press. Trim the backing close to the stitching. To add glitter to glamour on a cocktail dress, sew on a few sequins or beads by hand.

Outline Design

An outline design may be used in the same places as the geometric one. Prepare the work as described above. Select one of the open-spaced stitch patterns, and set the stitch length selector for satin stitching. Align the marking for the design with the center of the presser foot, and stitch. Guide the fabric with both hands, turning it as you sew. At the corners, stop with the needle in the fabric, raise the presser bar, and turn the fabric, pivoting on the needle. Lower the presser bar and continue the stitching. (On sharp curves, you may need to raise the presser bar slightly when the needle is in the fabric, and ease the fabric to the right or left.) When completed, pull the threads through to the underside and tie. Press. Either stitch the lines within the design, using a narrow, plain zig-zag stitch, or sew on beads. Trim the backing on the underside close to the stitching.

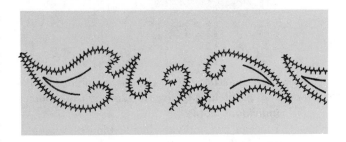

Scalloped Hems

Scalloped hems add interest to babies' and children's clothes, cotton dresses for adults, and household linens.

Fold and press the hem. Mark a 2-inch scallop about 1 inch below the top of the hem. Baste close to the marking to prevent the two layers of fabric from slipping.

Select an open-spaced stitch pattern, and set the stitch length selector for satin stitching. Position the work under the needle with the scallops to the right, and align the marking with the center of the presser foot. Stitch around the scallops, using both hands to guide the work and turning the fabric gradually as you sew. At the point of the scallop, and on the left swing of the needle, stop with the needle in the fabric. Raise the presser bar and turn the fabric, pivoting on the needle, then lower the presser bar and stitch the next scallop. (On sharp curves, it is sometimes necessary to raise the presser bar slightly when the needle is in the fabric and ease the fabric slightly to the right or left.) When completed, press. Trim the upper edge of the hem on the underside, close to the stitching.

Many of the decorative stitch patterns are adaptable to scallops that have a curve instead of a point between the scallops.

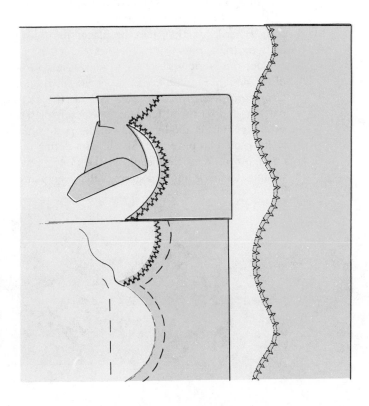

Pin Tucks, Lace, and Stitch Patterns

Groups of pin tucks combined with pattern stitching add a fashionable and delicate touch to blouses, babies' clothes, and children's dresses made of soft fabrics.

Pin-tuck the fabric as instructed on page 236. Then lightly mark the position for the decorative stitching midway between the groups of tucks. Select one of the open-spaced stitch patterns, and set the stitch length selector for satin stitching. Align the marking for the pattern with the center of the presser foot and stitch. Press.

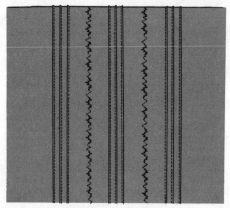

Lace insertion may also be combined with decorative stitching to give the same delicate touch.

Individual Motifs

You can give individuality to blouses, summer dresses, children's clothes, and place mats by grouping small designs made of such stitch patterns as the solid scallop or pyramid. The designs may form a border or they may be placed asymmetrically on the garment.

Dot the fabric with chalk to mark the position of the design. Prepare the work as described under *Geometric Design*, page 268. Select the stitch pattern, and set the stitch length selector for satin stitching. Start at the beginning of the pattern unit as instructed on page 266. Stitch, completing only one pattern. With the needle in the fabric, pivot, turning the fabric left 90 degrees. Stitch, completing

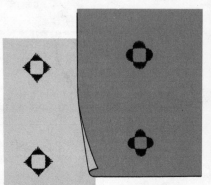

another stitch pattern, then pivot again. Continue in the same manner until the four sides are finished. Pull threads through to the underside and tie. Press.

Arrowheads as a Finish

The arrowhead provides a decorative and secure finish on fashion seams or darts that end within the garment, at the top of pleats, and at the ends of pockets in tailored clothes.

Start at the beginning of the arrowhead pattern. See page 266. Begin the stitching at the very end of the seam, dart, or pocket. When finished, pull threads to the underside and tie. Press.

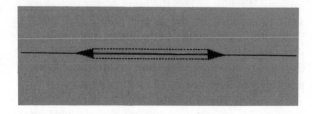

Flowerlike Design

Bar tacks may be placed in sequence to form flowerlike points—an exquisite touch in babies' and children's clothes, blouses, and summer dresses. The design may be used around the neckline, in a yoke, above the hem, or along each side of a front closing.

Dot the fabric with a pencil to mark the position of each flower. When the design borders a curved edge, such as a neckline, mark the cutting line instead of cutting the fabric. By not cutting the edge, you can prevent it from stretching as you stitch and guide the fabric.

Adjust the machine for a wide zig-zag stitch. Make the feed inoperative so that it will not move the fabric as you sew. (This is done by either raising the throat plate or lowering the feed. Check the instruction book accompanying your machine.)

When the needle is on the left stroke, position it in the fabric at the marking for the design. Lower

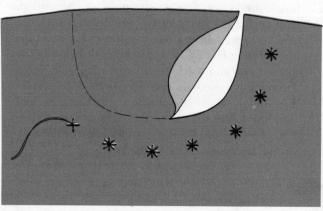

the presser foot and make four stitches, stopping with the left stroke of the needle in the fabric (center of the design). Raise the presser foot and turn the fabric left 180 degrees, pivoting on the needle. Lower the presser foot and make four stitches, again stopping with the needle in the fabric on the left stroke (center). Pivot again, turn the fabric left 90 degrees, and make four more stitches; then pivot, turn the fabric left 180 degrees, and make four stitches. You have now finished the first four points.

To make the remaining four points, pivot and turn the fabric on the needle far enough each time to place stitches midway between each of the four finished points. Take four stitches each time, stopping with the needle in the center of the design. When finished, use a needle to bring the thread through to the underside; then tie it with the bobbin thread. Press.

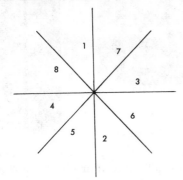

"Twin-Needle" Scallops

Scallops stitched with a twin needle add a delicate touch to dresses, blouses, and children's clothes.

Select the scallop pattern. The stitch length and stitch width vary the length and depth of the scallop; make the appropriate selection. If you are making several rows, start each row at the beginning of a scallop unit. See page 266. Press.

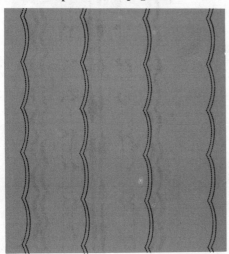

Appliquéd Designs

Interesting block designs lend distinction to curtains, place mats, and dresses. For a vivid note you can combine blocks contrasting in color with the fabric. Or you may appliqué a striped fabric to a solid-colored fabric for a simple, bright trim on blouses, dresses, and informal table linens. See *Appliqué*, page 250.

For the block design, first appliqué the blocks in position. Then lightly mark the lines for the crossbar stitching. Align the marking with the center of the presser foot and stitch, using a narrow, closely spaced zig-zag stitch. Press.

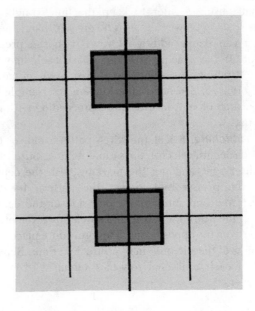

To appliqué a stripe to a solid color, mark a geometric or irregular design on the striped fabric and appliqué the striped fabric in place.

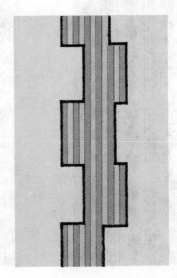

271

Border Designs

Border designs of unlimited variety can be created by combining several stitch patterns. Simple or elaborate, delicate or bold, they can be varied to suit the application. And they have many applications on dresses, blouses, children's clothes, men's or boys' sport shirts, curtains or linens. Use a border design as you would a braid—at the top of a hem, through the bodice and sleeve sections, in a yoke, and on collars, cuffs, belts, and pockets. The stitching may be placed on the horizontal, vertical, or bias line.

Preparation. Mark the center line for the first row of stitching with a light brush of pencil or chalk, using a ruler to keep the line straight. If the spacing between rows is no greater than ½ inch, you can gauge additional rows with the presser foot. If the spacing is wider, mark each line for the stitching. Use a backing of crisp lawn, organdy, or organza. See page 265. Make a test sample on a swatch of your fabric before proceeding with the actual work.

Stitching. Select the stitch pattern and set the stitch length selector for satin stitching. Stitch the center row, aligning the marking with the center of the presser foot. Select the pattern for the next row and stitch down one side of the center row; then turn the fabric and stitch down the other side from the opposite end. This procedure places the points of the stitching in opposite directions. Repeat it for each additional row of stitching used in the border.

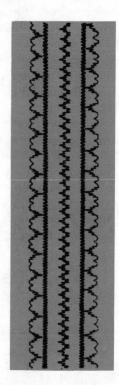

Borders may be made more glamorous by couching metallic thread or bouclé yarn with one of the open-spaced stitch patterns or by using the twin needle, as illustrated below. When finished, press. Trim the backing on the underside close to the stitching.

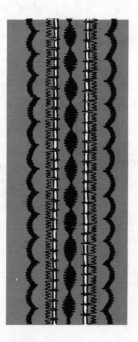

Fagoting

Seam edges joined with fagoting are a delicate addition to blouses, dresses, lingerie, and children's clothes. Two strips of bias binding joined with fagoting make an unusual yoke treatment.

Fold under the seam allowance and press. Baste the folded edges to onionskin paper or art tracing paper, allowing ⅛ inch between the edges.

Select either the multiple-stitch zig-zag or the fagoting stitch pattern. Use the widest stitch width and "fine" stitch length. Align the center of the work with the center of the presser foot. As you sew, the stitches will catch into the fabric fold on alternate sides.

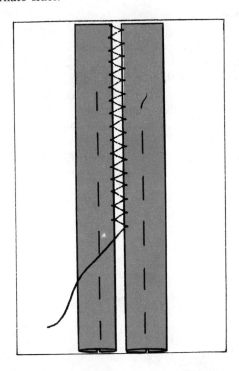

When completed, remove the bastings and gently pull the paper away from one side of the stitching, then from the other. Press.

Buttonholes for Lacing

Buttonholes, accented with decorative stitching, can be used to produce interesting lacing on clothing for children and teen-age girls as well as for adults.

Mark the position of each buttonhole. Use a backing of crisp lawn or organdy. Refer to the instruction book accompanying the machine, and work the buttonholes. Press. Add a row of decorative stitching above and below the buttonholes. Velvet ribbon, grosgrain ribbon, or braid may be laced through the buttonholes.

Drawn Work

Fabrics with a balanced weave are suitable for this decorative treatment, which may be used on informal table linens and scarves.

Draw a thread from the fabric to indicate each edge of the drawn work. Select the blindstitch zig-zag pattern, a "fine" stitch length, and medium stitch width. Stitch down the left side of the drawn work, then turn the fabric and stitch down the other side from the opposite end. This procedure places the point of the stitching in the solid fabric. Draw the remaining threads from the fabric to form the openwork between the rows of stitching.

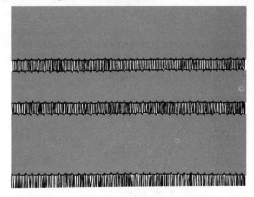

To fringe the edge, draw a thread from the fabric to mark the depth of the fringe. Stitch with this edge to the right. Draw the threads below the stitching to make the fringe. Press.

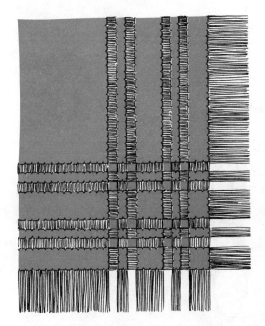

273

Shadow Design

A shadow effect is an interesting finish for collars and cuffs, facings, and yokes. It can be created easily on a double thickness of sheer fabric such as organdy, organza, voile, and sheer crisp nylon *when a closely spaced stitch pattern is used. Open-spaced stitch patterns are not suitable for this work.*

Cut the garment section by the pattern and construct it, using a hairline seam. See page 88 for instructions. Turn the section to the right side and press it, forming a sharp crease on the stitching line. Baste the two layers of fabric together just outside the line for the decorative stitching.

Select a closely spaced stitch pattern, such as the scallop in the illustration, and set the stitch length selector for satin stitching. Place two rows of stitches on the right side of the fabric—the first row about ⅜ inch from the edge, the second about ⅜ inch from the first. Carefully guide the fabric with both hands, turning it as you sew. Remove bastings and press. Cut away the undersection of fabric between the two rows of stitching to create a shadow effect. Use small, sharp-pointed scissors and trim close to the stitching.

reverse the ruler and draw the scallops facing the opposite direction, overlapping the first scallops about ¾ inch.

Prepare the work as described above. Stitch around the design. When completed, cut away the fabric on the underside between the rows of stitching.

Edgestitched Finish

Edgestitching is a delicate finish for babies' clothes, children's dresses, ruffles, and lingerie *when a closely spaced zig-zag stitch pattern is used. Open-spaced patterns are not suitable for this work.* Edgestitching may be used on many types of fabrics.

Mark the seamline, but instead of cutting on the seam edge, cut at least 1 inch from the seamline. When curved edges are not cut, the fabric is easier to guide and will not stretch during the stitching. If edgestitching is used on a single thickness of fabric, baste a backing of crisp lawn to the wrong side of the fabric for added body.

Select a closely spaced stitch pattern, and set the stitch length for satin stitching. Place the work under the needle so that the outer edge of the stitching will fall barely inside the seamline. Carefully guide the fabric with both hands, turning it as you sew. Remove bastings and press.

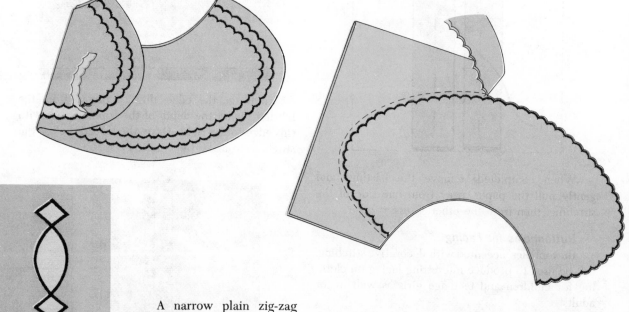

A narrow plain zig-zag stitch may also be used to obtain shadow effects. Set the stitch length selector for satin stitching. For the design illustrated, lightly draw the scallops on the fabric, using a 2-inch scallop ruler as a guide. Then

Trim the outer edge of fabric and backing close to the stitching, using embroidery scissors. Then trim the backing close to the inside edge of the stitching.

Ruffles. Edgestitching is a pleasing finish for ruffles. If the ruffle has a heading, finish each edge. After stitching the first edge, turn the fabric and stitch down the other side from the opposite end.

Large scallops. An edge of large scallops is appropriate for wearing apparel and linens when it is made with a narrow, plain, zig-zag stitch.

Lightly mark the scallops 2 inches from the edge of the fabric, using a 2-inch scallop ruler as a guide. *Do not cut.* For added body, baste a backing of crisp lawn on the underside of the scallops.

Select the plain zig-zag stitch, narrow stitch width; set the stitch length selector for satin stitching. Use a filler cord to prevent the scallops from stretching. Replace the presser foot with the Special Purpose Foot, and insert the filler cord into the eyelet. See *Hairline Seam,* page 88 for threading instructions. Position the work under the needle with the scallops to the right; align the marking with the center of the presser foot. Guide the fabric with both hands as you sew, turning it gradually, following the scallops. At the point of the scallop, and when the needle is in left position,

raise the presser bar and turn the fabric, pivoting on the needle. Then lower the presser bar and stitch the next scallop. When finished, press. Trim surplus border and backing close to the stitching. Then trim the backing close to the inside of the scallops.

Couching

You can achieve novel effects by couching gimp, yarn, or braid with zig-zag stitch patterns. Spaced patterns, such as the blindstitch zig-zag or narrow, open-spaced zig-zag, are most appropriate since they allow the decorative cord to show as part of the work. You may use either a single or twin needle in the machine.

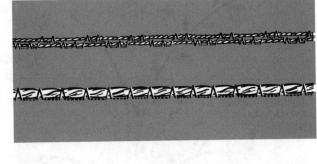

Lightly mark the position for the couching. Place the cord over the marking, and align it with the center of the presser foot. Stitch, allowing the stitches to form over the cord. Press.

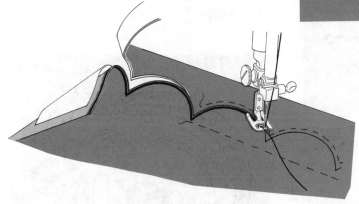

MOTIFS AND MONOGRAMS

Many of the decorative stitch patterns lend themselves perfectly to the creation of attractive and unusual motifs or monograms. Select a simple design from the many transfer patterns available, or sketch one to suit your purpose.

Motifs

Simulated Appliqué

A design for children's clothes similar to the one illustrated is a special decorative touch that looks like appliqué.

Trace the design lightly on the right side of the fabric. See page 251 for instructions. Baste a

backing of crisp organdy or lawn on the underside for added body. Set the stitch length selector

for satin stitching and use the following stitches: (1) A narrow, plain zig-zag stitch to outline the design; (2) the scallop stitch pattern for the eyebrows, hair, and lines within; (3) the ball stitch pattern for the eye and nose; and (4) the arrowhead for the bow at the neckline. Pull the threads through to the underside and tie them after stitching each section. When finished, trim the backing close to the stitching. Press.

Floral and Leaf Motifs

The floral motif illustrated is an excellent example of how you can combine several different stitch patterns and achieve pleasing results.

Prepare the work as described under *Simulated Appliqué*. Select the stitch pattern, and set the stitch length selector for satin stitching. Align the

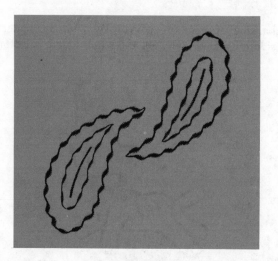

marking with the center of the presser foot, and stitch. To bring a stitch pattern to a point, as in the ends of the stems, flowers, and leaves, gradually move the stitch width selector to the narrowest width as you sew.

The leaflike motif is appropriate for dresses and table linens where a small design is required for the accent desired. Prepare the work and stitch as instructed in *Simulated Appliqué*.

Beads with Stitch Patterns

Beads combined with decorative stitches are an elegant way of enhancing cocktail and evening dresses, jackets, and stoles.

Prepare the work as described under *Simulated Appliqué* above. Set the stitch length selector for satin stitching. Select a closely spaced and an open-spaced stitch pattern to use within each leaf and a narrow, plain zig-zag stitch to outline the leaf. Pull the threads through to the underside and tie them after stitching each section. When completed, trim the backing close to the stitching. Press. To add a touch of glamour, arrange a few beads asymmetrically on the designs and hand-sew them in place.

Monograms

To monogram the "K" shown here, prepare the work as described under *Simulated Appliqué*, page 275. The first stitching is within the monogram. Select the stitch pattern, set the stitch length selector for satin stitching, and stitch. Then select a narrow, plain zig-zag stitch. Align the marking

Plate 9

Beading adds glitter to gala evenings

Right: Peau de soie leaves and bands in warm golden tones appliquéd on peau de soie obi. Hand-sewn bugle beads.

Below left: Beading applied with open-spaced zig-zag stitching in a design that explodes with the gaity of a sparkling fountain. Clusters of round beads sewn by hand.

Below right: Muted glimmer on a short evening dress. Satin band is decorated with zig-zag stitching, appliqué, and hand-sewn beads; then slip-stitched on dress and edged with beading.

Plate 10

Appliqué for all seasons

Above: Appliqué of gold synthetic leather (easier to handle than the real thing) forms an elegant jewel on deep blue velvet.

Left: Airy silk organza shadow-appliquéd with three colors. Different layers are cut away to obtain various shades.

Below: Gold synthetic leather appliqué highlights decorative stitching on taffeta.

for the monogram with the center of the presser foot, and stitch, outlining the outer edges. Pull the threads to the underside and tie them after stitching each section. When finished, trim the backing close to the stitching. Press.

For the "G W" monogram, prepare the work as described under *Simulated Appliqué*, page 275. Set the stitch length selector for satin stitching. First, work the individual flower petals, using the ball stitch pattern. To start stitching at the begin-

ning of the pattern unit see page 266. Then outline the monogram with a narrow, plain zig-zag stitch. Align the marking for the design with the center of the presser foot. Begin stitching at the point near the finished petals; gradually turn the fabric with both hands as you sew. When completed, pull the threads through to the underside and tie them. Trim the backing close to the stitching. Press.

EMBROIDERY

Script monograms and satin-stitched scallops that look like hand embroidery can be made with zig-zag stitching when you use the "free-motion" method.

In free-motion stitching, you sew without a presser foot and control the fabric movement (and hence, stitch length) yourself by means of embroidery hoop. Because you can move the hoop in any direction—forward or backward, from side to side, and even diagonally—free-motion stitching is well adapted to intricate embroidery designs.

To Prepare the Machine

Adjust the machine for a plain zig-zag stitch and either a medium or wide stitch width. Generally, a lighter needle thread tension is required. See page 266. Raise the stitch length selector to a short stitch. Remove the presser foot. Make the

feed inoperative so that it will not move the fabric. (This is done by either raising the throat plate or lowering the feed. Refer to the instruction book accompanying your machine.)

Monograms

Always make a test sample first to determine the correct stitch width, spacing, tension, and hoop movement.

Trace or mark the monogram on the right side of the fabric. See page 251. If the fabric is soft or loosely woven, add an underlay of crisp lawn or organdy slightly larger than the hoop used. Carefully baste the backing to the wrong side under the area where the stitching will be applied.

Center the work, right side up, in embroidery hoop large enough to encompass the entire design. Be sure that the fabric is held taut in the hoop.

Position the work under the needle. Lower the presser bar to activate the tension. Turn the hand wheel toward you and bring the bobbin thread up through the fabric to start the design.

Lower the needle into the fabric, hold both thread ends, and start stitching. Move the hoop slowly, following the outline of the design. To maintain parallel stitches, follow the monogram without turning; the work should remain straight in line with the feed at all times. The shading of stitches from wide to narrow is controlled by slowly moving the hoop to the right or left and at a slight angle. Where lines cross, make the first line of stitching less dense and the second line more prominent. This takes practice.

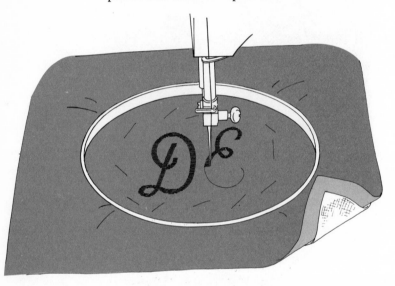

Run the machine at an even rate of speed so that the stitches are uniformly spaced. A slow motion of the hoop produces a close satin stitch; a more rapid movement produces an open stitch.

When finished, bring the threads through to the underside by means of a needle, and tie them. Cut away the backing close to the stitching. Press.

Monograms on Terry Cloth (Above right)

Monograms can easily be applied to bath and hand towels, beach robes, and other articles made of terry cloth.

Trace the monogram on a firm fabric, such as crisp lawn or organdy, slightly larger than the hoop used. Carefully position the lawn *on the right side of the terry cloth* and baste it in place. Then stitch, following the directions given above. When finished, cut away the lawn close to the stitching, using small, sharp scissors. Steam from the wrong side.

Satin-Stitched Scallops

Satin-stitched scallops provide a beautiful and durable finish for household linens as well as wearing apparel.

Trace the scallops on the *right side* of the fabric; *do not cut.* See page 251 for instructions. When scalloping is used as an edge finish, allow at least a 1-inch margin beyond the tracing. Machine-baste a strip of fabric to the cut edge so that the work is wide enough to fit in hoop.

If the fabric requires a backing, use crisp lawn or organdy cut slightly wider than the hoop. Machine-baste the marked scalloped edge over the

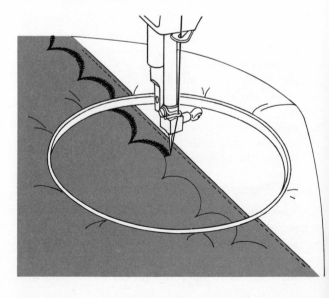

center of the backing. The lawn or organdy serves as an extension on the edge as well as a backing.

Center the work in embroidery hoop and position it under the needle the same as for monograms.

To maintain parallel stitches, follow the scallops without turning; the work remains straight in line with the feed at all times. Stitch slowly, moving the hoop to the right or left, so that the needle on its left swing follows the marking for the scallops. This produces the effect of a narrow stitch at the point between the scallops; the stitch widens to its full depth at the arc. Maintain an even rate of speed so that the stitches are uniformly spaced.

To cord scallops. A fine corded edge is used as an edge finish to complete satin-stitched scallops. Use the Special Purpose Foot on the machine,

and insert the filler cord into the right eyelet. See *Hairline Seam,* page 88 for threading instructions.

Position the needle close to the scalloped edge; lower the foot and stitch close to the scallops, covering the filler cord with narrow, closely spaced, plain zig-zag stitches. Crowd the stitches against the scallops all the way. Press.

If scallops border a hem, cut away the surplus of hem on the wrong side, close to the inside of the scallops. If scallops form an edge, cut away the surplus border and backing close to the cording stitches on the outside of the scallops. Then cut away the backing close to the inside of the scallops.

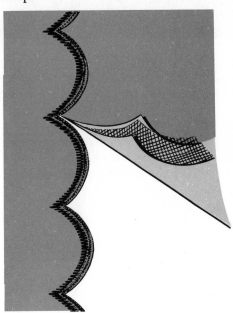

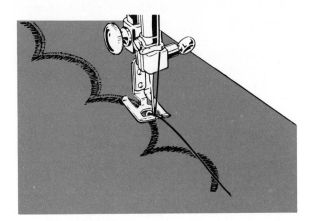

Using
Your Machine Accessories

ACCESSORIES ADD NEW DIMENSIONS to machine sewing. They enable you to accomplish quickly and expertly many finishing details that would be laborious and time consuming by hand.

Accessories are available for almost every phase of sewing. Many are standard and come with the machine; others can be purchased separately. This chapter explains how to use them all.

To Attach an Accessory

The accessories replace the regular presser foot on the machine. Refer to the instruction book accompanying the machine or accessory for complete information on how to place each one on your machine. If the accessory has a needle hole, be sure to draw the needle thread through it by taking a stitch in a swatch of fabric before starting to sew.

Zipper Foot, Seam Guide, and Quilter

These three accessories are illustrated elsewhere in the book. For pages giving instructions on their use, consult the alphabetical index.

The *Zipper Foot* simplifies zipper application and cording. It can be adjusted to the right or left of the needle and enables you to stitch close to the chain portion of a zipper or the bulk of a filler cord. It is a boon in dressmaking as well as in making home decorations.

The *Seam Guide* ensures accurate seam width and parallel lines of stitching for accent. It is in-valuable to the beginner and even to the experienced sewer.

The *Quilter*, with its short, open foot and adjustable and removable space guide, is especially adapted to stitching lightly padded fabrics.

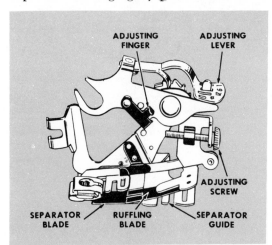

ADJUSTING FINGER · ADJUSTING LEVER · ADJUSTING SCREW · SEPARATOR BLADE · RUFFLING BLADE · SEPARATOR GUIDE

Ruffler

The Ruffler makes uniform gathered or pleated ruffles on light or medium-weight fabrics. The simple settings belie the variety of work possible.

For instructions on fabric requirements and cutting of ruffles, and for additional information, see *Ruffles*, page 240.

Gathering. Adjust the Ruffler for gathering. For maximum fullness, turn the adjusting screw clockwise; for less fullness, turn it counterclockwise. The stitch length also affects the fullness; a short stitch produces more fullness, a long stitch less.

Insert the fabric to be ruffled between the two blue blades. Bring the edge under the first guide to keep the seamline even. Stitch, guiding the fabric.

Ruffler and feed of the machine. Bring the fabric edge under the first guide. Stitch.

Correct Position for Fabric to be Ruffled

Correct Positions for Fabrics

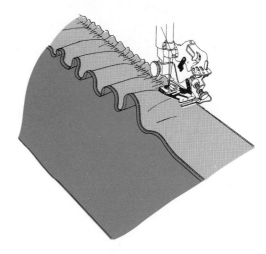

Ruffle with heading. Insert the fabric to be ruffled between the two blades, extending the right edge beyond the needle the width of the heading. As you sew, guide the fabric to keep the heading width even.

Pleating. Adjust the Ruffler for pleats, either six or twelve stitches apart. Turn the adjusting screw clockwise as far as it will go. A short stitch places the pleats close together; a long stitch places them farther apart. Insert the fabric to be pleated between the two blue blades as you did for gathering. Stitch; as each pleat is formed, finger-press it the full depth of the ruffle.

Correct Position for Fabric to be Ruffled

Correct Position for Fabric

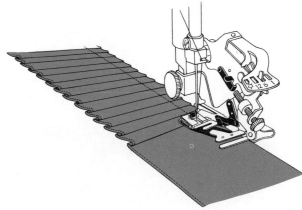

To form and attach a ruffle in one operation. Insert the ruffle strip, wrong side up, the same as for plain gathering. Place the fabric to which the ruffle is to be joined, right side up, between the

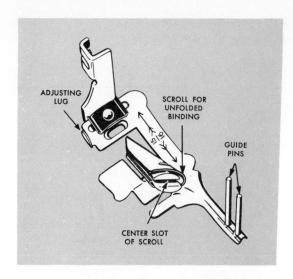

when you apply the binding, see *Zig-Zag Sewing* page 268.

Inside curves are straightened as they are fed into the Binder. If the fabric is soft and has a tendency to stretch, reinforce the edge with a single row of stitching before binding.

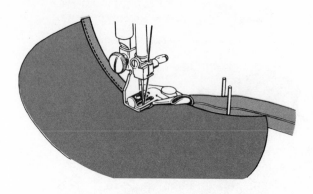

Binder

The Binder is used to apply commercial binding or self-fabric bias to an unfinished edge. Binding is a suitable finish for seam and hem edges that fray easily and a pretty trimming for ruffles, aprons, children's wear, curtains, and novelty items. Straight or zig-zag stitching may be used with the Binder.

Cut the binding diagonally to form a long point at the end. Insert the point in the slot in the Binder and pull it through the scroll until the evenly folded binding is under the needle. Stitch just far enough to place the stitching close to the edge. To do this, move the scroll to the right or left. Do not pull the binding as it feeds through the scroll. Do not raise the presser bar after the stitching is in the correct position.

Outside curves tend to lead away from the scroll. Guide the fabric to the left in line with the needle so that the full seam width is taken. Do not attempt to pull or straighten the fabric into the full length of the scroll.

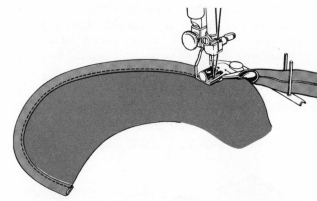

When rickrack braid is applied to an edge as it is bound, insert the edge and rickrack into the Binder at the same time, keeping the edges flush.

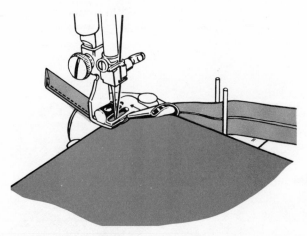

Insert the edge to be bound as far to the right as it will go in the center scroll, and stitch.

To use decorative or plain zig-zag stitching

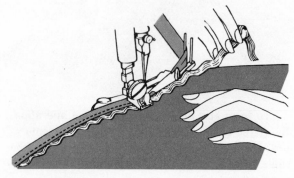

Hemmer Foot

With the Hemmer Foot you can turn and stitch narrow hems without basting or pressing. A time-saving accessory, it is especially suited to hemming ruffles, sashes, or any long edge where a narrow, machine-stitched hem is appropriate. Many yards may be finished as quickly as stitching a straight seam. Either straight or decorative stitching may be used. See *Narrow Hem Finishes*, page 195 for additional information.

Hemming. Form a ⅛-inch double fold at the very edge of the fabric and crease it for a distance of about 2 inches. Place the fabric under the foot and stitch through the creased fold for several stitches. Hold the thread ends in the left hand and

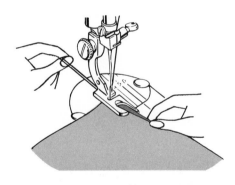

evenly guide the raw edge in front of the Hemmer into the scroll. Soft fabrics will enter the scroll best with the foot down; firm, crisp fabrics, with

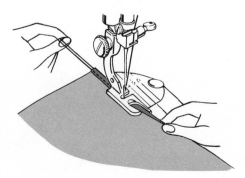

the foot raised. Even feeding is essential. As you sew, keep the same width of fabric in the scroll at all times.

Hemming with lace. You can form a hem and stitch lace edging in place with one line of stitching.

To apply lace over the hem, fold and start the hem in the usual way. Start about 1 inch down from the end of the lace and place the selvage under the needle; lower the needle to hold the lace firmly. Raise the foot slightly and slip the lace under the back portion of it. Stitch, guiding the hem with the right hand and the lace with the left.

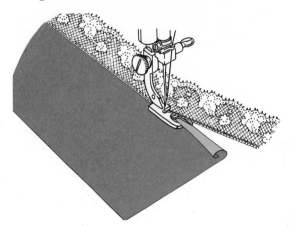

To apply lace under the hem, place the selvage of the lace ⅛ inch from the fabric edge; then fold and start the hem in the usual way. As you stitch, keep the lace ⅛ inch from the fabric edge, and form the hem over the lace selvage.

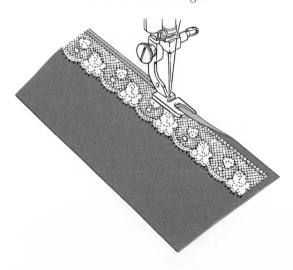

Hemmed seam. See page 85 for instructions.

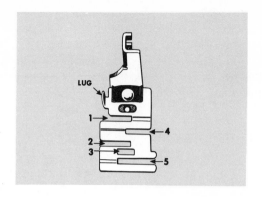

Edge Stitcher

The Edge Stitcher enables you to accurately place stitching on the extreme edge of a fabric. Using the numbered slots as your guide, you can join lace edges, fabric bands, and lace insertion; make French seams of uniform width; stitch tucks from pin width to ¼ inch; and edgestitch hems, facings, and seams.

The distance from the line of stitching to the edge of the fabric is regulated by the lug, which can be moved to the right or left. Test the adjustment on a swatch of fabric before working on the garment.

To edgestitch. Pink the edge of the seam allowance, facing, or hem. Fold the edge under from ⅛ to ¼ inch, and place it in slot 1. Adjust the lug to the left, far enough to position the stitching near the edge of the fold. Stitch, guiding the edge against the edge of the slot.

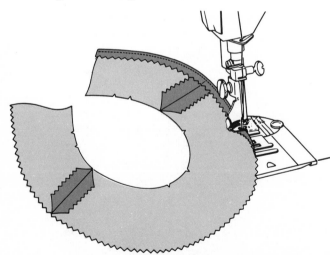

To join lace insertion and fabric bands. See page 261 for instructions.

To make a fine French seam. Trim the seam allowance to ¼ inch. See *French Seam*, page 86 for instructions on forming the seam. For the first row of stitching, place the seam in slot 1 with the lug adjusted to the left for a ⅛-inch seam.

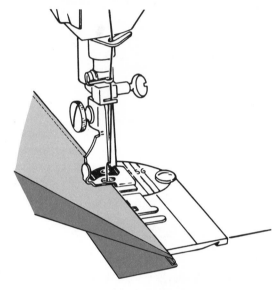

For the second row of stitching, use slot 1 with the lug adjusted to its extreme right. For a wider French seam, use slot 5 and move the lug to its extreme left for the second row of stitching.

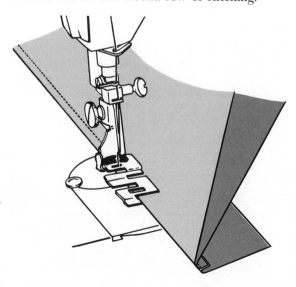

To make tucks from pin width to ¼ inch.
See *Tucks*, page 235 for instructions on marking the position of the tucks on the fabric and for other information. Fold and press the fabric on the drawn thread the entire length of each tuck. The Edge Stitcher keeps the tucks uniform in width.

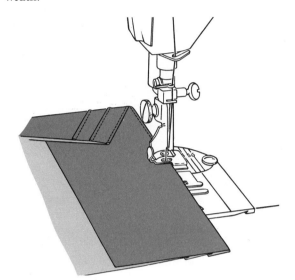

To make pin tucks, insert the creased fold in slot 1, and adjust the lug far enough to the left to position the stitching *just a few threads from the folded edge.* Guide the fold against the edge of the slot as you sew.

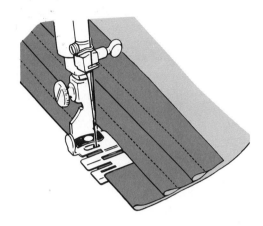

To make ¼-inch tucks, insert the. creased fold in slot 5 and move the lug to its extreme left position.
To make tucks with lace. See page 237 for instructions.

See *Shirring,* page 242 for instructions on marking the fabric, suggestions on fabrics that are appropriate for shirring, and additional information.

Rows of shirring spaced ¼ inch apart may be gauged by the edge of the foot. The center of the Gathering Foot is your stitching guide. Align it with the marking for the shirring.

Gathering Foot

The Gathering Foot enables you to place single or multiple rows of shirring quickly and expertly. Since the foot is designed to lock fullness into every stitch, it ensures evenly spaced shirring.

The stitch length on the sewing machine regulates the fullness of the shirring; a long stitch produces more fullness than a short one. Tension also affects fullness; your shirring will be fuller with heavy tensions than with light. Matching thread is generally used, but thread contrasting in color is quite acceptable for variety.

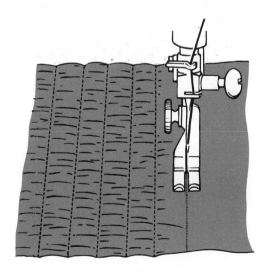

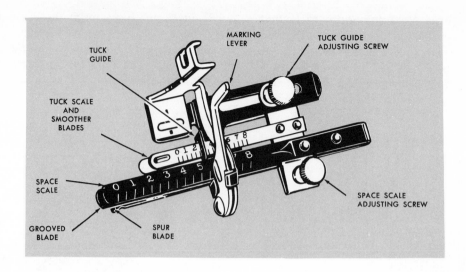

Tucker

The beauty of a tuck depends on absolutely accurate stitching. The Tucker enables you to achieve that for tucks from ⅛ to 1 inch in width. It carries two adjustable scales—a tuck guide and a space scale. *The tuck guide* is numbered from 0 to 8 at 1/8-inch intervals, with markings between the numbers spaced at 1/16-inch intervals; it ensures tucks of equal width from start to finish. *The space scale* is numbered from 0 to 8 at ¼-inch intervals, with marks between the numbers at ⅛-inch intervals; it ensures equal spacing between the tucks. The grooved blade and spur blade on the space scale mark the fabric for the fold of the next tuck while the present tuck is being stitched. Each scale is locked in position by means of an adjusting screw.

Before you begin, carefully study the material under *Tucks,* beginning on page 235. It will give you guides on fabric width required, marking the first tuck, proper stitch length, and additional information.

Adjust the tuck guide to the left or right for the desired width; move the space scale to the left or right for the desired space.

Fold and crease the fabric for the first tuck. Insert the creased fold between the grooved blade and spur blade on the space scale and between the two blades on the tuck scale. Place it far enough to the right to feed against the tuck guide. As you sew, the space scale marks the position for the next tuck.

Tucks and spaces may be equal, or the fold of the tuck may touch the previous tuck as in a blind tuck. Follow the suggested settings for tucking when adjusting the scales.

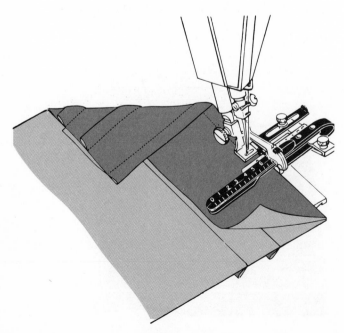

Suggested Settings for Tucking

	Tuck Guide	Space Scale
⅛" tucks with no space	1	1
⅛" tucks with ⅛" space	1	1½
¼" tucks with no space	2	2
¼" tucks with ¼" space	2	3
½" tucks with no space	4	4
½" tucks with ½" space	4	6
1" tucks with no space	8	8

Straight or decorative stitching may be used with the Tucker. See page 237.

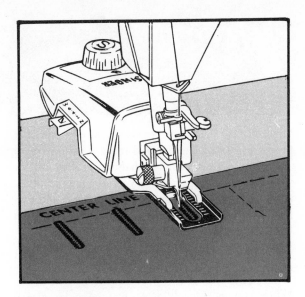

Buttonholer

The Buttonholer makes neat worked buttonholes in a variety of fabrics in a fraction of the time required by hand. The buttonholes are firmer and more durable than those made by hand—and also more regular. In addition, they are all the same length because a template controls the buttonhole length as well as style. The Buttonholer controls the stitch width and cutting space, which can be adjusted to accommodate fabric from sheer to heavy coating.

Five templates of varying lengths come with the Buttonholer—four for straight buttonholes and one for eyelet-end buttonholes for suits and coats. Five additional templates are available—three for straight buttonholes, one for an eyelet-end buttonhole, and one for eyelets for belts, studs, and lacings.

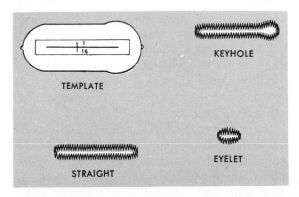

Determine the buttonhole length and position as described under *Worked Buttonhole*, page 116. Carefully mark the length and line of the buttonhole with chalk or hand basting along the thread of the fabric.

Place the fabric under the cloth clamp on the Buttonholer. (The cloth clamp will hold the fabric in position when the presser bar is lowered.) Align the buttonhole marking with the center front and back lines of the cloth clamp, and align the center line of the garment with the horizontal lines that are second from the back on both sides of the clamp. This alignment will accurately position the starting point of the buttonhole ⅛ inch beyond

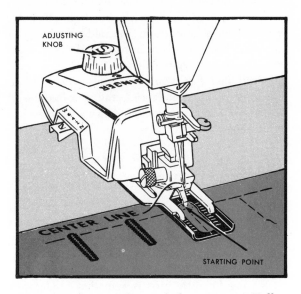

the center-line marking of the garment. Follow this procedure for all succeeding buttonholes so that they are the same distance from the garment edge.

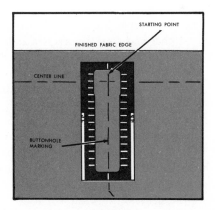

For guides on stitching the buttonholes, refer to the instruction book accompanying the Buttonholer. It gives you complete information.

Always make a test buttonhole on a swatch of your fabric to determine the correct settings of the stitch width and cutting space as well as the buttonhole length. Duplicate the number of fabric layers you will be using in the garment and include the same type of interfacing.

Sewing for Children

SOME OF THE GREATEST JOYS in sewing come from making well-fitting and becoming clothes for children and delicate dresses and articles for babies. Aside from your own satisfaction are other rewards, equally important: the individuality you can give your child's wardrobe and the money you can save. If your clothing budget is limited, you will find that you can outfit your children handsomely, in better fabrics, and at a fraction of the cost of ready-made clothes in expensive children's shops.

MAKING CLOTHES FOR BOYS AND GIRLS

Fashion is important to children. Little girls and boys know when they are smartly dressed and when a garment fits well. They begin at an early age to develop good taste and good grooming habits.

Sewing for little girls is a mother's delight—a pastime that may develop into a truly creative hobby as the girls grow older. Sewing for little boys generally continues until the boys reach the age where their shirts and pants require tailoring techniques.

Children's patterns are available in a variety of styles. Mother and daughter dresses and brother and sister outfits can be attractive and are often in the fashion picture. A word of caution here: Never make children's clothes too large, thinking they can be worn for a longer time. Both fit and fashion are lost along the way and generally the garment is worn out and discarded before the child grows to fit it. However, skirts may be made with deep hems so that they can be lengthened and worn a second year; the same is true of coats, including the sleeves.

Fabrics

Fabrics most suited for children's dresses, suits, and coats are gingham, broadcloth, chambray, poplin, percale, batiste, linen, dotted Swiss, organdy, organza, denim, sailcloth, piqué, seersucker, madras, flannel, lightweight wool, tweed, velveteen, corduroy, synthetic fabrics such as dacron and nylon, and bonded fabrics. Wash-and-wear and a blend of two fibers are practical and popular since they are easy to launder and require little ironing.

Always select a fabric that will withstand the wear and laundering necessary for children's clothes. Also, be certain that the fabric is tubfast and sunfast. If it is not preshrunk or Sanforized, shrink it before cutting. See page 15.

Color and Design

When sewing for children, you have an almost unlimited selection of colors from which to choose. Dark as well as pastel shades may be used. Let common sense be your guide. Select colors that are becoming to the child and practical for the outfit you are making.

As for design, solids, small plaids and prints, narrow stripes, little dots, and tiny checks all look charming on children.

Measurements

Measure the child accurately and record the measurements on the charts; girls' opposite, boys' on page 290. If the child is very young, it is advisable to measure a garment that fits the child correctly and record those measurements on the chart. To measure the crotch for slacks and shorts, see page 49.

Here are some rules to observe in measuring:

Sleeve seams should be at the shoulder line, not dropping over the shoulder.

A round neckline and collar should hug the neckline closely; a square or V neckline should fit the neckline closely over the shoulder line.

The waistline should be midway between the hip bone and the end of the ribs and should fit with a slight ease.

Short sleeves should end halfway between the shoulder and elbow; puffed sleeves should be shorter. Full-length sleeves extend to the wrist. Three-quarter length sleeves extend halfway between the elbow and wrist.

The skirt length must be correct for the dress to be fashionable. For a small girl, the skirt is short, usually midway between the knee and hipline. As a girl grows older, the skirt should generally be longer.

GIRL'S MEASUREMENTS

The illustrations below show you where to place the measuring tape
when taking each measurement. **Measurements are taken from right side.**
(Consider seam allowance in checking with pattern)

	CHILD'S MEASUREMENT	ALLOWANCE FOR EASE	PATTERN MEASUREMENT
1. **CHEST**	_____	1½″ to 2″	_____
2. **BREAST**	_____	1½″ to 2½″	_____
3. **WAIST**	_____	_____	_____
4. **HIP:** 3″ below waist	_____	_____	_____
5. **NECK CIRCUMFERENCE**	_____	_____	_____
6. **SHOULDER LENGTH:** Right	_____	_____	_____
Left	_____	_____	_____
7. **SHOULDER TO SHOULDER**	_____	½″ to 1″	_____
8. **WAIST LENGTH: a**—Front	_____	½″ to 1″	_____
b—Back	_____	½″ to 1″	_____
9. **SLEEVE LENGTH:**			
a—Shoulder to elbow	_____	_____	_____
b—Elbow to wrist	_____	_____	_____
c—Inside from underarm seam to wrist	_____	_____	_____
10. **SKIRT FINISHED LENGTH:**			
a—Front	_____	_____	_____
b—Back	_____	_____	_____
Plus allowance for hem (3″ to 5″)	_____	_____	_____
Plus allowance for "let-out tuck"			
(2″ if desired)	_____	_____	_____

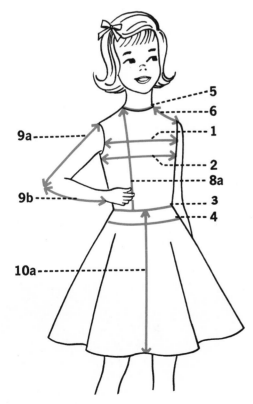

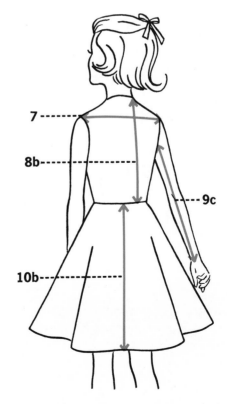

289

BOY'S MEASUREMENTS

The illustrations below show you where to place the measuring tape when taking each measurement. **Measurements are taken from right side.**

(Consider seam allowance in checking with pattern)

	CHILD'S MEASUREMENT	ALLOWANCE FOR EASE	PATTERN MEASUREMENT
1. **CHEST**	_____	5" to 7"	_____
2. **WAIST**	_____	_____	_____
3. **HIP**	_____	_____	_____
4. **HEIGHT:** Neckline to Floor	_____	_____	_____
5. **BACK LENGTH OF SHIRT** Neck to waistline plus "tuck-in"	_____	1½" to 2"	_____
6. **SHOULDER TO SHOULDER**	_____	½" to 1"	_____
7. **FINISHED LENGTH OF TROUSERS**	_____	_____	_____
8. **FINISHED LENGTH OF SHORTS**	_____	_____	_____
9. **FINISHED LENGTH OF JACKET:**			
a—Front	_____	_____	_____
b—Back	_____	_____	_____
10. **NECK CIRCUMFERENCE**	_____	_____	_____
11. **SLEEVE LENGTH**	_____	_____	_____

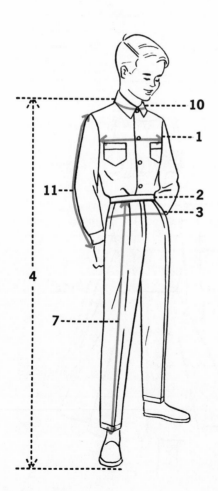

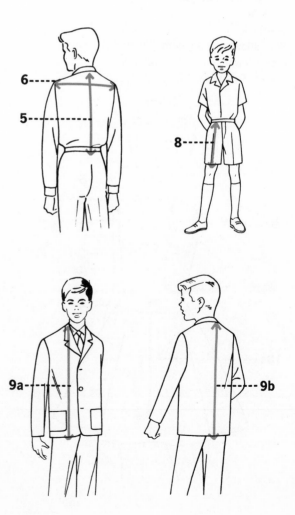

Patterns

Selecting Pattern Size

Before selecting the pattern, study the measurements on the back of the pattern envelope. For girls, select the pattern according to the breast measurement; for boys, chest measurement. *Never select a pattern by age.*

The size designated on the pattern will give the approximate age for which the pattern was designed. But children of the same age often differ in height, weight, and contour. A three-year-old child, for example, may require a size 4 or size 2 pattern. By using the breast and chest measurement as a guide, you will have to make very few, if any, adjustments in the pattern for a good fit.

The pattern allows sufficient ease for action; however, the ease may vary with the style and make of pattern. Buy the same size coat pattern as dress or shirt pattern since the necessary ease is included.

Checking the Pattern

Always measure the pattern and make any necessary adjustments. See *Checking the Pattern against Your Measurements,* page 37.

Pin the pattern pieces together and try the pattern on the right side of the figure if the child is not too young.

Adjusting the Pattern

The adjustments for children's patterns are essentially the same as for adults'. See *Adjusting the Pattern,* page 39. Shown here are adjustments for the *chubby child.*

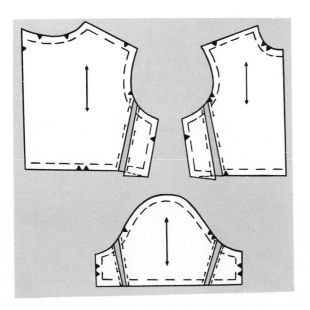

To add width across the chest, waistline, and sleeves. Slash the front and back bodice and sleeve from lower edge to armhole as illustrated. Place a piece of tissue paper underneath and spread the pattern to add one-fourth the width required. Pin the pattern to the tissue. Adjust the skirt in the same manner. Remember that only one-half the pattern is given; therefore, an adjustment of ½ inch in both the front and the back bodice sections will add 2 inches to the chest and waist measurement.

To add width across the shoulders, chest, and waistline. Slash the front and back bodice from the center of the dart at the lower edge to the shoulder line. Place a piece of tissue paper underneath and spread the pattern to add one-fourth the width required. Pin the pattern to the tissue. Adjust the skirt in the same manner. The shoulder width will be increased the amount of the adjustment; the chest and waistline will be increased four times the amount of the adjustment.

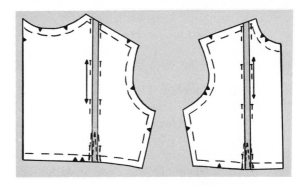

Decrease the darts the amount of the adjustment, as indicated by the dotted line. The darts should be in the correct position when the adjustment is made through their center.

Construction Tips

Good workmanship is essential. The construction tips listed below will guide you in your sewing for children. For specific instructions on each one, consult the alphabetical index.

Seams. Make sturdy seams that will withstand the many washings and rough wear to which the garment may be subjected. For little girls' dresses of washable cottons, wash-and-wear, and sheer fabrics, use French seams. For velveteen, corduroy, and linen, use plain seams pressed open, and finish the seam edges with overcasting.

Boys' shirts should be constructed with either a flat felled seam or a French seam. For shorts and pants, use a flat felled seam for play clothes and a plain seam pressed open for better clothes. Finish seam edges with binding, edgestitching, or overcasting.

Blend seams the same as you would in clothing for adults. See page 89.

Interfacings. Use a washable interfacing such as muslin, batiste, or lawn in boys' shirts, girls' dresses and blouses, and collars and cuffs. Always interface the waistband on shorts.

Plackets. The continuous bound placket is appropriate for the skirts of dresses and for boys' shirt sleeves with cuffs.

Hems. Always allow 3 or 4 inches for hems in full, gathered skirts and about 2 inches for hems in gored skirts. Hem finishes should be durable. Edgestitching is excellent for most fabrics. Finish velveteen, corduroy, and linen with seam binding. Hems blindstitched by machine are satisfactory for everyday dresses and shorts; for better clothes, finish hems by hand.

Closings. Buttons and worked buttonholes are used for most closings. On pajamas, coveralls, and boys' shirts, dot snappers may be substituted.

Decorative touches. To vary the look of often-used patterns, add something new. Dresses, for example, may be changed with the application of tucks, lace, ruffles, appliqué, lacing, rickrack, braid, bias folds, pockets, smocking, cording, or decorative zig-zag stitching. The neckline, waistline, and sleeve edge of little girls' dresses may be finished with a double-fold bias or covered cord; such details are found only in the better ready-made dresses. An organdy pinafore may be added for charm. Your machine accessories will simplify the stitching of many decorative details. (Refer to the alphabetical index for the listing of these finishes.)

Petticoats. When a dress has a full skirt, sew the petticoat to the waistline. Make the petticoat of net and cut it by the skirt pattern. Use a French seam to join the skirt sections. Gather the petticoat and skirt fabric separately, then join them to the bodice in a single seam. For instructions on gathering the skirt, see page 106.

After hemming the skirt, trim the petticoat to the same length and finish the edge with silk seam binding. Use decorative zig-zag stitching or straight stitching to sew the binding in place.

Special Features in Children's Clothes

Growth and Shrinkage Tucks

A tuck is frequently put into children's clothes to allow for growth or fabric shrinkage. The tuck *must be on the true grain of the fabric* and may be placed in the following sections, among others: (1) in the hem so that it is not visible on the right side; (2) on the right side just above the hem; (3) in the bodice near the waistline; and (4) vertically over the shoulder. Although you may use a regular

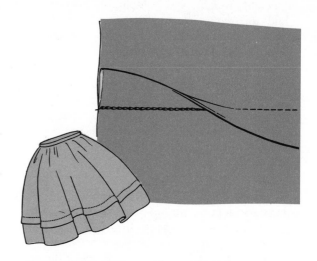

straight stitch, a chain stitch is ideal, for it makes "letting out" a simple task—you merely unlock the last loop of the chain formed on the underside of the tuck and pull out the stitching. (If your machine has Chain Stitch accessories, see page 63.)

Sash

The sash on a child's dress is often cut in two pieces and joined to the garment at each side seam.

To make the sash. Hem each side of the two pieces, using the Hemmer Foot. Hem one end of each piece by making a ⅝-inch double fold. Press, then stitch near the edge of the first fold.

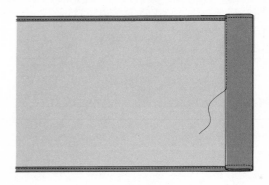

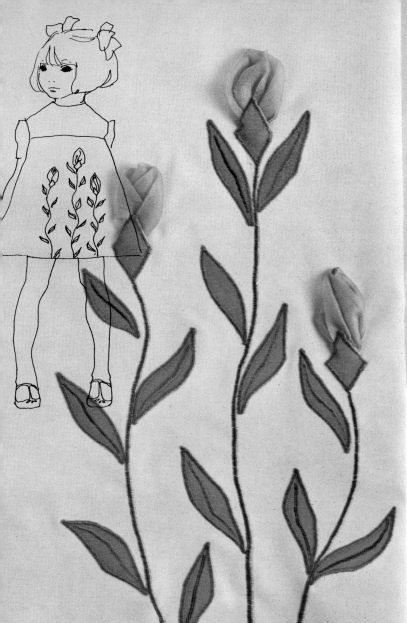

Plate 11

A girl's garden of roses

Above:
Roses cut out of a printed linen handkerchief, appliquéd to sheer fabric.

Below:
Flowered ribbon laced through two rows of buttonholes, as described on page 273.

Above:
Folded sheer fabric forms rosebuds, which are held in place by appliquéd leaves.

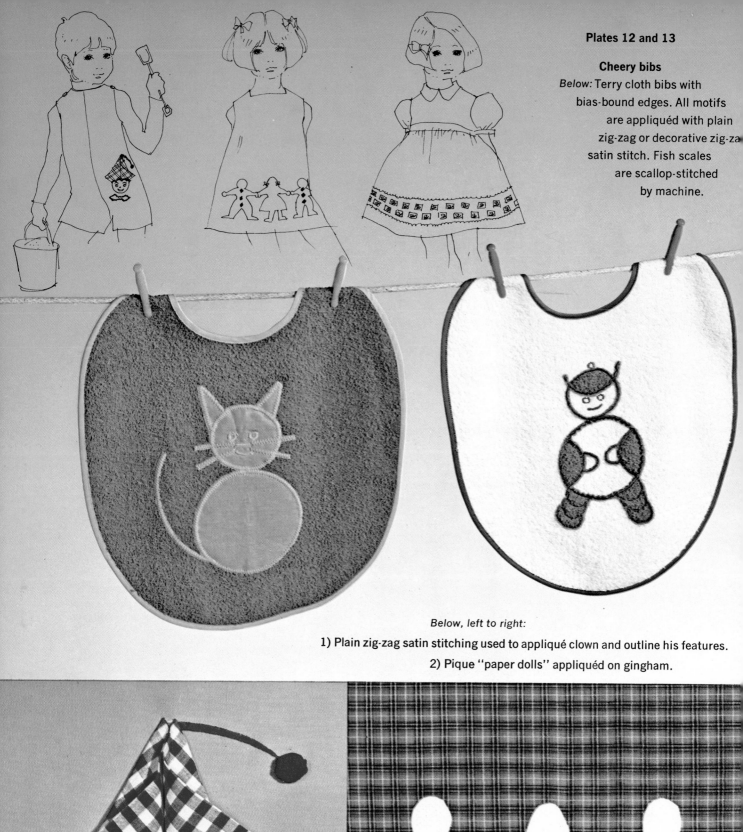

Cheery bibs

Below: Terry cloth bibs with bias-bound edges. All motifs are appliquéd with plain zig-zag or decorative zig-zag satin stitch. Fish scales are scallop-stitched by machine.

Below, left to right:

1) Plain zig-zag satin stitching used to appliqué clown and outline his features.

2) Piqué ''paper dolls'' appliquéd on gingham.

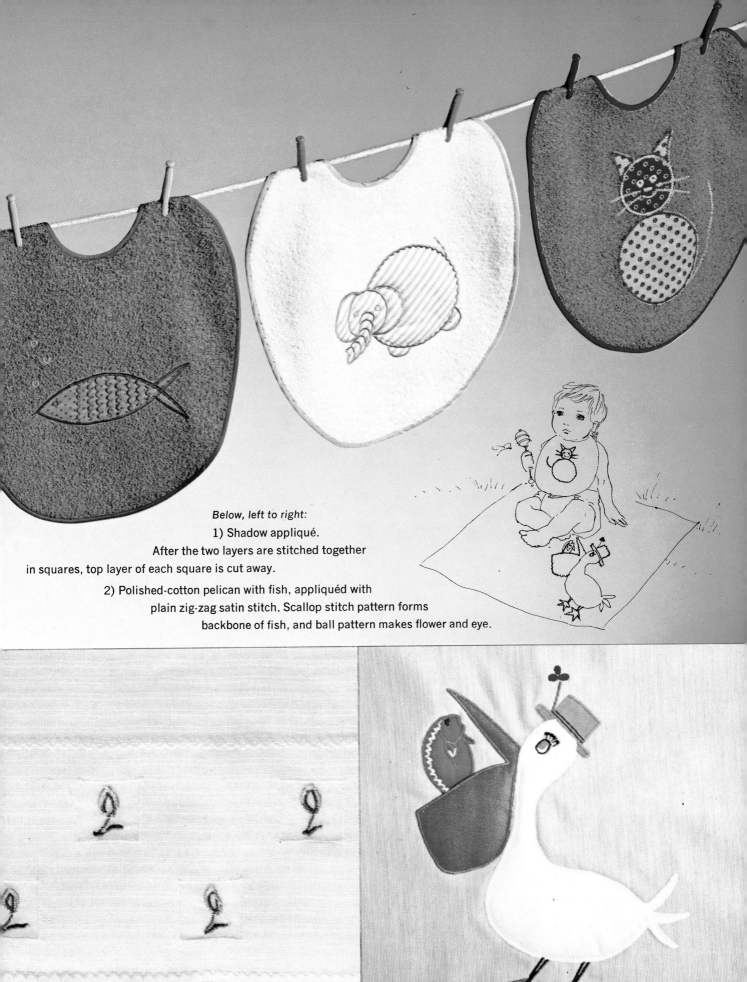

Below, left to right:

1) Shadow appliqué.
After the two layers are stitched together
in squares, top layer of each square is cut away.

2) Polished-cotton pelican with fish, appliquéd with
plain zig-zag satin stitch. Scallop stitch pattern forms
backbone of fish, and ball pattern makes flower and eye.

Plate 14

Fragile femininity

Above:
Rows of lace edging
applied with
scallop stitch pattern
form the yoke
of an organdy
party dress.

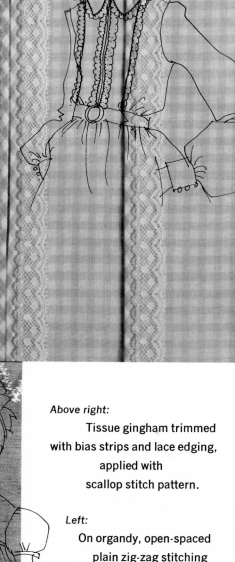

Above right:
Tissue gingham trimmed
with bias strips and lace edging,
applied with
scallop stitch pattern.

Left:
On organdy, open-spaced
plain zig-zag stitching
forms floral outline
with lace flower
tacked in center.
Rows of decorative
stitching trim
double-fold hem.

Another method is to form a point at the sash ends. Fold the end, right sides together, and stitch ¼ inch from the cut edge. Backstitch at each end. Clip off the corner at the folded edge, and press the seam open. Turn to the right side, forming a tie point.

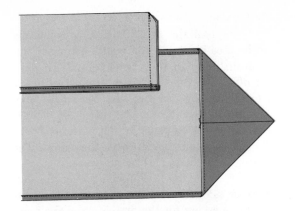

To join the sash to the bodice. Fold the unfinished ends of the sash into pleats and join them to the bodice, following one of the methods given below:

Method 1: Before stitching the side seams of the bodice. Pin the sash, right side up, to the right side of the back bodice, keeping the cut edges even at the side seam and the lower edge of the sash even with the waistline seamline. Stitch in place as the front and back bodice sections are seamed together.

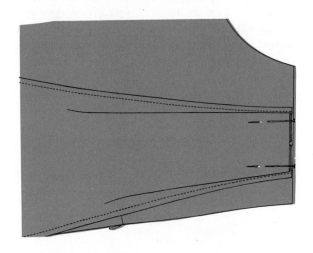

Method 2: After the dress is finished. On the right side, position the sash, right side up, at the side seam, keeping the cut edges to the front, the sash to the back, and the lower edge even with the waistline. Pin, then stitch ¼ inch from the cut edge; backstitch at each end. Trim the cut edge to ⅛ inch. Fold the sash to the front and stitch in place on the side seam. Backstitch at each end. This encases the cut edges and forms a finish similar to a French seam.

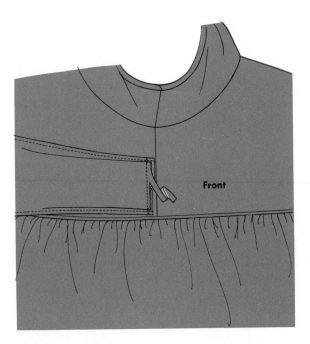

Front

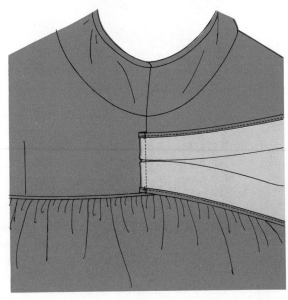

Fly Closing

For boys past the age of three, a fly closing should be used on shorts and pants. A trouser zipper is available in an 11-inch length only; it must be cut off at the top after it is stitched in place. A neckline zipper can be used for small boys' shorts and pants.

Cut the shorts or pants by the pattern. Transfer the notches and markings to the fabric. The fly closing is the first construction work.

Pin the facing for the opening over the left front, right sides together. Stitch from the waistline to the marking for the crotch. Trim the seam allowance to ¼ inch and clip into it on the curve. Press. Clip into the seam allowance ⅜ inch at the lower end of the opening. Turn the facing to the underside, fold on the stitching line, and press.

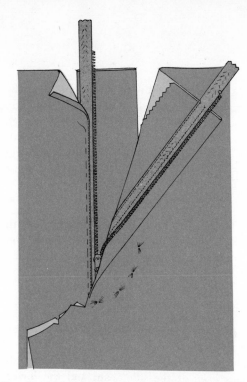

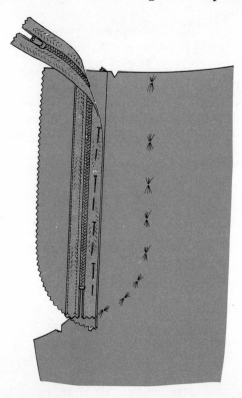

Turn the facing and seam allowance away from the garment. Place the closed zipper, face down, over the right side of the facing, with the edge of the tape even with the seamline and the bottom stop ¼ inch above the crotch seamline. Curve the tape to fit the lower end of the opening. Pin in place.

Adjust the Zipper Foot to the right of the needle and place two rows of stitching from the bottom to the waistline. Place the first row close to the chain portion of the zipper and the second row near the edge of the tape.

On the right front, clip into the seam allowance ⅜ inch at the lower end of the opening. Fold the edge of the opening under ¼ inch from the seamline. Open the zipper and pin the folded edge to the right side of the tape, with the bottom stop ¼ inch above the crotch seam and matching the left front at the end of the opening and at the waistline. Construct the fly shield, then pin it in place under the zipper, with the seam edges even. Baste through all thicknesses. Stitch in place from the bottom of the zipper to the waistline, close to the fold. Remove bastings.

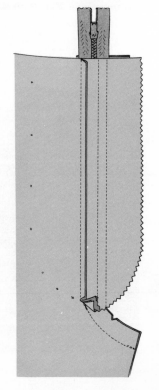

Pin the crotch seams together with the cut edges even. Stitch, joining the stitching of the left front facing seam. Backstitch at each end.

Turn the left front facing to the underside and pin. Baste in place, following the markings on the right side. Stitch on the right side, close to the basting, from the lower end to the waistline. (Do not catch the fly shield in the stitching.)

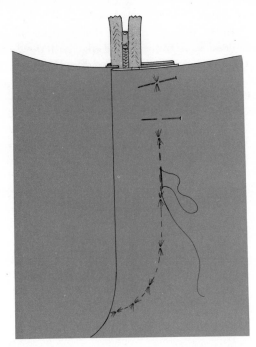

At the lower end, pull the threads through to the underside and tie. Make a bar tack through all thicknesses at the end of the opening. See page 337. This prevents ripping. Press the stitching, but do not press over the zipper.

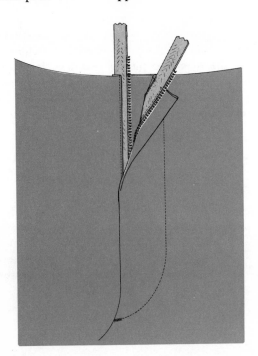

Interface the waistband with muslin, following the instructions under *Method 1*, page 154. Open the zipper and pin the waistband to the waistline, right sides together, extending the band ends ½ inch beyond the opening. Stitch. Trim the seam edges to ¼ inch and cut off the ends of the zipper if they extend beyond the waistline seam edge. Press. Turn the band away from the garment and press the seam allowance toward the band. Turn the ends of the band under ½ inch and press.

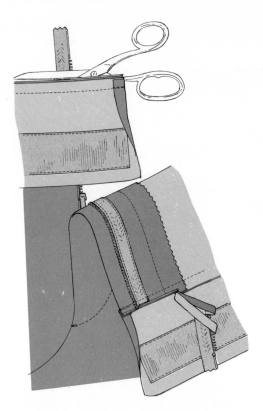

Turn under the free edge of the band and pin it in place on the underside, enclosing the seam allowances. Top-stitch around the band. Work buttonholes and sew on buttons.

Elastic Band on Boxer Shorts

To apply elastic to the waistline of boxer shorts you may use zig-zag stitching or straight stitching. Use conventional elastic or a woven elastic made especially for boxer shorts, pajamas, and underwear.

Fit the elastic band at the waistline for the desired snugness, allowing 1 inch for joining the ends. Lap the ends 1 inch, then fold one end under ¼ inch and join with two rows of narrow zig-zag stitching.

To attach the elastic to the waistline, use one of the methods described here—*Method 1* if the elastic is visible on the underside, and *Method 2* if the elastic is concealed between the hem and garment.

Method 1: Fold under the waistline seam allowance on the garment and press. Divide both the elastic circle and the garment waistline into quarters and pin-mark the garment and each edge of the elastic at these intervals.

Place the elastic circle over the wrong side of the garment, extending the fold for the seam ⅛ inch beyond the elastic. Pin each edge of the elastic to the garment at the quartered intervals.

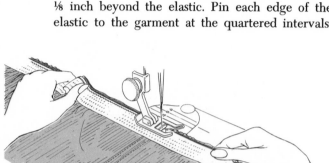

Join the two with a row of stitching placed near each edge of the elastic. Sew with the elastic up; as you stitch, stretch the elastic between the pins so that it will remain stretchable after the stitching is completed. Use a medium-width zig-zag stitch and a 10 stitch length. If you want a third row of stitching, space it evenly between the first two rows. Pull threads to the underside; tie and clip.

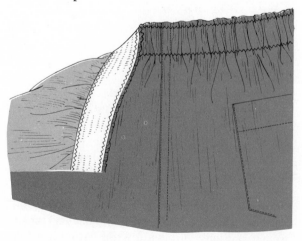

Method 2: Finish the cut edge of the waistline hem with the blindstitch zig-zag, or fold it under ¼ inch and edgestitch. Fold the waistline hem to the underside of the garment and press. Divide both the elastic circle and the garment waistline into quarters and pin-mark the garment and each edge of the elastic at these intervals.

Turn the hem away from the garment and, on the underside, align the elastic edge with the crease for the hem. Pin each edge of the elastic to the hem at the quartered intervals. Then, with the elastic up, stitch near the top edge of the elastic. Stretch the elastic between the pins as you stitch so that it will remain stretchable after the stitching is finished. Use a medium-width zig-zag stitch and a 10 stitch length.

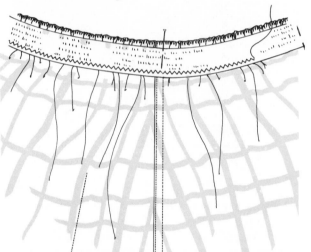

Fold the elastic and hem to the underside and pin to the garment at the quartered intervals. On the right side, place a row of zig-zag stitching close to each edge of the elastic, stretching the elastic between the pins as you sew. If you add the third row of stitching, space it evenly between the first two rows. Pull threads to the underside; tie and clip.

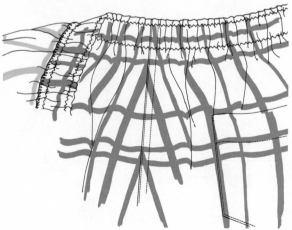

Shirt-Sleeve Opening

The opening. Finish the opening before stitching the sleeve seams. Slash the opening as marked on the pattern. Cut the pieces for the overlapping and the underlapping edges of the slash.

Bind the back edge of the slash with the narrow piece, taking a ¼-inch seam. Pin the overlap

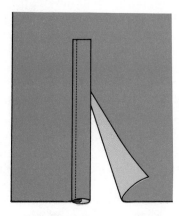

piece to the front edge of the slash with the right side next to the wrong side of the sleeve. Stitch, making a ¼-inch seam. Press, then press the seam edges toward the sleeve.

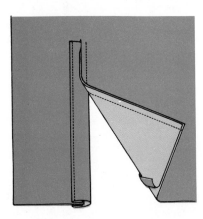

Turn the overlap to the right side of the sleeve. Turn under the cut edge and adjust the piece so

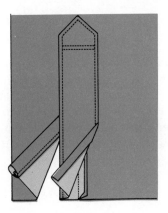

that it will overlap the back edge. Press. Top-stitch around the overlap and stitch twice across the point to hold the underlap in position.

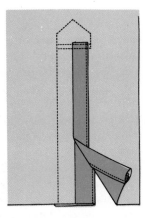

Stitch the sleeve seam, using a flat felled seam. Gather the lower edge. Turn the sleeve to the right side.

The cuff. Use a muslin interfacing. Make the cuff following the instructions on page 172, leaving the top edge open. Trim one seam edge and the interfacing to ⅛ inch and the other edge to ¼ inch. Press. Turn the cuff to the right side, and press. Pin the underside of the cuff and interfacing to the sleeve, matching markings. Adjust the gathers to fit the cuff, and stitch. Trim the seam allowance to ¼ inch, then press. Turn the cuff away from the sleeve and press the seam allowances toward the cuff. Turn the cut edge under on the top side of the cuff and pin it to the sleeve at the stitching line, enclosing the gathered seam allowance inside the cuff. Top-stitch as illustrated. Press. Work buttonholes and sew on buttons.

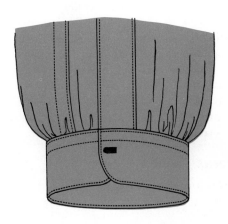

Sewing for babies brings you into a world of soft fabrics, fine seams, and dainty trimming. Choose soft cotton, silk, or woolen fabrics that will withstand frequent laundering. Kimono sleeves are practical in most infants' wear except dresses. They are simple to construct and their loose fit makes them comfortable for the baby and simplifies dressing for the mother.

A fine French seam, machine or hand-stitched, is preferred in garment construction. Your first stitching of the seam may be by machine and the second by hand. Since the fabric is delicate, the stitches should be short.

Trimming should be dainty. Narrow Val lace edging and insertion, entredeux, tiny pin tucks, dainty hand stitches, small appliquéd motifs, narrow hemstitching, smocking, scallops, and small zig-zag stitches that are lacy in design are all appropriate, decorative finishes for infant apparel.

Needle and Thread

The sewing thread should blend with the fabric in fiber, color, and size. In selecting a needle, consider both the fabric and the thread. Silk and woolen fabrics are stitched with silk thread and size 11 needle. Cottons, such as batiste, outing flannel, flannelette, piqué, pin wale corduroy, and cotton knits, are stitched with size 50 mercerized thread and size 14 needle. Threads used for embroidery stitches should be fine enough for you to make dainty stitches on the soft fabrics you will be working with.

Fastenings

Use tiny buttons and hand-made buttonholes or thread loops in dresses, slips, and diaper shirts; use string ties in sacques and kimonos. The hammer-on snap fastener is practical for the crotch opening of sleepers and crawlers. A narrow, ¼-inch, continuous bound placket or a hemmed placket is appropriate below the yoke of a garment. If the garment does not have a yoke, a hemmed placket is preferred.

Patterns

Basic layette patterns can be purchased at pattern counters. It is wise to select two or three and adapt them to your needs.

The seam allowance in layette patterns varies from ¼ to ½ inch, depending on the location of the seam and the make of the pattern. Observe the allowance indicated.

Pinning and Receiving Blankets

Pinning and receiving blankets are made of outing flannel and flannelette. Each blanket requires 1 yard of 36-inch fabric. Remove the selvages and finish the edges following one of the methods given here.

Method 1: Turn the cut edge under ¼ inch and press. Then fold a ¼- or ⅜-inch hem and baste. Finish the edge with a blanket stitch or buttonhole stitch. See page 231.

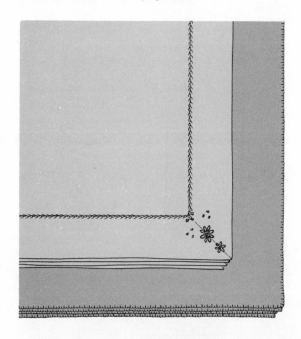

Method 2: For a wider hem, which is frequently used, turn the hem to the underside 2¼ inches and press. Fold the cut edge under ¼ inch; miter the corners as instructed on page 195. Baste the hem in place and finish on the top side, using a featherstitch near the inside edge of the hem. A group of French knots or a small lazy daisy stitch placed in each of the corners adds a touch of daintiness.

Gowns

Gowns are made of batiste, cotton crepe, nainsook, outing flannel, flannelette, and fine cotton jersey.

For sturdy seams that will withstand many washings, use a fine French seam throughout the construction. Finish the neckline and sleeves with a narrow hand-rolled hem, or face the edges with ⅝-inch lace insertion. Gather the lace and hand-sew it around the neckline and sleeves. If the fabric is white or a solid color, consider adding French knots near the neckline and sleeve edge. A small design, such as a duck, bunny, or kitten may be outlined with a cable stitch or small buttonhole stitch; use a pastel color and a single strand of six-strand floss.

Hem the lower edge by turning the cut edge under ¼ inch; then fold and baste the hem. Finish with a slip stitch.

If a drawstring is used at the bottom, leave one underarm seam open about ⅜ inch in the hem area. Turn the casing in the same manner as the hem and machine-stitch in place. Insert 1½ yards of ¼-inch twill tape in the casing.

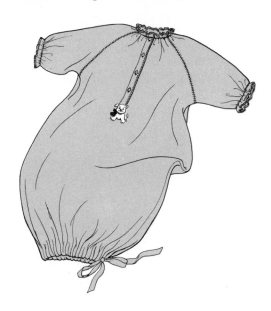

Sacques

Sacques are made of crepe de chine, challis, albatross, fine soft woolen, pin wale corduroy, outing flannel, and flannelette. Whites and pastel colors are appropriate; kimono sleeves are customary. Line silk and wool with China silk or crepe de chine; line cottons with batiste.

Lined Sacque

Cut the sacque and lining by the same pattern. Stitch the underarm seams separately in each. Clip

into the seam allowance at the underarm curve. Press the seams open and stay them at the curve of the underarm seam. See page 162.

Apply decorative detail around the neckline, front opening, lower edge, and sleeve—for example the featherstitch, French knots, lazy daisy stitch, or one of the lacy zig-zag machine stitches. A tiny appliqué may be placed near one side of the neckline or a very small pocket may be added as a finishing touch.

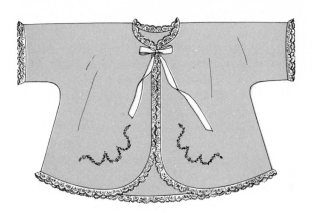

Turn the sacque to the wrong side. Place the lining inside, right sides together, matching seams and cut edges. Pin, then baste along the neckline, fronts, and lower edge. Stitch in a continuous line; make one stitch diagonally across the corners and overlap a few stitches at the starting point. Leave the sleeve edges open for turning the sacque to the right side. Trim the lining seam allowance to ⅛ inch and the sacque seam allowance to ¼ inch. Clip diagonally across the corners, close to the stitching, and clip into the seam allowance on the neckline curve. Notch the seam allowance of outside curves that may occur. Press.

(Continued)

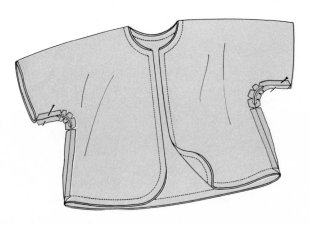

Turn the sacque through the sleeve opening to the right side. Fold on the seamline and baste. Press. To finish the sleeve edges, turn the seam allowance of the sacque to the underside and pin. Press. Turn the edge of the lining to the underside and pin it to the sacque. Slip-stitch the folded edges together.

Narrow lace edging may be gathered and hand-stitched to the outer edges.

Cut two 9-inch lengths of narrow ribbon for the ties. Fold one end to the right side ⅛ inch and pin to the underside of the neckline opening, overlapping the edges ⅛ inch. Hand-sew in place.

Zig-zag finished edge. The sacque in the illustration is made of albatross lined with China silk. The neckline is finished with a single bias fold that extends about 8 inches beyond each side of the opening for ties.

Stitch the underarm seams separately in the sacque and lining, following the instructions given above. Place the lining inside the sacque, wrong sides together, matching seams and keeping the cut edges even. Baste near all edges. Select the small scalloped zig-zag stitch on the machine and set the stitch length for satin stitching. See *Edge-stitched Finish*, page 274. From the right side, stitch down the front, around the lower edge, and up the opposite front. Stitch around the sleeve edges. Press. Trim the fabric close to the stitching.

center of the back neckline. Then pin around the neckline to the center fronts. When the neckline is finished, fold the tie ends under ¼ inch and press. Turn the long cut edges of the tie to the center and finger-press. Bring the folded edges together and pin; then slip-stitch. Do not draw the threads taut.

Unlined Sacque

Unlined sacques are made of cotton crepe, crepe de chine, and soft rayon. Ideal for summer wear, they are constructed in the same manner as unlined kimonos.

Kimonos

Kimonos are made of outing flannel, flannelette, pin wale corduroy, challis, cotton crepe, cotton jersey, and sheer cotton print. They may be lined or unlined. Batiste and fine terry cloth are appropriate fabrics for linings.

Lined Kimono with Raglan Sleeves

Cut the kimono and lining by the same pattern. Sew in the raglan sleeves and stitch the underarm seams separately in the kimono and in the lining. Press the seams open. Finish the lower edge of the kimono sleeve with a rolled hem and lace. See page 260. Gather the lower edge of the sleeve leaving a ½-inch heading, and gather the lining sleeve ½ inch from the edge.

Finish the neckline with a single-fold bias binding with ends long enough to tie. Cut off the seam allowance if binding is not specified on the pattern. Pin the neckline edges of the sacque and lining together and stitch a scant ⅛ inch from the edge.

Refer to *Single-Fold Bias Binding*, page 146, for instructions on finishing the neckline. Cut the true bias strip ¾ inch wide and 26 inches long. Begin by pinning the center of the binding to the

Turn the kimono to the wrong side. Place the lining inside, right sides together, matching seams and cut edges. Pin, baste, stitch, and blend the seams, following the instructions for the lined sacque; however, leave the lower edge open enough for turning the kimono to the right side.

Turn the kimono through the opening to the right side. Fold on the seamline and press. Slip-stitch the open edges together.

Trim the edge of the sleeve lining to within ¼ inch of the gathering stitches. Turn it under, barely beyond the stitching, and pin it to the gathering stitches of the kimono sleeve. Slip-stitch in place.

Gather the lace edging. See page 259. Hand-sew the lace to the edges of the neckline and front. Make buttonholes and sew on buttons.

Unlined Kimono

Cotton crepe, outing flannel, batiste, and sheer cotton print are appropriate fabrics for summer wear.

French-seam the underarm seams. Finish the neckline, fronts, lower edge, and sleeve edges with a single-fold bias binding (see page 146) or with a ⅛-inch rolled hem, hand-stitched in place. Gather narrow lace edging and sew it to the rolled hem, or use a blanket stitch in place of the lace. Appliqué a small design near the neckline, or use a fine featherstitch close to the hem. Use tiny buttons and thread loops for the closing.

Diaper Shirts

Diaper shirts are made of batiste, nainsook, outing flannel, flannelette, and cotton jersey.

Use a fine French seam at the shoulder and underarm. Finish the edge of the neckline, fronts, and sleeves with one of the decorative zig-zag stitch patterns (see *Edgestitched Finish*, page 274), with binding, or with the blanket stitch applied

over a ⅛-inch hem. Finish the lower edge with a ⅛-inch hem, hand-stitched in place. Place a dainty appliqué near one side of the neckline. Close with buttons and buttonholes.

Dresses

Dresses are made of batiste, organdy, and silk organza. A fine French seam is used throughout the construction. If the dress has a set-in sleeve, sew in the sleeve before stitching the underarm seam whenever possible. It is much easier to work with a flat surface than with a dress that is joined at these seams, especially when it is so small. Also, complete the placket before stitching the underarm and inside seams. Use tiny buttons and hand-worked buttonholes in the back opening.

Babies' clothes can be finished in so many beautiful ways that it is impossible to list them all; a few of the prettiest finishes are illustrated here.

Tucked Yoke Dress

Tiny pin tucks spaced 3/16 inch apart in groups of four, six, or eight, add a delicate beauty to the dress. Tucks may be hand- or machine-stitched. Fold, press, and stitch tucks in the front and back sections. See *Tucks*, page 235. At the lower end of the tucks, pull the threads to the underside and tie them together in a single knot.

Placket. Make a hemmed placket in the back of the dress. Slash down the center back to the end of the opening. At the end, clip diagonally into each side ⅛ inch. On one side, turn the hem on the marking and press. Then turn the cut edge under ⅛ inch and pin it to the dress. Slip-stitch

Seaming and pleating. Join dress front and back at the shoulder line and underarm, using a fine French seam.

Many patterns show an inverted pleat at the underarm. Lay in the pleat and press. Stitch in place at the armhole, barely outside the seamline.

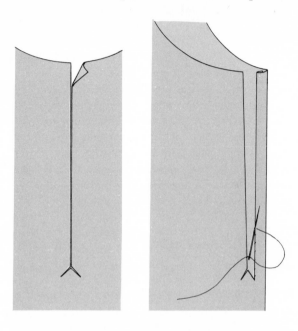

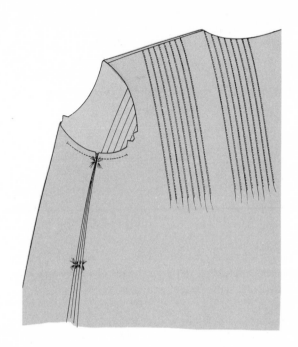

in place. Finish the opposite side in the same way. Lap the right hem over the left, and hand-stitch the lower ends together. This forms a soft pleat in the dress below the opening.

Neckline finish. Draw up the thread at the top edge of narrow lace edging and gather it to fit the neckline seam. Distribute the fullness evenly. Finish one end of the lace with a narrow hem. Baste the gathered lace, right side up, to the wrong side of the neckline seam. Finish the opposite end of the lace. Trim the neckline seam allowance to a scant ¼ inch. Roll the fabric edge over the seamline, and make small overhand stitches through the lace and rolled hem. Remove bastings. Turn the lace up over the edge, and press.

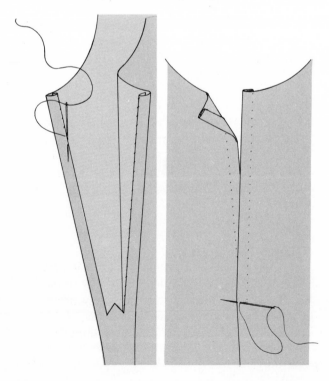

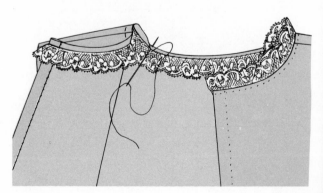

Sleeves. Finish the lower edge of the sleeves with narrow lace edging and a rolled hem the same as the neckline. Gather the lower edge of the

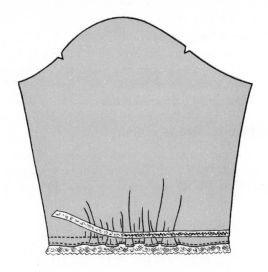

sleeve, leaving a ⅜-inch heading. Pin narrow lace insertion over the gathers and hand-sew each edge of the insertion, using a hemming stitch. Use a French seam to stitch the underarm seams.

Stitch the sleeve in the armhole. See *Set-In Sleeve*, page 158. Trim the seam allowance on the sleeve side to ⅛ inch, and on the armhole side to ¼ inch. Turn the edge of the armhole seam allowance under ⅛ inch; fold this seam allowance over the sleeve seam allowance to the stitching line, enclosing the cut edge. Pin. Slip-stitch in place.

Hem. A plain hem is generally used. Make it about 3 inches deep. Turn the hem to the underside and baste ¼ inch from the fold. Press. Turn the free edge under ⅛ inch and baste to the dress. Slip-stitch in place. On the top side, finish the hem with fine featherstitches or French knots.

Work buttonholes in the placket and sew on buttons.

Round Yoke Dress

The dainty, simple design of the yoke dress is traditionally favored for babies.

Yoke. Join the yoke sections at the shoulder line, using a fine French seam. Fold and hand-stitch the hems in the back opening. See *Placket*, page 302. Finish the neckline with gathered lace applied to a ⅛-inch rolled hem, as instructed on page 260.

Draw the thread at the top edge of lace insertion and shape it to fit around the seamline of the outer edge of the yoke. Press. Finish one end of the insertion with a hem the same width

as the yoke opening. On the right side of the yoke, baste the insertion, right side up, with the edge on the seamline. Finish the opposite end of the insertion. Trim the seam allowance under the lace to a scant ¼ inch. Roll the fabric edge and make small hand stitches through the rolled edge and lace.

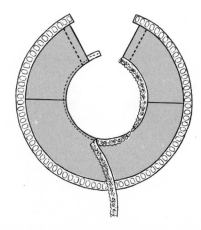

Joining yoke and dress. Join the shoulder seams of the dress, using a fine French seam; hem the placket, following the instructions for the tucked yoke dress. Gather the dress to fit the yoke. Pin, then baste the lace insertion on the yoke over the seam allowance of the dress. Trim the seam allowance under the lace to a scant ¼ inch. Roll the fabric edge and make small hand stitches through

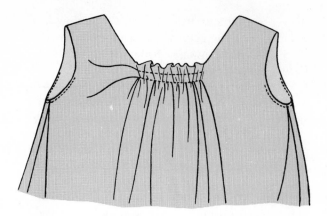

the lace and rolled edge. In the gathered section of the dress, sew the insertion in place from the top side, using small hand stitches over the lace edge; then overcast the fabric edges on the underside.

Sleeves. Stitch the sleeve seam, using a fine French seam. Sew gathered lace to the lower edge. See *Puffed Sleeve,* page 161. After you have stitched the sleeve in the armhole, finish the seam as instructed for the sleeve, page 303.

Hem. The scalloped hem is a dainty finishing touch. Transfer the scallop pattern to the lower edge of the dress, as illustrated. (The scallops will be reversed when the hem is turned.) Cut on the scalloped line. Turn the hem to the underside and baste ¼ inch from the fold. Press. On the free edge, clip ⅛ inch into the curve of the scallops at even intervals. Turn the edge under ⅛ inch, retaining the shape of the scallops, and baste. Baste

the scalloped edge to the dress. On the right side, finish the hem with a featherstitch or place French knots around the scallops. Gathered lace edging, hand-sewed on the right side of the scalloped edge, is also a lovely finish.

Christening Dress

Christening dresses may vary in length from 21 to 30 inches or longer. For this special occasion, the dress should be elaborate, yet dainty and delicate enough to belong to a baby.

Additional Dress Finishes

Make a tiny collar of a single thickness of fabric. Either roll the collar edge and hand-sew gathered lace around it as instructed on page 260, or use

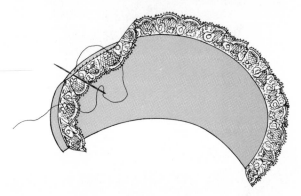

a small decorative zig-zag scallop on the edge. See *Edgestitched Finish,* page 274. Join the collar to the garment with a ½-inch bias facing, following the instructions on page 148. Or use narrow lace insertion instead of a bias strip—especially if you are hand-sewing the collar. Steam-press the lace and shape it to fit the curve of the neckline; pin it in place and finish by hand.

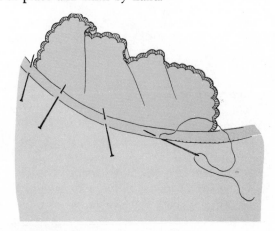

Instead of a hem, finish the lower edge of the baby's dress with edgestitching as you did the collar above.

Bassinet Cover and Skirt

The bassinet skirt illustrated has seven visible rows of shirring at the top and is finished with a tiny cord on the edge. Two 6-inch ruffles are sewed to the lower edge of the skirt. The skirt is held in place with dot-snap tape and can easily be removed for cleaning and storing.

A bassinet skirt may be made in any number of ways. The construction of the one illustrated is basic to all skirts.

There should be an *overskirt* and an *underskirt*. The overskirt may be of a sheer fabric, such as nylon net, organdy, eyelet embroidery, point d'esprit, or dotted Swiss. Taffeta, Glosheen, cotton satin, or chintz are suitable opaque fabrics for the underskirt. The overskirt may be white and the underskirt a pastel pink or blue, or both skirts may be white.

The inside of the basket should be lined with the same fabric used for the underskirt. The lining is quilted with a small cross-bar design.

The bassinet in the illustration is 90 inches in circumference and 27 inches from the top edge to the floor. The basket is 12 inches deep.

Fabric Requirements

The skirts should be gathered. Use triple fullness in the sheer overskirt and double fullness in the opaque underskirt. Fabric width may vary from 36 inches to 42 inches, and net may be 72 inches wide. In figuring your yardage requirements, therefore, consider the width of the fabric. In the bassinet illustrated, 40-inch fabric was used. Two inches were allowed for selvage and a French seam on each side, leaving a finished width of 38 inches.

Fabric requirements are determined as follows:

Overskirt. For the **width,** measure the circumference of the bassinet and multiply this figure by the amount of fullness required. *Example:* 90 inches (circumference) x 3 (fullness) = 270 inches after seaming. (Multiply the circumference by 2 when twice the fullness is required.)

For the **number of lengths** of fabric, divide the circumference plus fullness by the width of the fabric after seaming. *Example:* 270 inches (circumference plus fullness) ÷ 38 inches (width of fabric) = 7 lengths of fabric. (If the division results in a fraction of a length, buy another entire length.)

For the **skirt length,** measure from the top edge of the bassinet to the floor. (When the skirt is hemmed at the bottom and seamed at the top, it will be a scant 1 inch from the floor.) *Example:* 27 inches (length of skirt) x 7 (number of lengths) = 189 inches or 5¼ yards. Allow an additional ¾ yard for covering the cord and straightening the ends of the fabric; purchase 6 yards.

If the fabric has a design, remember to allow extra yardage for matching. See page 367.

The **two 6-inch ruffles** are twice as full as the overskirt. *Example:* 270 inches (fullness of skirt) x 2 (ruffle fullness) × 2 (number of ruffles) = 1080 inches, or 30 yards of ruffling. Six 6-inch widths, each 38 inches long, can be cut from 1 yard of fabric; therefore, buy an additional 5 yards of fabric for the ruffles.

Underskirt and bassinet lining. The fullness of the underskirt is twice the circumference of the bassinet. Multiply the circumference by 2 instead of 3, then figure the fabric requirements the same as you did for the overskirt. Five 27-inch lengths of 40-inch fabric, or 4 yards are required for the skirt in the example.

Line the inside of the bassinet with the same fabric as the underskirt. One and a half yards will be needed. Purchase an equal amount of outing flannel or sheet wadding to back the fabric for quilting.

The Lining

For the bassinet in the illustration, the lining must be 15 inches deep and 93 inches in circumference (including seams).

Straighten the ends of the fabric as described on page 14. Then cut strips of fabric on the lengthwise grain 15 inches long; cut as many strips as you will need for the 93 inches (about 2½ strips of 40-inch fabric). Join the strips with a ½-inch seam allowance; do not join the last ends together for the circle yet.

Cut the backing of outing flannel or sheet wadding the same size as the lining, and quilt the two pieces together. See *Diagonal Quilting,* page 256. When the quilting is finished, join the open ends with a ½-inch seam allowance.

Place the quilted lining inside the basket, wrong side out, with a seam at one corner, and extend the edge over the top rim of the bassinet about 2 inches. Shape the lining to fit smoothly by pinning a dart at each of the corners. Stitch the darts; then trim the dart width to within ½ inch of the stitching. Press the darts open. Sew ½-inch twill tape to the lower edge of the lining. Separate the dot-snap tape and stitch one half to the right side of the upper edge.

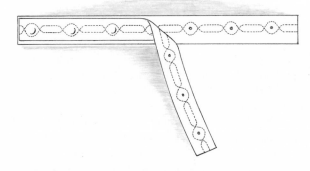

Place the lining smoothly inside the basket, right side out, and tack the twill tape to the bottom of the basket. Turn the upper edge over the top rim of the basket.

The Overskirt

Straighten the fabric. See page 14. Cut the required number of fabric lengths for the overskirt. Measure accurately and draw a thread from the fabric to indicate the cutting line and to ensure cutting on the true grain (see page 14).

Remove selvages and join the fabric on the lengthwise grain with a fine French seam. Press. Finish the lower edge with a narrow hem, using the Hemmer Foot. Press. If net is used, you need not hem it.

Cut 6-inch strips on the crosswise grain of the fabric for the ruffles. Draw a thread from the fabric for the cutting line. Join the strips; then hem each edge, using the Hemmer Foot. (Net need not be

hemmed.) Gather the ruffles with a ½-inch heading. Pin them to the skirt, keeping the lower edge of the first ruffle even with the lower edge of the skirt, and the lower edge of the second ruffle barely above the heading of the first ruffle. Stitch on the gathering stitches of the ruffles.

Gather the top edge of the skirt. Use heavy-duty mercerized or nylon thread on the bobbin because it will not break while you are easing the fullness across the width of the skirt. Follow the instructions for *Gathering to Control Fullness* on page 105. (Omit the pin tuck across the threads in this application.)

First divide the skirt into two sections and pin-mark. Then gather each section separately. After you have placed the first two rows of stitching in the seam allowance, place seven additional rows below the first, spacing them ¼ inch apart. Use the presser foot as a guide. To gather each skirt section, pull the bobbin thread at each end of the section and ease the fullness toward the center. Distribute the fullness evenly. Try the skirt on the bassinet to be sure it fits correctly. Pull the threads to the underside and join the broken lines of stitching by tying the four threads together in a single knot close to the stitching.

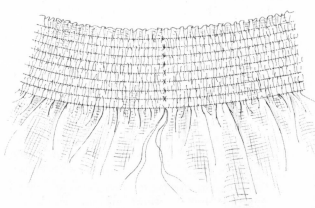

The Underskirt

Cut the required number of fabric lengths for the underskirt. Make them the same length as the overskirt and on the same grain. Remove the selvages, and join the fabric on the lengthwise grain, with a narrow French seam. Finish the lower edge with a narrow hem, using the Hemmer Foot.

Gather the underskirt in the same way as the overskirt. However, place only three rows of stitches below the first row; space them ½ inch apart.

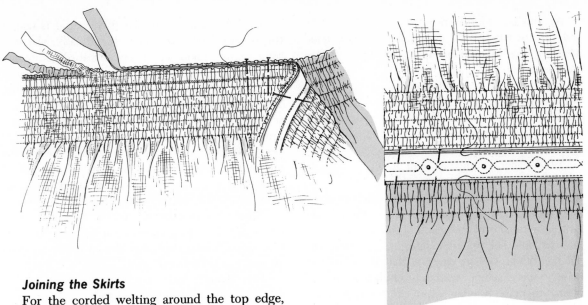

Joining the Skirts

For the corded welting around the top edge, cut a true bias of the sheer overskirt fabric and one of the opaque underskirt fabric. Cut enough lengths for the circumference of the gathered skirt plus seam allowances. Cover the cord, following the directions for sheer fabric on page 245.

Follow the instructions for cording a straight seam on page 245. Pin and stitch the cording to the right side of the overskirt. Join the ends of the cording as described on page 397. Then join the two skirt sections with the right side of the overskirt next to the wrong side of the underskirt.

Trim the corded seam allowance to ⅛ inch, and trim the seam allowance on both skirts to ¼ inch. Press. Turn the overskirt to the right side over the underskirt. The right sides of both skirts should face in the same direction. Fold on the seamline, and press.

Turn the underskirt and seam allowance away from the overskirt and pin the remaining side of the dot-snap tape to the underskirt, barely below the cording. Stitch on each side of the tape. Turn the underskirt back in place. Place the skirt around the bassinet, and fasten the dot-snap tape to hold the skirt in position.

CHILDREN CAN SEW TOO

While you are busy making dresses for your child or outfitting the nursery, there may be a pair of young eyes that enjoys watching you work and a pair of young hands that wants to stitch a seam too. This is the moment to lay your own sewing aside and to teach your child some simple sewing skills.

As an activity for children, sewing has much to recommend it. It brings out and stimulates children's innate creative talent, builds self-confidence, and gives them a sense of accomplishment.

Also not to be overlooked is the value of sewing in developing dexterity and coordination.

Sewing is an activity in which both boys and girls can express themselves easily and fluently. But keep it simple at first. The best beginning for small hands is hand sewing. Teach the child to make an X or sew on sequins and buttons, using a coarse needle and thread and following no particular pattern. A little later show the child how to thread a needle, to knot the end of the thread, and to baste two pieces of fabric together.

As you go along, teach the child that safety and care of her sewing equipment are two good friends. Needles, for example, belong in a pin cushion when not in use. Get her a pin cushion of her own and a small sewing box fitted with other supplies—a pair of small scissors, a small thimble, two or three needles with large eyes, several spools of colored thread, one lead pencil and one white pencil, and a ruler.

When your young beginner is old enough to sit at the sewing machine, teach her first how to stitch straight on lined tablet paper with the needle unthreaded, how to raise and lower the presser foot, how to control the speed of the machine, and how to keep her fingers a safe distance from the needle. When you are satisfied that the child can control the machine safely, teach her to thread it and to make a plain seam and hem. A sewer visualizes an idea, and the moving needle gives it shape and form. Thus real creativity is likely to manifest itself in each sewing project.

Sewing Machines for Children

If you have an eager young seamstress, you might consider the Little *Touch & Sew* sewing machine by Singer. Designed for the age level five to nine, it bridges the transition between hand sewing and real sewing.

The machine has a bobbin and bobbin winder, and it makes a lockstitch on real fabric. The presser foot has a guard that keeps little fingers out of the path of the needle.

Although the machine comes with batteries, you can remove them if your daughter is very young and let her begin sewing by using the hand crank. Later on, if you wish, you can buy an electrical adapter that converts the machine from battery or hand power to regular electric power.

Sewing Projects for Children

When children do begin to sew, they should start with simple projects—things they can make quickly and without much trouble. Nothing is more discouraging to a child than to undertake a project with excitement and anticipation and then find the details beyond her skill. But if the child is taught the details gradually and systematically, she will soon master them and enjoy the thrill of seeing real results.

Doll clothes are the first thought of many little girls. Save scraps of fabric for doll dresses and sequins, old buttons, and short lengths of lace, braid, and rickrack for trimmings. As your child progresses, she may want to try a real pattern for her doll's outfit. Pattern companies have created patterns for an entire wardrobe for dolls of all sizes.

To encourage individuality, let children be their own designers if they choose, cutting patterns when they need them. They may design items for gifts as well as for their own use.

Felt, flannel, and terry cloth are three fabrics that are easy for children to handle and that lend themselves to many gift articles. Some of the possibilities are listed below. They can all be made without patterns but do require accurate measuring and the drawing of straight lines or circles:

Apron	Mat for dog dish
Baby bib	Needle case
Bath mitt	Pencil and pad
Beanbag	holder
Bird cage cover	Pencil case
Book cover	Placemat
Bookmark	Potholder
Collar	Puppet
Dog's coat	Record tote bag
Doorknob cover	Scarf
Eyeglass case	Shoe bag
Marble bag	Tool case

When children reach the age of nine, they become more ambitious and adventuresome in their sewing projects. They are able to do neat finishing, and many are capable of making a simple dress, skirt, or blouse for themselves. They should be taught how to use a thimble and how to press. This may be the time when a young girl will wish to increase her sewing skills by studying sewing in school or taking a sewing course at the Singer Center during her summer vacation.

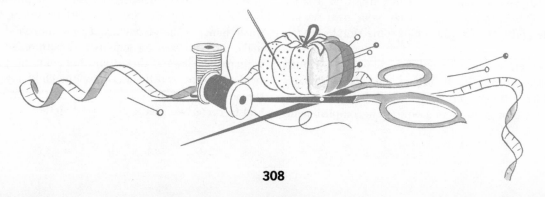

Plate 15

The animal kingdom at play

A part of each of these felt motifs was made with a PROFESSIONAL* buttonholer (note the owl's beak, the fish's scales, and the bulldog's nose.) Eyes are eyelets stitched with a buttonholer.

Other facial features are stitched with zig-zag patterns.

Children's clothes, tote bags and decorative cushions are just three of the many articles that would be brightened by these whimsical motifs.

Plate 16

A flight of fancy butterflies
Imaginative ways to combine
machine-worked buttonholes and eyelets
with decorative stitch patterns.

Any of these
gay butterflies
would add a delightful touch
to a gift wrapping,
could later serve
as a charming
button-on decoration
—on an apron, for example.

Tips on Mending

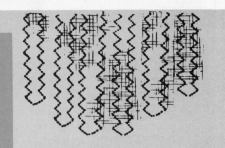

THE MENDING BASKET, like the ironing basket, is seldom empty. Just when you think you've reached the bottom, it disappears beneath an armful of socks and blue jeans and sheets.

Although mending is an unending task, it need not be an onerous one.

Mending is the term used to cover all types of fabric repairs—restitching ripped seams; darning socks; patching children's clothes; mending sheets and wearing apparel; replacing elastic in the waistline of lingerie, pajamas, and boxer shorts; repairing girdles; and replacing blanket binding. All the small jobs that prolong the life of worn but still usable articles can easily be taken care of by hand or by machine. Whenever possible, *mend by machine*. It is quicker, easier, and more durable than hand mending.

For machine mending, you may use the zig-zag machine with the presser foot or free-motion stitching. In free-motion stitching, the presser foot is removed, the feed is made inoperable, and the fabric to be mended is placed in embroidery hoop under the needle and moved manually in any direction you desire. Free-motion mending is usually best suited to a straight stitch machine.

Needle and Thread

Use a fine needle for both machine mending and hand mending. The thread should match the fabric in color and texture. You can use the warp threads of the fabric to darn small holes by hand, especially in woolens. When darning socks, separate the strands of darning thread and use only one or two in a fine darning needle.

Machine Darning with Embroidery Hoop

Free-motion darning is easier to do when the machine is designed with a throat plate that can be raised above the feed or with a feed that can be lowered below the throat plate.

Remove the presser foot and raise the throat plate or lower the feed. Set the stitch length lever in the "fine" area (above 20).

Darning an Open Area

Trim away any ragged edges from the area to be darned. Center the worn section, right side up, in embroidery hoop to hold it taut.

Position the work under the needle and lower the presser bar to activate the tension. Hold the needle thread loosely with the left hand, turn the hand wheel toward you, and draw the bobbin thread up through the fabric. Hold both thread ends and lower the needle into the fabric.

For reinforcement, outline the area to be darned with a line of stitching ⅛ to ¼ inch from the open edge. Stitch across the opening, moving the hoop backward and forward under the needle at a slight angle. Overlap the outline stitching at each end of the area; keep the lines of stitching closely spaced and even in length.

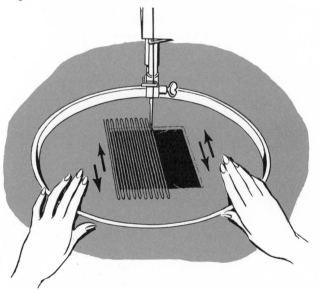

Run the machine at a moderate speed and control the hoop with a steady, continuous movement.

When the opening is filled, turn the work and cover the area with crosswise lines of stitching. Pull threads to the underside; tie and clip. Press.

Darning Rents or Tears

A straight tear may follow either the lengthwise or crosswise grain of the fabric. A three-cornered tear follows both grains.

Press the area around the tear. Cut an underlay, of the same fabric if possible, for reinforcement. Bring the edges of the tear together and pin the underlay to the wrong side. Baste.

Center the worn section, right side up, in embroidery hoop. Position the work under the needle and pull up the bobbin thread as instructed above. Move the hoop backward and forward under the needle, making about six stitches across the tear until the work is finished. In a three-cornered tear, cross the stitches at the corner for extra strength. Pull the threads through to the underside; tie and clip. Trim away the underlay close to the stitching. Press.

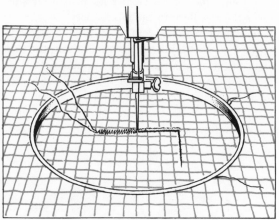

Machine Darning without Embroidery Hoop

With a little practice, you can darn worn or torn spots effortlessly and quickly without the aid of embroidery hoop.

Turn the pressure dial to D, which releases pressure and permits darning with the presser foot on the machine. See page 25. Set the selectors on the

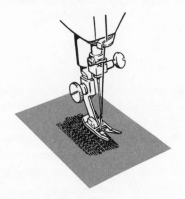

machine for straight stitching and 10 to 15 stitch length.

If the worn area is open, baste an underlay in place on the underside.

Place the area to be darned under the presser foot. Lower the presser foot and start stitching, alternately drawing the fabric gently away from you and pulling it gently toward you. Continue this forward and backward motion until the area is filled with parallel lines of stitching. For additional strength, turn the work and cover the area with crosswise lines of stitching.

Darning by Hand

Use a darning ball to darn socks and small embroidery hoop for flat work. Use a fine needle and do not knot the end of the thread.

Darn the sock over the darning ball, or place the flat work in the hoop. Make small running stitches, beginning about ¼ inch beyond the edge of the hole; work across to the opposite side, extending the stitches ¼ inch beyond the hole. Work back and forth, keeping the lines of stitching and the threads across the hole parallel and evenly spaced until the hole is covered. Then turn and work across the threads, weaving alternately over and under in parallel lines until the repair is completed. Be careful not to draw the threads taut; this will cause the work to pucker. Fasten the threads on the underside. Press.

Zig-Zag Mending without Embroidery Hoop

Zig-zag stitches are just as useful for mending as they are for creative sewing. The multiple-stitch zig-zag and plain zig-zag stitch provide a firm, flexible bond for repairing rents and tears, replacing elastic and blanket binding, and mending lingerie. Select the stitch length and stitch width suitable for the work. Use the presser foot on the machine.

Repairing Rents or Tears

Trim away the ragged edges. Cut an underlay, of the same fabric if possible, for reinforcement. Bring the edges of the tear together and pin the underlay to the wrong side. Baste.

Place the work under the presser foot with the needle directly over one end of the tear. Use the multiple-stitch zig-zag, and stitch along the line of the tear. Shorten the stitch length at the ends and cross the stitches at the corners for added strength.

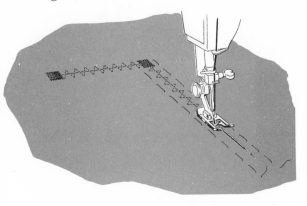

Pull threads to the underside; tie and clip. Trim away the underlay close to the stitching. Press.

Applying Elastic

Elastic is easily applied to the waistline of lingerie, pajamas, and boxer shorts with zig-zag stitching. The elasticity of the stitch prevents the stitches from breaking when the elastic is stretched.

Lingerie. Fit the elastic for the desired snugness at the waistline, allowing 1 inch for joining the ends. Lap the ends 1 inch, then fold one end under ¼ inch and join the two, using two rows of narrow zig-zag stitching.

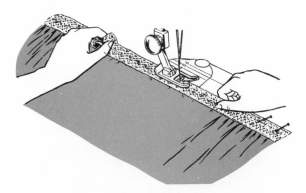

Remove the worn elastic, and press the garment. Divide the elastic circle and the garment waistline into quarters. From the right side, pin the two together at these intervals, lapping the elastic over the seam allowance of the garment. Join the layers with two rows of the multiple-stitch zig-zag or a narrow, plain zig-zag stitch; stretch the elastic between the pins as you stitch so that it will remain stretchable when the stitching is completed. Pull threads to the underside; tie and clip.

Boxer shorts. Remove the worn elastic and press the garment. To apply the new elastic, follow the instructions for *Elastic Band on Boxer Shorts*, page 295.

Girdle repairs. Either the multiple-stitch zig-zag or the plain zig-zag is appropriate for mending girdles. Both produce an elastic stitch that will not break when the girdle is stretched. If the repair requires elasticity in two directions—that is lengthwise and crosswise—the multiple-stitch zig-zag should be used, however.

Regulate the stitch length and stitch width according to the need. If you are sewing through several layers of elastic and fabric—for example, repairing the seams, garters, or waistband on foundation garments—use a needle slightly larger in size than that used for regular stitching.

Replacing Blanket Binding

Remove the worn binding and press the edges of the blanket. Fold under the cut ends of the new binding ½ inch, and pin and baste it securely in place. Stitch, using the multiple-stitch zig-zag. Adjust the pressure, if necessary, to accommodate the thickness of the blanket. Remove basting.

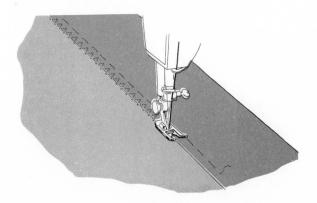

Patching

If a hole is large, a patch is preferred to darning. The fabric for the patch should be the same as the garment; if no scraps are available, cut the patch from the facing or pocket, or from the undercollar or cuff. If the fabric is a print, plaid, or stripe, match the design of the pattern.

Patching with Embroidery Hoop

Press the area around the hole. Cut the hole into a square or rectangle, following the thread of the fabric.

Cut the patch 1 inch larger than the hole and center it over the wrong side of the hole, matching the fabric grain and design. Baste.

Center the patch, right side up, in the embroidery hoop.

Prepare the machine and work as instructed in *Machine Darning with Embroidery Hoop*, page 309.

Work around the patch; move the hoop back and forth under the needle at a slight angle, making about six or eight small stitches across the cut edge. Turn the work at the corners, crossing the stitches for added reinforcement. Press. Trim the edges on the underside close to the stitching.

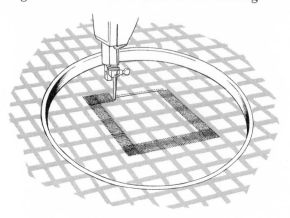

Tailored Patch

Press the area around the hole. Cut the hole into a square or rectangle, following the thread of the fabric. Clip diagonally into the corners about ¼ inch. Fold the cut edges under ¼ inch and baste. Press.

Cut the patch 1 inch larger than the hole and

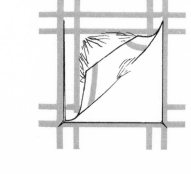

center it over the wrong side of the hole, carefully matching the fabric grain and design. Pin.

From the right side, slip-baste the folded edge to the patch. See *Slip Basting*, page 62.

Remove the pins and the first line of basting that was used to retain the fold.

On the wrong side, turn both the seam allowances away from the garment and stitch through the center of the short basting stitch in the fold. Stitch around the patch, pivoting the fabric on the needle at the corners; overlap a few stitches at the starting point. Pull threads to the underside; tie and clip. Press.

Stitch diagonally across the corners for reinforcement. Remove slip basting and press.

Catch-stitch the wide seam allowance to the garment as illustrated. Be sure that the stitches do not show on the right side. Press.

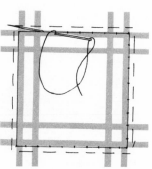 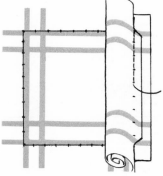 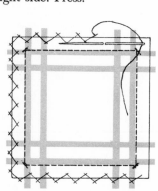

Top-Stitched Patch

Top stitching is often used to hold a patch in place.

Cut the fabric for the patch and baste it in place, following the instructions for the *Tailored Patch;* use regular basting instead of slip basting.

On the right side, stitch the patch in place near the folded edge. On the wrong side, fold under the cut edges of the patch and baste in place. Stitch again near the folded edge of the patch. Pull threads to the underside; tie and clip. Press.

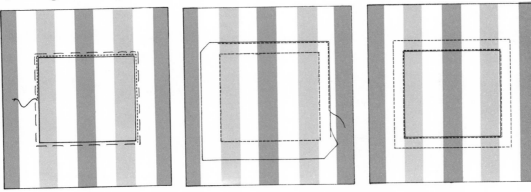

Reinforcing Worn Areas

You can add months of wear to a garment by reinforcing areas that are worn thin. Such areas occur most often at the elbow and underarm of a dress and at the knee and seat of boys' pants. Use a piece of the same fabric or a lightweight fabric such as chiffon, nylon net, or batiste. To reinforce the elbow and knee, select a fabric with some "give."

To Reinforce the Elbow or Underarm

Cut the reinforcement 1 inch larger than the worn spot. Center it over the wrong side of the worn section, and baste.

Use matching thread and a fine needle. Make small stitches by hand through the two layers of fabric, catching only a single thread of the fabric on the right side. Keep the rows of stitching parallel to the grain of the fabric and extend them slightly beyond the worn area. If extra body is needed, make several rows of stitches in the opposite direction. Fasten the threads on the underside; tie and clip. Press.

If the worn area is in the underarm of the garment, shape the upper edge of the reinforcement to fit the armhole and stitch it to the seam allowance.

To Reinforce Boys' Pants

Boys' pants last longer if the knees and seat are reinforced with zig-zag stitching when they are worn thin. The thread must match the fabric exactly in color.

Cut the reinforcement 1 inch larger than the worn area. Center it over the wrong side of the worn section, and baste.

Select the multiple-stitch zig-zag, medium stitch width, and short stitch length. Begin and end the work with backstitching. Stitch on the right side. To do this, turn the pants to the wrong side and work on the inside. If the reinforcement is to be placed at the knee, roll up the pants' leg to the stitching. Place several rows of stitching parallel to the grain of the fabric, extending them slightly beyond the worn area but not beyond the reinforcement. At the end of each row of stitching, stop with the needle in the fabric, raise the presser foot, and turn the fabric, pivoting on the needle. Lower presser foot and continue stitching.

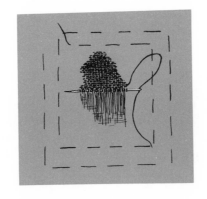

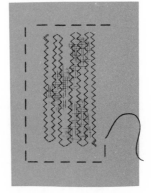

Graduate to Tailoring

TAILORING IS AT THE POST-GRADUATE END of sewing. To it you should bring a thorough knowledge of sewing techniques, flawless workmanship, and actual sewing experience. You must be able to sew with care, know how to handle fabric, respect tailor's tacks and bastings, and exercise care in fitting, seam blending, pressing, and hand finishing. In addition, tailoring requires that you be experienced in the use of underlining and interfacing, which are important in the molding and shaping of the garment. When you use fine fabrics, follow proper sewing techniques, and observe the rules of good workmanship, professional results will not be hard to achieve.

This chapter explains and illustrates the details of suit and coat construction. The principles given here are basic to tailoring and apply equally to other types of tailored apparel.

PRELIMINARIES

Pattern

Select the pattern with care. Choose one that is suitable for the fabric and classic enough to be fashionable for several years. Think of the pattern in relation to yourself and your needs and, above all, your figure proportions. Buy the same size suit and coat patterns as dress patterns since the necessary ease is included in the pattern.

Fabric

Firmly woven wool, tweed, flannel, wool broadcloth, knit fabric, raw silk, heavy cotton, linen, heavy silk, velveteen, corduroy, faille, rayon, a blend of natural and synthetic fibers, and many others are appropriate fabrics for suits. Coats are made of coating, flannel, cashmere, vicuna, wool broadcloth, and faille, to name a few. Although the fabric may be any one of a variety of weaves and weights, it must be heavy enough to prevent the interfacing, and the stitching securing it, from showing through, and sturdy enough to withstand several years of wear and many trips to the cleaners. See *Fabric*, page 7 for additional information.

As for color, select one that is becoming to you. Avoid plaids if you have not worked with them previously. Unless plaids are matched exactly at the seams, they destroy the harmony of the costume.

Lining and Interlining

To avoid bulk in suits, choose a lightweight fabric for the lining—for example, silk crepe, rayon crepe, or China silk—which matches the jacket fabric in color. Or, as a fashion note, choose a print or contrasting color for the lining and make a matching blouse.

Line coats with heavy silk or rayon crepe, satin, taffeta, Sunbak,[1] or Milium.[2] For warmth and added body, coats are generally interlined with wool or cotton interlining, lamb's wool or with cotton flannel. If Sunbak or Milium is used for the lining, interlining is not necessary. Sunbak lining has a rayon face and an acrylic back that has a fairly deep nap. Milium lining is an aluminum insulating treatment that increases warmth without increasing weight.

Interfacing and Underlining

Interfacing fabrics are available in many weights and textures. The weight of the garment fabric, the effect desired, and personal preference determine the choice. See *Interfacings*, page 16. For most coats and suits, hair canvas is appropriate. Lightweight suits may also be interfaced with Formite, Siri, or a similar fabric.

Underline jackets and coats designed to stand away from the figure. Hair canvas and pellon are two excellent fabrics that give the added body required for this effect. Loosely woven fabrics may be underlined with China silk, batiste, or voile to support the fabric and give added weight. Shrink batiste and voile before using them. See *Underlining and Lining*, page 20, for additional information.

Shrinking

Most quality fabrics are preshrunk and ready for cutting. They are usually labeled to that effect on the selvage or tag. If there is any doubt, shrink the fabric as instructed on page 15. Shrink interfacing fabrics except those that are nonwoven.

Pattern Adjustments

Select the pattern pieces for the version you have chosen. Measure and adjust the pattern to fit correctly. See *Fitting the Pattern to Your Figure*, page 37, and *Adjusting the Pattern*, page 39.

Pressing

Press out any wrinkles in the fabric before starting the construction work. See *Pressing as You Sew*, pages 66 and 67, for instructions on how to press the fabric you are using and how to press each construction detail. Before attaching the lining, press the jacket carefully on the wrong side; use the proper press cloth and the moisture the fabric requires. Do not press dry. Place the jacket on a hanger; lap and pin fronts and allow the jacket to dry completely before inserting the lining.

Muslin Shell

If you are a beginner in tailoring, or even an experienced sewer, it is a good idea to construct the suit jacket of muslin before cutting into the suit fabric. The muslin shell will ensure a perfect fit.

Use a good quality of unbleached muslin. After making the necessary pattern adjustments, cut the jacket of muslin. Transfer all notches and markings and mark the center lines on the front and back sections. (Use a tracing wheel and dressmaker's tracing paper to speed up the marking; on the jacket fabric, however, use tailor's tacks and bastings.) Mark the balance lines on the muslin. See page 77.

Stitch and press the darts, seams within the jacket, and shoulder and side seams. Apply the facings and undercollar. Blend all seams properly and press them open. Seam the sleeves and baste them into the armholes. Fold, baste, and press the hems at the lower edge of the jacket and sleeves.

A chain stitch is ideal for stitching the muslin shell for a fitting because the stitching can be ripped out in seconds if adjustments are necessary. If your machine has Chain Stitch Accessories, refer to the instruction book accompanying the machine, and to page 63.

Try on the jacket. For the muslin fitting, wear the blouse, lingerie and shoes you expect to wear with the finished jacket. Also wear a skirt made of a fabric similar in weight. If shoulder shapes or pads are used, slip them between the jacket and blouse. Lap the front opening, matching center

[1] Sunbak. Trademark of Wm. Skinner.
[2] Milium. Trademark of Deering Milliken & Co., Inc.

lines, and pin together at the buttonhole markings.

Check the position of the darts, buttonholes, and pockets; the length of shoulder and waist; the fit across the bustline, shoulder line, and hipline, allowing for the lining. Be sure that the waistline curve is in the correct position. The seams should hang straight from underarm. Check the position of the balance lines. See page 77. Check the fit, the "hang," and the length of the sleeves. The jacket length is important too; it may be necessary to lengthen or shorten the jacket, depending on your figure proportions. Pin-mark any adjustments.

Stitch the adjustments in the muslin shell and try it on again to prove them. Make the same adjustments in the tissue pattern before cutting the fabric.

Layout and Cutting

Straighten the ends of the fabric as instructed on page 14.

Study the instruction sheet accompanying the pattern and select the layout suited for the fabric width you are using. Lay all the pattern pieces on the fabric in the same direction so that the sheen and color will be uniform throughout the garment. Be sure to place the pieces on the correct grain, then pin them in place. Carefully cut out the garment, using dressmaker's shears.

Cut the notches and use tailor's tacks to mark the position of the buttonholes, pockets, darts, pleats, and any other joinings, such as slashes, gussets, and collars. Use different colored threads to designate each type of marking. Baste the center lines of the collar, skirt, and jacket, both front and back. See *Transferring Notches and Markings*, page 56.

Cut the interfacing, lining, and underlining and transfer the notches, markings, and center lines the same as above.

The Skirt

Make the skirt first and wear it each time you try on the jacket. Stitch the darts and underline or line the skirt, using the method appropriate for the fabric and style. See *Underlining and Lining*, page 95.

Baste the seams, then try on the skirt to check the fit. If you are satisfied, stitch and press the seams. Finish the seam edges according to the fabric. Use a hand finish for the final stitching of the zipper. See *Skirt Placket Zipper in Lapped Seam*, page 179.

Interface the skirt band; Method 2 on page 156 is excellent. Sew on hooks and eyes at the belt closing.

Try on the skirt, and mark the length. Finish the hem as required by the fabric. See *Hems and Hem Finishes*, page 187.

CONSTRUCTING THE JACKET

Pin, baste, and stitch the seams within the front and back sections, then press them open. It is not necessary to finish the jacket seams since the lining will cover them.

Baste all darts. Baste the front and back sections together at the shoulder and underarm seams. Baste the sleeve seams. If the sleeve has a center seam, stitch and press it open. Place a line of stitching around the sleeve cap between the notches for ease. Baste the sleeves in the armhole. Stitch the center seam of the undercollar. Pin the collar to the neckline in an overlapped seam, matching seamlines.

The Jacket Fitting

Try on the jacket with the finished skirt and the blouse and shoes that will be worn with the suit. If shoulder shapes or pads are used, slip them between the jacket and blouse. Lap the fronts so that the center lines coincide, and pin at the buttonhole markings.

Check the position of darts, buttonholes, and pockets; length of shoulder and waist; the fit across

the bustline, shoulder line, and hipline, allowing for the lining. Check the fit and "hang" of the sleeve. Be sure that the waistline curve is in the correct position. Check the position of the balance lines. Seams should hang straight from the underarm. Turn the jacket and sleeve hems to be certain of their length. Pin-mark any necessary adjustments, then pin-mark the roll line of the lapels and collar.

Remove the jacket and mark the adjustments with bastings. Try on the jacket again to prove the adjustments. If you are satisfied, continue with the other construction steps in the sequence given below.

Buttonholes

Bound buttonholes are preferred in better made suits. Place an underlay over the wrong side of the right front section where the buttonholes will be made. Then follow the instructions given under *Bound and Corded Buttonholes*, on page 108.

Darts

Stitch all darts. Underarm, shoulder, elbow, diagonal, and contour darts are used in making jackets. When they are made on the right side of the jacket, they become a styling point and the "continuous-thread" method should be used in

the stitching. If the fabric is heavy and the dart wide, slash through the center of the dart and press it open. See *Darts*, page 100.

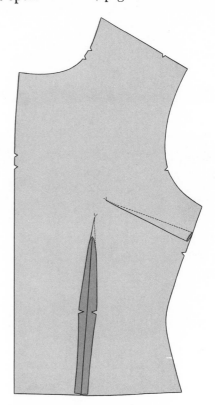

Back Underlining

Cut an underlining of preshrunk muslin, batiste, cotton broadcloth, or a similar fabric for the back section of the jacket. Use the jacket pattern as a guide. If the back has a center seam, pin the pattern pieces together with the seamlines meeting in the center. Cut the underlining in one piece about 10 inches deep at the center and shaped to fit around the armholes. Slash through the center of the shoulder darts. Lap one cut edge over the other with the seamline meeting in the center; stitch, using the multiple-stitch zig-zag. Backstitch at each end. Press.

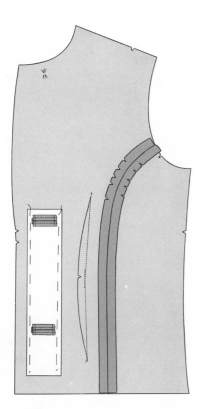

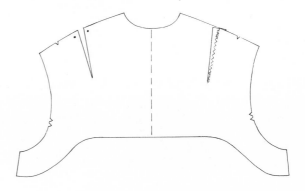

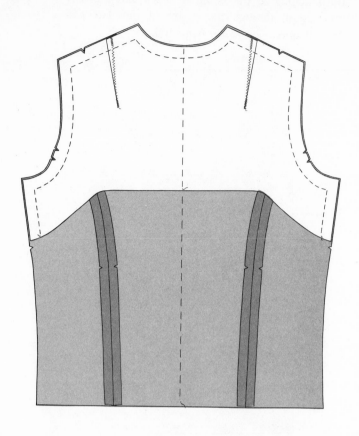

Place the underlining over the wrong side of the back section, matching center lines and seam edges. Pin, then baste in place about 1 inch from the edges.

Front Interfacing

Use *Method 1,* page 136, to treat the seam edge of the interfacing. It ensures a thin seam since the organza instead of the interfacing is included in the seam. If the interfacing has darts, read the instructions under *Interfacing Darts,* page 104.

Pin the interfacing over the wrong side of each front jacket section, keeping the organza strip and garment edges even.

Determine the roll line of the lapels from the neckline to the top button. Place a ruler between these points, and mark the interfacing with chalk. Pin the interfacing in place along this line. Stay it to the lapels with padding stitches, catching only one thread of the fabric under the interfacing. Use thread that matches the fabric. Begin each line of stitches at the top of the lapel and end at the seamline, working from roll line to seamline. As you work, roll the lapel over the first finger, and hold it firmly with the thumb. This will shape the lapels as they will be worn.

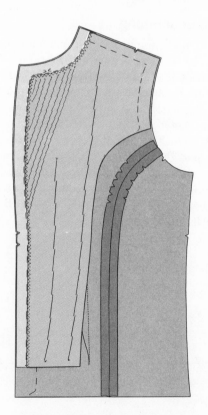

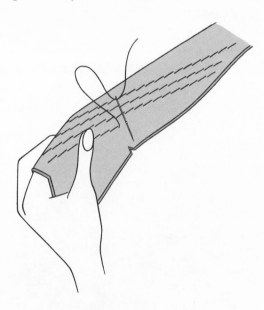

Baste the interfacing in place along the seamline; then make a few lines of long diagonal bastings within the interfacing to hold it in position as you work. Press the lapels over a tailor's ham or press mitt.

Shoulder Seams

Join the front and back sections at the shoulder line; make the seam through the garment fabric only. Clip off the corners of the dart in the seam allowance. Press, then press the seam open. Join the back underlining and front interfacing at the shoulder seam using either Method 1 or 2 below.

Method 1: Lap the back underlining and front interfacing over the shoulder seam and pin. Place the shoulder seam, right side up, over the hand to be certain that the interfacing and underlining fit smoothly on the underside. On the wrong side, catch-stitch the lapped seam from the neckline to within ¾ inch of the armhole, catching only the seam allowance of the garment.

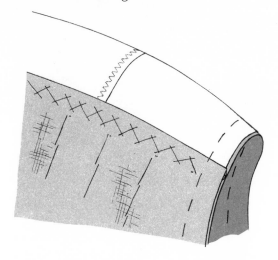

Method 2: Trim off the seam allowance on the back underlining and front interfacing, and slip the edges under the seam allowance of the jacket. Pin, then catch-stitch the seam edges to the back underlining and front interfacing.

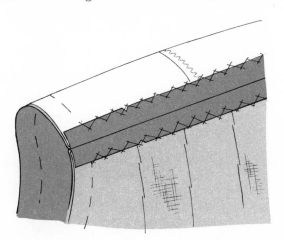

The Undercollar

Interfacing the Undercollar

Stitch the center seam of the undercollar and press it open. Lap the center seam of the interfacing, matching the seamlines, and stitch, using the multiple-stitch zig-zag. Mark the interfacing a measured ¾ inch from the edges. Place the markings close together to retain the shape of the collar. Trim on the marked line.

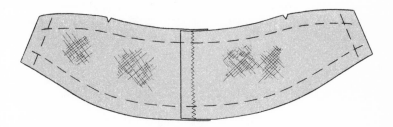

Cut a collar of organza, using the undercollar pattern and omitting the center seam. Center the interfacing over the organza and pin. (The organza should extend ¾ inch beyond all edges of the interfacing.) Clip off the corners of the interfacing to eliminate bulk when the collar is turned. Stitch, using the multiple-stitch zig-zag. Trim the organza under the interfacing ¼ inch from the stitching. Press.

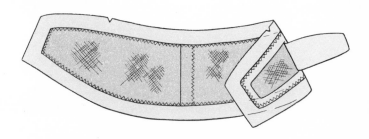

Pin the interfacing over the wrong side of the undercollar, keeping the organza and collar edges even. Baste along the roll line. Use thread matching the fabric. Stay the interfacing to the undercollar with padding stitches from the roll line to the neckline. Then stay the interfacing to the balance of the collar with rows of padding stitches as

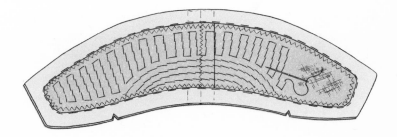

far as the seamline. As you work, roll the collar to shape it as you did the lapels. Baste the interfacing in place along the seamline. Press over a tailor's ham or press mitt.

Attaching the Undercollar to the Jacket

Pin the undercollar to the jacket, right sides together, matching markings. Work from the garment side. Pin at the center, shoulder, and front markings, then pin at intervals between, easing the collar between the markings. Baste. Try on the jacket to be sure that the collar fits properly.

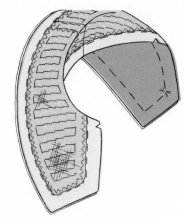

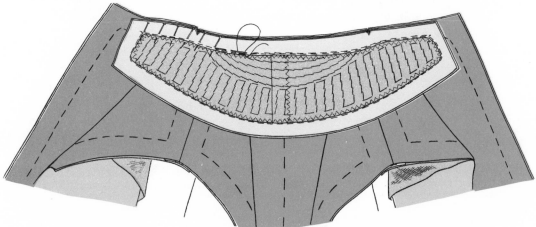

Stitch the undercollar to the jacket, beginning ⅝ inch from one collar edge and stitching to within ⅝ inch of the opposite edge. Backstitch at each end of the seam. (The open seam allowance at the ends prevents drawing when the facing is stitched and turned.) Remove bastings. Trim the seam allowance of the back underlining to ¼ inch and clip off corners where seams cross at the shoulder and center back. Press. Slash into the seam allowances at evenly spaced intervals so that they will lie flat when pressed. Press the seam open.

Buttonholes in Interfacing

Baste the interfacing smoothly around each buttonhole. Follow the instructions on page 110 and cut out the interfacing around the buttonholes.

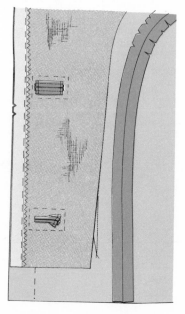

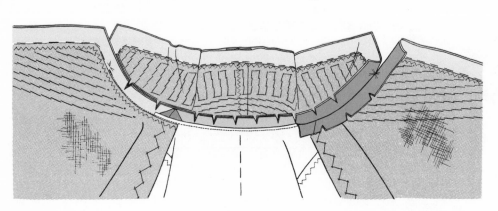

Facings and Top Collar

If a back neckline facing is not given with the pattern, cut one about 3½ inches deep, using the jacket tissue pattern to shape the neckline and shoulders.

Joining Facing to Top Collar

Join the front and back sections of the facing at the shoulder seams. Press the seams open.

Pin the top collar to the facing, right sides together, matching markings. Work from the collar side and pin at the center, shoulder, and front markings, then at intervals between, easing the collar between the markings. Baste. Stitch, beginning ⅝ inch from one collar edge and stitching to within ⅝ of the opposite edge. Pull threads through to the underside and tie. Clip off corners where seams cross at the shoulder. Remove bastings and press. Clip into the seam allowances at evenly spaced intervals so that the seam will lie flat. Press the seam open.

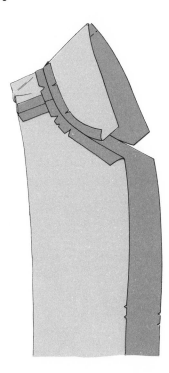

Attaching Facing and Top Collar to Jacket

Place the top collar and facing over the jacket, right sides together. Work from the top collar side and keep the seam edges even. Pin the collars together, first at the center, points, and notches. Match seams where the undercollar joins the jacket and the top collar joins the front facing. Then pin at intervals between, easing the top collar between the markings.

Pin the front facing in place, first at the lapel point, notches, and lower edge. Then pin at intervals between, easing the facing from the top button to the lapel point. Baste with silk thread but do not baste through the seam allowances of the crossing seams where the collars join.

To stitch the collar seam, turn the seam allowance on both the top side and the underside away from the collar. Carefully position the needle in the seamline, exactly at the end of the stitching that joins the collar and facing. Lower the presser foot and stitch around the collar to the same point on the opposite side. Make one or two stitches diagonally across the points to avoid bulk when the collar is turned.

To stitch the facing seam so that it will join the collar stitching perfectly, place a needle through the seam from the collar side to the facing side. The needle should come out at the end of the stitching that joins the collar and facing. Turn the seam allowance on both the top side and the underside away from the facing. Carefully lower the machine needle in the seamline at the needle marking and stitch. Make one or two stitches diagonally across the point. Stitch the opposite side in the same manner. Check the right side to be sure of an exact seam joining.

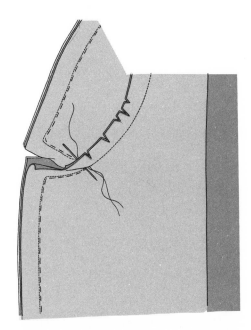

Pull the threads on the collar through to the underside and tie. Repeat the same procedure on the facing side, then use a needle to carry the threads through the seam to the collar side and fasten them in the interfacing with two backstitches. This gives added strength at the notch of the collar.

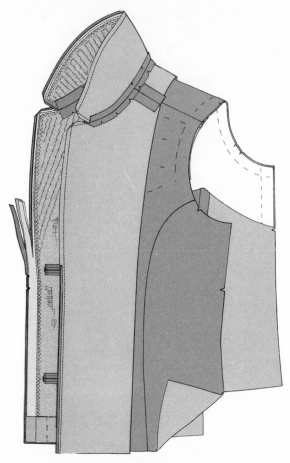

top of the lapel to the top button, trim the garment seam allowance to ⅛ inch and the facing seam allowance and organza strip to ¼ inch. Reverse the blending below the top button by trimming the facing seam allowance to ⅛ inch and the garment seam allowance and organza strip to ¼ inch. Cut diagonally across the points, close to the stitching, and clip off corners where seams cross at the outer edges. Press, then press the seams open.

Trim the seam allowances joining the undercollar and jacket to ⅜ inch from the outer edge to the shoulder line. Catch-stitch the open seam edges to the interfacing on each side.

Turn the facing to the underside. Ease out the corners of the collar and lapels. Baste, using diagonal basting and silk thread. As you work, ease the garment under slightly at the seamline along the lapels and collar, and ease the facing under slightly from the top button to the lower edge. Do not remove these bastings until the jacket is finished. Press, then press lapels and collar over a tailor's ham or press mitt.

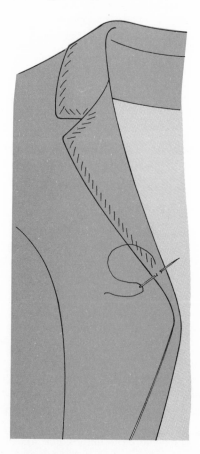

Remove the bastings and press. Trim the undercollar seam allowance to ⅛ inch and the top collar seam edge and organza strip to ¼ inch. Notch the seam allowances on the outside curve. From the

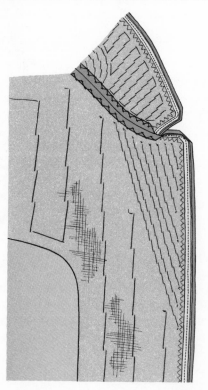

Roll the lapels and collar as they will be worn, allowing sufficient ease in the top collar and facing

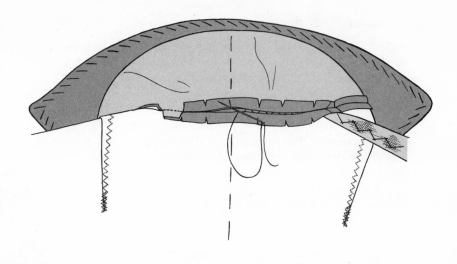

for them to fit smoothly over the roll. Pin the facing and top collar in place along the roll line, then near the neckline seam. Where the collars join the neckline across the back, stay the open seams together between the shoulders with loose hand stitches. (You will complete the work on the front facings after you have set in the sleeves.)

Sleeves

Before you sew in the sleeves, pin and baste the underarm seams of the jacket; include the back underlining in the seam. Try on the jacket to be sure that it fits correctly. Stitch the seams. Slash the seam allowances at the waistline just far enough so that they will lie flat. Press, then press the seam open.

Construct the sleeves. Refer to *Set-in-Sleeve*, page 158 for instructions on pinning and basting the sleeve in the armhole. Include the back underlining, but not the front interfacing in the seam.

Try on the jacket. Check the "hang" of the sleeve. Turn the hems in the sleeve and jacket and check their length. Pin-mark any adjustments.

Remove the jacket and adjust the sleeve if necessary. Baste the marking for the hemline of the sleeves and jacket.

Stitch the sleeve in the armhole, overlapping the stitching at the underarm seam. Remove bastings, clip off corners where seams cross at the underarm and shoulder. Trim the back underlining seam allowance to ¼ inch. Press. Turn the seam into the sleeve.

If the fabric is heavy and the armhole snug, trim the seam allowance on the sleeve side to ⅜ inch over the cap between the notches, then baste it to the garment side of the seam, using easy stitches. At the underarm, between the notches, trim the armhole seam allowance to ⅜ inch, then sew the edges together, using either the multiple-stitch zig-zag or the blindstitch zig-zag. Place the

stitching between the seamline and seam edge. Hand-sew the front interfacing to the sleeve seam, barely outside the previous line of stitching, using matching thread. Trim the interfacing to within ¼ inch of the hand stitching.

To maintain the roll of the sleeve cap, cut sheet wadding on the true bias 1¼ inches wide. Fold it through the center, then pin it to the sleeve side of the seam allowance over the cap between the notches, keeping the fold even with the stitching line. Hand-stitch the sheet wadding to the sleeve seam.

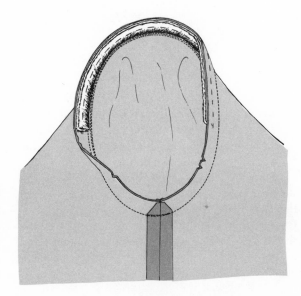

Shoulder Pads or Shapes

Suits with set-in sleeves require support at the shoulder line. If shoulder pads are not in fashion, use two layers of heavy felt or hair canvas to make shoulder shapes.

Use the jacket tissue pattern as a guide. Fold and pin the shoulder darts in the front and back bodice sections of the pattern. Cut a double thickness of felt the shape of the shoulder line and armhole as far as the notches. Remove the tissue pattern. On the back section, begin 1 inch from the neckline and cut the felt diagonally to the armhole notches. On the front section, begin 1 inch from the neckline and cut the felt straight down to the lower edge, then across to the armhole notches. Four front and back sections are required to make a pair of shoulder shapes.

Join the front and back sections at the shoulder line by lapping one edge over the other, with seamlines meeting in the center; pin. Stitch, using the multiple-stitch zig-zag. Join the two layers of

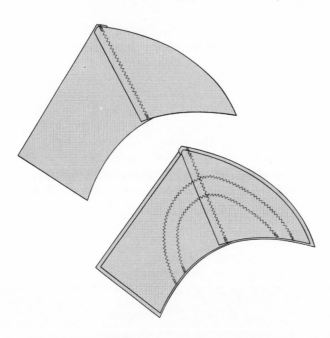

shapes with two lines of multiple-stitch zig-zag, as illustrated. Cut off the bottom layer of felt ¼ inch from the outer edge; remember to trim one shape for the right shoulder and one for the left.

Turn the jacket to the right side. Position the shoulder pads or shapes on the underside and pin them in place from the top side of the jacket. On the underside, tack the pads or shapes to the sleeve seam allowances between the notches and to the shoulder seam allowance at the neckline edge.

The Front Facings

Roll the lapels as they will be worn, allowing sufficient ease in the facing for it to fit smoothly over the roll. Carefully pin the free edge of the facing smoothly in place. Catch-stitch the facing to the interfacing from the shoulder to the point where the interfacing extends across the front; then baste it to the jacket down as far as the hemline.

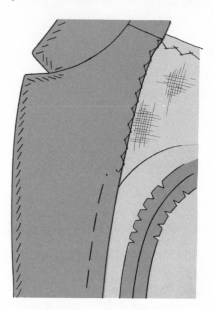

Jacket Hem

Compare the front edges of the jacket to be sure that they are the same length. Remove enough diagonal basting to fold the hem. Turn the facing away from the jacket. Fold the hem in the jacket and facing, and pin. Ease the hem down slightly at the seams to allow for the fold over the seam allowances. (The front interfacing should extend to the hem fold.) Baste with silk thread ¼ inch from the hem fold. Press. Trim the hem to an even width. Trim the hem across the facing and joining seam to ½ inch; trim all seam allowances to one-half their width from hem fold to edge. Press, shrinking out any fullness.

Interface the lower edge of the jacket with preshrunk muslin to give extra body and weight at the hem. Cut the interfacing on the true bias 1 inch wider than the hem and the length of the lower edge of the jacket plus 1 inch for seam allowances. Remove the bastings at the lower edge of the hem after pressing, and turn the hem away from the jacket. Place the interfacing between the hem and jacket; align the lower edge of the interfacing with the crease for the hem and extend the ends ½ inch over the front interfacing. Pin, baste, then catch-stitch the interfacing to the jacket along each edge, catching only one thread of the fabric outside the interfacing and only the interfacing on the opposite side. Use thread to match the fabric. Press.

Turn the hem over the interfacing and pin the free edge in place, matching seams. Hand-baste. Catch-stitch the hem to the interfacing as far as the facing seam. Make a stitch in the hem, then a stitch in the interfacing over the hem edge. Continue, alternating the stitches.

Turn the front facing to the underside; ease it under slightly at the lower edge and pin it to the hem. Slip-stitch in place, then catch-stitch over the cut edge the depth of the hem. (A soft hemline is described on page 194.)

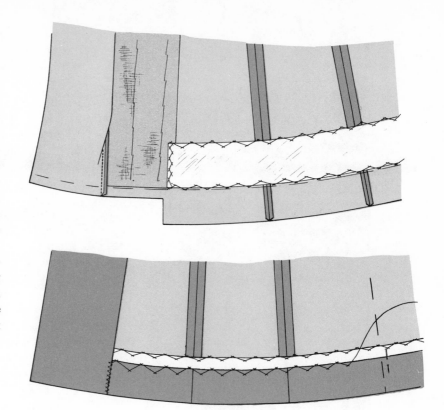

Sleeve Hem

Turn the sleeve hem and baste ¼ inch from the fold, using silk thread. Trim the seam allowances to one-half their width from the fold to the hem edge. Interface the hem of the sleeve the same as the jacket. Cut the interfacing ends on the lengthwise grain and join them, overlapping about ½ inch. Catch-stitch the interfacing in place, then hem the sleeve in the same way you hemmed the jacket.

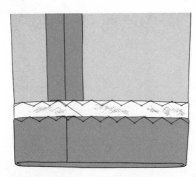

Buttonholes in Facing

Finish the back of the buttonholes, following the instructions on page 111.

Lining

Any adjustments you made in fitting the jacket must also be made in the lining.

Stay-stitch the back neckline of the lining ½ inch from the edge and stitch the shoulder darts. Fold and baste the release pleats and waistline darts in the front and back lining. Press.

Use a fine catch stitch to hold the release pleats and darts in position. Make the stitches through the three thicknesses, near the fold, on the right side of the lining. On the fronts, catch-stitch the release pleats from the shoulder to about 3 inches down, and the waistline darts about 1 inch above and below the waistline. On the back,

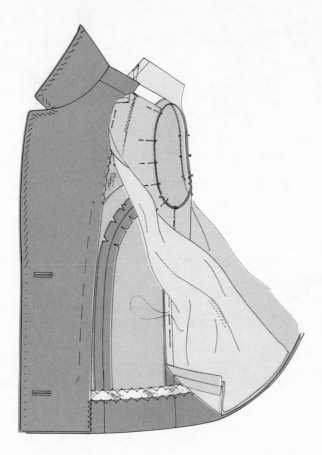

catch-stitch the release pleat from the neckline down about 2 inches, across the pleat at the waistline, and just above the hem.

Stitch the underarm seams. Clip into the seam allowances at the waistline. Press, then press the seams open. Stitch the sleeve lining seams and press them open. Press the lining thoroughly.

Joining Lining to Jacket

Place the lining inside the jacket, wrong sides together, matching all seams and center backs. Pin at the center back, underarm and around the armhole. Fold back the lining front and pin the lining and jacket seam allowances together at the underarm, matching markings. Sew with long basting stitches, starting below the armhole and ending 3 inches above the hem.

Turn under the seam allowance on the front edge of the lining and pin it over the free edge of the facing. Slip-stitch in place.

Pin and hand-sew the front lining over the shoulder seam. Turn under the back shoulder seam allowance, then lap it over the front lining and pin. Baste the lining to the seam allowance around the armhole. Clip into the lining seam allowance at the back neckline. Turn it under just beyond the stay stitching, and pin it to the neckline facing. Slip-stitch the lining in place from the outer edge of one shoulder to the other.

Place the jacket on a hanger, right side out. Smooth out the lining and pin it to the jacket 3 inches above the hem.

(Continued)

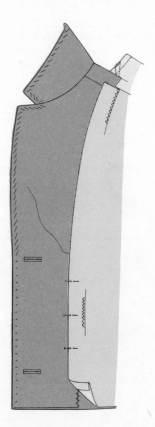

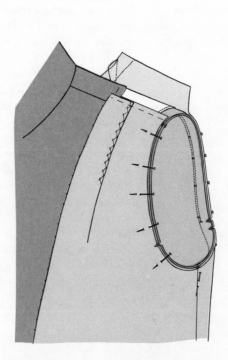

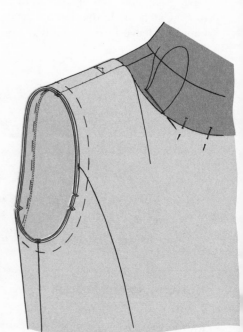

Allow ½ inch for ease in the lining length. Turn under the edge of the lining so that it overlaps the jacket hem 1 inch. Press. Pin the lining to the jacket hem, matching seams and darts, then baste it in place ½ inch above the fold. Turn back the lining on the basting line and slip-stitch it to the jacket hem, catching only the under layer of the lining.

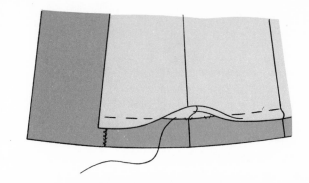

Lining the Sleeves

Place a line of stitching around the sleeve cap of the lining between the notches, ½ inch from the edge. Turn the sleeve to the wrong side.

Turn the jacket sleeve to the wrong side. Pin the lining and sleeve seam allowances together at the underarm seams, matching markings in the seams and armhole. Sew with long basting stitches, beginning about 3 inches below the armhole and ending 3 inches above the hem. If the sleeve is a two-piece one, hand-sew the back seams together.

Turn the lining sleeve to the right side over the jacket sleeve. Draw the bobbin thread around the sleeve cap and ease the lining to fit over the armhole seam allowance. Turn the seam edge under just beyond the stitching; overlap the armhole seam allowance and pin the sleeve lining in place at the shoulder, notches, and underarm seam, then at intervals between. Slip-stitch in place.

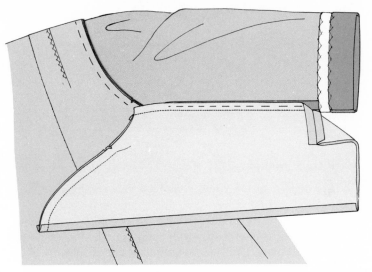

Allow ¼ inch for ease in the length of the sleeve lining. Turn under the lower edge and slip-stitch it to sleeve hem, following the instructions for the lower edge of the lining as described at the beginning of this page.

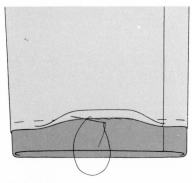

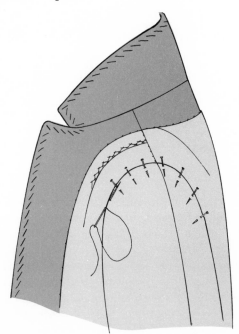

Chain Weight

To add weight at the hem and preserve the line of a jacket, hand-sew a chain weight to the jacket after you have sewed in the lining. The chain, made of flat links, is available for lightweight and heavyweight fabrics. If one chain is too long for your purpose, remove any links not required. If you need a longer weight, use two chains together.

(Continued)

Place the chain weight on the inside along the hem of the jacket, about 1½ inches above the hem fold. Extend the ends to the facings, or place the weight across the back between the side seams. Overcast the chain flat against the fabric at the ends, center, and about every 2 inches between. Make the hand stitches through the hem and interfacing only so that they will not be visible on the topside. The chain is exposed and can easily be removed when the garment is cleaned.

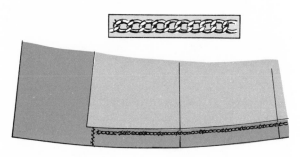

Fitted Jacket

In addition to front and collar interfacings, fitted jackets generally have an interfacing from the waistline to the hemline.

To shape interfacing darts and eliminate bulk, see the instructions under *Interfacing Darts,* page 104. Join the interfacing side seams with a lapped seam. See page 83.

Pin the interfacing in place over the wrong side of the jacket, with the lower edge aligned with the crease for the hem. Catch-stitch it in

place along the lower edge. Turn the hem over the interfacing and catch-stitch it in place, following the instructions for the jacket hem on page 324. If the hem is full, control the fullness with a line of stitching ¼ inch from the free edge before hemming.

Waistline Stay

To prevent stretching, stay the waistline of fitted and semifitted jackets and princessline coats with straight seam binding or ½-inch grosgrain ribbon. Work with the jacket in the shape it will be worn.

On the underside, pin the tape around the waistline, extending the ends ¾ inch beyond the front facings. Turn the ends of the tape under ¼ inch, and pin them to the front facings and interfacings. Tack the tape in place at the ends and at all seams and darts. When interfacing is used below the waistline, tack it in place with the tape.

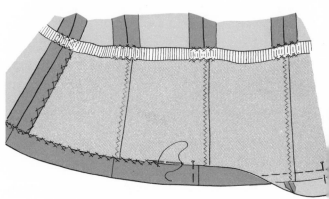

CONSTRUCTING A COAT

Basic Construction

Coat construction follows the same procedures and sequence as jacket construction up to the point of making the hem. Remember always to fit a coat over the type of dress or suit you will wear under it.

Sleeve styles vary. One comfortable and popular style is a sleeve that has a center seam with the back (or front) section cut-in-one with the bodice and the other section set into the armhole. Gussets are frequently used, so are raglan and regular set-in sleeves. Instructions on making the several types of sleeves are given under *Sleeve Styles and Finishes,* page 158.

Before you hem the coat, interface the sleeve

hem and finish it, following the directions for the jacket, page 325.

Coat Hem

Mark the coat length. Refer to *Hems and Hem Finishes,* page 187, and follow the first three steps in forming the hem. Turn the facing away from the coat and form the hem across it. The front interfacing should extend to the hem fold.

Hem Finishes

Finish the free edge as required by the fabric. The finishes most frequently used are the *Pinked Hem* for firmly woven fabrics and the *Bound Hem* for loosely woven fabrics that fray easily. See page 188. Baste the hem in place and finish it by hand, using a blind catch stitch. If the fabric is heavy or the hem wide, double-stitch the hem. See page 193.

Interfaced Hem

For added body and weight, interface the hem with a true bias strip of unbleached muslin or tailor's linen, cut the width of the hem.

Press the fold for the hem, shrinking out any fullness. Finish the free edge of the hem. Remove all bastings. Place the interfacing over the underside of the hem, extending the ends ½ inch beyond the front interfacings. Shape the interfacing to the hem and catch-stitch it to the hem near the fold and top edge. Press.

Hand-baste the free edge of the hem to the coat, and blind catch-stitch it in place. Press.

Lining and Interlining

Cut the lining and interlining by the same pattern; however, cut the interlining to extend to the turn of the lining hem at the bottom of the coat and sleeves. Be sure to make the same adjustments in the lining and interlining that you made in the coat after fitting it.

Place the interlining pieces over the wrong side of the lining pieces, matching markings; baste together along the edges. Place several rows of diagonal basting within the sections to hold the layers together. Handle as one in constructing the lining. See *Underlining a Dress*, page 95.

Stay-stitch ½ inch from the neckline edge. Stitch any seams within the lining; also stitch shoulder, underarm, and sleeve seams. Press, then press the seams open. Sew in the sleeves. Treat the darts and release pleats the same as in the jacket lining, page 325.

To Join the Lining to the Coat

Place the lining inside the coat, wrong sides together. Pin it in place at the center back, shoulders, sleeves, and underarm, matching seams and markings. Sew the lining and coat seam allowances together at the underarm and sleeve seams, following the instructions given for the jacket, page 326. Remove any pins necessary to sew the seam allowances together in the sleeves.

Clip into the lining seam allowance at the back neckline. Turn the edge under just beyond the stay stitching and pin it to the coat. Turn under the seam allowance on the front edge of the lining and pin it over the free edge of the facing. Slip-stitch in position.

Allow ½ inch for ease in the length of the sleeve lining. Turn under the lower edge and slip-stitch it to the sleeve hem, following the instructions for the jacket lining, page 327.

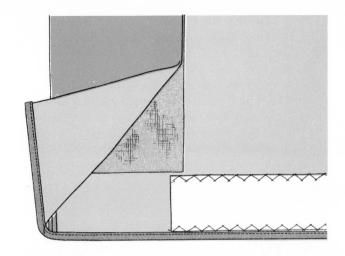

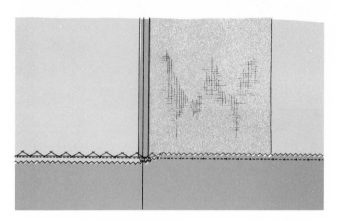

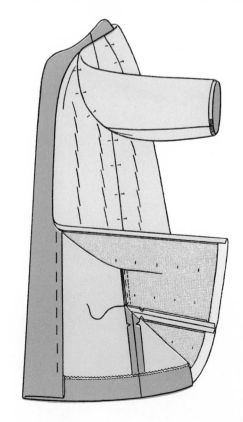

To Hem the Lining

Turn the hem in the lining so that it overlaps the coat hem 1 inch. (The interlining extends to the hem fold.) Press. Turn the free edge of the lining hem under ½ inch and pin it in place. Finish by hand, using a blind hemming stitch.

French-tack the lining to the coat at the seams, just above the hem; make the tacks about 1 inch in length. French-tack the free edge of the facing to the coat hem with a ¼-inch tack.

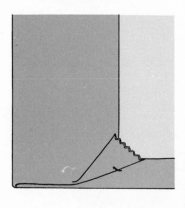 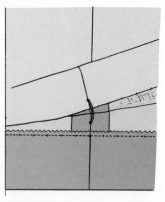

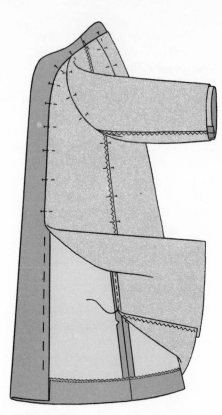

To Handle the Interlining Separately

The interlining and lining may be treated separately. Construct the interlining with lapped seams. See *Lapped Seam,* page 83. Sew in the sleeves, using a plain seam.

Slip the interlining into the coat. Match the seams and pin. Hand-sew the coat and interlining seam edges together at the underarm and sleeve, following the jacket lining instructions on page 326. Hand-sew the interlining to the facing edge.

Slip the lining into the coat and finish, following the lining instructions above.

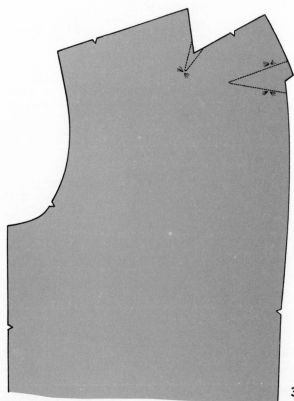

ADDITIONAL CONSTRUCTION TECHNIQUES

To Make a Notched Shawl Collar

In a shawl collar, the top collar and facing are cut-in-one with a center back seam. The tailoring technique is about the same as that for the jacket collar on page 321, except for the treatment of the notches.

Tailor-tack the position of the notches in the garment, facing, and interfacing. To retain the shape of the notches, do not cut them out until after the final stitching is completed.

Stay-stitch around the notched area of the garment and facing, barely outside the seamline. Use a 20 stitch length; take one or two stitches across the point. Press. (This stitching is not visible in the finished work.) Stay-stitch the slash in the neck-

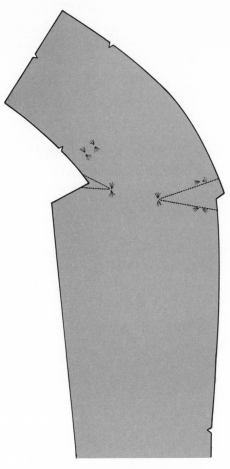

Cut a strip of organza wide enough to cover the notch; use the pattern to shape the neckline and front edges. Pin the organza strip over the interfacing, extending the edge ¾ inch beyond the interfacing. Cut out the notches in the interfacing only, ⅛ inch beyond the seamline. Clip off the corners of the interfacing to eliminate bulk when turned. Stitch, using the multiple-stitch zig-zag. Press.

Position the interfacing on the wrong side of the jacket or coat, keeping the organza strip and garment edge even. Be sure that the uncut notches in the garment coincide with those in the interfacing. Finish, following the instructions under *Front Interfacing*, on page 318. Join the shoulder seams, and interface the undercollar. See page 319.

Pin the undercollar to the neckline, matching markings, and slash the neckline seam at the inside corner. Baste, then stitch. Clip off the corners where seams cross, and slash into the seam allowances at evenly spaced intervals so that they will lie flat when pressed open. Remove the bastings and press the seam open. Trim the seam edges to ⅜ inch from the outer edge to the corner, then catch-stitch the open seam edges to the interfacing on each side. Press.

line seam allowance. Prepare the garment for a fitting as instructed on page 316.

Mark the neckline and front edges of the interfacing a measured ¾ inch from the edge (⅝ inch seam allowance plus ⅛ inch). Trim off along the marked line, *but do not cut out the notches.*

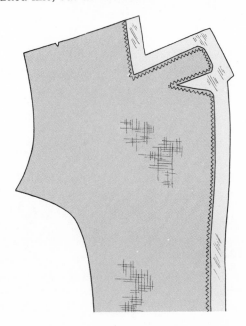

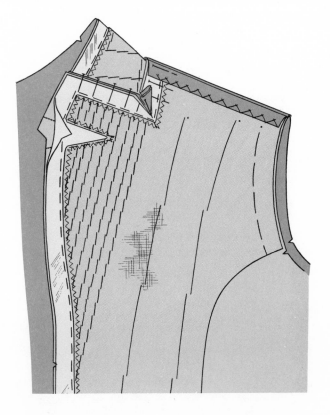

331

Stitch the center back seam of the top collar and facing, then press the seam open. Attach the back neckline facing in the same manner as the undercollar. Press the seam open.

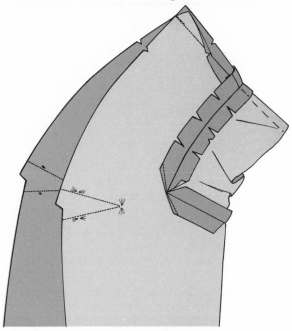

Place the facing over the jacket, or coat, right sides together. Pin together at center, points, and notches. Match seamlines of the uncut notches in the garment, interfacing, and facing, and pin together. Then pin at close intervals between, easing the top collar and lapel section of the facing between the markings. Baste. Stitch in one continuous line from one hem edge to the other. Take one or two stitches diagonally across the corners; stitch the notched area barely beyond the stay stitching, taking one or two stitches across the point. The width at the point provides space for cutting and prevents pulling at the point in the finished work. Remove bastings.

Trim the undercollar seam allowance to ⅛ inch and the top collar seam allowance and organza strip to ¼ inch. From the top of the lapel to the top button, trim the garment seam allowance to ⅛ inch and facing seam allowance and organza strip to ¼ inch. Reverse the blending below the top button by trimming the facing seam allowance to ⅛ inch and the garment seam allowance and organza to ¼ inch. Cut between the lines of stitching in the notch, almost to the point; then trim the garment seam allowance to ⅛ inch and the facing seam allowance and organza to ¼ inch. Clip diagonally across the corners at the lapel points and where seams cross. Press, then press the seams open.

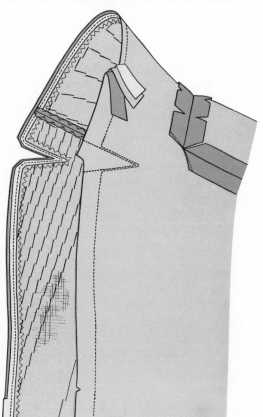

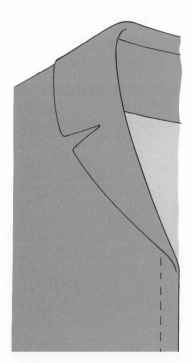

Turn facing to the underside and finish, following the instructions on page 322.

To Interface

You will probably prefer interfacing suits and coats according to the instructions given in the construction of the jacket. However, you may catch-stitch the interfacing in place as instructed under *Method 2*, on page 136. Or you may use the method explained here, which is appropriate for loosely woven fabrics such as tweed and heavy coating.

Mark the neckline and front edges of the interfacing a measured ¾ inch from the edge (⅝-inch seam allowance plus ¼ inch). Trim off on the markings. Clip off corners.

Place the interfacing over the wrong side of the garment front section with the fabric extending ¾ inch beyond the interfacing edge. Pin. Stay the interfacing to the lapels with padding stitches; then baste the interfacing in place, following the instructions on page 318.

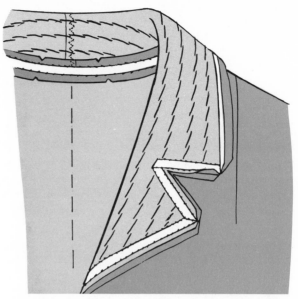

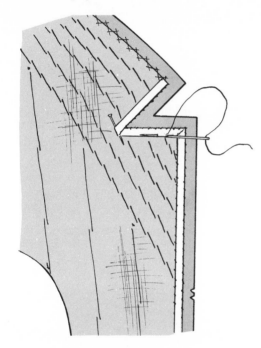

Tape the front opening, lapel, and front edge of the collar with ¼-inch twill tape. Shrink and shape the tape with steam pressing. Position the tape so that it overlaps the interfacing and the outer edge is 1/16 inch from the fabric seamline. Miter the tape at the corners. Sew the outer edge of the tape to the fabric, using a hemming stitch. Then sew the opposite edge in place, making the stitches through the interfacing and tape edge only. Press.

Apply the facing and top collar, following the instructions on page 321.

To Stay Neckline Seam

To prevent the back neckline seam from stretching, stay it with ¼-inch twill tape or straight seam binding folded and creased through the center. Steam-press the tape, shrinking and shaping it to fit the

neckline. After the undercollar is stitched in place and the seam pressed open, pin the tape over the open seam between the shoulders; then catch-stitch it to the seam allowance on each side.

To Stay Armhole Seam at Underarm

The armhole seam at the underarm of coats and suits is subject to extra strain. For added strength in tweed and loosely woven fabrics, tape the seam with ¼-inch twill tape (narrower, if possible) or straight seam binding folded through the center. Steam-press the tape, shrinking and shaping it to fit the armhole at the underarm.

Pin the tape over the right side of the seam allowance of the armhole, between the notches, with the lower edge barely above the seamline. Stitch it in place about 1/16 inch from the lower edge of the tape, using a 15 stitch length.

The seamline is just below the tape; therefore, when the sleeve is stitched in the armhole, the tape between the seam edges will carry the strain, not the seamline. Trim the armhole seam allowance at the underarm to ⅜ inch.

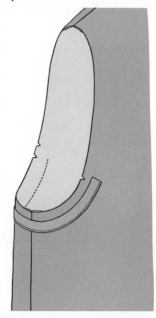

Tailored Binding

Suits, coats, and dresses occasionally carry a tailored binding as a finished edge on front openings, necklines, collars and cuffs, and pocket flaps. The binding is not difficult to apply if you follow the procedure given here.

A good quality of slipper satin is an excellent fabric for binding since it will not wear along the folded edge as quickly as other fabrics. Self-fabric may also be used if it is not too heavy. The finished width of the binding is generally ½ inch although it may be as wide as 1 inch. Buy enough fabric to cut long bias strips so that your binding will have a minimum of joinings.

Before applying the binding, finish the garment up to the point of attaching the interfacing. If the pattern does not specify binding, mark the edges to be bound ⅝ inch (seam allowance) from the edge and trim on the marked line. Treat the facing and interfacing the same. Baste the interfacing in place on the wrong side. Place the facing on the underside of the garment, wrong sides together, with the cut edges even; pin. Baste the layers of fabric together ⅝ inch from the edge. On a heavy fabric, it may be necessary to baste again ¼ inch from the edge.

Cut the binding on the true bias, four times the finished width. See *Cutting Bias Strips*, page 244. Fold the bias strip through the center, wrong sides together, and press lightly. Since this means pressing on the right side of the fabric, be sure to place a press cloth between the fabric and iron. Do not glide the iron, but merely lift it from one section to the other. Open the bias and fold the cut edges to the center, leaving a ⅛-inch space between the edges. Press. This spacing allows for folding the bias over the edge of the garment.

To Bind a Straight Edge or Curve

Open the binding and carefully pin it to the edge, right sides together, keeping the cut edges even. Extend the end of the binding ¼ inch beyond each end of the seam to allow for turning and finishing. Do not stretch the binding on straight edges; ease it slightly on outside curves and stretch it slightly on inside curves.

Carefully stitch in the folded crease of the binding. Trim the interfacing in the seam allowance close to the stitching. Press to the stitching, but not beyond.

Fold the ends of the binding under ¼ inch, then fold the binding over the seam edge to the stitching on the underside; pin. Finish by hand, using a slip stitch. Slip-stitch the folded ends of binding together.

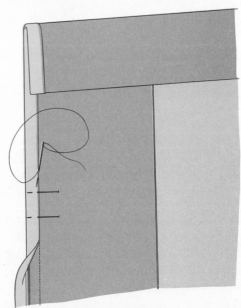

To Bind a Square Corner

Open the binding and pin it along *one* side, following the instructions above. Stitch in the folded crease from the outer edge to the intersecting seamline at the corner. Pull the threads to the

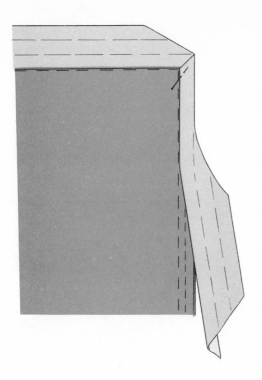

underside and tie them together in a single knot.

Fold the bias over the edge and miter the corner from the seamline to the center fold of the binding, as illustrated; pin. Turn the binding back over the garment, right sides together, and finish pinning the edge in place along the adjoining side. Carefully stitch in the folded crease of the binding. Press only the stitching.

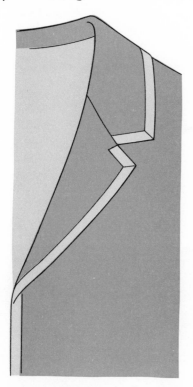

Finish, following the instructions for the straight edge. On the underside, miter the binding at the corner, folding it in the same direction as on the top side. Slip-stitch the folds of the miter together.

Top Stitching

Top stitching is a smart and practical way to accent the lines of a garment and at the same time add firmness. A single line of stitching on a heavy fabric, such as coating or a laminate, produces a welt effect. Single or multiple rows of parallel stitching on a lighter weight fabric lend importance to finished edges such as lapels, facing edges, collars, and pockets, as well as to style seams and hemlines.

For top stitching you may use either regular thread or buttonhole twist. Buttonhole twist is frequently preferred for medium-weight and heavy-weight fabrics. Use it for the needle thread and the regular thread for the bobbin. Select a size 18 needle and a slightly longer stitch than for the regular seaming. It is generally necessary to increase the needle thread tension when stitching with buttonhole twist. To determine the best stitch length and tension, make a stitching test on a swatch of your fabric; fold the fabric, duplicating the seam allowance, and include the same type of interfacing or underlining you are using in the garment.

Before applying top stitching to an edge, attach the interfacing and facing to the garment, blend the seams, and turn the facing and press as instructed on pages 318 and 321. Baste the layers of fabric together to prevent them from slipping during the stitching. Use diagonal basting and silk thread. One line of basting is sufficient if the top stitching will be close to the edge. Baste again just outside the stitching line if the stitching will be ½ inch or more from the edge.

Mark the stitching line with basting on the right side and use it as a guide in your machine stitching. Use a gauge to measure accurately, and take tiny stitches through all thicknesses of fabric. Space the stitches about 1 inch apart; keep the slack out of the thread between them. On curved edges and seams, place the basting stitches closer together, with the short thread on the top side and the long one on the underside.

On the right side of your garment, top-stitch very close to the basting but not on it. Stitch slowly, using the appropriate stitch length for the fabric. Additional rows of stitching may be gauged with the presser foot if the spacing is less than ¼ inch. For wider spacing, mark each stitching line the same as the first one. At corners, pivot and turn the fabric on the needle, following the directions on page 28.

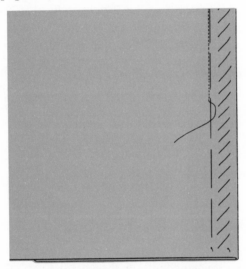

When the stitching ends at a finished edge, leave thread ends about 4 inches long. Then use a hand sewing needle to fasten them in the seam allowance between the facing and garment.

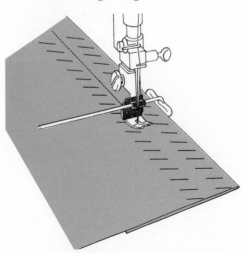

The Quilter and the Seam Guide are two aids in top stitching. The Quilter helps you gauge the stitching line and keep it straight and parallel to the edge or seam depression. See *Welt Seam*, page 88, for instructions on its use. As you sew, guide the finished edge or seam depression against the space guide of the Quilter. With the Seam Guide you can stitch parallel to the edge of the fabric at any distance from ⅛ inch to 1¼ inch from the edge.

The interesting use of top stitching in the style seams illustrated is simple to achieve. After stitching the seams, press them open. Then top-stitch on each side an equal distance from the seamline. The seam allowance on the underside must be wider than the distance between the top stitching and seamline.

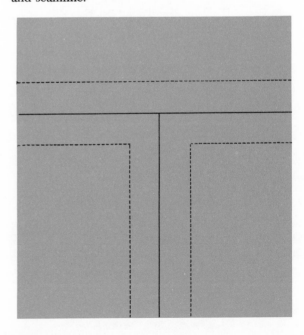

Arrowhead

The arrowhead is used in tailored costumes as a decorative and secure finish at the ends of pockets and top of pleats and on fashion seams that end within the garment.

Mark the triangular shape of the arrowhead with chalk or thread. Use buttonhole twist in the needle.

Make two small stitches, bringing the needle out at the lower left corner. At the upper corner, take a stitch from right to left. Insert the needle at the right corner and bring it out at the left corner, barely inside of the previous thread. Re-peat the procedure, placing the threads side by side until the triangle is completely filled in. Fasten the thread on the underside with two tiny back-stitches.

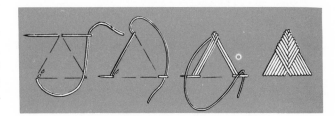

Crow's Foot

The crow's foot is used in the same places as the arrowhead. With thread or chalk, mark a triangle that is slightly curved on the sides. Use buttonhole twist in the needle.

Make two small stitches, bringing the needle out at the lower left corner. At the upper corner, take a horizontal stitch from right to left. At the lower right corner, take a diagonal stitch from left to right. Then at the lower left corner, make a diagonal stitch from left to right. Continue making stitches in the same sequence, placing them side by side until the center is filled in. Fasten the thread on the underside with two small backstitches.

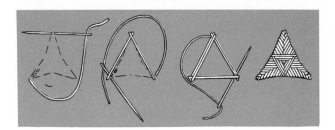

Bar Tack

Bar tacks are used to prevent ripping at the end of a fly opening and at the ends of pockets in shorts and slacks. They are also used to hold belt carriers in place. Make them by hand or by machine. Use mercerized, silk, or synthetic thread.

By Hand

Make two or three long stitches the length of the bar tack. Then make small overhand stitches across the threads and through the fabric. When the bar is finished, make tiny bar stitches across each end.

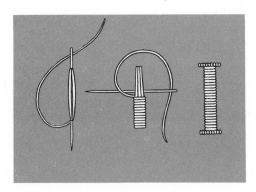

By Machine

Use a fine, closely spaced zig-zag stitch. Stitch the length of the bar tack. Pull the threads through to the underside and tie.

Introduction to Home Decorating

Home decorating is, in many ways, the most rewarding adventure in sewing. It offers you a perfect opportunity to express yourself—your sensitivity to design and proportion, your flair for color. In short, it brings out you—your personality and your creative talent.

Since the home you decorate is an intimate part of the life you share with your family, you want it to reflect as well as contribute to the charm and beauty of that life. Before you plunge into decorating, therefore, consult the several magazines available on the subject. They will give you many excellent ideas on style, color, and fabric. Consider fashion trends but do not let novelties or fads influence your judgment. Strive for harmony and unity, for beauty and comfort, and you will give your family a home they can enjoy for many years to come.

In making your decorating decisions, remember that fabric furnishings, should be planned in relation to the size and shape of the room, the height of the ceiling, the number and placement of windows, and the effect you wish to achieve. Fabric, color, and style, as well as construction, determine the end results.

This section of the book will guide you in choosing styles and fabrics and in planning color schemes. Its most valuable contribution, however, is the techniques it explains, through words and pictures, on construction. In custom-made fabric furnishings, it is not the price of the fabric that makes the greatest difference—it is the construction, the fit of a slipcover, or the fullness and "hang" of curtains and draperies.

PLANNING A COLOR SCHEME

The success of your entire decorating project may depend on how wisely you use color. But do not let this statement intimidate you. If you follow a few basic rules, you will find that it is not difficult to assemble colors harmoniously.

The Color System

To use color skillfully, you should have some knowledge of the color system. See color wheel, Plate 17 opposite page 340. The primary colors are red, yellow, and blue. They are pure colors and cannot be produced by mixing other colors. The secondary colors—orange, green, and violet—are produced by mixing equal amounts of two primary colors, as illustrated in the color wheel. The primary and secondary colors together comprise the six standard colors.

Intermediate colors or hues are produced by combining a primary color with the secondary color that flanks it in the color wheel. The six intermediate hues and the six standard colors are known as the twelve "true" colors because they are not diluted with white, black, or grey.

When true colors are diluted, a shade or tint results. A shade is produced by adding varying degrees of grey or black to the true color to give a color value darker than the true color. A tint is produced by adding varying degrees of white to the true color to give a color value lighter than the true color. Each true color has numerous shades and tints. A slight degree of color value is illustrated in the color wheel.

Warm and Cool Colors

The warm colors are red, orange, and yellow. All the hues in the color wheel containing these colors share in their warmth. The cool colors are blue and all the hues grouped around it in the color wheel. Green, which contains equal amounts of blue and yellow, and violet, which contains equal amounts of blue and red, are neither warm nor cool. As greater percentages of the warm colors are added to them, however, they gain in warmth; as the percentage of blue is increased, they grow cool.

Warm colors make the size of an object seem larger and the size of a room smaller. Cool colors behave in the opposite way, diminishing the apparent size of an object and giving an illusion of spaciousness in a room.

Neutral colors—white, grey, and beige—are frequently used in home decorating. Neutral walls, ceilings, windows, and floors provide an effective background for the bold, bright colors so often found in fabric furnishings. Colors appear darker than they actually are when placed against a light background, lighter against a dark background. Middle tones are less forceful than extreme light or dark tones.

Color Harmony

Color harmony is the art of grouping colors pleasingly in a room. Many ideas on color combinations can be gleaned from the beauty of nature. Study

a sunset or a rainbow; notice how subtly each color blends with and accents the other. Study color proportion, keeping in mind the colors nature used for the redbird and the elephant. In short, be aware of color!

Shades and tints are mainstays in home decorating. They make it possible for you to repeat a color, but to alter it slightly to retain interest without sacrificing unity and harmony. Strong contrasts may also be welcome in your decorating scheme. For example, red, blue, and yellow can produce a striking and still harmonious effect, provided the tints or shades are compatible.

Here are some suggestions for you in planning color schemes:

Think not only of the color value but also of color balance—that is, the placement and quantity of the colors you are using. Concentrating dark colors on one side of the room and light colors on the other upsets the balance of a room and prevents you from achieving the harmony you seek.

Prints or florals in fabric, rug, or wallpaper can add interest to the decorating scheme. However, do not mix two different figured or patterned fabrics; this creates a feeling of confusion. A wide assortment of coordinated colors is available to you. It is also possible to buy fabric in the identical pattern or color found in the wallpaper.

In decorating, the focal point of a room may be the window treatment or a picture, chair, or sofa. Plan your color scheme around one dominant color and use shades or tints of this color in moderate amounts to give interest. Select a third color for accent and contrast.

Slavish repetition of a color is monotonous, but judicious repetition is generally welcome. Draperies and walls of the same color or tone-on-tone are pleasing to the eye. White and gold produce a rich accent. Or, if you are using a print in the draperies, repeat one of the colors in the sofa, another in a chair. Keep the texture and weave of the fabrics compatible.

Consider the exposure of the room as well as the effect you wish to achieve. Some decorators advocate warm colors for north and east exposures and cool colors for south and west. Rooms that are distinctly feminine in character stress pale, pastel tints and shades; those that are masculine tend toward deep, strong colors. Family rooms and dens seem to require brighter colors. In planning color schemes for them, however, consider the family's living habits as well as the style and purpose of the room.

When your decorating project is confined to a

window treatment, a bedspread, or a chair or sofa covering, consider the colors and fabric textures now in the room.

Experiment with color. Drape swatches of various colors together to see whether they combine felicitously. If you wish to use red, choose shades or tints that harmonize with and complement the colors already selected.

SELECTING FABRICS

Fabrics today are interesting and exciting. Study them carefully when you are planning your room, for the variety at your disposal is bound to influence your decorating decisions. You can choose from the traditional natural fibers, man-made fibers, or a blend of natural and man-made fibers—each is offered in a variety of textures and weaves as well as colors. Often a metallic thread that will not tarnish is interwoven in a fabric for decorative effect.

The variation of weave may be the means of introducing pattern into the room. The weave may also determine where the fabric can be used—whether it will hang gracefully in draperies or be durable in slipcovers. (The tighter the weave, the more durable the fabric.) Both texture and weave should meet your functional needs as well as produce the decorative effect you desire. For more information on fabrics, see page 7.

In selecting a fabric, consider these facts about the room: its size and exposure; its purpose—whether formal or informal, whether for the entire family or only one of its members; its furniture—whether modern or traditional; and the effect you wish to achieve. Above all, be sure that the fabric is in keeping with family living as well as family likes and dislikes. Each style has its own way of achieving beauty.

For formal rooms, select antique satin, damask, etruscan, brocade, brocatelle, faille, antique taffeta, slipper satin, mohair, velvet, or velveteen. These fabrics may be of silk or man-made fibers, or a blend of two fibers.

For informal rooms, the selection is much greater—chintz, polished cotton, antique satin, gingham, sailcloth, burlap, denim, Indian Head†, hand-blocked linen, frisé, corduroy, poplin, and many synthetic fabrics such as fiberglass, nylon, and Dacron.

Curtains. Glass curtains are generally made of a soft, sheer fabric that softens and diffuses light without impeding it—for example, ninon, fiber-

†Indian Head

glass, Dacron, sheer nylon, theatrical gauze, marquisette, Orlon, and pongee. Ruffled tieback curtains should be made of crisp organdy, lawn, dotted Swiss, net, nylon, Dacron, unbleached muslin, marquisette, or gauze. Café curtains are made of gingham, Indian Head†, muslin, chintz, polished cotton, dotted Swiss, corduroy, and nylon, to name just a few.

Draperies are constructed of medium-weight and heavyweight fabrics, and the selection is unlimited. Some of the fabrics listed for glass curtains are also suitable for draw draperies.

Slipcovers should be made of a medium-weight or heavyweight, closely woven fabric so that they will retain their shape.

Lining. Draperies are frequently lined. A sateen lining is available in widths of 36 and 50 inches. Generally, white, light beige, eggshell, or soft grey is used to blend with the neutral color of the glass curtain.

When you contemplate changing only the window treatment, bedspread, or slipcover, carefully consider the function and existing design of the room before you choose a fabric. Harmony in texture as well as color must be maintained. Fabrics may be comparable in weight but may differ in light reflection.

If the entire room is to be redecorated, study it carefully before visiting the decorator's shop. Begin with your focal point of interest—a window, chair, sofa, picture, or lamp. For example, if windows are the focal point, select fabrics for the curtains and draperies, then blend and harmonize all other fabrics with this selection. Drape the fabrics together while you are still at the decorator's shop to be certain that the textures, weaves, and colors are compatible. Then try the fabrics in the room where they will be used. If swatches large enough for this purpose are not available on loan, it is advisable to buy yard lengths of the fabrics you are considering. In view of the ultimate investment, such a small expense is worthwhile.

To determine the yardage you will need, take the measurements of each project you are planning before you visit the decorator's shop. In making your purchase, be sure to consider the width of the fabric as well as the length.

Last, but not least, consider how the fabric will be cleaned. Must it be dry-cleaned? If washable, is it tubfast and colorfast? Will it shrink? Examine the labels for information on the properties of the fibers which will predict the performance of the fabric. Some fabrics are now chemically treated to resist soiling.

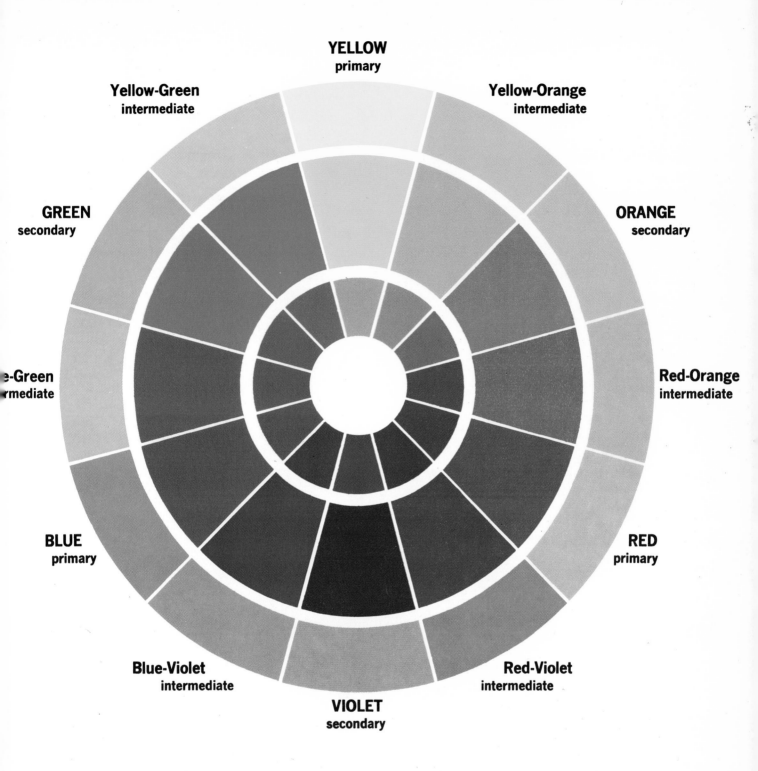

YELLOW
primary

Yellow-Green
intermediate

Yellow-Orange
intermediate

GREEN
secondary

ORANGE
secondary

e-Green
rmediate

Red-Orange
intermediate

BLUE
primary

RED
primary

Blue-Violet
intermediate

Red-Violet
intermediate

VIOLET
secondary

Plate 17

Color Wheel

The twelve true colors shown in the center (widest) ring,
can be varied to shades (inside ring) by adding black,
or to tints (outside ring) by adding white.
For an explanation of the color system, see pages 338 and 339.

From The American Home © 1964, The Curtis Publishing Co

Plate 18

Color brings the outdoors in

Brilliant floral linen slipcovers
reflect the garden atmosphere of the
patio. For privacy and convenience,
Roman shades, taped in red to echo
the red-beamed ceiling, solve the
drapery problem for the patio doors.

Romantic dining corner

Scalloped valance lends
an air of formality
to flowered cotton-satin draperies
in print to match wallpaper.
Pink ball fringe with tiny green
tassels adds finishing touches
to draperies, valance and tiebacks.

Courtesy of McCall's magazine

THREAD, NEEDLE, AND STITCH LENGTH

The selection of the thread depends on the fabric to be stitched. The thread should blend with the fabric in color, fiber, and size. Needle selection depends on both the thread and the fabric. The weight and texture of the fabric determine the stitch length.

Silk and wool fabrics are stitched with silk thread; cottons, linens, and some blended fabrics, with mercerized thread (however, fine linens may be stitched with silk thread). Synthetic fabrics and blends of natural and man-made fibers may be stitched with silk, mercerized, or synthetic thread. Use a size 14 needle with mercerized or silk thread and a size 11 needle for finer threads such as nylon.

Organdy, voile, dotted Swiss, marquisette, batiste, and similar fabrics used for glass curtains should be stitched with mercerized thread, size 14 needle, and 12 to 15 stitch length, depending on their weight. Nylon, Dacron, and similar synthetic fabrics may be stitched with either nylon or mercerized thread.

Damask, brocade, taffeta, satin, and similar fabrics appropriate for draperies and bedspreads should be stitched with silk or mercerized thread, size 14 needle, and 12 stitch length.

For lightweight or medium-weight fabrics like chintz, polished cotton, linen, percale, antique satin, corduroy, and faille, use mercerized thread, size 14 needle, and 12 stitch length.

Heavyweight fabric used in slipcovers—linen, cotton damask, sailcloth, ticking, denim, and the like—should be stitched with heavy-duty thread, size 16 needle, and 12 stitch length.

If the fabric you are working with is not listed above, check the chart on page 24.

A Look at Your Windows

WINDOWS BRING LIGHT AND AIR into your home. When you look at them with a homemaker's eye, your first thoughts are to ensure privacy without obstructing the sunlight or the view if it is a pleasing one. When you look at them with a decorator's eye, your concern is to create a window treatment that is in harmony with the other furnishings of the room and still captures the light and the view. The window treatment you decide on depends mainly on your plans for the room. True, the style of the window may suggest or even dictate the treatment, but even that can be changed by clever use of curtains and draperies or by simple carpentry tricks that alter inside window proportions.

The term "curtain" as used here refers to glass curtains and tieback curtains, which have a casing that fits around a rod, and to café curtains, which may have a casing, hooks, or clip-on rings. The term "drapery" designates hangings with pleated headings. Draperies may be of sheer or heavy fabric, lined or unlined. They are attached to rods by hooks.

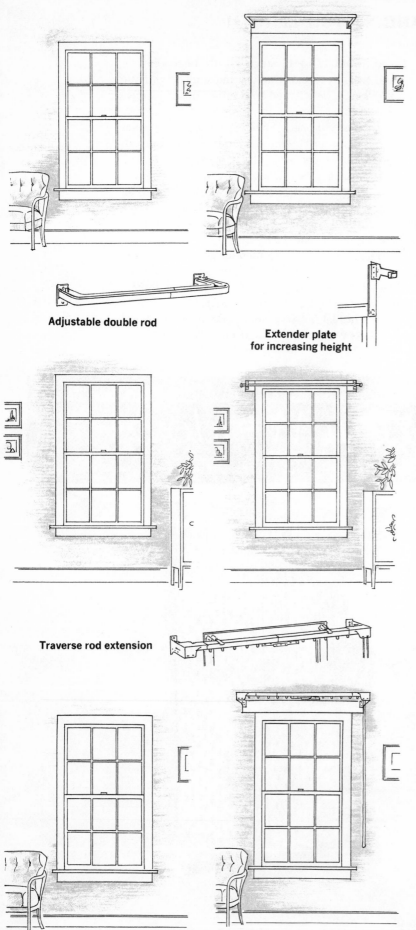

Adjustable double rod

**Extender plate
for increasing height**

Traverse rod extension

Changing Window Proportions

Window proportions can be changed to make them appear higher or wider or to create the illusion of an entire wall of windows.

To increase height. A window may be increased in height just a few inches or all the way to the ceiling by using either a board or an extender plate.

The board should be as thick as the window frame, at least 4 to 6 inches wide, and cut to the same length as the window width. Use the recommended method (opposite page) to attach the board to the wall above the frame. Then paint or finish the board to match the finish on either the frame or the wall, whichever will look better. When dry, mount the fixtures on the extreme ends of the board, 1 inch below the top.

Extender plates, available in three sizes, are mounted vertically on the window frame, and do not touch the wall or mar the paint.

To increase width. Narrow windows can be widened to bring them into proportion to the size of the room and to admit as much light as possible. Either boards or extender plates may be used to extend the top portion of the frame on each side.

Cut the boards, one for each side, to the desired increase in width. Use the recommended method (opposite page) to attach the boards to the wall on each side. Then paint or finish the boards to match either the finish on the frame or the wall, whichever will look better. When dry, mount the fixtures on the extreme ends of the boards, 1 inch below the top.

If the extender plates suggested above are to be used, mount them horizontally on the frame.

Extension rod and bracket

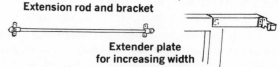

**Extender plate
for increasing width**

To increase both height and width. Often, a better proportion can be obtained by increasing both the height and the width. A board, cut to the required dimensions, can be mounted above the window frame using the method recommended on the opposite page. Mount the fixtures at the extreme ends of the board, 1 inch below the top.

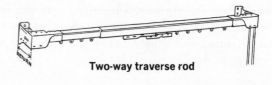

Two-way traverse rod

342

A **cornice board** may also be used to change window proportions. Mount it above the board you used to lengthen or widen the window. The cornice covers the top of the draperies.

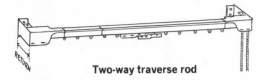

Two-way traverse rod

Rods and Fixtures

The type of rod and fixture you select depends on the style and weight of the curtains or draperies. The rod should be sturdy enough to prevent the curtains from sagging; it may be decorative or utilitarian. There is a rod available for every window treatment, and you can generally find the kind you need in shops that specialize in curtains and draperies.

Most rods have a return at each end. "Return" is the term used for the distance the rod projects from the wall. In the adjustable rod for glass curtains, the return is the distance from the curve of the rod to the wall. In the traverse rod, it is the depth of the bracket. Always measure the return, for its depth may vary from 3 to 4 inches, or more. Curtains and draperies extend around the returns.

The fixtures holding the rod in place should be mounted on the extreme ends of the window frame, 1 inch below the top, so that the curtains cover the entire window frame. Café curtains, however, may be recessed within the window frame and casement curtains are mounted on the window sash.

Since the measurements for your curtains and draperies are based on the position of the rod, the rod and fixtures should be fastened in place before you take any window measurements. In this way you will be sure of measuring accurately to determine the yardage required and the length and width of your curtains and draperies.

Installing Fixtures on a Wall

A moderate degree of skill with tools and some previous experience in mounting fixtures on walls are necessary if you expect to get a satisfactory result. If you do not have the skill or the experience, have the job done by a professional.

For the purpose of mounting drapery hardware or cornice boards on every type of wall construction, a **plastic anchor** used with a matching sheet-metal screw is the easiest to install. These anchors are available in many lengths and sizes, and your choice of the correct size will depend on the weight of your draperies. The heavier the drapery, the larger the anchor and screw should be.

Plastic anchor

Use the mounting bracket as a template, and mark the wall for the holes. Cover the mark with transparent tape (about an inch square) to prevent cracking the plaster. Use a drill bit of the size specified for the anchor with either an electric drill (750 revolutions per minute) or a hand drill (eggbeater type) and drill a hole in the plaster wall. Be sure to hold the drill steady at a right angle to the wall so as not to drill too large a hole. After the holes are drilled, tap the anchors into the holes, insert the matching sheet metal screws through the holes in the bracket, and turn in the screws with a screwdriver.

If the wall is hollow, the plastic anchor must be long enough to extend well into the hollow space so that it will expand when the screw is turned in.

The same procedure is followed for drilling holes in concrete or other masonry except that the bit must be tipped with tungsten carbide, and greater pressure must be exerted against the wall while drilling.

Caution: Do not touch the masonry bit when removing it from the hole. It will be hot enough to cause a burn on the skin.

This section explains how to measure different kinds of windows and how much to add for hems, headings, casings, seams, and shrinkage tucks. In all cases, the amount you should allow depends on the style of the window treatment. You will need these measurements later to estimate the yardage and to cut and construct your curtains and draperies.

Sash Windows

The curtain and drapery treatment possible for sash windows is practically unlimited. Any of the

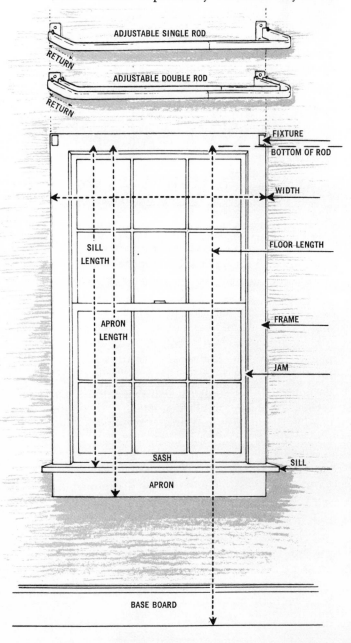

styles described in the chapters that follow can be used. When two or three windows are grouped together, they are treated as a single unit.

Living room and dining room curtains and draperies may be sill, apron, or floor length, depending on the style of the room and on whether there is an air conditioner in the window or a radiator below the window. Bedroom curtains and tiebacks may also be sill, apron, or floor length although here you will want to consider not only the effect desired but also the age and sex of the person occupying the room. Kitchen, bathroom, and breakfast room curtains generally extend to the sill or the lower edge of the apron.

To measure windows, use a steel tape or folding ruler if possible.

Length: Measure from the bottom of the rod to the sill, the lower edge of the apron, or the floor. (The finished length should be about ½ inch above the floor. The turning of the hems will take up the fabric slightly.)

Width: Measure from edge to edge of the window frame. To this width, add the depth of the return on each side. (The measurement for the return will be used later for positioning the end pleat in the drapery heading.)

This gives you your basic window measurements. To them you must add the allowances given below. Café curtains are an exception. For them, see page 358.

For Glass Curtains

Two panels are required for each window.

Length: To the measured length of your window, add 2 inches for casing, 2 inches for heading, ¼ inch for turning, 2 inches for shrinkage tuck

(1 inch per yard), and 3¼ inches for bottom hem and turning. If double bottom hems are used, and they are desirable for sheer fabrics, allow 6 inches for the bottom hem instead of 3¼ inches.

Width: Multiply the measured width of your window by 2½ or 3 for fullness. To this figure, add 8 inches for hems (1-inch double hem on each side of the two panels).

For Panel Draperies

A pair of drapery panels is required for each window or group of windows.

Length for lined draperies: To the measured length of your window, add 1 inch for rod, 2 inches for heading, 4 inches for top hem, and 3½ inches for bottom hem and turning.

Length for unlined draperies: Add an extra ½ inch for turning on the top hem.

Width: Determine how wide you want your finished drapery panel to be. To this measurement, add 4 inches for the depth of the return at one end, plus 5 inches for hems (2-inch hem and ½-inch seam allowance on each side), plus the amount required for pleats. See page 367.

For Draw Draperies

A pair of drapery panels is required for each window or group of windows. Use a two-way traverse rod. Measure the length as described above; however, since draw draperies cover the entire window, measure the width as instructed below for picture windows.

Picture Windows

Draw draperies are an attractive and practical treatment for picture windows. Use a two-way traverse rod. Install the brackets for the rods on the extreme ends of the window frame, 1 inch below the top of the frame or ceiling. (Use the ceiling-mounted track if feasible.)

Length for lined draperies: Measure from the bottom of the rod to the floor. To this measurement, add 1 inch for rod, 2 inches for heading, 4 inches for top hem, 3½ inches for bottom hem and turning.

Length for unlined draperies: Add an extra ½ inch for turning on the top hem. If double hems are used, and they are recommended for sheer fabrics, allow 8 inches for the top hem and 6 inches for the bottom hem.

If draperies extend from the ceiling, measure from the ceiling to the floor and add only the amounts stated for top and bottom hems.

Width: Measure across the window from one end of the rod to the other. To this measurement, add the depth of the return on each side, 10 inches for hems (2-inch hems and ½-inch seam allowance on each side of the two panels), 2½ inches for overlap, plus the amount required for pleats and seams within the drapery. See page 368.

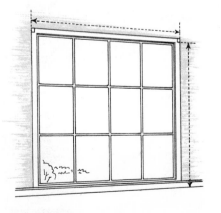

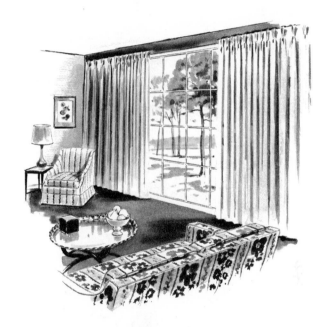

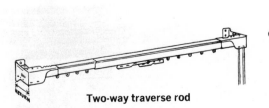

Two-way traverse rod

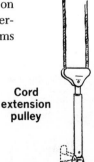

Cord extension pulley

Sliding Windows or Doors

Sliding windows or doors should be treated as a single unit. Draw draperies are an effective way to do this. Use either a two-way or one-way traverse rod, depending on the position of the window. Mount the brackets for the rod on the extreme ends of the window frame, 1 inch below the top of the frame or ceiling. Measure the length as instructed for the picture window and make the same allowances for top and bottom hems.

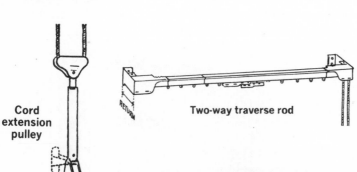

Cord extension pulley

Two-way traverse rod

Corner Windows

Corner windows are treated as a single unit; however, the draperies for each window should be an independent unit. Use two one-way traverse rods (a one-way left and a one-way right) and position them so that you draw each side drapery *away from the corner* when opening it. The rods may meet at the corner, or one rod may be fully in the corner and the second rod almost against the first, as illustrated. If the second installation is used, be sure to allow enough room for the drapery on the first rod to pass by the end of the second rod.

If a wall space intervenes between two windows that are near a corner, the windows may be treated separately or the wall and windows may be treated

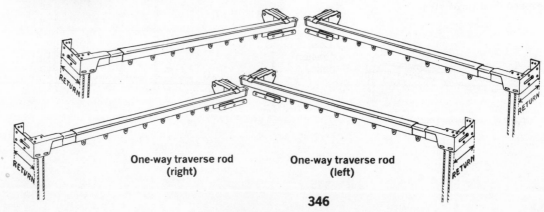

One-way traverse rod (right)　　　**One-way traverse rod (left)**

as a single unit as illustrated here. Install two one-way traverse rods the same as for the corner windows above, but reverse the rods so that you draw each side drapery *toward the corner* when you open it. With this positioning of the rods, the draperies cover the wall space at the corner whether they are opened or closed. Install one bracket for the rod on the wall in the corner and the other bracket on the extreme end of the window frame; position both brackets 1 inch below the top of the frame or ceiling.

Measure the length and width the same as instructed for picture windows on page 345; however, the length may be to the sill, the lower edge of the apron, or the floor.

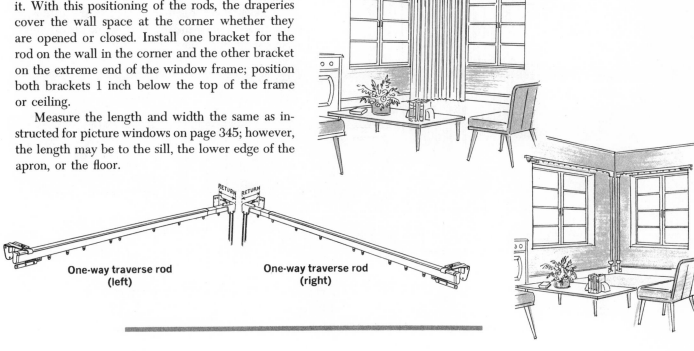

One-way traverse rod
(left)

One-way traverse rod
(right)

Casement Windows

If casement windows open inward, sheer casement curtains must be mounted on the window sash so that they will swing in with the window. The curtains have a heading and casing at the top and bottom and require two rods. They are stretched tightly over the glass.

Use the elbow bracket and rod. Place the brackets so that the curtain will cover the glass portion of the window.

Length: Measure from the bottom of the upper rod to the top of the lower rod. To this measurement add, to top and bottom, 1½ inches for heading, 1½ inches for easing, and ½ inch for turning, or 7 inches in all. Either shrink the fabric before cutting, or allow an additional 2 inches for a shrinkage tuck at the top.

Width: Measure across the window from one bracket edge to the other. Allow for double or triple fullness. To this figure, add 2 inches for hems (½-inch double-fold hem on each side).

If the windows open outward, the rods are mounted on the window frame so that the windows will swing free of the curtain or drapery. Draw draperies are an appropriate window treatment. They may be sill or floor length, depending on the style of the room and personal choice.

Elbow bracket

Elbow bracket and rod

347

Elbow bracket and rod

French Windows and Doors

French windows may swing either in or out. The window treatment is the same as for casement windows.

French doors open inward. Use the casement curtain and follow the instructions for the casement window opening inward.

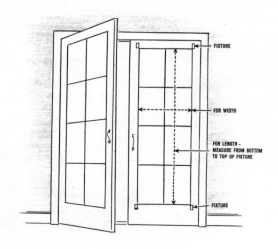

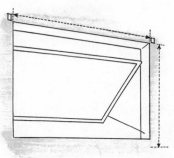

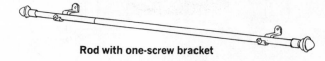

Rod with one-screw bracket

Projected Windows

Projected windows swing out and are generally placed high in a wall. Draw draperies are a customary treatment. A decorative two-way traverse rod with rings is shown in the illustration. Make the draperies in two panels that meet in the center of the window, and line them since the projected window usually has no venetian blind or window shade.

Install the brackets for the rod on the wall, 1 or 2 inches above the window and a few inches beyond each side of the window.

Length: Measure from the lower circle of the ring to about 2 inches below the window. To this measurement, add 5 inches for top and bottom hems (2-inch hem and ½ inch for turning).

Width: Measure from the edge of one bracket to the other. Multiply this measurement by 2 for fullness. To this figure, add 10 inches for hems (2-inch hem and ½ inch for turning on each side of the two panels).

One-screw bracket

Clip-on ring

Awning Windows

Café curtains are a pleasant informal treatment for awning windows. Draw draperies are also appropriate. In the illustration, café curtains are used and the tiers are uneven in length. They do not overlap and decorative rods and rings are visible above each tier. Two brass rods with sew-on or clip-on rings are required for this style of café.

Mount the brackets for the top rod on the wall, 1 or 2 inches above the window and a few inches beyond each side of the window. Mount the brackets for the second rod at the point where the top and second window sections meet; extend them the same distance beyond the window as the top brackets.

Length, top tier: Measure from the lower circle of the ring to the top of the second rod.

Bottom tier: Measure from the lower circle of the ring to 2 inches below the window. To these measurements, add 5 inches to each tier for top and bottom hems (2-inch hems plus ½ inch for turning).

Width: Follow the instructions for the projected window.

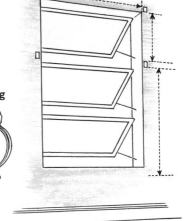

Clip-on ring

Two-screw bracket and rod

Two-screw bracket

Hopper Windows

Draw draperies and a two-way traverse rod should be selected for these windows so that the draperies can easily be drawn to the sides when you open or close the window. Position the bracket and measure the same way as for a projected window.

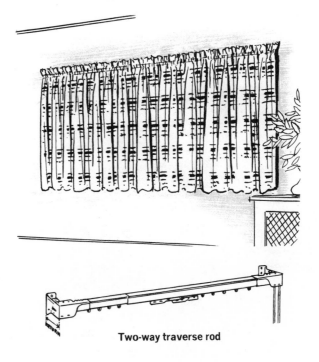

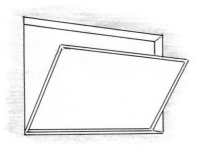

Two-way traverse rod

Bay or Bow Windows

A group of three or more windows placed at angles to each other and projecting outward, forming a recess or alcove in the wall, is known as a "bay window." If the window or windows are curved, they are call a "bow window." Many pleasing treatments are possible; however, the bay or bow should always be treated as a single unit.

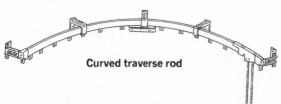

Curved traverse rod

Dormers

The dormer is a window in a gable rising from a sloping roof. Simple ruffled tiebacks, full sheer curtains hanging straight from a rod, or casement curtains, are all suitable.

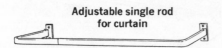

**Adjustable single rod
for curtain**

350

**Adjustable single rod
for curtain**

Success with Curtains

Your success with curtains depends on your accuracy in measuring your windows, in adding the allowances necessary for your curtain style, in estimating fabric requirements, in cutting your fabric, and in sewing. This chapter will guide you through those steps for four basic curtain styles: glass curtains, casement curtains, tieback curtains, and café curtains.

GLASS CURTAINS

Full, sheer curtains that hang straight from a rod against the glass are called "glass" curtains. They have a casing and heading at the top and are made in two panels, which are gathered on the curtain rod. Their purpose is to ensure privacy, to soften the interior, and to diffuse light. They also create a uniform appearance from the outside. Glass curtains may be used with panel or draw draperies. The curtains and draperies should be the same length and hung on separate rods.

Use an **adjustable curtain rod.** Secure the fixtures for the rod on the extreme ends of the window frame, 1 inch below the top.

Marquisette, ninon, fiberglass, theatrical gauze, Dacron, and other gossamer, or semi-sheer synthetics and blends are all appropriate fabrics for glass curtains. Neutral colors are generally used— beige, eggshell, white, or grey; however, pastels are seen occasionally.

Adding Allowances to Measurements

Glass curtains should hang in graceful, soft folds. To get the fullness necessary, you must allow from 2½ to 3 times the width of the window. Ready-made curtains are often skimpy and two pairs may be required for the desired fullness. If your budget is limited, choose less expensive fabric but *do not skimp on yardage.*

Length: To the measured length of the window (see page 344), add 2 inches for casing, 2 inches for heading, ¼ inch for turning, 2 inches for shrinkage tuck (1 inch per yard), plus 3¼ inches for the bottom hem and turning. *Example:* 72 inches (measured length) plus 9½ inches = 81½ inches. If double-fold bottom hems are used, and they are desirable in sheer fabrics to eliminate the turned raw edge that would normally show through, allow 6 inches for the bottom hem instead of 3¼ inches. 72 inches (measured length) plus 12¼ inches = 84¼ inches.

Width: Multiply the measured width (page 344) by 2½ or 3 for fullness. To this figure, add 8 inches for hems (1-inch double-fold hem on each side of the two panels). *Example:* 42 inches (measured width and returns) x 2½ (fullness) = 105 inches plus 8 inches (hems) = 113 inches. Each of the two panels is 56½ inches wide.

Estimating Yardage

To estimate yardage for each window, you must consider the fabric width. *Example:* Three lengths of 40-inch fabric are required for the 113-inch width in the example above. (Remember, lengths cannot be pieced. If your figures result in a fraction of a length, such as 2½, buy 3 full lengths.) 84¼ inches (length required for curtain with double bottom hem) x 3 (lengths of fabric) = 252¾ inches, or 7 yards and ¾ inch for each window. It is advisable to buy an extra 9 inches to allow for straightening the ends of the fabric.

Cutting the Curtains

Curtains must be cut on the true lengthwise and crosswise grains of the fabric so that they hang in straight, smooth lines.

Straighten the end of the fabric by drawing a single thread on the crosswise grain to indicate the cutting line. See page 14. Press the fabric and remove selvages.

Work on a flat surface and use a tape measure to measure the lengths for your curtain. Draw a thread on the crosswise grain to mark the cutting line of each length. Cut, do not tear, the fabric. Straighten the fabric grain, following the instructions on page 14.

Constructing the Curtains

Seams

If it is necessary to seam the fabric to gain the width you need, use a fine French seam. See page 86.

Suggestions for Folding and Pressing Hems

For convenience in folding and pressing hems and casings of your curtains, work on the ironing board. Reverse the direction of the board and place the iron on the small end so that you have a wider working area. If the height of the board is adjust-able, lower it so that you can work in a sitting position. Use a small gauge to measure each turn of the fabric; accuracy is extremely important. As you make each fold for the hem, pin straight through the fabric into the ironing board. Place the pins far enough from the fold so that they do not interfere with your pressing.

Side Hems

Finish the side hems first. Use a 1-inch double-fold hem on the side and center hems; then the panels will be interchangeable. (A 2-inch hem may be used if you prefer, but be sure to make the extra allowance when cutting the curtains.)

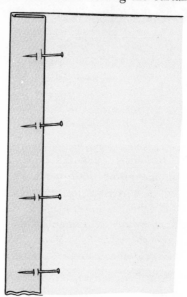

Turn a scant 1 inch to the underside and pin along the cut edge. Press the fold. Then make a second 1-inch turn and pin in place. Press the fold. Stitch as close to the first fold as possible. Backstitch at each end. Press.

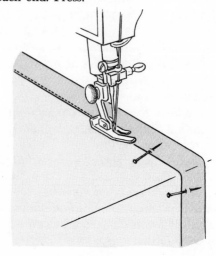

Casing and Heading

In the measurements, 4¼ inches were allowed for the casing, heading, and turning. At the top edge, turn ¼ inch to the underside and finger-press. Turn 2 inches to the underside and pin the free edge in place. Press along the top fold. Stitch close to the first fold. Backstitch at each end. Press.

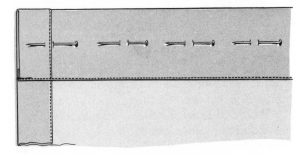

Divide the hem for the casing and heading by placing a row of pins midway between the stitching and top edge. Stitch along this line. Backstitch at each end. Press.

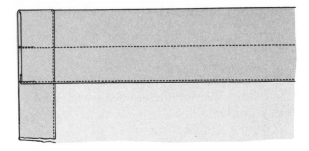

Shrinkage Tuck

On the right side (or wrong side, if you prefer), barely below the casing, fold and pin in a 1-inch tuck. Press. Stitch close to the previous line of stitching, using a long stitch. Backstitch at each end. If the curtain shrinks when laundered, let out the tuck the required length.

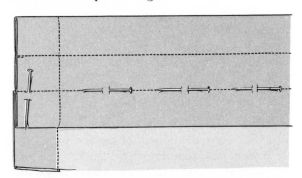

Note: If your machine is one with Chain Stitch Accessories, chain-stitch the shrinkage tuck. Then you can easily let out the tuck when necessary—merely unlock the last loop of the chain and pull out the stitching. Refer to the instruction book accompanying the machine, and to page 63.

Bottom Hem

Compare the panels to be sure that they are the same length. Place them wrong sides together, and check the length at the center and outside hems.

In the measurements, 6 inches were allowed for a 3-inch double-fold hem. Turn under a scant 3 inches and pin along the fold. Make a second 3-inch turn and pin the first fold to the curtain.

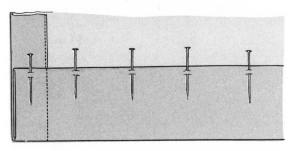

Before pressing and stitching the hem, hang the curtain on the rod. Adjust the fullness and check the length; the curtain should be about ½ inch above the floor. If your measurements were accurate, the length should be correct; however, if there is a slight difference in length, adjust the hem width accordingly.

Press the hem, then stitch it in place close to the fold. Backstitch at each end. Press.

Weights

Weight the bottom hems so that the curtains will hang evenly. A round-bead weighted tape is most suitable. Draw the weighted tape through the hem in back of the double turn and secure it on the underside with diagonal hand stitches. Make the stitches about ¼ or ⅜ inch apart, through a single thickness of the hem and the weights. Fasten each end of the thread with tiny backstitches. Remove the weights when laundering the curtains.

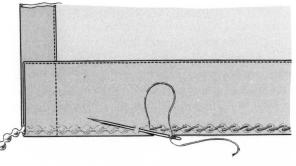

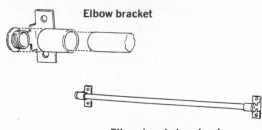

Elbow bracket

Elbow bracket and rod

CASEMENT CURTAINS

Casement curtains should be used on casement windows that open inward and on French windows and doors. They are tightly stretched over the glass portion of the window. Use the same types of fabrics suggested for glass curtains.

Mount elbow brackets and rods, then measure the window as instructed on page 347.

Adding Allowance to Measurements

Length: To the measured length (bottom of upper rod to top of lower rod), add to top and bottom, 1½ inches for heading, 1½ inches for casing, and ½ inch for turning. *Example:* 68 inches (measured length) plus 7 inches = 75 inches. Either

shrink the fabric before cutting, or allow an additional 2 inches for a shrinkage tuck at the top.

Width: Measure from bracket to bracket. Allow for double or triple fullness. To this figure, add 2 inches for hems (½-inch double hem on each side). *Example:* 26 inches (measured width) x 2 (fullness) = 52 inches plus 2 inches (hems) = 54 inches.

To estimate the yardage you will need, follow the guides given under *Glass Curtains,* page 352.

Cutting and Constructing the Curtains

Straighten and cut the fabric as instructed on page 352.

Side Hems.

Fold and press a ½-inch double-fold hem on each side, following the instructions for glass curtains on page 352.

Casing and Heading.

In the measurements, 7 inches (3½ inches for each end) were allowed for casing, heading, and turning. Turn under ½ inch at each end and press; then turn 1½ inches to the underside and press. Pin and stitch the casing and heading as instructed for glass curtains. See page 353.

TIEBACK CURTAINS

Informal, refreshing tieback curtains with ruffles brighten bedroom, breakfast room, kitchen, and bath, and may even be used in the living room. They are made in two panels that meet in the center or, in the case of crisscross curtains, overlap the width of the window as shown in illustration at top of opposite page.

Organdy, lawn, ninon, dotted Swiss, unbleached muslin, and similar fabrics are appropriate.

For crisscross curtains, use the adjustable crisscross or double rod. For tieback panels that meet in the center, use an adjustable curtain rod. Mount

the fixtures for the rod on the extreme ends of the window frame, 1 inch below the top.

Adding Allowances to Measurements

Measure from the bottom of the rod to the floor. See page 344. (Remember to consider the width of the finished ruffle in the measurement and when cutting the curtains.) To this measurement, add 2 inches for casing, 2 inches for heading, and ¼ inch for turning.

Allow 2½ to 3 times the width of the window

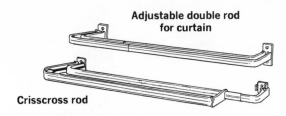

Adjustable double rod
for curtain

Crisscross rod

for fullness. If you are making crisscross curtains, double this figure since each gathered panel covers the entire window.

The width of the ruffle may be from 4 to 8 inches, depending on the texture of the fabric. Double or triple fullness may be required, depending on the width of the ruffle and the texture and weight of the fabric. Sheer fabrics require triple fullness; unbleached muslin may require only double fullness.

To estimate the yardage you will need, follow the guides given under *Glass Curtains,* page 352. Be sure to include the yardage for the ruffles.

Cutting the Curtains

Straighten and cut the fabric lengths as instructed on page 352. Generally, fabric for ruffling is cut on the crosswise grain. For curtains, however, cut the fabric on the lengthwise grain since you will need a great deal of yardage. Ruffles cut on the lengthwise grain require fewer seam joinings than those cut on the crosswise grain and will remain fluffy much longer when exposed to atmospheric conditions. It is always wise to cut and ruffle a little more length than your estimated requirement. If you are planning to make ruffled tiebacks, allow sufficient length for each pair.

Constructing the Curtains

Seams

Use a fine French seam if it is necessary to seam the fabric to gain the required width. See page 86. Join strips for the ruffles with a hemmed seam, using the Hemmer Foot.

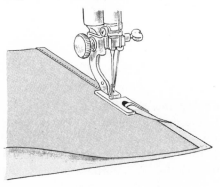

Making the Ruffle

Finish the edges of the ruffle with a narrow hem, using the Hemmer Foot. Hem each edge if there is a heading on the ruffle. One of the decorative zig-zag patterns may be used in the hemming.

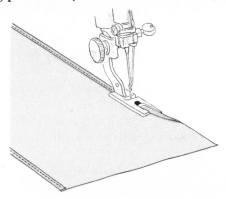

If crisp organdy or lawn is used, finished the edges with a decorative zig-zag stitch rather than a hem. See *Edgestitched Finish,* page 274.

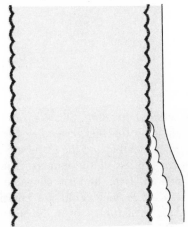

Use the Ruffler to gather the fabric. Always adjust the setting of the Ruffler and test the fullness of the ruffle on a swatch of your fabric. To ruffle organdy or chintz, dampen the fabric along the seamline with a small, moist sponge, and gather the fabric while it is still damp. Press when finished.

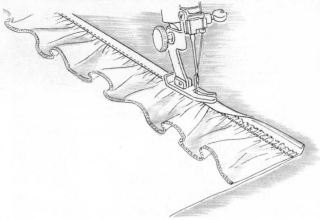

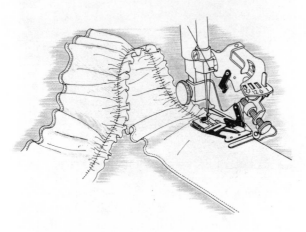

Joining Ruffle to Curtain
Ruffle with heading. First finish the center and lower edges of the curtain with a narrow hem. Use the Hemmer Foot or turn a ⅛-inch double hem to the underside and stitch. Press. Pin the ruffle, right side up, over the right side of the hemmed edge. Ease in extra fullness at the corners, beginning and ending about 1 inch from each side of the intersecting edge. Pin at close intervals. Stitch on the gathering stitches, with the ruffle side up.

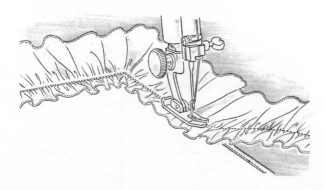

Ruffle without heading. Pin the ruffle to the curtain, right sides together, extending the curtain edge a scant ½ inch beyond the gathering stitches. Ease in extra fullness at the corners. Stitch with the ruffle side up. Trim the seam allowance on the ruffle to a scant ¼ inch. Fold the curtain edge under ⅛ inch, then fold it over the seam to the

stitching line, enclosing the raw edge; pin it in place. Stitch near the first fold. Press. Turn the ruffle away from the curtain and press the seam toward the curtain.

Side Hem
Finish the hem on the outer edge of the curtain and ruffle with a ½-inch double-fold hem. To do this, turn the cut edge under a scant ½ inch and press. Make a second ½-inch turn for the hem, and press. Pin the hem in place, then stitch. Backstitch at each end. Press.

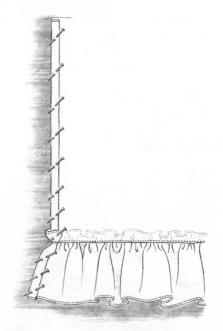

Casing and Heading
In the measurements, 4¼ inches were allowed for casing, heading, and turning. Turn, press and stitch the casing and heading now, following the instructions for glass curtains on page 353. However, extend the hem through the ruffle, making

sure that you keep it straight with the grain line of the ruffle.

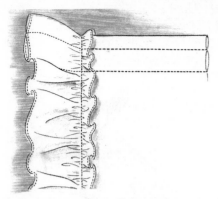

Ruffled Valance

Finish the ends of the ruffled valance with narrow hems to match those on the ruffle. Pin and stitch the ruffle to the curtain over the top line of stitching that forms the heading.

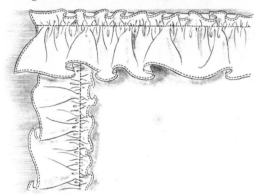

Casing and Cord for Draping

To ensure a consistently even drape in the curtains, you may use a cord with a casing on the underside of each panel.

Hang the curtains; then drape each side back, using a tape measure as a tieback. (At the same time, take the measurement for the length of the tiebacks.) Pin-mark each side of the curtain for the diagonal line of the drape.

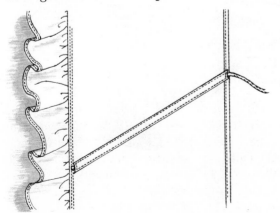

To make the casing. Cut a strip of the curtain fabric on the lengthwise grain the length of the diagonal line plus ½ inch for turning, and 1 inch wide. Fold under all edges ¼ inch and press. On the wrong side of the curtain, pin the strip on the diagonal line, from the ruffle to the outer edge. Stitch on each side of the strip to form a casing. Do not catch the ruffle heading in your stitching. Backstitch at each end. Press.

To add the cord. Insert a small cable cord (size 9) through the casing. Knot the end of the cord at the center edge of the curtain. Then stitch across the end of the cord and casing two or three times; do not catch the ruffled heading in the stitching. Tie the threads on the underside. Cut the opposite end of the cord to within ¼ inch of the curtain; then wind thread around the cord to keep it from raveling.

Hang the curtains. Draw the cord to gather the curtain the required amount. Tie a loop in the end of the cord so that the gathers may be released when the curtain is laundered. The tieback covers the casing.

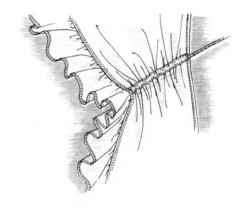

Instead of making a casing, you can purchase a shirring tape that has a woven-in cord. It is stitched in place the same way as the casing described above.

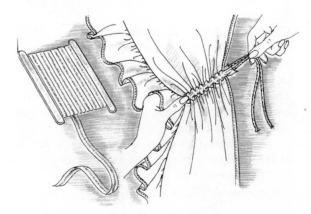

Tiebacks

A pair of tiebacks is used to hold the drape of the curtain in place. The position of the tieback depends on fashion as well as personal choice. Generally, however, it is at the center sash or below it.

The length of the tieback depends on the amount of fullness in the drape. For an average-sized window, the tiebacks are about 20 inches long; for a wide window, they may be 36 inches long. To determine the length necessary, hang the curtains, bring a tape measure around each curtain, and secure it with a thumbtack in the edge of the window frame. Drape the curtain, and adjust the tape measure for the length desired. Make one pair of tiebacks for each window.

Tieback with one ruffle. Cut the band for the tieback on the lengthwise grain the required length plus ½ inch for seam allowances, and 2½ inches wide. Crease the band through the center, wrong sides together. Cut the ruffle the same width as

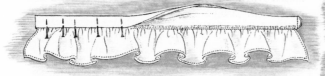

the curtain ruffle and the same length as the band. Finish each end of the ruffle with a ⅛-inch hem. Pin the wrong side of the ruffle to the right side of the band, extending the ends of the band ¼ inch beyond the ruffle. Stitch in place and backstitch at each end. Press the seam allowances toward the band. Turn under ¼ inch on the free side of the band and press. Turn the band, right

sides together, and stitch across each end, taking a ¼-inch seam. Clip diagonally across the corners. Turn the band to the right side and pin the folded edge in place at the stitching line, enclosing the seam allowance inside the band. Top-stitch close to the edge. Press.

Sew a small ring near each end of the tieback. Place a hook in the side edge of the window frame at the position for the tieback.

Tieback with ruffle on both edges. If the ruffle is no more than 3 inches wide and the fabric is crisp, you can stitch a ruffle on each side of the band. Cut two bands on the lengthwise grain the required length plus ½ inch for seam allowance, and 1½ inches wide. Cut two ruffles the length of the band and finish each end with a ⅛-inch hem. Lay the bands right sides together, and pin one ruffle between the two strips, extending the ends of the band ¼ inch beyond the ruffle at each end. Turn the ends of the band to the wrong side ¼ inch and press. Stitch, backstitching at each end. Pin the second ruffle to the

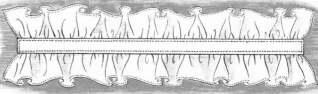

opposite edge of one band section, right sides together. Be sure the right sides of both ruffles face in the same direction. Stitch. Press the seam allowances toward the band. Turn the free edge of the band under ¼ inch and pin it in place at the stitching line, enclosing the seam allowances. Stitch around the band from the top side.

CAFÉ CURTAINS

Cafés are never full-length curtains. They may start at the center of the window or midway down on the upper half of the window, or they may be made in tiers that start from the top of the window. The tiers may be even or uneven in length. The bottom tier can be sill, apron, or floor length. Each tier must hang on a separate rod.

Café curtains are generally made in two panels. If the curtains begin at the center or upper half of the window, they are often used with a one-piece valance. (*Illustrated on left at top of opposite*

page.) The heading may be styled in several ways. Cafés may also be used in combination with draperies or tieback curtains.

Select such fabrics as chintz, sailcloth, Indian Head, gingham, dotted Swiss, organdy, muslin, nylon, corduroy, and polished cotton. Solid colors, plaids, prints, or stripes may be chosen for informal curtains, and antique satin, fiberglass, sheer silk, or taffeta for formal treatments.

Café curtains usually are not lined. They should be lined, however, when expensive fabric is chosen

or when no venetian blind or shade is used; the lining prevents the fabric from fading and ensures privacy. It also gives the window a uniform appearance from the outside.

Rods and Fixtures

Before taking measurements and purchasing fabric, you must decide what style and heading you are going to use for the curtains and what type of rod, fixture, and hooks you will need. Several types of rods and fixtures are illustrated. Also shown are two types of clip-on rings; they are ideal for hanging the curtains because they can be removed quickly when laundering is necessary.

(Continued on following page)

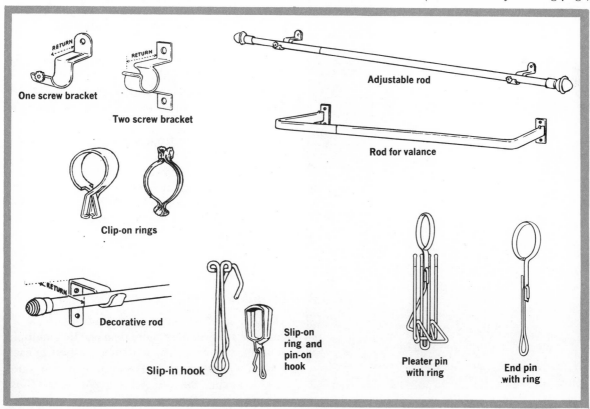

One screw bracket

Two screw bracket

Adjustable rod

Rod for valance

Clip-on rings

Decorative rod

Slip-in hook

Slip-on ring and pin-on hook

Pleater pin with ring

End pin with ring

If the curtains are to be pleated to control the fullness, they are constructed the same way as draperies and require both rings and drapery hooks.

Always position your rod (or rods) even with any horizontal strips between the glass panes or even with the center sash of the window.

Secure the brackets and rods before taking measurements. If you have chosen a valance for the top of your café curtains, mount the brackets for the first rod on the extreme ends of the window frame as close to the top as possible. (If you have recessed windows, see page 365.)

One-tier cafés. Place the brackets for the rod on the extreme ends of the window frame and at the center of the window (**C** in the illustration) or midway down on the upper half of the window (**B**).

Two-tier cafés. Place the brackets for the first rod on the extreme ends of the window frame as close to the top as possible. Position the rod for the second tier halfway between the first rod and sill, or lower edge of the apron (**A** in the illustration).

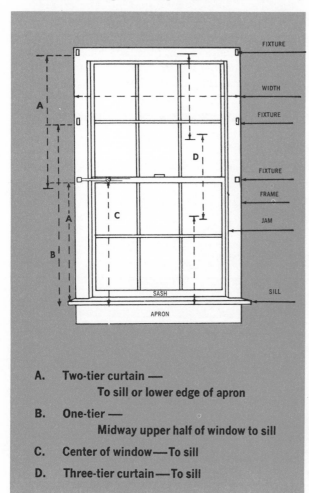

A.   Two-tier curtain —
         To sill or lower edge of apron

B.   One-tier —
         Midway upper half of window to sill

C.   Center of window—To sill

D.   Three-tier curtain—To sill

Three-tier cafés. Measure from the top of the first rod to the sill or lower edge of the apron. Divide the measurement by 3. Position the second and third rods at one-third intervals as shown in **D**.

Adding Allowances to Measurements

You must measure your windows and add allowances for hems, seams, and fullness. Make a note of your measurement and the allowances added and use them when you figure the yardage required and when you cut and make your curtains.

Measure each tier of the café as follows:

Length: Measure from the lower circle of the ring to the top of the next rod. To this measurement, add 5 inches for top and bottom hems (2-inch hems, plus ½ inch for turning). *Example:* 30 inches (measured length) plus 5 inches (hems) = 35 inches.

Width: Measure from the inside edge of one bracket to the other. Multiply this measurement by 2 for fullness. To this figure, add 10 inches for hems (2-inch hem and ½ inch for turning on each side of the two panels). *Example:* 36 inches (measured width) x 2 (fullness) = 72 inches plus 10 inches (for hems) = 82 inches. Each of the two panels is 41 inches wide.

The *valance* is one piece and the finished length may vary from 6 to 18 inches. Measure as follows:

Length: Decide on the length you wish. To this measurement, add 5 inches for top and botton hems (the same as for the tiers). *Example:* 12 inches (length of valance) plus 5 inches (hems) = 17 inches.

Width: Measure from one edge of the bracket to the other. Multiply this measurement by 2 for fullness. To this figure, add 5 inches for hems (2-inch hem and ½ inch for turning on each side of the valance). *Example:* 36 inches (measured width) x 2 (fullness) = 72 inches, plus 5 inches (hems) = 77 inches.

Estimating Yardage

The examples above are for a one-tier café. If your curtains will have more than one tier, multiply your measurements by the number of tiers in each curtain you are making. Then estimate your yardage, following the directions given under *Glass Curtains*, page 352.

360

Simple Café Curtains

Straighten and cut the fabric as instructed on page 352.

Side Hems.

Turn the edge under ½ inch and press. Turn under a 2-inch hem and press. Pin the hem in place. You may slip-stitch the hem by hand or machine-stitch it, using either straight stitching or blind-stitching. If hems are blindstitched, baste them in place, ¼ inch from the edge. With the wrong side

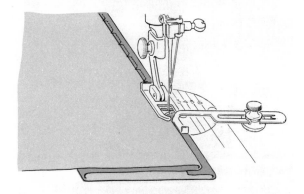

of the curtain up, turn the hem under on the basting line, forming a soft fold and exposing the ¼-inch hem edge. Select the blindstitch zig-zag, a medium stitch width, and 12 to 15 stitch length. Stitch so that the straight stitches are in the hem edge and the sideward stitches pierce only a few threads of the soft fold. Press.

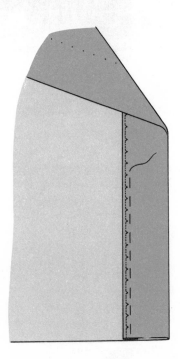

Top and Bottom Hems.

Turn the edge under ½ inch and press. Turn under a 2-inch hem and press. Pin the hem in place and miter the corners. Finish the same way

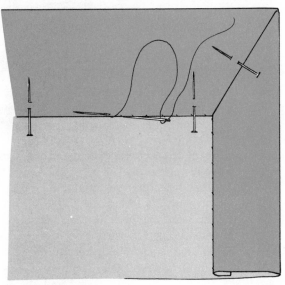

as the side hems. If you machine-stitch the hem, begin and end the stitching at the side hems using either straight stitching or blindstitching. Miter the corners and slip-stitch them in place. Press.

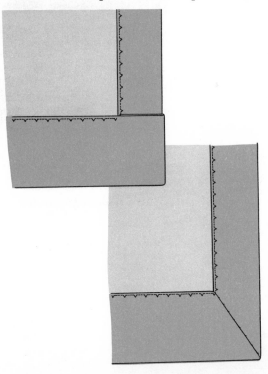

Clip rings to the top ends of each panel, then place additional rings between them at 4- or 5-inch intervals. Slip the rod through the rings and hang the curtains

Cafes with Decorative Trim

Bands of decorative zig-zag stitching glamorize the café curtains illustrated here. The bands extend above the finished heading, forming loops that slip over the rod.

Turn, press, and stitch the hems along the sides and top, following the instructions above. Cut 10 bands (5 for each panel) the length of the curtain plus 2½ inches for loops, and about 3 inches wide. Refer to *Border Designs*, page 272 for instructions on decorative stitching. When the stitching is completed, turn under each edge of the bands close to the stitching, and press.

Pin the bands to the right side of the curtain, extending the ends 2½ inches above the top hem, following this sequence: place the first band 1 inch from the outside edge; place the second band in the same position on the opposite edge; place the third band in the center; then place one band on each side, between the center band and the outside band. Space all bands an equal distance apart.

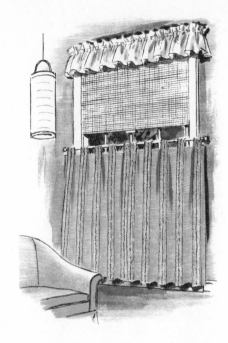

Stitch close to the folds, carrying the stitching to the end of each band.

To form the loops, fold under ¼ inch at the top of each band extension and hand-sew it to the curtain, ¼ inch below the finished edge.

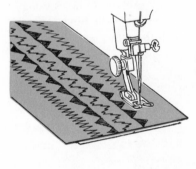

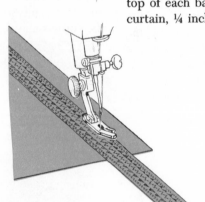

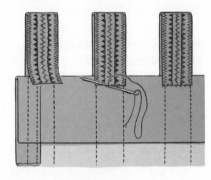

Finish the bottom hem, following the instructions, on page 361.

Ruffles are also an attractive addition to café curtains. For a decorative touch, finish the ruffles with zig-zag stitching. See *Edgestitched Finish*, page 274.

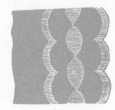

Cafés with Scalloped Heading and Pleats

The cafés in the illustration here alternate scallops and pleats in the heading. Select and position a decorative café rod and bracket with a return.

Length: Measure the length of the tier as instructed on page 360; however, allow 4½ inches instead of 2½ inches for the top hem and turning.

Width: Measure from the outside edge of one bracket to the other. Divide this measurement by 2 to determine the space each panel will cover. If the measurement is 36 inches, then 18 inches of the window will be covered by one panel. This width allows space for four scallops 4 inches wide, beginning 2 inches from the inside edge.

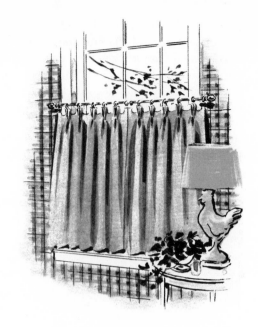

Adding Allowances to Measurements

For fullness, allow 4¾ inches for each pleat. Each panel in the illustration has five pleats. Place the first end pleat 2 inches from the inside edge and the second end pleat at the return, which is usually about 3 inches from the outside edge; then place three pleats between the four scallops. Five (pleats) x 4¾ inches (for each pleat) = 23¾ inch (required for pleats).

To one-half the measured width, add depth of return, 5 inches for hems (2-inch hem and ½ inch for turning on each side), plus the fullness required for pleats. *Example:* 18 inches (one-half window width) plus 3 inches (for return) plus 5 inches (for hems) plus 23¾ inches (for 5 pleats) = 49¾ inches. This is the width of one panel; you will need two panels for the window.

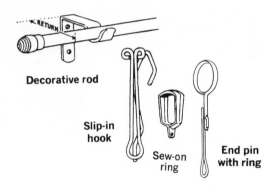

Decorative rod

Slip-in hook

Sew-on ring

End pin with ring

Cutting and Constructing the Curtains

Straighten the ends of the fabric and cut the length for the curtains as instructed on page 352.

Turn under the top edge of the curtain ½ inch and stitch close to the fold. Turn and press the side hems, following the instructions on page 361.

Cut 4-inch crinoline the length of the panel width. Mark the crinoline for the position of the return, pleats, and scallops, beginning 2 inches

from the inside edge as illustrated. Draw an outline for the scallops. See the example for pleats under *Adding Allowance to Measurements* above. Mark one strip of crinoline for the right panel and one for the left. Position the crinoline on the underside of the fabric, 4⅛ inches from the top edge and pin it in place.

Turn the top hem to the right side 4 inches,

(*Continued on following page*)

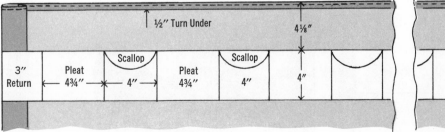

½″ Turn Under

4⅛″

| 3″ Return | Pleat 4¾″ | Scallop 4″ | Pleat 4¾″ | Scallop 4″ | 4″ | | Pleat 4¾″ | 2″ |

and pin. The fabric fold should be barely above the straight edge of the crinoline. Stitch the scallops, using a shorter stitch than that used in stitching the fabric. Backstitch at each end. Cut away the crinoline close to the stitching. Cut out the scallops ¼ inch from the stitching. Clip into the seam allowances at evenly spaced intervals for a smooth turning. Press. Slip the ends of the crinoline under the side hems. Turn the top hem to the underside, over the crinoline, and turn the scallops

smoothly on the stitching line; press.

Finish the side hems and the bottom hem by hand. Pin-mark the position for the pleats, allowing the same fullness and spacing as in your planning above. See *Adding Allowances to Measurements,* page 363. Make French pleats, following the instructions on page 380. Sew a drapery hook to the back of each pleat and at each end of the curtain. Fasten the hooks in the curtain rings of the rod.

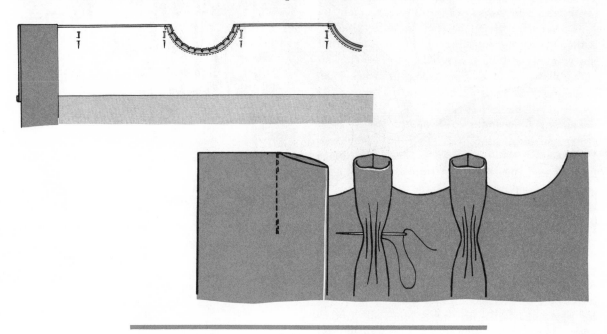

A ready-made scalloped pleater tape with woven-in pockets for pleater pins is available by the yard. To use it, follow these steps: Eliminate the allowance for the 4-inch top hem but allow ½ inch for turning. Arrange the cutout scallops

and space for pleats as instructed above. Pin the pleater tape to the right side of the curtain, ¼ inch from the edge. Stitch in place ¼ inch from the edge of the pleater tape. Cut out the scallops and turn the tape to the underside. Press. Stitch the lower edge of the tape to the curtain. Finish the side hems and bottom hem. Insert the prongs of the pleater pin into the woven pockets to form the pleat. Insert the end pins into woven pockets at each edge of the curtain.

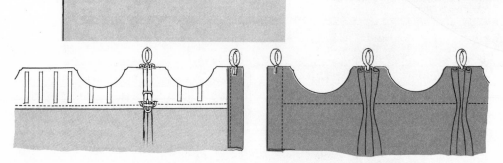

**Pleater pin
with ring**

Café Curtains for Recessed Windows

Curtains for a recessed window may hang flush with the wall. The illustration here shows where the rods are placed for a three-tier café in which the tiers overlap.

Rod and Fixtures

Select the spring-tension socket and round rigid rod, which must be cut to measurement. (In having this done, remember to allow for the spring in the socket.) A rod is required for each tier and is recessed between the sides of the window.

Measure the length inside the window recess. Divide the measurement by 3. Position the first rod in the recess close to the top; the middle rod at the one-third line; and the bottom rod at the two-thirds line. *Example:* If the window is 60 inches long, place the first rod at the top, the middle rod 20 inches from the top, and the bottom rod 20 inches above the sill.

Adding Allowances to Measurements

In a three-tier café with overlapping tiers, the visible lengths of all tiers should be the same. To achieve that, you must allow an extra 2 or 3 inches on the middle and bottom tiers for an overlap.

Measure the Window as Follows:

Length: Measure the top and middle tiers from the lower circle of the ring to the bottom of the next rod, and the bottom tier from the lower circle of the ring to the sill. To the measurement of each tier, add 5 inches for top and bottom hems (2-inch hems plus ½ inch for turning), and to the middle and bottom tiers, add an extra 2 inches for overlap. *Example:* Top tier, 20 inches (measured length) plus 5 inches (hems) = 25 inches. Middle and bottom tiers, each 20 inches (measured length) plus 5 inches (hems) plus 2 inches (overlap) = 27 inches.

Width: Measure the width inside the window recess. Multiply the measured width by 2 for fullness. To this figure, add 10 inches for hems (2-inch hem and ½ inch for turning on each side of the two panels). *Example:* 35 inches (measured width) x 2 inches (for fullness) = 70 inches plus 10 inches (for hems) = 80 inches. Each of the two panels is 40 inches wide.

Make a note of your measurements and the allowances added. Use them when you figure the yardage required and when you cut and make your café curtains.

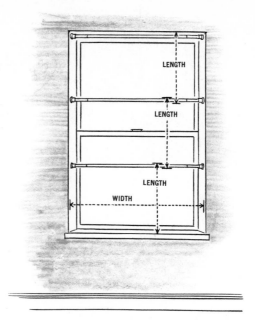

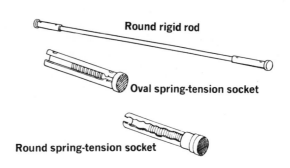

Round rigid rod

Oval spring-tension socket

Round spring-tension socket

Constructing the Curtains

Construct the curtains, following the instructions beginning on page 361.

Hanging the Curtains

Mark the position of the rods and remove them. It is simple to reposition them since spring-tension sockets are used.

Clip rings to the top ends of each panel, then place additional rings between them at 4- or 5-inch intervals. Slip the rod through the rings. Position the first rod at the top of the window flush with the wall, the middle rod 2 inches above the marking and into the window recess 1 inch from the wall, and the bottom rod 2 inches above the marking and into the window recess 2 inches from the wall.

Set the Stage
with Draperies

MAKING DRAPERIES LURES MANY WOMEN into sewing. The reason is not hard to find. Ready-made draperies are expensive and seldom completely satisfactory; often you have to compromise a little on color or fabric because you cannot find exactly what you want. Custom-made draperies from a decorator's shop may be absolutely lovely to the eye—but absolutely devastating to the purse. The solution: Make your own.

This chapter charts the course you should follow for panel draperies and draw draperies. As you embark on drapery construction, however, remember that your best ally is accuracy—accuracy in measuring, in estimating yardage, in cutting and in sewing.

PANEL DRAPERIES— PREPARATION

Draperies that hang on each side of a window and do not cover the full window are known as "panel draperies." They are generally used with glass curtains and both must be identical in length. A pair of draperies is required for each window or group of windows. When the drapery panels hang at either side of a group of windows, they should be connected across the top with a cornice board or valance unless a decorative rod is used.

The draperies should be full and hang in balanced, graceful folds. Their fullness is controlled by a pleated heading. The hem at the lower edge should be at least 3 inches deep; many decorators prefer one even wider. The deep hem gives added weight to the draperies and allows for lengthening them if the fabric shrinks.

Secure the fixture for the rod on the extreme ends of the window frame, 1 inch below the top. See page 343.

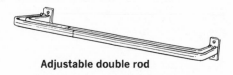

Adjustable double rod

Adding Allowances to Measurements

Length for lined draperies: To the measured length, as described on page 344, add 1 inch for rod, 2 inches for heading, 4 inches for top hem, and 3½ inches for bottom hem and turning. *Example:* 87 inches (measured length) plus 10½ inches = 97½ inches. *For unlined draperies* add an extra ½ inch for turning on the top hem. *Example:* 87 inches (measured length) plus 11 inches = 98 inches.

Width: For a single window 36 to 50 inches in width, the finished drapery heading after pleating should cover 12 to 15 inches of the window; however, this is a matter of choice. If you are changing the proportion of the window to make it appear wider, you will need wider panels, see page 342.

Determine how wide you want your finished drapery panels to be. To this measurement, add 4 inches for the depth of the return at one end plus 5 inches for hems (2-inch hem and ½-inch seam allowance on each side) plus the amount required for pleats.

At this point it is wise to decide what kind of pleat you intend to make. For cartridge and box pleats, the allowance for each pleat and the spacing are different from those given in the example below. See page 380.

An uneven number of pleats—5, 7, or 9 in each panel—is recommended. It is more pleasing to the eye than an even number, which tends to distract the observer and make him count the pleats in pairs. *Allow 5 to 6 inches for fullness in each pleat* and space the pleats about 4 inches apart. *Example:* 19 inches (measured width and 4-inch return at one end) plus 5 inches (hems) plus 25 inches (for 5 pleats) = 49 inches. This is the width of fabric required for each panel.

To determine the exact spacing between pleats, proceed as follows: Always locate one end pleat the depth of the return (4 inches) from the outside edge of each panel, and the other end pleat 2 inches from the inside edge; use the distance between these two pleats to figure the space between additional pleats. Since two end pleats are predetermined in each panel, the number of spaces is always one less than the number of pleats. *Example:* 19 inches (finished width) less 6 inches (depth of return and distance from inside edge) = 13 inches to be divided into spaces for additional pleats. For 5 pleats: 13 inches divided by 4 (spaces) = 3¼ inches (space between pleats). Page 379 describes how to measure and make pleats in the drapery heading.

Estimating Yardage

Most drapery fabric is 50 to 60 inches wide, and generally two widths are sufficient for each pair of draperies. *Example:* For two panels, 97½ inches (length of drapery) x 2 (lengths) = 195 inches, or 5 yards and 15 inches. Buy an additional 9 inches to allow for straightening the ends of the fabric.

If the fabric is only 36 inches wide, allow 1 inch for each seam within the drapery (½-inch seam allowance on each edge). Each pair of panels in the example above will require four lengths of fabric, or 10 yards and 30 inches.

These are yardage estimates for one window. Multiply them by the number of windows to arrive at your total requirements.

If you are treating a group of two or three windows, your draperies should be wider than those in the example and will require more fabric. Follow the directions for the example and add the amount required for each additional space (3¼ inches) and each additional pleat (5 inches). A pair of panels may require three lengths (one and one-half for each panel) or four lengths (two for each panel) of 50-inch fabric.

Matching the Design

If your fabric has a design, you will need extra yardage for matching since the design must fall in the same place in each panel. A full design should begin at the turn for the bottom hem. Measure from the center of one design to the center of the next one and allow this amount in each panel length for matching.

Estimating the Lining

The lining is 10 inches shorter and 8 inches narrower than the drapery fabric. In the example above, the lining for each panel is 87½ inches long, and 4 yards and 31 inches are required for each pair. Buy an extra 9 inches to allow for straightening the ends of the lining.

Turn to page 370 for cutting and construction.

DRAW DRAPERIES— PREPARATION

Draperies that can be drawn closed to cover the entire window are known as "draw draperies." They may be used on almost any type of window and are the preferred treatment for sliding windows or doors, picture windows, and casement windows that open out. They are also a handsome treatment for draping walls.

Draw draperies may be made of heavy or sheer fabric. Like panel draperies they should hang in balanced, graceful folds. Pleats are the most effective means of controlling their fullness.

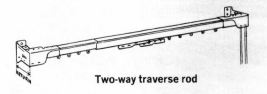

Two-way traverse rod

Rods and Fixtures

You will need a traverse rod for draw draperies. Select a two-way traverse rod if the draperies are made in two panels that overlap at the center.

See *Picture Windows,* page 345. Select a one-way traverse rod for corner windows and sliding doors, page 346, and other windows where the drapery is drawn to one side.

Install the brackets for the rods on the extreme ends of the window frame, 1 inch below the top of the window frame. If the draperies are to hang from the ceiling, use the ceiling-mounted track.

Adding Allowances to Measurements

Length: To the measured length (as described on page 345), add 1 inch for rod, 2 inches for heading, 4 inches for top hem, and 3½ inches for bottom hem and turning. *Example:* For lined draperies, 87 inches (measured length) plus 10½ inches = 97½ inches. For unlined draperies, add an extra ½ inch for turning on the top hem.

If double-fold hems are used, and they are preferred in sheer fabric, allow 8 inches for the top hem and 6 inches for the bottom hem. 87 inches (measured length) plus 17 inches (rod, heading, and double-fold hems) = 104 inches.

If draperies extend from the ceiling, measure from the ceiling to the floor and add only the amounts stated for top and bottom hems.

Width: Measure across the window from one end of the rod to the other. To this measurement, add the depth of the return on each side. *Example:* 92 inches (measured width) plus 8 inches (two 4-inch returns) = 100 inches. This is the width the draw draperies must cover; each finished panel must be one-half this width plus one-half the overlap.

To the measured width you must add the allowances for hems, overlap, seams, and pleats. But first you must determine the number of pleats and the space between the pleats.

Pleats in draw draperies must always be even in number although the number in each panel may be even or uneven. Allow 5 or 6 inches for fullness in each pleat, and space the pleats about 4 inches apart. (You may have to estimate the number of pleats several times before arriving at the exact spacing. The paper pattern suggested below will help you here.)

To determine the exact spacing between pleats, proceed as follows: Always locate an end pleat the depth of the return from the outside edge of each drapery panel; use the distance between these two pleats to figure the space between additional pleats. *Examples:* 100 inches (measured width and returns) less 8 inches (returns) = 92 inches (to be divided into space for additional pleats). Since two end pleats are predetermined, the number of spaces is one less than the number of pleats. For 24 pleats: 92 inches divided by 23 spaces = 4 inches (spaces between pleats). 24 (pleats) x 5 inches (for each pleat) = 120 inches (required for pleats). Page 379 describes how to measure and make pleats in the drapery heading.

The diagram here shows the 2½-inch overlap and the position of the first end pleat at the center edge of each panel. When the spacing of the pleats is figured before making the allowance for the overlap, the distance between pleats at the center overlap will be the same as that between all other pleats when the draperies are closed.

Making a Paper Pattern

You may feel more confident about your decisions if you make a pattern to fit your window and mark your spacings on that. Cut two strips of stiff paper about 6 inches wide and a few inches longer than the width of the window and return at each end. Lap the center edges the amount of the overlap—usually 2½ inches. Pin. Then mark paper 1¼ inches from one edge of the overlap to indicate the center line. Measure the window width and return at each end and cut the paper an equal distance from center line. *Example:* For the 100-inch width used above, the center is 50 inches from each edge of the pattern. Fit the pattern across the rod and around the return at each end to be certain that the width is correct. Mark the position of the returns and the spacing for pleats. Remember that the allowance for side hems, seams, and fullness for pleats has not been added to the pattern.

Now you are ready to determine the width required for the draperies. To do this, add your allowances to the window width plus the return at each end. *Example:* 92 inches (measured width) plus 8 inches (two 4-inch returns) plus 10 inches (2-inch hem and ½-inch seam allowance on each side of the two panels), 120 inches (pleats), and 2½ inches (overlap) = 232½ inches (width required). Each of the two panels is 116¼ inches wide plus seam allowances. For each seam within the drapery, allow 1 inch (½-inch seam allowance on each edge).

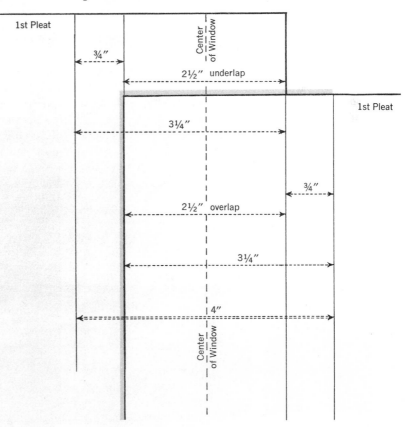

Estimating Yardage

In estimating yardage, consider first the width of the fabric. If 50-inch fabric is used, it will be 48 inches wide after you have removed the selvages and allowed for seaming. In the example, 232½ inches (width required) divided by 48 inches (fabric width) = 4 5/6 lengths. Buy 5 lengths. Remember, lengths cannot be pieced. If your figures result in a fraction, always buy the next full length.

Example: 97½ inches (length of drapery) x 5 (lengths) = 487½ inches or 13 yards 19½ inches. Buy an additional 9 inches to allow for straightening the ends of the fabric. If the fabric has a design, allow for matching. See page 367. If the draperies are sheer, add the allowances for double-fold hems. See page 368.

If you plan to place seams barely outside pleats, you will need extra width. This is explained below in *Making Seams.* How much extra depends on the width of your drapery panels.

Lining. The lining is 10 inches shorter and 8 inches narrower than the drapery fabric. For the example above, the lining is 87½ inches long, and 5 lengths of 50-inch lining, or 12 yards and 5½ inches, are required. Buy an additional 9 inches to allow for straightening the ends of the lining. Information on suitable lining fabric is given on page 340.

CUTTING THE DRAPERIES

Draperies must be cut on the true lengthwise and crosswise grains of the fabric so that they will hang straight, fall smoothly and gracefully, and clean satisfactorily.

Straighten the ends of the fabric by drawing a thread on the crosswise grain to indicate the cutting line. Steam-press the fabric, then remove the selvages.

For accuracy in cutting the draperies, work on a flat surface such as the dining room table, ping-pong table, or bedboard. *Use a tape measure to measure the lengths.* Draw a thread on the crosswise grain to mark the cutting line for each length; then cut the length. If the fabric has a design, match the pattern in each panel. See page 367.

Straighten the fabric grain as instructed on page 14.

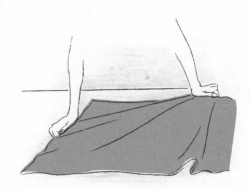

CONSTRUCTING THE DRAPERIES

Making Seams

Seaming is your first construction step if you are making draw draperies or wide panel draperies. Seams are placed barely outside pleats, where they are less noticeable than they would be if placed within a pleat or between pleats. To do this, measure and pin-mark the width of the center hem and turning, the distance of the first pleat from the hem edge, and then the amounts for as many pleats and spaces as the fabric width will allow, plus seam allowance. Draw a thread on the lengthwise grain to indicate the cutting line. Cut on the drawn thread. Use a French seam in unlined draperies so that the cut edges will be enclosed, and

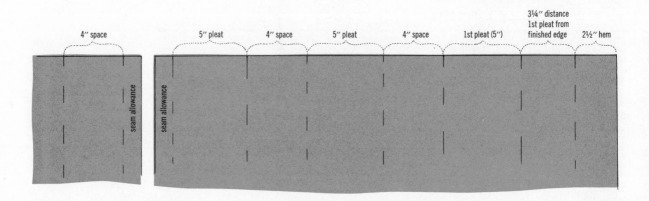

4″ space   5″ pleat   4″ space   5″ pleat   4″ space   1st pleat (5″)   3¼″ distance 1st pleat from finished edge   2½″ hem

seam allowance   seam allowance

a plain seam pressed open in lined draperies. Be sure to match designs at the seamline.

For convenience in folding and pressing hems in draperies, work on the ironing board during the construction steps that follow, as suggested for glass curtains, page 352.

Making Unlined Draperies

The informal mode of today's living has increased the popularity of unlined draperies. Many of the beautiful wonder fabrics do not require lining. The color and design of the fabric are visible from the outside.

The allowances for heading, side, and bottom hems referred to below are described on page 366 (for panel draperies) and page 368 (for draw draperies).

Heading Hem

To support the pleated heading, use crinoline of the same width as the hem at the top. In the measurements, 4½ inches were allowed for a top hem and turning. Turn 4½ inches to the underside and press.

Cut 4-inch crinoline 5 inches shorter than the width of the drapery. Place the crinoline over the underside of the hem, aligning one edge with the crease and extending the ends to within 2½ inches of the fabric edges. (This is the turn for the side hems.) Stitch the crinoline in place, ¼ inch from the crease for the hem. Turn the cut edge of fabric over the opposite edge of the crinoline and stitch. Press. Turn the hem to the underside and press again. Pin, then baste the hem in place. *Do not stitch the hem;* when the pleats are stitched, they will hold it in place. But be sure to leave the basting in until you have stitched the pleats.

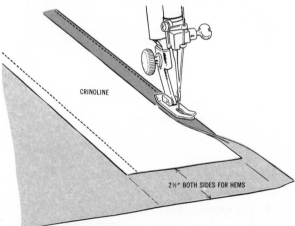

CRINOLINE

2½" BOTH SIDES FOR HEMS

Side Hems

To remove bulk, cut out the corner of the top hem edge. Begin 2½ inches from the outer edge (turn for the side hem) and cut upward to within ½ inch of the top fold; then cut diagonally to the top hem fold, and on the hem fold to the outer edge.

Turn ½ inch to the underside, and press. Turn a 2-inch hem and pin in place. Miter the corner at the top edge. Press.

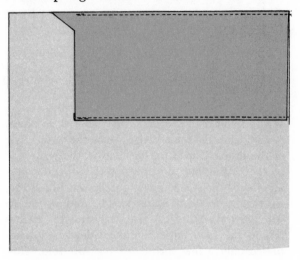

Hems may be slip-stitched by hand or machine-stitched, using either straight stitching or blind-stitching. If you finish the hem by hand, catch only a few threads of the fabric in the stitches so that they are invisible on the top side. If you machine-stitch the hem using straight stitching, place the stitching as close to the folded edge as possible.

(Continued on following page)

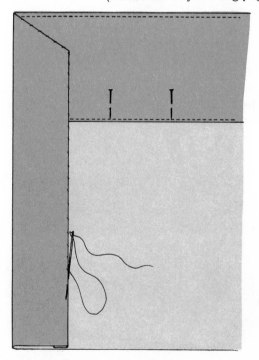

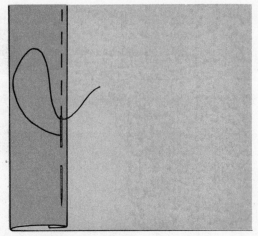

If you blindstitch the hem, first baste it in place, ¼ inch from the folded edge. With the wrong side of the drapery up, turn the hem to the right side on the basting line, creating a soft fold and exposing the ¼-inch hem edge. Select the blindstitch zig-zag, a medium stitch width, and about 15 stitch length. Stitch so that the straight stitches fall in the hem edge and the sideward stitches pierce only a few threads of the soft fold. Turn the hem down and press.

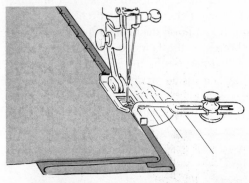

Bottom Hem

Compare the drapery panels, wrong sides together, and check the length at the center and outer side hems to be sure they are identical.

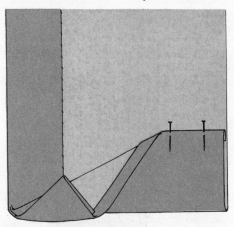

In the measurements, 3½ inches were allowed for the bottom hem and turning. Turn under ½ inch and press. Turn a 3-inch hem and pin in place. Miter the corners and ease the hem down slightly at this point to allow for the thicknesses of fabric and to square the corners. Baste the hem in place.

Before finishing the bottom hem, pleat the heading and attach the drapery hooks. See pages 379 and 381. Hang the draperies and check the length. The draperies should be ½ inch above the floor. If your measurements were accurate, the length should be correct and the change in hem, if any, will be slight.

The hem may be slip-stitched by hand or blindstitched by machine. If finished by hand, the work may be done after draperies are hung. If the hem is blindstitched, begin and end the stitching at the side hems. Then miter the corners and slip-stitch them in place, making the stitches through the hems only.

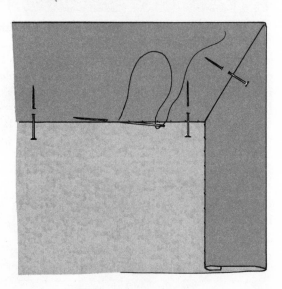

Making Draperies with Pleat Tape Heading

Ready-made pleat tape with woven-in pockets for pleater pins is available by the yard. If you use it instead of crinoline at the top, eliminate the allowance for the 4-inch top hem; however, allow ½ inch for turning. Consider the drapery return at each end and position the woven-in pockets so that a pleat falls at the turn of the rod.

Cut the pleat tape 5 inches shorter than the width of the drapery. Pin the tape across the top

Plate 19

Quilting for luxury

Right: A quilted print screen gives this bedroom a charming touch of distinction. The quilting outlines the handsome floral motif, giving the fabric an extra dimension of luxury. The fabric design is precisely matched in the pleated flounce. The simple coverlet can be varied for a quick change of color scheme or for laundering convenience.

Below: The smartly tailored bedspread's diamond-pattern quilting could be stitched by machine or bought by the yard. Luxurious blue draperies, hung on bright brass rods and held with braid and tassel tiebacks, create a Victorian feeling, which is softened by sheer, white glass-curtains.

Illustration above and below
from The American Home © 1964, The Curtis Publishing Company

Bands for elegance

Bands of fabric, cut from the striped pattern used for the flounce on the bed, add elegance to the brilliant orange and red tones of this room. Draperies, valance, coverlet and bolsters are all outlined with striking effect.

Plate 20   Pretty, practical and young

Above: In an attic room, the sloping ceiling provides a built-in base for a ruffled canopy of provincial print. Matching café curtain, placed low on the window, and gathered valance and draperies give a pleasing balance to the room.

Above: Sunny yellow brightens a small room. Semi-sheer patterned café curtains ensure privacy while letting in light. The same fabric is repeated in the flounce on the bed, which is topped with a quilted box coverlet.

Left: An Alice in Wonderland theme is created with printed fabric for draperies, bed flounce and headboard trim and is emphasized by cutouts from the fabric on the wall. Ball fringe makes a gay finish. The solid pink of the quilted coverlet blends perfectly with the print.

Plate 21

Light and airy

Right: Sheer, white draperies that let in lots of light while softening its glare are dramatically outlined in emerald green velvet ribbon, which also bands the white shades. Café curtains of the same sheer fabric cover the lower half of the window.

Quilted solid green bedspread and boldly patterned wallpaper provide an effective contrast to the delicate window treatment.

Cool and calm

Below: A wall-to-wall drapery provides a restful, unbroken wall treatment. Its refreshing blue roses are repeated in the quilted bedspread, on which corner underlays make a neat, tailored finish.

Plate 22

Twin-needle stitching
adds an expensive-looking
custom touch to
ruffled curtains.
Ruffle and heading
are both edged
with scallop stitching.

Appliqué adds decorative interest

Above: Solid on solid, leaves
and flower delineated with open
and closed zig-zag stitching.

Left: The simplest of all
appliqué methods, a cutout from
printed fabric appliquéd on a soli

Either of these treatments would
enhance a pillow or draperies.

of the drapery, right sides together, 5/16 inch from the fabric edge; extend the ends to within 2½ inches of the drapery edge. (This is the turn for the side hems.) Stitch the tape in place ½ inch from the fabric edge. Press.

Turn the pleat tape to the underside, fold the fabric on the stitching line, and press. Pin the lower edge of the pleat tape to the drapery and stitch ¼ inch from the edge. Press.

Form the side and bottom hems as instructed above. Then insert hooks into the woven-in pockets to form the pleats.

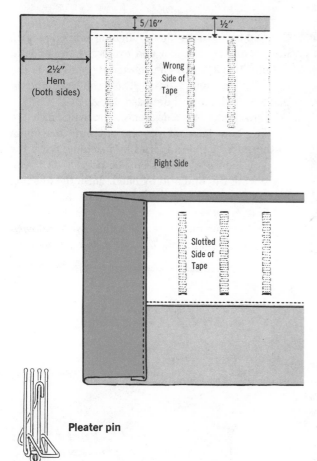

Pleater pin

Making Draperies of Sheer Fabric

Draw draperies of sheer fabric may be used alone or with glass curtains that are hung on a separate rod. The sheer over sheer imparts a cool, crisp look.

Refer to *Draw Draperies—Preparation*, page 368, for instructions on adding allowances to your measurements and estimating yardage. Remember that you should make double-fold hems in sheer fabrics.

Side Hems

The side hems are stitched first. In the measurements, 16 inches were allowed for a 2-inch double-fold hem on each side of the two panels. Fold, press, and stitch the double-fold hems, following instructions on page 352.

Heading Hem

Crinoline is used to support the pleated heading. It must be the same width as the heading hem. In the measurements, 8 inches were allowed for a 4-inch double-fold hem.

Cut 4-inch crinoline the exact length of the drapery width. Position the crinoline on the underside of the drapery hem, keeping the edges even, and pin. Stitch along the lower edge of the crinoline. Backstitch at each end. Press.

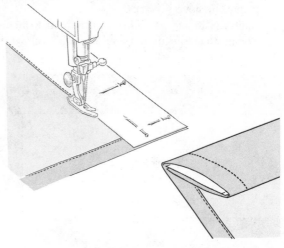

Turn the hem to the underside; fold along the edge of crinoline and press. Then turn again for a double-fold hem. Pin, press, and baste. Do not stitch the hem; the pleats will hold it in place when they are stitched. Do not remove this basting until you have stitched the pleats.

Bottom Hem

Compare the drapery panels, wrong sides together, and check the length at the center and outer side hems to be sure they are identical.

In the measurements, 6 inches were allowed for a 3-inch double-fold hem. Fold and pin the 3-inch double hem, following instructions on page 353. Before stitching the hem, pleat the heading and attach the drapery hooks as described on pages 379 and 381. Hang the draperies and check the length; it should be about ½ inch above the floor. If your measurements were accurate, the length should be correct and the hem width will require only a slight adjustment if any.

Machine-stitch the hem, then add weights. See page 353.

Making Lined Draperies

Draperies are lined to protect the drapery fabric. The lining also adds weight, ensures soft, graceful folds, and creates a uniform appearance from the outside. Sunfast sateen of light beige, eggshell, soft gray, or white is generally used as the lining fabric.

The allowances for heading, side, and bottom hems referred to below are described on page 366 (for panel draperies) and page 368 (for draw draperies).

The Lining

The lining fabric must be cut on the true lengthwise and crosswise grains the same as the drapery fabric. Straighten the ends by drawing a thread on the crosswise grain to indicate the cutting line. Remove selvages.

Cut the lining 10 inches shorter and 8 inches narrower than the drapery fabric. This allows ½

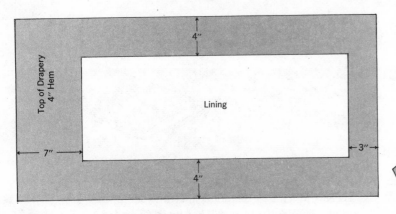

inch for seam allowance on each side, ½ inch for turning at the top, and 2 inches for the bottom hem plus ½ inch for turning. When the draperies are finished, the lining hem will overlap the drapery hem 1 inch.

Draw a thread on the crosswise grain to indicate the cutting line of each length. See page 370.

Bolts of sateen are often rolled tighter at one end of the board than the other, with the result that the fabric threads are drawn off grain. Straighten the fabric grain as described on page 14. Steam-press.

Heading Hem

In the measurements, 4 inches were allowed for the top hem of the drapery. Turn the 4-inch hem to the underside and press.

Cut 4-inch crinoline 5 inches shorter than the width of the drapery. Position the crinoline over

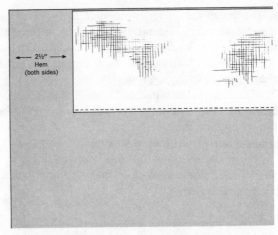

the underside of the hem, aligning one edge with the crease for the hem and extending the ends to within 2½ inches of the fabric edges. (This is the turn for the side hems.) Stitch the crinoline in place ¼ inch from the crease. Press.

Now make the side hems. You will finish the heading hem later: If you are stitching the lining to the sides of the draperies by machine, finish the heading hem *after* that step (see page 376); if you are sewing the lining in by hand, finish the heading hem *before* the hand sewing (see page 377).

Side Hems

In the measurements, 5 inches were allowed for a 2-inch hem and ½-inch seam allowance on

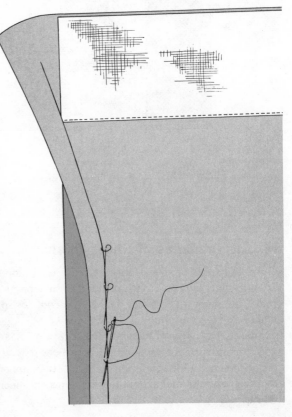

each side. Turn the side hems to the underside 2½ inches, and press. Pin the hem in place about 1½ inches from the fold. Place the pins parallel to the hem and leave them until you have sewed the lining in place. Turn the hem edge back on the pin line and stay the hem to the drapery. Make a stitch in the drapery about 8 inches below the top; loop the thread to the left; then, directly opposite the first stitch, make a stitch in the hem fold, bringing the needle out over the thread. Continue making the stitches, spacing them about 2 inches apart. Do not draw the threads too tight.

The next step is joining the lining to the drapery.

Methods of
Joining Lining to Drapery

The lining may be sewed to the drapery by machine as illustrated here or by hand as illustrated on page 377.

Method 1, Machine-Stitched:

Hem the lower edge of the lining as follows: Turn the edge under ½ inch and press; then turn the hem to the underside 2 inches, and press. Pin the hem in place, and stitch close to the top fold. Press.

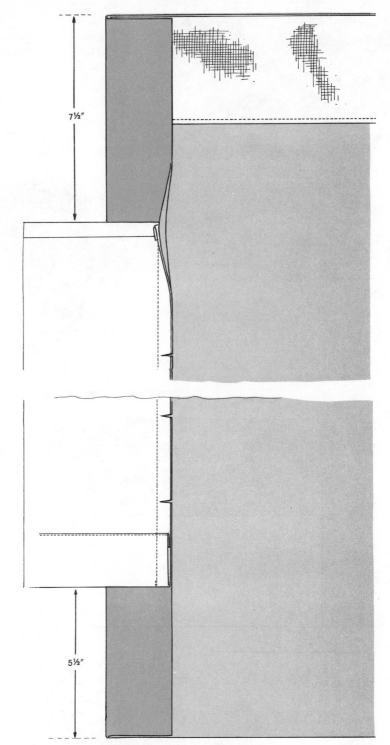

At the top of the lining, turn the ½-inch seam allowance to the underside and finger-press. Pin the lining to the drapery side hem, right sides together, keeping the top fold of the lining 7½ inches below the top edge of the drapery, and the bottom hem 5½ inches above the lower edge. Turn the seam allowance away from the drapery and stitch from the lining side, making a ½-inch seam.

Backstitch at each end. Stitch the lining to the hem on the opposite side of the drapery in the same way. Press, then press both seam edges toward the lining. Slash the seam allowances at 6-inch intervals. Turn to the right side. If measurements and seaming are accurate, the lining should fit smoothly over the drapery.

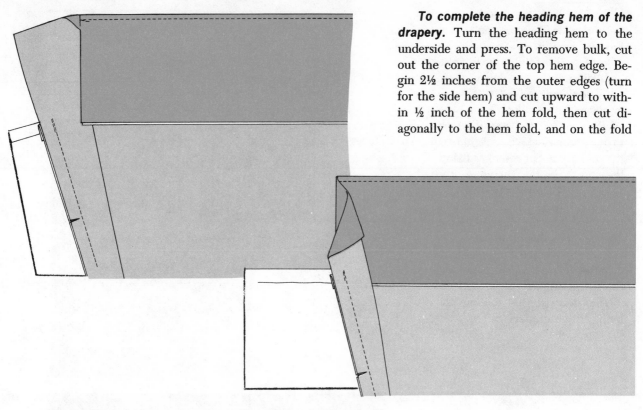

To complete the heading hem of the drapery. Turn the heading hem to the underside and press. To remove bulk, cut out the corner of the top hem edge. Begin 2½ inches from the outer edges (turn for the side hem) and cut upward to within ½ inch of the hem fold, then cut diagonally to the hem fold, and on the fold

to the outer edge. Miter the corners; turn under the side seam allowance on the drapery as far as the lining, and pin.

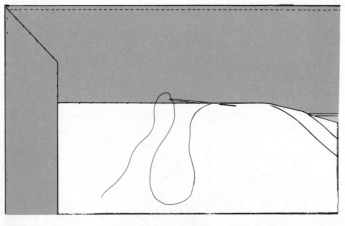

Lap the lining over the top hem edge ½ inch, and pin. Slip-stitch the mitered corners and lining in place, making the stitches through the hems and lining only. Press.

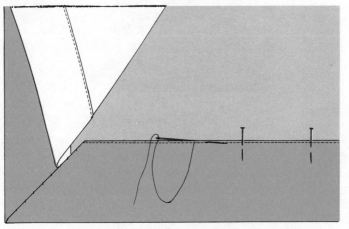

Finish the bottom hem in the drapery, following the instructions on page 378.

Method 2, Hand-Sewed: For draw draperies and wide panel draperies, it is advisable to hand-sew the lining to the drapery. This makes it possible to stay the lining to the drapery at even intervals, which prevents it from sagging below the drapery. Before you join the lining to the drapery, you must first finish the heading.

To complete the heading hem of the drapery. After you have cut and stitched the 4-inch crinoline to the heading as described under *Heading Hem* on page 374, turn the heading hem to the underside and press. To remove bulk, cut out the corner of the top hem edge. Begin 2½ inches from the outer edge (the turn for the side hem) and cut upward to within ½ inch of the hem fold; then cut diagonally to the hem fold, and on the fold to the outer edge. Miter the corners and turn under the seam allowance on the drapery as far as the lining; pin in place.

To sew the lining to the drapery. Fold, press, and slip-stitch the bottom hem of the lining. Along the top and side edges, turn the seam allowance to the underside ½ inch, and finger-press.

Lay the drapery, wrong side up, on a flat surface and smooth out the fabric. Place the lining over the drapery, wrong sides together, with the folded edges overlapping the heading and side

hems of the drapery ½ inch. The lining hem should extend to within 5½ inches of the lower edge of the drapery.

Now you must stay the lining to the drapery at about 24-inch intervals. Begin at the center. Pin the lining to the drapery on a vertical line, then turn the lining back on the pin line. Make a stitch in the drapery about 4 inches below the top hem, loop the thread to the left, then directly opposite the first stitch, make a stitch in the lining fold, bringing the needle out over the thread. Catch only one or two threads in the fabric so that the stitches will be invisible on the top side. Continue, spacing the stitches about 6 inches apart. Do not draw the thread taut. About 6 inches above the hem, fasten the thread in the lining with a tiny backstitch and leave a 4-inch thread end. Then pin and stitch additional vertical lines, working from the center toward each edge and spacing the rows about 24 inches apart.

Pin the lining to the drapery hems across the top and along each side, with the folded edges overlapping the drapery hems ½ inch. Slip-stitch the lining in place, making the stitches through the lining and drapery hems only so that the stitches will be invisible on the top side. Do not draw the thread tight.

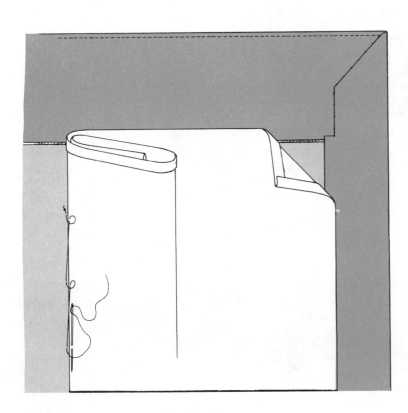
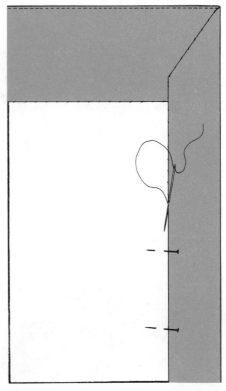

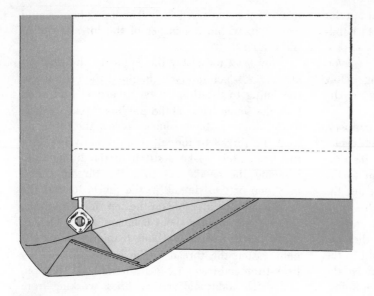

Bottom Hem

Compare the drapery panels, wrong sides together, and check the length at the center and outer side hems to be sure they are identical.

Turn the bottom edge of the drapery under ½ inch, and press. Stitch near the fold. (The lining will cover the stitching.) Turn a 3-inch hem to the underside, and pin in place. Miter the corners so that they fit smoothly under the lining. Ease the hem down slightly at this point to allow for the thicknesses of fabric and to square the corners. Sew weights at each side seam allowance to prevent drawing.

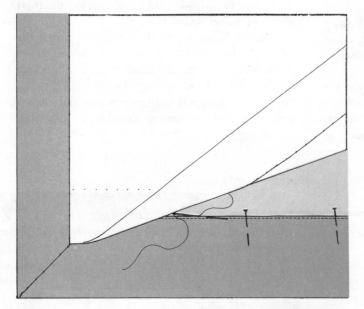

Before finishing the hem, pleat the heading and attach the drapery hooks. See pages 379 and 381. Hang the draperies and check the length, which should be about ½ inch above the floor. Let the draperies hang for two or three days before you sew the hem because some fabrics will shrink or stretch slightly. If your measurements are accurate, the length should be correct and the change in the hem width will be slight, if any.

The bottom hem may be finished after the draperies are hung. Slip-stitch the hem and mitered corners in place. Catch only one or two threads in the drapery and make the stitches through hems only at the mitered corners. The stitches should be invisible on the top side. Do not press this hem. If it is necessary to lengthen the draperies slightly after six months or so, there will be no crease to mar the fabric.

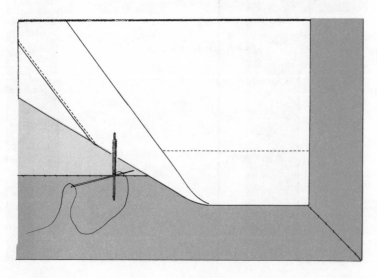

The lining hangs free of the drapery. To hold it in position, use French tacks spaced about 12 inches apart. See page 208.

Making the Pleated Heading

The most popular styles of pleats for draperies are the pinch pleat, box pleat, French pleat, and cartridge pleat.

Measuring for Pleats

Panel draperies should have an uneven number of pleats in each panel; draw draperies may have either an even or an uneven number in each, resulting in an even number in each pair. The number of pleats, the allowance for each pleat, and the spacing between pleats are matters you should decide before cutting the fabric for the drapery. See pages 367 and 369 for this information.

Always measure and pin-mark position of *all*

pleats and spaces before you begin any stitching.

In panel draperies, measure 2 inches from the center edge of the drapery and pin-mark. Then measure and pin-mark the width of the **first** end pleat. At the opposite edge, measure and pin-mark the depth of the return. Then measure and pin-mark the width of the **second** end pleat. Place the **third** pleat at the exact center between the **first** and **second** end pleats. Space the **remaining pleats** evenly between the first and third pleats and the second and third pleats. Compare the two panels, wrong sides together, to be sure the pin-marks correspond.

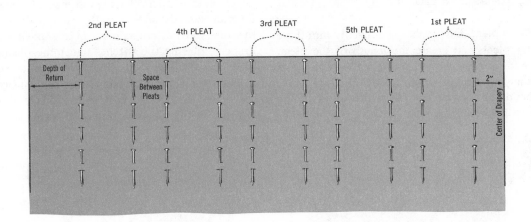

In draw draperies, the center edges overlap 2½ inches when a two-way traverse rod is used; therefore, the **first** end pleat must be farther from the center edge than in panel draperies. Using the measurements in the example on page 369, measure 3¼ inches from the center edge of the drapery and pin-mark. Then measure and pin-mark the width of the **first** end pleat. At the opposite

end, measure and pin-mark the depth of the return. Then measure and pin-mark the width of the **second** end pleat. Continue measuring and marking the space, then the width of each pleat. All spaces between the last and first pleats must be the same; and the width of all pleats must be the same. Compare the two panels, wrong sides together, to be sure the pin-marks correspond.

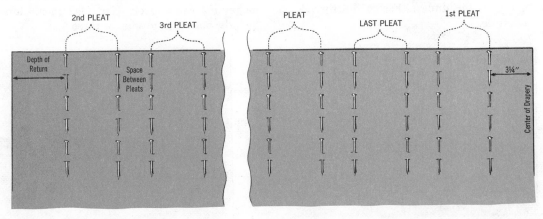

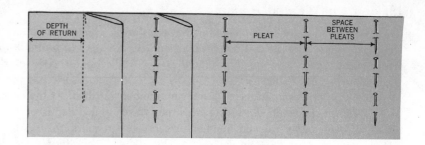

Forming the Pleats

Bring the pin-marks for each pleat together and pin. Stitch from the top edge to ½ inch below the heading hem, placing the stitching into the pleat about 1/16 inch from the pins (this allows for the width that is taken up by the layers of fabric). Backstitch at each end.

Pinch pleat. Divide the pleat evenly into three smaller pleats and crease the length of the pleat. At the lower edge, either hand-tack the three pleats together or machine-stitch across them. If they are hand-tacked, you can insert the shank of the drapery hook into the pleat.

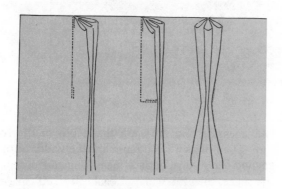

French pleat. At the lower edge of the heading, divide the pleat into three smaller pleats; then hand-sew through them several times before drawing tightly on the threads. Fasten the threads on the underside.

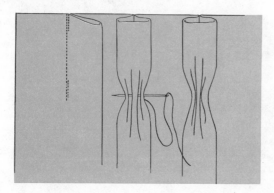

Box pleat. Slip two fingers inside the pleat and finger-press it open. Then press flat, keeping the folds an equal distance from the stitching line. Tack the top and bottom corners of the pleat to the drapery, placing the stitches under the pleat. Box pleats should be about 2 inches wide and require 4 inches of additional fabric for each pleat; the space between pleats is 4 inches. Make this allowance in the planning stage.

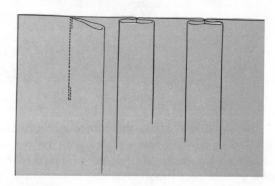

Cartridge pleat. This small, round pleat is filled with rolled stiff paper or crinoline, which holds its cartridge shape. In the planning stage, allow about 2 inches for each pleat and about 2 inches for each space. Cartridge pleats are frequently placed in groups of three.

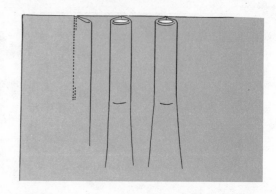

Selecting Drapery Hooks and Pins

Draperies are attached to the rod by hooks or pins, which are placed in the back of each pleat and at each end of the drapery. Most drapery hooks are available in several sizes. When buying them, be sure to consider the position of the hook part on the shank and the length of the prong. Examine them closely and get the type best suited for your purpose.

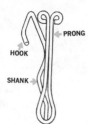

A few of the more popular hooks are illustrated.

Hook **A.** This popular and practical *slip-in hook* has a long two-piece prong that holds the heading erect. It requires no sewing. The long prong slips between the heading hem and drapery and around the pleat. Select hooks with the hook part near the bottom of the shank if the draperies hang from a traverse rod and the heading extends above the rod. Select hooks with the hook part at the top of the shank if draperies hang from a decorative rod with rings or a traverse rod mounted on the ceiling.

Hook **B.** The *pin-on hook* requires no sewing. It is available with a hook shaped to fit either over the adjustable curtain rod or in the traverse rod. The long prong pin holds the heading erect. If a different type of hook is used in the pleats, use this long prong pin at each end of the drapery where there are no pleats.

Hook **C.** The *sew-on hook* has a long prong to hold the heading erect. The position of the hook part on the shank is the same as hook A.

Hook **D.** The *slip-in hook* has a long two-piece prong that holds the heading erect. It requires no sewing. The hook part on the flat shaft can be adjusted for various headings. Insert it the same as hook A. This type of hook is popular with professional decorators.

Hook **E.** The *pleater pin* with *hook* or *ring* is used with ready-made pleat tape. Slip each prong into a woven-in pocket in the tape and fasten the hook to pinch the pleat in shape. Select the position of the hook part on the shank the same as hook A. Use hooks with rings when a decorative rod is visible above the drapery.

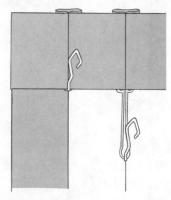

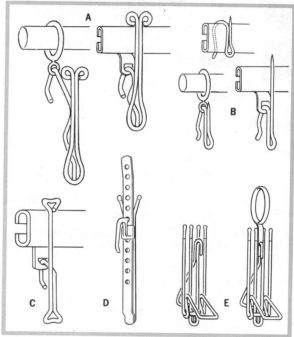

Whatever style of drapery hook you select, be sure to position the hook part correctly. If the drapery heading extends above the rod, measure the distance from the position of the hook part on the rod to 1 inch above the rod. Position the top edge of the hook (not the shank) this distance from the top of the draperies.

If draperies hang from a decorative rod that is visible or from a rod mounted on the ceiling, place the hook part at the top of the draperies.

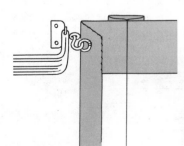

Anchoring Draperies

The outside edges of the draperies should hang against the wall in a straight, taut line. Sew small plastic rings to the heading hem in line with the rod, and to the bottom hem. Place cup hooks in the wall or baseboard in line with the rings. Fasten the rings over the hooks.

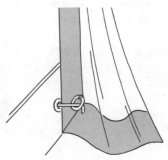

Top It Off
with a Valance
or Cornice

VALANCES AND CORNICES are decorative extras at the top of your draperies or curtains which put the stamp of individuality on your windows. They can also serve the more practical functions of connecting a group of windows, increasing window dimensions, and concealing the rods and fixtures on which draperies are hung. Good taste requires that the style of the valance or cornice conform to the decorative scheme of the room. Both have a tendency to make ceilings appear lower; use them with care in small rooms.

Although decoratively and functionally similar, valances and cornices differ in this way: Valances are made of fabric and tacked to a wood "shelf" or hung from a rod; the valances may be straight, shaped, pleated, or gathered. Cornices are made of wood that may be either covered with fabric or painted to match the draperies or walls, or used as the support for swags and cascades. Whichever you plan to use, you must first construct draperies with a finished heading and hang them as instructed in the previous chapter, beginning on page 366.

Next, determine how long the valance or cornice should be. Although the length of the valance is generally one-sixth the length of the drapery, that may not give the correct proportion to your window. Cut patterns of muslin or stiff paper the exact width of the window but of different lengths. Hold them up to the window to see which looks best.

The Valance Shelf and Cornice Board

The ends and top board of the valance shelf and cornice board should be made of ¾-inch pine, and the face board of the cornice of ¼-inch plywood. Before taking measurements for either, be sure the drapery rod is in position. See page 343. The width of the valance shelf or cornice board should be 4½ inches greater than the rod. After the ¾-inch wood is secured at the ends of the top board, there will be a space of 1½ inches between the rod and board at each end. The depth of the end sections should be 1½ inches greater than the distance from the wall to the rod (depth of the return). This allows space between the rod and the board for the draperies to hang freely and for draw draperies to be opened and closed easily.

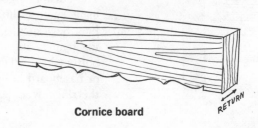

Cornice board

To make the valance shelf, join the end sections to the top board with finishing nails and a thin line of white glue. Keep the outer edges even. *To make the cornice board,* add a face board of ¼ inch plywood to the shelf with finishing nails and a thin line of white glue along both sides and top.

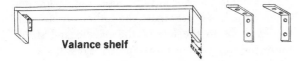

Valance shelf

Mount angle-iron brackets, top end extending forward, on the wall (see page 343) or frame at each end of the board. If the board is more than 40 inches across, mount extra brackets to give added support.

Although the valance shelf or cornice board merely rests on the brackets and is not fastened to them, it is advisable to hammer small finishing nails through one of the screw holes at each end to prevent the board from sliding forward. The covered board can then be lifted easily off the brackets for cleaning.

Straight and Shaped Valances

Straight and shaped valances are made over a stiff foundation such as buckram and are interlined and lined. If the fabric is quilted, you may omit the interlining.

Measuring the Valance Shelf

Place a tape measure across the return at one end, across the front, then across the return at the opposite end. This is the finished width of the valance.

Making a Paper Pattern

Cut a paper pattern this exact width and the length desired. If the lower edge is shaped, mark the depth of the return at each end; shape the valance between these markings, then at the returns. Fit the pattern to the valance shelf to be sure your measurements are correct.

Making the Valance

Cut buckram the exact measurements of the paper pattern. Press all fabrics before cutting. Cut cotton flannel interlining and drapery fabric 1 inch wider than the pattern on all edges to allow for seams. Cut the width on the crosswise grain and length on the lengthwise grain. Cut lining ¼ inch wider than the pattern on all sides for the seam allowances.

Lay the fabric on the table, wrong side up. Place the flannel interlining over the fabric and pin together along the edges. Center the buckram over the interlining. Turn the fabric and interlining

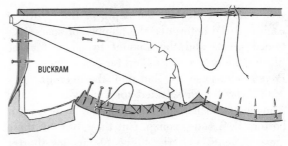

BUCKRAM

over the buckram edge 1 inch, and pin. Clip into the seam allowances at inside curves and notch them on outside curves. With a heavy needle and heavy-duty thread, catch-stitch the edges of the fabric to the buckram. Turn the lining edge under ½ inch and pin to the back of valance, ¼ inch from the edge. Slip-stitch in place. Hand-sew the top edge of ¾-inch twill tape near the top edge of the valance.

At the top and bottom edges of the valance, measure and pin-mark the depth of the return at each end. Fold the valance, wrong sides together, and crease the line of the return at each end.

Place the valance across the front and returns of the valance shelf with the twill tape over the top. Tack the tape to the shelf with upholsterer's tacks.

Pleated Valance

A pleated valance is made the same way as draperies except that it is in one piece. Also, it requires a separate rod. If the window treatment includes glass curtains as well as draperies and valance, triple rods are needed for the hangings.

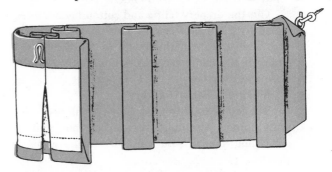

Position the rod. The depth of the return on the top rod is greater than on the other rod or rods.

Measure the length of the rod plus the depth of the return at each end. This is the finished width of the valance. To the measured width and depth of two returns, add the amount required for side hems, seam allowances, and pleats. This is the width required to make the valance. Always locate an end pleat at the depth of the return at each end. To determine the number of spaces between pleats and the amount to allow for the pleats, follow the instructions for *Draw Draperies—Preparation*, page 369, but omit the overlap.

To the length selected for your valance, add 7 inches (4 inches for top hem and 3 inches for bottom hem and turning). Cut the fabric by these measurements. Cut the lining 8½ inches shorter and 8 inches narrower than the top fabric and make a 2-inch bottom hem with a ½-inch turn.

To make the valance, see page 374, which describes how to make lined draperies, and page 379, which describes how to measure and make pleats in the heading. Select the proper hooks or pins for the heading. See page 381. Anchor the valance at the top the same as the drapery.

Fabric-Covered Cornice Board

A cornice may be covered with a fabric identical to that used in the drapery or, if the drapery is a print, the cornice board may be covered with a solid color that picks up one of the colors in the print. For an interesting contrast, the fabric may be quilted. The cornice board should be padded and interlining should be placed between the padding and drapery fabric.

Measuring the Cornice Board

Place a tape measure across the return at one end, across the front, and across the return at the opposite end. To this measurement, add 3 inches for turn-under. Measure the width at the widest and add 3 inches for turn-under.

Cut the drapery fabric and cotton flannel interlining by the measurements. Cut the width on the crosswise grain and the length on the lengthwise grain. If the fabric has a design, center it lengthwise and crosswise.

Making a Paper Pattern

The cornice illustrated has a scalloped edge with corded trimming. Before you cover it or something similar, you must first make a paper pattern.

Spread the paper flat and place the cornice board over it; then bring the paper around the returns and cut it the exact width of the cornice board. Draw the shape of the scallops on the paper; cut on the marking.

Place the pattern over the right side of the fabric, 1½ inches from the edge at the deepest point of the scallops and 1½ inches in from each end. Lightly mark the scallops on the fabric. *Do not cut.*

Covering the Cornice Board

Before you cover the cornice board, cover the cord and stitch it to the lower edge of the fabric as follows: Cut the bias strips as directed on page 244, but make the strips 2 inches wide plus three times the width of the filler cord. Bring the bias strip around the cord, right side out, with one edge 1 inch shorter than the other. Adjust the Zipper Foot to the left of the needle and stitch, following instructions on page 245. Press the seam.

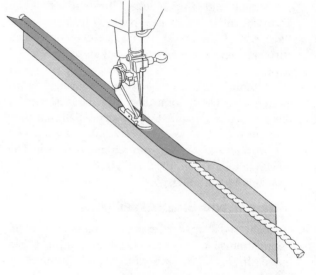

Pin the corded welting on the right side of the fabric, with the stitching on the welting over the scalloped marking. Stitch with the cording up, and crowd the stitching between the cord and previous line of stitching. Press. Trim the cornice fabric to within 1½ inches of the scallops.

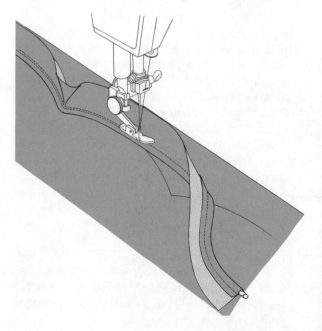

For the padding, place a layer of cotton batting, 1 inch thick, over the front and end sections of the cornice board. Trim the padding to within ¼ inch of the cornice edges. Lay the interlining and drapery fabric over the padding, right side up, extending all edges 1½ inch beyond the cornice board. Smooth out the fabric and thumb-tack it along all edges to hold it in place. (Do not push the tacks in too far since you will remove them when the cornice is finished.)

At the deepest point of the scallops, turn the fabric edges over the edge of the board and tack them to the underside with upholsterer's tacks. Be sure the cording follows the edge of the scallops. Clip into the seam allowances at the point of the scallops and finish tacking the edges to the underside of the board. Turn the fabric over the top edge of the board and tack it in place. Miter the corners. Across the returns, or end sections, turn the fabric over the edges of the board and tack it to the underside. Miter the corners. To finish the top of the board, tack ¾-inch twill tape over the fabric edges.

Lining the Cornice

Line the inside of the cornice so that it will have a finished look when viewed from the outside.

Use sateen lining. Cut the lining by the pattern you made for the top fabric and allow ½ inch

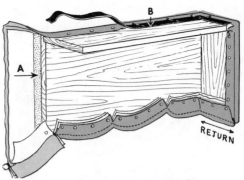

A. Layer of cotton batting
B. Cover edge of fabric with twill tape

on all edges for seam allowances.

Lay the cornice right side down. Place the lining over the inside of the cornice and use a few thumb tacks to hold the lining in place. (Do not push the tacks in too far because you will remove them after you have finished the edges.) Turn under the seam allowance and place the folded edge about ¼ inch in from the edge of the cornice; tack it in place with small upholsterer's tacks. First tack the lower edge in place, then the upper edge, and finally the ends. Place a few tacks along each corner to hold the lining securely in this area.

SWAGS AND CASCADES

Swags and cascades generally match the drapery fabric; the cascades may be faced with a contrasting fabric or self fabric. The edges are often adorned with decorative fringe. This touch is particularly attractive on swags and cascades made of a single thickness of sheer fabric.

A cornice board rather than a valance shelf should be used for the mounting. The shelf does not offer enough support to the swags and cascades and they tend to cup after hanging a short while. The finished swag and cascade are lapped over the top edge of the cornice board and tacked in place with carpet or upholsterer's tacks. Make the cornice board before you begin the swag. See page 382.

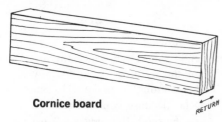

Cornice board

RETURN

Single Swag

For a single window of average width, one swag extending the width of the window is sufficient. For an oversized window, you will need two smaller swags overlapping at the center; and for a group of windows, three or more overlapping swags. The single swag is explained first.

Making a Muslin Pattern

Straighten the ends and cut the muslin 36 inches long on the lengthwise grain. Mark the center line along the entire length. Measure the width of the cornice. Subtract 10 inches from this measurement (5 inches from each end) and use this measurement to mark the top edge of the muslin. *Example:* 36 inches (width of cornice) less 10 inches = 26 inches. Center this measurement at the center line so that you have the same distance (13 inches) on each side of center. Then mark the muslin 1 inch from the top to indicate the lap over the top edge of the cornice. At the bottom edge, mark each side 8 inches wider than the top measurement; keep

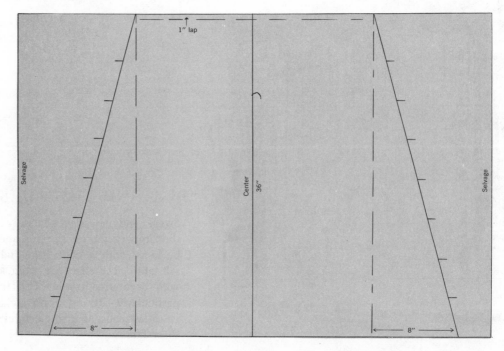

the markings an equal distance from the center line. On each side, draw a diagonal line between the top and bottom edges. Beginning 1 inch from the top, divide the diagonal lines into eight equal parts for seven folds and mark the muslin. (If five folds are used, divide the lines into six equal parts.)

Mark the center line on the top of the cornice board. Lap the straight top edge of the muslin 1 inch over the top of the cornice board, matching center lines; thumb-tack in place. Then tack the muslin at the **A** markings, which are 5 inches from the ends, and at intervals between. Fold the muslin at the first marking on the diagonal line and tack it to the top of the cornice at **A** on each side. Shape the fold smoothly from the center to each side and match the center line. Use pins

for tacking the folds; place them at an angle and drive them slightly into the wood with a hammer. Now make a fold at the second marking on the diagonal line and tack it to the board, ¼ inch from the previous fold. The fabric to the left and right of the diagonal lines lies in folds on top of the cornice board. Continue to follow the diagonal lines and tack each fold to the board, ¼ inch from the previous fold. When all folds are tacked in place, the muslin swag extends the entire width of the cornice board.

Cut off one end of the excess muslin across the top 1 inch above your pin tacks. Trim off the excess muslin along the lower curved edge 4 inches beyond the last fold, tapering gradually toward the center.

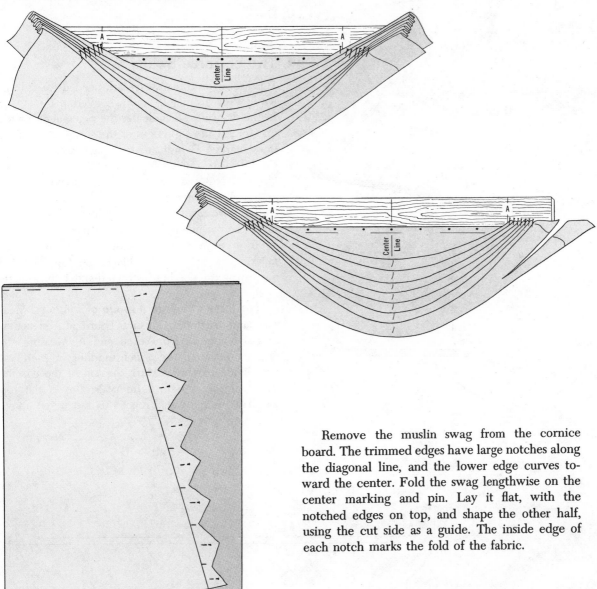

Remove the muslin swag from the cornice board. The trimmed edges have large notches along the diagonal line, and the lower edge curves toward the center. Fold the swag lengthwise on the center marking and pin. Lay it flat, with the notched edges on top, and shape the other half, using the cut side as a guide. The inside edge of each notch marks the fold of the fabric.

Making the Swag

Cut the drapery fabric by the muslin pattern, placing the center marking on the lengthwise grain of the fabric. If the fabric has a design, center it under the pattern. Baste the center line on the fabric. Cut a sateen lining by the same pattern but ¼ inch shorter.

Turn the lower edge of the top fabric under ½ inch and press. Lay the lining over the fabric,

wrong sides together; keep the top and notched edges even; pin. Turn the lower edge of the lining under ½ inch and pin it to the fabric ¼ inch from the edge. Slip-stitch in place. Sew the lining and fabric together along the notched edges and top, using the multiple-stitch zig-zag. Press.

Tack the swag to the top of the cornice board in the same way as the muslin pattern, matching center lines and markings. Fold the fabric at the inside cut of each notch on the diagonal lines, and tack it to the top of the board. As you tack each fold in place, shape it smoothly from the center to each side and match the center basting. Use upholsterer's tacks or webbing tacks that are long enough to go through the multiple layers of fabric and into the board far enough to hold the swag securely.

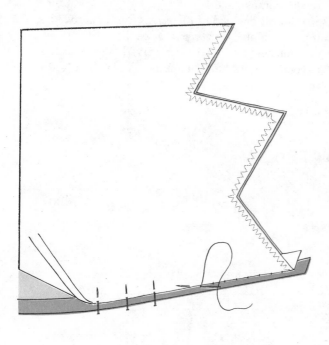

Two or Three Swags

When two or three swags are needed for a large window or group of windows, overlap the swags. In the diagrams, **A** indicates the placement for the first fold at the top edges of the swags; the curved lines marked **B** indicate the space covered when the folds are tacked in place and show the overlap, which is twice the 5 inches allowed at each end of the cornice board.

For two swags to a window. Measure and mark the cornice board at the center and 5 inches in from each end **A**. Measure from the 5-inch marking to the center; this is the top width of each swag. Proceed as instructed above for a single swag.

For three swags to a group of windows. Measure and mark the cornice board at the center and 5 inches in from each end **A**. Measure the distance between the 5-inch marking at each end and divide by three. Mark the top of the cornice board at the one-third intervals; this is the top width of each swag. Proceed as instructed above for a single swag.

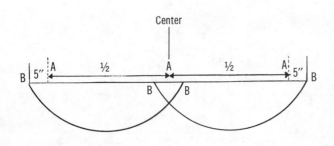

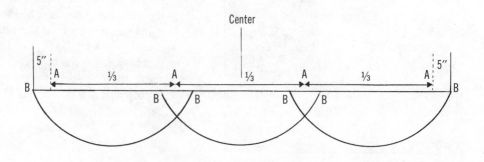

Cascades

Cascades extend around the returns of the cornice board and overlap the swag in front about 6 inches. The longest length is the outside edge, which is generally between 27 inches and 36 inches, depending on the height of the window; however, there is no set rule. The inside edge of the cascade matches the depth of the finished swag.

Making a Muslin Pattern

Straighten the ends and cut the muslin a few inches longer than the outside edge of the cascade. Measure the depth of the return across the end and add ½ inch for a seam allowance. Mark the top edge of the muslin this distance from the outer edge. Lay in the first pleat, bringing the fold to the inside edge of the return. Make the pleat 4 inches deep (8 inches of fabric). Form two more pleats of the same depth, overlapping the previous pleat about 3 inches. *Example:* 4½ inches (4-inch return and ½-inch seam allowance) plus 24 inches (3 pleats) plus 2 inches (1-inch space between two pleats) plus 4½ inches (from last fold to inside edge and seam) = 35 inches. If pleats are placed one on top of the other, make them at least 5 inches deep. Notch the folds at the top to mark the position of the folds for each pleat.

At the outside edge, 27 to 36 inches from the top, cut straight across the depth of the return and seam allowance. Mark the inside edge approximately 15 inches from the top, or the depth of the swag. Then draw a diagonal line between these two points. Cut on the drawn line.

Making the Cascade

Cut the drapery fabric by the muslin pattern, placing the top edge on the crosswise grain and the outside and inside edges on the lengthwise grain. Allow 1 inch on the top edge for the overlap on the cornice board and ½ inch on the lower edge for a seam allowance. Be sure to cut one cascade for the right side and one for the left. If your fabric has a design, it must fall in the same place on each cascade. Cut the facing the same size as the fabric.

Pin the facing to the fabric, right sides together. Stitch ½ inch from the edge, leaving the top edge open. Clip diagonally across the corners, ⅛ inch from the stitching. Press. Turn the fabric to the right side. Pull out the corners, fold on the seamline, and press. Lay in the pleats and pin them in place across the top edge. Lap the straight top edge over the top of the cornice board 1 inch, and tack it in place. The pleated section must overlap the swag across the front.

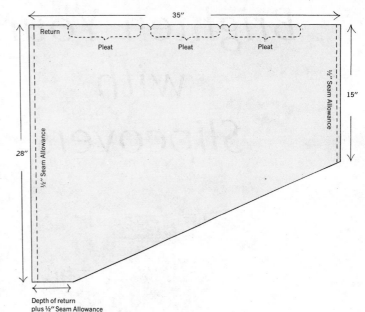

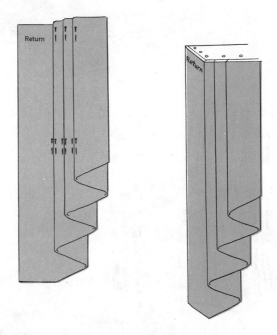

Finishing the Top

To finish the top of the cornice, cut self fabric 1 inch longer and 3 inches wider than the top of the cornice board. Spread the fabric over the top of the cornice. Turn the edges under ½ inch along the front and ends, overlap the cut edges of the swags and cascades 1 inch, and tack the cover to the board. Use steel furniture nails that are long enough to go through the multiple layers of fabric and into the board. Across the back, bring the fabric over the edge of the board and tack it to the underside.

Brighten Your Room with Slipcovers

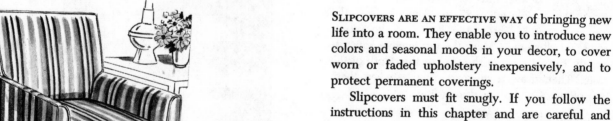

SLIPCOVERS ARE AN EFFECTIVE WAY of bringing new life into a room. They enable you to introduce new colors and seasonal moods in your decor, to cover worn or faded upholstery inexpensively, and to protect permanent coverings.

Slipcovers must fit snugly. If you follow the instructions in this chapter and are careful and accurate in measuring, cutting, and fitting, you will be able to achieve professional results.

Fabric and Color

Fabric selection is almost unlimited. But *choose closely woven fabric so that the slipcover will hold its shape.* Linen, chintz, velveteen, and many of the lovely cotton and synthetic fabrics are appropriate. Consider the texture, weave, color, and design of the fabric. Remember that massive designs belong in large rooms.

Solid colors are the easiest to work with because there is no design to match. Florals require a little extra care in cutting since they must be centered on each chair section, with the design running toward the top. Stripes must be matched on the lengthwise grain and plaids on both the lengthwise and the crosswise grains. Select even stripes and plaids because they are easier to match at the seamlines. See *Plaids,* page 53.

Measuring Your Chair

Record the measurements of your chair on the chart on page 392. Measure accurately, following the exact lines of the chair, and add seam allowances as indicated on the measurement chart. Always measure the lengths of the outside back, outside arms, and front section from seamline to floor; then deduct from these measurements the amount not required for finishing.

Estimating Yardage

After you have recorded the measurements of your chair on the chart, estimate the yardage required.

To estimate the yardage, add the *lengthwise* measurements of the sections and divide by 36 inches. If the fabric has a design that must be centered or matched, add an extra yard for matching. If you are cording the seams, add one yard of fabric to cover the cord. If you are going to make a flounce for the chair, add the yardage required. See page 400.

Preparing to Work

Conveniently arrange your sewing equipment. You will need a box of sharp pins, tape measure, colored pencil or chalk, hand sewing needles, heavy-duty thread, ironing board, iron, and of course your sewing machine. Place the chair to be covered on a card table or low table.

Pin-Fitting a Muslin Pattern or the Slipcover Fabric

Your first step is to pin-fit the chair. If you are a beginner or if the chair has an unusual shape, it is advisable to make a muslin pattern. If you have made slipcovers before and feel confident about your ability, you can begin with the slipcover fabric. The sequence of steps is the same in either case.

Cut all length measurements on the lengthwise grain of the fabric and all width measurements on the crosswise grain. Block the muslin or slipcover fabric to correspond with the measurements for each section of the chair, following the sequence in which the measurements were taken. Tear the muslin; however, if you are working with the slipcover fabric in this initial blocking, draw a thread on the lengthwise or crosswise grain to indicate

the cutting line, and cut the fabric along the drawn thread. As each section is cut, mark the center on the lengthwise grain with a small notch at each end. Pin-mark the center of the chair at the top and lower edges. Then pin the section in its proper place, using one or two pins to hold it to the chair.

To pin-fit the muslin pattern. Pin each section to the chair, following the sequence in which the measurements were taken. The dotted lines in the illustration indicate the lengthwise and crosswise grains of the fabric; these may be marked on the muslin but not on the fabric. Center the section on the chair and pin on the lengthwise grain and crosswise grain, then pin near the outer edges. Keep the crosswise grain parallel to the floor. At the widest points, the muslin extends 1 inch beyond the seamline on each side of the chair; at narrower points, however, the extension is greater. At rounded edges, place the pins crosswise and distribute the fullness evenly between them.

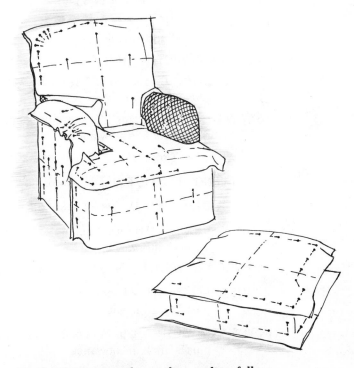

Pin the sections together at the seamline, following the lines of the chair. Begin at the center of the seams and work to the outer edges, placing
(Continued on page 394)

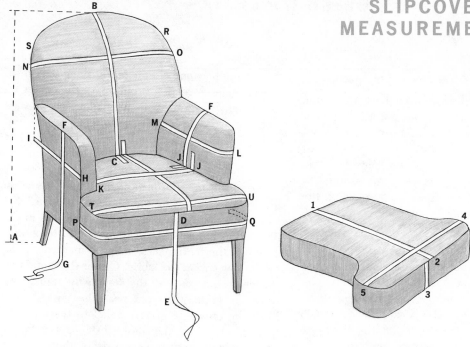

FOR YARDAGE

OUTSIDE BACK LENGTH (floor to top) — **A** to **B** plus
    1″ seam allowance   _____ inches   _____ inches

OUTSIDE BACK WIDTH — **R** to **S** plus 2″ seam allowances _____ inches

INSIDE BACK LENGTH — **B** to **C** plus 2″ seam allowances
    plus 3″ tuck-in allowance   _____ inches   _____ inches

INSIDE BACK WIDTH — **N** to **O** plus 2″ seam allowances _____ inches

SEAT LENGTH — **C** to **D** plus 2″ seam allowances
    plus 3″ tuck-in allowance   _____ inches   _____ inches

SEAT WIDTH — **J** to **K** plus 2″ seam allowances
    plus 6″ tuck-in allowances   _____ inches

SEAT WIDTH — **T** to **U** plus 2″ seam allowances _____ inches

FRONT LENGTH — **D** to **E** plus 1″ seam allowance   _____ inches   _____ inches

FRONT WIDTH — **P** to **Q** plus 2″ seam allowances _____ inches

OUTSIDE ARM LENGTH (arm to floor) — **F** to **G** plus
    1″ seam allowance   _____ inches   X 2 =   _____ inches

OUTSIDE ARM WIDTH — **H** to **I** plus 2″ seam allowances _____ inches

INSIDE ARM LENGTH — **F** to **J** plus 2″ seam allowances
    plus 3″ tuck-in allowance   _____ inches   X 2 =   _____ inches

INSIDE ARM WIDTH — **L** to **M** plus 2″ seam allowances
    plus 3″ tuck-in allowance   _____ inches

CUSHION —
    Length — **1** to **2** plus 2″ seam allowances   _____ inches   X 2 =   _____ inches
    Width — **4** to **5** plus 2″ seam allowances   _____ inches
    Depth of boxing — **2** to **3** plus 2″ seam allowances   _____ inches   _____ inches

Additional Measurements for Wing Chair

INSIDE WING LENGTH — **A-1** to **B-1** plus 2″ seam allowances _____ inches X 2 = _____ inches

INSIDE WING WIDTH — **C-1** to **D-1** plus 2″ seam allowances
plus 3″ tuck-in allowance _____ inches

OUTSIDE WING LENGTH — **A-1** to **B-2** plus 2″ seam allowances _____ inches X 2 = _____ inches

OUTSIDE WING WIDTH — **C-1** to **D-2** plus 2″ seam allowances _____ inches

FRONT ARM LENGTH — **E-1** to **F-1** plus 2″ seam allowances _____ inches X 2 = _____ inches

FRONT ARM WIDTH — **G-1** to **H-1** plus 2″ seam allowances _____ inches

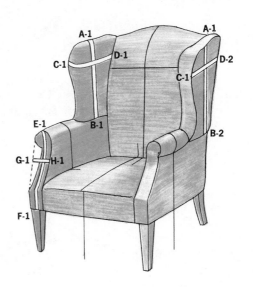

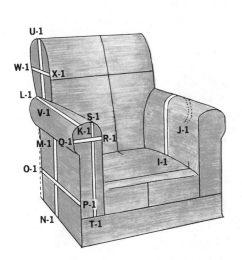

Measurements for Chair with Wide Rounded Arm and Front Section

(Take these measurements instead of arm measurements on preceding page.)

FOR YARDAGE

INSIDE ARM LENGTH — **I-1** to **J-1** plus 2″ seam allowances
plus 3″ tuck-in allowance _____ inches X 2 = _____ inches

INSIDE ARM WIDTH — **K-1** to **L-1** plus 2″ seam allowances _____ inches

OUTSIDE ARM LENGTH — **M-1** to **N-1** plus 1″ seam allowance _____ inches X 2 = _____ inches

OUTSIDE ARM WIDTH — **O-1** to **P-1** plus 2″ seam allowances _____ inches

FRONT ARM LENGTH — **S-1** to **T-1** plus 2″ seam allowances _____ inches X 2 = _____ inches

FRONT ARM WIDTH — **Q-1** to **R-1** plus 2″ seam allowances _____ inches

SIDE-BACK LENGTH — **U-1** to **V-1** plus 2″ seam allowances _____ inches X 2 = _____ inches

SIDE-BACK WIDTH — **W-1** to **X-1** plus 2″ seam allowances _____ inches

pins parallel to the seamline at close intervals. Observe the following sequence and fit the chair snugly but do not stretch the fabric:

A Pin the inside back and inside arm sections together with the seam fitting snugly over the round part of the arm and tapering to the full tuck-in allowance at the seat. Slash into the seam allowance on the curve for a smooth fit, then trim the seam allowance to 1 inch.

B Pin the inside and outside arm sections together, easing the fabric over the round part of the arm.

C Pin the front section to the seat.

D Pin the seat to the inside arm, fitting snugly at the outer edge and tapering to the full tuck-in allowance at the seat. Trim the seam allowance to 1 inch and slash into it for a smooth fit.

E Pin the outside arm to the front section.

F Join the seat to the inside arm and inside back sections, allowing for the full tuck-in allowance.

G Begin at the center and pin the outside back to the inside back and outside arm sections.

A wing chair or a *chair with front arm sections* requires additional seams:

H A tuck-in allowance should be made between the wing and the back, tapering from the 1-inch seam allowance at the top to the tuck-in at the seat.

I Pin small muslin or fabric pieces to the front of each arm section. As the seams are joined, ease the arm section slightly at the seamline.

Block the muslin for the cushion sections the same way as for the chair sections. Cut one continuous strip for the boxing, and place the seam in the center back. Pin the muslin or slipcover fabric sections in place, following the lines of the cushion.

When the pin-fitting is completed, examine the chair carefully to be sure that the slipcover fits snugly and that the seams are in the correct position. Make any necessary adjustments. Trim all seam allowances to 1 inch.

You can follow the above procedure for all types of chairs and sofas. The method of fitting and

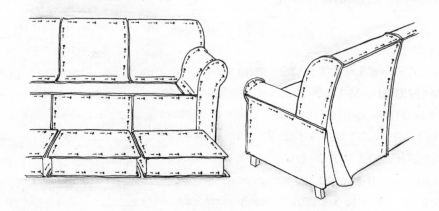

assembling the cover is the same regardless of the number of sections to be covered.

Before removing the pin-fitted cover from the chair, mark the seamlines and label each section.

Marking the Seamline

Cut small notches in the seam allowances at center points and on each side of the eased sections. Open the seams with the fingers and, with colored chalk, mark the seamline on the wrong side of the fabric over the parallel pins. Be sure to mark both sides of the seam allowance. Match these markings in seaming the slipcover fabric.

Label the muslin so that you can identify each section—for example, "inside back," "left inside arm," "right inside arm," and so on. If the slipcover fabric is pinned to the chair, write the identifications on pieces of paper and pin them to the fabric.

Leave all seam pins in place. Remove the pins holding the muslin or fabric to the upholstered chair. Mark the length of the opening at one back seam where inside and outside backs join, then remove the seamline pins in this area. Carefully remove the muslin pattern from the chair.

Cutting the Fabric

If you blocked and pin-fitted the slipcover fabric instead of the muslin, you are ready to proceed with the construction. If you made a muslin pattern, you are now ready to cut the fabric.

Remove the seamline pins. Lay the muslin pattern, right side up, on the right side of the slipcover fabric. Be sure the lengths of all sections are on the lengthwise grain. *Center floral designs and match strips on the lengthwise grain, and match plaids on both the lengthwise and the crosswise grains.* Pin the pattern in place along the edges, then cut. Notch the seam allowances to correspond with the pattern.

Pin-Fitting the Fabric

It is important to pin-fit the slipcover fabric even though you pin-fitted the muslin pattern. The texture and weight of the muslin differ from those of the fabric, and pin-fitting now may save time and trouble later.

Follow the same sequence of steps as for the muslin pattern. Pin-fit the cutout sections to the chair *right side out* to ensure proper matching of the design and a good fit. One arm of a chair or sofa may be slightly lower or fuller than the other. Match notches and place pins at close intervals, parallel to the 1-inch seams. Fit snugly, but do not stretch the fabric. Very few adjustments should be necessary.

Mark the seamlines as instructed above. Remove pins controlling the ease. With a needle and double strand of heavy-duty thread, place small running stitches on the seamline between the notches, and gather the fabric to fit the joining section. Fasten the thread ends.

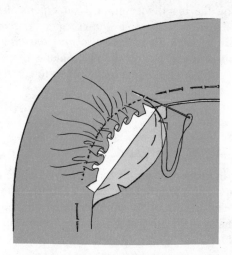

If darts are used instead of gathers to control the fullness, pin the darts to conform with the curve or corner of the chair. A word of caution: Darts may break the continuity of a striped or plaid design; avoid using them, therefore, if you can ease in the fullness.

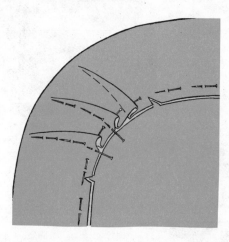

Before removing the pin-fitted cover from the chair, measure the seams to be decorated with cording or fringe to determine the yardage required. All seams should be decorated except those joining the seat and those with a tuck-in allowance. An arm chair or wing chair may require 12 to 14 yards; a sofa with three cushions, approximately 25 yards. Remember that the cushion has two decorated seams—those that join the top and bottom sections to the boxing; so double the measurement around the cushion. If cording is used at the top of the flounce, measure the circumference of the chair.

When you have completed the seam measurements, remove the pins holding the fabric to the upholstered chair; then remove the seamline pins in the zipper area only. Carefully remove the slipcover.

Accenting Seams

Seams in slipcovers are accented to emphasize the lines of the chair, to give added strength to the seam itself, and to ensure a professional finish.

Corded Seam

The most popular seam in slipcovers is the corded seam. Either self or contrasting fabric may be used. The size of the filler cord used depends on the size of the chair or sofa and the weight of the fabric covering the cord.

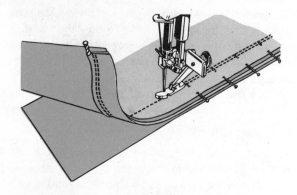

Cut the bias strips, cover the cord, and form the seams, following the instructions beginning on page 244. The width of the bias strips must be 2 inches plus three times the width of the filler cord. Straight and curved seams as well as square corners are used in slipcovers. Do not trim the seam allowances after stitching the corded welting in place but do slash them on inside curves and square corners and notch them on outside curves so that the cord will lie smoothly.

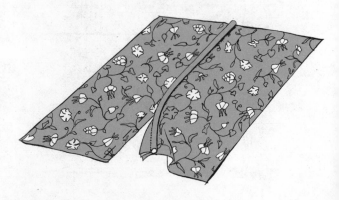

To join ends of cording in a seam. Overlap the ends of the corded welting 1 inch as you pin the cording to the single seamline. Cut the cord and bias fabric even at the first end. Pull out the cord at the second end and clip off 1 inch so that the ends of cord will just meet. Smooth the bias fabric back over the cord, then rip the stitching as far as the end of the cord. Turn the end of the bias fabric under ⅜ inch and lap it around the first end, with the ends of cord meeting; pin. Stitch the cording in place.

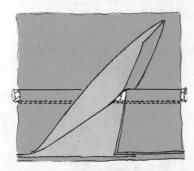

To match stripes and plaids. Join the seams from the right side of the fabric as follows: Stitch the corded welting to the seamline of one section; then turn the seam allowance of the second section to the underside, and pin. Lay both sections right side up, and lap the folded edge over the second seam allowance to the cording; pin in place. Slip-baste from the right side. See page 62. Stitch the seam from the wrong side, following the

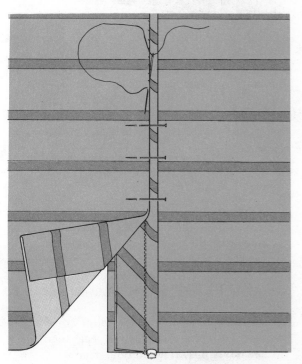

center of the short basting stitch. (Many women slip-baste the seams in *all* fabrics so that they can fit each section to the chair before stitching.)

Fringe Seam

Fringe may be used on almost any type of slipcover to lend interest and color. If the slipcover is casual, select fringe that is simple in style. Pin the fringe to the single seam allowance, right sides together, extending the heading slightly over the seamline. Stitch barely outside the seamline. Pin the second seam edge over the fringe with the fabric right sides together. Place the work under the needle with the first line of stitching up so that you can use it as a guide. Stitch on the seamline, barely beyond the previous stitching.

Bound Seam

This seam is an attractive finish for simple slipcovers where lightweight fabrics are used and where there is little stress or strain on the seam. Pin and stitch the seam, right sides together. Press. Then follow the instructions for *Plain Bound Seam*, page 93.

Seam Finish

After the seams of loosely woven fabrics are stitched, the edges should be finished to prevent

raveling. Use the blindstitch zig-zag on the machine, or overcast by hand. See page 93 and 94. Although seam edges are turned in the same direction, finish each edge separately.

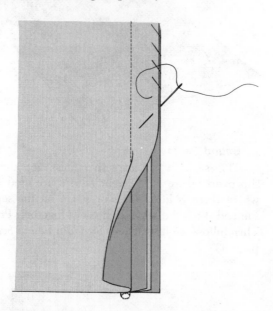

Constructing the Slipcover

Before you begin, be sure identifying labels are securely pinned to each section, as suggested on page 395.

Darts

If darts are used, mark the line on the wrong side of the fabric over the pins; then remove the pins. Fold the dart, right sides together, matching markings; pin and stitch, following the instructions on page 100.

Basic Rules for Seams

—Seams that will be crossed by other seams are stitched first.

—Always pin and stitch the corded welting or fringe to a single seam allowance; then pin and stitch to the joining section. Place the pins at right angles to the seamline with the heads toward the cut edge. Do not attempt to join sections and trimming in one operation.

—If striped or plaid fabric is used, slip-baste the sections together from the right side; then stitch from the wrong side. See page 397.

Sequence of Seams

Remove seamline pins and join the sections, right sides together, in the following sequence:

A Join the inside arm to the inside back, right sides together. Backstitch at each end. This seam fits snugly over the arm, then tapers to the full tuck-in allowance. Press.

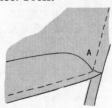

B Where the seat joins the front, pin the corded welting to the right side of the seat seam, keeping the line of stitching on the cording over the marking (on the wrong side of the fabric) for the seamline. Adjust the Zipper Foot to the right of needle and stitch. Pin the front section to the seat, right sides together, matching notches. Stitch, crowding the stitching between the previous line of stitching and the cord. Backstitch at each end. Press the seam. Fit this section on the chair.

C Join seat to inside arm, as instructed in "A" on opposite page.

D Pin; then stitch cording to the seamline of the inside arm and front sections, as instructed in "B" above. Join outside arm to inside arm and front sections, right sides together, matching notches.

Backstitch at each end. Press. Try the assembled sections on the chair; make any necessary adjustments.

E Pin, then stitch seat to inside arms and back sections, right sides together. Press.

F Pin cording to inside back and outside arms in a continuous line, as instructed in "B" above. Stitch, leaving the cording free in the zipper opening. Try assembled sections on the chair; make any necessary adjustments. Press.

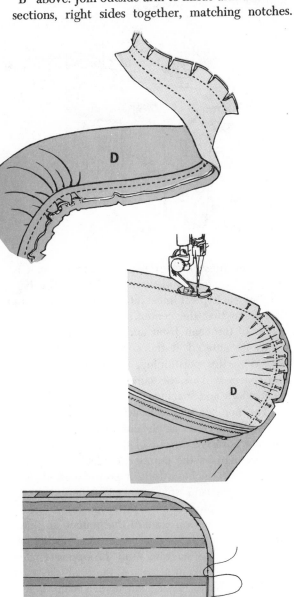

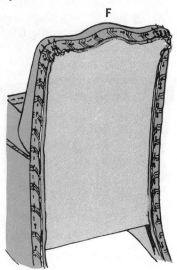

G Pin outside back to inside back and outside arm sections, right sides together. Stitch from the top of the zipper opening to the lower edge on the opposite side, as instructed in "B" above. Remove the pins holding the cording to the outside arm and inside back sections in the zipper opening; then pin and stitch the cording to the outside back section. Press. Try the slipcover on the chair for inspection.

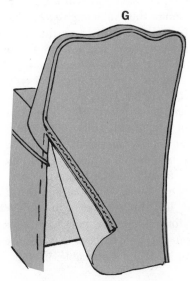

Adding a Skirt or Flounce

Preparatory Steps

Leave the slipcover on the chair until you are ready to stitch the flounce in place. Pin-mark the position of the flounce an even distance from the floor, using a 12-inch ruler. After the flounce has been stitched in place, cut off the excess fabric 1 inch below the marking for the flounce, and press the seam allowances of both the slipcover and the flounce toward the top of the slipcover to eliminate bulk. (Be sure to keep these seam allowances turned toward the top when the finished slipcover is placed on the chair.)

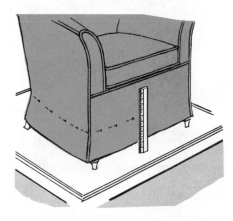

The flounce on the average chair is 7 or 8 inches deep and should clear the floor by approximately 1 inch. For a 7-inch flounce, pin-mark the slipcover 8 inches from the floor. To the depth of the flounce, add 1½ inches for hem and turning plus 1 inch for a top seam allowance. If you are planning to make a heading (as for spaced box pleats, described below), add an extra inch.

To determine the length required for the flounce, measure around the chair, over the pin line. To this measurement, add the amount for pleats or gathers, plus 6 to 8 inches for seaming of strips, ease, and hems at the opening. *Example:* If the circumference of the chair is 3 yards, twice this measurement, or 6 yards, plus 6 or 8 inches is required for evenly spaced box pleats; three times this measurement, or 9 yards, plus 6 or 8 inches is required for closed box pleats or side pleats.

Cut the flounce on the crosswise grain of the fabric. Draw a thread from the fabric to indicate the cutting line. Before you begin, study the instructions for the flounce you have selected so that you can determine where to place the seams. They should not be noticeable in the finished flounce.

Flounce with Spaced Box Pleats

The heading illustrated requires an extra inch in the depth of the flounce. Turn the top edge under 1 inch, and press.

In the illustration, the pleats and the spacing between pleats are identical in width. The back folds of each pleat meet at the center. Plan the flounce so that the center of a pleat falls at the center of the chair front and the spacing between pleats is centered at the corner, over each front leg. With this positioning, the number of pleats and spaces will be the same when you figure the pleat width and spacing.

The number of pleats across the front should be uneven. Decide on the number of pleats, then measure across the front of the chair. Divide this measurement by the number of pleats and spaces. *Example:* 28 inches (front measurement) divided by 14 (7 pleats, 7 spaces) = 2 inches (width of each finished pleat and width of spacing).

Pin-mark the top edge of the flounce at 2-inch intervals, beginning at the center. Lay in the box pleats, following diagram **A** on the opposite page. As seams are required, place them at the back folds of the pleat; use a plain ⅝-inch seam. Before stitching the seams, turn the top fold away from the flounce. Remove the pins holding the pleats, but not those at the 2-inch intervals.

Hem the flounce—either slip-stitch it by hand or machine-stitch it, using either straight stitching or blindstitching. See *Side Hems,* page 371.

Lay in the box pleats, following diagram **A**. Work on the ironing board and use *Method 3,* page 212. Hand-baste across the top of the pleats, a scant ½ inch from the edge. Pin the flounce to the right side of the slipcover, extending the heading ½ inch above the marking. Begin at the center

Diagram A for Box Pleats

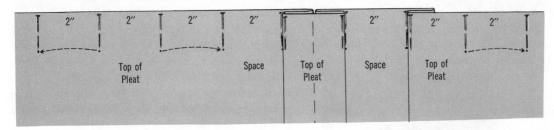

| 2" | 2" | 2" | 2" | | 2" | 2" | 2" |

Top of Pleat   Space   Top of Pleat   Space   Top of Pleat

Diagram B for Side Pleats

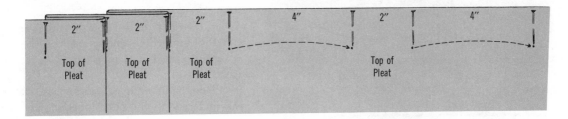

| 2" | 2" | 2" | 4" | 2" | 4" |

Top of Pleat   Top of Pleat   Top of Pleat   Top of Pleat

front and align the center of the pleat with the center of the slipcover. Ease the flounce slightly and extend the ends at least 2 inches beyond the sides of the opening. Stitch the flounce in place, ½ inch below the top edge of the flounce. Finish the seam edge on the slipcover.

Flounce with Side Pleats

The flounce illustrated here has no spacing between pleats. In the 28-inch measurement in the example for spaced box pleats, 14 pleats, 2 inches deep, will fit across the front of the chair. Pin-mark the top and bottom edges of the flounce alternately at 2- and 4-inch intervals. Lay in the pleats, following diagram **B** above. Work on the ironing board and use *Method 3*, page 212. Place the seams at the back fold of the pleats.

Sew corded welting to the right side of the flounce. Pin the flounce to the slipcover, right sides together, keeping the line of cording stitching

on the marking that designates the position of the flounce. Ease the flounce slightly and extend the ends about 2 inches beyond the sides of the opening. Place the work under the needle with the flounce and previous stitching uppermost so you can use the stitching as a guide. Stitch, crowding the stitching between the cord and previous line of stitching. Trim the seam allowance on the slipcover to 1 inch. Press the seam toward the top of the slipcover. Although seam edges are turned in the same direction, finish each edge separately.

Gathered Flounce

A gathered flounce is generally used for an informal effect in Early American rooms, summer cottages, or a family room. Allow one and one-half to two times the circumference of the chair for fullness, plus 6 or 8 inches for seaming of strips, ease, and a hem at the opening. Hem and gather the flounce. Stitch the flounce to the slipcover, following the instructions above.

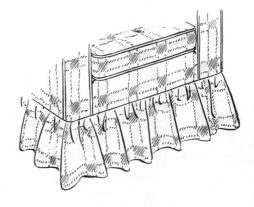

Skirt with Open Inverted Pleat

A straight skirt, with an open inverted pleat at each corner over the legs of the chair, is a neat, tailored finish. An underlay forms the underside of the open pleat. This means that each pleat has openings instead of back folds, and bulk is thus eliminated. The skirt is lined with matching sateen or batiste and needs no bottom hem.

Decide on the depth of the skirt. See page 400. To this measurement, add 1½ inches for top and bottom seams. For the length, take separate measurements for the front, sides, and back of the chair across the marking for the skirt. To each of these measurements, add 10 inches for pleat, seams, and ease. Cut the skirt in four sections, using these measurements. Pin a label to the right side of each section for identification; that is, front, back, and sides. Cut four underlays for the underside of the pleats, the depth of the flounce and 10 inches wide. Cut the lining the same as each skirt section and each underlay, but ¼ inch less in depth. Press the fabric.

Place the lining over the skirt sections and over the underlays, right sides together, and pin along the lower edge. Stitch, taking a ½-inch seam. Trim the seam allowance to ¼ inch. Press; then press the seam allowances toward the lining. Turn the right sides together again, fold the skirt and underlay fabric ¼ inch from the stitching line, and pin the lining in place across the ends. Stitch; then backstitch at each end. Trim the seam allowances to ¼ inch and clip diagonally across the corners. Turn to the right side and pull out the corners to square them. Fold the skirt and underlay fabric across the bottom ¼ inch from the stitching line and press. Fold the ends on the seamline and press.

Fold the ends of each skirt section under 4 inches to form the top folds of the pleats; pin. Do not press the folds at this time. Place the skirt

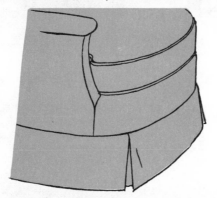

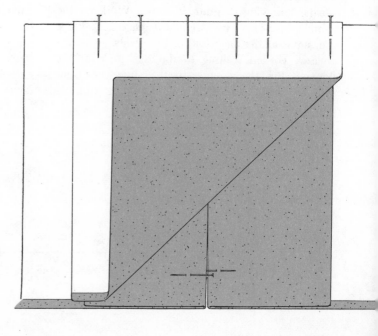

sections wrong side up. Bring the folded edges together in the following sequence: join sides to front skirt, and back to sides. Center the underlays over the joining folds, wrong side up, and pin in place across the top. The underlays should extend about ½ inch beyond the outer edges of the pleats.

Try the skirt on the chair, over the pin marking, to be sure it fits correctly. The inverted pleats should be centered over the legs and there should be a slight ease in the skirt to allow for the thicknesses of fabric. Make any necessary adjustments in the pleat folds. Press the pleats; then stitch the underlays in place a scant 1 inch from the top edge. At the side of the closing, stitch the underlay to the side skirt only.

Cut off the excess slipcover fabric 1 inch below the marking for the skirt. Before stitching the skirt in place, apply the zipper following the directions below; however, extend the open end of the zipper only to the seamline of the skirt.

Pin the skirt to the slipcover, right sides together, keeping the seam edge 1 inch below the marking on the slipcover. At each side of the zipper closing, the pleat folds extend to the seamline and the underlay on the side skirt extends beyond the seamline. Stitch with the skirt uppermost, taking a 1-inch seam. Backstitch at each end. Press the seam; then press the seam allowances toward the top of the slipcover. Although seam edges are turned in the same direction, finish each edge separately. Use snaps to hold the underlay in position under the back skirt.

Applying the Zipper

For an average chair, one closing on the left side is sufficient; for a sofa, two closings, one at each side, are necessary. Select either an 18-, 20- or 24-inch zipper, depending on the length of the closing required.

Side Closing

The following instructions explain how to apply the zipper when the closing is on the left side of the slipcover. When the closing is on the right side, reverse the right and left sides in the instructions as well as the adjustment of the Zipper Foot.

Trim the flounce even with the seam edge on the left side of the opening. If corded welting is used in the seam that joins the flounce to the slipcover, pull out the end of the cord and clip off 1 inch (width of the seam allowance). Turn the seam allowances toward the top of the slipcover.

On the left side of the opening, fold the seam

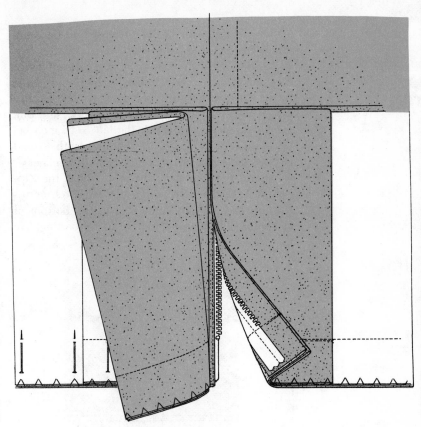

allowance under 3/16 inch from the seamline; carry the fold to the bottom of the flounce. Close the zipper. Pin; then baste the folded edge to the right side of the zipper tape, ⅛ inch from the chain; keep the pull-tab about 2 inches above the bottom of flounce. Adjust the Zipper Foot to the left of the needle and stitch near the fold from the top of the opening to the bottom of the flounce.

(Continued)

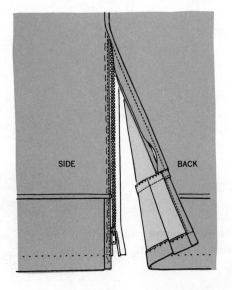

On the right side of the opening, fold the seam allowance under on the seamline; carry the fold to the bottom of the flounce. Press. In the flounce area, turn the cut edge under ½ inch and pin it to the flounce. Lap the folded edge over the zipper to the seamline on the opposite side, and pin. (The right side will overlap the left 5/16 inch beyond the zipper chain; the cording with extend beyond the seamline.) Baste through all thicknesses a measured ⅝ inch from the fold. Adjust the Zipper Foot to the right of the needle; stitch across the top end and down the side to the bottom of the flounce, following the even line of basting. Tie the threads on the underside.

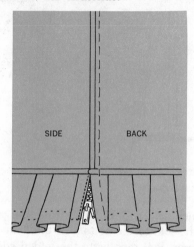

Blindstitching the final step of the zipper application gives a finish that is almost invisible. Follow the instructions on page 178.

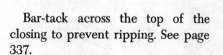

Bar-tack across the top of the closing to prevent ripping. See page 337.

Center Back Closing

A closing at the center back of the slipcover is frequently used in sofas and chairs that are placed against a wall or in a corner.

In a sofa the outside back section generally has one or two seams in which a zipper may be

inserted. In a chair the outside back is usually in one section and it is necessary to make a center back seam. Refer to the chart on page 392. Measure the *Outside Back Width—R to S*, and add 4 inches instead of 2 inches for seam allowances. The additional 2 inches are for the center seam allowances. Block the muslin or fabric as instructed on page 391. Fold the outside back lengthwise through the center, right sides together, then cut on the fold. Pin these edges together. Stitch from the top edge to the top of the zipper opening, making a 1-inch seam. Reinforce with backstitching. Machine-baste the seam in the opening. Press the seam; then press it open.

Construct the slipcover up to the point of applying the zipper; then follow the instructions given under *Neckline or Sleeve Zipper in Slot Seam*, page 181. However, place the open end of the zipper about ½ inch above the bottom of the flounce, and place the basting and stitching ½ inch from the center basted seam.

Plate 23

Two handsome monogram styles

Above: Modern block letters formed with decorative stitch patterns.

Below: A graceful satin monogram appliquéd on terry cloth. Cutout work.

Below left: Diamond-shaped cutouts, combined with decorative stitch
pattern, make an attractive pillowcase border.

Courtesy of Good Housekeeping magazine

Plate 24

Slipcovers can remake a room

Above:
Spirited red-white-and-blue
printed linen carries out
the Early American theme of this room
while contributing a contemporary glow.
Slipcovers made without skirt
show off the clean lines
of the wing chair and sofa.

Left:
The cheerful chintz chosen here for
slipcover and draperies is a lively addition
to this simple, restful room.
The love seat is covered in a fabric
much like the wall in color
and character, to blend
unobtrusively into the background,
yet add some textural
interest of its own.

Courtesy of Good Housekeeping magazine

Finishing a Slipcover without a Flounce

If you do not add a flounce or skirt to your slip-cover, allow 3 or 4 inches on the bottom edge for a turn-under. Mark the seamline across the legs, following the contour of the chair frame. Cut out the fabric over the legs to within ½ inch of the seam marking. Stitch cording on the ½-inch seam-line around the cutout, as illustrated. Slash into

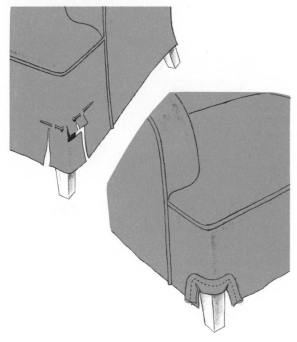

the corners, almost to the stitching. Press. Turn the seam allowance to the underside. Turn the cut edges of the slipcover under ½ inch and stitch near the fold.

Place the slipcover on the chair. Be sure the cover fits smoothly and the seams are straight. Close the zipper. Turn the bottom edge of the cover over the chair frame to the underside and tack it to the frame.

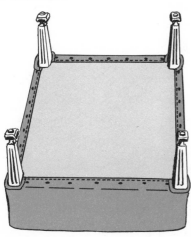

Holding the Slipcover Securely

Here are two suggestions:

—Sew ½-inch twill tape to the slipcover seams next to the chair legs. Cut the tape long enough to lap twice around the legs. Tie securely.

—Push a heavy cotton cord, ¾ to 1 inch in diameter, into the tuck-in to hold it in place. Or use a roll of cotton batting, 1½ to 2 inches in size, covered with muslin, or a roll of brown paper. Any one of these will help prevent the slipcover from sliding.

Covering the Cushion

Cushions should be reversible. Center floral designs on both sides of the cushion. Match stripes and plaids, on both sides of the cushion, with the inside back and front sections of the chair. Plaids must also match the inside arms. Match stripes and plaids across the front of the boxing with those on both sides of the cushion.

Constructing the Cover

Pin-fit the fabric to the cushion, right side out, following the instructions for the muslin pattern, page 391. Corners may be round or square; follow the exact contour of the cushion. Trim seam allowances to 1 inch; mark the seamline and stitch cording or fringe to the top and bottom sections, as in slipcovers. Pin the boxing to the top and bottom sections. Join the ends of boxing at the

back of the cushion. Stitch the boxing in place, but leave the seam open across the back and around the corners of the bottom section the entire length of the zipper. Backstitch at each end. Clip into the seam allowances on inside curves and notch them on outside curves. Press, then turn to the right side.

Applying the Zipper

Two methods of zipper application are explained here.

Method 1: Fold the boxing on the seamline of the opening and press. Open the zipper. Pin the corded seam to the zipper tape, right sides together, keeping the seamline about ⅛ inch from the chain or coil of the zipper. Stitch on the seamline. Close the zipper and turn it away from the seam. Lap the folded edge of the boxing over the zipper to the corded seam, and pin through all thicknesses. Open the zipper and baste a measured ⅝ inch from the fold. Stitch across the end, along the side, following the basting, and across the opposite end.

Method 2: Make a separate back section of the boxing and insert the zipper before joining the boxing to the top and bottom sections. To do this, cut the back section the length of the zipper, plus 2 inches for seam allowances and the same width as the boxing plus 2 inches for center seam

allowances. Fold lengthwise through the center, right sides together; then cut on the fold. Machine-baste the cut edges together, making a 1-inch seam. Press the seam, then press it open. Center the closed zipper over the wrong side of the basted seam, right side down, and pin through all thicknesses. Turn right side up and hand-baste, on each side, a measured ⅜ inch from the center seam. Adjust the Zipper Foot to the left of the needle and

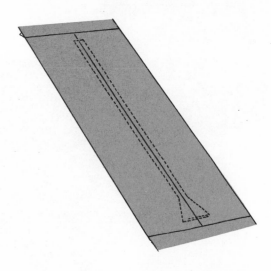

stitch around the zipper, following the basted line. Join the ends of this separate back section to the rest of the boxing with a 1-inch seam. Stitch the boxing in place as instructed above.

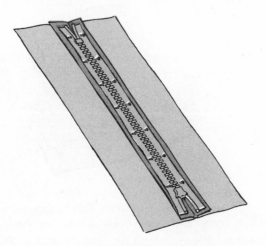

Slipcovers for a studio bed or couch may be styled to obtain almost any effect you want. A tailored cover is illustrated here.

In covering the mattress, treat it as the cushion for a chair or sofa—in other words, make it reversible. Make a separate fitted cover for the box spring. Center floral designs on both sides of the mattress. Match stripes or plaids on the boxing with those on both sides of the mattress; also match the stripes or plaids on the boxing and on the flounce for the box spring with those of the mattress. Cut each section on the true lengthwise and crosswise grains of the fabric. Draw a thread from the fabric to indicate the cutting line.

Covering the Mattress

Measure the length and width of the mattress and add 2 inches to each measurement for seam allowances. Cut two sections (one for each side of the mattress) by these measurements.

Measure the depth of the mattress and add 2 inches for seam allowances. Then measure around the mattress (both sides and ends) and add at least 8 inches for seam allowances. Cut the boxing on the lengthwise grain by these measurements; place seams at the back corners. If the fabric has a floral or one-way design, cut the boxing on the crosswise grain.

To Round the Corners

The corners of both top and bottom sections must be rounded to fit the mattress. Here is a simple and easy method:

Place a piece of cardboard (about 8 inches by 11 inches) between the mattress and box spring, with the edges extending about 1 inch beyond the side and end of the mattress. Hold the cardboard securely, and mark it to indicate the curve of the mattress corner as well as the straight line of the

side and end. Then cut off the cardboard edge along the marking.

Place the cardboard over the corners of the fabric (one at a time) with the fabric extending 1 inch (seam allowance) beyond the straight side and end of the cardboard. Hold the cardboard firmly in position and chalk-mark the shape of the corner on the fabric. *Do not cut.* This is the seamline in construction.

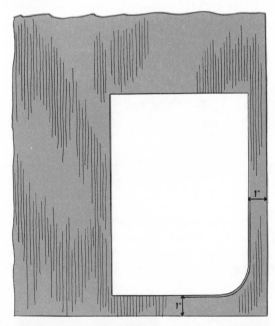

To Construct the Cover

Carefully study *Constructing the Slipcovers*, beginning on page 398; and *Covering the Cushion*, page 405. Then proceed with the construction of the mattress cover.

Stitch cording or fringe to the 1-inch seamline

of both the top and buttom sections of the cover. Join the ends of the cording at the center back, following the instructions on page 397. Try the sections over the mattress to be sure they fit correctly. Press. Join the boxing to the top and bottom sections, leaving the bottom seam open across the entire back and about 4 inches around the corners.

Trim the corner seam allowances to 1 inch. Press; then press the seam allowances toward the boxing. Use two zippers in the opening and place them so that the pull-tabs meet in the center back. Insert the zippers in the seam, following the instructions on page 406. Place the cover on the mattress and turn the seam allowances toward the boxing.

If you are not using zippers, turn under the 1-inch seam allowance on the boxing the length of the opening, and press. Place the cover on the mattress and turn the seam allowances toward the boxing. Lap the folded edge of the boxing over the second seam allowance to the cording, and pin at about 4-inch intervals. Slip-stitch in place, using a curved needle and heavy thread.

Covering the Box Spring

Measure the length and width of the box spring and add 2 inches to each measurement for seam allowances. Cut the fabric; then *round the corners* as instructed for the mattress. Stitch cording or fringe to the seamline.

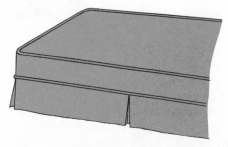

Measure the depth of the box spring and add 2 inches for seam allowances. Then measure around the box spring (both sides and ends) and add about 8 inches for seam allowances. Cut the boxing by these measurements. Join the boxing to the top section and try it over the box spring to be sure the fit is correct. Stitch cording or fringe to the free edge of the boxing.

Measure the depth of the flounce from the bottom of the box spring to the floor and add 1 inch for seam allowance plus 1½ inches for the bottom hem and turning. Measure the length around the box spring and add 12 inches for seam allowances plus the amount required for inverted pleats (16 inches for each) at the four corners and at the center front and back. Cut the flounce by these measurements; place the seams in the back fold of the pleats. Hem the lower edge. Join the flounce to the boxing, right sides together; lay in the inverted pleats, making each fold 4 inches deep.

Covering the Pillows

You can choose from several pillow styles—box or wedge pillows, or round or square bolsters. You may need two or three pillows of the same style. To cover the pillows, follow the instructions for the cushion, page 405. Decorative throw pillows may be added for color contrast.

Constructing a One-Piece Fitted Cover

Take measurements for the spread over sheets and blankets. Measure the top section of the mattress and boxing as instructed above; cut one section to cover the mattress top. Round the corners; then stitch cording or fringe to the seamline. See *Covering the Mattress,* page 407. Join the boxing to the top section. Stitch cording or fringe to the lower edge of the boxing.

Measure the depth of the flounce from the bottom of the mattress to the floor and add 1 inch for seam allowance plus 1½ inches for the bottom hem and turning. Measure the length around the mattress and add the amount required for pleats. Cut the flounce by these measurements. Construct the flounce; then join it to the boxing, right sides together.

Cover the pillows, following the instructions for the cushion, page 405.

Make Your Own Bedspreads

WHETHER AUSTERELY TAILORED or frivolously feminine, bedspreads are an essential element in your decorating scheme. The style of course depends on the other fabric furnishings in the bedroom. Bedspreads may match draperies or slipcovers, or they may introduce a new color note. Since bedspreads cover an article of furniture not easily overlooked, the texture and design of the fabric, as well as the styling and color, should all be harmoniously related.

BEDSPREAD PRELIMINARIES

What to Know before You Start

Many fabrics are appropriate for bedspreads. To name a few: rayon or silk taffeta, chintz, velveteen, polished cotton, antique satin, faille, sailcloth, hand-blocked linen, corduroy, fiberglass, gingham, and organdy. The fabric may consist of natural or synthetic fibers or a blend of two fibers such as Dacron and silk.

Bedspread are often underlined with taffeta, polished cotton, chintz, batiste, muslin, or the like. The selection depends on the fabric used in the bedpsread. If you are planning to use an underlining, select one that is as wide as the bedspread fabric so that the seams will fall in the same places. If lightweight or medium-weight fabric is used in the bedspread, only the center section covering the mattress may require underlining. If sheer fabric is used, the entire bedspread must be underlined. A style with a gathered ruffle is preferred in this case. The sheer fabric and underlining are hemmed and ruffled separately and then both ruffles are attached to the center section with one line of stitching.

A full width of fabric is always placed down the center of the bed, and the seams joining it to the other sections must fall in the same places on each side. When the bedspread has a flounce, the joining strips extend to the edge of the mattress, and the flounce extends from the top edge of the mattress to the floor; when the bedspread is plain, the strips joining the center section extend over the edge of the mattress to the floor. Whatever the style of the spread, most of the seams are straight lines of stitching, and a ⅝-inch seam allowance is adequate. The seams should be emphasized with cording, fringe, binding, or decorative bands of zig-zag stitching. See *Accenting Seams,* page 396.

409

To Measure the Bed

Before you take any measurements, be sure the bed is made up with sheets, blankets, and pillows. Decide on the style of bedspread, then measure accurately and add the amounts specified below. Pin-mark each edge of the mattress (**A, C,** and **D** in the illustration) to indicate the points of the measurements. Since the tape measure may not extend the entire length or width of the mattress, pin-mark the mattress at the point where the tape measure ends; then move the tape and continue your measurements.

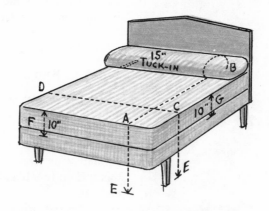

BEDSPREAD

LENGTH — **A** to **B.** Measure from the foot end, along the length of the mattress, over the pillow, and down well under the pillow. ADD 15″ for pillow tuck-in allowance plus ⅝″ for seam allowance plus 1″ for hem and turning at the headboard. . . . . _____inches

WIDTH — **C** to **D.** Measure from one side of the mattress to the other. Add 3¾″ for seam allowances. . . . . _____inches

FLOUNCE

DEPTH — **C** to **E.** Measure the side overhang from the top edge of the mattress to the floor. Add ⅝″ for seam allowance plus 1½″ for hem and turning. . . . . _____inches

LENGTH — **A** to **B.** Measure as for the bedspread length above. ADD 15″ for pillow tuck-in x 2 (sides) plus **C** to **D** (width across foot) plus allowances for pleats or gathers.

For Box Flounce—ADD depth of 2 inverted pleats (16″ each) plus 2½″ for seam allowances plus 2″ for hems and turnings at the headboard end. . . . . _____inches

For Gathered Flounce — Multiply the measured length by 2½ or 3 for fullness. ADD to this figure at least 8″ for seam allowances plus 2″ for hems and turnings at the headboard end. . . . . _____inches

COVERLET

LENGTH — **A** to **B.** Measure from the foot end, along the length of the mattress, over the pillow, and down well under the pillow. ADD 15″ for pillow tuck-in allowance plus 10″ for foot over-hang (indicated by **F**) plus ⅝″ for seam allowance plus 1″ for hem and turning at the headboard end. . . . .   _____inches

WIDTH — **C** to **D.** Measure from one side of the mattress to the other. ADD 20″ (10″ overhang on each side, indicated by **G**) plus 6¼″ for seam allowances. . . . .   _____inches

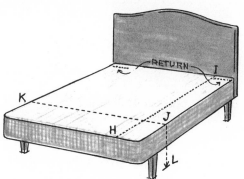

DUST RUFFLE COVERING FOR BOX SPRING
This is a covering that is placed between the mattress and box spring. Remove the mattress and measure the box spring.

LENGTH — **H** to **I.** Measure from one end of the box spring to the other. ADD ⅝″ for seam allowance at the foot end plus 1″ for hem and turning at the headboard end. . . . .   _____inches

WIDTH — **J** to **K.** Measure from one side of the box spring to the other. ADD 1¼″ for seam allowances. . . . .   _____inches

DUST RUFFLE

DEPTH — **J** to **L.** Measure the overhang from the top edge of the box spring to the floor. ADD ⅝″ for seam allowance plus 1½″ for hem and turning. . . . .   _____inches

LENGTH — **H** to **I.** Multiply the length measurement by 2 (sides) plus **J** to **K** (width across foot). ADD 12″ (6″ on each side) for returns at the headboard end; then multiply by 2½ or 3 for fullness. ADD to this figure at least 8″ for seam allowances plus 2″ for hems and turning at the headboard end. . . . .   _____inches

The average measurements of finished bedspreads are:

Full-size: 97 by 120 inches

Twin-size: 82 by 120 inches

Dual or King-size: 115 by 122 inches

Remember, the necessary allowances for seams and hems must be added to these finished measurements.
The average height of a bed (from top of mattress to floor) is 21 inches; however, it may vary from 19 to 22½ inches.

YARDAGE ESTIMATES FOR BEDSPREADS

	36″ Fabric	50″ Fabric

FULL-SIZE BED — 54″ x 75″ (or 78″ to 80″)

	36″ Fabric	50″ Fabric
Plain	10⅓ yards......	7 yards
Box Sides with Inverted Pleats at Corner	10¼ yards......	8½ yards
Gathered Flounce (2½ times length for fullness)	20½ yards......	13½ yards

TWIN-SIZE BED — 39″ x 75″ (or 78″)

	36″ Fabric	50″ Fabric
Plain	10⅓ yards......	7 yards
Box Sides with Inverted Pleats at Corner	10¼ yards......	7½ yards
Gathered Flounce (2½ times length for fullness)	19½ yards......	12½ yards

DUAL AND KING-SIZE BEDS — 78″ x 84″ (or 80″)
                                     or 72″ x 84″ (or 80″)

Plain	10½ yards
Box Sides with Inverted Pleats at Corner	10¼ yards
Gathered Flounce (2½ times length for fullness)	15⅓ yards

QUEEN-SIZE BED—60″ x 80″ .... Same yardage as King-Size Bed.

If you are planning to use corded seams, add an extra yard. If the fabric has a large floral design or plaid, allow one full length of the motif for each additional length required after cutting the center length.

The above figures are the approximate requirements. To be on the safe side, measure your own bed carefully. Remember it is better to have extra fabric than not enough.

412

MAKING THE BEDSPREAD

Box Bedspread

Refer to the *Bedspread Measurements* chart, page 410, and measurements **A** to **B, C** to **D,** and **C** to **E**. Check your measurements to be sure that they are accurate and that you have added the correct allowances for seams, hems, and pillow tuck-in.

The Center Section

Cut one length of fabric for the center section, using the full width. Remove selvages. Since the full width of the fabric is seldom as wide as the bed, cut two additional strips (one for each side) the length of the center section and wide enough to give the amount required to cover the top of the mattress plus 3¾ inches for seam allowances. If you have 50-inch fabric, cut both of these strips from one length, and use the remaining width for the end section of the flounce. If you have 36-inch fabric, cut the strips from two lengths of fabric so that sufficient width remains in each length for the flounce. If you are going to underline the bedspread, cut the underlining fabric the same length and width as each section. Pin the underlining to the top fabric, wrong sides together. Baste ½ inch from the edges if necessary.

Join a strip to each side of the center section, right sides together. Accent the seams with corded welting. See page 396. Try the section on the bed to be sure it fits properly. The ⅝-inch seam allowance should extend beyond the foot and each side of the mattress. Round the corners at the foot, following instructions on page 407. Pin corded welting, in a continuous line, to the right side of the ⅝-inch seamline: Begin at the headboard end and pin the cording in place along the side, across the end, and along the opposite side to the headboard. Stitch.

The Flounce

Cut the flounce in three sections: Cut two side sections (on the lengthwise grain) the length of the center section plus 12⅝ inches for pleat and seam allowances, and the depth of measurement **C** to **E** plus 2⅛ inches for seam allowances and hem; cut one end section (on the crosswise grain) the length of measurement **C** to **D** plus 9¼ inches for pleats and seam allowances, and the same depth as the side sections. This allows for two seams, one at the back fold of each corner pleat. If 50-inch fabric is used, cut both side lengths from one length of fabric; if 36-inch fabric is used, cut the side lengths from the fabric left from the strips that join the center section (see above).

Join the three sections of the flounce with a

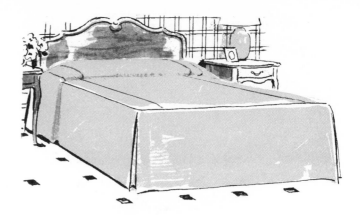

⅝-inch seam. Hem the bottom edge: Turn the edge to the underside ½ inch and press; then turn a 1-inch hem and press. The hem may be slip-stitched by hand or machine-stitched, using either straight stitching or blindstitching. See *Side Hems,* page 371.

To Join the Flounce and Center Section

Pin-mark the center of each of the following: the foot of the center section, the rounded corners, and the end section of the flounce. Pin the flounce to the center section, right sides together, matching the center pin marks. Lay in the inverted pleats at the corners, making each fold 4 inches deep. (Seams joining the sides of the flounce to the end section should fall at the back fold of the pleats.) Then pin each side of the flounce in place. Stitch, following the directions for *Corded Seams,* page 245. Finish the headboard end with a ½-inch double-fold hem.

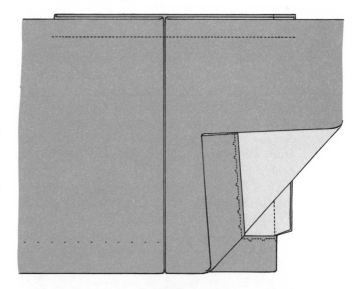

If the bed has a footboard, make an opening in the back seam of each corner pleat so that the flounce will fit over the frame joining the footboard.

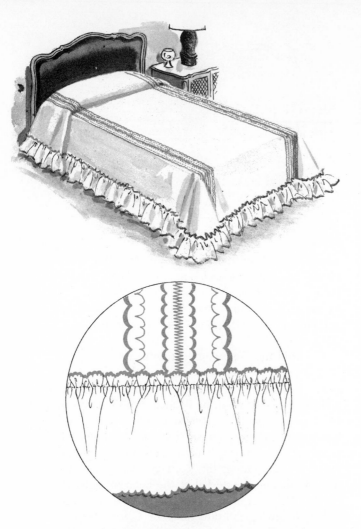

Plain Bedspread with Decorative Bands

For a plain bedspread, the entire length of the spread—that is from the floor to the headboard end (including tuck-in allowance)—is cut in one section. Refer to the *Bedspread Measurements* chart and illustration, page 410. Measure from **E** to **B**. Add 17 inches for a 15-inch pillow tuck-in and a 1-inch hem at each end. Measure the width from the floor, up and over the mattress, and down to the floor on the opposite side. Add 5 inches for seam allowances plus 2 inches for a 1-inch hem on each side.

Cut the center section the length required, using the full width of the fabric. Remove selvages.

The Decorative Bands

Cut two strips of fabric the length of the center section and about 3½ inches wide. Place the decorative stitching as explained in *Border Designs*, page 272. Allow ¾ inch on each side of the decorative stitching for a border.

Pin a band to each side of the center section, right sides together. Stitch, taking a ⅝-inch seam. Press the seams open.

The Side Sections

Cut two side sections the length of the center section and wide enough to complete the overhang on each side of the bedspread plus 2¼ inches for seam allowances and a hem at the bottom edge. (If you are adding a ruffle, make the allowance for its width.) Pin a side section to the band on each side of the center section, right sides together. Stitch, taking a ⅝-inch seam.

Place the spread on the bed; keep the edges even with the floor. *To round the corners* of the spread, pin-mark them in line with the floor. Remove the spread and check the evenness of the pin marks to be sure the curves are identical. Finish the lower edges with a narrow hem.

The Ruffle

The spread in the illustration has a ruffle at the bottom. Cut the ruffle on the lengthwise grain of the fabric, allowing for double or triple fullness. Finish each edge of the ruffle with decorative zig-zag. See *Edgestitched Finish*, page 274. Gather the ruffle with a ½-inch heading; then stitch it in place. See *Ruffle with Heading*, page 281. Finish the headboard end with a ½-inch double-fold hem.

Bedspread with Appliqué Monogram

A monogram is an individual and distinctive touch on a plain or tailored bedspread.

The center of the monogram should measure about 12 or 18 inches. Center the monogram in the center section of the bedspread and complete the appliqué before joining the flounce or overhang. See *Appliqué Monograms,* page 252.

Coverlet and Dust Ruffle

The overhang on a coverlet extends only a little below the mattress, not to the floor. The coverlet is used with a dust ruffle, which covers the box spring and extends to the floor.

For a pleasing contrast, the coverlet may be of a quilted or floral fabric and the dust ruffle of a solid color that matches the quilting or the background of the floral design. For instructions on quilting, see page 256.

The Coverlet

Refer to measurements **A** to **B** and **C** to **D** on the measurement chart on page 411. Be sure that your measurements are accurate and that you have added the correct allowances for seams, hems, and pillow tuck-in.

Cut and construct the center section of the coverlet, following the instructions for the box bedspread on page 413. Use corded seams, and stitch the cording to the outer edges. Try the section on the bed to check the fit. The ⅝-inch seam allowance should extend beyond the foot end and sides of the mattress.

The overhang in the coverlet illustrated is lined and has an open inverted pleat at each corner of the footboard end. An underlay forms the underside of the open pleat. This means that each pleat has openings instead of back folds so that bulkiness is eliminated. The edges of the overhang are finished with tailored binding.

Cut the overhang in three sections: Cut two side sections (on the lengthwise grain) the length of the center section and 10 inches deep (or more) plus ⅝ inch for seam allowances; cut one end section (on the crosswise grain) long enough to extend across the width of the center section and the same depth as the side sections. Cut two underlays 10 inches wide and 10 inches deep plus seam

allowance. Cut a sateen lining the same length and depth as each section of the overhang and underlap; then pin the lining to the fabric sections, wrong sides together. Finish these edges with tailored binding: the lower edge of the underlays; the lower edge and both ends of the end section; and the lower edge and end at foot end of each side section. Be sure to finish one section of the overhang for the right side and one for the left. For instructions on applying the binding, see *Tailored Binding,* page 334. Overcast the side edges of the underlays.

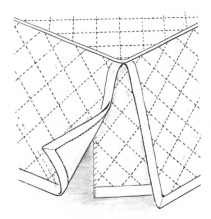

Pin the end section, then the side sections, of the overhang to the center section, right sides together, with the bound edges meeting at the corners. (Keep the ends the same depth.) Center an underlay, right side down, over each joining; pin. Refer to *Corded Seams,* page 245 and stitch. Finish the headboard end with a ½-inch double-fold hem.

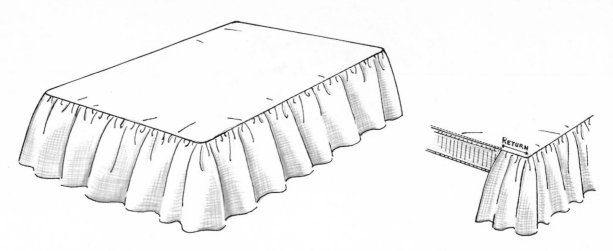

Dust Ruffle Covering for Box Spring

Refer to measurements **H** to **I, J** to **K,** and **J** to **L,** page 411. Measure accurately and add allowances for seams, hems, and returns at the headboard end.

The section covering the box spring, **H** to **I** and **J** to **K,** may be cut of good-quality muslin; it is placed between the box spring and mattress, and the coverlet overlaps the edges joining the dust ruffle. Round the four corners of the muslin, following the contours of the mattress. See the instructions on page 407. Pin-mark the center of the rounded corners.

Cut the dust ruffle on the crosswise grain the length and depth required. See *Dust Ruffle* on the chart, page 411. Seam the strips for the ruffle, using a French seam. Press. Hem the lower edge; then gather the ruffle. See page 280.

Pin the ruffle to the center section, right sides together, placing the gathering stitches on the seamline. Begin at the headboard end and extend the ruffle 7 inches around the corner (the return); pin along the side, across the end, along the opposite side, and 7 inches around the corner at the headboard end. (The returns at the headboard prevent the cover from slipping out of place.) Finish the ends of the ruffle with a ½-inch double-fold

hem. Stitch the ruffle in place, with the ruffle side up, barely beyond the gathering stitches. Hem the end of the muslin center section between the returns.

If the bed has a footboard, you must make an opening in the ruffle at each corner so that the ruffle will fit over the frame joining the footboard. Cut the ruffle as instructed above but add 20 inches to the length for the underlap and turn-under at the corners of the foot end.

Join the strips for the ruffle. Hem, then gather, the ruffle as instructed above.

Pin the gathered ruffle to one side of the center section, right sides together, extending it 7 inches around the corner (the return) at the headboard end. At the footboard end, extend the ruffle 5 inches beyond the corner; then cut it off at this point. Turn the end of the ruffle to the underside 5 inches. (The turn-under is not gathered.) Finish the cut end with a ½-inch double-fold hem. Pin the ruffle to the opposite side in the same manner. Pin the ruffle across the foot end, extending it 5 inches around each corner for the underlap. Finish the cut edges. Stitch the ruffle in place, and finish the headboard end between the returns with a ½-inch double-fold hem.

The Many Faces
of Knits

Table of Contents

About Knits

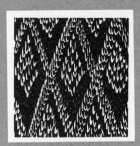

WHAT IS A KNIT?

KNITTED FABRICS FUNCTION DIFFERENTLY from woven fabrics. Woven fabrics are rigid; they resist stress. Knitted fabrics are mobile and "give" with stress. Good knitted fabrics are truly elastic in the sense that they can be stretched and will return to their original form.

Knitted and woven fabrics function differently because they are of two *different structures.* Woven fabrics are structured from two systems of yarns that cross each other and are interlaced. See page 10.

Knitted fabrics are structured from only one system of yarns. The single system of yarns is looped either in the lengthwise direction of the fabric (warp knitting) or across the width of the fabric (weft or circular knitting).

than weft knits. In warp knitting, multiple yarns (but all part of a single system of yarns) run vertically and parallel to each other. The fabric is constructed by manipulating all these warp yarns at the same time into interconnected loops.

The two most familiar types of warp knits are *tricot* and *raschel.* Until a few years ago, tricot was used mainly as a lingerie fabric or as backing for bonded fabrics, and raschel as lace for curtains. But today, so many advances have been made in both tricot and raschel knitting machines that the fashion fabric potential in warp knits is beyond simple classification.

Tricot: Warp knitting — yarns run up and down.

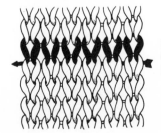

Plain Knit: Weft or circular knitting — yarns run across fabric.

Tricot: A system of vertical yarns interlocks loops vertically and horizontally, producing a smooth-surfaced fabric, resistant to runs, and with little lengthwise but considerable crosswise stretch.

Raschel: Rows of plain knit resembling chainstitch run vertically, interlocking crossing insertion yarns, to form lace-like or looped surface patterns.

Warp Knits, which are made on flat-bed machines, are generally tighter, flatter, and less elastic

Weft Knits, which are made on either circular or flat-bed knitting machines, are constructed in much the same way as hand knits. In weft knitting, the fabric is constructed with one yarn at a time running in a horizontal direction, with the needles forming loops in horizontal courses, building one on top of the other.

The most familiar types of weft knits are jersey, rib knits, double knits and jacquards. Double knits appear to have been knitted twice; the effect is produced by two-needle construction, which interlocks two fabrics into one. Double-knit fabrics have become familiar to most women who sew because they have become available in volume and have performed well in sewing and wearing.

The differences in knit fabrics come from many things, such as: the capabilities of the knitting machine; the design of the needle; the number of sets of needles; the gauge or number of needles per inch; the stitch formation or pattern; the type of yarn (filament, textured filament, or spun); the kind of fiber the yarn is made of; the size of yarn; and the finishing processes applied to the fabric.

To sew knitted fabrics successfully, you need to recognize that they have just as many different faces, textures, and characteristics as woven fabrics.

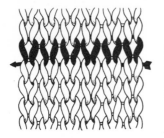

Jersey: A plain knit with a face of flat, smooth, vertical ribs and a back of horizontal loop segments.

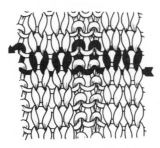

Rib Knit: A combination of sets of knit and purl stitches, which form prominent vertical ribs separated by receding spaces. The back of the fabric shows a reverse of the face ribs and spaces.

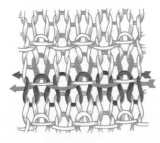

Double Knit: A smooth-surfaced face and back produced by interlocking stitches from two sets of both yarns and needles.

Jacquard: A figured surface produced by two or more sets of both yarns and needles working periodically together and separately to produce designed fabric.

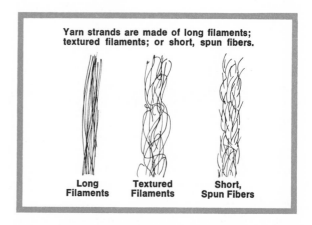

Yarn strands are made of long filaments; textured filaments; or short, spun fibers.

Long Filaments   Textured Filaments   Short, Spun Fibers

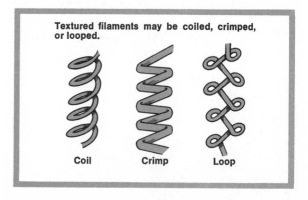

Textured filaments may be coiled, crimped, or looped.

Coil   Crimp   Loop

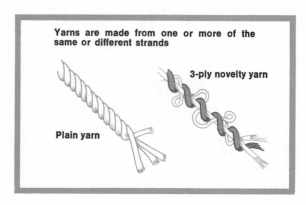

Yarns are made from one or more of the same or different strands

3-ply novelty yarn

Plain yarn

420

Knits place a greater demand on your sewing machine than wovens. Knowing more about your sewing machine and how it reacts to knits will help you to sew knits easily and well.

Machine Care

Because knits contain more yarn than wovens, they tend to drop more lint, fibers, and finishing granules into the machine; so frequent cleaning and light oiling are important. Your cleaning tools are: a lint brush; a piece of clean cheesecloth or any soft cloth; and a tube of SINGER* sewing machine oil. Disconnect the electric cord for safety and then brush out lint, wipe off residue or film, and oil lightly.

The upper threading points collect sticky film and fine lint because friction from the flow of thread creates heat and static electricity. To ensure an even flow of the needle thread, brush and wipe these threading points with a cloth, but do not oil them.

The *feed and bobbin-case area* collects a surprising amount of lint, fibers, and granules. A clean bobbin case is essential. Remove the throat plate and open the slide plate to expose the working

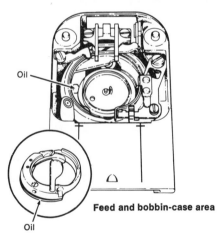

Feed and bobbin-case area

parts. Brush out all of the lint you can see. Then turn the hand wheel slowly, stop, and brush out additional lint as it appears. Remove the bobbin case and repeat the brushing procedure. Then, with a soft cloth, wipe the bobbin case and the surfaces it touches. If the metal parts feel sticky, put a little oil on the cloth to enable you to rub off the residue. Place a drop of oil at each point indicated in the instruction book for your machine. Replace the bobbin case and throat plate carefully when finished.

Open the face plate and brush out the small amount of lint that may have accumulated. Lightly oil the points indicated in the machine instruction book. Turn the hand wheel slowly to reveal the oiling points. Give special attention to the presser bar. Raise and lower the presser foot so that you can see which parts move. A freely moving presser bar improves the feeding of seam layers.

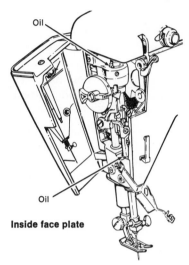

Inside face plate

When you have finished, close the face plate and wipe again around the lower part of the presser bar and needle bar to remove any excess oil. Then run the machine slowly to distribute the oil around the parts as they move.

The Needle

The importance of the sewing machine needle takes on a new dimension when one is sewing knits.

The correct *needle size* depends on the fabric thickness (consider both plain and crossing seams) and on the diameter of the needle thread. The needle should be large enough, and therefore strong enough, to penetrate seam layers without being deflected; also, it should have an eye large enough to allow the thread to pass through it freely.

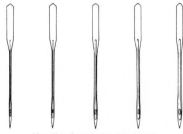

Needle sizes 9, 11, 14, 16, 18

Loosely constructed knits present no unusual problems; but closely constructed knits of nylon or polyester fibers, or those with a heat-set or fused surface, resist the needle's penetration. As a result, the needle forces the fabric downward, loosening it under the foot, before it penetrates; and this loosening of fabric may cause skipped stitches. Closely constructed fabrics also cling to the needle, choking off the flow of needle thread and causing skipped stitches. To overcome skipping from these causes, change to a finer needle and a finer but strong thread.

The **needle point** must be of a shape that will not damage the fabric. Sharp-pointed needles tend to pierce the yarns and sometimes cut them, whereas ball-point needles tend to separate the yarns when penetrating the fabric.

Regular 15 x 1, No. 2020, SINGER* needles have a modified point and thus are appropriate for all-purpose use on wovens and loosely constructed knits. SINGER needle No. 2021 has a ball point and thus is appropriate for many knits.

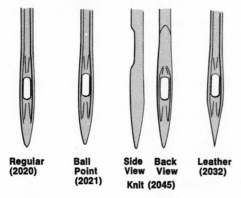

Regular (2020)   **Ball Point (2021)**   **Side View**   **Back View**   **Leather (2032)**

Knit (2045)

A **special needle for knits** is the SINGER ball-point needle No. 2045. In addition to the ball shape of the point, it has other features that make it stitch knits more dependably. It has a deeply cut flat side at the top, which brings the needle close to the point of the sewing hook and thus prevents skipped stitches; and it has a slanted crosswise groove just above the needle eye to let the hook pass without striking the needle as the stitch is being formed. The long groove on the opposite side of the needle is wider and deeper than on other needles to prevent the needle-thread supply from being choked off as the knitted fabric hugs the needle. These No. 2045 needles can be used only on SINGER sewing machine Models 750, 758, 737, 717, 719, 640 series, 413, 416, 418 and 252. On other models they are likely to strike the needle guard of the sewing hook.

Knit-backed vinyl, synthetic leather, or thermoplastic-coated fabrics should be sewn with a special **wedge-point needle,** style 15 x 2, No. 2032. These needles make a small, clean slash in the fabric. This kind of penetration is appropriate for leather and leather-like coated fabrics but not for other knits.

Blunt, bent, or out-of-set needles can cause stitching problems on knits. A needle is blunt when its point has been flattened or burred. Tightly constructed polyester or nylon knits wear off the needle point amazingly fast. A blunt needle will cause snagged or broken yarns and will make a thumping sound as you stitch.

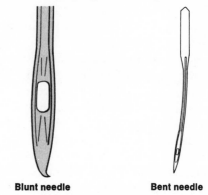

Blunt needle   **Bent needle**

A **bent needle** is usually caused by striking a pin, the presser foot, or a nonyielding crossing seam. Or it may be caused if fabric is removed from the machine by pulling it when the needle thread is above the presser foot. A needle can also be bent by changing from a straight-stitch to a zig-zag setting while the needle is in the fabric. A bent needle will cause skipped stitches and it may cause the seam to pull to the side as you stitch.

An **out-of-set needle** is one in which the lower part is angled in a different direction from the top part. To test for correct set, remove the needle from the machine and place it flat side down on the slide plate, holding it at the top. You should be able to see an even space between the needle and the plate for the full length of the needle blade. If the space is uneven, the needle will cause skipped stitches and should be replaced.

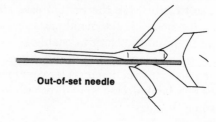

Out-of-set needle

A **sticky or coated needle** can cause skipped stitches after several seams have been stitched. The solutions used to stabilize the stretch in knits, or to impart permanent-press qualities, often remain in fabrics and rub off. (Excess finishing solutions can be removed by laundering before the fabric is cut.) Sometimes, the synthetic fibers themselves cause the needle to be coated. This coating results from the heat generated by the friction of the needle penetrating the fabric at a fast and constant speed.

Regardless of cause, the resulting skipped stitches can be corrected by cleaning or replacing the needle. To clean the needle, pass it repeatedly through an emery-filled cushion or wipe it with a cloth moistened with SINGER oil. Clean the long groove carefully and thoroughly.

The Thread

Knit sewing demands the correct size and kind of thread. Because of the overriding importance of thread size, however, you cannot always match the fiber of the thread with that of the fabric. The most reliable rule to follow is to use the strongest fine thread available so that you can use a fine needle for stitching. This rule is especially important when you sew firm, tightly constructed knits. The following comments on thread types will help you to make a wise choice.

Size A silk is often the best available thread for nylon and polyester knits; it is fine and strong, and it allows you to use a size 11, fine needle.

Size A nylon 3-cord thread is also fine and strong but not as widely available as silk.

Fine spun polyester, marked for lingerie sewing, is a little more wiry and harsh than silk or nylon, but it allows you to use a size 11, fine needle.

General-purpose spun polyester, which is suitable for heavier knits, must be used with a size 14 needle.

Polyester core that has a mercerized-cotton wrap is a general-purpose thread with stretch and strength, but it must be used with a size 14, medium needle.

Mercerized cotton, size 50, is generally available in all colors and should be used in a size 14,

medium needle. (Occasionally, you can break the rule and use mercerized thread in a size 11, fine needle, but the thread may fray or break.) Mercerized cotton lacks strength and stretch for knits. It is satisfactory only for seams that are stayed with tape or woven underlining, or seams that are stitched with the straight stretch stitch.

Size D silk, known also as buttonhole twist, should be used with a size 16 or 18 needle for top-stitching seams, collars, and faced edges where a heavy thread accent is desired.

The Stitch

A balanced straight stitch will produce a smooth, strong seam that will elongate slightly as the fabric stretches; when this stitch is made with silk or synthetic thread, it will stretch a little more.

By regulating the needle-thread tension, you can achieve a balanced straight stitch on almost every kind of fabric. A straight stitch is balanced if it looks the same on both sides.

Both tensions correct

Before making any change in your tension setting, however, make a test stitching on two layers of the fabric, using the thread and needle you have selected for stitching the garment. Start with a 12 stitch length and a straight-stitch setting. Inspect the stitching. Both sides should look the same. If the seam is puckered, shorten the stitch and test again. Seam pucker caused by too long a stitch should then disappear.

To correct an unbalanced stitch when the thread on the *upper* side of the fabric looks straight and tight, loosen the needle-thread tension by turning the dial to a lower number and test again.

Tight upper tension

To correct an unbalanced stitch when the thread on the *under* side looks straight and tight, tighten the needle-thread tension by turning the dial to a higher number and test again.

Loose lower tension

If thread loops appear on the underside, the needle-thread tension is too loose; tighten it and test again.

Very loose upper tension

Some nylon knits require a higher needle-thread tension than you would ordinarily choose for thin supple fabrics. The reason is that nylon hugs the needle and retards the flow of thread.

Once the bobbin-thread tension is set at a normal and versatile setting, you should seldom need to change it on most machines, and never on *Touch & Sew** machines.

There are some things you should not do. One is to attempt to test the bobbin-thread tension by pulling and feeling it. This test is invalid because every machine has a bobbin-thread pull-off device that supplies an increment of thread for each stitch; thus, what you feel is not the same tension as when the stitch is being formed. Neither should you set the needle-thread tension so low that there is no tension on it at all. With little or no tension on the needle thread, the take-up lever will pull thread from the spool instead of retrieving the thread loop from the bobbin case. The result, at best, is short thread loops on the underside of the seam and, at worst, a thread jam in the bobbin case.

Do not assume that seam pucker is caused by tensions balanced at too high a level. Seam pucker on knits is more often caused by too long a stitch, or too heavy a thread, or too coarse a needle.

Starting to Stitch

Many home sewers have formed careless habits for starting a seam. The combination of soft, tightly constructed knit fabric and strong synthetic thread makes it necessary to start seams carefully if you are to avoid having the machine stall from tangled threads on the underside of the seam or in the bobbin case. In extreme cases, threads will jam tightly under the bobbin case and pull the soft fabric down into the throat-plate needle hole.

When sewing on knits with strong synthetic threads, always place both bobbin thread and needle thread under the presser foot, across the feed diagonally to the right and back. Position the

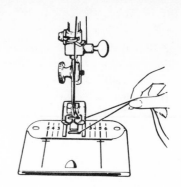

fabric and lower the needle into it *before* lower-the presser foot. The needle should enter the fabric at least ½ inch from the end of the seam. Before

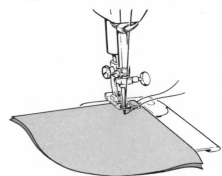

starting to stitch, grasp both the needle and bobbin threads; hold them securely in a position to the right and back of the presser foot; and then begin to stitch forward slowly for one or two stitches. When backstitching, stitch only to within ¼ inch of the end of the seam and then stitch forward.

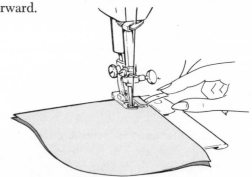

Handling the Fabric

"Fabric handling" refers to the way the seam layers pass under the presser foot. Three elements affect fabric handling: the selection of sewing machine accessories, the degree of presser-foot pressure, and the way you control the seam layers by hand when stitching.

Machine accessories. Select proper machine accessories for the work you are doing. (For the various types of stitches suitable for knits, see page 427.) Plain and stretch straight stitching on knits should be done with the straight-stitch

424

presser foot and throat plate. These accessories hold the fabric very close to the needle; the small opening in the throat plate supports the fabric upon penetration of the needle; and the presser foot strips the fabric from the needle as it is withdrawn.

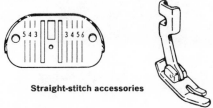

Straight-stitch accessories

Zig-zag stitching must be done with the zig-zag throat plate and the general-purpose presser foot or one of the special feet that accommodate the stitch width.

Zig-zag accessories

Loosely constructed knits—such as sweater, chenille, raschel, and novelty-yarn knits—sometimes catch over the toes of the general-purpose presser foot. To overcome this, simply cut a short strip of plastic transparent tape to ¼-inch width and wrap it around the foot, encasing both toes. Remove the tape after the project has been completed.

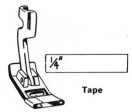

Tape

The *overedge foot* is designed for finishing edges or narrow seam allowances. (Available in the attachment set of many SINGER* sewing machines, the overedge foot is also available for separate purchase for both straight-needle and SINGER slant-needle zig-zag machines.) This foot may be used for a plain zig-zag stitch, an overedge stitch (use Disc 22 on slant-needle machines), or an overedge stretch stitch (available on SINGER sewing machine Models 750, 758, 737, 717, 719, 413, 416, and 418). The overedge foot is narrow and has a wire-like pin that extends from the front to beyond the needle. The stitch is formed over the pin, which prevents the seam edge from curling or crushing. The pin also holds the fabric down when the needle is being withdrawn and helps to prevent skipped stitches on tightly constructed knits. The overedge foot should be used with the zig-zag throat plate, and the needle should be set at "right" position to ensure that the needle straddles the pin.

Overedge foot

The *Even Feed sewing machine foot* is a very important accessory that solves many of the stitching problems presented by knits. By providing top feeding action, which works with the feed of the machine, it ensures that all seam layers feed evenly, with no puckers. At the same time, it prevents skipped stitches by providing a perfectly timed "hold" and "lift" action: the frame of the foot holds the fabric firmly when the needle is down and lifts on the feeding stroke. Finally, this foot eliminates the need to hold the fabric under tension during stitching.

The Even Feed foot can be used for straight and zig-zag stitching, as well as for forward and reverse stitching. Use it for stay stitching, machine basting, stitching seams, and topstitching through several layers of fabric. Use it also whenever instructions suggest a roller presser foot, because the Even Feed foot performs the same functions better.

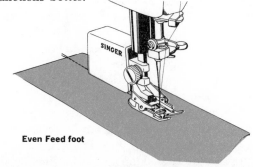

Even Feed foot

Presser-foot pressure is the force that the presser foot exerts against the seam layers. It is regulated by a dial inside the face plate or a dial or screw at the top of the presser bar. Presser-foot pressure holds the fabric in place while the stitch is being formed. When the pressure is correct, the top and bottom layers of fabric move as one layer under the presser foot.

When the pressure is too heavy, the top layer will lag behind the bottom layer, the bottom layer will pucker, and the seam will be uneven. Also, the presser foot or feed may make a permanent impression on the fabric. Pressure that is too light causes other problems. On heavy, spongy knits, the stitch length will be shorter than the setting indicates; the seam will not feel firm when you guide it; and crossing seams will stall under the foot. On firm, tightly constructed knits, the fabric will loosen under the foot, causing skipped stitches.

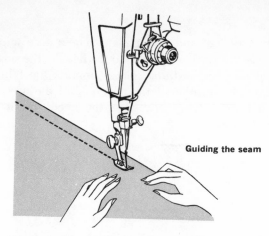

Guiding the seam

illustration indicates the hand position for guiding the seam and applying tension to the fabric while you stitch. This control does three things: 1) It prevents the fabric from loosening under the foot as the needle penetrates and is withdrawn from the fabric, thus preventing skips. 2) It stretches the seam while the stitch is being formed and puts more stretch into the seam when it is relaxed to its normal length. 3) It enables you to put ease in one seam layer and not the other when the construction calls for it. The recovery characteristic of most knits makes this method of handling ease possible; on woven fabrics, it is not appropriate.

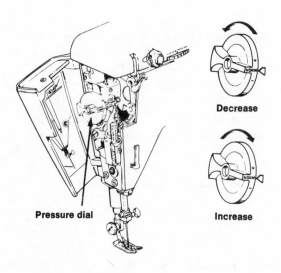

Pressure dial

Decrease

Increase

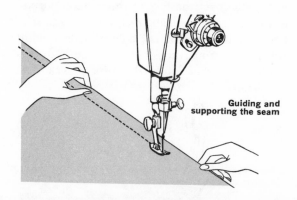

Guiding and supporting the seam

Most knits should be stitched at a normal or medium pressure setting, even those that appear soft and supple but are tightly constructed.

To arrive at the best pressure setting for a specific fabric, cut two 12-inch strips and "stitch" a seam without thread. If the two seam layers come out evenly at the ends, the pressure setting is correct for the feeding stroke. Then thread the machine and stitch with thread. If the stitch length is uniform, with no skipped stitches, the pressure setting is correct. However, if the seam ends come out unevenly in the first test, try decreasing the pressure a little at a time. If, on the second test with thread, there are skipped stitches, increase the pressure to see if skipping can be eliminated. If this does not work, check the other possible causes of skipping discussed earlier.

Manual control of the seam layers is sometimes necessary to improve stitching if you are not using the Even Feed sewing machine foot. Such control is called "guiding and supporting" the seam. The

The Nine Knit Groups

The following chapter gives sewing guidelines for four of the nine basic groups of knits; these four are the types traditionally thought of as knits, such as single and double knits, raschel knits, and sweater knits.

Guidelines for the five special groups —tricot, spandex, terry, fake leather, and fake fur—begin on page 455.

TYPES OF STITCHES

Today's sewing machines offer a wide variety of stitches that are appropriate for sewing knits. Take advantage of this variety for the special purposes described below.

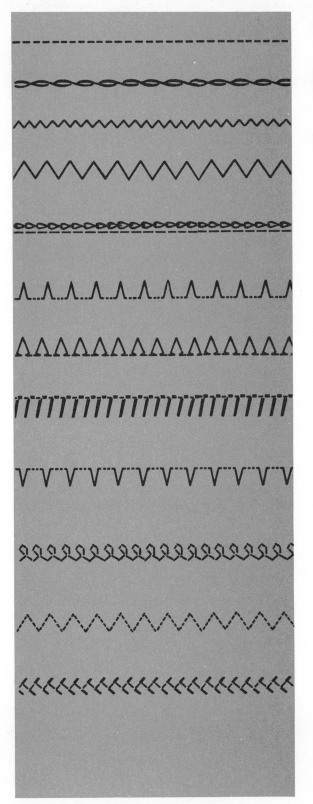

Straight stitch. Use with strong thread for stitching plain, pressed-open and double-stitched seams.

Straight stretch † stitch. Use for stitching plain, plain, pressed-open and double-stitched seams.

Narrow zig-zag, 1 to 2 stitch width. Use for stitch-pressed-open and double-stitched seams.

Wide, open zig-zag, 3 to 5 stitch width. Use for finishing seam, facing, and hem edges.

Chainstitch. Use double row, made from opposite directions, for double-stitching seams in thin knits. Use single row for stay stitching where some give is desired.

Overedge†† stitch. Use for finishing seam, hem, and facing edges and for seams stitched and finished with one row of stitching.

Overedge stretch † stitch. Use for finishing seam, hem, and facing edges and for seams stitched and finished with one row of stitching.

Slant overedge ††† stitch. Use for finishing seam, hem, and facing edges and for seams stitched and finished with one row of stitching.

Blindstitch. Use a 5 stitch width for finishing seam, hem, and facing edges; a 2 to 3 stitch width for blindstitching hems. When guided with seam allowance to left, the blindstitch duplicates the overedge stitch.

Multi-stretch† stitch. Use for finishing and flattening seam, hem, and facing edges and for topstitching seams in spandex power net for girdles and swimwear.

Multi-stitch zig-zag stitch. Use for finishing and flattening seam, hem, and facing edges and for topstitching seams in spandex power net for girdles and swimwear.

Featherstitch† for topstitching spandex power net for girdles and swimwear.

†Made with a *Flexi-Stitch** disc, built in or inserted.
††Can be obtained with disc 22 or 32, available separately for all SINGER slant- and straight-needle zig-zag machines with interchangeable *Fashion** discs.
†††Available on SINGER sewing machine Models 413 and 416.

Knits for Dressmaking

IDENTIFYING YOUR KNIT

Both the kind of garment and the characteristics of the knit fabric must be considered when selecting a pattern and a sewing procedure. It is important to consider the amount of stretch, recovery ability, thickness, loft, and surface texture of the fabric. The following four groups of fashion knits have both similarities and differences, and some fashion knits will fall on the borderline between groups. However, by treating knits in groups, instructions can be simplified and made easier to understand.

- Firm Dress- and Costume-Weight Knits and Bonded Knits
- Raschel and Rough-Textured, Medium-Firm Knits
- Sweater and Loose, Lofty, Stretchable Knits
- Single and Thin, Supple Knits

Determine the degree of stretch in your fabric so that you can identify the group into which it

falls. Measure and mark exactly 8 inches on the width of your fabric. Do this at least 6 inches from all edges. Mark each point with a thread marking, made with a single stitch, and tie the thread ends together. Hold the fabric at one width mark between the thumb and fingers of your left hand, and at the other width mark between the thumb and fingers of your right hand. Then gently stretch the fabric against a ruler, stretching the fabric only as far as it will go without distortion. Take a reading for the amount of stretch in the width. With the fabric relaxed, measure it again and take another reading; this will indicate the recovery ability in the width.

In another area of your fabric, mark 8 inches on the length, and follow the same procedure to determine the degree of stretch and recovery in the length.

Using the reading for the amount of stretch in the crosswise direction (width), classify your fabric according to the scale below.

If an 8-inch portion stretches in the crosswise direction:

—to 9¼ inches or less, it is a firm, stable knit;
—to more than 9¼ inches but less than 10½ inches, it has medium or moderate stretch;
—to 10½ inches or more, it is a stretchable knit.

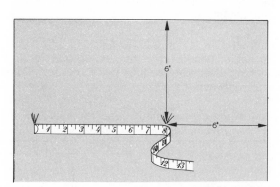

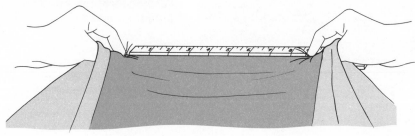

428

The amount of crosswise stretch is the primary factor in determining the suitable pattern classification, the amount of fitting ease needed, and the sewing methods to use.

Knowing the amount of lengthwise stretch will give you a clue as to how much lengthwise ease you may need to allow in the bodice of a garment with a waistline joining, or in the crotch length of pants. It will help you decide the kind of stitch, thread, and seam construction needed to prevent lengthwise seams from breaking, and it will guide you in deciding whether to tape seams.

Knowing the degree of recovery, or the ability of your fabric to return to its original length or width after being stretched, will tell you how well your fabric will hold its shape when you wear it. It will help you decide whether to line or underline it to prevent bagginess.

With respect to knits, *patterns* made by the four major companies may be classified in three categories:

Those that are designed primarily for woven fabrics but that list specific firm, stable knits that are also suitable. These patterns include standard basic ease allowances beyond actual body measurements and design ease allowances appropriate for the specific style.

Those designated as "Recommended for Knits" or "Suitable for Knits." These patterns have standard basic ease plus appropriate design ease allowances. They differ from the first group only in that the styling elements and lines are especially good for knits. They, too, will indicate specific knit fabrics on the pattern envelope.

Those designated for "Stretchable Knits Only." These patterns are smaller in comparison with other patterns of the same type and size. Less total ease, both basic and design, has been incorporated into the pattern; and shaping, normally achieved by seams and darts, is minimal. They are designed to utilize the stretchability of the fabric for both shaping and ease. These patterns should not be used for woven fabrics or firm and medium-firm knits. And they are suitable only for those with attractive body proportions.

PREPARING, CUTTING, AND PRESSING KNITS

Preparing Knits

Double knits and warp knits made of **polyester** or polyester and cotton have a permanent-press finish; therefore, they cannot be straightened by diagonal pulling. Simply fold, right side out, on a lengthwise rib. Place fold along table edge and cut crosswise ends square with the end of the

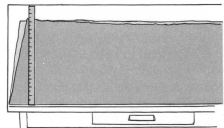

table. Baste crosswise ends together and lengthwise edges together. To shrink and to remove excess finish, launder the basted fabric in the same way you plan to launder the garment. Set your washing machine for gentle motion and warm water, and use a mild soap or detergent. An anti-static fabric softener is also recommended. After laundering, put the fabric and a dry Turkish towel in a dryer set for low temperature. (The towel will help to remove moisture from the fabric.)

Remove fabric from dryer before completely dry. If you do not have a washer with a gentle-motion cycle, wash fabric by hand. If you do not have a dryer, roll fabric in towels to take off most of the moisture and dry over a shower rod. Pressing before cutting is seldom necessary.

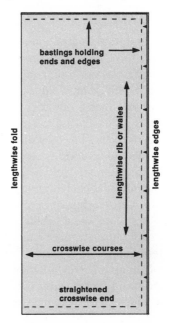

Wool jersey and double-knit fabrics can usually be straightened by pulling them diagonally. Fold, right side out, on a lengthwise rib. Lengthwise edges may not match exactly because tubular knits are sometimes cut crookedly. Single knits are more likely to be crooked than double knits. If the fabric is extremely crooked, there is no way to straighten it perfectly. Merely square the ends by placing the lengthwise fold along a table edge, and cut the crosswise ends square with the table end. Baste crosswise ends and lengthwise edges. Have the dry cleaner shrink the fabric.

If a knit that cannot be straightened has a **prominent crosswise** stripe or pattern, shrink it without squaring or basting the ends and edges.

Raschel knits with a soft finish are often made of acrylic fiber, which is washable. With right sides together, fold at center along a lengthwise chain. Lengthwise edges will be straight because they are knit on flat-bed machines. The crosswise yarns are very prominent and can be followed when cutting the ends straight.

Raschel knits with a sheen are usually polyester and can be treated the same way as acrylics.

Lace-patterned raschel knits should be handled in accordance with the fabric-label instructions. Some are washable; others must be dry-cleaned. Washable lace-patterned raschel knits should be shrunk before cutting; dry-cleanable ones should not.

Soft, loosely constructed raschel knits should be machine-stitched singly along crosswise edges before laundering to prevent raveling. Fold in center, baste ends and edges together, and launder.

Bonded knits should be straightened according to the rules for the face fabric. They are usually not labeled washable and usually do not need to be shrunk. Cut bonded knits folded right side out to make it easier to match designs.

Sweater knits labeled washable can be hand-laundered before cutting but they should be dried on a flat surface to prevent stretching out of shape. Wool sweater knits should not be laundered before cutting unless labeled otherwise. Machine-stitch along crosswise edges in a single layer to prevent raveling. If fabric is tubular, do not cut on lengthwise rib before shrinking or when laying out the pattern unless the layout calls for it.

Single knits that are labeled hand washable should be shrunk in warm water. Those labeled machine washable can be machine-washed. It is a good idea to test-launder a 6-inch square of the fabric to find out whether it shrinks and whether the colors run or fade. If there is no shrinkage, skip the shrinking step; if there is color fading, plan to dry-clean the garment rather than launder it.

Cutting

There are seven rules that apply to cutting all knits.

1. If knit fabric has a prominent lengthwise rib, fold the fabric right side out along a lengthwise rib.

2. If knit fabric has a prominent crosswise stripe, yarn, or pattern, treat it as you would a woven fabric with a crosswise stripe, matching stripes at corresponding notches.

3. Do not let fabric hang over the table edge because it will stretch out of shape.

4. Follow "with nap" pattern layout diagram. Because of their loop construction, knits have an up-and-down direction.

5. When pinning pattern to fabric, use ball-point pins. Pin sparingly and only within seam and dart allowances.

6. Use heavy, sharp shears and long cutting strokes.

7. Cut extended notches on firm knits and mark notches on loosely constructed knits with tailor's tacks.

If a **knit with a prominent crosswise stripe** or pattern cannot be straightened, cut it in a single layer, giving the crosswise detail precedence over the lengthwise rib. To reproduce the needed additional half of the pattern, cut duplicate pattern sections in plain tissue paper. Mark a crosswise grain line perpendicular to the lengthwise grain line on all pattern pieces and place the crosswise grain line parallel to the crosswise stripe. Match crosswise details at corresponding seam lines. To produce right and left sleeves, lay the sleeve pat-

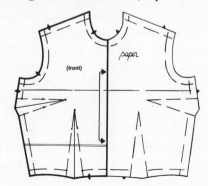

tern on the fabric twice, once face down and once face up.

Knits with a sharply pressed fold should be cut to avoid letting the fold fall within a pattern section. A sharply pressed fold can seldom be entirely removed with pressing. When parts of the pattern must be placed on a fold, create a new fold and place pattern edges on it.

Pressing

Pressing during construction is essential with all knits.

Iron temperature must be regulated according to the fiber content. When pressing blends, do not exceed the iron-temperature setting for the fiber that has the lowest heat tolerance. Always test-press a fabric scrap in which you have made a dart and a seam. Test for heat setting and amount of steam needed.

Never use the iron directly on the fabric. Protect the fabric with a dampened press cloth of thin cotton or cheesecloth; or use an attachment that covers the bottom of the iron and allows steam to escape through its perforated surface.

A softly padded ironing board is better for knits than a firmly padded one. Final pressing on the right side of the garment, and with the fabric protected from direct contact with the iron, will give a smoothly pressed surface because the impressions of seams, darts, and hems will be made in the soft surface of the ironing board rather than in the garment.

Trimming excess bulk from seam allowances and darts on knits is just as important as careful pressing. Slash narrow darts and press them open; then trim seam allowances diagonally within the crossing seam allowance. Press bustline darts

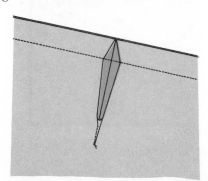

downward and trim the layer next to the garment to ½ inch; trim the other layer on the fold line. This method of trimming will hold the seam allowances of the dart in position and reduce bulk.

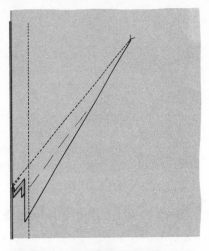

Square-cut the dart seam allowances at the crossing seam.

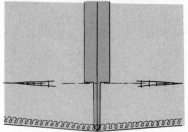

In hems, trim the seam allowances to half width from hem fold to hem edge.

On loose, lofty knits, use a blocking, rather than a conventional, pressing technique. "Blocking" means creating steam without iron pressure on the fabric. Cover the fabric with a moist cloth. Apply the iron to produce steam but do not allow the full weight of the iron to rest on the fabric. Move the iron from one position to another by lifting it rather than sliding it. Remove press cloth. Use a pounding block to flatten seams and eliminate steam. Do not move the garment section until it is dry.

Yarn-pulls may show up as you press. To repair a yarn-pull, grasp the fabric and stretch it along the pull to work as much yarn back in place as possible. Then insert the wire of a wire-loop needle threader through the fabric at the yarn-pull from the wrong side of the fabric. Pass the pulled yarn through the wire loop and draw it to the inside of the fabric.

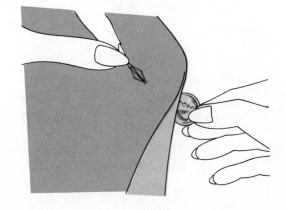

Conventional sewing and sweater construction methods, either singly or in combination, are used to sew knits. The method you select will depend on both the characteristics of your fabric and the type of garment you are making. This section will acquaint you with the various types of seams and construction methods called for in later instructions on various types of knits.

Plain and Double-Stitched Seams

Seam allowances in knits should be wide enough to support the structure of the garment, but they should not be too wide or they will roll and have excessive bulk. Seams should stretch and not break with the motion of the body. The strength and stretch of a seam are determined by the strength of the thread, the type of stitch, and the way the seam is handled. In the following instructions, wherever strong thread is indicated, use silk or synthetic thread.

Plain seam—straight stitch

• Straight stitch, 12 to 15 stitch length; or straight stretch stitch.
• Straight-stitch presser foot or Even Feed foot; straight-stitch throat plate.
• Strong thread; ball-point needle of appropriate size.

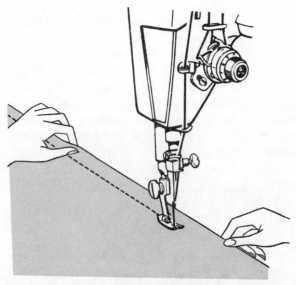

• Prepare seam with hand basting when necessary.
• Stitch seam under tension by guiding and supporting, except when using the Even Feed foot.

• Press seam as stitched, then press open; cut off notches and leave edges unfinished.

Plain seam—narrow zig-zag stitch

• Narrow zig-zag stitch, 1 to 2 width, 15 to 20 stitch length.
• General-purpose presser foot, overedge foot†, or Even Feed foot; zig-zag throat plate.
• Strong thread, ball-point needle of appropriate size.
• Prepare seam with hand basting if necessary.
• Stitch seam under tension by guiding and supporting, except when using the Even Feed foot.
• Press seam as stitched, then press open; cut off notches and leave edges unfinished.

†Use left needle position setting when using overedge foot. Test placement of zig-zag stitch over pin at left of foot before stitching.

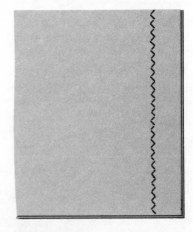

Double-stitched seam

• Stitch on seam line with straight, straight stretch, or narrow zig-zag stitch.
• Stitch again ⅛, ¼, or ⅜ inch outside seam line. Width depends on fabric weight, kind of garment, and desired width of finished seam allowance.

- Trim seam allowances near second stitching.
- Press seam as stitched, then toward the front on side and shoulder seams, and toward the sleeve on armhole seams.

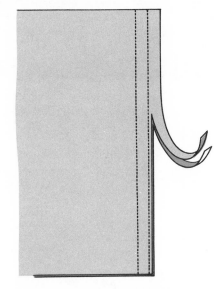

Double-stitched seam, mock-overedged
- Stitch on seam line with straight, straight stretch, or narrow zig-zag stitch.
- Stitch again ⅛†, ¼, or ⅜ inch outside seam line. Width depends on fabric weight, kind of garment, and the desired width of the finished seam allowance.

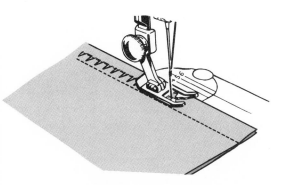

- Use blindstitch (illustrated) or one of the following stitches:

Overedge†	Multi-stretch zig-zag††
Overedge stretch†	Slant overedge †††
Multi-stitch zig-zag††	Plain zig-zag†

- Use zig-zag throat plate and general-purpose presser foot, overedge foot†, or Even Feed foot.
- Trim seam allowances near stitching and press.

†Use a stitch width less than 5 for seam-allowance widths less than ¼ inch and use left needle position with overedge foot.
††Use to finish and flatten seam allowances in bulky knits.
†††Available on SINGER sewing machine Models 413 and 416.

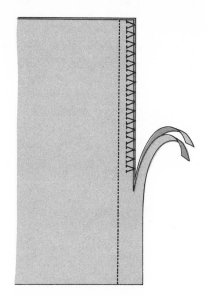

Double-stitched seam, overedged *(Above)*
- Stitch on seam line with straight, straight stretch, or narrow zig-zag stitch.
- Trim seam allowance to ⅛†, ¼, or ⅜ inch, depending on fabric weight and kind of garment.
- Use zig-zag throat plate and general-purpose or overedge foot.
- Stitch over the trimmed edges with overedge, slant overedge, or overedge stretch stitch.

†Use a stitch width less than 5 for seam widths less than ¼ inch and use left needle position with overedge foot.

Seams stitched and finished with one stitching
- Use only for seam allowances ¼ inch or less† in width.
- Hand-baste on seam line if necessary.
- Trim seam allowances to ¼ inch or less.††
- Use general-purpose throat plate and overedge foot.
- Stitch over seam-allowance edges, placing straight edge of overedge, slant overedge, or overedge stretch stitch on seam line.

†Use a stitch width less than 5 for seam-allowance widths less than ¼ inch and use left needle position with overedge foot. Seam-allowance widths less than ¼ inch are suitable for sheer nylon tricot only.
††Place seam allowance to left when stitching.

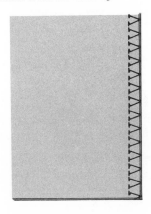

Stayed Seams

Neckline, shoulder, and waistline seams usually need to be stayed to prevent stretching and to support the shape of the garment. Other seams may also need to be stayed, depending on garment styling. Woven-edge seam binding and ¼-inch-wide twill tape are firm and do not stretch. Bias seam binding of rayon is pliable and allows for some stretch, and it prevents seam slippage on open knits of medium firmness. Shrink woven-edge seam binding and twill tape and, if seam line is curved, press it to shape before applying it.

Front shoulder seam. Baste seam line, center the stay tape, and stitch through stay and seam at the same time. Press seam as stitched, then press open.

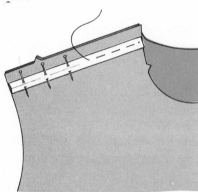

Neckline. Baste neckline including interfacing, garment facing, and stay tape (pressed to shape and centered on seam line). Stitch on seam line. Press. Then trim seam allowances to uneven widths. Press seam open, then turn and understitch facing to seam allowances.

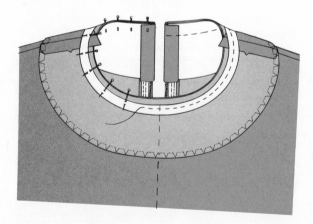

Waistline. Baste and stitch waistline seam. Position edge of stay tape near seam line and stitch along edge. Trim seam allowances even with out-

side edge of tape. Finish tape and seam allowances together with multi-stitch zig-zag.

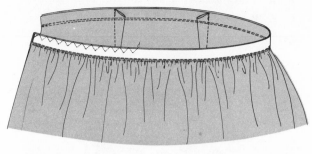

Bias stay for flexible seam. Cut rayon bias seam binding through center. Open fold, place it along the seam line, and stitch.

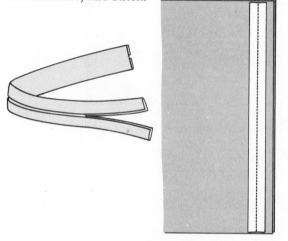

The seam may be a plain seam pressed open; and the edges may be finished or unfinished, depending on the fabric and construction. Or the seam edges may be trimmed even with the stay. Turn all edges toward seam edge and form a double-stitched seam with a blindstitch edge finish. This treatment is recommended for raschel knits and other open knits that tend to show seam slippage under strain.

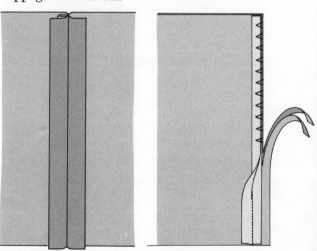

INTERFACING KNITS

Interfacing in collars and facings is just as important for firm and medium-firm knits that are constructed like conventional garments as it is for woven fabrics. You should omit interfacing only when you use sweater-knit construction methods. The interfacing fabric may be a soft woven fabric when you need only to increase the stability of the interfaced section. It may be a nonwoven fabric, such as all-bias, polyester nonwoven interfacing, when you need to increase the stability and add loft to the section. Or, it may be tailor's canvas or hair canvas when you want a crisp, tailored look in a lapel or collar detail. Handling the interfacing so as to eliminate seam bulk is especially important with knits.

Soft woven and nonwoven interfacing
• Baste interfacing (soft woven or all-bias polyester nonwoven) to wrong side of under collar.†
• Baste upper collar to under collar unit, right sides together, and ease upper collar slightly along seam line.

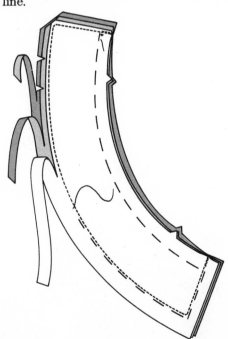

• Stitch on seam line, forming blunt corners by making one or two stitches diagonally across corners.
• Trim seam allowances to uneven widths, keeping the upper collar seam allowance widest. Notch seam allowances along outside curves.
• Press seam, then steam-press seam allowances open over a seam board.

• Turn seam allowances toward under collar and understitch from facing side through facing, interfacing, and all seam allowances.

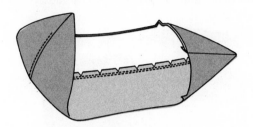

Tailor's canvas or hair canvas interfacing
Where a firm, crisp texture is desired—as in faced-front and open-neckline styles, collars, pockets, pocket flaps, and cuffs—either of the canvas interfacings can be handled in three different ways:

Method 1—organza strip
• Measure, mark, and cut the seam allowance from the interfacing.
• Attach canvas to a shaped section of organza (or crisp, thin underlining fabric), 1½ inches wide, with multi-stitch zig-zag stitching.
• Baste interfacing unit to wrong side of garment section and facing to right side with right sides together.
• Stitch on seam line near the edge of the interfacing.

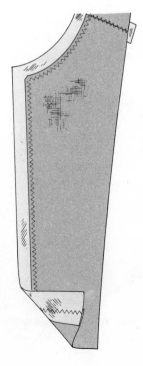

†To reduce collar thickness, under collar may be made of color-matched taffeta or another crisp, woven fabric.

Method 2—catch stitch

• Measure, mark, and cut the seam allowance from the interfacing.

• Baste interfacing to garment with the edge along the seam line.

• Catch-stitch interfacing to seam line.

• Baste and stitch facing as described in Method 1.

Method 3—fusibles

• Cut iron-on interfacing or interfacing and fusible web from pattern and carefully cut off all seam allowances.

• Fuse interfacing to the upper collar; to the upper side of cuff, pocket, or pocket flap; and to the facing of a neckline, lapel, or garment-front, depending on the design. Follow the instructions for the fusible material being used.

• Stitch facing and garment section on seam line near edge of fused interfacing.

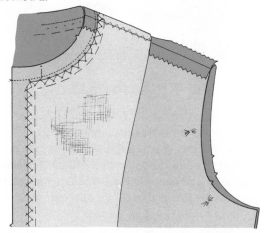

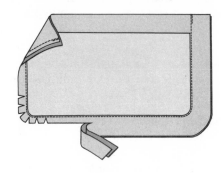

BOUND BUTTONHOLES

Bound, piped, or corded buttonholes are suitable for firm knits. Make them according to your favorite method. Finish them through the facing in a way that reduces the seam layers to a minimum. Baste the facing securely with a lengthwise basting along the inner edge. Make crosswise bastings above and below each buttonhole. Using a 20 stitch length and the straight-stitch presser foot, stitch around the buttonhole from the right side, letting the needle enter the crevice of the buttonhole stitching. Slash through the facing at the center of the buttonhole from the right side. Then turn the garment and trim the facing close to the stitching line on each side of the buttonhole. The result will be a smooth, sturdy finish on the facing side and almost invisible stitching on the right side.

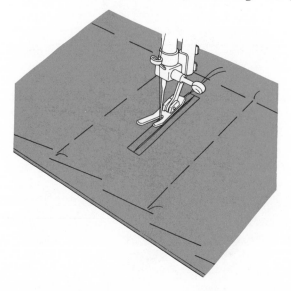

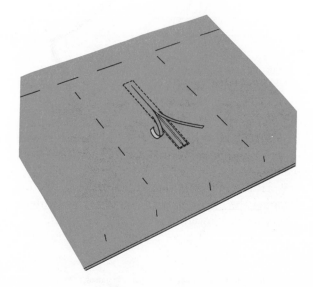

Fabric bands, shaped facings, and edge bindings are especially suited to knit fashions. They eliminate the bulk of conventional facings and add a special interest. Knowing how to apply them will enable you to vary simple patterns in ways that add a professional touch to your clothes.

Shaped bands

- Appropriate for firm, stable knits.
- Cut shaped band by pattern, $1\frac{1}{2}$ to $2\frac{1}{2}$ inches wide plus seam allowance.
- Cut interfacing for band from crisp, thin, color-matched fabric.
- Stitch and trim edge as illustrated. *(Below left)*

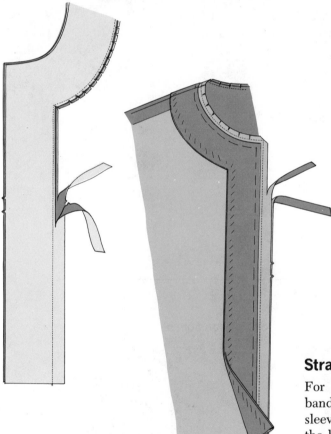

- Press and turn to place seam on inside of band. Then hold edge, favoring right side, with diagonal basting.
- Baste 1 inch from neckline and front edges through band and interfacing to keep edges in place.
- Trim seam allowance plus $\frac{1}{8}$ inch from interfacing near 1-inch basting line.

- Position band on wrong side of garment with right side of band facing the garment.
- Pin, baste, stitch, and trim neckline and front seam allowances. Press and turn band to right side of garment.
- Diagonally baste neckline and front edge.
- Baste free edge to garment and slip-stitch invisibly.
- Remove all basting and press.

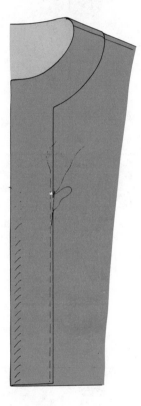

Straight bands

For firm and medium-firm knits, straight-cut bands form practical finishes for V necklines and sleeve ends. They can also substitute for a hem at the bottom edge of the garment. Cut the fabric lengthwise twice the width of the finished band plus two $\frac{1}{2}$-inch seam allowances.

V necklines

Three methods for completing the band at the point of a V neckline are: seamed and opened, hidden seam, and crossed. Regardless of method, the preparations are the same and start with cutting. Do not cut the front of a neckline on the seam line, but cut as a high round neckline.

Using a piece of pulpy paper, such as newspaper or practice-weight typing paper, mark the outline of the V, both the seam line and the cutting line,

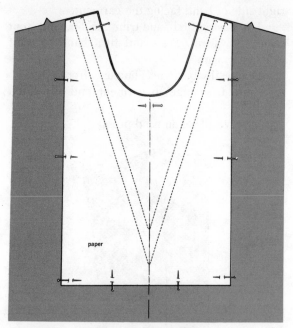

providing a ½-inch seam allowance. Pin the marked paper to the wrong side of the front section and stitch with a straight stitch, 15 stitch length, on both the seam line and the cutting line; pivot and blunt the point by making one stitch across it. Tear away the paper and slash the center

front as far as the cutting line, leaving the extra fabric beyond the seam line until the entire band is completed. Stay-stitch the back neckline exactly on the seam line and trim seam allowance to ½ inch. Then stitch and press shoulder seams. Be sure the V neckline is deep enough to allow the finished neckline to slip over your head without strain, or use a center-back zipper.

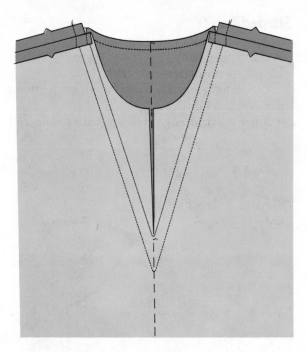

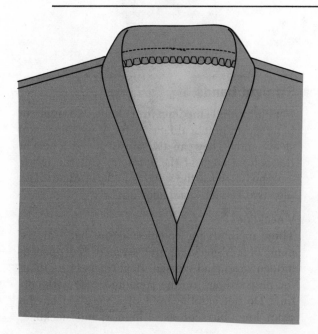

Seamed and opened

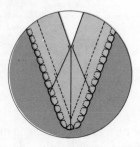

• Fold strip in center, right side out, to form band; press.
• Pin-mark center back of band.
• Starting at center of both back and band, with right sides together, pin together along seam

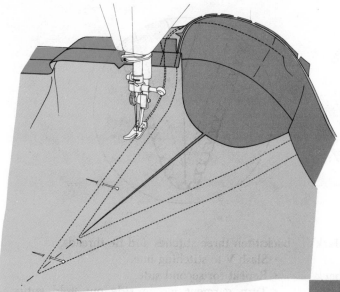

line. Slash back neckline seam allowance in several places almost to stay stitching. Do not ease or stretch. Continue pinning one side to V point. Baste if necessary.

• Stitch, garment side up, from center back to V just inside the seam-line stay stitching, stopping exactly at the end of the V. Carefully backstitch three stitches and tie threads.

• Slash V to stitching line.

• Repeat for second side.

• Place the front of garment right side up over the end of the ironing board. Extend folded edges of band toward neck opening and extend seam allowances toward garment. Let the ends of the band fold under, adjusting the fold to form a center line above the V point. Pin-mark the band at the edges where the centered folds meet.

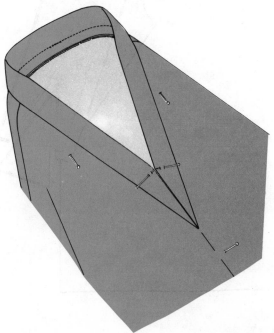

• Turn garment to wrong side and fold on center-front basting, carrying fold through the band matching the pin marks. The line should be straight from pin marks through point of V and along center-front fold. Baste band ends together along this line to form a miter.

• To stitch miter, lower needle ⅛ inch from point where band folds meet. Carefully backstitch two stitches, then forward only far enough to meet the seam-line stitching that joins the band at the V. Backstitch two stitches. Tie the thread ends at both ends of this stitching.

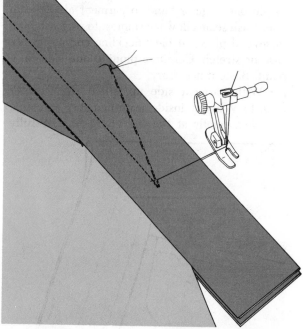

• Press band ends open along mitered seam and pin ends to seam allowances. Trim excess length from bands.

• Working with garment wrong side up, extend seam allowances and stitch 1/16 inch outside seam line through all layers including end of band. Do this on both sides of V. See detail in circle on opposite page.

• Trim seam allowances to uneven widths and finish with an overedge stitch.

• Press from right side over a padded surface to give a soft seam, being careful not to bring up the impression of the seam allowances. Do not press with iron directly on fabric; use a press cloth and light steam.

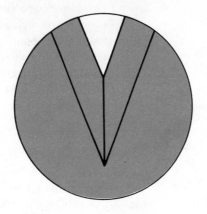

Miter, hidden seam

· Cut strip for band, but do not fold. Mark center back of band with basting.

· With right sides together, start at center back to pin one edge of band to garment along seam line. Slash seam allowance almost to stay stitching in several places at back neckline curve. Do not ease or stretch. Continue pinning one side to V point. Baste if necessary.

· With garment side up, stitch from center back to V barely inside seam-line stay stitching, stopping exactly at the end of the V. Carefully

backstitch three stitches and tie threads.

· Slash V to stitching line.

· Repeat for second side.

· Turn garment wrong side out, fold entire front on center basting, and pin. Extend band, letting seam allowances extend toward the garment. Cut off ends of band straight and even, ¼ inch beyond end of V. Pin seam lines of band together along V and pin unstitched edges of band together for 4 inches. Pin along exact center of band.

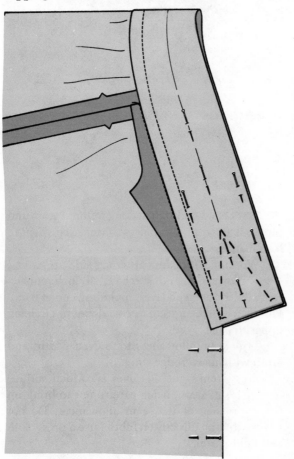

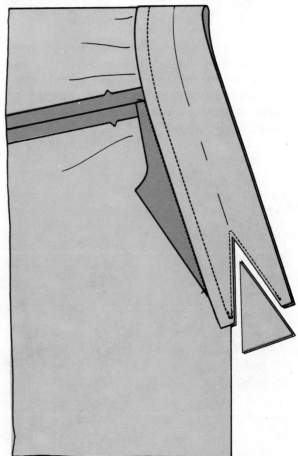

440

- To form a stitching line for the V miter, baste through the band in a straight line following the center-front fold, from point of V to center of band. Turn and continue basting from the center of band in a straight line to the seam line of the band (½ inch from outer edge, ¼ inch from end), forming a V.

- Stitch along basting, blunting V miter point by taking 1 stitch across point. Backstitch at both ends of this stitching.

- Trim seam allowance to ¼ inch and press seam open.

- Unpin and unfold garment.

- Pin bottom ends of band together with miter seams matching, and continue pinning the seam allowances of the band together along the entire neckline. Baste.

- Stitch through seam allowances of neckline and band, from wrong side of garment 1/16 inch outside neckline stitching.

- To reduce bulk, trim seam allowances to uneven widths—garment to ¼ inch, inside band seam edge to ⅛ inch, and outside band to ⅜ or ½ inch. Overedge seam allowances.

- Place garment right side up over a soft surface; cover with a press cloth and lightly steam-press the neckline.

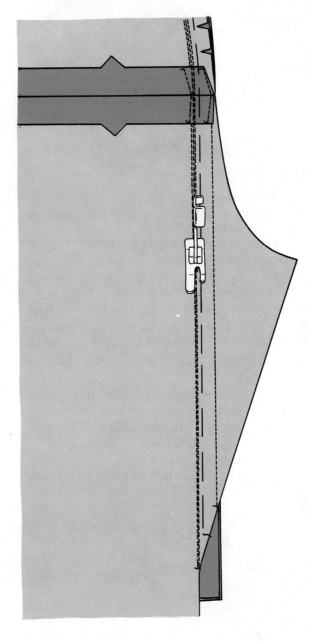

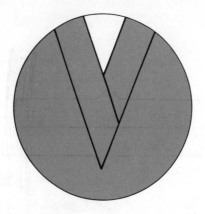

Crossed bands

• To form band, fold strip in center, right side out; press.

• Pin-mark center back of band.

• With right sides together, start at center back (on the right-hand side of a garment for a woman and the left-hand side of a garment for a man). Pin together along seam line. Slash seam allowance almost to stay stitching in several places at back neckline curve. Do not ease or stretch. Continue pinning one side to V point. Baste if necessary.

• With garment side up, stitch from center back to V barely inside the seam-line stay stitching. Stop exactly at the end of the V, carefully backstitch three stitches, and tie threads.

• Slash V to stitching line.

• Repeat for second side, but end the stitching about 1½ inches above point of the V.

• Turn the garment right side out and slip it over the end of the ironing board; let the band extend toward the neckline and the seam allowances toward the garment. Cross the ends of the band at the V point by letting the end of the band on the stitched side pass over the band on the unstitched side and into the unstitched seam.

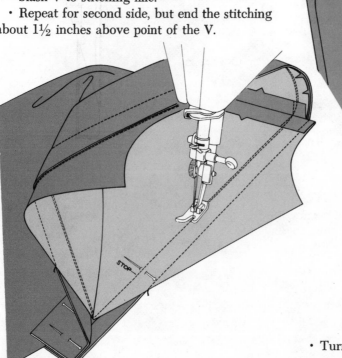

Arrange the garment front so that it is smooth and the V is not distorted. Place a pin through both layers of the band at the V. Using a press cloth and steam, press lightly along the stitched seam line, but avoid pressing over the pin and unstitched seam.

• Turn the garment inside out and stitch the open portion of the seam barely inside the stay stitching from the garment side to the point of the V. On second side, stitch 1/16 inch outside the seam line through all seam layers, including the extended portion of the crossed band.

• Trim seam allowances to uneven widths, leaving the bottom seam allowance widest.

• Finish with machine overedging. See detail of underside of neckline, in circle on opposite page.

to match cross seams. Leave ends unstitched until later. Band may be interfaced if desired.

• Fold band in center, right side out, and press lightly.

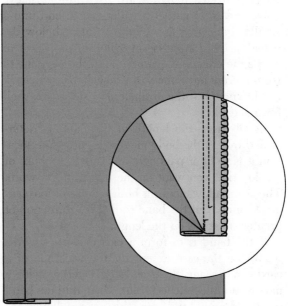

• Open band and, with right sides facing, pin one edge to the garment, starting with the center of the band. Do not ease or stretch. With garment side up, stitch to within 2 inches of the end of the band.

• Repeat for second side.

• Determine the exact location for seaming the ends of the band together (or the exact location for finishing each end of an open band). Stitch, trim seam allowances to ¼ inch, and press seam open.

• Stitch open portion of band, overlapping stitching lines.

• Press seam open and trim seam allowance of band to ¼ inch for bands wider than ½ inch. Do not trim seam allowance on ½-inch bands.

• Fold band along center crease, match the seam edges of the band and the garment, and pin them together. Baste through seam allowances only. Steam-press from right side, using a press cloth.

• Extend seam allowances and stitch from the wrong side, garment side up, through the seam allowances only, 1/16 inch outside the previous stitching.

• Machine-overedge the seam edges together or trim garment seam allowance to ¼ inch and overedge one edge only.

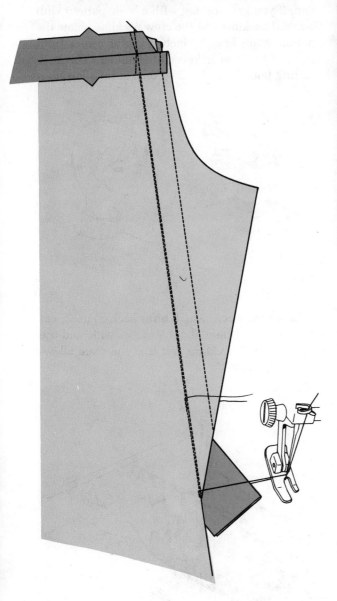

Open-front, sleeve, or hem edge finish

• Estimate length needed for band and add 1 inch. Width of finished band may be from ½ to 3 inches, depending on styling. To determine cutting width, add 1 inch to twice the finished width. Cut a continuous strip or plan locations of seams

Stretched Bands

Stretched bands, sold as "ribbing," are usually made of rib knit or a knit made of textured yarn that has a great deal of stretch and a strong recovery. Stretched bands are used: 1) at sleeve ends to ease or gather a wider sleeve end into a smaller band that fits snugly; 2) at or below the waistline of a sweater, overblouse, or jacket to shape the edge to the figure; 3) at the neckline to form a crew neck, mock turtleneck, or turtleneck finish; and 4) at the armhole of a sleeveless shell for a snug fit.

In all cases, the length of the band is determined by: 1) the body measurement at the location it is to fit or pass over and 2) the amount of tension that you want on the band as it is worn. The seam allowances for both band and garment are ¼ inch. Cut the band so that the direction of greater stretch is on the length of the band.

If the band is to form a closed circle (which would be the case except for the waistline of a cardigan), seam the band ends together with a narrow double-stitched seam. Then, fold the band right side out and pin the seam allowances together.

To ensure even distribution of fullness or ease, pin-mark both the band and the garment in four equal parts. Locate the joining where it will be noticed least and pin the band to the right side of garment, all seam edges even, matching pin locations of the equal parts.

Place garment under presser foot, band up, eased side toward feed. Set machine for a straight stretch stitch or an overedge stretch stitch, which seams and finishes at the same time. Stretch and stitch simultaneously; keep the work under tension by holding the seam both in back and in front of the presser foot, but allow the feed to carry the fabric. Stretch the band until the edge it is being applied to lies flat but is not stretched. Steam the seam by holding the iron above the fabric to assist the seam and band to recover to an unstretched length.

For a crew neck, cut the band 3 inches wide and, if you are working with a basic pattern with a round neckline, cut the crew neckline below the normal seam line, ¾ inch lower at center front tapered to ¼ inch lower at shoulder. This new cutting line allows for a ¼-inch seam allowance.

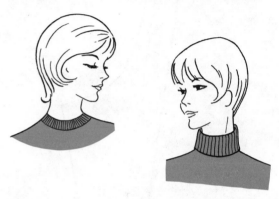

For a turtleneck, which turns back on itself, cut the band or ribbing about 9 inches wide and use a basic round neckline, but trim the seam allowance to ¼ inch.

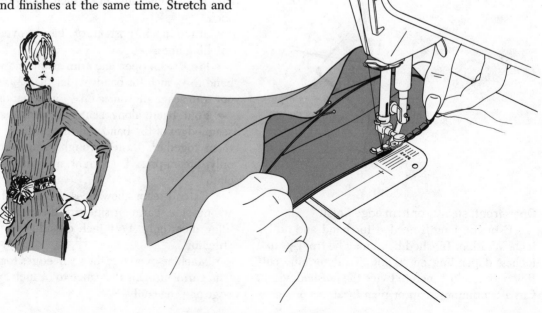

For a mock turtleneck, which does not turn back, cut the band or ribbing 4 to 4½ inches wide and use a basic round neckline, but trim the seam allowance to ¼ inch.

Blocked-to-shape Bands

Double knits of polyester, wool, or blends of these fibers, as well as some warp knits and single knits of these fibers, can be steam-pressed or blocked into shapes such as those used for accenting rounded pocket flaps, U necklines, rounded yokes, and patch pockets.

• Trace the outline of the finished edge on a large piece of laundered muslin or sheeting. Pin this to your ironing board cover to use as a shaping guide.

• Cut the strip for the shaped band twice the finished width plus two ½-inch seam allowances.

Cut either lengthwise or crosswise, after testing a short length to determine the best choice for shaping.

• Hand-baste edges of strip together, leaving one end of basting long and unknotted. Press lightly to form crease.

• Pin-mark band at center and position center of band at center of the marked shaping guide. Baste band to guide across center.

• Plan to use the surface of the band that is up as the underside in the garment in case some shine develops from pressing.

• Using a dampened cheesecloth over the band and working from the center basting, apply steam, stretch the band, and pin it along the cut edges, keeping the fold edge even with the marked line. Working with only a few inches of the band at a time, slightly ease the fold edge and stretch the cut edge. Place pins along the outside edge into the padding of the ironing board so that you can press over them without marring the band. When the entire band has been shaped and pinned, steam-press again to give a permanent set to the detail. Polyester knits will retain this shaping after laundering, as will wool after dry cleaning.

• Apply as described on page 443, Open-Front, Sleeve, or Hem-Edge Finish.

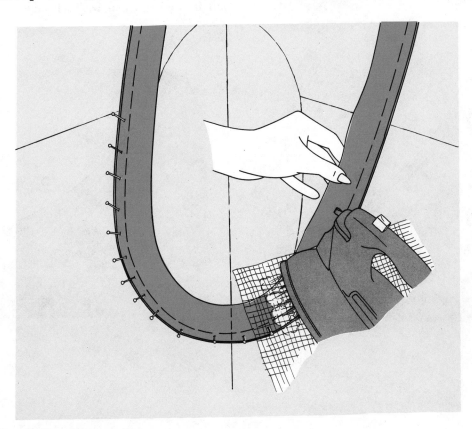

Bound, Piped, and Corded Edges

Bound, piped, and corded-edge finishes on knits differ from those on woven fabrics: on knits, the free edge may be finished with an overedge stitch; on wovens, the free edge is turned to the inside or covered with a facing. Fabric strips, which may be cut lengthwise, crosswise, or bias, are perfect for knits because they eliminate facings that often show an impression on the right side. These strips can be applied to an unstitched edge, to an edge that has been stay-stitched on the seam line for moderate control, or to an edge stayed with woven seam binding for firm control.

Bound Edge

For a ¼-inch-wide bound edge, cut a strip 1¼ inches wide and overedge one edge. Trim garment on seam line. Place bias strip over garment, edges even and right sides facing. Stitch ¼ inch from edges, as at **A**. Press seam allowances open. Turn strip over one seam allowance and hand-baste through center of binding, as in **B**. Turn garment wrong side up; extend both the seam allowance and the finished edge of strip. Stitch 1/16 inch outside first stitching line, as at **C**.

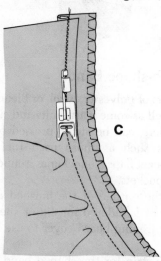

Remove basting and steam-press to shape binding and free edge, as in **D**. Tack edge at crossing seams.

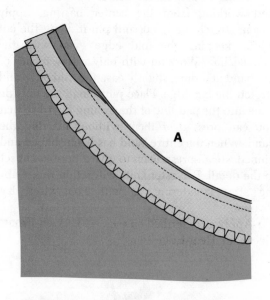

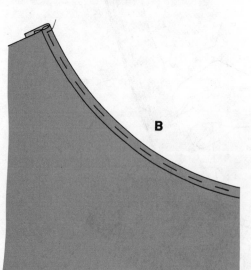

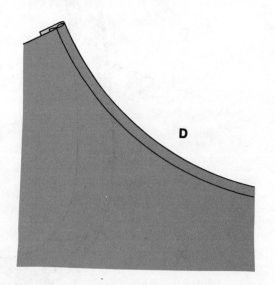

Piped Edge

For a piped edge, cut a strip 1½ inches wide and finish one edge with the overedge stitch. Fold back the unfinished edge ½ inch and steam-press, as in **E.** Trim garment on seam line. Place prepared strip right side down and garment edge over it, also right side down. Pin garment edge to strip, matching edges as at **F.** With general-purpose presser foot on machine, straight-stitch, 15 length, ¼ inch from edges, using edge of foot as a guide. See **G.** Remove pins before stitching over them. Fold strip to underside, letting piping extend from stitching line. See **H.** Steam-press to shape the piping and the free edge of strip. Tack edge at crossing seams.

Corded Edge

For a corded edge, cut strip 1½ to 2 inches wide, depending on diameter of cord. Fold strip over cord, right side out, near one edge of strip; allow ¼ inch to extend beyond the stitching line at the cord on one side and ¾ inch on the other. Machine-baste, using the cording foot, as in **I.** Finish the wider edge of the strip with machine overedging. Trim garment edge on seam line. Place prepared strip right side down with garment edge over it also right side down, edges matching as in **J.** Pin; then stitch, using the cording foot adjusted to the left of the needle and very

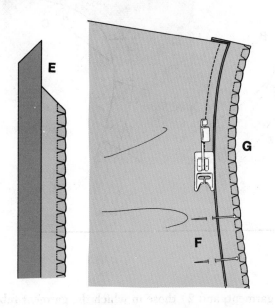

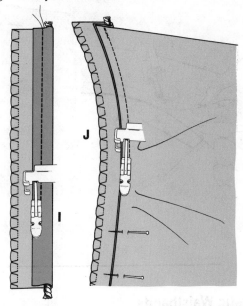

close to the cord as shown. Remove pins as you stitch. Fold strip to underside, letting the cording extend, as in **K.** Steam-press to shape the cording and the free edge of the strip. Tack edge at crossing seams.

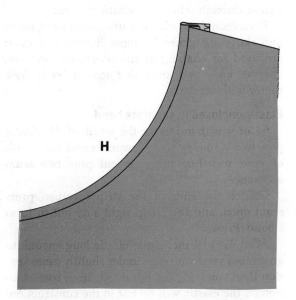

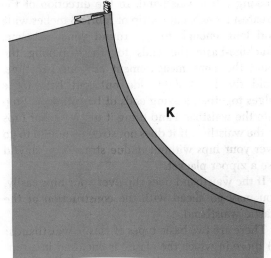

Soft-Roll Edge Finish

A bound edge with a bold, soft roll is an attractive finish for the neckline and armholes of tank tops and jumpers. Trim the garment edges to allow for a ½-inch seam allowance. Cut the strip for binding 2¾ inches wide on the crosswise direction of the knit. Set your sewing machine for a 15 stitch length and attach the straight-stitch presser foot. Then, with right sides together, stitch the binding strip to the garment ½ inch from edge; stretch the strip slightly at the curves, as in **A**.

Press seam allowances and stitching to remove any ripples along the curve. Then roll the binding over both seam allowances and place pins perpendicular to the edge along the crevice of the seam, catching the unfinished side of the binding, as in **B**.

Stitch in the crevice of the seam from the right side, using the zipper foot adjusted to the left side of the needle, and a 15 to 20 stitch length, as at **C**. When stitching is completed, trim the seam allowance of the binding close to the stitching.

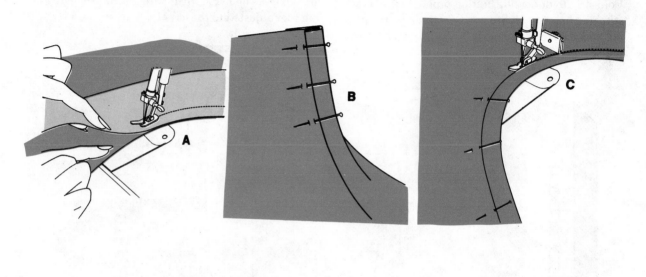

Elastic Waistbands

In most knit skirts and pants, you may omit the placket unless you have a larger-than-average difference between your waist and hip measurements. Test the knit fabric for suitability by making a test waistband. In the direction of the greatest stretch, cut a strip of fabric 3 inches wide and long enough to go around your waistline. Machine-baste the ends together, making the band the same measurement as your waistline. Fold the band right side out and hand-baste edges together, leaving ends of basting free. Step into the waistband and bring it up over your hips to the waistline. If it does not stretch enough to go over your hips without undue strain, you should use a zipper placket.

If the waistband does slip over your hips easily, you may go ahead with the construction of the elastic waistband.

There are two basic types of elastic waistbands: 1) those in which the elastic is enclosed in a separate band, which is then applied as a unit to the garment; and 2) those in which the garment fabric is cut to provide an allowance for a hem or casing through which the elastic will run.

Even though an elastic waistband is used, pants and skirts are generally more flattering if darts are used for shaping at the waistline; however, sweater knits and knits that stretch freely look better without darts.

Elastic enclosed in separate band

• Cut waistband twice the width of the elastic plus two ⅝-inch seam allowances and the length of your waistline measurement plus two seam allowances.

• Stitch the ends of the strip together, press seam open, and fold strip right side out to form a band. Press.

• Cut ¾- to 1-inch-wide elastic long enough to go around your waistline under slightly more tension than you need for a snug fit, since some tension on the elastic will be lost in the construction.

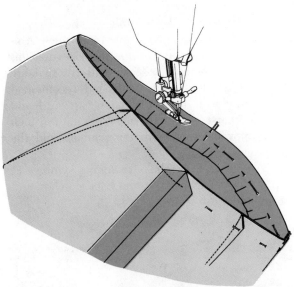

Add 1 inch to the length for an overlapped joining and then hand-whip the joining.

• Divide and pin-mark both the waistband and the garment into four equal portions.

• Place elastic inside band and pin seam allowances of band together at 2-inch intervals.

• Pin waistband unit to garment waistline, right sides together, matching the four points that divide the two edges into equal portions. Place waistband joining seam at center back or at a side seam.

• Equip machine with the zipper foot or the overedge foot, and set the machine for a narrow zig-zag or a straight stretch stitch. Test-stitch to see that machine settings are correct and that the needle does not strike the foot.

• Place garment under foot, right side down, with open edge of foot against the elastic.

• Stitch slowly, stretching the band if necessary and easing the garment seam to the band.

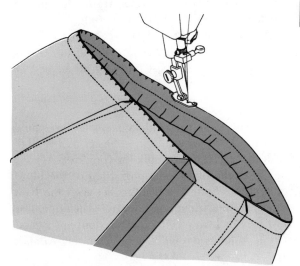

• Trim the center seam allowance to ¼ inch and machine-overedge the remaining seam allowances together. See illustration at bottom of previous column.

• Tack seam allowances to crossing seams.

Elastic enclosed in hem or casing

• Measure waistband elastic to fit snugly around your waistline and add 1 inch for overlapping ends. Hand-whip overlap of elastic together.

• Machine-overedge waistline seam allowance of garment.

• Turn garment hem over the elastic and pin at lower edge of elastic at 2-inch intervals. Hand-baste if necessary. Stitch with garment right side up, open side of zipper foot against elastic, and use a straight stretch stitch.

• To prevent elastic from turning, distribute ease evenly over the elastic, pinning through casing and elastic at crossing seams. Stitch in the crevice of each crossing seam through the casing and the elastic from the right side. Tie thread ends.

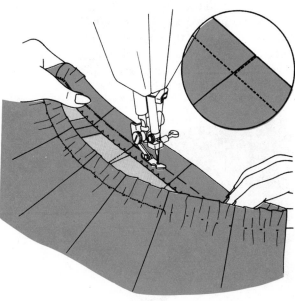

Elastic stitched to casing

• Measure and cut ¾-inch waistband elastic 1 inch less than your waist measurement.

• Overlap ends ½ inch and stitch joining.

• Divide elastic and waistline into 4 equal parts and mark with pins.

• Place top edge of the elastic ⅛ inch from edge on inside of the garment.

• Using the general-purpose presser foot and the straight stretch stitch, stitch near the lower edge of the elastic while holding the garment and elastic under enough tension to stretch the elastic to fit the fabric.

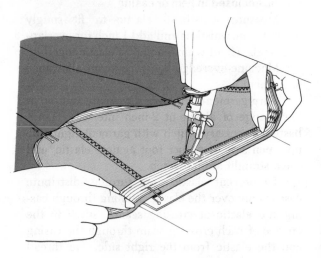

• Turn the elastic and fabric once to the inside. The elastic will then be covered.

• While holding the fabric and elastic under tension, stitch near the edge of the elastic through the turned fabric, the elastic, and the garment. Again, use the general-purpose presser foot and the straight stretch stitch.

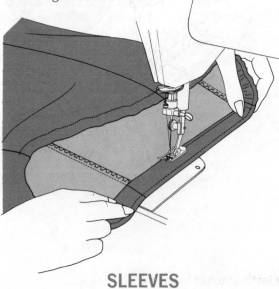

SLEEVES

Always set sleeves in firm and medium-firm knits by the conventional method for woven fabrics and finish the seam allowances, ⅜ inch wide, together.

On stretchable knits, follow the sweater method. Stitch the open sleeve to an open armhole and stitch the underarm and sleeve seams later as one continuous seam. Patterns that are designed for stretchable knits and recommend this method have a sleeve with less cap width and less ease than regular patterns. Work with ⅜-inch seam allowances on both the armhole and the sleeve cap.

• Pin sleeve to armhole, matching symbols at top of sleeve cap, at front and back notches, and at the underarm seams.

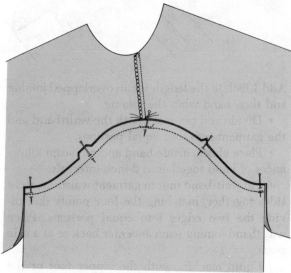

• Using the straight stretch stitch, straight-stitch presser foot and throat plate, and with garment side up, stitch from top of sleeve cap to underarm seam. Stretch the seam as you stitch.

• Overlap the stitching at the top of the sleeve cap and stitch the second side of the sleeve.

• Apply an overedge finish. On thin knits, where a narrower than ⅜-inch seam allowance is appropriate, trim seam, then overedge.

• Stitch underarm and sleeve seam the same way, matching crossing seams at the underarm.

• Apply steam to assist recovery of shape.

HEMS

Follow the same preparatory steps for hemming as for hemming woven fabrics. Select a hem-edge finish that has the least bulk for your knit. Always use either the blind hemming stitch or the blind catch stitch, both of which go between the hem edge and the garment and not over the edge. For most firm or heavy knits, use the double-stitched hem in which two rows of blind hemming stitches support the weight of the hem.

FABRICS

Characteristics. These knits are stable and have the hand of woven fabrics, minimum lengthwise stretch, and crosswise stretch of less than 1 1/4 inches in 8 inches.

Types. Double knits; bonded knits; firm, untextured warp knits; jacquard knits.

Fiber Content: All polyester, all wool, fiber blends and yarn mixtures of wool/nylon, wool/polyester, cotton/polyester, nylon/acrylic, etc.

PATTERN CHOICE

Dresses—look for simple style lines; darted or seamed shaping; pocket details; topstitched seams; soft pleats; collars, cuffs, facings; eased fullness; A-line, fitted one-piece styling; waistline joinings.

Also—separates, pants costumes, jackets, soft suits, children's wear, light- or medium-weight coats, some slacks and jackets for men.

PREPARATIONS

- Fold on lengthwise wale or rib, square ends, baste ends and edges for shrinking (unless fabric is labeled "preshrunk").
- Woolens—have shrunk by tailor or dry cleaner.
- Polyesters—launder to remove excess finishing solution.
- All other washables—launder by hand or machine according to label.
- Bonded knits—straighten according to face fabric; shrinking is usually not necessary.

PATTERN FITTING

- Purchase your regular pattern type and size.
- Allow no less than basic ease allowances.
- Fit pattern accurately to reduce garment fittings during construction.

CUTTING AND MARKING

- Fold fabric right side out on lengthwise rib.
- Follow "with nap" layout.
- Pin with ball-point or smooth, new pins.
- Cut with sharp shears.
- Cut notches outward.
- Mark center front and back lines with hand basting.
- Mark internal details with tailor's tacks.

STAY STITCHING

- Stay neckline and waistline seams with regular straight stitching (12 stitch length) or chain-stitching.
- Use Even Feed foot to avoid easing or stretching seam line.

STITCHING

- These fabrics are generally easy to stitch.
- Use size 14 regular or ball-point needle with polyester-core or spun-polyester thread.
- Use size 11 regular or ball-point needle with silk or nylon thread.
- Balance tensions.
- Use normal or regular presser-foot pressure.
- Set stitch length at 12 for straight seams, at 15 for curves.
- Kinds of stitches: regular straight stitch with strong thread; straight stretch stitch; narrow zig-zag (1-1 1/2 stitch width).
- Guide and gently support seam while stitching, holding it under tension with both hands, or
- Use the Even Feed foot.

SEAMS AND SEAM FINISHES

- For general use: Use plain seams pressed open, no seam finish.
- For unlined jackets, coats, pants, armhole of set-in sleeves: Use straight-stitched seam, pressed in one direction, cut to 3/8 inch or half-width, and edges finished together with machine overedge.
- To accent style lines: Topstitch seams with buttonhole twist or heavy thread. Use the Even Feed foot to reduce need for basting.
- For seams that must not stretch, such as shoulder and waistline seams: Use stayed seams.

FACINGS, INTERFACINGS, LININGS, UNDERLININGS

- Finish shaped facings with machine overedge stitch. Always understitch facing to seam allowances.
- Use lightweight woven or nonwoven interfacing for dresses.
- Use lightweight tailor's canvas in the conventional way to interface jackets or coats.
- For quick method, apply interfacing to facing with thermoplastic adhesive, but cut off seam allowances.
- Underlining or lining is optional for dresses, but recommended for tailored jackets or coats.

PRESSING

- Limit iron temperature to that for fiber with lowest heat requirement.
- Use damp cheesecloth to produce steam.
- Press at each construction step.
- Place heavy paper under seams and darts to keep them from marking the right side when pressed.

HEMS AND EDGE FINISHES

- For fashion garments—use blind hemming methods; consider also the double-stitched hem.
- For pants, sleeves, children's dresses and straight hems in fashion garments, use machine blind stitch.
- Edge finishes, such as folded straight-cut bands and cross- and diagonal-cut bindings, may be used instead of conventional hems.

FABRICS

Characteristics. These knits have:
—firmness without rigidity
—loft without cumbersome bulk
—soft, supple hand
—parallel rows of chainstitching on back of fabric, which hold filling yarns together.

Types. Raschel (often with embroidery-like surface) and other nubby knits that have medium stretch in both directions.

Fiber Content: Wool, polyester, acrylic cotton blend. Yarn may be smooth, looped, or chenille type.

PATTERN CHOICE

Dresses—look for simple lines, ease for shaping (gathers disappear as ease), soft unpressed pleats, set-in or raglan sleeves.

Pants—long and graceful or short.

Vests—long, sleeveless.

Skirts—wrap-around, gathered, or softly pleated.

Also—scarves, stoles, coats, hooded capes.

PREPARATIONS

- Fold lengthwise on chainstitch visible on back of fabric, right sides together.
- Cut ends crosswise along single filling yarn.
- Pull diagonally to square ends.
- Baste ends and edges for shrinking when necessary.
- Polyesters—launder to remove finishing solution.
- Woolens—have shrunk by tailor or dry cleaner.
- Acrylics—usually need no shrinking.
- Cottons—refer to label; should be easy-care and ready-to-sew.

PATTERN FITTING

- Purchase your regular pattern type and size.
- Allow no less than basic ease allowances. (Remember, these fabrics have minimum-to-medium stretch.)
- Fit pattern accurately, to reduce garment fittings during construction.

CUTTING AND MARKING

- Fold right sides together on lengthwise chain.
- Match patterns or designs.
- Determine which end of chain will unchain and use that end for tops of all pattern pieces.
- Lay out pattern according to "with nap" direction.
- Place pins close together; do not allow fabric to hang over table edge.
- Cut with long, even strokes, using sharp shears. Do not cut notches.
- Mark with basting lines and tailor's tacks.

STAY STITCHING

- Do **not** use conventional stay stitching.
- Through a single layer of fabric, stitch 1/4 inch from seam edges to prevent raveling, using straight stitch, 15 stitch length.
- Do this on all edges except bottom edges of sections before you begin any construction.

STITCHING

- These fabrics are generally easy to stitch.
- Use size 14 regular or ball-point needle with polyester-core or all-polyester thread.
- Use size 11 regular or ball-point needle with silk or nylon thread.
- Balance tensions.
- Set stitch length at 12 for straight seams, at 15 for curves.
- Use normal or regular presser-foot pressure.
- Encircle presser-foot toes with a 1/4-inch width of transparent tape to prevent loops of fabric yarn from catching on presser foot.

SEAMS AND SEAM FINISHES

- You do not need to stay seams that are stitched with the straight stretch stitch.
- Stay seams that are stitched with regular straight stitch to prevent pulling or "slipping." Use woven-edge or rayon bias seam binding, or twill tape. Shrink before using.
- Trim seam edges to eliminate frays.
- Finish seam edges separately when open, or together when pressed in one direction, with a zig-zag seam finish:
  1) overedge (Disc 22) and overedge foot.
  2) multi-stitch zig-zag.
  3) multi-stretch (Disc 55).
  4) blindstitch pattern.
  5) overedge stretch (Disc 59).

FACINGS, INTERFACINGS, LININGS, UNDERLININGS

- Facings—standard shaped facings for less bulky varieties; color-matched taffeta or soft-surfaced woven fabric for bulky knits. Understitching is appropriate. Optional: instead of using facings, finish edges with braid, bindings, or self-fabric bands.
- Interfacing—nonwoven or woven, soft or crisp, depending on styling. Test see-through effect and color-match interfacing to knit or underlined interfaced portion.
- Lining—optional, depending on styling.
- Underlining—optional, depending on styling. If you use underlining, preserve soft, supple hand of combined fabrics and color-match.

PRESSING

- Limit iron temperature to that for fiber with lowest heat requirement.
- Use damp cheesecloth to produce moisture.
- When pressing soft-surfaced raschels: stop pressing before fabric is dry; brush surface with soft brush or piece of same fabric; do not move fabric until dry.
- Press at each construction step.

HEMS AND EDGE FINISHES

- For fashion garments—use blind hemming methods; consider also the double-stitched hem.
- For casual garments—straight-stitch hem by machine, but hem edge should be machine-finished rather than turned.

Sweater and Loose, Lofty, Stretchable Knits

FABRICS

Characteristics. These knits look and act like hand knits; stretch freely in both directions; shape to the body; and have a loose, lofty look.

Types. Patterned, plain, or rib knits.

Fiber Content. Wool, polyester, or acrylic fibers or blends of these fibers.

PATTERN CHOICE

Choose patterns marked "for knits only" or with close-to-the-body styling.

Dresses—straight and slim with few or no darts, set-in or raglan sleeves, scoop or high neckline.

Vests—long, sleeveless.

Sweaters—cardigan or turtleneck.

Pants outfits—with sweater overblouse.

Scarves, ponchos.

Note: Sweater knits can also be used for couturier two-piece, tailored outfits if they are mounted over a firm, layered base of underlining, thin hair canvas, and lining. In this case, construction methods are the same as for woven fabrics.

PREPARATIONS

- Relax fabric by allowing it to lie flat on floor or table overnight.
- Cut ends along crosswise courses.
- Fold on lengthwise rib, right side out.
- Pull diagonally to straighten crosswise ends.
- Square ends with table edges.

PATTERN FITTING

- Pattern should accommodate body measurements only. All ease can come from the fabric itself for both length and girth measurements.
- Often, one size smaller than you normally wear is adequate.

CUTTING AND MARKING

- Observe grain-line principles.
- Pin sparingly.
- Do not let fabric hang over table edge.
- Lay out pattern according to "with nap" directions.
- Cut with strong, sharp shears.
- Do not cut notches.
- Mark with basting lines and tailor's tacks.

STAY STITCHING

- Do **not** use conventional stay stitching.
- Through a single layer of fabric, stitch 1/4 inch from seam edges to prevent raveling, using straight or chainstitch, 12 stitch length. Stitch slowly and neither ease nor stretch edges. The Even Feed foot helps with this stitching.
- Mount very loosely knit fabrics on tissue or pulpy paper for this stitching. Tear away paper after stitching.

STITCHING

- Requirements: 1) a stitch that will elongate, such as a straight stretch stitch, plain zig-zag (1/2-1 stitch width, 20 stitch length), or a plain straight stitch (15 stitch length) done under tension. 2) strong thread, such as polyester core or spun polyester with size 14 needle; or nylon or silk with size 11 needle.
- Use normal or regular presser-foot pressure.
- Balance tensions.
- Use ball-point needle to prevent snags.

SEAMS AND SEAM FINISHES

- Usually, seam edges are pressed and finished together. Pressed-open seam edges tend to roll.
- Most seams should **not** be stayed so that they will stretch with body movement.
- To prevent drawn seams, hand-baste. Leave bottom thread end long and free. Allow garment sections to hang overnight. Then stitch.
- Seams that should not stretch, such as some shoulder, back-of-neck, or waistline-joining seams, should be stayed with woven-edge seam binding or narrow twill tape (both shrunk).
- Seams that should stretch but need some support can be stayed with 1/4-inch "light soft" elastic.
- Select a seam-finishing stitch that will stretch, flatten, and retain the yarn ends but will not be harsh.
- Apply the seam-finishing stitch first, then trim seam allowance to 1/2-to-1/4-inch width. Heavy fabrics usually have wider seam allowances than medium-weight fabrics.

FACINGS, INTERFACINGS, LININGS, UNDERLININGS

- Not used, except for unusual styling; e.g., couturier 2-piece outfits are mounted over color-matched underlining, lightweight canvas interfacing, and a soft lining.

PRESSING

- Limit iron temperature to that for fiber with lowest heat requirement.
- Block rather than press. Steam, holding iron above the pressing surface, and allow fabric to dry before moving it with both hands.

HEMS AND EDGE FINISHES

- For dress hems—use a machine seam finish for edge and blind hemming for stitching hem; consider also the double-stitched hem.
- For sweater hems—use seam finish for edge and machine blindstitch for hemming.
- Apply finishing bands or folds of knit fabric, cut for greatest stretch, to finish neckline, sleeve ends, armhole, or bottom edge. These bands may be applied with or without being stretched, depending on styling.

FABRICS

Characteristics. Knits in this group are thin and supple; have moderate to maximum crosswise stretch and moderate lengthwise stretch; and tend to cling to the figure.

Types. Solid-color, printed, or knitted with a design. Surface may be brushed, dull or lustrous. Yarns may be filament, textured or crimped.

Fiber Content. Cotton, wool, triacetate, polyester, acrylic, or nylon.

PATTERN CHOICE

Fashion uses these fabrics for three distinctive "looks"—skinny and covered, elegantly draped, and comfortably supple.

Dresses—sportive, casual, dressy, or high-fashion.

Leisure Wear—turtleneck tops, gathered and scoop-neckline tops, shirts, draped jumpsuits. Children's dresses and fitted tops and men's shirts.

PREPARATIONS

- If fabric is tubular, cut on lengthwise rib.
- Plan not to use fold, which seldom will press out.
- Refold on lengthwise rib for cutting.
- Square and cut ends of fabric with table edges.
- Launder to shrink washable fabrics.
- Have dry cleaner shrink wool.
- Before cutting out pattern, relax fabric by allowing it to lie flat on table or floor overnight.

PATTERN FITTING

- Purchase your regular pattern type and size for supple or draped styling.
- Purchase patterns labeled "For stretchable knits only" for the skinny and covered look.
- Fit and alter pattern carefully before cutting to reduce number of fittings during construction.
- Handle design ease in accordance with the fashion look you intend to interpret.

CUTTING AND MARKING

- Cut on soft surface.
- Do not let fabric hang over table edge.
- Pin difficult-to-control fabrics to tissue for cutting.
- Use ball-point or fine, smooth pins, placed within seam allowances.
- Cut notches outward.
- Mark internal details with tailor's tacks.
- Use a whole pattern piece, rather than a half, for cutting crosswise stripes that cannot be squared.

STAY STITCHING

- Stay-stitch only neckline and waistline-joining seams.
- Use chainstitch or regular straight stitch, 15 stitch length. Even Feed foot eliminates the need for easing or stretching.

STITCHING

- For lightweight wool jersey, use silk thread, size 11 needle, regular straight stitch, 12 to 15 stitch length.

- For cotton knits, use fine spun polyester or polyester-core thread, size 11 needle, and regular straight stitch; or ball-point needle, straight stretch stitch and mercerized thread.
- For shiny-surfaced synthetics, use silk or nylon thread, ball-point needle or regular size 9 or 11 needle, and straight stretch stitch or regular straight stitch, 12 stitch length.
- Stitch all seams under tension by holding them in back and front of presser foot, or use the Even Feed foot.
- Normal or above-normal presser-foot pressure.
- Use straight-stitch presser foot and throat plate for all straight stitching.
- If you encounter stitching problems, remember: **Skips** result from too coarse needle, too heavy thread, too little tension on the fabric while stitching, or bent needle. **Fabric pulls** result from too heavy needle and thread or blunt needle. **Puckered seams** result from not supporting fabric while stitching, unbalanced tensions, too tight tensions, too long stitches. **Stitching through paper** next to feed helps to eliminate some puckering and skipping.

SEAMS AND SEAM FINISHES

- Kind of seaming depends on kind of garment.
- Fashion garments are made with plain, pressed-open seams with no seam finish.
- Casual garments are made with seam edges pressed in one direction, trimmed to 1/4-to-3/8-inch width and finished together.
- The overedge stretch stitch (*Flexi-Stitch* Disc 59) is preferred for seam finishing.
- Alternatives are: blindstitch, multi-stitch zig-zag, regular overedge (Disc 22), plain zig-zag (3 to 5 stitch width).

FACINGS, INTERFACINGS, LININGS, UNDERLININGS

- Skinny-look garments need none.
- Slim, straight-line dresses need none in body of garment but require soft interfacing in cuffs, collars, or faced necklines.
- Softly draped fashions usually require soft, firm underlining as a shape-builder.
- Loft is achieved with nonwoven all-polyester, all-bias interfacing.

PRESSING

- Limit iron temperature to that for fiber with lowest heat requirement.
- Pressing should be gentle and of a blocking nature.
- Use moist cheesecloth to produce steam.
- Do not over-press.

HEMS AND EDGE FINISHES

- For fashion garments—finish hem edge with straight stitching, 15 stitch length, placed 1/4 inch from straight cut edge, and use blind hemming stitch.
- For casual garments—machine-blindstitch hems.
- Folded bands may be substituted for hems.
- Narrow self bindings are suitable for necklines and armholes.

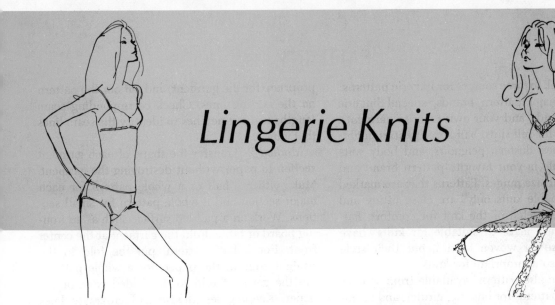

Lingerie Knits

NOW THAT NYLON TRICOT CAN BE PURCHASED by the yard, many women are finding that sewing lingerie can be both fun and economical.

Lingerie can be made amazingly fast because it requires little if any hand basting, pressing, or hand finishing. Most garments have very few seams, and the elastic and lace finishes are simple to apply with a zig-zag sewing machine.

The very simplicity of lingerie sewing may seem a little strange to you at first. You may have a tendency to overdo each step. But, once you relax, develop a light touch, and realize that a cut edge is acceptable (because tricot does not ravel), you will quickly learn to stitch seams and finishes on your machine without hand basting.

TRICOT FABRICS

Tricot is a two-thread warp knit that will not run or ravel because of its interlocking yarns. It has fine vertical ribs, or wales, on the right side and crosswise courses on the wrong side; the direction of greatest stretch is crosswise. The fabric is usually 108 inches wide although you may find it sold in narrower widths if the yardage has been split for easier handling.

The fiber content can be all nylon, a blend of nylon and acetate, or triacetate. Some stretch tricot fabrics contain spandex yarns to give light figure control. The surface may be smooth, satin-like, crepe-like, or napped, depending on the texture of the yarn used in knitting.

Tricot

Tricot comes in different weights, ranging from very sheer to heavy, depending on the size of the yarn and how closely it is knitted. Heavy tricots are used for robes, pajamas, and opaque slips. Medium tricots are used for panties, slips, nightgowns, pajamas, chemises, and the underlayer of nightgowns and peignoirs designed for two-layer construction. Sheer tricot resembles chiffon and is used for the outer layer of nightgowns and peignoirs, for underlining lace sections and insertions, and for edge trims. Brushed nylon, which has a napped surface, is suitable for warm robes and pajamas.

Stabilized nylon tricot has a special finish that limits its stretch and the amount of static it generates. Thus it is suitable for slips that are to be worn under knit dresses where noncling characteristics are essential.

Stretch tricot is usually made of nylon and spandex yarns and is used for light figure control in panties, briefs, bras, sections of bra-slips, and body suits.

PATTERNS

You can look to three sources for lingerie patterns: the four major pattern brands, special lingerie pattern brands, and your own favorite garments.

Patterns for full slips, half slips, panties, nightgowns, robes, dusters, peignoirs, and body suits are available in your favorite pattern brand and in the usual size ranges. Patterns that are marked "for stretchable knits only" are close fitting and rely on the stretch of the knit for comfort. Patterns that are marked "suitable for knits" have enough ease for woven fabrics, but their style lines are also appropriate for knits.

There are also patterns available from sources that make patterns for lingerie, girdles, and swimwear only. These are usually multi-size patterns that can be used for any size within a range of sizes, depending on which cutting line you use. Because these patterns usually have seam allowances other than the standard ⅝-inch width, it is wise to read the pattern instructions carefully.

The most challenging type of pattern is the one you cut yourself from a favorite garment. There are two ways to proceed.

Method 1. Cut apart a discarded garment. Cut on the seam lines and carefully lay each section on paper, keeping lengthwise and crosswise lines true. Mark the edges and then mark a ¼-, ½-, or ⅝-inch seam allowance, whichever is most ap-

propriate for the garment, and cut out the pattern on the cutting lines. Check corresponding seam lengths and cut notches to identify the seam lines that join.

Method 2. Transfer the shape of each garment section to paper without destroying the garment. Make either a half or a whole pattern for each major section and a whole pattern for small sections. Work on a padded surface such as an ironing board or table. Fold the garment at the center front. For a half pattern, pin the fold to the straight edge of the paper; for a whole pattern, pin the garment fold to the folded edge of the paper. Keeping lengthwise and crosswise lines straight, plunge pins through the garment seam lines into the paper and padded surface at short intervals (every ½ inch on straight seams; every ⅛ inch on curved seams). Remove the garment and draw the seam lines, following the pinholes in the paper. Add seam allowances and mark cutting lines. Follow the same procedure for each large section, and mark all edges for small sections.

Because tricot is so wide, you will usually be cutting two or more garments at one time; you will find this easier if you lay out whole, rather than half, patterns.

NOTIONS AND TRIMMINGS

Needles and thread must be fine; thread must also be strong. Nylon twist, silk, and fine spun polyester labeled "for lingerie" are the best threads for stitching tricot because they can be used with fine needles. Choose size 11 ball-point needles, Singer number 2021 or 2045. Size 11 regular needles will also work satisfactorily in many cases, but ball-point needles are recommended because they are especially designed for stitching knits.

Lace is an important edge finish for tricot garments and for decorative sections and insertions. Choose nylon or polyester lace because it requires no ironing and wears well. Lace comes in three forms. Lace for edging has one selvage edge and one decorative edge; it comes in widths from ½ inch to more than 3 inches. Lace for insertions

Edging   Insertion   Galloon

has two selvage edges and comes in widths from ½ inch to more than 3 inches. A third form, galloon lace, has two decorative edges and comes in a variety of widths.

Elastic in lingerie is primarily functional but it can also be decorative. The following descriptions of the different kinds of elastic and their uses will enable you to select the one that is best for your purpose.

Elastic braid (also called tunneling elastic) is the most familiar type. It looks the same on both sides and on both edges. It has lengthwise ridges of rubber or spandex. When stretched, elastic braid narrows. It comes in widths of ¼, ⅜, ⅓, ¾ and 1 inch. The yarn may be rayon, nylon, mercerized cotton or a blend. Rayon elastic braid relaxes when wet and should not be used for swimwear. Elastic braid is usually drawn through a hem or casing rather than stitched to an edge. Stitching should always be done between the lengthwise ridges; when stitching penetrates the lengthwise ridges, the rubber or spandex is damaged or broken and the elasticity is weakened.

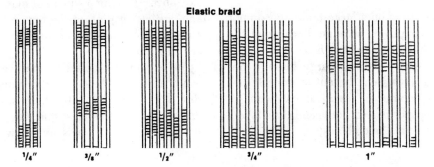

Elastic braid

¼"   ⅜"   ½"   ¾"   1"

Elastic edging for lingerie can be of either braid or web construction. Braid narrows when stretched; webbing does not. Edging always has one decorative edge that resembles a frill or picot. Widths of ⅝ or ½ inch are suitable for waist-bands of half-slips and panties; widths of ⅜ or ¼ inch, for legbands of panties and briefs. Elastic edging is not enclosed in a casing; it is applied to either the outside or the inside edge of the garment. Refer to page 465.

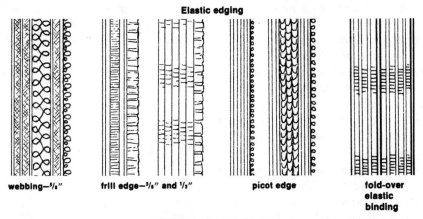

Elastic edging

webbing—⅝"   frill edge—⅜" and ½"   picot edge   fold-over elastic binding

PREPARATIONS

Launder nylon tricot before cutting the garment to prevent shrinkage later and to remove any finishing solution, which could cause stitching problems. Use an antistatic fabric softener to reduce the tendency of nylon tricot to cling to the needle during stitching. After laundering, place fabric and a dry Turkish towel in a dryer set at low temperature. (The towel will help to absorb moisture.) Remove fabric when not quite dry. If you do not have a low-heat dryer, roll the fabric in a Turkish towel to remove as much moisture as possible and finish drying by draping the fabric over a shower rod.

Pressing should not be necessary; but if there are wrinkles, press at a low temperature, moving the iron in a lengthwise direction only.

Prepare your pattern carefully. Patterns for tricot garments that fit the figure closely should measure at least as much as your figure and preferably 1 to 2 inches more at the hipline to allow ease. If you ordinarily need to increase or decrease the crotch depth on pants, apply the same alteration to lingerie pants patterns. Nightgowns should be roomy enough for comfort, and they look best with considerable ease. All fitting changes should be made at the pattern-alteration step so that construction can be completed without further fitting.

LAYOUT AND CUTTING

The right side of tricot is the side with fine length-wise ribs. On sheer tricot, it is sometimes difficult to see the ribs. For a quick test, stretch a crosswise edge. Tricot always rolls to the right side. Mark the wrong side with strips of magic transparent tape.

Lay out the fabric on a large table and do not let the fabric hang over the edge. Because of the 108-inch width, cutting on the floor or a bed is sometimes necessary when a large table is not available. Four layers can be cut at once if you are making a number of identical garments. A layer of tissue paper placed between fabric layers will help you to cut a smooth edge.

Tricot stretches most in the crosswise direction, always cut it with the stretch running across the figure. Cut crotch sections with the stretch running from back to front. Use ball-point pins and pin sparingly, preferably within seam allowances. Placing a square of magic transparent tape, instead of pins, at the top and bottom edge of each pattern piece is useful in holding the pattern on grain.

Cut extended notches to mark corresponding seams, and trim them off as you approach them when stitching. Cut with sharp scissors and be careful to cut all edges smoothly, especially if your pattern has narrow seam allowances.

PREPARING TO STITCH

Begin your sewing with a lint-free, carefully oiled sewing machine. Put in a new ball-point needle and thread it with fine, strong thread. Set the presser-foot pressure at normal or medium and the stitch length between 12 and 20, depending on the kind of stitch you have chosen to use. Refer to page 427 for appropriate stitches. If you are using a plain straight stitch or a straight stretch stitch, use the straight-stitch throat plate and the presser foot recommended for the kind of stitch and seam you will use. Regulate the needle-thread tension to produce a balanced stitch that looks the same on both sides. The best tension setting is usually a point or two lower than you regularly use for other fabrics. If your sewing machine has a "fast" and "slow" speed setting, use the slow setting because you should stitch slowly enough to control the unbasted seam edges. Remember to guide and support all lengthwise seams with one hand in front and one hand in back of the presser foot to keep the seam under tension during stitching.

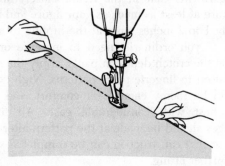

Test-stitch seams on fabric scraps before stitching your garment. This will enable you to get the feel of handling the fabric. Also, it will indicate whether your tension, pressure, stitch length, needle and thread sizes are correct.

Always position the needle in the fabric at the start of a seam, then lower the presser foot. Hold the thread ends until a few stitches have been made. This procedure is essential to prevent thread and fabric from jamming at the start. The softness of the fabric, coupled with the strength of the thread, makes this necessary.

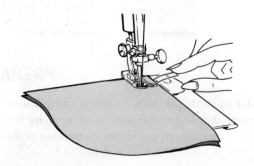

If skipped stitches appear, look first at thread and needle size and remember that "fine" is the requirement. To rule out the needle as the cause, it is always a good idea to change the needle. Presser-foot pressure may not be heavy enough, so increase it slightly and also increase the tension under which you are holding the fabric while stitching. Needle-thread tension, unless it is very high, is seldom a cause of skipped stitches.

If skipped stitches appear after you have been stitching for some time, the cause may be that the needle has lost its set and has become slanted away from the sewing-hook point, which picks up the thread loop from the needle. Sometimes you can correct an out-of-set needle by drawing your thumb down the long-groove side of the needle, exerting slight pressure to flex the needle back into its original position. *Do not* try to bend the needle; merely stroke it a few times, flexing the lower part back slightly. Before testing the stitching, turn the hand wheel by hand to make certain the needle enters the hole in the throat plate without rubbing or striking the edge. Then test-stitch on a fabric scrap.

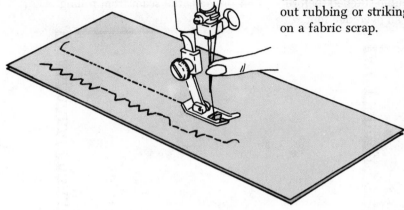

SEAMS AND DARTS

Seams

The following guidelines will help you to handle seams in tricot lingerie.

• Seams in tricot lingerie are always either double-stitched or stitched and finished with a single row of machine overedge stitching.

• Always stitch seams under tension by guiding and supporting the fabric.

• Almost all seams are lengthwise on both the fabric and the garment. The few exceptions are crotch seams in briefs and the horizontal seams at or above the waistline in slips and nightgowns.

• Pin short seams at notches and ends; long seams at 12-inch intervals.

• Finish crosswise edges with elastic, lace, or decorative edge finishes.

Double-stitched seams. The kind of double-stitched seam you select will depend on both the abilities of your sewing machine and personal preference. In the two seams where zig-zag or overedge stitches are placed over the seam edges, the straight stitching may be done either before or after the finishing stitch. When the straight stitching is done last, the zipper foot may be substituted for the straight-stitch presser foot.

Straight or straight stretch stitch. Use the straight-stitch presser foot and throat plate, center needle position, and a 15 stitch length or straight stretch settings. Stitch on the seam line and again ⅛ inch outside the seam line. Trim seam allowances near second stitching.

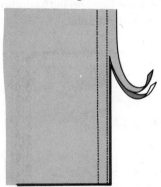

Straight and zig-zag stitches. Straight-stitch on the seam line as above. Trim seam allowances to ⅛ inch. Use zig-zag throat plate and overedge foot, a zig-zag stitch, right needle position, 2½ to 3 stitch width, and 20 stitch length. Guide seam edges along the right edge of the overedge foot.

Straight and overedge stitches. Straight-stitch on seam line as above. Trim seam allowances to ⅛ inch. Use zig-zag throat plate and overedge foot, overedge stitch or overedge stretch stitch, right needle position, 2½ to 3 stitch width, and 20 stitch length. Guide seam edges along right edge of foot. Seams may be double-stitched before trimming if you do not have an overedge foot.

Chainstitch. Use chainstitch accessories and 15 stitch length. Stitch on the seam line. Stitch second row close to first row, outside the seam line and in the opposite direction from the first stitching. Stitch the third row close to the second row, outside the seam line and in the opposite direction from the second stitching.

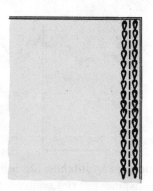

Seams stitched and finished with one stitching

Some sewing machines are capable of stitching and finishing in one step.

Overedge stretch stitch. Trim seam allowances to ¼ inch or slightly less for a seam narrower than ¼ inch. Use the overedge stretch stitch and either the overedge or the general-purpose presser foot. Set stitch width at 5 for a ¼-inch seam or between 3 and 5 for a narrower seam. Use right needle

position setting when using the overedge foot with a stitch width less than 5. Guide the edges of the seam along the right-hand edge of the overedge foot or under the general-purpose presser foot so that the needle goes over the right-hand seam edge rather than through it. The overedge foot prevents the seam from rolling.

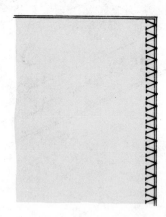

Overedge stitch. Follow the same procedure as described for the overedge stretch stitch above, but use a 15 to 20 stitch length and the overedge stitch.

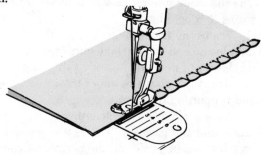

Slant overedge stitch. Some models of sewing machines make a slant overedge stitch instead of the overedge stretch stitch. Refer to your sewing machine instruction book for machine settings. Trim seam allowances to a scant ¼ inch. Place trimmed seam under general-purpose presser foot with seam edges to your left. For a slightly narrower seam, use a stitch width setting less than 5.

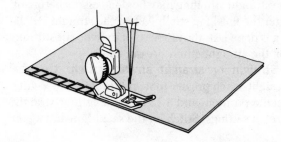

Darts

In tricot lingerie, darts are usually in the bodice sections of full slips, nightgowns, pajama tops, and bras. Trim away the fold of the dart by cutting a scant ¼ inch inside the stitching lines. Treat the stitching lines as seams. Where the darted section is of more than one layer, stitch all layers as one. With a seam-finishing stitch, stitch from the widest end of the dart to the point, then pivot on the needle and turn the fabric around half circle for the second stitching. Lower the presser foot and raise the needle. Set the machine for straight or straight stretch stitching, and stitch close to the inside of the first stitching. The reason for this procedure is that threads used for lingerie seldom remain knotted and in this way you can achieve neatness.

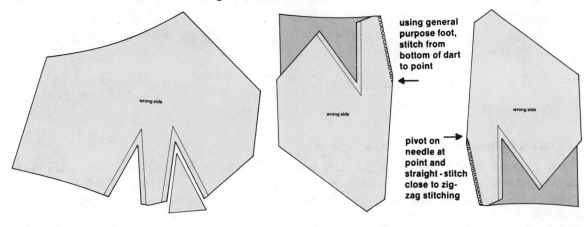

Seams in Pants

Crotch Seams in Briefs

Briefs are made from three pattern sections: front, back, and crotch. The crotch section is double with the lengthwise rib running across the section.

Stitch side seam first to ensure correct handling of right and wrong sides of these sections, which can easily be confused if crotch seams are made first.

Join front crotch seam, placing right sides of crotch sections next to the front section, front section in between. Stitch with straight stretch stitch and trim seam allowance to a scant ¼ inch; or trim seam allowances first and stitch with stretch overedge stitch.

Pin back seam of outside crotch section to the right side of the back.

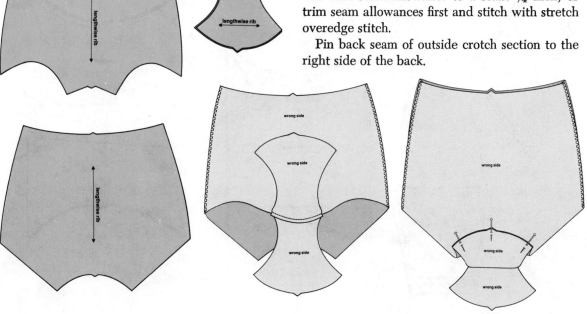

Pin back seam of inside crotch section to the wrong side of the back by bringing it entirely around the top of the briefs, crushing the fabric. Stitch in the same way as the front crotch seam.

Pull the body of the garment through one open side of the crotch section and turn it right side out. Seams will be concealed inside crotch sections.

To finish briefs, refer to *Elastic Finishes* on page 464.

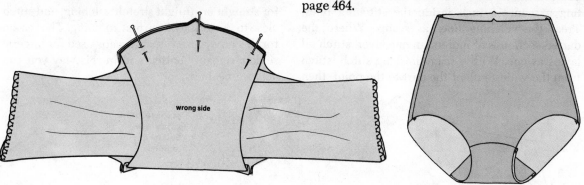

Crotch seams in flare-leg panties or petti-pants

These garments differ from briefs in that they are usually cut with center front and back seams instead of side seams. This makes the crotch section easy to insert and durable.

There are three shapes for crotch sections. One is a two-piece construction designed with a curved crotch seam from front to back. The other two shapes, the diamond and the modified diamond, are one-piece constructions. All styles have a double-layered crotch, and the sections are cut with the lengthwise rib running from side to side, placing the crosswise rib (the direction of greatest stretch) from front to back. All three crotch types are applied in the same way, but the two-piece crotch requires one preparatory step that the others do not.

To prepare the two-piece crotch, place the sections right sides together. Fold, matching the curved edges, which will form four seam layers. Stitch on the seam line, using the straight stretch stitch, and trim seam allowances to ⅛ inch or use the stretch overedge stitch. Grasp the two center layers and pull them out of one side opening; this places the seam allowances between the remaining two layers. Reverse the fold in the outside layers to flatten the seamed sections. The folds become the finished bottom edges of the inside portion of the legs. Apply lace to finish the outside leg sections of the panties before taking the next step.

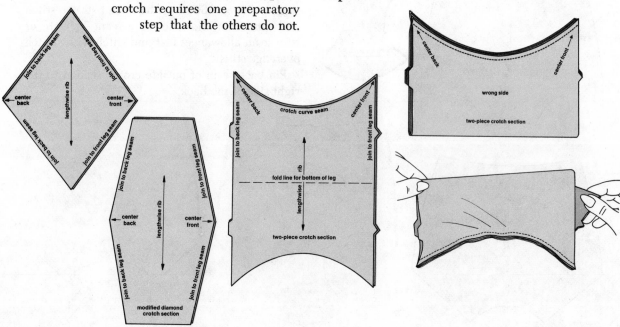

To assemble the crotch section and garment, stitch one leg front seam to the corresponding side of the crotch section. Then stitch the entire front seam, continuing across the seam joining and down the other leg seam, joining the remaining side of the crotch. Repeat the same steps at the back.

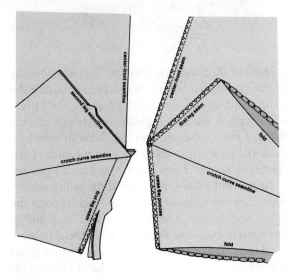

Seams in Pajama Pants

Tricot pajama pants are usually cut without side seams. If you need to lengthen or shorten a pattern above the crotch line for pants, you should do the same for pajamas, although pajamas should have at least 1 inch more ease at this point than pants. Stitch the center front and center back seams before stitching the leg seams, using one of the double-stitched seams or the overedge stretch seam. Then stitch the leg seams, starting at the crotch and stitching down one leg first and then the other. Hold the center back seam in one direction and the center front seam in the other, and overlap the stitching at least 1 inch. Finish the waistband with elastic (page 465). Finish the hem as outlined on page 470.

Setting in Sleeves

There are two ways to set in sleeves in robes, peignoirs, and pajamas. You may follow the conventional method of stitching the sleeve seams and side seams before putting in the sleeve, and trimming and finishing the seam allowances together to ¼ inch. Or, you may use the open construction method. Trim the seam allowances on both the armhole and the sleeve to ¼ inch. Stitch and finish the seam allowances together before the side and sleeve seams are stitched. Then stitch each side seam and sleeve seam as one continuous seam.

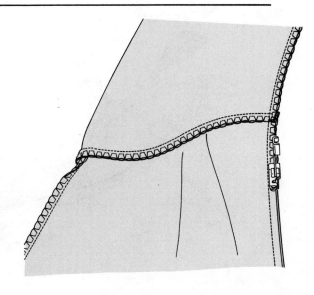

Elastic Braid in Casing

For children's panties, use ⅜-inch elastic for the waistline and ¼-inch elastic for the legs. For women's briefs or panties, use ⅝- or ½-inch elastic for waistline and ¼- or ⅜-inch elastic for legs. Measure elastic around waistline and legs at a comfortable degree of tension, allowing ½ inch for overlap.

Method 1. Overlap the elastic at the ends and hand-whip them together along the overlapped edges and ends. Fold top of garment over the

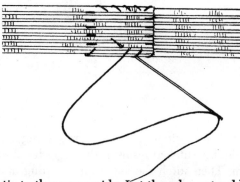

elastic to the wrong side. Let the edge extend beyond the elastic at least ¼ inch. The stitching may be done in one of two ways. Using the adjustable zipper foot and the straight stretch stitch, stitch through the tricot layers alongside the elastic. Or, using the overedge foot and a narrow zig-zag stitch (width 3, length 15, and right needle position), stitch along the elastic through the tricot layers. Trim the seam allowance close to the stitching. Finish the legs the same way.

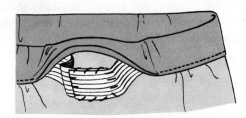

Method 2. Fold waistline or leg edge to the inside, and turn again to form a hem or casing the same width as the elastic. Stitch along the turned edge with a narrow zig-zag or straight stretch stitch. Leave a 1-inch opening through which to draw the elastic into the hem. Join the ends of the elastic as above. Then stitch the 1-inch opening.

To prevent elastic from twisting inside casing, distribute the fullness evenly and pin through the fabric and elastic at center front and back and at the centers between these points. Stitch, holding the fabric and elastic under tension, using plain zig-zag (5 stitch width, 12 stitch length) or multi-stitch zig-zag stitch (5 stitch width, 15 stitch length). Test this stitching on a scrap before stitching the garment because elastic braid with a heavy rib will cause stitching problems that prevent this step.

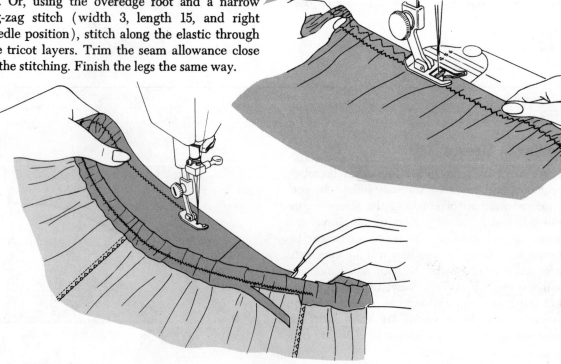

Nylon Elastic Lace Webbing

Measure elastic around waistline at a comfortable tension and allow 1 inch for joining. Machine-stitch across ends, wrong sides together. Open seam and stitch ¼ inch on each side of seam. Trim ends near stitching.

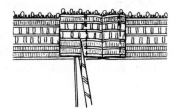

Place seam at center front. Divide elastic in four equal segments and mark with pins. Do the same to the garment. Then pin together at corresponding points, pinning elastic over right side of tricot, bottom edge on seam line. Stitch, using a 15 to 20 stitch length and a narrow zig-zag stitch (2 to 3 stitch width) that is just wide enough to cover the elastic ridge near the edge. Trim seam allowance near stitching.

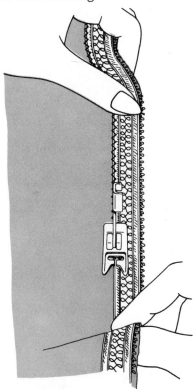

Cover elastic joining at center front with ½-inch satin ribbon folded over the elastic and top-stitched on the sides and the lower edge.

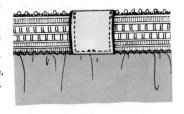

Frill- and Picot-Edge Elastic

Apply narrow elastic to the legs of briefs as described above. Allow 1 inch for overlapping the ends at the side seams for comfort. Catch the ends into the stitching as illustrated.

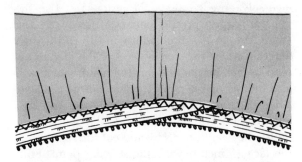

For a more feminine treatment at the waistline, the elastic may be concealed except for the decorative edge. Place the elastic with frill edge on seam line of garment, right sides together, elastic covering seam allowance. Stitch over the elastic rib nearest the frill, using the general-purpose presser foot and a narrow zig-zag stitch (2 stitch width and 18 stitch length). Hold elastic and tricot under tension as you stitch, and guide the stitching uniformly over the elastic rib. Trim seam

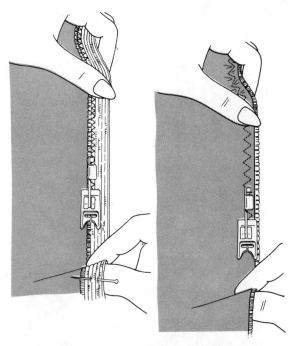

allowance to ¼ inch. Turn elastic to the inside of the garment and, using the multistitch zig-zag stitch (5 stitch width and 15 stitch length), topstitch through the tricot and the center of the elastic while holding it under tension.

Lace Edging

Method 1. The easiest and quickest way to apply lace edging is to hold it on top of the tricot, lace selvage edge along the seam line. Use the general-purpose presser foot and a narrow zig-zag stitch (1½ to 2½ stitch width and 15 to 18 stitch length). Allow the starting end of the lace to extend ¼ inch beyond the starting point, which will also be the joining point for the ends of the lace. After stitching all but 2 or 3 inches of the lace edging, and without removing the work from under the needle, measure and cut the free end of the lace ½ inch beyond the starting point. Fold ¼ inch of the lace over the first end and fold both ends another ¼ inch.

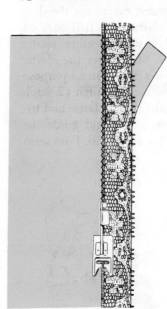

Whip overlapped lace seam edges together by hand. Continue the zig-zag stitching, overlapping the starting point a few stitches. Pull thread ends to underside and tie. Cut away tricot seam allowance near stitching on inside of garment.

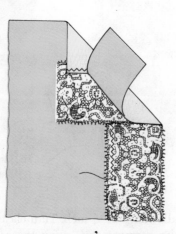

Lace without a selvage can be applied in the same way, but let the decorative edge extend slightly above the zig-zag stitching.

Method 2. Place lace over tricot, right sides together, with selvage of lace on seam line and decorative edge away from the seam edge. Stitch over selvage with a narrow zig-zag stitch (1½ to 2 stitch width, 15 stitch length) or along selvage with a 15 to 20 length straight stitch. Turn lace toward the edge, seam allowance toward garment, and topstitch along tricot fold with a narrow zig-zag or straight stitch. Trim seam allowance near stitching on underside. This method is also suitable for lace insertions.

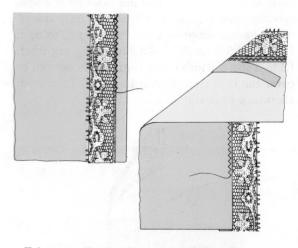

Tricot appliqué. Place tricot right side up over right side of lace and pin. Hand-baste, if neces-

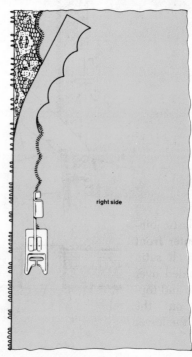

right side

sary. Stitch near selvage of lace, using a decorative satin stitch ("fine" stitch length, 5 stitch width), such as the open scallop or crescent pattern. Trim tricot seam allowance outside decorative stitching and trim lace inside decorative stitching from the underside. Any width of lace with or without a selvage may be used.

Sheer Footing
or Fold Tricot Appliqué

Net footing or a fold of sheer tricot may be used for an edge finish instead of lace. Hand-baste the fold underneath the tricot edge above the seam line. Using a decorative zig-zag stitch, such as the crescent pattern, stitch on the seam line. Trim tricot along the outside edge of the stitching, and trim the underneath edges of the applied fold straight along the top edge of the decorative stitching.

Applied Band

An applied 1- to 1½-inch band or false hem makes a sturdy, smooth, tailored finish for legbands and the hem edge of slips. Cut a lengthwise strip of tricot twice the finished width plus ⅜ inch for two seam allowances, and the length of the edge to be finished plus ⅜ inch for two seam allowances. Stitch ends of strip together with the overedge foot and the overedge stretch stitch. Fold band and place the edges even with the right side of the tricot edge. Offset seams slightly in band to reduce number of layers at a single point. Pin in at least four places to avoid stretching the garment edge and band unequally as you stitch. Stitch over the two edges of the band and one edge of the tricot, using the overedge foot and either the overedge or the stretch overedge stitch. Regulate stitch width to suit fabric weight. Turn band toward edge when completed.

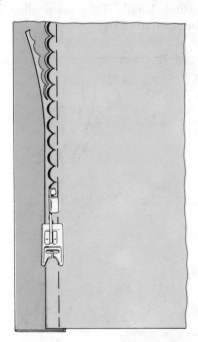

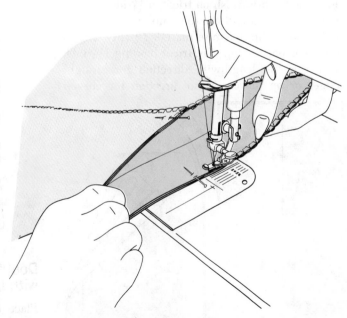

Shell Edge

The shell edge can be made with either the blind-stitch, *Flexi-Stitch* Disc 59, or Disc 22. Use the general-purpose presser foot; 5 stitch width; and 15 stitch length. Fold tricot edge to underside ½ inch. Guide edge to your right with *Flexi-Stitch* Disc 59 or Disc 22, and to the left with the blind-stitch. Stitch from the right side of the fabric, guiding it so that the needle passes over the fabric fold at the zig-zag stitch. Tighten needle-thread tension slightly if shell formation is indistinct.

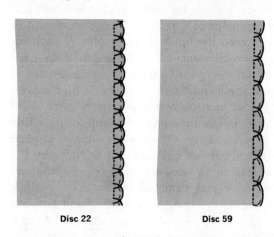

Disc 22   Disc 59

Tricot Bound Edge

For a self-fabric finish on tricot, a ¼-inch bound edge is tailored and durable and an appropriate finish on a slip, chemise, flare-leg panty, nightgown, or pajama top. Cut tricot binding 1¼ inch wide on the lengthwise direction for straight edges or on the crosswise direction for curved

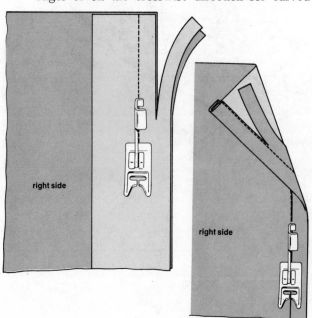

edges. With right sides together, place binding along garment edge and straight-stitch a ½-inch seam, using a 15 to 20 stitch length. Trim both seam allowances to an even ¼ inch. Fold the binding around the seam edges snugly, and stitch near the crevice of the first seam through the garment and the single free edge of the binding strip. Trim the seam allowance of the binding strip near the stitching. This finish is practical and durable for tricot because it does not ravel.

Simulated Rolled Edge

To finish the edge of a tricot ruffle or frill, turn the edge under ½ inch. Stitch over the turned edge from the right side, using the general-purpose presser foot, a plain zig-zag stitch, 3 stitch width, and 12 stitch length. Trim seam allowance on underside near stitching.

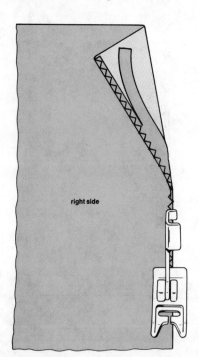

Double Collar with Decorative Edge

Place collar sections wrong sides together and stay-stitch ⅛ inch outside neckline seam line through both layers. If you prefer more firmness and loft than two layers of tricot give, use one layer of all-polyester, nonwoven interfacing between the layers. Hand-baste outer edges. Stitch

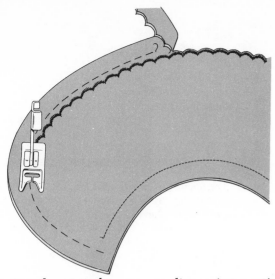

outer edges together on seam line, using a satin stitch, 5 stitch width, and open scallop or crescent stitch pattern. Trim seam allowances near outside edge of scallop.

There are many other decorative stitch patterns that can be used in place of the crescent. A bound edge and lace edging are also suitable finishes. The conventional faced collar is not as attractive as other finishes.

Tailored Hem

Appropriate for pajama sleeves and legs, the tailored hem is 1 to 1¼ inches wide and is formed after the sleeve and leg seams have been stitched. Turn and press the full hem width to the wrong side of the garment. Turn and press the full hem width again, keeping the edge inside the second fold. Stitch ¼ inch from the fold, hem side up, through the three thicknesses with a straight 15 length stitch and the general-purpose presser foot. Turn hem fold downward when stitching is completed.

Machine-Blindstitched Hem

Suitable for pajama tops, robes, nightgowns and general use where a hem is required; the machine-blindstitched hem is easy to make. Measure and fold hem the width desired. Press lightly. Hand-baste ¼ inch from top edge if desired. With garment right side out, fold hem to right side, forming a soft fold ¼ inch from top edge of hem. Place under the general-purpose presser foot with machine set for the blindstitch (2½ stitch width, 15 stitch length) and with the needle entering the single edge during the straight-stitching interval and just piercing the soft fold on the zig-zag stitch. When completed, trim edge near stitching and turn hem downward.

Buttonholes

Machine-stitched buttonholes are the most appropriate kind for tricot garments although bound buttonholes can be made in tricot. Those made by the manual method on a zig-zag machine are the most effective. The buttonhole foot or special-purpose foot will not mar the fabric surface, as sometimes happens with an attachment with a cloth clamp, and the stitch length can be set to space the stitches far enough apart to avoid stretching the buttonhole with too-dense stitching. Always use an interfacing of either nonwoven all-polyester or a crisp, fine woven fabric. Stitch width settings of 2½ and 4½ are appropriate on most machines.

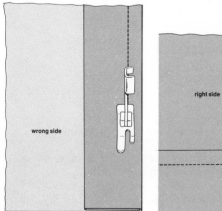

right side

wrong side

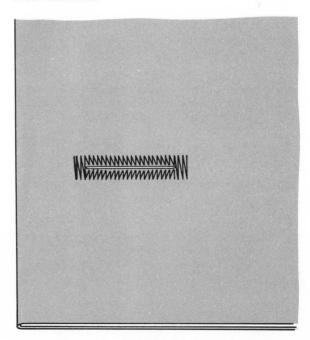

FABRICS

Characteristics. Crosswise is direction of greater stretch. Tricot is usually very wide, 108 inches.

Types. Tricot comes in different weights, depending on yarn size and number of loops per inch. 40-denier is a medium weight. 15-denier is a sheer, light weight.

Fiber Content. Nylon, acetate, triacetate.

PATTERN CHOICE

Choose from the growing selection of commercial patterns.

Or, cut apart a favorite discarded garment and make a pattern of its sections.†

Or, make a pattern from a favorite garment without cutting it apart. Lay each section, one at a time, over paper on a soft surface. Mark outline by plunging pins through fabric and paper along seam lines at short intervals; then cut paper along pin marks.†

†Add seam allowances when cutting new fabric.

PREPARATIONS

- Test-stitch a swatch before cutting to test ease of stitching. If stitches are skipped, launder yardage before cutting, using fabric softener to remove excess finish and static.
- Relax fabric by allowing it to lie flat on floor or table overnight.
- Fold, right sides together, and square and cut ends with table edge.
- To find right side, stretch a crosswise edge; tricot will roll to the right side.

PATTERN FITTING

- Purchase your regular pattern type and size.
- Alter pattern before cutting.
- Garments are usually sewn without fitting during construction.

CUTTING AND MARKING

- Fold fabric, right sides together.
- Since crosswise direction has greater stretch, cut with the stretch to encircle the figure and to run from front to back on crotch sections of panties or briefs.
- Use ball-point or sharp, smooth pins. Pin sparingly, within seam allowances.
- Patterns may be anchored with magic transparent tape instead of pins. (Some patterns allow only ¼-inch seam allowances; others ⅝-inch.)
- Do not let edges of fabric drape over table edge.
- Observe lengthwise grain-line markings on pattern and place on lengthwise rib.
- Cut with sharp shears and keep cut edges even and regular.
- Cut notches outward.
- Mark internal details with tailor's tacks.

STAY STITCHING

- Usually omitted.
- Used occasionally to hold 2 layers together.

STITCHING

- Use ball-point or size 11 needle and very fine thread (silk, nylon, or fine polyester).
- Balanced tensions.
- Normal to above-normal presser-foot pressure.
- For straight stitching, use straight-stitch (round-hole) throat plate and straight-stitch presser foot. (Rigid presser foot—not hinged—helps to prevent skipped stitches.)
- 15 stitch length for straight stitching.
- Guide and support fabric, keeping seam under tension while stitching.
- Kinds of stitches: regular straight, straight stretch, stretch overedge, plain zig-zag (narrow widths), chainstitch (2 or 3 rows in alternating directions), overedge with Disc 22 and overedge foot, or plain narrow zig-zag (right needle position with overedge foot).

SEAMS AND SEAM FINISHES

- Narrow, machine-finished seams are generally used.
- Choose from three different procedures: 1) stitch, finish, and trim; 2) stitch, trim, and finish; or 3) trim and stitch, using the stretch overedge (*Flexi-Stitch* Disc 59).
- Pin seams at ends and center; do not hand-baste; trim off notches before stitching; stretch short side of seam where ease is indicated.

FACINGS, INTERFACINGS, LININGS, UNDERLININGS

- Use double layer of same weight tricot for crotch.
- Underline lace inserts or sections with sheer tricot.
- Face collar with same weight tricot.
- Interfacing is often omitted.

PRESSING

- Limit iron temperature to that for nylon.
- Press lightly with moist cheesecloth to generate steam to remove stretched portions.

HEMS AND EDGE FINISHES

- Hems may be finished with:
  — Machine blindstitching (1- or 1½-inch hem).
  — Shell edging (½-inch hem).
  — Machine stitching with hemmer foot (⅛-inch hem).
- Hems or edges may be finished with:
  — Folded, cross-cut matching or sheer tricot.
  — Applied lace.
  — Appliquéd lace with finished selvage, sometimes underlined with sheet tricot.
  — Taffeta or satin binding cut on bias (suitable also for tubular straps or ties).
- Waistline may be finished with lingerie elastic encased or stitched and turned to underside with picot edge extending.

Spandex Knits

KNITS THAT INCLUDE SPANDEX YARN have an elastic-like ability to stretch and recover. Thus they are appropriate for action-wear clothing and figure-control lingerie.

Spandex knits that look like regular knits are usually used for garments worn for swimming, skiing, skating, gymnastics, and other active sports. These knits are cut and stitched in much the same way as stretch knits, but special attention must be given to retaining the stretch in the seams. Unlike other knits, on which strong thread and straight stitching are often adequate, knits that contain spandex require stretch stitches, such as the straight stretch stitch, the overedge stretch stitch, and the multi-stretch stitch.

Power net, stretch lace, and satin-faced tricot, all containing spandex, are primarily used for figure-control lingerie. The methods for sewing them are easy but quite different from other sewing.

Seams in Power Net

Almost all seams start with a plain seam, stitched with right sides together using the straight stretch stitch, the general-purpose presser foot or the Even Feed foot, lingerie thread of nylon or spun polyester, and a ball-point needle. If your sewing machine does not make the straight stretch stitch, you can substitute the narrow plain zig-zag stitch, 2½ stitch width and 15 stitch length. Topstitching is usually applied to hold the seam allowances in one position and to strengthen the seam. The featherstitch, *Flexi-Stitch* Disc 51, and the multi-stitch zig-zag are good choices for topstitching because they will stretch in all directions.

Featherstitch—centered. Finger-press plain

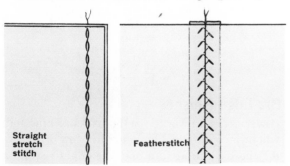

Straight stretch stitch

Featherstitch

seam open. Topstitch from right side of garment, centering the featherstitch over the seam line.

Featherstitch—double row. Finger-press plain seam open. Topstitch on each side of seam line from right side of garment through seam allowances.

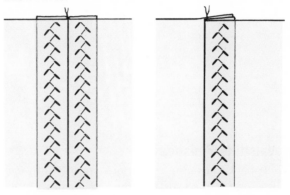

Featherstitch—welt seam. Finger-press seam allowances in the same direction and topstitch through garment and seam layers from the right side with the featherstitch.

Figure-Control Panels

For areas of the figure that need strong control, the degree of stretch can be decreased by using two or more layers of power net as an underlay. Power net does not ravel so a cut edge is acceptable and the application simple.

Pin panel in place on the underside of the girdle section. Set your machine for the featherstitch or the multi-stitch zig-zag, 5 stitch width, above-20 stitch length, and use the general-purpose presser foot. Stitch near the panel edge, from the right side of the garment section.

Crotch and Leg Seams

Seams that join the crotch and leg sections of panty girdles consist of two layers of nylon tricot and one layer of power net. Stitch these three-ply seams with ¼-inch allowances, using the overedge foot and the overedge stretch stitch, Flexi-Stitch Disc 59, which seams and finishes in one stitching.

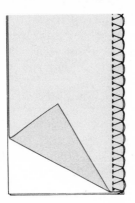

Waistline Finishes

Soft-back elastic in a wide or narrow width can be used for the waistline finish of girdles. Apply medium and narrow widths with hidden seam allowances; apply wide widths with a shaped and topstiched edge. Do not stretch or ease the girdle or the elastic.

Hidden-seam waistband. Place soft-back elastic, soft back up, frill edge extended, slightly below the seam line. Stitch with the general-purpose presser foot and a narrow zig-zag stitch, 2½ stitch width, 15 stitch length, over elastic rib nearest frill. Turn elastic to underside of garment and topstitch from the outside of the garment through the elastic near the bottom edge.

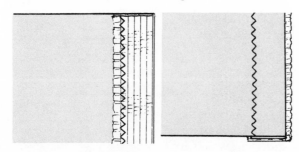

Shaped, topstitched waistband. Shape top edge of girdle by trimming on the seam line and pin wide, soft-back waistband elastic in position right side up underneath the shaped edge. Baste if necessary and do not stretch or ease either elastic or girdle. The firm waistline control comes from the greater strength of the waistband elastic.

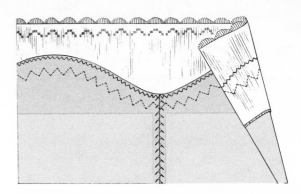

With a narrow plain zig-zag stitch (2½ stitch width, 15 stitch length) and the general-purpose presser foot, stitch near the shaped edge of the power net.

With the multi-stitch zig-zag (5 stitch width, above-20 stitch length) and the general-purpose presser foot, topstitch, guiding the edge of the foot along the bottom of the zig-zag stitching.

Leg Finishes

The legs of panty girdles can be finished with soft-back elastic applied in the same manner as described for the hidden-seam waistband. Or they can be finished with stretch lace.

Stitch ends of stretch-lace leg band with the stretch overedge stitch and topstitch seam from the outside.

Pin lace to overlap bottom edge of power net ½ inch. Do not stretch or ease either edge.

With leg turned wrong side out, topstitch the stretch lace near the edge, using the general-purpose presser foot and the featherstitch, multi-stitch zig-zag stitch, or plain zig-zag stitch.

Bra Edge Finishes

Power net is a favorite for the backs of bras and, whether you are making an entire bra or replacing the back in a worn one, the edges require a finish. The best finish is narrow soft-back elastic applied with a hidden seam as described for waistbands. An alternative finish is the bound edge of power net.

Cut a 1-inch-wide lengthwise strip of power net. With right sides together, using the straight stretch stitch and general-purpose presser foot, stitch a seam with a ¼-inch seam allowance. Turn the strip over the edge to the underside, letting the cut edge extend ¼ inch below the seam line. Stitch near the seam line below the binding with a narrow zig-zag stitch, 2½ stitch width, 15 stitch length.

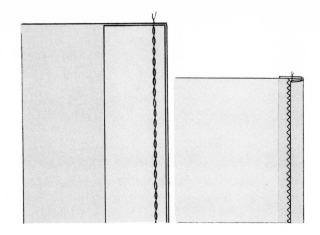

Spandex Stretch (Power Net)

FABRICS

Characteristics. Spandex yarns, combined with yarns of other fibers, impart stretch and recovery to any knit fabric.

Types. Many look like other knits but have elastic-like stretch. These are used for action sportswear and are handled like stretchable knits.

Power net, stretch lace, and satin-faced tricot with spandex are figure-control lingerie fabrics.

PATTERN CHOICE

- For figure-control lingerie, choose from the growing selection of commercial patterns.
- Or, cut apart a favorite discarded garment and make a pattern of its sections.†
- Or, make a pattern from a favorite garment without cutting it apart. Lay each section, one at a time, over paper on a soft surface. Mark outline by plunging pins through fabric and paper along seam lines at short intervals, then cut paper along pin marks.†

†Add seam allowances when cutting new fabric.

CUTTING AND MARKING

- Fold fabric right sides together on lengthwise rib.
- Use few pins, within seam allowances.
- Use ball-point or fine, smooth pins; or anchor pattern with magic transparent tape. Cut with sharp shears and keep edges even.
- Cut notches outward.
- Mark internal details with tailor's tacks.

STAY STITCHING

- Usually omitted. Used occasionally to hold 2 layers together.

STITCHING

- Use ball-point needle; fine, strong thread (nylon, polyester, or polyester-core).
- Balanced tensions.
- Normal presser-foot pressure.
- Select stitches that stretch, preferably in both lengthwise and crosswise directions.
- Kinds of stitches: straight stretch stitch, multi-stitch zig-zag, featherstitch, plain zig-zag, over-edge stretch, and multi-stitch stretch.

SEAMS AND SEAM FINISHES

- Power net does not require a seam finish.
- Seams are usually made as plain seams, stitched with straight stretch stitch, opened and finger-pressed, then stitched opened from right side with plain zig-zag, featherstitch, or multi-stitch zig-zag.
- Seam edges are sometimes finger-pressed in one direction and stitched decoratively as above.
- Underlays for strengthening figure control are pinned on the underside and stitched decoratively near the edge from the right side.
- Satin-like-surface lingerie fabrics with spandex are usually seamed with straight stretch stitching, trimmed to ¼ inch, and finished with over-edge stretch stitch.
- Seams may be strengthened on the underside with a stay of woven elastic applied with zig-zag stitching.
- Seams may be stiffened with featherboning, plastic, or metal foundation-garment stays.

FACINGS, INTERFACINGS, LININGS, UNDERLININGS

- Usually not used.

PRESSING

- Use an iron sparingly, if at all, and at low heat setting.
- Finger pressing is usually adequate.

HEMS AND EDGE FINISHES

Girdle edges — Finish with soft-back elastic. 1) Stitch elastic, soft side up, to right side of garment, using stretch stitch; 2) turn elastic to underside and stitch near unattached edge, using plain or decorative stretch stitch.

Terry and Stretch Terry

KNIT TERRY, WITH ITS LOOPED SURFACE and stretchable back, has become a favorite for all ages, from babies to grownups. It is a companion fabric to knit velour, which has a cut rather than a looped pile surface. There is considerable range within this fabric type, and the appearance and density can vary greatly, depending on the kinds and sizes of yarns, size and number of needles used in knitting and whether the fabric also contains spandex yarn, which strengthens its recovery after being stretched.

Preparing to Stitch

Use the general-purpose throat plate and presser foot, the overedge foot, or the Even Feed foot for most stitching. Use normal presser-foot pressure, a size 14 ball-point needle (catalogue 2021 or 2045), and strong thread such as polyester core, spun polyester, or nylon twist.

Unless you use an Even Feed foot, guide and support the seam layers by holding the seam taut in back of the presser foot with one hand and in front of the needle with the other.

If the looped surface catches over the toes of the general-purpose foot, wrap it with a ¼-inch width of magic transparent tape (see page 425).

Seams

When seaming knit terry or stretch terry, the important points to remember are: Most seams must stretch with the fabric. Seams that should not stretch should be stayed with twill tape or woven-edge seam binding. And seams should be made in ways to keep bulkiness to a minimum because pressing will not sharpen seams appreciably.

Stitched and finished in one stitching. The most frequently used seam for joining garment sections is the one that uses the overedge stretch stitch and the overedge foot. Stitch on the seam line while holding the seam taut. Trim the seam allowances near the outside edge of the stitching. The stitching-then-trimming sequence retains the garment shape better than the reverse sequence.

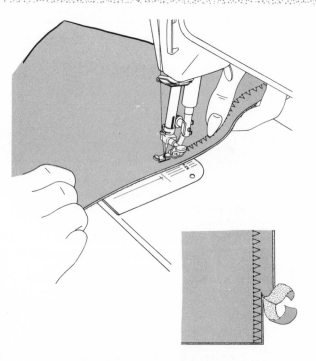

Stitched and finished in two steps. Another favorite is the narrow seam that is first stitched on the seam line with the straight stretch stitch and either the general-purpose presser foot or the Even Feed foot and then finished with a flattening stitch such as the multi-stretch as illustrated.

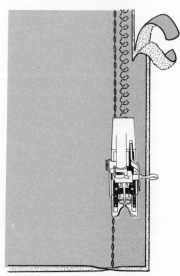

Alternative stitches are the regular straight stitch or a narrow zig-zag stitch (2 stitch width, 15 stitch length) instead of the straight stretch stitch, and multi-stitch zig-zag or wide plain zig-zag (5 stitch width, 12 stitch length) instead of the multi-stretch zig-zag stitch.

Mock flat-felled seam. For men's wear and baby clothes, a flat seam is sometimes preferred. Stitch first as a plain seam on the seam line, using the straight stretch stitch and the Even Feed foot, or the regular straight stitch and the general-purpose presser foot. (Hold seam taut if you use the general-purpose presser foot.) Finger-press both seam allowances in one direction and topstitch from the right side of the fabric an even distance (¼ to ⅜ inches) from the seam line through both seam allowances. Trim both seam allowances near the stitching. The seam may appear slightly stretched when finished, but it will recover after light steam pressing or when the garment is worn.

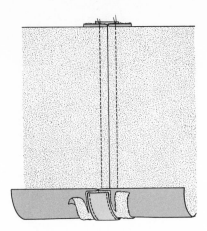

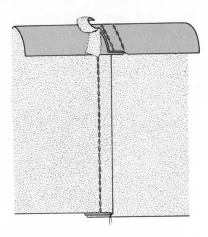

Plain seam, double topstitched. Where a flat and bulkless joining is necessary, a plain seam, topstitched ⅛ inch from the seam line on both sides, is preferred. Seam allowances can be trimmed near the topstitching to further reduce bulk.

Collars and Band Finishes

While garments of knit terry and velour should retain their soft, supple, stretchable characteristics, collars and finishes of some garments must have body and shape. Men's sport shirts, kimonos, V-neck pullovers, and girls' robes are a few examples. All-polyester, nonwoven featherweight interfacing will supply the shape and body needed in these areas without robbing the terry of its softness or washability.

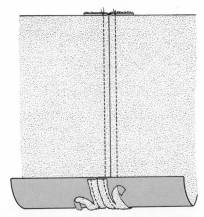

Plain seam, double topstitched, taped. For seams that should not stretch, such as the shoulder and back-of-neck or yoke seams, include woven-edge seam binding or twill tape on the underside when topstitching.

A firm band suitable for a kimono, V-neck pullover, or cardigan cover-up is cut twice the width of the finished band plus two ⅝-inch seam allowances on the lengthwise direction of the fabric. Cut the interfacing the same length and width. With a plain, straight-stitch seam, join one edge of the interfaced band to the garment edge. Finger-press seam allowances open and trim the seam

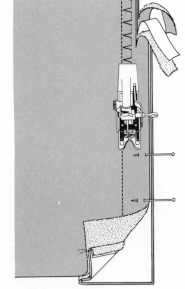

allowances of the band and interfacing band to ¼ inch. Pin free edges of interfaced band to the extended seam allowance of the garment. Stitch with either the Even Feed foot, or the general-purpose presser foot, using the blind stitch (5 stitch width, 15 stitch length). Place the stitching with the left edge slightly outside the seam line.

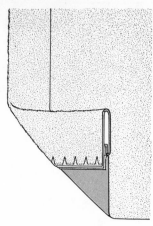

Trim the seam allowances near right-hand edge of the blind stitching.

Trim seam allowances on upper collar and interfacing to ¼ inch and on under collar and interfacing to ⅛ inch. Turn collar right side out, finger-press, and pin edges to turn sharply on seam line. Topstitch ⅜ inch from edge.

A round collar, interfaced with one layer of all-polyester, nonwoven interfacing and finished with a self-binding, makes a feminine finish. Cut two collar sections and one interfacing section. With collar sections right sides out, place the interfacing between them. Cut a binding strip, on crosswise direction of the fabric for greatest stretch, two times the width of the finished binding plus two seam allowances. Pin the binding to the collar unit, edges matching and binding stretched slightly. Stitch with multi-stitch zig-zag stitch (5 stitch width, 20 stitch length), inside edge of

A tailored collar will have shape and stay neat when interfacing is attached to both the upper and under collar sections. Cut both upper and under collar sections on the lengthwise rib from the upper-collar pattern. The fabric has adequate give for shaping. Cut also two collar sections of all-polyester nonwoven featherweight interfacing. Stitch one interfacing to the wrong side of each collar section ½ inch from all edges.

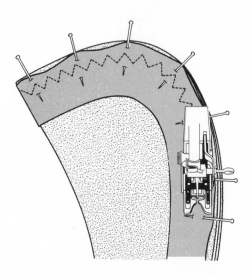

Place right sides of interfaced collar sections together; pin and stitch ⅝ inch from edges, blunting the collar points by taking 3 stitches diagonally across point.

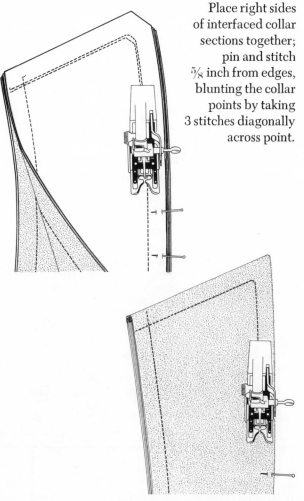

stitching on seam line. Trim all seam allowances near outside edge of stitching. Fold free edge of binding over seam allowances and pin. Topstitch with Even Feed foot and straight stitch, 15 stitch length, in the crevice of the seam line through collar layers and free edge of binding on under-

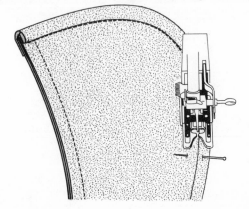

476

side. Trim binding seam allowance near the stitching.

Soft finishes applied as bands or bindings are appropriate for garments that should look unstructured and molded to the body. Remember that lengthwise-cut bands or bindings have greater control of an edge than crosswise-cut strips because knit terry stretches less lengthwise. Also, as on tricot, a cut edge near a line of stitching is acceptable. Many of the techniques suggested for lingerie apply to terry garments as well.

Hems

Machine-blindstitched hems are appropriate for terry, as are multi-row topstitched hems and applied bands instead of hems.

Buttonholes and Closures

Machine-stitched buttonholes are appropriate if made in an interfaced area and with uncrowded stitches, as in lingerie tricot. Metal snaps, which are attached with a tool, are preferred for young children.

Terry and Stretch Terry

FABRICS

Characteristics. Greater stretch in crosswise direction.

Types. Plain, printed, or striped. Some have a velour surface and terry back.

Fiber Content. All-cotton, nylon, polyester, or blends of these fibers; some include spandex yarn.

PATTERN CHOICE

Casual wear—Jumpsuits, long or short pants, swimwear, hooded cover-ups, robes, dresses.

Children's wear.

Men's wear.

PREPARATIONS

- Relax stretch terry by allowing it to lie flat on floor or table overnight.
- Pin crosswise edges of stretch terry to tissue to control, since they tend to roll.
- Cut ends on crosswise course.
- Pull diagonally to straighten.

PATTERN FITTING

- Purchase your regular pattern type and size.
- Patterns for "Stretchable Knits Only" are suitable.
- Alter pattern before cutting.
- Stretch terry may be fitted with no ease in the stretch direction.

CUTTING AND MARKING

- Fold most terry wrong side out.
- Cut heavy terry from single thickness.
- Stretch terry (crosswise stretch) may be cut in either direction, depending on where you want the stretch.
- Cut with sharp, rigid-blade shears.
- Mark notches with tailor's tacks.

STAY STITCHING

- Instead of using conventional stay stitching, stitch seam allowances with chainstitch or straight stitch, 12 to 15 stitch length, 1/4 inch from cut edge to keep crosswise-cut edge from raveling or rolling during construction.

STITCHING

- Use size 14 ball-point needle. Needles may blunt quickly because of yarn density.
- Spun polyester, polyester-core, or nylon threads.
- Normal presser-foot pressure.
- Guide and support seam by holding fabric taut behind and in front of presser foot, except with Even Feed foot.
- Wrap toes of presser foot with 1/4-inch strip of magic transparent tape to prevent snagging.
- Kinds of stitches: regular straight stitch, straight stretch stitch, or narrow zig-zag. For finishing: wide zig-zag, overedge stretch, multi-stretch stitch, multi-zig-zag stitch, blind stitch.
- Even Feed foot handles seam layers evenly.

SEAMS AND SEAM FINISHES

- Stitched and overedged seams, 1/4 to 3/8 inch wide, are generally used.
- Plain seams, opened and topstitched, are used to reduce bulk and, when taped, to give stability.
- Mock flat-felled seams are used for some men's wear.

FACINGS, INTERFACINGS, LININGS, UNDERLININGS

- Generally not used.
- For some garments, all-polyester, featherweight nonwoven interfacing is suitable.
- Facings are often cut as one with garment.
- Applied bands may replace facings.
- Ribbing is a popular finish.

PRESSING

- Press sparingly.
- Finger pressing is adequate in many situations.

HEMS AND EDGE FINISHES

- Finish hem edge with overedge stitch, turn once, and machine-stitch hem.
- Or, finish edge as above and machine-blindstitch hem.
- Or, finish edge as above and hand-whip hem.
- Or, finish edge with decorative braid or fabric binding.
- Use worked or bound buttonholes or fabric or cord button loops.

Shiny-Faced Knits

LEATHER-LIKE FABRICS HAVE REACHED A HIGH PLACE in fashion. Those with a knit back are more supple than those with a woven back. The knit-back fake leathers consist of a plastic layer of polyurethane or vinyl over a knitted base fabric. Polyurethane produces a soft, spongy fabric; vinyl tends to be more rigid. Whether made to look like patent or grained leather or like fabric, the new plastics are handled alike.

Preparing to Stitch

Stitch plastic-coated fabrics with spun polyester or polyester-core thread, a style 15 x 2 (catalogue 2032) needle, size 14, and a 10 stitch length.

Equip your sewing machine with the straight-stitch presser foot and throat plate for straight stitching, or the general-purpose presser foot and throat plate for zig-zag stitching, or the Even Feed machine foot for either straight or zig-zag stitching. The top feeding action of the Even Feed foot overcomes the natural tendency of plastic-coated fabrics to adhere to the underside of the presser foot and thus retard the movement of the top seam layer. When you do not use the Even Feed foot on polyurethane or vinyl fabrics for topstitching, use clear oil[†] or powder[††] as you stitch to keep the top layer from adhering to the underside of the presser foot. Test before applying to the garment for complete removal of oil or powder.

[†]–SINGER* oil or clear baby oil.
[††]–Talcum powder, cornstarch, or chalk spot remover.

Test-stitch seams. Usually, you will need to increase the needle-thread tension slightly to compensate for the lack of porosity of these materials. Medium or normal presser-foot pressure is usually adequate. However, if the stitch length appears shorter than set for, increase the pressure slightly; or if feed marks show on the underside and the machine runs hard, decrease the pressure. Use your test-stitched seams to test the new ways of treating seams that follow in the next section.

Darts and Seams

Preparations. Leave the pattern on the cut-out sections and defer marking until you are ready to use the section. Mark seam widths that vary from the standard ⅝ inch, and mark notches with short, perpendicular lines.

Darts. Fold right sides together, matching markings. If you use pins, place them within the dart allowance because of the permanent holes they will leave, or use paper clips over the fold.

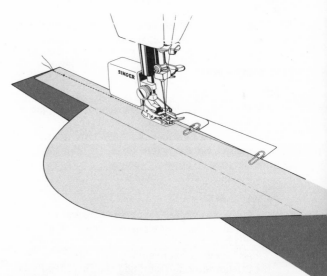

Darts, which are placed over rounded parts of the figure, should be stitched on a slight outward curve, and the last few stitches near the point should be on the edge of the fold. Tie threads at both ends. Slash through the fold as far as possible, finger-press the allowances open, and trim to ¼ inch.

Pounding, Rolling, and Gluing. Pounding seams open on leather-like fabrics is equivalent to pressing to embed the stitches and to pressing a seam open with the point of the iron. With the garment held over a padded and rounded hardwood surface (or a firm tailor's ham), use a wooden mallet to pound along the stitching line

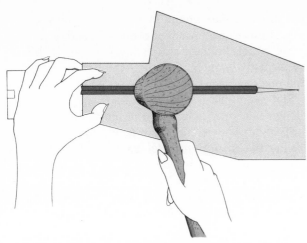

glue under the seam allowance slightly inside the seam edge. Finger-press the seam allowance against the garment. Pound lightly or roll to compress the two layers, and allow to dry.

Plan to do as much gluing at one time as possible. Be meticulous and avoid smears. A fine, stiff-point brush for applying the glue and a small glue cup will help you to do a neat job. To protect the shiny face of the fabric, work with the garment section over a Turkish towel.

with short, staccato strokes. Pound near the dart point to flatten the fold, distributing it equally on each side of the stitching:

Plain seam. Place garment sections right sides together. Match edges, if seam allowances are equal, or seam lines, if seam allowances are unequal. Match seam ends and notches first, and hold together with paper clips or small squares of magic transparent tape. Add clips or tape as needed.

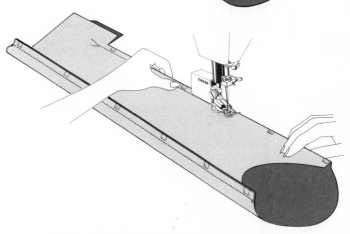

Rolling, another substitute for pressing leatherlike fabrics, is superior to pounding. Use a small roller similar to that used for sealing the edges of wallpaper. Hold the seam allowances open and run the roller back and forth, exerting pressure along the stitching line.

Gluing is the process by which seam allowances are held in an opened position. Use a glue, such as Sobo brand, or rubber cement. Place a thin line of

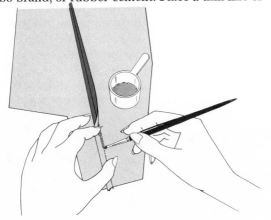

If there is slight ease in one layer of the seam, stitch with that side against the feed. Stitch slowly and keep a firm hold on the seam. Remember, you cannot remove stitches without leaving holes. Tie threads at both ends, remove tape, and finger-press seam open. Pound or roll along stitching line, and glue seam allowances open.

Taped seam. When extra strength is required, include pre-shrunk twill tape or woven-edge seam binding in the seam as you stitch. Pound or roll along the stitching line, and glue seam allowances open the same as a plain seam.

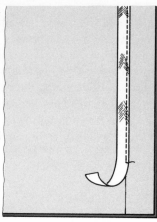

Double-Topstitched seam. Straight-stitch a plain seam, pound or roll it open, but do not glue. Topstitch an equal distance from center on each side through garment and seam allowance.

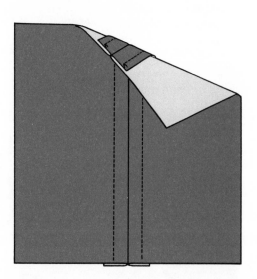

Welt seam. Seam allowances may be equal or unequal for the welt seam. Stitch a plain seam on

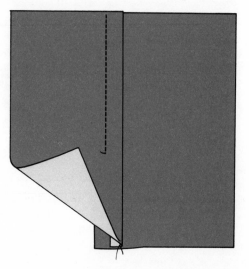

the stitching line. Pound or roll seam open first. Then turn seam allowances to one side and pound or roll again. Trim the seam allowance next to the garment to ¼ inch. Topstitch through garment and one seam layer. Use no glue.

Slot seam. Turn both seam allowances under along seam line. Pound or roll and glue. Cut a strip of fabric twice the seam width plus ½ inch. Center the strip, right side against one seam allowance, and topstitch one side. Hold the strip and abutted edges in place with strips of magic transparent tape or masking tape, as illustrated, and stitch second side. Do not stitch through the tape.

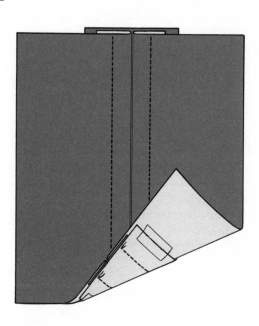

Clipping, notching and trimming seam allowances. Straight seam allowances present few problems in handling, but curved seam allowances must be carefully clipped or notched to form a smooth and continuous line. Clip small wedges to flatten seam allowances that ripple, and slash into seam allowances that draw too tightly and restrict the shape of the garment. Cut seam allowances diagonally at cross seams. Cut seam allowances that are inside faced edges to unequal widths, such as ¼ and ⅛ inch.

Pockets and Buttonholes

Pockets and bound or corded buttonholes should be completed before garment sections are interfaced and assembled; hand-worked buttonholes should be made after the garment is completed.

FABRICS

Characteristics. Thermoplastic or vinyl coating gives knit-backed fabrics a shiny, water-repellent surface and makes them highly stable, with little or no give. Supple and soft, they are easy to sew.

Types. Surface may be smooth, crinkled, or marked with reptile-skin pattern.

Fiber Content.
Face—Vinyl or polyurethane.
Back—Cotton, polyester.

PATTERN CHOICE

Select patterns with a tailored look.
- Avoid gathers, sharp pleats or tucks.
- Select styles with shaped seams rather than darts.
- Topstitching is a good fashion accent and is also functional (substitutes for pressing).
- Raglan sleeves are easiest to handle.

All-weather coats, capes, jackets, jumpers, pants outfits.

Children's wear.

Men's wear.

Home furnishings—cushions, chair covers, table-cloths, and mats.

PREPARATIONS

- Store rolled. Do not fold or crease.
- Fold face out.
- Square and cut ends with table edges.

PATTERN FITTING

- Purchase your regular pattern type and size.
- Fit pattern carefully, preserving standard basic ease and design ease.
- Test-fit in muslin or nonwoven interfacing fabric.
- Convert ease to darts.
- Eliminate seamed-on facings if possible.
- Remove excessive ease in sleeve cap.
- Once stitched, the garment cannot easily be refitted.

CUTTING AND MARKING

- Lay out pattern on grain of fabric.
- Observe pattern-matching rules required by the design.
- Avoid pinning into garment areas; pin marks will show.
- Pin only within seam allowances and sparingly.
- Weights and transparent tape can substitute for pins.
- Mark fabric back with chalk or marking pencil.

STAY STITCHING

- Do **not** stay-stitch.

STITCHING

- Use size 14 leather-sewing needle, style 15 x 2, and polyester-core or all-polyester thread.
- Increase needle-thread tension to balance stitch.
- 10 stitch length for straight stitching.
- Normal or regular presser-foot pressure.
- When stitched from right side, the shiny surface will adhere to presser foot. To prevent sticking, dust the surface with a thirsty powder such as talcum powder, cornstarch, or one of the powders used for spot cleaning. These brush off without stain.
- The Even Feed foot will enable you to stitch without need for the above precautions.

SEAMS AND SEAM FINISHES

- Pin only within seam allowances or hold edges together with paper clips.
- Topstitched seams and darts are best because they control and hold the seam allowances in place.
- Or, use a thin line of glue.
- No seam finish is required.
- Shoulder and neckline seams should usually be taped to prevent stretching.

FACINGS, INTERFACINGS, LININGS, UNDERLININGS

INTERFACING
- Hair canvas for sharp support.
- Nonwoven for soft support.
- Nonwoven fleece for loft and support.

LINING
- Line for comfort.
- Washable fabric that does not show soil.
- Fake fur for zip-out type.
- Interline for warmth and to prevent harsh seams from abrading lining.
- Machine-stitch lining to facing.

UNDERLINING
- Generally not used except at back across shoulders and in front to anchor interfacing.

PRESSING

- Do **not** press with an iron.
- Instead, finger-press, weight or topstitch.
- "Press" seams open with a small roller.

HEMS AND EDGE FINISHES

- Turn and topstitch.
- Use glue to hold hem.
- Or, stitch on a folded band for hem substitute.
- Bound or worked buttonholes and sewn-on buttons with protective, flat sew-through button on back make pleasing closures.

Furry-Faced Knits

MANY FUR FABRICS ARE OF KNIT CONSTRUCTION. Knit-back furs are more flexible, more drapable, and more responsive to easing and thus easier to sew than woven-back furs.

Cutting

Cut fur fabrics with sturdy shears and cut through the backing only, not the hairs. The way you cut is entirely different from the way you cut other fabrics. Cut with the tips of the shears only, taking one short snip at a time. Do not rest the shears on the table but hold them up enough to allow the underneath blade to separate the hairs. Fur fabrics can also be cut with a single-edge razor blade, an artist's knife or a regular fur-cutting knife, but most women find it far easier to cut them with shears.

Preparing to Stitch

For most fur fabrics, select strong thread, such as spun polyester, polyester core, or 3-cord nylon in general-purpose sizes. For lightweight fur fabrics, use size A silk thread.

For all knit-back fur fabrics, use a size 14 ball-point needle, style 15 x 1, catalogue 2021 or 2045.

The Even Feed sewing machine foot gives the best results on most fur fabrics for both zig-zag and straight stitching; on very thick varieties, however, the zipper foot is superior.

The straight-stitch or general-purpose presser foot also can be used for straight stitching and the general-purpose presser foot only for zig-zag stitching.

Stitch lengths of 10 to 12 are best for straight stitching. Use the shorter length, 12, for short-pile and 10 for long-pile fur fabrics. Stitch lengths of 12 to 15 are best for zig-zag stitching. Use the shorter length, 15, for short-pile and 12 for long-pile furs.

Needle-thread tension should be regulated to produce an evenly set stitch. In most fabrics, it must be regulated at a slightly higher setting than for fabrics of similar weight without pile.

Presser-foot pressure should be tested at a regular or normal setting first and then increased slightly if the stitch length appears shorter than the setting indicates or if the fabric is not firmly held under the presser foot.

Seams

For a lined garment, you have a choice of two basic types of seams: 1) plain, straight-stitch seams with ⅝-inch seam allowances pressed open and 2) zig-zag seams with seam allowances trimmed to narrow width before stitching. Procedures vary for making each of these basic types of seams, depending on the bulk and length of the fur pile and whether you use tape to support the seam.

For an unlined fur garment, you have a choice of straight-stitch or zig-zag seams with a decorative covering or a flat-felled seam.

Using scraps, test-stitch different kinds of seams and procedures described in this section in order to decide which ones are best for your fur. Two or more different kinds of seams may be used in a single garment because some seams function differently from others.

Plain straight-stitch seams
(⅝-inch seam allowances)

In short-pile furs, pin, hand-baste (optional), and stitch in the same direction as the pile.

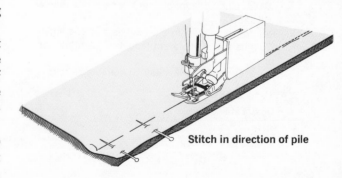

Stitch in direction of pile

Finger-press the seam open. Inspect the right side and, with the eye end of a heavy, long darning needle, raise hairs caught in the stitching. Then apply steam by holding the steam iron level, an inch or two above the fabric. Roll along the seam line to press. Use long, loose padding stitches to hold seam allowances open.

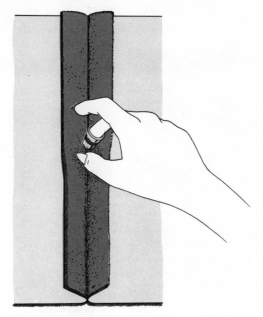

Finger-press seam open

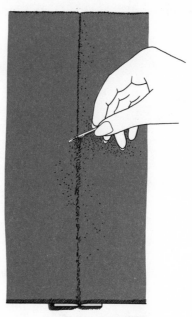

Raise hairs caught in stitching

**Steam,
holding iron above fabric**

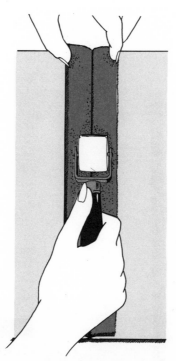

Roll along seam line

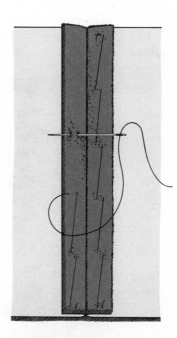

**Hold seam allowances
open with padding stitches**

In medium-length-pile furs, pin, hand-baste (optional), and stitch in the direction of the pile, working the pile away from the seam line with a long needle. Finger-press seam allowances open. Inspect both sides of the seam and raise the hairs caught in the stitching from both inside and out-

In long-pile furs, shear pile from ½ inch of the seam allowances and baste on the seam line. Inspect the outside and then raise hairs caught in the basting. Stitch on the seam line in the direction of the pile and, if necessary, use the zipper foot adjusted to the right of the needle to avoid the bulk of the fur. Finger-press seam allowances

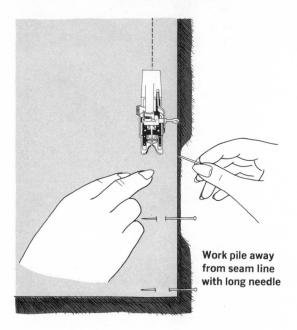

Work pile away from seam line with long needle

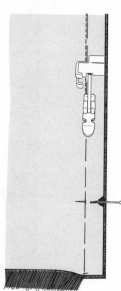

side. Shear pile from seam allowances with scissors, snipping the hairs close to the backing. Steam, holding the iron an inch or two above the fabric. Roll along the seam line to press.

Use long, loose padding stitches to hold seam allowances open.

open. From the outside, raise hairs along both sides of stitching with a long needle. Press seam allowances with steam iron, allowing it to rest on the two layers of seam allowance only. Cover the seam allowances with a thin press cloth if testing indicates a fiber content that needs protection.

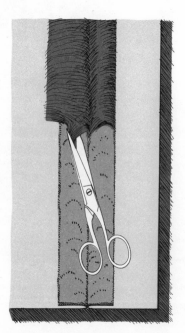

Open the seam allowances with your fingers and roll to hold them open temporarily. Use long, loose padding stitches to hold seam allowances open permanently.

To tape straight-stitch seams that should not stretch, include ¼-inch shrunk twill tape in the seam as it is being stitched. This procedure applies to furs of any pile length.

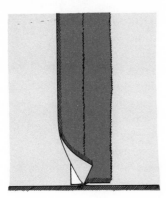

Zig-Zag seams (⅛-to-¼-inch seam allowances)

In sparsely covered, short-pile furs, do not use a zig-zag seam.

In short-but-dense-pile furs, trim seam allowances to ⅛-inch width, transferring notches to new seam-allowance edge. Pin edges together at seam ends and at notches. Use a plain zig-zag stitch, 3 stitch width, and 15 stitch length; stitch in the direction of the pile, letting the needle enter at the seam line on one side and beyond the seam edge on the other side. Backstitch at both the start and the finish of the seam. Finger-press seam allowances open. From the outside, raise hairs caught in the stitching. Steam, holding the iron above the inside of the fabric, and roll lightly.

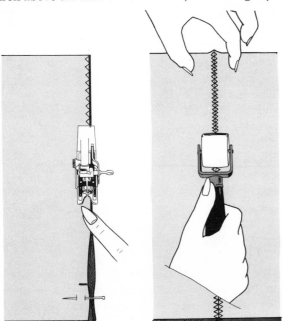

In medium- and long-pile furs, trim seam allowances to ¼-inch width, taking special care to snip with the points of shears through the backing only. Do not cut off the fur. Transfer notch markings as you work. Pin seam-allowance edges together at ends and notches, and at shorter intervals if necessary. Hand-baste with thread of matching color, with an overcasting stitch. From the outside, raise hairs caught in the basting. Stitch with the plain zig-zag stitch, 5 stitch width, and 12 stitch length, backstitching at both ends of the seam. Finger-press seam open. Raise hairs caught in stitching. Steam, holding the iron above the inside of the fabric, and roll lightly.

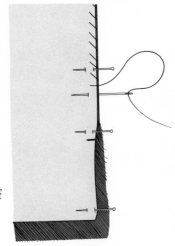

To tape zig-zag seams that should not stretch, add ¼-inch shrunk twill tape to the basting step of the above seam preparation, catching only the outside edge of the tape in the basting and allowing the greater width of the tape to extend toward the garment.

To cross a zig-zag seam, make sure that the stitching at the end of the seam being crossed is reinforced. Trimming the seam allowance before crossing is likely to remove the backstitching that reinforced the seam end. When this has happened, reinforce the seam end again. Position the seam under the needle ½ inch from the new seam end and stitch backward ½ inch, then forward ½ inch.

To cover seams with tape, use ½-inch shrunk twill tape and catch-stitch it over the seam. This taping method prevents abrasion of the lining and gives a slightly more flexible seam than the taping method described above. A covering is usually preferred for side seams and other major structural seams.

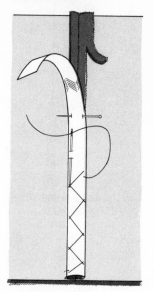 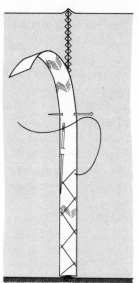

To tape folds, such as the fold of a soft pleat or the fold line of an in-seam pocket, catch-stitch ½-inch twill tape on the underside of the fabric, bringing the outside edge of the tape to the fold line. The purpose of taping is to prevent the fabric from stretching. For an in-seam pocket, tape both back and front sections alike for firmness, although only the front section is folded.

Seams in unlined furs

Straight-stitch or zig-zag seams can be covered with grosgrain ribbon, leather or leather-like fabric, braid, or folded bias-cut bands of fabric. Edges can be finished with contrasting ribbon that has been pressed to shape before being applied. This kind of detail is usually applied to the fabric side of fur fabric by hand or machine. Experiment with this creative construction and adapt the method to suit the specific situation.

Flat-fell seams can be used for unlined garments made from fur fabrics that are boldly printed on the back and have a matted lamb's wool face. The printed side is usually used as the outside of the garment so that the lamb's-wool side becomes the lining. Often, the lamb's wool is turned to the right side for trimming bands on front, sleeve, and hem.

To make a flat-fell seam, straight-stitch the

seam first. Trim the seam edge that will be covered to ¼ inch; shear the pile from it and from ½ inch of the garment area underneath it. Also, shear the pile from the wide seam allowance for ⅛ inch so that you can turn it under and top-stitch. These fabrics are often polyester and can be steam-pressed like other fabrics, using a moist cheesecloth to protect the fabric.

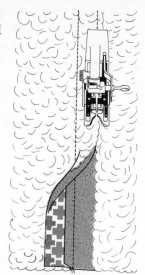

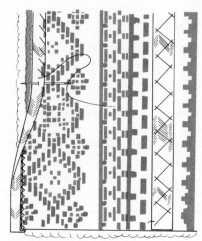

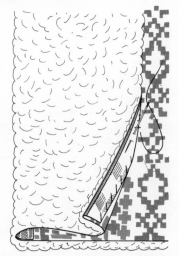

Above. Finish turned-back facing edges with twill tape. Apply the tape with a narrow zig-zag stitch. Turn tape and stitch it to the backing with an overcasting stitch.
Right. Slip-stitch the finished taped edge to the garment.

Darts

Darts can be straight-stitched in your fur fabric in the same way as the seams. However, in all except sparsely covered short-pile furs, narrow zig-zag stitching is preferred.

FABRICS

Characteristics. These fabrics are highly stable, with little give in either lengthwise or crosswise direction. Some are washable; others must be dry-cleaned.

Types. Range is great, from thin ones that handle like corduroy to long-haired ones that require special handling. Some are printed on the back, hence reversible.

Fiber Content. Backing—cotton, acrylic, or polyester. Face—rayon, modacrylic, polyester, acrylic, or wool.

PATTERN CHOICE

Look for simple lines, few seams, and raglan or set-in sleeves. Choose patterns recommended for fur fabrics, if possible. Remember, fur-lined garments must be cut generously to allow for fur on the inside. These fabrics combine well with leather, suede, tweed, or bulky wool knits.

Coats and capes—casual, country, or dressy; long vests.

Children's coats, capes, jackets.

Men's wear—car coats, jackets, vests.

PREPARATIONS

- Store suspended from a hanger.
- Relax fabric by allowing it to lie flat on floor or table overnight, fur side up.
- Notice stripes, animal-like markings, shadings and any special design or pile characteristics.
- Square and cut ends with table edge.

PATTERN FITTING

- Usually, purchase your regular pattern type and size.
- If using fur on inside, add up to $3/4$ inch to side and sleeve seams; or, use a pattern one size larger than usual; or, use a pattern designed for fur lining.
- Attach facing sections to garment sections where possible, to eliminate seams.
- Cut and fit garment of muslin.

CUTTING AND MARKING

- Plan for one-way cutting, fur running downward, except for sheared beaver or seal types, which should run upward.
- Plan for single-layer cutting. (Purchase two patterns or cut duplicate pattern sections from tissue, or cut from fitted muslin.)
- Be sure to cut pairs, not two for same side.
- Lay fabric fur side down.
- Lay pattern on fabric side, right side down.
- On patterned furs, observe pattern-matching procedures.
- Cut fur with cutting knife, razor-type cutter, or tips of shears, through backing only and with very short strokes.
- Mark notches with chalk or thread.
- With your vacuum cleaner, pick up fall-out of fur fabric as you cut.

STAY STITCHING

- Do **not** stay-stitch.

STITCHING

- Fur fabrics stitch quite easily.
- Use all-polyester or polyester-core threads.
- Size 14 ball-point needle for thinner weights.
- Needle-thread tension usually must be increased one or two points above normal to balance the stitch.
- Normal to heavy presser-foot pressure.
- Use a 10 stitch length for straight stitching, 12 to 15 for zig-zag stitching.
- Use Even Feed foot for best results.

SEAMS AND SEAM FINISHES

- For plain, pressed-open seams in lined garments, pin and stitch, using hands to put tension on seam, and withdraw pins as you stitch; or use Even Feed foot.
- On long-pile furs, stroke fur away from seam line as you stitch.
- Pull long hairs from seam on right side with coarse darning needle.
- To reduce seam-allowance bulk, shear fur.
- Stitch seam allowances to backing with padding stitches.
- For zig-zag seams, trim seam allowances to $1/4$ or $1/8$ inch; use plain zig-zag, 5 or 3 stitch width.
- For two-faced fur fabrics in unlined garments, use flat-felled seams and trim fur from all underlayers of the seam allowances. Hand-stitch the second stitching where stitching will not embed.

FACINGS, INTERFACINGS, LININGS, UNDERLININGS

- Fur fabrics styled for conventional construction —Use these fabrics in the regular way, except for underlining, which is seldom required.
- Two-faced fabrics—When using reverse side for trimming, stitch, turn back, and whip twill tape to edge of fur facing used for trimming, then slip-stitch to garment.

PRESSING

- Limit iron temperature to that for fiber with lowest heat requirement.
- Fur fabrics accept padding and inside tacking stitches without showing on outside.
- Many fur fabrics should not be pressed at all.
- Press only all-polyester lamb's-wool types with steam from moist cheesecloth and with low temperature.
- Embed stitching and shape seams with a small roller.
- Stitch sheared seam allowances to backing instead of pressing.

HEMS AND EDGE FINISHES

- Lined garments—Turn hem only 1 inch, stitch twill tape to edge, hand-whip to garment, and face hem with 2-inch bias of lining fabric.
- Edges may be finished decoratively with suede, leather, plastic or woven binding.
- For long furs, make closures of button loops, toggles, or metal fasteners rather than buttonholes.
- Reinforce sewn buttons with a protective, flat sew-through button on back.

GLOSSARY OF SEWING TERMS*

abutted seam—Two cut seam edges joined edge to edge with an underlay of a lightweight fabric. Usually used in interfacing and interlining.

appliqué—To sew a design of a small piece of fabric over the main fabric. The design or motif may be applied either by machine with a zig-zag stitch, or by hand with the blanket stitch.

armhole—The garment opening for the arm and sleeve. Formerly known as "armscye."

backstitch—1. The reverse stitch on the machine. Used to reinforce the stitching at the beginning and ending of seams. 2. A hand sewing stitch.

balance lines—The horizontal level on which the crosswise grain of the fabric falls at a right angle to the lengthwise grain in each dress section.

basting stitch—A long stitch made by hand or machine to hold two pieces of fabric together temporarily. Used to join garment sections before fitting and to prevent the fabric from slipping during stitching of seams.

belting—Stiffening used as interlining or backing in a belt and inside a waistband.

beveling seams—See Seam blending, beveling, or grading.

bias—The diagonal line of fabric that is on neither the lengthwise nor the crosswise grain. A "true bias" is the diagonal line formed when the lengthwise grain of the fabric is folded to the crosswise grain.

binding—A single or double bias finish used to encase raw edges. It may be applied without top stitching or with top stitching, using the Binder Foot.

blindstitch—1. A hand stitch used for hemming and finishing which is invisible on the right side. 2. A zig-zag machine stitch pattern. See Zig-Zag stitches.

block—To outline on muslin, paper, or fabric, the principle sections of a chair, sofa, or cushion before the slipcover fabric is cut. Sections of dress fabric also are often blocked to ensure a perfect matching of design.

bodkin—A heavy needle with a blunt point and large eye. Used to draw tape, elastic, ribbon, cord, etc., through a casing or heading; also used to help form a thread shank in button sewing.

boning—See Featherbone.

cable cord—Soft cotton cord used for cording and tubing; available in several sizes.

canopy—1. Fabric hung or draped over a frame attached to a four-poster. 2. A decorative treatment above a headboard.

casing—1. A hem or tuck through which ribbon, tape, cord, or elastic can be drawn. 2. Opening at the top of a curtain through which a rod is run.

center line—The vertical center of the bodice, skirt, or yoke section of a garment. It is designated on the pattern pieces and is transferred to the fabric sections with a basting thread.

clip—To cut a short distance into a seam allowance or selvage with the point of the scissors. Used in curved seams, square corners, buttonholes, and the like so that seams will lie flat when pressed.

controlled fullness—The gather-

ing necessary on a long seam edge so that it can be joined to a shorter seam edge.

crease—1. A line or mark made by folding the fabric and pressing the fold. 2. The line or mark that may result when the manufacturer folds the fabric and rolls it on the bolt.

crinoline—A coarse, stiff, cotton fabric used to hold the heading erect in curtains and draperies and to give body to contour belts, and similar constructions.

custom finish—Perfection in fit and construction of garments, slipcovers, bedspreads, draperies, and the like.

decorative stitching—1. A zig-zag machine stitch that is ornamental in design. 2. Hand embroidery stitches.

directional stitching—Stitching of seams in the correct direction of the grain so that the fabric will not stretch during the stitching.

drape—1. A property many fabrics have of falling easily into graceful folds; a soft silk, for example. 2. An attractive arrangement of folds in a garment or window drapery. The folds may be controlled by means of gathers, tucks, or pleats.

drop shoulder—Shoulder line located below the normal line.

ease—The even distribution of fullness when one section of a seam is joined to a slightly shorter section without forming gathers or tucks. Used to shape set-in sleeves, the shoulder line, and other areas.

ease allowance—That amount added to body measurements to make garments more comfortable and allow for action.

*Many of the terms defined here are explained more fully in the text. Consult the alphabetical index.

488

edgestitch—1. To stitch close to a finished edge or seam from the right side of the fabric. 2. To stitch close to the edge of a fold after the fabric edge is turned to the underside. Used to finish the edge of hems and facings.

emery cushion—Small bag filled with an abrasive. Used to sharpen needles and remove rust.

facing—The second layer of fabric used to finish necklines, front and back openings, sleeves, and the like.

featherbone—A narrow strip of boning used to stiffen the seams and edges of closely fitted garment sections to prevent them from slipping or rolling; for example, the bodice of strapless dresses and cummerbunds.

fibers—Natural or man-made filaments from which yarns are spun.

finishing—The sewing techniques used in garment construction to finish seams, facings, hems, necklines, and other sections.

fly—A finished closing that conceals the zipper or buttons. Generally used in shorts, men's pants, and topcoats.

footboard—The upright board at the foot of a bed.

grading seams—See Seam blending, beveling, or grading.

grain—In woven fabrics, the lengthwise and crosswise direction of the yarn. The lengthwise yarn forms the lengthwise grain; the crosswise yarn, the crosswise grain. When these two threads or grains are at right angles, the fabric is "on the true grain."

gusset—A small shaped piece of matching fabric set into a slash or seam for added width and ease. Often found at the underarm when sleeve and bodice are cut-in-one.

headboard—The upright board at the head of a bed.

heading—1. A fabric tuck above the casing or at the top edge of curtains. 2. A narrow edge above a line of gathers that form a ruffle.

hemline—The line on which the hem is marked and turned to the underside. This line is an even distance from the floor.

interfacing—A third thickness of carefully selected fabric which is placed between the garment and facing fabrics for added body, shaping, and support.

interlining—A fabric placed between the lining and outer fabric. Used in coats, jackets, and the like to add warmth or bulk; in bedspreads to give body; in draperies to add body and to prevent light from showing through and fading the fabric.

intersecting seams—Seams that cross one another when garment sections are joined together at the waistline, shoulder line, set-in sleeve, and similar points.

joinings—The points at which one garment section is joined to another, such as skirt and bodice.

lap—To extend or fold one piece of fabric or garment section over another.

lapel—The section of a garment which is turned back between the top button and collar.

layout—The position in which pattern pieces are laid on the fabric for cutting.

layering—Another term for blending or beveling. See Seam blending, beveling, or grading.

lining—A carefully selected fabric that covers the underside of another fabric, adding body to the article. 1. In dress construction, the lining is cut the

same as the dress fabric and constructed separately. It adds a finished look to the underside. 2. In tailoring, the lining is constructed to fit into the jacket or coat and prevents the unfinished seam allowance from showing. 3. In home decorating, the lining is used to finish the underside of draperies and protect the top fabric. It is also used in bedspreads.

markings—The symbols shown on the pattern for darts, buttonholes, tucks, and other construction details. They are transferred from the pattern to the fabric by means of tailor's tacks, chalk, bastings, or tracing wheel.

mercerized—A finish for cotton that adds strength and luster and makes the fabric more receptive of dyes.

miter—1. The diagonal line formed when fabric is joined at a square corner. After seaming, the excess fabric is generally cut away on the underside where the hems meet. Used where hems join at the corner as in a vent in a jacket, draperies, and linens. 2. The diagonal fold made when applying a band, lace, or the like to square or pointed shapes.

multiple-stitch zig-zag—See Zig-Zag stitches.

notches—V-shaped cutouts in the cut edge of the seam allowance that indicate which edges are to be seamed together. Matching notches are always joined.

notions—Small items used in sewing such as thread, needles, pins, buttons, and the like.

overlap—The part of the garment that extends over another part, as the opening of a blouse, jacket, coat, or waistband.

pattern layout guide—The instruction sheet that shows how

(Continued)

to arrange the pattern pieces on the fabric before cutting. It includes the most economical layout for different types and widths of fabrics and for the various pattern sizes.

pattern stitching—Zig-zag stitching of designs on a zig-zag machine which is made possible by setting selectors in a certain position or by inserting specific cams or discs.

pivot—To turn the fabric on the machine needle while the needle is still in the fabric. Used when stitching square corners such as in buttonholes, pockets, and notched sections.

placket—A finished opening that is generally closed by means of a zipper, snaps, or other fastening. Used in dresses, skirts, shorts, and other garments to make them easy to put on and to assure a good fit at the waistline, sleeve, etc.; also used in such fabric furnishings as slipcovers and cushions.

preshrunk—To shrink the fabric before cutting so that its dimensions will not be altered by laundering or dry cleaning. Many fabrics are preshrunk by the manufacturer.

pressure—The force the presser foot exerts on the fabric during the machine stitching. The pressure can—and should—be regulated to suit the fabric.

ravel—1. To separate or pull the woven threads away from the cut edges of the fabric, leaving long threads; to unweave. 2. To fray, as unfinished seam edges.

reinforce—To strengthen an area that will be subjected to strain. The area may be reinforced with an underlay or patch of fabric or with extra rows of stitching.

regular stitch—The machine stitch length best suited to the fabric being stitched;

usually applied to straight stitching.

return—In curtain and drapery fixtures, the distance from the curve of the rod to the wall. Curtains and draperies are constructed so that they extend around the return.

revers—Wide, shaped lapels on coats and suits.

reversible—Describing: 1. A fabric that is woven so that either side may be used for the right side—for example damask or double-faced wool. 2. A garment finished so that it may be worn with either side out.

rip—1. To remove machine stitching. 2. To tear, usually along the seam.

sag—To hang or droop below the normal line or level. A seam sags when it is stretched or pulled down from the normal position through weight of the fabric (for example, a bias seam).

seam allowance—The amount of fabric allowed for seams in joining sections of a garment or other article together—generally ⅝ inch.

seam blending, beveling, or grading—Trimming all seam allowances within a seam to different widths. Blending removes bulk so that the seam will lie flat.

seam edge—The cut edge of the seam allowance.

seam finish—The finish used on the edge of the seam allowance to prevent the fabric from raveling or fraying.

seamline—The line designated for stitching the seam—generally ⅝ inch from the cut edge.

selvage—The finished edges on all woven fabrics which parallel the lengthwise thread.

shank—The stem between the button and the garment to which the button is sewed. The shank can be made with thread or it can be a part of the button. It allows room for the buttonhole side of the garment to fit smoothly over the button.

shrink—To relax the fibers of the fabric through moisture or steam to prevent subsequent shrinking.

sizing—A finish applied to fabrics to add body and stiffness.

slash—A cut in the fabric along a straight line. A slash is longer than a clip. Examples are: a finished slit in a garment that is faced, and an opening into which a gusset is inserted.

spanking—Act of pounding or flattening fabric to shape a finished edge after it has been steam-pressed.

stay—A small piece of fabric or tape that is sewed to an area of the garment for reinforcement. Use at the point of a slash, under bound buttonholes, and at the waistline.

stitch pattern—See Pattern stitching.

tack—To attach one piece of fabric to another with tiny hand stitches—generally with several backstitches over the first stitch; for example, a facing to seam allowance.

tailoring—A method of sewing characterized by classic lines; encompasses suits, coats, dresses, and shorts.

tailor's tacks—Markings made of thread which are used to transfer symbols from the pattern to the fabric.

tension—The degree of looseness or tightness of the needle and bobbin threads that interlock to form the sewing machine stitch. There are two tensions

—the upper (needle thread) and the lower (bobbin thread). When the two are balanced, both the needle and the bobbin threads are drawn into the fabric to the same degree.

thread count—Number of threads (yarns) per inch in the warp and weft of woven fabric.

underlap—The edge of a garment that extends under another edge, as in the opening of a coat, jacket, or waistband.

underlay—1. A strip of fabric that is placed on the underside of the main fabric for reinforcement. Used in stitching buttonholes, pockets, and similar sections; in mending; in decorative zig-zag stitching. 2. A piece of fabric placed under finished shirring to prevent strain on the shirring stitches.

underlining—The second thickness of a carefully selected fabric which is cut by the same pattern as the garment and is stitched in place with the garment seams. Used to give added body and shape.

up and down—The direction of the nap, pile, or design of a fabric. On napped and pile fabrics, the shading varies depending on the angle from which the fabric is viewed. On prints, the design may run in one direction—for example, flowers with "heads up," or uneven plaids.

vent—A lapped opening. Used in hems of tailored jackets and sleeves and in other garment sections.

warp—The threads or yarns that run lengthwise in the weaving of the fabric.

weft (old term woof)—The threads or yarns that cross the warp. Also called "filler."

zig-zag stitches:

blindstitch zig-zag—A stitch pattern that produces four straight stitches separated by a single sideward stitch to the left. Used in finishing seam edges, in stitching hems, and in decorative stitching.

closely spaced stitch pattern—A decorative zig-zag stitch pattern that places all stitches close together when the stitch length selector is set for satin stitching.

multiple-stitch zig-zag—A stitch pattern that makes four stitches to the left, then four to the right in a zig-zag shape. Used to finish hem and seam edges, mend, stitch darts and seams in interfacing, and sew elastic and blanket binding in place; also used for decorative stitching and other sewing.

open-spaced stitch pattern—A decorative zig-zag stitch pattern that does not place the stitches close together although the stitch length selector is set for satin stitching.

plain zig-zag stitch—A regular zig-zag stitch where all stitches are of the same width and in a straight line. The stitch length and stitch width selectors may be set for various lengths and widths.

Index

(continued)

(continued)

(continued)

497

index for "the many faces of knits"

*Trademark of THE SINGER COMPANY

Copyright © 1987, 1986, 1985, 1984, 1983, 1982, 1981 by J. G. Ferguson Publishing Company
International Standard Book Number: 0-89434-057-3
LIBRARY OF CONGRESS CARD CATALOG NUMBER 84-6042
All rights reserved
Printed in the United States of America

K-7

The
LEGAL
GUIDE
for the Family

by

DONALD L. VERY

WINNER

AMERICAN BAR ASSOCIATION

CERTIFICATE OF MERIT

"for noteworthy contribution to public
understanding of the American
system of law and justice."

Editorial Consultant
EUGENE F. KEEFE
Attorney-at-Law

J. G. FERGUSON PUBLISHING C
Chicago

To Norma because...

Donald Leroy Very

Donald Leroy Very was born in Pittsburgh on August 19, 1933. He received his Bachelor of Arts Degree from Duquesne University in 1955 and his J.D. from the University of Notre Dame in 1958.

He was admitted to the Pennsylvania Bar in 1959; Partner in the law firm of Campbell, Thomas and Burke of Pittsburgh from 1959 to 1970; Partner in the law firm of Tucker, Arensberg, Very and Ferguson since 1971.

Assistant Director of In-Dev-Or, the Insurance Development Organization Business School; member Admiralty Rules Committee U.S. District Court of the Western District of Pennsylvania; examiner of Pennsylvania Board of Law Examiners; Adjunct Professor of Admiralty Law University of Pittsburgh; President—1978— Allegheny County Bar Association; member American Judicature Society; member American Trial Lawyers Association; member Maritime Law Association.

Mr. Very was the Editor-In-Chief of the Pittsburgh Legal Journal, and Editor of the Pennsylvania Bar Quarterly Publication.

Richard Dell
EDITORIAL DIRECTOR

Russell Primm
EDITOR

Harriet Helmer
PERMISSIONS AND RIGHTS

Pam Hori
INDEXER

Dick Flood
ILLUSTRATIONS

Herb Slobin
DESIGN

Foreword

I was impressed by the courage of the publisher when I was approached to read this book and write a foreword. There is as much art as science in the practice of law; in addition, attorneys, as with any other group, run a broad spectrum in their personal philosophies and approach to the practice of their profession. Moreover, the "law" in any particular area varies from state to state. Even where there is a "uniform" law such as the Uniform Commercial Code, there is not only an "Official" commentary but also an "Illinois" commentary to the official commentary to point out where the Illinois statute differs from the "model" statute. Finally, the law is constantly changing; witness the fact, that as this manuscript was going to press, Congress enacted the Economic Recovery Tax Act of 1981, thereby requiring last minute editorial work to ensure that various parts of the text reflected this latest development. Thus it is a bold stroke for a lawyer and a publisher to seek to present a book on the "law" to the public.

However, the strength of *The Legal Guide for the Family* is that it does not purport to be a definitive statement of the law in any particular area. Nor does it purport to be one of the "how to avoid a lawyer" type book; this latter category runs the risk of causing much mischief if people are encouraged to rely on superficial knowledge where expertise is required.

The purpose of Mr. Very's work is to offer the average reader a perspective on the legal system in general and upon particular aspects of that system with respect to which most individuals will be affected at some point in their lives. The book also provides a perspective for the reader upon the role of the attorney and the relationship between attorney and client. I would expect that a person who reads this book with awareness of the foregoing goals will not only have a better understanding of our legal system and the way it touches us in our daily lives but also will be in a better position to seek legal advice when appropriate and to work effectively, efficiently and harmoniously with an attorney when the attorney-client relationship is formed.

Dean Charles W. Murdock
Loyola University of Chicago
School of Law

EDITOR'S NOTE

The *Legal Guide for the Family* is an extraordinarily informative guide to the laws that affect all of us at one time or another during our normal business and social activities. It provides useful guidelines for the reader's assistance when he or she is entering into any venture covered by statutes, whether it is forming a partnership, signing a lease, building a patio, or planning a will. In this book the reader will find a wealth of helpful information simply and concisely outlined in language the layperson can understand. The book is not, however, meant to be a substitute for a lawyer, and, in fact, the book offers guidelines on when to seek a lawyer's help, what assistance a lawyer will provide, and why it is usually essential to have a lawyer's services.

It must be noted that laws and customs vary from state to state and what is a rule in one state will not necessarily be the rule in another. Lawyers who are licensed by states understand the application of the law within your state.

TABLE OF CONTENTS

Part I
INTRODUCTION

In the words of Oliver Wendell Holmes, Jr., "The law is the witness and external deposit of our moral life. Its history is the history of the moral development of the race."

Its value in the life of every citizen, one might add, lies in its capacity to serve every citizen. To serve, in this case, means to provide the protections that all bodies of law must give if they are to continue in existence.

To serve also means that the individual citizen has the right and privilege to call on the law, courts, and lawyers in case of need.

This book deals with ways in which the law can be used more effectively. This is a goal that can be achieved whether one uses a lawyer or not. More effective use of the law can be promoted in at least five ways:

(1) by gaining a better understanding of the nature of law;
(2) by using lawyers more effectively;
(3) by proceeding without a lawyer when that is appropriate;
(4) by planning one's personal affairs so as to prevent legal problems before they arise; and
(5) by changing the law where that becomes possible.

Chapters 1 and 2 are concerned mainly with the first two ways of using the law. Later sections deal with the other three ways to make the law work for you.

In understanding the law, one can better appreciate the issues that involve the law and its methods. For example, a news item may involve freedom of speech or freedom of the press. The citizen can decide how the issue involves him and what action should be taken, if any. Even if he chooses to take no action, he will have made an informed choice.

In trying to ascertain when a lawyer is needed and what he can do for a particular problem, the individual faces challenges. He or she needs to know several things: how to find a lawyer, how to agree on a proper fee, how to use one's time with the lawyer effectively, what to expect from him, and what to do if dissatisfied with fees or services.

In discussing these and related subjects, Chapters 1 and 2 provide stepping stones to use of the rest of this book.

1 WHAT IS "THE LAW"?

What is the law? It represents many things to many people. To a consumer seeking compensation for a faulty product, it stands for one thing. To a corporation executive seeking patent protection for a new product, it promises something else. To the person arrested on criminal charges, it may have yet another meaning. For the lawyer representing each of these individuals, the law has still different meanings.

The law, in short, is complex, and has many facets. The phrase, "the law," simply offers a convenient way to deal with that complexity.

The law even represents something different from laws. As a concept and a reality, the law refers to the great heritage on which the rights, benefits, and privileges of Americans are based. The laws are the specific statutes and provisions that guarantee these rights and privileges.

The different facets of the law have their own characteristics. Each facet has its own origins in history, deals with certain kinds of cases or situations, and has meaning in certain kinds of courts. And, in fact, not all cases even go to a courtroom. This suggests that the law is a flexible tool.

The law's flexibility points to another quality: continuous change and growth. New laws appear all the time; old laws disappear. The new laws help citizens to deal with new needs and problems as they arise. Supreme Court decisions provide one example of how the law grows. But the decisions of other courts, bills or pieces of legislation, and many other legal developments forward the process of growth.

A set of rules for the common good

No matter how much the law grows and changes, it has a definite, unchanging meaning: the law stands as a set of rules or principles of conduct designed for the common good. The law specifies what behavior is desired and not desired in specific situations. It frequently spells out what remedies to apply when undesirable behavior is encountered.

Law has been described as a set of do's and don'ts. But such rules and regulations do not exist for their own sake. They are not intended to place obstacles in the way of freedom or the pursuit of happiness. Rather, they are designed to remove or at least smooth out obstacles: to make freedom a reality. The obstacles arise inevitably when people live together in a society. Some of the more obvious of these obstacles are crimes and disputes between people.

The law tries to walk the fine line between the rights of one person to act and of another person to enjoy protection. In the words of the adage, "My right to swing my fist ends where your nose begins."

Laws are thus designed to serve and protect in two ways. First, they are designed to protect the individual's interests so long as no one else is harmed. Second, the laws are designed to protect society as a whole. Society, in turn, is protected in three ways:

1. Order is maintained and progress is ensured.
2. Society is protected from harmful acts by individuals.
3. The general welfare and justice are advanced.

Laws function in accordance with at least two principles. The first centers on fairness: if a wrong has been committed, the remedy prescribed should make amends for that wrong as much as is humanly possible. The second has universal application: all individuals, without exception, are to be treated alike under the law.

Far from being just a set of do's and don'ts, the law represents a practical instrument for individual use. A citizen of the United States of America has obligations and duties; but he also has rights under the Constitution. U.S. law is vitally concerned with preserving Constitutional rights.

THE ORIGINS OF MODERN LAW

Every society has some kind of law. In any social group the law survives because people accept and believe in it. Even the most ancient and primitive of societies have been lawful societies.

Law survives if it is accepted

The American system of law has carried forward and refined this legal approach to solving problems. Modern man's heritage of law can be traced back to ancient civilizations.

Ancient Developments

Among ancient legal developments, several have significance today. For example, the Code of Hammurabi appeared in 1900 B.C. Basically a set of criminal laws, the Code prescribed a punishment for each crime. The Ten Commandments of Moses, dating from about 1200 B.C., provide the basis for many modern laws. Here a moral element appears: rather than stress punishment and the fear of punishment, the Commandments proceed from a conviction that certain acts are wrong.

The moral precepts of the Ten Commandments have been accepted down to the present day. Laws, it is assumed, have a moral basis. Citizens may resist or rebel against a law if they feel that it is wrong, morally or otherwise.

The Greeks developed the philosophy that a country should be ruled by laws rather than by men. The American government functions according to that belief. Typically, Greek laws dealt with property and commerce, particularly contracts. They also held trials before citizens—what are now known as jury trials.

Roman law incorporated Greek law

Roman Law incorporated Greek Law in a complete set of moral precepts published in 450 B.C. The Roman Emperor Justinian I, a thousand years later, published the *Corpus Juris Civilis* ("Body of Civil Law"). Roman law became the basis for canon law in the Roman Catholic Church. Napoleon carried this tradition forward in the Napoleonic Code. Louisiana, once a French possession, still uses that code as the basis of its civil law.

The civil-law tradition exemplified by the Napoleonic Code had its counterpart in areas that were historically under Spanish control. The Spanish *fuero juzgo*, or legal court, stood as a code of laws for those areas. The *fuero juzgo* was replaced by U.S. law as the Spanish possessions came under American control.

English Common Law and the Constitution

The American legal system owes much of its character to the English Common Law. Most of the earlier developments involved establishing codes of conduct. The Common Law offered a method of establishing new laws in the courtroom. The judge, or the jury, reaches decisions on the basis of previous decisions—precedents—in similar cases.

The origin of the term common law

The name Common Law comes from the fact that this form of law was commonly practiced throughout England.

Common law developed when a group of king's judges began to "ride the circuit" to hear cases. When the judges could not find any known principle to apply in a given case, they created a new one. Staying at inns, these judges would share experiences and opinions with one another. Summaries of many proceedings were written into legal *Year Books*.

Sir Edward Coke (1552-1634) analyzed many of these cases and developed a set of rules or standards. Sir William Blackstone (1723-1780) carried these analyses further. His *Commentaries* formed the basis for legal training in England through the nineteenth century. Americans have carried on this tradition of commentaries. Thus, both court decisions and commentaries on them form central parts of the common law.

Growing out of the English traditions, the U.S. Bill of Rights—the first ten amendments to the Constitution—embodies ideas expressed long before Thomas Jefferson put them down in organized form. The principles to which Jefferson referred reached all the way back to ancient Greece.

Many other thinkers contributed ideas that helped form Jefferson's thinking—and thus our Bill of Rights. One was England's John Locke. Discussing human nature and natural law, Locke wrote:

> The State of Nature has a law of nature to govern it, which obliges everyone; and reason, which is that law, teaches all mankind, who will but consult it, that all begin equal and independent, no one aught harm another in his life, health, liberty or possession.

In discussing American law today, we are actually talking about two kinds of law: case law and statutory law. Case law utilizes the precedents reached by courts in similar situations. Statutory law functions on the basis of written laws, or acts of federal, state, or local legislative bodies.

Two kinds of American law

THE PURPOSES OF LAWS

The law today comprises a thorough, comprehensive body of precepts and regulations. Laws deal with every aspect of a person's life. Some ways in which the individual is affected by the law include:

Marriage and rights of the marriage partners
Relations between parent and child
Buying a house
Household loans
Wills and the disposal of property
The rights of employers and employees
Injuries to one's body, property, or reputation
Civil rights
Protection against crime
Rights if arrested

The law operates in these and other areas to achieve four different goals:

1. It serves to prevent and settle disputes.
2. It enforces standards of social conduct.
3. It establishes relations between the government and the society.
4. It distributes various kinds of resources within the society.

Preventing and Settling Disputes

Preventing and settling disputes, or conflict resolution, provides a rationale for civil lawsuits between individuals. Examples of such disputes include divorce proceedings and conflicting claims over property. In many disputes, the "case" may never come to court. Both attorneys may agree that one of the parties is entitled to all or part of his claim. For example, one party may be rewarded with ownership of a property ("have title") while the other can use it under the "easement" principle.

If the lawyers disagree, the case may go to court. "Going to court" represents an effort to obtain an impartial decision, or judgment. One or both parties may later appeal the verdict of the judge or jury. The party receiving a negative verdict may *appeal* to a higher court. The legal pathway for handling a dispute is clearly marked.

Social Conduct

Law in modern society

The law serves also as a way to enforce standards of acceptable social conduct. Society has both informal and formal means of enforcing standards of behavior. In primitive societies, informal means such as social pressure and opinion were used for the most part. Law, the formal means, became more important as society became more complex. Today's society, especially, could not live without the law.

This use of the law applies in many areas. For example, the control of crime requires enforcement of standards of acceptable behavior. The handling of disputes involves similar enforcement of rules.

Government and Society

The U.S. Constitution is concerned with establishing overarching relations between the government and society. "Society" here means individuals as well as the group. The fifth and fourteenth amendments to the Constitution established the right of the individual to "due process." This means that the government can only take legal actions toward individuals.

The application of due process

Two kinds of due process have been identified. The first is procedural, meaning that the methods the government uses to deal with its citizens must be acceptable. The second is concerned with the content of the laws passed by government. In the 1930s, for example, the Supreme Court rejected many New Deal laws passed by the Roosevelt administration.

Distribution of Resources

Finally, the law helps to determine how society's resources are distributed among its members. One way in which this is done is by regulating the actions of citizens. Such regulation, in turn, may be effected through control of the criminally greedy. Regulation also takes place through supervision of contractual relations. In both cases, standards of acceptable conduct are being enforced.

Another way of effecting the distribution of resources is through taxation. Here, the government (1) takes a portion of a citizen's money or (2) finds ways to spend it. People may be taxed either directly or indirectly. In the latter case, as with sales taxes, the tax is first paid to a merchant. Sometimes members of society see the ways in which resources are distributed as unfair or unjust. Individuals or groups may try to influence the government to use some of its tax money to remedy that injustice.

These four uses of the law overlap. For example, enforcing standards of conduct affects both the settlement of disputes and the relations between government and society. Poor allocation of resources can lead to social disorder and enforcement of standards. Such enforcement can prevent disputes, which maintains social order. Resolving conflicts can smooth out relations between individuals and the government.

THE TYPES OF LAW

"The law," as noted, is not a unitary thing. Laws exist at federal, state, and local levels. These, in turn, can be classified according to whether they deal with civil or criminal matters. Finally, the law may be considered with respect to its origins: whether a law was passed by a legislative body or shaped in the courtroom because of a judge's decision. Of special importance is whether a law is civil or criminal, and how it originated.

Civil and Criminal Law

Civil and criminal law differ according to the identity of the "injured" party. In civil law the injured party is another individual. In criminal law the injured party is considered to be society. Civil law may involve either common law or statutory law while criminal law usually involves only statutory law. Criminal statutes define the offenses that are considered grave enough to be regarded as crimes against society.

Differences between civil and criminal law

Civil law typically involves a plaintiff and his lawyer, and a defendant and his lawyer. Civil suits may involve any of the following: auto accidents, injuries at home, injuries on the job, and injuries to one's reputation.

In a criminal trial the defendant and his lawyer face a prosecuting attorney and his "client"—the state or federal government. Federal and state statutes describe the specific crimes and the permissible punishments for each. Violations of city ordinances are not classified as crimes, but can bring fines.

Some states have more than 200 crimes on their books. The most typical crimes are: murder, both first and second degree; voluntary manslaughter; criminal negligence; larceny; embezzlement; rape; robbery; receiving stolen goods; forgery; burglary; arson; perjury; kidnapping; accessory after fact; and assault.

Statutory and Common Law

In each state, legislatures pass laws, acts, or statutes from time to time. Cities, counties, townships, and other local municipal units have legislative bodies that pass ordinances. Nationally, the Congress passes laws which, as in the states, are called statutes.

Governments at all three levels have administrative agencies that make rules, regulations, and resolutions. These may have the force of law, and therefore are sometimes referred to as "administrative law." In each case, however, the agency's rulings have the backing or authorization of a specific statute or ordinance. Without that specific law, the ruling would be invalid. Thus, administrative law is often viewed as a branch of statutory law.

Administrative agencies control a wide variety of areas of public life. These include public utilities, insurance, banking, motor vehicles, taxation, and the regulation and licensing of professions and occupations.

The American system of courts The common law is centered in the systems of courts. Every state has its own system of courts. At the top is a State Supreme Court or a Court of Appeals. Lesser courts include Criminal Courts, Civil Courts, Alderman's Courts, Justice of the Peace Courts, Mayor's Courts, and City Courts. Each court has the duty of interpreting the law and enforcing it. They do this by imposing fines and penalties in criminal cases, or by awarding damages in civil cases.

Because courts rely on decisions made in previous cases involving similar conditions, an attorney can use his research into previous cases to advise his client of the present status of the law in a particular case.

Court Systems

The federal court system is headed by the Supreme Court of the United States. Lesser courts include the Circuit Courts of Appeal, U.S. District Courts, Tax Court, and the Court of Claims. Federal law, including statutory, administrative, and common, together with comparable kinds of law at state and local levels, comprises the sum total of what is called "the law."

Clearly, "the law" cannot be a simple thing. The average citizen may hesitate even to try to understand the total U.S. legal picture. But examination a little at a time can be helpful. For those concerned with civil matters, criminal law does not apply. If one is concerned with a federal matter, state and local matters have no immediate importance. If a case involves only statutory law, precedents may be of little concern.

Federal and State Courts

Two separate systems of courts, the state and federal systems, function side by side. State courts are established by state constitutions and state legislatures. Federal courts are established by the United States Constitution and the Congress. Both the state and federal systems have different levels of courts. These levels are classified according to their geographic jurisdiction and by the kinds of cases they try.

Federal Court System

The federal court system has three principal levels: (1) District Courts, (2) the Circuit Courts of Appeal, and (3) the United States Supreme Court.

The District Courts are known as the trial courts of the federal system. Every state in the nation is served by at least one District Court. Both Maine and Ohio have two district courts each.

District Courts hear cases involving federal laws, the U.S. Constitution, and problems between citizens of different states. All kinds of criminal cases are tried, including felonies and misdemeanors occurring under federal statutes. Civil suits include:

The role of district courts

- Matters governed by federal law, such as bankruptcies, patent and copyright cases, and admiralty cases, which involve laws of the seas and navigable waterways
- Suits involving the Constitution or federal statutes such as civil rights
- Suits to which the federal government is a party
- Suits by one state against another
- Trials involving citizens of different states and sums greater than $10,000

In the last instance, the kind of law used may vary with the case. For example, if a car accident occurred in Ohio between a resident of Ohio and a resident of Kentucky, Ohio law would be used. The reason for this is that the federal system has no common law of its own. It has only statutory laws and these do not cover accidents.

Each Circuit Court of Appeals covers one of the eleven "circuits" into which the country is divided. Such a court hears cases which have moved upward through the court system from a District Court within its circuit.

The Supreme Court is the highest U.S. court. The Supreme Court hears appeals of important cases from Circuit Courts. In addition, it may consent to hear appeals to decisions made in state Supreme Courts.

State Court Systems

State court systems vary from state to state. In Ohio, as one typical example, the court system functions on three levels: the Ohio Supreme Court, Ohio Court of Appeals, and Ohio trial courts. The last group includes Common Pleas Courts, Municipal and County Courts, Mayor's Courts, and the Court of Claims.

The differences among state court systems

Another state, Maine, has five distinct levels of courts. The Maine District Courts try traffic cases, civil cases involving less than $20,000, some adult criminal cases, and cases involving juvenile crimes. Small Claims Courts involve private disputes involving debt or damage of less than $800. Superior Courts try all state criminal and civil cases, and hear appeals of cases from District Courts and administrative agencies.

Maine has two other special courts. The Supreme Judicial Court of Maine, called the Law Court, hears appeals from Superior Courts. The Probate Court oversees the administration of estates of deceased persons.

THE ADVERSARY PROCEDURE

A court trial, in whatever court, is based on the "adversary procedure." The case may be either civil or criminal; the two "sides" contend. Each side tries to persuade a judge or jury that it is right.

In this contest the judge acts as a referee, or authority, on questions of law. The jury decides on questions of fact. A trial proceeds according to well-defined steps: (1) selection of a jury, where there is one; (2) opening statements by the attorneys; (3) presentation of witnesses and evidence, with the plaintiff or prosecutor appearing first; (4) closing arguments by the attorneys; (5) instructions by the judge to the jury; and (6) deliberation and jury decision.

The jury system

Parties to civil suits and defendants in criminal cases are entitled to a jury trial. A trial jury is called a petit (or petty) jury; a grand jury in Criminal Cases decides in advance whether a trial should be held on the basis of available evidence.

A party to a trial is not always entitled to a jury. Even where one is so entitled, it may not be provided unless it is demanded. Jury trials are not allowed in cases involving minor offenses calling for penalties up to $100. Felonies and major misdemeanors usually call for trials by jury. In felony cases, twelve jurors are normally used; in misdemeanor cases, eight.

RIGHTS

The Bill of Rights

Under the United States Constitution, each American has certain guaranteed rights. Briefly, these rights include: freedom of speech and freedom of the press; freedom of assembly; freedom of religion; the right to vote; the right to hold public office; the right to keep and bear arms; protection of individual privacy; full enjoyment of one's property; equal protection under the laws; privilege against self-incrimination; due process of law; the right of habeas corpus; protection against "double jeopardy" (two trials for one offense); and the right to a jury trial.

The first ten amendments to the Constitution make up the Bill of Rights. Other amendments have a bearing on rights, however. The Fourteenth Amendment, dealing with due process, incorporates many of the features of the first ten amendments.

The Constitution grows and changes constantly. The written document itself undergoes additions; but interpretations are made repeatedly by the Supreme Court. The Fourteenth Amendment, as indicated, has been selectively absorbing the Bill of Rights over a matter of years. Essentially, it guarantees that many of the rights provided at the federal level have also to be protected at the state level.

The rights of persons accused of crimes have been defined not only by the Constitution but by court decisions—most importantly, Supreme Court decisions. These rights fall into two main categories: substantive and procedural.

Substantive Rights

The word substantive refers to rights like freedom of speech and religion that have intrinsic or basic value to the individual.

No right, not even a substantive right, gives anyone absolute freedom. Where an act violates the rights of another individual, or runs counter to a law, it becomes illegal even though, in theory, it amounts to an exercise of a substantive right.

In democratic countries, including the United States and Canada, the courts protect substantive rights to the fullest possible extent. The courts do this by ordering agencies or governmental bodies to stop interfering with exercise of a specific right or by ordering that the individual be allowed to exercise a right.

Procedural Rights

The second kind of right protected by the Constitution is the procedural right. A defendant in a criminal trial in the United States today has the right to have counsel. The defendant also has the right to trial by jury. Both rights are procedural because they ensure that no one will be convicted unless evidence is fairly presented and impartially assessed.

While the First Amendment provides the main guarantees of substantive rights, three constitutional amendments in particular protect procedural rights. These three are the Fourth, Fifth, and Fourteenth

Amendments. The Fourth Amendment prohibits illegal searches of houses and other property and illegal seizures of papers and other effects. The Fifth Amendment states, among other things, that no person can be "deprived of life, liberty, or property, without due process of law...." The Fourteenth Amendment also guarantees "due process of law" to all citizens. The amendment also provides for equal protection of every citizen under the laws of the United States and of the separate states.

Enforcement of the Fourth Amendment may result in freedom or a new trial for an obviously guilty defendant. But the courts, including the Supreme Court, are not supposed to be influenced by the possible guilt or innocence of a single defendant. The courts try to interpret the Constitution and other laws in such a way as to protect all accused persons and make sure that each has the full protection of the law.

The Sixth Amendment also extends the concept of procedural rights. It provides that an accused "shall enjoy the right to a speedy and public trial ... , and ... have the Assistance of Counsel for his defence." But according to a 1984 Supreme Court ruling, the right to counsel does not become operative until there are both prosecutor and accused. Thus two prison inmates held in administrative segregation pending investigation of two prison murders did not, in *U.S.* v. *Gouveia*, have the right to legal representation while in detention even though they were held more than 90 days. Because no charges were brought, there was neither prosecutor nor defendant.

Juvenile Rights. All fifty states and the District of Columbia have laws that protect the rights of juveniles or minors—persons under certain ages—where a crime has been committed (see Chapter 18).

In noncriminal cases, the rights of children and minors have received similar new emphasis. Questions of freedom of speech and of the press have arisen in the educational and other contexts. The Supreme Court—and, following it, other courts—have given wide-ranging protection to minors.

However, in cases where a "serious risk" exists that a juvenile may commit a crime before coming to trial, police authorities may detain the young person for a period up to 17 days. Ruling in a 1984 case, the Supreme Court upheld a New York statute providing for such detention. The Court stated that detaining juveniles in serious risk cases does not violate the Fourteenth Amendment's due process clause.

2 LAWYERS AND THE LAW

As society becomes more complex, so does the law. As laws become more numerous, the need for lawyers grows. One can often conduct one's personal affairs without a lawyer. But it is important to know when a lawyer is needed and when one is not. Then more effective use can be made of lawyers. This chapter tells how and when to find and use a lawyer—and when not to. The nature of the legal profession is explained. Alternatives to the use of lawyers are noted, and the question of lawyers' fees receives attention. Finally, the reader learns what to do if he or she is dissatisfied with a lawyer's work.

WHAT IS A LAWYER?

In a single sentence, a lawyer is an officer of the court who is authorized to explain the law to clients and to represent them in and out of court. As an officer of the court, the lawyer swears that he will uphold the law and conduct himself according to appropriate court procedures. The court may discipline a lawyer who fails in either role.

A lawyer has expert knowledge within the field of law. Sometimes he has specialized knowledge within the many subfields of law. A nonlawyer may know some aspects of the law, and may even be able to help himself in some instances, as this book will show. But the lawyer's expert knowledge may prove to be indispensable. Because of the very complexity of the law, his intelligent guidance of his client may make the difference between great or little expense and inconvenience.

Regardless of where a lawyer represents his client—in court or out—or what kind of advice is given, the purpose is to help the client (1) safeguard his legal rights and (2) fulfill his legal obligations. A lawyer has primary loyalty, thus, to his client. However, as he is sworn to uphold the court and the law, he will never counsel a client to break the law.

Different kinds of lawyers

There are many different kinds of lawyers. *Family lawyers* are the "general practitioners" who help with leases, wills, estate planning, contracts, real estate transactions, and divorce. Family lawyers try to practice *preventive law*, keeping clients out of court if possible. *Trial lawyers* possess special skills in courtroom procedures and the presentation of evidence. *Corporate lawyers* are salaried employees of corporations who often specialize in legal subfields important to their employers. These subfields include labor law, patents, consumer protection, and many others. The corporate lawyer may or may not become involved in court cases.

Among the many specialties in law, the most common in addition to those named are:

Negligence

Tax law

Banking and business law

Wills, estate planning, and probate

Real estate

Criminal law

Domestic relations

What Lawyers Do

Lawyers perform in many different roles to help their clients. The lawyer's principal tasks are preparing documents and agreements, negotiating out-of-court settlements of disputes, and representing clients in court and before government agencies. Lawyers have to develop various skills, including:

- *Reading.* Lawyers must read constantly to keep informed. This is essential not only for a general knowledge of the law, but to prepare a client's case.

- *Writing.* A lawyer's writing must be clear, comprehensive, and persuasive.
- *Creative thinking.* Lawyers must be able to adapt their knowledge of the law to the particular client's needs. This may mean applying old precedents or trying to shape new ones.
- *Speaking.* This vital skill comes into use when lawyers represent clients in court or before agencies, boards, councils, commissions, and other governmental bodies.
- *Counseling.* Clients receive legal advice that can prevent legal problems and disputes.
- *Dealing with disputes.* Lawyers must anticipate legal arguments once disputes have developed.
- *Negotiation.* Lawyers try to settle legal disputes with an eye to preventing court appearances (litigation).
- *Serving the public.* Many lawyers try to improve the profession and engage in civic activities.

Their Training and Qualifications

Lawyers must meet certain requirements before they are permitted to practice law. Most or all of the following are required, with some variations among states:

Meeting requirements for practice

- Four years of college.
- Three years in an accredited law school.
- Specialization in a particular area of law (optional). In a state such as California, before lawyers can advertise themselves as specialists in specific areas, they must be certified by the state.
- Clerkship or internship in a law office. While sometimes optional, this phase of training is usually required.
- Passing a state bar examination, a rigorous test of all areas of legal knowledge, administered and graded by personnel appointed by the state Supreme Court.
- Membership in some bar association, usually the state bar association. Memberships may also include the American Bar Association, the county bar association for smaller communities, or the local bar association for larger cities. Membership is not essential to the practice of law.
- Evidence of good character, whether vouchers of character from associates or affidavits of character from practicing lawyers or both.
- Waiver of the above requirements in some states, including Kansas, if a lawyer has been practicing in another state for over five years.

- A license to practice, upon completing all other requirements, issued by the state Supreme Court.

Discipline and Ethics

Codes and Standards

Standards of conduct for lawyers are determined both ethically and legally. Standards seek to ensure prompt, adequate, and lawful assistance to clients. Key guidelines for the lawyer-client relationship appear below.

Various codes set standards for lawyers. The Supreme Court has adopted a Code of Professional Responsibility. The American Bar Association has its Canons of Professional Ethics that govern the behavior of members. In addition, individual state Supreme Courts and legislatures may have their own codes of conduct.

Bar associations work primarily in the public interest, not in the interest of individual lawyers. Offering voluntary memberships, such organizations also try to ensure high standards of ethics among lawyers and to improve the administration of justice. Most bar associations have a committee on *legal ethics* and *professional conduct*. Such a committee can recommend to a state Supreme Court the suspension, disbarment, or reprimand of a lawyer who has violated any standards or who has committed an act of moral turpitude.

Services provided by bar associations may include any of the following:

- Lawyer referral service or lawyer directory
- Continuing legal education
- Fee dispute arbitration
- Legal Aid
- Tel-Law, "Call for Action," and other free information and counseling services for the public

Professional Conduct

The American Bar Association in 1983 issued its Model Rules of Professional Conduct, a definitive statement of a lawyer's responsibilities. The preamble to the Rules spells out those responsibilities, including statements that a lawyer

- is an officer of the legal system, a representative of clients, and a public citizen with special responsibility for the quality of justice;
- should conform to the law both as a lawyer and as a private citizen;
- should serve the client's interests, but dissuade the client from wrongful acts against others;
- should be honest with any tribunal and respectful of the interests of other parties while asserting his client's position;

- should safeguard the client's interest when negotiating while showing fairness to others;
- may serve as intermediary between clients;
- is responsible to third parties where they exist;
- should act competently, promptly, and diligently;
- should seek improvement of the law and the administration of justice;
- is ethically bound to perform at his highest level of competence, to try to improve the law and his profession, and to try to meet the profession's ideals of public service; and
- should exercise his professional and moral judgment in resolving conflicts in his responsibilities where the Rules of Professional Conduct do not provide guidelines for such resolution.

The lawyer's obligations to the client are discussed more fully in a section below.

USING A LAWYER

How and when do lawyers become necessary? This section discusses why and when a lawyer is needed and how the citizen can utilize his or her services. The decision to use a lawyer is an individual matter, but some general considerations can help in making that decision.

Why a Lawyer May Be Needed

The individual may decide to hire a lawyer for at least three reasons. The law's complexity may require it, or the services of lawyers as officers of the court may be needed. Very importantly, lawyers can prevent bigger legal problems.

Law can be complex

The law's complexity may present too great a problem for the average citizen. Various laws may be relevant to a particular case. Moreover, as was noted in Chapter 1, the law has different sources—the Constitution, statutory law, common law, administrative law, and so on—and each kind has its own scope and effect. Certain kinds of cases may be relatively easy for a layman to handle without a lawyer—for example, small claims cases. In many situations, however, the "amateur lawyer" would be in over his head. An old adage holds that "the person who is his own lawyer has a fool for a client."

As officers of the court, lawyers understand the procedures and protocols of the courtroom. Not all cases need to go to court. When one does, however, the layman without a lawyer may needlessly delay proceedings. An "amateur lawyer" is also prohibited from representing persons in court; only an officer of the court may do that. Similarly, only a licensed lawyer can give "legal advice." So long as a person receives advice and representation from a lawyer, he has the court's protection because the lawyer remains accountable to the court. The court may protect the individual against his or her own lawyer!

Finally, lawyers serve both to prevent and to cure problems. What kinds of problems require the aid of a lawyer? Anyone faced with the following kinds of situations should absolutely hire a lawyer:

Being arrested for a crime
Facing a lawsuit
Wanting to sue someone else
Seeking a divorce
Filing for bankruptcy

Preventive law Practicing preventive law can save time, trouble, and money. The ways in which early consultation with a lawyer can help include these:

- Preventing some legal problems entirely, for instance by signing an important paper
- Consuming less time on a case by consulting a lawyer beforehand
- Making information and evidence (including witnesses) more readily available when prompt action needs to be taken
- Avoiding complications by advising a client what or what not to do, say, or sign
- Having a legal matter taken care of before a "statute of limitations" blocks action
- Settling a dispute in negotiation phase, rather than letting it mushroom into a typically more expensive court case

When a Lawyer Is Needed

At many other times in a person's life he or she should at least consider seeing a lawyer. These include:

Buying a house
Selling a house
Getting an opinion on a real estate title
Making or terminating a lease
Dealing with troubles with a landlord
Choosing the right insurance
A change in legal status, such as marriage or coming of age
Adoption
Retirement planning
Preparing and revising wills and estates
Deaths
Administering estates
Calculating taxes and dealing with tax disputes

Organizing, buying, selling, or dissolving a business
Employer-employee relations
Consumer problems
Business transactions, such as collecting debts
Money problems
A significant change in financial status
Accidents, when there is damage to property or person
Taking out copyrights and patents
Signing a contract or making a verbal agreement
When arrested for a crime
Dealing with a governmental agency on an important matter
When one's rights are threatened
When one is not certain of the need for a lawyer

Lawyers cannot, of course, solve every problem. Some problems are so minor that additional legal expenses would not be warranted—for example, in a dispute with a merchant involving less than $50. The best time to see a lawyer is in a preventive situation. Often, the individual can minimize problems by engaging a lawyer in advance. Still other legal problems can be handled by alternative means. Some disputes can be removed from the jurisdiction of the legal system, for example, and "kept out of court." *Minimizing problems*

What a Lawyer Can and Cannot Do

Examination of the extent of a lawyer's powers and capabilities may influence a final decision on hiring a lawyer. Such examination may also encourage more realistic expectations about the lawyer's future performance. But sometimes, clearly, only an initial consultation can provide an individual with information on whether to proceed further with a lawyer. Among the things that a lawyer can do are:
Confer with the client to pinpoint the problem
Gather and analyze all available facts and information
Interview those involved in the case
Study applicable laws and previous court decisions
Prepare legal arguments for presentation in court
Negotiate a settlement if both sides are agreeable
Present a client's arguments before the court
Appeal the decision of a court

Within that general framework, it is important to keep in mind the things a lawyer cannot do: *A lawyer cannot . . .*
- Contact a client about a new case or new legal matter before the client has requested advice. Exceptions to this rule include cases

in which a lawyer is specifically hired to handle all of a person's legal affairs at all times, and where a lawyer is a close relative or friend. If a lawyer who is a stranger approaches a person, that lawyer should be reported to the local bar association.

- Take action, for a client, that conflicts with a lawyer's duty to the court. A lawyer cannot introduce misleading or false evidence or assist a client in spiteful, malicious, stubborn, or obstructive actions. Nor can a lawyer represent a client where a conflict of interest exists between lawyer and client.

- Guarantee the outcome or result of a lawsuit.

- Speed up the time required by law for processing a lawsuit. A lawyer should, upon request, inform his client as to the time allotted by the court for each phase of the proceedings.

Thus, a lawyer can often achieve for a person what the person unaided could not achieve. At the same time, the lawyer is not all-powerful, since he must abide by his obligations to the court. He also has obligations to his client.

The Lawyer's Obligations to the Client

The lawyer's obligations In order to do his job effectively and to ensure client satisfaction, a lawyer has certain obligations to the client. A client has a right to expect that all of the following obligations will be fulfilled:

- To keep the client's personal legal matters confidential. The lawyer can reveal only those facts that must become public knowledge when he pleads his client's case and offers evidence and testimony.

- To account promptly and completely to the client for money and other things of value that the client has entrusted to him. A lawyer cannot mix a client's funds into his own personal account. If a client asks for a return of valuables or funds, they must be returned promptly, without delay or excuses.

- To remain absolutely loyal to the client and his cause. An exception would be where such loyalty conflicts with the lawyer's ethical duties and responsibilities. The lawyer should then advise his client of the conflict and what to do about it.

- To file the client's action, or response to an action filed against the client, within the prescribed time.

- To record in timely fashion other legal documents that are intended to notify the public as protection to the client.

- To counsel the client to obey the orders of the court. If a court order is erroneous, it should be challenged on appeal and not disobeyed or ignored.

- To keep up to date on developments in law and the latest methods and models of practice.
- To investigate thoroughly the facts and laws that are relevant to the client's legal problem.
- To analyze carefully the client's problems and give a candid opinion of the probability of success or failure of the case.
- To make a thorough effort to settle a case and avoid the risks and expense of a lawsuit.
- To make adequate and timely preparation of the client's case for trial and to prepare relevant documents and papers well in advance of a settlement or a closing of a transaction.

The Client's Obligations to the Lawyer

The relationship between a lawyer and a client is not one-sided. If a lawyer is to work effectively on the client's behalf, the client must fulfill certain obligations as well. These include: *The client's obligations*

- To give full and complete disclosure of all facts, particularly regarding the client's conduct in a case. All information given is protected by the lawyer's obligation of confidentiality. A client can even confess a crime to his lawyer; such a confession is considered privileged communication.
- To consult promptly when a problem first develops.
- To adhere strictly to a lawyer's advice. Disregarding instructions could result in loss of a case.
- To have faith in the lawyer's opinion and judgment. In short, "let the lawyer run the case."
- To give adequate time to render satisfactory service. After a client puts a matter into a lawyer's hands, he should wait for the lawyer to make return contact unless there is an important new development.
- To feel free to ask about any relevant matter in the case.
- To give prompt notice to the lawyer of any dissatisfaction with his conduct of the client's affairs.
- To pay a fair and reasonable fee.
- To compliment the lawyer and give a good recommendation when the client feels that he has received outstanding service.

How to Conduct a Relationship with a Lawyer

Guidelines such as those just listed are directed at helping the client in specific dealings with his lawyer. The following guidelines will help the *To work with your lawyer . . .*

client establish a good overall atmosphere that may ensure a successful working relationship with his lawyer.

- The client should view his lawyer as another human being, not a god. The lawyer is not all-powerful; like all persons, he can make mistakes. However, he remains accountable for living up to his obligations. The client need not feel intimidated. If a lawyer appears intimidating, the client should feel free to complain or find another lawyer.

- At the outset, the client should tell the lawyer what he expects of him. If any of those expectations are unreasonable, the lawyer should say so. Similarly, the client should ask what the lawyer expects of him.

- The client should ask what steps are involved in handling the case and what kind of time schedule may be expected. This can reduce or eliminate impatience.

- The fee arrangement should be discussed at the outset. It should be made clear when the fee is to be paid. The client should know if and how he will be charged for making phone calls to ask questions. Guidelines for keeping fees down are presented later in this chapter.

- The client should help in any way he can—for example, by providing papers and evidence and finding witnesses. If the lawyer has not suggested it, the client should offer such help. In this way time is saved; the lawyer's fees may be reduced.

- The client should always choose the lawyer, not the other way around. An exception may be the class-action suit for a group or category of clients.

- The client should call with any and all questions. He should make sure that making frequent calls will not result in a higher legal bill. If it will, the client should make his phone calls count, grouping questions together on a given call.

What to Expect and Do During the First Visit

That first visit   On first meeting with a lawyer, and not before, an individual will usually decide whether or not he wants to hire that lawyer. If he decides to hire the lawyer, the meeting should be used to establish the relationship. The first meeting should therefore be approached with those objectives in mind. The following pointers should help the individual in the first meeting:

- Before going to the meeting, the potential client makes notes about the problem. He can then go over the important points when talking to the lawyer.

- He should bring the names, addresses, and telephone numbers of everyone connected with the case. Some lawyers may ask to see certain papers even before a meeting takes place.
- He should ask the lawyer to tell him about cases like his that he may have handled. Note: a lawyer's ability to handle a particular case may have nothing to do with his age.
- When dealing with a law firm, the potential client should ask the lawyer conducting the interview whether he will conduct the case personally. If another lawyer in the firm will handle the case, it would be advisable to talk to the other lawyer as well.
- Beware the lawyer who guarantees results. Most lawsuits are not "sure things." A lawyer should assess the chances of success or failure, however.
- If the lawyer says something that is not clear, the individual should ask for an explanation in simpler language.
- The individual should not hurry into a decision on hiring. He can decide at the first meeting or he can "think about it."
- Considerations in the hiring decision should include: feeling comfortable with that lawyer, the lawyer's experience and skill at handling a particular type of case (insofar as these can be determined), understanding of the lawyer's explanation of what the case involves, and whether the fee seems reasonable. A "no" verdict on even one of these criteria may rule out a particular lawyer.
- If an individual has decided to hire the lawyer, he should then follow the guidelines for conducting the relationship.

Compromise or negotiate?

Most cases, it should be noted, do not end up in court. Notable exceptions are when one is being sued or when one is arrested for a crime. In a civil case, a lawyer may see a court fight as futile or expensive or both. Litigation can then be a luxury. The lawyer may therefore recommend compromise or negotiation.

How to Find a Lawyer

If an individual does not have a lawyer, he can take several routes to find one. These include:

Recommendations
Referral services
Advertisements
Lawyer directories
Public interest groups
Prepaid plans

Various free or low-cost services such as Legal Aid, public defenders, Public Interest Bar, and various special projects for the elderly and other groups

The individual should initially develop a list of candidates from which to choose a lawyer. It may turn out that the first lawyer a person finds proves to be satisfactory on the basis of the criteria listed above. On the other hand, it helps to have a list from which to select—if only to avoid feeling pressed to take the first lawyer one finds. The various sources of lawyers are described below.

Recommendations

A lawyer may be recommended by a friend or relative who has had similar legal work done. This person can provide information on the lawyer's competence, personality, and fees. Recommendations may come also from professionals such as clergy, doctors, business executives, or social workers. Such individuals may have had to deal with a similar problem in their lives or in their professional work.

Sources of recommendations
Other possibilities exist. At one's place of work, co-workers and employers can also be important sources of recommendations. One lawyer may recommend another who specializes in the particular kind of legal problem. Where a person has moved, a lawyer known or used earlier may be able to provide one or more names of lawyers in the new community. A lawyer who happens to be a neighbor might be another source.

Referral Services

Lawyer referral services are operated by state, county, and local bar associations. They may also be called attorney referral services or lawyer reference services. Such services put individuals who have legal problems in touch with attorneys; the latter may charge a modest fee for a first consultation.

Consulting a referral service is usually not a complicated process. The individual who thinks he has a legal problem contacts the lawyer referral service office, most often using a toll-free number; any information given is held in strict confidence. Office personnel will then place the individual in contact with an attorney in his area. If the problem is not a legal one, either the referral office or the lawyer will say so. If the caller has a legal problem, the individual can decide for himself whether to make another appointment or authorize the lawyer to take appropriate action.

These services are found in the Yellow Pages of the telephone directory under "Attorneys," "Lawyers," "Attorney Referral Services," or some similar entry. Some referral services deal with special problems of groups such as artists, Spanish-speaking people, or the elderly.

The lawyers obtained through referral services typically charge low fees for consultations. A typical fee would be $15. If a person thinks he cannot afford that much, he has other alternatives, such as Legal Aid and other legal services.

Low fees for consultations

Advertisements

The Yellow Pages and newspaper advertisements offer other sources of lawyers' names. Most lawyers, however, choose not to advertise except to be listed in the Yellow Pages. Lawyers can advertise in the Yellow Pages, in newspapers and magazines, on radio and television, on billboards, or elsewhere as desired. The single restriction that applies is that the information in an ad cannot be false or misleading.

In addition to fees, ads may specify the legal fields in which lawyers specialize. "Legal clinics," law firms that deal with typical problems, often on a high-volume basis, may advertise their services for adoptions, divorces, bankruptcies, and wills. If an ad uses phrases like "simple will" or "uncontested divorce," it is important to ask what the service includes and what additional charges are entailed for more complicated cases or for expenses.

If the ad appeared in print, it should be clipped and kept. It tells much in few words about the lawyer's practice. If the ad appeared as a radio or television commercial, it may be helpful to take notes.

Lawyer Directories

Some bar associations publish lawyer directories. These provide names and information, usually as furnished by the lawyers themselves. Included are educational background, fees (including those for initial consultations), areas of practice or specialization, office hours, and foreign languages spoken. Such directories are usually found in public libraries and bar association offices. A nationwide directory found in most public libraries is the seven-volume Martindale and Hubbell Law Directory, now in its 112th edition (Summit, N.J.: Martindale-Hubbell, Inc., 1980).

Lawyer directories

Public Interest Groups

Nonprofit public-interest organizations may either provide legal services in specific areas or refer persons to experienced lawyers specializing in those areas. The American Civil Liberties Union, for instance, can help if one's civil rights, such as freedom of speech or religion, are threatened or violated. The Women's Legal Defense Fund provides counseling and referral services for women with problems in domestic relations or sex discrimination. The National Association for the

Advancement of Colored People Legal Defense Fund handles individual and class-action cases of discrimination against minorities.

In general, such groups may be divided into those that help individuals and those that only help groups in class-action cases. These organizations may be found in a variety of ways, for example by calling a city agency or contacting the "consumer action line" of a local paper, radio station, or television station. Checking the Yellow Pages under "Associations," "Consumer Protection Organizations," "Social Service and Welfare Organizations," or other similar entries may also produce lawyers' names.

Prepaid Plans

Legal insurance plans

Legal services are sometimes provided under "legal insurance" plans sponsored by an employer, by a labor union or credit union, or through individual purchase. Such a plan involves a prepaid fee or premium. An employer may establish the program on behalf of all covered employees or as an employee benefit provided either voluntarily or under collective bargaining. In some companies, an individual may join the plan by authorizing a payroll deduction.

Other characteristics may be noted. The premiums may be paid to (1) a trust fund that then provides legal services, (2) an insurance company, or (3) a private entrepreneurial group. Staff lawyers may work exclusively for plan members, or one or more law firms may handle plan services. A large group of lawyers may contribute services under the plan. Some programs offer the services of any licensed lawyer anywhere. Most such plans pay for specific service to the individual beneficiary or group member; services not covered by the plan require additional fees from the individual.

Plans offer advantages

The advantages of such plans are many. Members have access to lawyers, especially for preventive services, without paying high initial consultation fees. Methods of payment are easier, and sometimes painless, depending on the plan's benefits. Fee schedules are published. In general, members are assured of quality services and good treatment. The possibility that a lawyer may lose group business has been said to motivate many plan lawyers to deliver uniformly high-quality services.

THE SHREVEPORT PLAN[1]

The Shreveport Plan was established in 1971. One of the first of the prepaid legal plans, it was created in recognition of the fact that middle-income Americans have typically been deprived of adequate legal protection: the poor could get government-financed legal aid while the rich could afford to pay lawyers.

In 1969, the American Bar Association decided to use Shreveport, Louisiana, as an experimental site for creating a prepaid legal plan. The local bar association was responsive to the idea. A local group of workers, Laborers' Local 229, joined in the experiment.

Local 229 negotiated an arrangement under which two cents an hour from the salary of each worker would be paid into the plan. The American Bar Association and the Ford Foundation also provided funds. Shreveport Legal Services Corporation, a nonprofit corporation, was formed.

The members of Local 229, mostly rural blacks, did not trust strangers, especially those representing the law. The law collected bills, repossessed furniture, or put people in jail. Officials of the Local had been giving advice on legal matters for years, but could not call it "legal advice."

Seeing a demand for real legal services and hearing about the American Bar Association's interest in starting a plan, a union official had contacted the local

attorney handling the project. As a result, Shreveport became the site for the experiment.

Many members of Local 229 have been aided by the plan. In one case, a man was confronted by local, state, and federal officials with another person's check, apparently endorsed with his signature. Calling an attorney, the victim received help; a handwriting expert was able to state that it was not the man's writing. A woman neighbor was identified as the culprit.

In 1974, Ford Foundation funding was terminated. The union membership voted overwhelmingly to retain the plan. Were it not for the plan, many workers would have suffered serious financial losses or invasions of personal liberties.

[1] Adapted from Philip J. Murphy, Ralph N. Jackson, and David Chandler, *Lawyers for Laborers* (American Bar Association, 1975).

Free or Low-Cost Services

Inexpensive legal services are available for those who need help but cannot afford ordinary attorneys' fees. Such services include Legal Aid, law school clinical programs, public defenders, the Public Interest Bar, and Pro Bono, elderly, and other special projects.

Legal Aid, also called Legal Services, offers services for the indigent under funding by the federal and state governments and by bar associations. Lawyers in Legal Aid offices can represent clients in most legal situations. However, since the demand for services usually exceeds the supply of lawyers, Legal Aid will not handle criminal cases or cases in which a person seeks a money award (*see* Contingency Fees, below). A person must also meet an eligibility requirement by proving that his income is below a certain level. The level varies from one community to another.

Law school clinical programs provide law students with practical experience with indigent clients. At any given law school, either the supervising lawyer or the program's referral individual may be contacted. Some programs make referrals to former students who are practicing in the area. Alternatively, the law school dean may provide the name of a faculty member specializing in the area of concern. That person may refer the potential client to other attorneys.

Law school clinical programs

State governments make *public defenders* available to individuals accused of crimes who cannot afford attorneys' fees. The public defender can be found in the White Pages of the phone book under Public Defender. If an area or community has no public defender, a judge may appoint a private attorney to take a case without charge.

Public interest groups, as noted, sometimes provide legal services for individuals. Other special programs for particular groups may be provided by bar associations. The Lawyer Referral Service may also be a source of inexpensive, if not free, help.

AIDS AND ALTERNATIVES

The individual has some alternatives to lawyers or law offices in resolving certain legal problems. For example, the Small Claims Court makes it possible to file claims below certain levels. Some of the specific alternatives are described in later chapters.

Tel-law tapes One aid is Tel-Law, a library of tape recordings that can be heard over the telephone. Such recordings are designed to convey an understanding of the justice system and of state laws, to aid in determining whether one has a legal problem, and to help in finding assistance. These tapes are not intended as legal advice or as a substitute for a lawyer; nor do they apply to all legal problems and situations. But diverse areas of law are covered, including adoption, bankruptcy, juvenile law, criminal law, civil law, public benefits, domestic relations, legal matters related to the handicapped, credit and consumer law, and estates and probate. The number of tapes may range from 50 to over 100 depending on the particular bar association.

WHEN A LAWYER MAY NOT BE NEEDED[1]

- When money is needed in an emergency; a better way is to consult a banker.

- Income tax problems; consult an accountant first.

- Routine purchase of a house from a reputable builder; use a real estate agent or title insurance company or an attorney for a lending institution (*see* Chapter 3).

- Problems receiving social security or unemployment compensation; see appropriate government agency officials (*see* Chapter 12).

- Claims for a relatively small amount of money under the limits set by the state; go to Small Claims Court (*see* Chapter 13).

- Traffic accident; in states with no-fault liability laws, conflict is minimized and matters are handled by the person's insurance company (*see* Chapter 17).

- Divorce; some states have no-fault divorce laws, making unnecessary the adversary procedure; elsewhere, do-it-yourself divorce kits may handle the problem without a hitch (*see* Chapter 8).

- Incorporation; in this area, do-it-yourself kits may have their pros and cons; indeed, incorporation may not even be the best way for some to organize a business (*see* Chapter 13).

- Consumer complaint; new consumer protection laws are being enforced by government agencies, and private consumer groups can exert pressure (*see* Chapter 14).

Another alternative to lawyers is do-it-yourself kits. These provide aid in such areas as wills, divorces, incorporation, and avoiding probate. In the case of probate, a group of lawyers sued the author of such a kit for illegally dispensing legal advice. The author successfully appealed the action, and has sold many copies of his plan along with the appropriate forms. The plan does successfully avoid the costs of probate. Even where a lawyer is used, the kit has features that are useful to both client and lawyer.

Not all alternatives may prove as useful or foolproof as the probate-avoidance plan. A kit may provide only minimum protection for the average person. But there is no average person as far as the law is concerned: each case is unique. A kit may not anticipate some kinds of legal problems. Consequently, one could end up with more cost and trouble than expected. The objective is to make an informed, thoughtful decision on whether and how to use a lawyer.

LAWYERS' FEES

Fees vary depending on the type of service provided. They vary also from lawyer to lawyer and community to community. Lawyers determine fees according to the following criteria:

Fees depend on services provided

- The fee customarily charged in the area for a particular type of service.
- The amount of time and labor invested.
- The skill of the lawyer, his experience, ability, specialties, and reputation.
- Business or office expenses, which vary from 35 to 50 per cent of the fee.
- Whether a fixed or contingent fee is established. Where a fee is contingent, the lawyer receives nothing if the case is lost.
- Results, in the case of the contingent fee.
- The amount involved in the settlement, in the case of a contingent fee.
- The complexity of the case.
- The nature and length of the relationship with the client. For example, a client doing casual business with a lawyer would be charged a higher rate than an old client doing steady business.

- Time limitations imposed by the client or by the circumstances of the case. If a lawyer is prevented from taking other employment that might have been available, he may charge more.

Types of Fees

Lawyers may charge different kinds of fees. In some instances, the client can negotiate the kind of fee; in others, it is already determined. Types include:

- *Fixed fees.* This constitutes a "standard" fee, used for routine legal matters such as drafting an uncomplicated will. Law clinics typically use this kind of fee.
- *Hourly fees.* Here, time determines the final cost. But the hourly rate varies from one lawyer and area to another. The client's objective is to obtain the best combination of hourly rate and efficiency in getting the work done more quickly.
- *Retainers.* A lawyer may ask for a retainer, or advance payment, to cover the fee or expenses. Clients requiring regular service pay monthly or annual retainers to ensure continuing service.
- *Contingency fees.* In cases where the client is suing for money, the lawyer receives a percentage of the award if he wins and nothing if he loses. The lawyer may assess his percentage according to the total amount or on the award after other costs are deducted. If the latter, the client keeps more of the award. The client should determine beforehand the lawyer's method of charging.
- *Statutory fees.* The cost of probate and other kinds of legal work is set by law, hence is "statutory." A probate court has a schedule of allowable fees. These are usually based on percentages of the value of different kinds of property.
- *Fees set by a judge.* Probate may fall under this heading. Considering the size of the estate and the amount of time the lawyer puts in, the judge determines the fee to be awarded.

Keeping Legal Fees Down

Keeping fees down Whatever the type of fee, the client can use a number of tactics to keep fees to a minimum. He can, for example:

- Write down the names, addresses, and phone numbers of all persons involved and all the relevant facts that he can recall
- Take any pertinent papers to the first interview
- Be as brief as possible in all interviews
- Keep emotion from coloring the facts
- Make a full and honest disclosure of all facts to the lawyer

- Avoid unnecessary phone calls to the lawyer
- Obtain legal advice before signing documents or taking legal action and then follow that advice
- Consider the financial pros and cons of a proposed legal action by discussing it with a lawyer

If the Fee Is Too High

If the client feels the fee is too high, he should tell his lawyer. Asking for an explanation may prove entirely satisfactory. Some states, including California, have arbitration services that are provided by the state bar association. The services charge set fees to determine whether the lawyer did the work he was supposed to do for the amount paid. Fees set by a court or by law are not subject to arbitration, however. Such a proceeding usually takes no more than 80 days and costs a maximum of $50. Lacking arbitration, a client may sue a lawyer.

Dissatisfaction with a Lawyer's Performance

Aside from fee disputes, a client may be dissatisfied with what the lawyer has delivered. Generally, a client does not have grounds for complaint unless the lawyer has violated standards of professional responsibility.

Before registering a complaint

A formal complaint can be damaging to a lawyer even if he is not at fault. For that reason, and because dissatisfaction often springs from misunderstanding or poor communication between client and lawyer, the client should thoroughly air his grievance with the lawyer. The state bar can only discipline the lawyer; it cannot remedy any loss to the client. For that, the client must sue.

Each state has its own procedures for handling client grievances. The state Supreme Court has the power to discipline lawyers. Such discipline may include disbarment as a type of sanction. It is worth remembering that losing a case does not automatically imply incompetence or malpractice.

Rating a lawyer's performance   Can you make your own independent judgment of your attorney's effectiveness? As of May 1984, the Supreme Court provided some guidelines for such assessment.

Ruling in a criminal case, *Strickland* v. *Washington*, the Court laid down three key standards for determining an attorney's "actual effectiveness." As the defendant who engaged the lawyer, you would, in order to prove ineffectiveness, have to show the following:

- that the attorney's performance failed to meet an objective standard of reasonableness;
- that the performance so prejudiced you that you were, in effect, denied a fair trial; and
- that the reasonable probability exists that the result of the proceeding would have been different but for the counsel's unprofessional errors.

Writing the Court's majority opinion, Justice Sandra Day O'Connor noted that the

> benchmark for judging any claim of ineffectiveness must be whether counsel's conduct so undermined the proper function of the adversarial process that the trial cannot be relied on as having produced a just result. . . . An error by counsel, even if professionally unreasonable, does not warrant setting aside the judgment of a criminal proceeding if the error has no effect on the judgment.

Part II
"ON THE STREET WHERE YOU LIVE"

The right to own real estate, or real property, provides the basis for many other rights in the American legal system. The Founding Fathers who framed the Constitution recognized that right. They believed that the "right of property" had to be secured or liberty could not exist.

Property rights remain a cornerstone of the entire complex of rights that Americans enjoy. But property rights have acquired public meanings. Where at one time a person's home and land were his castle, to be used as the owner saw fit, the situation has changed to a degree. The owner of land and buildings—real property—cannot use that property without considering his neighbors. He cannot, for example, befoul the environment unreasonably, pollute neighboring water or air, or violate zoning regulations and other restrictions.

Within those limitations, most of which are outgrowths of a developing awareness that every person has duties as well as rights where real property is concerned, the owner of property enjoys important kinds of protection. One of them received new emphasis as recently as 1967. In that year, the Supreme Court of the United States ruled that the owner of a home has immunity under the Fourth Constitutional Amendment against a property search without a warrant. The case, *Camara* v. *Municipal Court*, bore out the principle that an official inspection of a home constitutes a search under the Fourth Amendment. Therefore, the Court said, a search could not be conducted without a warrant.

What are the basic questions?

The Fourth Amendment, of course, guarantees the right of all citizens "to be secure in their persons, houses, papers, and effects, against unreasonable searches and seizures..."

So important is the body of law surrounding real property rights and duties that laws have been devised to cover many basic phases of the entire ownership process. In Part II, many of the ways in which those laws apply or can be put to work are described. Many common-sense rules and principles are also noted. Particular attention is given to the procedures by which real estate is bought or sold; to zoning and similar devices for controlling population density; to condemnation and other procedures involved in the assumption of property ownership by a public agency or body; and to renting and leasing.

35

3 "HOME, SWEET HOME"

Purchasing a home may be the largest investment that a person makes during his or her lifetime. Numerous legal questions relate to the purchase of an existing home, construction of a new home, various types of financing, the sale of a home, and similar transactions.

BUYING AN EXISTING HOME

Some persons find their "dream homes" the first time they go house hunting. Others, undoubtedly more typical, search for weeks or months before the perfect home turns up.

House hunting takes time, usually, because many factors, legal and other, enter into the purchase process. Every home buyer should make certain that he knows exactly what he is buying. That means questions and more questions—to both the seller and his real estate agent.

Finding the Right Property

Finding the home that suits your needs is vitally important. Finding the right home in a strange area or neighborhood may add up to a major challenge. When moving into a new area without prior knowledge of the neighborhood, however, the home seeker has several possible ways to find out about the new neighborhood and the types of homes there.

Some obvious options are open. A friend who lives in the new area can show a prospective buyer the various locations and perhaps take the time to make a circuit of the city or town. A telephone call or letter to the local Chamber of Commerce or Board of Realtors can produce information on the properties in the areas of interest. Nothing, however, takes the place of a personal inspection trip.

What are the basic questions? Some of the considerations that should be investigated are fairly self-evident. The size of the home; its price and how it fits with your budget; the area, especially with respect to schools, shopping, distance from work, and other such practical considerations—all have to be checked out. Often, consulting a real estate broker in the area found to be most attractive is the best method of finding property. In order to avoid wasting their own time and the time of the broker, house hunters should explain what they are looking for. Looking at photographs of various listings before making a personal inspection of the property can clarify key points.

Many persons make a very serious mistake in house hunting: they look only at the house itself. Naturally, if the house fits in with the buyer's needs, is structurally sound and of suitable size, and falls in the right price bracket, an offer to buy may be called for as promptly as possible. However, an inspection of the house alone is never enough. The owner or the broker should take the potential buyer on a "guided tour" of the property itself. An inspection trip should follow along the borders of the property. The property line should be defined at all points. The buyer should look up in the air to determine whether or not utility lines or other apparent uses or obstructions cross the air space over the property.

Most situations follow one or another pattern. Unless all utilities are underground, telephone and electric lines connect to the house from a pole or other utility installation bordering the street. But electric power lines or telephone lines may cross the property without connection to the house. That usually means that the utility company has an easement or right of way to cross the property. Such a use might be found later to constitute interference with the complete use and enjoyment of the property.

Don't forget to look down Walking over the property, the buyer should also look down to determine whether or not visible pathways or walkways indicate that people use the property as a shortcut. A path suggests a need for full investigation—possibly by an attorney. The law in most states holds that the public can gain an easement or right of way by continuous, uninterrupted use of someone else's property for shortcut purposes.

Manhole covers could indicate the existence of a sewage system across the property. The owner or broker should be asked to explain such facilities.

It is thus very important not to overlook a physical inspection, not only of the house itself but also of the surrounding property on which it sits, including the boundary lines, utility lines, both aboveground and underground, and any other easement or rights of way that may exist.

Hand Money Deposit

Assume that a piece of property fits within the buyer's means and satisfies all other needs and desires. It may be wise to prevent the seller from selling the property to someone else before a contract of sale can be signed. In this situation a *hand money deposit* is usually made. The seller then gives the would-be buyer a deposit receipt.

Because most states require that contracts for the sale of real estate be in writing, the deposit receipt that represents the amount of hand money or *earnest money* deposited by the buyer should contain some essential elements. With these, the receipt becomes a legally enforcible contract in the event that a later long-form agreement of sale is not signed.

The amount of the earnest money deposit is not set by law and is subject to negotiation between the parties. The deposit applies as part payment

Earnest money equals part payment

of the purchase price if the buyer later buys the land and completes the sale. Usually, the contract provides that the earnest money deposit may be retained by the seller if the buyer defaults and does not buy the land. Ordinarily a seller will require a sufficiently high earnest money deposit to cover the broker's commission and other expenses of the sale to the seller—including his loss of time and loss of opportunity to sell elsewhere if the buyer should default. The hand money deposit may be a percentage of the total purchase price, such as 5 per cent, 10 per cent, and so on.

THE PURCHASE AND SALE AGREEMENT: QUESTIONS THE BUYER SHOULD ASK BEFORE SIGNING[1]

The paper first given to a prospective buyer by a real estate broker is the purchase and sale agreement. Few people realize that this paper is the most important step in making the purchase of a home, for the details of this agreement determine what you buy and how you buy it. Before signing, read the agreement carefully and discuss with your family lawyer such items as the following:

1. Exactly what land, buildings, and furnishings are included in your offer? Are stove, refrigerator, and the like included?
2. What details regarding payments should be stated?
3. When can you take possession?
4. Is the seller to furnish you with a good, marketable title?
5. What kind of deed should the seller give?
6. Who pays for the examination of the title to the property in the event the offer is accepted? Who pays for the abstract of title or title insurance?
7. Have utilities been installed and paid for?
8. Should a surveyor be employed to determine whether the improvements are actually located on the property? Who should pay for the cost of the survey?
9. If a mortgage is to be given, who will pay the intangible tax on the mortgage?
10. If termite, water, or other damage is found, shall the seller pay the cost of repairs?
11. What are the zoning regulations, or restrictions, on the use of the property?
12. What is the time within which the purchase should be accepted or refused? Is the date of such acceptance to be vital to the offer?
13. If your offer is accepted, what steps should be taken with respect to insuring the improvements to protect you, the prospective purchaser, pending the final closing?
14. What persons (husbands and wives) should be required to sign and accept the offer?
15. Are boundary lines properly specified?
16. Are timber, mineral, and water rights, if any, properly covered?
17. Who is responsible for payment of taxes?
18. How should the agreement be executed to make it binding?
19. What are the remedies if the buyer or seller defaults?

[1] Adapted from *So You're Going to Buy a Home* (Tallahassee: The Florida Bar, February 1980).

The deposit receipt given by the seller to the buyer should at least identify by name the seller and the buyer. It should also describe the property so that it can be identified easily. As an exchange of promises between the seller and the buyer to purchase and sell the property, the receipt should state the full price. All parties to the deposit receipt should sign it to make certain that it stands as a legally enforcible contract.

A deposit receipt cannot substitute for an agreement of sale. The receipt only acknowledges deposit of the earnest money under all the basic terms. The deposit receipt should refer to the fact that an agreement of sale will be entered into by the parties as soon as possible after the earnest money has been paid.

The deposit receipt

The Agreement of Sale

All the essential elements in the sale and purchase of a home converge in the agreement of sale. All these elements, including full cost, description of the property, the type of title that the owner has and will convey to the buyer, and so on, must appear in the agreement. A checklist of those items that should be in the final agreement of sale would include at least the following:

- Date of the agreement. The agreement should contain the date on which it is made.

- The name and address of the seller. These should be stated clearly, and the marital status of the seller should be stated, such as "James Smith and Mary Smith, his wife, of 121 Jane Street, Center City, State X."

- The name of the buyer. "Name" should include marital status, mailing address, and so on.

If the buyers are not husband and wife, and want to take title jointly, the nature of the title that they wish to take should be stated in the agreement of sale. Many states recognize a form of title ownership known as "joint tenancy." If the two persons, not husband and wife, want to take title as "joint tenants," such should be stated in the agreement. If they want to take title as "tenants in common," also a recognized form of ownership, this should be stated.

Specify the kind of title

Agreement to Sell. The agreement of sale should contain a specific agreement by the seller to sell the property and the buyer to purchase it on a specified date. In other words, the agreement should state that the seller will "on or before 90 days from the date of this agreement, sell, and the buyer will buy" the property as described in the agreement.

JOINT TENANCY: PROS AND CONS[1]

Many misleading ideas about joint tenancy are passed from person to person, usually quite innocently. You have probably heard them—"Joint tenancy eliminates the necessity of a will" . . . "Joint tenancy saves probate costs" . . . "Joint tenancy reduces 'death taxes' " . . . "Jointly held property passes 'automatically' at death to the survivor" . . . "Your creditors can't reach jointly held property" . . . and so forth. To clear up misunderstandings on these and other misconceptions, read on.

What is joint tenancy? It is a way of holding title to personal property or real estate by two or more persons. There are three types of joint tenancy: "with rights of survivorship," "as tenants in common," and "as tenants by the entireties" (limited to husband and wife).

Why do many property owners favor joint tenancy? They think the "survivorship" feature will save the surviving owner probate costs and inheritance taxes. The only costs saved are the small probate court costs and not attorney fees or transfer expenses. There is no inheritance tax due on property passing to a spouse, whether in joint tenancy or otherwise, and no inheritance taxes are saved if the property is held jointly with anyone else.

Is it a substitute for a will? No. Joint tenancy with rights of survivorship will pass that particular property to the other named owner or owners, and do nothing else. A tenant in common's undivided interest, absent a will, will pass to his or her heirs-at-law. A properly drawn will covers a number of items in addition to passing property. For example, it designates who is to handle the estate, names a guardian for minor children, etc. Joint tenancy may be the right thing for you today but the wrong thing tomorrow, but you cannot change it easily—as you can a will—to fit tomorrow's situation.

Does jointly held property pass "automatically" at death to the other joint tenant? No. If the joint tenancy was "with rights of survivorship" or "as tenants by the entirety," the property does pass by operation of law (statute or contract), to the survivor, but not automatically. A Survivorship Affidavit with respect to real estate and Consents to Transfer (except for spouses), stock powers, affidavits of domicile and perhaps other documents are required to be prepared, signed and recorded or sent to banks and transfer agents to get the title placed in the name of the surviving owner.

Why is joint tenancy difficult to change? Because one co-owner may refuse.

Can a man compel his wife to give back a joint title he has conferred on her? No.

Can creditors reach jointly held property? Yes, except possibly for real estate held by a husband and wife as tenants by the entirety if only one spouse takes bankruptcy. On death, the creditors of the deceased joint tenant can reach that person's contributions into jointly held checking and savings accounts, certificates of deposit, and other accounts if necessary.

What is common danger in joint tenancy? Joint owners—even husband and wife—may disagree. After that it becomes difficult to make such necessary decisions as those concerning management, repairs, division of income from the property, public liability problems, insurance to be carried, and so forth. If tenants in common cannot agree on the sale of real estate, one party has to bring a partition suit which generally results in the court ordering the property to be sold at a time when the market may or may not be good.

What happens to a husband-wife joint tenancy in case of a divorce? If the parties cannot agree upon a split of the property between themselves, the tenancy is converted into a "tenants in common" type of joint tenancy.

Does joint tenancy reduce taxes? When one of two joint tenants dies, for federal estate taxes and many state inheritance taxes, the law presumes that the decedent was the owner of such property and taxes it in his or her estate, except to the extent that the survivor can prove his or her contribution to the cost thereof. Trouble may arise in perfecting the record title of the joint tenancy property. The real tax liability comes upon the death of the surviving spouse and often results in "double taxation" of some of the property.

Does joint tenancy save probate expense? Very seldom. If a deceased person owned other property besides that held in joint tenancy, the other property must be probated just the same. There is also expense in perfecting the record title to the property after the death of each joint owner.

If joint owners die simultaneously (as in an accident), what happens to their joint tenancy property? Without a will containing a "survivorship clause," the jointly held property is divided one-half into each joint tenant's estate, and probate proceedings are then required to pass the property on to the devisees or heirs-at-law of each joint tenant.

Does the creation of joint tenancy ever constitute a gift? Yes, if an appropriate election is made. If no election is made, the entire property will be taxed as a part of the estate of the first joint tenant to die, and then will be taxed again when the other joint tenant dies.

Is joint tenancy ever advisable? In some circumstances, and with respect to some types of property, but only after careful consideration of all the circumstances.

[1] Adapted from *Joint Tenancy: Does It Fit YOU?* (Indianapolis: The Indiana State Bar Association).

Type of Deed to be Delivered. The agreement should specify the type of deed that the seller will give to the buyer. A deed of *general warranty* is the highest form of deed that can be conveyed and ordinarily is utilized in the sale of a residence. Other forms of deed, such as deeds of special warranty, are used mainly in situations involving a sale from the estate of a deceased person and in other special situations.

Type of Title to be Conveyed. The agreement should provide that the seller will convey "fee simple title," the highest form of title. The statement indicates that the seller has all the elements of title to the property that he is agreeing to sell. By specific terms, the sale should be made clear of all liens and encumbrances except as noted in the agreement, thus assuring the buyer that the seller is agreeing to convey free of any liens or encumbrances except those noted in the contract itself.

Good and Marketable Title. The buyer wants to be certain that the title he is acquiring is good. He may later want to sell the property to someone else. The agreement should thus provide that the seller is conveying a good and marketable title, one that will be insurable by a title insurance company at its regular rates and that can be freely transferred in the marketplace.

The good and marketable title

Description. The agreement of sale should contain a full-length description by "metes and bounds" and by courses and distances. his

means that the description is the kind that a registered engineer would prepare from a survey of the property.

It is important that the buyer insist on a perimeter survey—one that examines the boundaries of the property only. The buyer should also insist on a survey showing the existence and location of all improvements on the lot, including the house, garage, swimming pool, toolshed, or any other building. These improvements should be located precisely on the lot. The surveys are important for determining:

(1) whether or not there are any encroachments onto the lot by an adjoining land owner;

(2) whether or not the buildings that exist on the property encroach on someone else's property; and

(3) whether or not the buildings and other improvements are consistent with local laws dealing with provisions for setback from the roadway, side-yard restrictions, open-space restrictions, and so on.

Who pays for surveys? The parties to the sale should agree between themselves, after negotiation, on who pays for the surveys. Usually, the seller will have a completed survey that can be used by the buyer. The seller simply attaches a certificate stating that no changes, additions to property, or other structures have been erected since the date of the survey.

Under any circumstances, the buyer should have a survey that conforms to local ordinances and that shows any private covenants and restrictions that may exist if the property is within a plan of lots as well as any recorded easements or rights of way.

The legal description contained in the agreement of sale should be prepared, if possible, in accordance with the survey made by the registered engineer.

Title Reference. The agreement of sale should contain the deed book volume and page record under which the seller acquired title to the property. In all counties, a register or recorder of deeds office makes a formal record after a transfer of property has taken place. To assist the buyer in a title examination, or to give him the opportunity to inspect the title to the property, the agreement of sale should contain a title reference showing where the current deed to the property can be found in the public records.

"Under and Subject." If the agreement of sale, after negotiation, indicates that the property is to be taken subject to certain restrictions, easements, or rights of way, these should be stated specifically in the agreement of sale. For example, if a right of way crosses the rear of the property, this should be stated specifically. The buyer should have an opportunity to decide whether or not he wants to buy the property with that right of way.

Buyer beware

Many agreements are signed with a provision like this: "Under and subject to all liens and encumbrances, easements, and rights of way that may appear of record." In this case the buyer should beware. In agreeing to such a provision, the buyer is agreeing to any liens, encumbrances, rights of way, or easements that might appear on the record before he has an opportunity to do a title search. Under no circumstances should a buyer—if he can avoid it—sign an agreement with such a provision in it except on advice of counsel. The covenant that the seller will deliver a good and marketable title gives the buyer a measure of protection in such a situation. All easements and rights of way should nonetheless be specifically itemized to the extent possible.

Any other special provisions should likewise be included in the agreement of sale. For example, if the buyer is taking the property subject to an existing mortgage—if he is assuming the mortgage of the seller—the agreement should so state. The assumption clause should be specific, should identify the mortgage and the name of the financial institution involved, the place where the mortgage is recorded, and the balance at the time of signature.

Appurtenance Clause. Why does an agreement of sale mention specifically such items as plumbing, heating fixtures and systems, laundry tubs and permanent fixtures, awnings, venetian blinds, and television antennas? Unfortunately, some sellers have removed from the property such things as blinds, fixtures, storm doors, and even light bulbs after the agreement of sale has been signed. The buyer moving into the property later finds a significantly different property from what he agreed to buy.

The agreement of sale should be specific. It should state that the sale includes all the buildings, improvements, and all plumbing and heating fixtures forming a part of the property. To be mentioned also: all built-in ranges, refrigerators, laundry tubs and other permanent fixtures, storm doors, windows and awnings if any, screens, shades, blinds, drapery rods and fixtures, television antennas, and all trees, shrubbery, and plants currently on the property.

Personal Property. Personal property includes items that are not normally considered part of the real estate. If any personal property items are to be transferred with the house, they should be separately listed, not included in the purchase price. Personal property may cover such items as wall-to-wall carpeting, rugs, drapes, mirrors, chandeliers, refrigerator, deep freeze, dishwasher, window air conditioners, fireplace items, lawnmower, garden tools, workbenches, water softeners, automatic door openers, and similar items. If any of these is being sold with the property, it should be specifically listed if it is to pass as part of the purchase price.

Listing personal property

A better alternative should be noted. Where personal property is being sold with real estate, a separate value should be given to the personal items. They can then be listed in a separate bill of sale. For example, if the wall-to-wall carpeting, drapes, chandelier, and refrigerator are included in the sale, and the parties agree that they are worth $3,000, then the agreement of sale for the house could reflect a purchase price of $27,000. A separate bill of sale ($3,000) would list the items of personal property passing to the buyer. Total price for the entire package: $30,000.

Here a distinction has been made between the real estate and the items of personal property. This becomes important later on since, in many cases, the real estate tax assessment on the land and the house is based on the price stated in the deed. If the price in the deed reflects items of personal property that are not really part of the real estate, the real estate tax assessment may be set at too high a rate—namely, on $30,000 instead of on $27,000.

Covenant to Buy. In the agreement the buyer consents to purchase the property. The price is stated. All terms of payment should also be stated, such as the amount of earnest money paid and the balance and how it is to be paid—whether in cash or certified funds or otherwise. For example, if the price of the property is $30,000 and $5,000 has already been deposited as earnest money, the agreement should provide that the buyer agrees to pay the sum of $30,000 payable as follows: $5,000 as earnest money on the signing of the agreement, receipt of which is acknowledged by the seller, and the balance of $25,000 to be payable in cash at the time of final closing.

The terms of payment

The contract must contain other provisions on payment of the purchase price if the buyer must sell his present home first in order to secure funds to buy the home. This is also true if the buyer must secure a mortgage himself to proceed with the purchase of the property. Too often a buyer signs without specifying that he has to sell his present house first to obtain money to buy the new house. If he cannot sell the old house in time—before the closing date—he may be in breach of his agreement with the seller.

A buyer might also have difficulty in getting a mortgage to finance the purchase of the new house. When the time comes to close, he cannot produce the money. In this case he can lose his earnest money deposit.

The buyer who has to sell his present home or obtain a mortgage to finance the new home, or both, should insist that the agreement of sale protect him. He needs *conditioned liability* under the contract: he has to be allowed to sell his existing home prior to the closing on the new home.

An element of uncertainty The seller may, of course, resist such a provision. It brings an element of uncertainty into the contract because the buyer may not be able to sell his home within the time limit set in the sale agreement. The seller should then insist on a time limitation. The buyer will have to sell his old home by a specified date or the agreement will be void, and the seller can proceed to sell to someone else.

If the buyer has to obtain a mortgage to buy the new home, he should make sure that the agreement contains a provision stating that purchase is subject to securing the mortgage. If agreeable to the seller, the interest rate should be indicated and the number of years to pay off the mortgage specified.

Such a provision is, of course, to the advantage of the buyer. It gives him an opportunity to "shop" for a mortgage that suits his situation. Again, the seller may raise the legitimate objection that this injects an element of uncertainty into the contract.

The seller who agrees to such a provision usually insists on a time limit by which the buyer has to secure a mortgage commitment in writing —to be shown to the seller. The seller is then assured that the sale will go through on schedule. If the buyer cannot procure the mortgage commitment within the time specified, the seller can offer the property to others.

Contract provisions conditioning the sale in any way should be negotiated matters in which both the seller and buyer have legitimate interests. Where possible, however, the buyer should insist, to the extent possible, on having these protections written into the contract. If they are not there, he is breaching the agreement if he cannot buy for those reasons at the time of closing.

THE CONTRACT[1]

The contract should be simple and complete, covering such items as:

- Legal description of the property (not just the street address)

- List of all items included in the sale, including removable items such as drapes and appliances

- Purchase price, including down payment and any special terms and provisions as to the types of financing the buyer will accept
- Date abstract is to be furnished to the buyer for examination by his attorney, or terms relating to title insurance
- Dates of payments
- Date possession is to be given
- Date deed is to be delivered
- Apportionment of taxes and special assessments
- Whether property is to be conveyed free and clear of all encumbrances (mortgages, taxes, and assessments)

- Who is to bear the loss if the property is damaged or destroyed before the sale is completed
- Damages to be paid if the contract is forfeited
- How the costs, legal and other, are to be apportioned between the parties

This list is not intended to be complete. It merely illustrates the basic items that should be included. Failure to include all necessary items could result in problems for both the buyer and seller.

[1] Adapted from *Tips on Buying a Home* (Montgomery: Alabama State Bar Assn., January 1978).

Settlement. The agreement should provide a specific closing date. The agreement can be closed or settled any time prior to that date. But a definite terminal date should be fixed in the contract so that all parties know what the time limitations are.

Any sale agreement should state that either party may, on written notice to the other, declare *time to be of the essence* of the contract and fix a date, time, and place for final settlement. In this way the parties are assured that a closing will eventually take place. Neither party can drag his feet or postpone the sale if the contract does not provide for such a contingency.

What are the time limitations?

If, after written notice is given, either party fails to proceed with the sale or purchase, that party is in default under the contract. The contract should also provide for a method of giving notice to the other party, such as certified or registered mail at the addresses set forth in the contract.

Possession. The contract should specify the date on which the buyer can take possession of the property or move into the property. The possession date is normally the same as the date of final closing. But this is not always the case.

To ensure a closing . . .

In a typical case, a seller may need additional time to move out of the property, and may request that the buyer take possession 30 days after the date of final closing. If the buyer agrees to the provision, the contract should provide for payment of rent or other form of payment for the 30-day waiting period. Alternatively, the buyer may want to move into the property before the closing in order to make repairs, paint, or do other work. In this case the seller should insist on some form of 30-day lease or other written agreement that would give him the right to eject the buyer

if the latter cannot proceed with the closing after moving into the property.

Where possession is granted before delivery of the deed, or where the seller remains in possession after delivery of the deed to the buyer, and the party in possession does not sell or buy as specified, the contract should provide for the right of ejectment by the innocent party.

Tenants.   If any part of the property included in the sale is occupied by a tenant, the sale agreement should specify this fact. The lease or leases under which the tenants are holding possession should be identified. There is need also to provide for the assignment and the proration of rent.

Proration of rent   The agreement of sale should thus provide that the leases will be assigned at the closing to the buyer and that rent for the month during which the sale takes place will be prorated between the seller and the buyer.

Prorated Items.   Normally, such things as real estate taxes, water and sewer charges, rents, and interest are prorated—divided proportionately—between seller and buyer as of the date of closing. For example, if the real estate taxes for the current year have already been paid by the seller, then he is entitled to a refund of those taxes for the balance of the year following the date of settlement. If the taxes have not been paid by the seller, the buyer is entitled to a credit for the seller's portion of the taxes for the part of the year during which the seller was the owner of the property.

Realty Transfer Taxes.   Many states and local municipalities impose taxes on the transfer of real estate by sale. This tax has various names; it is in fact a realty transfer tax.

The transfer tax is usually based on a percentage of the purchase price. The agreement of sale should provide how the tax is to be paid and by whom. The amounts of these taxes can be a significant factor in the purchase of real estate, and often can be prorated between the parties. If the buyer agrees to pay all the realty transfer taxes, the seller is receiving much more than the agreed purchase price for the real estate. Thus after negotiation it is usually agreed that the parties split or divide the realty tax between them.

Risk of Loss. It happens sometimes, after an agreement of sale has been signed, that the property then is destroyed by fire or some other accidental event. In many states the buyer may nevertheless be required to perform the contract and pay the purchase price even though the house is no longer in existence. *Accidental destruction*

Against that possibility, a *risk of loss* clause in the contract provides that if neither title nor possession of the property has been transferred to the buyer, and if all material part of the property is destroyed without the buyer's fault or is taken by condemnation proceedings, the seller cannot then enforce the contract. The buyer at his option can ask for return of the earnest money deposit.

Such an arrangement is fair to the seller. The real estate is ordinarily insured against fire or other casualty and the seller can recover the loss. If the property is condemned, the seller receives the condemnation proceeds awarded him. The buyer, however, needs the risk of loss clause so that he can get back his earnest money and declare the agreement void in the event of major loss.

Insurance. The agreement of sale must definitely provide for insurance coverage. The arrangement between the parties is usually one of two types. In one, the buyer agrees to take out adequate fire and casualty insurance on the property to protect his own interest starting with the effective date of the agreement. In the second, the seller agrees to add an endorsement to his own insurance policy to refer to the agreement, with a loss-payable clause making the proceeds payable to the seller and to the buyer "as their interests may appear." *Two types of arrangements*

Why is this insurance clause necessary? A buyer, when he signs a sale contract, becomes an owner of the property—what is known as the "equitable owner." This means that the buyer can go to court to force the seller to sell the property to him and deliver a deed—if the seller otherwise refuses to do so. As an owner, the buyer has an interest in the property; he can insure it and his interest must be protected.

The buyer may therefore want to place fire and casualty insurance on the property as of the date of the agreement, usually through a "binder" with his own insurance broker. As an alternative, the parties can agree that the seller will add an endorsement to his own policy making the proceeds payable to either the seller or the buyer or both as appropriate.

Of the two types, the first arrangement is to be preferred. The insurance proceeds would go directly to the buyer. They could not become involved in a possible legal quarrel between the seller and the buyer over entitlement to the proceeds of the policy.

"Fair ordinary wear and tear"

Maintenance and Repair. Ordinarily, the agreement of sale should contain a provision that the seller will continue to maintain and repair the property until final closing. "Fair ordinary wear and tear," casualty damages from causes insurable under a standard fire policy, or any other loss that occurs without the fault of the seller would not, however, be covered. This clause has importance because many sellers, after they have found a buyer, do not maintain the property, but let it deteriorate until final closing.

Seller's Expense. Ordinarily the seller pays to have the deed prepared, to have all matters of title clearance taken care of, including liens, and to have other restrictions taken off the property.

Statement of Zoning Classification and Uncorrected Violations of Ordinances. Many states require that an agreement of sale, especially in large cities, contain a statement on zoning classification. The buyer then knows, on reading the applicable zoning ordinance, what uses can be made of the property.

A property may also be sold while subject to uncorrected housing, fire, building, or safety violations. The agreement should provide for disclosure of such uncorrected violations. If the seller improperly indicates that there are no such violations when in reality these exist, the buyer has a cause of action or lawsuit against the seller for breach of the agreement.

It is very useful if the agreement of sale can specify the use to which the buyer wants to put the property. The seller should guarantee that the property is properly zoned for that use. For example, in a residential area a buyer may want to use one room on the first floor of the residence as an office for meeting customers or clients. The buyer should state that intention in the agreement of sale and request the seller to state that such a use is permitted under the applicable zoning laws. The buyer cannot complain if he does not indicate what use he wants to make of the property—if in fact he cannot use the property for that purpose after the purchase is completed.

Improvements by Municipality. In many cases, the municipality in which the property is situated has served notice on a seller that certain work or improvements have to be carried out on the property. An ordinance or resolution may have been passed authorizing work that will improve the property. For that work additional property assessments will be made. It comes as quite a surprise to a buyer, after he has purchased property, to receive a bill from the municipality for a sewer that was installed six months prior to his purchase.

Additional property assessments

To avoid such surprises, the buyer should insist that the seller state in the contract that he has no notice of any municipal demand that work be done on the property, or that no ordinance or other municipal resolution has been passed authorizing improvements to the property for which

an assessment might be made later. The buyer can then agree that any such notices or requirements received after the signing of the agreement of sale would be the buyer's responsibility.

Inspection of Premises. The buyer should have inspected the premises both inside and out, as noted. But the agreement should provide that the buyer has in fact made such an inspection. To protect the seller, the contract should also state that the purchase is being made with reliance on the inspection and that no representations were made except as stated in the contract. The buyer should be given the right, on reasonable notice, to enter the property to view it prior to closing.

Additional Provisions. If no construction or recent remodeling has taken place, the plans and specifications for the house should be given—if available—to the buyer. The buyer should also receive any useful survey that the seller may have in his possession along with any warranties on any equipment or structural parts of the property. A termite inspection may be necessary, particularly if the buyer's financing arrangement is being insured by a government agency. If a termite inspection is to be made, provision should be made for it and for payment for it by one or both of the parties.

The seller's options **Default of the Buyer.** The agreement should specifically protect the seller in the event that the buyer does not go through with the deal. Ordinarily the seller has certain options in the event of the buyer's breach of the agreement. He may, for example:

> (1) keep the earnest money and all monies paid toward the purchase price as liquidated damages, thus rendering the agreement null and void, and go on to sell the property to someone else;

> (2) apply the earnest money toward the purchase price and sue the buyer for the balance; or

> (3) apply the earnest money toward the seller's loss if he resells the property, then sue the buyer for any other damages sustained.

Default by Seller. If the seller breaches the contract by refusing to deliver the deed or close the sale, the buyer has the option to:

> (1) take back the earnest money from the seller and waive any claim for "loss of bargain" damages;

> (2) sue for delivery of a deed to the property; or

> (3) sue for damages sustained by the buyer as a result of the breach by the seller.

Avoiding future problems **No Other Warranties or Agreements.** In cases on record, one or both of the parties has later said that provisions were made or agreements entered into that were not included in the contract. For that reason an agreement usually specifies that the document constitutes the entire agreement between the parties and that no other oral or written understandings regarding the sale were entered into. This avoids any problems in the future concerning so-called oral agreements made with the contract.

Other provisions may, in some areas, be required in a contract of sale. These could include provisions covering mineral rights in Pennsylvania, West Virginia, and other coal-producing states; drilling rights in oil-producing states; and water rights in some of the states in the West. Such provisions are customarily inserted into agreements in those states or areas.

The above, however, constitutes a reasonably complete checklist of items that should be contained in an agreement of sale for real estate. The sheer number of these items should make it clear that the purchase of a piece of real estate is not a simple matter—that it requires considerable time and study. Negotiation and signing of an agreement of sale are only the first steps in the sale process. Some important additional steps essential to completion of the process should be noted.

Title Examination or Title Abstract. Depending on the state in which the property is located, either the seller or the buyer has to provide a title abstract, or title search, leading to the issuance of a title insurance policy. In some states, this obligation falls on the seller. The title abstract indicates the exact condition of the title, the existence of encumbrances, liens, easements and rights of way, whether or not the mineral rights on the property have been sold to others, and all other matters dealing with the quality of the title of the real estate.

In some states the buyer can decide to conduct a title search. In that case an attorney may issue a certificate of title or a title insurance company will draw a title insurance policy that preliminarily describes the quality of the title. If the title report or title abstract indicates deficiencies in the title, and if these can be corrected before the closing, the buyer has to notify the seller of the deficiencies at once. The seller then has the opportunity to correct those defects prior to closing. For example, a judgment may have been entered against the seller without his knowledge. Unless he learns of the judgment, he will not have an opportunity to do anything about it prior to closing.

Conducting a title search

Ordinarily, the copy of the preliminary title report or preliminary abstract should be delivered to the seller by the buyer sometime prior to the closing. The seller can then clear up the defects in the title.

Final Closing or Settlement of the Sale

At this point everything comes together. The deed and final evidence of good title are delivered to the buyer. The buyer pays the balance of the purchase price. The mortgages needed by the buyer to pay the purchase price are executed and the charges against the property are prorated between the parties.

No mystery in "closing"   Some mystery seems to surround the "closing" in the minds of people who have never bought or sold real estate. Such persons may view the whole question of a "closing" with some fear. However, if the agreement of sale has been properly prepared and executed, and if a title examination has been properly conducted, the closing merely represents the culmination of all the various steps.

The closing usually takes place in the offices of the financial institution that granted the buyer a mortgage. In some cases the closing is held in the office of the title insurance company—if title insurance is to be placed on the property—or in the offices of one of the attorneys for the seller or buyer. At the closing, a closing sheet is prepared which lists all the various items, including:

The purchase price

Earnest money paid

Various judgments paid

Taxes and other prorated items

Net balances due the seller

Proceeds received from the buyer

The method of final disbursement of all funds

At the closing the buyer should receive a signed deed for recording. Alternatively, the deed, after being shown to the buyer, is recorded on the buyer's behalf. The buyer also receives the following:

- A title report or title insurance policy or other evidence of good title
- A bill of sale on any personal property sold with the real estate
- A receipt for the purchase price of the personal property
- A survey of the property
- The insurance policies covering the property
- A statement from the mortgagee of the amount due on any existing seller's mortgage that has to be paid from the proceeds at the closing, or a release and satisfaction of the mortgage or other liens to be paid off and released from the property

What the buyer receives

A COST CHECKLIST[1]

You may want to use the following real estate cost checklist while discussing costs with your attorney:

Purchaser's Closing Cost

(a) Reimbursement for Disbursements for:

County search .... $

Municipal searches ....

Judgment search ....

Recording costs ....

Survey...

Mortgage policy of title insurance ....

Owner's policy of title insurance.............................

Other ....

Total Reimbursement for Disbursements .... $

(b) Attorney's Fee... $

(c) Funds Required by Lending Institution:

Application fee and credit report .... $

Taxes: month at $ per month interest from

   to ....

Review of documents, lender's counsel ....

Other ....

Total Funds Required by Lender............................. $

(d) Miscellaneous:

Premium, homeowner's insurance policy....................... $

Other, such as adjustments to seller for taxes, water and sewer

   charges, and fuel .... $

Total Miscellaneous .... $

Total Purchaser's Closing Costs (a, b, c, and d) .... $

Seller's Closing Costs

(a) Attorney's fee .... $

(b) Realtor's commission   % × price of $ .... $

(c) Realty transfer fee: $3.50 per $1,000.00 of price, or less if seller $

   qualifies for exemption ....

Total Seller's Closing Costs (a, b, and c) .... $

[1] Adapted from *New Jersey Real Estate, the Law, and You* (Trenton: New Jersey State Bar Assn., February 1977).

- Leases and assignments of leases
- Letters from the seller advising any tenants to pay future rents to the buyer
- Receipts for taxes for the last three years
- Receipts showing payment of all utilities to date, including water, gas, and electricity, and especially those utilities that under the law of the state are entitled to be liened against the property for nonpayment
- Keys to the home

At the closing, the seller should also receive the balance of the purchase price as adjusted in the closing statement. If the seller is taking a "purchase money mortgage" from the buyer, to be discussed later, the seller will also want evidence at the closing that the buyer has insurance naming the seller as mortgagee. This policy protects the seller in the event that a fire or other "act of God" causes loss to the dwelling.

IN A NUTSHELL: QUESTIONS TO ASK BEFORE SIGNING A CONTRACT[1]

As a precaution, you should know the answers to the following questions before you sign anything or pay any money for a piece of real estate:

- When should you sign a purchase contract?
- Is the price specified?
- Does the proposed contract provide for furnishing proper evidence of title?
- Does the seller agree to furnish possession?
- Does the contract provide for the property to be insured?
- Is there a good marketable title to the property?
- Does the contract specify who is to pay the real estate taxes?
- Have you had your own attorney check the title?

- Is there an "easement or restriction of record" clause in the contract?
- Have you checked for zoning restrictions affecting the use of the property?
- Have you decided whether to hold the property in one person's name or in more than one name?
- Are you relying on a warranty deed alone for title protection?
- Will you have to pay for the property even if you can't borrow the money?
- Can you get your down payment back?
- Who is to pay the escrow fees?
- When will the transaction be closed?
- Is someone else living on the property?
- Will you have to pay any hidden fees?

[1]Adapted from *Stop, Look and Check before Buying a Home* (Topeka: Kansas Bar Assn.)

What Is a Deed?

As noted, the owner or seller of the property has to give the buyer at the closing a properly executed deed on the property. The deed is the written instrument or document by which the owner of the property conveys the land, or some interest in the land, to the buyer.

A person may make a gift of real property by deed as well as sell property by deed. A father, for example, could make a gift of a piece of real estate to his son or other person by signing it, having it notarized before a notary public, and delivering the deed to the person receiving the property.

Making a gift by deed

At the time of sale the deed will identify the parties, state the price or consideration paid, and give a complete, accurate description of the property. The deed has to be signed by the seller—or sellers if there is more than one person involved—and must be acknowledged before a notary public. At the closing, the deed is delivered to the buyer for recording.

Recording the deed is very important to the buyer. That formality constitutes notice that the buyer now owns the property and that the seller no longer has an interest as of the date of recording. If the buyer does not record the deed, anyone with a claim against the seller who is unaware of the fact of the sale can put a lien on the property. The buyer may actually have paid the purchase price and may have a deed in his possession. For the buyer's protection, the deed should be recorded immediately following the settlement.

There are various types or classes of deeds. Two rank as important insofar as individual rights are concerned:

- The *warranty deed* transfers an interest in the property and guarantees to the buyer that such interest has in fact been transferred.
- The *quitclaim deed* merely transfers whatever interest, if any, the seller may have in the property.

The latter has a special purpose. For example, as a result of the title examination a third party may be found to have an interest in the property that the buyer intends to buy. The third party may have the right to use the property as a shortcut. In order to clear the title of that possible defect, the buyer would insist that the party who claims the right of way sign and deliver to the buyer a quitclaim deed. This transfers to the buyer whatever right the third party may have with respect to the property. In this way, the buyer is assured that the third party cannot later claim an interest in the property.

The quitclaim deed

At the closing the buyer should make certain that the deed conforms in all respects to the agreement of sale and all its provisions. The lawyer for the buyer should inspect the deed to make certain that all promises contained in the sale agreement are fulfilled.

After the closing, and after the deed has been recorded, the buyer should change to his own name all necessary utility services and the real estate tax records. In many instances, because the next billing cycle for the real estate taxes comes along before the ownership records are changed, a statement for real estate taxes may be sent to the former owner. The buyer should make sure he is informed when this occurs. He must obtain a statement for the tax bill or the taxes may be placed as a lien against the property. The buyer may never know that the taxes were liened.

If the seller does not pay the tax or deliver the tax bill to the buyer when he receives it, the buyer may have no way of knowing that the taxes for that year have been billed.

BUILDING A HOME

Building versus buying

Some of the problems and procedures involved in buying an existing home have been described. Methods of financing such a purchase and the types of mortgages that may be used will be discussed later.

Suppose now that a buyer wants to build a home on a particular lot. Building is a much more complicated matter, one that requires knowledge by the proposed buyer or builder of just what is involved.

First, of course, the person who wants to build a home has the problem of finding a suitable lot. He faces the same problems in connection with the title to the lot, and with making certain that the title is good, as the buyer of an existing home. Other concerns include the cost of construction, selection of a knowledgeable builder, protection against the claims of subcontractors whom he may never have met, supervision of the work as it progresses so that he "gets his money's worth," and his need for financing.

Assuming that he has found a lot on which he hopes to build a home, the buyer may proceed in several ways. If he is buying a lot from a developer, the latter may have sets of plans and specifications available for use by the buyer. The sale may proceed as a purchase of the lot only, with an agreement to build a house later. The sale may, as an alternative, be based on an agreement to purchase the lot and the house to be built upon it. The final closing would then be held when the house is completed.

Either of these two methods may be utilized depending on the circumstances of the case and the needs of the parties as regards financing.

If the buyer decides to utilize plans and specifications already prepared by the developer, certain dangers may arise. The buyer should find out the reputation of the builder or developer—and ask some questions. What other types of homes has he built? Are the homes structurally sound? Are the people who have purchased these homes satisfied with their homes and construction features?

No one who is building should hesitate to ask the developer or builder for references. Not only the people referred by the builder or developer, but other persons who have purchased a home constructed by this particular builder should be contacted.

Obtaining references

Most persons, it seems, will discuss such matters with people who inquire, especially if the homeowners are satisfied with their homes. A lukewarm response regarding a house built by the builder should touch off suspicions and should lead to further inquiries before buying or contracting to build.

It is very important that the plans and specifications should contain as much detail as possible so as to eliminate future problems. Some things the plans should do:

- Specify the kinds of materials and the brand names of the fixtures to be put in the house
- Be specific as far as colors are concerned
- Be very clear where specifications refer to the use of a certain type of material "or its equal"

Models, trade names, types

The latter clause, of course, gives the builder the right to substitute materials that he says are equal in quality to those specified, but that may not be or that the buyer would not want in the home. The buyer should for this reason investigate models of the desired types of lighting fixtures, kitchen fixtures, furnace, air-conditioning units, and even the types of faucets or commodes. The plans can be specific as to trade names and types.

The buyer should spend as much time as necessary in the review and preparation of the specifications for the building. He will be living in that home for a long time; if it is not exactly to his liking, he will always entertain some regret or some bitterness in connection with it. Such problems can be avoided by having the specifications reviewed by an attorney and by a construction adviser if the buyer has no architect.

The architect, the agreement with the general contractor, and other subjects deserve additional close attention from the buyer.

The Architect

If you are dissatisfied with the plans and specifications furnished by the builder or developer, you can utilize the services of an architect in the planning and designing phases. An architect will submit sketches, on request, of plans that will meet all requirements.

Architect's responsibilities, buyer's obligations

Ordinarily, a contract with an architect is based on the normal uniform architectural agreements that the American Institute of Architects distributes. These require payments based on a percentage of the total cost of the project. The agreement with the architect should be thoroughly discussed with him and with an attorney before it is signed—for one thing because it normally contains provisions for payment of architectural fees even if the buyer is not pleased with the architect's designs. The contract should specify the architect's responsibilities and the buyer's payment obligations.

The architect's services normally include drawing up the construction plans and specifications, including those relating to the architecture, structural details, all mechanical work such as electrical, heating, and plumbing installation, and all outside work on parking areas, walks, fences, landscaping, and so on.

An architect normally draws up preliminary plans for approval by the owner or buyer. If the latter approves the preliminary drawings, the architect proceeds with the final drawings or "detailed drawings." These plans may then be submitted for bids to various contractors. The preliminary plans often save unnecessary work because they make possible advance agreement on construction designs and plans.

THE PURCHASE AND SALE AGREEMENT: QUESTIONS THE BUYER SHOULD ASK BEFORE SIGNING[1]

The paper first given to a prospective buyer by a real estate broker is the purchase and sale agreement. Few people realize that this paper is the most important step in making the purchase of a home, for the details of this agreement determine what you buy and how you buy it. Before signing, read the agreement carefully and discuss with your family lawyer such items as the following:

1. Exactly what land, buildings, and furnishings are included in your offer? Are stove, refrigerator, and the like included?

2. What details regarding payments should be stated?

3. When can you take possession?

4. Is the seller to furnish you with a good, marketable title?

5. What kind of deed should the seller give?

6. Who pays for the examination of the title to the property in the event the offer is accepted? Who pays for the abstract of title or title insurance?

7. Have utilities been installed and paid for?

8. Should a surveyor be employed to determine whether the improvements are actually located on the property? Who should pay for the cost of the survey?

9. If a mortgage is to be given, who will pay the intangible tax on the mortgage?

10. If termite, water, or other damage is found, shall the seller pay the cost of repairs?

11. What are the zoning regulations, or restrictions, on the use of the property?

12. What is the time within which the purchase should be accepted or refused? Is the date of such acceptance to be vital to the offer?

13. If your offer is accepted, what steps should be taken with respect to insuring the improvements to protect you, the prospective purchaser, pending the final closing?

14. What persons (husbands and wives) should be required to sign and accept the offer?

15. Are boundary lines properly specified?

16. Are timber, mineral, and water rights, if any, properly covered?

17. Who is responsible for payment of taxes?

18. How should the agreement be executed to make it binding?

19. What are the remedies if the buyer or seller defaults?

[1] Adapted from *So You're Going to Buy a Home* (Tallahassee: The Florida Bar, February 1980).

The agreement with the architect should contain a provision that the plans and specifications belong to the buyer or person intending to build the home. Without such a provision the plans remain the property of the architect.

Supervision may guarantee performance

Depending on the size of the home and the amount of money involved, the owner may want also to retain the architect to supervise construction. Such supervision of the general contractor and all subcontractors serves often as a guarantee that the contractor will follow the plans and specifications. Normally, additional fees are required if the architect is to supervise, but it may well be worth the expense.

If no architect is used, someone with construction experience should be hired by the buyer to inspect the property from time to time and to make certain that the contractor is following the plans and specifications. Normally, the financial institution that granted the buyer a mortgage loan will have an inspector check the property before allowing any periodic payment of construction funds to the contractor. But this type of inspection is made by the financial institution primarily for its own benefit. It cannot be considered the complete type of inspection that an owner would want to ensure that high-quality materials and workmanship are going into the project.

Agreement with General Contractor

Agreement should be in writing

An architect can either place a project with several general contractors for bids or suggest a builder who meets the buyer's standards. In either case, the buyer is now in a position to enter into an agreement with a builder for the construction of the home.

For obvious reasons the agreement should be in writing. It will contain the basic agreement on the construction project. The contract must provide that the home and land will be free of all liens from all contractors, subcontractors, laborers, and persons supplying material to the general contractor.

Why is the latter assurance necessary? In most cases the buyer deals only with one general contractor. The contractor in turn enters into contracts with other people to supply him with materials and to do portions of the work, such as plastering, electrical, and plumbing. These are people the buyer may never meet or ever see. If, however, they perform services on the home site and are not paid, such subcontractors, suppliers of material, and workmen can, in most states, file liens against the property, called *mechanic's liens*, even though the buyer had no agreement with them.

In specific terms the building contract provides that the general contractor, on behalf of himself and all subcontractors, laborers, and suppliers of materials, will not lien the property for nonpayment. In some states a contract between the person building the home and the general contractor may specifically waive the right to file a mechanic's lien. This contract can be recorded in the courthouse so that any contractor or other "mechanic" dealing with the general contractor can know that the general contractor has waived the right to file mechanic's liens against the property. In those states where such a contract is permitted, the contract waiving the right to file mechanic's liens must be signed and filed before any work is done or any materials are supplied.

In rare cases general contractors will try to retain the right to file mechanic's liens by having supplies delivered to the project quickly, or by doing a minimal amount of work so that they can claim later that they started the work or supplied materials before the agreement waiving the mechanic's liens was filed. This is called "spiking the work."

To prevent "spiking"

To avoid spiking, many financial institutions, in lending money on new construction, will insist that photographs be taken on the site on the day the construction agreement is signed. The photos prove that no work has been done on the project, and that no supplies have been delivered.

Every buyer should make certain that the building contract provides that no liens can be filed. In states where they are permitted, contracts waiving the right to file a lien should be signed and filed as soon as possible—certainly before any work is done or any supplies delivered.

The sole judge of quality

The construction agreement will provide for payments to the general contractor in accordance with a fixed timetable. The latter is usually based on stages of completion of the dwelling. For example, one-fifth of the total price must be paid after the foundation is completed, and so on. Normally, such agreements should provide that no payment will be made until the architect or job supervisor is satisfied that the work has been completed to that stage and issues a certificate to that effect. In such agreements, too, the architect or job supervisor should be named as the sole judge of the quality of the work, of any damages that may have been incurred because of delays, of the timeliness with which the work is proceeding, and of the degree to which the plans and specifications have been followed.

The construction contract also provides for changes in the work, normally accomplished by a "written change order." To protect the buyer, the architect, and the general contractor, the construction contract should provide only for written change orders signed by all parties. The reason: change orders may increase or decrease in number depending on the circumstances and the type of payment due.

As an example, the builder may indicate that a certain type of furnace that was specified is no longer available. He may suggest a substitute. If the different model is available at a lower price, a written change order would be prepared indicating the substitution of the new furnace and a reduction in the cost of the dwelling.

Normally, of course, change orders call for an increase in the purchase price due to a change in market conditions. At that time the parties should decide whether or not the change order should be executed. The important thing to remember here is that provisions for change orders should be included in the original construction contract.

One of the most important parts of the building or construction contract is the clause that sets a completion date. Normally, the owner's permanent financing is based on completion of the dwelling before a certain date. The date agreed upon in the contract should make some provision for the unforeseen contingencies that may arise. For example, strikes may cause certain supplies to be delivered late to the site through no fault of the general contractor. Or bad weather might delay the contract completion date. If, however, a delay occurs through the fault of the contractor, the building and construction agreement should provide for damages to be paid by the contractor at a fixed rate per day.

The termination for cause

Finally, the construction contract should contain provisions giving the owner the right to terminate the contract for cause. That means the contractor is not doing the work properly or is not following the specifications.

These basic contract provisions and the advice of a family lawyer will protect the buyer and provide for remedies in the event the general contractor defaults. The provisions also protect the buyer if the general contractor, after receiving payment, fails to pay the subcontractors. The latter will not be able to file a lien against the property or force the buyer to pay twice for the same work.

Construction Bonds

A bond is a personal commitment by the principal, the general contractor, and the surety, usually an insurance company, that both are bound to the third party, the buyer or owner, in a certain amount. The bond is conditioned on proper performance of the contract and payment of all subcontractors and suppliers.

- In a *performance bond,* the general contractor and the insurance company guarantee that the contractor will perform properly his end of the contract. If he does not, and the owner has to find another contractor to complete the work, the insurance company will pick up the additional costs.
- The *labor and material payment bond* guarantees that the general contractor will pay all his subcontractors and material

suppliers. If he does not, the insurance company will step in and pay the claims.

While these bonds are normally used on large projects, they are available and may be required by contract in the construction of a home. While the premiums for these bonds are normally added to the contract price by the general contractor, the bonds are well worth the money because they give valuable added protection.

Caveat on construction bonds

A word of caution regarding construction bonds: when the construction contract or the building plans and specifications are altered or modified in any way, the written consent of the insurance company must be obtained on every change. If this is not done, and if the contractor does not perform properly, the insurance company can claim that the change increased the possibility that the company would have to pay without its consent. Since the risk was increased, the company is no longer liable on the bonds.

If the change in the plans does increase the risk to the insurance company, it will be relieved of liability under the bond. Consent to the change should be secured from the insurance company when change orders are made out. Consent may be obtained by an architect, job supervisor, or lawyer. But it must be obtained!

The construction contract should also require that the general contractor provide the owner with insurance certificates, issued by his insurance company, protecting all parties against accidents. The certificates state that the contractor has liability insurance and workers' compensation insurance in sufficient amounts to protect himself and the owner in case of a construction accident, injury, or death. The buyer should be named as an insured person in these policies. Also, obviously, materials will be delivered to the property and more and more value will be added to the structure as construction goes forward. These values could be lost if fire should destroy the incomplete home.

Fire insurance coverage

The construction contract itself should provide for fire insurance coverage in the event of loss by fire or some other casualty. Again, the buyer should be named as an insured. A conference with an insurance counselor on the appropriate coverage is well worth the time. It will pay off in peace of mind and in dollars and cents should a loss occur. The agreement should require that the general contractor provide the buyer with the insurance certificates so the buyer will be assured of having complete protection.

Common Disputes During Construction

Disputes arising between an owner and a contractor during construction of a dwelling usually center on whether the plans and specifications

are adequate. Other questions may arise: whether the land was in the condition represented by the owner, whether the contractor suffered additional costs because of stone encountered in excavating, whether extras claimed by the contractor were properly ordered and charged to the job, and whether the contractor deviated from the plans and specifications. Many of these disputes can be avoided by careful preparation of documents, a complete investigation of the contractor's reputation and prior performance, and a common-sense effort to be fair and understand the other guy's problems.

Protection in Making Payments

After the architect or job superintendent certifies that the work has been completed, the owner should make the final payment. A "retainage," a certain percentage of each periodic payment, is usually held back from earlier payments to ensure that the work will be done properly. The retainage is also paid over to the contractor on satisfactory completion of the work.

Before the final payment Before making final payment, the owner should obtain from the contractor statements signed by each subcontractor and supplier that he has been paid in full. No subcontractors or suppliers will then be able to file future claims. These statements, called "releases of liens," are standard documents.

The complicated process of building a home requires the owner's close attention. He will, after all, live there for many years. A little study and care can save much money, many headaches, and a great deal of heartache. To keep that dream house from becoming a nightmare, do not hesitate to insist that the construction contract include the provisions discussed here.

The best protection, however, is a solid, competent, reputable contractor who stands behind his work. Spend as much time as necessary to find the best contractor available.

FINANCING THE PURCHASE OR BUILDING OF YOUR HOME

No discussion of the purchase or construction of a home would be complete without some discussion of how one pays for it. Not everyone, unfortunately, is in a position to pay cash when purchasing a home. Most people have to give much thought to the ways in which they can pay for it.

The property becomes security

Mortgages have traditionally been used to finance the purchase of real estate. They are not the sole means; personal loans, with or without security, can also be utilized. But in most cases, mortgages are used. With a mortgage, the owner retains the benefits of ownership while offering the property as security for a loan from the lender. While mortgages are different in the various states, the lender's interest in all cases is solely to protect his loan.

Like a deed, a mortgage must be recorded. Then the mortgagee, the party holding the mortgage, has a protected security in the real estate against third parties who might not know of the mortgage loan. The mortgage represents a lien on the real estate; it creates no personal liability on the part of the owner of the land. The mortgage follows the land from one owner to another as long as it is not paid.

The owner may become personally liable for the total amount of the mortgage loan by means of a *note* or a *bond* that can accompany the mortgage. This means that the owner signs a personal promise to pay back the entire loan. He also, of course, signs the mortgage, which creates a *security lien* in the hands of the lender. These are different documents creating different rights and obligations.

Certain types of mortgages and ancillary documents are commonly used in buying or building a home. The federal government may insure a mortgage through the Federal Housing Administration (FHA) or guarantee a mortgage loan through the Veterans Administration (VA). The seller may give the home buyer a purchase money mortgage, also called a "take-back mortgage." Finally, the buyer may obtain a conventional mortgage, one that involves no government backing.

Government-Backed Mortgages

Established in 1934, the FHA makes possible low-down-payment loans. The federal agency assures the lender that the government will cover any losses if the buyer fails to keep up with the mortgage payments. By law, the FHA requires a down payment of 3 per cent on homes priced up to $50,000. On homes valued at more than $50,000, the FHA requires a down payment of 3 per cent on the first $25,000 and 5 per cent on the remainder.

Interest rates on FHA-insured mortgages are set by agreement between the lender and the borrower. An FHA loan cannot exceed a maximum limit, with the limit determined according to the location of the property. The maximum generally ranges from a base of $67,500 to a high of $90,000 in some high-cost areas. In Alaska and Hawaii the limit is $135,000. FHA loans are "assumable"—subsequent buyers may take on the payments.

The VA loan-guarantee program functions differently. Established at the end of World War II, the program provides for a guarantee to the lender of 60 per cent of the loan or $27,500, whichever is lower. To be eligible for a loan guarantee, veterans of the U.S. armed services must have been on active duty for at least 90 days during specified wartime periods or 181 days during peacetime. Also eligible are the unmarried surviving spouses of military personnel killed in action, of those who died from a service-related disability, or of those listed as missing in action (MIA).

To use the VA program, borrowers have to obtain a "certificate of eligibility" from the VA. On its reverse side the certificate notes the amount of the holder's guarantee. Having repaid a loan, the veteran can use the certificate again. Subsequent buyers can assume VA-guaranteed loans.

A third kind of government-backed mortgage is offered by the Farmers Home Administration (FmHA). This program provides for direct loans to low- and moderate-income applicants in rural areas with populations below 20,000. The FmHA sets income limits for borrowers based on median incomes in the area. Homes purchased under the program are modest in cost, design, and size.

Purchase Money Mortgage

Financing part of purchase price

Because of financial problems facing a buyer, he may be unable to secure financing to purchase a home from any conventional mortgage or finance company. At the same time the seller may be willing to finance part of the purchase price. In other words, the seller says to the buyer, "Look, if you can't come up with all the money you need, give me a down payment and I will take back monthly payments, at interest, over a term of X number of years. Give me a mortgage to that effect, and we'll go ahead with the deal."

What the seller is talking about is a *purchase money mortgage,* a mortgage running back to the seller that covers the balance of the purchase price after the down payment is made. The seller takes a position similar to that of a bank or financial institution. He gives the buyer an opportunity to pay the balance in monthly installments with interest over a term of years.

Like every other mortgage, a purchase money mortgage must be recorded. However, to protect the seller, many states, by statute, give priority to a purchase money mortgage if it is recorded within a certain number of days or weeks from the date of settlement. This is true even though there may be other liens filed on the real estate between the final closing and the date on which the purchase money mortgage is actually recorded.

The purchase money mortgage method is a very important method of financing for those buyers who cannot secure conventional mortgages. In some cases, too, buyers may obtain mortgage money from a financial institution for part of the purchase price. These buyers then need additional funds to complete their purchases. Where the seller will take back a purchase money mortgage, that becomes a "second mortgage"— second in priority to the first mortgage provided by the financial institution.

Conventional Mortgages

To qualify for a loan

Savings banks, commercial banks, savings and loan associations, building and loan groups, credit unions, and other private mortgage companies may grant *conventional mortgages* if the buyer qualifies for a loan as regards occupation, income, credit history, and so on. If a buyer goes into the mortgage department of a commercial bank seeking money to buy a dwelling, he must qualify for the loan under the rules of the individual bank. These rules touch on such things as the amount of money the buyer will put down in cash, the number of years the mortgage is to run, the interest rate to be paid on the mortgage, whether or not the buyer can afford the monthly payment in view of his monthly income, and whether or not he is a good credit risk.

In brief, the financial institution looks to the property to make certain it is sufficiently valuable to support a mortgage in the amount sought. The institution looks at the individual buyer to ensure that he is qualified for a mortgage under the rules and regulations.

The formats and terms of conventional mortgages change according to marketplace conditions. They undergo changes, for example, in the interest rates charged, in the periods specified for repayment, and in many other aspects. The state of the national and local economies affects the rise and fall of interest rates.

Much has been written in recent years of the so-called "prime rate," the rate of interest that financial institutions charge their most valued clients. If the prime rate of interest at Bank X is 10 per cent, then the rate of interest charged to secondary clients can be expected to be higher than that. The individual buying a home is usually not a prime client. The buyer seeking a conventional loan should, thus, "shop" for his or her mortgage at various financial institutions. That way, the home buyer can find the best possible "deal" insofar as interest rate and number of years are concerned.

Shopping for a mortgage makes sense, too, because lending became, by the middle 1980s, an immensely competitive field. Periods of inflation and deflation directly affected rates. Rather than simply stating their terms, many lending institutions looked for ways to fashion loan agreements that both borrowers and lenders could accept.

Mortgages may be deceptive. A mortgage at one bank or financial institution for a 25-year term may mean a monthly payment of principal and interest of $400 while a mortgage at a different bank for a 20-year term may cost $450 per month. While the monthly payment may be more in the latter case, the total amount paid over the life of the mortgage would be much greater on a 25-year basis than on a 20-year basis.

In "shopping" for a mortgage, the buyer should determine the exact cost of that mortgage over the entire term of the mortgage. Only then can he make an intelligent decision on the financing of the purchase.

Other factors have also to be considered. Whether or not the mortgage has a *prepayment privilege* becomes very important. Many mortgages have a penalty clause: the buyer pays a penalty if the mortgage is paid in full prior to its expiration date. This penalty is usually stated as a percentage of the total mortgage loan. Where possible, the buyer should secure a mortgage that allows prepayment without penalty.

The lender may insist, however, that the buyer both sign a bond or note, as mentioned, and allow other property to be covered by the mortgage in order to further secure the loan.

In the case of an existing dwelling, the amount of a conventional mortgage is ordinarily based on an appraisal of the property. Either by law or by its own policy, the financial institution involved will loan only up to a certain percentage of the appraised value, whether it be 75 per cent, 66⅔ per cent, 90 per cent, or whatever figure may be involved.

When money is "tight," the financial institution requires a much larger percentage of the total price as a deposit from the buyer and grants a lower percentage of the balance under the mortgage. In times of "easy money," a much larger mortgage can usually be found.

Home mortgage loans evolved in new directions in the 1980s. The new forms sought partly to adapt the traditional fixed-rate, fixed-term, level-payment mortgage to new conditions. The adjustable-rate mortgage (ARM) came into being as a complement to the fixed-rate mortgage (FRM). One such ARM, the *graduated payment mortgage* (GPM) accommodates payment levels to changing family income. The FRM cannot account for a young family's increasing income over the years; the GPM can and does. Under this plan the payments on the mortgage begin at lower than average levels and increase gradually over the years.

New mortgage formats also take into account some basic economic facts during periods of inflation and recession. The ARM seeks, for example, to protect lenders. It gives the lender the right to raise interest rates on existing mortgages as economic factors push interest rates up. Theoretically, rates can also fall if local regional rates drop.

At least nine of the more common types of new or experimental mortgages should be noted.

The Adjustable-Rate Mortgage (ARM). As indicated, the ARM carries an interest rate that is adjusted periodically according to a preselected index. The borrower and lender usually negotiate the loan terms, the adjustment schedule, and the index to be used. Adjustment schedules usually call for changes every one or three years; but adjustments can take place as frequently as every three months and as seldom as every five years. Commonly used indexes include the Federal Home Loan Bank Board's national average mortgage rate and the U.S. Treasury bill rate.

Two other forms of ARMs are the *renegotiable-rate mortgage* (RRM) and the *variable-rate mortgage* (VRM). The two are virtually identical to the basic ARM.

In many cases ARMs provide for "reverse amortization," a process that allows the borrower to add to the amount owed the lender. Negative amortization can also add to the normal 30-year loan term. Some lenders specify that they can call in the loan if, under reverse amortization, the loan increases to 125 per cent of its original amount. In that case the buyer may have to find alternative financing quickly.

Balloon Mortgage. The balloon mortgage requires periodic payments of installments of principal and interest. Because the regular payments do not fully amortize, or pay off, the loan, the borrower pays a lump sum at a specified date in the future, usually at the end of the mortgage term, to pay off the balance.

Biweekly-Payment Mortgage (BPM). A "quick-pay" mortgage calling for payments every two weeks of one-half of the regular monthly payment. A fixed-rate plan, the BPM loan can be amortized more quickly than, for example, a 30-year fixed-rate mortgage requiring monthly payments. As an illustration, a $70,000 loan at 13 per cent would be amortized in 18 years (with an interest saving of about $97,000) rather than the standard 30 years. As the borrower, you are making the equivalent of 13 payments a year rather than 12.

Graduated-Payment Mortgage (GPM). A mortgage whose terms specify that payments will increase for a specified period of time and then level off. The GPM is another kind of fixed-interest mortgage and enables younger buyers with lower incomes to qualify for loans. The GPM does this by providing lower monthly payments in the early years of the loan term. GPMs typically run for 30 years and monthly payments generally increase at the rate of 7.5 per cent a year for the first five years, then level off. GPMs involve deferred interest; thus the borrower pays more over the life of the loan.

Growing-Equity Mortgage (GEM). The GEM calls for payments that increase each year by a predetermined percentage. The annual increase can be anywhere from 2.5 per cent to 7.5 per cent of the monthly payment. With GEMs the interest rate is fixed. All increases in the monthly payments go toward reduction of the loan principal and increases may take place for a specified number of years or yearly throughout the life of the loan.

Land-Contract Loan. With a land-contract loan, a borrower takes out a loan and makes payments on it but does not get title or ownership until a specified number of payments have been made. The land-contract usually enables the borrower to make a smaller down payment than would otherwise be required. But missing a single payment may mean that the seller may take back the property. The buyer then loses the value of the down payment and all accumulated equity.

Pledged-Account Mortgage (PAM). A form of GPM, the PAM requires that part of the buyer's down payment go into a savings account. The buyer agrees that the funds in the account can be drawn to supplement the monthly payments during the early years of the loan.

Reverse-Annuity Mortgage (RAM). RAMs enable older homeowners to draw on the equity in their homes during their retirement years. The borrower does not take the loan in a lump sum, but receives the loan funds in regular monthly payments over several years. When these payments end, the borrower begins to repay the loan, which is amortized on a 30-year schedule. The balance of the loan must be repaid if the home is sold or the owner dies.

The RAM poses many questions, including: Does the homeowner

want to sacrifice part of his or her estate to pay back the loan after death, rather than leave it all to specified heirs? If Aunt Jenny dies leaving the homeowner half a million, can the RAM be paid off in full?

The questions do not mean that the RAM has no real value. In specific cases it obviously can help older persons, retired or not. A plus is that it can be adapted almost entirely to the situation of the borrower.

Shared-Appreciation Mortgage (SAM). SAMs give the borrower a below-market interest rate. In return, the lender receives part of the future appreciation in the value of the property. The lender's share is payable either when the home is sold or at a specified time five to ten years into the loan term.

SHOPPING BY COMPUTER

Because shopping for a mortgage can take substantial amounts of time, computerized mortgage shopping services have sprung up. These search services make available most of the data a potential buyer needs to evaluate the mortgage arrangements offered by subscribing financial institutions. Shoppers can therefore quickly and easily ascertain interest rates and other costs of borrowing.

STATE-SPONSORED MORTGAGES

Forty-eight states participate in programs designed to make possible home purchases by persons who might otherwise not be able to afford such investments. Buyers pay interest rates that are usually well below market rates. Down payments may be as low as 5 per cent of the purchase prices (well below the more normal 10 to 15 per cent). States fund these programs by issuing tax-free bonds at below-market yields. State-sponsored mortgages are fixed for 30-year terms.

SECOND MORTGAGES

Many home buyers or owners take out second mortgages or "equity loans" either to finance the purchases of houses they do not yet own or to draw on the equity in homes already owned. The second mortgage is "junior" to the first: it carries rights that are secondary to those of the first mortgage. In a foreclosure sale, the proceeds must go toward payment of the first mortgage before any funds can be used to pay off the second.

Typically, a homeowner may need funds to finance a college education, remodel his or her present home, invest in a business, or make a down payment on another house. The second mortgage offers a solution. The homeowner cashes in on the equity or appreciated value of his or her home without having to sell it. The borrower, however, usually pays a substantially higher rate of interest for a second mortgage than for the first. Lenders giving second mortgages justify the higher rates by pointing to the relatively greater risk in a second mortgage.

Commitment Letter

Once the terms of the mortgage have been agreed on, the lender will ordinarily issue a commitment letter. The letter states the terms of the mortgage, such as interest rate, number of years, and other relevant facts. The commitment letter from the financial institution usually remains in effect for a specified period of time, such as 90 days or 120 days. If the sale is not completed within that period, the financial institution is no longer committed to give the mortgage, and no other terms remain in effect. The insitution can refuse to proceed on the basis of its prior commitment letter. Where a conventional mortgage is secured, the sale should obviously be closed within the time limitation indicated in the commitment letter.

Financing the Construction of a Dwelling

Construction and permanent financing phases

Financing the construction of a dwelling differs from the financing of the purchase of an existing dwelling. In the typical case, financing a home to be built is divided into two stages: the construction phase and the permanent financing phase.

A short-term mortgage, for a year or 18 months, is normally written to finance the construction of a new dwelling or improvements on an existing dwelling. Some lenders cannot, by law, make short-term loans to finance construction; other lenders can do so. In other words, certain lenders can only issue commitment letters for "permanent" mortgages when the dwelling is completed.

Essentially, this distinction means that a construction mortgage involves a somewhat higher risk than a permanent mortgage obtained after the home has been completed. For example, the home may never be built; the contractor may default; the owner may run into difficulties; as a result, the financial institution may find itself with a home that is half built and a substantial investment already paid out.

Because of the higher risk, short-term construction loans are generally made at a higher interest rate than are permanent mortgages. Thus investors are attracted to this type of investment.

After preparing plans, specifications . . .

The buyer has his plans and specifications prepared. The next step is to approach the lender who, he feels, may give him a construction loan. The application for the loan usually requires financial information concerning the borrower, the architect, and others. Then come the appraisal of the property by the financial institution, inspection of the survey, and investigation of the credit ratings of the owner and the contractor.

The lender will also want to know where the balance of the construction money, if any, is coming from and who will be the "permanent" lender—who will provide the permanent mortgage after the home is built.

In many cases, the construction-loan lender and the permanent lender are one and the same institution. If so, the institution may simply advance funds from time to time on the basis of the mortgage. The mortgage may become permanent after completion of the entire project. The mortgage may also set forth the full amount needed at the beginning of the work, and funds may be advanced from time to time to complete the project; at final completion, a final settlement is made.

Construction-loan mortgages may differ from permanent mortgages in many details. But the principles mentioned above ordinarily govern. The builder can sometimes aid in the securing of financing, but if the builder does extensive business with the financial institution, the owner should have his own inspector or architect follow the progress of the work from beginning to end. Otherwise, the financial institution's inspector could intentionally or unintentionally favor the contractor in a dispute arising over a progress payment. The attorney, architect, or job superintendent can assist sometimes in securing financing and in determining the type of inspection and supervision of the work on a day-to-day basis.

Construction-loan mortgages

As noted, the financing institution will usually inspect only to determine whether or not, in its judgment, the progress of the work has proceeded sufficiently far to allow the next payment to be made to the contractor. The institution is not really as concerned as the owner with the day-to-day quality of the work. The owner should take all necessary steps to make sure the work is being done properly.

A commitment letter is issued by the financial institution on the construction-loan financing as well as on the permanent financing. Such a letter will spell out all the terms and conditions of the commitment on the construction loan.

Disclosure of Interest Rates

Recent federal and state laws, including the federal "truth-in-lending" and various state consumer-protection laws, require that mortgage and loan institutions disclose to the consumer all the terms of the sale insofar as financing is concerned. These terms include interest rates and annual percentage rate of interest charged. The borrower can then ascertain the exact amount and cost of securing a loan and making a purchase.

Making proper disclosure The owner-borrower may be asked to sign a "disclosure statement" at a closing on his loan. The statement indicates that he has received all the necessary disclosures required by law with respect to interest, time payment charges, and all other required information. Failure on the part of the financial institution to make proper disclosure in cases where such disclosure is required may render the entire transaction null and void. Such failure may even make the institution liable in damages or penalty to the borrower or consumer.

Because of the nature of this legislation and its importance, the advice of a lawyer is essential to anyone dealing with these problems. A detailed discussion of truth-in-lending laws follows in a later chapter.

THE SELLER'S PROBLEMS

You may at this point be asking, "Whatever happened to the seller?" Everything appearing so far in this chapter has had to do with the buyer's problems: finding the property, obtaining an agreement of sale, checking the title, closing the deal, getting a proper deed, and finding the proper financing for both the purchase of an existing home and the building of a new home. What about the seller?

The seller in most cases has much less to worry about than does a buyer. The seller owns the property, and is primarily concerned with finding a buyer who is ready, willing, and able to purchase the property on terms that are agreeable to him.

If the seller has set a realistic price on the property—and this is important because being unrealistic leads only to delays in finding a buyer—the seller can proceed to sell in two different ways. First, he can try to find a buyer himself. Second, he may make use of a real estate broker to find a buyer.

TAX BENEFITS

How can *the law work for you* in the purchase and sale of a home?

If you study the principles discussed in this chapter, you will be able to speak intelligently about real estate. You will also want to remember the changes that the Economic Recovery Tax Act of 1981 introduced. For example, starting in July 1981, the seller of a principal residence could qualify for a capital gains deferral if he bought another home costing as much as or more than the "old" one within two years after the sale. Previously, the seller had 18 months to purchase a new home. Also starting in July 1981, the seller over 55 years of age could claim a one-time

capital-gains exclusion of $125,000 when selling a home and buying a new residence. Earlier, the exclusion was $100,000.

If he tries to sell the property himself, the seller may be successful in a very short period of time. He may also have to walk many prospective buyers through his house on a regular basis. Some of these persons may only be incidentally interested in the property, or just curious.

Selection of a Real Estate Broker

If the seller decides to use the services of a broker, it is important to select a broker who is totally familiar with the area, who can answer the questions of prospective buyers, and who has a good record for moving properties.

Finding a broker

How do you find such a broker? Again, consult other persons who have recently sold property and who have had good experience with a particular broker. Consult the real estate brokers' local board for help in this regard. Don't be afraid to ask questions to find out whether or not a particular broker is sufficiently interested in your property and is sufficiently knowledgeable in the area.

In interviewing a broker, one useful method is to quote to the particular broker a price that the seller himself knows is too high for the property. If the broker readily agrees that the property is worth what is clearly an exorbitant price, chances are he is only after the *listing* of the property. He will later come back to report that the price is too high and that it has to come down.

The broker will already have the written listing agreement. He will not have to worry about losing the seller as a client for the period of time covered by the agreement.

When the broker objects validly

If the broker truthfully and sincerely indicates that the asking price is too high, the chances are that he is more reliable. The seller can

---

THE JARGON OF REAL ESTATE[1]

Here, courtesy of Sylvia Porter, is a guide to the bafflegab of buying and selling real estate.

ABSTRACT. Short legal history of a property tracing ownership over the years and noting such encumbrances as unpaid taxes and liens.

AMORTIZATION. Reduction of a debt through monthly mortgage payments (or some other schedule of repayment in which the loan principal is reduced), along with payments of interest and other loan costs.

APPRAISAL. Estimate, made by the Federal Housing Administration, the Veterans Administration, a private lender, or other qualified appraiser, of the current market value of a property.

ASSESSMENT. Special charge imposed by local government on homeowners to cover costs of special projects such as street paving or new sewer systems from which the homeowners presumably benefit.

BINDER. Tentative agreement, between a buyer and seller of real estate, to the terms of the transaction—usually involving a deposit of a small amount of money.

BROKER. Professional who is licensed by the state in which he works to assist buyers and sellers of property.

CERTIFICATE OF TITLE. Legal statement to the effect that property ownership is established by public records.

CLOSING. The occasion on which the buyer and seller of a property—or their representatives—meet to exchange payment for the deed to a property.

CLOSING COSTS. Costs, other than the basic purchase price of a piece of property, which are imposed at the time a real estate deal is closed. Closing costs can include lawyers' fees, title insurance, taxes, and several other items.

COMMISSION. Fee which a seller of property pays to a real estate agent for his services—usually amounting to six to ten per cent of the sale price.

CONDOMINIUM. Individually owned real estate consisting of a dwelling unit and an undivided interest in joint facilities and areas which serve the multiunit complex.

CO-OPERATIVE. A form of real estate ownership in which each individual owns stock in a corporation, giving him the right to live in one of the units owned and administered by the corporation.

DEED. Legal, written document used to transfer ownership of property from seller to buyer.

DEFAULT. In this context, failure by a buyer to meet a mortgage payment or other requirement of the sale—which may result in forfeiture of the property itself.

DEPOSIT (or "EARNEST MONEY"). Sum of money, normally a small fraction of the sale price of the property, which a prospective buyer gives to a seller to secure a sales contract. See "Binder."

DEPRECIATION. Decrease in the value of property due to wear and tear, obsolescence, or the action of the elements. Differs from deterioration, which signifies abnormal loss of quality.

EARNEST MONEY. A deposit. *See* above.

EASEMENT. Right granted to one property owner by another to use the grantor's land for certain purposes—for example, a right of way for an access road or for power lines.

ENCUMBRANCE (or DEFECT OF RECORD). Claim against the title of a parcel of real estate by a third party, other than the buyer or seller (e.g., a lien due to unpaid taxes or a mortgage delinquency), which challenges the property's ownership and tends to reduce its value.

EQUITY. In real estate terms, value built up in a property over the years, including the down payment, repaid portion of the mortgage principal, and appreciation (or depreciation) in the property's market value. The amount of equity in a property is the total current value of the property minus debts against the property.

ESCROW. The placing of money or other items of value in the custody of a bank or other third party until the terms of a real estate transaction are fulfilled by the two parties involved. Also, amounts paid by a homeowner into an account, usually administered by the mortgage lender, to provide for recurring expenses such as real restate taxes and homeowner insurance preminums. This type of escrow usually is included in the total monthly payments to the lender.

FHA. Federal Housing Administration, which insures mortgage holders against losses from default on loans made according to the Administration's policies.

FORECLOSURE. Sale by a bank or other lender of a property on which payments are seriously in default in order to satisfy the debt at least partially.

LIEN. Claim against a property which sometimes is kept as security for the repayment of a debt.

LISTING. Registration of a property with one or more real estate brokers or agents, entitling the broker who actually sells the property to a commission. An exclusive listing gives one individual broker the exclusive right to handle the sale of a property; a multiple listing permits a special group of brokers to handle the transaction.

MORTGAGE. Legal claim on property, given as security by a borrower to the lender of the funds in case repayment of the loan is not made.

OPTION. Often sold by a seller of property to prospective buyer, giving the latter the right to buy the property at a specified price within a specified period of time.

PLAT. Pictorial plan or map of a land subdivision or housing development.

POINTS. Part of the settlement costs of exchanging real estate. One point is 1 per cent of the amount of the mortgage. Points are paid to the mortgage lender. In some cases, the term simply means a service charge imposed by the lender to cover part of the administrative costs of processing the loan. In other cases, particularly when an FHA loan is involved, the points amount to an adjustment in the interest rate to bring an artificially administered rate up to the market rate at the time. Points, in this second sense, technically are paid by the seller of the property. However, since the price of the house normally is adjusted to allow for this, points always effectively increase the interest rate on the loan to the buyer. They tend to eliminate the interest rate advantage of government-insured or guaranteed loans.

PURCHASE MONEY MORTGAGE. Mortgage granted directly by a seller to the buyer of the seller's property, in which the seller may take back the property if the buyer does not pay off the mortgage as agreed. In brief, the seller of the house lends the buyer the money with which to buy the house.

QUITCLAIM DEED. Deed which releases any interest a seller or other individual may have in a given piece of land. *See* "Deed."

REAL ESTATE (REAL PROPERTY). Land, and any structures situated on it.

REALTOR. Real estate agent who is a member of the National Association of Realtors. A copyrighted word, always capitalized.

SETBACK. A common restriction provided under zoning ordinances specifing the distance a new house must be set back from a road or from the lot boundaries.

SURVEY. The determination, by means of examination of land records and also field measurements based on these records, of the exact boundaries and location of a property.

TITLE. Legal document containing all necessary facts to prove ownership of property.

TITLE DEFECT. Fact or circumstance which challenges such ownership.

---

[1] Selections from *Sylvia Porter's New Money Book for the 80's* by Sylvia Porter, copyright © 1975, 1979 by Sylvia Porter. Reprinted by permission of Doubleday & Company, Inc.

usually deal with him with a high degree of confidence. These are only assumptions, however. The seller's best protection is the reputation of the broker, his memberships in the professional real estate boards in the area, and his experience.

Exclusive Listing Agreements

Once the seller has found a broker, an "exclusive listing agreement" may come up for discussion. This means that the broker wants the property listed for sale with his firm exclusively for a fixed period of time, usually from 90 days to six months. The property cannot be sold through any other broker during that period.

Often, even though an exclusive agreement has been signed with Broker X, he will place the property on a so-called "multilist," a group of brokers who work together to sell a particular piece of property on a split commission basis. The multilist is also called a Multiple Listing Service (MLS). In this case the listing broker receives a percentage of the real estate commission regardless of which multilist broker actually sells the property.

Ordinarily, an exclusive real estate listing agreement contains a special clause. It provides that if the property is sold to someone who was introduced by the broker during the term of the exclusive listing agreement, then the broker earns his commission regardless of the fact that the property was sold directly to the buyer after the listing agreement had expired.

A hypothetical case A hypothetical case shows what this can mean. You sign a six-month exclusive real estate listing agreement with Broker Brown. After three months have gone by, Broker Brown brings Mr. Smith to look at your house. You hear nothing from Mr. Smith for another eight months. If Mr. Smith comes back after the listing agreement has expired and says he wants to buy the property, you will owe the broker a commission since Mr. Smith was introduced to the property by the broker during the exclusive listing agreement period.

From the standpoint of the broker, the special clause prevents the parties from agreeing among themselves not to deal until the exclusive listing agreement period has expired. From the seller's point of view, however, the clause creates a difficult situation. A lawsuit could result if the seller and the broker disagree as to whether or not the individual to whom the property was sold was in fact introduced to the property by the broker.

For the seller's protection Depending on the language used in the listing agreement, it becomes very important for the seller to protect himself in such a situation. Another provision in the exclusive listing agreement should require that the broker supply the seller with the names of all persons with whom the broker has discussed the property—or to whom he has shown the property during the term of the exclusive agreement. The list should be given to the seller at the end of the term of the agreement. This provision protects the seller in dealing with third parties after the expiration of the exclusive contract.

The requirement that the broker supply a list of names is fair to both the seller and the broker. It should not be objected to.

Multilist Plans

When a piece of property is placed on a multilist, the seller in effect engages the services of many more brokers whether he deals only through one or directly through the multilist. While some of these services have come under attack because of alleged antitrust problems, they do exist. They also bring in many brokers who will work to sell a property.

How long should an exclusive listing agreement run? Caution should be exercised. The period should not be too long. Six months, for example, is usually too long.

The circumstances of each particular case should, of course, be considered. A lawyer may be able to advise the seller. But in the normal situation, 90 to 120 days should be long enough. If more time is allowed on an exclusive agency agreement, the broker may have a tendency to push off the sale of the property while trying to "move" properties on which the listing agreements are about to expire. This is only human nature. But it may leave the seller with little activity on the sale of his property for a long time.

When Does a Broker Earn His Commission?

While the law differs from one state to another on this point, many states provide that a broker earns his commission once he finds a buyer who signs an agreement of sale. Even if the sale of the property does not go through because the buyer cannot qualify for the mortgage, or because he decides he does not want to buy for whatever reason, the broker nevertheless has earned his commission once a buyer signs an agreement.

Once again the seller should protect himself. The listing agreement should specify clearly that the broker earns his commission only when and if a final closing takes place. The buyer must of course have been introduced to the property by that broker.

Commission to be paid on closing

Where a seller decides to keep the earnest money as liquidated damages, as noted, disagreement over a broker's commission may be minimized. Many listing agreements provide that the earnest money be split between the broker and the seller where a sale falls through. Where, however, the broker's commission exceeds the amount of the earnest money paid, the seller may have to pay the commission to the broker from his own funds.

The
"nonexclusive"
agreement

Another form of listing agreement is the "nonexclusive" type. Here, the broker is given the right to sell the property on behalf of the seller, but other brokers have the same right. The nonexclusive agreement is similar to the multilist plans. But the seller can deal with several brokers individually, and each has the right to sell the property on his behalf. All this has been said before in connection with the exclusive agency agreement applies equally to the nonexclusive agreement.

Most real estate brokers work hard and diligently to secure buyers for residential property. While the commission earned in a particular case may seem high, usually 6 or 7 per cent, the broker may show the property to many persons before finding a buyer. Thus the selection of a qualified broker to assist in the sale of property can be of great help.

How can the law work for you in the purchase and sale of a home?

If you study the principles discussed in this chapter, you will be able to speak intelligently about real estate. You will also know what questions to ask, and can save money by understanding ahead of time what you are dealing with. You will be in a much stronger bargaining position, which, after all, is the name of the game.

Good luck in your new home!

4 "THEY WON'T LET ME ADD A PATIO TO MY HOME"

Every right that Americans possess under their system of laws has a corresponding duty. The right of free ownership of property carries with it the duty under the law not to interfere with the free use of someone else's property while exercising the right of ownership.

Under the policy power of the state to regulate the public health, safety, and morals for the general welfare, local governments enact and enforce "zoning regulations." As a result of zoning regulations, the free use of property is restricted. These restrictions, if reasonable, are deemed necessary for the public health, safety, and morals.

No matter where you live, you are affected by some form of zoning regulation. The regulations involve the determination by the governing body of the state, or the local government that receives its zoning authority from the state, that a zoning regulation is needed for a public purpose. That public purpose may be real or imagined in a particular case. While no clear-cut line separates arbitrary zoning from proper and legal zoning, the courts decide these issues as they arise.

COURT ACTIONS IN ZONING CASES: THE TEMPERING INFLUENCE

Court decisions have both upheld the zoning policies of local communities and attacked them. The net effect has been to moderate the social and other effects of zoning regulations.

Zoning that excludes certain groups of people, or people in certain socioeconomic categories, has come under attack. For example, the Supreme Court has stated its opposition to exclusionary zoning regulations that keep persons of low and moderate income out of specific portions of communities or entire areas. The Court has expressed the belief that developing communities have to make it possible for persons of widely diverse backgrounds and professions to reside within their boundaries.

By contrast, the Supreme Court refused in 1974 to hear the case of *Construction Industrial Association of Sonoma County* v. *City of Petaluma.* In so refusing, the Court in effect upheld the right of the City of Petaluma, California, to preserve its small-town character by passing zoning ordinances. The city also gained the right to grow at an orderly and deliberate rate and to preserve its open spaces and low-density population.

Preserving a town's character

The U.S. Court of Appeals had earlier ruled in the City of Petaluma case in favor of the city. The court said that "the concept of the public welfare is sufficiently broad to uphold Petaluma's desire" to preserve its basic character.

Other court cases can be expected both to underscore the rights of individuals to live where they want to and the municipality's right to establish plans for orderly community growth and development.

Zoning ordinances, to be valid and constitutional, must conform to a comprehensive plan of zoning in the area involved. The attacks on zoning ordinances that have been successful have been based on a community's failure to establish a comprehensive plan of development. Without such a plan, zoning restrictions can create undue hardship for the owner of particular real property, resulting in discrimination against that owner.

In addition, every zoning ordinance has to conform to the constitutional protections that keep a property owner from being deprived of his property without due process of law. If the ordinance bears no substantial relationship to the public health, safety, welfare, or morals, the ordinance can be attacked as unconstitutional.

Constitutional protections

Each particular case has to be decided upon its own facts. These include the circumstances surrounding the enactment of the ordinance, its purposes, the particular property involved, any undue hardship on the owner as a result of literal enforcement of the ordinance, and many other factors that go into determination of the validity of any ordinance.

DIVIDING PROPERTY INTO DISTRICTS

The purpose of a zoning ordinance is to divide a particular community into zoning districts. The ordinance specifies or limits the use to which property in that district can be put, and restricts or requires certain improvements and uses of land within the district. There are three main types of controls inherent in a typical zoning ordinance: control of population density, control of use of property, and control of height or other physical characteristics.

CONTROLLING POPULATION DENSITY

The ordinance will attempt to control population density by specifying the minimum lot area for a home or family, the number of square feet of open space required between structures, and the maximum number of homes per acre or per half acre or other given area.

Population density and zoning

The control of population density is a recent development in the law of zoning, and it has led to a method of developing property different from the normal, single-family residential dwelling-type development. The new developments, utilizing the townhouse or condominium-apartment ownership concept, have attempted to utilize a high-density population area with open space common to all the people living in the high-density housing development. For example, townhouses—individualized attached homes, sometimes on various levels but nevertheless having party or common walls—are built to include a common yard or parklike area immediately adjoining the residences. The net effect is to satisfy the total open-area requirement of the zoning ordinance and also permit high-density population within the area.

This concept will undoubtedly remain popular in future years if the cost of construction of single-family dwellings continues to rise and if the need for housing, at reasonable cost, continues to grow.

Control of population density becomes a matter of critical interest where an apartment building "goes condo," or is turned into a condominium. In this situation, a very common one in the cities in the 1970s, many apartment dwellers become homeowners. They usually have the opportunity to buy their apartments. Making such a purchase, most often by taking out a common type of mortgage, the new homeowner acquires a personal interest in limiting the population of his building or area.

Like the owner of a single-family home or townhouse, the condominium owner takes title to his unit by deed. He shares with other owners a common ownership of public areas. This means that each owner pays taxes on a prorated basis.

Each owner also contributes to the upkeep of common areas. Most condos are organized as corporations or associations. They have boards of directors, provide by-laws with which all owners have to comply, and decide on changes in the building or common areas.

Upkeep of common areas

Control of Use of Property

Zoning ordinance restrictions on use result in control of the particular type of activity or use that may be carried on in a building or on a piece of land. For example, a district may be limited to residential uses

only, such as single- or multifamily dwellings. Another district may be limited to commercial uses. The ordinance may specify by name the kinds of commercial uses that are permitted, such as bakery, professional offices, laundry, grocery store, and so on. Light manufacturing may be allowed in particular districts depending on the definitions contained in the ordinance itself.

Area and Height Restrictions

Area and height restrictions refer to the number of stories permitted in a building or dwelling by height in feet. The ordinance may also specify the minimum areas for side yard, front yard, and rear yard setback for any structures on the property. For example, if a particular district requires a 30-foot front yard, or 30-foot setback, the dwelling or building on any particular lot in that district must be at least 30 feet from the edge of the road or street right of way.

The side yard setback Side yard setback means that the side of the building must be at least the number of feet specified from the lotline or dividing line to the side of the building. Rear yard setback means that the building must be at least a specified number of feet from the rear property line, unobstructed by any other structure.

The area regulations may go still farther. They may provide that a number of square feet or a percentage of the total lot be utilized or covered by a structure or a building. In some cases the ordinance will set a minimum size for lots that may be used as single units or individually owned units, or a maximum size or height for all buildings in relationship to the width of the streets adjoining the lot.

The typical zoning ordinance contains a definition of permitted or excluded uses in given, clearly defined blocks, areas, or districts. There may be residential, commercial, light industrial, heavy industrial, or special development districts. Still other types may be defined in the ordinance, each district classification spelling out the particular uses permitted.

Accompanying each zoning ordinance is a zoning map that shows the boundaries of the various districts. Each area is colored or shaded to indicate the district classifications. For example, an R-1 (Residential-1) district shown on a municipal map may be color-coded in red, the R-2 (Residential-2) district in blue, the C-1 (Commercial-1) district in yellow, and so on.

How to determine zoning by area The color-coding or shading enables a prospective purchaser of real property to determine the zoning for the property. He simply goes to the

local municipal building, speaks to the zoning officer, and looks at the zoning ordinance and the zoning map.

Anyone buying real estate should follow that procedure. Unless the law requires the seller to note the zoning classification in the agreement of sale, a purchaser is taking a chance if he fails to make absolutely certain that the property is zoned properly for his intended use, or that the dwelling or other structure can be utilized for his intended use. Otherwise he may buy the property and find out too late that he cannot use the property as he wants to.

SPECIAL EXCEPTIONS AND VARIANCES

The zoning ordinance attempts to be comprehensive regarding district classifications and other details. But provisions have to be built into the ordinance for property that does not precisely fit in with the general scheme of the ordinance. The typical ordinance thus contains exceptions to the general zoning scheme where the circumstances warrant. These special arrangements for problem property fall ordinarily into two categories: the special exception and the variance.

The Special Exception

A use of property that is specifically denied in the zoning ordinance, but that may be allowed if certain conditions are fulfilled, ranks as a special exception. For example, a zoning ordinance may forbid an auto repair shop in a light commercial district. However, the ordinance may indicate that the auto repair shop will be allowed by special exception if the proposed user or owner of the property appears before the zoning commission of the municipality, shows his plans and specifications, and gives assurance concerning the elimination of noise, odors, and so on.

Public hearings on uses

A public hearing may be held to determine whether or not the proposed use would meet with criticism from the inhabitants of the area. If all the requirements are met, a special exception use for the auto repair shop may be granted.

The special exception, in brief, permits a use ordinarily denied if the owner or user submits all the necessary information and if the zoning body rules favorably on the request.

The Variance

A variance is a procedure by which the literal language of a zoning ordinance is not followed. Usually, strict compliance with the ordinance requirements would cause unreasonable and unnecessary hardship to the owner of the property involved.

The *variance procedure* involves an application for a variance by the owner or intended user of the property. The application is filed with the local zoning officer or building permit officer. The user will receive a formal denial of his application, since his use for some reason will not conform to the strict literal language of the ordinance. The user then, after receiving the denial, will appeal to the local zoning board of adjustment or zoning appeals board.

In order to establish the hardship that he must show, the owner has to be able to establish several details in his application for the variance.

- Because of the nature of the property, for example because it is irregular in size, grade, or other feature, development of the property in accordance with the strict requirements of the zoning ordinance is unreasonable or impossible. Here it is stressed that the physical features of the site do not allow its use as specified in the ordinance.

Unreasonable cost of development

- The nature of the site would involve an unreasonable cost of development. The reason may be the dimensions or shape of the property, its location, or the fact that strict adherence to the ordinance would make the property unprofitable.
- The owner has to show that he himself did not create the hardship problem. For example, a developer who lays out a plan

of lots, leaving one plot irregular, would be denied a zoning variance on the basis of hardship because he himself created the hardship situation.

- The owner must show that the character of the neighborhood would not be changed if the proposed variance were granted. A factory might change the neighborhood in a residential district, for example; a three-flat might not. Construction of a parking area in a residential district might not in and of itself change the residential nature of the district, and could possibly qualify for variance treatment.

- Finally, the owner must show he is applying for the minimum change from the strict, literal terms of the ordinance that will give him the relief he seeks. Sometimes this requires proof of what the return on an investment will be, involving the use of appraisals and expert testimony before the reviewing body. While difficult to establish because of possible alternative uses of the property, the fact of minimal deviation must generally be proved.

The reviewing board of a municipality may refuse a variance even after the owner establishes all five points. He may then appeal to the courts for relief, claiming that the negative decision is arbitrary and capricious and not in accordance with the law.

The zoning ordinance, to be effective, has to contain all necessary instructions on variance procedures and special exceptions. It must also provide for appeals procedures and the creation of zoning commissions and zoning boards of adjustment.

Instructions on variance procedures

NONCONFORMING USE

When a zoning ordinance is first enacted, it often affects existing structures. For example, a commercial retail bakery that may have been operating at a particular location for a long time may find that its continued use is not permitted under a new zoning ordinance.

Existing buildings that do not conform to the newly established requirements of a zoning ordinance are called "nonconforming uses." If they have been proper uses under the regulations that previously existed, these will usually be allowed to continue under the new zoning ordinance as "legal nonconforming uses."

The buyer of real property should nonetheless ascertain whether or not the property he wants to buy constitutes a nonconforming use. If it does—if its use can continue because it was valid prior to enactment of a later ordinance—he takes a substantial risk in buying that property for several reasons.

A method of
nullifying

First of all, the nonconforming use may be nullified through abandonment or discontinuance of the particular use. It may be nullified by provisions of the zoning ordinance that require discontinuance of the nonconforming use after a certain number of years. In another situation, a new owner may change the use, however slight, and in that way give the municipal authorities the opportunity to claim that the nonconforming use had been discontinued.

Another danger is that the property might be destroyed or damaged by fire or some other "act of God." In most cases, if more than 50 per cent of the property is destroyed, the zoning ordinance will not permit the owner to reconstruct the same structure for the same use. Destruction would terminate the nonconforming use. An owner would rarely be able to obtain a variance or other exception to permit continuance of the use after destruction of the property.

For such reasons the purchaser of property will always investigate the zoning requirements completely. If a use is nonconforming, the owner risks loss of a substantial investment.

AMENDMENT OR CHANGE OF THE ZONING ORDINANCE

In addition to the procedures for seeking a variance or establishing a special exception, the owner of property has another option. He may decide to seek a change in the zoning classifications for the area covered by his property. This involves a request for a change to the zoning commission or planning commission of the municipality. The owner has to prove that the change sought will benefit not only himself but the community in general. He also has to establish that the requested change is in conformity with the comprehensive plan of development for the entire community.

It may happen that the owner wants to make a change in a particular area of another district. That change will not affect the entire zoning district or even a substantial part of it. For example, he may want to erect a small shopping center in a residential district. The request may be attacked as "spot zoning," which means changing the classification only for a small area in a given zoning district.

"Spot zoning"

Where spot zoning takes place to any great extent, it destroys the entire zoning scheme. It can sometimes upset the comprehensive zoning plan of the municipality. As a result, spot zoning is rarely permitted. It may be allowed, however, if the owner can establish a need for the type of use in the area and can thus establish his right to have the zoning changed. The proof required of the owner in a case of spot zoning is very heavy, however; an owner should proceed only with that awareness.

A change in zoning ordinarily requires a public hearing before the municipal plan commission. The meeting is announced publicly so that other residents or owners in the area can raise any objections that they might have.

From a practical standpoint, many courts are reluctant to consider zoning problems because they are considered the bailiwick of the local governing body representing the people in the area. A denial of a zoning change by the plan commission, or by the board of councilmen, commissioners, or supervisors, will very likely not be reversed by a court in the absence of clear proof of the need for the change. A permitted rezoning, if attacked by area residents, has a better chance of being upset by the courts.

PROCEDURES FOR APPEALS UNDER ZONING ORDINANCES

Assume that you are the person in this chapter title who wants to add a patio to your home. You will have prepared plans and specifications showing the area of your property where the patio is to be located, the patio's size, and the materials to be used. You will then take these plans and specifications to the zoning officer of your municipality for a *building permit*.

*Two reasons
for refusal*
If the permit is refused, it will be for one of two reasons or both. The patio may come too close to, or impinge on, the rear yard, side yard, or front yard setback, or your specifications are not suitable under the building codes.

Refusal could be based on other factors. But once the refusal is made, you should insist that the zoning officer state his reasons in writing. Working with your family lawyer, you can decide whether you should apply for a special exception or for a variance under the terms of the ordinance. You may even decide to attack the ordinance on constitutional or other grounds; but since the law favors orderly development of property, you should make every attempt to bring your request within the terms of the ordinance rather than attack it.

You will next file the necessary appeal forms with the zoning officer. Attached to your application you should have the following, if available:

- *Consent of neighbors.* It is important that the zoning officials understand that your neighbors have no objection to your application. If you cannot obtain their consent, at least try to get their assurances that they will not actively object to your request. Then you can truthfully tell the zoning board that your neighbors will not raise any objections.

- *A listing of other locations* where zoning officials have granted a request similar to yours. If you can point out that your neighbor down the street added a patio to his home recently, this will help your case. But previous allowance of a use similar to yours is not necessarily binding on the board. The board will normally be influenced by the prior allowance, however.

- *Master plan.* Your presentation before the zoning board should show that your request is totally consistent with the master plan for the municipality. If you can establish this, your chances of success are greatly increased.

Presentation and master plan

- *Evidence produced at the hearing.* It usually helps at municipal hearings if diagrams, photographs, and other documents are used to establish the need for a proposed change. The more complicated the request, the greater the need for "visuals" to show your request to the best advantage. You may also consider bringing in an expert to state his opinion that your request will add to the value and appearance of the property and enhance the neighborhood.

- *Financial evidence.* It may be helpful to your case to show that you may not get a fair return on your investment in the property unless you secure the change you seek. This is true even where you are not trying to establish financial hardship because of the physical characteristics of the property. If adding a patio will add to the value of the property, enhance the beauty of the neighborhood, and conform to the master plan, you have presented a good case for the new use.

After the hearing, the zoning board is required to make its decision known within a specified time. In rezoning cases, final action is taken by the elected governing body of the municipality. If the planning commission to which the rezoning petition is referred recommends the rezoning, it will be brought before the governing body. Another public hearing may be held before final action is taken. Only after all appeals within the zoning ordinance have been unsuccessful can you appeal to a court.

The example of the addition of a patio as a zoning "problem" has been used only for convenience. The methods discussed here apply equally to any other zoning problem that you might have.

ZONING CONSIDERATIONS FOR THE PURCHASER OF PROPERTY

As indicated, a purchaser of property should make sure he is totally familiar with the zoning situation. More specifically, the buyer must be aware of the following:

Specific things to learn

- *The existing zoning status or classification.* He should be familiar with the zoning district in which the property is located; the uses permitted in the district; the height of structures permitted; the rear, side, and front yard setback provisions; the area or percentage of the lot that can be covered by the structure; and the minimum sizes of dwellings.

- *Variance.* The buyer should know whether or not a structure or use can continue because of a variance issued at some time in the past. If so, the terms and conditions of the variance must be studied. Variances are usually granted under strict conditions that may change. If the variance was issued for a limited time, this would affect the buyer's use of the property.
- *Nonconforming use.* The purchaser should know whether or not the present use of the property is nonconforming. If it is, the zoning ordinance may contain terms that may affect the expiration of the legal nonconforming use. In addition, the buyer will be taking the chance that the nonconforming use may expire because of abandonment, change of use, or destruction of a building by fire or some other cause.
- *Certificate of occupancy.* Many municipalities require that a certificate of occupancy be issued before a building or structure can be occupied. The certificate ensures that the applicable building codes and zoning regulations have been complied with. The buyer who does not obtain a certificate of occupancy may be required later to make expensive improvements or tear out part of the structure before he can occupy it.

No vested right
- *Statement that use is permissible.* No property owner has a vested right in the continuance of a particular zoning classification for a piece of property. The zoning classification of the property may be changed if all the requirements of notices, hearings, and other protections are satisfied.

It sometimes happens that a change of zoning classification takes place between the time when an agreement of sale is signed and the time of the final closing or settlement. The courts have decided that a buyer cannot escape from his obligation to buy the property if the zoning is changed unless the agreement provides for that kind of alternative. Very properly, the buyer can insist that the agreement contain statements by the seller of the then-existing zoning classification and of the buyer's right to void the agreement if the property cannot be used as intended.

Such factors are important where the buyer is purchasing *improved* property that already has a dwelling or some other structure on it. If the purchaser is buying *unimproved* property, intending to build on it at some time in the future, his concerns are slightly different:

- *Zoning of intended use.* The buyer should check the zoning ordinance to make certain that the intended or future use is permitted in the district. The size of the plot, the height of the intended structure, and the area covered by the structure are all important.

- *Variance.* If the buyer's intended use of the property requires a variance, the agreement with the seller should spell out clearly that "the deal is off" if the buyer cannot secure the variance before he completes the purchase. The application for the variance should be made in the seller's name because he is still holder of the legal title to the property. From a practical standpoint, his chances for success might be greater than the future owner's.

- *Statement that intended use is permissible.* The buyer should have the seller certify in the agreement that the intended use is permissible. Then zoning problems can be avoided.

The seller must certify

PRIVATE DEED RESTRICTIONS

Another form of control over the use of land, other than zoning regulations, is based on *private restrictions* on use specified in the deeds to the property. These private restrictions may be called "protective covenants" or "restrictive covenants." But they involve contracts between a buyer and seller stipulating how land may be used.

In most cases, the purpose of a protective covenant or private deed restriction is to protect or preserve the character of the neighborhood. Examples of these restrictions include covenants against the sale of intoxicating liquors on the premises and restrictions against commercial uses.

Many years ago, many large tracts of land were sold with restrictions against the use of the land by churches and houses of religious worship, or with prohibitions on its sale to members of certain racial groups. These restrictions have since been declared unconstitutional and void by the Supreme Court.

A common deed restriction

The more common form of private deed restriction limits the kinds of structure that can be erected on a lot. A developer may want to maintain a certain "tone" on the lots he sells; to ensure that this tone or atmosphere is maintained, he will insert restrictions into the deeds to the lots. For example, a clause will state that all dwellings erected must be "brick to grade," with minimum livable floor space of not less than 3,000 square feet, with integral garages that face to the rear of the lot, and so on.

Each deed that the developer delivers contains the same restrictions. As an alternative, the developer may list all of the restrictions in one document, record that document in the local register or recorder of deeds

office, and refer to that document in all deeds on all lots sold. In this way the developer can force restrictions on every property owner in the development.

These restrictions, if valid, may also be enforced by any owner of land that is subject to the restrictions. If the area has substantially changed from the conditions that existed when the restrictions were imposed, the court may, on application of one of the owners, set the restriction aside. This could occur where the deed restricts the use of the land to single-family dwellings in a situation where the area has become commercial in fact.

PROPERTY OWNERS' ASSOCIATIONS

Where cluster, condominium, or other high-density housing appears, a *maintenance association* may be established by the developer by means of the restrictive covenants contained in the deeds or in a separate document. These maintenance associations provide a vehicle for enforcement of the protective covenants in favor of all, for maintaining the open spaces and parks that are provided for all owners and residents, and for providing certain types of recreational activities. The latter could include swimming pools, community rooms, tennis courts, and club or meeting rooms.

An association of this kind can assess the owners of property in the development for benefits that the association provides. The association may be responsible for such tasks as paving sidewalks, painting common areas, paying taxes and assessments on property held for common use, and purchasing property from an owner desiring to sell. The latter applies if the restrictions require the owner to offer his property for sale to the association first. The association may also provide for garbage collection, snow removal, and even police and fire protection.

Ordered developed and individual rights

This discussion of zoning has focused on how zoning and master development plans of local municipalities have materially affected the rights of private landowners in the use of their property. But remember that while the orderly planning of a community is essential to the well-being and future value of the area, the right of private ownership must also be protected. The clash between the need for ordered development of land and the rights of the individual spotlights an area in which the law must find answers.

As the housing patterns of the country change, so will zoning regulations change to meet those changing patterns. The decrease in the United States birth rate that became particularly evident in the 1970s will undoubtedly lead to an increase in the high-density apartment-condominium type of construction and reduced construction of the single-family dwelling.

You, as a possible future buyer of real property, should be aware of the place of zoning in the scheme of land development. But you should also understand the principles and procedures used in the zoning process. As a possible investor in real estate, you should be aware of future housing trends to capitalize on those trends in seeking out available property. Then your decision to invest in land will be an informed decision.

In any event, good luck with your new patio!

5 "THEY WANT MY PROPERTY FOR THE NEW COURTHOUSE"

In the preceding chapter, it was shown that a comprehensive plan of development provided a community with a basic plan for growth. One of the considerations in community planning and development must include the right of governmental authority or other public body to "condemn" private property for public use. Condemnation, or "eminent domain," is the legal process by which a governmental body acquires private property from private citizens for public use on payment of reasonable and just compensation for the property. If no payment is made, the owner has been denied his right to his property without due process of law, an unconstitutional act.

Many typical condemnation situations could be cited. Additional property may be needed to widen a street. A new courthouse may have to be built on what was formerly private land. A limited-access highway

may have to pass across private property. A municipal park or a municipal sewer system may have to be expanded through condemnation of some private property.

How do you, a private owner of real property who paid good money for that property, who lives in it or on it, and who wants to keep it, react to the intent of some governmental body to take your property? What are your rights? If you don't agree with the amount they offer you, what can you do about it? These are some of the questions that are dealt with in this chapter.

WHAT IS A "PUBLIC USE"?

In order to be valid, a condemnation has to have a public-use purpose. That means, today, that the proposed use must be more of a public necessity than the present use.

A "public use" —originally Originally, "public use" meant a use that was clearly public: one that all citizens could enjoy, or in which all could take part. A good example would have been a highway system, or a new courthouse, or a municipal park. But in relatively recent times, the concept of a "public use" has grown. It now includes such things as a public parking garage for the use of a limited number of people, the rental of airspace over a public garage to private users, or even a low-income housing project. The theory is that "public" includes both uses for the general public and uses for a limited number of citizens, such as low-income families.

The redevelopment of blighted areas has become a key means by which communities upgrade properties or districts. Redevelopment generally involves condemnation of private property by a redevelopment agency or authority, the payment of condemnation damages for taking the property, and then resale to other private companies or developers for the purpose of erecting new or improved structures on the condemned land.

Parenthetically, it should be noted that condemnation also refers to a governing body's right to declare a building unsafe or unfit for use. Where a structure is condemned because it is a menace to individuals or the public safety, use is usually ended until the defects have been remedied.

Redevelopment authorities were attacked at first because they took private property for public use and resold it to other private interests. Where was the alleged public use? However, because of the social desirability of redevelopment, the propriety of condemnation for that purpose has been universally allowed.

Charters for redevelopment Redevelopment projects are usually undertaken by agencies under charter of state law. The agencies are called "authorities." By law, they have the right to issue bonds to finance their operations. By using these bonds and separately created authorities, a state can proceed with a program of redevelopment and rehabilitation without incurring any additional state debt.

WHAT IS INCLUDED IN THE "TAKING" OF PROPERTY?

When land is taken for a new highway, courthouse, or other public purpose, it is easy to see what land was actually taken and to acknowledge that the owner is entitled to compensation for it. But what about a situation in which a limited-access highway is built across a neighbor's land? The highway cuts off access to the property from one side. What if a flood control project results in the occasional flooding of a person's land even though none of his land is actually taken?

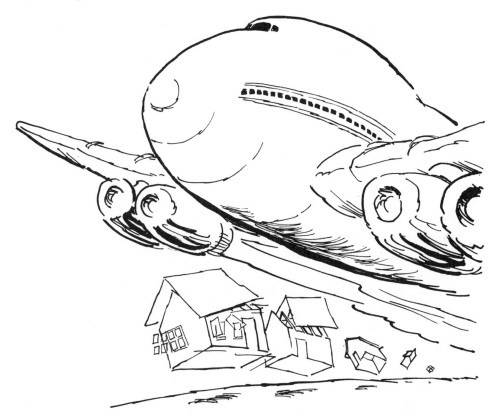

What if an airport is built near a residential area? On their approaches, the airplanes fly close to ground level, disturbing residents and interfering with the enjoyment and use of property for miles around.

The courts have said that the affected property owners in all such cases are entitled to compensation: they should be paid. The owner who cannot gain access to his property because of construction of a limited-access highway has sustained a definite loss in value of his own property even though his property was not formally condemned. The owner whose land

Interference with use or enjoyment

floods occasionally has had his land taken away—in the sense that he may not be able to use it or sell it under given circumstances. The owner who cannot enjoy his property because of low-flying airplanes is likewise entitled to damages for the "taking" of his property.

Even in the absence of a formal condemnation, if the use or enjoyment of property is interfered with by a condemnation or public construction on someone else's property, you may be able to make the law work for you. You may have the right to damages for the implicit taking of your property. A lawyer can find out if you have a valid claim.

PROCEDURES IN CONDEMNATION CASES

Depending on the nature of the improvement, the landowner will normally receive some form of notice. By mail or in a personal visit, he will learn that the improvement is on the drawing boards and that the property is in line for condemnation. Negotiations will follow regarding the amount of property to be taken and the compensation to be paid.

While these negotiations are going on, the condemnation body may file with the County Recorder, Register of Deeds, or other proper public official a condemnation plan showing the property to be condemned. Alternatively, a "Declaration of Taking," which amounts to the same thing, may be filed. The filing of this document, in whatever form is required by state law, constitutes the act of condemnation. It may be accompanied by a bond or some other type of security in the amount that the condemning body believes the property is worth.

The private owner will not necessarily agree with this figure; in fact, he usually does not. The bond or other security is posted to make sure that a fund will be available to pay the owner the amount of his award. The law of the state may require that the amount agreed to by the condemning authority be paid to the owner immediately rather than be posted in bond form.

After the condemnation plan or declaration of taking is filed, the legal title to the property vests in (passes to) the condemning body. But vesting is subject to any objections that the former owner may have regarding the right to take the property. There may be an error in the procedure used, or a question whether the use is a proper public use, or an objection that too much property was taken under the circumstances.

Five things to consider   The remaining considerations in a condemnation procedure normally number five:

1. Appointment of "viewers" or appraisers
2. Partial condemnation
3. Assessment of benefits
4. Recovery for additional items of damage

5. Condemnation of leased property

Appointment of "Viewers" or Appraisers

If the parties cannot agree on the value of the property taken, either the owner or the condemning authority may file a petition in court. The petition asks the court to determine the damages to which the owner is entitled. The court then appoints a group of citizens, usually called "viewers" or appraisers, whose duty is to go out, look at the property, and hold a hearing to determine the property's value.

While the viewers are looking at the property, the owner may be present to explain its features; representatives of the condemning body may also be present. At the follow-up hearing, evidence may be submitted by both parties regarding the value of the property immediately before the condemnation, unaffected by the condemnation. Expert real estate witnesses may also be called to give their opinions on values under oath. Documents such as deeds, plans, and photos may be used as evidence.

After the hearing, the viewers decide on the value of the property and hear any exceptions to their report. After disposing of the exceptions, they file their report in court. If one of the parties, or both, should be dissatisfied with the amount awarded, either or both may appeal—and may request a jury trial to determine the value of the land taken.

The test for determining the value of any condemned property is the highest and best or most profitable use for which the property is used or could be used in the reasonably near future. In testifying, a real estate expert would use this test.

A test of value

The property is valued as a unit. If there are different interests in the property, such as an owner, a tenant, and the holder of a mortgage, their individual interests, if any, will be decided after the value of the total property is fixed. In addition to the amount awarded, the owner may be entitled to interest from the date on which the property was taken.

Throughout all these proceedings, the owner and the condemning body may continue to negotiate on the value of the property. At any time they can settle the matter and end the proceedings.

Partial Condemnation

It sometimes happens that only a part of a piece of land is needed. That part may be condemned. Now a much more difficult problem arises. The damages for the owner's loss will involve the value of the part actually taken and may also include a substantial reduction in the value of the property remaining.

If part of a tract of land is condemned, the landowner will have to prove that the attractiveness of the part remaining has been reduced, that access has been interfered with, that the area remaining has been distorted in shape or area, that the cost of providing utilities such as gas, electricity, and water has been increased, or that the cost of constructing a building on the remaining property has been increased. The law will not allow mere speculation regarding damages of this kind, but demands clear proof.

TYPES OF REAL ESTATE VALUE[1]

Condemnation value represents only one kind of value placed on real estate. Experts in real estate law and practice recognize at least ten kinds of value, each of which is directly or indirectly related to the others. Also, each has its uses in specific contexts. The ten, including condemnation value:

Assessed value: a dollar amount assigned to taxable property by an assessor for the purpose of taxation; frequently a statutorily determined percentage of market value.

Condemnation value: value sought in condemnation proceedings is market value. In the instance of a partial taking, adjustments to the value of the part taken may be made for damages or special benefits to the remainder property.

Excess value: value over and above market value which is ascribable to a lease that guarantees contract rental income in excess of market rental at the time of appraisal.

Forced "value", liquidation "value": the price paid in forced sale or purchase when time is not sufficient to permit negotiations

resulting in the payment of market value; should be called "forced price" or "liquidation price."

Going concern value: the value of the business enterprise and the real estate it occupies; includes good will.

Insurable value: the value of the destructible portions of a property.

Intangible value: value not imputable to any part of the physical property, such as the excess value attributable to a favorable lease, or the value attributable to good will.

Leasehold value: the value of leasehold interest; the right to use, enjoyment, and profit existing by virtue of the rights granted under a lease instrument.

Mortgage value: value for mortgage lending purposes.

Stabilized value: a long-term value estimate which excludes from consideration an abnormal relation of supply and demand; or a value estimate which excludes from consideration any transitory condition that may cause excessive cost of construction and an excessive sale price.

[1] Adapted from *The Real Estate Handbook* edited by Maury Seldin, © Dow Jones-Irwin 1980. Reprinted by permission of Dow Jones-Irwin.

Assessment of Benefits

Public improvement and property values

An owner's property may actually benefit as a result of a public improvement. For example, the construction of a new municipal sewer system can involve the condemnation of easements across private property that entitles the owners to some compensation. The owners may at the same time benefit: they can now tap into a sewer system, thus increasing their property values.

Viewers or appraisers are used in such cases to determine the extent of such a benefit. The owner or owners will be assessed the value of the improvement. The procedures in the assessment of benefits are essentially the same as those involving the determination of damages.

Additional Items of Damage

While not all items of actual loss are recoverable in a condemnation case, landowners or tenants have in recent years been able to recover for additional items of loss. That trend will undoubtedly continue in the future. For example, assume that a person has owned and operated a small business for many years. He has built up extensive good will for the business. Then the building housing the business is condemned. The owner would be required to move to another location.

The owner might not be able to find a suitable building in an acceptable neighborhood at the same rental or value. He might have to start all over again to build up good will. In recognition of the problems the businessman faces in such a case, the eminent domain laws in many of the states now allow awards of *dislocation* and *relocation damages*.

Moving expenses traditionally have not been compensable in condemnation cases. But under recent statutes, moving expenses are recognized, and the cost of moving business fixtures and heavy equipment from the condemned property may be recovered up to a specified amount. Legal fees and the costs of professional appraisers and appraisals can now be recovered by owners in some states.

Moving expenses may be repaid

Condemnation of Leased Property

A tenant in possession of property can recover for the loss of his lease if a condemnation results in his losing the property. In most instances, however, a lease would specify for the owner that the lease terminates in the event of condemnation. In that case the owner would receive the entire award for the property.

The tenant, in such a case, would receive his moving expenses and relocation expenses if state laws recognize those damages. If the lease does not provide for termination in the event of condemnation, however, the tenant may have lost the opportunity to sublease the property at a higher rent than he was paying under the lease, or he may have to rent another location at a higher rent. Both of these events could involve substantial losses for the tenant. Where state law allows a tenant to recover for the loss of his lease, he could, of course, recover those losses.

The laws of the states are very different. Some state laws permit this and some permit that. This is as true in the field of eminent domain as in other fields.

Differing state laws

On receiving any notice whatsoever that property in which he has an interest is, or even might be, the subject of condemnation, the wise owner consults a lawyer. With the principles learned in this chapter, he knows what to expect, what the procedures will be, and what his rights are. But over and above that, if either the enjoyment or the use of property is interfered with because of a condemnation of another's property, the injured party may have the right to claim damages. The law can and should be used to protect property rights.

6 "LANDLORD, STAY AWAY FROM MY DOOR"

Suppose you have no desire to purchase or build a home. You would rather find a place to live on a somewhat temporary basis. In such a case, you will probably want to rent an apartment. This is particularly true of young married couples who may not have the means to purchase a home immediately.

What is involved in renting an apartment? What should the average tenant look for in the way of space, amount of rent, and other conditions of the lease? What is a lease and how does it operate?

FINDING THE RIGHT APARTMENT

Apartment-for-rent listings appear in the classified ad columns of local newspapers. A broker or real estate agent can often help in the

search for the right apartment. So can the various neighborhood or area services that exist for that purpose.

Is an entire home needed or only a part of a residence, such as the first or second floor of a duplex? Most persons know they need a certain number of rooms. Thus, in hunting for an apartment, they consider the amount of space available, the amount of rent to be paid, and whether or not the landlord is willing to renew the lease or will grant an option to renew the lease for a future term. Other lease provisions will be discussed later.

A CHECKLIST FOR APARTMENT HUNTERS[1]

	YES	NO

Is building sound, attractive, well built? . . . .
Is it well managed and maintained? . . . .
Are corridors and entranceways clean and well lighted? . . . .
Is protection from burglars provided? . . . .
Is there a doorman? . . . .
Is landscaping pleasant? . . . .
Is there enough outdoor space? . . . .
Are extras you want included (such as swimming pool, steam baths, a gym for men and women)? . . . .
Is there parking space, indoor or outdoor? . . . .
Is there a receiving room for packages? . . . .
Is laundry equipment available? . . . .
Are fire escapes adequate? . . . .
Are there fire extinguishers? . . . .
Is trash collected or disposed of? . . . .
Are there storage rooms or facilities? . . . .
Are there elevators? . . . .
Are mailboxes locked? . . . .
Is routine maintenance—window washing, decorating, painting—provided? . .
Are servicemen available for emergency repairs? . . . .
Is the floor plan convenient? . . . .
Is the apartment big enough? . . . .
Are rooms light enough? . . . .
Are wall spaces adequate for your furniture? . . . .
Is the apartment soundproof? . . . .
Is decorating (if any) attractive? . . . .
Are views attractive? . . . .
Are there enough windows, and are they well located? . . . .
Are there screens and storm windows? . . . .
Are major appliances you need installed? . . . .
Are appliances in good condition? . . . .
Is wiring sufficient? . . . .
Is ventilation adequate? . . . .
Will cleaning be easy? . . . .
Are there separate heat controls for each part of the apartment? . . . .
Are there enough electric outlets and are they well located? . . . .
Do windows and doors, including cabinet doors, open and close easily? . . . .

Is there air conditioning? . . . .
Is there a fireplace? Does it work? . . . .
Is there carpeting? . . . .
Is there a balcony? . . . .
Are there workable blinds or shades? . . . .

[1] Selections from *Sylvia Porter's New Money Book for the 80's* by Sylvia Porter, copyright ©
1975, 1979 by Sylvia Porter. Reprinted by permission of Doubleday & Company, Inc.

Having found the right apartment, the prospective tenant should understand the relationship that he or she will be entering into with the landlord. The lease establishes that relationship.

What Is a Lease?

A lease can be oral. Much more commonly, it is a written document that transfers the *right of possession* of real estate to a tenant for a specified term. The term of the lease may be a month, several months, a year, or more than one year. A lease may be *at sufferance*, meaning that it can be terminated by the landlord at any time.

The lease and the right of possession

The lease should set forth all the terms and conditions of the tenant's occupancy of the property for the entire term of the lease.

Provisions Usually Found in a Lease

Leases for residential uses or occupancy, not business leases, are considered here. The terms that are discussed below are limited primarily to leases for residential purposes, not those for commercial purposes.

Rental Payments. The apartment is perfect, and vacant. The first question that comes up is, typically, the amount of rent. It is important to understand that rent is the price paid for the occupancy of the space described in the lease. If the lease is to run for one year, the amount of rent is determined, normally, on a total yearly rental basis. In other words, the lease will provide that "for the total rent of X dollars, payable in monthly installments of X dollars a month, being one-twelfth of the annual rent, you, as tenant, have the right to occupy the premises." You become legally obligated for the entire year's rent, even though you pay rent on a monthly installment basis.

This becomes important if for some reason, before the year is up, the tenant wants to vacate the property or to get out of the lease. He has committed himself, however, to pay rent for the entire year. Unless the lease provides an "out," he may be required by the landlord to pay the whole amount.

It is possible to negotiate with the landlord the proper term of the lease. The recently married person who wants to have a place to live for a year

Negotiating a lease

should probably ask for a one-year lease. The landlord will want to know that the property will be rented for a reasonable time. The tenant usually wants a reasonable period so that he will have time to find another place—if he is looking for a permanent home. He will want a sufficiently long term to make it unnecessary to go looking for another apartment in the near future.

How likely is it that the landlord will be prepared and willing to negotiate the terms of a lease—including the period for which it will run? In practical fact, most landlords know they want tenants who will "stay for awhile." These landlords will offer the prospective tenant a one-year or two-year lease. The apartment seeker can then accept or reject.

The flat rental has just been described: a uniform monthly installment rate for the entire term of the lease. But other, less common forms of rental arrangements are available. Each of them, however, anticipates a total rent payable in some form of installment, perhaps in equal installments. The total amount of rent for the entire term is chargeable to the tenant and payable in various ways.

- A lease may provide for graduated rental payments at specified intervals. It is used normally to compensate the landlord for increasing expenses. Or it may be used where a tenant has inadequate funds in the beginning but expects to be able to pay a higher rent later.

Rent increases at specified intervals This type of lease provides for rent increases at specified intervals. For example, $250 a month may be charged for the first three months, $275 a month for the next three months, and so on to $325 or $350.

- A lease may provide that a specified portion of the real estate taxes, insurance, or costs of repairs be added periodically to the basic rent. This type of arrangement is normally part of a business lease; but residential leases also may provide for increases in the rent if the taxes on the property go up during the term of the lease. The rent may also go up with increases in utility charges caused by the tenant's use of the property.

The language of these leases usually provides that, "as additional rental," the tenant agrees to pay proportionate amounts of the real estate taxes or utilities. These charges are called "additional rental" to give the landlord the opportunity—if needed—to evict the tenant or sue for back rent.

- In a "cost-of-living lease," the tenant's rental obligation may fluctuate as the cost of living increases. More common in the commercial or business lease, this clause also finds its way into residential leases from time to time.

- Some leases call for a discount if the rent is paid before the tenth day of the month. This is designed to induce the tenant to make his payments promptly.

Discount for early payment

Whatever the total basic rent or the amount of the installments, the lease should specify the method of payment. If it is payable monthly, the lease should state where it is to be paid—at the home of the landlord or elsewhere. The date on which the initial rent payment is due should be set forth specifically. Then the tenant and the landlord know the date on which the rent is due every month.

Security Deposit. Most landlords try to protect themselves against a tenant's abandonment of the property, failure to maintain the property, nonpayment of rent, or other default. Usually, the tenant is required to deposit extra money with the landlord in advance: this security deposit is used to reimburse the landlord for any such default. In case of default, the lease usually authorizes the landlord to re-let the premises to someone else.

Most leases provide that the security deposit, if not applied by the landlord in the event of a default, will be treated as payment of rent for the last month or months of the lease. In other words, if two months' rent is required as a security deposit, this amount, if not utilized by the landlord because of any default or to pay for damages to the premises, will be refunded to the tenant upon termination of the lease.

Many states have considered or passed legislation concerning the so-called security deposit. Some of the possible questions are whether or not the landlord should be required to pay interest on the security deposit; whether or not security deposits should be allowed at all; and whether or not the landlord should be required to refund the security deposit without suit at the end of a lease.

Laws on security deposits

Any or all of these matters can be discussed with your lawyer where questions arise.

Options in Leases. An option in a lease is a right granted normally to the tenant. There are several types of options.

An *option to renew* is a right granted to the tenant to decide, within a specific period before the expiration of the original lease, whether or not he wants to renew it and, if so, to notify the landlord of that decision. For example, the original lease may provide that the tenant has the option to renew the lease for an additional term of one year. To exercise the option, the tenant has to notify the landlord of that decision at least three months before the expiration of the original one-year lease.

The renewal option is the most common type. The landlord will often require that the renewal term be at a higher rent level than the original

The renewal option

term so as to make certain that the rental covers increased costs, taxes, and other expenses.

The lease may contain an *option to purchase*. In this case the tenant rents part of a home that he would like to purchase but cannot for financial reasons. The owner may be willing to rent the property for one year, granting an option to buy the property at a stated price at the expiration of that year or during the term of the lease. The owner may even allow all the rental that has been paid to be applied as a down payment on the purchase of the property once the tenant is ready to proceed with the purchase.

All of this can be arranged in an "option to purchase" clause. However, if the tenant wants such a clause, he should make certain that the option to buy contains all the necessary provisions of an agreement of sale because exercise of the option to purchase turns the lease into an agreement of sale of real estate; therefore, the lease must contain all the necessary provisions of an agreement of sale, including the purchase price and the closing or settlement date.

INTEREST ON SECURITY DEPOSITS? YES, SOMETIMES

Some states, including Illinois, require landlords to pay interest on security deposits under certain conditions. The landlord of some residential real estate may, for example, have to pay 5 per cent interest on any security deposit held more than six months. This rule applies generally to landlords of larger buildings—containing, say, 25 or more units.

The "grace period" The landlord who is obligated to pay security deposit interest will have a "grace period" in which to make payment. The period may be 30 days from the end of the rental term. The landlord can pay the interest in cash or credit the interest to rent due.

Few tenants will go to court to recover security deposit interest—in the event that the landlord does not pay—while they are still tenants. But they have that right, and can recover not only the interest but court costs and attorneys' fees. After the tenant moves, a different situation prevails.

In some states, the landlord may have to return the entire security deposit within 45 days after the tenant moves. The landlord can deduct the costs of repairing damage to the apartment. But he may have to give the tenant an itemized bill for such damages. Then the landlord has to return the balance of the security deposit.

Two types of law may be involved in these cases. One covers payment of interest on security deposits. The second applies to refunds of security deposits.

In either case the tenant—in given states—has the right to sue if the landlord defaults or if the landlord "chisels" on the amount of interest due or the extent of damage to the apartment. A solution may be to go to a Small Claims Court, where no lawyer is required. But some states, as noted, require a defaulting or chiseling landlord to pay attorneys' fees as well as court costs.

Options for additional space or for cancellation may be specified in the lease. A tenant on a long-term lease commonly faces the problem of unexpected events that may require him to vacate before the end of the term. Also, what happens if additional space is needed because of additions to the family? These situations can both be solved by provisions in the lease—if the landlord is willing to include them.

Two types of options

A *cancellation option* gives the tenant the right, at a designated time and with adequate notice, to either cancel his lease with the landlord or eliminate certain space that he no longer needs. The *additional space option*, on the other hand, allows the tenant to take over additional space at designated times, as necessary.

These options, like all other provisions of the lease, must be negotiated with the landlord. If they are granted, they can substantially help the tenant to deal with an unknown future.

Sublease. The right to sublease allows the tenant to give possession of the premises to a *subtenant*. A tenant decides to allow someone else to live in the premises. The subtenant then pays rental to the tenant, who is still obligated under his original lease with the landlord.

Most residence leases contain provisions restricting the right of a tenant to sublease. The reason is that the landlord does not want "unsuitable" subtenants in the premises—persons whom the landlord has not been able to investigate. Usually this restriction states that the tenant cannot sublease all or part of the premises without the prior written consent of the landlord. Where possible, however, the tenant should try to include a sublease agreement, or at least a provision that the landlord will not unreasonably withhold his consent to a sublease.

Where the lease contains a clause against subleasing, the tenant should be prepared to remain on the premises under the lease for the full term—or pay the rent for the full term.

Prohibition of subleasing

Identify the Premises Leased. It is important that the lease be very specific about what actually is being leased. If an apartment is being leased, the number of rooms and the location of the apartment should be spelled out. If permission to use the basement washer and dryer is granted, this should be indicated. If the right to use a garage on the property is given, this should also be spelled out. If the right to use a yard or recreation area is part of the lease, this should be clearly indicated. Any other similar permitted uses should be noted.

Right to Make Alterations. This is a very important clause in the lease. If the landlord agrees to make alterations for the tenant before the tenant moves in, this should be spelled out in detail. Specifications on the type of alterations should be listed very clearly. The tenant's obligation to pay rent should be conditioned on the landlord's performance of these alterations. Then the tenant need not move into the property until the work is done.

Where the alterations are to be made by the tenant, they are usually subject to the landlord's prior approval. It is, after all, his property. The landlord should understand that the alterations will benefit the property. If that is the case, his consent will usually be given freely.

Questions regarding ownership of fixtures

Where alterations are made, questions may arise at the expiration of the lease regarding ownership of any fixtures attached or fixed to the property by the tenant. The normal lease provision states that such fixtures belong to the landlord unless he agrees otherwise. If possible, the tenant should seek to have the clause provide that he can take the specified fixtures away when he vacates the property.

The tenant may also want to leave specified alterations of fixtures because of the expense that removal involves. The lease should indicate that.

Alterations mean substantial changes in the premises or the addition of fixtures to the premises by a tenant.

Repairs. Perhaps no other provision of the lease causes more difficulty or more lawsuits than the one indicating who is required to repair and maintain the premises.

Normally, the lease provides that at the end of the term the tenant has to return the property to the landlord in the condition in which it was originally leased. Only normal wear and tear is allowed. So-called structural repairs—repairs to parts of the building itself, such as the roof and outside walls—are the responsibility of the landlord unless the lease states otherwise. Interior repairs, having to do with the use and occupancy of the premises, such as leaking faucets, interior plumbing, and a blown fuse, are normally the tenant's responsibility. However, the usual lease form provides that the tenant is responsible for damage resulting from such causes as short circuits, leakage of water, steam, gas, odors, frost, and bursting or leaking of pipes or plumbing.

A tenant signing such a lease is assuming a great deal of responsibility, especially where he may be occupying only a part of a dwelling rather than the entire building.

Where the tenant is in a good negotiating position, he should demand a clause providing that he is only obligated to make interior repairs of a minor nature, or only such repairs as might result from his own misuse of the property. All other repairs, structural or otherwise, will then be the responsibility of the landlord.

Minor interior repairs

Destruction or Condemnation of the Premises. What happens if, during the term of the lease, the property is destroyed or is condemned for public use? Strange as it may seem, in most states the liability of the tenant to pay rent may continue. To protect himself, therefore, the tenant should insist on a clause in the lease stating that in the event of destruction, the obligation of the tenant to pay any further rent ends immediately. The landlord ordinarily will want a provision specifying that, in the event of condemnation, the entire award for the loss of the property will go to the landlord. The tenant will then not share in the award at all.

While this clause is subject to negotiation in a residential lease, the landlord would normally have the right to claim the entire condemnation award. But it is important that the tenant should have the option to terminate the lease if the premises are destroyed.

Other Provisions of Residential Leases. Some other common clauses in leases deal with these questions:

Pets

Garbage or rubbish removal

Keeping the sidewalks free of snow and ice

Obstruction of sidewalks or doorways

Noises or disturbances in or around the building

The parties may negotiate other provisions from time to time.

DEFAULTS IN LEASES

Two kinds of defaults

If a tenant cannot perform under a lease, what happens? What rights does the landlord have in such a case? Normally, a residential lease contains provisions dealing with defaults by the tenant. These defaults fall in two main classes: (1) failure to pay rent or any other sum provided for under the lease, and (2) removal by the tenant of any of the landlord's goods from the premises—or expression of an intention to do so.

In a third type of case, a lien may be filed against the tenant, or bankruptcy proceedings may be begun against him. The tenant may become insolvent, or a receiver may be appointed for him—someone appointed by a court to take over the tenant's business.

Should any of these defaults occur, the landlord under the typical residential lease has the right, first of all, to declare the entire balance of the rent for the remaining term of the lease immediately due and payable. The landlord also can evict the tenant in case any of these defaults should occur. In those states that still recognize it, the landlord has the right to enter a "confession of judgment" for the balance of the rent.

Confession of judgment and the landlord's rights

The confession of judgment clause gives the landlord the right to go to court to get a judgment against the tenant for the balance of the rent. The landlord files a paper; he does not have to bring a regular lawsuit. The latter would involve filing a complaint, whereupon the tenant would file an answer to the complaint. In the normal course of events a trial would take place.

The confession of judgment has for some years been under attack in the courts. In some cases it has been declared unconstitutional. The legality of such a lease provision should always be questioned.

The landlord himself may be violating the lease agreement. This occurs most often in a situation known as "constructive eviction." The landlord, failing to make repairs or provide necessary services, such as utilities, renders the premises uninhabitable. The tenant can then claim that he has been unlawfully evicted because of the landlord's breach of the lease. If the tenant can substantiate his claim, his obligation to pay rent ceases until the landlord corrects the default.

At present, state statutes are under consideration regarding the landlord's duty to make the premises habitable. Some states have even adopted, by court decision, a rule that the landlord, in leasing property, delivers a *warranty* to the tenant that the premises are habitable. In these states a tenant can sue the landlord for breach of that warranty where "constructive eviction" occurs.

The tenant may not have to pay rent where a breach of warranty takes place or during the period of a constructive eviction. But the tenant may also have a claim for additional damages if he has to leave the premises or find other housing because of the landlord's breach.

IN THE TYPICAL STATE:
THE LANDLORD'S OBLIGATIONS[1]

Various states have their own laws dealing with landlord-tenant rights and obligations. A typical set of state laws specifies the following obligations of the landlord:

A. The landlord is obliged at all times during the tenancy:
   1) to comply with all applicable building, housing, or health codes, or
   2) in the absence of codes, to maintain all structural components (e.g., roofs, windows, floors, exterior walls, etc.) in good repair; and to maintain the plumbing in a reasonable working condition. The landlord may alter or modify these obligations with respect to a single-family home or duplex by stating so in writing to his tenant(s).

B. Unless otherwise agreed in writing, in addition to the above requirements, the landlord of a dwelling unit, other than a single-family home or duplex, shall also make reasonable provisions for extermination of rats and bugs; supplying locks and keys; removal of garbage; heat; running water and hot water. He must also maintain the common areas in a clean and safe condition.

C. The landlord must disclose in writing to the tenant his name and address, or that of someone authorized by him to act as his agent. He shall disclose this in writing at or before commencement of the tenancy.

D. The landlord may enter the dwelling unit at any time necessary to protect or preserve the premises under the following circumstances:
   1) with the tenant's consent;
   2) in the case of an emergency;
   3) when consent has been unreasonably withheld by the tenant; or
   4) if the legal presumption for abandonment has occurred. The landlord shall not abuse his right of access nor use it to harass the tenant.

E. The landlord must observe and comply with the requirements of the rental agreement. He cannot make any agreements with the tenant which would take away any of the rights of the tenant.

[1] Adapted from *Landlord-Tenant: The Law* (Tallahassee: Florida Department of Agriculture and Consumer Services).

THE SALE CLAUSE

Clause covering possible sale

Every residential lease should contain a clause regarding the possible sale of the property while a tenant is in possession. Ordinarily, any buyer of residential real estate buys subject to all existing leases; the buyer should find out who is in possession of the property and the basis on which that person is in possession before he completes the purchase. If a tenant has possession, the buyer should find out on what basis that tenant has possession. The buyer can then buy the property subject to the tenant's rights to remain on the property.

IN THE TYPICAL STATE:
THE TENANT'S OBLIGATIONS[1]

Various states have their own laws setting out the rights and obligations of the landlord and tenant. A typical body of state law specifies the following obligations of the tenant. Every tenant shall be responsible for:

A. Ensuring that he does nothing to cause the landlord to be in violation of building, housing, and health codes.

B. Keeping that part of the premises which he occupies clean and sanitary, removal of garbage, and keeping the plumbing clean and in working order. This includes not flushing anything down the toilet or washing foreign matter down the sink drain which would have a tendency to cause these units to malfunction.

C. Operating in a reasonable manner all electrical, plumbing, sanitary, heating, ventilating, air-conditioning, and other facilities and appliances, including elevators.

D. Not destroying, damaging, or removing any property belonging to the landlord.

E. Conducting himself, and requiring those who visit him to conduct themselves, in a manner which will not disturb others.

F. Allowing the landlord entrance to the premises for purposes of inspection, repairs, or to show the dwelling unit to someone else. The tenant may not unreasonably withhold access to the unit.

G. Living up to all provisions made with the landlord when the rental agreement was made, particularly paying the rent on time. The law itself does not directly address the issue of late charges; however, it is customary and common for landlords to require a late fee for delinquent rental payments.

[1] Adapted from *Landlord-Tenant: The Law* (Tallahassee: Florida Department of Agriculture and Consumer Services).

If the landlord wants to change that situation, the lease should provide that in the event of the sale of the property, the tenant agrees to vacate after receiving a certain number of days' or months' notice of the sale. If the lease does not contain a sale clause, then the tenant is guaranteed possession of the property for the full term of the lease, regardless of whether or not the property is ever sold.

Waiver of protection

Most printed form leases contain a waiver of this protection by the tenant. These forms are usually drawn by the landlord, and a prospective tenant should understand what it means to waive the right to remain on the premises in the event of a sale. The tenant would ordinarily want the sale clause removed from the lease; the landlord may want to keep it. This again is a negotiated item.

HOLDOVER BY TENANT

A tenant retaining possession beyond the original term of the lease is a "holdover." Depending on the law of the state, the lease may or may not be renewed automatically for another full term, whatever the original terms of the lease. In some states, the holdover status only means that the lease is renewed for another month.

Because of this difference in the laws of various states, most leases contain a provision covering tenant holdovers. The lease usually specifies that if a tenant lawfully occupies the premises after the end of the term, the lease will be enforced for another year, or month, or whatever period is agreed to by the parties. The lease continues from month to month or year to year so long as the relationship of landlord and tenant continues. Such a clause clarifies the legal relationship where the tenant holds over beyond the original term of the lease. The clause also indicates the duration of the additional term—whether a year, a month, or another period of time.

To keep the landlord away from your door, it is important to sign a lease agreement that you understand and that benefits you. In looking for an apartment, take advantage of the comments in this chapter. Study them before entering into any agreement.

Part III
FAMILY MATTERS

The family plays so many roles in modern society that the law takes a basic interest in nearly all types of family matters. The family ensures the biological reproduction of the next generation and takes responsibility for the child's maintenance and education. Child training or socialization also falls in the family's area of responsibility, as does the provision of sexual controls. In effect, the family constitutes society's most basic unit.

The family performs all its social functions at once. In doing so, it gains in effectiveness and makes a fundamental contribution to a nation's or a society's survival. There can be little wonder that the law concerns itself with the ways in which a family is formed and what happens to it afterward.

The family begins with marriage, a step that commits both partners to legal responsibilities of a serious nature. The responsibilities rest in a contract. Marriage actually involves a contract in which three parties have an interest: the bride, the bridegroom, and the state in which the marriage is performed. The state is a party because under its laws the partners to the marriage assume certain duties toward each other and the state itself. For example, the husband is viewed widely as taking the primary duty of support for his wife and children. But that obligation may fall on the wife under certain circumstances.

Marriage is a contract

The law girds the family around with both restrictions and protocols. Divorce or annulment requires specific procedures before the law recognizes any change—any formal dissolution of the marriage bonds. Insurance, the protection that can guarantee the family's survival in difficult times, is subject to close regulation under the law.

In one way or another, the law follows the family—and the individual who "goes it alone"—through life. The law safeguards personal security even after the individual's working years are done. Legislation has, for example, established the entire Social Security system. Other means of providing for the "golden years" come under the protective umbrella of the law, which seeks to ensure that pension, profit-sharing, and similar programs contribute to the comfort and dignity of older citizens.

All citizens share in the ambience created by the law. But in many cases the legal family is directly and deeply involved as a group, for example, where estate planning, wills, taxation, death, and burial are concerned. Part III examines all these areas of the law. By carefully reading this overview you can be better prepared to avoid many family-related problems and make the necessary adjustments in time.

7 "BE SURE, INSURE WITH SURE INSURANCE"

Think insurance for a moment. It has invaded every phase of the life of modern technological man.

The situations abound. A woman suddenly made a widow is asked, "How much insurance did he leave you?" Other similar questions may be asked:

- if someone slips and falls on the sidewalk in front of a friend's home;
- if the driver of a grocery truck runs into a pedestrian;

- if a bookkeeper absconds with money belonging to the firm or to others;
- if a fire destroys a home and/or its contents; or
- if a tenant fails to keep hallways clear and a visitor falls down the steps in the building.

In still another situation, a major illness strikes. Because of rapidly increasing medical care costs and ever higher charges for the delivery of medical services, a family's life savings can be wiped out by that one serious illness—unless insurance is available to meet the cost.

In this chapter, the normal types of insurance such as life, liability, and various types of business insurance come under examination. The typical provisions in these policies will be noted along with the risks covered. An attempt will be made to clarify the language of the policies. When deciding on more life insurance, or whether he has sufficient liability insurance, the individual should have an understanding of the basic terms used and the reason why a particular policy is needed to cover a particular risk. Everyone should be able to recognize a risk and know that insurance is available as protection against loss or disaster.

LIFE INSURANCE

Adequate life insurance is vital in any plan designed to provide for a family in the event of a parent's death. Insurance can give a family the means to live in an atmosphere of security. In addition to its normal use, life insurance can provide for the retirement of corporate stock or the purchase of a partnership interest from a deceased partner's estate.

Insurance can be utilized to provide funds for pension and profit-sharing plans and many other family and business arrangements.

In brief, life insurance is an agreement by an insurance company to pay an amount of money in the event of the death of the insured. The sum can be fixed, or based on some scale depending on either the age of the insured or some other element. Life insurance falls into three basic categories: term insurance, permanent or whole life insurance, and endowment insurance.

Payment in the event of death

So-called "term" insurance is insurance written for a "term" or "period," rather than on a permanent basis. Term insurance normally remains in effect for one year, and is renewable on continued payment of premiums. It involves either a fixed *premium* with benefits reducing as the years go by—"reducing or decreasing term insurance"—or a fixed *benefit* with annual or other periodic increases in premiums over a period of time ("increased premium or level term insurance").

In other words, the benefits decrease (decreasing term) or the premiums increase (level term) as time passes. With decreasing term insurance, a policy can eventually expire.

Whole life insurance is generally taken out to cover a person for the remainder of his life. Payments may be made for a specified number of years. For example, a "20-Pay-Life" policy calls for payments for 20 years. Afterward, the insured is covered under his *limited-payment life* to the full extent of the policy for the rest of his life. Under *straight life,* or *ordinary* or *whole life* insurance, the insured is not only covered for the rest of his life; he can borrow against the *cash value* of the policy and can sometimes simply "cash it in" and take a cash settlement.

The distinction between term and permanent life insurance also has to do with the question of *cash value.* Ordinarily, permanent insurance has a certain cash value after the policy has been in force for a certain period of time. That feature does not exist with term insurance. In purchasing term insurance, the insured is usually purchasing primary protection for his family. Whole life insurance has a cash feature that gives it some investment potential.

The question of cash value

An *endowment life insurance* policy is designed primarily for the person who wants to receive a certain amount of money at a specific time in the future. Until that time, the person also has normal life insurance protection. The policy provides that a sum of money or income payments will go to the insured if he or she reaches a certain age. If the policy owner dies before reaching that age, the death benefit is paid to the beneficiary.

Young couples with small children sometimes find it difficult to afford permanent life insurance. These couples should probably buy as much *convertible term* insurance as possible—term insurance that, for a limited premium, delivers a high degree of protection in the dollar amount of death benefits payable. At the same time, such a policy can contain a convertible feature that permits the insured to convert the term insurance into permanent life insurance at any time. The premium rates will be those charged by the insurance company for similar insurance.

Other kinds of life insurance This convertible feature ordinarily carries with it the right to convert without evidence of insurability: without taking a medical exam.

Three other kinds of life insurance should be identified:

Credit life insurance will pay the balance of a debt, such as a loan, if the insured dies or is disabled.

Annuity life insurance is based on a contract under which an insurance company provides a regular income to the insured starting at a certain age, usually 65. An alternative to this *deferred annuity* policy is the *immediate basis* policy under which the insured pays the company a lump sum and starts receiving income payments at once.

Group life insurance is the kind provided typically by companies, labor unions, trade associations, and other organizations. Generally written as a form of term insurance, group life almost always gives the individual insured the option of continuing the insurance by applying 30 to 60 days after termination of employment or membership.

The standard provisions of the whole or term life insurance policy are important. So are those elements that give protection under the typical life insurance policy.

Grace Period

Premium due dates Unless a policy is completely paid for, which may occur with some types of permanent insurance, premiums are due on a specified date. This is normally the anniversary of the date on which the policy was issued. Premiums are payable annually, semiannually, quarterly, or monthly. For accounting purposes and bookkeeping purposes the premium, if paid on an annual basis, is ordinarily slightly less than if the premium were paid on some other basis.

For situations in which the premium is not paid on the due date, the policy usually contains a "grace period" provision. That means the company will accept the premium if paid within, say, 31 days after the due date specified in the policy.

Automatic Premium Loan Provisions

If the premium is not paid within the grace period, under a permanent policy the insurance does not automatically expire. Rather, it ordinarily continues as term insurance for a period of time measured by the cash value earned by the policy over the years. In other words, if the permanent policy has cash value, that cash value will be utilized to pay the premium and keep the policy in force until the total cash value is exhausted.

The policy in that case will be treated as term insurance. No additional cash value will be earned as long as no premium is paid. Once the cash value is exhausted, the policy lapses for nonpayment of premium.

Many policies have an *automatic premium loan* provision. Such a clause provides that the insured can borrow, or request, against the cash value of the policy to pay premiums. This can be important if the insured is disabled and unable to pay the premiums as they come due.

In this situation the insured is billed periodically for interest on the loans that are being made as premium payments. But the cash value of the policy continues to build. By contrast, where premiums are paid out of the cash value and permanent insurance becomes term insurance, no cash value is earned during the period of nonpayment.

Billing for loan interest

In most cases, if a permanent policy's cash value is exhausted the policy can later be reinstated on payment of the unpaid premiums with interest. But the insured may have to show satisfactory evidence of good health. A physical examination may be required before the policy can be reinstated.

Death Benefit and Premium Adjustment

The amount of the death benefit is a matter of choice—and need. A young man with a wife and small children may want the highest death benefit at the least cost. For that reason convertible term insurance is usually a good buy in such a situation. Anyone "shopping" for permanent insurance should also consider the following:

- The premium base
- The amount of death benefit available for the particular premium
- The cost of various options or additions to the basic coverage
- The needs of the family after the insured's death
- Whether the amount of insurance selected fits the needs

More information on the last-cited point appears in the chapter on Wills and Estate Planning.

Death benefit and premium adjustment

In the event an insured dies, the beneficiary will receive not only the death benefit scheduled in the policy but also a *premium adjustment.* The latter is normally a refund of that portion of the paid premium that covers a period beyond the month of death. For example, if the policy runs from July to July and death occurs in September, the part of the premium representing the time from September to the following July will be refunded.

THE NEW LIFE INSURANCE: "GRADED DEATH BENEFITS" FOR HIGH-RISK CASES

In the recent past persons with serious health problems or risky jobs found it hard to buy life insurance. Today, by degrees, the picture is changing. The premiums paid on high-risk insurance may be 10 to 50 per cent higher than those on standard policies. But the individual may have no other source of protection.

Liberalized approaches to life insurance

The options open to diabetics, those undergoing psychotherapy, epileptics, and even persons with histories of cancer have increased substantially in number. People in high-risk jobs, including window washers and submarine testers, have encountered similar liberalization of life insurance underwriting.

A few companies today are offering "graded death benefit" coverage for individuals in high-risk categories. At those higher premium rates the companies offer "open enrollment" policies: they require no medical exams. The full face value of such a policy will not be paid if the insured dies from natural causes before a specified period of time elapses. By contrast, accidental death is covered in full at any time. The insurance policies generally take one of two forms:

- Those providing for an *elimination period.* If the insured dies after a certain number of years—usually three—from the date on which the policy became effective, the beneficiaries receive the policy's full face value. Before the lapse of three years, the insurance company would pay out only the money already paid in premiums plus interest. The interest rates run 5 or 6 per cent and up.

- Those providing for a *graded benefit.* Under this type of policy, payments to beneficiaries are tied to a rising percentage of the policy's face value. The total paid depends on how long the insured lives. If, for example, an insured were to die in the first year of coverage, the company might pay 5 per cent of the face value. The benefit might be 15 per cent if death occurs in the second year. The policy's full face value would be paid if the insured lives seven years.

Applications for graded benefit policies may ask some searching questions. The purpose is to avoid clear "deathbed" cases. As with other policies, the insurance company retains the right to cancel a graded benefit policy during the first two years of coverage.

Incontestability Clause

It used to be that an insurance company could refuse to pay benefits after the death of an insured, even though a substantial amount of time had passed since the policy was issued and substantial premiums had been paid. Because of this situation, the rule of *incontestability* was introduced into the laws dealing with insurance.

The incontestability clause specifies that after a life insurance policy has been in force for a period of time—usually two years—the beneficiary of the policy must receive the insurance proceeds upon the death of the insured. The company cannot contest payment. This applies even where misstatements were included in the application for insurance.

The beneficiary under the incontestability clause

Most often, insurance companies claimed that applications included misstatements regarding the health of the insured, his or her age, and similar factual questions. To avoid such defenses, the incontestability clause is required in all life insurance policies in all states. If the insured was actually older than was stated in the application, the benefits payable under the policy may be adjusted downward. On the other hand, if the insured was younger than was stated on the application, a slight adjustment upward will be made in the benefits.

Cash Value and Loan Value

As noted, permanent life insurance carries with it a cash value. The policy will contain a table showing the cash value of the policy for any given time in the life of the insured. In addition, the policy may set out various income options, giving the insured the opportunity to select one that will ordinarily provide for guaranteed installment payments for a fixed number of months or years. The payments start after a specified date.

A real advantage of permanent life insurance centers on the loans that can be made against the policy. The policy itself states the interest that will be charged on a loan against the cash value of the policy. The interest rate stated in the policy is usually substantially lower than the prevailing interest rate on bank or other marketplace loans.

Loans against life insurance policies

In times of high interest rates, as in the early 1980s, insurance companies usually report an extremely high number of loans against life insurance policies. Loans can be taken out at the lower interest rates stated in the policies and reinvested at rates that run more than double the policy rates. Thus the loan privilege becomes both a kind of resource for emergencies and a means of fighting inflation.

Surrender of Policy for Paid-Up Insurance

Most permanent life policies can be surrendered before the death of the insured. Rather than take the cash value, the insured elects to take a *paid-up policy* according to a table that is contained in the policy. For example, if he owns a policy insuring his life for $50,000, and at a given time he wants to surrender that policy for either its cash surrender value or an amount of paid-up insurance, he can select the paid-up policy as shown on the table rather than the cash surrender value. This means the insurance requires no further payment of any premium, but is paid up and has a cash value of its own.

In this case the insured no longer pays any premiums. But the insurance continues in force.

Ownership and Beneficiary Provisions

Naming the owner: a must

The owner of the policy is always named in it. The owner is usually the insured, but may be the beneficiary or some third party. In order to remove the proceeds of the insurance from the insured's estate, a common concern in the area of estate planning, the insured's wife or husband or a trust fund may be named as the owner of the policy.

The insured should always name a primary and a secondary or contingent beneficiary, usually specified as first and second beneficiaries. A third and even fourth beneficiary may be named.

Listing more than one beneficiary can avoid typical insurance problems. Many husbands, for example, name only their wives and forget about their children. If the wife dies before the husband, and the husband then dies, the insurance company has no named, living beneficiary to whom to make payment. The benefits then pass to the estate of the insured. The proceeds of the policy become subject to various death and inheritance taxes in many states. The taxes come out of the insurance.

You should review all your life insurance to make certain that you have named not only a primary beneficiary but a second and even a third. If you wish to protect your spouse and your children, your beneficiary designation should name your spouse as first beneficiary and your children, equally, as your secondary or contingent beneficiaries.

Dividend Options

The so-called "participating" life insurance policy entitles the policyholder or insured to dividends on earnings of the insurance company. These policies carry *dividend options*.

In applying for insurance, the individual who wants such options may face choices regarding the dividend payments and their application. For example, one person may want to have the dividends paid to him in cash. He selects that option and later receives checks representing dividends as these are declared by the company. In another case the dividends can be used to reduce the premium payments, or to pay for additions to the policy. These are then paid up and require no further premium.

Options involve choices

Dividends may also be utilized to pay interest on policy loans, to purchase additional term insurance, and to secure various other options available under the standard participating life insurance policy. The applicant chooses the desired option.

Conversion Privileges

Normally a life insurance policy will specify what other plans of insurance the existing policy can be converted into. The procedure to be followed to make such conversion will also be indicated.

Most term policies, as noted, contain a conversion clause that makes them very attractive. They can usually be converted into permanent insurance without a medical examination, unless the policyholder wants a lower premium program for the same or a higher death benefit. In the latter case the company may require a medical examination.

Assignment

The typical policy spells out the procedures under which it can be assigned or transferred to someone else. The company is normally not bound by any assignment of the policy until it receives written notice of the assignment. The assignment has to cover all the outstanding loans to which the policy is subject; the responsibility for making a valid assignment falls on the insured or owner and not on the company itself.

Assignment and written notice

In order to transfer ownership, the proper forms of assignment must be sent to the insurance company to make certain that the formalities have been satisfied.

Extra Coverages Available with a Basic Life Policy

Various endorsements can be added to the basic life insurance policy. Some or all of these may be very valuable. These endorsements, or "riders" to the policy, may entail extra charges, or they may be added without additional charge.

Ask your insurance advisor or agent

An insurance advisor or agent will know whether these coverages are available to an applicant for a policy. Depending on the purpose that the insurance is intended to serve—whether security, protection of one's family, retirement, or business—these special coverages may serve valid purposes and should be considered. The following are examples of some possible riders.

- *Accidental death benefit.* This endorsement provides that if the policyholder dies in an accident the company will pay the beneficiary an amount in excess of the face amount of the policy. This extra amount is usually some multiple of the policy's face value. For example, a double indemnity provision provides for payment of twice the amount of the face value if death occurs by accidental means.

  Some *exclusions* of accidental death benefits should be noted. As in all types of insurance coverage, these exclusions apply to deaths due to war, certain types of airline accidents, and accidents resulting from illness or disability. Death must occur within a fixed period of time following the accident. In some cases, the double indemnity provisions expire when the insured reaches a certain age. Premiums for the accidental death benefit are ordinarily based on a flat rate per $1,000 of coverage.

- *Waiver of premium.* If the policyholder becomes totally and permanently disabled, the insurance carrying a waiver of premium will remain in force without any further payment of premiums. A waiting period is required before this clause can take effect. Generally, the disability of the insured must occur prior to his reaching a specified age. A disability resulting from war or a self-inflicted wound is not covered and is specifically excluded.

A particular benefit of the waiver of premium provision is that the cash value of the policy continues to grow even though no further premiums are paid. As noted earlier, if the premiums on a permanent life policy are not paid the cash value may be used by the company to pay the premiums as if the policy were term insurance. Thus no further cash value accrues. With the waiver of premium provision, however, the cash value does grow even though no actual premiums are paid by the insured because of his disability. The disabled insured can also borrow against the cash value in such a case.

Ordinarily, the premium for this extra benefit is low in comparison with the benefits provided. In fact, some companies do not charge an extra premium for it, but include it in the basic premium charge.

Obviously, the waiver of premium can bring substantial benefits. It protects the insured if he is disabled and safeguards his family by keeping his insurance in force.

- *Guaranteed insurability endorsement.* Under this rider, the insured is guaranteed that he can take out additional insurance at standard rates without further evidence of insurability. That means he does not need to take an additional medical examination. Additional insurance would normally have to be purchased before the insured reaches certain age levels.

Guaranteed insurability can be a valuable addition to a policy. A young man may not be able to afford a great amount of life insurance at the beginning of his career. But he can obtain more insurance in the future at standard rates even if in the meantime he has contracted a serious illness that would prevent him from buying additional insurance on his own. The illness might cause him to be "rated"—meaning that the insurance would be much more expensive—if he did not have the guaranteed insurability endorsement.

In a typical case an insured may have guaranteed insurability to a maximum of $10,000 in additional coverage, if he applies before a certain age. He can apply for that additional coverage no matter how his health may have changed since he purchased the original policy. Premiums are inexpensive, and are payable, usually, until the insured turns 40 or up to the end of the basic policy payment period, whichever is earlier. Typically, the additional coverage has to be applied for within 60 days of the *option dates.*

- *Dismemberment benefits.* A typical group and association life insurance plan may contain, in addition to accidental death benefits, benefits for dismemberment—the loss of a limb, blindness, or other physical loss. Again, for an increase in premium payments the disability payoff provision may be included so that the face amount of the policy will be paid out in installments in the event of total disability.

Additional Add-On Riders for Term Insurance

The typical term life insurance policy may contain a great variety of riders and endorsements. These can provide additional low-cost insurance. Like those already mentioned, the *disability income rider* involves the payment of an additional premium, however small, for the additional coverage. The *automatic premium loan clause,* however, and those that follow it are free; no additional premium is charged. The add-on riders include the following.

Disability Income Rider. The disability income rider provides a monthly income to the insured if he becomes totally disabled. The amount of income is always stated in the policy. Some benefits are based on a percentage of the face amount of the policy—for example, 1 per cent, continuing to a stated age of the insured. A waiting period is usually required before disability payments begin.

HOW MUCH LIFE INSURANCE DO YOU NEED?

The somewhat bewildering world of life insurance changes constantly. New names for old policies make their ways into the marketplace. Some actually describe new life insurance gimmicks. Practically all of them confuse the issue and make choices difficult.

Questions and calculations

Remembering that there are two basic, popular kinds of life policy, ask yourself some questions and perform some calculations. The questions relate to what you want your life insurance to do—and for whom—and how many resources you have to play with. The calculations come out as rules of thumb:

- Estimate approximately how much income your family, close friend, or other beneficiary will need after your death. "Need" means enough to maintain a current or better standard of living.
- Estimate how much the significant other or others will receive from dividends, interest, salaries, Social Security, and other sources.

- Calculate the difference. That difference represents the post-mortem need that has to be met by life insurance or some other kind of protection.

Then ask yourself some additional questions to inject realism into the calculations and, if necessary, recalculate. Some of the questions:

- Have you figured in inflation, and, if so, at what rate?
- Will your beneficiary or beneficiaries be able to invest the insurance money made available after your death, and then live on the interest or dividends, or will they have to burrow into those benefits?
- What kind of interest will the insurance be able to earn?
- If a spouse survives, will he or she work? Be invalided? Handicapped? Will he or she need job training or education?
- Will the kids, if any, go to college? Can you estimate the costs of education in five years, or ten? Should there be special insurance for that purpose?
- And finally, is insurance the answer, or would investments be better, or something else you can more easily afford?

Automatic Premium Loan Clause. Under this clause the company is authorized to borrow against the policy to pay the premium if the policyholder fails to pay. The policy becomes lapse-proof while any cash value remains.

The lapse-proof policy

Settlement Agreement. Under the settlement agreement the method of payment of benefits is specified. The insured chooses one or more of the many payment options in an agreement that is attached to the policy.

Spendthrift Trust Clause. Some states have laws that automatically exclude life insurance proceeds from the claim of creditors. Other states require that a "spendthrift trust" clause be included in the policy to protect the proceeds against creditors' claims. The clause is designed to protect insurance proceeds that are to go, for example, to a trust fund for a spouse and children.

Where a policy contains a spendthrift trust clause, the creditors of the beneficiaries cannot reach the proceeds until they are actually paid over to the beneficiaries or their guardian, as the case may be.

Retirement Options. An insured may want to use the cash value of his policies and any accumulated dividends to build a retirement fund or to provide an annuity to be paid monthly after retirement. The insured can in this case choose a lifetime income or installments for a fixed period of time. Together with his spouse, he can establish a joint and survivor annuity that pays monthly benefits until husband and wife are deceased.

These retirement options are open to the insured while he lives. In planning his estate, he should consider the use of life insurance to provide such retirement income.

The choice of a settlement option

Settlement Options. Retirement options are available to a living insured who wants to use his cash policy value for retirement purposes. *Settlement options* refer to the options under which the beneficiaries of a deceased insured specify how they will take the proceeds of the policy.

The insured may select the kind of settlement option when he takes out the policy. Also he may select the option anytime during his life. After the death of the insured, the benefits can be paid in a lump sum. However, the insured may opt for other types of settlement to the spouse and children, trust fund, or another beneficiary.

These settlement options normally fall into several categories. *Interest only* settlements pay installments composed of only the interest earned by the available benefits. At the end of the specified installment period, the lump sum is payable. Under the *installment time option* installments are paid for a fixed period of time. At the end of that period, no further payment is made. The *installment amount option* pays a fixed amount until the total fund is exhausted. The *life income option* pays monthly checks for life. These life income options may be subdivided as follows:

- *Life income with definite guaranteed number of payments* provides income payable for the life of the beneficiary. But it provides for a definite number of payments. In the event of the death of the beneficiary before all the payments are made, payments are continued to the estate of the beneficiary.
- *Life annuity income plan.* Under this plan, no fixed number of payments is guaranteed. Monthly payments are made to the date of death of the beneficiary, but there is no guaranty of the total number of payments. Thus if the beneficiary dies shortly after the date for payment arrives, the insurance company is "off the hook" for any balance.
  Alternatively, the beneficiary may live so long that the total number of installments equals the face amount of the policy. In this case the company pays more money than it would have under the lump-sum payment option.
- *Cash refund life annuity income plan.* Under this plan, any amount not utilized under the life income annuity plan is refunded in cash to the estate of the beneficiary.

Annuity for the beneficiary and spouse jointly

- *Joint and survivorship annuity income plan.* An annuity is established in joint names of the beneficiary and his or her spouse. After the death of the primary beneficiary, the annuity

continues and the survivor collects payments until the benefits are used up.

Why would anyone select the life annuity income plan when the beneficiary might die shortly after the insured and no further payments would be made? The reason has to do with the amount of the monthly installments. The greater the risk that a beneficiary might not receive the full benefits because of a premature death, the higher the monthly payment. Many insured persons are only concerned with the primary beneficiary; they want him or her to get the highest possible monthly payment and to be secure during life.

**WHEN AN INSURANCE POLICY GOES TO COURT:
A CASE CALLED "CORDER WINS"[1]**

MATTHEW J. JASEN, Justice.
This is a motion by plaintiff for summary judgment.[2]

An insurance policy was issued to deceased Anna M. Corder in the amount of $5,000.00 on April 26, 1960. The beneficiaries listed in said policy were Wesley D. Corder, husband of the insured, if living, otherwise Willa Eakman, mother of the insured. On April 15, 1963, the named insured died. Subsequently, the plaintiff brought action to collect said proceeds from the insurance company who in turn interpleaded Willa Eakman as Administratrix of the Estate of Anna M. Corder. The administratrix answered the complaint herein and interposed a counterclaim that the proceeds of the insurance policy in question be paid to her.

It is the contention of the plaintiff that he is the named beneficiary and therefore entitled to the proceeds.

The mother-administratrix in opposing this motion proceeds upon two theories. First, by reason of fraud of the plaintiff the proceeds of the policy belong to the estate of the insured, and secondly, that plaintiff was not the husband of the insured and that therefore the insurance contract is void by virtue of the deceased's breach of warranty in representing him as her husband.

It is conceded that the Wesley D. Corder who brings this action is the Wesley D. Corder named as beneficiary by the deceased in the insurance policy, and that he is the particular person intended by the insured to be the beneficiary of said proceeds.

(1) Where the deceased effects the insurance upon her own life, it is well-established law that she can designate any beneficiary she desires without regard to relationship or consanguinity.

(2) Since the undisputed proof shows that the application for the policy was made by the insured deceased, there is no issue of insurable interest on the part of the plaintiff.

The use of the term "husband" in the connection was merely descriptive of the relationship which the insured claimed existed between her and the beneficiary. Even though the named beneficiary was not actually the insured's husband, it does not alter the basic fact that the plaintiff is the person to whom the deceased had intended that the proceeds of the policy be paid.

For the reasons stated, motion for summary judgment granted.

[1] *Corder* v. *Prudential Insurance Company*, 248 N.Y.S. (2d) 265 (1964). Adapted from *Law and the Life Insurance Contract* by Janice E. Greider and William T. Beadles, ©

Richard D. Irwin, Inc., 1960, 1968, 1974, and 1979. Reprinted by permission of Richard D. Irwin, Inc.

² An immediate judgment granted by the court without further proceedings, generally on the basis of the documents filed with the court and without the oral testimony of witnesses.

A choice of one of these settlement options will depend on many factors. The insurance shopper should pick that option that best fits with his estate plan and his family's needs in the event that he is not there to provide for them.

Federal Estate Tax Considerations and Life Insurance

As indicated, life insurance proceeds can be taxable to the estate of the insured. They thus become subject to the federal estate tax unless the insured puts the insurance benefits beyond the reach of the taxing authorities. This is usually done through transfer of ownership of the life insurance policy to the beneficiaries. This is how it works.

Transfer and update
Most importantly, the policy is transferred and the designation of the beneficiary is kept up to date. If the beneficiary is dead, and if no living person is named in the policy as beneficiary, the proceeds will be payable to the estate of the insured at his death and will be fully taxable.

But note: with a properly named, living beneficiary, the proceeds will still be taxable to the estate as long as the insured holds "incidents of ownership" in the policy at the time of his death. That means the insured remains the owner of the policy; he has the right to cancel it, surrender it, or cash it in, and can change the beneficiary or borrow on the policy. But if, prior to his death, the insured makes a complete transfer of ownership of the policy and does not retain any of these incidents of ownership, the proceeds will most likely not be taxable to his estate.

In sum, where an overall estate plan makes it advisable, it is possible to avoid a larger federal tax against an estate. More money will go to those loved ones if the insured makes an irrevocable assignment of ownership of the policy to the beneficiary, retaining no ownership rights. Starting in 1981, it should be noted, federal taxes were levied on all estates totaling, with insurance benefits, $175,000 or more.

INSURANCE AGAINST LIABILITY AND LOSS OR DAMAGE TO PROPERTY

Have you ever read one of your insurance policies? Be honest, now. If you have, you are the great exception. Perhaps you are turned off by the technical language used, or the small print. Whatever the reason, most people do not read their policies. They depend on what their agent tells them regarding coverages.

This section discusses the most important coverages that are available in the fields of *liability and property insurance*. An effort will be made to explain simply the technical language used in the policies. The goal is to enable the reader to understand and be able to discuss insurance problems intelligently.

Both the homeowner and the apartment dweller are constantly exposed to possible losses that could wipe out all savings and assets. The types of risks are usually divided into two types: risks involving *liability*, that is, that may make one liable to someone else because of what he, an employee, or an agent does or has done; and *property losses or damage*. The latter includes loss of income and credit—personal loss resulting from property losses caused by oneself or someone else.

Liability Insurance

The ownership of property or the operation of a business may involve exposure to liability for one's own acts or for the acts of employees performing normal services. In general, a liability policy provides protection only if the insured is legally liable to pay a claim resulting from an accident or other event. There is no protection:

(1) if the insured is not legally obligated to pay the claim;

(2) if he has voluntarily assumed the risk; or

(3) if the occurrence is not really an "accident" (for example, where the other person becomes ill through repeated exposure to someone who carried the illness).

In brief, there must usually be some unintended event causing damage or injury for which the insured is legally obligated. Then the liability policy provides coverage.

The basic policy is divided into two parts. One sets limits on the liability coverage for bodily injury claims—for example, claims by persons sustaining personal injuries while on one's property. The second sets limits on the coverage for damage to someone else's property.

The policy buyer chooses the desired limit of liability for each type of coverage: bodily injury or property damage. The many different kinds of policies available are designed to meet specific purposes and fulfill specific needs. The most important ones are noted below.

Owners', Landlords', and Tenants' (OLT) Liability Policy. This policy provides protection against claims that result from the ownership, leasing, and operation of property that is specifically listed in the policy. The property may include commercial buildings, both retail and wholesale, office buildings, and theaters. The policy lists the specific properties covered and the amonts of the bodily injury and property damage limits provided.

Comprehensive General Liability Policy. This is the broadest form of liability policy that can be purchased. It provides both bodily injury and property damage coverage, and may give additional protection against "personal injury" risks. These include such things as liability resulting from assault and battery, libel and slander, false imprisonment, and other types of "intentional" acts that may impose liability on the insured.

The "broad form" policy The comprehensive policy is a "broad form" policy. It differs from the Owners', Landlords' and Tenants' policy in that it does not specify each risk covered. Rather, it is written on an all-risk basis and specific exceptions are listed. More information on the broad form policy appears in the "Homeowners' Policy" and subsequent subsections.

Product Liability Policy. Product liability constitutes one of the most rapidly expanding areas of the law. If a soft drink bottle explodes, if a washing machine throws a bolt, causing injury to a member of the family, or if another manufactured product malfunctions and causes bodily injury or property damage, a claim can be brought against the manufacturer, wholesaler, or seller of the product.

In this area, liability insurance is essential today. The product liability policy provides coverage for what the manufacturer, wholesaler, or dealer may be legally liable to pay in damages for claims arising out of the handling or use of goods or products. The goods or products, of course, must be manufactured, handled, distributed, or sold by the insured. There must be a defect or unsafe condition in the product.

Product liability insurance can cover a service type of business as well as a manufacturing type. Those delivering services include barbers, painters, and contractors. A policy may insure against defects in installation as well as defects in equipment.

Like the product liability policy, the professional liability policy insures physicians, lawyers, accountants, architects, and other professionals against liability resulting from a defect in the performance of functions or the delivery of services. The malpractice insurance taken out by doctors is a typical professional liability policy format.

Contractual Liability. Certain obligations arising under contracts or agreements may result in legal liability. The contractual liability policy is intended to cover such liability; it usually involves manufacturers, distributors, and retailers of products as well as persons engaged in service businesses who, under their contracts, assume certain obligations.

An example may be noted. A homeowner may want to have work done on his home under a building agreement. The agreement would include a provision that the contractor agrees to *indemnify* the homeowner if anyone suffers bodily injury or property damage because of the contractor's performance of the work. In purchasing contract liability coverage, the contractor would protect himself against any claim against the homeowner. The latter simply refers the claim to the contractor under the contract.

For example . . . indemnification

Contractual liability coverage may be included in the comprehensive general liability policy mentioned above, usually for an additional premium. This assumption of liability, or an agreement to "hold harmless," appears in many different types of contracts, leases, and other arrangements. To be protected, the party making these promises of indemnity must have this coverage.

Owners' and Contractors' Protective Liability Policy. This policy is intended to give protection against claims arising out of work done by someone who is not under direct contract with the insured. An example is the subcontractor doing work for the insured, but under a contract with the general contractor.

In a typical case, homeowner Smith contracts to have contractor "X" put siding on his home. Contractor "X" may subcontract the work out to subcontractor "Y," who, in the process of doing the work, causes injury to another person. The protective liability policy will protect Smith against the claims of the injured person. Smith may have demanded that "X" provide this coverage as part of the contract, or Smith may secure this coverage himself.

Homeowners' Policy. The homeowners' policy is a relatively recent development in the field of insurance. Previously, a homeowner seeking protection against losses resulting from such events as fire, theft, or vandalism, or trying to protect himself against liability claims resulting from injury or property damage on his property, would have had to take out a series of separate policies to get total protection.

Homeowners' policy—a recent development

The homeowners' policy is designed to give the homeowner in one package all the necessary protections. If the mailman trips and falls over cracks in the sidewalk, if a dog bites someone, or if a piece of your roof falls and injures someone, the homeowners' policy, under its liability provisions, would give protection. It would provide protection for what the homeowner would be legally obligated to pay if he or a member of his family were at fault. The property loss provisions of the homeowners' policy come under discussion in the section dealing with property insurance.

In any liability policy, the type and amount of coverage depends on the risks that concern the insured. In these days of six- and seven-figure jury awards, everyone should protect his home and business with an adequate, comprehensive general liability policy and a homeowners' policy. Thus the law governing contracts works for the private individual.

Property Coverages. Eight different kinds of homeowners' policies are in current use. The policies and the kinds of coverages they provide are described in the following sections.

HO-1. The most basic policy, HO-1 was the original basic package policy. Because of diminishing demand, insurance companies were phasing it out in the 1980s. HO-1 provided protection against 11 specific perils: fire or lightning; loss of property removed from premises that were endangered by fire or other hazards; windstorm or hail; explosion; riot or civil commotion; aircraft; vehicles; smoke; vandalism and malicious mischief; theft; and breakage of door or window glass.

HO-2. The HO-2 policy (sometimes called the broad form) adds seven other risks to the HO-1 coverage. The seven: falling objects; weight of ice, snow, or sleet; collapse of the building or any part(s) of it; bursting of steam or other appliances or heating systems; leaks from plumbing, heating, or air-conditioning equipment; freezing of such systems; and accidental damage to electrical appliances because of overloads. The homeowner can usually obtain these additional coverages by paying premiums that are only moderately higher than those on HO-1 policies.

HO-3. Called a "special policy," HO-3 fits the needs of homeowners who want the broadest available coverage on a structure itself but do not want broad personal property coverage. HO-3 generally gives the "all-risk" dwelling protection provided by the HO-5 comprehensive form (see below) but gives only limited personal property coverage.

HO-4. Known as the "renter's policy," HO-4 is adapted to those who rent a home or apartment or who own a cooperative apartment. The policy offers the same broad protection against a wide range of risks to household goods and personal belongings that HO-2 provides.

HO-5. The "comprehensive policy," HO-5 covers all common perils except for a few that are specifically excluded. The latter usually include war, flood, earthquake, and nuclear accident. Premiums on HO-5 policies are uniformly higher than on other forms.

HO-6. Designed for the condominium unit owner, HO-6 basically duplicates HO-4 coverage. It is adapted, however, to meet the needs of unit owners who want coverage to supplement that provided by the condominium association.

HO-8. An "older-home" insurance, the HO-8 policy offers "no frills" coverage for older homes with market values substantially lower than replacement costs. Offering essentially the same coverage as HO-1,

HO-8 policies undertake to return properties to serviceable condition—but not necessarily by using the materials that went into the original structure.

Mobile-Homeowners' Policy. A recent addition to the family of standard policies, this form can be written to provide virtually the same coverages as HO-2. The mobile home, to qualify for the insurance, must be at least 10 feet by 40 feet in size.

Additional Benefits Available under Liability Insurance. Not only does the liability policy give protection and pay money claims for damages; the typical policy also provides for additional valuable coverages. Often overlooked by an insured, these include:

- *Lawsuit defenses.* Under a lawsuit clause the insurance company will defend the insured against all lawsuits brought against him, even where a suit is groundless and has no basis in fact or in law. It is essential, however, that the suit, if successful, would have been covered by the policy or would be considered a proper claim under the policy. In addition to paying any judgment or settlement falling within the policy limits, the company will pay attorneys' fees and other costs of defense, including those for investigation, securing witnesses, and other court costs. If required, the company would also pay interest on the judgment.

What the company pays

In defending an insured under an insurance policy, the company retains its own lawyer to handle the case. Where the amount of the possible recovery exceeds the amount of coverage, the lawyer for the company should so advise the insured. He should also suggest that the insured retain his own lawyer to protect him on the possible excess liability. This is another reason for making certain that coverage is adequate.

In a typical case, a policy would place a $50,000 limit on the insured liability. The amount that could be recovered might be $100,000 or more. The insured has the option of engaging his own lawyer to defend him against the amount of the claim in excess of $50,000.

- *Bond premiums.* The liability policy also provides for payment of bond premiums required in an appeal from an adverse decision, bonds to release legal attachments against property, and similar charges.
- *Reimbursement of expenses paid by insured.* If the insured incurs some expense at the request of the insurance company, such as travel or securing affidavits and notary fees, the policy may provide for full reimbursement.

■ *Inspection and reimbursement for immediate medical aid rendered.* The policy may provide for inspection services to minimize the risk as well as to reimburse the insured for medical and surgical services. These may have been rendered by the insured to an injured party at the time of an accident.

Covering the injured party

■ *Medical payments coverage.* This coverage provides protection against the cost of reasonable medical and surgical expenses incurred within a year after an accident. Each person who suffers bodily injury, illness, or disease as a result of an accident is covered regardless of whether the insured is legally liable or not. This protection covers the injured party, not the insured. It is usually limited to a specified amount per person and per accident. It is available under the liability policy for an additional premium.

Property Insurance

Property insurance protects the insured against direct damage to or losses of property such as real estate, furniture, fixtures, and equipment. The insurance can also cover loss of the use of damaged property. For an additional premium, consequential damages may also be covered— losses not to the physical property itself, but those resulting from losses to physical property of the insured or some other person. Consequential losses will be discussed in greater detail later.

There is no satisfactory way to list all the various types of property insurance. The modern trend is toward "package policies" providing multiple-peril insurance that incorporates many individual coverages into one package. However, as a help toward understanding the nature of property insurance, a basic listing follows.

Under the same policy . . .

Fire Insurance. Everyone knows about fire insurance that gives protection against direct losses caused by fire and lightning. The same insurance can cover certain types of damage caused by smoke where the damage results from a "hostile fire"—a fire not started by the insured in fireplace, stove, or other container. The latter is called a "friendly fire." Smoke damage caused by the fire in a fireplace is not covered because the fire is not "hostile." But smoke damage resulting from a hostile fire, whether on the insured's or someone else's property, would be covered.

Extended Coverage. Usually by endorsement, extended coverage can be added to the basic fire policy that covers risks of damage from windstorm, hail, explosion, riot, civil commotion, aircraft, smoke, and vehicle damage. Also, extended coverage may be provided for an additional premium against falling trees, glass breakage, malicious mischief and vandalism, and accidental discharge of water or steam from plumbing or heating fixtures.

Included also would be damage to vehicles owned or operated by the insured or his tenant as well as water damage and damage caused by ice, snow, and freezing.

The extended coverage endorsements do not increase the basic benefits of the fire policy. They only bring additional perils or risks under the coverage.

Endorsement Adding Earthquake Coverage. By special contract or by endorsement to the fire policy, protection can be obtained against earthquake, sprinkler leakage, hail that damages crops, and other risks.

Motor Vehicle Damage. Collision, comprehensive fire and theft, and similar policies can protect an insured against physical damage to his autos, trucks, and other motor vehicles. The types of coverage and the rates will vary from place to place and from time to time. They will be affected by the make, model, and the way the vehicle is used. Automobile insurance policies are examined at greater length in a later chapter.

Coverage and rates vary

Burglary and Theft. Various types of burglary and theft policies afford protection against losses due to burglary of merchandise, fixtures, and equipment. The same applies to losses of money, securities, or other property through burglary of a safe or storekeeper's office. Special robbery policies give "package" protection to various kinds of business.

An example of the broad-form comprehensive coverage mentioned earlier is the money and securities form that provides all-risk protection against losses of money or securities.

Fidelity Bonds. A fidelity bond may be used to protect an employer against dishonest employees. The bond gives protection against losses of money, securities, raw materials, equipment and real property. Depending on the kind of bond used, the bond can cover either named individuals, all the incumbents in certain positions, such as the board of directors or officers of a corporation, or all employees of a firm.

The type of business, the number of employees, and their duties determine the kind of fidelity bond used and who is covered under it. A business in which employees handle cash or securities should probably have these employees bonded for the employer's protection and that of his customer.

Determining the kind of fidelity bond

Package Policies and Floaters. In recent years, as indicated, multiple-peril, or package, policies have proliferated. The package policy has a major advantage: it eliminates overlapping coverages in separate policies and reduces expenses and costs. It is important, however, to distinguish multiple-peril policies providing all-risk protection with specific exclusions from other policies covering only specifically stated risks and excluding all others. An insurance agent and family lawyer should probably be consulted on the type of package policy that will best fit a business and family arrangement.

A package policy in widespread use today is the homeowners' policy that provides basic fire coverage, extended coverage, and other insurance for the home and its contents. The property aspects of the homeowners' policy will be reviewed later in this section. The liability protection has already been discussed.

The floater for risk coverages   A *floater* usually provides all risk coverages on specified personal property such as jewelry and furs. Many floaters require the specific listing of all articles insured, with a description and valuation based on an appraisal or bill of sale. The types of floaters available are too numerous to list. They depend on the risk and the type of property to be protected.

Surety Bonds. Many commercial transactions and contracts are guaranteed by the issuance of a surety bond. Here, the principal party guarantees that he will perform under a contract or the insurance company, as surety, will pay the party guaranteed. As indicated in the discussion of legal aspects of home construction, labor and material payment bonds and performance bonds are forms of surety bonds. There are others, however:

- *Contract bonds* guarantee the performance of a contract. These are written for the actual term of the contract and cannot be cancelled during the contract term.

- *Bid bonds* are bonds that accompany the bids of contractors for public and other types of contracts. The bond guarantees that the bidder, if awarded the contract, will sign it and furnish the prescribed performance, labor, and material payment bonds when required. If the bidding contractor defaults and fails to provide the necessary bonds later, the insurance company becomes liable for the difference between the amount of the bid of its contractor-principal and the next lowest bid.

- *Performance bonds,* such as construction bonds, guarantee the faithful performance of work by a construction contractor. The labor and material payment construction bond that guarantees that the contractor will pay all bills for labor and material is involved in almost every large construction project.

- *Maintenance bonds* guarantee that the work performed by the contractor will be free of defective workmanship or materials. The bond may be separate or may be included in the performance bond.

Homeowners' Insurance. As noted, this multiple-peril coverage provides liability protection as well as protection against losses directly caused to a home or its contents. The homeowners' insurance may include only the fire and extended coverage; but it may also include specific additional risks or may be written on an all-risk or all-property basis so long as no commercial property or use is involved. The premium, of course, depends on the type of homeowners' policy that the insured purchases.

Multi-peril coverage

The "all physical loss" form of the homeowners' policy is the broadest form available. It gives protection against all physical loss to the insured's property so long as it is a part of the insured's home and is not commercial in character.

Consequential Loss Coverages. Property insurance has been mentioned as providing coverage for direct physical loss to property. But with consequential loss coverage the insurance may also cover losses sustained by the insured as a direct result of property losses. For example, a business may be interrupted as a result of damage to property. The owner has then suffered a real loss over and above the loss incurred on the property.

This generally overlooked factor is very important. A restaurant that has been severely damaged by fire reveals obvious physical damage to fixtures and equipment. Will fire insurance alone take care of all the owner's losses? Of course not. Insurance may provide funds to replace and repair the damaged equipment; but what about the owner's loss of business and his obligation to continue to pay rent and other expenses while repairs are being made? As a rule, any property insurance is woefully inadequate if it has no consequential loss coverages. Such coverage comes in several different forms.

- *Business interruption insurance* covers losses resulting from the interruption of the insured's business because of fire or other accident.

- *Contingent business interruption insurance* covers losses resulting from the interruption of the business of a supplier or someone else whose activity or lack of activity directly affects the insured. A retailer may depend on a steady supply of goods from a wholesaler. If the wholesaler's business is interrupted by a fire, he may not be able to ship his goods to the retailer. The retailer then suffers losses that would be covered by the contingent business interruption policy.

When the insured is directly affected

- *Extra expense insurance* covers those expenses of a business that, because of its importance, cannot be interrupted and that produces additional expenses in remaining open during an emergency.

- *Leasehold insurance* covers a tenant's financial loss if he has a good lease from the standpoint of rent and loses it because of property damage. If the tenant has to rent other property at a higher rate, he has sustained a real loss that the insurance can cover.

On the other side of the fence, the landlord may have suffered a loss because his building was destroyed and he lost a tenant. Rent insurance or rental value insurance protects the landlord by covering the loss of rents while a building is unusable because of some insured peril or accident.

- *Other consequential insurance coverages* also can be purchased to cover particular risks.

Co-Insurance Clause. Suppose a homeowner has a policy on his home. He is insured against all physical losses to a total of $40,000. Suppose also that the policy contains a co-insurance clause. What is it? How does it work? Can this clause actually cut back the amount of your proceeds from the policy in the event of loss?

A misunderstood provision Without doubt the co-insurance clause is most totally unknown, or totally misunderstood, provision in insurance. The clause makes the insured a co-insurer with the insurance company. If the insured should suffer a loss and is underinsured, he will be required to bear part of the loss. The co-insurance clause requires that the insurance coverage total at least a stated percentage (usually 80 per cent) of the total insurable value of the insured property. If the coverage is less than 80 per cent of the insurable value, the insured shares in "paying" for the loss.

A case illustration will show how this works. Assume that a home has an insurable value of $50,000. The insurance policy provides $40,000 worth of coverage with an 80 per cent co-insurance clause. The homeowner has satisfied the requirements of the co-insurance clause since exactly 80 per cent of the insurable value of the home is covered.

The insurance company in this case will pay in full for any losses covered by the policy up to the amount of the total coverage, or $40,000.

Assume that the homeowner has insurance only in the amount of $20,000, however. A dramatically different result can be expected. If a loss is sustained, the company will pay only for one-half of the total loss up to the limit of coverage. If the total was $20,000, the company would only pay one-half of that amount, $10,000, and the homeowner would be the co-insurer with the company on the other $10,000: the homeowner bears that loss himself.

Note that the homeowner had coverage in the amount of $20,000, and that was the amount of the loss. But he should have had coverage in the amount of at least $40,000. He thus failed to satisfy the co-insurance requirements. If he had had the $40,000 coverage, the company would have paid the entire $20,000 loss.

Many persons with inadequate insurance are surprised by the amounts they collect on losses when those losses equal or are less than the coverage. In almost every region of the country, real estate values have increased tremendously. Most people carry fire or homeowners' policies on a three-year basis; few even think about the insurance on their homes until they receive the next three-year premium statement from their insurance agent.

Keeping up with inflated real estate values

Where a mortgage company collects the insurance premium out of the monthly mortgage payment and pays the premiums directly to the insurer, the homeowner never has occasion to think about the insurance. Many agents are reluctant to "push" for an increase in coverage because they fear that the insured may take offense. It is becoming more and more obvious, however, that the insurance agent has to keep his clients abreast of the increases in property values. He has to impress on them the need for periodic increases in coverage to protect the property adequately.

Another method of handling this problem is to use the "replacement value" formula. The property is continually updated by appraisals and the coverage amount is maintained to meet the appraised values and cover replacement costs.

Adequate coverage on property, particularly a home, is essential. Without such coverage, no one can escape the effect of the co-insurance clause.

MORTGAGEE AND OTHER CREDITOR RIGHTS

In purchasing your home, if you needed a mortgage your insurance policy on the home contained a mortgagee clause naming the company as "First Mortgagee." In the event of a loss, the mortgage company would be paid first from the insurance proceeds. You, as the insured, would receive the balance after the mortgage was paid. By this means a creditor such as a mortgagee is protected by your insurance.

Insurance pays the mortgage company first

The ways in which creditors' rights can be protected by property insurance can be itemized as follows:

- The creditor takes out or receives from the debtor a separate policy protecting the creditor's interest; the property owner takes out a separate policy protecting his ownership interest.

- The owner assigns his policy to the creditor, but the insurance company may insist on its right to approve the assignment before it is effective.

- A "loss payable" clause is inserted into the owner's policy to protect the creditor. By endorsement or in the body of the policy, it is provided that the loss, if any, is payable to "creditor X" or "as its interest may appear." The creditor usually keeps possession of the policy. The owner then receives a *memorandum of insurance* indicating that the policy has been issued with a loss payee clause.

"As their interests may appear"

- Where several people or business interests have an interest in the same property, they may all be protected as named insureds "as their interests may appear." For example, two farmers who store their grain in the same grain elevator may insure it in both names "as their interest may appear." They cannot really separate the grain and identify what each originally stored.

Where a creditor wants to preserve his rights by using the property insurance of a debtor, the creditor should insist on an agreement that spells out:

- who would secure the insurance;

- how the premiums are to be paid;

- who receives the policy and who receives the memorandum of insurance; and

- how the creditor is to be designated as loss payee.

The agreement should also specify clearly how the proceeds are to be distributed. The policy itself should have the creditor as the party to whom the benefits are first to be paid.

Insurance protection is vital. In private life, it serves to protect the homeowner—to insure him against loss and liability claims. But insurance also plays a major role in business. For example, it can be used to finance buy-sell agreements, provide key-man protection, and accomplish many other purposes. These will be discussed in the chapter dealing with business organizations.

Check your personal insurance program

The present chapter serves as a checklist of a personal insurance program. Do those liability policies provide adequate protection? Should the limits of the homeowners' policy be increased? Do the life insurance policies contain all the necessary options and additional coverages, many available for a slight or no increase in premium?

8 THE FAMILY THAT STAYS TOGETHER . . .

The field of law involving matrimonial matters—domestic relations law—is perhaps the most personal of all. It deals with the close personal relationships that exist between husband and wife and between parent and child. Key areas of the field include the questions that arise before marriage, the property rights of husband and wife, separation and dissolution of marriage, alimony, divisions of property, customary provisions for custody and visitation of children, and support payments.

Domestic relations law often deals with people under emotional stress. Who can be dispassionate when faced with a problem involving wife, husband, or children? Who can be objective when faced with a spouse who indicates he or she wants a divorce, or who has aroused a fear

of serious bodily harm as a result of his or her activities, or who is attempting to violate one's property rights?

Some solutions and answers are discussed in this chapter.

THE MARRIAGE CONTRACT: ISSUES AND ALTERNATIVES

Marriage as a civil contract has one aspect that sets it apart from other kinds of contracts: the parties cannot dissolve their marriage by themselves. They have to call on the sovereign power of the state if they want to obtain a divorce.

That fact suggests how important marriage is in the eyes of the law. The marriage contract brings legal consequences that can and often do affect the persons involved for the rest of their lives.

Valid and Invalid Marriages

Most states require that the parties to a marriage go through certain formalities before the ceremony. Typically, the following steps would be essential:

- A marriage license has to be issued. The license serves as legal permission to marry. Both the prospective partners have to sign an application at the offices of the appropriate local agency— Circuit Court, marriage license bureau, or other—to obtain the license.
- Before the license is issued, both applicants are required to undergo a standard laboratory blood test. The test certifies that each party is free of venereal disease.
- After the license is issued, most states require that the marriage be solemnized within a specified period. A judge, qualified clergyman, or other person appointed by a court can perform the marriage ceremony.

States specify marriageable ages Both parties to a marriage have to have reached a legally specified age to be validly married. The age varies from state to state. Persons who have not reached the specified age—minors—can marry in most states with their parents' consent. In a typical case a girl of 16 or 17 can marry with her parents' consent; at the age of 18 she has reached her majority and can marry without consent.

A minor who lies about his or her age to get married has contracted an invalid marriage. A parent or guardian can go to court to have the marriage *annulled*—declared legally invalid. The court can annul the marriage without the parties' consent.

Common-Law Marriages. Common-law marriages are legal and valid in some states. In others, they are not recognized. But even in the latter states, the common-law marriage contracted legally in another state will usually be recognized.

In a common-law marriage the two partners simply agree to be married and to live together as man and wife. They do not take out a license or go through a formal ceremony. They consider themselves to be married.

Living Together. Social conventions have changed to the point where more and more couples live together in arrangements that replace marriage or that serve as "trial marriages." Such arrangements have become increasingly acceptable in a social sense. Yet many states still make living-together relationships illegal.

The laws against illegal cohabitation, where they exist, are rarely enforced. Thus the couples are generally free to form agreements, in writing or orally, on property rights, household duties, child-rearing responsibilities, and other matters. Because no valid marriage has taken place, such agreements may be held to be unenforceable: many courts will refuse to sanction an agreement that has an illegal basis.

AGE AND OTHER MARRIAGE REQUIREMENTS BY STATE[1]

	Minimum Age With Parents' Consent		Minimum Age Without Parents' Consent		Blood Test Required	Waiting Period	Marriages Between First Cousins Prohibited	Common-Law Marriages Recognized
	Men	Women	Men	Women				
Alabama	17	14	18	18	yes	no	no	yes
Alaska	18	16		18	yes	no	no	no
Arizona	18	18	18	18	yes	no	yes	no
Arkansas	17	18	18	18	yes	3 days	yes	no
California					yes	no	no	no
Colorado	16	16	16	18	yes	no	no	yes
Connecticut	16	16	18	18	yes	4 days 24-96 hours	no	no
Delaware	18	16	18	18	yes			no
Florida	18	16	18	21	yes	3 days	no	no
Georgia	18	16	18	18	no	3 days	no	no
Hawaii	16	16	18	18	yes	3 days	yes	no
Idaho	15	15	18	18	yes	no	yes	yes
Illinois	16	16	18	18	yes	no	yes	no
Indiana	18	18	18	18	yes	3 days	yes	no
Iowa	18	18	18	18	yes	no	yes	yes
Kansas	14	12	18	18	yes	3 days	yes	yes
Kentucky	18	18	18	18	yes	3 days	yes	no
Louisiana	18	16	18	18	yes		yes	no
Maine	16	16	18	18	yes	5 days	yes	no
Maryland	16	16	18	18	no	48 hours	yes	no
Massachusetts	14	12	18	18	yes	5 days	no	no
Michigan	18	16		18	yes	no	yes	no
Minnesota	16	16	18	16	no	5 days	yes	no
Mississippi	no	no	17	15	yes	3 days	yes	no
Missouri	15	15	21	18	yes	3 days	yes	no
Montana			18	18	yes	5 days	yes	yes
Nebraska	18	18	18	18	yes	3 days	yes	yes

	Minimum Age With Parents' Consent		Minimum Age Without Parents' Consent		Blood Test Required	Waiting Period	Marriages Between First Cousins Prohibited	Common-Law Marriages Recognized
	Men	Women	Men	Women				
Nevada	18	18	18	18	no	no	yes	no
New Hampshire ...	18	18	18	18	yes	5 days	yes	no
New Jersey	18	18	18	18	yes	72 hours	no	no
New Mexico	18	18	18	18	yes	no	no	no
New York	16	14	18	18	yes	3 days	no	yes
North Carolina	16	16	18	18	yes	no	no	no
North Dakota	18	15	18	18	yes	no	yes	no
Ohio............	18	16	18	18	yes	5 days	yes	yes
Oklahoma	16	16	21	18	yes	no	yes	yes
Oregon	17	17	17	17	yes	7 days	yes	no
Pennsylvania	18	18	18	18	yes	3 days	yes	yes
Rhode Island	14	12	18	16	yes	no	no	yes
South Carolina....	14	16	18	18	no	24 hours	no	yes
South Dakota	18	16	18	18	yes	no	yes	no
Tennessee	16	16	18	18	yes	3 days	no	no
Texas	14	14	18	18	yes	no	no	yes
Utah.............	16	14	21	18	yes	no	yes	no
Vermont	18	16	18	18	yes	5 days	no	no
Virginia	16	16	18	18	yes	no	no	no
Washington	17	17	18	18	no	3 days	yes	no
West Virginia	18	16	18	18	yes	3 days	yes	no
Wisconsin	18	18	18	18	yes	5 days	yes	no
Wyoming	16	16	16	16	yes	no	yes	no

Legal Considerations

A number of other factors that can render a marriage void will be noted later. These factors rank among the legal considerations that the parties to a marriage should consider before the "knot is tied." Still other basic considerations that become important where a marriage is valid include the following:

- *Name change.* On marrying, the wife usually assumes her husband's last name. But she is not legally required to do so. For professional or other reasons a wife may keep her maiden name. Many wives today retain their maiden names because, among other reasons, they have developed lines of credit with stores or institutions, often over long periods of time and at considerable expense.

Hyphenated surnames   In other cases both husband and wife may assume hyphenated or combined surnames at the time of marriage. Mary Smith and John Jones become Mary and John Smith-Jones. The husband should usually enter a court petition for a legal name change; the wife can make such a change, often, without going through any formal legal procedures. Name changes

"*I now pronounce you Mr. Jones and Ms. Smith.*"

should of course be given as soon as possible to governmental agencies, including vehicle licensing authorities, and institutions such as banks and insurance companies.

- *Insurance.* Marriage represents a change in status. Thus insurance companies that may be affected should be notified immediately. Where life insurance is involved, a change of beneficiaries—from a parent to a spouse, for example—may be called for. Auto insurance rates may change in the married person's favor. Combining the hospitalization coverages of husband and wife will usually result in substantial savings.

- *Wills and estate planning.* Everyone, and particularly every married person, should have a will. Even for a young couple with limited assets, the will constitutes the first step in estate planning. Of equal importance, the will helps the partners in a marriage to protect one another and their children in the event of the wife's or husband's death.

- *Tax status.* Once married, the couple become eligible to file a joint income tax return with both their state and federal governments. The joint return should be studied carefully, however. In some cases it can save money; in others, it will mean a larger tax "bite." The advantages and disadvantages are determined by each couple's financial situation.

Sales contract determines legal obligations

- *Buying a home.* Many couples look forward to owning a home of their own. When they buy, they should remember that the sales contract, not the deed, determines their legal obligations. The aid and advice of a lawyer should be solicited. The lawyer can do more than advise; he can also, if necessary, draw up or review the sales contract and examine the title to the property.
- *Record keeping.* Records become important as soon as two people marry. Documents such as insurance policies, the marriage certificate, deeds, contracts, and birth certificates should be stored in a safe place. Almost inevitably, one partner or the other, or both, will have to refer to or use these documents. Even canceled checks should be retained for a period of time—if only as records for the Internal Revenue Service.
- *Children.* Obviously, the children born to a married couple introduce entirely new sets of legal considerations. The same applies if the couple adopts a child. The key questions touch on support obligations, inheritance, and many others.

REMARRIAGE

A man has lost his wife of many years. He is lonely, despondent; he seeks companionship. He has a family, both sons and daughters, that is deeply concerned about him.

A woman has lost her husband. The deceased, concerned about her welfare, has left her with sufficient insurance and property to provide for her well-being. She can live very comfortably. She can remain close to her children.

Remarriage and property rights

Assume that this fictional man and woman meet. They find a companionship that satisfies a distinct human need. But they both have families. Because of the nature of the law dealing with property rights in marriage, they are concerned that if they marry, their own children will not receive the property they want them to inherit. Both fear that the property that each owns individually will find its way to the other and not pass on to their children.

This couple's situation is a common one today. Many organizations exist to bring people together: Parents Without Partners, for example, and other organizations that help widows and widowers to adjust to the fact that they are alone.

In other cases, an older widower wants to marry someone much younger than himself. Less frequently, an older widow wants to marry a man younger than herself. The same considerations apply insofar as the older person's children are concerned.

Can widows or widowers in these situations have the benefit of the companionship and love that they seek? Can they protect the rights of their own children to inherit their property? The law, always adaptable, offers a method by which this can be done.

Prenuptial Agreements

An antenuptial agreement, or prenuptial agreement, is formulated before the marriage. It defines the interests that each will have in property of the other acquired before or during the marriage.

Defining interests before marriage

The prenuptial agreement might provide, first, that in contemplation of marriage and in consideration of a marriage to take place in the future, each party releases all the rights and interest he or she might have in the estate of the other. In other words, the widower would specifically release any rights or interest he might acquire by marriage in the property of the widow. The widow would do likewise.

The prenuptial agreement would also provide that if either partner dies, his or her property will pass under state law as if the person had died unmarried.

The prenuptial agreement requires a full disclosure by each party of the assets owned in his or her own right. Thus each knows clearly and specifically what he or she is releasing. If a prospective spouse does not reveal the total extent of his or her property holdings, the other spouse can later claim that full disclosure was not made. The prenuptial agreement would be rendered null and void. The lawsuits arising over prenuptial agreements have almost always been based on nondisclosure of assets at the time the agreement was signed.

Where there's nondisclosure of assets . . .

Postnuptial Agreements

A couple may marry before drawing up an agreement regarding money, property, or the rights of each spouse. These postnuptial agreements have traditionally performed functions similar to those of prenuptial agreements.

The postnuptial agreement serves as a useful estate planning technique—like the prenuptial agreement. But the agreement entered into after marriage may also help to resolve differences that may arise during marriage.

Postnuptial agreements are never separation agreements. The former are made while the marriage contract is binding on both the husband and wife; the latter are made in preparation for divorce or separation.

Validity of Agreements

Both the pre- and postnuptial forms of agreement have encountered some hostility among judges. Some confusion regarding the validity of such contracts had arisen by the mid-1980s. Judges in some cases seemed to feel that prenuptial agreements in particular tended to encourage divorce.

In public policy, agreements that promote divorce are unenforceable. For that reason, prenuptial agreements have been less effective than postnuptial agreements in the courts. Yet judges tend to uphold prenuptial agreements that do not impose undue hardships on the contracting parties.

State legislatures have generally accepted both pre- and postnuptial agreements. Laws on marriage and divorce assume, largely, that marriage agreements do not run contrary to the state's interest in marriage.

The Support Agreement

Where a widow or widower with property holdings marries someone who does not own property, the situation is somewhat different. As usual, the agreement will ordinarily consist of a release by the second party of all rights to the estate of the spouse. But the agreement may also require that one spouse make provision for the other in a will. A support agreement may provide for payments on a monthly or some other basis.

In this situation, as in that involving the widow and widower, full disclosure of assets is required to support the agreement.

The same type of agreement can be "postnuptial"—the parties can formulate it after the marriage. The full disclosure requirements still apply.

The agreement may provide for termination if the parties divorce or are separated. This is particularly important where the agreement provides for some form of monthly payments by one spouse to another—or where one spouse agrees to make out a will naming the other as a beneficiary.

Prenuptial and postnuptial agreements involve very serious federal estate and gift tax consequences. The family lawyer should be consulted regarding the method of preparation and the actual content of these agreements. They are important because they can protect the interest of children in the estates of their parents and give peace of mind to widows, widowers, and others. They can ensure that estates will be properly handled.

For protection and peace of mind

UNTIL DEATH US DO PART

The breakup of a marriage is a sad, sad thing. Psychologically, it affects the parties because they often feel they have failed in the most personal of human relationships. Practically, it means that they face a difficult period in their lives, economically and otherwise. Emotionally, it can mean a traumatic experience, especially if the marriage has lasted a long time and if children are involved.

Normally, divorce constitutes a last-resort measure, one to be taken only after all other means of saving the marriage have failed. The lawyer's first suggestion may be that the partners consult with their minister, priest, or rabbi. In many instances, this has already been attempted without success.

A next suggestion may indicate professional counseling by any of the excellent family or children's services supported by municipal governments, private foundations, and the United Fund and similar agencies. But, often, one or the other spouse refuses even to admit that a problem exists.

Mediation

By the mid-1980s, a new method of encouraging divorce-bound couples to agree on ways to structuring their settlements had come into widespread use. Called divorce mediation, the method involves the services of a professional mediator who confers with both parties in an effort to reach a solution before a court hearing.

In 1983 twenty-three states were using mediators as parts of court systems. California required couples who differed on questions of child custody to see a mediator before going to court. Around the country, social workers, trade-union negotiators, and some lawyers were becoming mediators.

Mediation has been found generally to bring couples to find their own —not court-assigned—solutions to their problems.

Mediation has proved to be a way to lighten caseloads. Critics have contended that the method may provide inadequate protection for one or the other spouse.

Some questions are commonly asked by a partner to a marriage that is breaking up. These include:

- *Who has to leave the house first?* If the property is owned jointly by the husband and wife, both have the right to remain on the property. Neither can be required to leave before the other. If one spouse fears that the other will inflict bodily injury or harm, the aid of a court should be sought to force the other party to leave the premises.

The obligation to support

- *Does the husband have to continue to support the wife?* The answer is yes. The husband's duty to support his wife continues until divorce. In those states that recognize alimony, the duty continues after the divorce decree is entered. Wives may also be required to support their husbands who may not have the same means. The same rules may apply equally to husband and wife.

- *What happens if one partner realistically and properly fears that the other may inflict serious bodily harm?* What about a wife beater? Practically, it may be impossible to deal with a wife beater. Counseling does not help; the only real protection for the spouse may be the protection that the law affords. Admittedly, this may not be adequate in all cases.

Where a wife seriously fears that her husband may injure her or her children—where she has a "reasonable apprehension of bodily harm"—she may have to face a very disagreeable, embarrassing confrontation. She may have to ignore what the neighbors may think. She may have to bring charges against her husband, and take whatever steps are necessary to show that she will not stand for physical abuse.

Extreme measures may become unavoidable. The wife in some cases packs her husband's clothes, throws them out on the porch, and locks the door, effectively driving him out. She should then be prepared to call the police immediately if he attempts to gain entrance to the home. While he may have a legal right to possession equal to hers, she has the right not to be assaulted, and may take steps to protect herself and her children.

Wives in such situations sometimes take the children and leave the house to seek refuge with a friendly neighbor or relative. The preservation of property rights becomes secondary to the safety of the wife and children.

A wife beater is generally recognized as a coward. When confronted by a defiant, angry wife, this husband usually loses heart. Many such husbands do not give their wives credit for having enough sense to consult a lawyer for legal advice in problem situations. The husbands are amazed to learn that their wives had enough "gumption" to seek legal advice. Often, the contact with a lawyer is enough to show the husband that the wife means business and will not stand being "pushed around" any more.

When legal advice may be needed

Some abusive husbands, of course, continue to act in the same boorish manner. In such cases the wife should make up her mind to resist; she should take any steps necessary to protect herself and her children.

The same considerations apply where a wife has been acting irrationally. It is always difficult for a husband to deal with a wife who shows no concern for the children, for him, or for herself; who stays out late at night; who drinks; or who otherwise appears incapable of taking care of herself or her family. The husband in such a case must assess how much unavoidable unpleasantness may result if he takes legal steps, particularly where the wife needs medical or psychiatric help.

Termination of a Marriage

In most states a marriage may be terminated in several ways. The marriage may be terminated by the death of one of the parties, of course. The marriage may also be terminated where a spouse is presumed to be dead after an unexplained absence for a fixed period of years. Here, the circumstances usually indicate that death is a reasonable explanation for the absence. The marital relationship may be suspended by separation, and it may be terminated by divorce or annulment.

Grounds for Absolute Divorce. The grounds for termination of the marriage relationship differ in those few states that still require proof of "fault" in one of the marriage partners. As a result, it is difficult to generalize in this area. However, certain common elements run through the state laws dealing with divorce as a way to terminate the marriage relationship.

Some states require proof of "fault"

Adultery. As a ground for divorce, adultery has essentially the same significance in all the "fault" states. Adultery occurs where one spouse has sexual relations with someone other than his or her wife or husband. It is generally not necessary to prove adultery by direct evidence. But it must at least be established that the spouse and the third party (corespondent) had the occasion and the inclination to perform the act.

Proof of a single act of adultery is enough to support a claim for divorce. But *condonation* may be raised as a defense. This becomes possible where the husband and wife have resumed marital relations after the other spouse has learned of the adultery.

Conviction of a Crime. Statutory provisions establishing grounds for divorce often include terms such as the conviction of an infamous crime, a crime involving moral turpitude, or conviction for the commission of a felony. Conviction of a crime may have to be accompanied by an extended prison sentence that will constitute cause for divorce. Service of a one-year or an 18-month prison term would typically justify a divorce.

Cruelty. Cruelty may still constitute grounds for divorce or separation. But cruelty may be either physical or mental. Some states, for example, have viewed physical violence or cruel and barbarous treatment as one kind of cruelty. "Mental cruelty," or what have been termed indignities to the person of the innocent spouse, or incompatibility, represent another form entirely.

A single act, a course of conduct

A basic factor distinguishes cruelty involving physical violence from mental cruelty, indignities, or incompatibility. In the former, only one single act of violence usually justifies divorce if it endangers the life of the other spouse. Mental cruelty, indignities, or similar causes must usually involve a course of conduct. The offending spouse must continually have performed such acts, leading to mental anguish on the part of the other spouse, or to an intolerable condition for that marriage partner.

Some mental cruelty grounds have appeared repeatedly in court cases. These include:

- Habitual drunkenness—not merely a single act of drunkenness
- Habitual intemperance
- Repeated insults to the spouse in front of other people
- False accusations of immorality
- Habitual refusal to communicate or treat the spouse as a marriage partner
- Cruel treatment of a child in the presence of the spouse

Desertion and Abandonment. Desertion or abandonment for a continuous statutory period of time is another ground for divorce. The period varies from one state to another. To establish desertion or abandonment, the suing spouse must establish the necessary intent on the part of the other partner. A separation to which the marriage partners validly agree will not constitute desertion or abandonment.

As noted, a marriage can be terminated where the unexplained absence of one spouse justifies a presumption of death. The circumstances must indicate that efforts to locate the spouse would be pointless. When the statutory period specified in state "Enoch Arden" laws expires, the remaining spouse may apply for a termination of the marriage. It is generally required, however, that the circumstances under which the missing spouse disappeared be shown. The remaining spouse must also have made efforts to locate him or her, unless the absent partner disappeared under circumstances indicating that efforts to locate him would be useless. For example, the absent spouse may have been last heard from in a war zone. No further word arrived throughout the statutory period. In this case the marriage relationship could be terminated under an Enoch Arden law without any further showing.

"Enoch Arden" laws

A spouse may remarry under an Enoch Arden law after the dissolution of the earlier marriage. If the first spouse later reappears, the validity of the second marriage would not be affected.

The Enoch Arden laws get their names from a poem, "Enoch Arden," by Alfred Lord Tennyson. The poem's hero, a sailor, is shipwrecked. Rescued after many years on a desert island, Enoch returns to find his wife happily remarried. He continues to live nearby, hiding his identity, and eventually dies of a broken heart.

Drunkenness. Habitual drunkenness constitutes another statutory ground for divorce. But the drunkenness must be habitual and not merely a single incident or a tendency toward occasional drunkenness. The spouse must have acquired the habit after the marriage. In some states, the habit must have continued for a specified period of time.

Fraud in the marriage contract

Fraud. Since marriage is a contract, the ordinary rules of valid contract apply in a marriage, and fraud that would make any contract void may also make a marriage contract void. The following are generally recognized as bases for an annulment for fraud:

- Misrepresentation or concealment of a prior marital status
- Misrepresentation of one's intent to go through a religious ceremony after a civil ceremony has taken place
- A secret intent not to have children or not to live with one's partner
- Concealment of a serious health impairment or a venereal disease
- Concealment at the time of the marriage of a pregnancy by someone other than the intended husband
- Misrepresentation as to prior morals

Insanity. A ground for divorce, insanity is also a ground for annulment in some states. If the sane spouse is seeking an annulment, he or she must prove that the condition of the insane spouse was unknown at the time of the marriage. If the wife is the insane partner, the court may require the husband to provide for her support.

Annulment

Annulment differs from divorce

An annulment differs from a divorce in a basic way. Where a divorce dissolves a valid marriage, an annulment states that a marriage is void—that it never legally existed. Some of the grounds for annulment may also be cited as grounds for divorce, as indicated. These include fraud and insanity or idiocy. In Indiana, a marriage will be held to be illegal or void if two Indiana residents are married in another state to avoid Indiana marriage license provisions. The same law applies in other states. A marriage to a minor, a person under the legal age of consent, can generally be annulled, as can an incestuous marriage. The latter is a marriage to a person within a specified degree of kinship.

Bigamy, a second marriage by a person who has a living spouse, will also render a marriage void. Because bigamy is not recognized in the United States, the second marriage can always be annulled, or held to be void.

In a few states, bigamy also constitutes grounds for an absolute divorce. Under any circumstances, a judicial decree of annulment will clear the record of the second marriage. Bigamy is also a crime, but ordinarily the bigamist can be prosecuted only in the state where the crime was committed. That means the state in which the second marriage was performed.

REQUIREMENTS OF RESIDENCE; SEPARATION AGREEMENTS

Most states require that a person who wants to bring a divorce action must reside in the state for a specified period of time before starting the suit. All states recognize separation agreements under which the parties agree to live apart without divorcing.

Residence requirements and state laws

"Public Policy"

Under each state's "public policy" regarding divorce, the residence requirement varies. For example, certain states seek divorce cases. These states have a residency requirement of several weeks to a month. Other states, however, take a different view, requiring at least a year's residence or more before the action can be started.

Residence requirements are strictly enforced because the state is said to have an interest in the marital contract. If for any reason the residency requirement is not met, any divorce can be set aside if attacked by one of the parties.

Separation Agreements

Under a separation agreement, the two parties to a marriage agree that they will live separately and not molest one another. In general, the agreement will provide for the disposition of the joint property of the parties and for support to be paid by one party to the other.

A separation agreement allows a husband and wife to live separate and apart from one another without getting a divorce. With an agreement, neither party has grounds for divorce on the basis of abandonment or desertion. The agreement spells out the parties' respective rights regarding shared property and, where children are involved, with respect to custody and visitation of the children.

A separation agreement requires all the legal steps that are involved in obtaining a divorce decree. Residence, grounds, pleadings, and court appearances become necessary. But a separation agreement leads to a *legal separation*, and the parties cannot remarry. Rights of inheritance and the duty to support may continue. A successful divorce proceeding leads to total dissolution of the marriage. The parties can remarry.

The partners in a marriage can separate immediately after signing an agreement. In most states, the agreement should not be conditioned on one of the parties getting a divorce. The reason is that many states have a

Separation after agreement

policy against any agreements that interfere with the marital relationship.

The separation agreement usually involves matters common also to divorce actions, including the obligation of support, custody of children and visitation rights, insurance and tax considerations, support payments or alimony, and methods of enforcing support provisions.

Obligation of Support. The support obligation has changed as a result of equal rights legislation and amendments to various state constitutions. Today, both husband and wife may be obligated to support one another during their joint lives even where, in a separation agreement, one of the parties agrees to pay a stipulated amount instead of support. Each party may be liable for the other's support at least to the extent of keeping the other party from becoming another statistic on the welfare roles.

Some states restrict the right of either party to be released from the obligation to support the other. Other states permit a separation agreement providing a regular and substantial payment that will relieve the other party of his or her duty to pay support.

Many separation agreements provide for a *lump-sum* settlement to cover property rights, provide for the transfer of real estate from one spouse to the other, or release one spouse's interest in real estate to the other. An agreement may also provide for the distribution of personal property such as stocks, bonds, cash, furniture, fixtures, equipment, automobiles, and any other property.

Danger in lump-sum settlement

It should be noted that a lump-sum settlement involves some danger. The receiving spouse may lose the lump sum through an unfortunate accident or bad investment, and may then bring a further claim against the paying spouse despite the agreement. The danger can be avoided by payment of a substantial lump sum and acceptance of an obligation to pay on a monthly or other periodic basis such additional amounts as may be agreed on by the parties.

Custody and Visitation Rights. By far the most important part of the separation agreement relates to child custody. Where an agreement has no provision for child custody, and where a court becomes involved in determining custody, the sole consideration will be the welfare of the child. Even if a divorce decree settles the question of custody, the court may alter the custodial provisions at any time because of changes in the circumstances of the parties. For example, a father who could not provide a home for a child when an agreement was signed may improve his status later. He may then go to court to try to obtain custody. He may ask for a writ of habeas corpus to have the child brought to court for determination of custody.

Before the equal rights movement gained momentum, courts usually favored the mother where the child was of "tender years"—12 years of age or younger. The father had to go to court to establish that the mother was "unfit." That meant the mother had mental, moral, or physical limitations that could endanger the health or welfare of the child.

Today the courts generally hold that the father has as much right to custody of a child under the age of 12 as does the mother. No longer, in most states, is there a presumption favoring the mother. The welfare of the child is the only criterion applied.

Where a child is old enough and reasonably mature, the court as a general rule will ask what the child's wishes are; but that alone will not affect the decision if other factors indicate that custody should be awarded to the other spouse. In some cases, depending on the circumstances, custody may

A child's wishes not necessarily binding

be awarded to another relative such as grandmother, aunt, or other third party.

A separation agreement may and should provide for custody. But such an agreement is not binding on the court. Normally it does carry considerable weight where custody is at issue.

Where a court awards custody to one parent, the other will be given visitation rights. Usually these rights of visitation will be limited to a particular time and place; or one spouse will have to give the one having custody notice as to when the visit will take place.

In many cases a court will allow a child to spend a summer vacation with the other spouse, perhaps for several weeks or a month. The child may be allowed to leave the jurisdiction of the court. In many cases, however, to avoid possible problems the court will direct that the child remain within its jurisdiction. One such problem is that the host parent may try to keep the child permanently.

If the spouse having custody of the child dies, the right of custody generally reverts to the surviving spouse. But that spouse must be able to provide a suitable home. Where the surviving spouse cannot provide a suitable home, custody awards may be made to other relatives or third parties.

The remarriage of either spouse does not automatically affect custody of children by a former marriage; but the remarried spouse may have acquired a proper home to replace the one broken by the divorce. Such arguments have been successful where the facts can be proved.

Joint Custody.   The early 1980s saw **joint custody** emerge as a widely used solution for custody problems. In joint custody the child of divorcing or separating parents spends specified amounts of time, alternately, with both the father and the mother. But joint custody may also mean that each parent has an equal say in a child's educational and medical care.

Shared-time joint custody has been available as an option for parents for many years. But by 1983, twenty-seven states had passed statutes making joint custody a definite option in divorce or separation situations. The laws varied widely. Where some states simply permitted parents to choose joint custody, others required judges to consider it before they examined other options.

As a solution to custody problems, joint custody has been widely praised. It gives a child the opportunity to grow up with both parents. Many persons say it helps fathers who want to help raise their children— and mothers who may face financial problems after divorce or separation.

The Rights of Children.   Parents have rights when they divorce or separate; but so do children. Increasingly, the states have enacted laws that protect children's rights. The laws seek mainly to safeguard the psychological and physical welfare of the child (see Chapter 1).

The standard for determining a child's rights is generally expressed as "the best interests of the child." Protecting these interests centers on maintenance of stability and continuity in the parent-child relationship. Among the factors that a court usually considers are these:

- The affection, love, and other emotional ties existing between the parents and the child
- The parents' capacity and desire to provide love, affection, guidance, and continued education and rearing of the child in its religion or creed, if any
- The parents' capacity to provide for the child's physical well-being: food, clothing, medical care, and any necessary remedial care
- The child's experiences, including the time spent in a satisfactory, stable environment
- The family unit or custodial home itself, in particular its permanence
- The "moral fitness" of the competing parties
- The child's home, school, and community record

Heartbreak and an emotion-charged atmosphere may mar a custody hearing in which children become pawns in the struggle between divorcing parents. For that reason a separation agreement should provide for child custody. All details of custody and visitation should be spelled out.

When children become pawns

Insurance. To protect the children, again, the separation agreement should deal with the question of insurance. One spouse may want to keep the insurance on the other spouse in effect. The spouse having custody, or the children, may be named as irrevocable beneficiaries. This is done to prevent the other from agreeing to keep the policy in force and then changing the beneficiary.

Usually, the agreement will provide that ownership of the insurance policies is to be transferred to the wife or the husband, as the case may be; the other spouse will agree to continue to make the premium payments to keep the insurance in force. In this case the spouse paying the premiums cannot change the beneficiaries because the policy is owned by the other spouse.

Alimony. Most states recognize alimony, either temporary or permanent, as a basic part of a divorce action. Alimony should not be confused with support payments. The same principles apply, however, to support payments under a separation agreement and to a divorce decree that includes alimony, or provision of support by one spouse for the other.

Temporary alimony may be awarded while an action for divorce is pending. In other words, the court will direct one spouse to pay temporary alimony to the other who may be in need before a final decree is entered.

Alimony while divorce action is pending

Again, it should be stressed that the court has to have jurisdiction over the paying party by valid service of process. That second party must have knowledge of the action, and have an opportunity to defend himself.

Temporary alimony is awarded where the court exercises its discretion in view of all the circumstances of the case. The award is usually based on the reasonable probability that the suing party will obtain the divorce. That party's needs and the ability of the other to pay also enter into the decision. Lawyers' fees, which the suing partner may want to have paid, are not treated the same as alimony payments and are separate and distinct from alimony.

Divorce decree and permanent alimony

Permanent alimony is generally awarded as a part of the divorce decree when all parties are present and in court. Where a separation agreement has previously been signed, the court may consolidate the separation agreement into the final divorce decree and make it a part of the decree. The separation agreement may then be enforced just as a direction to pay alimony would be.

The court considers various factors in determining the amount of permanent alimony. The factors include the financial status of the parties and their ability to pay, the anticipated future earnings of the parties, their social standing, the conduct of the parties, and which party was at fault. In most cases, permanent alimony will continue until the death of either spouse or the remarriage of the spouse receiving alimony. Where a separation agreement exists, it may spell out different conditions for termination.

Just as with provisions of a separation agreement dealing with custody of children, a decree of permanent alimony may be modified by the court on application by either party. But the circumstances must show substantially changed financial conditions, or one of the parties must be shown to have concealed assets at the time the original decree was entered. Any such modification must be made by the court that entered the original decree.

Support and temporary alimony

Not all states recognize permanent alimony, however. Some states hold that a final divorce decree terminates all duties of support between the parties. These states may recognize support payments while an action is pending, and may refer to such payments as "temporary alimony." But they do not recognize permanent alimony as such. The laws of the state should be checked before a marriage partner decides on a course of action.

Income Tax Aspects of Alimony. Important income tax considerations should be noted regarding alimony payments. Some of these include:

- Whether or not the person paying the alimony can deduct the alimony payments from his own personal income tax
- Whether these payments can be included in the gross income of the person receiving the alimony

- The tax result where alimony payments are contingent on the death or remarriage of the other spouse
- Whether or not the payments are in fact periodic
- The tax effect of insurance premiums paid by one spouse when the policies have been assigned to the other spouse

The separation agreement and the divorce decree raise similar tax and other problems. The family lawyer should be consulted to determine income tax consequences that may be considerable where a sizeable estate is involved. Division of the estate may be only one of those problems.

Some generalizations can be noted. The payments made as support by a husband under a written separation agreement will generally be taxed to the wife. But they will be deductible on the husband's tax returns where periodic payments are made and where the husband and wife file separate income tax forms. The parties may thus decide to take tax considerations into account in the separation agreement so that the wife will not have to report the support payments as income. At the same time the husband will not be able to claim tax deductions for those payments.

Enforcement of Support or Alimony Payments. A particular benefit emerges where a separation agreement is consolidated into the divorce decree, or where the divorce decree sets the alimony payments. Consolidation allows a court to enforce the decree through contempt proceedings. A separation agreement providing for support payments is a contract; it can be used as the basis of a suit, like any other contract, if one of the parties breaches it.

Legal effects of consolidation

A lawsuit may not always be the best remedy, however. The time involved in a lawsuit may, for example, be prohibitive if the other party defends. Where a separation agreement is part of a decree, a court can hold in contempt of court the party refusing to abide by its terms. The possibility of imprisonment for contempt constitutes a strong inducement to the other party to make the proper payments under the decree.

Imprisonment is actually unusual in such cases. The threat alone often convinces the offending party that he or she should meet the specified conditions.

A spouse may sue under a separation agreement. If that spouse secures a judgment, the judgment may be collected by the normal means. These include attachment of the property of the other spouse, garnishment of rents or other funds owed the other spouse by third parties, and other methods established by state law. Decrees for the support of a spouse or children can also be enforced from one state to another under laws known as reciprocal support laws. These laws provide a means of following the spouse who owes support but skips town to avoid payments.

Suit under a separation agreement

ALTERNATIVE TYPES OF DIVORCE

A divorce action normally begins, as noted, with a complaint by one party against the other. The time required for completion of the action will depend on many factors. These include the degree to which husband and wife have agreed on financial and other problems and the backlog of cases in divorce court. Typically, from two months to a year or more can elapse before the divorce decree becomes final.

In some states an *interlocutory decree* may precede a *final decree*. The interlocutory decree will not become final for a period of time—30, 60, or 90 days or more. The parties are not divorced until the final decree is entered.

"Quickie" and no-fault divorces

Many couples and some states have sought ways in which to speed divorce actions. Two such methods are the so-called "quickie" divorce and no-fault divorce. The latter had been legalized in most states by the early 1980s; only five states—Illinois, Massachusetts, Mississippi, Pennsylvania, and South Dakota—did not have some kind of no-fault divorce.

"Quickie" Divorce Decrees

So-called "quickie" divorce decrees can be obtained in countries or states having little or no residence requirements. Are these "quickie" divorce decrees recognized everywhere?

Under the federal Constitution, the "Full Faith and Credit" clause requires that the courts of one state give full faith and credit to the judgments and decrees of the courts of another state. However, in an exception to this general rule, the court entering the original decrees must have had jurisdiction over the parties to that action. If the court did not have such jurisdiction, the second court does not have to give the decree full faith and credit.

The requirement of residence has been mentioned in connection with divorce decrees. The courts in several states have held that residence requires more than merely being present in the state for the period required to get a divorce. Rather, residence means physical presence plus an intent to remain within the state on a permanent basis. For example, divorce decrees have been attacked in some cases because the spouse did not indicate an intent to remain in the state. He or she may nonetheless have been in the state long enough to meet the residence requirement for a divorce.

In effect, some states take a stricter view of residence requirements than do others. An important question centers on notice—whether personal notice was given to the other party regarding the filing of the divorce action.

Quickie or "overnight" divorces may be granted in a foreign country such as Mexico. Ads proclaim that "you can get a divorce overnight" by sending certain forms to the foreign country. The decree is allegedly granted the next day. Neither party has to be present. *The foreign country divorce*

The full faith and credit clause of the U.S. Constitution does not apply to judgments or decrees of a court in a foreign nation. Further, a foreign country's decrees must have a proper jurisdictional basis. Among nations, recognition of a foreign country's judgments and decrees is based in "comity," under which foreign courts will generally recognize the decrees of another country. But where the physical presence of the party is not required, American courts will almost universally refuse to recognize the foreign decree. That decree, after all, was not based on proper jurisdictional grounds.

A quickie divorce may not, in brief, be recognized in some states as a legal divorce. The situation varies from state to state.

Again, some generalizations may be made. If a state's residence requirements have been met insofar as the original decree is concerned, if the spouse suing for divorce is physically present in the state issuing the decree for the required residence period, and if that spouse indicates an intent to remain there, normally such a decree will be valid and binding if attacked in another state. If a foreign country's decree is based on residence and the physical presence of the suing spouse in that country for a specified period, normally the U.S. courts will recognize the foreign country's divorce decree. *Residence may change the situation*

One-Party Divorces. In many cases one party receives a divorce from another when there is no indication that the other party was present or even had notice of the divorce action. These "one-party" divorce actions are possible because the laws of some states make it unnecessary to give the other party actual notice of the pending action. The court where the action is pending, in essence, has jurisdiction over the marriage and can change the marital relationship without notice to the absent party.

Like any other court action, a one-party divorce suit begins with the filing of a complaint or petition. An effort must be made to serve that complaint or summons on the other party. Many state rules of procedure permit service of the complaint on the other party by publication—through an advertisement in a newspaper noting the last known address of the other party. Other rules seek to ensure as much as possible that actual notice is given. But that step is not always necessary. The laws of any given state should be consulted.

In other cases the second spouse must receive notice. This is true where a support order, an alimony decree, or any other decree or court order *Notice may be required* involving a judgment for money—or a direction to pay money to one's spouse—is concerned. The other party then has the opportunity to come in and defend.

No-Fault Divorce. The old "fault"-style divorce has been criticized because it encouraged deceit and lying for the purpose of obtaining a divorce. Beyond that, couples found it difficult to agree quietly to a divorce because one spouse had to prove guilt in the other. Unnecessary bitterness and resentment often resulted, forcing one person—where divorce was not a mutual decision—into a position of consenting to unreasonable terms.

How no-fault divorce differs
No-fault divorce, also known as no-fault dissolution, differs from the conventional divorce in the following respects:

No evidence of fault or misconduct on the part of either spouse is required in filing. Usually, the only ground needed is "irreconcilable differences," "irretrievable breakdown," or "incompatibility." Each state has its own standards for establishing the existence of this condition in a marriage. Some states require that a couple make an attempt, through counseling provided by the state or county, to repair the marital relationship. If that attempt fails, either party can file for dissolution. New York allows a spouse to file either under no-fault grounds or on the grounds of cruel and inhuman treatment, abandonment for one or more years, imprisonment for three or more years, or adultery.

Divorce settlements are not dictated by a finding on which spouse is "at fault" in a marriage. Alimony (or maintenance), property, child custody, and child support are based on need and other rational considerations rather than fault.

"THE GLEASON RULE"

In a variation of the "no-fault" rule, New York requires that the parties live apart for at least one year under the terms of a written, notarized agreement that is filed with the court. The so-called "Gleason Rule" states that it does not matter who filed for separation or whether fault was the ground for separation. Comedian-actor Jackie Gleason was granted a divorce on the ground that he lived apart even though his wife had obtained a separation based on a finding of fault against him.

A typical dissolution procedure
A typical no-fault dissolution procedure occurs through these steps:
- *An initial visit to a lawyer.* A spouse should provide his or her lawyer with the following: (1) a complete list of property owned by each spouse, jointly or with the children, including the value and how and when acquired; (2) an itemization of mortgages,

debts, insurance policies, or other financial factors; (3) information about the children that would be affected by divorce; and (4) a copy of the latest income tax return. One should also discuss legal fees, as in all dealings with a lawyer.

- *Reconciliation.* One or both parties must consult with a party having expertise in marital problems. If a lawyer feels that not all efforts at reconciliation have been made, he will suggest further counseling.
- *Filing the petition.* Failing reconciliation attempts, a petition for dissolution is filed. At least 60 days will normally be required between filing and court hearing. This time should be used by both parties to reach a settlement. One spouse may be granted temporary child custody, support, or alimony.
- *Reaching a settlement.* This is based on the present and future needs of each party and on their respective abilities to meet those needs. For example, the spouse who gains child custody may require funds for child care and other needs. Child custody may be dictated by any of these factors: ages and sexes of the children; compatibility with each parent; the ability of each parent to take care of each child; and the personal characteristics of each parent. Some states, such as California, may grant either sole custody or joint custody.
- *Changing the settlement.* Division of property is one aspect of the settlement that cannot be changed. As circumstances change, however, support provisions can be altered except where the original decree did not include alimony; that cannot be added later. Negotiating a settlement that is agreeable to both parties can save time and expense later.

No-fault divorce reduces the trauma and bitterness of a proceeding as well as the time involved. Neither party is legally at fault. Formerly, the wife would usually be given custody of children. With no-fault divorce, however, more men are being awarded custody. In this respect, women not receiving custody may see themselves as somehow "at fault." This is one possible negative consequence of no-fault divorce. With the increase in no-fault divorces, the number of annulments has declined.

Reducing trauma, saving time

DIVISION OF PROPERTY

Laws governing the division of property in divorce cases vary from state to state. In the so-called "community property" states—Arizona, California, Idaho, Nevada, New Mexico, Texas, and Washington—most income and property acquired during a marriage are considered jointly owned. Such income and property, including a home, automobile, personal savings, and even pension benefits, are usually divided relatively equally between the two parties.

Most other states have "equitable distribution" laws. Income and property, including pension rights, are generally divided on the basis of such factors as the age and employability of the divorcing parties.

The many state courts that hold that pension benefits are divisible upon divorce are actually ignoring provisions of the Employee Retirement Income Security Act, or ERISA (see p. 182). The Act specifically restricts to the pensioned person the assignment of pension rights. But courts have interpreted that clause as an effort to protect a pension plan from creditors, not a former spouse.

A trend toward recognition of a spouse's contributions to a marriage as "property" became visible in the mid-1980s. In a 1984 court decision the State of Washington decided that, in dividing marital property or awarding maintenance upon divorce, the contribution of a wife who worked to support a student spouse should be considered. With his wife's help the husband had earned a professional degree. "These sacrifices (for the sake of an education) are made in the mutual expectation of a higher standard of living," the Washington court held. "But dissolution of the marriage intervenes.... The student spouse has the degree and the increased earning potential that it represents, while the supporting spouse has only a dissolution decree."

The court refused, however, to consider the "somewhat metaphysical" question whether a professional degree was property.

Uniform Marital Property Act The American Bar Association in 1984 took a step toward standardization of state laws on division of property between divorcing parties. The ABA approved a model Uniform Marital Property Act, recommending that states adopt the law if they agreed with its substantive provisions.

9 "COME TO RETIREMENT CITY FOR THE REST OF YOUR LIFE"

With the rapid rise in American technology, more and more employers have adopted retirement policies that allow employees to retire at specified ages. The feeling seems to be that once an employee reaches a certain age, his capacity to produce for the company diminishes, and "new blood" should be brought in to take over his job. Many companies require that employees retire at a certain age.

There is by no means total agreement on whether a person's productivity drops when he reaches the age of 65 or any other age. Many men and women who are forced into retirement go into a new field and become very successful. Evidence to the contrary might also be cited.

From a practical standpoint, no employer should have a mandatory retirement age without some form of pension or profit-sharing plan that guarantees security to the retiring employee. So important has the whole question of pension and profit-sharing plans become that Congress has passed protective legislation, the Employee Retirement Income Security Act (ERISA) of 1974. The Act seeks to eliminate many of the problems resulting from the loss of benefits when employees change jobs or when they are fired or laid off just before they might qualify for pension benefits.

All too often an employee, feeling that he is secure in his pension rights, finds himself suddenly cast adrift when the company goes out of business, or is merged into another company. The employee may have no adequate provision for the future under existing pension plans.

The Employee Retirement Income Security Act guarantees greater security to the approximately 30 million workers who belong to private pension plans. But the Act also provides pension opportunities for an estimated 35 million other workers whose employers do not offer private pension plans. The self-employed person also benefits. By law, this person could in the tax year ending December 31, 1983, contribute either $15,000 a year or 15 per cent of all self-employment income, whichever is less. For the tax year ending December 31, 1984, and in subsequent years, any self-employed individual could contribute $30,000 or 25 per cent of all self-employment income.

The 1974 Act established age and length of service requirements. These entitle a worker who changes jobs or is fired before his retirement date to a part or all of the benefits he would have received after retirement—provided that he has put in at least five or ten years of service or that his age and years of service add up to 45. The employer has the option of which vesting procedure he wishes to choose for his plan and his employees.

Some ERISA provisions

Under the 1974 Act, if an employee quits, is fired, or changes employers after satisfying the minimum vesting requirements of the plan, he still retains his pension rights. His original employer will be required to pay him the pension benefits to which his service entitles him even though he has worked for someone else between his former employment and his retirement. If the company plan provides for it, the employee can take his vested or owned pension credits with him.

If his new employer agrees, the employee can invest the money from his former pension plan in the new company's plan. If not, the employee can invest that money in his own tax-free retirement account at a bank or other institution until he retires.

Additional important provisions of ERISA include funding standards. These ensure that there will be money in the plan to pay retirement benefits when they are due. Severe restrictions are placed on pension fund investment and management. All workers' pension plans are now insured against loss by the Federal Pension Benefit Guaranty Corporation, which is similar to the Federal Deposit Insurance Corporation that insures bank deposits against loss to the depositor.

ERISA is not the final word on the matter. But it represents a first attempt to prevent forfeiture of pension rights when an employee is not at fault. The Act marks a good beginning in pension reform, one that was desperately needed. In a later reform, the Supreme Court ruled in 1978 that an employer was violating the Civil Rights Act of 1964 if he charged women more than men for participation in a retirement plan. By 1980, efforts to update ERISA were under way in Congress. Critics charged that the Act's complexity was forcing thousands of employers to terminate pension plans. The goal of proposed new reforms is the simplification of ERISA.

A step toward pension reform

The standard private pension and profit-sharing plan and the federal Social Security laws require specific attention.

PRIVATE PENSION AND PROFIT-SHARING PLANS

A profit-sharing plan differs basically from a pension plan, particularly where employer contributions are concerned. The normal pension plan provides that the employer has a fixed commitment to make payments and contribute funds to the plan so that there will be sufficient funds to meet retirement claims. On the other hand, a profit-sharing plan contains no fixed commitment on the dollar amount to be contributed by an employer. Such a plan depends on the net profits of the company at the end of its fiscal year. A percentage is usually applied to the net profits to determine the amount to be contributed. If there are no net profits, no contribution is made.

Method of allocating funds differs

Another difference is the method of allocating funds to individual employees. Actuarial (age and life expectancy) calculations are required in a pension plan to make certain that the beneficiaries have the retirement funds needed at retirement. The 1974 Act provides for such adequate funding. Profit-sharing plans are normally based on the wages or salaries of employees, with some consideration given to length of service.

The actual forms that pension and profit-sharing plans take may also differ depending on investment objectives and the way the plan is administered. For example, an employer's plan may use mutual funds and direct stock investment (the so-called equity plans); it may also utilize annuities, life insurance, a combination of both, or debt obligations such as corporate, municipal, and treasury bonds and notes.

Administrators of pension and profit-sharing plans have to follow certain rules. Where investments are made in stocks or bonds, the plan will usually designate a trustee under a written trust agreement to hold and invest the plan's funds for the benefit of the employees. This agreement fixes the duties and obligations of the trustee. Where an annuity and life insurance program is used, a contract between the insurance company and the employer controls the method of administration.

Many people covered by pension or profit-sharing plans appear to have little understanding of their own plans. They may be aware that their employer has one and that he contributes to it, but other than that, they know nothing. Yet retirement security must be understood. How can you plan for your retirement if you don't know how your plan operates?

INCOME TAX BENEFITS

Study your own plan

Aside from providing a means of achieving retirement security, pension and profit-sharing plans have a distinct advantage for both the employer and the employee. A "qualified" pension or profit-sharing plan—one that fulfills all the requirements of the federal Internal Revenue Code—offers definite tax advantages.

Within limits specified in the tax laws, a corporate employer can claim current deductions from gross business income for all amounts contributed to a qualified plan. This remains true even though no benefits are currently payable to employees in the year in which a contribution is made.

The employee, on the other hand, does not have to include in his own individual income tax return the amount contributed to the plan by his employer. The contribution is not considered income until the employee has actually received the benefits. Thus the employee will be taxed at ordinary income rates or at capital gains rates depending on the year when the contributions were made to the plan, as represented by the benefits paid.

In sum, the employee pays no income tax on the contributions until he actually receives retirement benefits from the plan.

Other tax benefits may be noted. If the employer's contributions are paid into an investment trust fund, any income from the investments is exempt from income tax during the entire period in which these investments are effective. If the contributions to the trust fund are allowed to accumulate, tax free, over the period of an employee's service to a company, the rate of accumulation is much greater since there is no withdrawal from the fund to pay income tax.

Qualified Plans

To take advantage of the tax benefits for both employer and employee, the plan must be "qualified" under the Internal Revenue Code. The plan must fulfill the following requirements:

Four basic requirements

- The plan must be permanent, not temporary.
- It must be for the exclusive benefit of the employees and their designated beneficiaries under the plan.
- It must be primarily a deferred compensation plan, a plan that recognizes the service of employees and compensates them on their retirement.
- It must not discriminate among different classes of employees.

Regarding the latter, the plan cannot favor high-salaried employees over other employees. Nor can the plan discriminate with respect to benefits distributable to employees. In other words, one employee cannot receive an amount that bears no relationship to the amounts received by other similar employees.

If a trust plan is used, the trust agreement must prohibit the trustee from taking money from the plan to benefit other persons who are not beneficiaries. The plan must also require the trustee to follow the investment restrictions of the law. It is important that the plan be in writing. It must be distributed and explained fully to all employees, and the papers filed with the Internal Revenue Service to qualify the plan must contain copies of all pertinent documents. These include the notices and reports given to the employees to advise them of the existence and terms of the plan.

The SEP Plan

As an employee or self-employed person, you may have another alternative: the Simplified Employee Pension plan. Under this plan your employer, or you as a self-employed individual, would contribute to an IRA on your behalf—up to 15 percent of your annual earnings or $15,000, whichever is less.

Your employer may offer an SEP. To be eligible to join, you would have to be at least twenty-five years old. You would also need to have worked for that employer any time during three of the last five years. Every employee-participant has to deposit the same percentage of salary in contributions.

SEP plans are also available to employed persons who have an outside income apart from salary paid by an employer.

If you are in an SEP plan, you can donate up to $2,000 more of your own money to the plan or to another IRA. You can deduct that additional amount when you make out your federal income tax return. All basic IRA rules apply to all contributions made by you or your employer.

Integration with Social Security   In most pension and profit-sharing plans, the benefits payable will take into account the amount of Social Security benefits that the retired or disabled employee, or his beneficiary, may receive. Thus the plans are said to be "integrated" with the Social Security benefits. A profit-sharing plan must also have a formula for allocating the contributions to the beneficiaries and should indicate a method for determining the net profit based upon which the amount of the contribution is figured.

Self-Employment

Self-employed persons and persons whose companies have no retirement plans cannot claim all the technical benefits that are available under corporate pension and profit-sharing plans. But Keogh plans and Individual Retirement Accounts (IRAs) do offer similar tax advantages. The number of these plans for self-employed individuals has grown steadily as increased benefits are made available. But note: plans for self-employed persons must also "qualify" for special tax advantages.

Keogh plans and IRAs actually give self-employed persons such as doctors, lawyers, and sole proprietors a form of tax shelter. Others who are employed full-time but who earn money by "moonlighting" may also set up such programs with the extra funds they earn.

Under the Economic Recovery Tax Act of 1981, the Keogh plan tax shelter works as follows: Retirement funds are invested in mutual funds, trust accounts with banks, U.S. Treasury certificates, or other programs. Effective in 1982 and continuing in 1983, the individual could contribute as much as $15,000 to the plan out of gross self-employment income. The person cannot, however, contribute more than 15 per cent of that income. All such contributions are deductible from income. No taxes are paid on the funds until after retirement. At that time, taxes are usually paid at a reduced rate.

The Individual Retirement Account brings tax advantages similar to those provided by Keogh plans. But by 1983 the person with an existing IRA account could contribute up to $2,000 tax-free—or $2,250 if the person's spouse were unemployed. A working couple could invest $2,000 each, or a total of $4,000. The part-time teacher who in 1981 earned $5,000 and could put only $750 into an IRA could in 1983 contribute the maximum of $2,000.

At insured banks, savings and loan institutions, and credit unions, IRA savings were guaranteed up to $100,000. An individual's or couple's other accounts in the same bank or other institution would be insured separately to $100,000.

Participants in Keogh plans or Individual Retirement Accounts can start drawing on their investments—without penalty—at the age of 59½. They can defer retirement—and drawing benefits—until 70½.

Also available to the person planning for retirement is the Defined Benefit Plan (DBP), a type of Keogh. Contributions in this case are determined by the amount you want to receive annually during your retirement years.

You can generally contribute more under a DBP. But the rules governing DBPs are extremely complex. Experts suggest the need for a professional tax advisor before opening an account.

In Sum . . .

If you are an employee of a company with a pension or profit-sharing plan, you should read all the literature about the plan carefully. Learn what rights you possess, the manner in which your rights are protected, and other details. Remember that the tax act of 1981 specified that if you are making contributions to a "mandatory" retirement plan, with the company putting money away only if you do too, your contributions won't be deductible. *What to find out...*

If you are an employer without a company pension plan, you owe it to yourself and your employees to investigate the advantages of launching a plan. There is no better way to show your appreciation to your faithful, steady employees and give them the incentive to stay with you. The size of your company should make no difference; the tax savings and tax-deferred benefits that you may realize make it advantageous to examine the details immediately.

SOCIAL SECURITY BENEFITS

No discussion of pension and profit-sharing plans is complete without a discussion of the Social Security laws. As noted, private pension and profit-sharing plans take into account the Social Security benefits that the covered employee would receive on his retirement or disability. An understanding of the Social Security program fills in the picture regarding retirement benefits.

A series of programs offered by the federal government has the general heading of "Social Security." These include those programs operated directly by the federal government, such as the Old Age, Survivors' and Disability Insurance program and the health insurance program, including hospital and medical insurance for the aged.

State programs   In addition, programs involving unemployment insurance and public assistance and welfare services are operated by the several states. The programs include old age, aid to the blind, aid to needy families with children, aid to permanently and totally disabled individuals, medical assistance, maternal and child health services, services to crippled children, and child welfare services. The states run these programs with the cooperation and aid of the federal Department of Health and Human Services under the Social Security system.

A problem involving public assistance or welfare services can usually be solved by contacting a state or county public assistance agency.

This section deals with the benefits available under the program handled directly by the federal government under Social Security. Because benefits under other related programs change from time to time, no schedule of benefits will be cited. An up-to-date schedule can be obtained from any Social Security office.

Old Age, Survivors' and Disability Insurance Benefits

Key categories   The Old Age, Survivors' and Disability Insurance program involves
of beneficiaries   monthly Social Security cash payments made directly to beneficiaries. The following list shows the key categories of persons who can participate as beneficiaries:

- A disabled insured worker
- A retired insured worker age 62 or older
- The wife (including the divorced wife in some cases) of a retired or disabled worker entitled to benefits, if the wife is age 62 or over or is caring for a worker's child who is under 18 or who is disabled and entitled to Social Security benefits
- The dependent husband of a retired or disabled woman entitled to benefits if he is age 62 or over
- The dependent, unmarried child of a retired or disabled worker entitled to benefits, or of a deceased insured worker, if the child is under 18 years or is age 18 or over but under a disability which began before he or she reached 18 years, or if the child is age 18 or over but under age 22 and attending school on a full-time basis
- The widow (including the surviving divorced wife, in some cases) of a deceased insured worker if the widow is age 60 or over

- The disabled widow (including the surviving divorced wife, in some cases) of a deceased insured worker if the disabled widow is at least 50 but under 60 and becomes disabled within the period specified in the law
- The widow (including the surviving divorced wife, in some cases) of a deceased insured worker, regardless of her age, if she cares for a child of the deceased under age 18, or a disabled child who is entitled to benefits
- The dependent widower of a deceased insured worker age 62 or over
- The disabled dependent widower of a deceased insured worker if the widower is at least 50 but under 62 and becomes disabled within the period specified in the law
- The dependent parents of an insured worker who died at age 62 or over

In addition to the monthly cash payment made to a beneficiary, a lump-sum death payment may also be paid to the widow or widower who was living with the insured worker at the time of the worker's death. If there is no eligible widow or widower, the lump-sum death payment may be applied to pay the worker's funeral expenses. If the burial expenses are paid by someone other than the widow or widower, proof of payment must be made to the Social Security office before this payment can be made.

Monthly payment plus lump-sum

The rights to benefits depend on whether the worker was "insured" and became qualified during his lifetime. To be eligible for retirement, survivors' or disability benefits, the worker must have accumulated a certain number of "quarters of coverage." These are calendar quarters ending March 31, June 30, September 30, and December 31 of each calendar year in which a person has been paid $50 or more in wages for employment covered by the law. A self-employed person qualifies by earning $100 or more in self-employment income for a specified period. But, beginning after 1950, the self-employed person must earn at least $400 net in the taxable year before any quarters in the taxable year can be credited with self-employment income.

The method of computing the quarters of coverage needed under the program is very complicated. It is based on schedules and regulations in the law. Up-to-date information on the number of quarters of coverage required for qualification can be obtained from a local Social Security office.

"Retirement Test"

The Social Security Act provides for a "retirement test" for self-employed persons who have retired after contributing to Social Security.

The test limits the amount of income Social Security applicants can earn or receive after retirement without reducing or eliminating entirely their Old Age, Survivors, and Disability Insurance benefits.

Retirement planning with the retirement test in mind may make it unnecessary for self-employed persons to choose between part-time work and full employment.

Significantly, the Social Security Act and allied decisions exclude some types of income from the retirement test. Types that are not considered excess income and that need not be counted toward income that might reduce Social Security payments include:

- Retirement plan payments and annuities
- Bona fide dividends that would be judicially recognized as dividends from self-employment income
- Royalty payments made on publications issued or copyrighted before Social Security entitlement began
- Rentals from real estate—unless the claimant is a dealer in real estate

Health Insurance Program under Social Security

"Medicare" administration   The health insurance program, or "Medicare," is administered by the federal Social Security Administration with the assistance of "intermediaries" composed of insurance companies or the local Blue Cross agency. This program includes comprehensive hospital insurance and medical insurance features.

Medicare provides for payments for daily in-hospital benefits for persons 65 or over who are entitled to Social Security monthly cash benefits. The individual may not receive the payments for some reason. A person 65 or over who is a qualified railroad retirement beneficiary is also eligible. So are all persons 65 or over who do not meet the above two requirements but who have done some work covered by Social Security, are citizens of the United States or aliens who have been lawfully admitted to this country for permanent residence, and who have resided in the United States at least five years continuously before applying for benefits.

OLD AGE, SURVIVORS' AND DISABILITY INSURANCE:
WHAT KINDS OF BENEFITS AND WHO RECEIVES THEM?[1]

There are three basic types of benefits available:

RETIREMENT BENEFITS: When a worker retires, he or she can choose to receive benefits at age 62 or age 65. The worker's spouse and dependent children, including stepchildren and adopted children, can be eligible for benefits as well.

DISABILITY BENEFITS: When a worker becomes severely disabled, monthly benefits can start even before age 65. Disability, for Social Security purposes, means having a severe mental or physical condition which prevents work and (1) has lasted for at least one year, (2) is expected to last for at least a year, or (3) is expected to result in death. Benefits can start for the sixth full month of disability and continue as long as the disability. The spouse and dependent children can be eligible for benefits too.

SURVIVORS' BENEFITS: When a worker dies, benefits can go to certain family members as monthly payments and a lump-sum payment, usually to the surviving spouse.

OTHER BENEFITS: In addition to the monthly cash payments under retirement, disability, and survivors' benefits, Medicare helps persons 65 and older and severely disabled people under age 65 to pay the high cost of health care. In some instances, a monthly premium must be paid for Medicare benefits. In other cases, you may receive it without paying the premium. If you are 65 or older or under 65 and severely disabled and do not have Medicare coverage, you should contact your Social Security office for information.

In addition to those situations noted above, which entitle a person to benefits under

retirement, disability, and survivors' provisions, there are special situations which may apply to you:

COMMON-LAW MARRIAGES: Common-law spouses, widows, and widowers are eligible for benefits just as if there were a traditional ceremonial marriage.

ILLEGITIMATE CHILDREN: Illegitimate children are eligible for benefits just as legitimate children are, although there may be the additional problem of proving the relationship to the retired, disabled, or deceased parent.

GRANDCHILDREN: Unmarried grandchildren may be able to receive benefits if three requirements are met: (1) the child actually lives or lived with the grandparent, (2) the child receives or received at least half of his or her support from the grandparent, and (3) both parents are dead or totally disabled.

---

[1] Adapted from the brochure, *What Should I Know about Social Security?* Copyright June 1979, Pennsylvania Bar Association. Single copies of the brochure are available directly from the Association at the following address: Post Office Box 186, Harrisburg, PA 17108.

The law includes these transitional provisions for persons not otherwise entitled to hospital benefits. Benefits are not paid if the person has been convicted of treason or any other crime against the United States or is covered by a program providing health benefits to federal employees.

The Medicare coverage is provided on enrollment. In other words, application must be made specifically for the medical insurance coverage.

The amounts of Medicare benefits and the spans of coverage change from time to time. But the program does provide significant help to those individuals who have reached the required age and who do not have the means to maintain their own private hospitalization programs. In addition, certain insurance companies today provide hospitalization and medical coverages that supplement Medicare and provide longer spans of coverage.

Persons who do not qualify for monthly Social Security cash benefits may nevertheless qualify for Medicare coverage. They have to be age 65 or over and fall within the provisions of the law.

Qualifying for "Medicare"

The above represents an outline of private pension and profit-sharing plans and Social Security benefits available to retired or disabled persons and their survivors and beneficiaries. Additional questions should be referred to the administrators of a pension plan or to the local Social Security office. They are there to help; they are required to answer questions.

Future Social Security Changes

In 1983 Congress approved the Social Security Amendments of 1983. The amendments came from the bipartisan National Commission on Social Security. They were designed to ensure the solvency of the system over the next seventy-five years.

Most importantly, perhaps, the new law provides that, beginning in 1984, upper-income Social Security recipients could be taxed on parts of their benefits. Social Security taxes would be levied in addition to income taxes that retirees might pay on pensions or other income.

Computation of the new tax is not difficult. Retirees add up (1) their adjusted gross incomes, (2) any interest from tax-exempt obligations, and (3) one-half of all Social Security benefits. Depending on the total, the retiree will include in gross income the lesser of two sums: one-half the excess over a base amount or one-half the Social Security benefits received.

The base amount? The retiree would pay taxes as described if the total is more than $25,000 for a single person or $32,000 for a married couple filing jointly.

The new law introduced a number of other changes, including:

- It deferred the scheduled July 1983 cost-of-living (COL) adjustments in benefits to January 1, 1984. All future annual adjustments were to be made in January.
- Providing for "lean" years in which SS trust funds may be less than 15 per cent of the total needed for the year, the law provided for possible downward adjustments of COL increments in the years 1985 through 1988.
- It specified that over a period of years (ending in 2027) the normal retirement age would be increased to 67.
- It established a schedule of increases in employer and employee payroll taxes. Beginning in 1984, the tax was to rise from 6.7 per cent to 7 per cent.
- It also increased Social Security taxes for self-employed persons.
- It provided that federal employees hired after January 1, 1984, would come under the Social Security system. On the same date all employees of private, nonprofit organizations were "integrated" into the SS system.
- It prohibited state and local governments from withdrawing from the system and further reduced the benefits of workers who retire early.

10 "I DECLARE THIS TO BE MY LAST WILL AND TESTAMENT"

An elderly couple requested that a lawyer stop at their home to discuss the task of writing their wills. The gentleman was 85 years of age; his wife 83. They had raised 12 children, all of whom had children of their own.

The lawyer explained the processes involved in making a will and what the couple should be thinking about regarding their property. But the old gentleman had a puzzled expression on his face. When asked whether it

"How does this sound? Being of sound mind we are spending our money as fast as we can."

was his wish that all his property pass to his wife, the man said, "Yes, I leave everything to Mama, but if she marry again, she get *nothing!*"

Despite the fact that his wife had borne him 12 children and had been a good wife to him for many years, the old gentleman was worried about her marrying again. The case indicates the kinds of superstitions and fears that people entertain, even today, concerning the making of a will. The feeling occurs mostly among elderly people, but many younger persons do not appreciate the need for and importance of a will.

This chapter deals with the making of a will; what happens if you die without a will; what should be included in a will; and the process known as "estate planning" that is so much discussed today. This kind of planning seeks to ensure that your loved ones receive your property with a minimum of expense and taxes.

LAWS OF INTESTACY: DESCENT AND DISTRIBUTION

Every state has laws governing the ways in which property passes on the death of the owner who dies without a will. An "estate" is the sum total of all the property of a deceased individual. That property passes to the deceased's heirs at law, if he dies without a will, or to his beneficiaries under his will.

The laws of the various states differ regarding the transfer of property from a deceased person to his *heirs*, the persons who inherit from him under state law. If a man is survived by his wife and children, they become his primary heirs. However, in some states the wife does not inherit the entire estate of her husband if there are surviving children. Rather, she receives only a portion of the estate depending on the number of children. Or a wife may not inherit the entire estate if other relatives, such as brothers and sisters, parents, aunts and uncles, or cousins survive the deceased.

Wife may lose out No one can assume, in short, that if he dies without a will, leaving a wife and children or other relatives, the wife will inherit the entire estate. The will in fact has this advantage: it ensures that one's wishes are carried out regardless of the state law dealing with inheritance. A will may also substantially reduce tax liabilities in the handling of an estate.

Under the laws of some states, if a person dies without a will the person appointed by the court to handle the estate must post a bond to ensure faithful performance of his duties. But the person named in a will need not post a bond in some cases. Depending on the size of the estate, a bond may involve a substantial expense. That money goes to a bonding company and is thus lost to the heirs.

A will is essential to your peace of mind. It also provides your loved ones with proof of your concern for them and shows your intentions regarding the property passing to them.

WHAT IS A WILL AND HOW IS IT MADE?

A will is a written document in which the person making the will, called the "testator," specifies how and to whom his property will pass in the event of his death. It is commonly held that a will should be written, dated, and signed at the end. Some states require two or three witnesses to attest to the signing of the will by the testator. Other states do not require witnesses.

The will and disposition of property

For safety, witnesses should be present when any will is signed. A will may be made out in a state not requiring witnesses; then the testator may later die in a state which does require them. Without witnesses, the will would not be valid in the second state.

WHAT ARE THE ADVANTAGES OF A WILL?[1]

- You can choose the executor you wish to handle your estate.
- The expense of bond premiums, required of the person managing your estate, as well as some probate costs, can be avoided.
- You decide who gets your property instead of having the law decide for you. You may wish to provide a larger share for a young or sick child, leave something to charity, or give all your property to your spouse. You may take into consideration gifts that you have made.

- A trust may be created to keep your property intact for the benefit of your family.
- Minors can be cared for without the expense of guardianship proceedings.
- You may avoid the forced sale of your business.
- You can save estate and inheritance taxes. Only your will can place the burden on the right parties.
- Your will is the final document that completes your lifetime of planning for your family.

[1] Adapted from *Legal Facts about Wills* (Jefferson City: The Missouri Bar).

Kinds of Wills

The most common type of will is the *witnessed will.* Whether handwritten or typed, this will should be signed by the testator and witnessed by at least two, and if possible three, persons. The witnesses attest that the testator signed his own will on a specified date. Other types of wills include:

- The *holographic will* that is written out by the testator in his or her own handwriting. The holographic will may or may not be witnessed. In the former case, the will would normally be held to be valid. If the will has not been witnessed, as when a trapper in fear of death scribbles his "last will and testament" while alone, proving the will may be difficult.

- The *nuncupative will* involves an oral declaration by a testator in extreme circumstances of what he wants to do with his estate. The testator may be in grave danger; he makes his declaration in the presence of witnesses; and the will may or may not be written down later. A court may decide that such a will is valid because the testator could not put down his final wishes in any other way. But all courts examine nuncupative wills closely.
- A *joint will* is the kind made out by the husband and wife together. The joint will is rarely used today because it has proved relatively inflexible.
- The *mutual* or *reciprocal will* offers much greater flexibility. The husband and wife make out separate but complementary documents. Mutual wills make it possible for the couple to provide specifically for most family needs, including unusual ones.

Any will is effective only at death. It can be changed at any time during the life of the testator. No one has any rights under the will of a living person since the will is effective only on the death of the testator.

A will is effective at death

Once death takes place, probate, the process of putting the will, in particular the witnessed will, on record, begins. The will then controls the settlement of the deceased person's estate. The will becomes a public record when it is probated.

Because the laws require that the will be signed, dated, and witnessed, it is always dangerous to put together a "home-made" will. A violation of any of the legal requirements concerning wills will render it null and void.

Can you scratch a name out of a will and just leave it in that form? No. Scratching out a name may effect what is seen as a *material alteration*. The validity of the entire document may come into question. That means no erasures, no scratching out, no adding is permitted.

A caveat: beware of the so-called "form wills," and of those who claim that anyone can write his own will without the advice of counsel. Many lawsuits have arisen because people have attempted to write their own wills.

Information Needed to Prepare a Witnessed Will and Estate Plan

In order to draft a will properly, certain information should be made available to the family lawyer. A listing of all valuable papers, including birth certificates, deeds, mortgages, insurance policies, stocks and bonds, savings passbooks, and so on marks a beginning. This information or list is vital to the proper preparation of the will and should be kept with the will in a safe place. The information necessary is listed below in more specific form:

What information is needed?

1. Names, ages, and addresses of the testator and all relatives who might be beneficiaries under the will, including children, spouse, and others.

2. Details concerning the testator and his immediate family, with ages, financial status, and any personal facts that may bear on the estate plan. For example, where a child has a physical deformity, a larger distribution may be necessary for that child than for the others.

3. A complete list of all assets owned by the testator and spouse. The list should be complete and should include:

- Personal effects and household furnishings, with values; all real property and its value; all investments; names of corporations and denominations of stocks and bonds; bank accounts, both savings and checking; mortgages owned on other people's property; oil and gas properties owned; patents and copyrights owned; cash; and so on

- Property such as automobiles, work of art, libraries, coin or gun collections, and yachts
- All pension and profit-sharing plans to which the testator belongs, death benefits, any stock options that the testator may elect, and the Social Security benefits involved
- Life insurance payable at the time of the testator's death along with a listing of all policies by number and name of company, all annuities (monthly payment plans) and related policies
- A listing of all the testator's business interests, including any corporate, partnership, or sole proprietorship businesses, and all documents, stock certificates, profit and loss statements, and balance sheets connected with the business interests of the testator, for the purpose of determining the value of these interests
- Any interest in any estates or trusts created by others to which he is a beneficiary, and financial statements and back tax returns

This is a relatively exhaustive list. Putting it together serves a double purpose. First, the list shows all the assets that the will should cover. Second, drawing up the list necessitates a review of exactly what is owned and of the financial direction the testator is taking. The list should be complete and up to date.

Gathering documents for the family lawyer

All documents relating to property owned should be gathered for inspection by the family lawyer. The manner of ownership of property—by husband and wife, jointly with someone else, or otherwise—makes a big difference in planning an estate. The form of ownership of some properties may have to be changed.

To be complete, the list should include all debts and obligations of the testator, both personal and business. These would include mortgage obligations, long-term debts, short-term debts, charge accounts, and all currently payable items such as insurance premiums.

To assist the family lawyer, the listing should include the names and addresses of the testator's accountant, insurance agent or broker, bank trust officer, and stock broker. The lawyer can consult with these others as necessary in drawing up the total estate plan.

Goals of an estate plan

The testator should state his objectives clearly. What is the estate plan intended to do? If primary concerns are that the spouse and children remain secure, that children receive college educations, that funds be available to start them in business or buy them a home, and that their property be protected against the claims of creditors, the family lawyer should know that. He can then draft the will and estate plan with these objectives in mind.

Next some specific points should be considered:

1. *Specific instructions regarding funeral arrangements and burial.* These may be included in the will; but because the will is usually not read or probated until after the funeral arrangements have been completed, the instructions should usually be kept separate. A letter left with one's spouse and children specifying the testator's wishes regarding burial is usually a better method.

2. *Personal belongings.* Unless the testator makes specific reference to personal belongings, they will pass under the "residuary" clause of the will. This catchall section provides that anything left after specific bequests should go to the *residuary* beneficiary. An automobile, clothing, and any other specific personal property should be left to particular individuals. But if everything is left to the spouse, all personal belongings are covered. They should, however, be listed item by item.

3. *Cash gifts in the will.* A cash bequest can create problems. The executor—the person named in the will to handle the estate—may have to pay a specific amount of money despite the effect of that payment on the balance of the will. The executor may have to sell real property in order to obtain enough money to pay the specific cash bequests.

Bequests as percentages of the total estate

If an estate turns out to be smaller than anticipated, the cash bequests may exhaust the great bulk of the assets. Little or nothing may remain for distribution to other beneficiaries. Bequests can be made more appropriately in the form of parts or percentages of a total net estate rather than as specific dollar amounts. Thus the beneficiaries receive their percentages of whatever the total estate is when the testator dies.

4. *Real estate.* Various choices lie open to the testator in connection with real estate. He can leave it to his beneficiary outright, or direct that it be held in trust to provide income to a family member. He can have it sold, with the proceeds to go to the beneficiaries. The testator can give a *life estate*, the right of a beneficiary to live in the property or use it for life, with ownership automatically shifting to someone else after the death of the life tenant. Finally, disposition can be left to the discretion of the executor.

5. *The remainder of the estate.* Who receives the remainder of an estate after all individual bequests have been made? The testator makes that choice. But if more than one person is to receive the remaining portions, they should, again, be left shares (½ to X, ½ to Y).

6. *The guardian for minor children.* If assets are left to children under 18, on the testator's death a court has to appoint a guardian—usually a bank or trust company—for their persons and their property. As an alternative, the will can name a guardian for any minor children. The latter is often the preferred procedure.

Empowering the guardian

The terms of a will should give the guardian the power to use the property for the benefit of any minor children and to provide maintenance, support, and educational assistance.

Property left to minor children is their property. But because in the eyes of the law they are "under age," they cannot handle the property themselves. The guardian is needed to handle the property for them.

Another type of guardian should be named: the guardian of the person of each minor child. The guardian of the person takes physical charge of the children and raises them in the parent's absence. Serious consideration should be given to the appointment of someone who will raise the children, love them, and provide accommodations needed to keep them together in their younger years.

No guardians are required for adult beneficiaries. A testator who fears that an adult child will dissipate the assets received under a will can place that child's share in a special trust fund. The will in this case names a trustee to handle the property and provide for the beneficiary's maintenance, support, and education. The testator can specify the amounts to be distributed to him from time to time. The will can also include a special "spendthrift" provision that protects the trust assets from the claims of the child's creditors while the assets are being held for his benefit.

7. *The executor.* The executor, sometimes called an administrator or personal representative, is the person or firm named in the will to handle an estate to its conclusion. Depending on the state in which an estate is being settled, an executor can usually complete his work within a year of the date of death—or a year from the date on which the executor is appointed by the court. Some more complex estates, however, take years to settle.

An executor should have some understanding of financial matters. But he need not be an expert or a lawyer; nor does he have to be completely familiar with accounting or the handling of an estate. The more complicated the estate, however, the more important it is to select an executor who has experience in the handling of an estate. The best choice is, often, the trust department of a bank.

The executor and financial matters

Witnesses to the Will

As noted, witnesses should invariably be provided. If other conditions are met, a witnessed will is valid in all 50 states. Also, the presence of the witnesses becomes important if the "testamentary capacity" of the testator is questioned later—if anyone asks whether the testator had sufficient mental competence or other legal ability to make a will at the time it was made.

The attorney who draws up the will can appropriately act as a witness. He stands in an excellent position to know the testamentary capacity of the testator and the intent of the testator at the time he signs the will.

Importantly, three disinterested persons—three people who are not named as beneficiaries under the will—should serve as witnesses. In certain states, if a witness acts as a beneficiary under a will, he may lose his bequest to the extent that it exceeds the amount he would have received without a will. If, therefore, a will is signed and witnessed in a state which allows beneficiaries to be witnesses, but is later probated in a state which does not, problems can arise. It is much better to have disinterested persons, in all cases, as witnesses to the will.

Formalities for Signing a Will

The following is a list of protocols and formalities that should be observed in preparing and signing a will:

1. The will should first be written out.

2. The testator should sign it. If the testator cannot sign his name, he should place his "X" in the appropriate place. A witness should sign the testator's name and the words "his mark" over and below the "X". If the testator is physically incapable of even putting an "X" on the will, one

Protocols and formalities

of the witnesses should sign for him in his presence and at his request. The fact that a witness has signed should be noted in the clause immediately preceding the signature, sometimes called the "attestation" clause. This clause would state that the testator is unable to sign his name and that the witness signed for him.

3.   The signature of the testator or the person signing for him must follow the text of the will immediately, with nothing in between.

4.   The testator should expressly declare in the presence of the witnesses that he is signing his will. He should ask the witnesses to witness his signature.

5.   At least three witnesses should sign their names and addresses in the presence of the testator and of each other, stating that they saw the testator sign the will and that they are signing as witnesses at his request.

6.   The will should be dated by day, month, and year so that no question can arise as to when the will was signed.

Signing and "conforming" the will

7.   Only the original copy of the will should be signed by the testator and witnesses. If more than one copy is signed, the testator might later change his will but not destroy both copies of the earlier will. Also, all copies of the will should be "conformed" copies: the names of the testator and witnesses and their addresses should be typed or printed onto the copies so that the testator cannot at some future time sign a second copy.

8.   The original copy of the will should be kept in a safe place, such as a home safe or strongbox. Many testators keep the executed or original copy of the will in the office of their family lawyer so that it can be referred to at any time. It may also be appropriate to give the original copy of the will to the named executor for safekeeping.

Because bank and other institutional safety deposit boxes are usually locked when a testator dies, a will should never be kept in such a box. The will could effectively be out of reach. A representative of a state tax commission might have to be called to stand by while the box is opened by bank officers. The representative would make sure that nothing is removed but the will.

Now that we have discussed the formalities of a will and some of the factors that make the preparation of a will important to you, the planning of your total estate, as it relates to your will, will be discussed.

ESTATE PLANNING AND ESTATE TAXES

A twofold goal of estate planning

The concept of total estate planning has developed in relatively recent times. It attempts to bring together all the factors relating to a man's or woman's financial status, his or her desires regarding family members, and their security. Estate planning combines these considerations by taking into account all federal and state death, inheritance, estate, and income tax laws. The purpose of estate planning, therefore, is twofold:

- To establish a plan to meet specific objectives insofar as family needs are concerned, including as parts of the plan the will and other necessary legal documents
- To take full advantage of all available tax avoidance or tax savings provisions of the various tax laws

Proper estate planning gives the family an important protective tool.

The family will need income in the future. Liabilities will have to be settled. Income will have to be shifted from one person to another or others. An estate-planning survey may indicate that additional life insurance is needed to meet tax liabilities that may arise when the head of the family dies. Provision may have to be made for additional income over and above that immediately available. That means Social Security and other pension benefits may have to be augmented for the family's protection after the breadwinner's death.

SOME QUESTIONS TO ASK—AND ANSWER—ABOUT ESTATE PLANNING[1]

You want your assets and property to go to specific persons, or to fulfill specific purposes, after your death. You want to minimize the taxes that will be paid by your estate after you die. You want to leave enough assets that are readily convertible into cash to pay your death expenses and protect your family until your estate is settled. Why not consider these questions—and have them answered—NOW, while you can make plans for the disposition of your estate.

1. Is there any better way of holding my property to minimize my income taxes?

2. If I transfer some of my property to my spouse or children during my lifetime, will I be subject to gift taxes?

3. Are the beneficiaries properly designated in my life insurance policies?

4. Would my spouse be able to carry on my business in the event of my death?

5. In case of a partnership, do I have any arrangements for the survivor to buy my interests?

6. Does my estate have sufficient liquid assets to cover the costs of my death?

7. Have I adequately provided for the support and education of my children?

8. Would part of my estate pass to minor children and be subject to guardianship proceedings?

9. Do I have my estate arranged to minimize the death taxes?

[1] Adapted from *Estate Planning* (Des Moines: The Iowa State Bar Association, September 1978).

The complicated process of estate planning is usually approached in the following ways:

1. A complete inventory of all assets, current income, and any anticipated income is drawn up. Each asset should be listed with its cost, value, and projected future value. Insurance should be listed by its cash surrender value and face value. An "educated guess" should be made

regarding the value of your business interests. The planner should have all the information necessary to make an independent business survey, including balance sheets and profit and loss statements for the last three years.

2.   Cash, assets that can be readily converted to cash, and assets that are to be retained in their present form, such as real estate, should be specified. These should be analyzed to see whether noncash assets can readily be converted into cash or whether additional items should be listed.

3.   All debts and liabilities, including anticipated funeral and final medical expenses and the costs of handling the estate, are reviewed and deducted from the assets of the estate.

4.   After deducting all liabilities from total estate assets, the estate planner estimates the federal estate tax liability that will be charged to the estate under the value and ownership conditions that presently exist. The estate planner also projects the dollar amount needed for the federal estate tax and the state inheritance or death taxes to calculate how much cash will be needed to pay these taxes after death. The estate planner will also indicate how these taxes may be reduced through the use of the "marital deduction," available in the federal laws.

Deduction of expenses from assets
5.   The total expenses of the estate, including all taxes, costs of administration, and debts and liabilities, are deducted from the assets. If additional assets would be needed to meet various obligations, a forced sale of assets, usually at a loss, might be necessary to pay all the bills. Depending on the size of the estate, this comparison of assets and liabilities will usually reveal a need to make immediate cash available to meet postdeath expenses.

6.   After making this comparison, the estate planner will discuss the distribution of the estate. He will want to know about beneficiaries and what is to be provided for them. Knowing what will be available, the planner may suggest a reevaluation of either the assets or the method of disposition.

While a great part of estate planning has to do with saving taxes, that should never be the main concern. The main goal is to provide for family members and other survivors.

7.   A schedule is prepared to show the assets passing to each beneficiary and how much income is generated from those assets. The assets may be analyzed to ascertain whether they will be adequate to meet the living requirements of the beneficiaries.

8.   The estate planner will explain how to reduce federal estate and other death tax liabilities through the use of lifetime gifts, provision of additional insurance or additional investments, and other means of

increasing the net asset value of the estate. He may show how rearrangement of some assets may increase the value of assets passing to the beneficiaries and decrease taxes.

A key device in estate planning, lifetime giving offers a way to make gifts of assets to family members before death—to reduce the size of the estate, to provide for college educations, or for other purposes. Starting in 1982, the annual gift tax exclusion was increased from $3,000 to $10,000 per donee, with an unlimited exclusion for tuition and medical expenses. Gift taxes could also be paid on an annual rather than a quarterly basis. A husband could make the same gifts to his wife without incurring gift tax liability.

Under the 1981 tax-cut law, both spouses could make the same gifts to children or other family members, doubling the basic figures. The annual exclusion of gifts for any one person could then total $20,000.

The spouse's gift exclusion

The federal gift tax rates and the federal estate tax rates remain identical under the provisions of the 1981 law. But the top estate and gift tax rate was reduced from 70 percent to 65 percent as of 1982, to 60 percent in 1983, to 55 percent in 1984, and to 50 percent—the projected maximum—in 1985. Starting in 1985 the top rate would apply to gifts and estates of more than $2.5 million. Three cases illustrate the use of estate planning devices. In each case, the husband is assumed to be the person whose estate is being planned. He wants to provide for his wife and three children, all under the age of 18.

Estate Plan No. 1: $60,000 in Joint Assets

In this plan, the husband and wife have joint assets of $60,000. Because of the limited size of the estate, there is no federal estate tax liability at all. Under the 1981 Economic Recovery Tax Act, the total amounts of estate and gift transfers that would be exempt from estate and gift taxes would be $225,000 in 1982 (from the 1981 level of $175,625); $275,000 in 1983; $325,000 in 1984; $400,000 in 1985; $500,000 in 1986, and $600,000 in 1987.

The federal estate tax exemption

The plan for this individual includes a will providing that everything passes to his wife if she survives him for a specified period, usually 30 or 60 days. Should she fail to survive him for that period, everything passes in equal shares to his children. The reason for the 30- or 60-day survivorship requirement is to avoid a double tax if state law provides that the wife would take ownership under the husband's will if she survives him by even one moment. In this case, without a survivorship clause, state death taxes might have to be paid on both deaths. The survivorship clause eliminates that possibility by requiring the spouse to survive for the specified period of time; if he or she does not, the assets skip the estate of the spouse and go directly to the children. Only one death tax is imposed.

In Estate Plan No. 1, a witnessed will would be used to leave everything to the wife and, if she fails to survive, to the children equally. A guardian of the person must be named for the children. A guardian of the property should be named in case both parents die.

Estate Plan No. 2: Assets of $250,000

The "marital deduction" provisions

In this estate, the assets are considerably larger than those described in Plan No. 1. But basically the same strictures apply. Because of the changed "marital deduction" provisions of the federal estate tax laws, the estate would not be subject to any federal estate tax at all. The 1981 tax act simply repealed all limits on tax-free estate or gift transfers between spouses.

The plan for the individual here includes a will that leaves everything to the wife and, when she dies, to the children equally, with the same guardianship provisions mentioned in Plan No. 1. A trust may also be used for the benefit of the wife and children, or just for the children if both parents die.

In this testamentary trust, legal title to the estate assets passes to a trustee named in the will for the benefit of the spouse or children of the deceased. Unlike a guardianship, which ends when a child reaches the age of 18 or 21, depending on state law, a trust can continue beyond the age of 18 or 21 and even over the lifetime of the beneficiary if desired. The trustee generally has power to invest, sell, and handle the assets in the trust fund. He distributes the income to the beneficiaries at fixed intervals or at the trustee's discretion.

Distribution of principal

The trust provisions may also allow the trustee to distribute the principal of the fund to the beneficiaries at intervals or on termination of the trust. The trust has flexibility in other ways. For example, spendthrift protection can be built into the terms to keep the trust assets out of creditors' hands.

Under Plan No. 2, the testator may direct that the property pass to the wife. If she should fail to survive him, the assets go to a trustee for the benefit of the children. The property may be placed in trust for the wife's lifetime. On her death, the assets pass to the children.

The tax consequences of Plans 1 and 2 are basically the same. If the will in Plan 2 leaves everything outright to the wife and then in trust to the children, the property, beginning in 1983, would not be taxable at her death. If she has only a pure life estate in trust with no power to obtain any of the principal, but receives only what the trustee at his discretion may give her, and if, at her death, the trust assets are held for the benefit of the children, there would be no estate taxes to be paid at her death.

THOSE IMPORTANT PAPERS...
WHERE TO KEEP WHAT

Where do you keep important papers? The following checklist gives a basic breakdown of types of papers, including wills, and where they should normally be kept. Circumstances can, of course, dictate variations.

SAFE DEPOSIT BOX

1. Birth certificates
2. Citizenship papers
3. Marriage certificates
4. Adoption papers
5. Divorce decrees
6. Death certificates
7. Deeds
8. Automobile titles
9. Household inventory
10. Veteran's papers
11. Bonds and stock certificates
12. Important contracts

ACTIVE FILE

1. Tax receipts
2. Unpaid bills
3. Paid bill receipts
4. Current bank statements
5. Current canceled checks
6. Income tax working papers
7. Employment record

8. Health and life insurance information and policies
9. Credit card information
10. Copies of wills
11. Health records
12. Appliance manuals and warranties
13. Receipts of items under warranty
14. Education information
15. Inventory of safe deposit box (and key)
16. Loan statements
17. Loan payment books
18. Receipts of expensive items not yet paid for

LAWYER'S OR EXECUTOR'S SAFE

Wills

DEAD FILE

All active file papers over 3 years old

WHAT TO DISCARD

1. Salary statements (after checking on W-2 forms)
2. Canceled checks for cash or nondeductible expenses
3. Expired warranties.
4. Coupons after expiration date
5. Other records no longer needed

A trust problem

The problem with using a trust for the wife's life is that, to avoid a tax at her death, she may, depending on the type of trust, lose the right to control what she receives from the trustee. This may be too harsh and restrictive. It may prevent the wife from receiving what she needs to maintain her standard of living. Again: tax considerations have never been, and should not be, the sole concern if the family does not have the freedom that the testator desires. The trust instrument should at least give the wife the latitude to obtain part or all of the principal during her lifetime.

Estate Plan No. 3: Assets of $1.5 Million

The federal estate tax resembles the federal income tax in one way: it is not a fixed percentage tax but a graduated tax. Many state death or inheritance taxes, by contrast, are based upon a percentage of the net taxable estate. For example, if a state imposes a death tax of 6 per cent of the net taxable estate, the tax is determined by multiplying .06 times the net estate. No matter how big the net estate is, the tax rate remains the same. Under federal estate tax laws, the larger the estate, the higher the tax—up to 50 percent in 1985.

Defining taxable property

The federal tax also differs from state taxes as regards the definition of taxable property or assets. Some states do not tax such things as the jointly held property of husband and wife that passes to one spouse on the death of the other, life insurance proceeds owned by the deceased, or the share of the surviving person in jointly held property not owned by husband and wife. The federal estate tax, however, includes all this property in determining the taxable estate for federal estate tax purposes. In short, any property over which the deceased had ownership, control, or any indication of ownership is included in the federal estate tax evaluation.

Because the federal estate tax is so all-inclusive, it may include much more property than is subject to probate under the will. Most states provide that jointly held property passes automatically on death to the surviving spouse. Life insurance proceeds are payable directly to the named beneficiary without going through the probate proceedings. It may, therefore, be misleading when newspapers report that Mr. Gotrocks died leaving an estate valued in the probate proceedings at $400,000. The estate was probably much greater than that, since life insurance, joint property, and other assets under Mr. Gotrocks' control would not be reported in the state proceedings.

The "adjusted gross estate"

While the estate tax includes all those assets that are not included in state probate proceedings, it does allow for exemptions and deductions that reduce the tax considerably. Beginning with the "gross value" of your estate, it permits deductions of certain debts and expenses to arrive at the "adjusted gross estate." These include the costs of settling the estate, debts and taxes owned by the decedent at death, and funeral expenses and casualty losses suffered by the estate during administration. Also, in theory, all of the estate can—effective in 1982—be transferred, untaxed, to one's spouse or to his or her control.

Plan No. 3. In Plan No. 3 the total estate of husband and wife totals $1.5 million. The wife has no property of her own purchased solely from her own funds. Assume that $50,000 of debts and expenses are allowable. The adjusted gross estate becomes $1,450,000.

If the husband in his will leaves his entire estate to his wife, he may, according to experts, be walking into a trap. The trap works this way: Assume that the year is 1987. The husband who, in taking care of his wife's future needs, leaves his entire $1,450,000 estate to his wife may in effect be leaving his children $249,000 less than if he did two things:

- Left his wife $950,000 under his will, and
- Took advantage of the full $600,000 exclusion that will be in effect in 1987 to put the rest of the estate into a marital trust.

In so doing, the husband would be avoiding all federal taxes.

If the husband fails to make a will, the estate passes under the laws of intestacy. The wife will not receive the full $1,450,000. Depending on the laws of her state of residence, she may receive only a share of the estate. The estate will have lost the advantage of the marital deduction.

When the Wife Dies. What happens when the wife dies? What effect does her death have on the estate tax? If the wife dies shortly after the husband, her estate will include all the assets she received because of the husband's death less the taxes that were paid.

The husband in planning his estate must take into account the effect on his children if the wife should die retaining substantially the same assets that he leaves her. The sensible estate plan takes into account the effects of both deaths and the possibility of reducing the total federal estate taxes to be paid. All beneficiaries can be provided for at the same time. Two basic approaches involve the *testamentary* and the *inter vivos* or *living trust*.

Two Trusts. Trusts can take many specific forms depending on their terms. But all are either testamentary or living trusts. The former, as noted, is established in a will. The living trust is usually set up in a separate document made during the lifetime of the husband. The testamentary trust goes into effect when the testator dies. The living trust can become effective at once.

Testamentary and living trusts

Either basic kind of trust can utilize the marital deduction privilege. Whether the marital deduction is established by will or by a separate agreement, the method of distributing the property would have the following format:

- The husband directs in his will or in the inter vivos agreement that his estate or the insurance proceeds be divided into two parts, the part that qualifies for the marital deduction and the balance or residue.
- The husband then directs that the first part (Fund A) be placed in trust on his death for the benefit of his wife. The income from the property in the trust fund would be paid to the wife for life. She would have the absolute right to reach the principal of this part as well. She has the right to direct in her will how and to whom Fund A should be distributed at her death. But on the possibility that she may fail to exercise the right to direct to whom it should go at her death, the husband

may direct that the property in Fund A will pass to the second trust, Fund B, on the death of his wife or later.

- The husband directs that the second part of his estate, Fund B, be established as a second trust or separate fund. The income from this second trust is likewise to be paid to the wife for life. But the Fund B property is to be distributed to the children on his wife's death or some other date. The wife has no absolute right to take any part of the principal of that part of the estate.

Fund B not taxable on wife's death

Fund B thus remains outside the wife's estate on her death. She has no absolute right to any part of it. The balance remaining in the first trust, Fund A, is taxable to the wife on her death since she has the right to withdraw all or any part of it during her lifetime and can also specify in her will to whom the balance of that trust fund should pass.

Net Effect. The net effect of this plan is to divide the estate into two different parts. One part, if substantial enough, is taxed at the wife's death, the other part at the husband's death. The portion that is taxable at the death of the wife, Fund A, is the marital deduction portion of the estate. This portion is entitled to the deduction, without tax, from the husband's estate and is taxed at the death of the wife. Fund B, in which the wife has no absolute right, is taxable at the husband's death and passes tax free to the children after the death of the wife.

The more varied the types of property owned, the more involved will be the estate plan chosen. Competent counsel can play an important role in the planning of an estate. So, in many cases, can an insurance advisor, accountant, broker, and bank trust officer.

Federal Income Tax

The estate planning process should include consideration of federal income taxes as they affect the administration of the estate. Because of the complexities of the income tax laws, tax advice is usually needed to handle the tax problems that the family will face after a testator dies. If the estate is sizeable, the executor will probably be required to file income tax returns on the estate, and will be faced with many of the same problems that the testator faces in the filing of his own income tax returns. A very brief summary of some of these considerations follows:

Ordinary income and capital gains: differences

Ordinary Income and Capital Gains. Most persons are affected most directly by the two different types or categories of income, ordinary income and capital gains. Ordinary income includes such items as salary, dividends, interest, bonuses, commissions, and so on. Ordinary income is taxed on a progressive scale. Capital gains, on the other hand, receive preferential treatment.

With certain exceptions, everything one owns is a capital asset. Stock in trade for sale to customers, accounts receivable, and many other categories are included. If a capital asset is held for six months or less, its sale or exchange may result in a capital gain or loss.

Generally, any short-term (six months or less) capital gain is treated as ordinary income. Any short-term loss must first be used to offset short-term gains and then to offset long-term (more than six months) gains.

Executors' and Administrators' Tax Duties. Executors and administrators may have a number of tax-related duties. One of them is to pay any income taxes that are unpaid when the estate owner dies. Estate tax returns must be filed with both federal and state tax authorities. Heirs may have to be informed of the basis for computing capital gains on inherited property.

Procedure for computing value

The Tax Reform Act of 1976 changed the regulations governing computation of the tax basis for all inherited assets. Before the Act, the value of any asset was its value on the date of the owner's death. Afterward, the tax basis for the heirs on all assets acquired by the deceased before December 31, 1976, became the value as computed on that date. Marketable stocks and bonds were excepted because their market value fluctuated and could be determined at any time. Computation of the value of all other assets followed an established procedure:

- It was assumed that the *rate of appreciation* remained constant from the date on which the deceased acquired the asset and the date of his death.
- The proportion of gain in value or growth would be a determinable fraction of the overall growth.
- This fraction would be: the number of years and days between the purchase and December 31, 1976, divided by the number of years and days between the purchase and deceased's death.

Other regulations further complicated the problem facing executors and administrators trying to establish asset values for tax purposes. By 1980 the U.S. Congress was considering means of simplifying these laws, which placed heavy burdens on many trustees as well as executors and administrators. An executor might have hundreds of valuable items—from boats to paintings to stamp collections—on which, in effect, individual histories might have to be compiled.

In a relatively simple instance, an executor might have to inform an heir of the value of an oil painting purchased in 1966. The cost to the deceased at that time was $60,000. The deceased owned the painting for 10 years on December 31, 1976. The fraction by which the painting has appreciated in value is estimated at $20,000. The value of the painting would then be calculated at $80,000, the original purchase price plus

$20,000. The trustee, executor, or administrator would use that overall figure in computing capital gains of the estate.

The Economic Recovery Tax Act of 1981 introduced basic changes in the personal and business income tax rates. The trustee or executor would also have to take those new rates into consideration. The personal income tax reductions were to total 5 percent starting October 1, 1981, 10 percent additional on July 1, 1982, and a final 10 percent on July 1, 1983.

An estate is a taxpayer

Other Taxable Income. Executors, trustees, and administrators have to pay estate income taxes because an estate is considered a taxpayer. Thus taxes have to be paid on income from interest-yielding bonds, savings accounts, and other investments. Municipal bonds and similar securities that are tax free are usually excluded but may be taxable under state or local income tax laws.

The sale of a corporate bond may require payment of income taxes. The amount of appreciation will be taxed, for example, if the bond was held more than six months. The Internal Revenue Code contains a formula for determining the taxable gain or loss from the sale of a corporate bond where the issue price of the bond is different from its redemption value. Competent tax advice may be required where this situation obtains.

Income from securities issued by the U.S. government, such as Series E and Series H bonds, is taxable. But these securities have advantages because the owner can choose to take the interest income in a year in which he has a reduced income or losses that put him in a lower tax bracket. No one needs to pay taxes on the accrued interest on these bonds until they are redeemed or the interest actually received. One can also exchange Series E bonds for Series H bonds which pay cash interest on a regular basis.

What isn't taxable income?

Certain types of income are not includable in the definition of "income" under the tax laws. Social Security and veterans' benefits are not taxable. A relief provision applies to stock dividends, excluding the first $100 of corporate dividend income. If a joint return of husband and wife is filed and the stock is owned in both names, a stock dividend exclusion of up to $200 can be claimed.

Many of these provisions apply whether assets are held by the estate of a deceased person or by a living person. Extensive regulations involve the federal income tax laws as applied to estates and the filing of the "fiduciary" income tax returns by the executor.

THE ADMINISTRATION OF AN ESTATE

What happens when someone dies? What are the duties of the executor? How long does it take to settle the estate of a deceased person? What steps are taken to settle the estate?

Many persons recall that when "Uncle Joe" died, it only took the attorney six months to close the estate. When "Aunt Emma" died, it took over two years.

Obviously, the time involved in settling an estate depends on many factors:

- The size of the estate
- The identification of the beneficiaries if they are hard to find and if tracers are needed
- The presence of trust provisions that would require the services of a trustee
- The sale of assets to preserve the value of the estate (the timing of the sale is very important)
- Claims against the estate
- The filing of tax returns and payment of taxes. No two estates are alike, and the time spent in settling one estate has nothing to do with the time spent in settling another.

Some of the duties of the executor and family lawyer, who works closely with the executor, are as follows:

Some duties of executor and lawyer

- To notify all the savings institutions where the decedent may have had accounts and obtain the necessary account numbers and balances as of the date of death

- To arrange for the custody of the decedent's personal property
- To maintain and see that all the decedent's property is covered by insurance, and change the "insured" in the policies to the "estate" of the deceased person
- To estimate the size of the estate to determine whether the estate has to go through formal probate and administration proceedings or whether the estate can be settled under the "small estate" (usually under $5,000) provisions that apply in many states to short-cut the more involved, full administration
- To obtain additional copies of the will for distribution to the beneficiaries and arrange a meeting with all of the beneficiaries as soon as practical and proper after the funeral of the testator
- To advise the beneficiaries of their interest and assure them of his intent to keep them advised
- To inventory the contents of any safe deposit boxes held by the decedent, usually in the presence of state taxing authorities who may be required by law to be present
- To find out whether any beneficiary wants to take any asset "in kind," that is, in its present form, rather than have it sold and the proceeds distributed
- To have the beneficiary sign an "election to take the property in kind" as soon as possible, providing a choice in the event that the property—corporate stocks, for example—drops in value before it is sold

An executor needs information The executor has also to find out whether any beneficiaries want to renounce any gifts or object to any provisions of the will. He must, with the help of the family lawyer, prepare the petition to probate the will and file it in court, and make copies available to all parties. Copies of the death certificate have to be obtained; beneficiaries may need help in the collection of life insurance proceeds, including provision of any necessary forms from the insurance companies. The executor will need information on salaries, wages, or commissions owed to the deceased, and will inquire about the pension or profit-sharing plans of the company employing the deceased and the amounts due the estate, if any. Other duties:

- To decide on continuing the operations of any businesses of the deceased and to arrange for collection of loans, rents, dividends, or other obligations owed to the decedent
- To follow local requirements concerning advertising the estate and asking all debtors to pay claims and all creditors to present their claims
- To collect and keep all information needed for tax returns, file for Social Security and veterans' benefits, and assemble all data

on joint property, life insurance, trusts, and other assets for tax purposes

- To file any "fiduciary" bonds that may be required of him under local laws
- To obtain certified copies of his appointment for presentation to those requiring evidence of his authority to act for the estate

---

**"DEAR ANN LANDERS" LETTER
TELLS THE NO-WILL STORY[1]**

A letter to columnist Ann Landers tells the poignant story of "Thorns among the widow's weeds," a wife whose husband died leaving no will. The letter, and Ann's answer:

Dear Ann Landers:

Why would a bright, loving man who showed every consideration for his wife and children during his lifetime die without leaving them protected by a will?

It's too late for your answer to help us, but please, Ann, print this letter because both my attorney and funeral director have told me that an unbelievable number of men, responsible and competent in fiscal matters, behave as if they are going to live forever. They make no preparation whatever for the eventuality of death.

I am now faced with a financial mess beyond belief. Attorney fees and inheritance taxes are horrendous. I am also having heartbreaking problems with my husband's brother over some property—the ownership of which is unclear.

I know my husband loved me and the children with all his heart. Why didn't he take care of us properly?

Thorns among the widow's weeds

Dear Thorns:

Why? Because, like so many others, he hated to think about death—as if by ignoring it, it would ignore him.

I hope every man who reads this column will ask himself, "If I died tonight would my family be protected financially?" If the answer is yes, you deserve to sleep like a baby. If not, get busy and put your affairs in order. You owe it to those you love.

Ann Landers

[1] From *Your Will* (Lansing: State Bar of Michigan). Letters from Ann Landers' column in the *Detroit Free Press* reprinted by permission of Ann Landers and Field Newspaper Syndicate.

An important duty of the executor is to keep the beneficiaries advised of progress in settling the estate. More misunderstandings result from lack of communication in this area than from any other cause.

After his appointment, the executor must prepare an accurate inventory of all estate assets and then make certain that the property passes to the beneficiaries named in the will. He should secure receipts from each beneficiary showing that they have in fact received the property or the cash directed to them. Eventually, the executor has to account properly to a court, to the creditors, and to the beneficiaries of the estate for all payments, receipts, disbursements, and distributions made by him in settling the estate, including payment of taxes.

Working with your family lawyer

The executor should work closely with the family lawyer in handling an estate. The law of the particular state may require that the executor perform many functions; he should know what these obligations are. In practice, the lawyer prepares most of the papers for the executor and guides him in this process.

Where a testamentary trustee is named in a will, his duties begin where the executor's duties end. Most of the trustee's duties are specified in the will. State law gives the trustee certain powers and duties as well. But basically, a properly drawn will notes these powers and duties specifically.

Once the estate is closed and a final distribution of assets is made to the beneficiaries, the executor transfers the assets to be held in trust to the trustee and takes back a receipt. The trustee then takes over the administration of the trust property. In the ordinary case he is required to invest for income, pay taxes and expenses of the trust fund, exercise all obligations as set forth in the will or trust agreement, and exercise his discretion for the benefit of the trust assets and the beneficiaries.

The trustee also has to render accounts to the beneficiaries periodically. At the conclusion of the trust, he distributes the trust property to the beneficiaries. He must keep the trust property separate from his own, and pays any income from the trust assets to the beneficiaries as required by the will, trust agreement, or the law. A corporate trustee, such as the trust department of a bank, has the same rights and obligations as an individual trustee.

Compensation with court approval

Both the executor and trustee are entitled to compensation or commissions for handling estates and trust assets. The amount of compensation depends on the time spent and the work performed, and is subject to the approval of the court that has jurisdiction over the administration of estates and trusts.

Estate Tax Returns

As indicated, both the estate and the trust have to pay taxes. In some cases, the executor and trustee can be personally liable for taxes unpaid or improperly paid.

The returns that have to be filed may include:

Federal Estate Tax Return. The federal tax return must be filed within nine months from the date of death of a decedent who is a U.S. citizen and who leaves an estate in any given year whose gross worth exceeds the figures noted earlier. As indicated, the total amount of estate and gift transfers that would be exempt from estate and gift taxes in 1987 would be $600,000. Starting in 1985, the maximum estate and gift tax rate would be 50 percent, not the 70 percent of 1981.

Since federal estate taxes are levied on the *gross estate*, the executor or administrator has to account for all the assets and property owned by a decedent at the time of death—less, of course, debts and other obligations. The gross estate includes three main types of gifts:

Three types of gifts

- All gifts made outright after January 1, 1977

- Gifts over whose income the decedent has retained control for life, or those for which the decedent reserved the right to name the ultimate donee

- Gifts that remained revocable or amendable by the donor during his lifetime

Not included in the gross estate after 1981 are tax-free gifts of up to $10,000 a year per donee—or $20,000 if given jointly by husband and wife. Such gifts may have been made to anyone. They remain outside the gross estate under the 1981 Act.

Federal Income Tax Return. If the estate or trust during the period of administration has income in excess of $600, a federal income tax return must be filed. A taxable year for the estate or trust must be chosen and income reported accordingly. The year need not be a calendar year. The return must be filed by the fifteenth day of the fourth month following the end of the tax year. The choice of the proper fiscal year is very important and may have serious tax consequences. The federal law contains regulations concerning the proper taxable year.

Since the income tax return may show amounts that are distributable to beneficiaries, the executor or trustee should report these amounts to the beneficiaries for inclusion in their own personal income tax returns. The executor or administrator has also to report to the Internal Revenue Service all income distributed to the beneficiaries during the taxable year.

Reporting to the beneficiaries

Final Federal Income Tax Return. The executor must also file the final federal income tax return of the decedent along with any returns that the decedent had not filed in prior years. It may be difficult to reconstruct the affairs of the decedent for the year of death or for prior years, but the duty nonetheless falls on the executor. If the decedent was married at the time of his death, a joint return may be filed as his final return unless the surviving spouse remarries before the close of the tax year or if some other exception applies.

The executor or trustee has the task of making sure that all taxes are paid before he makes any distribution of the assets of the estate or trust to the beneficiaries. If he fails to do so, he can be held personally liable for those taxes, plus penalty and interest. The only exceptions would be payments of allowances to the widow or widower, the funeral expenses, and some others that the law allows the executor to pay out before payment of federal taxes due.

An executor normally takes a "clearance" from the Internal Revenue Service before making final distribution to the beneficiaries. He also requests a prompt audit of the returns filed on behalf of the estate and previous years' returns filed by the decedent to ensure that no later audit will result in a claim for additional taxes after the estate is closed.

Tax Planning by Executor and Beneficiaries

Certain steps can be taken by the executor and beneficiaries to reduce the tax impact on the estate and the beneficiaries. For example, as indicated, the correct choice of a taxable year for the estate may have a significant impact on the total tax liability. In addition, decisions regarding the timing of distributions of income from the estate to the beneficiaries may be vital. Income payable to beneficiaries and distributable to them is taxable to them personally. The individual tax status of the beneficiaries must therefore be considered by them and by the executor in deciding when to make distributions.

Tax avoidance, not evasion

A TEN-POINT CHECKLIST OF THE DUTIES NORMALLY PERFORMED BY AN EXECUTOR[1]

- Notify heirs and creditors of the probate proceedings.

- Take possession of, inventory, and preserve the probate assets of the decedent.

- Collect all income, such as rents, interest, and dividends, and make demand for and collect all debts, claims, and notes due the decedent.

- Determine the names, ages, residences, and degrees of relationship of all heirs at law and next of kin of the decedent.

- Complete any pending lawsuits in which the decedent has an interest and represent the estate of the decedent in any will contests.

- Determine, prepare returns for, and pay all state and federal inheritance, estate, and income taxes.

- Pay the valid claims of creditors of the decedent and, when necessary, sell property to raise funds to pay such claims as well as taxes and expenses of administration.

- Transfer decedent's title to real property to his or her beneficiaries through a decree of distribution (no deed or other formal document of transfer is required).

- Transfer decedent's title to certain personal property, such as stocks and bonds, to his or her beneficiaries.

- Distribute the remaining assets to the proper persons.

[1] Adapted from *Why Probate?* (Portland: Oregon State Bar).

The basic assets of the estate are not "income." No income tax is payable on those assets by the beneficiaries or by the estate. Only the income earned from these assets is taxable under the income tax laws.

The federal estate tax law contains provisions for an alternate valuation date. Under this provision the executor can select a date different from the date of death (six months later) for determination of the value of assets in the estate. The choice of a different valuation date is the most important means of saving on estate taxes, especially if the assets are mainly stocks, bonds, or other assets whose value is subject to shifts in value.

If the assets are worth less on the alternate valuation date than they were on the date of death, the executor will choose that date for determination of value. He thus reduces the tax liability. If the assets gain in value, he will use the date-of-death value.

Another method of tax planning to save on estate and income taxes has to do with the handling of deductions. The executor has a choice of deciding whether certain deductions should be taken against the gross estate value to reduce the federal estate tax or of taking the deductions against the estate's federal income tax liability. A correct choice may save considerable money for the estate or the beneficiaries.

Some allowable deductions The deductions that may be allowed from the gross estate include the following:

- Burial expenses
- Claims against the estate, including legitimate debts
- Unpaid mortgage balances on properties owned by the decedent
- The expenses of administration of the estate, which may include commissions
- Losses resulting from casualty or theft
- Charitable bequests within the limits imposed by federal and state laws

Special rules also deal with any income earned by the decedent prior to his death, referred to as "income in respect to a decedent." Such income should be included in the estate tax return and deducted by the beneficiaries on their income tax returns.

Obviously, a testator has to use care in selecting an executor. The executor may have to work closely with the family lawyer to ensure that the beneficiaries receive the highest amount possible from an estate. Tax evasion is a crime; but tax avoidance is perfectly legal and proper.

Dozens of articles, books, and pamphlets tell the world how easy it is to write one's own will, how estate plans can be handled without help, and so on. However, the people who try to act as their own lawyers, accountants, and insurance advisors only create additional needs for professional help once they get in trouble. The legal profession has a cliché that expresses the truth neatly: "The lawyer who handles his own case has a fool for a client."

11 "THE ONLY THINGS CERTAIN ARE DEATH AND TAXES"

From the point of view of the law, death is related in at least one way to coming of age, marriage, divorce, and retirement: it represents a change in status for the individual. Where Chapter 10 discussed ways of using "preventive law" to prepare for death, this chapter discusses other ways.

Death often involves severe stress for family members. Making burial arrangements ahead of time can eliminate one source of stress. Also, decisions made calmly frequently emerge as wiser decisions that bring fewer legal complications.

Death has many legal aspects. Advances in medical science have resulted in the prolongation of life. The problem is that in many cases it has become difficult to determine when death has occurred. Once death has occurred, the legal questions become paramount.

WHAT IS DEATH?

Death has been defined variously. Most commonly, it has been held to be the moment and state when:

- there is loss of spontaneous respiration and of respiratory effort;

- that loss becomes irreversible; and

- the loss occurs during a coma judged to be irreversible.

There are important reasons for developing comprehensive and workable policies to help in determining the moment of death. Four such reasons are:

- Prolonging "life" through medical devices beyond the point of real or actual death can result in needlessly high medical bills for the patient's family.

- Terminating medical attention before the "point of no return" may result in needless and grievous loss of a loved one.

- In cases where the dying patient had made a commitment to donate an organ for transplantation, his survival is more important than the welfare of a potential organ recipient.

- On the other hand, where the donor is truly dead, the donee's welfare is vital.

221

A Legal Definition

Death: a definition

For centuries human societies have accepted the common-sense definition of death as the cessation of breathing, heartbeat, and brain functioning. For most purposes, this definition was all that was necessary. With advances in medical science, especially in the use of organ transplants, people began to take a closer look at the moment of death. Some people who were incurably ill insisted that they had the right to take their own lives.

These trends have exerted pressure on state legislatures in the United States to draft new death statutes. Kansas, for example, adopted a new definition of death in 1971, and Maryland followed suit in 1972. The Kansas statute states that a person is medically and legally dead when, in the opinion of a physician and based on ordinary standards of medical practice, either of the following conditions is met:

- There is an absence of spontaneous respiration and heartbeat because of disease or, because of the passage of time since they stopped, attempts to resuscitate are considered hopeless.
- There is an absence of spontaneous brain function, and despite attempts to maintain circulation and breathing, it appears that further attempts will not restore the brain.

Under the Kansas law, death is to be pronounced before artificial breathing and circulation functions are terminated. Such pronouncement must be made before any vital organ can be removed for transplanting.

The Maryland law differs little in basic respects from the Kansas law. Both laws have been criticized for making it too easy for a surgeon to take an organ for transplant from a person who is still alive.

Medical Definitions

Ambiguity in the legal definition of death

The legal definition of death suffers clearly from some ambiguity. This comes into sharper focus when medical viewpoints are considered. One has to speak here of "viewpoints" because no single medical definition of death applies universally.

One medical definition holds that *total human death* is characterized by the death of every cell in the body. In this irreversible state, there is in each cell a total absence of chemical, physical, or electrical activity. But, admittedly, not all cells need to be dead before a person may be said to be essentially dead: the nails and hair may continue to grow after death.

Another definition seeks to describe *essential death*. Here, both the heart and the breathing system have stopped functioning. But, again, qualifications may be noted. In a state of essential death, people can still be resuscitated, especially where the organism has suffered no brain damage. The brain may appear to show no life; but this can occur when the body temperature drops or when some nervous system poison enters the body.

In the absence of low body temperature or poisoning, it is possible to consider *irreversible death*, which occurs at some point between essential death and total death. Here, the progress toward death is irreversible; so are final coma and loss of breathing.

Even irreversible death raises some ambiguities: the basis of an illness, along with its diagnosis and prognosis, may come into doubt. People pronounced dead have spontaneously "come back from the dead." Where breathing has stopped, death is usually considered irreversible only under these conditions:

"Coming back from the dead"

- A comatose patient cannot make an effort to breathe without mechanical assistance. In one test, a breathing apparatus may be removed for a specified period, perhaps two minutes.

GUIDELINES FOR PRONOUNCING DEATH[1]

In 1968, the major medical associations of the world convening at the twenty-second World Medical Assembly in Sydney, Australia, established the following guidelines for pronouncing a person dead:

- Total lack of response to external stimuli, even the most painful permissible

- Absence of all spontaneous muscular movements, notably breathing; a respirator can be turned off for three minutes to determine whether spontaneous breathing takes place

- Absence of reflexes; dilated pupils should not contract when a bright light is shown directly into them; the eyes must not move when ice water is poured into the ears; biceps, triceps, or quadriceps do not contract

- Flat electroencephalogram (EEG) or absence of brain waves

Other guidelines have been developed by committees at the Harvard Medical School and the Duquesne University Law School. These guidelines resemble those described above; but they also differ in some respects. This underlines the fact that no agreement exists on the exact moment when death takes place.

[1] Adapted from *The Right to Die* by Milton D. Heifetz, M.D. with Charles Mangel, copyright © 1975 by Milton D. Heifetz, M.D., and Charles Mangel. Reprinted by permission of the Putnam Publishing Group.

- There is no question of simple nerve damage or loss of control of the muscles used in breathing, as in polio.

- The possibility does not arise that the portion of the brain controlling breathing has irrevocably ceased to function.

The concept of irreversible death comes closest to serving both the medical and the legal requirements. It is important to know where each state stands, whether the irreversibility concept is used, and how that concept

Protecting the rights of the dying

is spelled out. Thus the rights of the dying patient are protected; alternatives become clearer for him and for his family.

CERTIFICATION OF THE CAUSE OF DEATH

Every state requires that a certificate of death be issued. Depending on the state, either the physician or a coroner may sign and issue the certificate. This document must then be filed either with the county registrar or with another public official, as designated, in the place where the death occurred. The certificate indicates the time, place, and cause of death.

Where the cause of death is unknown, a temporary certificate may be issued. Burial would not be prevented or delayed if the temporary certificate was issued by a coroner or medical examiner. Issuance by a private physician or hospital would, however, forestall immediate burial.

Generally, several copies of the death certificate are required. Some of the purposes to which copies of the death certificate are put include:

Arranging probate of a will

Securing Social Security benefits

Claiming life insurance proceeds, pensions, or other payments

The death certificate constitutes proof of death. Without it, it is impossible to proceed with any of the above arrangements. The certificate should be checked closely for errors.

A death certificate will always specify the cause of death. Possible entries include death by natural causes, by accident, by homicide, by suicide, and "by cause unknown."

Uncertainty as to Cause of Death

When the cause of death is unknown, it is usually necessary to make an effort to determine the cause. Depending on the state or locale, the coroner or medical examiner has this responsibility. Either an informal or a formal inquest may be held.

Powers and Duties of Coroner or Medical Examiner

The coroner is an elected official —usually

Coroners and medical examiners differ from one another as regards their required credentials and how they attain office. A *coroner* is an elected official in most places in the United States; he is appointed in others. The office of coroner originated almost 900 years ago in England, and originally meant "King's officer." As such, he not only investigated unexplained deaths but also disposed of property following a suicide or homicide.

A CHECKLIST ON WHAT TO DO AFTER A DEATH OCCURS[1]

—Obtain a death certificate from the attending physician or from the coroner or medical examiner.

—Determine whether the deceased wanted to donate his body or any organs for medical purposes; ask the lawyer to see if the will contains reference to such wishes.

—Engage a mortician to handle the body, or notify the burial society if deceased was a member of one.

—Notify the insurance company or agent if there is burial insurance; make a list of the burial allowances available from various government agencies or private associations and make applications for them.

—Obtain a burial plot, unless deceased already had one.

—Arrange for the funeral and interment.

—Inform friends and relatives of the date, time, and place of the funeral and interment.

—Locate the deceased's will and turn it over to the executor to start probate proceedings; it should be in a home strongbox or the family lawyer's vault, and the executor may already have a copy of it.

—Review documents left by the deceased with the executor and his lawyer; give them the ones they will need to set in motion the settlement of the estate.

[1] Adapted from *You and the Law,* Copyright © 1977 The Reader's Digest Association, Inc. Copyright © 1977 The Reader's Digest Association (Canada) Ltd. Copyright © 1977 Reader's Digest Association Far East Ltd. Philippine Copyright 1977 Reader's Digest Association Far East Ltd.

The common law heritage

As part of the heritage of Anglo-Saxon common law, the coroner's office eventually found its way to America. The office has been part of the formal law, and even of constitutional law, in many areas. No specific qualifications for the office existed for many years. A coroner may or may not have the professional expertise to carry out his job—either legal or medical.

For such reasons the office of *medical examiner* is becoming more important. The medical examiner is appointed by the chief executive of a city, county, or state jurisdiction. He may also be appointed by a commission. In order to qualify for the job, he must meet these qualifications:

- Pass a competitive examination, along with other applicants
- Have a medical degree and five years' residence in the fields of general pathology and forensic pathology, the fifth year to have been spent at one of 15 medical-legal training centers in the country
- Obtain formal recognition as a diplomate from the American Board of Pathology by passing a national examination
- Show achievements in the chosen profession
- Optionally, earn certification by the American Board of Pathology in forensic pathology

- Also optionally, have training in law

The coroner or medical examiner assumes jurisdiction in cases such as the following:

- Where a doctor was not in attendance
- Where a doctor is unable to certify the cause of death with certainty
- In all homicides, accidents, and suicides
- In all deaths of a sudden or suspicious nature
- Where deaths occur in prisons and similar governmental institutions
- In industrial deaths
- In unexpected deaths at hospitals, particularly if medical negligence is possible or suspected
- In poisonings
- In drug overdoses

Some post-mortem tests and analyses   Once the coroner or medical examiner assumes jurisdiction in a given case, he may decide to perform appropriate scientific studies. He may also see that such tests or studies are made. These include:

Autopsy

Toxicology tests

Microscopic slide examinations

Bacteriological tests

Chemical analyses

Blood and teeth tests

Physical measurement recordings

Fingerprinting

Any other tests deemed necessary

The coroner or medical examiner may also call in experts in these fields, as he sees fit. He then prepares his findings in an official way and makes them available to persons or institutions interested in them for one reason or another. These may include lawyers, hospitals, doctors, courts, law enforcement agencies, prosecuting and defense attorneys in criminal cases, families, and insurance companies.

All deaths from whatever causes are reported to the coroner or medical examiner by police, hospitals, doctors, and even private citizens. The coroner or medical examiner immediately conducts an investigation to determine whether an autopsy or other tests are necessary. It is usually necessary to conduct such tests. If the individual was under a doctor's care, the requirement may be waived.

Causes of Death

Inquests are formal legal examinations into the causes of death. They are usually not held in jurisdictions where medical examiners hold office. Where a coroner has local responsibility, he must conduct an inquest even when the possibility of a criminal charge exists. When a coroner conducts an inquest, he often appoints a six-man jury to render a verdict. Some jurisdictions, especially those in which a medical examiner serves, do not have inquests. A medical examiner may conduct an inquest with or without a jury, depending on the jurisdiction.

Coroner's inquest plus jury

The inquest constitutes a semijudicial proceeding. The coroner, the medical examiner, or the latter's lawyer may preside over it. Witnesses are called to testify. They may include law enforcement officers, the pathologist who performed the autopsy, any lay witnesses who can contribute information, and, in criminal cases, the defendant.

Where the coroner or jury determines that the death involved a criminal act, he or they will turn the suspect over to a grand jury for indictment. In some cases or jurisdictions, a preliminary hearing will achieve the same results as an inquest.

Whether a coroner or medical examiner has jurisdiction in a given case, the question of final disposition of the body remains. Even when the cause of death is unknown, a temporary death certificate may be issued, permitting funeral services and burial or other arrangements to be made. Where the identity of the body remains unknown, the local government will make final arrangements. This could include giving the body to a medical school for anatomical studies in cases where the body is not disfigured or decomposed.

The question of final disposition

FUNERALS AND FUNERAL DIRECTORS

The funeral director handles all aspects of a funeral from embalming to funeral services to interment or burial. He is trained to deal with all these final steps as well as to deal with people in their times of grief.

To be licensed, the funeral director must meet these requirements:

- Have at least a high school diploma
- Have completed one year of college (in four states)

- Have at least one year of study in a professional curriculum in a college of funeral service education or mortuary science

- Have completed a period of internship or apprenticeship, ranging from one to three years—usually one year

All states except Alabama require that funeral directors be licensed before they can practice. Embalmers must be licensed in every state. Most states provide a single license covering all aspects of the profession, excluding embalming. Some states include embalming in the single license. About three-fourths of all funeral directors have a license that covers embalming.

Four types of charges and fees The costs of a funeral can vary considerably. Some charges or fees contribute to the total of funeral costs. There are four main categories:

1. Those relating specifically to the funeral director: his professional services and those of his staff, the use of his premises and equipment, and the casket and vault selected by the family

2. Those involving disposition of the body: the cost of a grave if interred in the earth or the cost of cremation and of an urn if desired

3. The cost of memorialization: a grave monument or marker, or a niche in a columbarium for the cremation urn

4. Miscellaneous expenses paid by the family directly or through the funeral director: honoraria, flowers, newspaper death notices, additional limousines, burial clothing, and out-of-town transportation of the body

The costs of funerals may vary from community to community. They will also vary according to the ethnic and religious customs of the family involved. In discussions with the funeral director, it is usually possible to arrive at an agreeable price in advance. Prearranging or prefinancing a funeral may offer certain advantages:

- Those living alone will be assured that they will have the kind of funeral they want.

- Survivors will be relieved of some responsibility at the time of death.

- The survivors will thus be able to make last-minute arrangements under less pressure, possibly saving some expenses.

PROFESSIONAL CODE OF FUNERAL DIRECTORS

The National Funeral Directors Association, the largest group of its kind in the United States, has adopted a code that underscores the following provisions:

- A card or brochure is placed in each casket in the selection room.

- Such card or brochure lists the services offered; services not included should be listed as separate items.

- After a family decides on the kind of service they want, they are given a memorandum or agreement to approve or sign. It should include:

  1. The price of the service selected and what is included

  2. The price of each of the supplemental items of service and/or merchandise requested

  3. The amount involved in purchase of each of the items for which the funeral director will advance funds or credit as an accommodation to the family

  4. The method of payment agreed upon by the family and the funeral director

In prearranging and prefinancing a funeral, certain factors should be taken into consideration:

Before prearranging your funeral...

- The possible effect on survivors.

- The logic and economics of planning for a situation that may not occur for many years. For example, many persons feel that they have other expenses at the moment that are more important.

- Selection of a funeral director and burial merchandise for some future time must be tentative at best.

- Money paid in advance is governed by law in most states. Where it is not, the funeral agreement should include provision for a trust fund. The person paying should maintain control. The fund should include money already paid. The agreement should retain the right to terminate the contract without forfeiting any funds paid or interest accrued.

Importantly, the subject of financial resources for funeral and burial, whether prearranged or not, should be kept in mind. Money for these expenses can come from any of a number of sources:

- Some life insurance policies

- Allowances paid by governmental agencies, including Social Security, the Veterans Administration, worker's compensation, welfare, and others

- Union and fraternal organization benefits

- Savings and estate funds

- Specially designated insurance such as funeral insurance and burial insurance

BURIAL AND CREMATION

State laws on burial   Each state specifies the number of days within which a body must be buried or cremated. If a person's will indicates a wish that his body be disposed of in a particular way, his family is not legally bound to abide by those wishes. The law does honor the person's right to donate his body or any organs thereof for medical purposes.

A body left unclaimed for a specified time must be buried by the state or given to a medical institution. The bodies of people killed *en masse* in natural disasters are buried or cremated by local authorities to minimize the risk of contamination.

If a person wants to donate organs or his entire body to medicine, he should be guided by a number of considerations. For example, a donation agreement, properly signed and witnessed, is legally binding on the person's heirs. In actual practice, relatives may object. When this happens, medical institutions are reluctant to go to court. In any case, delay would likely render the donated organ useless.

A person who is determined to donate an organ should discuss the matter with his family. They may then accept the decision. An organ should be removed before embalming. Organ removal does not in any way interfere with a proper funeral.

Cremation

In cremation, a body is reduced to ashes in a high-temperature oven. An old custom, cremation is far more prevalent in some other countries than in the United States. Following cremation, the ashes may be disposed of in a variety of ways. The urn and the ashes may be placed in a columbarium. The urn may be placed in an earth grave, either in a family grave or in a special plot connected with a crematorium. The ashes may be strewn or scattered by one means or another. Whatever method is used, a final service may be held.

Legal controls on cremation   Special legal circumstances attach to the process of cremation. Where a suspicion of criminal involvement exists, a cremated body cannot be exhumed for examination. Cremation is therefore not permitted until the cause of death has been specifically determined. The waiting period before a cremation can take place varies from state to state. Moreover, some states require the permission of a medical examiner or health authority before cremation becomes permissible.

No state requires that a body be embalmed and placed in a casket before cremation. Yet funeral parlors and crematoria may insist on these processes—to raise the disposal costs. For this reason, cremation in the United States costs about the same as burial. Some localities forbid the scattering of ashes. The remains then have to be placed in a columbarium. The cost of a niche in such a memorial may be as expensive as a grave.

Under common law, the body of the deceased is regarded as being under the control of the next of kin. This usually, but not always, ensures that the body will receive proper treatment.

Burial Grounds

The law requires that a burial or *interment* take place in a plot of land officially designated as a cemetery or graveyard. By special permission, that requirement may be waived. All cemeteries are subject to regulation and supervision by local and state governments as well as federal authorities.

In terms of ownership, there are different kinds of cemeteries:

Different kinds of cemeteries

- Small churchyard cemeteries
- Mutual cemeteries, owned by the families who were using or going to use them and run by boards of trustees
- Municipal cemeteries, run by local governments for those residing within their jurisdictions
- Privately owned cemeteries established by philanthropic citizens desiring to meet a public need
- Cemeteries owned by religious and fraternal groups, ethnic groups, and craft organizations
- Memorial parks run as businesses, with perpetual care funds and memorials close to the ground, facilitating upkeep

Burial space or plots can be bought either in advance or at the time of death. Advance purchase has the same benefits as prearranging and prefinancing funerals. As with funerals, it is important to negotiate carefully to ensure fair treatment. In choosing a cemetery, the following considerations are important:

- The reputation of the cemetery
- The service it renders to the community
- How well it is maintained

- Whether it is guided by responsible citizens
- The availability of management with which to discuss problems
- How care funds are handled: whether money is set aside on a regular basis for care; whether the support fund is supervised by well-known and trustworthy citizens or banks; and whether accrued interest is used to provide care for grass and shrubbery

Once the purchase agreement is signed, the cemetery is obligated to live up to it. This applies in particular to care. Cemeteries often have rules about such matters as resale of burial space to the cemetery. A potential buyer should inquire if he will be permitted to do so, and at what price relative to the original purchase price.

Regulations on vaults and liners

Other cemetery regulations apply to the use of vaults and liners. These keep the earth from sinking as a casket deteriorates. Most cemeteries require them, and that adds to the burial costs. Here, the buyer has no choice. He should also remember that a memorial park permits only low markers; if he prefers a monument, he should look elsewhere.

In today's mobile society, the purchaser of a cemetery plot may move away from the locale of the burial plot. There are two main solutions. In one, the individual makes arrangements with a funeral home in his new location, perhaps his place of retirement. The undertaker can make arrangements with an undertaker in the old location. The body can then be sent back and buried.

A second solution requires an organization that will permit one to transfer ownership from the old burial lot to one in the new locale. One such organization, the National Exchange Trust (NET) of Beckley, West Virginia, can arrange acquisition of property comparable to the original purchase. The original must be in a cemetery belonging to NET. The new plot can be in any cemetery over 50 miles from the original cemetery.

Under the Lot Exchange Dollar Credit Plan of the National Association of Cemeteries of Arlington, Virginia, it is possible to transfer dollar-for-dollar credit up to $1,500 between member cemeteries. But the two cemeteries must be at least 75 miles apart. The organizations can supply details.

Part IV
ECONOMIC MATTERS

You've lost your job as a secretary in a large industrial plant.

The itch to get into business on your own has convinced you that now is the time. You're searching for ways to go about it.

That new water heater has konked out completely and you're wondering whether the warranty really means anything.

In America's business society each of those kinds of problems has become common. Nearly every American faces these or similar situations in the course of a lifetime. Hundreds of other economic problems and questions occupy the average citizen; many, or most, involve elementary or complex principles of law.

Understanding the principles that operate in four basic areas—the rights of the unemployed, starting a business of one's own, consumer affairs, and patents and copyrights—provides a basis for economic survival. Some knowledge of the background of modern legal dispensations takes one a step farther.

Key economic areas

In the field of unemployment compensation, to name one example, history indicates that the worker at one time had to deal with laws that protected his employer against lawsuits more than they protected him. The worker could be injured on the job, or on the business premises. He would have great difficulty recovering any kind of compensation. That situation began to change when Germany, in 1883, then England, in 1897, passed compensation laws. In 1911, the U.S. Congress passed a similar law protecting federal employees.

Similar changes have taken place in other economic areas. A new copyright law was passed in 1976 and became effective in 1978. The consumer has become a protected species in hundreds of ways. The person going into business for himself can still find the United States a land of great opportunity. Part IV details some key aspects of the laws in effect today.

12 "THE UNEMPLOYMENT RATE FOR THIS YEAR IS UP"

Most people spend a great part of their lives at work. While work ranks as a source of pleasure to many, it is a necessity for millions.

Work may equate with economic security: receiving a steady income from a job. But it also brings—or should bring—a feeling that one will continue to have a job. In times of depression or recession, that feeling can be threatened.

The person who loses his or her job may still have ways of salvaging the situation, or at least of making the best of it. This chapter deals with some of the key remedies.

WHO ARE THE UNEMPLOYED?

The term "unemployed" applies to many different types of people and many different situations. It makes sense, moreover, to distinguish between the *unemployed* and the *underemployed*. These categories, in turn, differ from that of the *disadvantaged*. Examples of people in these three situations are as follows:

- Underemployed people include workers employed below their skill level; people outside the labor force seeking work; and people engaged in involuntary part-time work.

- Unemployed people include workers laid off temporarily or permanently because of recession or other economic reasons; workers laid off because of low productivity or misconduct on the job; people who are injured or sick because of their job, temporarily or permanently; unskilled and uneducated workers; seasonal workers; and people who have traditionally had difficulty finding adequate employment in America, such as teenagers, older workers, and women workers.

- Disadvantaged workers include many members of minority groups, such as black Americans, Spanish-speaking Americans, and American Indians; ex-convicts; hard-core unemployed; and people who are handicapped, due either to congenital or early illness.

Factors causing unemployment   A variety of factors operate to create these various categories. Prejudice, population changes that create excess labor markets, and apathy may result in unemployment. Poor training or education may combine with poor guidance to make some persons almost unemployable. Unhealthy working conditions and economic cycles may simply force some people out of jobs.

EMPLOYER AND EMPLOYEE

Whether on the job or without a job, the worker under the common law had minimal protection in the past. Over the past several decades, however, organized labor has obtained protection for the worker through collective bargaining. Today, the worker can find various kinds of assistance in the private and public sectors to cope with unemployment or the threat of unemployment. A number of federal and state statutes also provide additional protection.

The Civil Rights Act of 1964, amended in 1972, prohibits employers, labor organizations, and employment agencies from discriminating in employment or membership on the grounds of race, religion, national origin, or sex. Enforcement of this law takes place through the Equal

Employment Opportunity Commission (EEOC) or through the appropriate state or local agency.

The Age Discrimination in Employment Act of 1967 prohibits discrimination against older workers because of age. Excepted are jobs where age is an important criterion, as where heavy physical work is required.

Age discrimination prohibited

FACTORS AFFECTING LAYOFFS DURING A RECESSION[1]

Based on statistics from the past few recessions, the chances of being laid off may be affected by any of the following factors:

- *How well a person does his or her job.* During a recession many companies weed out poor performers.
- *What field a person is in.* People working in manufacturing, mining, construction, agriculture, transportation, communications, and utilities will fare worse than those in wholesale and retail trades, personal and business services, finance, insurance, real estate, and government.
- *How much a person earns.* The chances of losing a job decline as one's salary rises. At the $28,000 to $30,000 levels and above, in 1979 the chances became minimal. Thus professional, technical, and administrative people are less vulnerable than others. Exceptions are salesmen on commission and executives receiving performance bonuses.

- *Where a person lives.* Key industries can be affected by recession. So can the communities in which they are located. Locations in which layoffs may become epidemic: Detroit and Flint, Michigan, auto industry; Cumberland County, New Jersey, the glass industry; Miami, construction; New England and San Diego, tourism; Pennsylvania's steel areas. Least vulnerable: the Sunbelt, Rocky Mountain states, and the midwestern farm belt.
- *A person's age.* People under 25 are especially vulnerable even in prosperous times. Seniority protects older employees on the job. Even where an employer hires college graduates, they are not immune to an ensuing recession.
- *A person's sex and race.* In previous recessions, women and blacks suffered disproportionately. Because of affirmative action hiring, and the consequent buildup of seniority, these groups may not today be so adversely affected.

[1] Adapted from "How Safe Is Your Job in a Slowdown?" by Patrick Flanagan, *Money* magazine, July 1979, by special permission, ©1979, Time Inc. All rights reserved.

The Rehabilitation Act of 1973, which became fully operative in 1978, encourages government agencies and institutions receiving federal funds to hire handicapped workers, provided they can perform. Many states have similar laws.

The Fair Labor Standards Act limits the kind of work children can do. People under 16 cannot, for example, work as public messengers, use power-driven machinery, work on construction jobs, or work in public utilities, transportation, mining, manufacturing, and other industries. Violators cannot sell their products in interstate or foreign commerce.

STATE LAWS PROTECTING WORKERS[1]

State	Fair Employment Practices Act	Civil or Human Rights Commission[2]	Right-to-Work Law	Workers' Compensation Act[3]
Alabama	No	No	Yes	Yes
Alaska	Yes	Yes	No	Yes
Arizona	Yes	Yes	Yes	Yes
Arkansas	Yes	Yes	Yes	Yes
California	Yes	Yes	No	Yes
Colorado	Yes	Yes	No	Yes
Connecticut	Yes	Yes	No	Yes
Delaware	Yes	Yes	No	Yes
D.C.	Yes	Yes	No	Yes
Florida	No	Yes	Yes	Yes
Georgia	Yes	No	Yes	Yes
Hawaii	Yes	No	No	Yes
Idaho	Yes	Yes	No	Yes
Illinois	Yes	Yes	No	Yes
Indiana	Yes	Yes	No	Yes
Iowa	Yes	Yes	Yes	Yes
Kansas	Yes	Yes	Yes	Yes
Kentucky	Yes	Yes	No	Yes
Louisiana	No	No	Yes	Yes[4]
Maine	Yes	Yes	No	Yes
Maryland	Yes	Yes	No	Yes
Massachusetts	Yes	Yes	No	Yes
Michigan	Yes	Yes	No	Yes
Minnesota	Yes	Yes	No	Yes
Mississippi	No	No	Yes	Yes
Missouri	Yes	Yes	No	Yes
Montana	Yes	Yes	No[5]	Yes
Nebraska	Yes	Yes	Yes	Yes
Nevada	Yes	Yes	Yes	Yes
New Hampshire	Yes	Yes	No	Yes
New Jersey	Yes	Yes	No	Yes
New York	Yes	Yes	No	Yes
North Carolina	Yes	Yes	Yes	Yes
North Dakota	Yes	No	Yes	Yes
Ohio	Yes	Yes	No	Yes
Oklahoma	Yes	Yes	No	Yes
Oregon	Yes	No[6]	Yes	Yes
Pennsylvania	Yes	Yes	No	Yes
Rhode Island	Yes	Yes	No	Yes
South Carolina	Yes[7]	Yes[8]	Yes	Yes
South Dakota	Yes	Yes	Yes	Yes
Tennessee	Yes	Yes	Yes	Yes
Texas	Yes[7]	Yes	Yes	Yes
Utah	Yes	No[9]	Yes	Yes
Vermont	Yes	Yes	No	Yes
Virginia	Yes	No[10]	Yes	Yes
Washington	Yes	Yes	No[11]	Yes
West Virginia	Yes	Yes	No	Yes
Wisconsin	Yes	Yes	No	Yes
Wyoming	Yes	Yes	Yes	Yes[12]

[1] Adapted from *You and the Law*, Copyright © 1977 The Reader's Digest Association, Inc. Copyright © 1977 The Reader's Digest Association (Canada) Ltd. Copyright © 1977 Reader's Digest Association Far East Ltd. Philippine Copyright 1977 Reader's Digest Association Far East Ltd.

[2] This includes Equal Opportunity Commission and Human Relations Council.

[3] Known in some states as industrial insurance.

[4] Not compulsory, but elected by employers and employees.

[5] A law prevents union interference with a sole proprietor or two-person partnership in the retail or amusement business.

[6] Complaints heard by the Commission of the Bureau of Labor.

[7] Only state employees are protected by a limited antidiscrimination law.

[8] The Human Affairs Commission deals only with discrimination against state employees.

[9] The antidiscrimination division of the Industrial Commission handles discrimination complaints.

[10] The Commission of Labor and Industry hears complaints.

[11] An agricultural laborer may not be denied work on the basis of whether he is or is not a union member.

[12] Applies only to workers in extra-hazardous industries.

The Wage and Hour Law, a 1974 amendment of the Fair Labor Standards Act, puts a ceiling on the number of hours worked and a minimum on wages. The law applies to all workers engaged in interstate or foreign commerce. The minimum wage is scheduled to go from $2.90 in 1979 to $3.35 in 1981. Exceptions include executives and administrative employees, outside salesmen, certain types of transportation employees, employees in seasonal industries, and handicapped workers and students, with government permission.

Violations of the Wage and Hour Law are handled by the Wage and Hour Division of the U.S. Department of Labor, which has field offices in most states. A worker may sue for double the wages not paid him, plus court costs and attorney's fees, but must do so within two years from the time of the violation. Serious violations can bring heavy fines or imprisonment by the Department of Labor. An employer may not fire an employee who files a complaint or suit. States that also have wage and hour laws should be consulted for details.

The Occupational Safety and Health Act (OSHA) of 1970 sets standards designed to minimize exposure to hazards on the job. All states have similar laws. Areas covered include buildings and furnishings, construction, equipment and machinery, fire hazards, and industrial safety.

Minimizing hazards on the job: OSHA

The National Labor Relations Act of 1935 was passed to help workers who were organizing unions and to prevent domination of those unions by employers. It also helped to obtain employer recognition of unions as collective bargaining agents. The NLRA is administered by the National Labor Relations Board (NLRB).

The Taft-Hartley Act of 1947 covers the same ground as the National Labor Relations Act, but goes farther, establishing prohibitions against the following:

Some provisions of Taft-Hartley

- Forcing workers to join a union. This is the so-called "closed shop" situation. In a "union shop," however, a nonunion member can be hired, but must join the union within a specified time period or risk losing his job.
- Forcing employers to discriminate against an employee.
- The refusal of a union to enter into collective bargaining with an employer.
- Jurisdictional work stoppages, secondary boycotts, or forcing an employer to assign certain work to certain unions.
- Featherbedding, or forcing an employer to pay for unperformed work.

- Excessive initiation fees or dues in union shop plants.

There are also laws requiring various kinds of insurance, as specified by federal or state statutes. These include workers' compensation insurance for disabilities incurred on the job; nonoccupational disability insurance, required by a few states; Social Security; and unemployment insurance (UI), paid for by employers and administered by state and federal governments. Federal employees and members of the armed services are also covered on discharge. These and other plans are covered in greater detail later in the chapter.

Common law protections
The law of employer and employee, under common law, deals with the contractual obligations of the two parties. Features include:

- The employer's right to fire with good cause, and to refuse to pay wages for the period beyond the time of firing even if there was a contract for a longer period of work
- The employer's obligation to ensure the safety of employees, provide suitable tools, and warn of hazards
- Liability for damages due to a worker's negligence where such negligence occurred outside the line of work
- The employee's rights to an invention only if he used his own time and materials
- The employer's obligation to withhold and deposit income and Social Security taxes
- The employee's right to know what kind of insurance coverage he has, and when that coverage changes

To sum up, these laws give workers various forms of protection. For example, they prevent discrimination in hiring or promotion on the basis of race, sex, age, or physical handicap and establish minimum levels of pay and maximum numbers of work hours, with suitable extra compensation for extra hours. The laws also seek to prevent exposure to occupational hazards, and safeguard the right to join or form a labor union and be represented by it in collective bargaining.

Today an employee cannot legally be fired because he joined a union or brought suit against an employer for violation of a law or for negligence. Workers are also protected against union abuses. Various kinds of insurance are provided, including unemployment and disability.

UNIONS AND STRIKES

Labor unions are worker organizations established to obtain higher wages and improved working conditions and generally to protect worker rights and interests.

Craft unions are composed of workers in a particular craft, trade, or occupation. *Industrial unions* are generally mass organizations of people who work in particular industries, irrespective of their own special crafts or occupations. Unions within a single plant, or *plant unions*, are founded by and for one group of employees. Unlike the first two types, these unions are not usually affiliated with larger national or international unions.

Three kinds of union organization

The National Labor Relations and Taft-Hartley acts govern the relations between management and unions. Under the rules of the National Labor Relations Board (NLRB), each side has certain rights while collective bargaining is in progress. Management, for example, can express its opinions to workers on each side's proposals. But in that expression management can never make threats or engage in intimidation. In particular, workers who disagree with management cannot be threatened with firing or disciplinary action. The union must also avoid intimidation—of both management and the workers.

In most cases, a collective bargaining agreement emerges from union-management negotiations. In the event that no agreement is reached, a strike may be called. In industries engaging in interstate commerce, a union must give 60 days' notice before calling a strike.

Unions were formed to protect workers from unjust firings and other prejudicial actions. A collective bargaining agreement usually includes a section dealing with firing with "just cause" as well as protocols for handling grievances. If a worker complains to his or her union, the union then weighs the merits of the case. If it feels the worker has a legitimate grievance, the union takes the responsibility of defending the worker or taking action against the employer. The law requires that the union handle the case even if the worker is not a union member.

Under the Taft-Hartley Act, *closed shops* are illegal. Firms engaged in interstate or foreign commerce cannot be required to hire union members. However, *union shops* are legal, and are permitted in most states. In these states, nonmembership cannot keep a person from being hired. But he must join the union within the time specified by the union-employer agreement, usually 60 to 120 days. If he does not join, the employer has to discharge him.

Union shops are legal in most states

Both closed and union shops are prohibited in *open shop* states that have "right-to-work" laws. In these states every worker has the *right to work* whether he wants to join a union or not. A worker moving to another state that has no such law is no longer free of union shop rules.

Unions make their own admission rules. However, most unions admit as members all eligible workers who apply. It is to the union's advantage to have as many members as possible. Where a union shop agreement is in force, the union has to accept all who are eligible and apply. Under the Taft-Hartley Act, if the union in this situation does not take all applicants, it cannot enforce the union shop clause. If a union expels a member, an employer must keep him on as an employee.

Many states have fair employment practices laws that prevent discrimination in granting union memberships. The Equal Employment Opportunity Commission (EEOC) handles individuals' grievances, but in the states that have fair employment laws, state authorities also handle them.

Starting with the union's grievance machinery

A person with a grievance against a union should first use the union's grievance machinery. The union should also make available a copy of the collective bargaining agreement with the company. Failure to do so entitles the complainant to file a complaint with the federal Department of Labor. If the union gives no satisfaction, the worker can sue the union or its officials, and he is protected against union retaliation.

NLRB rules applying to workers

Under NLRB rules, if a union goes on strike, the following strictures apply to workers:

1. Employees taking part in legal strikes remain employees. The NLRB can force an employer to take back an employee and to compensate him for any time he was not allowed to work after the settlement was reached. However, the employer does not have to rehire workers if new employees are legally engaged as replacements during the strike. The discharged workers retain voting rights in the union.

2. Employees in illegal strikes are not protected by the NLRB. An employer is not obliged to rehire them.

3. Employees of the federal government are not allowed to strike; most states also prohibit their employees from striking. Under the Taft-Hartley Act, a striking federal employee is subject to immediate discharge.

PROTECTION PLANS

Some of the laws described above indicate conditions under which a person may legally lose his job. These include incompetence, illegal strikes, and failure to join a union in a union shop. In still other situations, neither laws nor collective bargaining agreements can guarantee that a person will retain his job. Notable examples are conditions of recession or seasonal business.

Management and unions have developed a variety of protection plans in collective bargaining agreements. The federal and state governments have also devised plans and programs for the protection of workers in various categories. The remainder of this chapter deals with government programs and one private plan that dovetails with a government plan. The government plans include workers' compensation, nonoccupational disability, unemployment insurance (UI), veterans' rights under the GI Bill, and Social Security disability. The single private plan is known as supplemental unemployment benefits (SUB).

Workers' Compensation

Workers' compensation evolved as industrial injuries became an increasingly serious problem in the early twentieth century. Under common law, an employer had only to provide safe premises and equipment, competent fellow workers, and proper warnings of hazards. An employer could be held exempt from liability on the ground that the employee accepted the conditions of work when he accepted employment.

How workers' compensation was born

WHAT EMPLOYERS AND UNIONS CAN DO TO PROMOTE AN EMPLOYEE'S SECURITY[1]

Measures to promote group security
—Control over job functions, methods of production, technology
  ▪ work rules, including output or pace
  ▪ tight job definitions
  ▪ prohibitions on using some types of machinery
—Restrictions on management in directing production
  ▪ restrictions on subcontracting
  ▪ manning requirements
  ▪ required ratios of learners to journeymen
  ▪ controls on scheduling overtime, or other work scheduling
—Regulation of individual worker hours
  ▪ shorten workweek by
    —increasing daily breaks, ''make-ready'' time, union business time
    —altering shiftwork patterns; short shifts
    —shortening workday directly; reducing number of days in standard workweek

  ▪ shorten workyear by
    —increasing vacations or holidays
    —adding to paid weeks of training, jury duty, etc.
Measures to allocate and specify the individual's security
—Seniority control over layoff and recall, job assignment, transfers, bumping, etc.
—Special rights provided by contract to
  ▪ training and retraining, in order to remain on the payroll
  ▪ interplant transfer
  ▪ wage retention after bumping or transfer
Income security, after unemployment has occurred
—Severance pay
—Supplemental unemployment benefits (SUB)
—Individual account benefit plans
—Savings plans

[1] Adapted from Audrey Freedman, *Security Bargains Reconsidered: SUB, Severance Pay, Guaranteed Work* (New York: The Conference Board, 1978).

The federal government passed a workers' compensation act for federal employees in 1908. In 1911, New York became the first state to pass such a law. Most states had equivalent laws by 1921, and all states have them today.

Although state laws vary, all workers' compensation laws have characteristics in common, including:

- Employer negligence need not be shown.
- If an employee is injured in a work-related accident, injury or death is compensated according to a fixed schedule of benefits, no matter who may be at fault.
- Benefits are payable weekly for a set number of weeks, computed as a percentage of a person's weekly wages, with a maximum limit.
- Injuries subject to compensation include temporary and permanent disability (either partial or total), fractures, total or partial loss of use of various body parts, disfigurement, other permanent injuries, and many occupational diseases.
- Death benefits are payable to designated dependents.
- The employee, in addition to cash compensation, is entitled to all necessary medical care.

Filing a claim, notifying the employer

When injury or illness has occurred, the employee seeking compensation should file a claim with the appropriate administrative agency. The employer should be notified immediately. Neglecting to notify the employer or delaying such notification can result in denial of the claim.

A person needing medical attention can obtain it on his own even when the employer does not provide it. The claimant simply includes the medical bills with his request for compensation.

After a person notifies the administrative agency, an arbitrator makes an initial determination of whether the injury can be compensated, and in what amount. This decision is reviewed by an administrative board, followed by approval, disapproval, or modification. The worker who is dissatisfied with the decision can obtain a judicial ruling in the next step.

State restrictions on claims

Some states set restrictions on the payments for injuries incurred in especially hazardous occupations. Some states also set restrictions on claims arising from occupational diseases. These states list only those diseases that are covered. A person may not be covered where the particular type of illness or injury is not covered in a particular state or where the regulatory agency does not rule in a person's favor. Coverage may also be lacking where an employer has fewer than three people on his payroll. If a person is not covered, he can bring a suit against his employer for negligence.

A brief waiting period is usual before a person collects workers' compensation. Benefits are classified as *medical* and *income*. Some states make partial medical payments; some provide for full compensation. All states make provision for rehabilitation training as well as surgery and prosthetic devices designed to restore limb and other functions to the greatest degree possible.

Disabilities are generally classified as *permanent total*, *temporary total*, and *permanent partial* disabilities. Two-thirds of a person's average earnings usually establishes the limit for income benefits. Death benefits, in the form of a pension for beneficiaries, also have the same limitation. But they may be less than the two-thirds level.

Nonoccupational Disability

Nonoccupational disability insurance is provided in only four states: California, New Jersey, New York, and Rhode Island. About 90 per cent of all illness is non-job related, but can still keep a person from working. A separate nonoccupational insurance plan covers railroad workers. The unemployment insurance (UI) program in each of the four states administers nonoccupational disability insurance.

The core features of the typical program, regardless of the state, include:

- Both employer and employee contribute to the plan.
- The amount of compensation depends on regular weekly earnings within fixed minimum and maximum levels.
- Payments continue up to one year, commencing after a one-week waiting period.
- The right to benefits depends on the type of disability, on how many weeks one has worked, and on whether one has earned the minimum amount stipulated by the state.

Unemployment Insurance (UI)

UI constitutes the main form of compensation for unemployed workers. UI has historically ranked as the youngest member of the family of protective programs. Various countries have tended to establish programs for work injuries, old age, and sickness before they established forms of UI. When the United States established the Social Security system in 1935, the UI section came closest to being declared unconstitutional. UI still tends to enjoy least favored status among programs. The main objectives of UI are to:

provide cash during involuntary unemployment;

maintain a worker's standard of living;

give him time to locate or regain employment; and

UI—a main form of unemployment compensation

help him find a specific job.

In addition, UI serves to:

counteract the effects of business cycles;

improve the utilization of workers;

encourage employers to stabilize employment; and

maintain a skilled work force.

State and D.C. administration
UI is administered individually by each state and the District of Columbia. It is supported by taxes paid by employers and by federal funding. Eligibility of workers for UI stipulates a need to meet such requirements as qualifying wages or employment, ability to work and availability for work, and actively looking for work. Eligible employees have also to prove freedom from disqualifications. The latter may include quitting one's job, discharge for misconduct, and refusal of suitable work.

Taking part in labor disputes—strikes—may also disqualify a worker for UI. Other causes could include student unavailability for work because of class schedules, pregnancy (in 23 states), quitting to marry (in 15 states), and fraudulent misrepresentation.

When a worker loses a job covered by UI, he should apply immediately to his nearest state UI office to file a claim for benefits. Promptness is vital; several weeks may elapse before the first compensation payment arrives. The person filing should have with him his Social Security card and discharge notice. Payments last up to 26 weeks; under extra hardship conditions, they may last a year.

UNEMPLOYMENT INSURANCE:
THE STATE-BY-STATE PICTURE[1]

In these states the base period is the first four of the last five completed calendar quarters. Your earnings in your highest-paying quarter in that period become the basis for your benefit.

	weekly benefit amount minimum	maximum	weeks of entitlement minimum	maximum	high quarter earnings to qualify for minimum	maximum
Alabama	$15	$90	11	26	$ 348	$2,136
Arizona	30	90	12	26	625	2,238
Arkansas	15	124	10	26	118	3,198
California	30	120	12	26	188	1,160
Colorado	25	142	7	26	188	3,666
Connecticut	15-20	134-201	26	26	150	3,458
Delaware	20	150	11	26	520	3,874
District of Columbia	13-14	181	17	34	300	4,140
Georgia	27	90	4	26	275	2,225
Hawaii	5	144	26	26	38	3,575
Idaho	17	121	10	26	416	3,120
Illinois	15	133-177	26	26	250	3,445
Indiana	35	74-124	3	26	400	1,698
Iowa	17-18	131-148	15	26	400	2,803
Kansas	30	123	10	26	—	2,871
Kentucky	22	120	15	26	500	2,749

	weekly benefit amount		weeks of entitlement		high quarter earnings to qualify for	
	minimum	maximum	minimum	maximum	minimum	maximum
Louisiana	10	149	12	28	75	3,700
Maine	12-17	96-144	3	26	367	2,101
Maryland	10-13	106	26	26	192	2,520
Massachusetts	12-18	131-197	9	30	225	3,380
Mississippi...............	10	90	12	26	160	2,314
Missouri	15	105	8	26	300	2,311
Montana	30	119	12	26	767	3,081
Nebraska	12	106	17	26	200	2,550
Nevada	16	115	11	26	375	2,850
New Mexico	22	106	18	26	546	2,730
North Carolina...........	15	130	13	26	150	3,367
North Dakota.............	36	131	12	26	910	3,380
Oklahoma...............	16	132	20	26	250	3,275
Pennsylvania	13-18	162-170	30	30	120	3,988
Puerto Rico	7	72	20	20	75	1,846
South Carolina	10	111	10	26	180	2,860
South Dakota	28	109	13	26	600	2,376
Tennessee	14	100	12	26	338	2,970
Texas	18	105	9	26	125	2,600
Utah	10	137	10	36	175	3,536
Virginia	38	122	12	26	342	3,025
Virgin Islands	15	90	26	26	99	2,225
Washington	17	137	8	30	325	3,413
Wyoming................	24	131	12	26	600	3,250

[1] States listed here use as a base period either four of the last five quarters or another recent 52-week period, perhaps the 52 weeks before you lost your job. Your total earnings in the base period then become the benefit basis.

	weekly benefit amount		weeks of entitlement		high quarter earnings to qualify for	
	minimum	maximum	minimum	maximum	minimum	maximum
Alaska	$18-$28	$90-$120	14	28	$ 750	$8,500
New Hampshire	21	114	26	26	1,200	10,500
Oregon	35	127	6	26	700	10,120
West Virginia.............	18	166	28	28	1,150	15,650

These states use the 52-week system, too, but figure benefits roughly as a percentage of your average weekly wage during the base period. In Michigan, Minnesota and New York, for which a range of percentages is shown, the higher figures apply to those with lower earnings and vice versa.

	weekly benefit amount		weeks of entitlement		minimum earnings to qualify	% of average weekly wage
	minimum	maximum	minimum	maximum		
Florida	$10	$95	10	26	$ 400	50%
Michigan.................	16-18	97-136	11	26	350	63-55
Minnesota	30	150	11	26	750	60-50
New Jersey	20	123	15	26	600	66.6
New York...............	25	125	26	26	800	67-50
Ohio	10	128-202	20	26	400	50
Rhode Island.............	30-35	120-140	12	26	1,060	55
Vermont	18	115	26	26	700	50
Wisconsin...............	29	155	1	34	840	50

"Unemployed and looking for work"

Under UI regulations, the worker has to report regularly to the state employment service office to prove that he or she is both unemployed and looking for work. The compensation check has to be picked up in person. If a claimant is doing any work, the wages are deductible from benefits.

The unemployed worker earning less than his usual weekly pay may be entitled to partial benefits. To qualify, he should obtain a payroll voucher or other document showing the gross pay received. Benefits will nonetheless be determined according to regular-job earnings.

Refusal to accept a suitable full-time job can result in loss of benefits. Ineligibility may also result from acceptance of workers' compensation, dismissal payments (severance pay), a pension, or other remuneration. Refusal of benefits can be appealed; the UI office will provide guidance on the procedures to be followed.

The state employment service can provide assistance in finding a job. A given state can refer applicants to employers, administer tests, provide counseling, prepare individuals for job interviews, or refer applicants to training programs.

Generally, the more of these services provided, the better are the chances of finding a job. One survey has shown that workers not temporarily laid off and not due to be called back to their old jobs received more assistance. Younger workers received much more attention than older. The more skilled the worker, the more attention given by the employment service. The most crucial service provided for job seekers was referral to a job interview.

Supplementary Unemployment Benefits (SUB)

Criticism of UI

UI has been criticized for a number of reasons. Its coverage has been said to be incomplete and its benefits inadequate. Only a small proportion of unemployed have received benefits. Disqualification standards have been termed harsh. Benefits are exhausted too quickly and the taxable wage base is inadequate.

Disqualification can occur, as noted, when one receives other government benefits. This cannot occur, however, when supplemental unemployment benefits (SUB) are provided. SUB is intimately related to UI, both in administration and in what it provides. SUB was developed privately as a reaction to the inadequacies of UI.

Many labor unions initiated SUB plans to supplement UI benefits. The United Auto Workers started the first plan in 1955. A number of major industries, afflicted by recurring unemployment, now have SUB plans—for example, the auto and steel industries, in which the threat of unemployment is especially great during recessions. SUB plans have proved acceptable to employers because they reduce worker resistance to change and displacement. They tend to reinforce the uses for which UI was intended.

SUB plans are of two types:

- *Pooled funds.* The more common type, pooled funds "pool" losses on behalf of all eligible employees. The employer contributes so many cents for each hour worked to a central fund. Pooled SUB plans, combined with UI, can cover from 60 to 95 per cent of a worker's former salary. Payments can last up to 52 weeks.

- *Individual account plans.* Under an individual account plan, a separate account is established for each employee. The result is a form of compulsory saving. Plans vary in details. If an employer does not contribute to the plan, a higher wage may replace the benefit. In other plans, the employer matches the amount deducted from the worker's salary. Still other plans have profit-sharing funds from which withdrawals can be made during periods of unemployment.

Two kinds of SUB plans

SUB offsets unemployment benefit differences among states. In states with low UI payments, SUB makes up the difference with higher payments. The chances that UI benefits will increase are small. SUB therefore serves a useful purpose for a large number of unionized workers: meeting the threat of unemployment.

Veterans' Rights

Under the GI Bill, veterans are entitled to a number of benefits. These include:

- Educational assistance at various educational institutions at the rate of one and one-half months for each month served up to a limit of 45 months. For those serving after Vietnam, the ratio is two months for every month served. The Veterans Administration (VA) gives a monthly allowance varying according to the number of dependents. The allowance is designed to cover tuition, books, and living expenses. The wives and widows of disabled veterans are also eligible. The veteran has to use his or her benefits within 10 years after discharge.

- The right to reclaim a former job. A veteran is legally entitled to his former job after discharge. He even acquires seniority for the time spent in the service. A veteran must, however, apply for his old job within 90 days after discharge. Where an employer refuses to rehire, the Veterans Reemployment Rights Office of the U.S. Department of Labor should be contacted.

A veteran can reclaim his former job

- Home loan guarantee. The VA cannot guarantee the entire price of a property—home, mobile home, condominium, or farm—since the law limits the amount of the mortgage that the government will insure. In some rural areas where there are few lenders, the VA will make loans directly.
- Medical care for service-connected disabilities. Even for a disability that is not service-connected, a VA hospital will admit a veteran if he cannot pay for care elsewhere. VA clinics are also available, and a veteran can be authorized by the VA to be treated by his own physician.
- Compensation and pensions for disabled veterans. Eligibility for such benefits arises from disability incurred or disease contracted or aggravated while in the service. Payments vary with the kind of disability. Even if the disability was not incurred in the service, the veteran may still be eligible if he served 90 days or more.

Social Security Disability

Social Security is not supposed to provide retirement benefits only. A person working in a job covered by Social Security can acquire eligibility for disability benefits at any age. To be eligible, one has to be unable to earn a living. Also, the condition must have lasted, or be expected to last, for at least a year. The disability may be mental or physical. There must be sufficient credit in one's Social Security account and the applicant must have worked for five of ten years or ten of 20 quarters preceding the onset of the disability.

To claim benefits, one should contact a local Social Security office. A five-month waiting period elapses before issuance of the first monthly payment. Physicians involved in treatment will fill out forms provided by Social Security; hospitals can provide records. Disability benefits are the same as old-age benefits at age 65; benefits may be reduced if one is under 62 and receiving workers' compensation. Denials of benefits can be appealed.

Contacting the local Social Security office

13 "BUSINESS OPPORTUNITY— YOUNG COUPLE— MINIMUM INVESTMENT"

Everyone has read, at one time or another, that opportunities in the United States are less numerous than they used to be. Stories abound— about the small business person, his or her problems, the bankruptcies that occur with greater frequency, and other data that seem to support the basic proposition.

The Business Opportunity section in the daily newspaper nonetheless lists numbers of enterprises that appeal to the small businessman, the person who is thinking of adopting a new way of life, and others. Franchise operations offer just one example of a field that expanded rapidly, creating thousands of opportunities.

More and more professional and business people are changing their lifestyles and their occupations. Despite whatever business or financial success they may have achieved, they launch new searches for occupations with more meaning for them and their families. Not unusually, a husband

or wife may decide to start a family business and to make whatever adjustments in lifestyle may be necessary.

This chapter deals with the problems of the individual seeking to operate a small business or to start out on a new line of work. What form of business enterprise will be best suited for one's family or for others who may come into the business later? How to raise capital and do all the things that have to be done in order to make a business operation succeed. Some basic answers will provide guidelines.

THREE TYPES OF BUSINESS ORGANIZATIONS

Three forms that a business may take will be considered here: the sole proprietorship, the partnership, and the corporation. Other forms will be touched on passingly.

The Sole Proprietorship

The sole proprietorship is perhaps the most simple organizational format. It may be the best way for an individual to start out on a small scale.

In a typical situation, a person wants to operate a franchise. It is likely that he will be the sole owner. Just as likely, he will not need additional capital, at least in the beginning, and the business will probably not grow to the point where the owner will need outside help.

One company,
one boss
The sole proprietorship is the answer. One person is the boss; he has only himself to answer to. He can give orders freely if he has employees, and has only his own tax situation to worry about. If the business remains small, he can keep a finger on the growth pattern and operating costs. Many of the complicated matters that arise under the corporate form of doing business, or even the partnership form, can be controlled.

Under the laws of many states, operating a business under an assumed or fictitious name requires, initially, that the necessary information be filed with county and state authorities. The information includes the name to be used and the names and addresses of all persons interested in the business. Filing is required so that individuals dealing with the business will be able to ascertain which parties actually have an interest in the business should the need ever arise. Typically, a state law might be called an Assumed Names Act.

For example, to do business under the trade name "Acme Food Market," it would be necessary in most states to register the company name and the names and addresses of all persons interested in the name. If ownership changes, an amendment to the filing will have to be made. New information would include the name of the new owner, whether a partnership is created, and the names of any new partners.

The Partnership

A partnership is composed of two or more persons working together in a business enterprise, usually on the basis of a partnership agreement. A relatively simple way to do business, the partnership is not as complicated as the corporation. Also, the partnership has advantages and disadvantages vis-à-vis both the sole proprietorship and the corporation.

As in any new business venture, in the early stages capital will be needed. The partners may have to use their personal credit. Each partner is personally responsible for the debts and credit arrangements of any other partners and of the business itself. After a partnership has accumulated assets and can show an earnings history, credit will usually be extended to the enterprise without the personal guarantees of the principal parties.

When two or more work together

Each partner may act for all the others. The partnership form of doing business is governed in most states by statute. These laws set out, in detail, the rights and obligations of partners where no formal partnership agreement exists.

However, most partnerships do—and should—operate under the terms of a partnership agreement. The agreement spells out all the relative rights and obligations of the parties, describes the business in detail, enumerates its objectives, and indicates the investment or contributions of each partner.

General observations Some general observations can be made regarding the typical partnership as it is ordinarily set out in a partnership agreement.

Duration. The length of time a partnership will endure depends on the terms of the agreement. Ordinarily the agreement provides that the partnership will continue for an indefinite period until it is terminated by the death of a partner, by voluntary act of the partners, by the insolvency or bankruptcy of one of the partners, by improper activity on the part of a partner, or by other means.

THE THREE BASIC KINDS OF BUSINESS[1]

There are three basic kinds of business in our society. The first is the individual proprietorship or ownership, the second is the partnership, and the third is the corporation. Each of these types of business organization has unique characteristics that make it more or less suitable for a specific kind of operation.

The Individual Ownership

More than half the business concerns in this country are owned by a single person. This kind of business is known legally as an individual ownership or proprietorship. It may be small, like a newsstand or a candy store, or it may be a fairly large company. The individual owner has great flexibility; he is responsible only to himself and he alone reaps the rewards of a successful operation. By the same token, however, he is entirely responsible for any debts or losses his company incurs in the course of business. Many such businesses are started from scratch by the owner. Others are purchased from a previous owner. In either case, the individual owner may operate under his own name or under a company name.

The Partnership

A partnership is a more complicated form of business than an individual ownership. Any number of people may enter into a partnership (of course there must be at least two), investing their money or their services or both in the business of which they are co-owners. Usually there is a written partnership agreement between them that sets out their rights and duties under the partnership. Unless the agreement provides otherwise, the partners share equally in the profits or the losses of the company. In a general partnership all the partners are liable for any business debts, and they may be obliged to make up deficits out of their own personal property. A partnership may be for a limited or for an indefinite term.

The Corporation

While only a small percentage of American businesses are corporations, they are by far the largest and most important ones. The corporation is a group of people who have banded together to do business and who have been granted a charter by the government which gives them, as a unit, some of the legal rights and powers of an individual. In other words, the law regards a corporation as a person. A corporation may own, buy, sell and inherit property in its own name. It may even commit a crime and be tried and punished for it. Most corporations get the capital necessary for their operations by selling stock—units or shares in the ownership of the company. If the business is successful, the profits are distributed to the stockholders in the form of dividends.

The partnership agreement may specify that the partnership does not terminate or will not be dissolved on the death of a partner. Such a partnership continues so long as there are two or more partners. The remaining partners have the right to purchase the share of the deceased partner from his estate. Business insurance can help to facilitate the financing of the buy-out agreement in such a case.

Unlike a corporation, the partnership is not separate and distinct from the partners. The liability of the general partners in a partnership is individual to each of them and applies to all partnership obligations throughout the life of the agreement. *Limited partners* or other special partners may, however, have their liability limited to their investment only.

Changes and Limitations. If an existing partnership decides to take in a new partner, the "old" partnership should be terminated and a new one created. All of the former partners should give their consent. If one of the partners wants to retire, arrangements have to be made to protect him insofar as partnership debts are concerned. Thus no creditor can recover from the partner who has resigned or retired.

The partnership agreement must either provide for such contingencies or it must be amended. A new partnership agreement may have to be drawn up to incorporate changes.

Ring out the old . . .

The partnership can raise capital only in certain ways. Loans may involve the individual guarantees of all the partners. New partners may bring in additional capital. Additional contributions may be required of the present members of the partnership.

Management of the partnership ordinarily requires the unanimous agreement of all the partners. But one partner may be appointed *managing partner* under a partnership agreement, giving him responsibility for the day-to-day management decisions. Policy-making authority may thus reside in all the partners together or in the managing partner alone. Problems may, of course, arise, especially where the partners have equal management responsibility.

A partnership has a degree of flexibility in conducting business operations. But the basic agreement should specify the nature of the partnership and the work to be done. The partnership should not engage in any activity not specified in the agreement.

A partnership has flexibility

Taxation. Insofar as taxation is concerned, the partnership has only to file a federal *information return* for income tax purposes. The partnership itself pays no income tax, in brief. Rather, it distributes its income to the individual partners who are taxed on their own proportionate shares of the partnership income. That income may or may not be distributed to the partners during the taxable year.

Partners are taxed on distributed earnings, on accumulated earnings, and on their proportionate shares of all gains and losses of the partnership. Partners also use the same methods of determining capital gains and losses that they would use in individual sole proprietorships. The partnership return shows the amount distributable to the partners; they in turn report this income on their own individual income tax returns.

As regards charitable contributions, partners again figure in their proportionate shares of any partnership contributions when computing income. Pension and profit-sharing plans are available to partners, but only in the limited amount permitted to self-employed persons under the current federal income tax laws. An income tax deduction may be permitted for a limited pension and profit-sharing program (see Chapter 9).

Like self-employed persons, partners have to pay their own self-employment tax. If a partner wishes to sell his share, or assign income or interest in the partnership, he ordinarily has to have the consent of all the other partners. A new partnership may result.

Exemption from state income tax

With respect to state taxes, the same considerations usually apply. A partnership does not have to pay any state income tax. But again, income is distributable to the partners themselves, and they have to report it as income if the particular state has such a tax. Sales taxes and other business-type taxes may be chargeable to the partnership. These are paid, usually, as ordinary and necessary business expenses.

Caveats. A partnership implies a very close relationship. It should be entered into only with someone in whom you have the utmost confidence and faith, someone who gets along well with you and whose spouse gets along well with your spouse. Make no mistake: more partnerships have been dissolved for reasons of personal animosity that arises during the partnership period than through lack of business success.

Examples of partnerships that failed are numerous. Some famous show-business partnerships have been broken up because of conflicts between the spouses of the partners.

The human element is as important as the business element in the successful operation of any partnership. Before entering into such an arrangement, the potential partner should know the person he wants to enter into business with, know the spouse, and reach an affirmative conclusion after study of all the business and personal ramifications.

The Corporation

The corporate way of doing business is much more complicated than the sole proprietorship or partnership. But where the business is such that the corporate form makes sense, it can be very flexible.

Basically, a corporation is made up of its *shareholders*, who are the owners of the company; the *board of directors*, which handles the management and policy of the company; and *officers* who handle day-to-day affairs. This division between ownership and management gives the corporation its flexibility. In addition, the corporation guarantees limited liability to the shareholders: their liability is limited to their investment only. Ordinarily, the individual shareholders need not concern themselves with the possibility that they can be held personally liable for debts of the corporation over and above their investments.

The shareholders own the company

Does the corporate form of doing business apply only to a large enterprise, or to a large business operation? Not at all. The laws of many states provide for so-called "close" or "closed" corporations that have few shareholders, usually five or fewer. A corporation can have one or an unlimited number of shareholders. Thus a corporation format can be utilized by one person even if he is the only shareholder. He may thus have all the benefits of the corporate form, including these:

- A corporation may continue on a perpetual basis, until dissolved by law, unless a specific state statute limits the time. Ordinarily, however, a corporation can be organized to exist "forever."

- A corporation has an existence separate and apart from its owners, the stockholders. It has the legal capacity to sue and it can be sued, and it has the capacity to own property in its name.

- As far as liability is concerned, the corporation is liable for all of its own debts and obligations. But once its assets are exhausted by creditors, each shareholder's liability is limited to his capital contribution to the corporation.

Organizing. In organizing, a corporation as a creature of state law must adhere strictly to the laws of the state. Most states require that a corporate charter be issued after application to the appropriate state official. Usually, a corporate purpose must be stated in the charter. That purpose often sets limits on the activities of the corporation. In recent years, however, states have allowed corporations to include very broad statements of purpose in their charters.

Some states require that the prospective issuance of the charter or the application for the corporate charter be publicly announced. Once the charter is issued, the corporation is legally organized. The application for the charter is accompanied by necessary filing fees, initial tax statements, and other required documentation.

Announcing the corporate charter

Ordinarily, the first board of directors, or the first stockholders who will elect the board of directors, must also be identified in the application.

Some states require that all limitations on the transfer of stock or issuance of shares of stock, or classes of stock, be set forth in the charter.

Small Corporations. If the corporation is a closed one, the creditors may attempt to look beyond the corporation and go after the personal assets of individual shareholders. The creditors may claim that the corporation is merely a sham designed to protect the shareholders who are in fact the owners and managers of the company.

In many cases, clearly, the corporate officers may be the same as the corporate directors. They may even be the same as the shareholders: the same individuals hold all positions. Unless all corporate records are maintained accurately and precisely, according to law, the creditor may be able to support such contentions. All corporate state and federal tax returns must be filed and minutes of corporate stockholders' meetings, corporate board of directors' meetings, and executive committee meetings must be maintained.

Keeping minutes   Accurate minutes must also be kept on all actions required by law of the board of directors or the stockholders. Only in this way can a small corporation protect itself against claims that it is not operating according to law and that the shareholders should therefore be responsible for company debts.

Raising Funds. The corporate form of doing business has a very practical advantage when funds are needed for capital expansion. Also, since the ownership of the corporation is represented by shares of stock, ownership can be transferred simply by selling the shares of stock. Unless the company's by-laws contain *stock transfer restrictions*, the stock is ordinarily freely saleable.

Some stock transfer restrictions are relatively common. For example, a stockholder may be required to offer stock shares for sale to the corporation before selling to a third party.

In larger corporations whose stock is traded on a national or local exchange such as the American or New York stock exchanges, transfers are made by brokers, based on the average price of the stock on the day of transfer. Where a small company is involved, however, it becomes more difficult to assess the value of stock shares. A closely held corporation whose shares are to be sold may have to rely on company records, such as earnings and other financial reports, since there is no ready market for these shares.

Where stock is sold in this way, no new agreements need be filed. A change in stock ownership does not change such factors as corporate assets, the operation of the company, or its title to real estate.

Money-raising   In raising additional funds for a corporate business operation, the
options   corporation has several options. It can sell an issue of *new stock—stock*

that it issues for sale to the general public in addition to that already outstanding in the hands of stockholders. It can issue *bonds*, interest-bearing certificates of corporate debt, or other forms of securities such as preferred stock and debentures. The latter also represents corporate debt. With more options open to it than an individual proprietor or a partnership, the growth business established as a corporation can often provide periodically for expansion.

Management. The management of the corporation is in the hands of its board of directors, which ordinarily acts by majority agreement. The stockholders of the corporation elect the board of directors, usually on an annual basis at the annual stockholders' meeting. The board of directors normally appoints the top officers. Minutes of all meetings of the board of directors and stockholders are maintained. In some larger corporations, minutes are kept of all meetings of the executive committee and the officers.

As the legal owners, the stockholders may vote by proxy in electing the board of directors. The stockholders in effect give the right to vote to some other party who then votes for members of the board. However, the board of directors does not have the right to delegate its duties and must exercise its obligations directly. A director cannot, by proxy, give some other person or group his right to vote at the directors' meeting.

Taxes and Tax Reports. Many more state tax reports are ordinarily required of a corporation than of a partnership or a sole proprietorship. The various states have enacted different tax laws affecting corporations. Capital stock taxes, initial excise taxes, and a corporate net profits tax are usually levied. These may require the assistance of an experienced accountant.

Paying taxes directly on income

Unlike the partnership, the corporation pays taxes directly on its income. The stockholders pay taxes only on the dividend income they receive less the dividend tax credit. If the corporation does not distribute its dividends, and has a surplus available for payment of dividends over and above that allowed by law, a penalty or surtax may be charged for the accumulation of income beyond that permitted.

As a major advantage, the corporation under present tax laws can set up full-scale pension and profit-sharing plans. A current deduction is allowed for payments into the pension or profit-sharing fund. The members pay no taxes on the profit-sharing or pension benefits until they actually receive them—usually after retirement.

Pension/profit-sharing plan limitations

The tax laws limit the amounts that can be paid out under corporate pension and profit-sharing plans. But these benefits are much more liberal than those available to partners or other self-employed individuals. The sick-pay provisions of the tax laws typically allow regular employees a limited tax deduction on such payments. A corporation can also deduct its own charitable contributions up to a specified amount.

Officers and employees of a corporation are entitled to all the benefits enjoyed by employees. The corporation must withhold from the pay of officers and employees the necessary Social Security and other taxes, including income taxes. Even though they may also be shareholders, the officers are employees of the corporation and not self-employed individuals, and must report income as employees.

A final tax-related advantage is the ability of the corporation owner to make gifts of stock as part of an estate plan. A sole proprietor would find it very difficult to bring his children into his business in an ownership way. If he is incorporated, however, the individual can transfer shares of stock from himself to his children on a regular basis. In doing so, he reduces the size of his estate and increases each child's ownership interest in the business.

Things to Remember. Considering incorporation? Remember that the corporation is separate and apart. That remains true even if you are the sole stockholder and the president of the company. The corporation exists as an entity; it has a separate legal existence.

Remember also that even the owner-president of a small corporation has to have a working arrangement with the company. For example, he should have an *employment agreement* with the corporation that indicates his compensation and stock rights, his pension and profit-sharing rights, if any, and so on. It may seem unnecessary to have an employment agreement when there is only one stockholder. But the value of the agreement becomes clear if additional stockholders join the corporation later. The agreement protects the original owner's status as an officer of the company and his compensation level.

Mr. President's employment agreement

An employment agreement may have major impact on tax liability, particularly where a question arises involving the valuation of stock or the reasonableness of an officer's salary. In reviewing the income received by a corporate officer, and measuring it against the duties performed, the Internal Revenue Service sometimes finds that the officer is receiving a dividend, not compensation. The dividend could then be taxed twice—once while in the corporate account and again after it reaches the stockholder.

An employment agreement that specifies the total compensation to be paid to the officer and the duties required can often eliminate such problems.

Many other considerations relating to the corporate form of doing business should be kept in mind. These can depend on the nature of the business, the company's size, its growth potential, the degree of flexibility required, and so on. The need for competent legal and financial advice is ever-present. If set up properly, the corporation can serve as practical application of business principles to bring success to an enterprise.

OTHER FORMS OF BUSINESS ORGANIZATIONS

In addition to the sole proprietorship, the general partnership, and the corporation, there are other ways to go into business. These are combinations of some of the forms already noted. All should have a place in the process of determining the appropriate way to go into business.

From limited partnership to joint venture

The Limited Partnership

A limited partnership combines some of the elements of a general partnership with those of a corporation. A limited partner makes an investment in the partnership; but he ordinarily has nothing whatever to do with the management of the business and he enjoys a limitation on his liability for partnership debts. The limit is the amount of money that he has invested. The partnership form remains, but the limited partner has liability similar to that of a stockholder in a corporation.

The limited partnership is controlled by statute in the various states. The statutory requirements have to be followed very closely if each limited partner is to enjoy the advantage of limited liability. Major tax advantages can also be claimed by limited partners.

A limited partnership and a corporation may be joined in a single enterprise. Each of the entities performs a separate function. In such instances, it is important to keep all records of the two organizations separate and apart. All agreements, arrangements, and contracts between the two are treated as though the partnership and corporation were unrelated entities and totally separate business enterprises.

The limited partnership has been widely used as a vehicle for conducting long-range, risky, and costly operations of a highly technical nature. An example would be oil and gas exploration and drilling. The partners usually do not want to take a direct role in management. They have funds to invest; in making an investment, they see the risk of loss as secondary. More importantly, the investment usually gives them a *tax write-off*. The funds in many cases would have been paid to the government as income taxes.

One general partner required
Every limited partnership has to have at least one general partner who organizes and runs the partnership operations. One or more limited partners—up to dozens and even hundreds—join the partnership and invest in it. If the partnership makes a profit, it is distributed to the partners according to a formula set out in the limited partnership certificate that each partner receives.

The "Sub-Chapter S" Corporation

The federal tax laws permit the so-called "sub-chapter S" corporation to be treated as a partnership insofar as taxation is concerned. The requirements are that the corporation have no more than 10 stockholders to qualify. The corporation then retains all the advantages that make the corporation form advisable, such as limited liability of stockholders. At the same time the "sub-S" corporation is not taxed as a corporation.

Taxing Sub-S shareholders as partners
The shareholders of a sub-S corporation are taxed as partners. They include all the distributed income in their own income tax returns, reporting it as income.

Under the income tax laws a partnership or a sole proprietorship, if qualified, can elect to be treated as a corporation. Ordinarily, the purpose would be to reduce taxes. Typically, the corporation has unreasonably high income and wants to take advantage of certain lower tax rates.

The Joint Venture

A joint venture is similar to a partnership. Two or more individuals or a combination of individuals and companies undertake to perform certain services or do a certain job. Unlike a partnership, however, the joint venture is not a continuing arrangement. A joint venture is entered into only for one specific project. On termination or completion of that project, the joint venture terminates.

The parties to a joint venture enter into an agreement that spells out all rights and obligations and the nature of the work or project to be undertaken by the joint venture. The test of a joint venture is whether it has been formed for one specific project only.

CONTROL OF THE BUSINESS ENTERPRISE

A particular field of business has been selected. A specific form of organization—sole proprietorship, partnership, or corporation—has been decided on. How about the problem of control? How can you be assured that, having set up the business, you will be able to protect it—or keep out people whom you may not want to be in it? How do you keep the management and control of the business in your hands or subject to your approval?

The question of control involves a number of considerations. The type of business, the method by which interests can be transferred to others, restrictions on the transfer of ownership, employment contracts, and other factors become important. This is why the necessary agreements, contracts, charters, by-laws, and other documents should be prepared by a lawyer. All rights and obligations of the parties have to be spelled out clearly and precisely or questions of control may arise in the future. *The question of control*

The nonlawyer may not be able to assess the importance of some factors. Specific questions may turn on the provisions of state law regarding restrictions on transfers of shares, what can be included in the charter of a corporation, the attitudes of the local courts toward management, and restrictions on the transfer of control of the business. The wording of some documents may affect an owner's power to control his own business.

Some possible ways of maintaining control include the following:

1. *Restrictions on transfers of interest.* As noted, an absolute restriction on the transfer of an interest in a business enterprise may be considered unreasonable. The law generally does not favor restraints on the selling or assignment of business enterprise or property rights. This legal hurdle can be overcome, however, by a *stock transfer restriction agreement* among the shareholders. The agreement gives the other partners or stockholders an option or right of first refusal before stock shares can be sold to a third party outside the business. *Limiting transfers of interest*

An example may be noted. A partnership agreement could specify that a partnership interest could not be sold unless the partner wishing to sell first offered his partnership interest to the other partners. If the others refuse to buy under a formula established in the agreement, then the partner would be free to sell to someone else.

Other agreements might provide that before a shareholder can sell his stock to the general public, he must first offer it to the corporation itself—or to the other shareholders. The latter could buy the offered stock in proportion to the total number of shares each owns. If the stock is not purchased, the shareholder would have the right to sell to the general public.

Stock transfer restrictions: valid but not absolute Such stock transfer restrictions are valid and enforceable. They are not considered absolute restrictions on transfer of shares. This type of restriction is often set out in a clause in the agreement among the shareholders in a by-law provision, and in a statement on every stock certificate. Anyone who buys the stock in violation of the restriction is regarded as having been put on notice by the provision on the certificate.

2. *Employment contracts.* Continued control of a business can be assured by drawing up an employment agreement between a partnership and its partners or between a corporation and its officers. The agreement can specify the rights, duties, and obligations of the corporation or partnership and of the employee or officer.

3. *Voting rights.* Most business enterprises involve a number of people. Usually, the parties want some assurance that the business will go on as originally planned. Where the possibility exists that a majority could act contrary to the wishes of the founders and forget what the business was designed to do, voting provisions can be used to maintain control. Various approaches are utilized to protect the business operation in such cases:

- Arrangements may be made for voting and nonvoting stock, for voting rules that ensure that the minority group is represented on the board of directors, and for elections of different directors in different years.

- Shareholder agreements may be written so as to require the shareholders to vote their stock in a certain way. For example, the agreements could require all shareholders to elect each other as directors of the corporation and no one else. The stockholders would then be able to prevent others from taking control of the corporation. It should be noted, however, that such restrictions on voting or on transfers of shares will naturally inhibit someone else from buying that stock. If the intent of the corporation is to create a market for its stock and to attract additional shareholders, such restrictions will adversely affect that intent.

- Where a number of shareholders want to join together to give a lesser number the right to vote all the shares, a *voting trust agreement* may be utilized. The voting trustees are designated by the agreement. They themselves can agree on how the votes will be cast.

  Use of the voting trust agreement

- Depending on the law of the state, the charter and by-law provisions of the corporation may provide for the requirements as to quorums and the number of persons required to vote. Different percentages of the total number of shares may have to be represented at meetings before votes can be taken on certain acts. For example, a two-thirds vote of all shareholders may be needed to change the by-laws of the corporation. In a small corporation, the by-laws or a separate agreement among the shareholders may specify that all shareholders must agree to any change in the company by-laws.

- Arrangements may be made to provide for arbitration. Where disagreements arise, preventing the orderly operation of the business, the partnership agreement, the by-laws of the corporation, or a separate agreement among the shareholders should provide for some means of breaking any deadlock. Arbitration, dissolution of the company, or a provision allowing one party to buy out the other are all possible methods. All can be useful, especially where only a few shareholders or partners are involved.

  Arbitration to settle disagreements

Not uncommonly, a partnership agreement or stockholder agreement involving a few partners or stockholders will provide that one party offer his stock to another party at a certain price. The other person then decides whether to sell or buy depending on the price. One party sets the price, and the other party decides whether to sell his own stock at that price or to buy the other person's stock at the same price.

4. *Buy-sell agreements between shareholders in a corporation.* The founder of a corporation would usually want to ensure that on his death the corporation would have an opportunity to buy his interest for the benefit of his estate or beneficiaries. These *buy-sell agreements* ordinarily establish an obligation on the part of the corporation to buy. The estate of the deceased shareholder has to sell the stock.

Sometimes such agreements are called "options" to buy and sell. They may require that if the estate wants to sell the stock, the stock must first be offered to the corporation or to the other surviving shareholders before it can be offered to others.

In order to finance the purchase of the stock of a deceased shareholder, the corporation must have a *stock retirement program* providing funds for

Stock retirement and cross-purchase

this purpose. A *cross-purchase plan*, by contrast, gives the other stockholders the right to purchase the shares of the deceased. The corporation cannot then buy the shares.

One problem faced by a corporation in retiring stock is that under the laws of most states it must have funds for such purchases in its surplus account. It may be difficult for the company to set aside such funds. A cross-purchase plan for stockholders solves the problem. Funded through an insurance program, with each shareholder owning an insurance policy on the lives of the other shareholders, the plan makes it possible to buy the stock of a deceased shareholder with the insurance proceeds. Such funds go to the estate of the deceased to purchase his stock.

If the corporation buys the stock, the ownership interest of the other stockholders remains the same. No change has taken place in the numbers of shares owned by the surviving shareholders. If those survivors buy the decedent's stock, a change in the stock interest of the surviving shareholders does result.

How do you set the price of stock for the purpose of carrying out a corporate buy-sell agreement? If the stock is traded on a regional or national stock exchange, the price can be easily determined from the quotation for the day on which the stock is offered. In a close corporation, however, where there is no ready market for the stock, the problem of evaluation becomes critical. A mandatory buy-sell agreement must outline an effective method of determining the price of the stock or the agreement is not worth the paper it is written on.

Incidentally, an effective formula may help in determination of the value of a decedent's stock for federal estate tax purposes. The price as determined according to the agreement could be used to calculate the estate tax valuation.

Ways to establish the per-share value of stock A buy-sell agreement in a closely held corporation may utilize any of several different ways of determining the per-share value of stock. The shareholders can set a fixed price per share, adding provisions for revising the price on an annual or some other basis. Calculations of value would be based on the performance of the company and other criteria. The controlling price would be the last stated price set before the death of the stockholder.

Where stock values have not been updated under a buy-sell agreement, problems may arise. The stock may have inflated or deflated in value since the last stated price was set. Where a fixed price has not been calculated for more than a year, an *appraisal method* of pricing the stock may be used. Other methods are also available.

The appraisal method leaves the price of the stock open pending later appraisal by a disinterested appraiser. On the death of the stockholder, the appraiser comes in and evaluates the stock. That decision is binding on the several parties.

The *book value method* of determining stock values utilizes both the last corporate balance sheet prepared before the death of the stockholder and a "net worth" adjustment to the date of death. The book value method does not take into account the value of the business as a going concern. The net worth method, however, will serve adequately:

- if inventory, for example, is determined at its actual worth rather than at cost;

- where accounts receivable are adjusted to take care of those that are not collectible;

- where the book value of machinery and equipment adequately represents their fair value and present worth;

- where real estate and buildings reflect current market values; and

- where insurance proceeds are considered as part of the evaluation.

Various other methods combine different valuation techniques that attempt to average corporate proceeds over a period of time and either *capitalize* the proceeds or *average out* the proceeds to determine a fair price for each share of stock.

Where a valuation formula is limited to book value only, the fair market value of the depreciable assets will be ignored. Only the depreciated value will be determined. The beneficiaries may receive much less for the stock than it is actually worth.

5. *Partnership buy-sell agreement.* A partnership has problems similar to those of corporations. The partnership agreement should therefore establish the circumstances under which the surviving partners can buy the interest of the deceased partner. The obligation of the decedent's estate to offer the partnership interest for sale on agreed terms should be specified.

When survivors can buy the deceased partner's shares

All partners and the partners' spouses should sign the partnership agreement—or the separate buy-sell agreement if such exists.

The valuation of the partnership interest for purposes of the buy-sell agreement involves some of the same considerations as the valuation of corporate stock. A value for good will should be placed on the partnership interest in the agreement. Provisions for payment should be spelled out clearly. The income tax laws provide for different treatments of payments depending on how they are made and the nature of the agreement. Thus care should be used in preparing the agreement to take advantage of the best possible tax thinking of professional advisors.

Four elements of a life insurance buyout agreement

Where life insurance is used to fund the purchase of a partner's interest, the agreement should spell out at least the following:

- Exactly how much life insurance is to be purchased
- Whether the partnership or the other partners own the policies on the lives of individual partners
- How the premium is to be paid
- How the transfer of the policy held by the deceased to the survivors is to be handled

INSURANCE UTILIZED IN BUSINESS OPERATIONS

Chapter 12, on insurance problems, noted some situations in which the insurance advice of professionals is needed. Such advice is absolutely indispensable where business insurance is concerned.

The insurance industry has recognized its obligation to provide expert advice in a professional way in recent years. Programs have been set up to train agents and brokers. Continuing education programs of the insurance industry include programs, seminars, and courses leading to the certification of an individual as a *Chartered Life Underwriter* (CLU). Other programs lead to the professional designation of *Chartered Property and Casualty Underwriter* (CPCU). Thus the business community has available top-notch experts who have the ability, the training, and the experience to apply their knowledge to current problems.

Insurance advisors can analyze risks. They can also read a partnership agreement or an agreement among shareholders to determine whether insurance protection is needed. They can give advice on the kinds of protection required and on costs.

In many cases, insurance offers the most economical and feasible method of funding programs for the purchase of stock of a deceased shareholder or the partnership interest of a deceased partner. The insurance advisor can explain how such programs work. The method to be used depends on the nature of the plan involved and the needs of the parties. If the number of shareholders or partners is large enough to require one, a trustee may be named to own the insurance policies and see to the distribution of the proceeds. The trustee becomes the designated beneficiary under the insurance policies so that he can carry out the terms of the agreement.

The trustee becomes the beneficiary

In other respects the trustee plan works much the same as that involving ownership of the policy by other partners, stockholders, or the corporation. The trustee can, however, be helpful where a great number of persons is involved and where distribution may be difficult.

A key factor in determining the best method of using life insurance to retire or purchase the stock of a deceased shareholder relates to the older and the younger shareholder. In a cross-purchase plan, the younger shareholder may "take a beating." This shareholder may have to pay premiums on a policy on the life of an older shareholder. These premiums, of course, can be very high. Where this situation exists, a corporation may use a stock retirement plan rather than the cross-purchase arrangement.

Premiums paid by corporations or individuals on insurance carried on the lives of stockholders are generally not deductible from income under the federal income tax laws. But in each case the insurance proceeds will be received by the beneficiaries free of tax. In most cases the corporation will receive the proceeds from the insurance and then buy up the decedent's stock. Where the stockholders own insurance on one another, the individual stockholder receives the proceeds and then purchases the stock.

Partnership insurance is treated in similar fashion. The insurance policies can be owned by the partnership, which can later purchase the partnership interest of the deceased. Or the insurance can be owned, and the premiums paid, by the partners, who insure the other partners. Again, premium payments are not deductible by the partnership or by individual partners. But the proceeds are not includable in income or subject to income tax. *Partnership insurance*

The decision to go into business raises complex questions. These relate to the form of business organization, the element of control of the business operation by various lawful means, and the funding of various plans to protect the interest of the businessman and his estate in the event of his death. What emerges constitutes a complete business plan. The need for sound business planning goes hand in hand with the necessity for consultation and advice from those whose profession or business it is to provide such assistance.

CONTRACTS

Among the problem areas, whatever business you go into may involve contracts of one kind or another. Some basic information about contracts and contract law may enable you to protect yourself—and thrive.

Contract Terms

The written contract should contain all the important details of a transaction or agreement. The contract begins, usually, with the date on which it is entered into. It also gives the parties' precise names and addresses. If one of the contract's signers is a corporation, the firm's name should be given in full.

Other parts of the contract fill in the key details of the agreement. The details are sometimes summarized as the *Who, What, Why, Where, When,* and *How.* If all those essential questions are answered in full, the contract will usually be complete.

Good Faith, Fair Dealing

Depending on the amount of money involved and the state in which the contract is signed, the agreement may have to be in writing to be valid and enforceable. In most states, the purchase/sale of goods worth $500 or more requires a written contract.

The standards do not apply so much to consideration, the payment or reward for performance of a contract, or to other elements as to concepts such as good faith and fair dealing. In contract cases courts have increasingly tried to measure the extent to which the parties have applied these concepts. At least four basic standards have evolved:

- Good faith generally means the parties act in accordance with the contract's purpose and with each other's expectations.
- Good faith in negotiation refers to the duty of the parties to a contract to avoid fraud and duress. In some cases, such as the "Truth in Lending Act," a law or statute requires good faith in negotiation (see "Fair Disclosure of Contract Terms," p. 280).
- Good faith performance rules out any attempt to violate the spirit of the contract, delay performance without good reason, or otherwise evade or ignore the contract's terms.
- Good faith in enforcement means that courts will generally rule that the parties must show good faith in the settlement of contract claims.

14 CAVEAT VENDOR— THE AGE OF THE CONSUMER

Without doubt the age of the consumer has begun. The consumer is king. Until recently, the maxim "caveat emptor"—"let the buyer beware" —was the rule of the marketplace. The purchase of goods of any kind, or an application for any kind of credit, put a consumer on his or her guard. No special treatment, no warnings, no protective information could be expected.

The complaints of consumers in such areas as exorbitant interest rates, defective goods, repossession of purchased products in cases of minor defaults, and many others reached such a crescendo that something had to be done. Both Congress and the various state legislatures have now

passed laws protecting the consumer. The purpose of this chapter is to examine some of these laws and the citizen's rights as a consumer.

The consumer protection movement is based on the concept that the consumer is not in a position to protect himself against unfair practices. Because of their economic clout, companies can exert pressure against the consumer—or take advantage of him. He is vulnerable when buying goods, borrowing funds, or investing for financial gain. He also "consumes" the environment in which he lives—in various ways. In all these instances, he is today entitled by law to certain protections. If these protections are not honored, the consumer may have the right to a remedy against the party at fault.

The early 1980s saw far-reaching changes taking place in the consumer movement. From a relatively spectacular series of isolated controversies—car warranties, flammable children's underwear, dangerous drugs, and so on—consumerism has been transformed. It has become a true movement, one that seeks continually to generate legislation, change the ways in which institutions work, make companies responsive to popular needs.

How is the consumer protected? One need remains to be underscored more thoroughly: the consumer's need to know how he or she is protected and how the protections can be used.

CONSUMER PROTECTION

The citizen's protection as a consumer of goods reaches into many different areas. These include:

Methods of presentation of goods, among them advertising
Packaging and labeling of goods
Methods used in selling the goods
Sales on credit
Protection of consumer defenses

Many more such areas might be listed. Each can be discussed under a separate heading.

Deceptive Practices

The statutes, rules, and regulations of various governmental agencies forbid or restrict deceptive practices in the sale of consumer goods. Some of these practices are:

False or Misleading Endorsements. An endorsement of a product is a statement by someone, usually someone with high public exposure and identity, that he or she approves the product. The endorser may be an athlete, a movie performer, a TV personality, or anyone else known to the public. Where the person making the endorsement has no way of knowing whether the product endorsed lives up to the ad statement, deception may be involved.

In a typical example, a movie star endorses a lawn mower, claiming that it is safe in all respects. But the movie star has no way of knowing whether the product is in fact safe. The endorsement may then be deceptive. The public figure who has loaned his or her name, for a price, to a product or business in the hope of stimulating sales may have incurred liability if the product does not perform as advertised. The same is true if the advertising is otherwise deceptive.

Endorsement may involve liability

Deception in Advertising. Until recent years, only a fraudulent act on the part of the seller of goods could serve as the basis for a remedy on the part of the consumer. A period in which courts tended to hold that deception did not necessarily involve an intentional, fraudulent act has now led to an apparent revival of the older doctrine.

A ruling by the Federal Trade Commission in late 1983 heralded the return to the more traditional approach. The FTC announced that it would consider an act or practice "deceptive" only if there was misrepresentation, omission, or other offense that would likely mislead reasonable consumers to their deception. The ruling made "reasonableness" the test of deception. A seller's claims which convey more than one meaning—one of them false—to reasonable consumers may make the seller liable for the misleading interpretation. But practices unlikely to deceive consumers acting reasonably will not offend the FTC.

Retail advertising is policed by the Federal Trade Commission (FTC), which reviews advertising materials to see whether a buyer would likely be misled. The FTC's Bureau of Consumer Protection also "rides shotgun" on illegal sales tactics, violations of the federal Truth in Lending law, and many other fraudulent or deceptive practices. Claims that overstate the life of a product, the superiority of one product over another, and other characteristics are outlawed unless they can be proved. The advertiser has to maintain records to substantiate his advertised claims regarding the quality of the product, its safety, its comparative price, and its contents.

Challenging The FTC continually challenges advertisers regarding misleading or
advertisers deceptive advertising. In a 1970s case the FTC discovered that a national advertiser was making false claims to encourage sales. The FTC ordered the offending company to launch a $10 million advertising campaign to correct the false claims. In 1978 the Supreme Court upheld the FTC's right to issue such orders for the protection of consumers.

Governmental efforts to protect the consumer touch on many aspects of life. For example, the Public Health Cigarette Smoking Act requires that a health warning appear on each package of cigarettes sold. Cigarette advertising has been banned on radio and television, and other forms of cigarette advertising have to contain the health warning in conspicuous print. The cigarette companies are also required to state the exact nicotine and tar content of their products. They cannot simply give a general statement that the product is low in nicotine and tar.

Paying some attention to radio and TV commercials, and to the advertisements in newspapers and magazines, will pay dividends. An effort should be made to analyze exactly what the advertiser is saying. If it is not clear what the advertiser is saying, or if the ad states that the product is better, lighter, smoother, mellower, more fragrant, harder-working, the consumer has the right to ask: "[li] better, lighter, smoother than *what?*"

"Better, lighter, smoother than what?"

If the ad deceives you, you have the right to complain. In some cases, you may have a right of action against the advertiser.

"Bait and Switch" Tactics. The FTC has outlawed "bait and switch" advertising. In one case a food store advertised a "special" without having on hand a sufficient stock of the special item to meet anticipated demand. The advertiser knew that by "baiting" the customer into the store with the advertised special, he was probably selling something else. The customer would usually buy a substitute item while in the store.

A "bait and switch" variation involves a merchant who advertises a low-cost item to get the customer into the store. The merchant then disparages or "talks down" the low-cost item in favor of a higher-priced item.

Many states outlaw such tactics. For example, state laws may forbid the "going out of business sale" when the store is not actually going out of business. Also prohibited in some states: the "fire sale" when there has been no fire, the "water damage and fire damage sale," or the "lost our lease sale," when none of these has in fact occurred. The laws of states or municipalities may require special licenses to conduct such sales to ensure that they are legitimate.

Are you really going out of business?

Games, Drawings, and Similar Contests. An obvious and frequently used advertising method is the sweepstakes or game-type promotion. The merchant tries to induce the customer to enter a contest or drawing. Where a sales promotion plan is involved, as is usual, the FTC has taken the position that there must be disclosure of the numerical odds of winning a prize, the approximate values of the prizes, the fact that all announced prizes will be awarded, and that they have in fact been awarded.

Requirements of Packaging and Labeling

What appears on the product label or package may be as important from a consumer rights viewpoint as the advertising that promotes its sale. Many federal laws have dealt with this area in recent years. They include the Fair Packaging and Labeling Act; the Fair Products Labeling Act; the Food, Drug, and Cosmetics Act; the Cigarette Labeling and Advertising Act; and the Flammable Fabrics Act. In addition, various federal and state laws forbid the use of such deceptive terms as "full,"

"jumbo size," "giant size," or "family size" in describing package dimensions. Such terms, it is held, create the impression that more is contained in the package than is actually there.

Under pressure and as a result of legislation, merchants have increasingly dated their products. They have tended more and more to describe contents in terms of commonly understood weights and measures —to avoid deceiving the consumer.

Labels have to be specific

Legislation now requires specifics on labels. The Fair Products Labeling Act, for example, requires that a product bear a label stating the identity of the product, the name and place of business of the manufacturer, the packer or distributor, the net quantity of all of the contents, and the net quantity of one serving when the number of servings is stated on the label. In addition, the Act gives the FTC and the Department of Health and Human Services the authority to require more information or additional disclosures on a label.

Where food, drugs, and cosmetics are involved, the federal Food and Drug Administration (FDA) regulates labeling and packaging. "Quackery" in medicine and drugs and the so-called "miracle drug" claims also come under the policing power of the FDA.

Approval or Testing of Goods

What does the "seal of approval" mean?

Stop and think. How many products can you name that are sold with a guarantee, tag, or other indication that the product has been tested and approved by some testing agency or organization? If the product has a seal of approval, this ordinarily means that the product has been tested and approved for normal consumer uses. If it has not in fact been tested and approved, the seller has violated a warranty made to the consumer and may be liable for fraud.

Products involving fire and electrical safety features may be tested by manufacturers' associations and testing companies for insurance purposes. Successful testing indicates that the product has been manufactured in accordance with industry safety standards and will pass muster. The consumer can rely on tests made by someone who knows more about the product than the consumer does, and thus is assured that the product is safe.

Some private and industry testing agencies report factually what the tests reveal but draw no conclusions. This is true also of private consumer organizations that report test results in various consumer magazines. On the other hand, certain magazines accept product advertising and agree to refund product costs or replace an item if it should prove defective.

Such approval would usually carry only the liability to refund a price or replace a defective article. But if the consumer is injured by the defective article, there may be liability in the expanding area of *product liability.* The magazine or organization giving its approval or guarantee might be held liable. The buyer might have a right of action against the seller as well. Should deception or injury result from a defective, guaranteed product, it is usually wise to consult a lawyer.

Control of Methods of Selling Goods

The methods used by merchants in selling their products have been sharply limited in recent years. The reason: those methods may involve violations of consumer rights.

The sale-closers

Read the classified ads section of the daily newspaper. Various ads call for salesmen who are specialists in closing a sale, called "closers." These are people who are trained to get the customer to sign on the dotted line. Many of them can take a "lead," the name of a prospective customer secured from someone else, and close the sale with a minimum investment of time and effort. These closers, who are highly trained and experienced, usually work on a straight commission basis. They try to induce the lead to sign immediately, rather than allow him or her to think about the purchase before signing.

Because the law seeks both to protect the consumer and to punish the fraudulent or unlawful merchant, various selling practices have been either placed under legal controls or outlawed.

Fair Disclosure of Contract Terms. The person taking out a loan and paying interest, points, service charges, or any other extra charge must have full disclosure of such charges. The person buying furniture, an automobile, or home improvements on the installment plan, or charging meals, gasoline costs, or repair charges is entitled to full disclosure of all contract terms. So is the buyer of hundreds of other items who buys on time or credit and pays interest. The law does not apply if no interest or other charges are added to the basic cost of the item even if installment payments are allowed.

The Consumer Credit Protection Act, better known as the "Truth in Lending Act," is the source of such protection. It is designed to let the consumer know exactly what the credit offered by the merchant will cost. Comparisons of the credit arrangements of other credit sources can then be made. The consumer can shop for the best "deal."

Finance charges and annual percentage rates

The landmark Truth in Lending Act guarantees the availability of information on the two most important factors in the cost of credit—the *finance charge,* or the amount paid to obtain credit, and the *annual percentage rate* (APR), the percentage of interest paid over a year's time. Both the finance charge and the annual percentage rate must be prominently displayed on the forms used by the merchant, banker, or

---

**THINK BEFORE YOU BORROW
OR BUY ON TIME![1]**

The wise borrower or buyer on time will pause a moment before signing anything. He or she will ask questions: Is it necessary to buy now? Can the loan be taken out later—when more cash will be available to repay or reduce it? Can interest or carrying charges be reduced in other ways?

Whatever the answers, some steps should be followed for one's own protection.

—Read and understand the contract; don't rush.

—Never sign a contract with blank spaces.

—Be sure the contract spells out in plain language:

 ▪ exactly what you are buying (make, model, size, type)

 ▪ purchase price

 ▪ down payment and trade-in allowances, if any

 ▪ amount borrowed

 ▪ total amount due

 ▪ interest and service charge in dollars and annual percentage rate

—Know to whom and where you make payments, as well as when the payments are due. What happens if you can't pay on time? Or if you pay ahead?

—What are the seller's obligations for delivery, maintenance, service, or replacement?

—Do you get a copy of the contract to keep?

—Do you suspect a violation of the Truth in Lending Act? It should be reported to the Bureau of Consumer Protection, Federal Trade Commission, Washington, D.C. 20580, or to a local consumer protection group.

[1] Reprinted with permission of Macmillan Publishing Co., Inc. from *Consumer Complaint Guide 1979* by Joseph Rosenbloom, copyright© 1979, Joseph Rosenbloom.

other lender. With that information, the consumer can exactly compute what he or she will be paying.

How does this work in practice? Suppose you borrowed $100 for one year and paid $6 in interest. If you had the full use of all of that money for a full year and did not have to repay it until the end of that year, you would be paying an annual percentage rate of 6 per cent. The finance charge would be $6. But if you repay the total $106 in 12 equal monthly installments, you would not have the full use of the $100 over the entire year. You would have an average of about one-half of the full amount. The $6 interest charged for the credit extended to you thus becomes an annual percentage rate of 11 per cent.

Some creditors apply a service charge or carrying charge instead of interest or in addition to interest. Whatever they call them, they must total up all of these charges, including interest, and call the total amount the "finance charge." Then they have to list the annual percentage rate on the total cost of credit.

Remember that the Truth in Lending Act is not designed to establish interest rates or other charges. Most states have laws that set the legal rates of interest for various types of transactions. The Act does apply to all business and financial institutions dealing in consumer credit.

An important subfeature of the law deals with advertising. If a business mentions one feature of credit in its advertising, such as the amount of the down payment, it must also mention all the other important terms. These range from the amount of each installment payment to the total number of such payments.

A violation of the Truth in Lending law by a lender can result in criminal penalties as well as civil money damages. The consumer can sue if the lender fails to make the proper disclosures, claiming an amount that is twice the finance charge or a minimum of $100 to a maximum of $1,000 for each violation. The lender may also have to pay court costs and reasonable attorney's fees.

Sales by Mail. More and more goods and services are being offered to the consuming public through the mails. If the mails are used to defraud, however, federal laws protect the consumer.

State statutes may also forbid deceptive practices by companies that use the mail as the primary means of advertising or delivering their products. Because the amounts involved in mail-order sales may be small, the consumer may find himself unable to recover the amount lost on the sale. If there is no attempt to defraud on the part of the seller, federal law would not ordinarily give any relief to the party buying by mail-order.

The consumer has the right, in mail-order sales, to know or do certain things. He is entitled, for example:
- to know when he can expect shipment of the merchandise;
- to have the merchandise shipped within 30 days;
- to cancel an order where merchandise is not shipped as promised or within 30 days;
- to be notified of delays and have a free means to reply, such as a postage-free postcard;
- to agree to a new shipping date; and
- to have any payments returned if 30 days elapse and the merchandise is not shipped.

Free sample and charitable mailings

Only two kinds of merchandise can be sent through the mail without the recipient's consent or agreement. The two are free samples, clearly marked as such, and items mailed by charitable organizations seeking contributions. In either case the merchandise can, at the option of the recipient, be regarded as a gift.

Control of Methods of Payment

The methods by which payment may be made or demanded by a creditor on a consumer sale comprise another area in which protective laws are common. Under the laws of some states, if a creditor accepts payment in a form other than cash or check, the creditor takes a chance. For example, if he has to sell the sales contract to a bank or finance company, the consumer can raise various defenses against the bank or finance company to block collection. A check gives the consumer adequate protection since he can stop payment if an item appears defective.

Application of Payments. In addition to payment by cash or check, *application* of the payments to the debt becomes important.

In the past it appeared proper for a creditor to require payment on any item on a continuous charge basis. Payments were to be applied in any way he wished. The result: if a debtor who was three months delinquent on his open credit account sent in a monthly payment, the creditor could apply that payment to the newest monthly charge. He could then hold the debtor in default on the payment due three months ago.

Today, the laws of a number of states provide that in the event of default, any right of repossession by the creditor is limited to the later unpaid items. He must apply the payment to the oldest monthly installment due. *Right of repossession limited*

Accelerated and Large Final Payments. Under consumer credit contracts, the final payment in a monthly installment series could at one time have been larger than any of the previous monthly payments. In this way, unscrupulous creditors tried to make the last payment in the series larger than the debtor could pay. The debtor would then be in default on the last payment.

The laws of various states now ban this type of practice. The laws provide that if the final payment is double the average of the earlier scheduled payments, the debtor has a right to refinance the final payment on terms similar to those of the original transaction. The creditor is thus required to accept the refinancing of the final payment and cannot claim a default.

Federal law has similar provisions. Under these, the creditor has to identify any large final payments and provide in the contract for the terms under which the financing of this last payment may be handled.

Acceleration of payments refers to provisions in contracts that give creditors the right to declare an unpaid balance entirely due and payable in the event of default of one installment. In other words, the creditor can say, "All right, Tom, now you owe me the entire balance because you missed the August payment."

While the creditor still has the right to accelerate payments, most states require that the acceleration be based on a good faith decision by the creditor that a substantial default has actually occurred. This eliminates the "trivial" default that previously could militate against consumers. All *Default must really have occurred* earlier payments were lost in many cases because of some minor deviation from the contract. In sales of furniture, appliances, and many other categories of products, the buyer even today should study both the fine and the large print.

Control of Credit Card Sales

Commentators have noted that American society is rapidly becoming "cashless." This means that instead of cash, transactions are increasingly being handled by such things as credit cards, entries in bank records, and so on. Cash appears to be going out of style.

Credit cards may now be used for just about everything, including travel, entertainment, and purchases of furniture and appliances. Certain credit cards can be used for all of the above and for loans, deposits to other accounts, check cashing, and many other bank transactions. Yet controls on the issuance, use, and liabilities of credit cards exist—and necessarily. Users of cards should be aware of these controls for their own protection.

Limits on credit card issuance and use

A credit card can no longer be issued to someone who has not applied for it. When the push for cards first began, the bank, store, or other issuer would commonly flood their customer lists. Credit cards were sent to almost anyone. There was little or no control over who actually ended up with the cards, and signed applications for cards were rarely on record. Tremendous problems resulted. The prohibition against issuance without an application resulted.

You lose a credit card. Someone else uses it without your permission. You are not liable for the purchases made on the card beyond the sum of $50.00. Even then, to hold you liable for that amount, the company issuing the card must show that the card was accepted by you, either through your use of the card or your application for it. You must also have been given notice that you might be liable up to $50.00; you must have been given a self-addressed, prestamped form to notify the issuer of the loss or theft of the card; and the issuing company must have provided a method of identifying you as the authorized user of the card—by providing a space on the card for your signature, photograph, fingerprint, or some other form of identification.

To hold you liable for the first $50.00, of course, the improper use of the card by someone else must have occurred before you notified the issuing company of the loss or theft. If the use occurs after you notify the company, you are not liable even for the first $50.00.

To protect yourself against any such claim, notify the issuing company immediately on discovery that your credit card has been lost or stolen. Send the notification by certified mail, return receipt requested.

Then you have proof that you sent the notice and that the company in fact received it.

In one ripoff scheme of recent years, credit card holders could buy insurance against loss of a card—and subsequent misuse of it by unauthorized persons. Because of the $50 limitation of liability, the insurance is no longer necessary—if it ever was.

Credit card insurance unnecessary

Defenses of the Consumer

Because the consumer and the merchant have had unequal bargaining positions, the merchant at one time could include provisions in a contract under which the consumer waived many protections that the law then provided. If the consumer could not understand what he was surrendering, the merchant could point to the "small print" on the reverse side, indicating that the consumer had given up many legal defenses he might have had.

A buyer cannot waive some defenses under recent consumer's statutes. For example, specific provisions permit the buyer to protect himself against the seller or against a financial institution that purchased the installment sales contract from the seller. Where a household appliance is defective, under the consumer protection statutes of many states the buyer has the right to withdraw from the contract. This is the case regardless of what the terms of the contract provide.

State law must be investigated to determine the rights or defenses that a consumer cannot waive. The methods used to defend against a third party who has purchased a sales contract from a seller should also be studied. The state laws are not uniform.

Control of the Sales Contract

The consumer protection laws are not designed to interfere with the rights of people to enter into contracts with others. But the laws do attempt to override certain terms or clauses in sales contracts that tend to deceive the consumer or place him in an unfortunate position as opposed to the merchant. For example, in some states the "confession of judgment" clauses in sales and other contracts have been outlawed. These clauses attempt to give the creditor the right to obtain an immediate judgment against the debtor in the event of an alleged default in payment. The creditor need not file a formal complaint in court and go through the normal trial procedures.

Some "confession of judgment" clauses outlawed

Under the confession of judgment procedure, the debtor has to come forward and try to have the judgment opened. Such clauses are still valid in some states—or can be valid depending on the circumstances. Where a sales contract contains a confession of judgment clause, the buyer should at least know what it means and make an intelligent decision on signing or not signing.

A court may declare other kinds of sales contracts invalid. For example, a contract involving grossly exorbitant prices would show clearly that the consumer was cheated. On application of the consumer, a court could rule against the seller.

Protecting the right to earn a living

Wages and salaries comprise yet another sensitive area. Both are considered so important to the individual and his family's well-being that state statutes in most states forbid or restrict the attachment of wages for payment of debts. The controlling public policy in such cases is the protection of the right to earn a living. For the same reason, most states hold that no one can assign his wages or direct that they be paid to someone other than his spouse or dependents. In those states that forbid assignment, no creditor can claim a person's wages before they are paid to the employee.

Finally, consumer protection laws sometimes require that sales contracts include certain clauses or fulfill certain conditions. The consumer may not be legally allowed to sign a blank contract. All the terms may have to be filled in completely before the contract is signed and delivered to the consumer. The contract may have to show exactly what the payments are composed of—the amount of the principal payment, the amount of interest, total finance costs, and the annual percentage rate of interest charged. The number of installments, the total amounts due, and the due dates may have to be specified.

Such laws may apply to credit card invoices, charge account invoices, and other credit invoices of any kind.

Control of the Methods of Collection

Notice of lawsuit or collection letter?

Who has not received in the mail an apparent notice that a lawsuit has been filed against him to collect a debt? Close study would probably reveal that the notice was nothing more than a cleverly worded collection letter from a creditor or collection agency. Such billing and collection practices have become the targets of consumer protection laws such as the federal Fair Debt Collection Practices Act of 1977.

Fair Treatment Guaranteed. Enforced by the FTC, the Fair Debt Collection Practices Act is designed to ensure that people are treated fairly by debt collectors. The debts covered are personal, household, and family debts. These could be contracted in purchasing a car, using a charge account, obtaining medical care, and buying literally hundreds of items or services.

Under the Act, the consumer has the right to receive a written notice of the indebtedness within five days after a debt collector contacts him.

The notice has to state the amount owed and the name of the creditor. The notice must also contain instructions on what the recipient can do if he or she believes that no debt exists.

Many financial institutions that lend money to the public have to be licensed by the state. The licenses can be suspended or revoked for abuses of credit laws. This is, of course, an excellent way to control the loan business, if properly policed. If you have any information concerning abusive collection or billing activities, or deceptive practices engaged in by such companies, the state agency involved with the licensing of the institution should be notified.

Licensing of lenders

Improper Billing and Collection. Like the collection letter that looks like a court summons, any deceptive method of debt collection is unlawful. To the extent that they are also unreasonable, those methods may involve the invasion of the *right of privacy* and result in legal action by the debtor. Notifying a debtor's employer of a debt or indicating that he is a "deadbeat," using the telephone to harass the debtor and his family, and hiring private investigators to follow, embarrass, and intimidate the debtor—all these are unlawful.

Many other methods of billing and collecting have been attempted. Today the consumer has the right to complain—and may have a right of action against the party employing such practices.

Control of Credit Reporting

Modern economies place great stress on a person's credit rating. The ability to get a job, to purchase what one wants or needs, and to live the good life may, consequently, depend on one's credit rating.

Is it wise to pay cash for everything purchased? The experts say No. More appropriately, young people, when starting out, are advised to borrow a minimum amount of money from a bank or other financial institution. They can pay the loan back as soon as possible. In the meantime they have a credit reference that they can use when applying for credit at a later date.

Until recently, a person applying for credit never knew that he might be investigated by a financial institution or a merchant. He would hear from his neighbors or his employer that someone was asking questions about him at home or at work. But he never knew what was said or what was finally reported to the company requesting the report.

Many private agencies were engaged in securing credit information and supplying it, for a fee, to interested persons or companies. Naturally, abuses arose in the system. Primarily, the person who was being investigated did not know what was in his credit report. No one could know for

Abuses by credit agencies

certain whether he was ever denied a job, credit, or something else because of a bad credit rating—even though the credit report may have contained incorrect information.

In an attempt to correct the abuses, Congress enacted the Fair Credit Reporting Act in 1970. The Act applies only to personal, family, and household credit, and not to business or commercial credit. Nevertheless, it gives the individual some protection with regard to his credit rating.

Right to Proper Information. When an applicant for a job, insurance, or credit is refused because of a negative credit report, the law requires that he or she be advised of the name and address of the agency supplying the report. If no agency was involved, the person must be given a summary of the information received. The applicant then knows at least the name of the agency or the basis on which his application was refused.

Right of Privacy. Under federal law, credit bureaus and investigative agencies cannot disclose information about a person's credit to persons who have no lawful use for it. The person being investigated must be advised of the fact that he is being investigated and of his right to know the results of the investigation. No longer can the report in such cases be kept secret from him. On request, a credit agency must also tell the consumer the names and addresses of the persons to whom it gave credit reports during a six-month period before the request. The agency must indicate to what employers such reports were given during a two-year period previous to the request.

Attack on Credit Report for Errors. Specification of the right to correct errors in a credit report is perhaps the most important provision of the law dealing with fair credit reporting. The information contained in the credit report is ordinarily supplied by friends, neighbors, employers, and others who may or may not know what they are talking about. Thus these reports may be incorrect and even downright false. If not corrected, a bad report may follow an individual and cause him problems for years.

A limited right to require disclosure

At one time the consumer had no way to correct a report. Today he has a limited right to have an agency disclose to him, on request, the information in its files.

When a consumer claims that his report contains incorrect information, the agency must try to determine whether or not the claim is correct. If the claim is verified, the information in the agency's report must be amended. Corrections must be sent to all persons to whom the agency sent reports in the preceding six months and to employers who received reports during the preceding two years.

If the consumer and the agency cannot agree on the accuracy of an item in a report, the consumer has the right to submit a written statement of his position to the agency. The agency must send the statement with the report to anyone requesting information concerning the consumer. Again, the consumer's written statement must be sent to all to whom the agency had sent a report during the previous six months and to employers who received reports during the previous two years.

Finally, the law provides for the elimination of old, stale items that are no longer applicable and which, if allowed to remain, could harm the consumer without justification. For example, a report containing information adverse or harmful to the individual's credit cannot be given out after three months from the date of the report unless it is determined that the report is still accurate. In addition, with certain exceptions dealing with loans, life insurance, and employment applications, any reference to lawsuits involving the consumer must be eliminated after seven years. Any reference to a bankruptcy must be eliminated after 14 years.

References to bankruptcy

An agency must, in brief, maintain up-to-date records of court proceedings and inspect public records on a regular basis to ensure that the information it supplies is accurate.

What does this all mean? Simply this: the person denied a job, credit, or insurance should ask whether the denial was based, in any degree, on an adverse credit report. If it was, the consumer should immediately ask for the name and address of the credit agency supplying the information. The agency should be asked about the general nature of the information furnished—and correction of erroneous items and the elimination of stale items can be demanded. The consumer can then submit a written statement of 100 words or less if the agency will not correct the report as demanded; the agency must send that statement to all who received the report earlier, as outlined above.

The lesson: don't allow your credit rating to suffer because of inaccurate information.

Control of Issued Securities

Most of the consumer protection laws were enacted recently. Others were enacted some time ago. In the latter group are laws governing the issuance of corporate stock and other securities. Some of these merit attention here.

State Blue Sky Laws. To protect the public from the sale of worthless stocks or other securities, many states have adopted "blue sky laws." These outlaw fraudulent practices in the issue and sale of stock; require the licensing of brokers, dealers, and others dealing in securities; and mandate the approval of a state securities agency or commission before a stock can be sold to the public. Engaging in fraudulent activities involving corporate securities is a criminal offense under these laws.

Those "blue sky laws"

Federal Regulation. In addition to the state laws, federal law recognized the need for regulation of the securities field as early as 1933. While the state laws deal only with transactions within a state, the Federal Securities Act of 1933 was adopted to control the interstate sale of, or dealing in, corporate stocks and bonds.

To make an intelligent decision . . . The federal Act requires the filing and registering of a *prospectus*, a written statement about a stock to be issued, the company and its financial situation, and the company's officers and directors. Government regulations specify what information is to be included in the prospectus; serious penalties are imposed for violations of the requirements. A detailed review of these regulations is outside the scope of this book. But, essentially, they are intended to prevent anyone from selling or dealing in corporate securities, by use of the mails or otherwise, in interstate commerce without full disclosure of all information that an investor would need to make an intelligent decision to invest. This information is to be supplied in the prospectus.

There are some limitations on the applicability of the federal securities laws. These have to do with the number of shares to be issued, the number of persons who are offered the stock, and the total assets of the company involved. The limitations may eliminate a particular stock offering from the requirements of the federal laws. But in most large stock offerings federal registration is required.

Protection against the issuance of worthless securities was one thing; but it became evident that the public also needed protection against abuses by stock exchanges and certain stock brokers. In 1934 Congress passed the Federal Securities Exchange Act. Under that law, it became unlawful for any broker, dealer, or stock exchange to use the mails or any means of communication to effect any security transaction without proper registration of the particular stock exchange with the Securities and Exchange Commission.

The Act permits some exemptions, and certain activities are outlawed. The latter include fraudulent rumors to affect the price of a stock, continuous trading in a particular stock to create the impression of great activity and boost the stock's price, and similar practices. Restrictions on speculation in stock are also imposed. The Federal Reserve Board has the right to establish *margin requirements*—the extent to which money can be borrowed to finance stock transactions and the percentage that the total amount borrowed must bear to the total price. Control of the use of "inside information," which restricts insiders from making a profit on information that is not given to the public, is also mandated.

Full disclosure is not a guarantee of performance These restrictions have been imposed on corporations, stock exchanges, and dealers. They also affect the consumer's rights. The consumer can obtain full disclosure of all information on a particular stock, bond, or other security so as to make an intelligent decision regarding investment. The law, of course, was not designed to guarantee the performance of any stock.

Control of Mutual Funds. The average investor is not in a position to investigate the past performances of corporations to determine whether to purchase their stocks. For that reason, mutual funds have stirred widespread interest among small investors. In recent years, the large institutional investors such as banks, trust companies, pension plans, and labor unions have also turned to mutual funds in increasing numbers.

The attraction of mutual funds lies in the fact that investment decisions are made for the investor by someone with more sophisticated knowledge of the stock market. Thus the risk of loss is spread over a broad range of investments. For example, the typical mutual fund portfolio includes stocks and bonds of utility companies, insurance companies, transportation companies, and manufacturing companies, among others. The investor purchases shares in the mutual fund itself. The fund then uses that money to purchase shares in the entire wide range of companies selected for investment.

Since mutual funds use investment counselors, it has sometimes appeared as if the fees charged by the counselors were excessive in comparison to the services rendered. The Investment Company Act Amendments of 1970 were designed to place restrictions on charges to investors for these services.

Another feature of mutual fund purchasing that aroused some criticism was the "front load." A consumer might agree to purchase mutual funds over a period of time, paying in annual or monthly installments. The funds with "front loads" would then take all commissions and other charges out of the front or early payments. If the investor cancelled out, or withdrew from the fund before completing his long-term purchase plan, he would have lost the entire amount paid as commissions or charges at the outset. *"Front loading" criticized*

Under the present law, mutual funds cannot charge more than 50 per cent of the total charges and commissions against payments made by an investor in his first year in the fund. If the fund charges the maximum 50 per cent allowed by law in the first year, the investor has a graduated right of rescission. If he rescinds the contract within 45 days after notification of the charges, he can get back the value of his account and all amounts charged to its administration. *The 50 per cent limit*

Regulation and control of the entire securities field will undoubtedly continue. The complex nature of the U.S. economy demands such controls.

But investors and consumers should insist on full disclosure of the facts in all stock transactions. Anyone receiving false or misleading information should complain about it to the broker or company issuing the stock. If no action results, the securities agency or commission in the particular state will investigate the complaint. A lawyer can help if court action becomes necessary to recover a loss.

Stock markets involve risks. The risks make investing an exciting pastime. The laws seek only to eliminate fraud and misrepresentation.

Control of Insurance Companies. Insurance companies come under regulation in all 50 states. By statute, insurance company regulation is accomplished through control of their financing, the maintenance of reserves of money to meet policy owners' claims, control of companies incorporated in other states, and control of the performance of insurers within the state. Control and regulation are handled through state insurance departments.

Licensing of insurance brokers, agents Statutes also provide for control over insurance agents and brokers in the advertising and soliciting of policies. Agents and brokers have to be licensed. Deceptive practices and other practices that may cause losses to the consumer, such as failure of a broker or agent to forward policy owners' premiums to the company, are prohibited. In some instances, these may be declared criminal activities.

Fraudulent insurance activity should be reported to state agencies. The many honest agents and brokers will not be affected, but will be able to maintain the professionalism of their field and organizations.

Control of Insurance Settlement and Claim Procedures. The test of a really good insurance company—whatever its field of specialization—is the method by which it handles claims and settlements. Advertising blurbs may have stated that the company pays all claims promptly and without a lot of red tape. In the event of a loss, the company's real character emerges.

Fortunately, the vast majority of insurance companies realize their responsibilities. They are reasonable and fair in their claims procedures. The number of fraudulent claims presented to insurance companies every year makes caution in the settlement of claims a must; but sometimes an overabundance of caution works to the disadvantage of the policy owner.

Liability may exceed policy coverage In recent years the law has developed methods by which it forces companies to be fair. In effect, the law holds insurance companies liable to the policyholder for more than the coverage of the policy.

How is this done? Normally, the company's liability under any policy is strictly set at the limits specified in the policy. If an automobile policy has liability limits of $10,000 for each person injured, the company's liability to pay a claim against the policyholder for one person's injury cannot exceed $10,000. But suppose the injury is very serious. Suppose the company nevertheless refuses to settle a claim within the $10,000 limit despite the willingness of the injured person to settle.

In this case the policyholder may be sued and forced to go to trial. If a judgment is secured against him for more than the $10,000 coverage, he may be able to hold his insurance company liable for the entire amount of the judgment. But the defendant has to establish that the company's refusal to settle was unreasonable under the circumstances and opened the door to the greater judgment eventually awarded.

In another case a company, under a liability policy, refuses to defend a policyholder becasue the claim is not protected by the policy. the policyholder then has to hire a lawyer and defend himself. Whatever the result of the lawsuit, if it can be established that the company's refusal to defend was fraudulent or unreasonable, the policyholder can sue the company and recover the amount of any judgment plus any other loss suffered, including lawyer's fees. This is true even if the total amount exceeds the limits of coverage under the policy.

Claims under insurance policies are investigated by adjusters. These persons work directly for insurance companies or as independent claims adjusters retained on contract by the companies to handle certain types of cases. In rare cases an adjuster does such a poor job investigating a claim, or treats the person making the claim so shabbily, that the individual suffers frustration and even physical or emotional injury. In a 1970s court case, a widow sustained the loss of her home by fire. Because the company, through its adjuster, failed to investigate the loss properly, the company offered the widow only a fraction of the real value of the loss. The widow brought suit for the value of her home and for the physical and emotional injuries that she had suffered because of the company's unreasonable conduct. In a landmark decision, the court allowed a judgment in the total amount of the claim.

"Adjusting" insurance claims

Consumers can and should continue to exert efforts to make the law work for them and to assert and win their claims. While faced with many fraudulent claims, insurance companies must accord to the valid claim the law's full right and protection.

The Poor as Consumers. Recent legislation enacted by Congress and some states, and backed by court decisions, has attempted to make certain that the law does not "favor the rich." Court decisions have sought to place the poor, insofar as their rights are concerned, in the same relative position as those better able to pay for legal advice.

Assistance to the poor has taken many forms. For example, the Supreme Court has decided that an attorney must be appointed for a poor or indigent defendant unable to pay for his own counsel. Even in less serious cases, including misdemeanors that may call for jail sentences, the court has to appoint an attorney for the poor defendant. This is a constitutional right.

A 1963 Supreme Court case underscored the right of every defendant to have legal counsel. In *Gideon* v. *Wainwright,* the Supreme Court reversed the decision of a Florida court because of the court's failure to provide counsel for a poor defendant. The decision holds the various states to the requirements set down in the Sixth Amendment regarding the right to defense counsel. The case became famous because the defendant, Clarence Gideon, wrote personally to the Supreme Court when the Florida court refused both to allow him to defend himself and to appoint counsel for him. On trial for burglary, Gideon was later acquitted.

Other types of protection for the poor involve the requirement of a public hearing before welfare payments can be discontinued, the requirement of counsel in divorce cases where the complaining spouse cannot afford a lawyer, and the elimination of the requirement of a jail sentence if the defendant cannot pay a fine. At one time the poor person faced with a "$60 or 60 days" judgment would have found himself in jail if he could not produce the $60. The person with funds would go free. Thus the constitutional rights of the poor were violated in such cases.

Other examples of how the law attempts to give equal protection to the poor might be cited. Public service corporations have been created to provide legal services for the poor. Neighborhood Legal Services agencies have been funded by federal and state grants for this purpose. Legal Aid Societies and Public Defender Associations have sought to provide adequate counsel for the poor, to educate the public in the need for such protection, and to seek continuing support from the government. Thus the fact that one person has less money than the next will not usually affect the right to protection. Local bar associations provide the names of lawyers and agencies that can help the needy.

Enforcement of the Rights of the Consumer

Laws protecting the rights of the consumer have developed rapidly. But the expanded concepts of rights mean little if the consumer cannot or will not enforce those rights. A person who buys a small item costing little may hesitate to enter a complaint or bring suit because of the cost involved. To remedy this situation, the law has placed the responsibility for enforcement with various agencies and individuals.

The consumer himself has the right to bring a lawsuit that may involve refunds and even penalties against an offending merchant. In some instances, the consumer can bring a class action suit—a lawsuit on behalf of himself and all members of the particular group of consumers who have suffered similar losses.

Local consumer protection agencies and state attorneys general can help in determining exactly what assistance may be expected in pressing a complaint.

Some states have laws barring claims against manufacturers and sellers after a stated period of time has passed. But upper-court rulings on such "statutes of limitations" have shown little agreement. Some courts or judges have upheld the limitations while others have invalidated them.

A rule of thumb may be that a product liability statute of limitations is invalid where it appears to nullify the possibility of consumer action before such action can be logically or legally considered. Pertinent cases in this category have involved the drug *diethylstilbestrol* (DES), a synthetic hormone designed to prevent miscarriages. Injuries resulting from use of the drug may not become evident for fifteen, twenty, or more years; thus a ten- or twelve-year statute of limitations may violate a consumer's equal protection guarantee.

Federal agencies

Reports of false advertising claims, mislabeling of products, and other deceptive practices should go to the FTC, which has both regional and field offices throughout the United States. The offices are listed under "Federal Trade Commission" in telephone directories. The FTC headquarters is located at 6th Street and Pennsylvania Avenue, N.W., Washington, D.C. 20580.

If you have been victimized by medical quacks, health claims, or mislabeled foods, drugs, or cosmetics, contact the Food and Drug Administration, listed in major telephone directories under "United States, Department of Health and Human Services." Or you can contact the FDA at its headquarters office at 5600 Fishers Lane, Rockville, Maryland 20852.

If meat and poultry products are involved in your complaint, contact the local office of the U.S. Department of Agriculture.

If the problem centers on the lack of proper sanitation of a restaurant or other business, contact your local health agency.

If you suspect that illegal sales or distribution of drugs or narcotics, such as stimulants, depressants or hallucinogens, are taking place, contact the local office of the United States Department of Justice, Drug Enforcement Section.

Help is usually available

To stop the receipt of unwanted mail, contact your local post office.

To report suspected violations of the Truth in Lending laws, contact the local Federal Reserve Board office. You will be directed to the proper agency to which you should complain.

The consumer has another remedy. He can contact a lawyer to find out what he, as an individual, can do to make the legal maxim, "caveat vendor"—"let the seller beware"—take on added meaning.

ENVIRONMENTAL PROTECTION:
NO MAN IS AN ISLAND

As recently as the middle 1960s, it would have been unthinkable to claim that a large industrial plant should be told to bank its furnaces because it was poisoning the atmosphere, or because of the amount of smoke boiling from its smokestacks. The need for a free and prosperous industrial society was held to be paramount. Little real thought was given to the problems of the environment—or to the pollution caused by wastes, smoke, noise, and other pollutants.

WHERE TO GO FOR HELP
ON A CONSUMER PROBLEM[1]

Hundreds of agencies and organizations across the country provide help on consumer complaints and problems. Some are local, some statewide. Some, including those listed below with their areas of specialization, are nationwide.

Bureau of Consumer Protection, Federal Trade Commission, Washington, D.C. 20580. Deceptive advertising, illegal sales tactics, violations of the Truth in Lending law, and a host of other consumer frauds, deceptions, unfair sales, and trade practices.

Center for Science in the Public Interest, 1755 S Street N.W., Washington, D.C. 20009. Food and health safety, energy conservation, and good nutrition through publications and participation in government proceedings.

Center for the Study of Responsive Law, P.O. Box 19367, Washington, D.C. 20036. From mental health to aviation to coal mining.

Common Cause, 2030 M Street N.W., Washington, D.C. 20036. "Structure and process" issues to improve function and accountability of government. Also, in the early 1980s, tax reform, energy policy, consumer and environmental protection.

Congress Watch, 133 C Street S.E., Washington, D.C. 20003. Voting records, committee performance, and responsiveness by senators and representatives to their constituents and to the public generally.

Consumer Federation of America, Suite 406, 1012 14th Street N.W., Washington, D.C. 20005. Helps groups organize and act, testifies and lobbies on any proposed consumer legislation, and publicizes important issues.

Consumers Opposed to Inflation in the Necessities (COIN), Suite 413, 2000 P Street N.W., Washington, D.C. 20036. Fights inflation in food, energy, health, and housing.

Consumers Union, 256 Washington Street, Mount Vernon, New York, 10550. Publishes *Consumer Reports* magazine on products ranging from cars to contraceptives—for safety, convenience, effectiveness. Also participates in lawsuits on behalf of consumers.

Corporate Accountability Research Group, 1346 Connecticut Avenue N.W., Washington, D.C. 20036. Contests corporate power, violation of antitrust laws, seeks to make corporations accountable to shareowners and the public.

Council of Better Business Bureaus, 1150 17th Street N.W., Washington, D.C. 20036. Headquarters of the well-known Better Business Bureaus. Provides local BBB contacts.

Disability Rights Center, 1346 Connecticut Avenue N.W., Washington, D.C. 20036.

Rights of the disabled through legal action and monitoring of federal actions.

Energy Action, 1523 L Street N.W., Washington, D.C. 20005. Watches federal energy legislation and publishes a newsletter.

Office of Consumer Affairs, 626 Reporters Building, Washington, D.C. 20201.

Government agency concerned with all kinds of consumer problems, consumer education, and legislation.

Public Citizen Litigation Group, 7th Floor, 2000 P Street N.W., Washington, D.C. 20036. Lawsuits against corporations, government agencies on behalf of the public.

That situation changed, to some extent at least, because of a book and a court case. The book was *Silent Spring* by Rachel Carson. Published in 1962, *Silent Spring* brought a powerful indictment against Americans' disregard of their country's ecology. The book found special fault with the wholesale use of pesticides, in particular DDT. The author painted a grim picture of an American earth denuded of much of its wildlife, of fields and streams poisoned by chemicals, of technology running destructively rampant.

A book and a court case

In the court case, decided in 1965, a major utility was told to consider the environment when drawing up plans for a new plant. The Federal

Power Commission had granted New York's Consolidated Edison Company a license to build the plant at Storm King Mountain. An appeals court ordered a reversal, noting that the company's plans had to "include as a basic concern the preservation of natural beauty and of national historic shrines."

It is recognized today that the impact of pollution on the environment directly affects each citizen at every moment of his life. If the air is polluted, if a next door neighbor's air conditioner keeps someone awake at night, if the property owner living on a higher street dumps water that erodes others' soil, everyone is eventually affected. Everyone has cause for real concern.

Young people first recognized the need for regulation and protection of the environment. They acknowledged first that the "quality of life" may be more important than the economics of a given situation. As the environment became a cause, small communities began to forbid the erection of large shopping centers within their boundaries. The shopping centers would have resulted in increased tax revenues, but they would also have had an adverse effect on the quality of life in the community. Changes in community planning, changes in zoning regulations, and many other changes indicated that the environment was receiving solid consideration. Principles were turned into law.

Environmentally, everyone is a "consumer"

Each individual is a "consumer" of his environment. Everyone uses it to bring quality into his life. As a consumer, each citizen has the right to an environment that is clean, enjoyable, and appropriate to the manner in which he lives. The resident of a congested city cannot, of course, expect that he could live in the same environment as someone living on a farm. Certain restrictions are imposed by society; but with those restrictions, consumers have a right to expect protection of their environments.

The federal Environmental Protection Agency (EPA) was formed in 1970 to give concrete form to many basic environmental concerns. The Agency has acted as a clearinghouse and headquarters for the national effort to ensure pure water and clean air. The Agency also works with state environmental commissions to enforce a long list of congressional mandates relating to ecology and the environment.

Control of Groundspace and Airspace

Unless given the right by the landowner, it is unlawful for someone to mine for coal or dig for oil under another's land. It is also unlawful for someone to build a house that projects over another's property line. A person owns to the center of the earth under his own property and up to the heavens—unless these rights have been conveyed away.

The right of flight over the land of another does exist. But the flight may not interfere with the proper use of the land or do damage to the structures on the land. This principle has led to many cases involving the condemnation or "taking" of property near airports, where the descent paths of landing planes bring planes so close to the ground that considerable noise pollution results. Farmers have complained that airplane noise may interfere with hens laying eggs, or cause injury to skittish livestock, or produce vibration damage in buildings. Noise may, in effect, destroy an owner's enjoyment of his property.

On airplanes and hens

The courts have held airports and others liable in damages for such noise pollution and for "taking" the property from the owners in such cases.

Weather studies have brought other problems. Hurricane and tornado investigations, seeding clouds to produce rain, and other attempts at scientific control of the weather have been said to be altering normal weather patterns. The effects on the environment will undoubtedly be accompanied by problems of damage to the owners of land. In fact, many people believe that severe storms or drought may today rank as one result of tampering with the weather.

Control of Water Rights

American history suggests that the availability of clear, unpolluted water has immense environmental importance. The development of the

West depended heavily on the availability of water. In consequence, laws were developed early to protect the sources and supply of water against waste pollution or appropriation by some persons to the exclusion of others.

The need for guaranteed supplies of water continues in many parts of the country. The continuing disputes over the Colorado River give evidence of deep concern.

How water practices and regulations differ

Water practices and regulations may differ depending on need. The person living on a lake or river usually has the right to use the water reasonably for his needs. But the person owning property above another on a river may interfere with the quality of the water or the quantity of flow, causing damage to the lower owner's property. In this case the lower owner may have the right to bring legal action for damages against the higher owner. Because of a lack of water, some states have permitted the use of water for irrigation or for watering cattle even though that use may affect others' enjoyment of the water supply.

The water pollution problem has been attacked by many state authorities. For example, dumping waste materials into waterways is restricted, as in voluntary spillage of oil from tankers off the seashore. Various federal statutes deal with this problem. The laws uniformly try to limit the negative effects of pollution on the water supply, on public and private beaches, on marine life, and on other areas of the environment.

Related problems involve the disposal of waste materials. Man today generates tremendous amounts of waste—throw-away containers, rubber and plastic materials, and other products. Laws have been passed to encourage recycling of such wastes and their reprocessing into other useful materials. Laws have restricted the use of nonreturnable containers. They have also encouraged and funded local and state pilot projects dealing with waste disposal, sanitary land fills, and treatment facilities under the guidance of the Department of Health and Human Services.

Pollution problems should normally be brought to the attention of local pollution control agencies.

Private Nuisance—The Neighbor's Air Conditioner

One person's free use of his land cannot, today, unreasonably interfere with another person's possession and enjoyment of his or her property. If it does interfere, a private nuisance may result.

Note a typical example. If, while excavation is under way on adjoining property, an explosion occurs, throwing rocks and soil onto your land, a physical trespass may have occurred for which you can recover damages. Continuation of the activity would constitute a *private nuisance* that you can stop by bringing suit for an injunction to prevent further blasting—and for any money damages you may have incurred.

Physical trespass through excavation

The trespass does not have to be a physical one, however. A nuisance can take the form of any prejudicial use of property. Your neighbor's air conditioner that interferes with your sleep at night, or his high-fidelity record system which plays into the wee hours of the morning, are cases in point. A nuisance may also involve the more serious problem of smoke, smells, or fumes from industrial plants that interfere with your use and enjoyment of your property.

The mere fact that you are annoyed by someone else's use of his property is not enough to create a personal, private nuisance. The law looks for damage to your property or your enjoyment of life, and balances that against the need to continue the problem activity for social or economic reasons. Thus, while you might be annoyed by smoke from the utility plant nearby, unless the amount of smoke is unreasonable, and the cost of abating the smoke is minimal, a balancing of interests may result in your inability to stop the smoke condition.

Annoyance may not constitute damage

Since interest in environmental protection has increased tremendously in recent years, various governmental agencies have been given the authority to direct plant shut-downs because of extreme pollution of the atmosphere. Where private suits are brought against such companies, the courts may award damages while leaving the question of shut-down or continued operation to the local or other governmental agencies having specific authority. An appeal from a court decision is always possible, as is an appeal from an agency's ruling.

Often, an offending company can reduce the amount of interference or pollution without totally stopping operations. Where this is possible, a workable solution can usually be found. Where individuals have suffered physical damage to person or property, a lawyer should be consulted regarding the possibility of bringing suit.

Public Nuisance

A *public nuisance* involves harm done to the general public as opposed to an individual person. The general public in an entire area is affected; the usual remedy will be an injunction and an award of damages. A generally accepted condition for a public nuisance is that the public health, safety, or morals suffer damage. Sewage disposal areas that emit foul odors, disposal of industrial wastes in rivers, lakes, and streams, and similar activities have all been found to be public nuisances.

To reduce pollution by auto and truck engines . . . Recognizing the need for controls over public nuisances, Congress has enacted legislation such as the Clean Air Act and the National Motor Vehicles Emissions Standards Act. The aim has been to reduce pollution by auto and truck engines. In response, the automobile industry has moved toward production of an automobile engine that is substantially pollution-free. In addition, standards have been adopted with respect to various types of emissions, techniques, and devices to control emissions. The Environment Protection Agency is charged with general overall review and control of the program.

The EPA has not, for the most part, acted ruthlessly. For example, it has required auto manufacturers to install antipollution devices in cars. But it has delayed implementation of some standards to give the manufacturers more time for research and development.

State laws have also been enacted to control nuisances such as air pollution. Both state and local agencies are involved in air pollution control. A common indication of this concern is the inclusion of air quality reports in the weather forecasts distributed by the National Weather Service and by private forecasting services.

Control of the Right of Land Support

Because all land depends on adjoining land for support, the law requires that no excavation on neighboring land can cause a lot to subside or fall away from its natural position. The neighbor has to brace and support the excavation to prevent damage to the lot in its natural state. The neighbor will be liable for any damage, in most states, even though he has done everything possible to prevent subsidence or cave-ins.

A different rule may apply where a building stands on Lot A. This land is not regarded as being in its natural state. In order to hold a neighbor, owner of Lot B, liable if Lot A subsides, it must be established that the neighbor performed the excavation negligently.

Some states and local municipalities require that an adjoining landowner receive notice that an excavation will be begun on the property and that possible subsidence may result. This gives the property owner an opportunity to try to protect his property from damage. Where soil conditions are such that a landslide may carry away land, the excavator is required to take practical precautions. In urban areas, an excavator customarily conducts core boring tests, using soil experts, to determine whether a danger of subsidence exists before starting an excavation. Failure to do this can easily be found to be negligence, making the excavator liable for damage to the adjoining property.

Notice of excavation

Control of Natural Conditions on Land

Formerly, a landowner was not required to do anything with his land in terms of its effects on his neighbors so long as it remained in its natural state. For example, land on which a natural pond served as a breeding ground for mosquitos did not have to be filled in or drained.

Under current law, many states and municipalities require that grass and weeds be cut, that wet areas where bugs, flies, and mosquitos can breed be filled in, and that the hazards of infection and fire be reduced. Not uncommonly, the owner of an unimproved lot will receive a notice from the local municipality directing that he cut the weeds, trim the trees, or fill in water holes. The reason may be that rodents or insects breed there, or that dandelion pollen is blowing onto the lawns of neighbors.

Defenses against weeds, bugs, fire, infection

These new requirements have come about because of changes in public policies. The owner of property now has certain responsibilities to his neighbors even though his property is not improved, or built upon.

A property owner should make every attempt to "get along" with his neighbors. But he should insist on what is rightfully his.

Control of Noise

Noise as a pollutant? Yes! With the rise of commercial aviation, and the arrival of "jumbo jets" and supersonic transports, noise pollution has become a significant concern of federal and state policy makers. Noise is now considered a type of interference with the environment that requires controls.

The Federal Aviation Act attempts to control noise pollution by aircraft. Also, states have regulations on the noise from vehicles such as autos and motorcycles. Studies of the effects of noise on property values and the enjoyment of life are continuing under federal auspices. Undoubtedly, the entire issue of noise pollution will continue to influence the laws to be passed in the future.

The Right of the Consumer to Sue

Harm and the right to sue Federal laws allow suits by private parties in federal courts to stop violations of federal legislation against air pollution. Suits are permitted even where the individual cannot show a particular harm to himself that differs from the harm done to any other member of the public.

In addition, various states have brought suits against other states, or citizens of other states, to end pollution in specific cases. The use of satellites to photograph pollution of waterways has proved effective in locating sources of pollution.

The citizen who wants to take an active role in the protection of his environment should attend meetings of the local zoning board. He can then be sure that the community in which he lives will develop as it should. Complaints can be directed to the state or federal environmental protection offices.

PROTECTION AGAINST PERSONAL INJURY
OR PROPERTY DAMAGE

The entire subject of consumer protection presumes that a fundamental right of the consumer is to be free from bodily injury or property damage resulting from defects in manufactured products. The rapidly expanding field of law known as "product liability" has to do with the liability of a manufacturer or dealer for injury or damage caused by defective products. The subject has been discussed in Chapter 7 from the point of view of insurance. It requires some additional analysis from the consumer-protection aspect.

A manufacturer or seller can be held liable for a defective product in various ways.

Liability for defective products

Breach of Express and Implied Warranty

A person selling a product may give a form of guarantee that the goods will be of a certain kind, or operate in a certain way, or obtain certain results. He may advertise his goods in such a way as to lead the consumer to believe that the product will function as advertised. For example, where a merchant advertises a properly insulated electric motor, and the consumer receives electric shocks when using the motor, the merchant has breached his express warranty of proper insulation.

Responsibility for the quality of the product may be binding on the seller even though the implied warranty or guarantee came from the manufacturer. A parallel case would be the statements made on the label on a can of food.

Implied and express warranties: differences
An *implied warranty*, as opposed to an express warranty, is not made expressly. Rather, the law infers that it has been made by reason of the sale. The law reads the warranty into the sale. A merchant, in selling a product, implicitly warrants that it is fit for normal use and will pass freely in the marketplace. The merchant may regularly deal in soda pop. He warrants that the soda pop he sells is fit for normal use—consumption by the consumer. If a foreign body is found in the soda, or if the bottle explodes, causing injury to the consumer, a breach of the implied warranty of fitness for normal use can be presumed.

To avoid any question of liability for breach of an implied warranty, a merchant normally gives an *express warranty*. The warranty includes the stipulation that no implied warranties are made. However, unless the disclaimer of implied warranties is phrased precisely as required by state law, the disclaimer may not be valid and the consumer may retain his right to claim breach of implied warranty.

At one time, only the direct buyer could sue the direct seller for a breach of implied warranty. A husband who purchased an item that injured his wife would not be able to recover damages. Today, however, most states permit members of the buyer's family, his household, and certain other persons not directly involved in the sale to sue for breach of warranty, particularly where food, beverages, or drugs are concerned.

By statute in many states, the requirement of a direct sales relationship between seller and the person injured or damaged has been abolished —to the extent that a suit for breach of warranty can be brought by members of the buyer's family, his household, and guests. A wife could recover for the defect in the product bought by her husband. So could other members of the family and guests on the premises, if they were injured. Recent trends in the law also indicate that the requirement of a direct sales relationship between the seller and the owner of damaged property is no longer necessary to make the seller liable for the property damage.

Court cases appear to have placed definite limits on the consumer's rights to sue for damages—at least where economic injury is involved. In one 1977 case, *Illinois Brick Co.* v. *Illinois,* the Supreme Court held that a manufacturer could not be sued for price-fixing by anyone but the direct purchaser or purchasers. The consumer who bought a product from a middleman—a plumber, retailer, or other source—could not "go over the middleman's head" and sue the manufacturer directly.

Limits on the right to sue for economic injury

By the early 1980s Congress had begun work on bills that would restore the consumer's right to sue manufacturers directly. The bills were viewed as aspects of the federal government's continuing antitrust activities. The consumer, it was reasoned, usually paid higher prices that covered artificially "fixed" product costs. The middleman then escaped unharmed. If the consumer could not sue, manufacturers might fix prices with impunity.

Strict Liability for Harm Caused by a Product

In many states, the law permits a purchaser, consumer, bystander, or anyone else who is injured by a defective product to bring an action against the manufacturer or dealer of the product. In other words, once a defective or dangerous product causes harm, the manufacturer, wholesaler, or dealer has liability for any harm done. It does not matter that negligence may not be shown, or that a component part secured from another manufacturer was the defective part. The liability rule is strictly enforced if the product was defective and caused injury.

Manufacturer and dealer liable for defective products

An example will show how this strict liability concept works. If the blade on a rotary mower breaks off, flies across the yard, and strikes a neighbor or breaks his large picture window, he may have a good claim against the manufacturer and seller of the mower. He need not show that the manufacturer or seller was negligent in the making of the mower. Nor does it matter that he did not buy the mower.

This strict liability protection applies also to people who are injured by defective leased property. Recent court decisions hold that all forms of rental equipment, such as automobiles, trucks, power tools, and gardening equipment, are subject to the strict liability rules. Thus if a neighbor is helping you load a rental truck and is injured when the hydraulic tailgate malfunctions, he may have a right of action against the truck rental company and the manufacturer of the truck. He may not have to establish negligence or breach of warranty.

A disclaimer of warranty made by a manufacturer on specific goods has no effect on the right of the injured person to sue on the basis of strict liability. While the disclaimer may eliminate certain warranties from the sale, it has no effect in the strict liability case.

Liability for Negligence

The consumer may also sue the dealer or manufacturer for negligence—for failing to exercise due care in the preparation, manufacture, instructions, or other aspects of an item or product. Warnings have to be given regarding dangerous characteristics. Where the manufacturer should have understood that if he was negligent a person or class of persons would have been injured, then he may be held liable for negligence.

Safety regulations for consumers Safety regulations have been drawn up for consumers in certain instances. Legislation involving safety features on automobiles—on seat belts, bumpers that absorb impact without damage, and so on—furnishes examples of safety regulations issued by governmental agencies that have the force of law. Violations of these safety regulations may be evidence of negligence. Without more proof, they may entitle the consumer or other person to recover for personal injury or property damage resulting from the safety violation.

Often a manufacturer will sell a product in a disassembled state and give instructions for its assembly and proper use. If the consumer puts the item together in accordance with the instructions and suffers an injury because of a malfunction, liability may be claimed for negligent instructions. If the consumer, using the product as directed, suffers injury or property damage, he may be able to recover for negligent instructions regarding use.

In summary, a consumer or other person injured by a defective product that was purchased from a manufacturer, wholesaler, or retailer may have a right to sue for property damage or personal injuries. Three theories underlie that right: the strict liability theory that is by far the easiest insofar as proof is concerned; the theory of breach of warranty, if the party injured falls within the appropriate group that, under local law, has the right to sue for breach of warranty; and the theory of negligence, if proof of negligence can be established.

Time limits may be imposed by local law on claims against manufacturers or dealers. These limits have to be met and satisfied. A lawyer can help a claimant determine the best procedures by which to enforce specific rights.

THE ULTIMATE PROTECTION: BANKRUPTCY AND ALTERNATIVES

The harried consumer has one other means of protecting himself. When his indebtedness gets out of control, he can declare bankruptcy. Alternatively, he can work out a personal repayment plan.

Article 1 of the U.S. Constitution empowers Congress to enact uniform bankruptcy laws. In 1978, acting under that power, Congress passed the Bankruptcy Reform Act that became effective October 1, 1979. The bankruptcy laws are adjudicated by federal judges. Under the laws, debtors have a choice between two forms of voluntary bankruptcy: Chapter 7 and Chapter 13, both parts of the Bankruptcy Reform Act.

The uniform bankruptcy laws

Chapter 7: "Straight Bankruptcy"

Under Chapter 7, a debtor declares what is called "straight bankruptcy," or liquidation. A portion of his assets is converted into cash that his creditors share. The debtor then receives a discharge that relieves him of further obligations.

The federal Bankruptcy Act allows the debtor to retain some of his assets. In fact, the Act for the first time lists the types of assets that would be exempt. They include:

—A $7,500 interest in a home and/or burial plot ($15,000 for a married couple). What if you don't own a home or burial plot? Federal law says you still can use the $7,500 exemption. In fact, you can add $400 to it and claim $7,900 worth of additional exemptions in any kind of property. Even if you do have a house and burial plot worth $7,500, you can claim $400 worth of extra exemptions in other property. You can use this exemption, too, to keep a refund on income taxes that you paid before the year you file bankruptcy.

—A $1,200 interest in *one* car or other motor vehicle.

—Any items worth up to $200 *each* in these categories: household goods and furnishings, clothing, appliances, books, animals, crops, or musical instruments.

—$500 in jewelry.

—$750 worth of books or tools that you need for your work.

—A life insurance policy.

—Health items, such as a hearing aid, that were prescribed for you.

—Social Security and veteran's benefits.

—Unemployment insurance proceeds.

—Pension and profit sharing plans.

Bankruptcy not the total solution Straight bankruptcy cannot, of course, solve all the problems facing an individual or family with an intolerable load of debt. But it can give you a new lease on life. The new lease will last only six years—no one can file again to have his debts discharged until six years have elapsed.

The federal bankruptcy laws provide that discharged debts must have been contracted in good faith. But it is often impossible to say which have been contracted in good faith and which in bad. It should also be noted that some states have in effect restricted the types and values of the assets that the debtor can exempt when declaring straight bankruptcy. In these states, the feeling is that the federal laws are too generous.

Chapter 13: Alternative Approaches

Chapter 13 of the Bankruptcy Reform Act offers alternatives that many persons view as superior to straight bankruptcy. Using Chapter 13, the debtor can rearrange his debt load so as to emerge with a more reasonable credit rating than he would have under straight bankruptcy.

Features of a Chapter 13 repayment plan Chapter 13 makes possible a budgetary plan. Called a "wage earner's plan," Chapter 13 actually applies to anyone whose principal source of income is derived from a salary, wages, or commissions. Filing under Chapter 13, the debtor is required to work out a repayment plan including the following features:

—A listing of all normal expenses each month.

—A compilation of total debts.

—Addition of 10 per cent to the debts to cover court costs.

—Dividing the total by 36 to ascertain what would be owing if the total were spread over 36 months.

—Adding in the monthly installments on all debts not covered in the second item above.

—Adding to the toal debts normal monthly living expenses.

—Calling all creditors and telling them about the plan—and obtaining verbal agreements to the plan from most of the unsecured creditors or *one* secured creditor.

The debtor can then file. Before the Reform Act, a debtor had to obtain approval of a repayment plan from a majority of his creditors. Because most creditors, naturally, wanted 100 percent repayment—or as close as possible to 100 percent—Chapter 13 was seldom used before 1979. Today, any plan is acceptable if it meets two conditions: the creditors have to receive at least as much in payments as they would in a straight bankruptcy after exemptions, and the plan has to represent a good faith effort by a debtor.

What valuations are placed on a debtor's possessions? A "fair market value" standard applies. That means a Chapter 13 plan allows the debtor to pay off unsecured installment debts at low rates, without interest. Reduced payments may also be made on secured debts other than home mortgages.

Small Claims Courts

The consumer who has a complaint against a merchant, and cannot settle it amicably, can take his case to a small claims court. The limited-jurisdiction small claims court typically handles disputes over accidents and contracts as well as such problems as clothing ruined by cleaners, differences between landlords and tenants, and damages caused by movers.

Your local bar association can tell you where the small claims court in your area or community is located. The association can also tell you the maximum claim that the court will hear—usually $500 but running in some states as high as $3,000. Generally you can file suit in these courts if you are over eighteen. If you win your case, the court usually requires the defendant to pay the claim and all court costs.

Small claims courts in different jurisdictions may have different rules. A few allow the plaintiff to be represented by a lawyer. These courts make available claim or complaint forms that are available from the Clerk of Court. The form indicates the nature of the claim, the reason why it is being filed, who is filing it, and the exact name and address of the defendant. Some other points to note about claim forms:

- Variable information to be provided by the plaintiff or the clerk should be kept to a minimum. Many forms have preprinted phrases that simplify the task of completion.

- The form should serve as notice to the defendant regarding the action and should give the defendant information on how to proceed or answer the charge or complaint. The form becomes, in effect, a summons. It provides such information as the name, address, and telephone number of the court clerk and a brief explanation of the consequences of a default judgment—a judgment issued if the defendant fails to respond.

- The complaint form should have some proof of service—proof that it was delivered to the defendant. In most small claims cases the plaintiff sends a copy of the form to the defendant by certified mail. A process-server may also handle delivery. Generally, the form comes in three parts, one for the plaintiff, one for the defendant, and one for the court.

- The Clerk of Court usually assigns a first appearance or trial date when the complaint is filed and that information goes on the complaint form with an identifying case number. The date, in most cases, is two to four weeks from the date of filing.

Given these elements, the small claims court offers a quick, fair, cheap, and informal way of settling money disputes to the consumer's satisfaction. Some small claims courts hear cases in the evening. Others may refuse to hear cases brought by corporations, preferring to serve the individual only. In some courts, a corporate defendant must be represented by an attorney.

In the few states that have no small claims courts, other courts may serve the same purpose and have similar methods of operation. The consumer may, for example, be able to bring his complaint before a conciliation or a magistrate's court.

Arbitration

Consumers with complaints against shop owners or manufacturers may decide to arbitrate their problems. Among the organizations that provide help in such cases is the American Arbitration Association (AAA). The Association has regional offices throughout the United States.

In an arbitration proceeding, the parties to a dispute voluntarily choose an arbitrator or judge. They then submit the problem to a tribunal rather than a court. Both sides have to consent to arbitration, but having done so they may obtain a quick and inexpensive decision.

The AAA has established general rules on the conduct of an arbitration proceeding. The rules require that you, as the claimant or plaintiff, tell the potential defendant that you plan to seek arbitration. To do so, you fill out a demand form that gives details on your complaint or claim, the amount involved, and the amount sought.

The arbitrator's decision, reached after a hearing, is final and binding.

15 THE GREAT AMERICAN NOVEL AND THE BETTER MOUSETRAP

The classic cartoon shows two gentlemen sitting outside a patent office. Each holds on his lap an identical strange-looking package. Each stares at the other with suspicion.

The cartoon symbolizes one aspect of American inventiveness and the problems involved in protecting that inventiveness against use by others. Writing the great American novel or building a better mousetrap takes much more than developing an idea and then transforming that idea into substance. Fortunately, the private enterprise system has created an atmosphere in which inventiveness has flourished. American-made products are copied, purchased, and utilized everywhere. The law has a definite place in the protection of the inventive genius of authors, composers, critics, novelists, engineers, technicians, and others.

This chapter deals with the questions of copyright and patent protection that the law affords individuals and companies. It also deals briefly

with trademarks. The protection extends to the creation of ideas, the utilization of ideas, and the production of an end product.

COPYRIGHTS

Under the Federal Copyright Act of 1976, an author or artist can obtain protection for his ideas and the exclusive right to control, publish, and sell his literary or artistic production. In addition to the copyright provided by federal law, copyright exists in the absence of statute. In this case any author, composer, or artist may retain the exclusive right to an idea or a composition until it is published. Once it is published, however, in the absence of a statutory copyright provided by Congress the exclusive right is lost forever. Publication involves the placing of the material before the general public for sale or for other use.

The copyright granted by statute to an artistic or literary creator protects him against appropriation of his ideas or work of art for his entire lifetime plus 50 years. All forms of literary or artistic expression, including records, musical compositions, plays, novels, sermons, pictures, and similar works, can enjoy copyright protection.

How to obtain a copyright

To obtain a copyright, the creator of an artistic or intellectual work places a notice of copyright, his name, and the year of first copyright on the first and all other copies of the work. He can then publish the work and apply for a certificate of registration on forms provided by the Register of Copyrights, Library of Congress. As an alternative, he can apply for a certificate of registration on the unpublished work. A specific number of copies should accompany the application along with a small fee.

The "copyright seal" is a small letter "c" enclosed in a circle. Thus a typical copyright line would read:

© John J. Doe, 1980

Sound recordings are protected by placing a special notice on the label:

℗ Jones Recording Co., 1980

Using the © symbol in the copyright notice, the owner obtains simultaneous copyright protection in more than 60 countries that adhere to the Universal Copyright Convention.

While the work must be original with the author, it does not have to be absolutely new in the sense that it has never been thought of before. In order to be copyrighted, works must be the independent result of a mental or creative exercise.

If you have in your attic an old song that you wrote in your college days, it is possible that it might be saleable. To find out, write the song on paper, place a *copyright notice* on the bottom, publish the song, register for a copyright, and file the necessary documents with the Register of

Copyrights in Washington. Following these steps should give you protection against anyone else who might copy the work.

Remember the cartoon. Copyright does not give protection against someone else who may independently create a similar or identical product. If two works are identical, the person claiming originality in the later work has a difficult time proving originality.

When copyright protects

Infringement of copyright occurs when a second work has copied, or plagiarized, from a previously copyrighted work. Since the copyright owner has the exclusive right to print, copy, adapt, and perform the composition, any action of anyone else in printing, copying, or publishing the work without proper permission constitutes infringement. The copyright owner then has the right to sue. To succeed in such an action, proof must be presented that the party sued had access to the copyrighted material and actually infringed it.

The Federal Copyright Act recognizes that most cases of infringement of copyright are innocent ones. Thus the Act provides for minimum damages in such cases. If the infringer is notified of the alleged infringement but does not discontinue the infringing activities, he will lose the benefit of the minimal damage provisions of the law. He may become subject to the full range of damages allowed.

If effect, when a claim of infringement is made, the party involved must decide whether to withdraw his material from publication or subject himself to possibly extensive damage claims.

In order to promote the use of materials without undue restrictions, the law dealing with copyright has developed what is known as the "fair use" rule. Under the rule, the moderate use of copyrighted material by other than the author is permitted.

The "fair use" rule

What constitutes "fair use" under the circumstances of any particular case has to be decided on the merits of each case. Generally, if the alleged infringer uses the previously copyrighted work in an attempt to substitute for it or take its place, and thus reduces the profits accruing to the copyright owner from the original work, there can be no valid claim to fair use. Beyond such a clear case, however, lies a vast area in which circumstances suggest what may be considered fair use.

A literary or artistic work can be promoted and exploited in many different ways. Newspapers, reprints, dramatic presentations, radio and television reproductions, musicals and other stage productions, recordings, hard- and soft-cover publications, reruns, and residual rights belong on the list. Thus the production and protection of artistic works involve much more than just their creation.

Lawyers, publishers, and other professionals can help ensure that an author or composer is properly protected, receives the royalties, and maintains ownership rights. Later adaptations of a work should not affect those rights.

That song up in the attic may find its way into a stage presentation, a musical comedy, a gold record, a folio of piano favorites, or, possibly, a movie.

The growing computer industry and the "videotaping fad" that swept the United States in the early 1980s gave rise to two far-reaching decisions by the U.S. higher courts.

Copyrighting in Computerville

As background to the computer decision, a major manufacturer of computers and the software that goes with them sued a smaller competitor. The charge: the competitor was copying the larger company's operating systems programs and was selling them as its own. The operating systems programs control the computer's inner workings.

The U.S. Court of Appeals in Philadelphia noted in its opinion that copyright protection extends not only to famous novels; it may also extend to such items as computer software.

The defendant company had admitted in court that it had copied the programs. But, it maintained, such programs were not protected by U.S. copyright laws. The judges, however, ruled that software can be copyrighted just as a book or an opera can be.

And in TV-Land . . .

A similarly critical decision by the U.S. Supreme Court in early 1984 affected the millions of Americans who owned videocassette recorders (VCRs), also called videotape recorders (VTRs).

In this suit the plaintiff companies charged that home taping of copyrighted programs, including films and special programs, violated the copyright holders' rights. Such taping deprived the copyright holders of extensive revenues. The plaintiffs asked that a surcharge or royalty be required on sales of VCRs or blank tapes.

The court cited the "fair use" rule in its opinion. Home taping, it said, did not violate copyright laws unless the material so taped was later used for a "commercial or profit-making purpose." Owners of VCRs could continue to use the equipment without paying extra fees.

PATENTS

The new or different mousetrap

A patent involves the protection of a physical expression of an idea or invention, usually for a period of 17 years. Unlike a copyright, a patent is not renewable without a special act of Congress. To be eligible for patent protection, the invention must consist of a new and useful article, a combination of materials, or a machine not previously known or used.

The better mousetrap must, therefore, contain a combination of materials or design that makes it, in fact, a new or different mousetrap.

WHEN SENDING A PATENT APPLICATION . . .

A patent application must be filed with the United States Patent and Trademark Office. The patent application must include:

- an abstract, which is a form of summary of the entire disclosure;
- a detailed description that would allow one skilled in the art to practice the invention;
- the claims which describe the distinguishing aspects of the invention; and
- drawings, if possible, showing the preferred embodiment of practicing the invention.

U.S. patents are of three kinds. They include:

1. "Utility" patents, the ordinary electrical, mechanical, or chemical patents on processes, machines, manufactured articles, compositions of matter, or improvements on any of those kinds of items

2. "Design" patents covering the ornamental or artistic appearance of manufactured articles, machines, and so on

3. "Plant" patents covering an originally discovered, developed, and asexually reproduced new and distinct variety of plant

Utility, design, and plant patents

Utility and plant patents are granted for terms of 17 years. Design patents are granted for periods of three and a half, seven, or 14 years. The inventor can specify how long he wants the design patent to run.

If an idea has merit as an invention, the inventor should give it concrete form by designing it on paper. He should then describe the invention in words, including all its components and what it is designed to do. This description must go into minute detail; it will form the basis of the patent application. Nothing should be left out. The components and mechanics of the invention should be described from beginning to end.

After the preliminary work is completed, the sketches and written description of the invention should be placed in the hands of a *patent lawyer*. A family lawyer can usually recommend a patent specialist who will review both the sketches and the description and conduct a "patent search."

The patent search will determine whether any existing, previously issued patent involves the same (or similar) ideas, methods, or material compositions as the "new" invention. Costing, usually, $250 and up, the search will determine whether a new invention will infringe on any other valid patent already issued. The lawyer can also conduct searches to find out which patents have been issued to other inventors and who owns a particular patent at the time of the search.

A patent application should be filed within a year after the invention is described, used, or put up for sale by the inventor. The first inventor to file a patent application for the same or a similar invention will usually prevail where there is a contest. While it is sometimes difficult to establish the date of an invention, the inventor should maintain all his notes and records to show the progress of the invention, how it was conceived, and the method by which it was reduced to a practical, physical object.

Damages for patent infringement   In the event of patent infringement, damages are collectible for a period of six years preceding the suit. Triple damages may be awarded for intentional or willful infringement. Under some circumstances, an injunction may be issued against the infringer to prevent additional damage.

A physical device may not be patentable. But it may have a definite use for which the inventor may want protection. He may be able to license others to use the product, perhaps utilizing his own engineering talents or other know-how. Leasing or licensing should be provided for under strict agreements. Covenants would be included to indicate that the party using the object will not reveal or take it for his own use and will return it and all specifications and plans concerning it after the lease or license expires.

The subjects of copyright and patents, the protection of trade secrets, technological information, artistic and literary works, and similar matters are highly complex. They require the assistance of qualified professionals. The genius of American industry and the inventiveness of the American personality indicate that the need for this kind of protection will continue.

If you have written that song, if you have a short story that you have always wanted to publish, or if you have an idea for a better mousetrap, why not do something with it? Fortunes have been made on less.

Part V
SPECIAL PROBLEMS

The law as a general concept has been viewed as preserving society's fabric. But the law also enables people to adjust to new and different situations; it emerges in many cases as a tool that every citizen can use to cope with special problems.

As a coping mechanism, law does not lose its regulatory function. It has still to serve as that moderating influence that keeps the rights of one person inviolate while guaranteeing the rights of others to enjoy "life, liberty, and the pursuit of happiness"—within limits. In at least three different categories of situations, the law projects itself into many people's lives at one time or another:

- Defamation, which arises when one person attacks or limits the right of another to be free of unwarranted, untruthful assaults on his or her character
- Automobile accidents
- Involvement with the law because of a crime or misdemeanor

Of these areas, the one involving auto accidents holds the lead insofar as numbers of cases are concerned. In fact, experts indicate that automobile accident cases take up a large proportion of all the court time in American courts at all levels. Auto accidents are traumatic in themselves. But they also lead under specific circumstances to civil or criminal actions, serious financial loss, and jail sentences.

Auto accidents and court time

What a person does and says immediately after an accident may determine entirely what happens to him later. It may even determine whether and how much he can recover for an injury or other loss. Thus Chapter 17 has special importance. But Chapter 16 should also be read with care if only because liability for libel or slander can be incurred unintentionally. The operations of the courts in criminal and other cases require some understanding, too, if the citizen is to remain up-to-date on some basic legal processes.

16 "IF YOU CAN'T SAY ANYTHING GOOD ABOUT A PERSON . . ."

In a crowded meat market, a woman customer says loudly that the market sells contaminated meat.

A man draws a recognizable picture of a neighbor, writes the name of a neighbor and the word "murderer" under it, and circulates it through the neighborhood.

A newspaper carries an item to the effect that a local department store is in financial straits.

The three hypothetical cases provide examples of libel and slander. Together, these two offenses constitute the offense of defamation of

character. In most instances, defamation ranks as a civil offense, or *tort*. The injured party can bring suit for damages. Less frequently, defamation may be a criminal offense, a misdemeanor, that is viewed by the law as a threat to the peace.

Before the invention of the printing press, the principal means of defaming a person was through the spoken word, or *slander*. With printed or written defamation, the legal concept of libel made its appearance. Today, *libel* is both a more serious and a more common offense than slander.

Libel and slander underscore some possible conflicts in the protections that the U.S. Constitution affords the American citizen. On the one hand, each person has the rights of freedom of speech and the press. On the other hand, those rights can interfere with another person's good reputation, privacy, or ability to earn a living. In trying to resolve this conflict, the laws of defamation are sometimes extremely complex.

This chapter will attempt to guide the reader through this complexity. The reader should remember that if he commits an act of defamation, he may be sued. At the same time a person who thinks he has been defamed should understand that he can bring legal action if he so chooses.

THE LAW OF DEFAMATION

When is a communication defamatory? A communication is defamatory when it has the effect of, or tends to have the effect of:

> harming the reputation of another;
>
> lowering that person's esteem or standing in the community;
>
> causing any persons to stop associating or dealing with him;
>
> exposing a person to scorn, ridicule, or contempt; or
>
> depriving a person of his job, or of his business if he is self-employed in a business, craft, or profession.

The content of a defamatory communication may take either of two forms. It may question a person's morality or integrity or it may brand the person with a loathsome disease that could cause people to avoid him. From another point of view, defamation may be either a statement of fact that charges a person with performance of a particular act or an expression of opinion about facts known or unknown, but which imply the commission of an act.

In general, before a suit can be brought because of a defamatory statement, all three of the following conditions must be met:

1. there must be publication, or communication, spoken or written, to a third party;

2. that communication must identify the particular individual either by name or in words that point to the person's identity; and

3. the communication must have a harmful effect that need not be tangible, as in provable financial loss, but may be merely an intangible affront to one's good name.

A defamatory publication need not have malicious intent. But proof of such intent would strengthen a lawsuit. A defendant in a civil defamation suit cannot escape responsibility for his actions by claiming mental incompetence, as he could in a criminal case.

Two kinds of damages

A defamed person usually tries to recover damages. In the normal case, he can then see himself as vindicated. Either of two kinds of damages may be awarded:

- General damages, where loss of reputation is presumed. In this situation, a case is called *actionable per se*: no special losses beyond a loss of reputation need to be shown. The loss of reputation is presumed to exist simply by virtue of the fact that the defamatory statement was published. General damages are typically token in nature, sometimes amounting to no more than six cents. The principle does matter.

- Special damages, where the person defamed can show he has suffered a particular loss, such as a loss of income or the prevention of a marriage. Special damages are awarded in addition to general damages. In order to receive special damages, however, a defamed person must show that special losses were incurred.

LYING DOWN ON THE JOB: A LIE?[1]

In the 1950s, his friends played a joke on John Cardiff of Brooklyn. The Brooklyn *Eagle* had published an announcement of John's death. He sued the paper on the basis that it not only falsely said he had died, but also said that he was lying "in state at 566-4th Avenue," which was his saloon. Still the court held that there was no libel. "At its worst, the publication might cause some amusement to the plaintiff's friends," the court said. "But it is difficult to see where his reputation would be impaired in the slightest degree and the law of defamation is concerned only with injuries thereto."

[1] From *Libel: Rights, Risks, Responsibilities* by Robert H. Phelps and E. Douglas Hamilton, revised edition. Copyright © 1966, 1978 by Robert H. Phelps and E. Douglas Hamilton. Reprinted with permission from Dover Publications, Inc.

He typically demands special damages in a specified amount at the time of filing suit. A jury may award special damages up to the amount specified by the plaintiff, but never more than that amount. Also, as long as the issue of defamation remains unresolved, the trial—according to a 1984 decision of the New Jersey Supreme Court—may continue even if a plaintiff dies before final adjudication.

Differences Between Libel and Slander

Libel more serious than slander

Libel is generally considered more serious than slander because the written or printed word has permanence while the spoken word does not. In addition, the commission of libel typically involves a more deliberate, studied attempt to defame. Slander is more subject to impulse. For these reasons, higher judgments for damages are awarded in cases of libel than in cases of slander.

Slander has, of course, been defined as spoken defamation. But with the advent of radio and television, the distinction between libel and slander has become somewhat hazy. The traditional definition of libel states that it involves publication of defamatory matter in the form of written or printed words, pictures, caricatures, statues, or other representations. These may appear in letters, circulars, petitions, newspapers, books, or other published works.

Spoken libel: a new phenomenon

The electronic and other media have led to broader definitions of libel. Today, in fact, "libel" includes spoken libel. In one form of spoken libel, defamatory matter is broadcast or telecast—issued over radio or television. The speaker or actor must, however, read or follow a prepared script or written notes. In some cases ad libs can constitute spoken libel.

A second form of spoken libel involves an orally transmitted defamation to a reporter. Publication may take place in a press conference, an interview, or a telephone conversation. The speaker may be liable even where the printed account differs somewhat from the spoken communication—if the substance of the communication is essentially accurate. The speaker may be liable even if he did not ask the reporter to print his remarks.

The Right to Be Protected from Defamatory Statements

The right to protection against defamatory publications is rooted in the U.S. Constitution and in most state constitutions. Every individual is guaranteed freedom from unwarranted and untruthful attacks upon his character. An attack that is warranted or true may be another matter.

The law normally labels any allegedly defamatory story as libelous even if the plaintiff does not recover damages. Likewise, a libel can be true and still be defamatory. The law makes the same point in another way. At the beginning of a court case, the court assumes that the libel is false.

Defamatory Words

The words used in a defamatory publication establish the principal criterion for determining whether such publication is actionable. Various qualifications of this criterion should be noted:
    the clear identification of the injured party
    the kinds of acts attributed to that party
    the social standing of the party
    the occupation held by the party
    the moral standards of the community at the time

Words That Are Defamatory Regardless of Actual Damage Done. A line may be drawn between general and special damages. A presumption that general damages are proper and deserved always exists in a defamation case. Proof of harm or loss must be shown before special damages will be awarded.

General and special damages

The distinction between libel and slander can be made more specific. In a case of libel, almost any publication is *actionable*—suit can be brought—for the recovery of general damages. In the case of slander, however, a publication is actionable without proof of damages under four specific circumstances:

When no proof of damages is needed

- When a person falsely and unjustifiably suggests that another person is guilty of a crime that is chargeable by indictment and punishable by death or imprisonment
- When a person suggests that another person has a loathsome disease
- When a person accuses another of improper conduct of a business or profession
- When one imputes unchastity to a woman

Unless one of these conditions is present, a slandered person must prove injury or harm meriting special damages. For example, he must prove a specific loss in terms of income or opportunity.

Words That Impute the Commission of a Crime or Status of Immorality. Crime is the most common subject matter of defamation. It can result in the most comprehensive kind of damage to a person: to his personal reputation, his right to enjoy social contacts, and his ability to make a living.

The accusation or suggestion of a crime is clear-cut; it must refer to a criminal act that is subject to indictment and to imprisonment or the death penalty. Any act that does not meet that criterion is libelous. For example, if a man kills in self-defense, he has not committed murder. If someone accuses him of murder, the accuser can be sued for libel.

To say that a person has committed a crime is much more serious than to say that he has been accused or is suspected of a crime. A libelous reference can mention a crime by name, telling of pertinent facts, or it can simply describe a punishment. Thus, to say that a person is an ex-convict indicates that he was guilty of a crime.

Moral standards change, vary

References to immoral acts may be still more ambiguous. Moral standards change from one year or decade to another. They also vary from one community to another, and from one group or social stratum in a community to another.

The phrase "the general public" admittedly expresses a fiction. However, it serves as a basis on which to decide what is libelous. In general, if a publication is intended to produce an unfavorable opinion in the minds of a large segment of a community's average, fair-minded people, that may constitute libel.

In 1900, describing a woman as a singer in a dance hall might have impugned her morality and would therefore have been libelous—if in fact she was not such a singer.

Words Tending to Injure a Person in a Profession or Business. Defamatory statements about persons in a profession or business may impute to them either criminal or immoral behavior. Such libels or slanders may injure not only individuals but partnerships and corporations as well. If a law office consisting of several partners is defamed, for example, the firm may sue. But individual partners may also bring suit. A defamation need not actually harm the reputation or business of a person; it may only tend, or be calculated, to do so.

Business or occupational defamations may take several forms:

- Charging a professional man with acts that are a breach of professional ethics

- Charging a person with general unfitness or with inefficiency in his occupation or business
- Charging a person or business with bankruptcy, insolvency, or other financial distress or embarrassment, whether past, present, or future
- Accusing a person or firm of fraud or dishonesty in one's line of work, in which case suspicion has the same effect as an outright charge of guilt

When can a person bring suit for this kind of defamation? Generally, the right to sue faces limitation in three kinds of situation:

Three limiting situations

- When the injured party has made, or is accused of making, a single mistake. "Anyone can make a mistake," and while it is held to be unfair to criticize a person for such an imperfection, it is also held that such a criticism does no real damage. However, an exception may be made to the general rule: the nature of the mistake may be such as to be open to criticism. If, for instance, a lawyer is accused of disclosing confidential information, an act that does not rank as a permissible mistake, that lawyer may sue for damages.
- When the act is illegal. If a person is accused of being an incompetent criminal, he may seek damages only for the imputed criminality, not for incompetence.
- When a person is not legally engaged in an occupation. A person not licensed as a physician cannot sue on the basis of a charge of incompetence.

In addition to individuals and corporations, nonprofit corporations and unincorporated groups can sue for defamation. Thus labor unions can sue; if they could not sue as organizations, each union member would have to sue separately.

Business or occupational defamations are the hardest to defend against. Because of the financial losses that may be involved, a business or professional person can seek compensatory damages from the defendant.

Damages for financial losses

Words Imputing Unfitness or Misconduct in a Public Office. Federal, state and local governments can legally be made the targets of defamatory statements. So can public officials in the act of carrying out government business. In their capacities as private citizens, however, public officials enjoy the same protections against defamation as do other citizens.

One exception to the latter protection may be noted: when some aspect of an official's personal or family life may have a serious bearing on his or her conduct in office. Thus the press did not libel Senator Eagleton of Missouri, a former vice-presidential candidate, when newspapers published reports that he had received psychiatric treatment for depression. The reports nonetheless cost Eagleton his candidacy.

Neither individuals nor the media stand under a legal restriction on criticisms of public officials or governments. Even if criticism consists entirely of lies, and the critic both knows he is lying and acts out of malice, he is still free to do so. Only one limitation exists: individual officials may not be named.

Third party involvement

Necessity of Certainty Regarding the Person Defamed. A person cannot be sued for defamation unless he directs his damaging remarks toward particular individuals or groups. Aside from the person being defamed, only one other person needs to be involved—to identify the person being defamed. It is not even necessary that a so-called "average person" be exposed to the publication—only a specific person, or any person. Nor is it necessary that the audience—one person or many—personally know or be acquainted with the defamed person.

FAIR COMMENT AND CRITICISM:
A NEWS AGENCY'S GUIDELINES[1]

The doctrine of *fair comment* has grown up in connection with slander and libel of public figures and elected and appointed officials. In essence, the rule holds that such persons have to expect more—and harsher—criticism of their performance on the job than private citizens.

A newspaper may charge a city official with inefficient or incompetent handling of public funds. Because the official's performance is a matter of public interest and concern, the criticism would probably fall under the fair comment rule. But the comments must be truly stated, must be based in some kind of fact, and must be honest expressions of opinion.

So important is libel to newspapers, news agencies, and other information media that many of them instruct their employees in basic principles. Especially sensitive are those relating to fair comment. The Associated Press, for example, warns its employees that ". . . whatever facts are stated, must be true" where comment and opinion are used with reference to matters of public interest or importance.

The AP also provides a summary of the fair comment rule:

Everyone has a right to comment on matters of public interest and concern, provided they do so fairly and with an honest purpose. Such comments or criticism are not libelous, however severe in their terms, unless they are written maliciously. Thus it has been held that books, prints, pictures and statuary publicly exhibited, and the architecture of public buildings, and actors and exhibitors are all the legitimate subjects of newspapers' criticism, and such criticism fairly and honestly made is not libelous, however strong the terms of censure may be. (*Hoeppner v. Dunkirk Printing Co.*, 254 N.Y. 95)

[1] From *The Associated Press Stylebook and Libel Manual* edited by Howard Angione. Copyright © 1977 by The Associated Press. Reprinted with permission from The Associated Press.

Establishing the Identity of the Person Defamed

You have gone hunting with old friend Jim. In the heat of pursuit you accuse Jim of murder. No third party hears the charge. You have not published slander.

The identity of a person can be established in a publication in a number of ways. These include, typically, a name, a nickname, a pen name, initials, or circumstances. Regarding the latter, pieces of information presented in a publication might enable a reader to arrive at the defamed person's identity with certainty. Identity is thus established circumstantially.

Direct and circumstantial identification

Similarity of names may mean similarity of identifications. For instance, if one chooses a fictitious name for the person being defamed, another person with that name could sue. If one accidentally used the wrong name, and another person happened to have that name, he could sue in every state but Illinois.

It may take more than one publication to connect a particular individual with a defamation. A newspaper one day may describe a police raid on a house of prostitution. The next day the same paper reports that a particular woman resides at that address. The woman may be able to sue on the ground that a reader can "put two and two together." This is an ambiguous area, however. Some courts will permit such a suit and others will not.

In defamation law, mention of a large group does not identify individuals. Under the law, defamatory talk is allowed where a professional, occupational, racial, religious, or ethnic group is concerned. One may refer to lawyers en masse in strongly negative terms, or use the traditional defamatory words for racial or ethnic groups.

A rule of thumb holds that when a group numbers fewer than 100, it is best not to refer to all members of the group even if no names are named. Qualifiers such as "some," or "many," or "most," or "certain" persons are preferable—and safer.

The Meanings of the Words Used. A publication may have more than one meaning. One meaning may be defamatory; another may not. As noted, standards vary with the times, the geographic area, and groups within a community. The first question is: What would the majority of average, reasonable citizens think of a particular publication?

If the words in a publication can have only one meaning—a defamatory one—the judge will usually be able to make the ruling on the case. If the judge decides that the meaning is not defamatory, then of course the trial ends.

The jury may decide Some judges let juries decide whether publications are defamatory. This may happen when the words are capable of having two or more meanings, a relatively rare occurrence.

Necessity for Intent and Malice. In defamation, intent constitutes an essential element, and that intent must be malicious. Evidence of malice may be either expressed or implied. Where a person publishes a communication that appears defamatory on its face, malicious intent is presumed. A plaintiff does not have to prove the existence of other circumstances showing malice.

Defamation thus differs from other torts—minor offenses—in that intent and malice are presumed elements. However, the person who composes a defamation and the person who publishes it may be two different persons. The editor of a newspaper publishing a libel has the same liability as the reporter who wrote it. If he knew nothing of the publication, the newspaper owner is free of liability.

Another aspect of defamation law involves repetition of a defamation. The person who repeats or republishes a defamation has the same liability as the originator of the defamation. If a defamatory newspaper article is syndicated to various newspapers, each of these newspapers may be sued for libel. Each republication of a defamation constitutes a new offense even if the originator is named.

An innocent mistake on the part of a publisher, committed without malice, will not excuse him. But a defendant remains liable if he publishes a defamation without malice. In this case he may have any award of damages reduced if he can prove that he acted with proper motives and with a belief in the truth of what he published. The bad reputation of the plaintiff may also mitigate damages.

"Innocent mistake" no excuse

Necessity of Publication to Other People. Publication has some technical meanings. The sale of even one newspaper constitutes publication. Proof of distribution of that paper would be viewed as evidence of publication.

A sealed letter or other communication delivered to the plaintiff's spouse constitutes a publication.

In the case of letters, a libel becomes criminal rather than civil if it appears in a letter addressed to another. In criminal libel, a prosecutor rather than the injured party seeks damages. As in all crimes, the state has become, at law, the injured party.

Civil libel may be established if:

- the letter was forwarded to the plaintiff during his absence;
- the letter was intended for the eyes of the plaintiff's family and/or employees; or
- the letter was in fact read by them.

If it was not read by those persons, it cannot be considered a publication.

When the person defamed is deceased, defamation may nonetheless take place on publication. This is a case of criminal libel, however, as the peace of the community is at stake. For example, if a president who died in office is called a traitor after his death, such a publication may incite riots. In general, criminal defamation is extremely rare.

Defamation after death: criminal libel

DEFENSES IN DEFAMATION CASES

Certain defenses can be used to avoid liability for either civil or criminal defamation. One such defense, the statute of limitations, means that a plaintiff cannot bring suit after a specified period of time has elapsed. Among other defenses are:

- the defense of consent, where the defamed person actually consented to have the statement published;
- the defense of husband and wife, where spouses can publish defamations about one another (by common law, husband and wife are one person);
- the defense of privilege; and
- the defense of truth.

The last two appear most commonly in defamation cases. Privilege may be either absolute—without restriction—or qualified.

Absolute Privilege

Two kinds of absolute privilege

Privilege as an absolute defense renders immaterial the motive of the publisher or the purpose of the publication. The two principal types of defenses arising out of absolute privilege are (1) statements made in court and (2) the official acts, reports, and records of public officials.

In the first instance, every participant in a court proceeding has the right to make, with impunity, any statement about a person regardless of intent or effect. Comments can touch on the judge, jurors, attorneys, prosecutor, witnesses, plaintiff, and defendant. The court setting provides complete freedom of speech.

In the second instance, a public official can make any statement about any person, regardless of intent or effect, while performing his official duties. If that condition is not fulfilled, the defense cannot be used. One official may be accused by another official of wrongful acts while both are taking part in legislative hearings. If the second official later makes the same statement off the floor, he may be compromising himself legally.

Qualified Privilege

Qualified privilege applies to persons not involved as described above. Qualified privilege cannot be used as a plea when malice is present. This kind of defense is typically employed by news media in two situations:

- Presenting authentic news reports of legislative, judicial, or legal proceedings of which there are official records

- Presenting fair comment or criticism of elected or appointed officials or of candidates for public office—as distinguished from reporting official activities

The so-called "*New York Times* rule" has a bearing on qualified privilege. It stipulates that publishing a defamatory statement about a public official justifies a lawsuit only when the writer knew it was false or wrote with reckless disregard of its truth or falsity. The news media also enjoy protection against suits by private parties where published statements involve issues of "public or general concern."

In the 1984 case of *Bose Corp.* v. *Consumer's Union of the United States, Inc.*, the Supreme Court reaffirmed the 20-year-old *New York Times* rule. The Court held that *Consumer Reports* magazine had not acted with actual malice when it criticized a loudspeaker manufactured by the plaintiff.

Truth as Justification

Truth constitutes the most complete, or perfect, defense in a suit. It is rooted in the right to free speech. But truth has not always been allowed as a defense. At one time, it could be used in civil cases more

STATUTES OF LIMITATION FOR STARTING A CIVIL ACTION AGAINST LIBEL OR SLANDER (IN YEARS)[1]

State	Libel	Slander	State	Libel	Slander
Alabama	1	1	Montana	2	2
Alaska	2	2	Nebraska	1	1
Arizona	1	1	Nevada	2	2
Arkansas	3	1	New Hampshire	2	2
California	1	1	New Jersey	1	1
Colorado	1	1	New Mexico	3	3
Connecticut	2	2	New York	1	1
Delaware	2	2	North Carolina	1	1
District of Columbia	1	1	North Dakota	2	2
Florida	4	4	Ohio	1	1
Georgia	1	1	Oklahoma	1	1
Hawaii	2	2	Oregon	1	1
Idaho	2	2	Pennsylvania	1	1
Illinois	1	1	Rhode Island	10	1
Indiana	2	2	South Carolina	2	2
Iowa	2	2	South Dakota	2	2
Kansas	1	1	Tennessee	1	½
Kentucky	1	1	Texas	1	1
Louisiana	1	1	Utah	1	1
Maine	2	2	Vermont	3	3
Maryland	1	1	Virginia	2	2
Massachusetts	3	3	Washington	2	2
Michigan	1	1	West Virginia	1	1
Minnesota	2	2	Wisconsin	2	2
Mississippi	1	1	Wyoming	1	1
Missouri	2	2			

[1] Adapted from *You and the Law,* Copyright© 1977 The Reader's Digest Association, Inc. Copyright© 1977 The Reader's Digest Association (Canada) Ltd. Copyright© 1977 Reader's Digest Association Far East Ltd. Philippine Copyright© 1977 Reader's Digest Association Far East Ltd.

readily than in criminal cases. Today, truth may be raised as a defense in both civil and criminal defamation cases.

In most states truth ranks as a complete defense even where malice is involved. By the early 1980s, the following states held that malice could not be an issue in civil cases: Delaware, Florida, Illinois, Maine, Massachusetts, Nebraska, New Hampshire, Pennsylvania, Rhode Island, West Virginia, and Wyoming. But even in those states truth would probably serve as an adequate defense.

To be effective as a plea, truth must be proved in all its essential particulars. Half-truths will not exonerate a defendant. Accusing a man of perjury, for example, means not only that he testified falsely under oath, but that he did so willfully and knowingly. A publication containing errors may nonetheless be held to be truthful if it is true in its essentials. If a publication accurately reproduces a defamatory charge, the defense of truth will not apply even though the reproduction was accurate.

Evidence that proves truth Truth can be proved only through presentation of hard evidence such as documents or the statements of witnesses. Because most people and organizations—including newspapers—lack the powers of the police to ferret out such evidence, the defense of truth is seldom used.

CENSORSHIP

The year 1982 brought a number of cases involving local censorship questions. A Virginia school official tried to remove Mark Twain's *The Adventures of Huckleberry Finn* from a school's reading curriculum. In Texas the State Board of Education decided not to buy a particular dictionary for use in schools because the book contained a number of "objectionable" words. In a third case, a citizen attempted to have two novels removed from a local public library.

A fourth famous case went to the U.S. Supreme Court. The court decided in *Board of Education, Island Trees Free School District* v. *Pico* that members of a school board or faculty can be sued in federal courts if they remove books from school libraries. In *Pico* a group of high school students had sued the school board after the board ordered removal of nine books from the school library.

A Constitutional Question

The cases appeared to mark a trend toward censorship of school and public libraries through removal or non-purchase of books and other materials. Two constitutional rights, freedom of speech and freedom of the press, seemed to come into conflict with the basic right of a school district or community to decide which books its libraries should contain.

The law provides no clear guidelines. The Supreme Court's decision in the *Pico* case does not clear up the confusion, primarily because the Court said only that school officials could be sued if they removed books from school libraries. The Court did not prohibit such removal; nor did it say that the school officials were automatically guilty of illegal censorship, or that they would be violating students' rights if they refused to buy certain books.

What does the Supreme Court's decision in *Pico* contribute? The Court has said, in effect, that censorship (by removal or other means) for political reasons stands in violation of the First Amendment—but that censorship designed to remove reading or other materials for obscenity reasons may be justified.

17 "DID YOU GET THE NUMBER OF THAT TRUCK?"

America has always been a nation on the move. The early movements westward, the drive for new horizons, and the ability of Americans to adjust to different climates and ways of life have been, perhaps, the most significant aspects of American traditions and history. Today, companies routinely move their executives or workers to new locations; the transferees have to make new plans, establish new roots, and find new homes. Millions of others move at whim, to find new jobs, or to relocate in retirement.

The automobile has played a distinct and dominant role in the development of the United States and its ways of life. The old "Model T" brought the automobile to the common man. That trend, continued, has probably had a greater influence on America's mobile society than any other factor.

America manufactures and uses more automobiles than any other nation of the world. Almost every American family has an automobile. More of the capital budgets of the various states go to road maintenance and construction than perhaps any other item on the budget. The possible exception may be welfare.

Inevitably, the passenger miles driven in any given year result in a high incidence of automobile accidents. Expectably, the automobile figures more than any other factor in accidental deaths and injuries. In

consequence, trials of automobile accident cases have taken up a substantial portion of the time of American courts for many years. Various plans and programs have been designed to reduce the numbers of auto accidents tried in the courts. But today and for the foreseeable future the auto accident case will continue to be the most typical one appearing on the nation's court calendars.

What should a person do if he is involved in an auto accident? What should he do if he witnesses an accident? What protection can the individual purchase to protect himself in the event he is sued for an accident in which someone else is hurt or injured?

In the event of an auto accident . . .

This chapter deals with the automobile accident, the procedures to follow in the event of an accident, and the types of protection which you can purchase to protect yourself against money claims.

AUTOMOBILE ACCIDENT PROCEDURES

Where an auto accident occurs, certain procedures are required by both common sense and the laws of most states. Regardless of who is at fault, both drivers in a two-car accident have to stop at the scene of the accident and supply names and addresses. They also give the names and addresses of the insurance agents and companies providing their liability insurance. Once this information has been exchanged, depending on the seriousness of the accident, the police may question the parties.

The Police Report

The police investigation at the scene of the accident is very important. The police report may be used in any lawsuit deriving from the accident. Thus the information supplied to the police officer has to be as accurate, clear, and complete as possible.

What the police report contains

The police report will normally include all pertinent details:
- The accident and its location
- A diagram of the scene and the locations of the vehicles immediately following the accident
- Any skid marks or debris that appear on the roadway
- The weather and road conditions
- The names and other information on all persons injured
- The approximate amount of any damage to the vehicles
- The various versions of the accident from the viewpoints of the drivers and passengers

A copy of the police report on a serious accident can and should be obtained from the local police, usually at minimum cost. The police version should be checked to make sure it is consistent with the facts. If it is not, a certified letter, return receipt requested, should be sent immediately to the police. The letter provides a correct statement of how the accident occurred as reported to the investigating officer.

The letter should contain a request that it be attached to the police report in the police files. If the police report is later used in court, the letter, written to correct an error in the report, can on request be used at the trial.

Many states require that an accident report be filed with the state public safety or motor vehicle department within a certain number of days following the accident. In these cases the accident will have involved personal injuries or property damage up to a stated amount. The report includes all the information set out in the police report along with information on the existence of liability insurance.

Most states provide that the information contained in these reports is confidential and cannot be used in any court trial that may arise out of the accident. Insurance information helps to fulfill the requirements of various state financial responsibility laws.

Reporting the Accident to the Insurance Company

An accident should be reported immediately to an individual's insurance agent or company. This is particularly important where "the other person" may bring a claim for vehicle or personal injury. The accident should be reported even if no one appears to be hurt—or even if no one says he is injured. Waiting too long may mean that the insurance company will be unable to investigate properly. The company may even refuse to defend its client against the claim of a second party. Failure to report the accident promptly may actually violate a requirement of the policy.

To be safe, call your insurance company or agent

**A CHECKLIST OF THINGS TO DO
IN CASE OF AN ACCIDENT[1]**
MAKE SURE YOU PROTECT YOURSELF
What to do in case of an accident. How you act after an accident may strongly influence the settlement of the insurance claim, so it's important to observe certain procedures. Here are key things you should try to do, according to the Professional Insurance Agents of Iowa, an association of agents who sell property and other insurance.
—Seek medical attention for anyone who is injured.
—Don't discuss who is at fault. Admitting guilt might jeopardize your rights.
—Don't discuss the kind of insurance coverage you have.

—Obtain the following information: operator's license number; license plate number; year and make of car; name, address and telephone numbers of driver, passengers and witnesses, if any; car owner's name, address and telephone number if driver is not the owner; name, address and telephone number of the other driver's insurance agent and company. Give the same information about yourself to the other driver.

—If police come to the scene, get their names, badge numbers, and the office where the report will be filed.

—While the accident is still fresh in your mind, jot down details about road and weather conditions and other relevant circumstances.

—Notify your insurance agent and consult with him on how to proceed with your claim.

—Make copies of accident reports, if needed (see list below). Some states require the agent to sign the form. Make sure the form is sent to the proper agency within the prescribed period.

When you have to report an accident. In all states and the District of Columbia, any accident involving physical injury or death must be reported to the authorities. If there are no injuries, an accident report has to be filed when the estimated property damage exceeds the following amounts (in most states the minimum applies to the combined damage to all vehicles):

Ala.	$ 50	Ill.	$250	Mont.	$250	R.I.	$200
Alaska	500	Ind.	200	Neb.	250	S.C.	200
Ariz.	300	Iowa	250	Nev.	250	S.D.	250
Ark.	250	Kan.[2]	300	N.H.	300	Tenn.	200
Cal.	500	Ky.	200	N.J.	200	Texas	250
Colo.	250	La.	200	N.M.	100	Utah	400
Conn.	400	Me.	300	N.Y.	400	Vt.	200
Del.[2]	250	Md.	100	N.C.[2]	200	Va.	350
D.C.	100	Mass.	200	N.D.	400	Wash.	300
Fla.	100	Mich.[2]	200	Ohio	150	W.Va.	250
Ga.	250	Minn.	300	Okla.	100	Wis.	400
H.I.	300	Miss.	250	Ore.	200	Wyo.	250
Ida.[2]	250	Mo.	500	Pa.[3]	—		

[1] Reprinted with permission from the Professional Insurance Agents of Iowa.

[2] Accident report filed by police officer only.

[3] Damage limit has been replaced by the following requirements: "If an accident involves death, injury or any vehicle involved cannot be driven away under its own power without further damage or hazard to the vehicle or other vehicles on the roadway, the police must be notified. If police are unable to investigate accident, driver must report accident to the Bureau of Accident Analysis within 5 days."

Photographs and Injury Diary

Photographs and an injury diary may make it possible to reconstruct details later. If you are the party injured or damaged, and feel that you have a claim against the other driver, you should take photographs of both cars to establish their condition immediately following the collision. The photos would become important in a lawsuit to show the cars' physical condition and assist in arriving at a determination of how the accident happened.

The importance of photos   Photos should also be taken at the scene of the accident from various angles. The photos should show the directions in which the vehicles were traveling, the point of impact, the general neighborhood, the traffic controls in the area, including traffic lights and stop signs, and speed limit signs or other warning signs.

If you have suffered injury, you should maintain a diary. Entries should provide a record of all hospital stays by dates; every inpatient and outpatient visit; the names of all physicians, on staff or otherwise, who treated you; the dates and times of all visits to doctors' offices; the types of medicines prescribed; all your doctor bills, hospital bills, and drug and medication bills; the amounts of lost wages or earnings; the number of days you were laid up at home; the days you were totally or partially incapacitated and unable to perform your normal work; and the number of days or amount of time lost because of doctor visits or outpatient treatment at the hospital.

The diary can be very important. It obviously records facts. But it also serves to refresh memories of the accident and later events. Several years may elapse before a case comes up for trial. Remembering incidental things with the aid of a diary may make the difference between an adequate and a good recovery for injuries.

Medical and Hospital Benefits

Insurance under Blue Shield, Blue Cross, or some other private medical or hospital policy provided by an employer does not necessarily restrict claims for medical and hospital expenses. The injured party's insurance company may even have paid all basic claims. The laws of many states do not allow the party at fault to escape liability for these expenses by claiming that the injured party had provided himself with private insurance to pay his bills. The reason for this is that the person at fault ought not to be able to take advantage of the foresight of the injured person.

Personal accident records should therefore include every single bill even though all the bills were covered by insurance. These amounts should be included in the total amount of the claim.

Including all bills

Dealing with the Insurance Adjuster

The injured party should give written notice of a claim to the other party. Shortly afterward, if the party at fault has insurance, the adjuster for his insurance company will contact the injured party to make an adjustment or settlement of the claim as soon as possible for the lowest possible amount. This is his job; no one should be offended if the first offer in settlement is far below what is deserved or demanded. In this case negotiations should continue.

The adjuster needs a statement from the injured party as quickly as possible. But it is usually better not to give any statement to the adjuster before consulting with a lawyer.

Dangers in giving statements Most people make the serious mistake of believing that they can "handle it themselves." They try to give statements that will not adversely affect their cases. They forget that taking a statement is an art, and that a trained adjuster can see things in a person's statement that the person himself would never see. In too many cases a statement comes back to haunt an accident victim at a trial. The statement may be written, put on tape, or given over the telephone. In each case the effect is the same.

If a statement must be given, it should be a written statement that can be checked thoroughly. All necessary corrections should be made before it is dated and signed. Taped statements, or those given over the phone, should be avoided because they cannot be corrected—or even replayed to ensure that they are accurate.

What, then, do you do when an adjuster calls you on the phone and asks if you mind if he records the conversation? You tell him, "Yes, I do indeed mind," and refuse to allow the conversation to be recorded. Any recording of the conversation after your refusal would be unlawful.

If the adjuster is advised that the injured party is represented by an attorney, he is required to deal with the lawyer through all phases of the claim. He cannot deal directly with the injured party without express instructions.

Cooperation with an Insurance Company

If contacted by the lawyer for the person injured, the party at fault should refer the lawyer to his insurance company. The party at fault should not deal directly with the other side. Nor should he give any statements to anyone representing the party injured. To do so could jeopardize his own protection under a liability policy.

A family lawyer might be brought into the case if the possible liability for the accident could exceed the limits of the policy. In such a case, the family lawyer will work with the insurance company lawyer. But the party at fault will have to pay for this lawyer's services.

When to Settle a Claim

Don't rush to settle a claim No one should rush to settle a claim. That rule of thumb has particular validity if an accident has resulted in personal injury. Unfortunately, many serious injuries do not become noticeable until many months after an accident has occurred.

Insurance adjusters are trained to secure settlements as quickly as is reasonably and fairly possible. In a clear case of liability, an adjuster may make an offer in the hope that the offer will be accepted, settling the case. The offer may be quite fair insofar as the condition of the injured person is known at that time. If final settlement is made, however, and if serious additional injury is discovered later, the injured person may have no right to recover anything further.

A formal, written "Release of All Claims" is normally required by the insurance company. The release is signed by the injured party and acknowledged before a notary public. It usually contains language that releases the party at fault and his insurance company from any further claims for any personal injury or property damage that may be discovered in the future.

It is important to realize that an adequate waiting period permits any additional medical problems to become evident. Normally, an injured person should wait until he or she is released from further medical treatment by the physician who has been treating the accident injuries. No claim should be settled without consultation with a lawyer first.

Waiting has a purpose

Statutes of Limitations

How can one decide when to sue or settle a claim? Most states have either a one-year or a two-year "statute of limitations" on personal injury cases. This means that a lawsuit to recover for injuries has to be started within one or two years from the date on which the accident occurred. Failure to bring suit within the time limit established in the particular state will normally terminate the right to sue. The period can, however, be extended if the party at fault waives the defense of the statute of limitations. Such a waiver is very difficult to establish.

In some states, suits based on certain types of claims must be filed within 100 days after the accident.

An injured party should have a pretty good idea before a year passes just how serious his condition is. He should know whether he can settle without a lawsuit. But his negotiations with the adjuster should not mislead him into believing that he does not have to file a suit in time to protect a claim.

Safety first: a suit can be discontinued once it is filed, but if not filed in time, the suit can never be filed.

A suit can be discontinued

Insurance policies typically require the insured to cooperate with the insurance company. If he is served with suit papers, the party at fault should immediately deliver them to the company so that it can prepare the necessary defense. The insured may also be required to sign various defense papers, to discuss the case with the attorneys for the insurance company, and to appear at pre-trial depositions. The latter are interviews, under oath, conducted by the attorney for the opposing party, with a court reporter present who transcribes all the questions and answers.

The insured may have to testify in court as part of his obligation to cooperate with the insurance company. Failure or refusal to cooperate may give the company a reason to deny any further coverage.

Elements of Damages

Four elements of a claim

By 1980, 16 states had no-fault insurance laws of various kinds. In the other 34 states and the District of Columbia, the basic elements on which a claim should be based, or damages sought, include the following:

1. Out-of-pocket expenses, such as medical bills, the cost of drugs and medicines, nursing costs, and all other expenses.
2. Lost wages or lost profits and earnings (if self-employed).
3. An amount representing the pain, suffering, and inconvenience that were sustained.
4. An amount representing future disability and loss of earning power. If the injury results in a permanent disability, either full or partial, this amount represents the total loss of earnings anticipated over one's working life, measured by income at the time of the accident, work expectancy in years as determined by mortality or work expectancy tables, and, in certain cases, by experts concerning future earnings and increments in income that could normally be expected in the future.

While these are the basic factors in a claim, there are others. For example, pain and suffering may be expected to continue over one's entire life span. The laws of a given state may indicate that this should be taken into account.

Depending on state laws, it may be possible to demand a specific amount in a lawsuit—a sum representing all the elements noted above. Some states, however, do not permit demands in specific amounts. These states leave it to the jury to place a value on the claim as part of its verdict.

HOW TO PUT A VALUE ON YOUR CLAIM

Determination of what a claim is worth constitutes the most difficult aspect of any suit for personal injury damages. Establishing liability may, of course, be equally difficult. But how can a dollar value be placed on pain and suffering?

State laws affect PI claims

What follows are some very general rules that apply to the basic personal injury claim. Each case, however, has its own peculiar facts that may change any basic formula. The laws of the several states will certainly affect these rules as they apply in any given case.

An example will serve to illustrate the basic rules. Suppose, as the result of an accident for which someone else is responsible, you accumulate $1,000 in total medical, hospital, and drug bills and $250 in lost wages. Your physician has discharged you from further treatment and has assured you that you should suffer no further discomfort or disability. In fact you feel fine. What is your claim worth?

You can rule out any claim for future disability or loss of earnings. Thus you can recover your out-of-pocket "special damages" of $1,000, as well as your lost wages of $250. For pain, suffering, and inconvenience, where there is no permanent pain, suffering, disability or loss of future earnings or earning power, and where the liability of the party at fault is clear, you can usually use the factor of two to four times the amount of the "special damages." That ratio is generally accepted by insurance adjusters as being reasonable.

The factor, it should be noted, can be different in different parts of the country. For example, the factor would be somewhat lower if the accident case is being tried in a rural area. It might be slightly higher in a large metropolitan area. The basic claim might thus be valued generally as follows:

Total medical expenses	$1,000
Lost wages	250
Pain, suffering and inconvenience:	
2 to 4 times $1,000	2,000 to 4,000
TOTAL	$3,250 to $5,250

Changing the facts, and considering that the other party's liability is not clear, the settlement value for a plaintiff is reduced accordingly. If, however, permanent disability is involved, either complete or partial, reducing future earning power, the value of the claim would substantially increase. Loss of a limb or eyesight, disfigurement, or other serious, enduring problems would increase the value of the claim.

If earning power is reduced . . .

Assume that an accident victim suffered a 25 per cent disability that will be permanent. A physician will give testimony to that effect. The victim was earning $15,000 per year at the time of the accident; he could assume a working life expectancy of 20 years. The calculation of the claim could be made as follows:

Medical expenses	$1,000
Lost wages	250
Loss of future earnings, pain, suffering and inconvenience, 30 years x $15,000 = $450,000; 25% disability x $450,000 = $112,500, reduced to present worth	

Note that the total claim, because it reaches into the future, must be "reduced to present worth." This involves a calculation to determine what amount, if invested at the time of the trial or settlement at the then-legal rate of interest in the state, would yield the sum of $112,500 after 30 years. Some states require that this calculation be made by an actuary or other expert.

The above example does not take into account any permanent pain and suffering. Nor does it allow for normal increments in income over the 30 years of the victim's working life. But it illustrates the vast difference in the value of the claim where disability or permanent injury is involved.

Huge awards may be deceptive

Newspaper accounts of huge sums awarded in personal injury cases can be deceptive. They can rarely be used as measures of the worth of other claims. Each case is different. One can only say, in general, that the more serious the injury, the higher the award.

THE TRIAL OF A PERSONAL INJURY LAWSUIT

Unlike radio and television programs that deal with courtroom trials, the trial of a lawsuit involving personal injuries is not, for the most part, dramatic or spectacular. Rather, the process unfolds as an orderly and, ideally, interesting presentation of facts and evidence. Rarely does a defendant break down on the stand and confess that he was not watching where he was going and that he caused the accident.

The trial of any lawsuit, like so many things in life, is not won or lost in the courtroom but in the painstaking preparation that must precede the trial. This includes complete investigation of the facts of the accident. It also includes interviews with witnesses and doctors, inspection of photographs and diagrams, expert witnesses, securing hospital records, and many similar tasks. The client can be of great help to the lawyer in his preparation of the case.

Before the Trial

Preparing to go to trial

As the trial date approaches, the victim may become impatient with the manner in which cases are called. Since personal injury cases make up the great bulk of the trial calendars in many courts, the trial schedules may be congested. Often, cases do not move as rapidly as they should.

In order to bring cases to trial as quickly as possible, judges may insist—either by rule of court or in practice—that attorneys be ready to go to trial immediately when their cases are called. However, neither the judges nor the attorneys can be absolutely sure when a case will actually be called. Other cases may take longer to complete than expected, or may be settled "on the courthouse steps," thereby moving up a later case faster than expected. This means that the lawyers must have all the witnesses lined up to come to court on short notice—a great inconvenience to many participants, particularly the medical witnesses.

Each county may, of course, have a slightly different system. But the basic problems with trial schedules are the same. They require the sympathetic cooperation of the principals and witnesses in each case.

Once a case is ready for trial, it will be assigned to a particular courtroom and judge. Before the start of the case, assuming it is a jury case, the attorneys will take part in the selection of a jury. In most states, juries of 12 persons are chosen for all civil cases. In the federal courts, a jury of six is common.

Assignment to a courtroom and judge

THE TRIAL

With the jury selected, the trial begins. In the normal case the attorney for the plaintiff, the party bringing the action, introduces himself, the other attorney, and the judge to the jury, then delivers his opening statement. Here he outlines the case that he is about to present. After he has finished, the defense attorney may make his opening remarks. He may, however, wait until the plaintiff's case has been presented in full.

The plaintiff's attorney calls his witnesses in order. After the "direct examination" of his witness is completed, the defense attorney begins the "cross-examination." After the cross-examination is completed, the plaintiff's attorney may ask additional questions on "re-direct examination." "Re-cross-examination" by the defense counsel may follow. The trial continues in this way until both attorneys and the judge—who also may put questions to the witnesses—have no further questions. The witness is then excused.

From "direct" to "re-cross-examination"

After the plaintiff's attorney has called all his witnesses and introduced into evidence all the exhibits, photos, and other documents, he *rests his case.* That means his part of the case, to that point, is concluded. The defense attorney then begins his case, makes his opening statement, and goes through the same procedures with his witnesses and exhibits. After he rests his part of the case, rebuttal witnesses may be called for the plaintiff, followed by any rebuttal witnesses for the defense.

After all witnesses and all exhibits have been heard or introduced into evidence, the closing arguments take place. These constitute a review of all the evidence and arguments in favor of the particular party. In some states, the defense attorney must give his closing argument first; other states require that the plaintiff's attorney speak first. After these arguments are concluded, the lawyers and the judge consult on the judge's instructions to the jury.

Since the jury decides on the facts that are in dispute, the judge must instruct the jury on the law to be applied to those facts. The attorneys may submit to the judge those instructions that they want to be included in the judge's instructions. At this time the judge rules on these requests and permits or denies some or all of the requested instructions.

The importance of instructions to the jury

Proper instructions to the jury are very important. If the judge makes a mistake and disallows a proper instruction, or gives an improper instruction, he may be establishing the basis for a reversal of the verdict and judgment on appeal to a higher court. The lawyers generally spend a great deal of time in preparing these instructions to the jury—and in trying to convince the judge that he should give the instructions they prepared.

Following his conference with the attorneys, the judge instructs the jury on the law. If the circumstances warrant, the judge reviews the evidence presented at the trial. The jury then goes to the jury room to consider its verdict in private. On reaching a verdict, the jury members return and state their verdict in open court in the presence of the judge, the attorneys, and, sometimes, the parties to the suit.

After the verdict, motions may be entered for a new trial, or for judgment in one principal's favor regardless of the jury's verdict. A judgment is then entered by the court in favor of the winning party. The motions are formal proceedings in which a party states his position that some error was committed in the trial of the case. The error presumably prejudiced him in the result reached by the jury. After the court makes a decision on these motions, the losing party has the right of appeal.

Where Death Occurs

Suits for "wrongful death"

Where personal injuries incurred in an accident have resulted in death, an action may be brought in most states for the "wrongful death" of the person killed. In this kind of lawsuit, beneficiaries such as a spouse, children, or the parents of the deceased, as identified under the laws of the state, sue to recover for the losses sustained through the death of the loved one.

Suits may also be brought on behalf of the estate of the deceased person to recover for losses that the deceased himself suffered and for losses to his estate resulting from the death. The laws of the various states differ as regards the amounts that can be recovered, and the beneficiaries who can recover, in wrongful death cases. Anyone faced with a situation involving the accidental death of a close relative should immediately consult a lawyer to ascertain what the laws say on these very important points.

INSURANCE AGAINST LIABILITY

The chapter on insurance dealt in general terms with liability insurance covering automobiles. This section will deal in more detail with the basic automobile liability policy and what it covers, whom it covers, and what protections are available under the policy.

First, in some of the states, and particularly since the passage of the "no-fault" insurance laws, it has become impossible to obtain a driver's license without evidence that the applicant has liability insurance coverage. In those states that do not have such requirements, financial responsibility laws on the books require the driver to provide proof that he is financially able to pay for any damages that he may cause in an accident. Sometimes some form of security, such as a bond, has to be posted. The bond would cover any judgment that might be rendered against the applicant.

A problem exists with both of these methods of establishing financial responsibility. Essentially, they do not protect the victim if the party at fault does not have the means to post bond or carry insurance. That party may lose his driving privileges, but that will be small consolation to the victim.

Limits of Liability

Automobile liability insurance protects the owner or driver against claims by third parties for property damage or personal injuries resulting from the use of the auto. The policy is stated in terms of limits of liability—for example, $10,000 for each person and $20,000 for each occurrence. That means that the coverage provided will not exceed $20,000 for all injuries resulting from one accident, regardless of the total number of persons injured. No more than $10,000 can be paid for each person injured.

Protection against third-party claims

Payment by the company is made directly to the injured party and is not paid to the insured. The company pays if the insured is liable. Under the typical policy, the insurance company is required to defend any claims brought against the insured. If the insured has insufficient coverage, however, the victim retains the right to sue for a judgment for the total amount of damage. If an injured party exhausts the total amount of insurance coverage carried by the party at fault, he can attempt to collect the balance directly from the insured.

Covered damages under auto liability policies extend to deaths and injuries as well as to physical damage to cars or other property. A policy may be described as 100/300/25. In the shorthand of the insurance industry, that means the insurance company will pay:

- up to $100,000 for injury to, or the death of, one person;

- up to $300,000 in the aggregate if more than one person is injured or killed in a single accident; and
- up to $25,000 for property damage.

Insurance experts believe that a good liability policy in the early 1980s should provide at least 100/300/25 coverage. Inflation could, of course, indicate a need for upward revision of those figures in coming years.

The auto liability policy protects the owner of the vehicle when he is operating it and anyone else operating it with the owner's permission. The policy may also protect the insured or his spouse, when either is driving someone else's vehicle, under "drive other car" coverage. Members of the household of the insured are normally covered by the policy. The courts liberally interpret the language of these policies to find that the individual involved was a resident or a member of the insured's household. Thus the policy would usually provide protection.

Exclusions from coverage

As with any other liability policy, there are exceptions or exclusions from coverage that generally appear in an auto policy. These include claims covered by the workers' compensation laws and claims involving areas in which certain commercial vehicles may be used.

The policy provision binding the insurance company to defend any claim made against the insured applies even though the company finds that the claim is false or fraudulent. If the company refuses to defend and the insured has to hire a lawyer, the company may have to pay both the amount of any judgment against the insured and the insured's costs and attorney's fees.

In addition to the liability insurance that is included in the standard auto policy, the insured can also elect to carry collision insurance. A form of property insurance, collision coverage pays for damage to the insured's own vehicle. "Collision" refers to the unintentional striking of another object, even if it is not another vehicle. Normally the collision coverage is purchased with a deductible feature: the first $100 or $250 of collision loss is paid by the insured and the insurance company picks up the balance.

Exclusions are usually written into the standard collision provisions. Among those are damages occurring when the vehicle is being operated in violation of the law, loss of personal property in the auto, and loss of use of the auto. As property insurance, collision coverage does not depend on fault on the part of the insured; the loss must merely be unintended.

The family and special package policies

The auto insurance policy may come in the form of a *family automobile policy* or a *special package automobile policy*. The first of these is the basic liability policy, which may contain various types of special coverage. Some of these are:

- *Medical payments.* Since most people have separate medical and hospital insurance, additional coverage is generally unnecessary. But in no-fault states, every policy has provisions for medical payments.
- *Uninsured motorist coverage.* The auto owner and his passengers are protected in the event of injuries incurred in an accident with a hit-and-run or an uninsured driver.
- *Comprehensive coverage.* A policy with "comp" covers damage resulting from an event other than a collision. Examples are fire, vandalism, theft, and so on.
- *Wage loss and substitute service.* In no-fault states insurers are required to include wage loss coverage for the loss of working time or services due to accident.
- *Safe-driving or merit-rating policies.* Some companies provide for discounts on premiums for persons with clean driving records. But the system works in reverse too: persons with poor records find their premiums going up for the next three years.

No-Fault Insurance

A relatively recent development in the law dealing with personal injury liability caused by auto accidents is the "no-fault" insurance concept. No-fault began partly as an attempt to reduce the load of auto accident cases that are taking up so much of the nation's courtroom time. In 1970, Massachusetts became the first state to adopt no-fault insurance.

The more common system of determining liability is based on a finding of fault on the part of one of the parties to an accident. For example, it is necessary to show that one of the parties was negligent and that his negligence caused the accident. If he is not found to be negligent, then he is not responsible. His liability insurance company will not have to pay. It often takes a lawsuit to determine the question of fault; as a result, if the party at fault refuses to settle or admit his fault a trial becomes necessary.

The "fault" system: more common

No-fault insurance programs seek to eliminate fault from consideration in auto accident injury cases. The no-fault statutes require that every auto liability policy provide no-fault coverage. When an insured is injured while using the insured auto, the company providing the coverage will make payment directly to the insured without regard to whether or not he or the other driver was at fault.

The "threshold" in no-fault programs

No-fault insurance covers medical expenses and losses of wages suffered by an insured. But it does not provide for payment for pain and suffering, inconvenience, or disability or disfigurement except in certain cases. Most no-fault programs have built into them a "threshold," the amount of medical expenses that must be incurred before the insured can bring a lawsuit against the party at fault to recover damages for pain, suffering, disability, disfigurement, and other claims that can be brought under the present fault system of liability.

An example may be noted. A no-fault system in a given state contains a threshold of $2,000. This means that before the insured can sue the party at fault to recover for all his claims, the amount of his medical expenses incurred as the result of the accident must exceed $2,000. Some no-fault programs allow suit if serious permanent injury, disability, or disfigurement results regardless of the threshold.

Each no-fault system is different from all the others. Whatever the differences, each system has a threshold amount. Other factors of significance:

- All of them restrict the right to sue.
- All of them attempt to eliminate lawsuits for personal injuries stemming from auto accidents.
- Some of them require arbitration of disputes between the insured and the company concerning the no-fault coverage.
- Some of them direct that some reduction in auto insurance premiums be made by the companies, at least in the first year or two of the system.

It is difficult to generalize further about no-fault insurance. The system will probably, in time, find its way in some form into the laws of most states. No-fault may be enacted into law by Congress as well—as a means of pushing the states into adopting their own plans. But no-fault has been attacked because it "unconstitutionally" deprives individuals of their right to use the courts for redress of their grievances.

The Problem of the Uninsured Motorist

What happens if an insured owner and driver is struck by a vehicle driven by someone who does not carry liability insurance?

"Uninsured motorist" coverage

In order to protect the insured person, the statutes of many states provide for a particular type of insurance called "uninsured motorist" coverage. As noted, the policy containing this coverage provides that one's own insurance company will pay if the insured is injured by a motorist who does not have liability insurance. It must, however, be established that the uninsured motorist was at fault and would be held liable in a lawsuit. Uninsured motorist coverage differs, thus, from no-fault coverage and collision coverage because fault on the part of the uninsured motorist must be shown.

Some policies offer "underinsured motorist" coverage. It pays off if the other driver's insurance is too low to cover injury losses.

The driver who leaves the scene of an accident before he can be identified is also considered an uninsured motorist. The typical policy contains a provision that an injured party, if struck by a "hit-and-run" motorist, must report the accident to the police within 24 hours. A search for the driver must also be made. This requirement is intended to prevent the filing of fraudulent claims. The conditions must be fulfilled or the insured will not qualify for the coverage.

Generally, liability in uninsured motorist coverage is limited to a maximum of $10,000. Only personal injury claims are covered. There must have been actual contact with the uninsured vehicle; the coverage does not apply if there was no such contact.

Only PI claims are covered

In the event of a dispute with the company regarding the claim or the amount to be paid, the policy normally provides for arbitration.

The victim of a hit-and-run accident, or the person struck by someone who does not carry insurance, should check his policy immediately. If he has uninsured motorist or "medical payments" coverage, he has some protection and can enter a claim if the other driver was at fault. If he does not have such coverage, he should probably get it right away.

LOSS OF DRIVING PRIVILEGES

Once considered a privilege, driving an automobile has become a virtual necessity. The salesman who delivers the milk every morning, the mail truck driver who brings the mail, the salesman who drives hundreds of miles a day all rely on their ability to drive to earn a living. For these and millions of others, suspension or revocation of driving privileges can qualify as a serious and very personal concern.

The statutes that control motor vehicle usage in the various states provide for the suspension and revocation of driving privileges under specified circumstances. While these laws differ from state to state, such suspensions or revocations usually hinge on the violations of the laws dealing with vehicle operation—"moving violations" such as speeding, reckless driving, and driving too fast for conditions.

Suspension or revocation of driving privileges

One little-understood aspect of this problem can lead to very serious consequences. To avoid going to court and losing time, people often voluntarily pay the fine when they receive a ticket for a serious moving violation. Rather than pay the fine, they should attend the hearing and contest the fine. They should do so especially if they believe they did not exceed the speed limit or otherwise violate any laws.

TEN RULES FOR SAFER DRIVING[1]

Speed. Observe posted limits but remember: most laws require lower speeds when maximum is dangerous.

Lanes. Keep right except when passing.

Right-of-Way. If no traffic signals, first vehicle entering intersection has it. In case of a tie, vehicle on your right has it. If no traffic signals, pedestrians have it at cross walks. Children conducted by school patrols have it. Emergency vehicles and funeral processions always have it.

Signals. Obey all traffic control signs; pedestrians and other drivers act on the assumption that you will.

Turning. Turn right only from the right lane, left from lane nearest center of road (except on one-way roadway). Always signal stops and turns.

Lights. Lower them when approaching another car. (It is courteous to lower them when following another car.)

Equipment. Keep lights, brakes, steering gear, tires, windshield wipers, mirror in good condition. Keep windshield, windows clear.

School buses. Stop when they load or unload.

Driver's license. Be ready to show it at all times.

Intersections. Always slow down and look to right and left regardless of signals.

[1] From *The Automobile Accident—What Should You Do?*, a pamphlet prepared and issued by Kansas Bar Association, 1334 Topeka Avenue, Topeka, Kansas.

Two separate proceedings

What is little understood is that a serious moving violation may involve two different proceedings. One is the criminal complaint for the violation, represented by the ticket. The other is a separate proceeding to suspend or revoke their driving privileges. Voluntarily paying the fine for the criminal moving violation may be treated as an admission of guilt in a later proceeding to suspend or revoke the driver's license.

Paying a moving violation fine is not necessarily the end of it. A notice may arrive later, asking the driver to appear before an examiner of the state motor vehicle department to determine whether cause exists for the suspension or revocation of his or her driver's license.

Paying a fine may also affect one's chances of collecting damages from the other driver later.

Fines and "point systems"

Many states have adopted "point systems." These assess points against an individual's driving record for violations. After amassing a certain number of points, the person may find that his driving privileges have been suspended or revoked. He may be required to attend safe driving classes as a condition of keeping the license or getting it back.

The intent of such laws is to control the reckless driver. But they affect deeply and directly those who depend on their ability to drive.

If you must drive to earn a living, before you pay a fine for a moving violation consult your lawyer to find out the effect of payment on any future proceeding that may affect your driving privileges. Despite the time and effort required, it may be better to attend a hearing on whether or not you did in fact violate the law.

To say that the automobile figures importantly in American life is to grossly understate the case. Production of the automobile creates and maintains jobs; its distribution and sales strengthen the economy; its repair and maintenance provide markets for many other products; the repair and maintenance of the highways it uses represent major parts of state budgets; and its ownership and use present problems to the motorist involving liability and livelihood. This discussion has been intended to pinpoint some of the problem areas.

This discussion was also intended to make it clear that there is, today, no such thing as a simple automobile accident. Claims and counter-claims can come out of the simplest "fender-bender."

18 "DAD, I'M CALLING FROM GRAND CROSSING POLICE STATION . . ."

Most parents have lived in dread of receiving a phone call like that mentioned in the title of this chapter. The newspapers, radio, and television are filled with stories of young people getting in trouble with the law, acquiring criminal records that could haunt them throughout their lives, and ruining their lives because of criminal activity.

What does a parent do when a child, relative, or close friend is accused of a crime? Where does he turn? What is involved in a criminal accusation and how is a child or adult released from custody? These questions are discussed in this chapter. Also included are basic rules that have to do with criminal procedures and practical pointers on how to handle the situation if it ever arises.

Supreme Court decisions have in recent years changed the entire complexion of criminal matters. The decisions touch on the need to involve the police, on apprehension of a suspect, on advice to be given the person regarding his rights to remain silent and to have an attorney

represent him. Legal representation may be called for in serious felony cases, and in less serious misdemeanor cases if they involve a possible jail term as a penalty.

The rules of several states and the federal courts require that the arrested person be taken before a committing magistrate without unreasonable delay after the arrest. Many other protections are available to the accused person.

It has been said that so much is done to protect the alleged criminal that the victim of the crime is ignored. Some maintain that something must be done to protect the victim. Some states have already taken steps in this direction by providing forms of compensation for the innocent person who has suffered serious personal injury or serious loss of property. Other states are considering similar legislation.

Under the American system of law a person is deemed innocent until proven guilty beyond a reasonable doubt. The laws, rules, and regulations devised over the years by legislatures and enforced by the courts have had as their primary objective observance of that fundamental rule.

Unreasonable detention is prohibited

In honoring the presumption of innocence, criminals may go free because of lack of evidence or because an accused did not have counsel. Evidence may be suppressed because of police failure to advise suspects properly of their rights. Other procedural factors may lead to an acquittal. The law does, in fact and in principle, deny to police the right to detain a suspect for an unreasonable length of time. Statements cannot be taken without advising the suspect of his rights. Both physical abuse and the subtle pressures of confinement without counsel degrade the presumption of innocence and create an atmosphere in which innocent persons may find themselves without protection.

It is, in sum, too facile to make generalizations that society protects criminals at the expense of innocent victims of crime. If that is your feeling, you might do two things. First, visit a jail or penitentiary in which people convicted of serious crimes are committed. You will most likely come out of that institution with a feeling of dread and a feeling of the hopelessness of the inmates there. Imagine, if you will, what it would be like for an innocent person to be committed to such an institution for any length of time.

Second, talk to the prison officials, prison chaplain, and others who are involved with the penal system. Many recommendations have been made regarding the rehabilitation of convicts, and some states have gone farther than others in this area. While prison officials will tell you that nearly every inmate claims to be innocent, the same officials will be the first ones to admit that the penal system is not perfect. Innocent people have been convicted of crime and have spent many years behind bars.

Protection of the innocent must be paramount. Conviction of the criminal must, in the American system, remain secondary. By utilizing the protections provided for accused persons, and by recognizing the difficulties facing the police daily, we can minimize the chance of an unjust conviction of an innocent person. The procedures involved in arresting and convicting the guilty may at the same time be improved. *Conviction may be secondary to protection*

No system is perfect. Citizens have to live within the system as it develops and attempt to perfect it through experience and by continual study and investigation.

POLICE
DOCTOR — 312-2
FIRE — 207-
LAWYER — 302
312.

PRACTICAL INFORMATION TO REMEMBER

A phone call comes from your son. He says he is being held by the police for a crime. Your first concern must be to get him released from custody. Beside every person's home telephone, in plain view, should be the numbers of the fire and police departments, the family doctor, and the family lawyer. The lawyer can provide the telephone number of a bail bondsman who is both reputable and available on short notice.

Why is all this necessary? Pending the posting of the bond, and depending on the seriousness of the alleged crime, a suspect will normally be held. He should be released as soon as possible because it is a terrifying experience to spend even one night in a jail or prison. Many individuals who have spent only a single night in jail have been beaten and robbed, had their clothes stolen, and been sexually assaulted. Such experiences can stay with the victim for a long time.

That single phone call The police will allow the detained person to make one phone call. The parent or other person receiving the call should immediately call his or her lawyer and then the bondsman. The attorney will talk to the police and will visit the suspect, advise him of his rights, and caution him to make no statement until the lawyer can find out what he is charged with, the circumstances of the arrest, and so on.

The lawyer's interview with the detainee will take place at the police station or lock-up where he is being detained. The lawyer will need the following information:

What the lawyer needs to know
- All the facts of the incident
- Whatever the suspect knows of the alleged crime
- The names and addresses of anyone who might be a witness
- The manner in which the arrest was made
- What was said to him by the police concerning his rights
- Whether the suspect gave any oral or written statement to the police at any time
- Details of any prior criminal record that the detainee might have
- Information regarding his job and where he works
- The identities of persons who might serve as alibi or character witnesses
- If no bondsman is available, the names of relatives or friends who could post bail
- Whether any personal business has to be attended to while the detainee is in jail or awaiting bond

What is Bail?

With bail, the authorities attempt to assure the presence or appearance of the accused person at a later date—in court, at a preliminary hearing, or at an arraignment—after his release from custody. Under the federal system, a person accused of a non-capital offense is entitled to bail. Eligibility for bail may, however, depend on the severity of the crime. In some states where the right to bail is governed by statute, the police official at the station where the accused is "booked" may release the accused on bail immediately.

Where bail is excessive and arbitrary The amount of bail is based on similar considerations. The severity of the crime and the circumstances of the particular case have a bearing on the amount. If the amount of bail is excessive and arbitrary, the constitutional rights of the accused will have been violated and the bail may be released or reduced on application to the court.

Other considerations may be important. Those include:

- The circumstances under which the accused was arrested
- How severe a penalty might be imposed
- The general weight of the evidence against the accused
- The likelihood that the accused might attempt flight
- The probability of guilt
- The accused's ability to post bond (what is reasonable for the rich may be unreasonable for the poor)
- The physical condition of the accused and whether he would face serious health hazards if jailed
- The accused's prior record, if any, and his general character

ARREST AND THE BILL OF RIGHTS

In the United States people are governed by laws, not men. Three separate sections of the U.S. Constitution, the fifth, sixth, and eighth amendments of the Bill of Rights, protect the basic rights of the citizen under arrest.

Amendment V—No person shall be held to answer for a capital, or otherwise infamous crime, unless on a presentment or indictment of a Grand Jury, except in cases arising in the land or naval forces, or in the Militia, when in actual service in time of War or public danger; nor shall any person be subject for the same offence to be twice put in jeopardy of life or limb; nor shall be compelled in any criminal case to be a witness against himself, nor be deprived of life, liberty, or property, without due process of law; nor shall private property be taken for public use, without just compensation.

Amendment VI—In all criminal prosecutions, the accused shall enjoy the right to a speedy and public trial, by an impartial jury of the State and district wherein the crime shall have been committed, which district shall have been previously ascertained by law, and to be informed of the nature and cause of the accusation; to be confronted with the witnesses against him; to have compulsory process for obtaining witnesses in his favor, and to have the Assistance of Counsel for his defence...

Amendment VIII—Excessive bail shall not be required, nor excessive fines imposed, nor cruel and unusual punishments inflicted.

Bail usually takes the form of a bail bond issued by an insurance company. Some of the states specify by statute the exact bond forms. In addition to requiring the payment of a premium for the bond, some bonding companies require other security to ensure the appearance of the

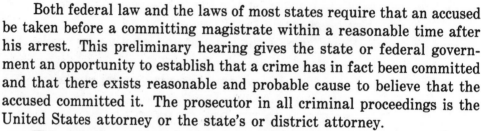

Cash deposit may be acceptable

accused at the later proceedings. A cash deposit or deposit of other property may be acceptable as a substitute for a bail bond depending on the nature of the crime involved. Where real estate is used as bail, a record to that effect is filed in the office of the county recorder of deeds.

The title of the real estate then shows that it is subject to a possible lien for the amount of bail specified. If the accused "jumps bail" and does not appear, the real estate remains subject to the lien.

The Preliminary Hearing

Both federal law and the laws of most states require that an accused be taken before a committing magistrate within a reasonable time after his arrest. This preliminary hearing gives the state or federal government an opportunity to establish that a crime has in fact been committed and that there exists reasonable and probable cause to believe that the accused committed it. The prosecutor in all criminal proceedings is the United States attorney or the state's or district attorney.

The state is not required, at the preliminary hearing, to establish that the accused committed the crime. There must only be sufficient basis for holding him.

The lawyer for the accused has the right to cross-examine the state's witnesses. But he need not call any witnesses to defend against the charges. Some states require that certain defenses that may be used at the trial of the accused, such as alibi or insanity, be raised at the preliminary hearing—or that notice be given to the prosecution that these defenses will be relied on later.

At the preliminary hearing the state may rely on a confession or admission of the accused. The defense that the confession or admission was secured by force or coercion, or resulted from delay in bringing the accused before a magistrate, should then be raised at once so that the same defense can be used at the trial. Some states require that these defenses go into the record as early as possible. The laws of other states may be more lenient.

In the 1980s voluntary, videotaped confessions became increasingly common. They provided what lawyers and district attorneys held were clear, tamper-proof records for the use of all principals in a trial. They also showed whether the defendant had been read the "Miranda rules" (see p. 362), saved days or weeks of pretrial hearings, and speeded trials substantially.

The defense of illegal search and seizure

State laws differ, again, where an accused wishes to use the defense of illegal search and seizure by the police. The claim may be made that the accused's property or home was searched without a warrant in violation of his constitutional rights. The accused's person may have been searched illegally. Depending on the state, the evidence for such a claim may be suppressed. But state law may require that this defense be raised at the preliminary hearing or at the arraignment that follows.

A trend toward relaxation of rules relating to some illegal searches, arrests, and seizures became evident in the middle 1980s. The "exclusionary rule" that forbids the use of illegally obtained evidence remained in force; but in one case the U.S. Supreme Court made it easier for police to obtain search warrants. In a second case, arising in 1983, Houston plainclothes officers using an invalid warrant—in the belief it was valid—arrested a man who subsequently confessed to racketeering offenses. The defendant's later efforts to have the confession suppressed were denied.

Two 1984 cases, *U.S.* v. *Leon* and *Massachusetts* v. *Sheppard*, confirmed the Supreme Court's sense of the validity of the limited "good faith" exception to the exclusionary rule. In still another case, a police officer searched a suspect and his car on what the Supreme Court held was a "reasonable suspicion" that the person was armed and dangerous. The evidence found was held to be admissible as evidence.

In the 1984 case of *Nix* v. *Williams*, the Supreme Court made a further exception to the exclusionary rule. The defendant in the case had led police to the body of his murder victim after a detective had spoken of the victim's right to a Christian burial. Citing a theory of "inevitable discovery," the Supreme Court held unanimously that the evidence of the location and condition of the body was admissible even though the defendant's right to counsel had been violated.

Some legislation, such as the "no knock" laws, allows the police to enter premises and make a search without knocking if they believe a crime is being committed or is about to be committed. This right is not unqualified, however.

The Grand Jury and Its Functions

Certain classifications of crimes are minor in nature. State laws normally allow these crimes to be handled at the magistrate, justice of the peace, or city court level. Minor crimes usually involve fines only and are usually misdemeanors. If, however, the crime is a serious one involving a possible imprisonment, or if the crime is a felony under the laws of the state, the case will generally be submitted to a grand jury for "indictment."

Handling minor crimes

The indictment constitutes an accusation by a grand jury that the accused has committed the crime charged in the indictment. The grand jury is composed of citizens of the county or district where the accused is to be tried. Jury members listen to sworn testimony and review other evidence. They then determine whether or not the state, acting through the proper county official or the federal government, has made out an adequate case that a crime has been committed and that the accused person should stand trial. The crime needs to be established only in broad terms. The details of the crime are left for presentation at the trial.

In some instances the accused may want to appear before the grand jury in an effort to avoid the issuance of an indictment. This may be permitted where the accused has agreed to waive immunity from prosecution for his testimony. The accused has no absolute right to appear before the grand jury unless state law gives him that right.

Besides returning indictments against persons accused of crimes, the grand jury serves another important function. It may also be convened to investigate, on a broad scale, various types of criminal activity in the community. The jury then has the power to issue *subpoenas* to compel witnesses to attend and testify before it.

To avoid self-incrimination . . .   An accused has the constitutional right to avoid self-incrimination if he is subpoenaed to testify before a grand jury. Even in states where an accused must appear, he can refuse to answer incriminating questions unless he has been granted immunity from prosecution for the alleged crime. After the grand jury has considered the evidence, it will either return an indictment or refuse to do so.

If indicted, the accused becomes the defendant. He faces arraignment, the next step in the criminal procedure.

THE MIRANDA RULES:
ADVICE BEFORE INTERROGATION

In the 1966 case of *Miranda* v. *Arizona*, the U.S. Supreme Court reversed a state conviction because of the use at a trial of statements given to police during an interrogation. The high court specified that an accused had to be told before interrogation of four basic rights. The four:

- the right to remain silent

- the right to know that anything he might say could be used against him

- the right to have an attorney present during questioning

- the right, if he has no money, to be provided with a lawyer without charge

The so-called "Miranda warnings" came to be used nationwide after the 1966 decision. The effect has been that admissions or a confession made by a suspect during police interrogation are not admitted as evidence at a subsequent trial —unless the four warnings were given.

The Supreme Court has slowly moved away from strict adherence to the Miranda rules. In some lower-court cases confessions obtained without following the rules have been admitted in evidence on technical grounds. In 1984, in an express relaxation of the Miranda ruling, the Supreme Court said "overriding considerations of public safety" might render the warnings unnecessary. The police officer or officers, the high court added in *New York* v. *Quarles*, must "reasonably" be said to have been motivated by a concern for public safety.

The Arraignment

At the formal court proceeding called the arraignment, the indictment is presented and read to the defendant. The defendant has an opportunity to plead to the indictment.

Where any doubt exists in the mind of the court regarding the defendant's understanding of the charges against him, the court may only accept a plea of "not guilty." Where, however, the defendant is represented by counsel and understands the nature of the charges against him, the court will usually accept whatever plea he makes.

The "not guilty" plea

Before the arraignment, however, the attorney for the defendant usually talks to the state's attorney to find out how strong the state's case actually is and—sometimes—whether the state would accept a plea of guilty to a lesser crime. This practice, called "plea bargaining," has been attacked by some as a means of allowing a criminal to escape the law's full penalty by pleading guilty to a lesser crime. Both the defense and the prosecution find the practice acceptable in many cases. It is not illegal. Also, it allows for the completion of criminal proceedings without a full-scale trial, and enables the state to obtain a conviction when the evidence to convict a defendant of a more serious crime is weak.

Charges of plea bargaining are raised in many cases that receive wide public notoriety. But in fact the great majority of criminal cases are terminated in some manner before trial.

The defendant has, of course, the right to plead not guilty to any and all charges and to take his chances before the jury. In most cases a defendant who agrees to plead guilty to a lesser charge will want some idea of the sentence to be imposed by the court. Some judges refuse, however, to commit themselves in advance on a sentence; others may be willing to do so. Only with the assistance of an experienced criminal lawyer can the defendant estimate his chances to plea bargain and ascertain the probable sentence to be imposed.

Various considerations go into a decision on whether the state will accept a plea to a lesser crime than that charged in the indictment. The factors include the character of the defendant, the strength of the state's case, the defendant's prior criminal record, if any, the views and opinions of character witnesses, the reports of the behavior from parole officers, and the reports of other social welfare agencies. The latter may be used by the court to determine the questions of sentence and probation.

A plea of *nolo contendere* indicates, in effect, "no contest." With such a plea the defendant states that he is not going to defend himself against the charge. It amounts to a plea of guilty in a criminal case. In a civil case, where a suit is brought for money damages suffered by others because of a criminal act, the defendant's liability may be reduced.

"Nolo contendere" in criminal and civil cases

Proceedings Before Trial

A defendant who has pleaded not guilty to the charges in the indictment pending trial and who is out on bail, in most states, can make some requests. In preparing his case, for example, he may ask for the grand jury's minutes to see if any of his rights have been violated, can attempt to have the indictment set aside for some violation of the law, and may request a statement of the particulars of the crime charged. He may also demand that the court dismiss the charges as inadequate to sustain indictment.

Request for change of venue

A crime may have caused sufficient public outrage to raise the question whether the defendant could receive a fair trial in that area. The defendant may then move for a "change of venue"—meaning that he requests that the trial be held in another location away from the area where the crime was committed. He may also request a separate trial where he has been indicted for more than one crime, or where he has been indicted with another accused person if a joint trial of the defendants would work against him. He may also seek, during this period before trial, the reports of such experts as medical examiners. He may ask to be shown the physical evidence: the books, records, and photographs that the police have gathered.

Whether such requests will be granted depends on the laws of the state in which the case is pending. State laws differ markedly on what portions of the state's case a defendant may inspect.

DEFENSES AND PRE-TRIAL PROCEDURES

In most criminal cases, as noted, the defenses usually have to be indicated as promptly as possible. The preliminary hearing or immediately thereafter is not too soon. The first of these is the defense of *insanity.*

Four kinds of defense

1. Insanity as a defense to a criminal charge constitutes a legal matter, not a psychological one. In other words the law defines "insanity" for its own purposes. A defendant must be found to have been within the legal definition of insanity at the time of the crime.

In a few words, insanity has been held to be a defect of reason resulting from a mental disease. That defect must prevent the accused from understanding the nature and quality of his act and the fact that it was wrong.

Most states follow that definition or some similar one. Other states hold simply that insanity means that the criminal act was the result of mental disease or mental defect.

The difference between the "right or wrong" test and the "mental disease or illness" test is highly important. Psychologists say that a defendant may be aware that what he is doing is wrong but nonetheless be unable, because of mental disease or defect, to resist performing the act.

Whatever the law of the state on this point, insanity must be raised as a defense early in the proceedings. Once it has been raised, the state has to attempt to establish the defendant's sanity. If an acquittal because of insanity results, the defendant may be committed to an institution rather than freed.

Such an acquittal verdict, reached in the 1981 case of John W. Hinckley, Jr., would-be assassin of President Ronald Reagan, brought a public outcry. Efforts to limit the uses of the insanity plea got under way. The federal government itself sought to persuade a Connecticut District Court to abolish the plea entirely.

In late 1983 the government's efforts were adjudged failures. But they had spotlighted key questions, including these:

- Does the insanity defense serve a legitimate purpose in the criminal justice system?
- Is a practical consequence of the plea the release of dangerous individuals from any form of control or restraint?
- May the successful use of the plea undermine or sap public confidence in the nation's courts?
- Does the plea, as such, encourage the "endless proliferation" of new varieties of mental illness?

In an earlier decision, the U.S. Supreme Court ruled that once acquitted by reason of insanity, a defendant might be held in a mental hospital almost indefinitely. Such incarceration would not deny the defendant due process if it continued until the individual had regained sanity or is no longer dangerous. The possibility exists that confinement could last longer than incarceration could or would have.

2. Like other defenses, an *alibi* must be raised as soon as possible. Some states require that this defense be specified by the defendant at or before the preliminary hearing. In some cases it may be submitted in writing to the state's attorney. Once the defense is properly raised, the state must prove the alibi false.

3. Illegally obtained evidence constitutes a common defense in criminal cases. Except as in cases already noted, evidence obtained as a result of an illegal search and seizure has to be excluded from a trial: the "exclusionary rule" applies. The definition of illegally obtained evidence varies according to the laws of the particular state. But the Supreme Court of the United States has placed definite restrictions on illegally obtained evidence and the use of such evidence in court.

Federal laws allow wiretaps where authorized by the Attorney General in writing. But the wiretap information, to be admissible as evidence, must have been secured in the precise way authorized by the statute. Some states have adopted procedures requiring a court order before telephones can be tapped to obtain evidence. With such an order or warrant wiretapping becomes legal. The information gathered can be used as evidence.

Wiretapping for evidence

4. *Double jeopardy* can serve as a valid defense where the defendant alleges that he has already been tried for the same offense. The test is whether or not the prior trial of the defendant did in fact place him in jeopardy of conviction. If he was not, the defense fails. Where the prior proceedings had gone so far that testimony was heard after a jury was empanelled, that would constitute a previous "jeopardy" and serve as a defense to the later action.

The Writ of Habeas Corpus

Uses of habeas corpus

The great triumph of the English Common Law, from which American law is derived, is the *writ of habeas corpus*. Historically, this writ has been used to require the production of the person or "body" of the defendant. The writ was and is used:

- to prevent injustice;
- to prevent the continued imprisonment of persons who have not been charged formally with a crime;
- to test the validity of the criminal prosecution in all of its stages;
- to test the arrest warrant; and
- to test the right of the police or state's attorney to refuse to allow the defendant's attorney to interview his client.

The writ is generally issued when the defendant's attorney makes application to a judge in a court of record in the district where the defendant is being held. A "court of record" is a court that has a clerk to keep a record of all its proceedings. The judge signs and issues the writ. A hearing is held on the facts stated in the writ regarding the allegedly illegal or improper acts of the authorities.

The writ of habeas corpus is entitled to top priority to bring the defendant before the court on the basis of some illegal detention. Under the federal system, federal judges may issue writs where a defendant alleges that his federal constitutional rights have been violated by his detention by state authorities. But usually the federal court will require that all of the defendant's remedies in the state courts be exhausted first, including his application to a state judge for a writ.

Extradition

In a typical case a person charged with a crime in one state flees that state and is later found in another state. The federal Constitution requires that the accused be extradited at the request of the executive authority of the accusing state. In this process the accused is moved to the state having jurisdiction of the crime.

Certain formalities have to be observed in extradition. These include certification of the indictment or charge and signature by the governor or chief judicial officer of the state demanding the return of the fugitive.

Formalities for extradition

Extradition of accused felons is provided for by treaty among the nations of the world. The nation to which the felon has escaped is required to surrender him to the nation demanding his return for trial. Not all countries have extradition treaties with the United States, however. Thus fugitives, including political dissidents, may escape to those countries so that they cannot be forced to return against their will.

TRIAL, SENTENCING, AND AFTER

Assume that a defendant has been convicted of a crime in a proper trial. He may then enter a motion for a new trial for one or all of the following reasons, as they apply to his case:

- The jury received improper evidence in or out of court.
- The jury itself did not act properly, as where a juror argued with counsel during the trial.
- The court did not properly instruct the jury on the law governing the case and on the effect of the law on the evidence after the defendant's attorney took the necessary exceptions to the court's instructions to the jury.
- The jury verdict is clearly against the evidence and the law.
- The defendant can show by affidavit that he has found new evidence that would have produced a different verdict—if the evidence was not available at the trial and was discovered after the trial ended.

Reasons for moving for a new trial

These motions for a new trial are argued by the lawyers before the court. They may result in an appeal by the defendant if he is refused a new trial. In many cases the lawyer for the accused has to take exceptions—or raise objections—during the trial to procedural or other matters. Without the objections, a later appeal may be impossible.

While new trial motions or an appeal is pending, the court may withhold sentencing the defendant until the motion or appeal is decided. In such a case the defendant will remain free on bond. However, sentence may be imposed, depending on the seriousness of the crime, while the motion or appeal is pending.

The Sentencing Process

A major problem area in criminal law focuses on sentencing. The judges who pass sentences are human beings. Since they have different temperaments, personalities, and views of the seriousness of various crimes, no uniformity exists among them as regards sentencing.

Judge has latitude in sentencing

This situation has led to much criticism. To their credit, criminal court judges have formed professional associations and have attended seminars and educational programs on the subject of proper sentencing. The problem continues to exist because the laws of the states are not the same. The laws usually give the judge wide latitude in imposing sentences consistent with specific crimes and the records of defendants. If the law, for example, sets the penalty for second degree murder at five to 20 years in prison, the judge is free to impose any term within that framework.

Some states require that judges sentence only to the maximum period of the penalty. The state correctional department can then determine the actual length of the sentence, up to the maximum imposed, depending on the record and behavior of the defendant.

The pre-sentence report

Whatever the procedure, the judge has help, in most states, in the difficult job of sentencing. State probation departments and behavior clinics will make pre-sentence investigations of the defendant, look into his or her background, find out whatever it can about the defendant, and file a report with the court. This report often becomes the basis of the sentence that is imposed on the defendant. If the report is favorable, the defendant can usually expect to receive a minimum sentence.

In this area the defendant's attorney can also be of significant help. So can the defendant's family, even after conviction. The family lawyer and the family should work closely with the probation office or behavior clinic to make available all needed information on the defendant. The pre-sentence report will then be entirely fair to the defendant.

In some states the attorney for the defendant is permitted to see the pre-sentence report before it is given to the judge. In other states the attorney cannot read the report. At the sentence hearing, the judge will have the report before him. Usually he will allow counsel and the defendant himself to make any statement they may wish to make that might affect the sentence. A statement may touch on the defendant's character, his family's need for support, his lack of a prior criminal record, and any other facts that might favorably affect the sentence.

Probation lasts a specified period

If all these factors bear strongly in the defendant's favor, and if his prior record allows it, the judge may suspend the sentence. The defendant is then placed on probation for a specified period during which he will be required to report to the probation office and stay out of trouble.

SEVEN MAIN STEPS IN A CRIMINAL JURY TRIAL[1]

Criminal trials held before juries generally follow a well-established pattern. They begin with selection of the jury and proceed through six other steps—to sentencing if the verdict is guilty. The seven steps or stages:

SELECTION OF JURY
- a. Challenges
    1. Cause
    2. Peremptory
- b. Completion of jury
- c. Oath

THE TRIAL
- a. Opening statements by counsel (not evidence)
- b. Evidence
    1. Testimony of witnesses
    2. Exhibits
    3. Depositions
- c. Closing arguments by counsel (not evidence)

JUDGE'S ADMONITIONS TO THE JURORS DURING TRIAL
- a. Admonitions to jurors not to discuss the case among themselves or with anyone else, until the case is finally submitted to the jury for verdict

JUDGE'S INSTRUCTIONS ON THE LAW
- a. Instructions to jurors on the law after completion of testimony and arguments

DELIBERATIONS BY JURY
- a. Selects foreman
- b. Weighs evidence
- c. "Beyond reasonable doubt" must characterize guilty finding

THE VERDICT
- a. Criminal case—unanimous

SENTENCING
- a. Judge pronounces sentence

[1] Adapted from *Juror's Manual*, State Bar of Michigan, 306 Townsend St., Lansing, MI 48933.

The Parole Process

Once a defendant has been convicted and imprisoned, he may become eligible for parole, or conditional release from prison, after serving a minimum sentence. Most states have parole boards that pass on the eligibility of convicted persons for parole. In many cases, the application for parole is made by the convict. But it may also be made by the attorney, prison social worker, or others.

The parole board will consider such things as the convict's behavior in prison, whether or not he has a job waiting for him, and whether he has shown that he can rehabilitate himself in civilian life.

The parole board hearing may consider medical, psychological, and other evidence. It may consider evidence offered by the state in opposition to the parole request. If the convict is then paroled, his activities will be restricted. He will be required to remain in the area and he will be required to report periodically to the parole officer assigned to his case. He cannot associate with known criminals or carry any weapons. A violation of any of these restrictions may result in the termination of parole and the parolee's return to prison to serve the balance of his sentence.

THE YOUTHFUL OFFENDER AND THE JUVENILE DELINQUENT

Delinquency age established by state

Special consideration has been given in criminal law to the youthful offender and the *juvenile delinquent*. Traditionally, the law has presumed that a person below a certain age—14, 16, or some other age established by state law—was not capable of committing a crime. Thus when a juvenile is apprehended for a crime, he is not charged with a particular crime. Rather he is charged with being a juvenile delinquent.

The juvenile delinquency laws help to prevent the minor from acquiring a criminal record. A hearing is usually held before a juvenile court judge. In former years, this hearing was not considered a criminal trial, and the juvenile was not given all the constitutional protections accorded an adult defendant. However, the Supreme Court has decided that a juvenile delinquent has the same constitutional rights as an adult accused. Among these rights is the right to counsel at the hearing to determine whether he is in fact a delinquent.

The juvenile delinquency procedure does not emphasize punishment. Rather, it seeks to help the delinquent child to adjust. Thus the juvenile court judge has considerable discretion in sentencing the juvenile. He may be placed in the custody of parents, sent to a reform school or similar institution, or sent to a foster home or a school operated by or for the state or county. Such an arrangement is intended to encourage rehabilitation. In imposing sentence, the judge will consider the offense involved, the juvenile's background, home life, past trouble with the law, and the institutions to which the juvenile can be sent.

A "youthful offender," by contrast, is a person who, in the eyes of the law, is old enough to be capable of committing a crime but whose age indicates that he should not be treated as an adult criminal. This treatment depends on the age of the accused, the nature of the crime, his background, and, often, the results of physical and mental examinations.

The preliminary hearing

The laws of most states provide for a preliminary hearing to decide whether an accused person should be treated as a youthful offender. The accused may be required to make formal application to the court for such treatment. But the court may, on its own, treat the person as a youthful offender.

To ensure privacy, the trial of a youthful offender is usually held in the judge's chambers rather than in open court. The offender must previously have waived the right to a jury trial and agreed to such a procedure.

A child or juvenile charged with an act that would be a crime if the offender were an adult may be tried *as an adult*. A jury will not be called to weigh the evidence; but the juvenile court judge will apply the standards of proof required in criminal cases. Proof of guilt must be established beyond a reasonable doubt.

In a case involving a serious crime such as murder or rape, a juvenile may be tried as an adult in criminal court. Such trials usually take place where the penalty, on a finding of guilt, could be death or life imprisonment.

By the early 1980s some states, including Florida, were launching programs that would more fully utilize both state and private-sector resources in the treatment of juvenile delinquency. One plan called for state contracts with a private-sector agency that would run state institutions for incarcerated delinquents. A Colorado program brought teens into court to serve as "juvenile juries." The juries take part in informal trials. They then draw up "contracts" with young offenders that require those charged and found guilty to carry out specific terms. In many cases the offenders take part-time jobs to pay a victim for damages.

The Court Trial

A court trial generally proceeds according to a set pattern. The trial may or may not call for selection of a jury, but in many civil suits and most criminal cases a jury is selected, or impaneled, to sit in judgment of the evidence.

Jurors

U.S. courts use three kinds of juries: the petit jury (or petty), the common trial jury; the grand jury, which usually decides whether there is enough evidence to justify bringing formal charges in a criminal case; and a coroner's jury, the jury that conducts an inquest when doubt exists as to the causes of death.

Jury Duty. Typically a jury in either a civil or a criminal case is made up of twelve persons. Prospective jurors' names are listed on a jury panel. From this panel court officials draw names until the jury box is filled.

Jurors have a serious responsibility. They may be deciding on a money award (in a civil case) or on a person's guilt or innocence (in a criminal case).

Once the trial has ended, jurors select a foreman. The foreman acts as a chairman, making certain that discussion proceeds in a fair and orderly way. When the jurors have reached a unanimous decision, the foreman records it and reports it to the court.

INDEX

E